PREFACE

This edition of the *McKinney's New York Rules of Court, Federal, 2009,* pamphlet replaces the 2008 edition. This volume provides in convenient form court rules governing federal practice in New York and is current with amendments received through September 15, 2008.

THE PUBLISHER

October, 2008

*

RELATED PRODUCTS
FROM WEST

WEST'S McKINNEY'S FORMS

Civil Practice Law and Rules

Uniform Commercial Code

Business Corporation Law

Matrimonial and Family Law

Real Property Practice

Estates and Surrogate Practice

Criminal Procedure Law

Not–For–Profit Corporation Law

Tax Practice and Procedure

Local Government Forms

Selected Consolidated Law Forms

McKinney's Consolidated Laws of New York Annotated

McKinney's Consolidated Laws of New York, Compact Edition

West's New York Legal Update

New York Digest

New York Law Finder

New York Official Reports, 3d Series

New York Pattern Jury Instructions—Civil

New York Forms, Legal and Business

New York Supplement, 2d Series

New York Practice 4th Edition
David D. Siegel

New York Court of Appeals on Criminal Law 2d Edition
William C. Donnino

Charges to the Jury and Requests to Charge in a Criminal Case in New York
Howard Leventhal

RELATED PRODUCTS

Criminal Law in New York, 4th Edition
Gary Muldoon, Esq.

Hon. Karen Morris

Nicole L. Black, Esq.

Criminal Procedure in New York, 2d Edition
Hon. Robert G. Bogle

Handling a Criminal Case in New York
Gary Muldoon, Esq.

Handling the DWI Case in New York
Peter Gerstenzang

Eric H. Sills

Modern New York Discovery, 2d
Abraham Fuchsberg, et al.

New York Driving While Intoxicated, 2d Edition
Edward Louis Fiandach

New York DWI Defense Forms
Michael S. Taheri, Esq.

James F. Orr

New York Vehicle and Traffic Law, 2d Edition
James M. Rose

Trial Handbook for New York Lawyers, 3d Edition
Aaron J. Broder

Village, Town and District Courts in New York
Hon. James E. Morris

RELATED PRODUCTS

Hon. Robert G. Bogle

Hon. Thomas F. Liotti

Maryita Dobiel, Esq.

WEST'S NEW YORK PRACTICE SERIES

Vol. 1

New York Limited Liability Companies and Partnerships
Walker, et al.

Vols. 2–4B

Commercial Litigation in New York State Courts 2d
Haig, et al.

Vol. 5

Evidence in New York State and Federal Courts
Barker and Alexander

Vol. 6

New York Criminal Law 3d
Greenberg, Marcus, Fahey and Cary

Vol. 7

New York Pretrial Criminal Procedure 2d
Marks, et al.

Vol. 8

New York Civil Appellate Practice 2d
Davies, Stecich and Gold

Vol. 9

Environmental Law and Regulation in New York
Ginsberg, Weinberg, et al.

Vol. 10

New York Family Court Practice
Sobie, et al.

Vols. 11–12

New York Law of Domestic Relations
Scheinkman

Vol. 13

Employment Litigation in New York
Taber, et al.

RELATED PRODUCTS

Vol. 13A
Employment Law in New York
Stiller

Vols. 14–16
New York Law of Torts
Kreindler, Rodriguez, et al.

Vols. 20–25
General Practice in New York
Ostertag, Benson, et al.

Vol. 26
New York Administrative Procedure and Practice
Borchers and Markell

Vol. 27
New York Workers' Compensation
Minkowitz

Vol. 28
New York Contract Law
Banks

Vol. A
Enforcing Judgments and Collecting Debts in New York
Borges, et al.

Vols. B–C
Personal Injury Practice in New York
Bensel, Frank, McKeon, et al.

Vols. D–E
Trusts and Estates Practice in New York
Preminger, et al.

Vols. F–G
Landlord and Tenant Practice in New York
Finkelstein and Ferrara

PAMPHLETS

McKinney's Criminal and Motor Vehicle Law
McKinney's Law and the Family—New York
McKinney's New York Rules of Court—State, Federal and Local Civil
McKinney's New York Civil Practice Law and Rules
McKinney's New York Estate and Surrogate Practice
New York Sentence and Related Law Charts

McKINNEY'S
NEW YORK
RULES OF COURT
2009 EDITION

FEDERAL

THOMSON
*
WEST

Mat#40580503

ISBN 978–0–314–97436–5

WESTLAW ELECTRONIC RESEARCH GUIDE

Westlaw—Expanding the Reach of Your Library

Westlaw is West's online legal research service. With Westlaw, you experience the same quality and integrity that you have come to expect from West books, plus quick, easy access to West's vast collection of statutes, case law materials, public records, and other legal resources, in addition to current news articles and business information. For the most current and comprehensive legal research, combine the strengths of West books and Westlaw.

When you research with westlaw.com you get the convenience of the Internet combined with comprehensive and accurate Westlaw content, including exclusive editorial enhancements, plus features found only in westlaw.com such as ResultsPlus™ or StatutesPlus.™

Accessing Databases Using the Westlaw Directory

The Westlaw Directory lists all databases on Westlaw and contains links to detailed information relating to the content of each database. Click Directory on the westlaw.com toolbar. There are several ways to access a database even when you don't know the database identifier. Browse a directory view. Scan the directory. Type all or part of a database name in the Search these Databases box. The Find a Database Wizard can help you select relevant databases for your search. You can access up to ten databases at one time for user-defined multibase searching.

Retrieving a Specific Document

To retrieve a specific document by citation or title on westlaw.com click **Find&Print** on the toolbar to display the Find a Document page. If you are unsure of the correct citation format, type the publication abbreviation, e.g., **xx st** (where xx is a state's two-letter postal abbreviation), in the Find this document by citation box and click **Go** to display a fill-in-the-blank template. To retrieve a specific case when you know one or more parties' names, click **Find a Case by Party Name**.

KeyCite®

KeyCite, the citation research service on Westlaw, makes it easy to trace the history of your case, statute, administrative decision or regulation to determine if there are recent updates and to find other documents that cite your document. KeyCite will also find pending legislation relating to federal or state statutes. Access the powerful features of KeyCite from the westlaw.com toolbar, the **Links** tab, or KeyCite flags in a document display. KeyCite's red and yellow warning flags tell you at a glance whether your document has negative history. Depth-of-treatment stars help you focus on the most important citing references. KeyCite Alert allows you to monitor the status of your case, statute or rule, and automatically sends you updates at the frequency you specify.

ResultsPlus™

ResultsPlus is a Westlaw technology that automatically suggests additional information related to your search. The suggested materials are accessible by a set of links that appear to the right of your westlaw.com search results:

- Go directly to relevant ALR® articles and Am Jur® annotations.
- Find on-point resources by key number.
- See information from related treatises and law reviews.

StatutesPlus™

When you access a statutes database in westlaw.com you are brought to a powerful Search Center which collects, on one toolbar, the tools that are most useful for fast, efficient retrieval of statutes documents:

- Have a few key terms? Click **Statutes Index**.
- Know the common name? Click **Popular Name Table**.
- Familiar with the subject matter? Click **Table of Contents**.
- Have a citation or section number? Click **Find by Citation**.
- Interested in topical surveys providing citations across multiple state statutes? Click **50 State Surveys.**
- Or, simply search with **Natural Language** or **Terms and Connectors.**

When you access a statutes section, click on the **Links** tab for all relevant links for the current document that will also include a KeyCite section with a description of the KeyCite status flag. Depending on your document, links may also include administrative, bill text, and other sources that were previously only available by accessing and searching other databases.

Additional Information

Westlaw is available on the Web at westlaw.com.

For search assistance, call the West Reference Attorneys at
1–800–REF–ATTY (1–800–733–2889).

For technical assistance, call West Customer Technical Support at
1–800–WESTLAW (1–800–937–8529).

TABLE OF CONTENTS

FEDERAL COURTS

	Page
FEDERAL RULES OF CIVIL PROCEDURE	1
Appendix of Forms	59
Supplemental Rules for Admiralty or Maritime Claims and Asset Forfeiture Actions	81
Index	91
FEDERAL RULES OF EVIDENCE	109
Index	128
FEDERAL RULES OF APPELLATE PROCEDURE	131
Appendix of Forms	159
Index	165
LOCAL RULES OF THE COURT OF APPEALS FOR THE SECOND CIRCUIT	169
Forms	197
Appendix	229
Selected Orders	270
Selected Notices	270
Index	271
RULES OF THE BANKRUPTCY APPELLATE PANEL SERVICE OF THE SECOND CIRCUIT	273
UNITED STATES DISTRICT COURTS, SOUTHERN AND EASTERN DISTRICTS	275
Local Civil Rules	277
Local Admiralty and Maritime Rules	302
Local Criminal Rules	304
Southern District Supplemental Materials	308
Eastern District Supplemental Materials	344
Administrative Orders—Eastern District	368
Rules for the Division of Business Among District Judges	374
Chapter 12 Bankruptcy Rules Supplement	385
UNITED STATES BANKRUPTCY COURT, SOUTHERN DISTRICT	405
General Orders	446
UNITED STATES BANKRUPTCY COURT, EASTERN DISTRICT	505
Appendix	534
Selected Orders	534
UNITED STATES DISTRICT COURT, NORTHERN DISTRICT	549
Local Rules of Practice	552
Criminal Procedure	595
Local Rules of Procedure for Admiralty and Maritime Cases	603
Electronic Case Filing	609
Chapter 12 Bankruptcy Rules Supplement	619
UNITED STATES BANKRUPTCY COURT, NORTHERN DISTRICT	621
Appendices	657
Administrative Orders	661
Interim Bankruptcy Rules	684
UNITED STATES DISTRICT COURT, WESTERN DISTRICT	713
Local Rules of Civil Procedure	714

TABLE OF CONTENTS

Page

Local Rules of Criminal Procedure 742
Electronic Case Filing Procedures 750
Appendices 759
Chapter 12 Bankruptcy Rules Supplement 785
UNITED STATES BANKRUPTCY COURT, WESTERN DISTRICT 787
Appendices 804
Electronic Case Filing Procedures 807
Administrative Orders 820
Standing Orders 824
RULES OF PROCEDURE OF THE JUDICIAL PANEL ON MULTIDISTRICT
    LITIGATION 829
FEDERAL COURTS MISCELLANEOUS FEE SCHEDULES 841

FEDERAL RULES OF CIVIL PROCEDURE

Effective September 16, 1938

Including Amendments Effective December 1, 2008, Absent Contrary Congressional Action

---

Research Note

These rules may be searched electronically on Westlaw in the US–RULES database; updates to these rules may be found on Westlaw in US–RULES-UPDATES. For search tips, and a detailed summary of database content, consult the Westlaw Scope Screen of each database.

Table of Rules

TITLE I. SCOPE OF RULES; FORM OF ACTION

Rule
1. Scope and Purpose.
2. One Form of Action.

TITLE II. COMMENCING AN ACTION; SERVICE OF PROCESS, PLEADINGS, MOTIONS, AND ORDERS

3. Commencing an Action.
4. Summons.
4.1 Serving Other Process.
5. Serving and Filing Pleadings and Other Papers.
5.1 Constitutional Challenge to a Statute—Notice, Certification, and Intervention.
5.2 Privacy Protection for Filings Made With the Court.
6. Computing and Extending Time; Time for Motion Papers.

TITLE III. PLEADINGS AND MOTIONS

7. Pleadings Allowed; Form of Motions and Other Papers.
7.1 Disclosure Statement.
8. General Rules of Pleading.
9. Pleading Special Matters.
10. Form of Pleadings.
11. Signing Pleadings, Motions, and Other Papers; Representations to the Court; Sanctions.
12. Defenses and Objections: When and How Presented; Motion for Judgment on The Pleadings; Consolidating Motions; Waiving Defenses; Pretrial Hearing.
13. Counterclaim and Crossclaim.
14. Third–Party Practice.
15. Amended and Supplemental Pleadings.
16. Pretrial Conferences; Scheduling; Management.

TITLE IV. PARTIES

17. Plaintiff and Defendant; Capacity; Public Officers.
18. Joinder of Claims.

Rule
19. Required Joinder of Parties.
20. Permissive Joinder of Parties.
21. Misjoinder and Nonjoinder of Parties.
22. Interpleader.
23. Class Actions.
23.1 Derivative Actions.
23.2 Actions Relating to Unincorporated Associations.
24. Intervention.
25. Substitution of Parties.

TITLE V. DISCLOSURES AND DISCOVERY

26. Duty to Disclose; General Provisions Governing Discovery.
27. Depositions to Perpetuate Testimony.
28. Persons Before Whom Depositions May Be Taken.
29. Stipulations About Discovery Procedure.
30. Depositions By Oral Examination.
31. Depositions By Written Questions.
32. Using Depositions in Court Proceedings.
33. Interrogatories to Parties.
34. Producing Documents, Electronically Stored Information, and Tangible Things, or Entering Onto Land, for Inspection and Other Purposes.
35. Physical and Mental Examinations.
36. Requests for Admission.
37. Failure to Make Disclosures or to Cooperate in Discovery; Sanctions.

TITLE VI. TRIALS

38. Right to a Jury Trial; Demand.
39. Trial By Jury or By the Court.
40. Scheduling Cases for Trial.
41. Dismissal of Actions.
42. Consolidation; Separate Trials.
43. Taking Testimony.
44. Proving an Official Record.
44.1 Determining Foreign Law.

Rule

45. Subpoena.
46. Objecting to a Ruling or Order.
47. Selecting Jurors.
48. Number of Jurors; Verdict.
49. Special Verdict; General Verdict and Questions.
50. Judgment as a Matter of Law in a Jury Trial; Related Motion for a New Trial; Conditional Ruling.
51. Instructions to the Jury; Objections; Preserving a Claim of Error.
52. Findings and Conclusions By the Court; Judgment on Partial Findings.
53. Masters.

TITLE VII. JUDGMENT

54. Judgment; Costs.
55. Default; Default Judgment.
56. Summary Judgment.
57. Declaratory Judgment.
58. Entering Judgment.
59. New Trial; Altering or Amending a Judgment.
60. Relief From a Judgment or Order.
61. Harmless Error.
62. Stay of Proceedings to Enforce a Judgment.
63. Judge's Inability to Proceed.

TITLE VIII. PROVISIONAL AND FINAL REMEDIES

64. Seizing a Person or Property.
65. Injunctions and Restraining Orders.
65.1 Proceedings Against a Surety.
66. Receivers.
67. Deposit into Court.
68. Offer of Judgment.
69. Execution.
70. Enforcing a Judgment for a Specific Act.
71. Enforcing Relief for or Against a Nonparty.

TITLE IX. SPECIAL PROCEEDINGS

71.1. Condemning Real or Personal Property.
72. Magistrate Judges: Pretrial Order.
73. Magistrate Judges: Trial By Consent; Appeal.
74. Method of Appeal From Magistrate Judge to District Judge Under Title 28, U.S.C. § 636(c)(4) and Rule 73(d) [Abrogated].
75. Proceedings on Appeal From Magistrate Judge to District Judge Under Rule 73(d) [Abrogated].
76. Judgment of the District Judge on the Appeal Under Rule 73(d) and Costs [Abrogated].

TITLE X. DISTRICT COURTS AND CLERKS: CONDUCTING BUSINESS; ISSUING ORDERS

77. Conducting Business; Clerk's Authority; Notice of an Order or Judgment.
78. Hearing Motions; Submission on Briefs.
79. Records Kept By the Clerk.
80. Stenographic Transcript as Evidence.

Rule

TITLE XI. GENERAL PROVISIONS

81. Applicability of the Rules in General; Removed Actions.
82. Jurisdiction and Venue Unaffected.
83. Rules By District Courts; Judge's Directives.
84. Forms.
85. Title.
86. Effective Dates.

APPENDIX OF FORMS

Form

1. Caption.
2. Date, Signature, Address, E–Mail Address, and Telephone Number.
3. Summons.
4. Summons on a Third–Party Complaint.
5. Notice of a Lawsuit and Request to Waive Service of a Summons.
6. Waiver of the Service of Summons.
7. Statement of Jurisdiction.
8. Statement of Reasons for Omitting a Party.
9. Statement Noting a Party's Death.
10. Complaint to Recover a Sum Certain.
11. Complaint for Negligence.
12. Complaint for Negligence when the Plaintiff Does Not Know Who Is Responsible.
13. Complaint for Negligence Under the Federal Employers' Liability Act.
14. Complaint for Damages Under the Merchant Marine Act.
15. Complaint for the Conversion of Property.
16. Third–Party Complaint.
17. Complaint for Specific Performance of a Contract to Convey Land.
18. Complaint for Patent Infringement.
19. Complaint for Copyright Infringement and Unfair Competition.
20. Complaint for Interpleader and Declaratory Relief.
21. Complaint On a Claim for a Debt and to Set Aside a Fraudulent Conveyance Under Rule 18(b).
30. Answer Presenting Defenses Under Rule 12(b).
31. Answer to a Complaint for Money Had and Received with a Counterclaim for Interpleader.
40. Motion to Dismiss Under Rule 12(b) for Lack of Jurisdiction, Improper Venue, Insufficient Service of Process, or Failure to State a Claim.
41. Motion to Bring in a Third–Party Defendant.
42. Motion to Intervene as a Defendant Under Rule 24.
50. Request to Produce Documents and Tangible Things, or to Enter Onto Land Under Rule 34.
51. Request for Admissions Under Rule 36.
52. Report of the Parties' Planning Meeting.
60. Notice of Condemnation.
61. Complaint for Condemnation.
70. Judgment on a Jury Verdict.
71. Judgment By the Court Without a Jury.
80. Notice of a Magistrate Judge's Availability.
81. Consent to an Assignment to a Magistrate Judge.
82. Order of Assignment to a Magistrate Judge.

SUPPLEMENTAL RULES FOR ADMIRALTY OR MAR-
ITIME CLAIMS AND ASSET FORFEITURE ACTIONS
Rule
A. Scope of Rules.
B. In Personam Actions; Attachment and Garnishment.
C. In Rem Actions: Special Provisions.

Rule
D. Possessory, Petitory, and Partition Actions.
E. Actions In Rem and Quasi In Rem: General Provisions.
F. Limitation of Liability.
G. Forfeiture Actions In Rem.

INDEX

TITLE I. SCOPE OF RULES; FORM OF ACTION

RULE 1. SCOPE AND PURPOSE

These rules govern the procedure in all civil actions and proceedings in the United States district courts, except as stated in Rule 81. They should be construed and administered to secure the just, speedy, and inexpensive determination of every action and proceeding.

[Amended December 29, 1948, effective October 20, 1949; February 28, 1966, effective July 1, 1966; April 22, 1993, effective December 1, 1993; April 30, 2007, effective December 1, 2007.]

RULE 2. ONE FORM OF ACTION

There is one form of action—the civil action.

[Amended April 30, 2007, effective December 1, 2007.]

TITLE II. COMMENCING AN ACTION; SERVICE OF PROCESS, PLEADINGS, MOTIONS, AND ORDERS

RULE 3. COMMENCING AN ACTION

A civil action is commenced by filing a complaint with the court.

[Amended April 30, 2007, effective December 1, 2007.]

RULE 4. SUMMONS

(a) Contents; Amendments.

(1) *Contents.* A summons must:

  (A) name the court and the parties;

  (B) be directed to the defendant;

  (C) state the name and address of the plaintiff's attorney or—if unrepresented—of the plaintiff;

  (D) state the time within which the defendant must appear and defend;

  (E) notify the defendant that a failure to appear and defend will result in a default judgment against the defendant for the relief demanded in the complaint;

  (F) be signed by the clerk; and

  (G) bear the court's seal.

(2) *Amendments.* The court may permit a summons to be amended.

(b) Issuance. On or after filing the complaint, the plaintiff may present a summons to the clerk for signature and seal. If the summons is properly completed, the clerk must sign, seal, and issue it to the plaintiff for service on the defendant. A summons—or a copy of a summons that is addressed to multiple defendants—must be issued for each defendant to be served.

(c) Service.

(1) *In General.* A summons must be served with a copy of the complaint. The plaintiff is responsible for having the summons and complaint served within the time allowed by Rule 4(m) and must furnish the necessary copies to the person who makes service.

(2) *By Whom.* Any person who is at least 18 years old and not a party may serve a summons and complaint.

(3) *By a Marshal or Someone Specially Appointed.* At the plaintiff's request, the court may order that service be made by a United States marshal or deputy marshal or by a person specially appointed by the court. The court must so order if the plaintiff is authorized to proceed in forma pauperis under 28 U.S.C. § 1915 or as a seaman under 28 U.S.C. § 1916.

(d) Waiving Service.

(1) *Requesting a Waiver.* An individual, corporation, or association that is subject to service under Rule 4(e), (f), or (h) has a duty to avoid unnecessary expenses of serving the summons. The plaintiff may notify such a defendant that an action has been commenced and request that the defendant waive service of a summons. The notice and request must:

(A) be in writing and be addressed:

(i) to the individual defendant; or

(ii) for a defendant subject to service under Rule 4(h), to an officer, a managing or general agent, or any other agent authorized by appointment or by law to receive service of process;

(B) name the court where the complaint was filed;

(C) be accompanied by a copy of the complaint, two copies of a waiver form, and a prepaid means for returning the form;

(D) inform the defendant, using text prescribed in Form 5, of the consequences of waiving and not waiving service;

(E) state the date when the request is sent;

(F) give the defendant a reasonable time of at least 30 days after the request was sent—or at least 60 days if sent to the defendant outside any judicial district of the United States—to return the waiver; and

(G) be sent by first-class mail or other reliable means.

(2) *Failure to Waive.* If a defendant located within the United States fails, without good cause, to sign and return a waiver requested by a plaintiff located within the United States, the court must impose on the defendant:

(A) the expenses later incurred in making service; and

(B) the reasonable expenses, including attorney's fees, of any motion required to collect those service expenses.

(3) *Time to Answer After a Waiver.* A defendant who, before being served with process, timely returns a waiver need not serve an answer to the complaint until 60 days after the request was sent—or until 90 days after it was sent to the defendant outside any judicial district of the United States.

(4) *Results of Filing a Waiver.* When the plaintiff files a waiver, proof of service is not required and these rules apply as if a summons and complaint had been served at the time of filing the waiver.

(5) *Jurisdiction and Venue Not Waived.* Waiving service of a summons does not waive any objection to personal jurisdiction or to venue.

(e) Serving an Individual Within a Judicial District of the United States. Unless federal law provides otherwise, an individual—other than a minor, an incompetent person, or a person whose waiver has been filed—may be served in a judicial district of the United States by:

(1) following state law for serving a summons in an action brought in courts of general jurisdiction in the state where the district court is located or where service is made; or

(2) doing any of the following:

(A) delivering a copy of the summons and of the complaint to the individual personally;

(B) leaving a copy of each at the individual's dwelling or usual place of abode with someone of suitable age and discretion who resides there; or

(C) delivering a copy of each to an agent authorized by appointment or by law to receive service of process.

(f) Serving an Individual in a Foreign Country. Unless federal law provides otherwise, an individual—other than a minor, an incompetent person, or a person whose waiver has been filed—may be served at a place not within any judicial district of the United States:

(1) by any internationally agreed means of service that is reasonably calculated to give notice, such as those authorized by the Hague Convention on the Service Abroad of Judicial and Extrajudicial Documents;

(2) if there is no internationally agreed means, or if an international agreement allows but does not specify other means, by a method that is reasonably calculated to give notice:

(A) as prescribed by the foreign country's law for service in that country in an action in its courts of general jurisdiction;

(B) as the foreign authority directs in response to a letter rogatory or letter of request; or

(C) unless prohibited by the foreign country's law, by:

(i) delivering a copy of the summons and of the complaint to the individual personally; or

(ii) using any form of mail that the clerk addresses and sends to the individual and that requires a signed receipt; or

(3) by other means not prohibited by international agreement, as the court orders.

(g) Serving a Minor or an Incompetent Person. A minor or an incompetent person in a judicial district of the United States must be served by following state law for serving a summons or like process on such a defendant in an action brought in the courts of general jurisdiction of the state where service is made. A minor or an incompetent person who is not within any judicial district of the United States must be served in the manner prescribed by Rule 4(f)(2)(A), (f)(2)(B), or (f)(3).

(h) Serving a Corporation, Partnership, or Association. Unless federal law provides otherwise or the defendant's waiver has been filed, a domestic or foreign corporation, or a partnership or other unincorporated association that is subject to suit under a common name, must be served:

(1) in a judicial district of the United States:

(A) in the manner prescribed by Rule 4(e)(1) for serving an individual; or

(B) by delivering a copy of the summons and of the complaint to an officer, a managing or general agent, or any other agent authorized by appointment or by law to receive service of process and—if the agent is one authorized by statute and the statute so requires—by also mailing a copy of each to the defendant; or

(2) at a place not within any judicial district of the United States, in any manner prescribed by Rule 4(f) for serving an individual, except personal delivery under (f)(2)(C)(i).

(i) Serving the United States and Its Agencies, Corporations, Officers, or Employees.

(1) *United States.* To serve the United States, a party must:

(A)(i) deliver a copy of the summons and of the complaint to the United States attorney for the district where the action is brought—or to an assistant United States attorney or clerical employee whom the United States attorney designates in a writing filed with the court clerk—or

(ii) send a copy of each by registered or certified mail to the civil-process clerk at the United States attorney's office;

(B) send a copy of each by registered or certified mail to the Attorney General of the United States at Washington, D.C.; and

(C) if the action challenges an order of a nonparty agency or officer of the United States, send a copy of each by registered or certified mail to the agency or officer.

(2) *Agency; Corporation; Officer or Employee Sued in an Official Capacity.* To serve a United States agency or corporation, or a United States officer or employee sued only in an official capacity, a party must serve the United States and also send a copy of the summons and of the complaint by registered or certified mail to the agency, corporation, officer, or employee.

(3) *Officer or Employee Sued Individually.* To serve a United States officer or employee sued in an individual capacity for an act or omission occurring in connection with duties performed on the United States' behalf (whether or not the officer or employee is also sued in an official capacity), a party must serve the United States and also serve the officer or employee under Rule 4(e), (f), or (g).

(4) *Extending Time.* The court must allow a party a reasonable time to cure its failure to:

(A) serve a person required to be served under Rule 4(i)(2), if the party has served either the United States attorney or the Attorney General of the United States; or

(B) serve the United States under Rule 4(i)(3), if the party has served the United States officer or employee.

(j) Serving a Foreign, State, or Local Government.

(1) *Foreign State.* A foreign state or its political subdivision, agency, or instrumentality must be served in accordance with 28 U.S.C. § 1608.

(2) *State or Local Government.* A state, a municipal corporation, or any other state-created governmental organization that is subject to suit must be served by:

(A) delivering a copy of the summons and of the complaint to its chief executive officer; or

(B) serving a copy of each in the manner prescribed by that state's law for serving a summons or like process on such a defendant.

(k) Territorial Limits of Effective Service.

(1) *In General.* Serving a summons or filing a waiver of service establishes personal jurisdiction over a defendant:

(A) who is subject to the jurisdiction of a court of general jurisdiction in the state where the district court is located;

(B) who is a party joined under Rule 14 or 19 and is served within a judicial district of the United States and not more than 100 miles from where the summons was issued; or

(C) when authorized by a federal statute.

(2) *Federal Claim Outside State–Court Jurisdiction.* For a claim that arises under federal law, serving a summons or filing a waiver of service establishes personal jurisdiction over a defendant if:

(A) the defendant is not subject to jurisdiction in any state's courts of general jurisdiction; and

(B) exercising jurisdiction is consistent with the United States Constitution and laws.

(l) Proving Service.

(1) *Affidavit Required.* Unless service is waived, proof of service must be made to the court. Except for service by a United States marshal or deputy marshal, proof must be by the server's affidavit.

(2) *Service Outside the United States.* Service not within any judicial district of the United States must be proved as follows:

(A) if made under Rule 4(f)(1), as provided in the applicable treaty or convention; or

(B) if made under Rule 4(f)(2) or (f)(3), by a receipt signed by the addressee, or by other evidence satisfying the court that the summons and complaint were delivered to the addressee.

(3) *Validity of Service; Amending Proof.* Failure to prove service does not affect the validity of service. The court may permit proof of service to be amended.

(m) Time Limit for Service. If a defendant is not served within 120 days after the complaint is filed, the court—on motion or on its own after notice to the plaintiff—must dismiss the action without prejudice against that defendant or order that service be made within a specified time. But if the plaintiff shows good cause for the failure, the court must extend the time for service for an appropriate period. This subdivision (m) does not apply to service in a foreign country under Rule 4(f) or 4(j)(1).

(n) Asserting Jurisdiction over Property or Assets.

(1) *Federal Law.* The court may assert jurisdiction over property if authorized by a federal statute. Notice to claimants of the property must be given as provided in the statute or by serving a summons under this rule.

(2) *State Law.* On a showing that personal jurisdiction over a defendant cannot be obtained in the district where the action is brought by reasonable efforts to serve a summons under this rule, the court may assert jurisdiction over the defendant's assets found in the district. Jurisdiction is acquired by seizing the assets under the circumstances and in the manner provided by state law in that district.

[Amended January 21, 1963, effective July 1, 1963; February 28, 1966, effective July 1, 1966; April 29, 1980, effective August 1, 1980; amended by Pub.L. 97-462, § 2, January 12, 1983, 96 Stat. 2527, effective 45 days after January 12, 1983; amended March 2, 1987, effective August 1, 1987; April 22, 1993, effective December 1, 1993; April 17, 2000, effective December 1, 2000; April 30, 2007, effective December 1, 2007.]

RULE 4.1   SERVING OTHER PROCESS

(a) In General. Process—other than a summons under Rule 4 or a subpoena under Rule 45—must be served by a United States marshal or deputy marshal or by a person specially appointed for that purpose. It may be served anywhere within the territorial limits of the state where the district court is located and, if authorized by a federal statute, beyond those limits. Proof of service must be made under Rule 4(*l*).

(b) Enforcing Orders: Committing for Civil Contempt. An order committing a person for civil contempt of a decree or injunction issued to enforce federal law may be served and enforced in any district. Any other order in a civil-contempt proceeding may be served only in the state where the issuing court is located or elsewhere in the United States within 100 miles from where the order was issued.

[Adopted April 22, 1993, effective December 1, 1993; amended April 30, 2007, effective December 1, 2007.]

RULE 5.   SERVING AND FILING PLEADINGS AND OTHER PAPERS

(a) Service: When Required.

(1) *In General.* Unless these rules provide otherwise, each of the following papers must be served on every party:

(A) an order stating that service is required;

(B) a pleading filed after the original complaint, unless the court orders otherwise under Rule 5(c) because there are numerous defendants;

(C) a discovery paper required to be served on a party, unless the court orders otherwise;

(D) a written motion, except one that may be heard ex parte; and

(E) a written notice, appearance, demand, or offer of judgment, or any similar paper.

(2) *If a Party Fails to Appear.* No service is required on a party who is in default for failing to appear. But a pleading that asserts a new claim for relief against such a party must be served on that party under Rule 4.

(3) *Seizing Property.* If an action is begun by seizing property and no person is or need be named as a defendant, any service required before the filing of an appearance, answer, or claim must be made on the person who had custody or possession of the property when it was seized.

(b) Service: How Made.

(1) *Serving an Attorney.* If a party is represented by an attorney, service under this rule must be made on the attorney unless the court orders service on the party.

(2) *Service in General.* A paper is served under this rule by:

(A) handing it to the person;

(B) leaving it:

(i) at the person's office with a clerk or other person in charge or, if no one is in charge, in a conspicuous place in the office; or

(ii) if the person has no office or the office is closed, at the person's dwelling or usual place of abode with someone of suitable age and discretion who resides there;

(C) mailing it to the person's last known address—in which event service is complete upon mailing;

(D) leaving it with the court clerk if the person has no known address;

(E) sending it by electronic means if the person consented in writing—in which event service is complete upon transmission, but is not effective if the serving party learns that it did not reach the person to be served; or

(F) delivering it by any other means that the person consented to in writing—in which event service is complete when the person making service delivers it to the agency designated to make delivery.

(3) *Using Court Facilities.* If a local rule so authorizes, a party may use the court's transmission facilities to make service under Rule 5(b)(2)(E).

(c) Serving Numerous Defendants.

(1) *In General.* If an action involves an unusually large number of defendants, the court may, on motion or on its own, order that:

(A) defendants' pleadings and replies to them need not be served on other defendants;

(B) any crossclaim, counterclaim, avoidance, or affirmative defense in those pleadings and replies to them will be treated as denied or avoided by all other parties; and

(C) filing any such pleading and serving it on the plaintiff constitutes notice of the pleading to all parties.

(2) *Notifying Parties.* A copy of every such order must be served on the parties as the court directs.

(d) Filing.

(1) *Required Filings; Certificate of Service.* Any paper after the complaint that is required to be served—together with a certificate of service—must be filed within a reasonable time after service. But disclosures under Rule 26(a)(1) or (2) and the following discovery requests and responses must not be filed until they are used in the proceeding or the court orders filing: depositions, interrogatories, requests for documents or tangible things or to permit entry onto land, and requests for admission.

(2) *How Filing Is Made—In General.* A paper is filed by delivering it:

(A) to the clerk; or

(B) to a judge who agrees to accept it for filing, and who must then note the filing date on the paper and promptly send it to the clerk.

(3) *Electronic Filing, Signing, or Verification.* A court may, by local rule, allow papers to be filed, signed, or verified by electronic means that are consistent with any technical standards established by the Judicial Conference of the United States. A local rule may require electronic filing only if reasonable exceptions are allowed. A paper filed electronically in compliance with a local rule is a written paper for purposes of these rules.

(4) *Acceptance by the Clerk.* The clerk must not refuse to file a paper solely because it is not in the form prescribed by these rules or by a local rule or practice.

[Amended January 21, 1963, effective July 1, 1963; March 30, 1970, effective July 1, 1970; April 29, 1980, effective August 1, 1980; March 2, 1987, effective August 1, 1987; April 30, 1991, effective December 1, 1991; April 22, 1993, effective December 1, 1993; April 23, 1996, effective December 1, 1996; April 17, 2000, effective December 1, 2000; April 23, 2001, effective December 1, 2001; April 12, 2006, effective December 1, 2006; April 30, 2007, effective December 1, 2007.]

RULE 5.1 CONSTITUTIONAL CHALLENGE TO A STATUTE—NOTICE, CERTIFICATION, AND INTERVENTION

(a) Notice by a Party. A party that files a pleading, written motion, or other paper drawing into question the constitutionality of a federal or state statute must promptly:

(1) file a notice of constitutional question stating the question and identifying the paper that raises it, if:

(A) a federal statute is questioned and the parties do not include the United States, one of its agencies, or one of its officers or employees in an official capacity; or

(B) a state statute is questioned and the parties do not include the state, one of its agencies, or one of its officers or employees in an official capacity; and

(2) serve the notice and paper on the Attorney General of the United States if a federal statute is questioned—or on the state attorney general if a state statute is questioned—either by certified or registered mail or by sending it to an electronic address designated by the attorney general for this purpose.

(b) Certification by the Court. The court must, under 28 U.S.C. § 2403, certify to the appropriate attorney general that a statute has been questioned.

(c) Intervention; Final Decision on the Merits. Unless the court sets a later time, the attorney general may intervene within 60 days after the notice is filed or after the court certifies the challenge, whichever is earlier. Before the time to intervene expires, the court may reject the constitutional challenge, but may not enter a final judgment holding the statute unconstitutional.

(d) No Forfeiture. A party's failure to file and serve the notice, or the court's failure to certify, does not forfeit a constitutional claim or defense that is otherwise timely asserted.

[Effective December 1, 2006; amended April 30, 2007, effective December 1, 2007.]

RULE 5.2 PRIVACY PROTECTION FOR FILINGS MADE WITH THE COURT

(a) Redacted Filings. Unless the court orders otherwise, in an electronic or paper filing with the court that contains an individual's social-security number, taxpayer-identification number, or birth date, the name of an individual known to be a minor, or a financial-account number, a party or nonparty making the filing may include only:

(1) the last four digits of the social-security number and taxpayer-identification number;

(2) the year of the individual's birth;

(3) the minor's initials; and

(4) the last four digits of the financial-account number.

(b) Exemptions from the Redaction Requirement. The redaction requirement does not apply to the following:

(1) a financial-account number that identifies the property allegedly subject to forfeiture in a forfeiture proceeding;

(2) the record of an administrative or agency proceeding;

(3) the official record of a state-court proceeding;

(4) the record of a court or tribunal, if that record was not subject to the redaction requirement when originally filed;

(5) a filing covered by Rule 5.2(c) or (d); and

(6) a pro se filing in an action brought under 28 U.S.C. §§ 2241, 2254, or 2255.

(c) Limitations on Remote Access to Electronic Files; Social–Security Appeals and Immigration Cases. Unless the court orders otherwise, in an action for benefits under the Social Security Act, and in an action or proceeding relating to an order of removal, to relief from removal, or to immigration benefits or detention, access to an electronic file is authorized as follows:

(1) the parties and their attorneys may have remote electronic access to any part of the case file, including the administrative record;

(2) any other person may have electronic access to the full record at the courthouse, but may have remote electronic access only to:

(A) the docket maintained by the court; and

(B) an opinion, order, judgment, or other disposition of the court, but not any other part of the case file or the administrative record.

(d) Filings Made Under Seal. The court may order that a filing be made under seal without redaction. The court may later unseal the filing or order the person who made the filing to file a redacted version for the public record.

(e) Protective Orders. For good cause, the court may by order in a case:

(1) require redaction of additional information; or

(2) limit or prohibit a nonparty's remote electronic access to a document filed with the court.

(f) Option for Additional Unredacted Filing Under Seal. A person making a redacted filing may also file an unredacted copy under seal. The court must retain the unredacted copy as part of the record.

(g) Option for Filing a Reference List. A filing that contains redacted information may be filed together with a reference list that identifies each item of redacted information and specifies an appropriate identifier that uniquely corresponds to each item listed. The list must be filed under seal and may be amended as of right. Any reference in the case to a listed identifier will be construed to refer to the corresponding item of information.

(h) Waiver of Protection of Identifiers. A person waives the protection of Rule 5.2(a) as to the person's own information by filing it without redaction and not under seal.

[Adopted April 30, 2007, effective December 1, 2007.]

RULE 6. COMPUTING AND EXTENDING TIME; TIME FOR MOTION PAPERS

(a) Computing Time. The following rules apply in computing any time period specified in these rules or in any local rule, court order, or statute:

(1) *Day of the Event Excluded.* Exclude the day of the act, event, or default that begins the period.

(2) *Exclusions from Brief Periods.* Exclude intermediate Saturdays, Sundays, and legal holidays when the period is less than 11 days.

(3) *Last Day.* Include the last day of the period unless it is a Saturday, Sunday, legal holiday, or—if the act to be done is filing a paper in court—a day on which weather or other conditions make the clerk's office inaccessible. When the last day is excluded, the period runs until the end of the next day that is not a Saturday, Sunday, legal holiday, or day when the clerk's office is inaccessible.

(4) *"Legal Holiday" Defined.* As used in these rules, "legal holiday" means:

(A) the day set aside by statute for observing New Year's Day, Martin Luther King Jr.'s Birthday, Washington's Birthday, Memorial Day, Independence Day, Labor Day, Columbus Day, Veterans' Day, Thanksgiving Day, or Christmas Day; and

(B) any other day declared a holiday by the President, Congress, or the state where the district court is located.

(b) Extending Time.

(1) *In General.* When an act may or must be done within a specified time, the court may, for good cause, extend the time:

(A) with or without motion or notice if the court acts, or if a request is made, before the original time or its extension expires; or

(B) on motion made after the time has expired if the party failed to act because of excusable neglect.

(2) *Exceptions.* A court must not extend the time to act under Rules 50(b) and (d), 52(b), 59(b), (d), and (e), and 60(b), except as those rules allow.

(c) Motions, Notices of Hearing, and Affidavits.

(1) *In General.* A written motion and notice of the hearing must be served at least 5 days before the time specified for the hearing, with the following exceptions:

    (A) when the motion may be heard ex parte;

    (B) when these rules set a different time; or

    (C) when a court order—which a party may, for good cause, apply for ex parte—sets a different time.

(2) *Supporting Affidavit.* Any affidavit supporting a motion must be served with the motion. Except as Rule 59(c) provides otherwise, any opposing affidavit must be served at least 1 day before the hearing, unless the court permits service at another time.

(d) Additional Time After Certain Kinds of Service. When a party may or must act within a specified time after service and service is made under Rule 5(b)(2)(C), (D), (E), or (F), 3 days are added after the period would otherwise expire under Rule 6(a).

[Amended December 27, 1946, effective March 19, 1948; January 21, 1963, effective July 1, 1963; February 28, 1966, effective July 1, 1966; December 4, 1967, effective July 1, 1968; March 1, 1971, effective July 1, 1971; April 28, 1983, effective August 1, 1983; April 29, 1985, effective August 1, 1985; March 2, 1987, effective August 1, 1987; April 29, 1999, effective December 1, 1999; April 23, 2001, effective December 1, 2001; April 25, 2005, effective December 1, 2005; April 30, 2007, effective December 1, 2007.]

TITLE III. PLEADINGS AND MOTIONS

RULE 7. PLEADINGS ALLOWED; FORM OF MOTIONS AND OTHER PAPERS

(a) Pleadings. Only these pleadings are allowed:

(1) a complaint;

(2) an answer to a complaint;

(3) an answer to a counterclaim designated as a counterclaim;

(4) an answer to a crossclaim;

(5) a third-party complaint;

(6) an answer to a third-party complaint; and

(7) if the court orders one, a reply to an answer.

(b) Motions and Other Papers.

(1) *In General.* A request for a court order must be made by motion. The motion must:

    (A) be in writing unless made during a hearing or trial;

    (B) state with particularity the grounds for seeking the order; and

    (C) state the relief sought.

(2) *Form.* The rules governing captions and other matters of form in pleadings apply to motions and other papers.

[Amended December 27, 1946, effective March 19, 1948; January 21, 1963, effective July 1, 1963; April 28, 1983, effective August 1, 1983; April 30, 2007, effective December 1, 2007.]

RULE 7.1 DISCLOSURE STATEMENT

(a) Who Must File; Contents. A nongovernmental corporate party must file two copies of a disclosure statement that:

(1) identifies any parent corporation and any publicly held corporation owning 10% or more of its stock; or

(2) states that there is no such corporation.

(b) Time to File; Supplemental Filing. A party must:

(1) file the disclosure statement with its first appearance, pleading, petition, motion, response, or other request addressed to the court; and

(2) promptly file a supplemental statement if any required information changes.

[Adopted April 29, 2002, effective December 1, 2002; April 30, 2007, effective December 1, 2007.]

RULE 8. GENERAL RULES OF PLEADING

(a) Claim for Relief. A pleading that states a claim for relief must contain:

(1) a short and plain statement of the grounds for the court's jurisdiction, unless the court already has jurisdiction and the claim needs no new jurisdictional support;

(2) a short and plain statement of the claim showing that the pleader is entitled to relief; and

(3) a demand for the relief sought, which may include relief in the alternative or different types of relief.

(b) Defenses; Admissions and Denials.

(1) *In General.* In responding to a pleading, a party must:

    (A) state in short and plain terms its defenses to each claim asserted against it; and

    (B) admit or deny the allegations asserted against it by an opposing party.

(2) *Denials—Responding to the Substance.* A denial must fairly respond to the substance of the allegation.

(3) *General and Specific Denials.* A party that intends in good faith to deny all the allegations of

pleading—including the jurisdictional grounds—may do so by a general denial. A party that does not intend to deny all the allegations must either specifically deny designated allegations or generally deny all except those specifically admitted.

(4) *Denying Part of an Allegation.* A party that intends in good faith to deny only part of an allegation must admit the part that is true and deny the rest.

(5) *Lacking Knowledge or Information.* A party that lacks knowledge or information sufficient to form a belief about the truth of an allegation must so state, and the statement has the effect of a denial.

(6) *Effect of Failing to Deny.* An allegation—other than one relating to the amount of damages—is admitted if a responsive pleading is required and the allegation is not denied. If a responsive pleading is not required, an allegation is considered denied or avoided.

(c) Affirmative Defenses.

(1) *In General.* In responding to a pleading, a party must affirmatively state any avoidance or affirmative defense, including:

- accord and satisfaction;
- arbitration and award;
- assumption of risk;
- contributory negligence;
- discharge in bankruptcy;
- duress;
- estoppel;
- failure of consideration;
- fraud;
- illegality;
- injury by fellow servant;
- laches;
- license;
- payment;
- release;
- res judicata;
- statute of frauds;
- statute of limitations; and
- waiver.

(2) *Mistaken Designation.* If a party mistakenly designates a defense as a counterclaim, or a counterclaim as a defense, the court must, if justice requires, treat the pleading as though it were correctly designated, and may impose terms for doing so.

(d) Pleading to Be Concise and Direct; Alternative Statements; Inconsistency.

(1) *In General.* Each allegation must be simple, concise, and direct. No technical form is required.

(2) *Alternative Statements of a Claim or Defense.* A party may set out 2 or more statements of a claim or defense alternatively or hypothetically, either in a single count or defense or in separate ones. If a party makes alternative statements, the pleading is sufficient if any one of them is sufficient.

(3) *Inconsistent Claims or Defenses.* A party may state as many separate claims or defenses as it has, regardless of consistency.

(e) Construing Pleadings. Pleadings must be construed so as to do justice.

[Amended February 28, 1966, effective July 1, 1966; March 2, 1987, effective August 1, 1987; April 30, 2007, effective December 1, 2007.]

RULE 9.   PLEADING SPECIAL MATTERS

(a) Capacity or Authority to Sue; Legal Existence.

(1) *In General.* Except when required to show that the court has jurisdiction, a pleading need not allege:

(A) a party's capacity to sue or be sued;

(B) a party's authority to sue or be sued in a representative capacity; or

(C) the legal existence of an organized association of persons that is made a party.

(2) *Raising Those Issues.* To raise any of those issues, a party must do so by a specific denial, which must state any supporting facts that are peculiarly within the party's knowledge.

(b) Fraud or Mistake; Conditions of Mind. In alleging fraud or mistake, a party must state with particularity the circumstances constituting fraud or mistake. Malice, intent, knowledge, and other conditions of a person's mind may be alleged generally.

(c) Conditions Precedent. In pleading conditions precedent, it suffices to allege generally that all conditions precedent have occurred or been performed. But when denying that a condition precedent has occurred or been performed, a party must do so with particularity.

(d) Official Document or Act. In pleading an official document or official act, it suffices to allege that the document was legally issued or the act legally done.

(e) Judgment. In pleading a judgment or decision of a domestic or foreign court, a judicial or quasi-judicial tribunal, or a board or officer, it suffices to plead the judgment or decision without showing jurisdiction to render it.

(f) Time and Place. An allegation of time or place is material when testing the sufficiency of a pleading.

(g) Special Damages. If an item of special damage is claimed, it must be specifically stated.

(h) Admiralty or Maritime Claim.

(1) *How Designated.* If a claim for relief is within the admiralty or maritime jurisdiction and also within the court's subject-matter jurisdiction on some other ground, the pleading may designate the claim as an admiralty or maritime claim for purposes of Rules 14(c), 38(e), and 82 and the Supplemental Rules for Admiralty or Maritime Claims and Asset Forfeiture Actions. A claim cognizable only in the admiralty or maritime jurisdiction is an admiralty or maritime claim for those purposes, whether or not so designated.

(2) *Designation for Appeal.* A case that includes an admiralty or maritime claim within this subdivision (h) is an admiralty case within 28 U.S.C. § 1292(a)(3).

[Amended February 28, 1966, effective July 1, 1966; December 4, 1967, effective July 1, 1968; March 30, 1970, effective July 1, 1970; March 2, 1987, effective August 1, 1987; April 11, 1997, effective December 1, 1997; April 12, 2006, effective December 1, 2006; April 30, 2007, effective December 1, 2007.]

RULE 10.   FORM OF PLEADINGS

(a) Caption; Names of Parties. Every pleading must have a caption with the court's name, a title, a file number, and a Rule 7(a) designation. The title of the complaint must name all the parties; the title of other pleadings, after naming the first party on each side, may refer generally to other parties.

(b) Paragraphs; Separate Statements. A party must state its claims or defenses in numbered paragraphs, each limited as far as practicable to a single set of circumstances. A later pleading may refer by number to a paragraph in an earlier pleading. If doing so would promote clarity, each claim founded on a separate transaction or occurrence—and each defense other than a denial—must be stated in a separate count or defense.

(c) Adoption by Reference; Exhibits. A statement in a pleading may be adopted by reference elsewhere in the same pleading or in any other pleading or motion. A copy of a written instrument that is an exhibit to a pleading is a part of the pleading for all purposes.

[Amended April 30, 2007, effective December 1, 2007.]

RULE 11. SIGNING PLEADINGS, MOTIONS, AND OTHER PAPERS; REPRESENTATIONS TO THE COURT; SANCTIONS

(a) Signature. Every pleading, written motion, and other paper must be signed by at least one attorney of record in the attorney's name—or by a party personally if the party is unrepresented. The paper must state the signer's address, e-mail address, and telephone number. Unless a rule or statute specifically states otherwise, a pleading need not be verified or accompanied by an affidavit. The court must strike an unsigned paper unless the omission is promptly corrected after being called to the attorney's or party's attention.

(b) Representations to the Court. By presenting to the court a pleading, written motion, or other paper—whether by signing, filing, submitting, or later advocating it—an attorney or unrepresented party certifies that to the best of the person's knowledge, information, and belief, formed after an inquiry reasonable under the circumstances:

(1) it is not being presented for any improper purpose, such as to harass, cause unnecessary delay, or needlessly increase the cost of litigation;

(2) the claims, defenses, and other legal contentions are warranted by existing law or by a nonfrivolous argument for extending, modifying, or reversing existing law or for establishing new law;

(3) the factual contentions have evidentiary support or, if specifically so identified, will likely have evidentiary support after a reasonable opportunity for further investigation or discovery; and

(4) the denials of factual contentions are warranted on the evidence or, if specifically so identified, are reasonably based on belief or a lack of information.

(c) Sanctions.

(1) *In General.* If, after notice and a reasonable opportunity to respond, the court determines that Rule 11(b) has been violated, the court may impose an appropriate sanction on any attorney, law firm, or party that violated the rule or is responsible for the violation. Absent exceptional circumstances, a law firm must be held jointly responsible for a violation committed by its partner, associate, or employee.

(2) *Motion for Sanctions.* A motion for sanctions must be made separately from any other motion and must describe the specific conduct that allegedly violates Rule 11(b). The motion must be served under Rule 5, but it must not be filed or be presented to the court if the challenged paper, claim, defense, contention, or denial is withdrawn or appropriately corrected within 21 days after service or within another time the court sets. If warranted, the court may award to the prevailing party the reasonable expenses, including attorney's fees, incurred for the motion.

(3) *On the Court's Initiative.* On its own, the court may order an attorney, law firm, or party to show cause why conduct specifically described in the order has not violated Rule 11(b).

(4) *Nature of a Sanction.* A sanction imposed under this rule must be limited to what suffices to deter repetition of the conduct or comparable conduct by others similarly situated. The sanction may include nonmonetary directives; an order to pay a penalty into court; or, if imposed on motion and warranted for

effective deterrence, an order directing payment to the movant of part or all of the reasonable attorney's fees and other expenses directly resulting from the violation.

(5) *Limitations on Monetary Sanctions.* The court must not impose a monetary sanction:

(A) against a represented party for violating Rule 11(b)(2); or

(B) on its own, unless it issued the show-cause order under Rule 11(c)(3) before voluntary dismissal or settlement of the claims made by or against the party that is, or whose attorneys are, to be sanctioned.

(6) *Requirements for an Order.* An order imposing a sanction must describe the sanctioned conduct and explain the basis for the sanction.

(d) Inapplicability to Discovery. This rule does not apply to disclosures and discovery requests, responses, objections, and motions under Rules 26 through 37.

[Amended April 28, 1983, effective August 1, 1983; March 2, 1987, effective August 1, 1987; April 22, 1993, effective December 1, 1993; April 30, 2007, effective December 1, 2007.]

RULE 12. DEFENSES AND OBJECTIONS: WHEN AND HOW PRESENTED; MOTION FOR JUDGMENT ON THE PLEADINGS; CONSOLIDATING MOTIONS; WAIVING DEFENSES; PRETRIAL HEARING

(a) Time to Serve a Responsive Pleading.

(1) *In General.* Unless another time is specified by this rule or a federal statute, the time for serving a responsive pleading is as follows:

(A) A defendant must serve an answer:

(i) within 20 days after being served with the summons and complaint; or

(ii) if it has timely waived service under Rule 4(d), within 60 days after the request for a waiver was sent, or within 90 days after it was sent to the defendant outside any judicial district of the United States.

(B) A party must serve an answer to a counterclaim or crossclaim within 20 days after being served with the pleading that states the counterclaim or crossclaim.

(C) A party must serve a reply to an answer within 20 days after being served with an order to reply, unless the order specifies a different time.

(2) *United States and Its Agencies, Officers, or Employees Sued in an Official Capacity.* The United States, a United States agency, or a United States officer or employee sued only in an official capacity must serve an answer to a complaint, counterclaim, or crossclaim within 60 days after service on the United States attorney.

(3) *United States Officers or Employees Sued in an Individual Capacity.* A United States officer or employee sued in an individual capacity for an act or omission occurring in connection with duties performed on the United States' behalf must serve an answer to a complaint, counterclaim, or crossclaim within 60 days after service on the officer or employee or service on the United States attorney, whichever is later.

(4) *Effect of a Motion.* Unless the court sets a different time, serving a motion under this rule alters these periods as follows:

(A) if the court denies the motion or postpones its disposition until trial, the responsive pleading must be served within 10 days after notice of the court's action; or

(B) if the court grants a motion for a more definite statement, the responsive pleading must be served within 10 days after the more definite statement is served.

(b) How to Present Defenses. Every defense to a claim for relief in any pleading must be asserted in the responsive pleading if one is required. But a party may assert the following defenses by motion:

(1) lack of subject-matter jurisdiction;

(2) lack of personal jurisdiction;

(3) improper venue;

(4) insufficient process;

(5) insufficient service of process;

(6) failure to state a claim upon which relief can be granted; and

(7) failure to join a party under Rule 19.

A motion asserting any of these defenses must be made before pleading if a responsive pleading is allowed. If a pleading sets out a claim for relief that does not require a responsive pleading, an opposing party may assert at trial any defense to that claim. No defense or objection is waived by joining it with one or more other defenses or objections in a responsive pleading or in a motion.

(c) Motion for Judgment on the Pleadings. After the pleadings are closed—but early enough not to delay trial—a party may move for judgment on the pleadings.

(d) Result of Presenting Matters Outside the Pleadings. If, on a motion under Rule 12(b)(6) or 12(c), matters outside the pleadings are presented to and not excluded by the court, the motion must be treated as one for summary judgment under Rule 56. All parties must be given a reasonable opportunity to present all the material that is pertinent to the motion.

(e) Motion for a More Definite Statement. A party may move for a more definite statement of a pleading to which a responsive pleading is allowed but which is so vague or ambiguous that the party cannot reasonably prepare a response. The motion must be made before filing a responsive pleading and must point out the defects complained of and the details desired. If the court orders a more definite statement and the order is not obeyed within 10 days after notice of the order or within the time the court sets, the court may strike the pleading or issue any other appropriate order.

(f) Motion to Strike. The court may strike from a pleading an insufficient defense or any redundant, immaterial, impertinent, or scandalous matter. The court may act:

(1) on its own; or

(2) on motion made by a party either before responding to the pleading or, if a response is not allowed, within 20 days after being served with the pleading.

(g) Joining Motions.

(1) *Right to Join.* A motion under this rule may be joined with any other motion allowed by this rule.

(2) *Limitation on Further Motions.* Except as provided in Rule 12(h)(2) or (3), a party that makes a motion under this rule must not make another motion under this rule raising a defense or objection that was available to the party but omitted from its earlier motion.

(h) Waiving and Preserving Certain Defenses.

(1) *When Some Are Waived.* A party waives any defense listed in Rule 12(b)(2)-(5) by:

(A) omitting it from a motion in the circumstances described in Rule 12(g)(2); or

(B) failing to either:

(i) make it by motion under this rule; or

(ii) include it in a responsive pleading or in an amendment allowed by Rule 15(a)(1) as a matter of course.

(2) *When to Raise Others.* Failure to state a claim upon which relief can be granted, to join a person required by Rule 19(b), or to state a legal defense to a claim may be raised:

(A) in any pleading allowed or ordered under Rule 7(a);

(B) by a motion under Rule 12(c); or

(C) at trial.

(3) *Lack of Subject–Matter Jurisdiction.* If the court determines at any time that it lacks subject-matter jurisdiction, the court must dismiss the action.

(i) Hearing Before Trial. If a party so moves, any defense listed in Rule 12(b)(1)-(7)—whether made in a pleading or by motion—and a motion under Rule 12(c) must be heard and decided before trial unless the court orders a deferral until trial.

[Amended December 27, 1946, effective March 19, 1948; January 21, 1963, effective July 1, 1963; February 28, 1966, effective July 1, 1966; March 2, 1987, effective August 1, 1987; April 22, 1993, effective December 1, 1993; April 17, 2000, effective December 1, 2000; April 30, 2007, effective December 1, 2007.]

RULE 13. COUNTERCLAIM AND CROSSCLAIM

(a) Compulsory Counterclaim.

(1) *In General.* A pleading must state as a counterclaim any claim that—at the time of its service—the pleader has against an opposing party if the claim:

(A) arises out of the transaction or occurrence that is the subject matter of the opposing party's claim; and

(B) does not require adding another party over whom the court cannot acquire jurisdiction.

(2) *Exceptions.* The pleader need not state the claim if:

(A) when the action was commenced, the claim was the subject of another pending action; or

(B) the opposing party sued on its claim by attachment or other process that did not establish personal jurisdiction over the pleader on that claim, and the pleader does not assert any counterclaim under this rule.

(b) Permissive Counterclaim. A pleading may state as a counterclaim against an opposing party any claim that is not compulsory.

(c) Relief Sought in a Counterclaim. A counterclaim need not diminish or defeat the recovery sought by the opposing party. It may request relief that exceeds in amount or differs in kind from the relief sought by the opposing party.

(d) Counterclaim Against the United States. These rules do not expand the right to assert a counterclaim—or to claim a credit—against the United States or a United States officer or agency.

(e) Counterclaim Maturing or Acquired After Pleading. The court may permit a party to file a supplemental pleading asserting a counterclaim that matured or was acquired by the party after serving an earlier pleading.

(f) Omitted Counterclaim. The court may permit a party to amend a pleading to add a counterclaim if it was omitted through oversight, inadvertence, or excusable neglect or if justice so requires.

(g) Crossclaim Against a Coparty. A pleading may state as a crossclaim any claim by one party against a coparty if the claim arises out of the transaction or occurrence that is the subject matter of the original action or of a counterclaim, or if the claim relates to any property that is the subject matter of the original action. The crossclaim may include a claim that the coparty is or may be liable to the cross-claimant for all or part of a claim asserted in the action against the cross-claimant.

(h) Joining Additional Parties. Rules 19 and 20 govern the addition of a person as a party to a counterclaim or crossclaim.

(i) Separate Trials; Separate Judgments. If the court orders separate trials under Rule 42(b), it may enter judgment on a counterclaim or crossclaim under Rule 54(b) when it has jurisdiction to do so, even if the opposing party's claims have been dismissed or otherwise resolved.

[Amended December 27, 1946, effective March 19, 1948; January 21, 1963, effective July 1, 1963; February 28, 1966, effective July 1, 1966; March 2, 1987, effective August 1, 1987; April 30, 2007, effective December 1, 2007.]

RULE 14. THIRD–PARTY PRACTICE

(a) When a Defending Party May Bring in a Third Party.

(1) *Timing of the Summons and Complaint.* A defending party may, as third-party plaintiff, serve a summons and complaint on a nonparty who is or may be liable to it for all or part of the claim against it. But the third-party plaintiff must, by motion, obtain the court's leave if it files the third-party complaint more than 10 days after serving its original answer.

(2) *Third–Party Defendant's Claims and Defenses.* The person served with the summons and third-party complaint—the "third-party defendant":

    (A) must assert any defense against the third-party plaintiff's claim under Rule 12;

    (B) must assert any counterclaim against the third-party plaintiff under Rule 13(a), and may assert any counterclaim against the third-party plaintiff under Rule 13(b) or any crossclaim against another third-party defendant under Rule 13(g);

    (C) may assert against the plaintiff any defense that the third-party plaintiff has to the plaintiff's claim; and

    (D) may also assert against the plaintiff any claim arising out of the transaction or occurrence that is the subject matter of the plaintiff's claim against the third-party plaintiff.

(3) *Plaintiff's Claims Against a Third–Party Defendant.* The plaintiff may assert against the third-party defendant any claim arising out of the transaction or occurrence that is the subject matter of the plaintiff's claim against the third-party plaintiff. The third-party defendant must then assert any defense under Rule 12 and any counterclaim under Rule 13(a),

and may assert any counterclaim under Rule 13(b) or any crossclaim under Rule 13(g).

(4) *Motion to Strike, Sever, or Try Separately.* Any party may move to strike the third-party claim, to sever it, or to try it separately.

(5) *Third–Party Defendant's Claim Against a Nonparty.* A third-party defendant may proceed under this rule against a nonparty who is or may be liable to the third-party defendant for all or part of any claim against it.

(6) *Third–Party Complaint In Rem.* If it is within the admiralty or maritime jurisdiction, a third-party complaint may be in rem. In that event, a reference in this rule to the "summons" includes the warrant of arrest, and a reference to the defendant or third-party plaintiff includes, when appropriate, a person who asserts a right under Supplemental Rule C(6)(a)(i) in the property arrested.

(b) When a Plaintiff May Bring in a Third Party. When a claim is asserted against a plaintiff, the plaintiff may bring in a third party if this rule would allow a defendant to do so.

(c) Admiralty or Maritime Claim.

(1) *Scope of Impleader.* If a plaintiff asserts an admiralty or maritime claim under Rule 9(h), the defendant or a person who asserts a right under Supplemental Rule C(6)(a)(i) may, as a third-party plaintiff, bring in a third-party defendant who may be wholly or partly liable—either to the plaintiff or to the third-party plaintiff—for remedy over, contribution, or otherwise on account of the same transaction, occurrence, or series of transactions or occurrences.

(2) *Defending Against a Demand for Judgment for the Plaintiff.* The third-party plaintiff may demand judgment in the plaintiff's favor against the third-party defendant. In that event, the third-party defendant must defend under Rule 12 against the plaintiff's claim as well as the third-party plaintiff's claim; and the action proceeds as if the plaintiff had sued both the third-party defendant and the third-party plaintiff.

[Amended December 27, 1946, effective March 19, 1948; January 21, 1963, effective July 1, 1963; February 28, 1966, effective July 1, 1966; March 2, 1987, effective August 1, 1987; April 17, 2000, effective December 1, 2000; April 12, 2006, effective December 1, 2006; April 30, 2007, effective December 1, 2007.]

RULE 15. AMENDED AND SUPPLEMENTAL PLEADINGS

(a) Amendments Before Trial.

(1) *Amending as a Matter of Course.* A party may amend its pleading once as a matter of course:

    (A) before being served with a responsive pleading; or

(B) within 20 days after serving the pleading if a responsive pleading is not allowed and the action is not yet on the trial calendar.

(2) *Other Amendments.* In all other cases, a party may amend its pleading only with the opposing party's written consent or the court's leave. The court should freely give leave when justice so requires.

(3) *Time to Respond.* Unless the court orders otherwise, any required response to an amended pleading must be made within the time remaining to respond to the original pleading or within 10 days after service of the amended pleading, whichever is later.

(b) Amendments During and After Trial.

(1) *Based on an Objection at Trial.* If, at trial, a party objects that evidence is not within the issues raised in the pleadings, the court may permit the pleadings to be amended. The court should freely permit an amendment when doing so will aid in presenting the merits and the objecting party fails to satisfy the court that the evidence would prejudice that party's action or defense on the merits. The court may grant a continuance to enable the objecting party to meet the evidence.

(2) *For Issues Tried by Consent.* When an issue not raised by the pleadings is tried by the parties' express or implied consent, it must be treated in all respects as if raised in the pleadings. A party may move—at any time, even after judgment—to amend the pleadings to conform them to the evidence and to raise an unpleaded issue. But failure to amend does not affect the result of the trial of that issue.

(c) Relation Back of Amendments.

(1) *When an Amendment Relates Back.* An amendment to a pleading relates back to the date of the original pleading when:

(A) the law that provides the applicable statute of limitations allows relation back;

(B) the amendment asserts a claim or defense that arose out of the conduct, transaction, or occurrence set out—or attempted to be set out—in the original pleading; or

(C) the amendment changes the party or the naming of the party against whom a claim is asserted, if Rule 15(c)(1)(B) is satisfied and if, within the period provided by Rule 4(m) for serving the summons and complaint, the party to be brought in by amendment:

(i) received such notice of the action that it will not be prejudiced in defending on the merits; and

(ii) knew or should have known that the action would have been brought against it, but for a mistake concerning the proper party's identity.

(2) *Notice to the United States.* When the United States or a United States officer or agency is added as a defendant by amendment, the notice requirements of Rule 15(c)(1)(C)(i) and (ii) are satisfied if, during the stated period, process was delivered or mailed to the United States attorney or the United States attorney's designee, to the Attorney General of the United States, or to the officer or agency.

(d) Supplemental Pleadings. On motion and reasonable notice, the court may, on just terms, permit a party to serve a supplemental pleading setting out any transaction, occurrence, or event that happened after the date of the pleading to be supplemented. The court may permit supplementation even though the original pleading is defective in stating a claim or defense. The court may order that the opposing party plead to the supplemental pleading within a specified time.

[Amended January 21, 1963, effective July 1, 1963; February 28, 1966, effective July 1, 1966; March 2, 1987, effective August 1, 1987; April 30, 1991, effective December 1, 1991; amended by Pub.L. 102–198, § 11, December 9, 1991, 105 Stat. 1626; amended April 22, 1993, effective December 1, 1993; April 30, 2007, effective December 1, 2007.]

RULE 16. PRETRIAL CONFERENCES; SCHEDULING; MANAGEMENT

(a) Purposes of a Pretrial Conference. In any action, the court may order the attorneys and any unrepresented parties to appear for one or more pretrial conferences for such purposes as:

(1) expediting disposition of the action;

(2) establishing early and continuing control so that the case will not be protracted because of lack of management;

(3) discouraging wasteful pretrial activities;

(4) improving the quality of the trial through more thorough preparation; and

(5) facilitating settlement.

(b) Scheduling.

(1) *Scheduling Order.* Except in categories of actions exempted by local rule, the district judge—or a magistrate judge when authorized by local rule—must issue a scheduling order:

(A) after receiving the parties' report under Rule 26(f); or

(B) after consulting with the parties' attorneys and any unrepresented parties at a scheduling conference or by telephone, mail, or other means.

(2) *Time to Issue.* The judge must issue the scheduling order as soon as practicable, but in any event within the earlier of 120 days after any defendant has been served with the complaint or 90 days after any defendant has appeared.

(3) *Contents of the Order.*

(A) Required Contents. The scheduling order must limit the time to join other parties, amend the pleadings, complete discovery, and file motions.

(B) *Permitted Contents.* The scheduling order may:

(i) modify the timing of disclosures under Rules 26(a) and 26(e)(1);

(ii) modify the extent of discovery;

(iii) provide for disclosure or discovery of electronically stored information;

(iv) include any agreements the parties reach for asserting claims of privilege or of protection as trial-preparation material after information is produced;

(v) set dates for pretrial conferences and for trial; and

(vi) include other appropriate matters.

(4) *Modifying a Schedule.* A schedule may be modified only for good cause and with the judge's consent.

(c) Attendance and Matters for Consideration at a Pretrial Conference.

(1) *Attendance.* A represented party must authorize at least one of its attorneys to make stipulations and admissions about all matters that can reasonably be anticipated for discussion at a pretrial conference. If appropriate, the court may require that a party or its representative be present or reasonably available by other means to consider possible settlement.

(2) *Matters for Consideration.* At any pretrial conference, the court may consider and take appropriate action on the following matters:

(A) formulating and simplifying the issues, and eliminating frivolous claims or defenses;

(B) amending the pleadings if necessary or desirable;

(C) obtaining admissions and stipulations about facts and documents to avoid unnecessary proof, and ruling in advance on the admissibility of evidence;

(D) avoiding unnecessary proof and cumulative evidence, and limiting the use of testimony under Federal Rule of Evidence 702;

(E) determining the appropriateness and timing of summary adjudication under Rule 56;

(F) controlling and scheduling discovery, including orders affecting disclosures and discovery under Rule 26 and Rules 29 through 37;

(G) identifying witnesses and documents, scheduling the filing and exchange of any pretrial briefs, and setting dates for further conferences and for trial;

(H) referring matters to a magistrate judge or a master;

(I) settling the case and using special procedures to assist in resolving the dispute when authorized by statute or local rule;

(J) determining the form and content of the pretrial order;

(K) disposing of pending motions;

(L) adopting special procedures for managing potentially difficult or protracted actions that may involve complex issues, multiple parties, difficult legal questions, or unusual proof problems;

(M) ordering a separate trial under Rule 42(b) of a claim, counterclaim, crossclaim, third-party claim, or particular issue;

(N) ordering the presentation of evidence early in the trial on a manageable issue that might, on the evidence, be the basis for a judgment as a matter of law under Rule 50(a) or a judgment on partial findings under Rule 52(c);

(O) establishing a reasonable limit on the time allowed to present evidence; and

(P) facilitating in other ways the just, speedy, and inexpensive disposition of the action.

(d) Pretrial Orders. After any conference under this rule, the court should issue an order reciting the action taken. This order controls the course of the action unless the court modifies it.

(e) Final Pretrial Conference and Orders. The court may hold a final pretrial conference to formulate a trial plan, including a plan to facilitate the admission of evidence. The conference must be held as close to the start of trial as is reasonable, and must be attended by at least one attorney who will conduct the trial for each party and by any unrepresented party. The court may modify the order issued after a final pretrial conference only to prevent manifest injustice.

(f) Sanctions.

(1) *In General.* On motion or on its own, the court may issue any just orders, including those authorized by Rule 37(b)(2)(A)(ii)-(vii), if a party or its attorney:

(A) fails to appear at a scheduling or other pretrial conference;

(B) is substantially unprepared to participate—or does not participate in good faith—in the conference; or

(C) fails to obey a scheduling or other pretrial order.

(2) *Imposing Fees and Costs.* Instead of or in addition to any other sanction, the court must order the party, its attorney, or both to pay the reasonable expenses—including attorney's fees—incurred because of any noncompliance with this rule, unless the noncompliance was substantially justified or other circumstances make an award of expenses unjust.

[Amended April 28, 1983, effective August 1, 1983; March 2, 1987, effective August 1, 1987; April 22, 1993, effective December 1, 1993; April 12, 2006, effective December 1, 2006; April 30, 2007, effective December 1, 2007.]

TITLE IV. PARTIES

RULE 17. PLAINTIFF AND DEFENDANT; CAPACITY; PUBLIC OFFICERS

(a) Real Party in Interest.

(1) *Designation in General.* An action must be prosecuted in the name of the real party in interest. The following may sue in their own names without joining the person for whose benefit the action is brought:

   (A) an executor;

   (B) an administrator;

   (C) a guardian;

   (D) a bailee;

   (E) a trustee of an express trust;

   (F) a party with whom or in whose name a contract has been made for another's benefit; and

   (G) a party authorized by statute.

(2) *Action in the Name of the United States for Another's Use or Benefit.* When a federal statute so provides, an action for another's use or benefit must be brought in the name of the United States.

(3) *Joinder of the Real Party in Interest.* The court may not dismiss an action for failure to prosecute in the name of the real party in interest until, after an objection, a reasonable time has been allowed for the real party in interest to ratify, join, or be substituted into the action. After ratification, joinder, or substitution, the action proceeds as if it had been originally commenced by the real party in interest.

(b) Capacity to Sue or Be Sued. Capacity to sue or be sued is determined as follows:

(1) for an individual who is not acting in a representative capacity, by the law of the individual's domicile;

(2) for a corporation, by the law under which it was organized; and

(3) for all other parties, by the law of the state where the court is located, except that:

   (A) a partnership or other unincorporated association with no such capacity under that state's law may sue or be sued in its common name to enforce a substantive right existing under the United States Constitution or laws; and

   (B) 28 U.S.C. §§ 754 and 959(a) govern the capacity of a receiver appointed by a United States court to sue or be sued in a United States court.

(c) Minor or Incompetent Person.

(1) *With a Representative.* The following representatives may sue or defend on behalf of a minor or an incompetent person:

   (A) a general guardian;

   (B) a committee;

   (C) a conservator; or

   (D) a like fiduciary.

(2) *Without a Representative.* A minor or an incompetent person who does not have a duly appointed representative may sue by a next friend or by a guardian ad litem. The court must appoint a guardian ad litem—or issue another appropriate order—to protect a minor or incompetent person who is unrepresented in an action.

(d) Public Officer's Title and Name. A public officer who sues or is sued in an official capacity may be designated by official title rather than by name, but the court may order that the officer's name be added.

[Amended December 27, 1946, effective March 19, 1948; December 29, 1948, effective October 20, 1949; February 28, 1966, effective July 1, 1966; March 2, 1987, effective August 1, 1987; April 25, 1988, effective August 1, 1988; amended by Pub.L. 100–690, Title VII, § 7049, November 18, 1988, 102 Stat. 4401 (although amendment by Pub.L. 100–690 could not be executed due to prior amendment by Court order which made the same change effective August 1, 1988); April 30, 2007, effective December 1, 2007.]

RULE 18. JOINDER OF CLAIMS

(a) In General. A party asserting a claim, counterclaim, crossclaim, or third-party claim may join, as independent or alternative claims, as many claims as it has against an opposing party.

(b) Joinder of Contingent Claims. A party may join two claims even though one of them is contingent on the disposition of the other; but the court may grant relief only in accordance with the parties' relative substantive rights. In particular, a plaintiff may state a claim for money and a claim to set aside a conveyance that is fraudulent as to that plaintiff, without first obtaining a judgment for the money.

[Amended February 28, 1966, effective July 1, 1966; March 2, 1987, effective August 1, 1987; April 30, 2007, effective December 1, 2007.]

RULE 19. REQUIRED JOINDER OF PARTIES

(a) Persons Required to Be Joined if Feasible.

(1) *Required Party.* A person who is subject to service of process and whose joinder will not deprive the court of subject-matter jurisdiction must be joined as a party if:

   (A) in that person's absence, the court cannot accord complete relief among existing parties; or

   (B) that person claims an interest relating to the subject of the action and is so situated that disposing of the action in the person's absence may:

(i) as a practical matter impair or impede the person's ability to protect the interest; or

(ii) leave an existing party subject to a substantial risk of incurring double, multiple, or otherwise inconsistent obligations because of the interest.

(2) *Joinder by Court Order.* If a person has not been joined as required, the court must order that the person be made a party. A person who refuses to join as a plaintiff may be made either a defendant or, in a proper case, an involuntary plaintiff.

(3) *Venue.* If a joined party objects to venue and the joinder would make venue improper, the court must dismiss that party.

(b) When Joinder Is Not Feasible. If a person who is required to be joined if feasible cannot be joined, the court must determine whether, in equity and good conscience, the action should proceed among the existing parties or should be dismissed. The factors for the court to consider include:

(1) the extent to which a judgment rendered in the person's absence might prejudice that person or the existing parties;

(2) the extent to which any prejudice could be lessened or avoided by:

(A) protective provisions in the judgment;

(B) shaping the relief; or

(C) other measures;

(3) whether a judgment rendered in the person's absence would be adequate; and

(4) whether the plaintiff would have an adequate remedy if the action were dismissed for nonjoinder.

(c) Pleading the Reasons for Nonjoinder. When asserting a claim for relief, a party must state:

(1) the name, if known, of any person who is required to be joined if feasible but is not joined; and

(2) the reasons for not joining that person.

(d) Exception for Class Actions. This rule is subject to Rule 23.

[Amended February 28, 1966, effective July 1, 1966; March 2, 1987, effective August 1, 1987; April 30, 2007, effective December 1, 2007.]

RULE 20. PERMISSIVE JOINDER OF PARTIES

(a) Persons Who May Join or Be Joined.

(1) *Plaintiffs.* Persons may join in one action as plaintiffs if:

(A) they assert any right to relief jointly, severally, or in the alternative with respect to or arising out of the same transaction, occurrence, or series of transactions or occurrences; and

(B) any question of law or fact common to all plaintiffs will arise in the action.

(2) *Defendants.* Persons—as well as a vessel, cargo, or other property subject to admiralty process in rem—may be joined in one action as defendants if:

(A) any right to relief is asserted against them jointly, severally, or in the alternative with respect to or arising out of the same transaction, occurrence, or series of transactions or occurrences; and

(B) any question of law or fact common to all defendants will arise in the action.

(3) *Extent of Relief.* Neither a plaintiff nor a defendant need be interested in obtaining or defending against all the relief demanded. The court may grant judgment to one or more plaintiffs according to their rights, and against one or more defendants according to their liabilities.

(b) Protective Measures. The court may issue orders—including an order for separate trials—to protect a party against embarrassment, delay, expense, or other prejudice that arises from including a person against whom the party asserts no claim and who asserts no claim against the party.

[Amended February 28, 1966, effective July 1, 1966; March 2, 1987, effective August 1, 1987; April 30, 2007, effective December 1, 2007.]

RULE 21. MISJOINDER AND NONJOINDER OF PARTIES

Misjoinder of parties is not a ground for dismissing an action. On motion or on its own, the court may at any time, on just terms, add or drop a party. The court may also sever any claim against a party.

[Amended April 30, 2007, effective December 1, 2007.]

RULE 22. INTERPLEADER

(a) Grounds.

(1) *By a Plaintiff.* Persons with claims that may expose a plaintiff to double or multiple liability may be joined as defendants and required to interplead. Joinder for interpleader is proper even though:

(A) the claims of the several claimants, or the titles on which their claims depend, lack a common origin or are adverse and independent rather than identical; or

(B) the plaintiff denies liability in whole or in part to any or all of the claimants.

(2) *By a Defendant.* A defendant exposed to similar liability may seek interpleader through a crossclaim or counterclaim.

(b) Relation to Other Rules and Statutes. This rule supplements—and does not limit—the joinder of parties allowed by Rule 20. The remedy this rule provides is in addition to—and does not supersede or limit—the remedy provided by 28 U.S.C. §§ 1335, 1397, and 2361. An action under those statutes must be conducted under these rules.

[Amended December 29, 1948, effective October 20, 1949; March 2, 1987, effective August 1, 1987; April 30, 2007, effective December 1, 2007.]

RULE 23.   CLASS ACTIONS

(a) Prerequisites. One or more members of a class may sue or be sued as representative parties on behalf of all members only if:

(1) the class is so numerous that joinder of all members is impracticable;

(2) there are questions of law or fact common to the class;

(3) the claims or defenses of the representative parties are typical of the claims or defenses of the class; and

(4) the representative parties will fairly and adequately protect the interests of the class.

(b) Types of Class Actions. A class action may be maintained if Rule 23(a) is satisfied and if:

(1) prosecuting separate actions by or against individual class members would create a risk of:

(A) inconsistent or varying adjudications with respect to individual class members that would establish incompatible standards of conduct for the party opposing the class; or

(B) adjudications with respect to individual class members that, as a practical matter, would be dispositive of the interests of the other members not parties to the individual adjudications or would substantially impair or impede their ability to protect their interests;

(2) the party opposing the class has acted or refused to act on grounds that apply generally to the class, so that final injunctive relief or corresponding declaratory relief is appropriate respecting the class as a whole; or

(3) the court finds that the questions of law or fact common to class members predominate over any questions affecting only individual members, and that a class action is superior to other available methods for fairly and efficiently adjudicating the controversy. The matters pertinent to these findings include:

(A) the class members' interests in individually controlling the prosecution or defense of separate actions;

(B) the extent and nature of any litigation concerning the controversy already begun by or against class members;

(C) the desirability or undesirability of concentrating the litigation of the claims in the particular forum; and

(D) the likely difficulties in managing a class action.

(c) Certification Order; Notice to Class Members; Judgment; Issues Classes; Subclasses.

(1) *Certification Order.*

(A) Time to Issue. At an early practicable time after a person sues or is sued as a class representative, the court must determine by order whether to certify the action as a class action.

(B) Defining the Class; Appointing Class Counsel. An order that certifies a class action must define the class and the class claims, issues, or defenses, and must appoint class counsel under Rule 23(g).

(C) Altering or Amending the Order. An order that grants or denies class certification may be altered or amended before final judgment.

(2) *Notice.*

(A) For (b)(1) or (b)(2) Classes. For any class certified under Rule 23(b)(1) or (b)(2), the court may direct appropriate notice to the class.

(B) For (b)(3) Classes. For any class certified under Rule 23(b)(3), the court must direct to class members the best notice that is practicable under the circumstances, including individual notice to all members who can be identified through reasonable effort. The notice must clearly and concisely state in plain, easily understood language:

(i) the nature of the action;

(ii) the definition of the class certified;

(iii) the class claims, issues, or defenses;

(iv) that a class member may enter an appearance through an attorney if the member so desires;

(v) that the court will exclude from the class any member who requests exclusion;

(vi) the time and manner for requesting exclusion; and

(vii) the binding effect of a class judgment on members under Rule 23(c)(3).

(3) *Judgment.* Whether or not favorable to the class, the judgment in a class action must:

(A) for any class certified under Rule 23(b)(1) or (b)(2), include and describe those whom the court finds to be class members; and

(B) for any class certified under Rule 23(b)(3), include and specify or describe those to whom the Rule 23(c)(2) notice was directed, who have not requested exclusion, and whom the court finds to be class members.

(4) *Particular Issues.* When appropriate, an action may be brought or maintained as a class action with respect to particular issues.

(5) *Subclasses.* When appropriate, a class may be divided into subclasses that are each treated as a class under this rule.

(d) Conducting the Action.

(1) *In General.* In conducting an action under this rule, the court may issue orders that:

(A) determine the course of proceedings or prescribe measures to prevent undue repetition or complication in presenting evidence or argument;

(B) require—to protect class members and fairly conduct the action—giving appropriate notice to some or all class members of:

(i) any step in the action;

(ii) the proposed extent of the judgment; or

(iii) the members' opportunity to signify whether they consider the representation fair and adequate, to intervene and present claims or defenses, or to otherwise come into the action;

(C) impose conditions on the representative parties or on intervenors;

(D) require that the pleadings be amended to eliminate allegations about representation of absent persons and that the action proceed accordingly; or

(E) deal with similar procedural matters.

(2) *Combining and Amending Orders.* An order under Rule 23(d)(1) may be altered or amended from time to time and may be combined with an order under Rule 16.

(e) Settlement, Voluntary Dismissal, or Compromise. The claims, issues, or defenses of a certified class may be settled, voluntarily dismissed, or compromised only with the court's approval. The following procedures apply to a proposed settlement, voluntary dismissal, or compromise:

(1) The court must direct notice in a reasonable manner to all class members who would be bound by the proposal.

(2) If the proposal would bind class members, the court may approve it only after a hearing and on finding that it is fair, reasonable, and adequate.

(3) The parties seeking approval must file a statement identifying any agreement made in connection with the proposal.

(4) If the class action was previously certified under Rule 23(b)(3), the court may refuse to approve a settlement unless it affords a new opportunity to request exclusion to individual class members who had an earlier opportunity to request exclusion but did not do so.

(5) Any class member may object to the proposal if it requires court approval under this subdivision (e);

the objection may be withdrawn only with the court's approval.

(f) Appeals. A court of appeals may permit an appeal from an order granting or denying class-action certification under this rule if a petition for permission to appeal is filed with the circuit clerk within 10 days after the order is entered. An appeal does not stay proceedings in the district court unless the district judge or the court of appeals so orders.

(g) Class Counsel.

(1) *Appointing Class Counsel.* Unless a statute provides otherwise, a court that certifies a class must appoint class counsel. In appointing class counsel, the court:

(A) must consider:

(i) the work counsel has done in identifying or investigating potential claims in the action;

(ii) counsel's experience in handling class actions, other complex litigation, and the types of claims asserted in the action;

(iii) counsel's knowledge of the applicable law; and

(iv) the resources that counsel will commit to representing the class;

(B) may consider any other matter pertinent to counsel's ability to fairly and adequately represent the interests of the class;

(C) may order potential class counsel to provide information on any subject pertinent to the appointment and to propose terms for attorney's fees and nontaxable costs;

(D) may include in the appointing order provisions about the award of attorney's fees or nontaxable costs under Rule 23(h); and

(E) may make further orders in connection with the appointment.

(2) *Standard for Appointing Class Counsel.* When one applicant seeks appointment as class counsel, the court may appoint that applicant only if the applicant is adequate under Rule 23(g)(1) and (4). If more than one adequate applicant seeks appointment, the court must appoint the applicant best able to represent the interests of the class.

(3) *Interim Counsel.* The court may designate interim counsel to act on behalf of a putative class before determining whether to certify the action as a class action.

(4) *Duty of Class Counsel.* Class counsel must fairly and adequately represent the interests of the class.

(h) Attorney's Fees and Nontaxable Costs. In a certified class action, the court may award reasonable attorney's fees and nontaxable costs that are authorized by law or by the parties' agreement. The following procedures apply:

(1) A claim for an award must be made by motion under Rule 54(d)(2), subject to the provisions of this subdivision (h), at a time the court sets. Notice of the motion must be served on all parties and, for motions by class counsel, directed to class members in a reasonable manner.

(2) A class member, or a party from whom payment is sought, may object to the motion.

(3) The court may hold a hearing and must find the facts and state its legal conclusions under Rule 52(a).

(4) The court may refer issues related to the amount of the award to a special master or a magistrate judge, as provided in Rule 54(d)(2)(D).

[Amended February 28, 1966, effective July 1, 1966; March 2, 1987, effective August 1, 1987; April 24, 1998, effective December 1, 1998; March 27, 2003, effective December 1, 2003; April 30, 2007, effective December 1, 2007.]

RULE 23.1   DERIVATIVE ACTIONS

(a) **Prerequisites.** This rule applies when one or more shareholders or members of a corporation or an unincorporated association bring a derivative action to enforce a right that the corporation or association may properly assert but has failed to enforce. The derivative action may not be maintained if it appears that the plaintiff does not fairly and adequately represent the interests of shareholders or members who are similarly situated in enforcing the right of the corporation or association.

(b) **Pleading Requirements.** The complaint must be verified and must:

(1) allege that the plaintiff was a shareholder or member at the time of the transaction complained of, or that the plaintiff's share or membership later devolved on it by operation of law;

(2) allege that the action is not a collusive one to confer jurisdiction that the court would otherwise lack; and

(3) state with particularity:

(A) any effort by the plaintiff to obtain the desired action from the directors or comparable authority and, if necessary, from the shareholders or members; and

(B) the reasons for not obtaining the action or not making the effort.

(c) **Settlement, Dismissal, and Compromise.** A derivative action may be settled, voluntarily dismissed, or compromised only with the court's approval. Notice of a proposed settlement, voluntary dismissal, or compromise must be given to shareholders or members in the manner that the court orders.

[Adopted February 28, 1966, effective July 1, 1966; amended March 2, 1987, effective August 1, 1987; April 30, 2007, effective December 1, 2007.]

RULE 23.2   ACTIONS RELATING TO UNINCORPORATED ASSOCIATIONS

This rule applies to an action brought by or against the members of an unincorporated association as a class by naming certain members as representative parties. The action may be maintained only if it appears that those parties will fairly and adequately protect the interests of the association and its members. In conducting the action, the court may issue any appropriate orders corresponding with those in Rule 23(d), and the procedure for settlement, voluntary dismissal, or compromise must correspond with the procedure in Rule 23(e).

[Adopted February 28, 1966, effective July 1, 1966; amended April 30, 2007, effective December 1, 2007.]

RULE 24.   INTERVENTION

(a) **Intervention of Right.** On timely motion, the court must permit anyone to intervene who:

(1) is given an unconditional right to intervene by a federal statute; or

(2) claims an interest relating to the property or transaction that is the subject of the action, and is so situated that disposing of the action may as a practical matter impair or impede the movant's ability to protect its interest, unless existing parties adequately represent that interest.

(b) **Permissive Intervention.**

(1) *In General.* On timely motion, the court may permit anyone to intervene who:

(A) is given a conditional right to intervene by a federal statute; or

(B) has a claim or defense that shares with the main action a common question of law or fact.

(2) *By a Government Officer or Agency.* On timely motion, the court may permit a federal or state governmental officer or agency to intervene if a party's claim or defense is based on:

(A) a statute or executive order administered by the officer or agency; or

(B) any regulation, order, requirement, or agreement issued or made under the statute or executive order.

(3) *Delay or Prejudice.* In exercising its discretion, the court must consider whether the intervention will unduly delay or prejudice the adjudication of the original parties' rights.

(c) **Notice and Pleading Required.** A motion to intervene must be served on the parties as provided in Rule 5. The motion must state the grounds for intervention and be accompanied by a pleading that sets out the claim or defense for which intervention is sought.

[Amended December 27, 1946, effective March 19, 1948; December 29, 1948, effective October 20, 1949; January 21, 1963, effective July 1, 1963; February 28, 1966, effective July 1, 1966; March 2, 1987, effective August 1, 1987; April 30, 1991, effective December 1, 1991; April 12, 2006, effective December 1, 2006; April 30, 2007, effective December 1, 2007.]

RULE 25. SUBSTITUTION OF PARTIES

(a) Death.

(1) *Substitution if the Claim Is Not Extinguished.* If a party dies and the claim is not extinguished, the court may order substitution of the proper party. A motion for substitution may be made by any party or by the decedent's successor or representative. If the motion is not made within 90 days after service of a statement noting the death, the action by or against the decedent must be dismissed.

(2) *Continuation Among the Remaining Parties.* After a party's death, if the right sought to be enforced survives only to or against the remaining parties, the action does not abate, but proceeds in favor of or against the remaining parties. The death should be noted on the record.

(3) *Service.* A motion to substitute, together with a notice of hearing, must be served on the parties as provided in Rule 5 and on nonparties as provided in

Rule 4. A statement noting death must be served in the same manner. Service may be made in any judicial district.

(b) Incompetency. If a party becomes incompetent, the court may, on motion, permit the action to be continued by or against the party's representative. The motion must be served as provided in Rule 25(a)(3).

(c) Transfer of Interest. If an interest is transferred, the action may be continued by or against the original party unless the court, on motion, orders the transferee to be substituted in the action or joined with the original party. The motion must be served as provided in Rule 25(a)(3).

(d) Public Officers; Death or Separation from Office. An action does not abate when a public officer who is a party in an official capacity dies, resigns, or otherwise ceases to hold office while the action is pending. The officer's successor is automatically substituted as a party. Later proceedings should be in the substituted party's name, but any misnomer not affecting the parties' substantial rights must be disregarded. The court may order substitution at any time, but the absence of such an order does not affect the substitution.

[Amended December 29, 1948, effective October 20, 1949; April 17, 1961, effective July 19, 1961; January 21, 1963, effective July 1, 1963; March 2, 1987, effective August 1, 1987; April 30, 2007, effective December 1, 2007.]

TITLE V. DISCLOSURES AND DISCOVERY

RULE 26. DUTY TO DISCLOSE; GENERAL PROVISIONS GOVERNING DISCOVERY

(a) Required Disclosures.

(1) *Initial Disclosure.*

(A) In General. Except as exempted by Rule 26(a)(1)(B) or as otherwise stipulated or ordered by the court, a party must, without awaiting a discovery request, provide to the other parties:

(i) the name and, if known, the address and telephone number of each individual likely to have discoverable information—along with the subjects of that information—that the disclosing party may use to support its claims or defenses, unless the use would be solely for impeachment;

(ii) a copy—or a description by category and location—of all documents, electronically stored information, and tangible things that the disclosing party has in its possession, custody, or control and may use to support its claims or defenses, unless the use would be solely for impeachment;

(iii) a computation of each category of damages claimed by the disclosing party—who must also

make available for inspection and copying as under Rule 34 the documents or other evidentiary material, unless privileged or protected from disclosure, on which each computation is based, including materials bearing on the nature and extent of injuries suffered; and

(iv) for inspection and copying as under Rule 34, any insurance agreement under which an insurance business may be liable to satisfy all or part of a possible judgment in the action or to indemnify or reimburse for payments made to satisfy the judgment.

(B) Proceedings Exempt from Initial Disclosure. The following proceedings are exempt from initial disclosure:

(i) an action for review on an administrative record;

(ii) a forfeiture action in rem arising from a federal statute;

(iii) a petition for habeas corpus or any other proceeding to challenge a criminal conviction or sentence;

(iv) an action brought without an attorney by a person in the custody of the United States, a state, or a state subdivision;

(v) an action to enforce or quash an administrative summons or subpoena;

(vi) an action by the United States to recover benefit payments;

(vii) an action by the United States to collect on a student loan guaranteed by the United States;

(viii) a proceeding ancillary to a proceeding in another court; and

(ix) an action to enforce an arbitration award.

(C) Time for Initial Disclosures—In General. A party must make the initial disclosures at or within 14 days after the parties' Rule 26(f) conference unless a different time is set by stipulation or court order, or unless a party objects during the conference that initial disclosures are not appropriate in this action and states the objection in the proposed discovery plan. In ruling on the objection, the court must determine what disclosures, if any, are to be made and must set the time for disclosure.

(D) Time for Initial Disclosures—For Parties Served or Joined Later. A party that is first served or otherwise joined after the Rule 26(f) conference must make the initial disclosures within 30 days after being served or joined, unless a different time is set by stipulation or court order.

(E) Basis for Initial Disclosure; Unacceptable Excuses. A party must make its initial disclosures based on the information then reasonably available to it. A party is not excused from making its disclosures because it has not fully investigated the case or because it challenges the sufficiency of another party's disclosures or because another party has not made its disclosures.

(2) *Disclosure of Expert Testimony.*

(A) In General. In addition to the disclosures required by Rule 26(a)(1), a party must disclose to the other parties the identity of any witness it may use at trial to present evidence under Federal Rule of Evidence 702, 703, or 705.

(B) Written Report. Unless otherwise stipulated or ordered by the court, this disclosure must be accompanied by a written report—prepared and signed by the witness—if the witness is one retained or specially employed to provide expert testimony in the case or one whose duties as the party's employee regularly involve giving expert testimony. The report must contain:

(i) a complete statement of all opinions the witness will express and the basis and reasons for them;

(ii) the data or other information considered by the witness in forming them;

(iii) any exhibits that will be used to summarize or support them;

(iv) the witness's qualifications, including a list of all publications authored in the previous 10 years;

(v) a list of all other cases in which, during the previous four years, the witness testified as an expert at trial or by deposition; and

(vi) a statement of the compensation to be paid for the study and testimony in the case.

(C) Time to Disclose Expert Testimony. A party must make these disclosures at the times and in the sequence that the court orders. Absent a stipulation or a court order, the disclosures must be made:

(i) at least 90 days before the date set for trial or for the case to be ready for trial; or

(ii) if the evidence is intended solely to contradict or rebut evidence on the same subject matter identified by another party under Rule 26(a)(2)(B), within 30 days after the other party's disclosure.

(D) Supplementing the Disclosure. The parties must supplement these disclosures when required under Rule 26(e).

(3) *Pretrial Disclosures.*

(A) In General. In addition to the disclosures required by Rule 26(a)(1) and (2), a party must provide to the other parties and promptly file the following information about the evidence that it may present at trial other than solely for impeachment:

(i) the name and, if not previously provided, the address and telephone number of each witness—separately identifying those the party expects to present and those it may call if the need arises;

(ii) the designation of those witnesses whose testimony the party expects to present by deposition and, if not taken stenographically, a transcript of the pertinent parts of the deposition; and

(iii) an identification of each document or other exhibit, including summaries of other evidence—separately identifying those items the party expects to offer and those it may offer if the need arises.

(B) Time for Pretrial Disclosures; Objections. Unless the court orders otherwise, these disclosures must be made at least 30 days before trial. Within 14 days after they are made, unless the court sets a different time, a party may serve and promptly file a list of the following objections: any objections to the use under Rule 32(a) of a deposition designated by another party under Rule 26(a)(3)(A)(ii); and any objection, together with the grounds for it, that may be made to the admissibility of materials identified under Rule 26(a)(3)(A)(iii). An objection not so made—except for one under Federal Rule of Evidence 402 or 403—is waived unless excused by the court for good cause.

(4) *Form of Disclosures.* Unless the court orders otherwise, all disclosures under Rule 26(a) must be in writing, signed, and served.

(b) Discovery Scope and Limits.

(1) *Scope in General.* Unless otherwise limited by court order, the scope of discovery is as follows:

Parties may obtain discovery regarding any nonprivileged matter that is relevant to any party's claim or defense—including the existence, description, nature, custody, condition, and location of any documents or other tangible things and the identity and location of persons who know of any discoverable matter. For good cause, the court may order discovery of any matter relevant to the subject matter involved in the action. Relevant information need not be admissible at the trial if the discovery appears reasonably calculated to lead to the discovery of admissible evidence. All discovery is subject to the limitations imposed by Rule 26(b)(2)(C).

(2) *Limitations on Frequency and Extent.*

(A) When Permitted. By order, the court may alter the limits in these rules on the number of depositions and interrogatories or on the length of depositions under Rule 30. By order or local rule, the court may also limit the number of requests under Rule 36.

(B) Specific Limitations on Electronically Stored Information. A party need not provide discovery of electronically stored information from sources that the party identifies as not reasonably accessible because of undue burden or cost. On motion to compel discovery or for a protective order, the party from whom discovery is sought must show that the information is not reasonably accessible because of undue burden or cost. If that showing is made, the court may nonetheless order discovery from such sources if the requesting party shows good cause, considering the limitations of Rule 26(b)(2)(C). The court may specify conditions for the discovery.

(C) When Required. On motion or on its own, the court must limit the frequency or extent of discovery otherwise allowed by these rules or by local rule if it determines that:

(i) the discovery sought is unreasonably cumulative or duplicative, or can be obtained from some other source that is more convenient, less burdensome, or less expensive;

(ii) the party seeking discovery has had ample opportunity to obtain the information by discovery in the action; or

(iii) the burden or expense of the proposed discovery outweighs its likely benefit, considering the needs of the case, the amount in controversy,

the parties' resources, the importance of the issues at stake in the action, and the importance of the discovery in resolving the issues.

(3) *Trial Preparation: Materials.*

(A) Documents and Tangible Things. Ordinarily, a party may not discover documents and tangible things that are prepared in anticipation of litigation or for trial by or for another party or its representative (including the other party's attorney, consultant, surety, indemnitor, insurer, or agent). But, subject to Rule 26(b)(4), those materials may be discovered if:

(i) they are otherwise discoverable under Rule 26(b)(1); and

(ii) the party shows that it has substantial need for the materials to prepare its case and cannot, without undue hardship, obtain their substantial equivalent by other means.

(B) Protection Against Disclosure. If the court orders discovery of those materials, it must protect against disclosure of the mental impressions, conclusions, opinions, or legal theories of a party's attorney or other representative concerning the litigation.

(C) Previous Statement. Any party or other person may, on request and without the required showing, obtain the person's own previous statement about the action or its subject matter. If the request is refused, the person may move for a court order, and Rule 37(a)(5) applies to the award of expenses. A previous statement is either:

(i) a written statement that the person has signed or otherwise adopted or approved; or

(ii) a contemporaneous stenographic, mechanical, electrical, or other recording—or a transcription of it—that recites substantially verbatim the person's oral statement.

(4) *Trial Preparation: Experts.*

(A) Expert Who May Testify. A party may depose any person who has been identified as an expert whose opinions may be presented at trial. If Rule 26(a)(2)(B) requires a report from the expert, the deposition may be conducted only after the report is provided.

(B) Expert Employed Only for Trial Preparation. Ordinarily, a party may not, by interrogatories or deposition, discover facts known or opinions held by an expert who has been retained or specially employed by another party in anticipation of litigation or to prepare for trial and who is not expected to be called as a witness at trial. But a party may do so only:

(i) as provided in Rule 35(b); or

(ii) on showing exceptional circumstances under which it is impracticable for the party to obtain facts or opinions on the same subject by other means.

(C) Payment. Unless manifest injustice would result, the court must require that the party seeking discovery:

(i) pay the expert a reasonable fee for time spent in responding to discovery under Rule 26(b)(4)(A) or (B); and

(ii) for discovery under (B), also pay the other party a fair portion of the fees and expenses it reasonably incurred in obtaining the expert's facts and opinions.

(5) *Claiming Privilege or Protecting Trial-Preparation Materials.*

(A) Information Withheld. When a party withholds information otherwise discoverable by claiming that the information is privileged or subject to protection as trial-preparation material, the party must:

(i) expressly make the claim; and

(ii) describe the nature of the documents, communications, or tangible things not produced or disclosed—and do so in a manner that, without revealing information itself privileged or protected, will enable other parties to assess the claim.

(B) Information Produced. If information produced in discovery is subject to a claim of privilege or of protection as trial-preparation material, the party making the claim may notify any party that received the information of the claim and the basis for it. After being notified, a party must promptly return, sequester, or destroy the specified information and any copies it has; must not use or disclose the information until the claim is resolved; must take reasonable steps to retrieve the information if the party disclosed it before being notified; and may promptly present the information to the court under seal for a determination of the claim. The producing party must preserve the information until the claim is resolved.

(c) Protective Orders.

(1) *In General.* A party or any person from whom discovery is sought may move for a protective order in the court where the action is pending—or as an alternative on matters relating to a deposition, in the court for the district where the deposition will be taken. The motion must include a certification that the movant has in good faith conferred or attempted to confer with other affected parties in an effort to resolve the dispute without court action. The court may, for good cause, issue an order to protect a party or person from annoyance, embarrassment, oppression, or undue burden or expense, including one or more of the following:

(A) forbidding the disclosure or discovery;

(B) specifying terms, including time and place, for the disclosure or discovery;

(C) prescribing a discovery method other than the one selected by the party seeking discovery;

(D) forbidding inquiry into certain matters, or limiting the scope of disclosure or discovery to certain matters;

(E) designating the persons who may be present while the discovery is conducted;

(F) requiring that a deposition be sealed and opened only on court order;

(G) requiring that a trade secret or other confidential research, development, or commercial information not be revealed or be revealed only in a specified way; and

(H) requiring that the parties simultaneously file specified documents or information in sealed envelopes, to be opened as the court directs.

(2) *Ordering Discovery.* If a motion for a protective order is wholly or partly denied, the court may, on just terms, order that any party or person provide or permit discovery.

(3) *Awarding Expenses.* Rule 37(a)(5) applies to the award of expenses.

(d) Timing and Sequence of Discovery.

(1) *Timing.* A party may not seek discovery from any source before the parties have conferred as required by Rule 26(f), except in a proceeding exempted from initial disclosure under Rule 26(a)(1)(B), or when authorized by these rules, by stipulation, or by court order.

(2) *Sequence.* Unless, on motion, the court orders otherwise for the parties' and witnesses' convenience and in the interests of justice:

(A) methods of discovery may be used in any sequence; and

(B) discovery by one party does not require any other party to delay its discovery.

(e) Supplementing Disclosures and Responses.

(1) *In General.* A party who has made a disclosure under Rule 26(a)—or who has responded to an interrogatory, request for production, or request for admission—must supplement or correct its disclosure or response:

(A) in a timely manner if the party learns that in some material respect the disclosure or response is incomplete or incorrect, and if the additional or corrective information has not otherwise been made known to the other parties during the discovery process or in writing; or

(B) as ordered by the court.

(2) *Expert Witness.* For an expert whose report must be disclosed under Rule 26(a)(2)(B), the party's duty to supplement extends both to information in-

cluded in the report and to information given during the expert's deposition. Any additions or changes to this information must be disclosed by the time the party's pretrial disclosures under Rule 26(a)(3) are due.

(f) Conference of the Parties; Planning for Discovery.

(1) *Conference Timing.* Except in a proceeding exempted from initial disclosure under Rule 26(a)(1)(B) or when the court orders otherwise, the parties must confer as soon as practicable—and in any event at least 21 days before a scheduling conference is to be held or a scheduling order is due under Rule 16(b).

(2) *Conference Content; Parties' Responsibilities.* In conferring, the parties must consider the nature and basis of their claims and defenses and the possibilities for promptly settling or resolving the case; make or arrange for the disclosures required by Rule 26(a)(1); discuss any issues about preserving discoverable information; and develop a proposed discovery plan. The attorneys of record and all unrepresented parties that have appeared in the case are jointly responsible for arranging the conference, for attempting in good faith to agree on the proposed discovery plan, and for submitting to the court within 14 days after the conference a written report outlining the plan. The court may order the parties or attorneys to attend the conference in person.

(3) *Discovery Plan.* A discovery plan must state the parties' views and proposals on:

(A) what changes should be made in the timing, form, or requirement for disclosures under Rule 26(a), including a statement of when initial disclosures were made or will be made;

(B) the subjects on which discovery may be needed, when discovery should be completed, and whether discovery should be conducted in phases or be limited to or focused on particular issues;

(C) any issues about disclosure or discovery of electronically stored information, including the form or forms in which it should be produced;

(D) any issues about claims of privilege or of protection as trial-preparation materials, including—if the parties agree on a procedure to assert these claims after production—whether to ask the court to include their agreement in an order;

(E) what changes should be made in the limitations on discovery imposed under these rules or by local rule, and what other limitations should be imposed; and

(F) any other orders that the court should issue under Rule 26(c) or under Rule 16(b) and (c).

(4) *Expedited Schedule.* If necessary to comply with its expedited schedule for Rule 16(b) conferences, a court may by local rule:

(A) require the parties' conference to occur less than 21 days before the scheduling conference is held or a scheduling order is due under Rule 16(b); and

(B) require the written report outlining the discovery plan to be filed less than 14 days after the parties' conference, or excuse the parties from submitting a written report and permit them to report orally on their discovery plan at the Rule 16(b) conference.

(g) Signing Disclosures and Discovery Requests, Responses, and Objections.

(1) *Signature Required; Effect of Signature.* Every disclosure under Rule 26(a)(1) or (a)(3) and every discovery request, response, or objection must be signed by at least one attorney of record in the attorney's own name—or by the party personally, if unrepresented—and must state the signer's address, e-mail address, and telephone number. By signing, an attorney or party certifies that to the best of the person's knowledge, information, and belief formed after a reasonable inquiry:

(A) with respect to a disclosure, it is complete and correct as of the time it is made; and

(B) with respect to a discovery request, response, or objection, it is:

(i) consistent with these rules and warranted by existing law or by a nonfrivolous argument for extending, modifying, or reversing existing law, or for establishing new law;

(ii) not interposed for any improper purpose, such as to harass, cause unnecessary delay, or needlessly increase the cost of litigation; and

(iii) neither unreasonable nor unduly burdensome or expensive, considering the needs of the case, prior discovery in the case, the amount in controversy, and the importance of the issues at stake in the action.

(2) *Failure to Sign.* Other parties have no duty to act on an unsigned disclosure, request, response, or objection until it is signed, and the court must strike it unless a signature is promptly supplied after the omission is called to the attorney's or party's attention.

(3) *Sanction for Improper Certification.* If a certification violates this rule without substantial justification, the court, on motion or on its own, must impose an appropriate sanction on the signer, the party on whose behalf the signer was acting, or both. The sanction may include an order to pay the reasonable expenses, including attorney's fees, caused by the violation.

[Amended December 27, 1946, effective March 19, 1948; January 21, 1963, effective July 1, 1963; February 28, 1966, effective July 1, 1966; March 30, 1970, effective July 1, 1970; April 29, 1980, effective August 1, 1980; April 28, 1983, effective August 1, 1983; March 2, 1987, effective August 1,

1987; April 22, 1993, effective December 1, 1993; April 17, 2000, effective December 1, 2000; April 12, 2006, effective December 1, 2006; April 30, 2007, effective December 1, 2007.]

RULE 27. DEPOSITIONS TO PERPETUATE TESTIMONY

(a) Before an Action Is Filed.

(1) *Petition.* A person who wants to perpetuate testimony about any matter cognizable in a United States court may file a verified petition in the district court for the district where any expected adverse party resides. The petition must ask for an order authorizing the petitioner to depose the named persons in order to perpetuate their testimony. The petition must be titled in the petitioner's name and must show:

(A) that the petitioner expects to be a party to an action cognizable in a United States court but cannot presently bring it or cause it to be brought;

(B) the subject matter of the expected action and the petitioner's interest;

(C) the facts that the petitioner wants to establish by the proposed testimony and the reasons to perpetuate it;

(D) the names or a description of the persons whom the petitioner expects to be adverse parties and their addresses, so far as known; and

(E) the name, address, and expected substance of the testimony of each deponent.

(2) *Notice and Service.* At least 20 days before the hearing date, the petitioner must serve each expected adverse party with a copy of the petition and a notice stating the time and place of the hearing. The notice may be served either inside or outside the district or state in the manner provided in Rule 4. If that service cannot be made with reasonable diligence on an expected adverse party, the court may order service by publication or otherwise. The court must appoint an attorney to represent persons not served in the manner provided in Rule 4 and to cross-examine the deponent if an unserved person is not otherwise represented. If any expected adverse party is a minor or is incompetent, Rule 17(c) applies.

(3) *Order and Examination.* If satisfied that perpetuating the testimony may prevent a failure or delay of justice, the court must issue an order that designates or describes the persons whose depositions may be taken, specifies the subject matter of the examinations, and states whether the depositions will be taken orally or by written interrogatories. The depositions may then be taken under these rules, and the court may issue orders like those authorized by Rules 34 and 35. A reference in these rules to the court where an action is pending means, for purposes of this rule, the court where the petition for the deposition was filed.

(4) *Using the Deposition.* A deposition to perpetuate testimony may be used under Rule 32(a) in any later-filed district-court action involving the same subject matter if the deposition either was taken under these rules or, although not so taken, would be admissible in evidence in the courts of the state where it was taken.

(b) Pending Appeal.

(1) *In General.* The court where a judgment has been rendered may, if an appeal has been taken or may still be taken, permit a party to depose witnesses to perpetuate their testimony for use in the event of further proceedings in that court.

(2) *Motion.* The party who wants to perpetuate testimony may move for leave to take the depositions, on the same notice and service as if the action were pending in the district court. The motion must show:

(A) the name, address, and expected substance of the testimony of each deponent; and

(B) the reasons for perpetuating the testimony.

(3) *Court Order.* If the court finds that perpetuating the testimony may prevent a failure or delay of justice, the court may permit the depositions to be taken and may issue orders like those authorized by Rules 34 and 35. The depositions may be taken and used as any other deposition taken in a pending district-court action.

(c) Perpetuation by an Action. This rule does not limit a court's power to entertain an action to perpetuate testimony.

[Amended December 27, 1946, effective March 19, 1948; December 29, 1948, effective October 20, 1949; March 1, 1971, effective July 1, 1971; March 2, 1987, effective August 1, 1987; April 25, 2005, effective December 1, 2005; April 30, 2007, effective December 1, 2007.]

RULE 28. PERSONS BEFORE WHOM DEPOSITIONS MAY BE TAKEN

(a) Within the United States.

(1) *In General.* Within the United States or a territory or insular possession subject to United States jurisdiction, a deposition must be taken before:

(A) an officer authorized to administer oaths either by federal law or by the law in the place of examination; or

(B) a person appointed by the court where the action is pending to administer oaths and take testimony.

(2) *Definition of "Officer".* The term "officer" in Rules 30, 31, and 32 includes a person appointed by the court under this rule or designated by the parties under Rule 29(a).

(b) In a Foreign Country.

(1) *In General.* A deposition may be taken in a foreign country:

(A) under an applicable treaty or convention;

(B) under a letter of request, whether or not captioned a "letter rogatory";

(C) on notice, before a person authorized to administer oaths either by federal law or by the law in the place of examination; or

(D) before a person commissioned by the court to administer any necessary oath and take testimony.

(2) *Issuing a Letter of Request or a Commission.* A letter of request, a commission, or both may be issued:

(A) on appropriate terms after an application and notice of it; and

(B) without a showing that taking the deposition in another manner is impracticable or inconvenient.

(3) *Form of a Request, Notice, or Commission.* When a letter of request or any other device is used according to a treaty or convention, it must be captioned in the form prescribed by that treaty or convention. A letter of request may be addressed "To the Appropriate Authority in [name of country]." A deposition notice or a commission must designate by name or descriptive title the person before whom the deposition is to be taken.

(4) *Letter of Request—Admitting Evidence.* Evidence obtained in response to a letter of request need not be excluded merely because it is not a verbatim transcript, because the testimony was not taken under oath, or because of any similar departure from the requirements for depositions taken within the United States.

(c) Disqualification. A deposition must not be taken before a person who is any party's relative, employee, or attorney; who is related to or employed by any party's attorney; or who is financially interested in the action.

[Amended December 27, 1946, effective March 19, 1948; January 21, 1963, effective July 1, 1963; April 29, 1980, effective August 1, 1980; March 2, 1987, effective August 1, 1987; April 22, 1993, effective December 1, 1993; April 30, 2007, effective December 1, 2007.]

RULE 29. STIPULATIONS ABOUT DISCOVERY PROCEDURE

Unless the court orders otherwise, the parties may stipulate that:

(a) a deposition may be taken before any person, at any time or place, on any notice, and in the manner specified—in which event it may be used in the same way as any other deposition; and

(b) other procedures governing or limiting discovery be modified—but a stipulation extending the time for any form of discovery must have court approval if

it would interfere with the time set for completing discovery, for hearing a motion, or for trial.

[Amended March 30, 1970, effective July 1, 1970; April 22, 1993, effective December 1, 1993; April 30, 2007, effective December 1, 2007.]

RULE 30. DEPOSITIONS BY ORAL EXAMINATION

(a) When a Deposition May Be Taken.

(1) *Without Leave.* A party may, by oral questions, depose any person, including a party, without leave of court except as provided in Rule 30(a)(2). The deponent's attendance may be compelled by subpoena under Rule 45.

(2) *With Leave.* A party must obtain leave of court, and the court must grant leave to the extent consistent with Rule 26(b)(2):

(A) if the parties have not stipulated to the deposition and:

(i) the deposition would result in more than 10 depositions being taken under this rule or Rule 31 by the plaintiffs, or by the defendants, or by the third-party defendants;

(ii) the deponent has already been deposed in the case; or

(iii) the party seeks to take the deposition before the time specified in Rule 26(d), unless the party certifies in the notice, with supporting facts, that the deponent is expected to leave the United States and be unavailable for examination in this country after that time; or

(B) if the deponent is confined in prison.

(b) Notice of the Deposition; Other Formal Requirements.

(1) *Notice in General.* A party who wants to depose a person by oral questions must give reasonable written notice to every other party. The notice must state the time and place of the deposition and, if known, the deponent's name and address. If the name is unknown, the notice must provide a general description sufficient to identify the person or the particular class or group to which the person belongs.

(2) *Producing Documents.* If a subpoena duces tecum is to be served on the deponent, the materials designated for production, as set out in the subpoena, must be listed in the notice or in an attachment. The notice to a party deponent may be accompanied by a request under Rule 34 to produce documents and tangible things at the deposition.

(3) *Method of Recording.*

(A) Method Stated in the Notice. The party who notices the deposition must state in the notice the method for recording the testimony. Unless the court orders otherwise, testimony may be recorded by audio, audiovisual, or stenographic means. The noticing party bears the recording costs. Any party may arrange to transcribe a deposition.

(B) Additional Method. With prior notice to the deponent and other parties, any party may designate another method for recording the testimony in addition to that specified in the original notice. That party bears the expense of the additional record or transcript unless the court orders otherwise.

(4) *By Remote Means.* The parties may stipulate—or the court may on motion order—that a deposition be taken by telephone or other remote means. For the purpose of this rule and Rules 28(a), 37(a)(2), and 37(b)(1), the deposition takes place where the deponent answers the questions.

(5) *Officer's Duties.*

(A) Before the Deposition. Unless the parties stipulate otherwise, a deposition must be conducted before an officer appointed or designated under Rule 28. The officer must begin the deposition with an on-the-record statement that includes:

(i) the officer's name and business address;

(ii) the date, time, and place of the deposition;

(iii) the deponent's name;

(iv) the officer's administration of the oath or affirmation to the deponent; and

(v) the identity of all persons present.

(B) Conducting the Deposition; Avoiding Distortion. If the deposition is recorded non-stenographically, the officer must repeat the items in Rule 30(b)(5)(A)(i)-(iii) at the beginning of each unit of the recording medium. The deponent's and attorneys' appearance or demeanor must not be distorted through recording techniques.

(C) After the Deposition. At the end of a deposition, the officer must state on the record that the deposition is complete and must set out any stipulations made by the attorneys about custody of the transcript or recording and of the exhibits, or about any other pertinent matters.

(6) *Notice or Subpoena Directed to an Organization.* In its notice or subpoena, a party may name as the deponent a public or private corporation, a partnership, an association, a governmental agency, or other entity and must describe with reasonable particularity the matters for examination. The named organization must then designate one or more officers, directors, or managing agents, or designate other persons who consent to testify on its behalf; and it may set out the matters on which each person designated will testify. A subpoena must advise a nonparty organization of its duty to make this designation. The persons designated must testify about information known or reasonably available to the organization. This paragraph (6) does not preclude a deposition by any other procedure allowed by these rules.

(c) Examination and Cross–Examination; Record of the Examination; Objections; Written Questions.

(1) *Examination and Cross–Examination.* The examination and cross-examination of a deponent proceed as they would at trial under the Federal Rules of Evidence, except Rules 103 and 615. After putting the deponent under oath or affirmation, the officer must record the testimony by the method designated under Rule 30(b)(3)(A). The testimony must be recorded by the officer personally or by a person acting in the presence and under the direction of the officer.

(2) *Objections.* An objection at the time of the examination—whether to evidence, to a party's conduct, to the officer's qualifications, to the manner of taking the deposition, or to any other aspect of the deposition—must be noted on the record, but the examination still proceeds; the testimony is taken subject to any objection. An objection must be stated concisely in a nonargumentative and nonsuggestive manner. A person may instruct a deponent not to answer only when necessary to preserve a privilege, to enforce a limitation ordered by the court, or to present a motion under Rule 30(d)(3).

(3) *Participating Through Written Questions.* Instead of participating in the oral examination, a party may serve written questions in a sealed envelope on the party noticing the deposition, who must deliver them to the officer. The officer must ask the deponent those questions and record the answers verbatim.

(d) Duration; Sanction; Motion to Terminate or Limit.

(1) *Duration.* Unless otherwise stipulated or ordered by the court, a deposition is limited to 1 day of 7 hours. The court must allow additional time consistent with Rule 26(b)(2) if needed to fairly examine the deponent or if the deponent, another person, or any other circumstance impedes or delays the examination.

(2) *Sanction.* The court may impose an appropriate sanction—including the reasonable expenses and attorney's fees incurred by any party—on a person who impedes, delays, or frustrates the fair examination of the deponent.

(3) *Motion to Terminate or Limit.*

(A) Grounds. At any time during a deposition, the deponent or a party may move to terminate or limit it on the ground that it is being conducted in bad faith or in a manner that unreasonably annoys, embarrasses, or oppresses the deponent or party. The motion may be filed in the court where the action is pending or the deposition is being taken. If the objecting deponent or party so demands, the deposition must be suspended for the time necessary to obtain an order.

(B) Order. The court may order that the deposition be terminated or may limit its scope and manner as provided in Rule 26(c). If terminated, the deposition may be resumed only by order of the court where the action is pending.

(C) Award of Expenses. Rule 37(a)(5) applies to the award of expenses.

(e) Review by the Witness; Changes.

(1) *Review; Statement of Changes.* On request by the deponent or a party before the deposition is completed, the deponent must be allowed 30 days after being notified by the officer that the transcript or recording is available in which:

(A) to review the transcript or recording; and

(B) if there are changes in form or substance, to sign a statement listing the changes and the reasons for making them.

(2) *Changes Indicated in the Officer's Certificate.* The officer must note in the certificate prescribed by Rule 30(f)(1) whether a review was requested and, if so, must attach any changes the deponent makes during the 30-day period.

(f) Certification and Delivery; Exhibits; Copies of the Transcript or Recording; Filing.

(1) *Certification and Delivery.* The officer must certify in writing that the witness was duly sworn and that the deposition accurately records the witness's testimony. The certificate must accompany the record of the deposition. Unless the court orders otherwise, the officer must seal the deposition in an envelope or package bearing the title of the action and marked "Deposition of [witness's name]" and must promptly send it to the attorney who arranged for the transcript or recording. The attorney must store it under conditions that will protect it against loss, destruction, tampering, or deterioration.

(2) *Documents and Tangible Things.*

(A) Originals and Copies. Documents and tangible things produced for inspection during a deposition must, on a party's request, be marked for identification and attached to the deposition. Any party may inspect and copy them. But if the person who produced them wants to keep the originals, the person may:

(i) offer copies to be marked, attached to the deposition, and then used as originals—after giving all parties a fair opportunity to verify the copies by comparing them with the originals; or

(ii) give all parties a fair opportunity to inspect and copy the originals after they are marked—in which event the originals may be used as if attached to the deposition.

(B) Order Regarding the Originals. Any party may move for an order that the originals be attached to the deposition pending final disposition of the case.

(3) *Copies of the Transcript or Recording.* Unless otherwise stipulated or ordered by the court, the officer must retain the stenographic notes of a deposition taken stenographically or a copy of the recording of a deposition taken by another method. When paid reasonable charges, the officer must furnish a copy of the transcript or recording to any party or the deponent.

(4) *Notice of Filing.* A party who files the deposition must promptly notify all other parties of the filing.

(g) Failure to Attend a Deposition or Serve a Subpoena; Expenses. A party who, expecting a deposition to be taken, attends in person or by an attorney may recover reasonable expenses for attending, including attorney's fees, if the noticing party failed to:

(1) attend and proceed with the deposition; or

(2) serve a subpoena on a nonparty deponent, who consequently did not attend.

[Amended January 21, 1963, effective July 1, 1963; March 30, 1970, effective July 1, 1970; March 1, 1971, effective July 1, 1971; November 20, 1972, effective July 1, 1975; April 29, 1980, effective August 1, 1980; March 2, 1987, effective August 1, 1987; April 22, 1993, effective December 1, 1993; April 17, 2000, effective December 1, 2000; April 30, 2007, effective December 1, 2007.]

RULE 31. DEPOSITIONS BY WRITTEN QUESTIONS

(a) When a Deposition May Be Taken.

(1) *Without Leave.* A party may, by written questions, depose any person, including a party, without leave of court except as provided in Rule 31(a)(2). The deponent's attendance may be compelled by subpoena under Rule 45.

(2) *With Leave.* A party must obtain leave of court, and the court must grant leave to the extent consistent with Rule 26(b)(2):

(A) if the parties have not stipulated to the deposition and:

(i) the deposition would result in more than 10 depositions being taken under this rule or Rule 30 by the plaintiffs, or by the defendants, or by the third-party defendants;

(ii) the deponent has already been deposed in the case; or

(iii) the party seeks to take a deposition before the time specified in Rule 26(d); or

(B) if the deponent is confined in prison.

(3) *Service; Required Notice.* A party who wants to depose a person by written questions must serve them on every other party, with a notice stating, if known, the deponent's name and address. If the name is unknown, the notice must provide a general description sufficient to identify the person or the particular

class or group to which the person belongs. The notice must also state the name or descriptive title and the address of the officer before whom the deposition will be taken.

(4) *Questions Directed to an Organization.* A public or private corporation, a partnership, an association, or a governmental agency may be deposed by written questions in accordance with Rule 30(b)(6).

(5) *Questions from Other Parties.* Any questions to the deponent from other parties must be served on all parties as follows: cross-questions, within 14 days after being served with the notice and direct questions; redirect questions, within 7 days after being served with cross-questions; and recross-questions, within 7 days after being served with redirect questions. The court may, for good cause, extend or shorten these times.

(b) **Delivery to the Officer; Officer's Duties.** The party who noticed the deposition must deliver to the officer a copy of all the questions served and of the notice. The officer must promptly proceed in the manner provided in Rule 30(c), (e), and (f) to:

(1) take the deponent's testimony in response to the questions;

(2) prepare and certify the deposition; and

(3) send it to the party, attaching a copy of the questions and of the notice.

(c) **Notice of Completion or Filing.**

(1) *Completion.* The party who noticed the deposition must notify all other parties when it is completed.

(2) *Filing.* A party who files the deposition must promptly notify all other parties of the filing.

[Amended March 30, 1970, effective July 1, 1970; March 2, 1987, effective August 1, 1987; April 22, 1993, effective December 1, 1993; April 30, 2007, effective December 1, 2007.]

RULE 32. USING DEPOSITIONS IN COURT PROCEEDINGS

(a) **Using Depositions.**

(1) *In General.* At a hearing or trial, all or part of a deposition may be used against a party on these conditions:

(A) the party was present or represented at the taking of the deposition or had reasonable notice of it;

(B) it is used to the extent it would be admissible under the Federal Rules of Evidence if the deponent were present and testifying; and

(C) the use is allowed by Rule 32(a)(2) through (8).

(2) *Impeachment and Other Uses.* Any party may use a deposition to contradict or impeach the testimony given by the deponent as a witness, or for any

other purpose allowed by the Federal Rules of Evidence.

(3) *Deposition of Party, Agent, or Designee.* An adverse party may use for any purpose the deposition of a party or anyone who, when deposed, was the party's officer, director, managing agent, or designee under Rule 30(b)(6) or 31(a)(4).

(4) *Unavailable Witness.* A party may use for any purpose the deposition of a witness, whether or not a party, if the court finds:

(A) that the witness is dead;

(B) that the witness is more than 100 miles from the place of hearing or trial or is outside the United States, unless it appears that the witness's absence was procured by the party offering the deposition;

(C) that the witness cannot attend or testify because of age, illness, infirmity, or imprisonment;

(D) that the party offering the deposition could not procure the witness's attendance by subpoena; or

(E) on motion and notice, that exceptional circumstances make it desirable—in the interest of justice and with due regard to the importance of live testimony in open court—to permit the deposition to be used.

(5) *Limitations on Use.*

(A) Deposition Taken on Short Notice. A deposition must not be used against a party who, having received less than 11 days' notice of the deposition, promptly moved for a protective order under Rule 26(c)(1)(B) requesting that it not be taken or be taken at a different time or place—and this motion was still pending when the deposition was taken.

(B) Unavailable Deponent; Party Could Not Obtain an Attorney. A deposition taken without leave of court under the unavailability provision of Rule 30(a)(2)(A)(iii) must not be used against a party who shows that, when served with the notice, it could not, despite diligent efforts, obtain an attorney to represent it at the deposition.

(6) *Using Part of a Deposition.* If a party offers in evidence only part of a deposition, an adverse party may require the offeror to introduce other parts that in fairness should be considered with the part introduced, and any party may itself introduce any other parts.

(7) *Substituting a Party.* Substituting a party under Rule 25 does not affect the right to use a deposition previously taken.

(8) *Deposition Taken in an Earlier Action.* A deposition lawfully taken and, if required, filed in any federal- or state-court action may be used in a later action involving the same subject matter between the same parties, or their representatives or successors in interest, to the same extent as if taken in the later

action. A deposition previously taken may also be used as allowed by the Federal Rules of Evidence.

(b) Objections to Admissibility. Subject to Rules 28(b) and 32(d)(3), an objection may be made at a hearing or trial to the admission of any deposition testimony that would be inadmissible if the witness were present and testifying.

(c) Form of Presentation. Unless the court orders otherwise, a party must provide a transcript of any deposition testimony the party offers, but may provide the court with the testimony in nontranscript form as well. On any party's request, deposition testimony offered in a jury trial for any purpose other than impeachment must be presented in nontranscript form, if available, unless the court for good cause orders otherwise.

(d) Waiver of Objections.

(1) *To the Notice.* An objection to an error or irregularity in a deposition notice is waived unless promptly served in writing on the party giving the notice.

(2) *To the Officer's Qualification.* An objection based on disqualification of the officer before whom a deposition is to be taken is waived if not made:

(A) before the deposition begins; or

(B) promptly after the basis for disqualification becomes known or, with reasonable diligence, could have been known.

(3) *To the Taking of the Deposition.*

(A) Objection to Competence, Relevance, or Materiality. An objection to a deponent's competence— or to the competence, relevance, or materiality of testimony—is not waived by a failure to make the objection before or during the deposition, unless the ground for it might have been corrected at that time.

(B) Objection to an Error or Irregularity. An objection to an error or irregularity at an oral examination is waived if:

(i) it relates to the manner of taking the deposition, the form of a question or answer, the oath or affirmation, a party's conduct, or other matters that might have been corrected at that time; and

(ii) it is not timely made during the deposition.

(C) Objection to a Written Question. An objection to the form of a written question under Rule 31 is waived if not served in writing on the party submitting the question within the time for serving responsive questions or, if the question is a recross-question, within 5 days after being served with it.

(4) *To Completing and Returning the Deposition.* An objection to how the officer transcribed the testimony—or prepared, signed, certified, sealed, endorsed, sent, or otherwise dealt with the deposition— is waived unless a motion to suppress is made prompt-

ly after the error or irregularity becomes known or, with reasonable diligence, could have been known.

[Amended March 30, 1970, effective July 1, 1970; November 20, 1972, effective July 1, 1975; April 29, 1980, effective August 1, 1980; March 2, 1987, effective August 1, 1987; April 22, 1993, effective December 1, 1993; April 30, 2007, effective December 1, 2007.]

RULE 33. INTERROGATORIES TO PARTIES

(a) In General.

(1) *Number.* Unless otherwise stipulated or ordered by the court, a party may serve on any other party no more than 25 written interrogatories, including all discrete subparts. Leave to serve additional interrogatories may be granted to the extent consistent with Rule 26(b)(2).

(2) *Scope.* An interrogatory may relate to any matter that may be inquired into under Rule 26(b). An interrogatory is not objectionable merely because it asks for an opinion or contention that relates to fact or the application of law to fact, but the court may order that the interrogatory need not be answered until designated discovery is complete, or until a pretrial conference or some other time.

(b) Answers and Objections.

(1) *Responding Party.* The interrogatories must be answered:

(A) by the party to whom they are directed; or

(B) if that party is a public or private corporation, a partnership, an association, or a governmental agency, by any officer or agent, who must furnish the information available to the party.

(2) *Time to Respond.* The responding party must serve its answers and any objections within 30 days after being served with the interrogatories. A shorter or longer time may be stipulated to under Rule 29 or be ordered by the court.

(3) *Answering Each Interrogatory.* Each interrogatory must, to the extent it is not objected to, be answered separately and fully in writing under oath.

(4) *Objections.* The grounds for objecting to an interrogatory must be stated with specificity. Any ground not stated in a timely objection is waived unless the court, for good cause, excuses the failure.

(5) *Signature.* The person who makes the answers must sign them, and the attorney who objects must sign any objections.

(c) Use. An answer to an interrogatory may be used to the extent allowed by the Federal Rules of Evidence.

(d) Option to Produce Business Records. If the answer to an interrogatory may be determined by examining, auditing, compiling, abstracting, or summarizing a party's business records (including electronically stored information), and if the burden of deriving or ascertaining the answer will be substantially the same for either party, the responding party may answer by:

(1) specifying the records that must be reviewed, in sufficient detail to enable the interrogating party to locate and identify them as readily as the responding party could; and

(2) giving the interrogating party a reasonable opportunity to examine and audit the records and to make copies, compilations, abstracts, or summaries.

[Amended December 27, 1946, effective March 19, 1948; March 30, 1970, effective July 1, 1970; April 29, 1980, effective August 1, 1980; April 22, 1993, effective December 1, 1993; April 12, 2006, effective December 1, 2006; April 30, 2007, effective December 1, 2007.]

RULE 34. PRODUCING DOCUMENTS, ELECTRONICALLY STORED INFORMATION, AND TANGIBLE THINGS, OR ENTERING ONTO LAND, FOR INSPECTION AND OTHER PURPOSES

(a) In General. A party may serve on any other party a request within the scope of Rule 26(b):

(1) to produce and permit the requesting party or its representative to inspect, copy, test, or sample the following items in the responding party's possession, custody, or control:

(A) any designated documents or electronically stored information—including writings, drawings, graphs, charts, photographs, sound recordings, images, and other data or data compilations—stored in any medium from which information can be obtained either directly or, if necessary, after translation by the responding party into a reasonably usable form; or

(B) any designated tangible things; or

(2) to permit entry onto designated land or other property possessed or controlled by the responding party, so that the requesting party may inspect, measure, survey, photograph, test, or sample the property or any designated object or operation on it.

(b) Procedure.

(1) *Contents of the Request.* The request:

(A) must describe with reasonable particularity each item or category of items to be inspected;

(B) must specify a reasonable time, place, and manner for the inspection and for performing the related acts; and

(C) may specify the form or forms in which electronically stored information is to be produced.

(2) *Responses and Objections.*

(A) Time to Respond. The party to whom the request is directed must respond in writing within

30 days after being served. A shorter or longer time may be stipulated to under Rule 29 or be ordered by the court.

(B) Responding to Each Item. For each item or category, the response must either state that inspection and related activities will be permitted as requested or state an objection to the request, including the reasons.

(C) Objections. An objection to part of a request must specify the part and permit inspection of the rest.

(D) Responding to a Request for Production of Electronically Stored Information. The response may state an objection to a requested form for producing electronically stored information. If the responding party objects to a requested form—or if no form was specified in the request—the party must state the form or forms it intends to use.

(E) Producing the Documents or Electronically Stored Information. Unless otherwise stipulated or ordered by the court, these procedures apply to producing documents or electronically stored information:

(i) A party must produce documents as they are kept in the usual course of business or must organize and label them to correspond to the categories in the request;

(ii) If a request does not specify a form for producing electronically stored information, a party must produce it in a form or forms in which it is ordinarily maintained or in a reasonably usable form or forms; and

(iii) A party need not produce the same electronically stored information in more than one form.

(c) Nonparties. As provided in Rule 45, a nonparty may be compelled to produce documents and tangible things or to permit an inspection.

[Amended December 27, 1946, effective March 19, 1948; March 30, 1970, effective July 1, 1970; April 29, 1980, effective August 1, 1980; March 2, 1987, effective August 1, 1987; April 30, 1991, effective December 1, 1991; April 22, 1993, effective December 1, 1993; April 12, 2006, effective December 1, 2006; April 30, 2007, effective December 1, 2007.]

RULE 35. PHYSICAL AND MENTAL EXAMINATIONS

(a) Order for an Examination.

(1) *In General.* The court where the action is pending may order a party whose mental or physical condition—including blood group—is in controversy to submit to a physical or mental examination by a suitably licensed or certified examiner. The court has the same authority to order a party to produce for examination a person who is in its custody or under its legal control.

(2) *Motion and Notice; Contents of the Order.* The order:

(A) may be made only on motion for good cause and on notice to all parties and the person to be examined; and

(B) must specify the time, place, manner, conditions, and scope of the examination, as well as the person or persons who will perform it.

(b) Examiner's Report.

(1) *Request by the Party or Person Examined.* The party who moved for the examination must, on request, deliver to the requester a copy of the examiner's report, together with like reports of all earlier examinations of the same condition. The request may be made by the party against whom the examination order was issued or by the person examined.

(2) *Contents.* The examiner's report must be in writing and must set out in detail the examiner's findings, including diagnoses, conclusions, and the results of any tests.

(3) *Request by the Moving Party.* After delivering the reports, the party who moved for the examination may request—and is entitled to receive—from the party against whom the examination order was issued like reports of all earlier or later examinations of the same condition. But those reports need not be delivered by the party with custody or control of the person examined if the party shows that it could not obtain them.

(4) *Waiver of Privilege.* By requesting and obtaining the examiner's report, or by deposing the examiner, the party examined waives any privilege it may have—in that action or any other action involving the same controversy—concerning testimony about all examinations of the same condition.

(5) *Failure to Deliver a Report.* The court on motion may order—on just terms—that a party deliver the report of an examination. If the report is not provided, the court may exclude the examiner's testimony at trial.

(6) *Scope.* This subdivision (b) applies also to an examination made by the parties' agreement, unless the agreement states otherwise. This subdivision does not preclude obtaining an examiner's report or deposing an examiner under other rules.

[Amended March 30, 1970, effective July 1, 1970; March 2, 1987, effective August 1, 1987; amended by Pub.L. 100–690, Title VII, § 7047(b), November 18, 1988, 102 Stat. 4401; amended April 30, 1991, effective December 1, 1991; April 30, 2007, effective December 1, 2007.]

RULE 36.   REQUESTS FOR ADMISSION

(a) Scope and Procedure.

(1) *Scope.* A party may serve on any other party a written request to admit, for purposes of the pending action only, the truth of any matters within the scope of Rule 26(b)(1) relating to:

(A) facts, the application of law to fact, or opinions about either; and

(B) the genuineness of any described documents.

(2) *Form; Copy of a Document.* Each matter must be separately stated. A request to admit the genuineness of a document must be accompanied by a copy of the document unless it is, or has been, otherwise furnished or made available for inspection and copying.

(3) *Time to Respond; Effect of Not Responding.* A matter is admitted unless, within 30 days after being served, the party to whom the request is directed serves on the requesting party a written answer or objection addressed to the matter and signed by the party or its attorney. A shorter or longer time for responding may be stipulated to under Rule 29 or be ordered by the court.

(4) *Answer.* If a matter is not admitted, the answer must specifically deny it or state in detail why the answering party cannot truthfully admit or deny it. A denial must fairly respond to the substance of the matter; and when good faith requires that a party qualify an answer or deny only a part of a matter, the answer must specify the part admitted and qualify or deny the rest. The answering party may assert lack of knowledge or information as a reason for failing to admit or deny only if the party states that it has made reasonable inquiry and that the information it knows or can readily obtain is insufficient to enable it to admit or deny.

(5) *Objections.* The grounds for objecting to a request must be stated. A party must not object solely on the ground that the request presents a genuine issue for trial.

(6) *Motion Regarding the Sufficiency of an Answer or Objection.* The requesting party may move to determine the sufficiency of an answer or objection. Unless the court finds an objection justified, it must order that an answer be served. On finding that an answer does not comply with this rule, the court may order either that the matter is admitted or that an amended answer be served. The court may defer its final decision until a pretrial conference or a specified time before trial. Rule 37(a)(5) applies to an award of expenses.

(b) Effect of an Admission; Withdrawing or Amending It. A matter admitted under this rule is conclusively established unless the court, on motion, permits the admission to be withdrawn or amended. Subject to Rule 16(e), the court may permit withdrawal or amendment if it would promote the presentation of the merits of the action and if the court is not persuaded that it would prejudice the requesting party in maintaining or defending the action on the merits. An admission under this rule is not an admission for any other purpose and cannot be used against the party in any other proceeding.

[Amended December 27, 1946, effective March 19, 1948; March 30, 1970, effective July 1, 1970; March 2, 1987, effective August 1, 1987; April 22, 1993, effective December 1, 1993; April 30, 2007, effective December 1, 2007.]

RULE 37. FAILURE TO MAKE DISCLOSURES OR TO COOPERATE IN DISCOVERY; SANCTIONS

(a) Motion for an Order Compelling Disclosure or Discovery.

(1) *In General.* On notice to other parties and all affected persons, a party may move for an order compelling disclosure or discovery. The motion must include a certification that the movant has in good faith conferred or attempted to confer with the person or party failing to make disclosure or discovery in an effort to obtain it without court action.

(2) *Appropriate Court.* A motion for an order to a party must be made in the court where the action is pending. A motion for an order to a nonparty must be made in the court where the discovery is or will be taken.

(3) *Specific Motions.*

(A) To Compel Disclosure. If a party fails to make a disclosure required by Rule 26(a), any other party may move to compel disclosure and for appropriate sanctions.

(B) To Compel a Discovery Response. A party seeking discovery may move for an order compelling an answer, designation, production, or inspection. This motion may be made if:

(i) a deponent fails to answer a question asked under Rule 30 or 31;

(ii) a corporation or other entity fails to make a designation under Rule 30(b)(6) or 31(a)(4);

(iii) a party fails to answer an interrogatory submitted under Rule 33; or

(iv) a party fails to respond that inspection will be permitted—or fails to permit inspection—as requested under Rule 34.

(C) Related to a Deposition. When taking an oral deposition, the party asking a question may complete or adjourn the examination before moving for an order.

(4) *Evasive or Incomplete Disclosure, Answer, or Response.* For purposes of this subdivision (a), an evasive or incomplete disclosure, answer, or response must be treated as a failure to disclose, answer, or respond.

(5) *Payment of Expenses; Protective Orders.*

(A) If the Motion Is Granted (or Disclosure or Discovery Is Provided After Filing). If the motion is granted—or if the disclosure or requested discovery is provided after the motion was filed—the court must, after giving an opportunity to be heard, require the party or deponent whose conduct necessitated the motion, the party or attorney advising that conduct, or both to pay the movant's reasonable expenses incurred in making the motion, including attorney's fees. But the court must not order this payment if:

(i) the movant filed the motion before attempting in good faith to obtain the disclosure or discovery without court action;

(ii) the opposing party's nondisclosure, response, or objection was substantially justified; or

(iii) other circumstances make an award of expenses unjust.

(B) If the Motion Is Denied. If the motion is denied, the court may issue any protective order authorized under Rule 26(c) and must, after giving an opportunity to be heard, require the movant, the attorney filing the motion, or both to pay the party or deponent who opposed the motion its reasonable expenses incurred in opposing the motion, including attorney's fees. But the court must not order this payment if the motion was substantially justified or other circumstances make an award of expenses unjust.

(C) If the Motion Is Granted in Part and Denied in Part. If the motion is granted in part and denied in part, the court may issue any protective order authorized under Rule 26(c) and may, after giving an opportunity to be heard, apportion the reasonable expenses for the motion.

(b) Failure to Comply with a Court Order.

(1) *Sanctions in the District Where the Deposition Is Taken.* If the court where the discovery is taken orders a deponent to be sworn or to answer a question and the deponent fails to obey, the failure may be treated as contempt of court.

(2) *Sanctions in the District Where the Action Is Pending.*

(A) For Not Obeying a Discovery Order. If a party or a party's officer, director, or managing agent—or a witness designated under Rule 30(b)(6) or 31(a)(4)—fails to obey an order to provide or permit discovery, including an order under Rule 26(f), 35, or 37(a), the court where the action is pending may issue further just orders. They may include the following:

(i) directing that the matters embraced in the order or other designated facts be taken as established for purposes of the action, as the prevailing party claims;

(ii) prohibiting the disobedient party from supporting or opposing designated claims or defenses, or from introducing designated matters in evidence;

    (iii) striking pleadings in whole or in part;

    (iv) staying further proceedings until the order is obeyed;

    (v) dismissing the action or proceeding in whole or in part;

    (vi) rendering a default judgment against the disobedient party; or

    (vii) treating as contempt of court the failure to obey any order except an order to submit to a physical or mental examination.

(B) For Not Producing a Person for Examination. If a party fails to comply with an order under Rule 35(a) requiring it to produce another person for examination, the court may issue any of the orders listed in Rule 37(b)(2)(A)(i)-(vi), unless the disobedient party shows that it cannot produce the other person.

(C) Payment of Expenses. Instead of or in addition to the orders above, the court must order the disobedient party, the attorney advising that party, or both to pay the reasonable expenses, including attorney's fees, caused by the failure, unless the failure was substantially justified or other circumstances make an award of expenses unjust.

(c) Failure to Disclose, to Supplement an Earlier Response, or to Admit.

(1) *Failure to Disclose or Supplement.* If a party fails to provide information or identify a witness as required by Rule 26(a) or (e), the party is not allowed to use that information or witness to supply evidence on a motion, at a hearing, or at a trial, unless the failure was substantially justified or is harmless. In addition to or instead of this sanction, the court, on motion and after giving an opportunity to be heard:

    (A) may order payment of the reasonable expenses, including attorney's fees, caused by the failure;

    (B) may inform the jury of the party's failure; and

    (C) may impose other appropriate sanctions, including any of the orders listed in Rule 37(b)(2)(A)(i)-(vi).

(2) *Failure to Admit.* If a party fails to admit what is requested under Rule 36 and if the requesting party later proves a document to be genuine or the matter true, the requesting party may move that the party who failed to admit pay the reasonable expenses, including attorney's fees, incurred in making that proof. The court must so order unless:

    (A) the request was held objectionable under Rule 36(a);

    (B) the admission sought was of no substantial importance;

    (C) the party failing to admit had a reasonable ground to believe that it might prevail on the matter; or

    (D) there was other good reason for the failure to admit.

(d) Party's Failure to Attend Its Own Deposition, Serve Answers to Interrogatories, or Respond to a Request for Inspection.

(1) *In General.*

    (A) Motion; Grounds for Sanctions. The court where the action is pending may, on motion, order sanctions if:

        (i) a party or a party's officer, director, or managing agent—or a person designated under Rule 30(b)(6) or 31(a)(4)—fails, after being served with proper notice, to appear for that person's deposition; or

        (ii) a party, after being properly served with interrogatories under Rule 33 or a request for inspection under Rule 34, fails to serve its answers, objections, or written response.

    (B) Certification. A motion for sanctions for failing to answer or respond must include a certification that the movant has in good faith conferred or attempted to confer with the party failing to act in an effort to obtain the answer or response without court action.

(2) *Unacceptable Excuse for Failing to Act.* A failure described in Rule 37(d)(1)(A) is not excused on the ground that the discovery sought was objectionable, unless the party failing to act has a pending motion for a protective order under Rule 26(c).

(3) *Types of Sanctions.* Sanctions may include any of the orders listed in Rule 37(b)(2)(A)(i)-(vi). Instead of or in addition to these sanctions, the court must require the party failing to act, the attorney advising that party, or both to pay the reasonable expenses, including attorney's fees, caused by the failure, unless the failure was substantially justified or other circumstances make an award of expenses unjust.

(e) Failure to Provide Electronically Stored Information. Absent exceptional circumstances, a court may not impose sanctions under these rules on a party for failing to provide electronically stored information lost as a result of the routine, good-faith operation of an electronic information system.

(f) Failure to Participate in Framing a Discovery Plan. If a party or its attorney fails to participate in good faith in developing and submitting a proposed discovery plan as required by Rule 26(f), the court may, after giving an opportunity to be heard, require that party or attorney to pay to any other party the reasonable expenses, including attorney's fees, caused by the failure.

[Amended December 29, 1948, effective October 20, 1949; March 30, 1970, effective July 1, 1970; April 29, 1980, effective August 1, 1980; amended by Pub.L. 96–481, Title II, § 205(a), October 21, 1980, 94 Stat. 2330, effective October 1, 1981; amended March 2, 1987, effective August 1, 1987; April 22, 1993, effective December 1, 1993; April 17,

2000, effective December 1, 2000; April 12, 2006, effective December 1, 2006; April 30, 2007, effective December 1, 2007.]

TITLE VI. TRIALS

RULE 38. RIGHT TO A JURY TRIAL; DEMAND

(a) Right Preserved. The right of trial by jury as declared by the Seventh Amendment to the Constitution—or as provided by a federal statute—is preserved to the parties inviolate.

(b) Demand. On any issue triable of right by a jury, a party may demand a jury trial by:

(1) serving the other parties with a written demand—which may be included in a pleading—no later than 10 days after the last pleading directed to the issue is served; and

(2) filing the demand in accordance with Rule 5(d).

(c) Specifying Issues. In its demand, a party may specify the issues that it wishes to have tried by a jury; otherwise, it is considered to have demanded a jury trial on all the issues so triable. If the party has demanded a jury trial on only some issues, any other party may—within 10 days after being served with the demand or within a shorter time ordered by the court—serve a demand for a jury trial on any other or all factual issues triable by jury.

(d) Waiver; Withdrawal. A party waives a jury trial unless its demand is properly served and filed. A proper demand may be withdrawn only if the parties consent.

(e) Admiralty and Maritime Claims. These rules do not create a right to a jury trial on issues in a claim that is an admiralty or maritime claim under Rule 9(h).

[Amended February 28, 1966, effective July 1, 1966; March 2, 1987, effective August 1, 1987; April 22, 1993, effective December 1, 1993; April 30, 2007, effective December 1, 2007.]

RULE 39. TRIAL BY JURY OR BY THE COURT

(a) When a Demand Is Made. When a jury trial has been demanded under Rule 38, the action must be designated on the docket as a jury action. The trial on all issues so demanded must be by jury unless:

(1) the parties or their attorneys file a stipulation to a nonjury trial or so stipulate on the record; or

(2) the court, on motion or on its own, finds that on some or all of those issues there is no federal right to a jury trial.

(b) When No Demand Is Made. Issues on which a jury trial is not properly demanded are to be tried by the court. But the court may, on motion, order a jury trial on any issue for which a jury might have been demanded.

(c) Advisory Jury; Jury Trial by Consent. In an action not triable of right by a jury, the court, on motion or on its own:

(1) may try any issue with an advisory jury; or

(2) may, with the parties' consent, try any issue by a jury whose verdict has the same effect as if a jury trial had been a matter of right, unless the action is against the United States and a federal statute provides for a nonjury trial.

[Amended April 30, 2007, effective December 1, 2007.]

RULE 40. SCHEDULING CASES FOR TRIAL

Each court must provide by rule for scheduling trials. The court must give priority to actions entitled to priority by a federal statute.

[Amended April 30, 2007, effective December 1, 2007.]

RULE 41. DISMISSAL OF ACTIONS

(a) Voluntary Dismissal.

(1) *By the Plaintiff.*

(A) Without a Court Order. Subject to Rules 23(e), 23.1(c), 23.2, and 66 and any applicable federal statute, the plaintiff may dismiss an action without a court order by filing:

(i) a notice of dismissal before the opposing party serves either an answer or a motion for summary judgment; or

(ii) a stipulation of dismissal signed by all parties who have appeared.

(B) Effect. Unless the notice or stipulation states otherwise, the dismissal is without prejudice. But if the plaintiff previously dismissed any federal-or state-court action based on or including the same claim, a notice of dismissal operates as an adjudication on the merits.

(2) *By Court Order; Effect.* Except as provided in Rule 41(a)(1), an action may be dismissed at the plaintiff's request only by court order, on terms that the court considers proper. If a defendant has pleaded a counterclaim before being served with the plaintiff's motion to dismiss, the action may be dismissed over

the defendant's objection only if the counterclaim can remain pending for independent adjudication. Unless the order states otherwise, a dismissal under this paragraph (2) is without prejudice.

(b) Involuntary Dismissal; Effect. If the plaintiff fails to prosecute or to comply with these rules or a court order, a defendant may move to dismiss the action or any claim against it. Unless the dismissal order states otherwise, a dismissal under this subdivision (b) and any dismissal not under this rule—except one for lack of jurisdiction, improper venue, or failure to join a party under Rule 19—operates as an adjudication on the merits.

(c) Dismissing a Counterclaim, Crossclaim, or Third–Party Claim. This rule applies to a dismissal of any counterclaim, crossclaim, or third-party claim. A claimant's voluntary dismissal under Rule 41(a)(1)(A)(i) must be made:

(1) before a responsive pleading is served; or

(2) if there is no responsive pleading, before evidence is introduced at a hearing or trial.

(d) Costs of a Previously Dismissed Action. If a plaintiff who previously dismissed an action in any court files an action based on or including the same claim against the same defendant, the court:

(1) may order the plaintiff to pay all or part of the costs of that previous action; and

(2) may stay the proceedings until the plaintiff has complied.

[Amended December 27, 1946, effective March 19, 1948; January 21, 1963, effective July 1, 1963; February 28, 1966, effective July 1, 1966; December 4, 1967, effective July 1, 1968; March 2, 1987, effective August 1, 1987; April 30, 1991, effective December 1, 1991; April 30, 2007, effective December 1, 2007.]

RULE 42. CONSOLIDATION; SEPARATE TRIALS

(a) Consolidation. If actions before the court involve a common question of law or fact, the court may:

(1) join for hearing or trial any or all matters at issue in the actions;

(2) consolidate the actions; or

(3) issue any other orders to avoid unnecessary cost or delay.

(b) Separate Trials. For convenience, to avoid prejudice, or to expedite and economize, the court may order a separate trial of one or more separate issues, claims, crossclaims, counterclaims, or third-party claims. When ordering a separate trial, the court must preserve any federal right to a jury trial.

[Amended February 28, 1966, effective July 1, 1966; April 30, 2007, effective December 1, 2007.]

RULE 43. TAKING TESTIMONY

(a) In Open Court. At trial, the witnesses' testimony must be taken in open court unless a federal statute, the Federal Rules of Evidence, these rules, or other rules adopted by the Supreme Court provide otherwise. For good cause in compelling circumstances and with appropriate safeguards, the court may permit testimony in open court by contemporaneous transmission from a different location.

(b) Affirmation Instead of an Oath. When these rules require an oath, a solemn affirmation suffices.

(c) Evidence on a Motion. When a motion relies on facts outside the record, the court may hear the matter on affidavits or may hear it wholly or partly on oral testimony or on depositions.

(d) Interpreter. The court may appoint an interpreter of its choosing; fix reasonable compensation to be paid from funds provided by law or by one or more parties; and tax the compensation as costs.

[Amended February 28, 1966, effective July 1, 1966; November 20, 1972, and December 18, 1972, effective July 1, 1975; March 2, 1987, effective August 1, 1987; April 23, 1996, effective December 1, 1996; April 30, 2007, effective December 1, 2007.]

RULE 44. PROVING AN OFFICIAL RECORD

(a) Means of Proving.

(1) *Domestic Record.* Each of the following evidences an official record—or an entry in it—that is otherwise admissible and is kept within the United States, any state, district, or commonwealth, or any territory subject to the administrative or judicial jurisdiction of the United States:

(A) an official publication of the record; or

(B) a copy attested by the officer with legal custody of the record—or by the officer's deputy—and accompanied by a certificate that the officer has custody. The certificate must be made under seal:

(i) by a judge of a court of record in the district or political subdivision where the record is kept; or

(ii) by any public officer with a seal of office and with official duties in the district or political subdivision where the record is kept.

(2) *Foreign Record.*

(A) In General. Each of the following evidences a foreign official record—or an entry in it—that is otherwise admissible:

(i) an official publication of the record; or

(ii) the record—or a copy—that is attested by an authorized person and is accompanied either by a final certification of genuineness or by a certification under a treaty or convention to which the United States and the country where the record is located are parties.

(B) Final Certification of Genuineness. A final certification must certify the genuineness of the signature and official position of the attester or of any foreign official whose certificate of genuineness relates to the attestation or is in a chain of certificates of genuineness relating to the attestation. A final certification may be made by a secretary of a United States embassy or legation; by a consul general, vice consul, or consular agent of the United States; or by a diplomatic or consular official of the foreign country assigned or accredited to the United States.

(C) Other Means of Proof. If all parties have had a reasonable opportunity to investigate a foreign record's authenticity and accuracy, the court may, for good cause, either:

(i) admit an attested copy without final certification; or

(ii) permit the record to be evidenced by an attested summary with or without a final certification.

(b) Lack of a Record. A written statement that a diligent search of designated records revealed no record or entry of a specified tenor is admissible as evidence that the records contain no such record or entry. For domestic records, the statement must be authenticated under Rule 44(a)(1). For foreign records, the statement must comply with (a)(2)(C)(ii).

(c) Other Proof. A party may prove an official record—or an entry or lack of an entry in it—by any other method authorized by law.

[Amended February 28, 1966, effective July 1, 1966; March 2, 1987, effective August 1, 1987; April 30, 1991, effective December 1, 1991; April 30, 2007, effective December 1, 2007.]

RULE 44.1 DETERMINING FOREIGN LAW

A party who intends to raise an issue about a foreign country's law must give notice by a pleading or other writing. In determining foreign law, the court may consider any relevant material or source, including testimony, whether or not submitted by a party or admissible under the Federal Rules of Evidence. The court's determination must be treated as a ruling on a question of law.

[Adopted February 28, 1966, effective July 1, 1966; amended November 20, 1972, effective July 1, 1975; March 2, 1987, effective August 1, 1987; April 30, 2007, effective December 1, 2007.]

RULE 45. SUBPOENA

(a) In General.

(1) *Form and Contents.*

(A) Requirements—In General. Every subpoena must:

(i) state the court from which it issued;

(ii) state the title of the action, the court in which it is pending, and its civil-action number;

(iii) command each person to whom it is directed to do the following at a specified time and place: attend and testify; produce designated documents, electronically stored information, or tangible things in that person's possession, custody, or control; or permit the inspection of premises; and

(iv) set out the text of Rule 45(c) and (d).

(B) Command to Attend a Deposition—Notice of the Recording Method. A subpoena commanding attendance at a deposition must state the method for recording the testimony.

(C) Combining or Separating a Command to Produce or to Permit Inspection; Specifying the Form for Electronically Stored Information. A command to produce documents, electronically stored information, or tangible things or to permit the inspection of premises may be included in a subpoena commanding attendance at a deposition, hearing, or trial, or may be set out in a separate subpoena. A subpoena may specify the form or forms in which electronically stored information is to be produced.

(D) Command to Produce; Included Obligations. A command in a subpoena to produce documents, electronically stored information, or tangible things requires the responding party to permit inspection, copying, testing, or sampling of the materials.

(2) *Issued from Which Court.* A subpoena must issue as follows:

(A) for attendance at a hearing or trial, from the court for the district where the hearing or trial is to be held;

(B) for attendance at a deposition, from the court for the district where the deposition is to be taken; and

(C) for production or inspection, if separate from a subpoena commanding a person's attendance, from the court for the district where the production or inspection is to be made.

(3) *Issued by Whom.* The clerk must issue a subpoena, signed but otherwise in blank, to a party who requests it. That party must complete it before service. An attorney also may issue and sign a subpoena as an officer of:

(A) a court in which the attorney is authorized to practice; or

(B) a court for a district where a deposition is to be taken or production is to be made, if the attorney is authorized to practice in the court where the action is pending.

(b) Service.

(1) *By Whom; Tendering Fees; Serving a Copy of Certain Subpoenas.* Any person who is at least 18 years old and not a party may serve a subpoena. Serving a subpoena requires delivering a copy to the named person and, if the subpoena requires that person's attendance, tendering the fees for 1 day's attendance and the mileage allowed by law. Fees and mileage need not be tendered when the subpoena issues on behalf of the United States or any of its officers or agencies. If the subpoena commands the production of documents, electronically stored information, or tangible things or the inspection of premises before trial, then before it is served, a notice must be served on each party.

(2) *Service in the United States.* Subject to Rule 45(c)(3)(A)(ii), a subpoena may be served at any place:

(A) within the district of the issuing court;

(B) outside that district but within 100 miles of the place specified for the deposition, hearing, trial, production, or inspection;

(C) within the state of the issuing court if a state statute or court rule allows service at that place of a subpoena issued by a state court of general jurisdiction sitting in the place specified for the deposition, hearing, trial, production, or inspection; or

(D) that the court authorizes on motion and for good cause, if a federal statute so provides.

(3) *Service in a Foreign Country.* 28 U.S.C. § 1783 governs issuing and serving a subpoena directed to a United States national or resident who is in a foreign country.

(4) *Proof of Service.* Proving service, when necessary, requires filing with the issuing court a statement showing the date and manner of service and the names of the persons served. The statement must be certified by the server.

(c) Protecting a Person Subject to a Subpoena.

(1) *Avoiding Undue Burden or Expense; Sanctions.* A party or attorney responsible for issuing and serving a subpoena must take reasonable steps to avoid imposing undue burden or expense on a person subject to the subpoena. The issuing court must enforce this duty and impose an appropriate sanction—which may include lost earnings and reasonable attorney's fees—on a party or attorney who fails to comply.

(2) *Command to Produce Materials or Permit Inspection.*

(A) Appearance Not Required. A person commanded to produce documents, electronically stored information, or tangible things, or to permit the inspection of premises, need not appear in person at the place of production or inspection unless also commanded to appear for a deposition, hearing, or trial.

(B) Objections. A person commanded to produce documents or tangible things or to permit inspection may serve on the party or attorney designated in the subpoena a written objection to inspecting, copying, testing or sampling any or all of the materials or to inspecting the premises—or to producing electronically stored information in the form or forms requested. The objection must be served before the earlier of the time specified for compliance or 14 days after the subpoena is served. If an objection is made, the following rules apply:

(i) At any time, on notice to the commanded person, the serving party may move the issuing court for an order compelling production or inspection.

(ii) These acts may be required only as directed in the order, and the order must protect a person who is neither a party nor a party's officer from significant expense resulting from compliance.

(3) *Quashing or Modifying a Subpoena.*

(A) When Required. On timely motion, the issuing court must quash or modify a subpoena that:

(i) fails to allow a reasonable time to comply;

(ii) requires a person who is neither a party nor a party's officer to travel more than 100 miles from where that person resides, is employed, or regularly transacts business in person—except that, subject to Rule 45(c)(3)(B)(iii), the person may be commanded to attend a trial by traveling from any such place within the state where the trial is held;

(iii) requires disclosure of privileged or other protected matter, if no exception or waiver applies; or

(iv) subjects a person to undue burden.

(B) When Permitted. To protect a person subject to or affected by a subpoena, the issuing court may, on motion, quash or modify the subpoena if it requires:

(i) disclosing a trade secret or other confidential research, development, or commercial information;

(ii) disclosing an unretained expert's opinion or information that does not describe specific occurrences in dispute and results from the expert's study that was not requested by a party; or

(iii) a person who is neither a party nor a party's officer to incur substantial expense to travel more than 100 miles to attend trial.

(C) Specifying Conditions as an Alternative. In the circumstances described in Rule 45(c)(3)(B), the court may, instead of quashing or modifying a subpoena, order appearance or production under specified conditions if the serving party:

(i) shows a substantial need for the testimony or material that cannot be otherwise met without undue hardship; and

(ii) ensures that the subpoenaed person will be reasonably compensated.

(d) Duties in Responding to a Subpoena.

(1) *Producing Documents or Electronically Stored Information.* These procedures apply to producing documents or electronically stored information:

(A) Documents. A person responding to a subpoena to produce documents must produce them as they are kept in the ordinary course of business or must organize and label them to correspond to the categories in the demand.

(B) Form for Producing Electronically Stored Information Not Specified. If a subpoena does not specify a form for producing electronically stored information, the person responding must produce it in a form or forms in which it is ordinarily maintained or in a reasonably usable form or forms.

(C) Electronically Stored Information Produced in Only One Form. The person responding need not produce the same electronically stored information in more than one form.

(D) Inaccessible Electronically Stored Information. The person responding need not provide discovery of electronically stored information from sources that the person identifies as not reasonably accessible because of undue burden or cost. On motion to compel discovery or for a protective order, the person responding must show that the information is not reasonably accessible because of undue burden or cost. If that showing is made, the court may nonetheless order discovery from such sources if the requesting party shows good cause, considering the limitations of Rule 26(b)(2)(C). The court may specify conditions for the discovery.

(2) *Claiming Privilege or Protection.*

(A) Information Withheld. A person withholding subpoenaed information under a claim that it is privileged or subject to protection as trial-preparation material must:

(i) expressly make the claim; and

(ii) describe the nature of the withheld documents, communications, or tangible things in a manner that, without revealing information itself privileged or protected, will enable the parties to assess the claim.

(B) Information Produced. If information produced in response to a subpoena is subject to a claim of privilege or of protection as trial-preparation material, the person making the claim may notify any party that received the information of the claim and the basis for it. After being notified, a party must promptly return, sequester, or destroy the specified information and any copies it has;

must not use or disclose the information until the claim is resolved; must take reasonable steps to retrieve the information if the party disclosed it before being notified; and may promptly present the information to the court under seal for a determination of the claim. The person who produced the information must preserve the information until the claim is resolved.

(e) Contempt. The issuing court may hold in contempt a person who, having been served, fails without adequate excuse to obey the subpoena. A nonparty's failure to obey must be excused if the subpoena purports to require the nonparty to attend or produce at a place outside the limits of Rule 45(c)(3)(A)(ii).

[Amended December 27, 1946, effective March 19, 1948; December 29, 1948, effective October 20, 1949; March 30, 1970, effective July 1, 1970; April 29, 1980, effective August 1, 1980; April 29, 1985, effective August 1, 1985; March 2, 1987, effective August 1, 1987; April 30, 1991, effective December 1, 1991; April 25, 2005, effective December 1, 2005; April 12, 2006, effective December 1, 2006; April 30, 2007, effective December 1, 2007.]

RULE 46. OBJECTING TO A RULING OR ORDER

A formal exception to a ruling or order is unnecessary. When the ruling or order is requested or made, a party need only state the action that it wants the court to take or objects to, along with the grounds for the request or objection. Failing to object does not prejudice a party who had no opportunity to do so when the ruling or order was made.

[Amended March 2, 1987, effective August 1, 1987; April 30, 2007, effective December 1, 2007.]

RULE 47. SELECTING JURORS

(a) Examining Jurors. The court may permit the parties or their attorneys to examine prospective jurors or may itself do so. If the court examines the jurors, it must permit the parties or their attorneys to make any further inquiry it considers proper, or must itself ask any of their additional questions it considers proper.

(b) Peremptory Challenges. The court must allow the number of peremptory challenges provided by 28 U.S.C. § 1870.

(c) Excusing a Juror. During trial or deliberation, the court may excuse a juror for good cause.

[Amended February 28, 1966, effective July 1, 1966; April 30, 1991, effective December 1, 1991; April 30, 2007, effective December 1, 2007.]

RULE 48. NUMBER OF JURORS; VERDICT

A jury must initially have at least 6 and no more than 12 members, and each juror must participate in the verdict unless excused under Rule 47(c). Unless the parties stipulate otherwise, the verdict must be unanimous and be returned by a jury of at least 6 members.

[Amended April 30, 1991, effective December 1, 1991; April 30, 2007, effective December 1, 2007.]

RULE 49. SPECIAL VERDICT; GENERAL VERDICT AND QUESTIONS

(a) Special Verdict.

(1) *In General.* The court may require a jury to return only a special verdict in the form of a special written finding on each issue of fact. The court may do so by:

(A) submitting written questions susceptible of a categorical or other brief answer;

(B) submitting written forms of the special findings that might properly be made under the pleadings and evidence; or

(C) using any other method that the court considers appropriate.

(2) *Instructions.* The court must give the instructions and explanations necessary to enable the jury to make its findings on each submitted issue.

(3) *Issues Not Submitted.* A party waives the right to a jury trial on any issue of fact raised by the pleadings or evidence but not submitted to the jury unless, before the jury retires, the party demands its submission to the jury. If the party does not demand submission, the court may make a finding on the issue. If the court makes no finding, it is considered to have made a finding consistent with its judgment on the special verdict.

(b) General Verdict with Answers to Written Questions.

(1) *In General.* The court may submit to the jury forms for a general verdict, together with written questions on one or more issues of fact that the jury must decide. The court must give the instructions and explanations necessary to enable the jury to render a general verdict and answer the questions in writing, and must direct the jury to do both.

(2) *Verdict and Answers Consistent.* When the general verdict and the answers are consistent, the court must approve, for entry under Rule 58, an appropriate judgment on the verdict and answers.

(3) *Answers Inconsistent with the Verdict.* When the answers are consistent with each other but one or more is inconsistent with the general verdict, the court may:

(A) approve, for entry under Rule 58, an appropriate judgment according to the answers, notwithstanding the general verdict;

(B) direct the jury to further consider its answers and verdict; or

(C) order a new trial.

(4) *Answers Inconsistent with Each Other and the Verdict.* When the answers are inconsistent with each other and one or more is also inconsistent with the general verdict, judgment must not be entered; instead, the court must direct the jury to further consider its answers and verdict, or must order a new trial.

[Amended January 21, 1963, effective July 1, 1963; March 2, 1987, effective August 1, 1987; April 30, 2007, effective December 1, 2007.]

RULE 50. JUDGMENT AS A MATTER OF LAW IN A JURY TRIAL; RELATED MOTION FOR A NEW TRIAL; CONDITIONAL RULING

(a) Judgment as a Matter of Law.

(1) *In General.* If a party has been fully heard on an issue during a jury trial and the court finds that a reasonable jury would not have a legally sufficient evidentiary basis to find for the party on that issue, the court may:

(A) resolve the issue against the party; and

(B) grant a motion for judgment as a matter of law against the party on a claim or defense that, under the controlling law, can be maintained or defeated only with a favorable finding on that issue.

(2) *Motion.* A motion for judgment as a matter of law may be made at any time before the case is submitted to the jury. The motion must specify the judgment sought and the law and facts that entitle the movant to the judgment.

(b) Renewing the Motion After Trial; Alternative Motion for a New Trial. If the court does not grant a motion for judgment as a matter of law made under Rule 50(a), the court is considered to have submitted the action to the jury subject to the court's later deciding the legal questions raised by the motion. No later than 10 days after the entry of judgment—or if the motion addresses a jury issue not decided by a verdict, no later than 10 days after the jury was discharged—the movant may file a renewed motion for judgment as a matter of law and may include an alternative or joint request for a new trial under Rule 59. In ruling on the renewed motion, the court may:

(1) allow judgment on the verdict, if the jury returned a verdict;

(2) order a new trial; or

(3) direct the entry of judgment as a matter of law.

(c) Granting the Renewed Motion; Conditional Ruling on a Motion for a New Trial.

(1) *In General.* If the court grants a renewed motion for judgment as a matter of law, it must also conditionally rule on any motion for a new trial by determining whether a new trial should be granted if the judgment is later vacated or reversed. The court

must state the grounds for conditionally granting or denying the motion for a new trial.

(2) *Effect of a Conditional Ruling.* Conditionally granting the motion for a new trial does not affect the judgment's finality; if the judgment is reversed, the new trial must proceed unless the appellate court orders otherwise. If the motion for a new trial is conditionally denied, the appellee may assert error in that denial; if the judgment is reversed, the case must proceed as the appellate court orders.

(d) Time for a Losing Party's New–Trial Motion. Any motion for a new trial under Rule 59 by a party against whom judgment as a matter of law is rendered must be filed no later than 10 days after the entry of the judgment.

(e) Denying the Motion for Judgment as a Matter of Law; Reversal on Appeal. If the court denies the motion for judgment as a matter of law, the prevailing party may, as appellee, assert grounds entitling it to a new trial should the appellate court conclude that the trial court erred in denying the motion. If the appellate court reverses the judgment, it may order a new trial, direct the trial court to determine whether a new trial should be granted, or direct the entry of judgment.

[Amended January 21, 1963, effective July 1, 1963; March 2, 1987, effective August 1, 1987; April 30, 1991, effective December 1, 1991; April 22, 1993, effective December 1, 1993; April 27, 1995, effective December 1, 1995; April 12, 2006, effective December 1, 2006; April 30, 2007, effective December 1, 2007.]

RULE 51. INSTRUCTIONS TO THE JURY; OBJECTIONS; PRESERVING A CLAIM OF ERROR

(a) Requests.

(1) *Before or at the Close of the Evidence.* At the close of the evidence or at any earlier reasonable time that the court orders, a party may file and furnish to every other party written requests for the jury instructions it wants the court to give.

(2) *After the Close of the Evidence.* After the close of the evidence, a party may:

(A) file requests for instructions on issues that could not reasonably have been anticipated by an earlier time that the court set for requests; and

(B) with the court's permission, file untimely requests for instructions on any issue.

(b) Instructions. The court:

(1) must inform the parties of its proposed instructions and proposed action on the requests before instructing the jury and before final jury arguments;

(2) must give the parties an opportunity to object on the record and out of the jury's hearing before the instructions and arguments are delivered; and

(3) may instruct the jury at any time before the jury is discharged.

(c) Objections.

(1) *How to Make.* A party who objects to an instruction or the failure to give an instruction must do so on the record, stating distinctly the matter objected to and the grounds for the objection.

(2) *When to Make.* An objection is timely if:

(A) a party objects at the opportunity provided under Rule 51(b)(2); or

(B) a party was not informed of an instruction or action on a request before that opportunity to object, and the party objects promptly after learning that the instruction or request will be, or has been, given or refused.

(d) Assigning Error; Plain Error.

(1) *Assigning Error.* A party may assign as error:

(A) an error in an instruction actually given, if that party properly objected; or

(B) a failure to give an instruction, if that party properly requested it and—unless the court rejected the request in a definitive ruling on the record— also properly objected.

(2) *Plain Error.* A court may consider a plain error in the instructions that has not been preserved as required by Rule 51(d)(1) if the error affects substantial rights.

[Amended March 2, 1987, effective August 1, 1987; March 27, 2003, effective December 1, 2003; April 30, 2007, effective December 1, 2007.]

RULE 52. FINDINGS AND CONCLUSIONS BY THE COURT; JUDGMENT ON PARTIAL FINDINGS

(a) Findings and Conclusions.

(1) *In General.* In an action tried on the facts without a jury or with an advisory jury, the court must find the facts specially and state its conclusions of law separately. The findings and conclusions may be stated on the record after the close of the evidence or may appear in an opinion or a memorandum of decision filed by the court. Judgment must be entered under Rule 58.

(2) *For an Interlocutory Injunction.* In granting or refusing an interlocutory injunction, the court must similarly state the findings and conclusions that support its action.

(3) *For a Motion.* The court is not required to state findings or conclusions when ruling on a motion under Rule 12 or 56 or, unless these rules provide otherwise, on any other motion.

(4) *Effect of a Master's Findings.* A master's findings, to the extent adopted by the court, must be considered the court's findings.

(5) *Questioning the Evidentiary Support.* A party may later question the sufficiency of the evidence supporting the findings, whether or not the party requested findings, objected to them, moved to amend them, or moved for partial findings.

(6) *Setting Aside the Findings.* Findings of fact, whether based on oral or other evidence, must not be set aside unless clearly erroneous, and the reviewing court must give due regard to the trial court's opportunity to judge the witnesses' credibility.

(b) Amended or Additional Findings. On a party's motion filed no later than 10 days after the entry of judgment, the court may amend its findings—or make additional findings—and may amend the judgment accordingly. The motion may accompany a motion for a new trial under Rule 59.

(c) Judgment on Partial Findings. If a party has been fully heard on an issue during a nonjury trial and the court finds against the party on that issue, the court may enter judgment against the party on a claim or defense that, under the controlling law, can be maintained or defeated only with a favorable finding on that issue. The court may, however, decline to render any judgment until the close of the evidence. A judgment on partial findings must be supported by findings of fact and conclusions of law as required by Rule 52(a).

[Amended December 27, 1946, effective March 19, 1948; January 21, 1963, effective July 1, 1963; April 28, 1983, effective August 1, 1983; April 29, 1985, effective August 1, 1985; April 30, 1991, effective December 1, 1991; April 22, 1993, effective December 1, 1993; April 27, 1995, effective December 1, 1995; April 30, 2007, effective December 1, 2007.]

RULE 53. MASTERS

(a) Appointment.

(1) *Scope.* Unless a statute provides otherwise, a court may appoint a master only to:

(A) perform duties consented to by the parties;

(B) hold trial proceedings and make or recommend findings of fact on issues to be decided without a jury if appointment is warranted by:

(i) some exceptional condition; or

(ii) the need to perform an accounting or resolve a difficult computation of damages; or

(C) address pretrial and posttrial matters that cannot be effectively and timely addressed by an available district judge or magistrate judge of the district.

(2) *Disqualification.* A master must not have a relationship to the parties, attorneys, action, or court that would require disqualification of a judge under 28 U.S.C. § 455, unless the parties, with the court's approval, consent to the appointment after the master discloses any potential grounds for disqualification.

(3) *Possible Expense or Delay.* In appointing a master, the court must consider the fairness of imposing the likely expenses on the parties and must protect against unreasonable expense or delay.

(b) Order Appointing a Master.

(1) *Notice.* Before appointing a master, the court must give the parties notice and an opportunity to be heard. Any party may suggest candidates for appointment.

(2) *Contents.* The appointing order must direct the master to proceed with all reasonable diligence and must state:

(A) the master's duties, including any investigation or enforcement duties, and any limits on the master's authority under Rule 53(c);

(B) the circumstances, if any, in which the master may communicate ex parte with the court or a party;

(C) the nature of the materials to be preserved and filed as the record of the master's activities;

(D) the time limits, method of filing the record, other procedures, and standards for reviewing the master's orders, findings, and recommendations; and

(E) the basis, terms, and procedure for fixing the master's compensation under Rule 53(g).

(3) *Issuing.* The court may issue the order only after:

(A) the master files an affidavit disclosing whether there is any ground for disqualification under 28 U.S.C. § 455; and

(B) if a ground is disclosed, the parties, with the court's approval, waive the disqualification.

(4) *Amending.* The order may be amended at any time after notice to the parties and an opportunity to be heard.

(c) Master's Authority.

(1) *In General.* Unless the appointing order directs otherwise, a master may:

(A) regulate all proceedings;

(B) take all appropriate measures to perform the assigned duties fairly and efficiently; and

(C) if conducting an evidentiary hearing, exercise the appointing court's power to compel, take, and record evidence.

(2) *Sanctions.* The master may by order impose on a party any noncontempt sanction provided by Rule 37 or 45, and may recommend a contempt sanction against a party and sanctions against a nonparty.

(d) Master's Orders. A master who issues an order must file it and promptly serve a copy on each party. The clerk must enter the order on the docket.

(e) Master's Reports. A master must report to the court as required by the appointing order. The master must file the report and promptly serve a copy on each party, unless the court orders otherwise.

(f) Action on the Master's Order, Report, or Recommendations.

(1) *Opportunity for a Hearing; Action in General.* In acting on a master's order, report, or recommendations, the court must give the parties notice and an opportunity to be heard; may receive evidence; and may adopt or affirm, modify, wholly or partly reject or reverse, or resubmit to the master with instructions.

(2) *Time to Object or Move to Adopt or Modify.* A party may file objections to—or a motion to adopt or modify—the master's order, report, or recommendations no later than 20 days after a copy is served, unless the court sets a different time.

(3) *Reviewing Factual Findings.* The court must decide de novo all objections to findings of fact made or recommended by a master, unless the parties, with the court's approval, stipulate that:

(A) the findings will be reviewed for clear error; or

(B) the findings of a master appointed under Rule 53(a)(1)(A) or (C) will be final.

(4) *Reviewing Legal Conclusions.* The court must decide de novo all objections to conclusions of law made or recommended by a master.

(5) *Reviewing Procedural Matters.* Unless the appointing order establishes a different standard of review, the court may set aside a master's ruling on a procedural matter only for an abuse of discretion.

(g) Compensation.

(1) *Fixing Compensation.* Before or after judgment, the court must fix the master's compensation on the basis and terms stated in the appointing order, but the court may set a new basis and terms after giving notice and an opportunity to be heard.

(2) *Payment.* The compensation must be paid either:

(A) by a party or parties; or

(B) from a fund or subject matter of the action within the court's control.

(3) *Allocating Payment.* The court must allocate payment among the parties after considering the nature and amount of the controversy, the parties' means, and the extent to which any party is more responsible than other parties for the reference to a master. An interim allocation may be amended to reflect a decision on the merits.

(h) Appointing a Magistrate Judge. A magistrate judge is subject to this rule only when the order referring a matter to the magistrate judge states that the reference is made under this rule.

[Amended February 28, 1966, effective July 1, 1966; April 28, 1983, effective August 1, 1983; March 2, 1987, effective August 1, 1987; April 30, 1991, effective December 1, 1991; April 22, 1993, effective December 1, 1993; March 27, 2003, effective December 1, 2003; April 30, 2007, effective December 1, 2007.]

TITLE VII. JUDGMENT

RULE 54. JUDGMENT; COSTS

(a) Definition; Form. "Judgment" as used in these rules includes a decree and any order from which an appeal lies. A judgment should not include recitals of pleadings, a master's report, or a record of prior proceedings.

(b) Judgment on Multiple Claims or Involving Multiple Parties. When an action presents more than one claim for relief—whether as a claim, counterclaim, crossclaim, or third-party claim—or when multiple parties are involved, the court may direct entry of a final judgment as to one or more, but fewer than all, claims or parties only if the court expressly determines that there is no just reason for delay. Otherwise, any order or other decision, however designated, that adjudicates fewer than all the claims or the rights and liabilities of fewer than all the parties does not end the action as to any of the claims or parties and may be revised at any time before the entry of a judgment adjudicating all the claims and all the parties' rights and liabilities.

(c) Demand for Judgment; Relief to Be Granted. A default judgment must not differ in kind from, or exceed in amount, what is demanded in the pleadings. Every other final judgment should grant the relief to which each party is entitled, even if the party has not demanded that relief in its pleadings.

(d) Costs; Attorney's Fees.

(1) *Costs Other Than Attorney's Fees.* Unless a federal statute, these rules, or a court order provides otherwise, costs—other than attorney's fees—should be allowed to the prevailing party. But costs against the United States, its officers, and its agencies may be imposed only to the extent allowed by law. The clerk may tax costs on 1 day's notice. On motion served within the next 5 days, the court may review the clerk's action.

(2) *Attorney's Fees.*

(A) Claim to Be by Motion. A claim for attorney's fees and related nontaxable expenses must be made by motion unless the substantive law requires those fees to be proved at trial as an element of damages.

(B) Timing and Contents of the Motion. Unless a statute or a court order provides otherwise, the motion must:

(i) be filed no later than 14 days after the entry of judgment;

(ii) specify the judgment and the statute, rule, or other grounds entitling the movant to the award;

(iii) state the amount sought or provide a fair estimate of it; and

(iv) disclose, if the court so orders, the terms of any agreement about fees for the services for which the claim is made.

(C) Proceedings. Subject to Rule 23(h), the court must, on a party's request, give an opportunity for adversary submissions on the motion in accordance with Rule 43(c) or 78. The court may decide issues of liability for fees before receiving submissions on the value of services. The court must find the facts and state its conclusions of law as provided in Rule 52(a).

(D) Special Procedures by Local Rule; Reference to a Master or a Magistrate Judge. By local rule, the court may establish special procedures to resolve fee-related issues without extensive evidentiary hearings. Also, the court may refer issues concerning the value of services to a special master under Rule 53 without regard to the limitations of Rule 53(a)(1), and may refer a motion for attorney's fees to a magistrate judge under Rule 72(b) as if it were a dispositive pretrial matter.

(E) Exceptions. Subparagraphs (A)-(D) do not apply to claims for fees and expenses as sanctions for violating these rules or as sanctions under 28 U.S.C. § 1927.

[Amended December 27, 1946, effective March 19, 1948; April 17, 1961, effective July 19, 1961; March 2, 1987, effective August 1, 1987; April 22, 1993, effective December 1, 1993; April 29, 2002, effective December 1, 2002; March 27, 2003, effective December 1, 2003; April 30, 2007, effective December 1, 2007.]

RULE 55. DEFAULT; DEFAULT JUDGMENT

(a) **Entering a Default.** When a party against whom a judgment for affirmative relief is sought has failed to plead or otherwise defend, and that failure is shown by affidavit or otherwise, the clerk must enter the party's default.

(b) **Entering a Default Judgment.**

(1) *By the Clerk.* If the plaintiff's claim is for a sum certain or a sum that can be made certain by computation, the clerk—on the plaintiff's request, with an affidavit showing the amount due—must enter judgment for that amount and costs against a defendant who has been defaulted for not appearing and who is neither a minor nor an incompetent person.

(2) *By the Court.* In all other cases, the party must apply to the court for a default judgment. A default judgment may be entered against a minor or incompetent person only if represented by a general guardian, conservator, or other like fiduciary who has appeared. If the party against whom a default judgment is sought has appeared personally or by a representative, that party or its representative must be served with written notice of the application at least 3 days before the hearing. The court may conduct hearings or make referrals—preserving any federal statutory right to a jury trial—when, to enter or effectuate judgment, it needs to:

(A) conduct an accounting;

(B) determine the amount of damages;

(C) establish the truth of any allegation by evidence; or

(D) investigate any other matter.

(c) **Setting Aside a Default or a Default Judgment.** The court may set aside an entry of default for good cause, and it may set aside a default judgment under Rule 60(b).

(d) **Judgment Against the United States.** A default judgment may be entered against the United States, its officers, or its agencies only if the claimant establishes a claim or right to relief by evidence that satisfies the court.

[Amended March 2, 1987, effective August 1, 1987; April 30, 2007, effective December 1, 2007.]

RULE 56. SUMMARY JUDGMENT

(a) **By a Claiming Party.** A party claiming relief may move, with or without supporting affidavits, for summary judgment on all or part of the claim. The motion may be filed at any time after:

(1) 20 days have passed from commencement of the action; or

(2) the opposing party serves a motion for summary judgment.

(b) **By a Defending Party.** A party against whom relief is sought may move at any time, with or without supporting affidavits, for summary judgment on all or part of the claim.

(c) **Serving the Motion; Proceedings.** The motion must be served at least 10 days before the day set for the hearing. An opposing party may serve opposing affidavits before the hearing day. The judgment sought should be rendered if the pleadings, the discovery and disclosure materials on file, and any affidavits show that there is no genuine issue as to any material fact and that the movant is entitled to judgment as a matter of law.

(d) Case Not Fully Adjudicated on the Motion.

(1) *Establishing Facts.* If summary judgment is not rendered on the whole action, the court should, to the extent practicable, determine what material facts are not genuinely at issue. The court should so determine by examining the pleadings and evidence before it and by interrogating the attorneys. It should then issue an order specifying what facts—including items of damages or other relief—are not genuinely at issue. The facts so specified must be treated as established in the action.

(2) *Establishing Liability.* An interlocutory summary judgment may be rendered on liability alone, even if there is a genuine issue on the amount of damages.

(e) Affidavits; Further Testimony.

(1) *In General.* A supporting or opposing affidavit must be made on personal knowledge, set out facts that would be admissible in evidence, and show that the affiant is competent to testify on the matters stated. If a paper or part of a paper is referred to in an affidavit, a sworn or certified copy must be attached to or served with the affidavit. The court may permit an affidavit to be supplemented or opposed by depositions, answers to interrogatories, or additional affidavits.

(2) *Opposing Party's Obligation to Respond.* When a motion for summary judgment is properly made and supported, an opposing party may not rely merely on allegations or denials in its own pleading; rather, its response must—by affidavits or as otherwise provided in this rule—set out specific facts showing a genuine issue for trial. If the opposing party does not so respond, summary judgment should, if appropriate, be entered against that party.

(f) When Affidavits Are Unavailable. If a party opposing the motion shows by affidavit that, for specified reasons, it cannot present facts essential to justify its opposition, the court may:

(1) deny the motion;

(2) order a continuance to enable affidavits to be obtained, depositions to be taken, or other discovery to be undertaken; or

(3) issue any other just order.

(g) Affidavit Submitted in Bad Faith. If satisfied that an affidavit under this rule is submitted in bad faith or solely for delay, the court must order the submitting party to pay the other party the reasonable expenses, including attorney's fees, it incurred as a result. An offending party or attorney may also be held in contempt.

[Amended December 27, 1946, effective March 19, 1948; January 21, 1963, effective July 1, 1963; March 2, 1987, effective August 1, 1987; April 30, 2007, effective December 1, 2007.]

RULE 57. DECLARATORY JUDGMENT

These rules govern the procedure for obtaining a declaratory judgment under 28 U.S.C. § 2201. Rules 38 and 39 govern a demand for a jury trial. The existence of another adequate remedy does not preclude a declaratory judgment that is otherwise appropriate. The court may order a speedy hearing of a declaratory-judgment action.

[Amended December 29, 1948, effective October 20, 1949; April 30, 2007, effective December 1, 2007.]

RULE 58. ENTERING JUDGMENT

(a) Separate Document. Every judgment and amended judgment must be set out in a separate document, but a separate document is not required for an order disposing of a motion:

(1) for judgment under Rule 50(b);

(2) to amend or make additional findings under Rule 52(b);

(3) for attorney's fees under Rule 54;

(4) for a new trial, or to alter or amend the judgment, under Rule 59; or

(5) for relief under Rule 60.

(b) Entering Judgment.

(1) *Without the Court's Direction.* Subject to Rule 54(b) and unless the court orders otherwise, the clerk must, without awaiting the court's direction, promptly prepare, sign, and enter the judgment when:

(A) the jury returns a general verdict;

(B) the court awards only costs or a sum certain; or

(C) the court denies all relief.

(2) *Court's Approval Required.* Subject to Rule 54(b), the court must promptly approve the form of the judgment, which the clerk must promptly enter, when:

(A) the jury returns a special verdict or a general verdict with answers to written questions; or

(B) the court grants other relief not described in this subdivision (b).

(c) Time of Entry. For purposes of these rules, judgment is entered at the following times:

(1) if a separate document is not required, when the judgment is entered in the civil docket under Rule 79(a); or

(2) if a separate document is required, when the judgment is entered in the civil docket under Rule 79(a) and the earlier of these events occurs:

(A) it is set out in a separate document; or

(B) 150 days have run from the entry in the civil docket.

(d) Request for Entry. A party may request that judgment be set out in a separate document as required by Rule 58(a).

(e) Cost or Fee Awards. Ordinarily, the entry of judgment may not be delayed, nor the time for appeal extended, in order to tax costs or award fees. But if a timely motion for attorney's fees is made under Rule 54(d)(2), the court may act before a notice of appeal has been filed and become effective to order that the motion have the same effect under Federal Rule of Appellate Procedure 4(a)(4) as a timely motion under Rule 59.

[Amended December 27, 1946, effective March 19, 1948; January 21, 1963, effective July 1, 1963; April 22, 1993, effective December 1, 1993; April 29, 2002, effective December 1, 2002; April 30, 2007, effective December 1, 2007.]

RULE 59. NEW TRIAL; ALTERING OR AMENDING A JUDGMENT

(a) In General.

(1) *Grounds for New Trial.* The court may, on motion, grant a new trial on all or some of the issues—and to any party—as follows:

(A) after a jury trial, for any reason for which a new trial has heretofore been granted in an action at law in federal court; or

(B) after a nonjury trial, for any reason for which a rehearing has heretofore been granted in a suit in equity in federal court.

(2) *Further Action After a Nonjury Trial.* After a nonjury trial, the court may, on motion for a new trial, open the judgment if one has been entered, take additional testimony, amend findings of fact and conclusions of law or make new ones, and direct the entry of a new judgment.

(b) Time to File a Motion for a New Trial. A motion for a new trial must be filed no later than 10 days after the entry of judgment.

(c) Time to Serve Affidavits. When a motion for a new trial is based on affidavits, they must be filed with the motion. The opposing party has 10 days after being served to file opposing affidavits; but that period may be extended for up to 20 days, either by the court for good cause or by the parties' stipulation. The court may permit reply affidavits.

(d) New Trial on the Court's Initiative or for Reasons Not in the Motion. No later than 10 days after the entry of judgment, the court, on its own, may order a new trial for any reason that would justify granting one on a party's motion. After giving the parties notice and an opportunity to be heard, the court may grant a timely motion for a new trial for a reason not stated in the motion. In either event, the court must specify the reasons in its order.

(e) Motion to Alter or Amend a Judgment. A motion to alter or amend a judgment must be filed no later than 10 days after the entry of the judgment.

[Amended December 27, 1946, effective March 19, 1948; February 28, 1966, effective July 1, 1966; April 27, 1995, effective December 1, 1995; April 30, 2007, effective December 1, 2007.]

RULE 60. RELIEF FROM A JUDGMENT OR ORDER

(a) Corrections Based on Clerical Mistakes; Oversights and Omissions. The court may correct a clerical mistake or a mistake arising from oversight or omission whenever one is found in a judgment, order, or other part of the record. The court may do so on motion or on its own, with or without notice. But after an appeal has been docketed in the appellate court and while it is pending, such a mistake may be corrected only with the appellate court's leave.

(b) Grounds for Relief from a Final Judgment, Order, or Proceeding. On motion and just terms, the court may relieve a party or its legal representative from a final judgment, order, or proceeding for the following reasons:

(1) mistake, inadvertence, surprise, or excusable neglect;

(2) newly discovered evidence that, with reasonable diligence, could not have been discovered in time to move for a new trial under Rule 59(b);

(3) fraud (whether previously called intrinsic or extrinsic), misrepresentation, or misconduct by an opposing party;

(4) the judgment is void;

(5) the judgment has been satisfied, released or discharged; it is based on an earlier judgment that has been reversed or vacated; or applying it prospectively is no longer equitable; or

(6) any other reason that justifies relief.

(c) Timing and Effect of the Motion.

(1) *Timing.* A motion under Rule 60(b) must be made within a reasonable time—and for reasons (1), (2), and (3) no more than a year after the entry of the judgment or order or the date of the proceeding.

(2) *Effect on Finality.* The motion does not affect the judgment's finality or suspend its operation.

(d) Other Powers to Grant Relief. This rule does not limit a court's power to:

(1) entertain an independent action to relieve a party from a judgment, order, or proceeding;

(2) grant relief under 28 U.S.C. § 1655 to a defendant who was not personally notified of the action; or

(3) set aside a judgment for fraud on the court.

(e) Bills and Writs Abolished. The following are abolished: bills of review, bills in the nature of bills of review, and writs of coram nobis, coram vobis, and audita querela.

[Amended December 27, 1946, effective March 19, 1948; December 29, 1948, effective October 20, 1949; March 2, 1987, effective August 1, 1987; April 30, 2007, effective December 1, 2007.]

RULE 61. HARMLESS ERROR

Unless justice requires otherwise, no error in admitting or excluding evidence—or any other error by the court or a party—is ground for granting a new trial, for setting aside a verdict, or for vacating, modifying, or otherwise disturbing a judgment or order. At every stage of the proceeding, the court must disregard all errors and defects that do not affect any party's substantial rights.

[Amended April 30, 2007, effective December 1, 2007.]

RULE 62. STAY OF PROCEEDINGS TO ENFORCE A JUDGMENT

(a) Automatic Stay; Exceptions for Injunctions, Receiverships, and Patent Accountings. Except as stated in this rule, no execution may issue on a judgment, nor may proceedings be taken to enforce it, until 10 days have passed after its entry. But unless the court orders otherwise, the following are not stayed after being entered, even if an appeal is taken:

(1) an interlocutory or final judgment in an action for an injunction or a receivership; or

(2) a judgment or order that directs an accounting in an action for patent infringement.

(b) Stay Pending the Disposition of a Motion. On appropriate terms for the opposing party's security, the court may stay the execution of a judgment—or any proceedings to enforce it—pending disposition of any of the following motions:

(1) under Rule 50, for judgment as a matter of law;

(2) under Rule 52(b), to amend the findings or for additional findings;

(3) under Rule 59, for a new trial or to alter or amend a judgment; or

(4) under Rule 60, for relief from a judgment or order.

(c) Injunction Pending an Appeal. While an appeal is pending from an interlocutory order or final judgment that grants, dissolves, or denies an injunction, the court may suspend, modify, restore, or grant an injunction on terms for bond or other terms that secure the opposing party's rights. If the judgment appealed from is rendered by a statutory three-judge district court, the order must be made either:

(1) by that court sitting in open session; or

(2) by the assent of all its judges, as evidenced by their signatures.

(d) Stay with Bond on Appeal. If an appeal is taken, the appellant may obtain a stay by supersedeas bond, except in an action described in Rule 62(a)(1) or (2). The bond may be given upon or after filing the notice of appeal or after obtaining the order allowing the appeal. The stay takes effect when the court approves the bond.

(e) Stay Without Bond on an Appeal by the United States, Its Officers, or Its Agencies. The court must not require a bond, obligation, or other security from the appellant when granting a stay on an appeal by the United States, its officers, or its agencies or on an appeal directed by a department of the federal government.

(f) Stay in Favor of a Judgment Debtor Under State Law. If a judgment is a lien on the judgment debtor's property under the law of the state where the court is located, the judgment debtor is entitled to the same stay of execution the state court would give.

(g) Appellate Court's Power Not Limited. This rule does not limit the power of the appellate court or one of its judges or justices:

(1) to stay proceedings—or suspend, modify, restore, or grant an injunction—while an appeal is pending; or

(2) to issue an order to preserve the status quo or the effectiveness of the judgment to be entered.

(h) Stay with Multiple Claims or Parties. A court may stay the enforcement of a final judgment entered under Rule 54(b) until it enters a later judgment or judgments, and may prescribe terms necessary to secure the benefit of the stayed judgment for the party in whose favor it was entered.

[Amended December 27, 1946, effective March 19, 1948; December 29, 1948, effective October 20, 1949; April 17, 1961, effective July 19, 1961; March 2, 1987, effective August 1, 1987; April 30, 2007, effective December 1, 2007.]

RULE 63. JUDGE'S INABILITY TO PROCEED

If a judge conducting a hearing or trial is unable to proceed, any other judge may proceed upon certifying familiarity with the record and determining that the case may be completed without prejudice to the parties. In a hearing or a nonjury trial, the successor judge must, at a party's request, recall any witness whose testimony is material and disputed and who is available to testify again without undue burden. The successor judge may also recall any other witness.

[Amended March 2, 1987, effective August 1, 1987; April 30, 1991, effective December 1, 1991; April 30, 2007, effective December 1, 2007.]

TITLE VIII. PROVISIONAL AND FINAL REMEDIES

RULE 64. SEIZING A PERSON OR PROPERTY

(a) Remedies Under State Law—In General. At the commencement of and throughout an action, every remedy is available that, under the law of the state where the court is located, provides for seizing a person or property to secure satisfaction of the potential judgment. But a federal statute governs to the extent it applies.

(b) Specific Kinds of Remedies. The remedies available under this rule include the following—however designated and regardless of whether state procedure requires an independent action:

- arrest;
- attachment;
- garnishment;
- replevin;
- sequestration; and
- other corresponding or equivalent remedies.

[Amended April 30, 2007, effective December 1, 2007.]

RULE 65. INJUNCTIONS AND RESTRAINING ORDERS

(a) Preliminary Injunction.

(1) *Notice.* The court may issue a preliminary injunction only on notice to the adverse party.

(2) *Consolidating the Hearing with the Trial on the Merits.* Before or after beginning the hearing on a motion for a preliminary injunction, the court may advance the trial on the merits and consolidate it with the hearing. Even when consolidation is not ordered, evidence that is received on the motion and that would be admissible at trial becomes part of the trial record and need not be repeated at trial. But the court must preserve any party's right to a jury trial.

(b) Temporary Restraining Order.

(1) *Issuing Without Notice.* The court may issue a temporary restraining order without written or oral notice to the adverse party or its attorney only if:

(A) specific facts in an affidavit or a verified complaint clearly show that immediate and irreparable injury, loss, or damage will result to the movant before the adverse party can be heard in opposition; and

(B) the movant's attorney certifies in writing any efforts made to give notice and the reasons why it should not be required.

(2) *Contents; Expiration.* Every temporary restraining order issued without notice must state the date and hour it was issued; describe the injury and state why it is irreparable; state why the order was issued without notice; and be promptly filed in the clerk's office and entered in the record. The order expires at the time after entry—not to exceed 10 days—that the court sets, unless before that time the court, for good cause, extends it for a like period or the adverse party consents to a longer extension. The reasons for an extension must be entered in the record.

(3) *Expediting the Preliminary–Injunction Hearing.* If the order is issued without notice, the motion for a preliminary injunction must be set for hearing at the earliest possible time, taking precedence over all other matters except hearings on older matters of the same character. At the hearing, the party who obtained the order must proceed with the motion; if the party does not, the court must dissolve the order.

(4) *Motion to Dissolve.* On 2 days' notice to the party who obtained the order without notice—or on shorter notice set by the court—the adverse party may appear and move to dissolve or modify the order. The court must then hear and decide the motion as promptly as justice requires.

(c) Security. The court may issue a preliminary injunction or a temporary restraining order only if the movant gives security in an amount that the court considers proper to pay the costs and damages sustained by any party found to have been wrongfully enjoined or restrained. The United States, its officers, and its agencies are not required to give security.

(d) Contents and Scope of Every Injunction and Restraining Order.

(1) *Contents.* Every order granting an injunction and every restraining order must:

(A) state the reasons why it issued;

(B) state its terms specifically; and

(C) describe in reasonable detail—and not by referring to the complaint or other document—the act or acts restrained or required.

(2) *Persons Bound.* The order binds only the following who receive actual notice of it by personal service or otherwise:

(A) the parties;

(B) the parties' officers, agents, servants, employees, and attorneys; and

(C) other persons who are in active concert or participation with anyone described in Rule 65(d)(2)(A) or (B).

(e) Other Laws Not Modified. These rules do not modify the following:

(1) any federal statute relating to temporary restraining orders or preliminary injunctions in actions affecting employer and employee;

(2) 28 U.S.C. § 2361, which relates to preliminary injunctions in actions of interpleader or in the nature of interpleader; or

(3) 28 U.S.C. § 2284, which relates to actions that must be heard and decided by a three-judge district court.

(f) Copyright Impoundment. This rule applies to copyright-impoundment proceedings.

[Amended December 27, 1946, effective March 19, 1948; December 29, 1948, effective October 20, 1949; February 28, 1966, effective July 1, 1966; March 2, 1987, effective August 1, 1987; April 23, 2001, effective December 1, 2001; April 30, 2007, effective December 1, 2007.]

RULE 65.1 PROCEEDINGS AGAINST A SURETY

Whenever these rules (including the Supplemental Rules for Admiralty or Maritime Claims and Asset Forfeiture Actions) require or allow a party to give security, and security is given through a bond or other undertaking with one or more sureties, each surety submits to the court's jurisdiction and irrevocably appoints the court clerk as its agent for receiving service of any papers that affect its liability on the bond or undertaking. The surety's liability may be enforced on motion without an independent action. The motion and any notice that the court orders may be served on the court clerk, who must promptly mail a copy of each to every surety whose address is known.

[Adopted February 28, 1966, effective July 1, 1966; amended March 2, 1987, effective August 1, 1987; April 12, 2006, effective December 1, 2006; April 30, 2007, effective December 1, 2007.]

RULE 66. RECEIVERS

These rules govern an action in which the appointment of a receiver is sought or a receiver sues or is sued. But the practice in administering an estate by a receiver or a similar court-appointed officer must accord with the historical practice in federal courts or with a local rule. An action in which a receiver has been appointed may be dismissed only by court order.

[Amended December 27, 1946, effective March 19, 1948; December 29, 1948, effective October 20, 1949; April 30, 2007, effective December 1, 2007.]

RULE 67. DEPOSIT INTO COURT

(a) Depositing Property. If any part of the relief sought is a money judgment or the disposition of a sum of money or some other deliverable thing, a party—on notice to every other party and by leave of court—may deposit with the court all or part of the money or thing, whether or not that party claims any of it. The depositing party must deliver to the clerk a copy of the order permitting deposit.

(b) Investing and Withdrawing Funds. Money paid into court under this rule must be deposited and withdrawn in accordance with 28 U.S.C. §§ 2041 and 2042 and any like statute. The money must be deposited in an interest-bearing account or invested in a court-approved, interest-bearing instrument.

[Amended December 29, 1948, effective October 20, 1949; April 28, 1983, effective August 1, 1983; April 30, 2007, effective December 1, 2007.]

RULE 68. OFFER OF JUDGMENT

(a) Making an Offer; Judgment on an Accepted Offer. More than 10 days before the trial begins, a party defending against a claim may serve on an opposing party an offer to allow judgment on specified terms, with the costs then accrued. If, within 10 days after being served, the opposing party serves written notice accepting the offer, either party may then file the offer and notice of acceptance, plus proof of service. The clerk must then enter judgment.

(b) Unaccepted Offer. An unaccepted offer is considered withdrawn, but it does not preclude a later offer. Evidence of an unaccepted offer is not admissible except in a proceeding to determine costs.

(c) Offer After Liability Is Determined. When one party's liability to another has been determined but the extent of liability remains to be determined by further proceedings, the party held liable may make an offer of judgment. It must be served within a reasonable time—but at least 10 days—before a hearing to determine the extent of liability.

(d) Paying Costs After an Unaccepted Offer. If the judgment that the offeree finally obtains is not more favorable than the unaccepted offer, the offeree must pay the costs incurred after the offer was made.

[Amended December 27, 1946, effective March 19, 1948; February 28, 1966, effective July 1, 1966; March 2, 1987, effective August 1, 1987; April 30, 2007, effective December 1, 2007.]

RULE 69. EXECUTION

(a) In General.

(1) *Money Judgment; Applicable Procedure.* A money judgment is enforced by a writ of execution, unless the court directs otherwise. The procedure on execution—and in proceedings supplementary to and in aid of judgment or execution—must accord with the procedure of the state where the court is located, but a federal statute governs to the extent it applies.

(2) *Obtaining Discovery.* In aid of the judgment or execution, the judgment creditor or a successor in interest whose interest appears of record may obtain discovery from any person—including the judgment debtor—as provided in these rules or by the procedure of the state where the court is located.

(b) Against Certain Public Officers. When a judgment has been entered against a revenue officer in the circumstances stated in 28 U.S.C. § 2006, or against an officer of Congress in the circumstances stated in 2 U.S.C. § 118, the judgment must be satisfied as those statutes provide.

[Amended December 29, 1948, effective October 20, 1949; March 30, 1970, effective July 1, 1970; March 2, 1987 effective August 1, 1987; April 30, 2007, effective December 1, 2007.]

RULE 70. ENFORCING A JUDGMENT FOR A SPECIFIC ACT

(a) Party's Failure to Act; Ordering Another to Act. If a judgment requires a party to convey land, to deliver a deed or other document, or to perform any other specific act and the party fails to comply within the time specified, the court may order the act to be done—at the disobedient party's expense—by another person appointed by the court. When done, the act has the same effect as if done by the party.

(b) Vesting Title. If the real or personal property is within the district, the court—instead of ordering a conveyance—may enter a judgment divesting any party's title and vesting it in others. That judgment has the effect of a legally executed conveyance.

(c) Obtaining a Writ of Attachment or Sequestration. On application by a party entitled to performance of an act, the clerk must issue a writ of attachment or sequestration against the disobedient party's property to compel obedience.

(d) Obtaining a Writ of Execution or Assistance. On application by a party who obtains a judgment or order for possession, the clerk must issue a writ of execution or assistance.

(e) Holding in Contempt. The court may also hold the disobedient party in contempt.

[Amended April 30, 2007, effective December 1, 2007.]

RULE 71. ENFORCING RELIEF FOR OR AGAINST A NONPARTY

When an order grants relief for a nonparty or may be enforced against a nonparty, the procedure for enforcing the order is the same as for a party.

[Amended March 2, 1987, effective August 1, 1987; April 30, 2007, effective December 1, 2007.]

TITLE IX. SPECIAL PROCEEDINGS

RULE 71.1 CONDEMNING REAL OR PERSONAL PROPERTY

(a) Applicability of Other Rules. These rules govern proceedings to condemn real and personal property by eminent domain, except as this rule provides otherwise.

(b) Joinder of Properties. The plaintiff may join separate pieces of property in a single action, no matter whether they are owned by the same persons or sought for the same use.

(c) Complaint.

(1) *Caption.* The complaint must contain a caption as provided in Rule 10(a). The plaintiff must, however, name as defendants both the property—designated generally by kind, quantity, and location—and at least one owner of some part of or interest in the property.

(2) *Contents.* The complaint must contain a short and plain statement of the following:

(A) the authority for the taking;

(B) the uses for which the property is to be taken;

(C) a description sufficient to identify the property;

(D) the interests to be acquired; and

(E) for each piece of property, a designation of each defendant who has been joined as an owner or owner of an interest in it.

(3) *Parties.* When the action commences, the plaintiff need join as defendants only those persons who have or claim an interest in the property and whose names are then known. But before any hearing on compensation, the plaintiff must add as defendants all those persons who have or claim an interest and whose names have become known or can be found by a reasonably diligent search of the records, considering both the property's character and value and the interests to be acquired. All others may be made defendants under the designation "Unknown Owners."

(4) *Procedure.* Notice must be served on all defendants as provided in Rule 71.1(d), whether they were named as defendants when the action commenced or were added later. A defendant may answer as provided in Rule 71.1(e). The court, meanwhile, may order any distribution of a deposit that the facts warrant.

(5) *Filing; Additional Copies.* In addition to filing the complaint, the plaintiff must give the clerk at least one copy for the defendants' use and additional copies at the request of the clerk or a defendant.

(d) Process.

(1) *Delivering Notice to the Clerk.* On filing a complaint, the plaintiff must promptly deliver to the clerk joint or several notices directed to the named defendants. When adding defendants, the plaintiff must deliver to the clerk additional notices directed to the new defendants.

(2) *Contents of the Notice.*

(A) Main Contents. Each notice must name the court, the title of the action, and the defendant to whom it is directed. It must describe the property sufficiently to identify it, but need not describe any property other than that to be taken from the named defendant. The notice must also state:

(i) that the action is to condemn property;

(ii) the interest to be taken;

(iii) the authority for the taking;

(iv) the uses for which the property is to be taken;

(v) that the defendant may serve an answer on the plaintiff's attorney within 20 days after being served with the notice;

(vi) that the failure to so serve an answer constitutes consent to the taking and to the court's authority to proceed with the action and fix the compensation; and

(vii) that a defendant who does not serve an answer may file a notice of appearance.

(B) Conclusion. The notice must conclude with the name, telephone number, and e-mail address of the plaintiff's attorney and an address within the district in which the action is brought where the attorney may be served.

(3) *Serving the Notice.*

(A) Personal Service. When a defendant whose address is known resides within the United States or a territory subject to the administrative or judicial jurisdiction of the United States, personal service of the notice (without a copy of the complaint) must be made in accordance with Rule 4.

(B) Service by Publication.

(i) A defendant may be served by publication only when the plaintiff's attorney files a certificate stating that the attorney believes the defendant cannot be personally served, because after diligent inquiry within the state where the complaint is filed, the defendant's place of residence is still unknown or, if known, that it is beyond the territorial limits of personal service. Service is then made by publishing the notice—once a week for at least three successive weeks—in a newspaper published in the county where the property is located or, if there is no such newspaper, in a newspaper with general circulation where the property is located. Before the last publication, a copy of the notice must also be mailed to every defendant who cannot be personally served but whose place of residence is then known. Unknown owners may be served by publication in the same manner by a notice addressed to "Unknown Owners."

(ii) Service by publication is complete on the date of the last publication. The plaintiff's attorney must prove publication and mailing by a certificate, attach a printed copy of the published notice, and mark on the copy the newspaper's name and the dates of publication.

(4) *Effect of Delivery and Service.* Delivering the notice to the clerk and serving it have the same effect as serving a summons under Rule 4.

(5) *Amending the Notice; Proof of Service and Amending the Proof.* Rule 4(a)(2) governs amending the notice. Rule 4(*l*) governs proof of service and amending it.

(e) Appearance or Answer.

(1) *Notice of Appearance.* A defendant that has no objection or defense to the taking of its property may serve a notice of appearance designating the property in which it claims an interest. The defendant must then be given notice of all later proceedings affecting the defendant.

(2) *Answer.* A defendant that has an objection or defense to the taking must serve an answer within 20 days after being served with the notice. The answer must:

(A) identify the property in which the defendant claims an interest;

(B) state the nature and extent of the interest; and

(C) state all the defendant's objections and defenses to the taking.

(3) *Waiver of Other Objections and Defenses; Evidence on Compensation.* A defendant waives all objections and defenses not stated in its answer. No other pleading or motion asserting an additional objection or defense is allowed. But at the trial on compensation, a defendant—whether or not it has previously appeared or answered—may present evidence on the amount of compensation to be paid and may share in the award.

(f) Amending Pleadings. Without leave of court, the plaintiff may—as often as it wants—amend the complaint at any time before the trial on compensation. But no amendment may be made if it would result in a dismissal inconsistent with Rule 71.1(i)(1) or (2). The plaintiff need not serve a copy of an amendment, but must serve notice of the filing, as provided in Rule 5(b), on every affected party who has appeared and, as provided in Rule 71.1(d), on every affected party who has not appeared. In addition, the plaintiff must give the clerk at least one copy of each amendment for the defendants' use, and additional copies at the request of the clerk or a defendant. A defendant may appear or answer in the time and manner and with the same effect as provided in Rule 71.1(e).

(g) Substituting Parties. If a defendant dies, becomes incompetent, or transfers an interest after being joined, the court may, on motion and notice of hearing, order that the proper party be substituted.

Service of the motion and notice on a nonparty must be made as provided in Rule 71.1(d)(3).

(h) Trial of the Issues.

(1) *Issues Other Than Compensation; Compensation.* In an action involving eminent domain under federal law, the court tries all issues, including compensation, except when compensation must be determined:

(A) by any tribunal specially constituted by a federal statute to determine compensation; or

(B) if there is no such tribunal, by a jury when a party demands one within the time to answer or within any additional time the court sets, unless the court appoints a commission.

(2) *Appointing a Commission; Commission's Powers and Report.*

(A) Reasons for Appointing. If a party has demanded a jury, the court may instead appoint a three-person commission to determine compensation because of the character, location, or quantity of the property to be condemned or for other just reasons.

(B) Alternate Commissioners. The court may appoint up to two additional persons to serve as alternate commissioners to hear the case and replace commissioners who, before a decision is filed, the court finds unable or disqualified to perform their duties. Once the commission renders its final decision, the court must discharge any alternate who has not replaced a commissioner.

(C) Examining the Prospective Commissioners. Before making its appointments, the court must advise the parties of the identity and qualifications of each prospective commissioner and alternate, and may permit the parties to examine them. The parties may not suggest appointees, but for good cause may object to a prospective commissioner or alternate.

(D) Commission's Powers and Report. A commission has the powers of a master under Rule 53(c). Its action and report are determined by a majority. Rule 53(d), (e), and (f) apply to its action and report.

(i) Dismissal of the Action or a Defendant.

(1) *Dismissing the Action.*

(A) By the Plaintiff. If no compensation hearing on a piece of property has begun, and if the plaintiff has not acquired title or a lesser interest or taken possession, the plaintiff may, without a court order, dismiss the action as to that property by filing a notice of dismissal briefly describing the property.

(B) By Stipulation. Before a judgment is entered vesting the plaintiff with title or a lesser interest in or possession of property, the plaintiff and affected defendants may, without a court order, dismiss the action in whole or in part by filing a stipulation of dismissal. And if the parties so stipulate, the court may vacate a judgment already entered.

(C) By Court Order. At any time before compensation has been determined and paid, the court may, after a motion and hearing, dismiss the action as to a piece of property. But if the plaintiff has already taken title, a lesser interest, or possession as to any part of it, the court must award compensation for the title, lesser interest, or possession taken.

(2) *Dismissing a Defendant.* The court may at any time dismiss a defendant who was unnecessarily or improperly joined.

(3) *Effect.* A dismissal is without prejudice unless otherwise stated in the notice, stipulation, or court order.

(j) Deposit and Its Distribution.

(1) *Deposit.* The plaintiff must deposit with the court any money required by law as a condition to the exercise of eminent domain and may make a deposit when allowed by statute.

(2) *Distribution; Adjusting Distribution.* After a deposit, the court and attorneys must expedite the proceedings so as to distribute the deposit and to determine and pay compensation. If the compensation finally awarded to a defendant exceeds the amount distributed to that defendant, the court must enter judgment against the plaintiff for the deficiency. If the compensation awarded to a defendant is less than the amount distributed to that defendant, the court must enter judgment against that defendant for the overpayment.

(k) Condemnation Under a State's Power of Eminent Domain. This rule governs an action involving eminent domain under state law. But if state law provides for trying an issue by jury—or for trying the issue of compensation by jury or commission or both—that law governs.

(*l*) Costs. Costs are not subject to Rule 54(d).

[Adopted April 30, 1951, effective August 1, 1951; amended January 21, 1963, effective July 1, 1963; April 29, 1985, effective August 1, 1985; March 2, 1987, effective August 1, 1987; April 25, 1988, effective August 1, 1988; amended by Pub.L. 100–690, Title VII, § 7050, November 18, 1988, 102 Stat. 4401 (although amendment by Pub.L. 100–690 could not be executed due to prior amendment by Court order which made the same change effective August 1, 1988); amended April 22, 1993, effective December 1, 1993; March 27, 2003, effective December 1, 2003; April 30, 2007, effective December 1, 2007.]

RULE 72. MAGISTRATE JUDGES: PRETRIAL ORDER

(a) Nondispositive Matters. When a pretrial matter not dispositive of a party's claim or defense is referred to a magistrate judge to hear and decide, the magistrate judge must promptly conduct the required proceedings and, when appropriate, issue a written order stating the decision. A party may serve and file objections to the order within 10 days after being served with a copy. A party may not assign as error a defect in the order not timely objected to. The district judge in the case must consider timely objections and modify or set aside any part of the order that is clearly erroneous or is contrary to law.

(b) Dispositive Motions and Prisoner Petitions.

(1) *Findings and Recommendations.* A magistrate judge must promptly conduct the required proceedings when assigned, without the parties' consent, to hear a pretrial matter dispositive of a claim or defense or a prisoner petition challenging the conditions of confinement. A record must be made of all evidentiary proceedings and may, at the magistrate judge's discretion, be made of any other proceedings. The magistrate judge must enter a recommended disposition, including, if appropriate, proposed findings of fact. The clerk must promptly mail a copy to each party.

(2) *Objections.* Within 10 days after being served with a copy of the recommended disposition, a party may serve and file specific written objections to the proposed findings and recommendations. A party may respond to another party's objections within 10 days after being served with a copy. Unless the district judge orders otherwise, the objecting party must promptly arrange for transcribing the record, or whatever portions of it the parties agree to or the magistrate judge considers sufficient.

(3) *Resolving Objections.* The district judge must determine de novo any part of the magistrate judge's disposition that has been properly objected to. The district judge may accept, reject, or modify the recommended disposition; receive further evidence; or return the matter to the magistrate judge with instructions.

[Former Rule 72 abrogated December 4, 1967, effective July 1, 1968; new Rule 72 adopted April 28, 1983, effective August 1, 1983; amended April 30, 1991, effective December 1, 1991; April 22, 1993, effective December 1, 1993; April 30, 2007, effective December 1, 2007.]

RULE 73. MAGISTRATE JUDGES: TRIAL BY CONSENT; APPEAL

(a) Trial by Consent. When authorized under 28 U.S.C. § 636(c), a magistrate judge may, if all parties consent, conduct a civil action or proceeding, including a jury or nonjury trial. A record must be made in accordance with 28 U.S.C. § 636(c)(5).

(b) Consent Procedure.

(1) *In General.* When a magistrate judge has been designated to conduct civil actions or proceedings, the clerk must give the parties written notice of their opportunity to consent under 28 U.S.C. § 636(c). To signify their consent, the parties must jointly or separately file a statement consenting to the referral. A district judge or magistrate judge may be informed of a party's response to the clerk's notice only if all parties have consented to the referral.

(2) *Reminding the Parties About Consenting.* A district judge, magistrate judge, or other court official may remind the parties of the magistrate judge's availability, but must also advise them that they are free to withhold consent without adverse substantive consequences.

(3) *Vacating a Referral.* On its own for good cause—or when a party shows extraordinary circumstances—the district judge may vacate a referral to a magistrate judge under this rule.

(c) Appealing a Judgment. In accordance with 28 U.S.C. § 636(c)(3), an appeal from a judgment entered at a magistrate judge's direction may be taken to the court of appeals as would any other appeal from a district-court judgment.

[Former Rule 73 abrogated December 4, 1967, effective July 1, 1968; new Rule 73 adopted April 28, 1983, effective August 1, 1983; amended March 2, 1987, effective August 1, 1987; April 22, 1993, effective December 1, 1993; April 11, 1997, effective December 1, 1997; April 30, 2007, effective December 1, 2007.]

RULE 74. METHOD OF APPEAL FROM MAGISTRATE JUDGE TO DISTRICT JUDGE UNDER TITLE 28, U.S.C. § 636(c)(4) AND RULE 73(d) [ABROGATED]

[Former Rule 74 abrogated December 4, 1967, effective July 1, 1968; new Rule 74 adopted April 28, 1983, effective August 1, 1983; amended April 22, 1993, effective December 1, 1993; abrogated April 11, 1997, effective December 1, 1997; April 30, 2007, effective December 1, 2007.]

RULE 75. PROCEEDINGS ON APPEAL FROM MAGISTRATE JUDGE TO DISTRICT JUDGE UNDER RULE 73(d) [ABROGATED]

[Former Rule 75 abrogated December 4, 1967, effective July 1, 1968; new Rule 75 adopted April 28, 1983, effective August 1, 1983; amended March 2, 1987, effective August 1, 1987; April 22, 1993, effective December 1, 1993; abrogated April 11, 1997, effective December 1, 1997; April 30, 2007, effective December 1, 2007.]

RULE 76. JUDGMENT OF THE DISTRICT JUDGE ON THE APPEAL UNDER RULE 73(d) AND COSTS [ABROGATED]

[Former Rule 76 abrogated December 4, 1967, effective July 1, 1968; new Rule 76 adopted April 28, 1983, effective August 1, 1983; amended April 22, 1993, effective December 1, 1993; abrogated April 11, 1997, effective December 1, 1997; April 30, 2007, effective December 1, 2007.]

TITLE X.   DISTRICT COURTS AND CLERKS: CONDUCTING BUSINESS; ISSUING ORDERS

RULE 77.   CONDUCTING BUSINESS; CLERK'S AUTHORITY; NOTICE OF AN ORDER OR JUDGMENT

(a) When Court Is Open. Every district court is considered always open for filing any paper, issuing and returning process, making a motion, or entering an order.

(b) Place for Trial and Other Proceedings. Every trial on the merits must be conducted in open court and, so far as convenient, in a regular courtroom. Any other act or proceeding may be done or conducted by a judge in chambers, without the attendance of the clerk or other court official, and anywhere inside or outside the district. But no hearing—other than one ex parte—may be conducted outside the district unless all the affected parties consent.

(c) Clerk's Office Hours; Clerk's Orders.

(1) *Hours.* The clerk's office—with a clerk or deputy on duty—must be open during business hours every day except Saturdays, Sundays, and legal holidays. But a court may, by local rule or order, require that the office be open for specified hours on Saturday or a particular legal holiday other than one listed in Rule 6(a)(4)(A).

(2) *Orders.* Subject to the court's power to suspend, alter, or rescind the clerk's action for good cause, the clerk may:

(A) issue process;

(B) enter a default;

(C) enter a default judgment under Rule 55(b)(1); and

(D) act on any other matter that does not require the court's action.

(d) Serving Notice of an Order or Judgment.

(1) *Service.* Immediately after entering an order or judgment, the clerk must serve notice of the entry, as provided in Rule 5(b), on each party who is not in default for failing to appear. The clerk must record the service on the docket. A party also may serve notice of the entry as provided in Rule 5(b).

(2) *Time to Appeal Not Affected by Lack of Notice.* Lack of notice of the entry does not affect the time for appeal or relieve—or authorize the court to relieve—a party for failing to appeal within the time allowed, except as allowed by Federal Rule of Appellate Procedure (4)(a).

[Amended December 27, 1946, effective March 19, 1948; January 21, 1963, effective July 1, 1963; December 4, 1967, effective July 1, 1968; March 1, 1971, effective July 1, 1971; March 2, 1987, effective August 1, 1987; April 30, 1991, effective December 1, 1991; April 23, 2001, effective December 1, 2001; April 30, 2007, effective December 1, 2007.]

RULE 78.   HEARING MOTIONS; SUBMISSION ON BRIEFS

(a) Providing a Regular Schedule for Oral Hearings. A court may establish regular times and places for oral hearings on motions.

(b) Providing for Submission on Briefs. By rule or order, the court may provide for submitting and determining motions on briefs, without oral hearings.

[Amended March 2, 1987, effective August 1, 1987; April 30, 2007, effective December 1, 2007.]

RULE 79.   RECORDS KEPT BY THE CLERK

(a) Civil Docket.

(1) *In General.* The clerk must keep a record known as the "civil docket" in the form and manner prescribed by the Director of the Administrative Office of the United States Courts with the approval of the Judicial Conference of the United States. The clerk must enter each civil action in the docket. Actions must be assigned consecutive file numbers, which must be noted in the docket where the first entry of the action is made.

(2) *Items to be Entered.* The following items must be marked with the file number and entered chronologically in the docket:

(A) papers filed with the clerk;

(B) process issued, and proofs of service or other returns showing execution; and

(C) appearances, orders, verdicts, and judgments.

(3) *Contents of Entries; Jury Trial Demanded.* Each entry must briefly show the nature of the paper filed or writ issued, the substance of each proof of service or other return, and the substance and date of entry of each order and judgment. When a jury trial has been properly demanded or ordered, the clerk must enter the word "jury" in the docket.

(b) Civil Judgments and Orders. The clerk must keep a copy of every final judgment and appealable order; of every order affecting title to or a lien on real or personal property; and of any other order that the court directs to be kept. The clerk must keep these in the form and manner prescribed by the Director of the Administrative Office of the United States Courts with the approval of the Judicial Conference of the United States.

(c) Indexes; Calendars. Under the court's direction, the clerk must:

(1) keep indexes of the docket and of the judgments and orders described in Rule 79(b); and

(2) prepare calendars of all actions ready for trial, distinguishing jury trials from nonjury trials.

(d) Other Records. The clerk must keep any other records required by the Director of the Administrative Office of the United States Courts with the approval of the Judicial Conference of the United States.

[Amended December 27, 1946, effective March 19, 1948; December 29, 1948, effective October 20, 1949; January 21, 1963, effective July 1, 1963; April 30, 2007, effective December 1, 2007.]

RULE 80.   STENOGRAPHIC TRANSCRIPT AS EVIDENCE

If stenographically reported testimony at a hearing or trial is admissible in evidence at a later trial, the testimony may be proved by a transcript certified by the person who reported it.

[Amended December 27, 1946, effective March 19, 1948; April 30, 2007, effective December 1, 2007.]

TITLE XI.   GENERAL PROVISIONS

RULE 81.   APPLICABILITY OF THE RULES IN GENERAL; REMOVED ACTIONS

(a) Applicability to Particular Proceedings.

(1) *Prize Proceedings.* These rules do not apply to prize proceedings in admiralty governed by 10 U.S.C. §§ 7651–7681.

(2) *Bankruptcy.* These rules apply to bankruptcy proceedings to the extent provided by the Federal Rules of Bankruptcy Procedure.

(3) *Citizenship.* These rules apply to proceedings for admission to citizenship to the extent that the practice in those proceedings is not specified in federal statutes and has previously conformed to the practice in civil actions. The provisions of 8 U.S.C. § 1451 for service by publication and for answer apply in proceedings to cancel citizenship certificates.

(4) *Special Writs.* These rules apply to proceedings for habeas corpus and for quo warranto to the extent that the practice in those proceedings:

(A) is not specified in a federal statute, the Rules Governing Section 2254 Cases, or the Rules Governing Section 2255 Cases; and

(B) has previously conformed to the practice in civil actions.

(5) *Proceedings Involving a Subpoena.* These rules apply to proceedings to compel testimony or the production of documents through a subpoena issued by a United States officer or agency under a federal statute, except as otherwise provided by statute, by local rule, or by court order in the proceedings.

(6) *Other Proceedings.* These rules, to the extent applicable, govern proceedings under the following laws, except as these laws provide other procedures:

(A) 7 U.S.C. §§ 292, 499g(c), for reviewing an order of the Secretary of Agriculture;

(B) 9 U.S.C., relating to arbitration;

(C) 15 U.S.C. § 522, for reviewing an order of the Secretary of the Interior;

(D) 15 U.S.C. § 715d(c), for reviewing an order denying a certificate of clearance;

(E) 29 U.S.C. §§ 159, 160, for enforcing an order of the National Labor Relations Board;

(F) 33 U.S.C. §§ 918, 921, for enforcing or reviewing a compensation order under the Longshore and Harbor Workers' Compensation Act; and

(G) 45 U.S.C. § 159, for reviewing an arbitration award in a railway-labor dispute.

(b) Scire Facias and Mandamus. The writs of scire facias and mandamus are abolished. Relief previously available through them may be obtained by appropriate action or motion under these rules.

(c) Removed Actions.

(1) *Applicability.* These rules apply to a civil action after it is removed from a state court.

(2) *Further Pleading.* After removal, repleading is unnecessary unless the court orders it. A defendant who did not answer before removal must answer or present other defenses or objections under these rules within the longest of these periods:

(A) 20 days after receiving—through service or otherwise—a copy of the initial pleading stating the claim for relief;

(B) 20 days after being served with the summons for an initial pleading on file at the time of service; or

(C) 5 days after the notice of removal is filed.

(3) *Demand for a Jury Trial.*

(A) As Affected by State Law. A party who, before removal, expressly demanded a jury trial in accordance with state law need not renew the demand after removal. If the state law did not require an express demand for a jury trial, a party need not make one after removal unless the court orders the parties to do so within a specified time. The court must so order at a party's request and may so order on its own. A party who fails to make a demand when so ordered waives a jury trial.

(B) Under Rule 38. If all necessary pleadings have been served at the time of removal, a party entitled to a jury trial under Rule 38 must be given one if the party serves a demand within 10 days after:

(i) it files a notice of removal; or

(ii) it is served with a notice of removal filed by another party.

(d) Law Applicable.

(1) *State Law.* When these rules refer to state law, the term "law" includes the state's statutes and the state's judicial decisions.

(2) *District of Columbia.* The term "state" includes, where appropriate, the District of Columbia. When these rules provide for state law to apply, in the District Court for the District of Columbia:

(A) the law applied in the District governs; and

(B) the term "federal statute" includes any Act of Congress that applies locally to the District.

[Amended December 28, 1939, effective April 3, 1941; December 27, 1946, effective March 19, 1948; December 29, 1948, effective October 20, 1949; April 30, 1951, effective August 1, 1951; January 21, 1963, effective July 1, 1963; February 28, 1966, effective July 1, 1966; December 4, 1967, effective July 1, 1968; March 1, 1971, effective July 1, 1971; March 2, 1987, effective August 1, 1987; April 23, 2001, effective December 1, 2001; April 29, 2002, effective December 1, 2002; April 30, 2007, effective December 1, 2007.]

RULE 82. JURISDICTION AND VENUE UNAFFECTED

These rules do not extend or limit the jurisdiction of the district courts or the venue of actions in those courts. An admiralty or maritime claim under Rule 9(h) is not a civil action for purposes of 28 U.S.C. §§ 1391–1392.

[Amended December 29, 1948, effective October 20, 1949; February 28, 1966, effective July 1, 1966; April 23, 2001, effective December 1, 2001; April 30, 2007, effective December 1, 2007.]

RULE 83. RULES BY DISTRICT COURTS; JUDGE'S DIRECTIVES

(a) Local Rules.

(1) *In General.* After giving public notice and an opportunity for comment, a district court, acting by a majority of its district judges, may adopt and amend rules governing its practice. A local rule must be consistent with—but not duplicate—federal statutes and rules adopted under 28 U.S.C. §§ 2072 and 2075, and must conform to any uniform numbering system prescribed by the Judicial Conference of the United States. A local rule takes effect on the date specified by the district court and remains in effect unless

amended by the court or abrogated by the judicial council of the circuit. Copies of rules and amendments must, on their adoption, be furnished to the judicial council and the Administrative Office of the United States Courts and be made available to the public.

(2) *Requirement of Form.* A local rule imposing a requirement of form must not be enforced in a way that causes a party to lose any right because of a nonwillful failure to comply.

(b) Procedure When There Is No Controlling Law. A judge may regulate practice in any manner consistent with federal law, rules adopted under 28 U.S.C. §§ 2072 and 2075, and the district's local rules. No sanction or other disadvantage may be imposed for noncompliance with any requirement not in federal law, federal rules, or the local rules unless the alleged violator has been furnished in the particular case with actual notice of the requirement.

[Amended April 29, 1985, effective August 1, 1985; April 27, 1995, effective December 1, 1995; April 30, 2007, effective December 1, 2007.]

RULE 84. FORMS

The forms in the Appendix suffice under these rules and illustrate the simplicity and brevity that these rules contemplate.

[Amended December 27, 1946, effective March 19, 1948; April 30, 2007, effective December 1, 2007.]

RULE 85. TITLE

These rules may be cited as the Federal Rules of Civil Procedure.

[Amended April 30, 2007, effective December 1, 2007.]

RULE 86. EFFECTIVE DATES

(a) In General. These rules and any amendments take effect at the time specified by the Supreme Court, subject to 28 U.S.C. § 2074. They govern:

(1) proceedings in an action commenced after their effective date; and

(2) proceedings after that date in an action then pending unless:

(A) the Supreme Court specifies otherwise; or

(B) the court determines that applying them in a particular action would be infeasible or work an injustice.

(b) December 1, 2007 Amendments. If any provision in Rules 1–5.1, 6–73, or 77–86 conflicts with another law, priority in time for the purpose of 28 U.S.C. § 2072(b) is not affected by the amendments taking effect on December 1, 2007.

[Amended December 27, 1946, effective March 19, 1948; December 29, 1948, effective October 20, 1949; April 17, 1961, effective July 19, 1961; January 21, 1963, and March 18, 1963, effective July 1, 1963; April 30, 2007, effective December 1, 2007.]

APPENDIX OF FORMS

FORM 1. CAPTION

(Use on every summons, complaint, answer, motion, or other document.)

United States District Court
for the
_____ District of _____

A B, Plaintiff	)	
	)	
v.	)	
	)	Civil Action No. _____
C D, Defendant	)	
	)	
v.	)	
	)	
E F, Third–Party Defendant	)	
(Use if needed.)	)	

(Name of Document)

[Effective December 1, 2007.]

FORM 2. DATE, SIGNATURE, ADDRESS, E–MAIL ADDRESS, AND TELEPHONE NUMBER

(Use at the conclusion of pleadings and other papers that require a signature.)

Date _____ _____

_____
(Signature of the attorney or unrepresented party)

_____
(Printed name)

_____
(Address)

_____
(E-mail address)

_____
(Telephone number)

[Effective December 1, 2007.]

FORM 3. SUMMONS

(Caption—See Form 1.)

To *name the defendant*:

A lawsuit has been filed against you.

Within 20 days after service of this summons on you (not counting the day you received it), you must serve on the plaintiff an answer to the attached complaint or a motion under Rule 12 of the Federal Rules of Civil Procedure. The answer or motion must be served on the plaintiff's attorney, _____, whose address is _____. If you fail to do so, judgment by default will be entered against you for the relief demanded in the complaint. You also must file your answer or motion with the court.

Date _____

_____
Clerk of Court

(Court Seal)

(*Use 60 days if the defendant is the United States or a United States agency, or is an officer or employee of the United States allowed 60 days by Rule 12(a)(3).*)

[Effective December 1, 2007.]

FORM 4. SUMMONS ON A THIRD–PARTY COMPLAINT

(Caption—See Form 1.)

To *name the third-party defendant*:

A lawsuit has been filed against defendant _____, who as third-party plaintiff is making this claim against you to pay part or all of what [he] may owe to the plaintiff _____.

Within 20 days after service of this summons on you (not counting the day you received it), you must serve on the plaintiff and on the defendant an answer to the attached third-party complaint or a motion under Rule 12 of the Federal Rules of Civil Procedure. The answer or motion must be served on the defendant's attorney, _____, whose address is, _____, and also on the plaintiff's attorney, _____, whose address is, _____. If you fail to do so, judgment by default will be entered against you for the relief demanded in the third-party complaint. You also must file the answer or motion with the court and serve it on any other parties.

A copy of the plaintiff's complaint is also attached. You may—but are not required to—respond to it.

Date _____

_____
Clerk of Court

(Court Seal)

[Effective December 1, 2007.]

FORM 5. NOTICE OF A LAWSUIT AND REQUEST
TO WAIVE SERVICE OF A SUMMONS

(Caption—See Form 1.)

To (*name the defendant—or if the defendant is a corporation, partnership, or association name an officer or agent authorized to receive service*):

Why are you getting this?

A lawsuit has been filed against you, or the entity you represent, in this court under the number shown above. A copy of the complaint is attached.

This is not a summons, or an official notice from the court. It is a request that, to avoid expenses, you waive formal service of a summons by signing and returning the enclosed waiver. To avoid these expenses, you must return the signed waiver within (*give at least 30 days or at least 60 days if the defendant is outside any judicial district of the United States*) from the date shown below, which is the date this notice was sent. Two copies of the waiver form are enclosed, along with a stamped, self-addressed envelope or other prepaid means for returning one copy. You may keep the other copy.

What happens next?

If you return the signed waiver, I will file it with the court. The action will then proceed as if you had been served on the date the waiver is filed, but no summons will be served on you and you will have 60 days from the date this notice is sent (see the date below) to answer the complaint (or 90 days if this notice is sent to you outside any judicial district of the United States).

If you do not return the signed waiver within the time indicated, I will arrange to have the summons and complaint served on you. And I will ask the court to require you, or the entity you represent, to pay the expenses of making service.

Please read the enclosed statement about the duty to avoid unnecessary expenses.

I certify that this request is being sent to you on the date below.

(Date and sign—See Form 2.)

[Effective December 1, 2007.]

FORM 6. WAIVER OF THE SERVICE OF SUMMONS

(Caption—See Form 1.)

To *name the plaintiff's attorney or the unrepresented plaintiff*:

I have received your request to waive service of a summons in this action along with a copy of the complaint, two copies of this waiver form, and a prepaid means of returning one signed copy of the form to you.

I, or the entity I represent, agree to save the expense of serving a summons and complaint in this case.

I understand that I, or the entity I represent, will keep all defenses or objections to the lawsuit, the court's jurisdiction, and the venue of the action, but that I waive any objections to the absence of a summons or of service.

I also understand that I, or the entity I represent, must file and serve an answer or a motion under Rule 12 within 60 days from _____, the date when this request was sent (or 90 days if it was sent outside the United States). If I fail to do so, a default judgment will be entered against me or the entity I represent.

(Date and sign—See Form 2.)

(Attach the following to Form 6.)

Duty to Avoid Unnecessary Expenses of Serving a Summons

Rule 4 of the Federal Rules of Civil Procedure requires certain defendants to cooperate in saving unnecessary expenses of serving a summons and complaint. A defendant who is located in the United States and who fails to return a signed waiver of service requested by a plaintiff located in the United States will be required to pay the expenses of service, unless the defendant shows good cause for the failure.

"Good cause" does *not* include a belief that the lawsuit is groundless, or that it has been brought in an improper venue, or that the court has no jurisdiction over this matter or over the defendant or the defendant's property.

If the waiver is signed and returned, you can still make these and all other defenses and objections, but you cannot object to the absence of a summons or of service.

If you waive service, then you must, within the time specified on the waiver form, serve an answer or a motion under Rule 12 on the plaintiff and file a copy with the court. By signing and returning the waiver form, you are allowed more time to respond than if a summons had been served.

[Effective December 1, 2007.]

FORM 7. STATEMENT OF JURISDICTION

    a. (*For diversity-of-citizenship jurisdiction.*) The plaintiff is [a citizen of *Michigan*] [a corporation incorporated under the laws of *Michigan* with its principal place of business in *Michigan*]. The defendant is [a citizen of *New York*] [a corporation incorporated under the laws of *New York* with its principal place of business in *New York*]. The amount in controversy, without interest and costs, exceeds the sum or value specified by 28 U.S.C. § 1332.

    b. (*For federal-question jurisdiction.*) This action arises under [the United States Constitution, *specify the article or amendment and the section*] [a United States treaty *specify*] [a federal statute, ___U.S.C. § ___].

    c. (*For a claim in the admiralty or maritime jurisdiction.*) This is a case of admiralty or maritime jurisdiction. (*To invoke admiralty status under Rule 9(h) use the following:* This is an admiralty or maritime claim within the meaning of Rule 9(h).)

[Effective December 1, 2007.]

FORM 8. STATEMENT OF REASONS FOR OMITTING A PARTY

(If a person who ought to be made a party under Rule 19(a) is not named, include this statement in accordance with Rule 19(c).)

    This complaint does not join as a party *name* who [is not subject to this court's personal jurisdiction] [cannot be made a party without depriving this court of subject-matter jurisdiction] because *state the reason.*

[Effective December 1, 2007.]

FORM 9. STATEMENT NOTING A PARTY'S DEATH

(Caption—See Form 1.)

    In accordance with Rule 25(a) *name the person,* who is [a party to this action] [a representative of or successor to the deceased party] notes the death during the pendency of this action of *name,* [*describe as party* in this action].

(Date and sign—See Form 2.)

[Effective December 1, 2007.]

FORM 10. COMPLAINT TO RECOVER A SUM CERTAIN

(Caption—See Form 1.)

1. (Statement of Jurisdiction–See Form 7.)

(Use one or more of the following as appropriate and include a demand for judgment.)

(a) On a Promissory Note

2. On *date*, the defendant executed and delivered a note promising to pay the plaintiff on *date* the sum of $ _____ with interest at the rate of __ percent. A copy of the note [is attached as Exhibit A] [is summarized as follows: _____.]

3. The defendant has not paid the amount owed.

(b) On an Account

2. The defendant owes the plaintiff $ _____ according to the account set out in Exhibit A.

(c) For Goods Sold and Delivered

2. The defendant owes the plaintiff $ _____ for goods sold and delivered by the plaintiff to the defendant from *date* to *date*.

(d) For Money Lent

2. The defendant owes the plaintiff $ _____ for money lent by the plaintiff to the defendant on *date*.

(e) For Money Paid by Mistake

2. The defendant owes the plaintiff $ _____ for money paid by mistake to the defendant on *date* under these circumstances: *describe with particularity in accordance with Rule 9(b).*

(f) For Money Had and Received

2. The defendant owes the plaintiff $ _____ for money that was received from *name* on *date* to be paid by the defendant to the plaintiff.

Demand for Judgment

Therefore, the plaintiff demands judgment against the defendant for $ _____, plus interest and costs.

(Date and sign—See Form 2.)

[Effective December 1, 2007.]

FORM 11.   COMPLAINT FOR NEGLIGENCE

(Caption—See Form 1.)

1.   (Statement of Jurisdiction–See Form 7.)

2.   On *date*, at *place*, the defendant negligently drove a motor vehicle against the plaintiff.

3.   As a result, the plaintiff was physically injured, lost wages or income, suffered physical and mental pain, and incurred medical expenses of $ _____.

Therefore, the plaintiff demands judgment against the defendant for $ _____, plus costs.

(Date and sign—See Form 2).

[Effective December 1, 2007.]

FORM 12.   COMPLAINT FOR NEGLIGENCE WHEN THE PLAINTIFF DOES NOT KNOW WHO IS RESPONSIBLE

(Caption—See Form 1.)

1.   (Statement of Jurisdiction–See Form 7.)

2.   On *date*, at *place*, defendant *name* or defendant *name* or both of them willfully or recklessly or negligently drove, or caused to be driven, a motor vehicle against the plaintiff.

3.   As a result, the plaintiff was physically injured, lost wages or income, suffered mental and physical pain, and incurred medical expenses of $ _____.

Therefore, the plaintiff demands judgment against one or both defendants for $ _____, plus costs.

(Date and sign—See Form 2.)

[Effective December 1, 2007.]

FORM 13.   COMPLAINT FOR NEGLIGENCE UNDER THE FEDERAL EMPLOYERS' LIABILITY ACT

(Caption—See Form 1.)

1. (Statement of Jurisdiction—See Form 7.)

2. At the times below, the defendant owned and operated in interstate commerce a railroad line that passed through a tunnel located at _____.

3. On *date*, the plaintiff was working to repair and enlarge the tunnel to make it convenient and safe for use in interstate commerce.

4. During this work, the defendant, as the employer, negligently put the plaintiff to work in a section of the tunnel that the defendant had left unprotected and unsupported.

5. The defendant's negligence caused the plaintiff to be injured by a rock that fell from an unsupported portion of the tunnel.

6. As a result, the plaintiff was physically injured, lost wages or income, suffered mental and physical pain, and incurred medical expenses of $ _____.

Therefore, the plaintiff demands judgment against the defendant for $ _____, and costs.

(Date and sign—See Form 2.)

[Effective December 1, 2007.]

FORM 14.   COMPLAINT FOR DAMAGES UNDER THE MERCHANT MARINE ACT

(Caption—See Form 1.)

1. (Statement of Jurisdiction—See Form 7.)

2. At the times below, the defendant owned and operated the vessel *name* and used it to transport cargo for hire by water in interstate and foreign commerce.

3. On *date*, at *place*, the defendant hired the plaintiff under seamen's articles of customary form for a voyage from _____ to _____ and return at a wage of $ _____ a month and found, which is equal to a shore worker's wage of $ _____ a month.

4. On *date*, the vessel was at sea on the return voyage. (*Describe the weather and the condition of the vessel.*)

5. (*Describe as in Form 11 the defendant's negligent conduct.*)

6. As a result of the defendant's negligent conduct and the unseaworthiness of the vessel, the plaintiff was physically injured, has been incapable of any gainful activity, suffered mental and physical pain, and has incurred medical expenses of $ _____.

Therefore, the plaintiff demands judgment against the defendant for $, plus costs.

(Date and sign—See Form 2.)

[Effective December 1, 2007.]

FORM 15. COMPLAINT FOR THE CONVERSION OF PROPERTY

(Caption—See Form 1.)

1. (Statement of Jurisdiction—See Form 7.)

2. On *date*, at *place*, the defendant converted to the defendant's own use property owned by the plaintiff. The property converted consists of *describe*.

3. The property is worth $ _____.

Therefore, the plaintiff demands judgment against the defendant for $ _____, plus costs.

(Date and sign—See Form 2.)

[Effective December 1, 2007.]

FORM 16.   THIRD–PARTY COMPLAINT

(Caption—See Form 1.)

1. Plaintiff *name* has filed against defendant *name* a complaint, a copy of which is attached.

2. (*State grounds entitling defendant's name to recover from third-party defendant's name for (all or an identified share) of any judgment for plaintiff's name against defendant's name.*)

Therefore, the defendant demands judgment against *third-party defendant's name* for *all or an identified share* of sums that may be adjudged against the defendant in the plaintiff's favor.

(Date and sign—See Form 2.)

[Effective December 1, 2007.]

FORM 17. COMPLAINT FOR SPECIFIC PERFORMANCE OF A CONTRACT TO CONVEY LAND

(Caption—See Form 1.)

1. (Statement of Jurisdiction–See Form 7.)

2. On *date*, the parties agreed to the contract [attached as Exhibit A][summarize the contract].

3. As agreed, the plaintiff tendered the purchase price and requested a conveyance of the land, but the defendant refused to accept the money or make a conveyance.

4. The plaintiff now offers to pay the purchase price.

Therefore, the plaintiff demands that:

(a) the defendant be required to specifically perform the agreement and pay damages of $ _____, plus interest and costs, or

(b) if specific performance is not ordered, the defendant be required to pay damages of $ _____, plus interest and costs.

(Date and sign—See Form 2.)

[Effective December 1, 2007.]

FORM 18. COMPLAINT FOR PATENT INFRINGEMENT

(Caption—See Form 1.)

1. (Statement of Jurisdiction—See Form 7.)

2. On *date*, United States Letters Patent No. _____ were issued to the plaintiff for an invention in an *electric motor*. The plaintiff owned the patent throughout the period of the defendant's infringing acts and still owns the patent.

3. The defendant has infringed and is still infringing the Letters Patent by making, selling, and using *electric motors* that embody the patented invention, and the defendant will continue to do so unless enjoined by this court.

4. The plaintiff has complied with the statutory requirement of placing a notice of the Letters Patent on all *electric motors* it manufactures and sells and has given the defendant written notice of the infringement.

Therefore, the plaintiff demands:

(a) a preliminary and final injunction against the continuing infringement;

(b) an accounting for damages; and

(c) interest and costs.

(Date and sign—See Form 2.)

[Effective December 1, 2007.]

FORM 19.   COMPLAINT FOR COPYRIGHT INFRINGEMENT
AND UNFAIR COMPETITION

(Caption—See Form 1.)

1.   (Statement of Jurisdiction–See Form 7.)

2.   Before *date*, the plaintiff, a United States citizen, wrote a book entitled _____.

3.   The book is an original work that may be copyrighted under United States law. A copy of the book is attached as Exhibit A.

4.   Between *date* and *date*, the plaintiff applied to the copyright office and received a certificate of registration dated _____ and identified as *date, class, number*.

5.   Since *date*, the plaintiff has either published or licensed for publication all copies of the book in compliance with the copyright laws and has remained the sole owner of the copyright.

6.   After the copyright was issued, the defendant infringed the copyright by publishing and selling a book entitled _____, which was copied largely from the plaintiff's book. A copy of the defendant's book is attached as Exhibit B.

7.   The plaintiff has notified the defendant in writing of the infringement.

8.   The defendant continues to infringe the copyright by continuing to publish and sell the infringing book in violation of the copyright, and further has engaged in unfair trade practices and unfair competition in connection with its publication and sale of the infringing book, thus causing irreparable damage.

Therefore, the plaintiff demands that:

(a) until this case is decided the defendant and the defendant's agents be enjoined from disposing of any copies of the defendant's book by sale or otherwise;

(b) the defendant account for and pay as damages to the plaintiff all profits and advantages gained from unfair trade practices and unfair competition in selling the defendant's book, and all profits and advantages gained from infringing the plaintiff's copyright (but no less than the statutory minimum);

(c) the defendant deliver for impoundment all copies of the book in the defendant's possession or control and deliver for destruction all infringing copies and all plates, molds, and other materials for making infringing copies;

(d) the defendant pay the plaintiff interest, costs, and reasonable attorney's fees; and

(e) the plaintiff be awarded any other just relief.

(Date and sign—See Form 2.)

[Effective December 1, 2007.]

FORM 20. COMPLAINT FOR INTERPLEADER
AND DECLARATORY RELIEF

(Caption—See Form 1.)

1. (Statement of Jurisdiction–See Form 7.)

2. On *date*, the plaintiff issued a life insurance policy on the life of *name* with *name* as the named beneficiary.

3. As a condition for keeping the policy in force, the policy required payment of a premium during the first year and then annually.

4. The premium due on *date* was never paid, and the policy lapsed after that date.

5. On *date*, after the policy had lapsed, both the insured and the named beneficiary died in an automobile collision.

6. Defendant *name* claims to be the beneficiary in place of *name* and has filed a claim to be paid the policy's full amount.

7. The other two defendants are representatives of the deceased persons' estates. Each defendant has filed a claim on behalf of each estate to receive payment of the policy's full amount.

8. If the policy was in force at the time of death, the plaintiff is in doubt about who should be paid.

Therefore, the plaintiff demands that:

(a) each defendant be restrained from commencing any action against the plaintiff on the policy;

(b) a judgment be entered that no defendant is entitled to the proceeds of the policy or any part of it, but if the court determines that the policy was in effect at the time of the insured's death, that the defendants be required to interplead and settle among themselves their rights to the proceeds, and that the plaintiff be discharged from all liability except to the defendant determined to be entitled to the proceeds; and

(c) the plaintiff recover its costs.

(Date and sign—See Form 2.)

[Effective December 1, 2007.]

FORM 21. COMPLAINT ON A CLAIM FOR A DEBT AND TO SET ASIDE A FRAUDULENT CONVEYANCE UNDER RULE 18(b)

(Caption—See Form 1.)

1. (Statement of Jurisdiction—See Form 7.)

2. On _date_, defendant _name_ signed a note promising to pay to the plaintiff on _date_ the sum of $ _____ with interest at the rate of ___ percent. [The pleader may, but need not, attach a copy or plead the note verbatim.]

3. Defendant _name_ owes the plaintiff the amount of the note and interest.

4. On _date_, defendant _name_ conveyed all defendant's real and personal property _if less than all, describe it fully_ to defendant _name_ for the purpose of defrauding the plaintiff and hindering or delaying the collection of the debt.

Therefore, the plaintiff demands that:

(a) judgment for $ _____, plus costs, be entered against defendant(s) _name(s)_; and

(b) the conveyance to defendant _name_ be declared void and any judgment granted be made a lien on the property.

(Date and sign—See Form 2.)

[Effective December 1, 2007.]

FORM 30. ANSWER PRESENTING DEFENSES UNDER RULE 12(b)

(Caption—See Form 1.)

Responding to Allegations in the Complaint

1. Defendant admits the allegations in paragraphs _____.

2. Defendant lacks knowledge or information sufficient to form a belief about the truth of the allegations in paragraphs _____.

3. Defendant admits *identify part of the allegation* in paragraph _____ and denies or lacks knowledge or information sufficient to form a belief about the truth of the rest of the paragraph.

Failure to State a Claim

4. The complaint fails to state a claim upon which relief can be granted.

Failure to Join a Required Party

5. If there is a debt, it is owed jointly by the defendant and *name* who is a citizen of _____. This person can be made a party without depriving this court of jurisdiction over the existing parties.

Affirmative Defense—Statute of Limitations

6. The plaintiff's claim is barred by the statute of limitations because it arose more than _____ years before this action was commenced.

Counterclaim

7. (*Set forth any counterclaim in the same way a claim is pleaded in a complaint. Include a further statement of jurisdiction if needed.*)

Crossclaim

8. (*Set forth a crossclaim against a coparty in the same way a claim is pleaded in a complaint. Include a further statement of jurisdiction if needed.*)

(Date and sign—See Form 2.)

[Effective December 1, 2007.]

FORM 31. ANSWER TO A COMPLAINT FOR MONEY HAD AND RECEIVED WITH A COUNTERCLAIM FOR INTERPLEADER

(Caption—See Form 1.)

Response to the Allegations in the Complaint
(See Form 30)

Counterclaim for Interpleader

1.   The defendant received from *name* a deposit of $ _____.

2.   The plaintiff demands payment of the deposit because of a purported assignment from *name*, who has notified the defendant that the assignment is not valid and who continues to hold the defendant responsible for the deposit.

Therefore, the defendant demands that:

(a) *name* be made a party to this action;

(b) the plaintiff and *name* be required to interplead their respective claims;

(c) the court decide whether the plaintiff or *name* or either of them is entitled to the deposit and discharge the defendant of any liability except to the person entitled to the deposit; and

(d) the defendant recover costs and attorney's fees.

(Date and sign—See Form 2.)

[Effective December 1, 2007.]

FORM 40. MOTION TO DISMISS UNDER RULE 12(b) FOR LACK OF JURISDICTION, IMPROPER VENUE, INSUFFICIENT SERVICE OF PROCESS, OR FAILURE TO STATE A CLAIM

(Caption—See Form 1.)

The defendant moves to dismiss the action because:

1.   the amount in controversy is less than the sum or value specified by 28 U.S.C. § 1332;

2.   the defendant is not subject to the personal jurisdiction of this court;

3.   venue is improper (this defendant does not reside in this district and no part of the events or omissions giving rise to the claim occurred in the district);

4.   the defendant has not been properly served, as shown by the attached affidavits of _____; or

5.   the complaint fails to state a claim upon which relief can be granted.

(Date and sign—See Form 2.)

[Effective December 1, 2007.]

FORM 41.   MOTION TO BRING IN A THIRD–PARTY DEFENDANT

(Caption—See Form 1.)

The defendant, as third-party plaintiff, moves for leave to serve on *name* a summons and third-party complaint, copies of which are attached.

(Date and sign—See Form 2.)

[Effective December 1, 2007.]

FORM 42.   MOTION TO INTERVENE AS A DEFENDANT UNDER RULE 24

(Caption—See Form 1.)

1.   *Name* moves for leave to intervene as a defendant in this action and to file the attached answer.

(State grounds under Rule 24(a) or (b).)

2.   The plaintiff alleges patent infringement. We manufacture and sell to the defendant the articles involved, and we have a defense to the plaintiff's claim.

3.   Our defense presents questions of law and fact that are common to this action.

(Date and sign—See Form 2.)

[An Intervener's Answer must be attached. See Form 30.]

[Effective December 1, 2007.]

FORM 50.   REQUEST TO PRODUCE DOCUMENTS AND TANGIBLE THINGS, OR TO ENTER ONTO LAND UNDER RULE 34

(Caption—See Form 1.)

The plaintiff *name* requests that the defendant *name* respond within _____ days to the following requests:

1.   To produce and permit the plaintiff to inspect and copy and to test or sample the following documents, including electronically stored information:

(Describe each document and the electronically stored information, either individually or by category.)

(State the time, place, and manner of the inspection and any related acts.)

2.   To produce and permit the plaintiff to inspect and copy—and to test or sample—the following tangible things:

(Describe each thing, either individually or by category.)

(State the time, place, and manner of the inspection and any related acts.)

3.   To permit the plaintiff to enter onto the following land to inspect, photograph, test, or sample the property or an object or operation on the property.

(Describe the property and each object or operation.)

(State the time and manner of the inspection and any related acts.)

(Date and sign—See Form 2.)

[Effective December 1, 2007.]

FORM 51.   REQUEST FOR ADMISSIONS UNDER RULE 36

(Caption—See Form 1.)

The plaintiff *name* asks the defendant *name* to respond within 30 days to these requests by admitting, for purposes of this action only and subject to objections to admissibility at trial:

1.   The genuineness of the following documents, copies of which [are attached] [are or have been furnished or made available for inspection and copying].

(List each document.)

2.   The truth of each of the following statements:

(List each statement.)

(Date and sign—See Form 2.)

[Effective December 1, 2007.]

FORM 52. REPORT OF THE PARTIES' PLANNING MEETING

(Caption—See Form 1.)

1. The following persons participated in a Rule 26(f) conference on _date_ by _state the method of conferring_:

(_e.g._, _name_ representing the plaintiff.)

2. Initial Disclosures. The parties [have completed] [will complete by _date_] the initial disclosures required by Rule 26(a)(1).

3. Discovery Plan. The parties propose this discovery plan:

(_Use separate paragraphs or subparagraphs if the parties disagree._)

(a) Discovery will be needed on these subjects: (_describe._)

(b) (Dates for commencing and completing discovery, including discovery to be commenced or completed before other discovery.)

(c) (Maximum number of interrogatories by each party to another party, along with the dates the answers are due.)

(d) (Maximum number of requests for admission, along with the dates responses are due.)

(e) (Maximum number of depositions by each party.)

(f) (Limits on the length of depositions, in hours.)

(g) (Dates for exchanging reports of expert witnesses.)

(h) (Dates for supplementations under Rule 26(e).)

4. Other Items:

(a) (A date if the parties ask to meet with the court before a scheduling order.)

(b) (Requested dates for pretrial conferences.)

(c) (Final dates for the plaintiff to amend pleadings or to join parties.)

(d) (Final dates for the defendant to amend pleadings or to join parties.)

(e) (Final dates to file dispositive motions.)

(f) (State the prospects for settlement.)

(g) (Identify any alternative dispute resolution procedure that may enhance settlement prospects.)

(h) (Final dates for submitting Rule 26(a)(3) witness lists, designations of witnesses whose testimony will be presented by deposition, and exhibit lists.)

(i) (Final dates to file objections under Rule 26(a)(3).)

(j) (Suggested trial date and estimate of trial length.)

(k) (Other matters.)

(Date and sign—see Form 2.)

[Effective December 1, 2007.]

FORM 60. NOTICE OF CONDEMNATION

(Caption—See Form 1.)

To *name the defendant*.

1. A complaint in condemnation has been filed in the United States District Court for the _____District of _____, to take property to use for *purpose*. The interest to be taken is *describe*. The court is located in the United States courthouse at this address: _____.

2. The property to be taken is described below. You have or claim an interest in it.

(*Describe the property.*)

3. The authority for taking this property is *cite*.

4. If you want to object or present any defense to the taking you must serve an answer on the plaintiff's attorney within 20 days [after being served with this notice][from (insert the date of the last publication of notice)]. Send your answer to this address: _____.

5. Your answer must identify the property in which you claim an interest, state the nature and extent of that interest, and state all your objections and defenses to the taking. Objections and defenses not presented are waived.

6. If you fail to answer you consent to the taking and the court will enter a judgment that takes your described property interest.

7. Instead of answering, you may serve on the plaintiff's attorney a notice of appearance that designates the property in which you claim an interest. After you do that, you will receive a notice of any proceedings that affect you. Whether or not you have previously appeared or answered, you may present evidence at a trial to determine compensation for the property and share in the overall award.

(Date and sign—See Form 2.)

[Effective December 1, 2007.]

FORM 61. COMPLAINT FOR CONDEMNATION

(Caption—See Form 1; name as defendants the property and at least one owner.)

1. (Statement of Jurisdiction—See Form 7.)

2. This is an action to take property under the power of eminent domain and to determine just compensation to be paid to the owners and parties in interest.

3. The authority for the taking is _____.

4. The property is to be used for _____.

5. The property to be taken is (describe in enough detail for identification—or attach the description and state "is described in Exhibit A, attached.")

6. The interest to be acquired is _____.

7. The persons known to the plaintiff to have or claim an interest in the property are: _____. (For each person include the interest claimed.)

8. There may be other persons who have or claim an interest in the property and whose names could not be found after a reasonably diligent search. They are made parties under the designation "Unknown Owners."

Therefore, the plaintiff demands judgment:

    (a) condemning the property;

    (b) determining and awarding just compensation; and

    (c) granting any other lawful and proper relief.

(Date and sign—See Form 2.)

[Effective December 1, 2007.]

FORM 70. JUDGMENT ON A JURY VERDICT

(Caption—See Form 1.)

This action was tried by a jury with Judge _____ presiding, and the jury has rendered a verdict.

It is ordered that:

[the plaintiff *name* recover from the defendant *name* the amount of $ _____ with interest at the rate of __%, along with costs.]

[the plaintiff recover nothing, the action be dismissed on the merits, and the defendant *name* recover costs from the plaintiff *name*.]

Date _____ _____

_____
               Clerk of Court

[Effective December 1, 2007.]

FORM 71. JUDGMENT BY THE COURT WITHOUT A JURY

(Caption—See Form 1.)

This action was tried by Judge _____ without a jury and the following decision was reached:

It is ordered that [the plaintiff _name_ recover from the defendant _name_ the amount of $ _____, with prejudgment interest at the rate of _____%, postjudgment interest at the rate of _____%, along with costs.] [the plaintiff recover nothing, the action be dismissed on the merits, and the defendant _name_ recover costs from the plaintiff _name_.]

Date _____

_____
Clerk of Court

[Effective December 1, 2007.]

FORM 80. NOTICE OF A MAGISTRATE JUDGE'S AVAILABILITY

1. A magistrate judge is available under title 28 U.S.C. § 636(c) to conduct the proceedings in this case, including a jury or nonjury trial and the entry of final judgment. But a magistrate judge can be assigned only if all parties voluntarily consent.

2. You may withhold your consent without adverse substantive consequences. The identity of any party consenting or withholding consent will not be disclosed to the judge to whom the case is assigned or to any magistrate judge.

3. If a magistrate judge does hear your case, you may appeal directly to a United States court of appeals as you would if a district judge heard it.

A form called _Consent to an Assignment to a United States Magistrate Judge_ is available from the court clerk's office.

[Effective December 1, 2007.]

FORM 81.   CONSENT TO AN ASSIGNMENT TO A MAGISTRATE JUDGE

(Caption—See Form 1.)

I voluntarily consent to have a United States magistrate judge conduct all further proceedings in this case, including a trial, and order the entry of final judgment. (Return this form to the court clerk—not to a judge or magistrate judge.)

Date _____

_____

Signature of the Party

[Effective December 1, 2007.]

FORM 82.   ORDER OF ASSIGNMENT TO A MAGISTRATE JUDGE

(Caption—See Form 1.)

With the parties' consent it is ordered that this case be assigned to United States Magistrate Judge _____ of this district to conduct all proceedings and enter final judgment in accordance with 28 U.S.C. § 636(c).

Date _____

_____

United States District Judge

[Effective December 1, 2007.]

SUPPLEMENTAL RULES FOR ADMIRALTY OR MARITIME CLAIMS AND ASSET FORFEITURE ACTIONS

Effective July 1, 1966

Including Amendments Effective December 1, 2008, Absent Contrary Congressional Action

RULE A. SCOPE OF RULES

(1) These Supplemental Rules apply to:

(A) the procedure in admiralty and maritime claims within the meaning of Rule 9(h) with respect to the following remedies:

(i) maritime attachment and garnishment,

(ii) actions in rem,

(iii) possessory, petitory, and partition actions, and

(iv) actions for exoneration from or limitation of liability;

(B) forfeiture actions in rem arising from a federal statute; and

(C) the procedure in statutory condemnation proceedings analogous to maritime actions in rem, whether within the admiralty and maritime jurisdiction or not. Except as otherwise provided, references in these Supplemental Rules to actions in rem include such analogous statutory condemnation proceedings.

(2) The Federal Rules of Civil Procedure also apply to the foregoing proceedings except to the extent that they are inconsistent with these Supplemental Rules.

[Amended effective December 1, 2006.]

RULE B. IN PERSONAM ACTIONS; ATTACHMENT AND GARNISHMENT

(1) When Available; Complaint, Affidavit, Judicial Authorization, and Process. In an in personam action:

(a) If a defendant is not found within the district when a verified complaint praying for attachment and the affidavit required by Rule B(1)(b) are filed, a verified complaint may contain a prayer for process to attach the defendant's tangible or intangible personal property—up to the amount sued for—in the hands of garnishees named in the process.

(b) The plaintiff or the plaintiff's attorney must sign and file with the complaint an affidavit stating that, to the affiant's knowledge, or on information and belief, the defendant cannot be found within the district. The court must review the complaint and affidavit and, if the conditions of this Rule B appear to exist,

enter an order so stating and authorizing process of attachment and garnishment. The clerk may issue supplemental process enforcing the court's order upon application without further court order.

(c) If the plaintiff or the plaintiff's attorney certifies that exigent circumstances make court review impracticable, the clerk must issue the summons and process of attachment and garnishment. The plaintiff has the burden in any post-attachment hearing under Rule E(4)(f) to show that exigent circumstances existed.

(d)(i) If the property is a vessel or tangible property on board a vessel, the summons, process, and any supplemental process must be delivered to the marshal for service.

(ii) If the property is other tangible or intangible property, the summons, process, and any supplemental process must be delivered to a person or organization authorized to serve it, who may be (A) a marshal; (B) someone under contract with the United States; (C) someone specially appointed by the court for that purpose; or, (D) in an action brought by the United States, any officer or employee of the United States.

(e) The plaintiff may invoke state-law remedies under Rule 64 for seizure of person or property for the purpose of securing satisfaction of the judgment.

(2) Notice to Defendant. No default judgment may be entered except upon proof—which may be by affidavit—that:

(a) the complaint, summons, and process of attachment or garnishment have been served on the defendant in a manner authorized by Rule 4;

(b) the plaintiff or the garnishee has mailed to the defendant the complaint, summons, and process of attachment or garnishment, using any form of mail requiring a return receipt; or

(c) the plaintiff or the garnishee has tried diligently to give notice of the action to the defendant but could not do so.

(3) Answer.

(a) *By Garnishee.* The garnishee shall serve an answer, together with answers to any interrogatories served with the complaint, within 20 days after service of process upon the garnishee. Interrogatories to the garnishee may be served with the complaint without leave of court. If the garnishee refuses or neglects to answer on oath as to the debts, credits, or effects of the defendant in the garnishee's hands, or any interrogatories concerning such debts, credits, and effects that may be propounded by the plaintiff, the court may award compulsory process against the garnishee. If the garnishee admits any debts, credits, or effects, they shall be held in the garnishee's hands or paid into the registry of the court, and shall be held in either case subject to the further order of the court.

(b) *By Defendant.* The defendant shall serve an answer within 30 days after process has been executed, whether by attachment of property or service on the garnishee.

[Amended April 29, 1985, effective August 1, 1985; March 2, 1987, effective August 1, 1987; April 17, 2000, effective December 1, 2000; April 25, 2005, effective December 1, 2005.]

RULE C. IN REM ACTIONS: SPECIAL PROVISIONS

(1) When Available. An action in rem may be brought:

(a) To enforce any maritime lien;

(b) Whenever a statute of the United States provides for a maritime action in rem or a proceeding analogous thereto.

Except as otherwise provided by law a party who may proceed in rem may also, or in the alternative, proceed in personam against any person who may be liable.

Statutory provisions exempting vessels or other property owned or possessed by or operated by or for the United States from arrest or seizure are not affected by this rule. When a statute so provides, an action against the United States or an instrumentality thereof may proceed on in rem principles.

(2) Complaint. In an action in rem the complaint must:

(a) be verified;

(b) describe with reasonable particularity the property that is the subject of the action; and

(c) state that the property is within the district or will be within the district while the action is pending.

(3) Judicial Authorization and Process.

(a) *Arrest Warrant.*

(i) The court must review the complaint and any supporting papers. If the conditions for an in rem action appear to exist, the court must issue an order directing the clerk to issue a warrant for the arrest of the vessel or other property that is the subject of the action.

(ii) If the plaintiff or the plaintiff's attorney certifies that exigent circumstances make court review

impracticable, the clerk must promptly issue a summons and a warrant for the arrest of the vessel or other property that is the subject of the action. The plaintiff has the burden in any post-arrest hearing under Rule E(4)(f) to show that exigent circumstances existed.

(b) *Service.*

(i) If the property that is the subject of the action is a vessel or tangible property on board a vessel, the warrant and any supplemental process must be delivered to the marshal for service.

(ii) If the property that is the subject of the action is other property, tangible or intangible, the warrant and any supplemental process must be delivered to a person or organization authorized to enforce it, who may be: (A) a marshal; (B) someone under contract with the United States; (C) someone specially appointed by the court for that purpose; or, (D) in an action brought by the United States, any officer or employee of the United States.

(c) *Deposit in Court.* If the property that is the subject of the action consists in whole or in part of freight, the proceeds of property sold, or other intangible property, the clerk must issue—in addition to the warrant—a summons directing any person controlling the property to show cause why it should not be deposited in court to abide the judgment.

(d) *Supplemental Process.* The clerk may upon application issue supplemental process to enforce the court's order without further court order.

(4) Notice. No notice other than execution of process is required when the property that is the subject of the action has been released under Rule E(5). If the property is not released within 10 days after execution, the plaintiff must promptly—or within the time that the court allows—give public notice of the action and arrest in a newspaper designated by court order and having general circulation in the district, but publication may be terminated if the property is released before publication is completed. The notice must specify the time under Rule C(6) to file a statement of interest in or right against the seized property and to answer. This rule does not affect the notice requirements in an action to foreclose a preferred ship mortgage under 46 U.S.C. §§ 31301 et seq., as amended.

(5) Ancillary Process. In any action in rem in which process has been served as provided by this rule, if any part of the property that is the subject of the action has not been brought within the control of the court because it has been removed or sold, or because it is intangible property in the hands of a person who has not been served with process, the court may, on motion, order any person having possession or control of such property or its proceeds to show cause why it should not be delivered into the custody of the marshal or other person or organization having a warrant for the arrest of the property, or paid into court to abide the judgment; and, after hearing, the court may enter such judgment as law and justice may require.

(6) Responsive Pleading; Interrogatories.

[Text of paragraph (6)(a) effective until December 1, 2008. For text of paragraph (6)(a) effective December 1, 2008, absent contrary Congressional action, see, post.]

(a) *Maritime Arrests and Other Proceedings.*

(i) a person who asserts a right of possession or any ownership interest in the property that is the subject of the action must file a verified statement of right or interest:

(A) within 10 days after the execution of process, or

(B) within the time that the court allows;

(ii) the statement of right or interest must describe the interest in the property that supports the person's demand for its restitution or right to defend the action;

(iii) an agent, bailee, or attorney must state the authority to file a statement of right or interest on behalf of another; and

(iv) a person who asserts a right of possession or any ownership interest must serve an answer within 20 days after filing the statement of interest or right.

[Text of paragraph (6)(a) effective December 1, 2008, absent contrary Congressional action. For text of paragraph (6)(a) effective until December 1, 2008, see, ante.]

(a) *Statement of Interest; Answer.* In an action in rem:

(i) a person who asserts a right of possession or any ownership interest in the property that is the subject of the action must file a verified statement of right or interest:

(A) within 10 days after the execution of process, or

(B) within the time that the court allows;

(ii) the statement of right or interest must describe the interest in the property that supports the person's demand for its restitution or right to defend the action;

(iii) an agent, bailee, or attorney must state the authority to file a statement of right or interest on behalf of another; and

(iv) a person who asserts a right of possession or any ownership interest must serve an answer within 20 days after filing the statement of interest or right.

(b) *Interrogatories.* Interrogatories may be served with the complaint in an in rem action without leave of court. Answers to the interrogatories must be served with the answer to the complaint.

[Amended April 29, 1985, effective August 1, 1985; March 2, 1987, effective August 1, 1987; April 30, 1991, effective December 1, 1991; April 17, 2000, effective December 1, 2000; April 29, 2002, effective December 1, 2002; April 25, 2005, effective December 1, 2005; April 12, 2006, effective December 1, 2006; April 23, 2008, effective December 1, 2008, absent contrary Congressional action.]

RULE D. POSSESSORY, PETITORY, AND PARTITION ACTIONS

In all actions for possession, partition, and to try title maintainable according to the course of the admiralty practice with respect to a vessel, in all actions so maintainable with respect to the possession of cargo or other maritime property, and in all actions by one or more part owners against the others to obtain security for the return of the vessel from any voyage undertaken without their consent, or by one or more part owners against the others to obtain possession of the vessel for any voyage on giving security for its safe return, the process shall be by a warrant of arrest of the vessel, cargo, or other property, and by notice in the manner provided by Rule B(2) to the adverse party or parties.

RULE E. ACTIONS IN REM AND QUASI IN REM: GENERAL PROVISIONS

(1) Applicability. Except as otherwise provided, this rule applies to actions in personam with process of maritime attachment and garnishment, actions in rem, and petitory, possessory, and partition actions, supplementing Rules B, C, and D.

(2) Complaint; Security.

(a) *Complaint.* In actions to which this rule is applicable the complaint shall state the circumstances from which the claim arises with such particularity that the defendant or claimant will be able, without moving for a more definite statement, to commence an investigation of the facts and to frame a responsive pleading.

(b) *Security for Costs.* Subject to the provisions of Rule 54(d) and of relevant statutes, the court may, on the filing of the complaint or on the appearance of any defendant, claimant, or any other party, or at any later time, require the plaintiff, defendant, claimant, or other party to give security, or additional security, in such sum as the court shall direct to pay all costs and expenses that shall be awarded against the party by any interlocutory order or by the final judgment, or on appeal by any appellate court.

(3) Process.

(a) In admiralty and maritime proceedings process in rem or of maritime attachment and garnishment may be served only within the district.

(b) *Issuance and Delivery.* Issuance and delivery of process in rem, or of maritime attachment and garnishment, shall be held in abeyance if the plaintiff so requests.

(4) Execution of Process; Marshal's Return; Custody of Property; Procedures for Release.

(a) *In General.* Upon issuance and delivery of the process, or, in the case of summons with process of attachment and garnishment, when it appears that the defendant cannot be found within the district, the marshal or other person or organization having a warrant shall forthwith execute the process in accordance with this subdivision (4), making due and prompt return.

(b) *Tangible Property.* If tangible property is to be attached or arrested, the marshal or other person or organization having the warrant shall take it into the marshal's possession for safe custody. If the character or situation of the property is such that the taking of actual possession is impracticable, the marshal or other person executing the process shall affix a copy thereof to the property in a conspicuous place and leave a copy of the complaint and process with the person having possession or the person's agent. In furtherance of the marshal's custody of any vessel the marshal is authorized to make a written request to the collector of customs not to grant clearance to such vessel until notified by the marshal or deputy marshal or by the clerk that the vessel has been released in accordance with these rules.

(c) *Intangible Property.* If intangible property is to be attached or arrested the marshal or other person or organization having the warrant shall execute the process by leaving with the garnishee or other obligor a copy of the complaint and process requiring the garnishee or other obligor to answer as provided in Rules B(3)(a) and C(6); or the marshal may accept for payment into the registry of the court the amount owed to the extent of the amount claimed by the plaintiff with interest and costs, in which event the garnishee or other obligor shall not be required to answer unless alias process shall be served.

(d) *Directions With Respect to Property in Custody.* The marshal or other person or organization having the warrant may at any time apply to the court for directions with respect to property that has been attached or arrested, and shall give notice of such application to any or all of the parties as the court may direct.

(e) *Expenses of Seizing and Keeping Property; Deposit.* These rules do not alter the provisions of Title 28, U.S.C., § 1921, as amended, relative to the expenses of seizing and keeping property attached or arrested and to the requirement of deposits to cover such expenses.

(f) *Procedure for Release From Arrest or Attachment.* Whenever property is arrested or attached,

any person claiming an interest in it shall be entitled to a prompt hearing at which the plaintiff shall be required to show why the arrest or attachment should not be vacated or other relief granted consistent with these rules. This subdivision shall have no application to suits for seamen's wages when process is issued upon a certification of sufficient cause filed pursuant to Title 46, U.S.C. §§ 603 and 604* or to actions by the United States for forfeitures for violation of any statute of the United States.

(5) Release of Property.

(a) *Special Bond.* Whenever process of maritime attachment and garnishment or process in rem is issued the execution of such process shall be stayed, or the property released, on the giving of security, to be approved by the court or clerk, or by stipulation of the parties, conditioned to answer the judgment of the court or of any appellate court. The parties may stipulate the amount and nature of such security. In the event of the inability or refusal of the parties so to stipulate the court shall fix the principal sum of the bond or stipulation at an amount sufficient to cover the amount of the plaintiff's claim fairly stated with accrued interest and costs; but the principal sum shall in no event exceed (i) twice the amount of the plaintiff's claim or (ii) the value of the property on due appraisement, whichever is smaller. The bond or stipulation shall be conditioned for the payment of the principal sum and interest thereon at 6 per cent per annum.

(b) *General Bond.* The owner of any vessel may file a general bond or stipulation, with sufficient surety, to be approved by the court, conditioned to answer the judgment of such court in all or any actions that may be brought thereafter in such court in which the vessel is attached or arrested. Thereupon the execution of all such process against such vessel shall be stayed so long as the amount secured by such bond or stipulation is at least double the aggregate amount claimed by plaintiffs in all actions begun and pending in which such vessel has been attached or arrested. Judgments and remedies may be had on such bond or stipulation as if a special bond or stipulation had been filed in each of such actions. The district court may make necessary orders to carry this rule into effect, particularly as to the giving of proper notice of any action against or attachment of a vessel for which a general bond has been filed. Such bond or stipulation shall be indorsed by the clerk with a minute of the actions wherein process is so stayed. Further security may be required by the court at any time.

If a special bond or stipulation is given in a particular case, the liability on the general bond or stipulation shall cease as to that case.

(c) *Release by Consent or Stipulation; Order of Court or Clerk; Costs.* Any vessel, cargo, or other property in the custody of the marshal or other person or organization having the warrant may be released forthwith upon the marshal's acceptance and approval of a stipulation, bond, or other security, signed by the party on whose behalf the property is detained or the party's attorney and expressly authorizing such release, if all costs and charges of the court and its officers shall have first been paid. Otherwise no property in the custody of the marshal, other person or organization having the warrant, or other officer of the court shall be released without an order of the court; but such order may be entered as of course by the clerk, upon the giving of approved security as provided by law and these rules, or upon the dismissal or discontinuance of the action; but the marshal or other person or organization having the warrant shall not deliver any property so released until the costs and charges of the officers of the court shall first have been paid.

(d) *Possessory, Petitory, and Partition Actions.* The foregoing provisions of this subdivision (5) do not apply to petitory, possessory, and partition actions. In such cases the property arrested shall be released only by order of the court, on such terms and conditions and on the giving of such security as the court may require.

(6) Reduction or Impairment of Security. Whenever security is taken the court may, on motion and hearing, for good cause shown, reduce the amount of security given; and if the surety shall be or become insufficient, new or additional sureties may be required on motion and hearing.

(7) Security on Counterclaim.

(a) When a person who has given security for damages in the original action asserts a counterclaim that arises from the transaction or occurrence that is the subject of the original action, a plaintiff for whose benefit the security has been given must give security for damages demanded in the counterclaim unless the court, for cause shown, directs otherwise. Proceedings on the original claim must be stayed until this security is given, unless the court directs otherwise.

(b) The plaintiff is required to give security under Rule E(7)(a) when the United States or its corporate instrumentality counterclaims and would have been required to give security to respond in damages if a private party but is relieved by law from giving security.

(8) Restricted Appearance. An appearance to defend against an admiralty and maritime claim with respect to which there has issued process in rem, or process of attachment and garnishment, may be expressly restricted to the defense of such claim, and in that event is not an appearance for the purposes of any other claim with respect to which such process is not available or has not been served.

(9) Disposition of Property; Sales.

(a) *Interlocutory Sales; Delivery.*

(i) On application of a party, the marshal, or other person having custody of the property, the court may order all or part of the property sold—with the sales proceeds, or as much of them as will satisfy the judgment, paid into court to await further orders of the court—if:

(A) the attached or arrested property is perishable, or liable to deterioration, decay, or injury by being detained in custody pending the action;

(B) the expense of keeping the property is excessive or disproportionate; or

(C) there is an unreasonable delay in securing release of the property.

(ii) In the circumstances described in Rule E(9)(a)(i), the court, on motion by a defendant or a person filing a statement of interest or right under Rule C(6), may order that the property, rather than being sold, be delivered to the movant upon giving security under these rules.

(b) *Sales, Proceeds.* All sales of property shall be made by the marshal or a deputy marshal, or by other person or organization having the warrant, or by any other person assigned by the court where the marshal or other person or organization having the warrant is a party in interest; and the proceeds of sale shall be forthwith paid into the registry of the court to be disposed of according to law.

(10) Preservation of Property. When the owner or another person remains in possession of property attached or arrested under the provisions of Rule E(4)(b) that permit execution of process without taking actual possession, the court, on a party's motion or on its own, may enter any order necessary to preserve the property and to prevent its removal.

* Law Revision Counsel Note: Repealed by Pub.L. 98–89, § 4(b), August 26, 1983, 97 Stat. 600, section 1 of which enacted Title 46, Shipping.

[Amended April 29, 1985, effective August 1, 1985; March 2, 1987, effective August 1, 1987; April 30, 1991, effective December 1, 1991; April 17, 2000, effective December 1, 2000; April 12, 2006, effective December 1, 2006.]

RULE F. LIMITATION OF LIABILITY

(1) Time for Filing Complaint; Security. Not later than six months after receipt of a claim in writing, any vessel owner may file a complaint in the appropriate district court, as provided in subdivision (9) of this rule, for limitation of liability pursuant to statute. The owner (a) shall deposit with the court, for the benefit of claimants, a sum equal to the amount or value of the owner's interest in the vessel and pending freight, or approved security therefor, and in addition such sums, or approved security therefor, as the court may from time to time fix as necessary to carry out the provisions of the statutes as amended; or (b) at the owner's option shall transfer to a trustee to be appointed by the court, for the benefit of claimants, the owner's interest in the vessel and pending freight, together with such sums, or approved security therefor, as the court may from time to time fix as necessary to carry out the provisions of the statutes as amended. The plaintiff shall also give security for costs and, if the plaintiff elects to give security, for interest at the rate of 6 percent per annum from the date of the security.

(2) Complaint. The complaint shall set forth the facts on the basis of which the right to limit liability is asserted and all facts necessary to enable the court to determine the amount to which the owner's liability shall be limited. The complaint may demand exoneration from as well as limitation of liability. It shall state the voyage if any, on which the demands sought to be limited arose, with the date and place of its termination; the amount of all demands including all unsatisfied liens or claims of lien, in contract or in tort or otherwise, arising on that voyage, so far as known to the plaintiff, and what actions and proceedings, if any, are pending thereon; whether the vessel was damaged, lost, or abandoned, and, if so, when and where; the value of the vessel at the close of the voyage or, in case of wreck, the value of her wreckage, strippings, or proceeds, if any, and where and in whose possession they are; and the amount of any pending freight recovered or recoverable. If the plaintiff elects to transfer the plaintiff's interest in the vessel to a trustee, the complaint must further show any prior paramount liens thereon, and what voyages or trips, if any, she has made since the voyage or trip on which the claims sought to be limited arose, and any existing liens arising upon any such subsequent voyage or trip, with the amounts and causes thereof, and the names and addresses of the lienors, so far as known; and whether the vessel sustained any injury upon or by reason of such subsequent voyage or trip.

(3) Claims Against Owner; Injunction. Upon compliance by the owner with the requirements of subdivision (1) of this rule all claims and proceedings against the owner or the owner's property with respect to the matter in question shall cease. On application of the plaintiff the court shall enjoin the further prosecution of any action or proceeding against the plaintiff or the plaintiff's property with respect to any claim subject to limitation in the action.

(4) Notice to Claimants. Upon the owner's compliance with subdivision (1) of this rule the court shall issue a notice to all persons asserting claims with respect to which the complaint seeks limitation, admonishing them to file their respective claims with the clerk of the court and to serve on the attorneys for the plaintiff a copy thereof on or before a date to be named in the notice. The date so fixed shall not be less than 30 days after issuance of the notice. For cause shown, the court may enlarge the time within which claims may be filed. The notice shall be published in such newspaper or newspapers as the court may direct once a week for four successive weeks prior to the date fixed for the filing of claims. The

plaintiff not later than the day of second publication shall also mail a copy of the notice to every person known to have made any claim against the vessel or the plaintiff arising out of the voyage or trip on which the claims sought to be limited arose. In cases involving death a copy of such notice shall be mailed to the decedent at the decedent's last known address, and also to any person who shall be known to have made any claim on account of such death.

(5) Claims and Answer. Claims shall be filed and served on or before the date specified in the notice provided for in subdivision (4) of this rule. Each claim shall specify the facts upon which the claimant relies in support of the claim, the items thereof, and the dates on which the same accrued. If a claimant desires to contest either the right to exoneration from or the right to limitation of liability the claimant shall file and serve an answer to the complaint unless the claim has included an answer.

(6) Information to Be Given Claimants. Within 30 days after the date specified in the notice for filing claims, or within such time as the court thereafter may allow, the plaintiff shall mail to the attorney for each claimant (or if the claimant has no attorney to the claimant) a list setting forth (a) the name of each claimant, (b) the name and address of the claimant's attorney (if the claimant is known to have one), (c) the nature of the claim, i.e., whether property loss, property damage, death, personal injury etc., and (d) the amount thereof.

(7) Insufficiency of Fund or Security. Any claimant may by motion demand that the funds deposited in court or the security given by the plaintiff be increased on the ground that they are less than the value of the plaintiff's interest in the vessel and pending freight. Thereupon the court shall cause due appraisement to be made of the value of the plaintiff's interest in the vessel and pending freight; and if the court finds that the deposit or security is either insufficient or excessive it shall order its increase or reduction. In like manner any claimant may demand that the deposit or security be increased on the ground that it is insufficient to carry out the provisions of the statutes relating to claims in respect of loss of life or bodily injury; and, after notice and hearing, the court may similarly order that the deposit or security be increased or reduced.

(8) Objections to Claims: Distribution of Fund. Any interested party may question or controvert any claim without filing an objection thereto. Upon determination of liability the fund deposited or secured, or the proceeds of the vessel and pending freight, shall be divided pro rata, subject to all relevant provisions of law, among the several claimants in proportion to the amounts of their respective claims, duly proved, saving, however, to all parties any priority to which they may be legally entitled.

(9) Venue; Transfer. The complaint shall be filed in any district in which the vessel has been attached or arrested to answer for any claim with respect to which the plaintiff seeks to limit liability; or, if the vessel has not been attached or arrested, then in any district in which the owner has been sued with respect to any such claim. When the vessel has not been attached or arrested to answer the matters aforesaid, and suit has not been commenced against the owner, the proceedings may be had in the district in which the vessel may be, but if the vessel is not within any district and no suit has been commenced in any district, then the complaint may be filed in any district. For the convenience of parties and witnesses, in the interest of justice, the court may transfer the action to any district; if venue is wrongly laid the court shall dismiss or, if it be in the interest of justice, transfer the action to any district in which it could have been brought. If the vessel shall have been sold, the proceeds shall represent the vessel for the purposes of these rules.

[Amended March 2, 1987, effective August 1, 1987.]

RULE G. FORFEITURE ACTIONS IN REM

(1) Scope. This rule governs a forfeiture action in rem arising from a federal statute. To the extent that this rule does not address an issue, Supplemental Rules C and E and the Federal Rules of Civil Procedure also apply.

(2) Complaint. The complaint must:

(a) be verified;

(b) state the grounds for subject-matter jurisdiction, in rem jurisdiction over the defendant property, and venue;

(c) describe the property with reasonable particularity;

(d) if the property is tangible, state its location when any seizure occurred and—if different—its location when the action is filed;

(e) identify the statute under which the forfeiture action is brought; and

(f) state sufficiently detailed facts to support a reasonable belief that the government will be able to meet its burden of proof at trial.

(3) Judicial Authorization and Process.

(a) *Real Property.* If the defendant is real property, the government must proceed under 18 U.S.C. § 985.

(b) *Other Property; Arrest Warrant.* If the defendant is not real property:

(i) the clerk must issue a warrant to arrest the property if it is in the government's possession, custody, or control;

(ii) the court—on finding probable cause—must issue a warrant to arrest the property if it is not in the government's possession, custody, or control and is not subject to a judicial restraining order; and

(iii) a warrant is not necessary if the property is subject to a judicial restraining order.

(c) *Execution of Process.*

(i) The warrant and any supplemental process must be delivered to a person or organization authorized to execute it, who may be: (A) a marshal or any other United States officer or employee; (B) someone under contract with the United States; or (C) someone specially appointed by the court for that purpose.

(ii) The authorized person or organization must execute the warrant and any supplemental process on property in the United States as soon as practicable unless:

(A) the property is in the government's possession, custody, or control; or

(B) the court orders a different time when the complaint is under seal, the action is stayed before the warrant and supplemental process are executed, or the court finds other good cause.

(iii) The warrant and any supplemental process may be executed within the district or, when authorized by statute, outside the district.

(iv) If executing a warrant on property outside the United States is required, the warrant may be transmitted to an appropriate authority for serving process where the property is located.

(4) Notice.

(a) *Notice by Publication.*

(i) When Publication Is Required. A judgment of forfeiture may be entered only if the government has published notice of the action within a reasonable time after filing the complaint or at a time the court orders. But notice need not be published if:

(A) the defendant property is worth less than $1,000 and direct notice is sent under Rule G(4)(b) to every person the government can reasonably identify as a potential claimant; or

(B) the court finds that the cost of publication exceeds the property's value and that other means of notice would satisfy due process.

(ii) Content of the Notice. Unless the court orders otherwise, the notice must:

(A) describe the property with reasonable particularity;

(B) state the times under Rule G(5) to file a claim and to answer; and

(C) name the government attorney to be served with the claim and answer.

(iii) Frequency of Publication. Published notice must appear:

(A) once a week for three consecutive weeks; or

(B) only once if, before the action was filed, notice of nonjudicial forfeiture of the same property was published on an official internet government forfeiture site for at least 30 consecutive days, or in a newspaper of general circulation for three consecutive weeks in a district where publication is authorized under Rule G(4)(a)(iv).

(iv) Means of Publication. The government should select from the following options a means of publication reasonably calculated to notify potential claimants of the action:

(A) if the property is in the United States, publication in a newspaper generally circulated in the district where the action is filed, where the property was seized, or where property that was not seized is located;

(B) if the property is outside the United States, publication in a newspaper generally circulated in a district where the action is filed, in a newspaper generally circulated in the country where the property is located, or in legal notices published and generally circulated in the country where the property is located; or

(C) instead of (A) or (B), posting a notice on an official internet government forfeiture site for at least 30 consecutive days.

(b) *Notice to Known Potential Claimants.*

(i) Direct Notice Required. The government must send notice of the action and a copy of the complaint to any person who reasonably appears to be a potential claimant on the facts known to the government before the end of the time for filing a claim under Rule G(5)(a)(ii)(B).

(ii) Content of the Notice. The notice must state:

(A) the date when the notice is sent;

(B) a deadline for filing a claim, at least 35 days after the notice is sent;

(C) that an answer or a motion under Rule 12 must be filed no later than 20 days after filing the claim; and

(D) the name of the government attorney to be served with the claim and answer.

(iii) Sending Notice.

(A) The notice must be sent by means reasonably calculated to reach the potential claimant.

(B) Notice may be sent to the potential claimant or to the attorney representing the potential claimant with respect to the seizure of the property or in a related investigation, administrative forfeiture proceeding, or criminal case.

(C) Notice sent to a potential claimant who is incarcerated must be sent to the place of incarceration.

(D) Notice to a person arrested in connection with an offense giving rise to the forfeiture who is not incarcerated when notice is sent may be sent to the address that person last gave to the agency that arrested or released the person.

(E) Notice to a person from whom the property was seized who is not incarcerated when notice is sent may be sent to the last address that person gave to the agency that seized the property.

(iv) When Notice Is Sent. Notice by the following means is sent on the date when it is placed in the mail, delivered to a commercial carrier, or sent by electronic mail.

(v) Actual Notice. A potential claimant who had actual notice of a forfeiture action may not oppose or seek relief from forfeiture because of the government's failure to send the required notice.

(5) Responsive Pleadings.

(a) *Filing a Claim.*

(i) A person who asserts an interest in the defendant property may contest the forfeiture by filing a claim in the court where the action is pending. The claim must:

(A) identify the specific property claimed;

(B) identify the claimant and state the claimant's interest in the property;

(C) be signed by the claimant under penalty of perjury; and

(D) be served on the government attorney designated under Rule G(4)(a)(ii)(C) or (b)(ii)(D).

(ii) Unless the court for good cause sets a different time, the claim must be filed:

(A) by the time stated in a direct notice sent under Rule G(4)(b);

(B) if notice was published but direct notice was not sent to the claimant or the claimant's attorney, no later than 30 days after final publication of newspaper notice or legal notice under Rule G(4)(a) or no later than 60 days after the first day of publication on an official internet government forfeiture site; or

(C) if notice was not published and direct notice was not sent to the claimant or the claimant's attorney:

(1) if the property was in the government's possession, custody, or control when the complaint was filed, no later than 60 days after the filing, not counting any time when the complaint was under seal or when the action was stayed before execution of a warrant issued under Rule G(3)(b); or

(2) if the property was not in the government's possession, custody, or control when the complaint was filed, no later than 60 days after the government complied with 18 U.S.C. § 985(c) as to real property, or 60 days after process was executed on the property under Rule G(3).

(iii) A claim filed by a person asserting an interest as a bailee must identify the bailor, and if filed on the bailor's behalf must state the authority to do so.

(b) *Answer.* A claimant must serve and file an answer to the complaint or a motion under Rule 12 within 20 days after filing the claim. A claimant waives an objection to in rem jurisdiction or to venue if the objection is not made by motion or stated in the answer.

(6) Special Interrogatories.

(a) *Time and Scope.* The government may serve special interrogatories limited to the claimant's identity and relationship to the defendant property without the court's leave at any time after the claim is filed and before discovery is closed. But if the claimant serves a motion to dismiss the action, the government must serve the interrogatories within 20 days after the motion is served.

(b) *Answers or Objections.* Answers or objections to these interrogatories must be served within 20 days after the interrogatories are served.

(c) *Government's Response Deferred.* The government need not respond to a claimant's motion to dismiss the action under Rule G(8)(b) until 20 days after the claimant has answered these interrogatories.

(7) Preserving, Preventing Criminal Use, and Disposing of Property; Sales.

(a) *Preserving and Preventing Criminal Use of Property.* When the government does not have actual possession of the defendant property the court, on motion or on its own, may enter any order necessary to preserve the property, to prevent its removal or encumbrance, or to prevent its use in a criminal offense.

(b) *Interlocutory Sale or Delivery.*

(i) Order to Sell. On motion by a party or a person having custody of the property, the court may order all or part of the property sold if:

(A) the property is perishable or at risk of deterioration, decay, or injury by being detained in custody pending the action;

(B) the expense of keeping the property is excessive or is disproportionate to its fair market value;

(C) the property is subject to a mortgage or to taxes on which the owner is in default; or

(D) the court finds other good cause.

(ii) Who Makes the Sale. A sale must be made by a United States agency that has authority to sell the property, by the agency's contractor, or by any person the court designates.

(iii) Sale Procedures. The sale is governed by 28 U.S.C. §§ 2001, 2002, and 2004, unless all parties, with the court's approval, agree to the sale, aspects of the sale, or different procedures.

(iv) Sale Proceeds. Sale proceeds are a substitute res subject to forfeiture in place of the property that was sold. The proceeds must be held in an interest-bearing account maintained by the United States pending the conclusion of the forfeiture action.

(v) Delivery on a Claimant's Motion. The court may order that the property be delivered to the claimant pending the conclusion of the action if the claimant shows circumstances that would permit sale under Rule G(7)(b)(i) and gives security under these rules.

(c) *Disposing of Forfeited Property.* Upon entry of a forfeiture judgment, the property or proceeds from selling the property must be disposed of as provided by law.

(8) Motions.

(a) *Motion To Suppress Use of the Property as Evidence.* If the defendant property was seized, a party with standing to contest the lawfulness of the seizure may move to suppress use of the property as evidence. Suppression does not affect forfeiture of the property based on independently derived evidence.

(b) *Motion To Dismiss the Action.*

(i) A claimant who establishes standing to contest forfeiture may move to dismiss the action under Rule 12(b).

(ii) In an action governed by 18 U.S.C. § 983(a)(3)(D) the complaint may not be dismissed on the ground that the government did not have adequate evidence at the time the complaint was filed to establish the forfeitability of the property. The sufficiency of the complaint is governed by Rule G(2).

(c) *Motion To Strike a Claim or Answer.*

(i) At any time before trial, the government may move to strike a claim or answer:

(A) for failing to comply with Rule G(5) or (6), or

(B) because the claimant lacks standing.

(ii) The motion:

(A) must be decided before any motion by the claimant to dismiss the action; and

(B) may be presented as a motion for judgment on the pleadings or as a motion to determine after a hearing or by summary judgment whether the claimant can carry the burden of establishing standing by a preponderance of the evidence.

(d) *Petition To Release Property.*

(i) If a United States agency or an agency's contractor holds property for judicial or nonjudicial forfeiture under a statute governed by 18 U.S.C. § 983(f), a person who has filed a claim to the property may petition for its release under § 983(f).

(ii) If a petition for release is filed before a judicial forfeiture action is filed against the property, the petition may be filed either in the district where the property was seized or in the district where a warrant to seize the property issued. If a judicial forfeiture action against the property is later filed in another district—or if the government shows that the action will be filed in another dis-

trict—the petition may be transferred to that district under 28 U.S.C. § 1404.

(e) *Excessive Fines.* A claimant may seek to mitigate a forfeiture under the Excessive Fines Clause of the Eighth Amendment by motion for summary judgment or by motion made after entry of a forfeiture judgment if:

(i) the claimant has pleaded the defense under Rule 8; and

(ii) the parties have had the opportunity to conduct civil discovery on the defense.

(9) Trial. Trial is to the court unless any party demands trial by jury under Rule 38.

[Effective December 1, 2006.]

INDEX TO FEDERAL RULES OF CIVIL PROCEDURE

Abatement of actions, public officers and employees, **FRCVP 25**
Absence, joinder of parties, **FRCVP 19**
Abstracts, business records, interrogatories, **FRCVP 33**
Accord and satisfaction, affirmative defenses, **FRCVP 8**
Accounts and accounting,
    Default judgments, **FRCVP 55**
    Masters, **FRCVP 53**
    Stay of proceedings, **FRCVP 62**
Addresses,
    Forms, **FRCVP Form 2**
    Summons, **FRCVP 4**
Adjournment, masters, **FRCVP 53**
Administrative Office of the United States Courts, **FRCVP 79**
Administrators, **FRCVP 17**
Admiralty,
    Application of rules, **FRCVP A**
    Arrest, **FRCVP C**
        Third parties, **FRCVP 14**
        Warrants, **FRCVP D**
    Attachment, **FRCVP A et seq.**
        In personam actions, **FRCVP B**
        In rem, **FRCVP E**
        Quasi in rem, **FRCVP E**
    Complaints, **FRCVP B et seq.**
        Derivative actions, **FRCVP 23.1**
        Injunctions, **FRCVP 65**
    Condemnation, supplemental rules, **FRCVP A**
    Costs,
        In rem, **FRCVP E**
        Quasi in rem, **FRCVP E**
        Security, **FRCVP E, F**
    Deposits,
        Liability, **FRCVP F**
        Searches and seizures, **FRCVP E**
    Eminent domain, **FRCVP A**
    Exoneration, **FRCVP A, F**
    Expenses and expenditures, **FRCVP E**
    Filing,
        In rem, **FRCVP C**
        Liability, **FRCVP F**
    Fines, penalties and forfeitures, **FRCVP A, C, G**
    Garnishment, **FRCVP A et seq.**
        In personam actions, **FRCVP B**
        In rem, **FRCVP E**
        Quasi in rem, **FRCVP E**
    In personam actions, **FRCVP B, C, E**
    In rem, **FRCVP A**
        Fines, penalties and forfeitures, **FRCVP G**
        Process, **FRCVP C, E, G**
        Quasi in rem, **FRCVP E**
        Special matters, **FRCVP C**
    Interrogatories, **FRCVP B, C, G**
    Joinder, **FRCVP 18**
    Judgments and decrees,
        In rem, **FRCVP C**
        Quasi in rem, **FRCVP C**
        Release, **FRCVP E**
    Jury, **FRCVP 38**

Admiralty—Cont'd
    Liability, **FRCVP A, F**
    Marshals,
        Process, **FRCVP 4.1; FRCVP E**
        Property, powers and duties, **FRCVP C**
    Masters, **FRCVP 53**
    Motions,
        Fines, penalties and forfeitures, **FRCVP G**
        Liability, **FRCVP F**
        Property, payment, **FRCVP C, E**
    Notice,
        Attachment, **FRCVP B**
        Clearance, vessels, **FRCVP E**
        Custody, **FRCVP E**
        Fines, penalties and forfeitures, **FRCVP G**
        Garnishment, **FRCVP B**
        Liability, **FRCVP F**
        Petitory actions, **FRCVP D**
        Possessory actions, **FRCVP D**
        Release, **FRCVP C, E**
        Vessels, clearance, **FRCVP E**
    Oaths and affirmations,
        Depositions, **FRCVP 28**
        Garnishment, **FRCVP B**
        In lieu of oath, **FRCVP 43**
        In rem, **FRCVP C**
    Orders of court,
        Liability, **FRCVP F**
        Notice, **FRCVP C**
        Sales, **FRCVP E**
    Partition, **FRCVP A**
        In rem, **FRCVP E**
        Notice, **FRCVP D**
        Process, **FRCVP D**
        Quasi in rem, **FRCVP E**
        Release, **FRCVP E**
    Payment, **FRCVP C, E**
    Permissive joinder, **FRCVP 20**
    Plea or answer,
        Garnishment, **FRCVP B**
        In rem, **FRCVP C, E**
        Liability, **FRCVP F**
        Quasi in rem, **FRCVP C, E**
    Pleading, **FRCVP 9**
        Fines, penalties and forfeitures, **FRCVP G**
    Prize proceedings, **FRCVP 81**
    Process,
        Attachment, **FRCVP B**
        Garnishment, **FRCVP B**
        In rem, **FRCVP C, E, G**
        Liability, **FRCVP F**
        Petitory actions, **FRCVP D**
        Possessory actions, **FRCVP D**
        Quasi in rem, **FRCVP C, E**
    Quasi in rem, **FRCVP E**
    Sales, **FRCVP C, E, G**
    Searches and seizures, **FRCVP E**
        United States vessels, **FRCVP C**
    Security interest, **FRCVP D et seq.**
    Third parties, **FRCVP 14**

Admiralty—Cont'd
    Time,
        In rem, **FRCVP C**
        Liability, **FRCVP F**
    Trial, fines, penalties and forfeitures, **FRCVP G**
    Trusts and trustees, **FRCVP F**
    Venue, **FRCVP 82**
Admissions,
    Amendments, **FRCVP 36**
    Answers, requests, **FRCVP 36**
    Expenses and expenditures, requests, **FRCVP 36, 37**
    Forms, requests, **FRCVP Form 51**
    Pending actions, **FRCVP 36**
    Pleading, **FRCVP 8**
    Requests, **FRCVP 36, 37**
        Forms, **FRCVP Form 51**
        Stipulations, **FRCVP 29**
        Supplementation, **FRCVP 26**
    Stipulations, requests, **FRCVP 29**
    Summary judgment, **FRCVP 56**
    Supplementation, requests, **FRCVP 26**
    Withdrawal, **FRCVP 36**
Adverse or pecuniary interest, depositions, **FRCVP 28**
Advisory juries, **FRCVP 39, 52**
Affidavits,
    Admiralty, **FRCVP B**
    Bad faith, **FRCVP 56**
    Contempt, **FRCVP 56**
    Default judgments, **FRCVP 55**
    Hearings, **FRCVP 43**
    New trial, **FRCVP 59**
    Service, **FRCVP 6**
        Proof, **FRCVP 4**
    Summary judgment, **FRCVP 56**
    Temporary restraining orders, **FRCVP 65**
Affirmative defenses,
    Pleading, **FRCVP 8**
        Service, **FRCVP 5**
    Service, pleading, **FRCVP 5**
Age,
    Depositions, **FRCVP 32**
    Service of process, **FRCVP 4**
Agents and agencies, admiralty, **FRCVP E**
Alterations,
    Class actions, **FRCVP 23**
    Judgments and decrees,
        Motions, **FRCVP 59**
        Stay of proceedings, **FRCVP 62**
Amendments,
    Admissions, **FRCVP 36**
    Class actions, **FRCVP 23**
    District courts, **FRCVP 83**
    New trial, **FRCVP 59**
    Service, probf, **FRCVP 4**
    Summons, **FRCVP 4**
    Time, **FRCVP 86**
Ancillary process, admiralty, **FRCVP C**
Appeal and review,
    Admiralty, **FRCVP E**
    Application of rules, **FRCVP 81**
    Bonds (officers and fiduciaries), **FRCVP 62**
    Class actions, **FRCVP 23**
    Clerical errors, **FRCVP 60**
    Costs, **FRCVP 54**
    Depositions, **FRCVP 27**
    District of Columbia, **FRCVP 81**
    Dockets and docketing, **FRCVP 6, 60**

Appeal and review—Cont'd
    Entry of judgment, **FRCVP 77**
    Extension of time, **FRCVP 6**
    Federal agencies, **FRCVP 62**
    Final judgments, **FRCVP 79**
    Findings, **FRCVP 52**
    Habeas corpus, **FRCVP 81**
    Injunctions, **FRCVP 62**
    Longshoremen and harbor workers, workers compensation, **FRCVP 81**
    Magistrate judges, **FRCVP 73**
    Pending appeals, **FRCVP 62**
    Records and recordation, **FRCVP 5**
    Stay of proceedings, **FRCVP 62**
    Time,
        Costs, **FRCVP 54**
        Entry of judgment, **FRCVP 77**
        Extension of time, **FRCVP 6**
        Stay of proceedings, **FRCVP 62**
Appearances,
    Admiralty, **FRCVP E**
    Dockets and docketing, **FRCVP 79**
    Eminent domain, **FRCVP 71.1**
    Service, **FRCVP 5**
Applications, **FRCVP 81**
    Injunctions, **FRCVP 65**
    Intervention, **FRCVP 24**
Appointment,
    Class actions, attorneys, **FRCVP 23**
    Interpreters, **FRCVP 43**
    Masters, **FRCVP 53**
    Process servers, **FRCVP 4**
Arbitration, **FRCVP 81**
    Affirmative defenses, **FRCVP 8**
Arrest, satisfaction of judgment, **FRCVP 64**
Assessments, masters, **FRCVP 53**
Assistance, writ of assistance, **FRCVP 70**
Associations and societies,
    Business associations, summons, **FRCVP 4**
    Capacity, **FRCVP 9, 17**
    Cross examination, **FRCVP 43**
    Depositions, **FRCVP 32, 37**
    Examinations and examiners, **FRCVP 43**
    Interrogatories, **FRCVP 33**
    Summons, **FRCVP 4**
    Witnesses, **FRCVP 43**
Assumption of risk, affirmative defenses, **FRCVP 8**
Attachment, **FRCVP 64**
    Compulsory counterclaims, **FRCVP 13**
    Disobeying judgments, **FRCVP 70**
Attestation, official records, **FRCVP 44**
Attorney General, parties, changes, **FRCVP 15**
Attorneys,
    Admiralty, **FRCVP F**
    Class actions, **FRCVP 23**
    Depositions, **FRCVP 32**
        Fees, **FRCVP 30, 37**
    Disclosure, **FRCVP 37**
    Discovery, **FRCVP 37**
    Documents, genuineness, **FRCVP 37**
    Entry upon land, **FRCVP 37**
    Fees,
        Class actions, **FRCVP 23**
        Depositions, **FRCVP 30, 37**
        Disclosure, **FRCVP 37**
        Discovery, **FRCVP 37**
        Documents, genuineness, **FRCVP 37**

Attorneys—Cont'd
  Fees—Cont'd
    Entry upon land, **FRCVP 37**
    Interrogatories, **FRCVP 37**
    Judgments and decrees, **FRCVP 58**
    Motions, **FRCVP 54**
    Orders, **FRCVP 37**
    Pleading, **FRCVP 11**
    Pretrial conferences, **FRCVP 16**
    Pretrial orders, **FRCVP 16**
    Production of documents or things, **FRCVP 37**
    Sanctions, **FRCVP 11**
    Summary judgment, **FRCVP 56**
    Summons, **FRCVP 4**
  Interrogatories,
    Fees, **FRCVP 37**
    Signatures, **FRCVP 33**
  Judgments and decrees, **FRCVP 58**
  Jury, instructions, **FRCVP 51**
  Masters, **FRCVP 53**
  Motions,
    Fees, **FRCVP 54**
    Signatures, **FRCVP 11**
  Orders, fees, **FRCVP 37**
  Pleading,
    Fees, **FRCVP 11**
    Service, **FRCVP 5**
    Signatures, **FRCVP 11**
  Pretrial conferences, fees, **FRCVP 16**
  Pretrial orders, fees, **FRCVP 16**
  Production of documents or things, fees, **FRCVP 37**
  Sanctions, fees, **FRCVP 11, 16**
  Signatures,
    Admissions, **FRCVP 36**
    Discovery, **FRCVP 26**
    Pleading, **FRCVP 11**
  Summary judgment, fees, **FRCVP 56**
  Summons, fees, **FRCVP 4**
  Temporary restraining orders, **FRCVP 65**
Audiovisual media, depositions, **FRCVP 30**
Audita querela, abolition of writ, **FRCVP 60**
Audits and auditors,
  Business records, **FRCVP 33**
  Masters, **FRCVP 53**
Authentication, official records, **FRCVP 44**
Avoidance, pleading, **FRCVP 5, 8**
Bad faith, depositions, sanctions, **FRCVP 30**
Bailment, **FRCVP 17**
Bankruptcy,
  Affirmative defenses, discharge, **FRCVP 8**
  Discharge, affirmative defenses, **FRCVP 8**
Bills of review, abolition, **FRCVP 60**
Boards and commissions,
  Eminent domain, **FRCVP 71.1**
  Masters, **FRCVP 53**
  Pleading, **FRCVP 9**
Bonds (officers and fiduciaries), **FRCVP 65.1**
  Admiralty, **FRCVP E**
  Appeal and review, **FRCVP 62**
  Injunctions, **FRCVP 62**
Books and papers,
  Delivery, **FRCVP 70**
  Discovery, **FRCVP 26**
  Masters, **FRCVP 53**
  Pleading, **FRCVP 9**
  Retention, **FRCVP 79**
  Subpoenas, **FRCVP 45**

Business associations, summons, **FRCVP 4**
Business records, interrogatories, **FRCVP 33**
Calendars,
  Declaratory judgments, **FRCVP 57**
  Preparation, **FRCVP 79**
  Pretrial calendar, **FRCVP 16**
  Trial, **FRCVP 40**
Capacity, **FRCVP 9, 17**
Captions,
  Forms, **FRCVP Form 1**
  Motions, **FRCVP 7**
  Pleading, **FRCVP 10**
Certificates and certification,
  Class actions, **FRCVP 23**
  Constitutional challenges, statutes, **FRCVP 5.1**
  Depositions, **FRCVP 30**
  Discovery, attorneys, **FRCVP 26**
  Habeas corpus, probable cause, **FRCVP 81**
  Official records, authentication, **FRCVP 44**
  Service of process, **FRCVP 5**
  Temporary restraining orders, attorneys, **FRCVP 65**
Certified copies, summary judgment, **FRCVP 56**
Certified public accountants, masters, **FRCVP 53**
Challenges, jury, **FRCVP 47**
Chambers, **FRCVP 77**
Children and minors,
  Default judgments, **FRCVP 55**
  Depositions, **FRCVP 27**
  Parties, **FRCVP 17**
  Summons, **FRCVP 4**
Citations,
  Federal Rules of Civil Procedure, **FRCVP 85**
  Local district rules, **FRCVP 83**
Citizens and citizenship, admission to citizenship, **FRCVP 81**
Civil commitment, orders, **FRCVP 4.1**
Class actions, **FRCVP 23**
  Joinder, **FRCVP 19**
  Shares and shareholders, derivative actions, **FRCVP 23.1**
  Unincorporated associations, **FRCVP 23.2**
Clerical mistakes, corrections, **FRCVP 60**
Clerks of courts,
  Admiralty, release, **FRCVP E**
  Appeal and review, costs, **FRCVP 54**
  Books and papers, **FRCVP 79**
  Business hours, **FRCVP 77**
  Calendars, **FRCVP 79**
  Chambers, **FRCVP 77**
  Copies, **FRCVP 79**
  Costs, taxation, **FRCVP 54**
  Default judgments, **FRCVP 55**
  Entry of judgment, **FRCVP 58**
  Executions, **FRCVP 70**
  Masters, **FRCVP 53**
  Notice, **FRCVP 77**
  Office hours, **FRCVP 77**
  Orders of court, **FRCVP 77, 79**
  Pleading, **FRCVP 5**
  Records and recordation, **FRCVP 79**
  Service of process, **FRCVP 65.1**
  Summons, **FRCVP 4**
  Writ of assistance, **FRCVP 70**
Committees, incompetents, **FRCVP 17**
Commonwealth, official records, authentication, **FRCVP 44**

Compensation and salaries,
    Eminent domain, **FRCVP 71.1**
    Interpreters, **FRCVP 43**
    Masters, **FRCVP 53**
Complaints,
    Conversion, **FRCVP Form 15**
    Copyrights, infringement, **FRCVP Form 19**
    Eminent domain, **FRCVP 71.1; FRCVP Form 61**
    Filing, **FRCVP 3**
    Fraudulent conveyances, **FRCVP Form 21**
    Interpleader, **FRCVP Form 20**
    Merchant Marine Act, **FRCVP Form 14**
    Money, sum certain, **FRCVP Form 10**
    Negligence, **FRCVP Form 11 et seq.**
    Patents, infringement, **FRCVP Form 18**
    Specific performance, **FRCVP Form 17**
    Summons, **FRCVP 4**
    Third parties, **FRCVP 7; FRCVP Form 16**
    Title of action, **FRCVP 10**
Complicated issues, masters, **FRCVP 53**
Compromise and settlement,
    Class actions, **FRCVP 23**
    Derivative actions, **FRCVP 23.1**
    Unincorporated associations, **FRCVP 23.2**
Compulsory counterclaims, pleading, **FRCVP 13**
Compulsory process, admiralty, **FRCVP B**
Computation, time, **FRCVP 6**
Conciseness, pleading, **FRCVP 8**
Conclusions of law, **FRCVP 52 et seq.**
    Masters, **FRCVP 53**
    New trial, **FRCVP 59**
Conditional rulings, motions, **FRCVP 50**
Conditions, pleading, **FRCVP 9**
Conferences, pretrial conferences, **FRCVP 16**
Confidential or privileged information, discovery, **FRCVP 26**
Conflict of interest, depositions, **FRCVP 28**
Conflict of laws, capacity, **FRCVP 17**
Consent,
    Admiralty, release, **FRCVP E**
    Court trial, **FRCVP 39**
    Jury trial, **FRCVP 39**
        Withdrawal, **FRCVP 38**
    Magistrate judges, jurisdiction, **FRCVP 73; FRCVP Form 81**
Conservators and conservatorship, **FRCVP 17**
Consideration, pleading, defenses, **FRCVP 8**
Constitutional challenges, statutes, **FRCVP 5.1**
Contempt,
    Depositions, **FRCVP 37**
    Discovery, **FRCVP 37**
    Masters, **FRCVP 53**
    Service of order, **FRCVP 4.1**
    Subpoenas, **FRCVP 45**
    Summary judgment, **FRCVP 56**
Continuances,
    Pleading, **FRCVP 15**
    Summary judgment, **FRCVP 56**
Contradicting testimony, depositions, **FRCVP 32**
Contribution, admiralty, third parties, **FRCVP 14**
Contributory negligence, affirmative defenses, **FRCVP 8**
Conversion, complaints, **FRCVP Form 15**
Copies,
    Admiralty, **FRCVP E**
    Admissions, documents, **FRCVP 36**
    Business records, **FRCVP 33**
    Eminent domain, **FRCVP 71.1**

Copies—Cont'd
    Foreign official records, authentication, **FRCVP 44**
    Masters, **FRCVP 53**
    Orders of court, **FRCVP 27**
    Written instruments, **FRCVP 10**
Copyrights,
    Application of rules, **FRCVP 81**
    Infringement, complaints, **FRCVP Form 19**
Coram nobis, writ abolished, **FRCVP 60**
Coram vobis, writ abolished, **FRCVP 60**
Corporations,
    Admiralty, security, **FRCVP E**
    Capacity, **FRCVP 17**
    Depositions, **FRCVP 32, 37**
    Disclosure, statements, **FRCVP 7.1**
    Interrogatories, **FRCVP 33**
    Shares and shareholders, derivative actions, **FRCVP 23.1**
    Statements, disclosure, **FRCVP 7.1**
    Summons, **FRCVP 4**
Correctional institutions,
    Depositions, **FRCVP 30 et seq.**
    Habeas corpus, **FRCVP 81**
Corrections, clerical errors, **FRCVP 60**
Costs,
    Default judgments, **FRCVP 55**
    Depositions, **FRCVP 30**
    Disclosure, parties, refusal, **FRCVP 37**
    Discovery, **FRCVP 26**
    Injunctions, **FRCVP 65**
    Interpreters, **FRCVP 43**
    Judgments and decrees, **FRCVP 58**
    Offer of judgment, **FRCVP 68**
    Pretrial conferences, sanctions, **FRCVP 16**
    Pretrial orders, sanctions, **FRCVP 16**
    Previously dismissed actions, **FRCVP 41**
    Service of process, **FRCVP 4**
    Signatures, sanctions, **FRCVP 11**
    Summary judgment, **FRCVP 56**
    Summons, **FRCVP 4**
Courts of appeals,
    Extension of time, **FRCVP 6**
    Time, extension of time, **FRCVP 6**
Cross claims, **FRCVP 8, 13**
    Answers, **FRCVP 7, 12**
    Dismissal and nonsuit, **FRCVP 41**
    Entry of judgment, **FRCVP 54**
    Joinder, **FRCVP 18**
    Judgments and decrees, **FRCVP 54**
    Separate trial, **FRCVP 42**
    Service, **FRCVP 5**
    Third parties, **FRCVP 14**
    Time, answers, **FRCVP 12**
Cross examination, depositions, **FRCVP 30**
Cross questions, depositions, **FRCVP 31**
Custody, admiralty, **FRCVP E**
Customs, admiralty, vessels, clearance, **FRCVP E**
Damages,
    Admiralty, **FRCVP E**
    Default judgments, **FRCVP 55**
    Discovery, **FRCVP 26**
    Injunctions, **FRCVP 65**
    Masters, **FRCVP 53**
    Special damages, **FRCVP 9**
    Summary judgment, **FRCVP 56**
Date, forms, **FRCVP Form 2**

Death,
 Admiralty, **FRCVP F**
 Parties,
  Statements, **FRCVP Form 9**
  Substitution, **FRCVP 25**
 Public officers and employees, substitution, **FRCVP 25**
 Witnesses, depositions, **FRCVP 32**
Declaratory judgments and decrees, **FRCVP 57**
 Class actions, **FRCVP 23**
Default judgment, **FRCVP 54, 55**
 Admiralty, **FRCVP B**
 Demands, **FRCVP 54**
 Discovery, **FRCVP 37**
 Pleading, **FRCVP 54, 55**
 Summons, **FRCVP 4**
Definitions, filing, **FRCVP 5**
Delays,
 Depositions, **FRCVP 30**
 Discovery, **FRCVP 26**
Delivery,
 Admiralty, process, **FRCVP E**
 Examinations and examiners, reports, **FRCVP 35**
 Pleadings, copies, **FRCVP 5**
 United States, process, **FRCVP 15**
Demand, judgments and decrees, **FRCVP 8, 54**
Denials, **FRCVP 8**
 Conditions precedent, **FRCVP 9**
Depositions, **FRCVP 26 et seq.**
 Admissibility of evidence, **FRCVP 32**
 Adverse or pecuniary interest, **FRCVP 28**
 Age, attendance, **FRCVP 32**
 Alterations, **FRCVP 26**
 Associations and societies, **FRCVP 32, 37**
 Audiovisual media, **FRCVP 30**
 Certificates and certification, **FRCVP 30**
 Compelling answers, **FRCVP 37**
 Competency, **FRCVP 32**
 Completion, notice, **FRCVP 31**
 Conflict of interest, **FRCVP 28**
 Contradicting testimony, **FRCVP 32**
 Corporations, **FRCVP 32, 37**
 Correctional institutions, **FRCVP 30 et seq.**
 Costs, **FRCVP 30**
 Cross questions, **FRCVP 31**
 Death, **FRCVP 32**
 Delays, **FRCVP 30**
 Disqualification, **FRCVP 28, 32**
 Errors, **FRCVP 32**
 Evasive answers, **FRCVP 37**
 Exhibits, **FRCVP 30**
 Expenses and expenditures, **FRCVP 37**
 Expert witnesses, **FRCVP 26**
 Federal agencies, **FRCVP 32, 37**
 Foreign countries, **FRCVP 28**
 Forms, **FRCVP 32**
 Hearings, **FRCVP 32**
 Illness, attendance, **FRCVP 32**
 Incomplete answers, **FRCVP 37**
 Interrogatories, **FRCVP 31, 33**
 Irregularities, **FRCVP 32**
 Letters of request, foreign countries, **FRCVP 28**
 Mental examinations, **FRCVP 35**
 Motions, compelling answers, **FRCVP 37**
 Multiple depositions, leave of court, **FRCVP 30, 31**
 Nonattendance, **FRCVP 37**
 Notice, **FRCVP 28 et seq.**

Depositions—Cont'd
 Notice—Cont'd
  Completion, **FRCVP 31**
  Errors, **FRCVP 32**
  Foreign countries, **FRCVP 28**
  Irregularities, **FRCVP 32**
  Oral examinations, **FRCVP 30**
  Stipulations, **FRCVP 29**
  Written questions, **FRCVP 31**
 Oaths and affirmations, **FRCVP 28**
  Oral examinations, **FRCVP 30**
 Objections and exceptions, **FRCVP 26**
  Depositions, **FRCVP 30**
  Errors, **FRCVP 32**
  Irregularities, **FRCVP 32**
  Subpoenas, **FRCVP 45**
 Officers and employees, **FRCVP 28, 30**
 Oral examinations, **FRCVP 30 et seq.**
 Orders of court, **FRCVP 27, 37**
 Outside United States, **FRCVP 32**
 Partnership, **FRCVP 32, 37**
 Pending appeals, **FRCVP 27**
 Petitions, **FRCVP 27**
 Physical examinations, **FRCVP 35**
 Place, **FRCVP 32**
 Prior actions, **FRCVP 32**
 Prisoners, **FRCVP 30 et seq.**
 Protective orders, **FRCVP 32**
 Records and recordation, **FRCVP 30**
 Recross questions, **FRCVP 31**
 Redirect questions, **FRCVP 31**
 Returns, **FRCVP 32**
 Sanctions, **FRCVP 30**
 Service, **FRCVP 27**
 Sound recordings, **FRCVP 30**
 Stipulations, **FRCVP 29**
 Subpoenas, **FRCVP 45**
  Nonattendance, **FRCVP 32**
  Written questions, **FRCVP 31**
 Substitution, parties, **FRCVP 32**
 Summary judgment, **FRCVP 56**
 Supplementation, **FRCVP 26**
 Termination, **FRCVP 30**
 Time, **FRCVP 27**
  Stipulations, **FRCVP 29**
  Written questions, **FRCVP 31**
 Trial, **FRCVP 32**
 Venue, **FRCVP 32, 37**
 Written questions, **FRCVP 31 et seq.**
Deposits,
 Court of appeals, **FRCVP 73**
 Courts, **FRCVP 67**
 Eminent domain, **FRCVP 71.1**
Derivative actions, shares and shareholders, **FRCVP 23.1**
Diagnoses, reports, **FRCVP 35**
Disclosure,
 Corporations, statements, **FRCVP 7.1**
 Electronically stored information, **FRCVP 16, 26, 33 et seq.**
 Motions, **FRCVP 37**
Discovery, **FRCVP 26 et seq.**
 Attorneys, fees, **FRCVP 37**
 Conferences, **FRCVP 26**
 Executions, **FRCVP 69**
 Expenses and expenditures, **FRCVP 37**
 Foreign countries, **FRCVP 37**
 Modification, **FRCVP 16**

Discovery—Cont'd
    Orders of court, **FRCVP 37**
    Plans and specifications, **FRCVP 26**
    Pretrial conferences, **FRCVP 16**
    Pretrial disclosures, **FRCVP 26**
    Protective orders, **FRCVP 26, 37**
    Sanctions, **FRCVP 37**
    Service, **FRCVP 5**
    Signatures, **FRCVP 26**
    Stipulations, **FRCVP 29**
    Summary judgment, **FRCVP 56**
    Supplementation, **FRCVP 26**
    Time,
        Modification, **FRCVP 16**
        Pretrial disclosures, **FRCVP 26**
        Stipulations, **FRCVP 29**
    Trial preparation materials, exemptions, **FRCVP 26**
    Witnesses, **FRCVP 26 et seq.**
Discretion of court,
    Interpreters, **FRCVP 43**
    Jury trial, **FRCVP 39**
    Masters, **FRCVP 53**
Dismissal and nonsuit, **FRCVP 41**
    Admiralty, **FRCVP F**
    Class actions, **FRCVP 23**
    Derivative actions, **FRCVP 23.1**
    Discovery, **FRCVP 37**
    Eminent domain, **FRCVP 71.1**
    Forms, motions, **FRCVP Form 40**
    Joinder, **FRCVP 19**
    Motions,
        Conclusions of law, **FRCVP 52**
        Findings, **FRCVP 52**
        Forms, **FRCVP Form 40**
        Pleading, **FRCVP 12**
    Real party in interest, **FRCVP 17**
    Receivers and receivership, **FRCVP 66**
    Substitution, parties, **FRCVP 25**
    Summons, **FRCVP 4**
    Third parties, **FRCVP 41**
    Unincorporated associations, **FRCVP 23.2**
    Voluntary dismissal, **FRCVP 41**
Dispositions, admiralty, property, **FRCVP E**
Distributions,
    Admiralty, funds, **FRCVP F**
    Eminent domain, **FRCVP 71.1**
District courts,
    Depositions, **FRCVP 37**
    Hearings, **FRCVP 77**
    Local rules, **FRCVP 83**
        Time, **FRCVP 6**
    Motion day, **FRCVP 78**
    Official records, authentication, **FRCVP 44**
    Time, local rules, **FRCVP 6**
District of Columbia, **FRCVP 81**
Dockets and docketing,
    Appeal and review, **FRCVP 6, 60**
    Entries, **FRCVP 79**
    Jury trial, **FRCVP 39**
    Notice, **FRCVP 77**
Domestic official records, authentication, **FRCVP 44**
Domicile and residence, parties, capacity, **FRCVP 17**
Duress, pleading, affirmative defenses, **FRCVP 8**
Dwellings,
    Pleading, service, **FRCVP 5**
    Summons, service, **FRCVP 4**
E-mail, forms, **FRCVP Form 2**

Electronic filing, **FRCVP 5**
Electronically stored information, disclosure, **FRCVP 16, 26, 33 et seq.**
Eminent domain, **FRCVP 71.1**
    Admiralty, supplemental rules, **FRCVP A**
    Complaints, **FRCVP 71.1; FRCVP Form 61**
    Forms,
        Complaints, **FRCVP Form 61**
        Notice, **FRCVP Form 60**
    Notice, **FRCVP 71.1; FRCVP Form 60**
Entry upon land, **FRCVP 34**
    Forms, requests, **FRCVP Form 50**
    Requests, **FRCVP 34; FRCVP Form 50**
    Sanctions, **FRCVP 37**
    Stipulations, **FRCVP 29**
Equity,
    Joinder, **FRCVP 18, 19**
    Pleading, **FRCVP 8**
Estoppel, pleading, affirmative defenses, **FRCVP 8**
Evidence,
    Admiralty, default judgments, **FRCVP B**
    Affidavits, **FRCVP 43**
    Compelling testimony, **FRCVP 81**
    Costs, **FRCVP 68**
    Eminent domain, **FRCVP 71.1**
    Foreign laws, **FRCVP 44.1**
    Forms, **FRCVP 43**
    Harmless error, **FRCVP 61**
    Injunctions, **FRCVP 65**
    Interpreters, **FRCVP 43**
    Letters of request, **FRCVP 28**
    Masters, **FRCVP 53**
    Motions, **FRCVP 43**
    Oaths and affirmations, **FRCVP 43**
    Objections and exceptions, **FRCVP 52**
    Official records, **FRCVP 44**
    Perpetuating testimony, **FRCVP 27**
    Pleading, amendments, **FRCVP 15**
    Pretrial procedure, **FRCVP 16**
    Process, **FRCVP 4, 4.1**
    Stenographers, **FRCVP 80**
    Subpoenas, **FRCVP 45**
    United States, **FRCVP 55**
    Voluntary dismissal, **FRCVP 41**
Ex parte proceedings, masters, **FRCVP 53**
Examinations and examiners, **FRCVP 35, 37**
    Business records, **FRCVP 33**
    Jury, **FRCVP 47**
    Masters, **FRCVP 53**
    Mental health, **FRCVP 35, 37**
    Physical examinations, **FRCVP 35, 37**
    Sanctions, **FRCVP 37**
Excusable neglect, **FRCVP 6, 60**
Execution,
    Admiralty, **FRCVP E**
    Discovery, **FRCVP 69**
    Dockets and docketing, **FRCVP 79**
    Masters, **FRCVP 53**
    Possession, **FRCVP 70**
    Stay of proceedings, **FRCVP 62**
    Time, **FRCVP 62**
Executors and administrators, **FRCVP 17**
Exemptions,
    Depositions, **FRCVP 32**
    U.S. vessels, arrest, supplemental rules, **FRCVP C**
Exhibits,
    Depositions, **FRCVP 30**

Exhibits—Cont'd
    Discovery, **FRCVP 26**
    Masters, **FRCVP 53**
    Written instruments, **FRCVP 10**
Exoneration, admiralty, **FRCVP A, F**
Expenses and expenditures,
    Admiralty, **FRCVP E**
    Admissions, requests, **FRCVP 36**
    Depositions, **FRCVP 37**
    Discovery, **FRCVP 37**
    Documents, genuineness, **FRCVP 37**
    Entry upon land, **FRCVP 37**
    Interrogatories, **FRCVP 37**
    Production of documents or things, **FRCVP 37**
Experts, **FRCVP 43**
    Depositions, **FRCVP 26**
    Discovery, **FRCVP 26**
    Pretrial conferences, **FRCVP 16**
Facsimile transmissions, **FRCVP 5**
Fair conduct, class actions, **FRCVP 23**
Federal agencies,
    Answers, **FRCVP 12**
    Appeal and review, **FRCVP 62**
    Depositions, **FRCVP 32, 37**
    Injunctions, **FRCVP 65**
    Interrogatories, **FRCVP 33**
    Process, **FRCVP 15**
    Subpoenas, **FRCVP 45, 81**
Federal Employers Liability Act, negligence, complaints,
    FRCVP Form 13
Federal officers and employees,
    Answer, **FRCVP 12**
    Appeal and review, **FRCVP 62**
    Compelling testimony, **FRCVP 81**
    Definitions, **FRCVP 81**
    Injunctions, **FRCVP 65**
    Process, **FRCVP 15**
    Subpoenas, **FRCVP 45**
Fellow servant, pleading, affirmative defenses, **FRCVP 8**
Filing,
    Complaints, **FRCVP 3**
    Definitions, **FRCVP 5**
    Electronic filing, **FRCVP 5**
    Eminent domain, **FRCVP 71.1**
    Facsimile transmissions, **FRCVP 5**
    Masters, **FRCVP 53**
    Numbers and numbering, dockets and docketing,
        FRCVP 79
    Pleading, **FRCVP 3 et seq.**
    Privacy protection, **FRCVP 5.2**
Findings, **FRCVP 52, 53**
    Admiralty, **FRCVP F**
    Amendments,
        Extension of time, **FRCVP 6**
        New trial, motions, **FRCVP 59**
        Stay of proceedings, **FRCVP 62**
    Class actions, **FRCVP 23**
    Jury, unanimity, **FRCVP 48**
    New trial, **FRCVP 59**
    Special verdict, **FRCVP 49**
    Stay of proceedings, **FRCVP 62**
Fines, penalties and forfeitures,
    Admiralty, **FRCVP A, C, G**
    Conferences, **FRCVP 16**
    Depositions, **FRCVP 30**
    Disclosure, parties, **FRCVP 37**
    Discovery, **FRCVP 37**

Fines, penalties and forfeitures—Cont'd
    Motions, **FRCVP 11**
    Pleading, **FRCVP 11**
    Pretrial conferences, **FRCVP 16**
    Pretrial orders, **FRCVP 16**
    Subpoenas, **FRCVP 45**
    Witnesses, **FRCVP 53**
Foreign countries,
    Depositions, **FRCVP 28**
    Discovery, **FRCVP 37**
    Judgments and decrees, **FRCVP 9**
    Laws, **FRCVP 44.1**
    Official records, authentication, **FRCVP 44**
    Subpoenas, **FRCVP 45**
    Summons, **FRCVP 4**
Foreign diplomatic and consular officers,
    Authentication, **FRCVP 44**
    Depositions, **FRCVP 28**
Forms, **FRCVP Form 1 et seq.**
    Addresses, **FRCVP Form 2**
    Admissions, requests, **FRCVP Form 51**
    Appendix forms, **FRCVP 84**
    Captions, **FRCVP Form 1**
    Conversion, complaints, **FRCVP Form 15**
    Copyrights, infringement, complaints, **FRCVP Form 19**
    Date, **FRCVP Form 2**
    Defenses, plea or answer, **FRCVP Form 30**
    Depositions, **FRCVP Form 32**
    Dismissal and nonsuit, motions, **FRCVP Form 40**
    E-mail, **FRCVP Form 2**
    Eminent domain,
        Complaints, **FRCVP Form 61**
        Notice, **FRCVP Form 60**
    Entry upon land, requests, **FRCVP Form 50**
    Evidence, **FRCVP 43**
    Fraudulent conveyances, complaints, **FRCVP Form 21**
    Interpleader, complaints, **FRCVP Form 20**
    Intervention, **FRCVP Form 42**
    Judgments and decrees, **FRCVP Form 71**
    Jurisdiction, statements, **FRCVP Form 7**
    Magistrate judges, jurisdiction, **FRCVP Form 80 et seq.**
    Masters, **FRCVP 53**
    Merchant Marine Act, complaints, **FRCVP Form 14**
    Money,
        Had and received, plea or answer, **FRCVP Form 31**
        Sum certain, complaints, **FRCVP Form 10**
    Motions, **FRCVP Form 40 et seq.**
    Negligence, complaints, **FRCVP Form 11 et seq.**
    Notice, **FRCVP Form 5 et seq.**
    Patents, infringement, complaints, **FRCVP Form 18**
    Pleading, **FRCVP 10; FRCVP Form 10 et seq.**
    Production of books and papers, requests, **FRCVP Form 50**
    Public policy, **FRCVP 84**
    Sanctions, nonuse, **FRCVP 83**
    Signatures, **FRCVP Form 2**
    Specific performance, complaints, **FRCVP Form 17**
    Subpoenas, **FRCVP 45**
    Telephone numbers, **FRCVP Form 2**
    Verdict, **FRCVP Form 70**
Fraud,
    Judgments and decrees, **FRCVP 60**
    Pleading, **FRCVP 9**

Fraudulent conveyances,
    Complaints, **FRCVP Form 21**
    Joinder, **FRCVP 18**
Garnishment, **FRCVP 64**
Good cause,
    Electronically stored information, access, **FRCVP 26**
    Examinations and examiners, **FRCVP 35**
Grounds, new trial, **FRCVP 59**
Guardian and ward, **FRCVP 17**
Habeas corpus, **FRCVP 81**
Harmless error, **FRCVP 61**
Hearings,
    Admiralty, **FRCVP E, F**
    Consolidation and merger, **FRCVP 42**
    Depositions, motions, **FRCVP 32**
    Discovery, **FRCVP 37**
    Injunctions, **FRCVP 65**
    Judges or justices, inability to proceed, **FRCVP 63**
    New trial, **FRCVP 59**
    Nonoral hearings, motions, **FRCVP 78**
    Notice, **FRCVP 6**
    Outside district, **FRCVP 77**
    Preliminary hearings, **FRCVP 12**
    Subpoenas, **FRCVP 45**
    Successor judges, **FRCVP 63**
    Temporary restraining orders, **FRCVP 65**
    Voluntary dismissal, **FRCVP 41**
Holidays,
    Clerks of courts, business hours, **FRCVP 77**
    Definitions, **FRCVP 6**
    Time, computation, **FRCVP 6**
Houses,
    Pleading, service, **FRCVP 5**
    Summons, service, **FRCVP 4**
Illegality, pleading, affirmative defenses, **FRCVP 8**
Illness, depositions, **FRCVP 32**
Immigration, privacy protection, **FRCVP 5.2**
Impeachment, depositions, **FRCVP 32**
Imprisonment, depositions, **FRCVP 32**
In forma pauperis, process, **FRCVP 4**
In personam actions, admiralty, **FRCVP B, C, E**
Inadvertence, judgments and decrees, **FRCVP 60**
Incompetency, **FRCVP 17**
    Default judgments, **FRCVP 55**
    Depositions, **FRCVP 27**
    Substitution, **FRCVP 25**
    Summons, **FRCVP 4**
Indexes, **FRCVP 79**
Indorsement,
    Admiralty, **FRCVP E**
    Temporary restraining orders, **FRCVP 65**
Infirmities, depositions, **FRCVP 32**
Infringement, stay of proceedings, accounts and accounting, **FRCVP 62**
Initial discovery, **FRCVP 26**
Injunctions, **FRCVP 65**
    Admiralty, **FRCVP F**
    Appeal and review, **FRCVP 62**
    Class actions, **FRCVP 23**
Inspection and inspectors,
    Business records, **FRCVP 33**
    Orders, **FRCVP 27**
Instructions, jury, **FRCVP 49, 51**
Insular possessions, official record, authentication, **FRCVP 44**
Insurance, discovery, **FRCVP 26**
Intangible property, admiralty, **FRCVP C, E**

Intent, pleading, **FRCVP 9**
Interest, admiralty, **FRCVP F**
Interested parties,
    Class actions, **FRCVP 23**
    Depositions, **FRCVP 28**
    Intervention, **FRCVP 24**
    Joinder, **FRCVP 19**
Interlocutory proceedings,
    Admiralty, **FRCVP E**
    Injunctions, **FRCVP 52**
Internal Revenue Service, judgments and decrees, **FRCVP 69**
International agreements, summons, **FRCVP 4**
Interpleader, **FRCVP 22**
    Complaints, **FRCVP Form 20**
    Injunctions, **FRCVP 65**
Interpreters, **FRCVP 43**
Interrogatories, **FRCVP 33**
    Admiralty, **FRCVP B, C, G**
    Alterations, **FRCVP 26**
    Business records, **FRCVP 33**
    Compelling answers, **FRCVP 37**
    Electronically stored information, **FRCVP 33**
    Evasive answers, **FRCVP 37**
    Experts, **FRCVP 26**
    General verdicts, **FRCVP 49**
    Incomplete answers, **FRCVP 37**
    Jury, **FRCVP 49**
    Masters, **FRCVP 53**
    Motions, **FRCVP 33 et seq.**
    Objections and exceptions, **FRCVP 33**
    Orders of court, **FRCVP 33, 37**
    Sanctions, **FRCVP 37**
    Service, **FRCVP 33**
    Stipulations, **FRCVP 29**
    Summary judgment, **FRCVP 56**
    Supplementation, **FRCVP 26**
    Time, **FRCVP 33**
    Trial, **FRCVP 33**
    Written interrogatories, **FRCVP 49**
Intervention, **FRCVP 24**
    Constitutional challenges, statutes, **FRCVP 5.1**
    Forms, **FRCVP Form 42**
    Motions, **FRCVP 24; FRCVP Form 42**
Investigations,
    Admiralty, **FRCVP E**
    Foreign official records, **FRCVP 44**
Involuntary plaintiffs, joinder, **FRCVP 19**
Issues,
    Court trial, **FRCVP 39**
    Jury trial, **FRCVP 38, 39**
    Pretrial procedure, **FRCVP 16**
    Separate trials, **FRCVP 42**
Joinder,
    Claims, **FRCVP 18**
    Eminent domain, **FRCVP 71.1**
    Fraudulent conveyances, **FRCVP 18**
    Remedies, **FRCVP 18**
Joint hearings, **FRCVP 42**
Judges or justices,
    Filing, **FRCVP 5**
    Inability to proceed, **FRCVP 63**
    Masters, **FRCVP 53**
    Official records, authentication, **FRCVP 44**
    Successor judges, **FRCVP 63**
Judgment as a matter of law, **FRCVP 50**
    Extension of time, **FRCVP 6**

Judgment as a matter of law—Cont'd
    Stay of proceedings, **FRCVP 62**
Judgments and decrees,
    Amendments,
        Findings, **FRCVP 52**
        Stay of proceedings, **FRCVP 62**
        Time, **FRCVP 59**
    Attachment, **FRCVP 70**
    Attorneys, fees, **FRCVP 58**
    Audita querela, **FRCVP 60**
    Bills of review, **FRCVP 60**
    Class actions, **FRCVP 23**
    Clerical mistakes, corrections, **FRCVP 60**
    Compulsory counterclaims, **FRCVP 13**
    Copies, **FRCVP 79**
    Coram nobis, **FRCVP 60**
    Costs, **FRCVP 58**
    Cross claims, **FRCVP 13, 54**
    Definitions, **FRCVP 54**
    Demand, **FRCVP 8, 54**
    Discovery, **FRCVP 69**
    Dockets and docketing, entries, **FRCVP 79**
    Entry of judgment, **FRCVP 58**
        Advisory juries, **FRCVP 52**
        General verdicts, **FRCVP 49**
        Multiple claims, **FRCVP 54**
        Multiple parties, **FRCVP 54**
        New trial, **FRCVP 59**
        Partial findings, **FRCVP 52**
    Excusable neglect, **FRCVP 60**
    Finality, **FRCVP 60**
    Forms, **FRCVP Form 71**
    Fraud, **FRCVP 60**
    Inadvertence, **FRCVP 60**
    Indexes, **FRCVP 79**
    Joinder, **FRCVP 19**
    Masters, reports, **FRCVP 54**
    Misconduct, **FRCVP 60**
    Mistake, **FRCVP 60**
    Modifications, **FRCVP 61**
    Motions,
        Amendments, **FRCVP 6, 59**
        Clerical mistakes, **FRCVP 60**
        Conclusions of law, **FRCVP 52**
        Excusable neglect, **FRCVP 60**
        Findings, **FRCVP 52**
        Matter of law, **FRCVP 50**
        Mistake, **FRCVP 60**
        Multiple claims, **FRCVP 54**
        Multiple parties, **FRCVP 54**
        Objections and exceptions, **FRCVP 52**
        Pleading, judgment on the pleading, **FRCVP 12**
        Stay of proceedings, **FRCVP 62**
    New trial, **FRCVP 59, 62**
    Newly discovered evidence, **FRCVP 60**
    Notwithstanding the verdict, judgment as a matter of law, **FRCVP 50**
    Offer of judgment, **FRCVP 5, 68**
    Partial findings, **FRCVP 52**
    Possession, **FRCVP 70**
    Prior proceedings, records and recordation, **FRCVP 54**
    Recitals, **FRCVP 54**
    Requests, entry of judgment, **FRCVP 58**
    Reversals, **FRCVP 60**
    Satisfaction, **FRCVP 60**
        Admiralty, **FRCVP E**

Judgments and decrees—Cont'd
    Separate judgments, **FRCVP 54**
    Sequestration, property, **FRCVP 70**
    Set-off and counterclaim, **FRCVP 13**
        Entry of judgment, **FRCVP 54**
    Specific performance, **FRCVP 70**
    State laws, enforcement, **FRCVP 62**
    Stay of proceedings, **FRCVP 62**
    Surprise, **FRCVP 60**
    Suspension, **FRCVP 60**
    Third parties, **FRCVP 54**
        Admiralty, **FRCVP 14**
    Time,
        Enforcement, **FRCVP 62**
        Entry of judgment, **FRCVP 58**
        Excusable neglect, **FRCVP 60**
        Extension of time, **FRCVP 6**
        Mistake, **FRCVP 60**
    Title to property, **FRCVP 70**
    United States, **FRCVP 62**
    Vacating or setting aside, **FRCVP 60, 61**
    Void judgment, **FRCVP 60**
    Written interrogatories, jury, verdicts, **FRCVP 49**
Jurisdiction,
    Application of rules, **FRCVP 82**
    Defenses, **FRCVP 12**
    Dismissal and nonsuit, **FRCVP 41**
        Subject matter jurisdiction, **FRCVP 12**
    Forms, statements, **FRCVP Form 7**
    Objections and exceptions, **FRCVP 4**
    Personal jurisdiction, **FRCVP 4, 12**
    Pleading, **FRCVP 9**
    Searches and seizures, **FRCVP 4**
    Statements, **FRCVP Form 7**
    Subject matter jurisdiction, dismissal and nonsuit, **FRCVP 12**
    Summons, **FRCVP 4**
    Sureties and suretyship, **FRCVP 65.1**
Jury, **FRCVP 38 et seq.**
    Admiralty, **FRCVP 38**
    Advisory juries, **FRCVP 39, 52**
    Calendars, **FRCVP 79**
    Declaratory judgments, **FRCVP 57**
    Default judgments, **FRCVP 55**
    Demand, **FRCVP 38 et seq.**
        Dockets and docketing, **FRCVP 79**
        Removal of cases or causes, **FRCVP 81**
    Disclosure, parties, **FRCVP 37**
    Dockets and docketing, demand, **FRCVP 79**
    Examinations and examiners, **FRCVP 47**
    Excusing jurors, **FRCVP 47**
    Findings, unanimity, **FRCVP 48**
    Injunctions, **FRCVP 65**
    Instructions, **FRCVP 49, 51**
    Issues, **FRCVP 38**
    Judgment as a matter of law, **FRCVP 50**
    Masters, **FRCVP 53**
    Numbers and numbering, **FRCVP 48**
    Peremptory challenges, **FRCVP 47**
    Removal of cases or causes, **FRCVP 81**
    Separate trials, **FRCVP 42**
    Stipulations, **FRCVP 39**
    Waiver, **FRCVP 38**
        Instructions, omissions, **FRCVP 49**
        Removal of cases or causes, **FRCVP 81**
    Withdrawal of demand, **FRCVP 38**
Knowledge, pleading, **FRCVP 9**

Laches, pleading, affirmative defenses, **FRCVP 8**

Lawsuits, notice, **FRCVP Form 5**

Leave of court,
   Admissions, requests, **FRCVP 36**
   Depositions, **FRCVP 30**

Legal representatives, judgments and decrees, **FRCVP 60**

Letters of request, foreign countries, depositions, **FRCVP 28**

Liability, admiralty, **FRCVP A, F**

Licenses and permits, pleading, affirmative defenses, **FRCVP 8**

Liens and incumbrances, admiralty, **FRCVP C**

Limitation of actions, pleading, affirmative defenses, **FRCVP 8**

Longshoremen and harbor workers, workers compensation, **FRCVP 81**

Magistrate judges, **FRCVP 72 et seq.**
   Appeal and review, **FRCVP 73**
   Attorney, fees, **FRCVP 54**
   Consent, jurisdiction, **FRCVP 73; FRCVP Form 81**
   Forms, jurisdiction, **FRCVP Form 80 et seq.**
   Jurisdiction, **FRCVP 72, 73**
      Forms, **FRCVP Form 80 et seq.**
   Masters, **FRCVP 53**
   Notice, jurisdiction, **FRCVP 73; FRCVP Form 80**
   Orders of court, assignments, **FRCVP Form 82**
   Pretrial matters, **FRCVP 72**
   Trial, **FRCVP 72, 73**
      Forms, **FRCVP Form 80 et seq.**

Mail and mailing,
   Admiralty, **FRCVP F**
   Business associations, summons, **FRCVP 4**
   Corporations, summons, **FRCVP 4**
   Masters, **FRCVP 53**
   Notice,
      Admiralty, **FRCVP F**
      Judgments and decrees, entries, **FRCVP 77**
      Orders of court, entries, **FRCVP 77**
   Process, **FRCVP 4 et seq.**
      Admiralty, **FRCVP B**
      Foreign countries, **FRCVP 4**
      Pleadings, **FRCVP 5**
      Sureties and suretyship, **FRCVP 65.1**
      Time, **FRCVP 6**
      United States, **FRCVP 4**
   United States, summons, **FRCVP 4**

Malice, pleading, **FRCVP 9**

Mandamus, writ abolished, **FRCVP 81**

Marshals, process, **FRCVP 4, 4.1**

Master and servant, injunctions, **FRCVP 65**

Masters, **FRCVP 52 et seq.**
   Attorneys, fees, **FRCVP 54**
   Compensation and salaries, **FRCVP 53**
   Definitions, **FRCVP 53**
   Findings, **FRCVP 52, 53**
   Reports, **FRCVP 53, 54**

Mental health,
   District of Columbia, **FRCVP 81**
   Examinations and examiners, **FRCVP 35, 37**

Merchant Marine Act, complaints, **FRCVP Form 14**

Merger and consolidation,
   Defenses, **FRCVP 12**
   Hearings, **FRCVP 42**
   Injunctions, **FRCVP 65**
   Trial, **FRCVP 42**

Mileage, subpoenas, **FRCVP 45**

Misconduct, judgments and decrees, **FRCVP 60**

Misjoinder, parties, **FRCVP 21**

Misnomers, public officers and employees, substitution, **FRCVP 25**

Mistake,
   Clerical mistakes, **FRCVP 60**
   Depositions, **FRCVP 32**
   Judgments and decrees, **FRCVP 60**
   Jury, instructions, **FRCVP 51**

Modification,
   Discovery, **FRCVP 29**
   Masters, **FRCVP 53**

Money,
   Complaints, sum certain, **FRCVP Form 10**
   Had and received, plea or answer, **FRCVP Form 31**

Motions,
   Additional findings, **FRCVP 52**
   Admissions, **FRCVP 36**
   Adoption by reference, **FRCVP 10**
   Advisory juries, **FRCVP 39**
   Amendments, findings, **FRCVP 52**
   Applications, orders of court, **FRCVP 7**
   Clerical mistakes, corrections, **FRCVP 60**
   Compelling discovery, **FRCVP 37**
   Conclusions of law, **FRCVP 52**
   Days, **FRCVP 78**
   Defenses, consolidation and merger, **FRCVP 12**
   Depositions, **FRCVP 32, 37**
   Disclosure, parties, **FRCVP 37**
   Entry upon land, **FRCVP 37**
   Examinations and examiners, reports, **FRCVP 35**
   Extension of time, **FRCVP 6**
   Findings, **FRCVP 52**
   Forms, **FRCVP Form 40 et seq.**
      Technical forms, **FRCVP 8**
   Interrogatories, **FRCVP 33 et seq.**
   Intervention, **FRCVP 24; FRCVP Form 42**
   Jury trial, **FRCVP 39**
   Masters, **FRCVP 53**
   More definite statement, pleading, **FRCVP 12**
   Notice,
      Clerical mistakes, corrections, **FRCVP 60**
      Discovery, **FRCVP 37**
      Sureties and suretyship, **FRCVP 65.1**
   Oral hearing, **FRCVP 78**
   Particularity, **FRCVP 7**
   Process, **FRCVP 5 et seq.**
      Intervention, **FRCVP 24**
      Judgments and decrees,
         Modification, **FRCVP 59**
         Summary judgment, **FRCVP 56**
      Substitution, parties, **FRCVP 25**
      Summary judgment, **FRCVP 56**
   Sanctions, **FRCVP 11**
   Severance, third parties, **FRCVP 14**
   Signatures, **FRCVP 7**
      Sanctions, **FRCVP 11**
   Striking,
      Pleading, **FRCVP 12**
      Third parties, **FRCVP 14**
   Substitution, parties, **FRCVP 25**
   Summary judgment, **FRCVP 12, 56**
   Suppression, depositions, **FRCVP 32**
   Sureties and suretyship, **FRCVP 65.1**
   Technical forms, **FRCVP 8**
   Temporary restraining orders, **FRCVP 65**
   Third parties,
      Complaints, service, **FRCVP 14**

Motions—Cont'd
    Third parties—Cont'd
        Forms, **FRCVP Form 41**
    Time,
        Excusable neglect, judgments and decrees,
            FRCVP 60
        Inadvertence, judgments and decrees, **FRCVP 60**
        Judgment on the pleadings, **FRCVP 12**
        Mistake, judgments and decrees, **FRCVP 60**
        New trial, **FRCVP 59**
        Pleading, responsive pleadings, **FRCVP 12**
        Service, **FRCVP 6**
        Summary judgment, **FRCVP 56**
        Surprise, judgments and decrees, **FRCVP 60**
    Writings, **FRCVP 7**
Multiple claims or parties,
    Judgments and decrees, **FRCVP 54, 62**
    Stay of proceedings, **FRCVP 62**
    Summons, **FRCVP 4**
Municipal corporations, Foreign States, summons,
    FRCVP 4
Names,
    Depositions, **FRCVP 28**
    Discovery, **FRCVP 26**
    Nonjoinder, **FRCVP 19**
    Pleading, **FRCVP 10, 19**
National Labor Relations Board, **FRCVP 81**
Naturalization, **FRCVP 81**
Negligence,
    Complaints, **FRCVP Form 11 et seq.**
    Federal Employers Liability Act, **FRCVP Form 13**
    Unknown defendants, **FRCVP Form 12**
New trial, **FRCVP 59**
    Affidavits, **FRCVP 59**
    Alternative motion, judgment as a matter of law,
        FRCVP 50
    Courts own initiative, **FRCVP 59**
    Harmless error, **FRCVP 61**
    Judgment as a matter of law, alternative motion,
        FRCVP 50
    Judgments and decrees, **FRCVP 59, 62**
    Motions, **FRCVP 59**
        Additional findings, **FRCVP 52**
        Alternative motion, judgment as a matter of law,
            FRCVP 50
        Amended findings, **FRCVP 52**
        Extension of time, **FRCVP 6**
        Judgment as a matter of law, alternative motion,
            FRCVP 50
        Time, **FRCVP 59**
    Orders of court, **FRCVP 59**
        Extension of time, **FRCVP 6**
    Stay of proceedings, **FRCVP 62**
    Written interrogatories, answers, inconsistencies,
        FRCVP 49
Newly discovered evidence, judgments and decrees,
    FRCVP 60
Newspapers, admiralty, notice, **FRCVP C, F**
Next friend, claims, **FRCVP 17**
Nonjoinder, pleading, **FRCVP 19**
Nonresidents, depositions, **FRCVP 45**
Notice,
    Amended rules, **FRCVP 83**
    Class actions, **FRCVP 23**
    Constitutional challenges, statutes, **FRCVP 5.1**
    Costs, **FRCVP 54**

Notice—Cont'd
    Default judgments,
        Applications, **FRCVP 55**
        Summons, **FRCVP 4**
    Derivative actions, **FRCVP 23.1**
    Dismissal and nonsuit, **FRCVP 41**
    Dockets and docketing, **FRCVP 77**
    Eminent domain, **FRCVP 71.1; FRCVP Form 60**
    Examinations and examiners, **FRCVP 35**
    Extension of time, **FRCVP 6**
    Forms, **FRCVP Form 5 et seq.**
    Injunctions, **FRCVP 65**
    Lawsuits, **FRCVP Form 5**
    Magistrate judges, jurisdiction, **FRCVP 73; FRCVP
        Form 80**
    Masters, **FRCVP 53**
    New trial, **FRCVP 59**
    Offer of judgment, acceptance, **FRCVP 68**
    Orders of court, **FRCVP 77**
    Process, **FRCVP 5 et seq.**
        Default judgments, **FRCVP 55**
        Depositions, **FRCVP 27**
        Hearings, **FRCVP 6**
        Orders of court, **FRCVP 77**
        Third parties, **FRCVP 14**
    Service, waiver, **FRCVP 4**
    Temporary restraining orders, **FRCVP 65**
    Time,
        Admiralty, **FRCVP F**
        Costs, **FRCVP 54**
        Extension of time, **FRCVP 6**
        Service, **FRCVP 6**
    Writings, **FRCVP 7**
Numbers and numbering,
    Claims, **FRCVP 42**
    Cross claims, **FRCVP 42**
    Experts, pretrial conferences, **FRCVP 16**
    Jury, **FRCVP 48**
    Separate trials, **FRCVP 42**
Objections and exceptions,
    Admiralty, **FRCVP F**
    Admissions, requests, **FRCVP 36**
    Electronically stored information, **FRCVP 34**
    Eminent domain, **FRCVP 71.1**
    Entry upon land, **FRCVP 34**
    Evidence, **FRCVP 52**
    Findings, **FRCVP 52**
    Formal exceptions, **FRCVP 46**
    Interrogatories, **FRCVP 33**
    Jury, instructions, **FRCVP 51**
    Magistrates, **FRCVP 72**
    Masters, **FRCVP 53**
    Motions, **FRCVP 12**
    Pleading, **FRCVP 12**
    Production of documents and things, **FRCVP 34**
    Service, **FRCVP 37**
    Sufficiency, **FRCVP 36**
Offer of judgment, **FRCVP 5, 68**
Officers and employees,
    Parties, substitution, **FRCVP 25**
    Pleading, **FRCVP 9**
    Records and recordation, **FRCVP 44**
Official acts, pleading, **FRCVP 9**
One form of action, **FRCVP 2**
Open court, trial, **FRCVP 77**
Opinions and decisions,
    Court trial, **FRCVP 52**

Opinions and decisions—Cont'd
    Formal exceptions, **FRCVP 46**
    Pleading, **FRCVP 9**
Oral examinations, depositions, **FRCVP 30 et seq.**
Orders of court,
    Admissions, requests, **FRCVP 36, 37**
    Class actions, **FRCVP 23**
    Clerical mistakes, corrections, **FRCVP 60**
    Clerks of courts, **FRCVP 77, 79**
    Consolidations and mergers, **FRCVP 65**
    Depositions, **FRCVP 27, 37**
    Discovery, **FRCVP 37**
    Dockets and docketing, **FRCVP 79**
    Documents, genuineness, **FRCVP 37**
    Entry upon land, **FRCVP 37**
    Examinations and examiners, **FRCVP 35**
    Fraud, **FRCVP 60**
    Interrogatories, **FRCVP 33, 37**
    Joinder, **FRCVP 19**
    Judgments and decrees, **FRCVP 54**
    Magistrate judges, assignments, **FRCVP Form 82**
    Masters, **FRCVP 53**
    Mental examinations, **FRCVP 27**
    Misconduct of party, relief from order, **FRCVP 60**
    Multiple claims or parties, **FRCVP 54**
    Newly discovered evidence, **FRCVP 60**
    Notice, **FRCVP 77**
    Objections and exceptions, **FRCVP 46**
    Parties, substitution, **FRCVP 25**
    Physical examinations, **FRCVP 35**
    Pretrial orders, **FRCVP 16**
    Production of documents and things, **FRCVP 37**
    Receivers and receivership, **FRCVP 66**
    Service, **FRCVP 5**
    Time, computation, **FRCVP 6**
    Unincorporated associations, **FRCVP 23.2**
    Voluntary dismissal, **FRCVP 41**
Owners and ownership, admiralty, **FRCVP F**
Paragraphs, pleading, **FRCVP 10**
Partial findings, judgments and decrees, **FRCVP 52**
Parties,
    Additional parties, **FRCVP 13**
    Capacity, **FRCVP 17**
    Children and minors, **FRCVP 17**
    Class actions, **FRCVP 23**
    Compelling discovery, **FRCVP 37**
    Corporations, **FRCVP 17**
    Cross claims, **FRCVP 13**
    Death,
        Statements, **FRCVP Form 9**
        Substitution, **FRCVP 25**
    Default judgments, **FRCVP 55**
    Discovery, **FRCVP 26 et seq.**
    Eminent domain, **FRCVP 71.1**
    Forms,
        Death, statements, **FRCVP Form 9**
        Meetings, planning meetings, reports, **FRCVP Form 52**
        Omissions, reasons, statements, **FRCVP Form 8**
    Incompetency, **FRCVP 17, 25**
    Indispensable parties, dismissal and nonsuit, **FRCVP 41**
    Joinder, **FRCVP 19 et seq.**
        Cross claims, **FRCVP 13**
        Dismissal and nonsuit, **FRCVP 41**
        Misjoinder, **FRCVP 12, 21**
        Nonjoinder, **FRCVP 12, 21**

Parties—Cont'd
    Joinder—Cont'd
        Set-off and counterclaim, **FRCVP 13**
        Summons, **FRCVP 4**
    Jurisdiction, **FRCVP 12**
    Jury trial, consent, **FRCVP 38**
    Masters, **FRCVP 53**
    Meetings, planning meetings, reports, **FRCVP Form 52**
    Misjoinder, **FRCVP 12, 21**
    Nonjoinder, **FRCVP 12, 21**
    Partnerships, **FRCVP 17**
    Planning meetings, reports, **FRCVP Form 52**
    Process, **FRCVP 71**
    Public officers and employees, **FRCVP 17**
        Substitution, **FRCVP 25**
    Real party in interest, **FRCVP 17**
    Receivers and receivership, **FRCVP 17**
    Reports, planning meetings, **FRCVP Form 52**
    Representatives, **FRCVP 17**
    Service, **FRCVP 5**
    Statements,
        Death, **FRCVP Form 9**
        Omissions, reasons, **FRCVP Form 8**
    Substitution, **FRCVP 25**
        Depositions, **FRCVP 32**
        Eminent domain, **FRCVP 71.1**
    United States, **FRCVP 17**
    Voluntary dismissal, **FRCVP 41**
Partnership,
    Capacity, **FRCVP 17**
    Depositions, **FRCVP 32, 37**
    Interrogatories, **FRCVP 33**
    Summons, **FRCVP 4**
Patents,
    Infringement, complaints, **FRCVP Form 18**
    Stay of proceedings, **FRCVP 62**
Payment, **FRCVP 67**
    Admiralty, **FRCVP C, E**
    Pleading, affirmative defenses, **FRCVP 8**
Pending actions,
    Discovery, **FRCVP 37**
    Set-off and counterclaim, **FRCVP 13**
Peremptory challenges, jury, **FRCVP 47**
Permissive counterclaims, pleading, **FRCVP 13**
Permissive intervention, parties, **FRCVP 24**
Permissive joinder, parties, **FRCVP 20**
Perpetuation of testimony, **FRCVP 27**
Personal jurisdiction, **FRCVP 4, 12**
Personal representatives, **FRCVP 81**
Personal service, summons, **FRCVP 4**
Petroleum control boards, orders, appeal and review, **FRCVP 81**
Photography and pictures,
    Court orders, **FRCVP 27**
    Orders of court, **FRCVP 27**
Physical examinations, **FRCVP 35, 37**
Place,
    Depositions, **FRCVP 29**
    Examinations and examiners, **FRCVP 35**
    Pleading, averments, **FRCVP 9**
Plans and specifications,
    Discovery, **FRCVP 26**
    Parties, planning meetings, reports, **FRCVP Form 52**
Plea or answer,
    Admissions, requests, **FRCVP 36**
    Defenses, **FRCVP Form 30**

Plea or answer—Cont'd
    Depositions, **FRCVP 37**
    Eminent domain, **FRCVP 71.1**
    Evasive answers, **FRCVP 37**
    General verdict, interrogatories, answers, **FRCVP 49**
    Incomplete answers, **FRCVP 37**
    Removed actions, **FRCVP 81**
    Service, **FRCVP 12**
Pleading, **FRCVP 7 et seq.**
    Additional claims, **FRCVP 5**
    Admissions, **FRCVP 8**
    Adoption by reference, **FRCVP 10**
    Affirmative defenses, **FRCVP 8**
    Alternative statements, **FRCVP 8**
    Ambiguity, **FRCVP 12**
    Amendments, **FRCVP 15**
        Eminent domain, **FRCVP 71.1**
        Evidence, **FRCVP 15**
        Omissions, **FRCVP 12**
        Pretrial procedure, **FRCVP 16**
        Relation back, **FRCVP 15**
    Associations and societies, **FRCVP 9**
    Boards and commissions, **FRCVP 9**
    Capacity, **FRCVP 9**
    Captions, **FRCVP 7, 10**
    Class actions, **FRCVP 23**
    Compulsory counterclaims, **FRCVP 13**
    Conciseness, **FRCVP 8**
    Conditions precedent, **FRCVP 9**
    Consistency, **FRCVP 8**
    Consolidations and mergers, **FRCVP 12**
    Damages, special damages, **FRCVP 9**
    Default judgments, **FRCVP 54, 55**
    Defects, supplemental pleading, **FRCVP 15**
    Defenses, **FRCVP 8, 12**
        Discovery, **FRCVP 37**
        Eminent domain, **FRCVP 71.1**
        Forms, **FRCVP Form 30**
        Paragraphs, **FRCVP 10**
        Removed actions, **FRCVP 81**
        Summary judgment, **FRCVP 56**
        Third parties, **FRCVP 14**
    Denials, **FRCVP 8**
        Conditions precedent, **FRCVP 9**
    Directness, **FRCVP 8**
    Dismissal and nonsuit, **FRCVP 41**
    Eminent domain, **FRCVP 71.1**
    Evidence, amendments, **FRCVP 15**
    Exhibits, **FRCVP 10**
    Filing, **FRCVP 3 et seq.**
    Foreign judgments, **FRCVP 9**
    Foreign laws, **FRCVP 44.1**
    Forms, **FRCVP 10; FRCVP Form 10 et seq.**
        Technical forms, **FRCVP 8**
    Fraud, **FRCVP 8, 9**
    Fraudulent conveyances, **FRCVP 18**
    General denials, **FRCVP 8**
    Hypothetical statements, **FRCVP 8**
    Insufficiency, **FRCVP 7**
    Intent, **FRCVP 9**
    Joinder, **FRCVP 18**
    Judgments and decrees, **FRCVP 9**
        Demand, **FRCVP 8**
        Recitals, **FRCVP 54**
    Jurisdiction, **FRCVP 9**
    Knowledge, **FRCVP 9**
    Mail and mailing, service, **FRCVP 5**

Pleading—Cont'd
    Malice, **FRCVP 9**
    Mental condition, **FRCVP 9**
    Mistake, **FRCVP 9**
        Amendments, relation back, **FRCVP 15**
        Set-off and counterclaim, **FRCVP 8**
    Motions,
        Defenses, **FRCVP 12**
        Judgment on the pleading, **FRCVP 12**
        More definite statement, **FRCVP 12**
        Responsive pleadings, **FRCVP 12**
        Striking, **FRCVP 12**
        Summary judgment, **FRCVP 12**
        Supplemental pleadings, **FRCVP 15**
    Names, **FRCVP 10, 19**
    Negative averments, **FRCVP 9**
    Negligence, **FRCVP Form 11 et seq.**
    New claims, **FRCVP 5**
    Nonjoinder, **FRCVP 12**
    Notice,
        Filing, **FRCVP 5**
        Foreign laws, **FRCVP 44.1**
        Parties, amendments, relation back, **FRCVP 15**
    Numerous defendants, **FRCVP 5**
    Objections and exceptions, **FRCVP 12**
    Official documents, **FRCVP 9**
    Outside matters, **FRCVP 12**
    Paragraphs, numbers and numbering, **FRCVP 10**
    Particularity, conditions precedent, **FRCVP 9**
    Parties,
        Amendments, relation back, **FRCVP 15**
        Captions, names, **FRCVP 10**
        Defects, **FRCVP 12**
        Defenses, **FRCVP 12**
        Title of action, **FRCVP 10**
    Permissive counterclaims, **FRCVP 13**
    Place, **FRCVP 9**
    Preliminary hearings, **FRCVP 12**
    Quasi-judicial tribunals, **FRCVP 9**
    Removed cases, **FRCVP 81**
    Set-off and counterclaim, **FRCVP 13**
    Signatures,
        Motions, **FRCVP 7**
        Sanctions, **FRCVP 11**
        Statements, **FRCVP 8**
    Special matters, **FRCVP 9**
    Summary judgment, **FRCVP 12, 56**
    Supplemental pleadings, **FRCVP 12, 15**
    Third parties, **FRCVP 8**
    Time, **FRCVP 9**
        Amendment, **FRCVP 15**
        Dismissal of action, **FRCVP 41**
        Service, **FRCVP 12**
        Summary judgment, **FRCVP 56**
    Title of action, **FRCVP 10**
    United States,
        Reply, time, **FRCVP 12**
        Set-off and counterclaim, **FRCVP 13**
    Waiver, defenses, **FRCVP 8**
Political subdivisions, Foreign States, summons, **FRCVP 4**
Possession,
    Admiralty, **FRCVP D**
    Judgments and decrees, **FRCVP 70**
Preliminary hearings, pleading, **FRCVP 12**
Preliminary injunctions, **FRCVP 65**
Preservation of defenses, **FRCVP 12**

Pretrial conferences, **FRCVP 16**
Pretrial disclosures, **FRCVP 26**
Prevailing parties, costs, **FRCVP 54**
Priorities and preferences,
    Admissions, requests, **FRCVP 36**
    Declaratory judgments, **FRCVP 57**
    Interrogatories, **FRCVP 33**
    Trial, calendar, **FRCVP 40**
Privacy protection, **FRCVP 5.2**
Privileges and immunities, subpoenas, **FRCVP 45**
Prize proceedings, admiralty, **FRCVP 81**
Process, **FRCVP 4 et seq.**
    Admissions, **FRCVP 36**
    Age, servers, **FRCVP 4**
    Answer, **FRCVP 12, 36**
    Appearance, **FRCVP 5**
    Attorneys, **FRCVP 5**
    Certificates and certification, **FRCVP 5**
    Compulsory counterclaims, **FRCVP 13**
    Defenses, **FRCVP 12**
    Demand, **FRCVP 5**
        Jury trial, **FRCVP 38**
    Depositions, objections and exceptions, **FRCVP 32**
    Discovery, **FRCVP 5**
    Dockets and docketing, **FRCVP 79**
    Eminent domain, **FRCVP 71.1**
    Evidence, **FRCVP 4, 4.1**
    Federal agencies, **FRCVP 15**
    In forma pauperis, **FRCVP 4**
    Interrogatories, **FRCVP 33, 37**
    Joinder of parties, **FRCVP 19**
    Multiple defendants, **FRCVP 5**
    Nonparties, **FRCVP 71**
    Offer of judgment, **FRCVP 5, 68**
    Orders of court, **FRCVP 5**
    Parties, substitution, **FRCVP 25**
    Pleadings, **FRCVP 5, 11 et seq.**
    Process servers, **FRCVP 4**
    Production of books and papers, **FRCVP 34**
    Records and recordation, appeal and review, **FRCVP 5**
    Searches and seizures, **FRCVP 5**
    Substitution, parties, **FRCVP 25**
    Sureties and suretyship, **FRCVP 65.1**
    Third parties, **FRCVP 14**
    Time, **FRCVP 6 et seq.**
    United States Marshals, **FRCVP 4**
Production of books and papers, **FRCVP 34**
    Application of rules, **FRCVP 81**
    Compelling production, **FRCVP 37, 45**
    Depositions, **FRCVP 27**
    Forms, requests, **FRCVP Form 50**
    Nonparties, **FRCVP 34**
    Objections and exceptions, **FRCVP 34**
    Requests, **FRCVP 34; FRCVP Form 50**
    Sanctions, **FRCVP 37**
    Service, requests, **FRCVP 34**
    Stipulations, **FRCVP 29**
    Subpoenas, **FRCVP 45**
    Supplementation, **FRCVP 26**
Property, admiralty, disposition, **FRCVP E**
Protective orders,
    Depositions, **FRCVP 32**
    Discovery, **FRCVP 26, 37**
    Privacy protection, **FRCVP 5.2**
Psychologists and psychology, examinations and examiners, **FRCVP 35**

Public officers and employees,
    Parties, **FRCVP 17**
    Substitution, **FRCVP 25**
Public policy, **FRCVP 1**
    Forms, **FRCVP 84**
Publication, official records, evidence, **FRCVP 44**
Quasi in rem, admiralty, **FRCVP E**
Quasi-judicial tribunals, pleading, **FRCVP 9**
Questions of law or fact,
    Class actions, **FRCVP 23**
    Foreign laws, **FRCVP 44.1**
    Sanctions, **FRCVP 37**
Quo warranto, **FRCVP 81**
Railroads, labor disputes, **FRCVP 81**
Real party in interest, **FRCVP 17**
Receipts, service, **FRCVP 4**
Receivers and receivership, **FRCVP 66**
    Capacity, **FRCVP 17**
    Stay of proceedings, **FRCVP 62**
Recitals, judgments and decrees, **FRCVP 54**
Records and recordation,
    Authentication, **FRCVP 44**
    Business records, **FRCVP 33**
    Clerical mistakes, corrections, **FRCVP 60**
    Clerks of court, **FRCVP 79**
    Depositions, **FRCVP 30**
    Discovery, **FRCVP 26**
    Evidence, **FRCVP 44**
    Findings, **FRCVP 52**
    Injunctions, **FRCVP 65**
    Judgments and decrees, **FRCVP 54**
    Magistrates, **FRCVP 72, 73**
    Masters, **FRCVP 5, 53**
Recross questions, depositions, **FRCVP 31**
Redacted filings, **FRCVP 5.2**
Redirect questions, depositions, **FRCVP 31**
Redundancy, pleading, **FRCVP 12**
References,
    Default judgments, **FRCVP 55**
    Magistrates, **FRCVP 73**
    Masters, **FRCVP 53**
    Pleading, adoption by reference, **FRCVP 10**
Release,
    Admiralty, **FRCVP E**
        Notice, **FRCVP C**
    Pleading, affirmative defenses, **FRCVP 8**
Removal of cases or causes, **FRCVP 81**
Repleading, removed cases, **FRCVP 81**
Replevin, **FRCVP 64**
Reply, **FRCVP 7 et seq.**
    Admissions, **FRCVP 8**
    Discovery, **FRCVP 29**
    New trial, **FRCVP 59**
    Omissions, **FRCVP 12**
    Time, **FRCVP 12**
Reports,
    Discovery, **FRCVP 26**
    Mental examinations, **FRCVP 35**
    Parties, planning meetings, **FRCVP Form 52**
    Physical examinations, **FRCVP 35**
Representatives and representation,
    Capacity, **FRCVP 17**
    Children and minors, **FRCVP 17**
    Death, substitution, **FRCVP 25**
    Incompetents, **FRCVP 17**
Requests,
    Electronically stored information, **FRCVP 34**

Requests—Cont'd
 Entry upon land, **FRCVP 34; FRCVP Form 50**
 Examinations and examiners, **FRCVP 35**
 Findings, **FRCVP 52**
 Judgments and decrees, entries, **FRCVP 58**
 Jury, instructions, **FRCVP 51**
 Masters, **FRCVP 53**
 Production of books and papers, **FRCVP 34; FRCVP Form 50**
Res judicata, pleading, **FRCVP 8**
Restraining orders, **FRCVP 65**
Returns,
 Admiralty, marshals, **FRCVP E**
 Habeas corpus, **FRCVP 81**
Reversals,
 Judgments and decrees, **FRCVP 60**
 New trial, **FRCVP 50**
Sales, admiralty, **FRCVP C, E, G**
Sanctions,
 Attorneys, fees, **FRCVP 11, 16**
 Depositions, **FRCVP 30**
 Discovery, **FRCVP 37**
 Electronically stored information, **FRCVP 37**
 Entry upon land, **FRCVP 37**
 Forms, nonuse, **FRCVP 83**
 Interrogatories, **FRCVP 37**
 Pretrial conferences, **FRCVP 16**
 Pretrial orders, **FRCVP 16**
 Production of books and papers, **FRCVP 37**
 Signatures, **FRCVP 11**
Satisfaction, judgments and decrees, **FRCVP 60**
 Admiralty, **FRCVP E**
Saturday,
 Business hours, **FRCVP 77**
 Time, computation, **FRCVP 6**
Scandalous matter, motion to strike, **FRCVP 12**
Scire facias, abolition of writ, **FRCVP 81**
Seals (official seals),
 Records and recordation, authentication, **FRCVP 44**
 Summons, **FRCVP 4**
Seamen, process, service, **FRCVP 4**
Searches and seizures, **FRCVP 64**
 Admiralty, **FRCVP E**
  United States vessels, **FRCVP C**
 Service, **FRCVP 4, 5**
 United States vessels, **FRCVP C**
Secretary of Agriculture, **FRCVP 81**
Secretary of embassy, official records, authentication, **FRCVP 44**
Secretary of the Interior, **FRCVP 81**
Security interest,
 Admiralty, **FRCVP D et seq.**
 Injunctions, **FRCVP 62, 65**
 Masters, **FRCVP 53**
 Stay of proceedings, **FRCVP 62**
 Sureties and suretyship, **FRCVP 65.1**
Sequestration, property, **FRCVP 70**
Set-off and counterclaim, **FRCVP 7 et seq.**
 Admiralty, **FRCVP E**
 Compulsory counterclaims, **FRCVP 13**
 Dismissal and nonsuit, **FRCVP 41**
 Entry of judgment, **FRCVP 54**
 Joinder, **FRCVP 18**
 Judgments and decrees, **FRCVP 13, 54**
 Mistake, **FRCVP 8**
 Money had and received, interpleader, **FRCVP Form 31**

Set-off and counterclaim—Cont'd
 Omissions, **FRCVP 13**
 Permissive counterclaims, **FRCVP 13**
 Reply, **FRCVP 7**
  Time, service, **FRCVP 12**
 Separate trials, **FRCVP 42**
 Service, **FRCVP 5**
 Third parties, **FRCVP 14**
 United States, **FRCVP 12, 13**
 Voluntary dismissal, **FRCVP 41**
Shares and shareholders, derivative actions, **FRCVP 23.1**
Ships and shipping, mortgages, foreclosure, **FRCVP C**
Show cause orders, admiralty, **FRCVP C**
Signatures,
 Admiralty,
  Affidavits, **FRCVP B**
  Release, **FRCVP E**
 Admissions, **FRCVP 36**
 Discovery, **FRCVP 26**
 Electronic signatures, **FRCVP 5**
 Foreign official records, authentication, **FRCVP 44**
 Forms, **FRCVP Form 2**
 Interrogatories, **FRCVP 33**
 Summons, **FRCVP 4**
Social security, privacy protection, **FRCVP 5.2**
Sound recordings, depositions, **FRCVP 30**
Special pleadings, **FRCVP 9**
Special verdict, **FRCVP 49**
Specific performance,
 Complaints, **FRCVP Form 17**
 Execution, **FRCVP 70**
Statements,
 Corporations, disclosure, **FRCVP 7.1**
 Defenses, **FRCVP 12**
 Jurisdiction, **FRCVP Form 7**
 Official records, **FRCVP 44**
 Parties,
  Death, **FRCVP Form 9**
  Omissions, reasons, **FRCVP Form 8**
States,
 Admiralty, **FRCVP B**
 Execution, **FRCVP 69**
 Jury trial, **FRCVP 81**
 Official records, authentication, **FRCVP 44**
 Prior actions, **FRCVP 32**
 Summons, **FRCVP 4**
Statute of frauds, pleading, **FRCVP 8**
Statute of limitations, pleading, **FRCVP 8**
Statutes,
 Admiralty, **FRCVP C**
 Capacity, **FRCVP 17**
 Constitutional challenges, **FRCVP 5.1**
 Intervention, **FRCVP 24**
 Time, **FRCVP 6**
Stay of proceedings,
 Admiralty, **FRCVP E**
 Appellate courts, **FRCVP 62**
 Bonds (officers and fiduciaries), **FRCVP 62**
 Class actions, **FRCVP 23**
 Discovery, **FRCVP 37**
 Execution, **FRCVP 62**
 Injunctions, **FRCVP 62**
 Judgments and decrees, **FRCVP 62**
 Patents, accounts and accounting, **FRCVP 62**
 Previously dismissed actions, costs, **FRCVP 41**
 Receivers and receivership, **FRCVP 62**
 State laws, **FRCVP 62**

Stay of proceedings—Cont'd
United States, **FRCVP 62**
Stenographers, evidence, **FRCVP 80**
Stipulations,
Admiralty, **FRCVP E**
Court trials, **FRCVP 39**
Depositions, **FRCVP 29, 30**
Discovery, **FRCVP 29**
Dismissal and nonsuit, **FRCVP 41**
Jury verdict, **FRCVP 48**
Masters, **FRCVP 53**
New trial, **FRCVP 59**
Production of books and papers, **FRCVP 29**
Sureties and suretyship, **FRCVP 65.1**
Striking of pleadings, **FRCVP 12**
Discovery, **FRCVP 37**
Motions, more definite statement, **FRCVP 12**
Third parties, **FRCVP 14**
Subclasses, class actions, **FRCVP 23**
Subject matter, jurisdiction, defenses, **FRCVP 12**
Subpoena duces tecum, **FRCVP 30**
Subpoenas, **FRCVP 45**
Electronically stored information, **FRCVP 45**
Federal agencies, **FRCVP 45, 81**
Foreign countries, **FRCVP 37**
Forms, **FRCVP 45**
Masters, **FRCVP 53**
Objections and exceptions, **FRCVP 45**
Production of books and papers, **FRCVP 81**
United States, **FRCVP 45, 81**
Substantial rights, mistake, **FRCVP 61**
Successors, parties, **FRCVP 25**
Summaries,
Business records, **FRCVP 33**
Foreign official records, **FRCVP 44**
Summary judgment, **FRCVP 56**
Motions, **FRCVP 12, 52, 56**
Pretrial conferences, **FRCVP 16**
Time, **FRCVP 41**
Summons, **FRCVP 4 et seq.**
Admiralty, **FRCVP B, C**
Forms, **FRCVP 4; FRCVP Form 3 et seq.**
Third parties, **FRCVP Form 4**
Waiver, **FRCVP Forms 5, 6**
States, **FRCVP 4**
Third parties, **FRCVP 14; FRCVP Form 4**
Time, **FRCVP 4**
Waiver, **FRCVP 4; FRCVP Forms 5, 6**
Sundays,
Clerks of court, business hours, **FRCVP 77**
Time, computation, **FRCVP 6**
Supplemental pleadings, **FRCVP 12, 15**
Supplemental process, admiralty, **FRCVP C**
Supplementary proceedings, execution, **FRCVP 69**
Supplementation, discovery, **FRCVP 26**
Surprise, judgments and decrees, **FRCVP 60**
Telecommunications,
Depositions, **FRCVP 30**
Telephone numbers, forms, **FRCVP Form 2**
Temporary restraining orders, **FRCVP 65**
Territories, official record, authentication, **FRCVP 44**
Third parties, **FRCVP 14**
Admiralty, **FRCVP 14**
Answers, **FRCVP 7**
Complaints, **FRCVP 7; FRCVP Form 16**
Dismissal and nonsuit, **FRCVP 41**
Entry of judgment, **FRCVP 54**

Third parties—Cont'd
Forms,
Complaints, **FRCVP Form 16**
Motions, **FRCVP Form 41**
Summons, **FRCVP Form 4**
Joinder, **FRCVP 18**
Judgments and decrees, **FRCVP 54**
Admiralty, **FRCVP 14**
Motions,
Complaints, service, **FRCVP 14**
Forms, **FRCVP Form 41**
Pleading, **FRCVP 8**
Separate trials, **FRCVP 42**
Summons, **FRCVP Form 4**
Three judge court, injunctions, **FRCVP 62**
Time, **FRCVP 6**
Admissions, **FRCVP 36**
Amendments, **FRCVP 86**
Appearance, **FRCVP 4**
Complaints, **FRCVP 3**
Computation, **FRCVP 6**
Dismissal and nonsuit, **FRCVP 17**
Electronically stored information, **FRCVP 34**
Entry upon land, **FRCVP 34**
Execution, **FRCVP 62**
Filing, **FRCVP 5**
Habeas corpus, **FRCVP 81**
Interrogatories, **FRCVP 33**
Involuntary dismissal, **FRCVP 41**
Masters, **FRCVP 53**
Mental health, examinations and examiners, **FRCVP 35**
New trial, affidavits, **FRCVP 59**
Offer of judgment, **FRCVP 68**
Original rules, **FRCVP 86**
Physical examinations, **FRCVP 35**
Production of documents or things, **FRCVP 34**
Summary judgment, **FRCVP 56**
Summons, **FRCVP 4**
Supersedeas bonds, **FRCVP 62**
Temporary restraining orders, **FRCVP 65**
Third parties, **FRCVP 14**
United States, **FRCVP 4**
Voluntary dismissal, **FRCVP 41**
Title, **FRCVP 85**
Pleading, **FRCVP 10**
Title to property, judgments and decrees, **FRCVP 70**
Trade secrets,
Protective orders, **FRCVP 26**
Subpoenas, **FRCVP 45**
Transcripts,
Depositions, **FRCVP 30**
Stenographers, evidence, **FRCVP 80**
Traveling expenses, subpoenas, **FRCVP 45**
Treaties, depositions, **FRCVP 28**
Trial,
Admiralty, fines, penalties and forfeitures, **FRCVP G**
Advisory juries, **FRCVP 52**
Assignments, **FRCVP 40**
Consolidations and mergers, **FRCVP 42, 65**
Court trials, **FRCVP 52**
Dismissal and nonsuit, motions, **FRCVP 41**
Issues, **FRCVP 39**
Judgment and decrees, forms, **FRCVP Form 71**
Magistrates, **FRCVP 72**
Motions, dismissal and nonsuit, **FRCVP 41**
Stipulations, **FRCVP 39**

Trial—Cont'd
  Cross claims, separate trials, **FRCVP 13**
  Depositions, **FRCVP 32**
  Discovery, preparation material, **FRCVP 26**
  Dismissal and nonsuit, court trials, motions, **FRCVP 41**
  Eminent domain, **FRCVP 71.1**
  Interrogatories, **FRCVP 33**
  Issues, court trials, **FRCVP 39**
  Joinder, separate trials, **FRCVP 20**
  Judges or justices, inability to proceed, **FRCVP 63**
  Masters, **FRCVP 53**
  Motions, court trials, dismissal and nonsuit, **FRCVP 41**
  Open court, **FRCVP 77**
  Orders of court, separate trials, **FRCVP 42**
  Pretrial conferences, separate trials, **FRCVP 16**
  Pretrial procedure, **FRCVP 16**
  Separate trials,
    Cross claims, **FRCVP 13**
    Joinder, **FRCVP 20**
    Orders of court, **FRCVP 42**
    Pretrial conferences, **FRCVP 16**
    Set-off and counterclaims, **FRCVP 13**
    Third parties, **FRCVP 14**
  Set-off and counterclaims, separate trials, **FRCVP 13**
  Stipulations, court trials, **FRCVP 39**
  Subpoenas, **FRCVP 45**
  Successor judges, **FRCVP 63**
  Third parties, separate trials, **FRCVP 14**
  Voluntary dismissal, **FRCVP 41**
Trusts and trustees, **FRCVP 17**
  Admiralty, **FRCVP F**
Uniform numbering system, local rules, **FRCVP 83**
Unincorporated associations, **FRCVP 23.2**
  Derivative actions, shares and shareholders, **FRCVP 23.1**
  Shares and shareholders, derivative actions, **FRCVP 23.1**
  Summons, **FRCVP 4**
United States,
  Admiralty, **FRCVP E**
  Answers, **FRCVP 12**
  Appeal and review, **FRCVP 62**
  Bonds (officers and fiduciaries), **FRCVP 62**
  Costs, **FRCVP 54**
  Depositions, **FRCVP 28, 55**
    Leave of court, **FRCVP 30**
    Outside country, **FRCVP 32**
  Discovery, **FRCVP 37**
  Names, **FRCVP 17**
  Official records, authentication, **FRCVP 44**
  Process, **FRCVP 15**
  Set-off and counterclaim, **FRCVP 12, 13**
  Stay of proceedings, **FRCVP 62**
  Subpoenas, **FRCVP 45, 81**
  Summons, **FRCVP 4**
United States attorneys,
  Pleading, amendments, parties, changes, **FRCVP 15**
  Service, **FRCVP 4, 12**
United States laws, calendar, **FRCVP 40**

Unknown defendants, negligence, complaints, **FRCVP Form 12**
Vacating or setting aside,
    Default judgments, **FRCVP 55**
    Findings, **FRCVP 52**
    Judgments and decrees, **FRCVP 60, 61**
    Verdict, **FRCVP 61**
Vacation of judgments, judgment as a matter of law, alternative new trial motion, **FRCVP 50**
Venue,
    Admiralty, **FRCVP 82; FRCVP F**
    Defenses, **FRCVP 12**
    Depositions, **FRCVP 32, 37**
    Discovery, **FRCVP 37**
    Dismissal and nonsuit, **FRCVP 41**
    Joinder, **FRCVP 19**
    Objections and exceptions, **FRCVP 4**
Verdict,
    Dockets and docketing, **FRCVP 79**
    Forms, **FRCVP Form 70**
    General verdict, interrogatories, **FRCVP 49**
    Harmless error, **FRCVP 61**
    Special verdicts, **FRCVP 49**
    Unanimity of jurors, **FRCVP 48**
Verification,
    Admiralty, **FRCVP C**
    Electronic verification, **FRCVP 5**
Vice consul, official records, authentication, **FRCVP 44**
Void judgment, **FRCVP 60**
Voluntary dismissal, **FRCVP 41**
Waiver,
    Affirmative defenses, **FRCVP 8**
    Defenses, **FRCVP 12**
    Depositions, **FRCVP 32**
    Eminent domain, **FRCVP 71.1**
    Examinations and examiners, **FRCVP 35**
    Privacy protection, **FRCVP 5.2**
    Summons, **FRCVP 4; FRCVP Forms 5, 6**
Withdrawal,
    Admissions, **FRCVP 36**
    Deposits, **FRCVP 67**
    Jury trial, **FRCVP 38**
    Offer of judgment, **FRCVP 68**
Witnesses,
    Compelling testimony, **FRCVP 81**
    Discovery, **FRCVP 26 et seq.**
    Masters, **FRCVP 53**
    Oaths and affirmations, **FRCVP 43**
    Pretrial conferences, **FRCVP 16**
    Successor judges, **FRCVP 63**
Writings,
    Admissions, requests, **FRCVP 36**
    Depositions, **FRCVP 32**
    Discovery, stipulations, **FRCVP 29**
    Examinations and examiners, **FRCVP 35**
    Motions, **FRCVP 7**
    Subpoenas, **FRCVP 45**
Writs, **FRCVP 81**
    Abolished writs, **FRCVP 60**
    Assistance, **FRCVP 70**
Written interrogatories, **FRCVP 49**
Written questions, depositions, **FRCVP 31 et seq.**

*

FEDERAL RULES OF EVIDENCE

Effective July 1, 1975

Including Amendments Effective
September 19, 2008

Research Note

These rules may be searched electronically on Westlaw in the US–RULES database; updates to these rules may be found on Westlaw in US–RULES-UPDATES. For search tips, and a detailed summary of database content, consult the Westlaw Scope Screen of each database.

Table of Rules

ARTICLE I. GENERAL PROVISIONS

Rule
101. Scope.
102. Purpose and Construction.
103. Rulings on Evidence.
104. Preliminary Questions.
105. Limited Admissibility.
106. Remainder of or Related Writings or Recorded Statements.

ARTICLE II. JUDICIAL NOTICE

201. Judicial Notice of Adjudicative Facts.

ARTICLE III. PRESUMPTIONS IN CIVIL ACTIONS AND PROCEEDINGS

301. Presumptions in General in Civil Actions and Proceedings.
302. Applicability of State Law in Civil Actions and Proceedings.

ARTICLE IV. RELEVANCY AND ITS LIMITS

401. Definition of "Relevant Evidence."
402. Relevant Evidence Generally Admissible; Irrelevant Evidence Inadmissible.
403. Exclusion of Relevant Evidence on Grounds of Prejudice, Confusion, or Waste of Time.
404. Character Evidence Not Admissible to Prove Conduct; Exceptions; Other Crimes.
405. Methods of Proving Character.
406. Habit; Routine Practice.
407. Subsequent Remedial Measures.
408. Compromise and Offers to Compromise.
409. Payment of Medical and Similar Expenses.
410. Inadmissibility of Pleas, Plea Discussions, and Related Statements.
411. Liability Insurance.

Rule
412. Sex Offense Cases; Relevance of Alleged Victim's Past Sexual Behavior or Alleged Sexual Predisposition.
413. Evidence of Similar Crimes in Sexual Assault Cases.
414. Evidence of Similar Crimes in Child Molestation Cases.
415. Evidence of Similar Acts in Civil Cases Concerning Sexual Assault or Child Molestation.

ARTICLE V. PRIVILEGES

501. General Rule.
502. Attorney–Client Privilege and Work Product; Limitations on Waiver.

ARTICLE VI. WITNESSES

601. General Rule of Competency.
602. Lack of Personal Knowledge.
603. Oath or Affirmation.
604. Interpreters.
605. Competency of Judge as Witness.
606. Competency of Juror as Witness.
607. Who May Impeach.
608. Evidence of Character and Conduct of Witness.
609. Impeachment by Evidence of Conviction of Crime.
610. Religious Beliefs or Opinions.
611. Mode and Order of Interrogation and Presentation.
612. Writing Used to Refresh Memory.
613. Prior Statements of Witnesses.
614. Calling and Interrogation of Witnesses by Court.
615. Exclusion of Witnesses.

ARTICLE VII. OPINIONS AND EXPERT TESTIMONY

701. Opinion Testimony by Lay Witnesses.
702. Testimony by Experts.
703. Bases of Opinion Testimony by Experts.
704. Opinion on Ultimate Issue.

Rule
705. Disclosure of Facts or Data Underlying Expert Opinion.
706. Court Appointed Experts.

ARTICLE VIII.　HEARSAY

801. Definitions.
802. Hearsay Rule.
803. Hearsay Exceptions;　Availability of Declarant Immaterial.
804. Hearsay Exceptions;　Declarant Unavailable.
805. Hearsay Within Hearsay.
806. Attacking and Supporting Credibility of Declarant.
807. Residual Exception.

ARTICLE IX.　AUTHENTICATION AND IDENTIFICATION

901. Requirement of Authentication or Identification.

Rule
902. Self-Authentication.
903. Subscribing Witness' Testimony Unnecessary.

ARTICLE X.　CONTENTS OF WRITINGS, RECORDINGS, AND PHOTOGRAPHS

1001. Definitions.
1002. Requirement of Original.
1003. Admissibility of Duplicates.
1004. Admissibility of Other Evidence of Contents.
1005. Public Records.
1006. Summaries.
1007. Testimony or Written Admission of Party.
1008. Functions of Court and Jury.

ARTICLE XI.　MISCELLANEOUS RULES

1101. Applicability of Rules.
1102. Amendments.
1103. Title.

INDEX

ARTICLE I.　GENERAL PROVISIONS

RULE 101.　SCOPE

These rules govern proceedings in the courts of the United States and before the United States bankruptcy judges and United States magistrate judges, to the extent and with the exceptions stated in rule 1101.

[Amended March 2, 1987, effective October 1, 1987; April 25, 1988, effective November 1, 1988; April 22, 1993, effective December 1, 1993.]

RULE 102.　PURPOSE AND CONSTRUCTION

These rules shall be construed to secure fairness in administration, elimination of unjustifiable expense and delay, and promotion of growth and development of the law of evidence to the end that the truth may be ascertained and proceedings justly determined.

RULE 103.　RULINGS ON EVIDENCE

(a) Effect of Erroneous Ruling.　Error may not be predicated upon a ruling which admits or excludes evidence unless a substantial right of the party is affected, and

(1) *Objection.*　In case the ruling is one admitting evidence, a timely objection or motion to strike appears of record, stating the specific ground of objection, if the specific ground was not apparent from the context; or

(2) *Offer of Proof.*　In case the ruling is one excluding evidence, the substance of the evidence was made known to the court by offer or was apparent from the context within which questions were asked.

Once the court makes a definitive ruling on the record admitting or excluding evidence, either at or before trial, a party need not renew an objection or offer of proof to preserve a claim of error for appeal.

(b) Record of Offer and Ruling.　The court may add any other or further statement which shows the character of the evidence, the form in which it was offered, the objection made, and the ruling thereon. It may direct the making of an offer in question and answer form.

(c) Hearing of Jury.　In jury cases, proceedings shall be conducted, to the extent practicable, so as to prevent inadmissible evidence from being suggested to the jury by any means, such as making statements or offers of proof or asking questions in the hearing of the jury.

(d) Plain Error.　Nothing in this rule precludes taking notice of plain errors affecting substantial rights although they were not brought to the attention of the court.

[Amended April 17, 2000, effective December 1, 2000.]

RULE 104.　PRELIMINARY QUESTIONS

(a) Questions of Admissibility Generally.　Preliminary questions concerning the qualification of a person to be a witness, the existence of a privilege, or the admissibility of evidence shall be determined by the court, subject to the provisions of subdivision (b). In making its determination it is not bound by the rules of evidence except those with respect to privileges.

(b) Relevancy Conditioned on Fact. When the relevancy of evidence depends upon the fulfillment of a condition of fact, the court shall admit it upon, or subject to, the introduction of evidence sufficient to support a finding of the fulfillment of the condition.

(c) Hearing of Jury. Hearings on the admissibility of confessions shall in all cases be conducted out of the hearing of the jury. Hearings on other preliminary matters shall be so conducted when the interests of justice require, or when an accused is a witness and so requests.

(d) Testimony by Accused. The accused does not, by testifying upon a preliminary matter, become subject to cross-examination as to other issues in the case.

(e) Weight and Credibility. This rule does not limit the right of a party to introduce before the jury evidence relevant to weight or credibility.

[Amended March 2, 1987, effective October 1, 1987.]

RULE 105. LIMITED ADMISSIBILITY

When evidence which is admissible as to one party or for one purpose but not admissible as to another party or for another purpose is admitted, the court, upon request, shall restrict the evidence to its proper scope and instruct the jury accordingly.

RULE 106. REMAINDER OF OR RELATED WRITINGS OR RECORDED STATEMENTS

When a writing or recorded statement or part thereof is introduced by a party, an adverse party may require the introduction at that time of any other part or any other writing or recorded statement which ought in fairness to be considered contemporaneously with it.

[Amended March 2, 1987, effective October 1, 1987.]

ARTICLE II. JUDICIAL NOTICE

RULE 201. JUDICIAL NOTICE OF ADJUDICATIVE FACTS

(a) Scope of Rule. This rule governs only judicial notice of adjudicative facts.

(b) Kinds of Facts. A judicially noticed fact must be one not subject to reasonable dispute in that it is either (1) generally known within the territorial jurisdiction of the trial court or (2) capable of accurate and ready determination by resort to sources whose accuracy cannot reasonably be questioned.

(c) When Discretionary. A court may take judicial notice, whether requested or not.

(d) When Mandatory. A court shall take judicial notice if requested by a party and supplied with the necessary information.

(e) Opportunity to Be Heard. A party is entitled upon timely request to an opportunity to be heard as to the propriety of taking judicial notice and the tenor of the matter noticed. In the absence of prior notification, the request may be made after judicial notice has been taken.

(f) Time of Taking Notice. Judicial notice may be taken at any stage of the proceeding.

(g) Instructing Jury. In a civil action or proceeding, the court shall instruct the jury to accept as conclusive any fact judicially noticed. In a criminal case, the court shall instruct the jury that it may, but is not required to, accept as conclusive any fact judicially noticed.

ARTICLE III. PRESUMPTIONS IN CIVIL ACTIONS AND PROCEEDINGS

RULE 301. PRESUMPTIONS IN GENERAL IN CIVIL ACTIONS AND PROCEEDINGS

In all civil actions and proceedings not otherwise provided for by Act of Congress or by these rules, a presumption imposes on the party against whom it is directed the burden of going forward with evidence to rebut or meet the presumption, but does not shift to such party the burden of proof in the sense of the risk of nonpersuasion, which remains throughout the trial upon the party on whom it was originally cast.

RULE 302. APPLICABILITY OF STATE LAW IN CIVIL ACTIONS AND PROCEEDINGS

In civil actions and proceedings, the effect of a presumption respecting a fact which is an element of a claim or defense as to which State law supplies the rule of decision is determined in accordance with State law.

ARTICLE IV. RELEVANCY AND ITS LIMITS

RULE 401. DEFINITION OF "RELEVANT EVIDENCE"

"Relevant evidence" means evidence having any tendency to make the existence of any fact that is of consequence to the determination of the action more probable or less probable than it would be without the evidence.

RULE 402. RELEVANT EVIDENCE GENERALLY ADMISSIBLE; IRRELEVANT EVIDENCE INADMISSIBLE

All relevant evidence is admissible, except as otherwise provided by the Constitution of the United States, by Act of Congress, by these rules, or by other rules prescribed by the Supreme Court pursuant to statutory authority. Evidence which is not relevant is not admissible.

RULE 403. EXCLUSION OF RELEVANT EVIDENCE ON GROUNDS OF PREJUDICE, CONFUSION, OR WASTE OF TIME

Although relevant, evidence may be excluded if its probative value is substantially outweighed by the danger of unfair prejudice, confusion of the issues, or misleading the jury, or by considerations of undue delay, waste of time, or needless presentation of cumulative evidence.

RULE 404. CHARACTER EVIDENCE NOT ADMISSIBLE TO PROVE CONDUCT; EXCEPTIONS; OTHER CRIMES

(a) **Character Evidence Generally.** Evidence of a person's character or a trait of character is not admissible for the purpose of proving action in conformity therewith on a particular occasion, except:

(1) *Character of Accused.* In a criminal case, evidence of a pertinent trait of character offered by an accused, or by the prosecution to rebut the same, or if evidence of a trait of character of the alleged victim of the crime is offered by an accused and admitted under Rule 404(a)(2), evidence of the same trait of character of the accused offered by the prosecution;

(2) *Character of Alleged Victim.* In a criminal case, and subject to the limitations imposed by Rule 412, evidence of a pertinent trait of character of the alleged victim of the crime offered by an accused, or by the prosecution to rebut the same, or evidence of a character trait of peacefulness of the alleged victim offered by the prosecution in a homicide case to rebut evidence that the alleged victim was the first aggressor;

(3) *Character of Witness.* Evidence of the character of a witness, as provided in Rules 607, 608, and 609.

(b) **Other Crimes, Wrongs, or Acts.** Evidence of other crimes, wrongs, or acts is not admissible to prove the character of a person in order to show action in conformity therewith. It may, however, be admissible for other purposes, such as proof of motive, opportunity, intent, preparation, plan, knowledge, identity, or absence of mistake or accident, provided that upon request by the accused, the prosecution in a criminal case shall provide reasonable notice in advance of trial, or during trial if the court excuses pretrial notice on good cause shown, of the general nature of any such evidence it intends to introduce at trial.

[Amended March 2, 1987, effective October 1, 1987; April 30, 1991, effective December 1, 1991; April 17, 2000, effective December 1, 2000; April 12, 2006, effective December 1, 2006.]

RULE 405. METHODS OF PROVING CHARACTER

(a) **Reputation or Opinion.** In all cases in which evidence of character or a trait of character of a person is admissible, proof may be made by testimony as to reputation or by testimony in the form of an opinion. On cross-examination, inquiry is allowable into relevant specific instances of conduct.

(b) **Specific Instances of Conduct.** In cases in which character or a trait of character of a person is an essential element of a charge, claim, or defense, proof may also be made of specific instances of that person's conduct.

[Amended March 2, 1987, effective October 1, 1987.]

RULE 406. HABIT; ROUTINE PRACTICE

Evidence of the habit of a person or of the routine practice of an organization, whether corroborated or not and regardless of the presence of eyewitnesses, is relevant to prove that the conduct of the person or organization on a particular occasion was in conformity with the habit or routine practice.

RULE 407. SUBSEQUENT REMEDIAL MEASURES

When, after an injury or harm allegedly caused by an event, measures are taken that, if taken previously, would have made the injury or harm less likely to occur, evidence of the subsequent measures is not admissible to prove negligence, culpable conduct, a defect in a product, a defect in a product's design, or a need for a warning or instruction. This rule does not require the exclusion of evidence of subsequent measures when offered for another purpose, such as proving ownership, control, or feasibility of precautionary measures, if controverted, or impeachment.

[Amended April 11, 1997, effective December 1, 1997.]

RULE 408. COMPROMISE AND OFFERS TO COMPROMISE

(a) Prohibited Uses. Evidence of the following is not admissible on behalf of any party, when offered to prove liability for, invalidity of, or amount of a claim that was disputed as to validity or amount, or to impeach through a prior inconsistent statement or contradiction:

(1) furnishing or offering or promising to furnish—or accepting or offering or promising to accept—a valuable consideration in compromising or attempting to compromise the claim; and

(2) conduct or statements made in compromise negotiations regarding the claim, except when offered in a criminal case and the negotiations related to a claim by a public office or agency in the exercise of regulatory, investigative, or enforcement authority.

(b) Permitted Uses. This rule does not require exclusion if the evidence is offered for purposes not prohibited by subdivision (a). Examples of permissible purposes include proving a witness's bias or prejudice; negating a contention of undue delay; and proving an effort to obstruct a criminal investigation or prosecution.

[Amended effective December 1, 2006.]

RULE 409. PAYMENT OF MEDICAL AND SIMILAR EXPENSES

Evidence of furnishing or offering or promising to pay medical, hospital, or similar expenses occasioned by an injury is not admissible to prove liability for the injury.

RULE 410. INADMISSIBILITY OF PLEAS, PLEA DISCUSSIONS, AND RELATED STATEMENTS

Except as otherwise provided in this rule, evidence of the following is not, in any civil or criminal proceeding, admissible against the defendant who made the plea or was a participant in the plea discussions:

(1) a plea of guilty which was later withdrawn;

(2) a plea of nolo contendere;

(3) any statement made in the course of any proceedings under Rule 11 of the Federal Rules of Criminal Procedure or comparable state procedure regarding either of the foregoing pleas; or

(4) any statement made in the course of plea discussions with an attorney for the prosecuting authority which do not result in a plea of guilty or which result in a plea of guilty later withdrawn.

However, such a statement is admissible (i) in any proceeding wherein another statement made in the course of the same plea or plea discussions has been introduced and the statement ought in fairness be considered contemporaneously with it, or (ii) in a criminal proceeding for perjury or false statement if the statement was made by the defendant under oath, on the record and in the presence of counsel.

[Amended by Pub.L. 94–149, § 1(9), December 12, 1975, 89 Stat. 805; amended April 30, 1979, effective December 1, 1980 (effective date pursuant to Pub.L. 96–42, July 31, 1979, 93 Stat. 326).]

RULE 411. LIABILITY INSURANCE

Evidence that a person was or was not insured against liability is not admissible upon the issue whether the person acted negligently or otherwise wrongfully. This rule does not require the exclusion of evidence of insurance against liability when offered for another purpose, such as proof of agency, ownership, or control, or bias or prejudice of a witness.

[Amended March 2, 1987, effective October 1, 1987.]

RULE 412. SEX OFFENSE CASES; RELEVANCE OF ALLEGED VICTIM'S PAST SEXUAL BEHAVIOR OR ALLEGED SEXUAL PREDISPOSITION

(a) Evidence Generally Inadmissible. The following evidence is not admissible in any civil or criminal proceeding involving alleged sexual misconduct except as provided in subdivisions (b) and (c):

(1) Evidence offered to prove that any alleged victim engaged in other sexual behavior.

(2) Evidence offered to prove any alleged victim's sexual predisposition.

(b) Exceptions.

(1) In a criminal case, the following evidence is admissible, if otherwise admissible under these rules:

(A) evidence of specific instances of sexual behavior by the alleged victim offered to prove that a person other than the accused was the source of semen, injury or other physical evidence;

(B) evidence of specific instances of sexual behavior by the alleged victim with respect to the person accused of the sexual misconduct offered by the accused to prove consent or by the prosecution; and

(C) evidence the exclusion of which would violate the constitutional rights of the defendant.

(2) In a civil case, evidence offered to prove the sexual behavior or sexual predisposition of any alleged victim is admissible if it is otherwise admissible under these rules and its probative value substantially outweighs the danger of harm to any victim and of unfair prejudice to any party. Evidence of an alleged vic-

tim's reputation is admissible only if it has been placed in controversy by the alleged victim.

(c) Procedure to Determine Admissibility.

(1) A party intending to offer evidence under subdivision (b) must—

(A) file a written motion at least 14 days before trial specifically describing the evidence and stating the purpose for which it is offered unless the court, for good cause, requires a different time for filing or permits filing during trial; and

(B) serve the motion on all parties and notify the alleged victim or, when appropriate, the alleged victim's guardian or representative.

(2) Before admitting evidence under this rule the court must conduct a hearing in camera and afford the victim and parties a right to attend and be heard. The motion, related papers, and the record of the hearing must be sealed and remain under seal unless the court orders otherwise.

[Adopted by Pub.L. 95–540, § 2(a), October 28, 1978, 92 Stat. 2046, applicable to trials that begin more than 30 days after October 28, 1978; amended by Pub.L. 100–690, Title VII, § 7046(a), November 18, 1988, 102 Stat. 4400; amended April 29, 1994, effective December 1, 1994; amended by Pub.L. 103–322, Title IV, § 40141(b), September 13, 1994, 108 Stat. 1919, effective December 1, 1994.]

RULE 413. EVIDENCE OF SIMILAR CRIMES IN SEXUAL ASSAULT CASES

(a) In a criminal case in which the defendant is accused of an offense of sexual assault, evidence of the defendant's commission of another offense or offenses of sexual assault is admissible, and may be considered for its bearing on any matter to which it is relevant.

(b) In a case in which the Government intends to offer evidence under this rule, the attorney for the Government shall disclose the evidence to the defendant, including statements of witnesses or a summary of the substance of any testimony that is expected to be offered, at least fifteen days before the scheduled date of trial or at such later time as the court may allow for good cause.

(c) This rule shall not be construed to limit the admission or consideration of evidence under any other rule.

(d) For purposes of this rule and Rule 415, "offense of sexual assault" means a crime under Federal law or the law of a State (as defined in section 513 of title 18, United States Code) that involved—

(1) any conduct proscribed by chapter 109A of title 18, United States Code;

(2) contact, without consent, between any part of the defendant's body or an object and the genitals or anus of another person;

(3) contact, without consent, between the genitals or anus of the defendant and any part of another person's body;

(4) deriving sexual pleasure or gratification from the infliction of death, bodily injury, or physical pain on another person; or

(5) an attempt or conspiracy to engage in conduct described in paragraphs (1)–(4).

[Adopted by Pub.L. 103–322, Title XXXII, § 320935(a), September 13, 1994, 108 Stat. 2135, applicable to proceedings commenced on or after July 9, 1995, including all trials commenced on or after July 9, 1995 (Pub.L. 103–322, Title XXXII, § 320935(e), September 13, 1994, 108 Stat. 2137, as amended by Pub.L. 104–208, Div. A, Title I, § 101(a) [Title I, § 120], September 30, 1996, 110 Stat. 3009–25).]

RULE 414. EVIDENCE OF SIMILAR CRIMES IN CHILD MOLESTATION CASES

(a) In a criminal case in which the defendant is accused of an offense of child molestation, evidence of the defendant's commission of another offense or offenses of child molestation is admissible, and may be considered for its bearing on any matter to which it is relevant.

(b) In a case in which the Government intends to offer evidence under this rule, the attorney for the Government shall disclose the evidence to the defendant, including statements of witnesses or a summary of the substance of any testimony that is expected to be offered, at least fifteen days before the scheduled date of trial or at such later time as the court may allow for good cause.

(c) This rule shall not be construed to limit the admission or consideration of evidence under any other rule.

(d) For purposes of this rule and Rule 415, "child" means a person below the age of fourteen, and "offense of child molestation" means a crime under Federal law or the law of a State (as defined in section 513 of title 18, United States Code) that involved—

(1) any conduct proscribed by chapter 109A of title 18, United States Code, that was committed in relation to a child;

(2) any conduct proscribed by chapter 110 of title 18, United States Code;

(3) contact between any part of the defendant's body or an object and the genitals or anus of a child;

(4) contact between the genitals or anus of the defendant and any part of the body of a child;

(5) deriving sexual pleasure or gratification from the infliction of death, bodily injury, or physical pain on a child; or

(6) an attempt or conspiracy to engage in conduct described in paragraphs (1)–(5).

[Adopted by Pub.L. 103–322, Title XXXII, § 320935(a), September 13, 1994, 108 Stat. 2135, applicable to proceedings commenced on or after July 9, 1995, including all trials commenced on or after July 9, 1995 (Pub.L. 103–322, Title XXXII, § 320935(e), September 13, 1994, 108 Stat. 2137, as amended by Pub.L. 104–208, Div. A, Title I, § 101(a) [Title I, § 120], September 30, 1996, 110 Stat. 3009–25).]

RULE 415. EVIDENCE OF SIMILAR ACTS IN CIVIL CASES CONCERNING SEXUAL ASSAULT OR CHILD MOLESTATION

(a) In a civil case in which a claim for damages or other relief is predicated on a party's alleged commission of conduct constituting an offense of sexual assault or child molestation, evidence of that party's commission of another offense or offenses of sexual assault or child molestation is admissible and may be considered as provided in Rule 413 and Rule 414 of these rules.

(b) A party who intends to offer evidence under this Rule shall disclose the evidence to the party against whom it will be offered, including statements of witnesses or a summary of the substance of any testimony that is expected to be offered, at least fifteen days before the scheduled date of trial or at such later time as the court may allow for good cause.

(c) This rule shall not be construed to limit the admission or consideration of evidence under any other rule.

[Adopted by Pub.L. 103–322, Title XXXII, § 320935(a), September 13, 1994, 108 Stat. 2135, applicable to proceedings commenced on or after July 9, 1995, including all trials commenced on or after July 9, 1995 (Pub.L. 103–322, Title XXXII, § 320935(e), September 13, 1994, 108 Stat. 2137, as amended by Pub.L. 104–208, Div. A, Title I, § 101(a) [Title I, § 120], September 30, 1996, 110 Stat. 3009–25).]

ARTICLE V. PRIVILEGES

RULE 501. GENERAL RULE

Except as otherwise required by the Constitution of the United States or provided by Act of Congress or in rules prescribed by the Supreme Court pursuant to statutory authority, the privilege of a witness, person, government, State, or political subdivision thereof shall be governed by the principles of the common law as they may be interpreted by the courts of the United States in the light of reason and experience. However, in civil actions and proceedings, with respect to an element of a claim or defense as to which State law supplies the rule of decision, the privilege of a witness, person, government, State, or political subdivision thereof shall be determined in accordance with State law.

RULE 502. ATTORNEY-CLIENT PRIVILEGE AND WORK PRODUCT; LIMITATIONS ON WAIVER

The following provisions apply, in the circumstances set out, to disclosure of a communication or information covered by the attorney-client privilege or work-product protection.

(a) Disclosure Made in a Federal Proceeding or to a Federal Office or Agency; Scope of a Waiver. When the disclosure is made in a Federal proceeding or to a Federal office or agency and waives the attorney-client privilege or work-product protection, the waiver extends to an undisclosed communication or information in a Federal or State proceeding only if:

(1) the waiver is intentional;

(2) the disclosed and undisclosed communications or information concern the same subject matter; and

(3) they ought in fairness to be considered together.

(b) Inadvertent Disclosure. When made in a Federal proceeding or to a Federal office or agency, the disclosure does not operate as a waiver in a Federal or State proceeding if:

(1) the disclosure is inadvertent;

(2) the holder of the privilege or protection took reasonable steps to prevent disclosure; and

(3) the holder promptly took reasonable steps to rectify the error, including (if applicable) following Federal Rule of Civil Procedure 26(b)(5)(B).

(c) Disclosure Made in a State Proceeding. When the disclosure is made in a State proceeding and is not the subject of a State-court order concerning waiver, the disclosure does not operate as a waiver in a Federal proceeding if the disclosure:

(1) would not be a waiver under this rule if it had been made in a Federal proceeding; or

(2) is not a waiver under the law of the State where the disclosure occurred.

(d) Controlling Effect of a Court Order. A Federal court may order that the privilege or protection is not waived by disclosure connected with the litigation pending before the court—in which event the disclosure is also not a waiver in any other Federal or State proceeding.

(e) Controlling Effect of a Party Agreement. An agreement on the effect of disclosure in a Federal proceeding is binding only on the parties to the agreement, unless it is incorporated into a court order.

(f) Controlling Effect of This Rule. Notwithstanding Rules 101 and 1101, this rule applies to State proceedings and to Federal court-annexed and Federal court-mandated arbitration proceedings, in the circumstances set out in the rule. And notwithstanding Rule 501, this rule applies even if State law provides the rule of decision.

(g) Definitions. In this rule:

(1) "attorney-client privilege" means the protection that applicable law provides for confidential attorney-client communications; and

(2) "work-product protection" means the protection that applicable law provides for tangible material (or its intangible equivalent) prepared in anticipation of litigation or for trial.

Effective September 19, 2008.

ARTICLE VI. WITNESSES

RULE 601. GENERAL RULE OF COMPETENCY

Every person is competent to be a witness except as otherwise provided in these rules. However, in civil actions and proceedings, with respect to an element of a claim or defense as to which State law supplies the rule of decision, the competency of a witness shall be determined in accordance with State law.

RULE 602. LACK OF PERSONAL KNOWLEDGE

A witness may not testify to a matter unless evidence is introduced sufficient to support a finding that the witness has personal knowledge of the matter. Evidence to prove personal knowledge may, but need not, consist of the witness' own testimony. This rule is subject to the provisions of rule 703, relating to opinion testimony by expert witnesses.

[Amended March 2, 1987, effective October 1, 1987; April 25, 1988, effective November 1, 1988.]

RULE 603. OATH OR AFFIRMATION

Before testifying, every witness shall be required to declare that the witness will testify truthfully, by oath or affirmation administered in a form calculated to awaken the witness' conscience and impress the witness' mind with the duty to do so.

[Amended March 2, 1987, effective October 1, 1987.]

RULE 604. INTERPRETERS

An interpreter is subject to the provisions of these rules relating to qualification as an expert and the administration of an oath or affirmation to make a true translation.

[Amended March 2, 1987, effective October 1, 1987.]

RULE 605. COMPETENCY OF JUDGE AS WITNESS

The judge presiding at the trial may not testify in that trial as a witness. No objection need be made in order to preserve the point.

RULE 606. COMPETENCY OF JUROR AS WITNESS

(a) At the Trial. A member of the jury may not testify as a witness before that jury in the trial of the case in which the juror is sitting. If the juror is called so to testify, the opposing party shall be afforded an opportunity to object out of the presence of the jury.

(b) Inquiry Into Validity of Verdict or Indictment. Upon an inquiry into the validity of a verdict or indictment, a juror may not testify as to any matter or statement occurring during the course of the jury's deliberations or to the effect of anything upon that or any other juror's mind or emotions as influencing the juror to assent to or dissent from the verdict or indictment or concerning the juror's mental processes in connection therewith. But a juror may testify about (1) whether extraneous prejudicial information was improperly brought to the jury's attention, (2) whether any outside influence was improperly brought to bear upon any juror, or (3) whether there was a mistake in entering the verdict onto the verdict form. A juror's affidavit or evidence of any statement by the juror may not be received on a matter about which the juror would be precluded from testifying.

[Amended by Pub.L. 94–149, § 1(10), December 12, 1975, 89 Stat. 805; amended March 2, 1987, effective October 1, 1987; April 12, 2006, effective December 1, 2006.]

RULE 607. WHO MAY IMPEACH

The credibility of a witness may be attacked by any party, including the party calling the witness.

[Amended March 2, 1987, effective October 1, 1987.]

RULE 608. EVIDENCE OF CHARACTER AND CONDUCT OF WITNESS

(a) Opinion and Reputation Evidence of Character. The credibility of a witness may be attacked or supported by evidence in the form of opinion or reputation, but subject to these limitations: (1) the evidence may refer only to character for truthfulness or untruthfulness, and (2) evidence of truthful character is admissible only after the character of the witness for truthfulness has been attacked by opinion or reputation evidence or otherwise.

(b) Specific Instances of Conduct. Specific instances of the conduct of a witness, for the purpose of attacking or supporting the witness' character for truthfulness, other than conviction of crime as provided in rule 609, may not be proved by extrinsic evidence. They may, however, in the discretion of the court, if probative of truthfulness or untruthfulness, be inquired into on cross-examination of the witness (1) concerning the witness' character for truthfulness or untruthfulness, or (2) concerning the character for truthfulness or untruthfulness of another witness as to which character the witness being cross-examined has testified.

The giving of testimony, whether by an accused or by any other witness, does not operate as a waiver of the accused's or the witness' privilege against self-incrimination when examined with respect to matters that relate only to character for truthfulness.

[Amended March 2, 1987, effective October 1, 1987; April 25, 1988, effective November 1, 1988; March 27, 2003, effective December 1, 2003.]

RULE 609. IMPEACHMENT BY EVIDENCE OF CONVICTION OF CRIME

(a) General Rule. For the purpose of attacking the character for truthfulness of a witness,

(1) evidence that a witness other than an accused has been convicted of a crime shall be admitted, subject to Rule 403, if the crime was punishable by death or imprisonment in excess of one year under the law under which the witness was convicted, and evidence that an accused has been convicted of such a crime shall be admitted if the court determines that the probative value of admitting this evidence outweighs its prejudicial effect to the accused; and

(2) evidence that any witness has been convicted of a crime shall be admitted regardless of the punishment, if it readily can be determined that establishing the elements of the crime required proof or admission of an act of dishonesty or false statement by the witness.

(b) Time Limit. Evidence of a conviction under this rule is not admissible if a period of more than ten years has elapsed since the date of the conviction or of the release of the witness from the confinement imposed for that conviction, whichever is the later date, unless the court determines, in the interests of justice, that the probative value of the conviction supported by specific facts and circumstances substantially outweighs its prejudicial effect. However, evidence of a conviction more than 10 years old as calculated herein, is not admissible unless the proponent gives to the adverse party sufficient advance written notice of intent to use such evidence to provide the adverse party with a fair opportunity to contest the use of such evidence.

(c) Effect of Pardon, Annulment, or Certificate of Rehabilitation. Evidence of a conviction is not admissible under this rule if (1) the conviction has been the subject of a pardon, annulment, certificate of rehabilitation, or other equivalent procedure based on a finding of the rehabilitation of the person convicted, and that person has not been convicted of a subsequent crime that was punishable by death or imprisonment in excess of one year, or (2) the conviction has been the subject of a pardon, annulment, or other equivalent procedure based on a finding of innocence.

(d) Juvenile Adjudications. Evidence of juvenile adjudications is generally not admissible under this rule. The court may, however, in a criminal case allow evidence of a juvenile adjudication of a witness other than the accused if conviction of the offense would be admissible to attack the credibility of an adult and the court is satisfied that admission in evidence is necessary for a fair determination of the issue of guilt or innocence.

(e) Pendency of Appeal. The pendency of an appeal therefrom does not render evidence of a conviction inadmissible. Evidence of the pendency of an appeal is admissible.

[Amended March 2, 1987, effective October 1, 1987; January 26, 1990, effective December 1, 1990; April 12, 2006, effective December 1, 2006.]

RULE 610. RELIGIOUS BELIEFS OR OPINIONS

Evidence of the beliefs or opinions of a witness on matters of religion is not admissible for the purpose of showing that by reason of their nature the witness' credibility is impaired or enhanced.

[Amended March 2, 1987, effective October 1, 1987.]

RULE 611. MODE AND ORDER OF INTERROGATION AND PRESENTATION

(a) Control by Court. The court shall exercise reasonable control over the mode and order of interrogating witnesses and presenting evidence so as to (1) make the interrogation and presentation effective for the ascertainment of the truth, (2) avoid needless consumption of time, and (3) protect witnesses from harassment or undue embarrassment.

(b) Scope of Cross-Examination. Cross-examination should be limited to the subject matter of the direct examination and matters affecting the credibility of the witness. The court may, in the exercise of discretion, permit inquiry into additional matters as if on direct examination.

(c) Leading Questions. Leading questions should not be used on the direct examination of a witness except as may be necessary to develop the witness' testimony. Ordinarily leading questions should be permitted on cross-examination. When a party calls a hostile witness, an adverse party, or a witness identified with an adverse party, interrogation may be by leading questions.

[Amended March 2, 1987, effective October 1, 1987.]

RULE 612. WRITING USED TO REFRESH MEMORY

Except as otherwise provided in criminal proceedings by section 3500 of title 18, United States Code, if a witness uses a writing to refresh memory for the purpose of testifying, either—

(1) while testifying, or

(2) before testifying, if the court in its discretion determines it is necessary in the interests of justice,

an adverse party is entitled to have the writing produced at the hearing, to inspect it, to cross-examine the witness thereon, and to introduce in evidence those portions which relate to the testimony of the witness. If it is claimed that the writing contains matters not related to the subject matter of the testimony the court shall examine the writing in camera, excise any portions not so related, and order delivery of the remainder to the party entitled thereto. Any portion withheld over objections shall be preserved and made available to the appellate court in the event of an appeal. If a writing is not produced or delivered pursuant to order under this rule, the court shall make any order justice requires, except that in criminal cases when the prosecution elects not to comply, the order shall be one striking the testimony or, if the court in its discretion determines that the interests of justice so require, declaring a mistrial.

[Amended March 2, 1987, effective October 1, 1987.]

RULE 613. PRIOR STATEMENTS OF WITNESSES

(a) **Examining Witness Concerning Prior Statement.** In examining a witness concerning a prior statement made by the witness, whether written or not, the statement need not be shown nor its contents disclosed to the witness at that time, but on request the same shall be shown or disclosed to opposing counsel.

(b) **Extrinsic Evidence of Prior Inconsistent Statement of Witness.** Extrinsic evidence of a prior inconsistent statement by a witness is not admissible unless the witness is afforded an opportunity to explain or deny the same and the opposite party is afforded an opportunity to interrogate the witness thereon, or the interests of justice otherwise require. This provision does not apply to admissions of a party-opponent as defined in rule 801(d)(2).

[Amended March 2, 1987, effective October 1, 1987; April 25, 1988, effective November 1, 1988.]

RULE 614. CALLING AND INTERROGATION OF WITNESSES BY COURT

(a) **Calling by Court.** The court may, on its own motion or at the suggestion of a party, call witnesses, and all parties are entitled to cross-examine witnesses thus called.

(b) **Interrogation by Court.** The court may interrogate witnesses, whether called by itself or by a party.

(c) **Objections.** Objections to the calling of witnesses by the court or to interrogation by it may be made at the time or at the next available opportunity when the jury is not present.

RULE 615. EXCLUSION OF WITNESSES

At the request of a party the court shall order witnesses excluded so that they cannot hear the testimony of other witnesses, and it may make the order of its own motion. This rule does not authorize exclusion of (1) a party who is a natural person, or (2) an officer or employee of a party which is not a natural person designated as its representative by its attorney, or (3) a person whose presence is shown by a party to be essential to the presentation of the party's cause, or (4) a person authorized by statute to be present.

[Amended March 2, 1987, effective October 1, 1987; April 25, 1988, effective November 1, 1988; amended by Pub.L. 100–690, Title VII, § 7075(a), November 18, 1988, 102 Stat. 4405 (although amendment by Pub.L. 100–690 could not be executed due to prior amendment by Court order which made the same change effective November 1, 1988); amended April 24, 1998, effective December 1, 1998.]

ARTICLE VII. OPINIONS AND EXPERT TESTIMONY

RULE 701. OPINION TESTIMONY BY LAY WITNESSES

If the witness is not testifying as an expert, the witness' testimony in the form of opinions or inferences is limited to those opinions or inferences which are (a) rationally based on the perception of the witness, (b) helpful to a clear understanding of the witness' testimony or the determination of a fact in issue, and (c) not based on scientific, technical, or other specialized knowledge within the scope of Rule 702.

[Amended March 2, 1987, effective October 1, 1987; April 17, 2000, effective December 1, 2000.]

RULE 702. TESTIMONY BY EXPERTS

If scientific, technical, or other specialized knowledge will assist the trier of fact to understand the evidence or to determine a fact in issue, a witness qualified as an expert by knowledge, skill, experience, training, or education, may testify thereto in the form of an opinion or otherwise, if (1) the testimony is based upon sufficient facts or data, (2) the testimony is the product of reliable principles and methods, and (3) the witness has applied the principles and methods reliably to the facts of the case.

[Amended April 17, 2000, effective December 1, 2000.]

RULE 703. BASES OF OPINION TESTIMONY BY EXPERTS

The facts or data in the particular case upon which an expert bases an opinion or inference may be those perceived by or made known to the expert at or before the hearing. If of a type reasonably relied upon by experts in the particular field in forming opinions or inferences upon the subject, the facts or data need not be admissible in evidence in order for the opinion or inference to be admitted. Facts or data that are otherwise inadmissible shall not be disclosed to the jury by the proponent of the opinion or inference unless the court determines that their probative value in assisting the jury to evaluate the expert's opinion substantially outweighs their prejudicial effect.

[Amended March 2, 1987, effective October 1, 1987; April 17, 2000, effective December 1, 2000.]

RULE 704. OPINION ON ULTIMATE ISSUE

(a) Except as provided in subdivision (b), testimony in the form of an opinion or inference otherwise admissible is not objectionable because it embraces an ultimate issue to be decided by the trier of fact.

(b) No expert witness testifying with respect to the mental state or condition of a defendant in a criminal case may state an opinion or inference as to whether the defendant did or did not have the mental state or condition constituting an element of the crime charged or of a defense thereto. Such ultimate issues are matters for the trier of fact alone.

[Amended by Pub.L. 98–473, Title II, § 406, October 12, 1984, 98 Stat. 2067.]

RULE 705. DISCLOSURE OF FACTS OR DATA UNDERLYING EXPERT OPINION

The expert may testify in terms of opinion or inference and give reasons therefor without first testifying to the underlying facts or data, unless the court requires otherwise. The expert may in any event be required to disclose the underlying facts or data on cross-examination.

[Amended March 2, 1987, effective October 1, 1987; April 22, 1993, effective December 1, 1993.]

RULE 706. COURT APPOINTED EXPERTS

(a) Appointment. The court may on its own motion or on the motion of any party enter an order to show cause why expert witnesses should not be appointed, and may request the parties to submit nominations. The court may appoint any expert witnesses agreed upon by the parties, and may appoint expert witnesses of its own selection. An expert witness shall not be appointed by the court unless the witness consents to act. A witness so appointed shall be informed of the witness' duties by the court in writing, a copy of which shall be filed with the clerk, or at a conference in which the parties shall have opportunity to participate. A witness so appointed shall advise the parties of the witness' findings, if any; the witness' deposition may be taken by any party; and the witness may be called to testify by the court or any party. The witness shall be subject to cross-examination by each party, including a party calling the witness.

(b) Compensation. Expert witnesses so appointed are entitled to reasonable compensation in whatever sum the court may allow. The compensation thus fixed is payable from funds which may be provided by law in criminal cases and civil actions and proceedings involving just compensation under the fifth amendment. In other civil actions and proceedings the compensation shall be paid by the parties in such proportion and at such time as the court directs, and thereafter charged in like manner as other costs.

(c) Disclosure of Appointment. In the exercise of its discretion, the court may authorize disclosure to the jury of the fact that the court appointed the expert witness.

(d) Parties' Experts of Own Selection. Nothing in this rule limits the parties in calling expert witnesses of their own selection.

[Amended March 2, 1987, effective October 1, 1987.]

ARTICLE VIII. HEARSAY

RULE 801. DEFINITIONS

The following definitions apply under this article:

(a) Statement. A "statement" is (1) an oral or written assertion or (2) nonverbal conduct of a person, if it is intended by the person as an assertion.

(b) Declarant. A "declarant" is a person who makes a statement.

(c) Hearsay. "Hearsay" is a statement, other than one made by the declarant while testifying at the trial or hearing, offered in evidence to prove the truth of the matter asserted.

(d) Statements Which Are Not Hearsay. A statement is not hearsay if—

(1) *Prior Statement by Witness.* The declarant testifies at the trial or hearing and is subject to cross-examination concerning the statement, and the statement is (A) inconsistent with the declarant's testimony, and was given under oath subject to the penalty of perjury at a trial, hearing, or other proceeding, or in a deposition, or (B) consistent with the declarant's testimony and is offered to rebut an express or implied charge against the declarant of recent fabrication or improper influence or motive, or (C) one of identification of a person made after perceiving the person; or

(2) *Admission by Party-Opponent.* The statement is offered against a party and is (A) the party's own statement, in either an individual or a representative capacity or (B) a statement of which the party has manifested an adoption or belief in its truth, or (C) a statement by a person authorized by the party to make a statement concerning the subject, or (D) a statement by the party's agent or servant concerning a matter within the scope of the agency or employment, made during the existence of the relationship, or (E) a statement by a coconspirator of a party during the course and in furtherance of the conspiracy. The contents of the statement shall be considered but are not alone sufficient to establish the declarant's authority under subdivision (C), the agency or employment relationship and scope thereof under subdivision (D), or the existence of the conspiracy and the participation therein of the declarant and the party against whom the statement is offered under subdivision (E).

[Amended by Pub.L. 94–113, § 1, October 16, 1975, 89 Stat. 576; amended March 2, 1987, effective October 1, 1987; April 11, 1997, effective December 1, 1997.]

RULE 802. HEARSAY RULE

Hearsay is not admissible except as provided by these rules or by other rules prescribed by the Supreme Court pursuant to statutory authority or by Act of Congress.

RULE 803. HEARSAY EXCEPTIONS; AVAILABILITY OF DECLARANT IMMATERIAL

The following are not excluded by the hearsay rule, even though the declarant is available as a witness:

(1) Present Sense Impression. A statement describing or explaining an event or condition made while the declarant was perceiving the event or condition, or immediately thereafter.

(2) Excited Utterance. A statement relating to a startling event or condition made while the declarant was under the stress of excitement caused by the event or condition.

(3) Then Existing Mental, Emotional, or Physical Condition. A statement of the declarant's then existing state of mind, emotion, sensation, or physical condition (such as intent, plan, motive, design, mental feeling, pain, and bodily health), but not including a statement of memory or belief to prove the fact remembered or believed unless it relates to the execution, revocation, identification, or terms of declarant's will.

(4) Statements for Purposes of Medical Diagnosis or Treatment. Statements made for purposes of medical diagnosis or treatment and describing medical history, or past or present symptoms, pain, or sensations, or the inception or general character of the cause or external source thereof insofar as reasonably pertinent to diagnosis or treatment.

(5) Recorded Recollection. A memorandum or record concerning a matter about which a witness once had knowledge but now has insufficient recollection to enable the witness to testify fully and accurately, shown to have been made or adopted by the witness when the matter was fresh in the witness' memory and to reflect that knowledge correctly. If admitted, the memorandum or record may be read into evidence but may not itself be received as an exhibit unless offered by an adverse party.

(6) Records of Regularly Conducted Activity. A memorandum, report, record, or data compilation, in any form, of acts, events, conditions, opinions, or diagnoses, made at or near the time by, or from information transmitted by, a person with knowledge, if kept in the course of a regularly conducted business activity, and if it was the regular practice of that business activity to make the memorandum, report, record, or data compilation, all as shown by the testimony of the custodian or other qualified witness, or by certification that complies with Rule 902(11), Rule 902(12), or a statute permitting certification, unless the source of information or the method or circumstances of preparation indicate lack of trustworthiness. The term "business" as used in this paragraph includes business, institution, association, profession, occupation, and calling of every kind, whether or not conducted for profit.

(7) Absence of Entry in Records Kept in Accordance With the Provisions of Paragraph (6). Evidence that a matter is not included in the memoranda reports, records, or data compilations, in any form, kept in accordance with the provisions of paragraph (6), to prove the nonoccurrence or nonexistence of the matter, if the matter was of a kind of which a memorandum, report, record, or data compilation was regularly made and preserved, unless the sources of information or other circumstances indicate lack of trustworthiness.

(8) Public Records and Reports. Records, reports, statements, or data compilations, in any form, of public offices or agencies, setting forth (A) the activities of the office or agency, or (B) matters observed pursuant to duty imposed by law as to which matters there was a duty to report, excluding, however, in criminal cases matters observed by police officers and other law enforcement personnel, or (C) in civil actions and proceedings and against the Government in criminal cases, factual findings resulting from an investigation made pursuant to authority granted by law, unless the sources of information or other circumstances indicate lack of trustworthiness.

(9) Records of Vital Statistics. Records or data compilations, in any form, of births, fetal deaths, deaths, or marriages, if the report thereof was made to a public office pursuant to requirements of law.

(10) Absence of Public Record or Entry. To prove the absence of a record, report, statement, or data compilation, in any form, or the nonoccurrence or nonexistence of a matter of which a record, report, statement, or data compilation, in any form, was regularly made and preserved by a public office or agency, evidence in the form of a certification in accordance with rule 902, or testimony, that diligent search failed to disclose the record, report, statement, or data compilation, or entry.

(11) Records of Religious Organizations. Statements of births, marriages, divorces, deaths, legitimacy, ancestry, relationship by blood or marriage, or other similar facts of personal or family history, contained in a regularly kept record of a religious organization.

(12) Marriage, Baptismal, and Similar Certificates. Statements of fact contained in a certificate that the maker performed a marriage or other ceremony or administered a sacrament, made by a clergyman, public official, or other person authorized by the rules or practices of a religious organization or by law to perform the act certified, and purporting to have been issued at the time of the act or within a reasonable time thereafter.

(13) Family Records. Statements of fact concerning personal or family history contained in family Bibles, genealogies, charts, engravings on rings, inscriptions on family portraits, engravings on urns, crypts, or tombstones, or the like.

(14) Records of Documents Affecting an Interest in Property. The record of a document purporting to establish or affect an interest in property, as proof of the content of the original recorded document and its execution and delivery by each person by whom it purports to have been executed, if the record is a record of a public office and an applicable statute authorizes the recording of documents of that kind in that office.

(15) Statements in Documents Affecting an Interest in Property. A statement contained in a document purporting to establish or affect an interest in property if the matter stated was relevant to the purpose of the document, unless dealings with the property since the document was made have been inconsistent with the truth of the statement or the purport of the document.

(16) Statements in Ancient Documents. Statements in a document in existence twenty years or more the authenticity of which is established.

(17) Market Reports, Commercial Publications. Market quotations, tabulations, lists, directories, or other published compilations, generally used and relied upon by the public or by persons in particular occupations.

(18) Learned Treatises. To the extent called to the attention of an expert witness upon cross-examination or relied upon by the expert witness in direct examination, statements contained in published treatises, periodicals, or pamphlets on a subject of history, medicine, or other science or art, established as a reliable authority by the testimony or admission of the witness or by other expert testimony or by judicial notice. If admitted, the statements may be read into evidence but may not be received as exhibits.

(19) Reputation Concerning Personal or Family History. Reputation among members of a person's family by blood, adoption, or marriage, or among a person's associates, or in the community, concerning a person's birth, adoption, marriage, divorce, death, legitimacy, relationship by blood, adoption, or marriage, ancestry, or other similar fact of personal or family history.

(20) Reputation Concerning Boundaries or General History. Reputation in a community, arising before the controversy, as to boundaries of or customs affecting lands in the community, and reputation as to events of general history important to the community or State or nation in which located.

(21) Reputation as to Character. Reputation of a person's character among associates or in the community.

(22) Judgment of Previous Conviction. Evidence of a final judgment, entered after a trial or upon a plea of guilty (but not upon a plea of nolo contendere), adjudging a person guilty of a crime punishable by death or imprisonment in excess of one year, to prove any fact essential to sustain the judgment, but not including, when offered by the Government in a criminal prosecution for purposes other than impeachment, judgments against persons other than the accused. The pendency of an appeal may be shown but does not affect admissibility.

(23) Judgment as to Personal, Family, or General History, or Boundaries. Judgments as proof of matters of personal, family or general history, or boundaries, essential to the judgment, if the same would be provable by evidence of reputation.

(24) [Transferred to Rule 807.]

[Amended by Pub.L. 94–149, § 1(11), December 12, 1975, 89 Stat. 805; amended March 2, 1987, effective October 1, 1987; April 11, 1997, effective December 1, 1997; April 17, 2000, effective December 1, 2000.]

RULE 804. HEARSAY EXCEPTIONS; DECLARANT UNAVAILABLE

(a) Definition of Unavailability. "Unavailability as a witness" includes situations in which the declarant—

(1) is exempted by ruling of the court on the ground of privilege from testifying concerning the subject matter of the declarant's statement; or

(2) persists in refusing to testify concerning the subject matter of the declarant's statement despite an order of the court to do so; or

(3) testifies to a lack of memory of the subject matter of the declarant's statement; or

(4) is unable to be present or to testify at the hearing because of death or then existing physical or mental illness or infirmity; or

(5) is absent from the hearing and the proponent of a statement has been unable to procure the declarant's attendance (or in the case of a hearsay exception under subdivision (b)(2), (3), or (4), the declarant's attendance or testimony) by process or other reasonable means.

A declarant is not unavailable as a witness if exemption, refusal, claim of lack of memory, inability, or absence is due to the procurement or wrongdoing of the proponent of a statement for the purpose of preventing the witness from attending or testifying.

(b) Hearsay Exceptions. The following are not excluded by the hearsay rule if the declarant is unavailable as a witness:

(1) *Former Testimony.* Testimony given as a witness at another hearing of the same or a different proceeding, or in a deposition taken in compliance with law in the course of the same or another proceeding, if the party against whom the testimony is now offered, or, in a civil action or proceeding, a predecessor in interest, had an opportunity and similar motive to develop the testimony by direct, cross, or redirect examination.

(2) *Statement Under Belief of Impending Death.* In a prosecution for homicide or in a civil action or proceeding, a statement made by a declarant while believing that the declarant's death was imminent, concerning the cause or circumstances of what the declarant believed to be impending death.

(3) *Statement Against Interest.* A statement which was at the time of its making so far contrary to the declarant's pecuniary or proprietary interest, or so far tended to subject the declarant to civil or criminal liability, or to render invalid a claim by the declarant against another, that a reasonable person in the declarant's position would not have made the statement unless believing it to be true. A statement tending to expose the declarant to criminal liability and offered to exculpate the accused is not admissible unless corroborating circumstances clearly indicate the trustworthiness of the statement.

(4) *Statement of Personal or Family History.*

(A) A statement concerning the declarant's own birth, adoption, marriage, divorce, legitimacy, relationship by blood, adoption, or marriage, ancestry, or other similar fact of personal or family history, even though declarant had no means of acquiring personal knowledge of the matter stated; or

(B) a statement concerning the foregoing matters, and death also, of another person, if the declarant was related to the other by blood, adoption, or marriage or was so intimately associated with the other's family as to be likely to have accurate information concerning the matter declared.

(5) *[Transferred to Rule 807.]*

(6) *Forfeiture by Wrongdoing.* A statement offered against a party that has engaged or acquiesced in wrongdoing that was intended to, and did, procure the unavailability of the declarant as a witness.

[Amended by Pub.L. 94–149, § 1(12) and (13), December 12, 1975, 89 Stat. 806; amended March 2, 1987, effective October 1, 1987; amended by Pub.L. 100–690, Title VII, § 7075(b), November 18, 1988, 102 Stat. 4405; amended April 11, 1997, effective December 1, 1997.]

RULE 805. HEARSAY WITHIN HEARSAY

Hearsay included within hearsay is not excluded under the hearsay rule if each part of the combined statements conforms with an exception to the hearsay rule provided in these rules.

RULE 806. ATTACKING AND SUPPORTING CREDIBILITY OF DECLARANT

When a hearsay statement, or a statement defined in Rule 801(d)(2)(C), (D), or (E), has been admitted in evidence, the credibility of the declarant may be attacked, and if attacked may be supported, by any evidence which would be admissible for those purposes if declarant had testified as a witness. Evidence of a statement or conduct by the declarant at any time, inconsistent with the declarant's hearsay statement, is not subject to any requirement that the declarant may have been afforded an opportunity to deny or explain. If the party against whom a hearsay statement has been admitted calls the declarant as a witness, the party is entitled to examine the declarant on the statement as if under cross-examination.

[Amended March 2, 1987, effective October 1, 1987; April 11, 1997, effective December 1, 1997.]

RULE 807. RESIDUAL EXCEPTION

A statement not specifically covered by Rule 803 or 804 but having equivalent circumstantial guarantees of trustworthiness, is not excluded by the hearsay rule, if the court determines that (A) the statement is offered as evidence of a material fact; (B) the statement is more probative on the point for which it is offered than any other evidence which the proponent can procure through reasonable efforts; and (C) the general purposes of these rules and the interests of justice will best be served by admission of the statement into evidence. However, a statement may not be admitted under this exception unless the proponent of it makes known to the adverse party sufficiently in advance of the trial or hearing to provide the adverse party with a fair opportunity to prepare to meet it, the proponent's intention to offer the statement and the particulars of it, including the name and address of the declarant.

[Adopted April 11, 1997, effective December 1, 1997.]

ARTICLE IX. AUTHENTICATION AND IDENTIFICATION

RULE 901. REQUIREMENT OF AUTHENTICATION OR IDENTIFICATION

(a) **General Provision.** The requirement of authentication or identification as a condition precedent to admissibility is satisfied by evidence sufficient to support a finding that the matter in question is what its proponent claims.

(b) **Illustrations.** By way of illustration only, and not by way of limitation, the following are examples of authentication or identification conforming with the requirements of this rule:

(1) *Testimony of Witness With Knowledge.* Testimony that a matter is what it is claimed to be.

(2) *Nonexpert Opinion on Handwriting.* Nonexpert opinion as to the genuineness of handwriting, based upon familiarity not acquired for purposes of the litigation.

(3) *Comparison by Trier or Expert Witness.* Comparison by the trier of fact or by expert witnesses with specimens which have been authenticated.

(4) *Distinctive Characteristics and the Like.* Appearance, contents, substance, internal patterns, or other distinctive characteristics, taken in conjunction with circumstances.

(5) *Voice Identification.* Identification of a voice, whether heard firsthand or through mechanical or electronic transmission or recording, by opinion based upon hearing the voice at any time under circumstances connecting it with the alleged speaker.

(6) *Telephone Conversations.* Telephone conversations, by evidence that a call was made to the number assigned at the time by the telephone company to a particular person or business, if (A) in the case of a person, circumstances, including self-identification, show the person answering to be the one called, or (B) in the case of a business, the call was made to a place of business and the conversation related to business reasonably transacted over the telephone.

(7) *Public Records or Reports.* Evidence that a writing authorized by law to be recorded or filed and in fact recorded or filed in a public office, or a purported public record, report, statement, or data compilation, in any form, is from the public office where items of this nature are kept.

(8) *Ancient Documents or Data Compilation.* Evidence that a document or data compilation, in any form, (A) is in such condition as to create no suspicion concerning its authenticity, (B) was in a place where it, if authentic, would likely be, and (C) has been in existence 20 years or more at the time it is offered.

(9) *Process or System.* Evidence describing a process or system used to produce a result and showing that the process or system produces an accurate result.

(10) *Methods Provided by Statute or Rule.* Any method of authentication or identification provided by Act of Congress or by other rules prescribed by the Supreme Court pursuant to statutory authority.

RULE 902. SELF–AUTHENTICATION

Extrinsic evidence of authenticity as a condition precedent to admissibility is not required with respect to the following:

(1) **Domestic Public Documents Under Seal.** A document bearing a seal purporting to be that of the United States, or of any State, district, Commonwealth, territory, or insular possession thereof, or the Panama Canal Zone, or the Trust Territory of the Pacific Islands, or of a political subdivision, department, officer, or agency thereof, and a signature purporting to be an attestation or execution.

(2) **Domestic Public Documents Not Under Seal.** A document purporting to bear the signature in the official capacity of an officer or employee of any entity

included in paragraph (1) hereof, having no seal, if a public officer having a seal and having official duties in the district or political subdivision of the officer or employee certifies under seal that the signer has the official capacity and that the signature is genuine.

(3) Foreign Public Documents. A document purporting to be executed or attested in an official capacity by a person authorized by the laws of a foreign country to make the execution or attestation, and accompanied by a final certification as to the genuineness of the signature and official position (A) of the executing or attesting person, or (B) of any foreign official whose certificate of genuineness of signature and official position relates to the execution or attestation or is in a chain of certificates of genuineness of signature and official position relating to the execution or attestation. A final certification may be made by a secretary of an embassy or legation, consul general, consul, vice consul, or consular agent of the United States, or a diplomatic or consular official of the foreign country assigned or accredited to the United States. If reasonable opportunity has been given to all parties to investigate the authenticity and accuracy of official documents, the court may, for good cause shown, order that they be treated as presumptively authentic without final certification or permit them to be evidenced by an attested summary with or without final certification.

(4) Certified Copies of Public Records. A copy of an official record or report or entry therein, or of a document authorized by law to be recorded or filed and actually recorded or filed in a public office, including data compilations in any form, certified as correct by the custodian or other person authorized to make the certification, by certificate complying with paragraph (1), (2), or (3) of this rule or complying with any Act of Congress or rule prescribed by the Supreme Court pursuant to statutory authority.

(5) Official Publications. Books, pamphlets, or other publications purporting to be issued by public authority.

(6) Newspapers and Periodicals. Printed materials purporting to be newspapers or periodicals.

(7) Trade Inscriptions and the Like. Inscriptions, signs, tags, or labels purporting to have been affixed in the course of business and indicating ownership, control, or origin.

(8) Acknowledged Documents. Documents accompanied by a certificate of acknowledgment executed in the manner provided by law by a notary public or other officer authorized by law to take acknowledgments.

(9) Commercial Paper and Related Documents. Commercial paper, signatures thereon, and documents relating thereto to the extent provided by general commercial law.

(10) Presumptions Under Acts of Congress. Any signature, document, or other matter declared by Act of Congress to be presumptively or prima facie genuine or authentic.

(11) Certified Domestic Records of Regularly Conducted Activity. The original or a duplicate of a domestic record of regularly conducted activity that would be admissible under Rule 803(6) if accompanied by a written declaration of its custodian or other qualified person, in a manner complying with any Act of Congress or rule prescribed by the Supreme Court pursuant to statutory authority, certifying that the record—

(A) was made at or near the time of the occurrence of the matters set forth by, or from information transmitted by, a person with knowledge of those matters;

(B) was kept in the course of the regularly conducted activity; and

(C) was made by the regularly conducted activity as a regular practice.

A party intending to offer a record into evidence under this paragraph must provide written notice of that intention to all adverse parties, and must make the record and declaration available for inspection sufficiently in advance of their offer into evidence to provide an adverse party with a fair opportunity to challenge them.

(12) Certified Foreign Records of Regularly Conducted Activity. In a civil case, the original or a duplicate of a foreign record of regularly conducted activity that would be admissible under Rule 803(6) if accompanied by a written declaration by its custodian or other qualified person certifying that the record—

(A) was made at or near the time of the occurrence of the matters set forth by, or from information transmitted by, a person with knowledge of those matters;

(B) was kept in the course of the regularly conducted activity; and

(C) was made by the regularly conducted activity as a regular practice.

The declaration must be signed in a manner that, if falsely made, would subject the maker to criminal penalty under the laws of the country where the declaration is signed. A party intending to offer a record into evidence under this paragraph must provide written notice of that intention to all adverse parties, and must make the record and declaration available for inspection sufficiently in advance of their offer into evidence to provide an adverse party with a fair opportunity to challenge them.

[Amended March 2, 1987, effective October 1, 1987; April 25, 1988, effective November 1, 1988; April 17, 2000, effective December 1, 2000.]

RULE 903. SUBSCRIBING WITNESS' TESTIMONY UNNECESSARY

The testimony of a subscribing witness is not necessary to authenticate a writing unless required by the laws of the jurisdiction whose laws govern the validity of the writing.

ARTICLE X. CONTENTS OF WRITINGS, RECORDINGS, AND PHOTOGRAPHS

RULE 1001. DEFINITIONS

For purposes of this article the following definitions are applicable:

(1) **Writings and Recordings.** "Writings" and "recordings" consist of letters, words, or numbers, or their equivalent, set down by handwriting, typewriting, printing, photostating, photographing, magnetic impulse, mechanical or electronic recording, or other form of data compilation.

(2) **Photographs.** "Photographs" include still photographs, X-ray films, video tapes, and motion pictures.

(3) **Original.** An "original" of a writing or recording is the writing or recording itself or any counterpart intended to have the same effect by a person executing or issuing it. An "original" of a photograph includes the negative or any print therefrom. If data are stored in a computer or similar device, any printout or other output readable by sight, shown to reflect the data accurately, is an "original".

(4) **Duplicate.** A "duplicate" is a counterpart produced by the same impression as the original, or from the same matrix, or by means of photography, including enlargements and miniatures, or by mechanical or electronic re-recording, or by chemical reproduction, or by other equivalent techniques which accurately reproduces the original.

RULE 1002. REQUIREMENT OF ORIGINAL

To prove the content of a writing, recording, or photograph, the original writing, recording, or photograph is required, except as otherwise provided in these rules or by Act of Congress.

RULE 1003. ADMISSIBILITY OF DUPLICATES

A duplicate is admissible to the same extent as an original unless (1) a genuine question is raised as to the authenticity of the original or (2) in the circumstances it would be unfair to admit the duplicate in lieu of the original.

RULE 1004. ADMISSIBILITY OF OTHER EVIDENCE OF CONTENTS

The original is not required, and other evidence of the contents of a writing, recording, or photograph is admissible if—

(1) **Originals Lost or Destroyed.** All originals are lost or have been destroyed, unless the proponent lost or destroyed them in bad faith; or

(2) **Original Not Obtainable.** No original can be obtained by any available judicial process or procedure; or

(3) **Original in Possession of Opponent.** At a time when an original was under the control of the party against whom offered, that party was put on notice, by the pleadings or otherwise, that the contents would be a subject of proof at the hearing, and that party does not produce the original at the hearing; or

(4) **Collateral Matters.** The writing, recording, or photograph is not closely related to a controlling issue.

[Amended March 2, 1987, effective October 1, 1987.]

RULE 1005. PUBLIC RECORDS

The contents of an official record, or of a document authorized to be recorded or filed and actually recorded or filed, including data compilations in any form, if otherwise admissible, may be proved by copy, certified as correct in accordance with rule 902 or testified to be correct by a witness who has compared it with the original. If a copy which complies with the foregoing cannot be obtained by the exercise of reasonable diligence, then other evidence of the contents may be given.

RULE 1006. SUMMARIES

The contents of voluminous writings, recordings, or photographs which cannot conveniently be examined in court may be presented in the form of a chart, summary, or calculation. The originals, or duplicates, shall be made available for examination or copying, or both, by other parties at reasonable time and place. The court may order that they be produced in court.

RULE 1007. TESTIMONY OR WRITTEN ADMISSION OF PARTY

Contents of writings, recordings, or photographs may be proved by the testimony or deposition of the party against whom offered or by that party's written admission, without accounting for the nonproduction of the original.

[Amended March 2, 1987, effective October 1, 1987.]

RULE 1008. FUNCTIONS OF COURT AND JURY

When the admissibility of other evidence of contents of writings, recordings, or photographs under these rules depends upon the fulfillment of a condition of fact, the question whether the condition has been fulfilled is ordinarily for the court to determine in accordance with the provisions of rule 104. However, when an issue is raised (a) whether the asserted writing ever existed, or (b) whether another writing, recording, or photograph produced at the trial is the original, or (c) whether other evidence of contents correctly reflects the contents, the issue is for the trier of fact to determine as in the case of other issues of fact.

ARTICLE XI. MISCELLANEOUS RULES

RULE 1101. APPLICABILITY OF RULES

(a) Courts and Judges. These rules apply to the United States district courts, the District Court of Guam, the District Court of the Virgin Islands, the District Court for the Northern Mariana Islands, the United States courts of appeals, the United States Claims Court, and to United States bankruptcy judges and United States magistrate judges, in the actions, cases, and proceedings and to the extent hereinafter set forth. The terms "judge" and "court" in these rules include United States bankruptcy judges and United States magistrate judges.

(b) Proceedings Generally. These rules apply generally to civil actions and proceedings, including admiralty and maritime cases, to criminal cases and proceedings, to contempt proceedings except those in which the court may act summarily, and to proceedings and cases under title 11, United States Code.

(c) Rule of Privilege. The rule with respect to privileges applies at all stages of all actions, cases, and proceedings.

(d) Rules Inapplicable. The rules (other than with respect to privileges) do not apply in the following situations:

(1) *Preliminary Questions of Fact.* The determination of questions of fact preliminary to admissibility of evidence when the issue is to be determined by the court under rule 104.

(2) *Grand Jury.* Proceedings before grand juries.

(3) *Miscellaneous Proceedings.* Proceedings for extradition or rendition; preliminary examinations in criminal cases; sentencing, or granting or revoking probation; issuance of warrants for arrest, criminal summonses, and search warrants; and proceedings with respect to release on bail or otherwise.

(e) Rules Applicable in Part. In the following proceedings these rules apply to the extent that matters of evidence are not provided for in the statutes which govern procedure therein or in other rules prescribed by the Supreme Court pursuant to statutory authority: the trial of misdemeanors and other petty offenses before United States magistrate judges; review of agency actions when the facts are subject to trial de novo under section 706(2)(F) of title 5, United States Code; review of orders of the Secretary of Agriculture under section 2 of the Act entitled "An Act to authorize association of producers of agricultural products" approved February 18, 1922 (7 U.S.C. 292), and under sections 6 and 7(c) of the Perishable Agricultural Commodities Act, 1930 (7 U.S.C. 499f, 499g(c)); naturalization and revocation of naturalization under sections 310–318 of the Immigration and Nationality Act (8 U.S.C. 1421–1429); prize proceedings in admiralty under sections 7651–7681 of title 10, United States Code; review of orders of the Secretary of the Interior under section 2 of the Act entitled "An Act authorizing associations of producers of aquatic products" approved June 25, 1934 (15 U.S.C. 522); review of orders of petroleum control boards under section 5 of the Act entitled "An Act to regulate interstate and foreign commerce in petroleum and its products by prohibiting the shipment in such commerce of petroleum and its products produced in violation of State law, and for other purposes", approved February 22, 1935 (15 U.S.C. 715d); actions for fines, penalties, or forfeitures under part V of title IV of the Tariff Act of 1930 (19 U.S.C. 1581–1624), or under the Anti-Smuggling Act (19 U.S.C. 1701–1711); criminal libel for condemnation, exclusion of imports, or other proceedings under the Federal Food, Drug, and Cosmetic Act (21 U.S.C. 301–392); disputes between seamen under sections 4079, 4080, and 4081 of the Revised Statutes (22 U.S.C. 256–258); habeas corpus under sections 2241–2254 of title 28, United States Code; motions to vacate, set aside or correct sentence under section 2255 of title 28, United States Code; actions for penalties for refusal to transport destitute seamen under section 4578 of the Revised Statutes (46 U.S.C. 679);* actions against the United States under the Act entitled "An Act authorizing suits against the United States in admiralty for damage caused by and salvage service rendered to public vessels belonging to the United States, and for other purposes", approved March 3, 1925 (46 U.S.C. 781–790), as implemented by section 7730 of title 10, United States Code.

* Law Revision Counsel Note: Repealed and reenacted as 46 U.S.C. 11104(b)-(d) by Pub.L. 98–89, §§ 1, 2(a), 4(b), August 26, 1983, 97 Stat. 500.

[Amended by Pub.L. 94–149, § 1(14), December 12, 1975, 89 Stat. 806; Pub.L. 95–598, Title II, § 251, November 6, 1978, 92 Stat. 2673, effective October 1, 1979; Pub.L. 97–164, Title I, § 142, April 2, 1982, 96 Stat. 45, effective October 1, 1982; amended March 2, 1987, effective October 1, 1987; April 25, 1988, effective November 1, 1988; amended by Pub.L. 100–690, Title VII, § 7075(c)(1), November 18, 1988, 102 Stat. 4405 (although amendment by Pub.L. 100-690 could not be executed due to prior amendment by Court order which made the same change effective November 1, 1988); amended April 22, 1993, effective December 1, 1993.]

RULE 1102. AMENDMENTS

Amendments to the Federal Rules of Evidence may be made as provided in section 2072 of title 28 of the United States Code.

[Amended April 30, 1991, effective December 1, 1991.]

RULE 1103. TITLE

These rules may be known and cited as the Federal Rules of Evidence.

INDEX TO FEDERAL RULES OF EVIDENCE

Absence and absentees,
Accidents, evidence of other crimes or wrongs, **FRE 404**
Hearsay rule, exception, **FRE 804**
Mistakes, evidence of other crimes or wrongs, **FRE 404**
Accidents, absence and absentees, evidence of other crimes or wrongs, **FRE 404**
Actions and proceedings,
Child molestation, relevancy of similar cases, **FRE 415**
Sexual assault, relevancy of similar cases, **FRE 415**
Acts of Congress, self-authentication, **FRE 902**
Admiralty, **FRE 1101**
Amendments, **FRE 1102**
Ancient documents,
Authentication, **FRE 901**
Hearsay rule, exceptions, **FRE 803**
Annulment, conviction of crime, impeachment, **FRE 609**
Appeal and review, conviction of crime, impeachment, pending appeals, **FRE 609**
Application of rules, **FRE 101, 1101**
Arrest warrants, **FRE 1101**
Attorneys, privileges and immunities, **FRE 502**
Authentication, **FRE 901 et seq.**
Bail, **FRE 1101**
Baptismal certificates, hearsay rule, exception, **FRE 803**
Bases of opinions, opinion and expert testimony, **FRE 703**
Best evidence rule, **FRE 1001 et seq.**
Bias and prejudice, exclusion, prejudicial evidence, **FRE 403**
Books and papers, best evidence, **FRE 1001 et seq.**
Boundaries,
Judgments and decrees, hearsay rule, exception, **FRE 803**
Reputation, hearsay rule, exception, **FRE 803**
Burden of proof, presumptions, **FRE 301**
Capital punishment, impeachment, conviction of crime, **FRE 609**
Character and reputation,
Conviction of crime, **FRE 609**
Hearsay rule, exception, **FRE 803**
Methods of proof, **FRE 405**
Relevancy, **FRE 404**
Witnesses, **FRE 404, 608**
Children and minors, molestation, relevancy of similar crimes, **FRE 414, 415**
Citation of rules, **FRE 1102**
Collateral matters, **FRE 1004**
Commercial paper, self-authentication, **FRE 902**
Commercial publications, hearsay rule, exception, **FRE 803**
Compensation and salaries, court-appointed experts, **FRE 706**
Compromise and settlement, relevancy, **FRE 408**
Confessions, admissibility, **FRE 104**
Confusing evidence, exclusion, **FRE 403**
Contempt, **FRE 1101**
Copies,
Admissibility, **FRE 1003**
Public records, self-authentication, **FRE 902**
Credibility,
Conviction of crime, **FRE 609**
Preliminary determinations, **FRE 104**

Crimes and offenses,
Conviction of crime,
Judgments and decrees, hearsay rule, exception, **FRE 803**
Witnesses, credibility, **FRE 609**
Judgments and decrees, conviction of crime, hearsay rule, exceptions, **FRE 803**
Other crimes or wrongs, relevancy, **FRE 404**
Relevancy, other crimes or wrongs, **FRE 404**
Witnesses, conviction of crime, credibility, **FRE 609**
Cross examination, **FRE 611**
Impeachment, conviction of crime, **FRE 609**
Preliminary matters, **FRE 104**
Cumulative evidence, exclusion, **FRE 403**
Death penalty, impeachment, conviction of crime, **FRE 609**
Definitions,
Attorney-client privilege, **FRE 502**
Best evidence, **FRE 1001**
Courts, **FRE 1101**
Hearsay, **FRE 801, 804**
Judges or justices, **FRE 1101**
Relevant evidence, **FRE 401**
Work product protection, **FRE 502**
Disclosure, attorneys, privileges and immunities, **FRE 502**
Dishonesty, impeachment, conviction of crime, **FRE 609**
Domestic public documents, self-authentication, **FRE 902**
Emotional condition then existing, hearsay rule, exception, **FRE 803**
Excited utterances, hearsay rule, exception, **FRE 803**
Exclusion, witnesses, **FRE 615**
Exemptions, impeachment, conviction of crime, **FRE 609**
Extradition, **FRE 1101**
False statements, impeachment, conviction of crime, **FRE 609**
Family history,
Judgments and decrees, hearsay rule, exception, **FRE 803**
Statements, hearsay rule, exception, **FRE 804**
Foreign public documents, self-authentication, **FRE 902**
Forfeiture by wrongdoing, hearsay rule, **FRE 804**
Former testimony, hearsay rule, exception, **FRE 804**
General history,
Judgments and decrees, hearsay rule, exception, **FRE 803**
Reputation, hearsay rule, exceptions, **FRE 803**
Grand jury, application of rules, **FRE 1101**
Habits, relevancy, **FRE 406**
Handwriting, authentication, **FRE 901**
Hearsay, **FRE 801 et seq.**
Admissibility, **FRE 802**
Credibility of declarant, **FRE 806**
Definitions, **FRE 801**
Exceptions,
Declarant availability immaterial, **FRE 803**
Declarant unavailable, **FRE 804**
Hearsay within hearsay, **FRE 805**
Residual exception, **FRE 807**
History,
Judgments and decrees, hearsay rule, exception, **FRE 803**
Reputation, hearsay rule, exception, **FRE 803**

Identity and identification, **FRE 901 et seq.**
    Other crimes or wrongs, **FRE 404**
Impending death, statement made under belief, hearsay rule, exception, **FRE 804**
Indictment and information, validity, jurors as witnesses, **FRE 606**
Instructions,
    Judicial notice, jury, **FRE 201**
    Jury,
        Judicial notice, **FRE 201**
        Limited admissibility, **FRE 105**
    Limited admissibility, jury, **FRE 105**
Insurance, liability insurance, relevancy, **FRE 411**
Intent, evidence of other crimes or wrongs, **FRE 404**
Interpreters, witnesses, **FRE 603**
Judges or justices, competency as witnesses, **FRE 605**
Judgments and decrees, conviction of crime, hearsay rule, exception, **FRE 803**
Judicial notice, **FRE 201**
Jury,
    Competency as witnesses, **FRE 606**
    Instructions,
        Judicial notice, **FRE 201**
        Limited admissibility, **FRE 105**
    Photographs, **FRE 1008**
    Preliminary determinations, **FRE 104**
    Recordings, **FRE 1008**
    Rulings, **FRE 103**
    Writings, **FRE 1008**
Juvenile delinquents and dependents, impeachment, conviction of crime, **FRE 609**
Knowledge, evidence of other crimes or wrongs, **FRE 404**
Leading questions, witnesses, **FRE 611**
Learned treatises, hearsay rule, exception, **FRE 803**
Liability insurance, relevancy, **FRE 411**
Limited admissibility, instructions to jury, **FRE 105**
Lost or destroyed originals, other proof, admissibility, **FRE 1004**
Maritime cases, **FRE 1101**
Market reports, hearsay rule, exception, **FRE 803**
Marriage certificates, hearsay rule, exception, **FRE 803**
Medical care and treatment,
    Payment, relevancy, **FRE 409**
    Statements, hearsay rule, exception, **FRE 803**
Mental condition then existing, hearsay rule, exception, **FRE 803**
Mistakes,
    Absence and absentees, evidence of other crimes or wrongs, **FRE 404**
    Rulings, **FRE 103**
Motive, evidence of other crimes or wrongs, **FRE 404**
Newspapers, self-authentication, **FRE 902**
Notice,
    Crimes or wrongs, **FRE 404**
    Impeachment, conviction of crime, **FRE 609**
Opinions and expert testimony, **FRE 701 et seq.**
    Bases of opinion, **FRE 703**
    Character evidence, **FRE 405**
    Court-appointed experts, **FRE 706**
    Facts or data underlying expert opinion, disclosure, **FRE 705**
    Lay witnesses, **FRE 701**
    Ultimate issues, **FRE 704**
    Witnesses, **FRE 608**
Opportunity, evidence of other crimes or wrongs, **FRE 404**
Original writings, recordings, or photographs, **FRE 1002**
Other crimes or wrongs, relevancy, **FRE 404**

Pardons, impeachment, **FRE 609**
Parties, writings, recordings, or photographs, **FRE 1004, 1007**
Past sexual history or predisposition, sex offenses, victims, relevancy, **FRE 412**
Pending appeals, impeachment, conviction of crime, **FRE 609**
Periodicals, self-authentication, **FRE 902**
Personal history,
    Judgments and decrees, hearsay rule, exception, **FRE 803**
    Statements, hearsay rule, exception, **FRE 804**
Personal knowledge, witnesses, competency, **FRE 602**
Photography and pictures, best evidence, **FRE 1001 et seq.**
Physical condition then existing, hearsay rule, exception, **FRE 803**
Plain errors, **FRE 103**
Plans and specifications, evidence of other crimes or wrongs, **FRE 404**
Pleas, relevancy, **FRE 410**
Prejudice or bias, exclusion, prejudicial evidence, **FRE 403**
Preliminary examination, **FRE 104**
    Facts, **FRE 1101**
Preparation, evidence of other crimes or wrongs, **FRE 404**
Present sense impressions, hearsay rule, exception, **FRE 803**
Presumptions, **FRE 301**
    State laws, **FRE 302**
Previous conviction of crime, hearsay rule, exception, **FRE 803**
Prior conviction, impeachment, conviction of crime, **FRE 609**
Prior inconsistent statements of witnesses, **FRE 613**
Privileges and immunities, **FRE 501**
    Application of rules, **FRE 1101**
    Attorneys, **FRE 502**
    Preliminary determinations, **FRE 104**
Probation, **FRE 1101**
Procurement, witnesses, hearsay rule, exception, **FRE 804**
Property, records and recordation, hearsay rule, exception, **FRE 803**
Purpose of rules, **FRE 102**
Rape shield, victims of crime, past sexual history or predisposition, **FRE 412**
Recorded recollections, hearsay rule, exception, **FRE 803**
Records and recordation,
    Absence of entry, hearsay rule, exception, **FRE 803**
    Authentication, **FRE 901**
    Best evidence, **FRE 1001 et seq.**
    Copies, admissibility, **FRE 1005**
    Extrinsic evidence of contents, **FRE 1005**
    Hearsay rule, exception, **FRE 803**
    Offers of evidence, **FRE 103**
    Self-authentication, **FRE 902**
Refreshing memory, witnesses, writings, **FRE 612**
Regularly conducted activities, records and recordation,
    Hearsay rule, exception, **FRE 803**
    Self-authentication, **FRE 902**
Rehabilitation certificates, conviction of crime, impeachment, **FRE 609**
Related writings, **FRE 106**
Relevancy, **FRE 401 et seq.**
    Admissibility, **FRE 402**
    Character evidence, **FRE 404, 405**
    Compromise and settlement, **FRE 408**
    Conditioned on fact, preliminary determinations, **FRE 104**
    Confusing evidence, **FRE 403**
    Cumulative evidence, **FRE 403**
    Definitions, **FRE 401**

Relevancy—Cont'd
    Habit, **FRE 406**
    Liability insurance, **FRE 411**
    Medical care and treatment, payment, **FRE 409**
    Pleas, **FRE 410**
    Prejudicial evidence, **FRE 403**
    Routine practices, **FRE 406**
    Subsequent remedial measures, **FRE 407**
Religion, impeachment, **FRE 610**
Religious organizations and societies, records and recordation, hearsay rule, exception, **FRE 803**
Remainder of writings, **FRE 106**
Rendition, **FRE 1101**
Reports,
    Authentication, **FRE 901**
    Public reports, hearsay rule, exception, **FRE 803**
Routine, relevancy, **FRE 406**
Rulings, **FRE 103**
Scope of rules, **FRE 101**
Searches and seizures, warrants, **FRE 1101**
Self-authentication, **FRE 902**
Sentence and punishment, application of rules, **FRE 1101**
Settlement and compromise, relevancy, **FRE 408**
Sex offenses, **FRE 412 et seq.**
    Child molestation, similar crimes, **FRE 414**
    Civil cases, similar crimes, **FRE 415**
    Relevancy, **FRE 412 et seq.**
        Child molestation, similar crimes, **FRE 414**
        Civil cases, similar crimes, **FRE 415**
        Similar crimes, **FRE 413 et seq.**
        Victims past sexual behavior or predisposition, **FRE 412**
    Similar crimes, **FRE 413 et seq.**
    Victims past sexual behavior or predisposition, **FRE 412**
Specific instances of conduct,
    Character evidence, **FRE 405**
    Witnesses, **FRE 608**
Statements against interest, hearsay rule, exception, **FRE 804**
Subsequent remedial measures, relevancy, **FRE 407**
Summaries, writings, recordings, or photographs, admissibility, **FRE 1006**
Summons, criminal cases, **FRE 1101**
Telecommunications, authentication, **FRE 901**
Time,
    Conviction of crime, impeachment, **FRE 609**

Time—Cont'd
    Judicial notice, **FRE 201**
Title of rules, **FRE 1102**
Trade inscriptions, self-authentication, **FRE 902**
Ultimate issues, opinion and expert testimony, **FRE 704**
Unobtainable originals, other proof, admissibility, **FRE 1004**
Verdicts, validity, jurors as witnesses, **FRE 606**
Victims of crime,
    Character evidence, **FRE 404**
    Sex offenses, past sexual behavior or predisposition, relevancy, **FRE 412**
Vital statistics, records and recordation, hearsay rule, exception, **FRE 803**
Voices, authentication, **FRE 901**
Waiver, attorneys, privileges and immunities, **FRE 502**
Weight of evidence, preliminary determinations, **FRE 104**
Witnesses,
    Calling by court, **FRE 614**
    Character and reputation, **FRE 404, 608**
    Competency, **FRE 601 et seq.**
        Judges and justices, **FRE 605**
        Jurors, **FRE 606**
        Personal knowledge, **FRE 602**
    Conviction of crime, credibility, **FRE 609**
    Cross examination, **FRE 611**
    Exclusion, **FRE 615**
    Impeachment, **FRE 607 et seq.**
        Character and reputation, **FRE 608**
        Conviction of crime, **FRE 609**
        Religious beliefs or opinions, **FRE 610**
        Specific instances of conduct, **FRE 608**
    Interpreters, **FRE 603**
    Interrogation, **FRE 611, 614**
    Leading questions, **FRE 611**
    Opinions, **FRE 608**
    Presentation, **FRE 611**
    Prior statements, **FRE 613**
    Qualifications, preliminary determinations, **FRE 104**
    Refreshing memory, writings, **FRE 612**
    Specific instances of conduct, **FRE 608**
    Writings, refreshing memory, **FRE 612**
Work product, **FRE 502**
Writings,
    Original writings, recordings, or photographs, **FRE 1002**
    Refreshing memory, witnesses, **FRE 612**

FEDERAL RULES OF APPELLATE PROCEDURE

Adopted Effective July 1, 1968

**Including Amendments Effective
December 1, 2007**

Research Note

These rules may be searched electronically on Westlaw in the US–RULES database; updates to these rules may be found on Westlaw in US–RULES-UPDATES. For search tips, and a detailed summary of database content, consult the Westlaw Scope Screen of each database.

Table of Rules

TITLE I. APPLICABILITY OF RULES

Rule
1. Scope of Rules; Title.
2. Suspension of Rules.

TITLE II. APPEAL FROM A JUDGMENT OR ORDER OF A DISTRICT COURT

3. Appeal as of Right—How Taken.
3.1 Appeal From a Judgment of a Magistrate Judge in a Civil Case [Abrogated].
4. Appeal as of Right—When Taken.
5. Appeal by Permission.
5.1 Appeal by Permission Under 28 U.S.C. § 636(c)(5) [Abrogated].
6. Appeal in a Bankruptcy Case From a Final Judgment, Order, or Decree of a District Court or Bankruptcy Appellate Panel.
7. Bond for Costs on Appeal in a Civil Case.
8. Stay or Injunction Pending Appeal.
9. Release in a Criminal Case.
10. The Record on Appeal.
11. Forwarding the Record.
12. Docketing the Appeal; Filing a Representation Statement; Filing the Record.

TITLE III. REVIEW OF A DECISION OF THE UNITED STATES TAX COURT

13. Review of a Decision of the Tax Court.
14. Applicability of Other Rules to the Review of a Tax Court Decision.

TITLE IV. REVIEW OR ENFORCEMENT OF AN ORDER OF AN ADMINISTRATIVE AGENCY, BOARD, COMMISSION, OR OFFICER

15. Review or Enforcement of an Agency Order—How Obtained; Intervention.

Rule
15.1 Briefs and Oral Argument in a National Labor Relations Board Proceeding.
16. The Record on Review or Enforcement.
17. Filing the Record.
18. Stay Pending Review.
19. Settlement of a Judgment Enforcing an Agency Order in Part.
20. Applicability of Rules to the Review or Enforcement of an Agency Order.

TITLE V. EXTRAORDINARY WRITS

21. Writs of Mandamus and Prohibition, and Other Extraordinary Writs.

TITLE VI. HABEAS CORPUS; PROCEEDINGS IN FORMA PAUPERIS

22. Habeas Corpus and Section 2255 Proceedings.
23. Custody or Release of a Prisoner in a Habeas Corpus Proceeding.
24. Proceeding In Forma Pauperis.

TITLE VII. GENERAL PROVISIONS

25. Filing and Service.
26. Computing and Extending Time.
    (a) Computing Time.
    (b) Extending Time.
    (c) Additional Time After Service.
26.1 Corporate Disclosure Statement.
27. Motions.
28. Briefs.
28.1 Cross-Appeal.
29. Brief of an Amicus Curiae.
30. Appendix to the Briefs.
31. Serving and Filing Briefs.
32. Form of Briefs, Appendices, and Other Papers.
32.1 Citing Judicial Dispositions.

Rule

33. Appeal Conferences.
34. Oral Argument.
35. En Banc Determination.
36. Entry of Judgment; Notice.
37. Interest on Judgment.
38. Frivolous Appeal—Damages and Costs.
39. Costs.
40. Petition for Panel Rehearing.
41. Mandate: Contents; Issuance and Effective Date; Stay.
42. Voluntary Dismissal.
43. Substitution of Parties.
44. Case Involving a Constitutional Question When the United States or the Relevant State is Not a Party.
45. Clerk's Duties.
46. Attorneys.
47. Local Rules by Courts of Appeals.
48. Masters.

APPENDIX OF FORMS

Form

1. Notice of Appeal to a Court of Appeals From a Judgment or Order of a District Court.
2. Notice of Appeal to a Court of Appeals From a Decision of the United States Tax Court.
3. Petition for Review of Order of an Agency, Board, Commission or Officer.
4. Affidavit Accompanying Motion for Permission to Appeal In Forma Pauperis.
5. Notice of Appeal to a Court of Appeals From a Judgment or Order of a District Court or a Bankruptcy Appellate Panel.
6. Certificate of Compliance With Rule 32(a).

INDEX

TITLE I. APPLICABILITY OF RULES

FRAP 1. SCOPE OF RULES; TITLE

(a) Scope of Rules.

(1) These rules govern procedure in the United States courts of appeals.

(2) When these rules provide for filing a motion or other document in the district court, the procedure must comply with the practice of the district court.

(b) [Abrogated].

(c) Title. These rules are to be known as the Federal Rules of Appellate Procedure.

[Amended April 30, 1979, effective August 1, 1979; April 25, 1989, effective December 1, 1989; former Rule 48 renumbered as Rule 1(c) April 29, 1994, effective December 1, 1994; April 24, 1998, effective December 1, 1998; April 29, 2002, effective December 1, 2002.]

FRAP 2. SUSPENSION OF RULES

On its own or a party's motion, a court of appeals may—to expedite its decision or for other good cause—suspend any provision of these rules in a particular case and order proceedings as it directs, except as otherwise provided in Rule 26(b).

[Amended April 24, 1998, effective December 1, 1998.]

TITLE II. APPEAL FROM A JUDGMENT OR ORDER OF A DISTRICT COURT

FRAP 3. APPEAL AS OF RIGHT— HOW TAKEN

(a) Filing the Notice of Appeal.

(1) An appeal permitted by law as of right from a district court to a court of appeals may be taken only by filing a notice of appeal with the district clerk within the time allowed by Rule 4. At the time of filing, the appellant must furnish the clerk with enough copies of the notice to enable the clerk to comply with Rule 3(d).

(2) An appellant's failure to take any step other than the timely filing of a notice of appeal does not affect the validity of the appeal, but is ground only for the court of appeals to act as it considers appropriate, including dismissing the appeal.

(3) An appeal from a judgment by a magistrate judge in a civil case is taken in the same way as an appeal from any other district court judgment.

(4) An appeal by permission under 28 U.S.C. § 1292(b) or an appeal in a bankruptcy case may be taken only in the manner prescribed by Rules 5 and 6, respectively.

(b) Joint or Consolidated Appeals.

(1) When two or more parties are entitled to appeal from a district-court judgment or order, and their interests make joinder practicable, they may file a joint notice of appeal. They may then proceed on appeal as a single appellant.

(2) When the parties have filed separate timely notices of appeal, the appeals may be joined or consolidated by the court of appeals.

(c) Contents of the Notice of Appeal.

(1) The notice of appeal must:

(A) specify the party or parties taking the appeal by naming each one in the caption or body of the notice, but an attorney representing more than one party may describe those parties with such terms as "all plaintiffs," "the defendants," "the plaintiffs A, B, et al.," or "all defendants except X";

(B) designate the judgment, order, or part thereof being appealed; and

(C) name the court to which the appeal is taken.

(2) A pro se notice of appeal is considered filed on behalf of the signer and the signer's spouse and minor children (if they are parties), unless the notice clearly indicates otherwise.

(3) In a class action, whether or not the class has been certified, the notice of appeal is sufficient if it names one person qualified to bring the appeal as representative of the class.

(4) An appeal must not be dismissed for informality of form or title of the notice of appeal, or for failure to name a party whose intent to appeal is otherwise clear from the notice.

(5) Form 1 in the Appendix of Forms is a suggested form of a notice of appeal.

(d) Serving the Notice of Appeal.

(1) The district clerk must serve notice of the filing of a notice of appeal by mailing a copy to each party's counsel of record—excluding the appellant's—or, if a party is proceeding pro se, to the party's last known address. When a defendant in a criminal case appeals, the clerk must also serve a copy of the notice of appeal on the defendant, either by personal service or by mail addressed to the defendant. The clerk must promptly send a copy of the notice of appeal and of the docket entries—and any later docket entries—to the clerk of the court of appeals named in the notice. The district clerk must note, on each copy, the date when the notice of appeal was filed.

(2) If an inmate confined in an institution files a notice of appeal in the manner provided by Rule 4(c), the district clerk must also note the date when the clerk docketed the notice.

(3) The district clerk's failure to serve notice does not affect the validity of the appeal. The clerk must note on the docket the names of the parties to whom the clerk mails copies, with the date of mailing. Service is sufficient despite the death of a party or the party's counsel.

(e) Payment of Fees. Upon filing a notice of appeal, the appellant must pay the district clerk all required fees. The district clerk receives the appellate docket fee on behalf of the court of appeals.

[Amended April 30, 1979, effective August 1, 1979; March 10, 1986, effective July 1, 1986; April 25, 1989, effective Decem-

ber 1, 1989; April 22, 1993, effective December 1, 1993; April 29, 1994, effective December 1, 1994; April 24, 1998, effective December 1, 1998.]

FRAP 3.1 APPEAL FROM A JUDGMENT OF A MAGISTRATE JUDGE IN A CIVIL CASE [ABROGATED]

[Adopted March 10, 1986, effective July 1, 1986; amended April 22, 1993, effective December 1, 1993; abrogated effective December 1, 1998.]

FRAP 4. APPEAL AS OF RIGHT— WHEN TAKEN

(a) Appeal in a Civil Case.

(1) *Time for Filing a Notice of Appeal.*

(A) In a civil case, except as provided in Rules 4(a)(1)(B), 4(a)(4), and 4(c), the notice of appeal required by Rule 3 must be filed with the district clerk within 30 days after the judgment or order appealed from is entered.

(B) When the United States or its officer or agency is a party, the notice of appeal may be filed by any party within 60 days after the judgment or order appealed from is entered.

(C) An appeal from an order granting or denying an application for a writ of error coram nobis is an appeal in a civil case for purposes of Rule 4(a).

(2) *Filing Before Entry of Judgment.* A notice of appeal filed after the court announces a decision or order—but before the entry of the judgment or order—is treated as filed on the date of and after the entry.

(3) *Multiple Appeals.* If one party timely files a notice of appeal, any other party may file a notice of appeal within 14 days after the date when the first notice was filed, or within the time otherwise prescribed by this Rule 4(a), whichever period ends later.

(4) *Effect of a Motion on a Notice of Appeal.*

(A) If a party timely files in the district court any of the following motions under the Federal Rules of Civil Procedure, the time to file an appeal runs for all parties from the entry of the order disposing of the last such remaining motion:

(i) for judgment under Rule 50(b);

(ii) to amend or make additional factual findings under Rule 52(b), whether or not granting the motion would alter the judgment;

(iii) for attorney's fees under Rule 54 if the district court extends the time to appeal under Rule 58;

(iv) to alter or amend the judgment under Rule 59;

(v) for a new trial under Rule 59; or

(vi) for relief under Rule 60 if the motion is filed no later than 10 days after the judgment is entered.

(B)(i) If a party files a notice of appeal after the court announces or enters a judgment—but before it disposes of any motion listed in Rule 4(a)(4)(A)—the notice becomes effective to appeal a judgment or order, in whole or in part, when the order disposing of the last such remaining motion is entered.

(ii) A party intending to challenge an order disposing of any motion listed in Rule 4(a)(4)(A), or a judgment altered or amended upon such a motion, must file a notice of appeal, or an amended notice of appeal—in compliance with Rule 3(c)—within the time prescribed by this Rule measured from the entry of the order disposing of the last such remaining motion.

(iii) No additional fee is required to file an amended notice.

(5) *Motion for Extension of Time.*

(A) The district court may extend the time to file a notice of appeal if:

(i) a party so moves no later than 30 days after the time prescribed by this Rule 4(a) expires; and

(ii) regardless of whether its motion is filed before or during the 30 days after the time prescribed by this Rule 4(a) expires, that party shows excusable neglect or good cause.

(B) A motion filed before the expiration of the time prescribed in Rule 4(a)(1) or (3) may be ex parte unless the court requires otherwise. If the motion is filed after the expiration of the prescribed time, notice must be given to the other parties in accordance with local rules.

(C) No extension under this Rule 4(a)(5) may exceed 30 days after the prescribed time or 10 days after the date when the order granting the motion is entered, whichever is later.

(6) *Reopening the Time to File an Appeal.* The district court may reopen the time to file an appeal for a period of 14 days after the date when its order to reopen is entered, but only if all the following conditions are satisfied:

(A) the court finds that the moving party did not receive notice under Federal Rule of Civil Procedure 77(d) of the entry of the judgment or order sought to be appealed within 21 days after entry;

(B) the motion is filed within 180 days after the judgment or order is entered or within 7 days after the moving party receives notice under Federal Rule of Civil Procedure 77(d) of the entry, whichever is earlier; and

(C) the court finds that no party would be prejudiced.

(7) *Entry Defined.*

(A) A judgment or order is entered for purposes of this Rule 4(a):

(i) if Federal Rule of Civil Procedure 58(a)(1) does not require a separate document, when the judgment or order is entered in the civil docket under Federal Rule of Civil Procedure 79(a); or

(ii) if Federal Rule of Civil Procedure 58(a)(1) requires a separate document, when the judgment or order is entered in the civil docket under Federal Rule of Civil Procedure 79(a) and when the earlier of these events occurs:

- the judgment or order is set forth on a separate document, or

- 150 days have run from entry of the judgment or order in the civil docket under Federal Rule of Civil Procedure 79(a).

(B) A failure to set forth a judgment or order on a separate document when required by Federal Rule of Civil Procedure 58(a)(1) does not affect the validity of an appeal from that judgment or order.

(b) Appeal in a Criminal Case.

(1) *Time for Filing a Notice of Appeal.*

(A) In a criminal case, a defendant's notice of appeal must be filed in the district court within 10 days after the later of:

(i) the entry of either the judgment or the order being appealed; or

(ii) the filing of the government's notice of appeal.

(B) When the government is entitled to appeal, its notice of appeal must be filed in the district court within 30 days after the later of:

(i) the entry of the judgment or order being appealed; or

(ii) the filing of a notice of appeal by any defendant.

(2) *Filing Before Entry of Judgment.* A notice of appeal filed after the court announces a decision, sentence, or order—but before the entry of the judgment or order—is treated as filed on the date of and after the entry.

(3) *Effect of a Motion on a Notice of Appeal.*

(A) If a defendant timely makes any of the following motions under the Federal Rules of Criminal Procedure, the notice of appeal from a judgment of conviction must be filed within 10 days after the entry of the order disposing of the last such remaining motion, or within 10 days after the entry of the judgment of conviction, whichever period ends later. This provision applies to a timely motion:

(i) for judgment of acquittal under Rule 29;

(ii) for a new trial under Rule 33, but if based on newly discovered evidence, only if the motion is made no later than 10 days after the entry of the judgment; or

    (iii) for arrest of judgment under Rule 34.

    (B) A notice of appeal filed after the court announces a decision, sentence, or order—but before it disposes of any of the motions referred to in Rule 4(b)(3)(A)—becomes effective upon the later of the following:

    (i) the entry of the order disposing of the last such remaining motion; or

    (ii) the entry of the judgment of conviction.

    (C) A valid notice of appeal is effective—without amendment—to appeal from an order disposing of any of the motions referred to in Rule 4(b)(3)(A).

(4) *Motion for Extension of Time.* Upon a finding of excusable neglect or good cause, the district court may—before or after the time has expired, with or without motion and notice—extend the time to file a notice of appeal for a period not to exceed 30 days from the expiration of the time otherwise prescribed by this Rule 4(b).

(5) *Jurisdiction.* The filing of a notice of appeal under this Rule 4(b) does not divest a district court of jurisdiction to correct a sentence under Federal Rule of Criminal Procedure 35(a), nor does the filing of a motion under 35(a) affect the validity of a notice of appeal filed before entry of the order disposing of the motion. The filing of a motion under Federal Rule of Criminal Procedure 35(a) does not suspend the time for filing a notice of appeal from a judgment of conviction.

(6) *Entry Defined.* A judgment or order is entered for purposes of this Rule 4(b) when it is entered on the criminal docket.

(c) Appeal by an Inmate Confined in an Institution.

(1) If an inmate confined in an institution files a notice of appeal in either a civil or a criminal case, the notice is timely if it is deposited in the institution's internal mail system on or before the last day for filing. If an institution has a system designed for legal mail, the inmate must use that system to receive the benefit of this rule. Timely filing may be shown by a declaration in compliance with 28 U.S.C. § 1746 or by a notarized statement, either of which must set forth the date of deposit and state that first-class postage has been prepaid.

(2) If an inmate files the first notice of appeal in a civil case under this Rule 4(c), the 14–day period provided in Rule 4(a)(3) for another party to file a notice of appeal runs from the date when the district court dockets the first notice.

(3) When a defendant in a criminal case files a notice of appeal under this Rule 4(c), the 30–day period for the government to file its notice of appeal runs from the entry of the judgment or order appeal-ed from or from the district court's docketing of the defendant's notice of appeal, whichever is later.

(d) Mistaken Filing in the Court of Appeals. If a notice of appeal in either a civil or a criminal case is mistakenly filed in the court of appeals, the clerk of that court must note on the notice the date when it was received and send it to the district clerk. The notice is then considered filed in the district court on the date so noted.

[Amended April 30, 1979, effective August 1, 1979; amended by Pub.L. 100–690, Title VII, § 7111, November 18, 1988, 102 Stat. 4419; amended April 30, 1991, effective December 1, 1991; April 22, 1993, effective December 1, 1993; April 27, 1995, effective December 1, 1995; April 24, 1998, effective December 1, 1998; April 29, 2002, effective December 1, 2002; April 25, 2005, effective December 1, 2005.]

FRAP 5.   APPEAL BY PERMISSION

(a) Petition for Permission to Appeal.

(1) To request permission to appeal when an appeal is within the court of appeals' discretion, a party must file a petition for permission to appeal. The petition must be filed with the circuit clerk with proof of service on all other parties to the district-court action.

(2) The petition must be filed within the time specified by the statute or rule authorizing the appeal or, if no such time is specified, within the time provided by Rule 4(a) for filing a notice of appeal.

(3) If a party cannot petition for appeal unless the district court first enters an order granting permission to do so or stating that the necessary conditions are met, the district court may amend its order, either on its own or in response to a party's motion, to include the required permission or statement. In that event, the time to petition runs from entry of the amended order.

(b) Contents of the Petition; Answer or Cross–Petition; Oral Argument.

(1) The petition must include the following:

    (A) the facts necessary to understand the question presented;

    (B) the question itself;

    (C) the relief sought;

    (D) the reasons why the appeal should be allowed and is authorized by a statute or rule; and

    (E) an attached copy of:

        (i) the order, decree, or judgment complained of and any related opinion or memorandum, and

        (ii) any order stating the district court's permission to appeal or finding that the necessary conditions are met.

(2) A party may file an answer in opposition or a cross-petition within 7 days after the petition is served.

(3) The petition and answer will be submitted without oral argument unless the court of appeals orders otherwise.

(c) Form of Papers; Number of Copies. All papers must conform to Rule 32(c)(2). Except by the court's permission, a paper must not exceed 20 pages, exclusive of the disclosure statement, the proof of service, and the accompanying documents required by Rule 5(b)(1)(E). An original and 3 copies must be filed unless the court requires a different number by local rule or by order in a particular case.

(d) Grant of Permission; Fees; Cost Bond; Filing the Record.

(1) Within 10 days after the entry of the order granting permission to appeal, the appellant must:

(A) pay the district clerk all required fees; and

(B) file a cost bond if required under Rule 7.

(2) A notice of appeal need not be filed. The date when the order granting permission to appeal is entered serves as the date of the notice of appeal for calculating time under these rules.

(3) The district clerk must notify the circuit clerk once the petitioner has paid the fees. Upon receiving this notice, the circuit clerk must enter the appeal on the docket. The record must be forwarded and filed in accordance with Rules 11 and 12(c).

[Amended April 30, 1979, effective August 1, 1979; April 29, 1994, effective December 1, 1994; April 24, 1998, effective December 1, 1998; April 29, 2002, effective December 1, 2002.]

FRAP 5.1 APPEAL BY PERMISSION UNDER 28 U.S.C. § 636(c)(5) [ABROGATED]

[Adopted March 10, 1986, effective July 1, 1986; amended April 22, 1993, effective December 1, 1993; April 29, 1994, effective December 1, 1994; abrogated effective December 1, 1998.]

FRAP 6. APPEAL IN A BANKRUPTCY CASE FROM A FINAL JUDGMENT, ORDER, OR DECREE OF A DISTRICT COURT OR BANKRUPTCY APPELLATE PANEL

(a) Appeal From a Judgment, Order, or Decree of a District Court Exercising Original Jurisdiction in a Bankruptcy Case. An appeal to a court of appeals from a final judgment, order, or decree of a district court exercising jurisdiction under 28 U.S.C. § 1334 is taken as any other civil appeal under these rules.

(b) Appeal From a Judgment, Order, or Decree of a District Court or Bankruptcy Appellate Panel Exercising Appellate Jurisdiction in a Bankruptcy Case.

(1) *Applicability of Other Rules.* These rules apply to an appeal to a court of appeals under 28 U.S.C.

§ 158(d) from a final judgment, order, or decree of a district court or bankruptcy appellate panel exercising appellate jurisdiction under 28 U.S.C. § 158(a) or (b). But there are 3 exceptions:

(A) Rules 4(a)(4), 4(b), 9, 10, 11, 12(b), 13–20, 22–23, and 24(b) do not apply;

(B) the reference in Rule 3(c) to "Form 1 in the Appendix of Forms" must be read as a reference to Form 5; and

(C) when the appeal is from a bankruptcy appellate panel, the term "district court," as used in any applicable rule, means "appellate panel."

(2) *Additional Rules.* In addition to the rules made applicable by Rule 6(b)(1), the following rules apply:

(A) Motion for rehearing.

(i) If a timely motion for rehearing under Bankruptcy Rule 8015 is filed, the time to appeal for all parties runs from the entry of the order disposing of the motion. A notice of appeal filed after the district court or bankruptcy appellate panel announces or enters a judgment, order, or decree—but before disposition of the motion for rehearing—becomes effective when the order disposing of the motion for rehearing is entered.

(ii) Appellate review of the order disposing of the motion requires the party, in compliance with Rules 3(c) and 6(b)(1)(B), to amend a previously filed notice of appeal. A party intending to challenge an altered or amended judgment, order, or decree must file a notice of appeal or amended notice of appeal within the time prescribed by Rule 4—excluding Rules 4(a)(4) and 4(b)—measured from the entry of the order disposing of the motion.

(iii) No additional fee is required to file an amended notice.

(B) The record on appeal.

(i) Within 10 days after filing the notice of appeal, the appellant must file with the clerk possessing the record assembled in accordance with Bankruptcy Rule 8006—and serve on the appellee—a statement of the issues to be presented on appeal and a designation of the record to be certified and sent to the circuit clerk.

(ii) An appellee who believes that other parts of the record are necessary must, within 10 days after being served with the appellant's designation, file with the clerk and serve on the appellant a designation of additional parts to be included.

(iii) The record on appeal consists of:

● the redesignated record as provided above;

● the proceedings in the district court or bankruptcy appellate panel; and

● a certified copy of the docket entries prepared by the clerk under Rule 3(d).

(C) Forwarding the record.

(i) When the record is complete, the district clerk or bankruptcy appellate panel clerk must number the documents constituting the record and send them promptly to the circuit clerk together with a list of the documents correspondingly numbered and reasonably identified. Unless directed to do so by a party or the circuit clerk, the clerk will not send to the court of appeals documents of unusual bulk or weight, physical exhibits other than documents, or other parts of the record designated for omission by local rule of the court of appeals. If the exhibits are unusually bulky or heavy, a party must arrange with the clerks in advance for their transportation and receipt.

(ii) All parties must do whatever else is necessary to enable the clerk to assemble and forward the record. The court of appeals may provide by rule or order that a certified copy of the docket entries be sent in place of the redesignated record, but any party may request at any time during the pendency of the appeal that the redesignated record be sent.

(D) Filing the record. Upon receiving the record—or a certified copy of the docket entries sent in place of the redesignated record—the circuit clerk must file it and immediately notify all parties of the filing date.

[Former Rule 6 amended April 30, 1979, effective August 1, 1979; repealed and new Rule 6 adopted April 25, 1989, effective December 1, 1989; caption amended April 30, 1991, effective December 1, 1991; caption and text amended April 22, 1993, effective December 1, 1993; April 24, 1998, effective December 1, 1998.]

FRAP 7. BOND FOR COSTS ON APPEAL IN A CIVIL CASE

In a civil case, the district court may require an appellant to file a bond or provide other security in any form and amount necessary to ensure payment of costs on appeal. Rule 8(b) applies to a surety on a bond given under this rule.

[Amended April 30, 1979, effective August 1, 1979; April 24, 1998, effective December 1, 1998.]

FRAP 8. STAY OR INJUNCTION PENDING APPEAL

(a) **Motion for Stay.**

(1) *Initial Motion in the District Court.* A party must ordinarily move first in the district court for the following relief:

(A) a stay of the judgment or order of a district court pending appeal;

(B) approval of a supersedeas bond; or

(C) an order suspending, modifying, restoring, or granting an injunction while an appeal is pending.

(2) *Motion in the Court of Appeals; Conditions on Relief.* A motion for the relief mentioned in Rule 8(a)(1) may be made to the court of appeals or to one of its judges.

(A) The motion must:

(i) show that moving first in the district court would be impracticable; or

(ii) state that, a motion having been made, the district court denied the motion or failed to afford the relief requested and state any reasons given by the district court for its action.

(B) The motion must also include:

(i) the reasons for granting the relief requested and the facts relied on;

(ii) originals or copies of affidavits or other sworn statements supporting facts subject to dispute; and

(iii) relevant parts of the record.

(C) The moving party must give reasonable notice of the motion to all parties.

(D) A motion under this Rule 8(a)(2) must be filed with the circuit clerk and normally will be considered by a panel of the court. But in an exceptional case in which time requirements make that procedure impracticable, the motion may be made to and considered by a single judge.

(E) The court may condition relief on a party's filing a bond or other appropriate security in the district court.

(b) **Proceeding Against a Surety.** If a party gives security in the form of a bond or stipulation or other undertaking with one or more sureties, each surety submits to the jurisdiction of the district court and irrevocably appoints the district clerk as the surety's agent on whom any papers affecting the surety's liability on the bond or undertaking may be served. On motion, a surety's liability may be enforced in the district court without the necessity of an independent action. The motion and any notice that the district court prescribes may be served on the district clerk, who must promptly mail a copy to each surety whose address is known.

(c) **Stay in a Criminal Case.** Rule 38 of the Federal Rules of Criminal Procedure governs a stay in a criminal case.

[Amended March 10, 1986, effective July 1, 1986; April 27, 1995, effective December 1, 1995; April 24, 1998, effective December 1, 1998.]

FRAP 9. RELEASE IN A CRIMINAL CASE

(a) Release Before Judgment of Conviction.

(1) The district court must state in writing, or orally on the record, the reasons for an order regarding the release or detention of a defendant in a criminal case. A party appealing from the order must file with the court of appeals a copy of the district court's order and the court's statement of reasons as soon as practicable after filing the notice of appeal. An appellant who questions the factual basis for the district court's order must file a transcript of the release proceedings or an explanation of why a transcript was not obtained.

(2) After reasonable notice to the appellee, the court of appeals must promptly determine the appeal on the basis of the papers, affidavits, and parts of the record that the parties present or the court requires. Unless the court so orders, briefs need not be filed.

(3) The court of appeals or one of its judges may order the defendant's release pending the disposition of the appeal.

(b) Release After Judgment of Conviction.

A party entitled to do so may obtain review of a district-court order regarding release after a judgment of conviction by filing a notice of appeal from that order in the district court, or by filing a motion in the court of appeals if the party has already filed a notice of appeal from the judgment of conviction. Both the order and the review are subject to Rule 9(a). The papers filed by the party seeking review must include a copy of the judgment of conviction.

(c) Criteria for Release.

The court must make its decision regarding release in accordance with the applicable provisions of 18 U.S.C. §§ 3142, 3143, and 3145(c).

[Amended April 24, 1972, effective October 1, 1972; amended by Pub.L. 98–473, Title II, § 210, October 12, 1984, 98 Stat. 1987; April 29, 1994, effective December 1, 1994; April 24, 1998, effective December 1, 1998.]

FRAP 10. THE RECORD ON APPEAL

(a) Composition of the Record on Appeal.

The following items constitute the record on appeal:

(1) the original papers and exhibits filed in the district court;

(2) the transcript of proceedings, if any; and

(3) a certified copy of the docket entries prepared by the district clerk.

(b) The Transcript of Proceedings.

(1) *Appellant's Duty to Order.* Within 10 days after filing the notice of appeal or entry of an order disposing of the last timely remaining motion of a type specified in Rule 4(a)(4)(A), whichever is later, the appellant must do either of the following:

(A) order from the reporter a transcript of such parts of the proceedings not already on file as the appellant considers necessary, subject to a local rule of the court of appeals and with the following qualifications:

    (i) the order must be in writing;

    (ii) if the cost of the transcript is to be paid by the United States under the Criminal Justice Act, the order must so state; and

    (iii) the appellant must, within the same period, file a copy of the order with the district clerk; or

(B) file a certificate stating that no transcript will be ordered.

(2) *Unsupported Finding or Conclusion.* If the appellant intends to urge on appeal that a finding or conclusion is unsupported by the evidence or is contrary to the evidence, the appellant must include in the record a transcript of all evidence relevant to that finding or conclusion.

(3) *Partial Transcript.* Unless the entire transcript is ordered:

(A) the appellant must—within the 10 days provided in Rule 10(b)(1)—file a statement of the issues that the appellant intends to present on the appeal and must serve on the appellee a copy of both the order or certificate and the statement;

(B) if the appellee considers it necessary to have a transcript of other parts of the proceedings, the appellee must, within 10 days after the service of the order or certificate and the statement of the issues, file and serve on the appellant a designation of additional parts to be ordered; and

(C) unless within 10 days after service of that designation the appellant has ordered all such parts, and has so notified the appellee, the appellee may within the following 10 days either order the parts or move in the district court for an order requiring the appellant to do so.

(4) *Payment.* At the time of ordering, a party must make satisfactory arrangements with the reporter for paying the cost of the transcript.

(c) Statement of the Evidence When the Proceedings Were Not Recorded or When a Transcript Is Unavailable.

If the transcript of a hearing or trial is unavailable, the appellant may prepare a statement of the evidence or proceedings from the best available means, including the appellant's recollection. The statement must be served on the appellee, who may serve objections or proposed amendments within 10 days after being served. The statement and any objections or proposed amendments must then be submitted to the district court for settlement and approval. As settled and approved, the statement must be included by the district clerk in the record on appeal.

(d) Agreed Statement as the Record on Appeal. In place of the record on appeal as defined in Rule 10(a), the parties may prepare, sign, and submit to the district court a statement of the case showing how the issues presented by the appeal arose and were decided in the district court. The statement must set forth only those facts averred and proved or sought to be proved that are essential to the court's resolution of the issues. If the statement is truthful, it—together with any additions that the district court may consider necessary to a full presentation of the issues on appeal—must be approved by the district court and must then be certified to the court of appeals as the record on appeal. The district clerk must then send it to the circuit clerk within the time provided by Rule 11. A copy of the agreed statement may be filed in place of the appendix required by Rule 30.

(e) Correction or Modification of the Record.

(1) If any difference arises about whether the record truly discloses what occurred in the district court, the difference must be submitted to and settled by that court and the record conformed accordingly.

(2) If anything material to either party is omitted from or misstated in the record by error or accident, the omission or misstatement may be corrected and a supplemental record may be certified and forwarded:

(A) on stipulation of the parties;

(B) by the district court before or after the record has been forwarded; or

(C) by the court of appeals.

(3) All other questions as to the form and content of the record must be presented to the court of appeals.

[Amended April 30, 1979, effective August 1, 1979; March 10, 1986, effective July 1, 1986; April 30, 1991, effective December 1, 1991; April 22, 1993, effective December 1, 1993; April 27, 1995, effective December 1, 1995; April 24, 1998, effective December 1, 1998.]

FRAP 11. FORWARDING THE RECORD

(a) Appellant's Duty. An appellant filing a notice of appeal must comply with Rule 10(b) and must do whatever else is necessary to enable the clerk to assemble and forward the record. If there are multiple appeals from a judgment or order, the clerk must forward a single record.

(b) Duties of Reporter and District Clerk.

(1) *Reporter's Duty to Prepare and File a Transcript.* The reporter must prepare and file a transcript as follows:

(A) Upon receiving an order for a transcript, the reporter must enter at the foot of the order the date of its receipt and the expected completion date and send a copy, so endorsed, to the circuit clerk.

(B) If the transcript cannot be completed within 30 days of the reporter's receipt of the order, the reporter may request the circuit clerk to grant additional time to complete it. The clerk must note on the docket the action taken and notify the parties.

(C) When a transcript is complete, the reporter must file it with the district clerk and notify the circuit clerk of the filing.

(D) If the reporter fails to file the transcript on time, the circuit clerk must notify the district judge and do whatever else the court of appeals directs.

(2) *District Clerk's Duty to Forward.* When the record is complete, the district clerk must number the documents constituting the record and send them promptly to the circuit clerk together with a list of the documents correspondingly numbered and reasonably identified. Unless directed to do so by a party or the circuit clerk, the district clerk will not send to the court of appeals documents of unusual bulk or weight, physical exhibits other than documents, or other parts of the record designated for omission by local rule of the court of appeals. If the exhibits are unusually bulky or heavy, a party must arrange with the clerks in advance for their transportation and receipt.

(c) Retaining the Record Temporarily in the District Court for Use in Preparing the Appeal. The parties may stipulate, or the district court on motion may order, that the district clerk retain the record temporarily for the parties to use in preparing the papers on appeal. In that event the district clerk must certify to the circuit clerk that the record on appeal is complete. Upon receipt of the appellee's brief, or earlier if the court orders or the parties agree, the appellant must request the district clerk to forward the record.

(d) [Abrogated.]

(e) Retaining the Record by Court Order.

(1) The court of appeals may, by order or local rule, provide that a certified copy of the docket entries be forwarded instead of the entire record. But a party may at any time during the appeal request that designated parts of the record be forwarded.

(2) The district court may order the record or some part of it retained if the court needs it while the appeal is pending, subject, however, to call by the court of appeals.

(3) If part or all of the record is ordered retained, the district clerk must send to the court of appeals a copy of the order and the docket entries together with the parts of the original record allowed by the district court and copies of any parts of the record designated by the parties.

(f) Retaining Parts of the Record in the District Court by Stipulation of the Parties. The parties may agree by written stipulation filed in the district court that designated parts of the record be retained in the district court subject to call by the court of appeals or request by a party. The parts of the record so designated remain a part of the record on appeal.

(g) Record for a Preliminary Motion in the Court of Appeals. If, before the record is forwarded, a party makes any of the following motions in the court of appeals:

- for dismissal;
- for release;
- for a stay pending appeal;
- for additional security on the bond on appeal or on a supersedeas bond; or
- for any other intermediate order—

the district clerk must send the court of appeals any parts of the record designated by any party.

[Amended April 30, 1979, effective August 1, 1979; March 10, 1986, effective July 1, 1986; April 24, 1998, effective December 1, 1998.]

FRAP 12.　DOCKETING THE APPEAL; FILING A REPRESENTATION STATEMENT; FILING THE RECORD

(a) Docketing the Appeal. Upon receiving the copy of the notice of appeal and the docket entries from the district clerk under Rule 3(d), the circuit clerk must docket the appeal under the title of the district-court action and must identify the appellant, adding the appellant's name if necessary.

(b) Filing a Representation Statement. Unless the court of appeals designates another time, the attorney who filed the notice of appeal must, within 10 days after filing the notice, file a statement with the circuit clerk naming the parties that the attorney represents on appeal.

(c) Filing the Record, Partial Record, or Certificate. Upon receiving the record, partial record, or district clerk's certificate as provided in Rule 11, the circuit clerk must file it and immediately notify all parties of the filing date.

[Amended April 30, 1979, effective August 1, 1979; March 10, 1986, effective July 1, 1986; April 22, 1993, effective December 1, 1993; April 24, 1998, effective December 1, 1998.]

TITLE III.　REVIEW OF A DECISION OF THE UNITED STATES TAX COURT

FRAP 13.　REVIEW OF A DECISION OF THE TAX COURT

(a) How Obtained; Time for Filing Notice of Appeal.

(1) Review of a decision of the United States Tax Court is commenced by filing a notice of appeal with the Tax Court clerk within 90 days after the entry of the Tax Court's decision. At the time of filing, the appellant must furnish the clerk with enough copies of the notice to enable the clerk to comply with Rule 3(d). If one party files a timely notice of appeal, any other party may file a notice of appeal within 120 days after the Tax Court's decision is entered.

(2) If, under Tax Court rules, a party makes a timely motion to vacate or revise the Tax Court's decision, the time to file a notice of appeal runs from the entry of the order disposing of the motion or from the entry of a new decision, whichever is later.

(b) Notice of Appeal; How Filed. The notice of appeal may be filed either at the Tax Court clerk's office in the District of Columbia or by mail addressed to the clerk. If sent by mail the notice is considered filed on the postmark date, subject to § 7502 of the Internal Revenue Code, as amended, and the applicable regulations.

(c) Contents of the Notice of Appeal; Service; Effect of Filing and Service. Rule 3 prescribes the contents of a notice of appeal, the manner of service, and the effect of its filing and service. Form 2 in the

Appendix of Forms is a suggested form of a notice of appeal.

(d) The Record on Appeal; Forwarding; Filing.

(1) An appeal from the Tax Court is governed by the parts of Rules 10, 11, and 12 regarding the record on appeal from a district court, the time and manner of forwarding and filing, and the docketing in the court of appeals. References in those rules and in Rule 3 to the district court and district clerk are to be read as referring to the Tax Court and its clerk.

(2) If an appeal from a Tax Court decision is taken to more than one court of appeals, the original record must be sent to the court named in the first notice of appeal filed. In an appeal to any other court of appeals, the appellant must apply to that other court to make provision for the record.

[Amended April 30, 1979, effective August 1, 1979; April 29, 1994, effective December 1, 1994; April 24, 1998, effective December 1, 1998.]

FRAP 14.　APPLICABILITY OF OTHER RULES TO THE REVIEW OF A TAX COURT DECISION

All provisions of these rules, except Rules 4–9, 15–20, and 22–23, apply to the review of a Tax Court decision.

[Amended April 24, 1998, effective December 1, 1998.]

TITLE IV.   REVIEW OR ENFORCEMENT OF AN ORDER OF AN ADMINISTRATIVE AGENCY, BOARD, COMMISSION, OR OFFICER

FRAP 15.   REVIEW OR ENFORCEMENT OF AN AGENCY ORDER—HOW OBTAINED; INTERVENTION

(a) Petition for Review; Joint Petition.

(1) Review of an agency order is commenced by filing, within the time prescribed by law, a petition for review with the clerk of a court of appeals authorized to review the agency order. If their interests make joinder practicable, two or more persons may join in a petition to the same court to review the same order.

(2) The petition must:

(A) name each party seeking review either in the caption or the body of the petition—using such terms as "et al.," "petitioners," or "respondents" does not effectively name the parties;

(B) name the agency as a respondent (even though not named in the petition, the United States is a respondent if required by statute); and

(C) specify the order or part thereof to be reviewed.

(3) Form 3 in the Appendix of Forms is a suggested form of a petition for review.

(4) In this rule "agency" includes an agency, board, commission, or officer; "petition for review" includes a petition to enjoin, suspend, modify, or otherwise review, or a notice of appeal, whichever form is indicated by the applicable statute.

(b) Application or Cross–Application to Enforce an Order; Answer; Default.

(1) An application to enforce an agency order must be filed with the clerk of a court of appeals authorized to enforce the order. If a petition is filed to review an agency order that the court may enforce, a party opposing the petition may file a cross-application for enforcement.

(2) Within 20 days after the application for enforcement is filed, the respondent must serve on the applicant an answer to the application and file it with the clerk. If the respondent fails to answer in time, the court will enter judgment for the relief requested.

(3) The application must contain a concise statement of the proceedings in which the order was entered, the facts upon which venue is based, and the relief requested.

(c) Service of the Petition or Application. The circuit clerk must serve a copy of the petition for review, or an application or cross-application to enforce an agency order, on each respondent as prescribed by Rule 3(d), unless a different manner of service is prescribed by statute. At the time of filing, the petitioner must:

(1) serve, or have served, a copy on each party admitted to participate in the agency proceedings, except for the respondents;

(2) file with the clerk a list of those so served; and

(3) give the clerk enough copies of the petition or application to serve each respondent.

(d) Intervention. Unless a statute provides another method, a person who wants to intervene in a proceeding under this rule must file a motion for leave to intervene with the circuit clerk and serve a copy on all parties. The motion—or other notice of intervention authorized by statute—must be filed within 30 days after the petition for review is filed and must contain a concise statement of the interest of the moving party and the grounds for intervention.

(e) Payment of Fees. When filing any separate or joint petition for review in a court of appeals, the petitioner must pay the circuit clerk all required fees.

[Amended April 22, 1993, effective December 1, 1993; April 24, 1998, effective December 1, 1998.]

FRAP 15.1   BRIEFS AND ORAL ARGUMENT IN A NATIONAL LABOR RELATIONS BOARD PROCEEDING

In either an enforcement or a review proceeding, a party adverse to the National Labor Relations Board proceeds first on briefing and at oral argument, unless the court orders otherwise.

[Adopted March 10, 1986, effective July 1, 1986; April 24, 1998, effective December 1, 1998.]

FRAP 16.   THE RECORD ON REVIEW OR ENFORCEMENT

(a) Composition of the Record. The record on review or enforcement of an agency order consists of:

(1) the order involved;

(2) any findings or report on which it is based; and

(3) the pleadings, evidence, and other parts of the proceedings before the agency.

(b) Omissions From or Misstatements in the Record. The parties may at any time, by stipulation, supply any omission from the record or correct a misstatement, or the court may so direct. If necessary, the court may direct that a supplemental record be prepared and filed.

[Amended April 24, 1998, effective December 1, 1998.]

FRAP 17.   FILING THE RECORD

(a) Agency to File; Time for Filing; Notice of Filing. The agency must file the record with the circuit clerk within 40 days after being served with a petition for review, unless the statute authorizing review provides otherwise, or within 40 days after it files an application for enforcement unless the respondent fails to answer or the court orders otherwise. The court may shorten or extend the time to file the record. The clerk must notify all parties of the date when the record is filed.

(b) Filing—What Constitutes.

(1) The agency must file:

(A) the original or a certified copy of the entire record or parts designated by the parties; or

(B) a certified list adequately describing all documents, transcripts of testimony, exhibits, and other material constituting the record, or describing those parts designated by the parties.

(2) The parties may stipulate in writing that no record or certified list be filed. The date when the stipulation is filed with the circuit clerk is treated as the date when the record is filed.

(3) The agency must retain any portion of the record not filed with the clerk. All parts of the record retained by the agency are a part of the record on review for all purposes and, if the court or a party so requests, must be sent to the court regardless of any prior stipulation.

[Amended April 24, 1998, effective December 1, 1998.]

FRAP 18.   STAY PENDING REVIEW

(a) Motion for a Stay.

(1) *Initial Motion Before the Agency.* A petitioner must ordinarily move first before the agency for a stay pending review of its decision or order.

(2) *Motion in the Court of Appeals.* A motion for a stay may be made to the court of appeals or one of its judges.

(A) The motion must:

(i) show that moving first before the agency would be impracticable; or

(ii) state that, a motion having been made, the agency denied the motion or failed to afford the relief requested and state any reasons given by the agency for its action.

(B) The motion must also include:

(i) the reasons for granting the relief requested and the facts relied on;

(ii) originals or copies of affidavits or other sworn statements supporting facts subject to dispute; and

(iii) relevant parts of the record.

(C) The moving party must give reasonable notice of the motion to all parties.

(D) The motion must be filed with the circuit clerk and normally will be considered by a panel of the court. But in an exceptional case in which time requirements make that procedure impracticable, the motion may be made to and considered by a single judge.

(b) Bond. The court may condition relief on the filing of a bond or other appropriate security.

[Amended April 24, 1998, effective December 1, 1998.]

FRAP 19.   SETTLEMENT OF A JUDGMENT ENFORCING AN AGENCY ORDER IN PART

When the court files an opinion directing entry of judgment enforcing the agency's order in part, the agency must within 14 days file with the clerk and serve on each other party a proposed judgment conforming to the opinion. A party who disagrees with the agency's proposed judgment must within 7 days file with the clerk and serve the agency with a proposed judgment that the party believes conforms to the opinion. The court will settle the judgment and direct entry without further hearing or argument.

[Amended March 10, 1986, effective July 1, 1986; April 24, 1998, effective December 1, 1998.]

FRAP 20.   APPLICABILITY OF RULES TO THE REVIEW OR ENFORCEMENT OF AN AGENCY ORDER

All provisions of these rules, except Rules 3–14 and 22–23, apply to the review or enforcement of an agency order. In these rules, "appellant" includes a petitioner or applicant, and "appellee" includes a respondent.

[Amended April 24, 1998, effective December 1, 1998.]

TITLE V. EXTRAORDINARY WRITS

FRAP 21. WRITS OF MANDAMUS AND PROHIBITION, AND OTHER EXTRAORDINARY WRITS

(a) Mandamus or Prohibition to a Court: Petition, Filing, Service, and Docketing.

(1) A party petitioning for a writ of mandamus or prohibition directed to a court must file a petition with the circuit clerk with proof of service on all parties to the proceeding in the trial court. The party must also provide a copy to the trial-court judge. All parties to the proceeding in the trial court other than the petitioner are respondents for all purposes.

(2)(A) The petition must be titled "In re [name of petitioner]."

(B) The petition must state:

(i) the relief sought;

(ii) the issues presented;

(iii) the facts necessary to understand the issue presented by the petition; and

(iv) the reasons why the writ should issue.

(C) The petition must include a copy of any order or opinion or parts of the record that may be essential to understand the matters set forth in the petition.

(3) Upon receiving the prescribed docket fee, the clerk must docket the petition and submit it to the court.

(b) Denial; Order Directing Answer; Briefs; Precedence.

(1) The court may deny the petition without an answer. Otherwise, it must order the respondent, if any, to answer within a fixed time.

(2) The clerk must serve the order to respond on all persons directed to respond.

(3) Two or more respondents may answer jointly.

(4) The court of appeals may invite or order the trial-court judge to address the petition or may invite an amicus curiae to do so. The trial-court judge may request permission to address the petition but may not do so unless invited or ordered to do so by the court of appeals.

(5) If briefing or oral argument is required, the clerk must advise the parties, and when appropriate, the trial-court judge or amicus curiae.

(6) The proceeding must be given preference over ordinary civil cases.

(7) The circuit clerk must send a copy of the final disposition to the trial-court judge.

(c) Other Extraordinary Writs. An application for an extraordinary writ other than one provided for in Rule 21(a) must be made by filing a petition with the circuit clerk with proof of service on the respondents. Proceedings on the application must conform, so far as is practicable, to the procedures prescribed in Rule 21(a) and (b).

(d) Form of Papers; Number of Copies. All papers must conform to Rule 32(c)(2). Except by the court's permission, a paper must not exceed 30 pages, exclusive of the disclosure statement, the proof of service, and the accompanying documents required by Rule 21(a)(2)(C). An original and 3 copies must be filed unless the court requires the filing of a different number by local rule or by order in a particular case.

[Amended April 29, 1994, effective December 1, 1994; April 23, 1996, effective December 1, 1996; April 24, 1998, effective December 1, 1998; April 29, 2002, effective December 1, 2002.]

TITLE VI. HABEAS CORPUS; PROCEEDINGS IN FORMA PAUPERIS

FRAP 22. HABEAS CORPUS AND SECTION 2255 PROCEEDINGS

(a) Application for the Original Writ. An application for a writ of habeas corpus must be made to the appropriate district court. If made to a circuit judge, the application must be transferred to the appropriate district court. If a district court denies an application made or transferred to it, renewal of the application before a circuit judge is not permitted. The applicant may, under 28 U.S.C. § 2253, appeal to the court of appeals from the district court's order denying the application.

(b) Certificate of Appealability.

(1) In a habeas corpus proceeding in which the detention complained of arises from process issued by a state court, or in a 28 U.S.C. § 2255 proceeding, the applicant cannot take an appeal unless a circuit justice or a circuit or district judge issues a certificate of appealability under 28 U.S.C. § 2253(c). If an applicant files a notice of appeal, the district judge who rendered the judgment must either issue a certificate of appealability or state why a certificate should not issue. The district clerk must send the certificate or statement to the court of appeals with the notice of appeal and the file of the district-court proceedings. If the district judge has denied the certificate, the

applicant may request a circuit judge to issue the certificate.

(2) A request addressed to the court of appeals may be considered by a circuit judge or judges, as the court prescribes. If no express request for a certificate is filed, the notice of appeal constitutes a request addressed to the judges of the court of appeals.

(3) A certificate of appealability is not required when a state or its representative or the United States or its representative appeals.

[Amended by Pub.L. 104–32, § 103, April 24, 1996, 110 Stat. 1218; amended April 24, 1998, effective December 1, 1998.]

FRAP 23. CUSTODY OR RELEASE OF A PRISONER IN A HABEAS CORPUS PROCEEDING

(a) Transfer of Custody Pending Review. Pending review of a decision in a habeas corpus proceeding commenced before a court, justice, or judge of the United States for the release of a prisoner, the person having custody of the prisoner must not transfer custody to another unless a transfer is directed in accordance with this rule. When, upon application, a custodian shows the need for a transfer, the court, justice, or judge rendering the decision under review may authorize the transfer and substitute the successor custodian as a party.

(b) Detention or Release Pending Review of Decision Not to Release. While a decision not to release a prisoner is under review, the court or judge rendering the decision, or the court of appeals, or the Supreme Court, or a judge or justice of either court, may order that the prisoner be:

(1) detained in the custody from which release is sought;

(2) detained in other appropriate custody; or

(3) released on personal recognizance, with or without surety.

(c) Release Pending Review of Decision Ordering Release. While a decision ordering the release of a prisoner is under review, the prisoner must—unless the court or judge rendering the decision, or the court of appeals, or the Supreme Court, or a judge or justice of either court orders otherwise—be released on personal recognizance, with or without surety.

(d) Modification of the Initial Order on Custody. An initial order governing the prisoner's custody or release, including any recognizance or surety, continues in effect pending review unless for special reasons shown to the court of appeals or the Supreme Court, or to a judge or justice of either court, the order is modified or an independent order regarding custody, release, or surety is issued.

[Amended March 10, 1986, effective July 1, 1986; April 24, 1998, effective December 1, 1998.]

FRAP 24. PROCEEDING IN FORMA PAUPERIS

(a) Leave to Proceed In Forma Pauperis.

(1) *Motion in the District Court.* Except as stated in Rule 24(a)(3), a party to a district-court action who desires to appeal in forma pauperis must file a motion in the district court. The party must attach an affidavit that:

(A) shows in the detail prescribed by Form 4 of the Appendix of Forms the party's inability to pay or to give security for fees and costs;

(B) claims an entitlement to redress; and

(C) states the issues that the party intends to present on appeal.

(2) *Action on the Motion.* If the district court grants the motion, the party may proceed on appeal without prepaying or giving security for fees and costs, unless a statute provides otherwise. If the district court denies the motion, it must state its reasons in writing.

(3) *Prior Approval.* A party who was permitted to proceed in forma pauperis in the district-court action, or who was determined to be financially unable to obtain an adequate defense in a criminal case, may proceed on appeal in forma pauperis without further authorization, unless:

(A) the district court—before or after the notice of appeal is filed—certifies that the appeal is not taken in good faith or finds that the party is not otherwise entitled to proceed in forma pauperis and states in writing its reasons for the certification or finding; or

(B) a statute provides otherwise.

(4) *Notice of District Court's Denial.* The district clerk must immediately notify the parties and the court of appeals when the district court does any of the following:

(A) denies a motion to proceed on appeal in forma pauperis;

(B) certifies that the appeal is not taken in good faith; or

(C) finds that the party is not otherwise entitled to proceed in forma pauperis.

(5) *Motion in the Court of Appeals.* A party may file a motion to proceed on appeal in forma pauperis in the court of appeals within 30 days after service of the notice prescribed in Rule 24(a)(4). The motion must include a copy of the affidavit filed in the district court and the district court's statement of reasons for its action. If no affidavit was filed in the district court, the party must include the affidavit prescribed by Rule 24(a)(1).

(b) Leave to Proceed In Forma Pauperis on Appeal or Review of an Administrative Agency Pro-

ceeding. When an appeal or review of a proceeding before an administrative agency, board, commission, or officer (including for the purpose of this rule the United States Tax Court) proceeds directly in a court of appeals, a party may file in the court of appeals a motion for leave to proceed on appeal in forma pauperis with an affidavit prescribed by Rule 24(a)(1).

(c) Leave to Use Original Record. A party allowed to proceed on appeal in forma pauperis may request that the appeal be heard on the original record without reproducing any part.

[Amended April 30, 1979, effective August 1, 1979; March 10, 1986, effective July 1, 1986; April 24, 1998, effective December 1, 1998; April 29, 2002, effective December 1, 2002.]

TITLE VII. GENERAL PROVISIONS

FRAP 25. FILING AND SERVICE

(a) Filing.

(1) *Filing With the Clerk.* A paper required or permitted to be filed in a court of appeals must be filed with the clerk.

(2) *Filing: Method and Timeliness.*

(A) In General. Filing may be accomplished by mail addressed to the clerk, but filing is not timely unless the clerk receives the papers within the time fixed for filing.

(B) A Brief or Appendix. A brief or appendix is timely filed, however, if on or before the last day for filing, it is:

(i) mailed to the clerk by First–Class Mail, or other class of mail that is at least as expeditious, postage prepaid; or

(ii) dispatched to a third-party commercial carrier for delivery to the clerk within 3 calendar days.

(C) Inmate Filing. A paper filed by an inmate confined in an institution is timely if deposited in the institution's internal mailing system on or before the last day for filing. If an institution has a system designed for legal mail, the inmate must use that system to receive the benefit of this rule. Timely filing may be shown by a declaration in compliance with 28 U.S.C. § 1746 or by a notarized statement, either of which must set forth the date of deposit and state that first-class postage has been prepaid.

(D) Electronic Filing. A court of appeals may by local rule permit or require papers to be filed, signed, or verified by electronic means that are consistent with technical standards, if any, that the Judicial Conference of the United States establishes. A local rule may require filing by electronic means only if reasonable exceptions are allowed. A paper filed by electronic means in compliance with a local rule constitutes a written paper for the purpose of applying these rules.

(3) *Filing a Motion With a Judge.* If a motion requests relief that may be granted by a single judge, the judge may permit the motion to be filed with the judge; the judge must note the filing date on the motion and give it to the clerk.

(4) *Clerk's Refusal of Documents.* The clerk must not refuse to accept for filing any paper presented for that purpose solely because it is not presented in proper form as required by these rules or by any local rule or practice.

(5) *Privacy Protection.* An appeal in a case whose privacy protection was governed by Federal Rule of Bankruptcy Procedure 9037, Federal Rule of Civil Procedure 5.2, or Federal Rule of Criminal Procedure 49.1 is governed by the same rule on appeal. In all other proceedings, privacy protection is governed by Federal Rule of Civil Procedure 5.2, except that Federal Rule of Criminal Procedure 49.1 governs when an extraordinary writ is sought in a criminal case.

(b) Service of All Papers Required. Unless a rule requires service by the clerk, a party must, at or before the time of filing a paper, serve a copy on the other parties to the appeal or review. Service on a party represented by counsel must be made on the party's counsel.

(c) Manner of Service.

(1) Service may be any of the following:

(A) personal, including delivery to a responsible person at the office of counsel;

(B) by mail;

(C) by third-party commercial carrier for delivery within 3 calendar days; or

(D) by electronic means, if the party being served consents in writing.

(2) If authorized by local rule, a party may use the court's transmission equipment to make electronic service under Rule 25(c)(1)(D).

(3) When reasonable considering such factors as the immediacy of the relief sought, distance, and cost, service on a party must be by a manner at least as expeditious as the manner used to file the paper with the court.

(4) Service by mail or by commercial carrier is complete on mailing or delivery to the carrier. Service by electronic means is complete on transmission, unless the party making service is notified that the paper was not received by the party served.

(d) Proof of Service.

(1) A paper presented for filing must contain either of the following:

(A) an acknowledgment of service by the person served; or

(B) proof of service consisting of a statement by the person who made service certifying:

(i) the date and manner of service;

(ii) the names of the persons served; and

(iii) their mail or electronic addresses, facsimile numbers, or the addresses of the places of delivery, as appropriate for the manner of service.

(2) When a brief or appendix is filed by mailing or dispatch in accordance with Rule 25(a)(2)(B), the proof of service must also state the date and manner by which the document was mailed or dispatched to the clerk.

(3) Proof of service may appear on or be affixed to the papers filed.

(e) Number of Copies. When these rules require the filing or furnishing of a number of copies, a court may require a different number by local rule or by order in a particular case.

[Amended March 10, 1986, effective July 1, 1986; April 30, 1991, effective December 1, 1991; April 22, 1993, effective December 1, 1993; April 29, 1994, effective December 1, 1994; April 23, 1996, effective December 1, 1996; April 24, 1998, effective December 1, 1998; April 29, 2002, effective December 1, 2002; April 12, 2006, effective December 1, 2006; April 30, 2007, effective December 1, 2007.]

FRAP 26. COMPUTING AND EXTENDING TIME

(a) Computing Time. The following rules apply in computing any period of time specified in these rules or in any local rule, court order, or applicable statute:

(1) Exclude the day of the act, event, or default that begins the period.

(2) Exclude intermediate Saturdays, Sundays, and legal holidays when the period is less than 11 days, unless stated in calendar days.

(3) Include the last day of the period unless it is a Saturday, Sunday, legal holiday, or—if the act to be done is filing a paper in court—a day on which the weather or other conditions make the clerk's office inaccessible.

(4) As used in this rule, "legal holiday" means New Year's Day, Martin Luther King, Jr.'s Birthday, Washington's Birthday, Memorial Day, Independence Day, Labor Day, Columbus Day, Veterans' Day, Thanksgiving Day, Christmas Day, and any other day declared a holiday by the President, Congress, or the state in which is located either the district court that rendered the challenged judgment or order, or the circuit clerk's principal office.

(b) Extending Time. For good cause, the court may extend the time prescribed by these rules or by its order to perform any act, or may permit an act to be done after that time expires. But the court may not extend the time to file:

(1) a notice of appeal (except as authorized in Rule 4) or a petition for permission to appeal; or

(2) a notice of appeal from or a petition to enjoin, set aside, suspend, modify, enforce, or otherwise review an order of an administrative agency, board, commission, or officer of the United States, unless specifically authorized by law.

(c) Additional Time After Service. When a party is required or permitted to act within a prescribed period after a paper is served on that party, 3 calendar days are added to the prescribed period unless the paper is delivered on the date of service stated in the proof of service. For purposes of this Rule 26(c), a paper that is served electronically is not treated as delivered on the date of service stated in the proof of service.

[Amended March 1, 1971, effective July 1, 1971; March 10, 1986, effective July 1, 1986; April 25, 1989, effective December 1, 1989; April 30, 1991, effective December 1, 1991; April 23, 1996, effective December 1, 1996; April 24, 1998, effective December 1, 1998; April 29, 2002, effective December 1, 2002; April 25, 2005, effective December 1, 2005.]

FRAP 26.1 CORPORATE DISCLOSURE STATEMENT

(a) Who Must File. Any nongovernmental corporate party to a proceeding in a court of appeals must file a statement that identifies any parent corporation and any publicly held corporation that owns 10% or more of its stock or states that there is no such corporation.

(b) Time for Filing; Supplemental Filing. A party must file the Rule 26.1(a) statement with the principal brief or upon filing a motion, response, petition, or answer in the court of appeals, whichever occurs first, unless a local rule requires earlier filing. Even if the statement has already been filed, the party's principal brief must include the statement before the table of contents. A party must supplement its statement whenever the information that must be disclosed under Rule 26.1(a) changes.

(c) Number of Copies. If the Rule 26.1(a) statement is filed before the principal brief, or if a supplemental statement is filed, the party must file an original and 3 copies unless the court requires a different number by local rule or by order in a particular case.

[Adopted April 25, 1989, effective December 1, 1989; amended April 30, 1991, effective December 1, 1991; April 29, 1994, effective December 1, 1994; April 24, 1998, effective December 1, 1998; April 29, 2002, effective December 1, 2002.]

FRAP 27. MOTIONS

(a) In General.

(1) *Application for Relief.* An application for an order or other relief is made by motion unless these rules prescribe another form. A motion must be in writing unless the court permits otherwise.

(2) *Contents of a Motion.*

(A) Grounds and relief sought. A motion must state with particularity the grounds for the motion, the relief sought, and the legal argument necessary to support it.

(B) Accompanying documents.

(i) Any affidavit or other paper necessary to support a motion must be served and filed with the motion.

(ii) An affidavit must contain only factual information, not legal argument.

(iii) A motion seeking substantive relief must include a copy of the trial court's opinion or agency's decision as a separate exhibit.

(C) Documents barred or not required.

(i) A separate brief supporting or responding to a motion must not be filed.

(ii) A notice of motion is not required.

(iii) A proposed order is not required.

(3) *Response.*

(A) Time to file. Any party may file a response to a motion; Rule 27(a)(2) governs its contents. The response must be filed within 8 days after service of the motion unless the court shortens or extends the time. A motion authorized by Rules 8, 9, 18, or 41 may be granted before the 8–day period runs only if the court gives reasonable notice to the parties that it intends to act sooner.

(B) Request for affirmative relief. A response may include a motion for affirmative relief. The time to respond to the new motion, and to reply to that response, are governed by Rule 27(a)(3)(A) and (a)(4). The title of the response must alert the court to the request for relief.

(4) *Reply to Response.* Any reply to a response must be filed within 5 days after service of the response. A reply must not present matters that do not relate to the response.

(b) Disposition of a Motion for a Procedural Order.

The court may act on a motion for a procedural order—including a motion under Rule 26(b)—at any time without awaiting a response, and may, by rule or by order in a particular case, authorize its clerk to act on specified types of procedural motions. A party adversely affected by the court's, or the clerk's, action may file a motion to reconsider, vacate, or modify that action. Timely opposition filed after the motion is granted in whole or in part does not constitute a request to reconsider, vacate, or modify the disposition; a motion requesting that relief must be filed.

(c) Power of a Single Judge to Entertain a Motion.

A circuit judge may act alone on any motion, but may not dismiss or otherwise determine an appeal or other proceeding. A court of appeals may provide by rule or by order in a particular case that only the court may act on any motion or class of motions. The court may review the action of a single judge.

(d) Form of Papers; Page Limits; and Number of Copies.

(1) *Format.*

(A) Reproduction. A motion, response, or reply may be reproduced by any process that yields a clear black image on light paper. The paper must be opaque and unglazed. Only one side of the paper may be used.

(B) Cover. A cover is not required, but there must be a caption that includes the case number, the name of the court, the title of the case, and a brief descriptive title indicating the purpose of the motion and identifying the party or parties for whom it is filed. If a cover is used, it must be white.

(C) Binding. The document must be bound in any manner that is secure, does not obscure the text, and permits the document to lie reasonably flat when open.

(D) Paper Size, Line Spacing, and Margins. The document must be on 8½ by 11 inch paper. The text must be double-spaced, but quotations more than two lines long may be indented and single-spaced. Headings and footnotes may be single-spaced. Margins must be at least one inch on all four sides. Page numbers may be placed in the margins, but no text may appear there.

(E) Typeface and Type Styles. The document must comply with the typeface requirements of Rule 32(a)(5) and the type-style requirements of Rule 32(a)(6).

(2) *Page Limits.* A motion or a response to a motion must not exceed 20 pages, exclusive of the corporate disclosure statement and accompanying documents authorized by Rule 27(a)(2)(B), unless the court permits or directs otherwise. A reply to a response must not exceed 10 pages.

(3) *Number of Copies.* An original and 3 copies must be filed unless the court requires a different number by local rule or by order in a particular case.

(e) Oral Argument.

A motion will be decided without oral argument unless the court orders otherwise.

[Amended April 30, 1979, effective August 1, 1979; April 25, 1989, effective December 1, 1989; April 29, 1994, effective December 1, 1994; April 24, 1998, effective December 1,

1998; April 29, 2002, effective December 1, 2002; April 25, 2005, effective December 1, 2005.]

FRAP 28. BRIEFS

(a) Appellant's Brief. The appellant's brief must contain, under appropriate headings and in the order indicated:

(1) a corporate disclosure statement if required by Rule 26.1;

(2) a table of contents, with page references;

(3) a table of authorities—cases (alphabetically arranged), statutes, and other authorities—with references to the pages of the brief where they are cited;

(4) a jurisdictional statement, including:

(A) the basis for the district court's or agency's subject-matter jurisdiction, with citations to applicable statutory provisions and stating relevant facts establishing jurisdiction;

(B) the basis for the court of appeals' jurisdiction, with citations to applicable statutory provisions and stating relevant facts establishing jurisdiction;

(C) the filing dates establishing the timeliness of the appeal or petition for review; and

(D) an assertion that the appeal is from a final order or judgment that disposes of all parties' claims, or information establishing the court of appeals' jurisdiction on some other basis;

(5) a statement of the issues presented for review;

(6) a statement of the case briefly indicating the nature of the case, the course of proceedings, and the disposition below;

(7) a statement of facts relevant to the issues submitted for review with appropriate references to the record (see Rule 28(e));

(8) a summary of the argument, which must contain a succinct, clear, and accurate statement of the arguments made in the body of the brief, and which must not merely repeat the argument headings;

(9) the argument, which must contain:

(A) appellant's contentions and the reasons for them, with citations to the authorities and parts of the record on which the appellant relies; and

(B) for each issue, a concise statement of the applicable standard of review (which may appear in the discussion of the issue or under a separate heading placed before the discussion of the issues);

(10) a short conclusion stating the precise relief sought; and

(11) the certificate of compliance, if required by Rule 32(a)(7).

(b) Appellee's Brief. The appellee's brief must conform to the requirements of Rule 28(a)(1)–(9) and (11), except that none of the following need appear unless the appellee is dissatisfied with the appellant's statement:

(1) the jurisdictional statement;

(2) the statement of the issues;

(3) the statement of the case;

(4) the statement of the facts; and

(5) the statement of the standard of review.

(c) Reply Brief. The appellant may file a brief in reply to the appellee's brief. Unless the court permits, no further briefs may be filed. A reply brief must contain a table of contents, with page references, and a table of authorities—cases (alphabetically arranged), statutes, and other authorities—with references to the pages of the reply brief where they are cited.

(d) References to Parties. In briefs and at oral argument, counsel should minimize use of the terms "appellant" and "appellee." To make briefs clear, counsel should use the parties' actual names or the designations used in the lower court or agency proceeding, or such descriptive terms as "the employee," "the injured person," "the taxpayer," "the ship," "the stevedore."

(e) References to the Record. References to the parts of the record contained in the appendix filed with the appellant's brief must be to the pages of the appendix. If the appendix is prepared after the briefs are filed, a party referring to the record must follow one of the methods detailed in Rule 30(c). If the original record is used under Rule 30(f) and is not consecutively paginated, or if the brief refers to an unreproduced part of the record, any reference must be to the page of the original document. For example:

- Answer p. 7;
- Motion for Judgment p. 2;
- Transcript p. 231.

Only clear abbreviations may be used. A party referring to evidence whose admissibility is in controversy must cite the pages of the appendix or of the transcript at which the evidence was identified, offered, and received or rejected.

(f) Reproduction of Statutes, Rules, Regulations, etc. If the court's determination of the issues presented requires the study of statutes, rules, regulations, etc., the relevant parts must be set out in the brief or in an addendum at the end, or may be supplied to the court in pamphlet form.

(g) [Reserved].

(h) [Reserved].

(i) Briefs in a Case Involving Multiple Appellants or Appellees. In a case involving more than one appellant or appellee, including consolidated cases, any number of appellants or appellees may join in a brief, and any party may adopt by reference a part of another's brief. Parties may also join in reply briefs.

(j) Citation of Supplemental Authorities. If pertinent and significant authorities come to a party's attention after the party's brief has been filed—or after oral argument but before decision—a party may promptly advise the circuit clerk by letter, with a copy to all other parties, setting forth the citations. The letter must state the reasons for the supplemental citations, referring either to the page of the brief or to a point argued orally. The body of the letter must not exceed 350 words. Any response must be made promptly and must be similarly limited.

[Amended April 30, 1979, effective August 1, 1979; March 10, 1986, effective July 1, 1986; April 25, 1989, effective December 1, 1989; April 30, 1991, effective December 1, 1991; April 22, 1993, effective December 1, 1993; April 29, 1994, effective December 1, 1994; April 24, 1998, effective December 1, 1998; April 29, 2002, effective December 1, 2002; April 1, 2005, effective December 1, 2005.]

FRAP 28.1 CROSS–APPEALS

(a) Applicability. This rule applies to a case in which a cross-appeal is filed. Rules 28(a)–(c), 31(a)(1), 32(a)(2), and 32(a)(7)(A)–(B) do not apply to such a case, except as otherwise provided in this rule.

(b) Designation of Appellant. The party who files a notice of appeal first is the appellant for the purposes of this rule and Rules 30 and 34. If notices are filed on the same day, the plaintiff in the proceeding below is the appellant. These designations may be modified by the parties' agreement or by court order.

(c) Briefs. In a case involving a cross-appeal:

(1) *Appellant's Principal Brief.* The appellant must file a principal brief in the appeal. That brief must comply with Rule 28(a).

(2) *Appellee's Principal and Response Brief.* The appellee must file a principal brief in the cross-appeal and must, in the same brief, respond to the principal brief in the appeal. That appellee's brief must comply with Rule 28(a), except that the brief need not include a statement of the case or a statement of the facts unless the appellee is dissatisfied with the appellant's statement.

(3) *Appellant's Response and Reply Brief.* The appellant must file a brief that responds to the principal brief in the cross-appeal and may, in the same brief, reply to the response in the appeal. That brief must comply with Rule 28(a)(2)–(9) and (11), except that none of the following need appear unless the appellant is dissatisfied with the appellee's statement in the cross-appeal:

(A) the jurisdictional statement;

(B) the statement of the issues;

(C) the statement of the case;

(D) the statement of the facts; and

(E) the statement of the standard of review.

(4) *Appellee's Reply Brief.* The appellee may file a brief in reply to the response in the cross-appeal. That brief must comply with Rule 28(a)(2)–(3) and (11) and must be limited to the issues presented by the cross-appeal.

(5) *No Further Briefs.* Unless the court permits, no further briefs may be filed in a case involving a cross-appeal.

(d) Cover. Except for filings by unrepresented parties, the cover of the appellant's principal brief must be blue; the appellee's principal and response brief, red; the appellant's response and reply brief, yellow; the appellee's reply brief, gray; an intervenor's or amicus curiae's brief, green; and any supplemental brief, tan. The front cover of a brief must contain the information required by Rule 32(a)(2).

(e) Length.

(1) *Page Limitation.* Unless it complies with Rule 28.1(e)(2) and (3), the appellant's principal brief must not exceed 30 pages; the appellee's principal and response brief, 35 pages; the appellant's response and reply brief, 30 pages; and the appellee's reply brief, 15 pages.

(2) *Type-Volume Limitation.*

(A) The appellant's principal brief or the appellant's response and reply brief is acceptable if:

(i) it contains no more than 14,000 words; or

(ii) it uses a monospaced face and contains no more than 1,300 lines of text.

(B) The appellee's principal and response brief is acceptable if:

(i) it contains no more than 16,500 words; or

(ii) it uses a monospaced face and contains no more than 1,500 lines of text.

(C) The appellee's reply brief is acceptable if it contains no more than half of the type volume specified in Rule 28.1(e)(2)(A).

(3) *Certificate of Compliance.* A brief submitted under Rule 28.1(e)(2) must comply with Rule 32(a)(7)(C).

(f) Time to Serve and File a Brief. Briefs must be served and filed as follows:

(1) the appellant's principal brief, within 40 days after the record is filed;

(2) the appellee's principal and response brief, within 30 days after the appellant's principal brief is served;

(3) the appellant's response and reply brief, within 30 days after the appellee's principal and response brief is served; and

(4) the appellee's reply brief, within 14 days after the appellant's response and reply brief is served, but at least 3 days before argument unless the court, for good cause, allows a later filing.

[Amended April 25, 2005, effective December 1, 2005.]

FRAP 29. BRIEF OF AN AMICUS CURIAE

(a) When Permitted. The United States or its officer or agency, or a State, Territory, Commonwealth, or the District of Columbia may file an amicus-curiae brief without the consent of the parties or leave of court. Any other amicus curiae may file a brief only by leave of court or if the brief states that all parties have consented to its filing.

(b) Motion for Leave to File. The motion must be accompanied by the proposed brief and state:

(1) the movant's interest; and

(2) the reason why an amicus brief is desirable and why the matters asserted are relevant to the disposition of the case.

(c) Contents and Form. An amicus brief must comply with Rule 32. In addition to the requirements of Rule 32, the cover must identify the party or parties supported and indicate whether the brief supports affirmance or reversal. If an amicus curiae is a corporation, the brief must include a disclosure statement like that required of parties by Rule 26.1. An amicus brief need not comply with Rule 28, but must include the following:

(1) a table of contents, with page references;

(2) a table of authorities—cases (alphabetically arranged), statutes and other authorities—with references to the pages of the brief where they are cited;

(3) a concise statement of the identity of the amicus curiae, its interest in the case, and the source of its authority to file;

(4) an argument, which may be preceded by a summary and which need not include a statement of the applicable standard of review; and

(5) a certificate of compliance, if required by Rule 32(a)(7).

(d) Length. Except by the court's permission, an amicus brief may be no more than one-half the maximum length authorized by these rules for a party's principal brief. If the court grants a party permission to file a longer brief, that extension does not affect the length of an amicus brief.

(e) Time for Filing. An amicus curiae must file its brief, accompanied by a motion for filing when necessary, no later than 7 days after the principal brief of the party being supported is filed. An amicus curiae that does not support either party must file its brief no later than 7 days after the appellant's or petitioner's principal brief is filed. A court may grant leave for later filing, specifying the time within which an opposing party may answer.

(f) Reply Brief. Except by the court's permission, an amicus curiae may not file a reply brief.

(g) Oral Argument. An amicus curiae may participate in oral argument only with the court's permission.

[Amended April 24, 1998, effective December 1, 1998.]

FRAP 30. APPENDIX TO THE BRIEFS

(a) Appellant's Responsibility.

(1) *Contents of the Appendix.* The appellant must prepare and file an appendix to the briefs containing:

(A) the relevant docket entries in the proceeding below;

(B) the relevant portions of the pleadings, charge, findings, or opinion;

(C) the judgment, order, or decision in question; and

(D) other parts of the record to which the parties wish to direct the court's attention.

(2) *Excluded Material.* Memoranda of law in the district court should not be included in the appendix unless they have independent relevance. Parts of the record may be relied on by the court or the parties even though not included in the appendix.

(3) *Time to File; Number of Copies.* Unless filing is deferred under Rule 30(c), the appellant must file 10 copies of the appendix with the brief and must serve one copy on counsel for each party separately represented. An unrepresented party proceeding in forma pauperis must file 4 legible copies with the clerk, and one copy must be served on counsel for each separately represented party. The court may by local rule or by order in a particular case require the filing or service of a different number.

(b) All Parties' Responsibilities.

(1) *Determining the Contents of the Appendix.* The parties are encouraged to agree on the contents of the appendix. In the absence of an agreement, the appellant must, within 10 days after the record is filed, serve on the appellee a designation of the parts of the record the appellant intends to include in the appendix and a statement of the issues the appellant intends to present for review. The appellee may, within 10 days after receiving the designation, serve on the appellant a designation of additional parts to which it wishes to direct the court's attention. The appellant must include the designated parts in the appendix. The parties must not engage in unnecessary designation of parts of the record, because the entire record is available to the court. This paragraph applies also to a cross-appellant and a cross-appellee.

(2) *Costs of Appendix.* Unless the parties agree otherwise, the appellant must pay the cost of the appendix. If the appellant considers parts of the record designated by the appellee to be unnecessary, the appellant may advise the appellee, who must then advance the cost of including those parts. The cost of the appendix is a taxable cost. But if any party causes unnecessary parts of the record to be included in the appendix, the court may impose the cost of those parts on that party. Each circuit must, by local rule, provide for sanctions against attorneys who unreasonably and vexatiously increase litigation costs by including unnecessary material in the appendix.

(c) Deferred Appendix.

(1) *Deferral Until After Briefs Are Filed.* The court may provide by rule for classes of cases or by order in a particular case that preparation of the appendix may be deferred until after the briefs have been filed and that the appendix may be filed 21 days after the appellee's brief is served. Even though the filing of the appendix may be deferred, Rule 30(b) applies; except that a party must designate the parts of the record it wants included in the appendix when it serves its brief, and need not include a statement of the issues presented.

(2) *References to the Record.*

(A) If the deferred appendix is used, the parties may cite in their briefs the pertinent pages of the record. When the appendix is prepared, the record pages cited in the briefs must be indicated by inserting record page numbers, in brackets, at places in the appendix where those pages of the record appear.

(B) A party who wants to refer directly to pages of the appendix may serve and file copies of the brief within the time required by Rule 31(a), containing appropriate references to pertinent pages of the record. In that event, within 14 days after the appendix is filed, the party must serve and file copies of the brief, containing references to the pages of the appendix in place of or in addition to the references to the pertinent pages of the record. Except for the correction of typographical errors, no other changes may be made to the brief.

(d) Format of the Appendix. The appendix must begin with a table of contents identifying the page at which each part begins. The relevant docket entries must follow the table of contents. Other parts of the record must follow chronologically. When pages from the transcript of proceedings are placed in the appendix, the transcript page numbers must be shown in brackets immediately before the included pages. Omissions in the text of papers or of the transcript must be indicated by asterisks. Immaterial formal matters (captions, subscriptions, acknowledgments, etc.) should be omitted.

(e) Reproduction of Exhibits. Exhibits designated for inclusion in the appendix may be reproduced in a separate volume, or volumes, suitably indexed. Four copies must be filed with the appendix, and one copy must be served on counsel for each separately represented party. If a transcript of a proceeding before an administrative agency, board, commission, or officer was used in a district-court action and has been designated for inclusion in the appendix, the transcript must be placed in the appendix as an exhibit.

(f) Appeal on the Original Record Without an Appendix. The court may, either by rule for all cases or classes of cases or by order in a particular case, dispense with the appendix and permit an appeal to proceed on the original record with any copies of the record, or relevant parts, that the court may order the parties to file.

[Amended March 30, 1970, effective July 1, 1970; March 10, 1986, effective July 1, 1986; April 30, 1991, effective December 1, 1991; April 29, 1994, effective December 1, 1994; April 24, 1998, effective December 1, 1998.]

FRAP 31. SERVING AND FILING BRIEFS

(a) Time to Serve and File a Brief.

(1) The appellant must serve and file a brief within 40 days after the record is filed. The appellee must serve and file a brief within 30 days after the appellant's brief is served. The appellant may serve and file a reply brief within 14 days after service of the appellee's brief but a reply brief must be filed at least 3 days before argument, unless the court, for good cause, allows a later filing.

(2) A court of appeals that routinely considers cases on the merits promptly after the briefs are filed may shorten the time to serve and file briefs, either by local rule or by order in a particular case.

(b) Number of Copies. Twenty-five copies of each brief must be filed with the clerk and 2 copies must be served on each unrepresented party and on counsel for each separately represented party. An unrepresented party proceeding in forma pauperis must file 4 legible copies with the clerk, and one copy must be served on each unrepresented party and on counsel for each separately represented party. The court may by local rule or by order in a particular case require the filing or service of a different number.

(c) Consequence of Failure to File. If an appellant fails to file a brief within the time provided by this rule, or within an extended time, an appellee may move to dismiss the appeal. An appellee who fails to file a brief will not be heard at oral argument unless the court grants permission.

[Amended March 30, 1970, effective July 1, 1970; March 10, 1986, effective July 1, 1986; April 29, 1994, effective December 1, 1994; April 24, 1998, effective December 1, 1998; April 29, 2002, effective December 1, 2002.]

FRAP 32. FORM OF BRIEFS, APPENDICES, AND OTHER PAPERS

(a) Form of a Brief.

(1) *Reproduction.*

(A) A brief may be reproduced by any process that yields a clear black image on light paper. The paper must be opaque and unglazed. Only one side of the paper may be used.

(B) Text must be reproduced with a clarity that equals or exceeds the output of a laser printer.

(C) Photographs, illustrations, and tables may be reproduced by any method that results in a good copy of the original; a glossy finish is acceptable if the original is glossy.

(2) *Cover.* Except for filings by unrepresented parties, the cover of the appellant's brief must be blue; the appellee's, red; an intervenor's or amicus curiae's, green; any reply brief, gray; and any supplemental brief, tan. The front cover of a brief must contain:

(A) the number of the case centered at the top;

(B) the name of the court;

(C) the title of the case (see Rule 12(a));

(D) the nature of the proceeding (e.g., Appeal, Petition for Review) and the name of the court, agency, or board below;

(E) the title of the brief, identifying the party or parties for whom the brief is filed; and

(F) the name, office address, and telephone number of counsel representing the party for whom the brief is filed.

(3) *Binding.* The brief must be bound in any manner that is secure, does not obscure the text, and permits the brief to lie reasonably flat when open.

(4) *Paper Size, Line Spacing, and Margins.* The brief must be on 8½ by 11 inch paper. The text must be double-spaced, but quotations more than two lines long may be indented and single-spaced. Headings and footnotes may be single-spaced. Margins must be at least one inch on all four sides. Page numbers may be placed in the margins, but no text may appear there.

(5) *Typeface.* Either a proportionally spaced or a monospaced face may be used.

(A) A proportionally spaced face must include serifs, but sans-serif type may be used in headings and captions. A proportionally spaced face must be 14–point or larger.

(B) A monospaced face may not contain more than 10½ characters per inch.

(6) *Type Styles.* A brief must be set in a plain, roman style, although italics or boldface may be used for emphasis. Case names must be italicized or underlined.

(7) *Length.*

(A) Page limitation. A principal brief may not exceed 30 pages, or a reply brief 15 pages, unless it complies with Rule 32(a)(7)(B) and (C).

(B) Type-volume limitation.

(i) A principal brief is acceptable if:

● it contains no more than 14,000 words; or

● it uses a monospaced face and contains no more than 1,300 lines of text.

(ii) A reply brief is acceptable if it contains no more than half of the type volume specified in Rule 32(a)(7)(B)(i).

(iii) Headings, footnotes, and quotations count toward the word and line limitations. The corporate disclosure statement, table of contents, table of citations, statement with respect to oral argument, any addendum containing statutes, rules or regulations, and any certificates of counsel do not count toward the limitation.

(C) Certificate of Compliance.

(i) A brief submitted under Rules 28.1(e)(2) or 32(a)(7)(B) must include a certificate by the attorney, or an unrepresented party, that the brief complies with the type-volume limitation. The person preparing the certificate may rely on the word or line count of the word-processing system used to prepare the brief. The certificate must state either:

● the number of words in the brief; or

● the number of lines of monospaced type in the brief.

(ii) Form 6 in the Appendix of Forms is a suggested form of a certificate of compliance. Use of Form 6 must be regarded as sufficient to meet the requirements of Rules 28.1(e)(3) and 32(a)(7)(C)(i).

(b) Form of an Appendix.
An appendix must comply with Rule 32(a)(1), (2), (3), and (4), with the following exceptions:

(1) The cover of a separately bound appendix must be white.

(2) An appendix may include a legible photocopy of any document found in the record or of a printed judicial or agency decision.

(3) When necessary to facilitate inclusion of odd-sized documents such as technical drawings, an appendix may be a size other than 8½ by 11 inches, and need not lie reasonably flat when opened.

(c) Form of Other Papers.

(1) *Motion.* The form of a motion is governed by Rule 27(d).

(2) *Other Papers.* Any other paper, including a petition for panel rehearing and a petition for hearing or rehearing en banc, and any response to such a petition, must be reproduced in the manner prescribed by Rule 32(a), with the following exceptions:

(A) A cover is not necessary if the caption and signature page of the paper together contain the information required by Rule 32(a)(2). If a cover is used, it must be white.

(B) Rule 32(a)(7) does not apply.

(d) Signature. Every brief, motion, or other paper filed with the court must be signed by the party filing the paper or, if the party is represented, by one of the party's attorneys.

(e) Local Variation. Every court of appeals must accept documents that comply with the form requirements of this rule. By local rule or order in a particular case a court of appeals may accept documents that do not meet all of the form requirements of this rule.

[Amended April 24, 1998, effective December 1, 1998; April 29, 2002, effective December 1, 2002; April 25, 2005, effective December 1, 2005.]

FRAP 32.1 CITING JUDICIAL DISPOSITIONS

(a) Citation Permitted. A court may not prohibit or restrict the citation of federal judicial opinions, orders, judgments, or other written dispositions that have been:

(i) designated as "unpublished," "not for publication," "non-precedential," "not precedent," or the like; and

(ii) issued on or after January 1, 2007.

(b) Copies Required. If a party cites a federal judicial opinion, order, judgment, or other written disposition that is not available in a publicly accessible electronic database, the party must file and serve a copy of that opinion, order, judgment, or disposition with the brief or other paper in which it is cited.

Effective December 1, 2006.

FRAP 33. APPEAL CONFERENCES

The court may direct the attorneys—and, when appropriate, the parties to participate in one or more conferences to address any matter that may aid in disposing of the proceedings, including simplifying the issues and discussing settlement. A judge or other person designated by the court may preside over the conference, which may be conducted in person or by telephone. Before a settlement conference, the attorneys must consult with their clients and obtain as much authority as feasible to settle the case. The court may, as a result of the conference, enter an order controlling the course of the proceedings or implementing any settlement agreement.

[Amended April 29, 1994, effective December 1, 1994; April 24, 1998, effective December 1, 1998.]

FRAP 34. ORAL ARGUMENT

(a) In General.

(1) *Party's Statement.* Any party may file, or a court may require by local rule, a statement explaining why oral argument should, or need not, be permitted.

(2) *Standards.* Oral argument must be allowed in every case unless a panel of three judges who have examined the briefs and record unanimously agrees that oral argument is unnecessary for any of the following reasons:

(A) the appeal is frivolous;

(B) the dispositive issue or issues have been authoritatively decided; or

(C) the facts and legal arguments are adequately presented in the briefs and record, and the decisional process would not be significantly aided by oral argument.

(b) Notice of Argument; Postponement. The clerk must advise all parties whether oral argument will be scheduled, and, if so, the date, time, and place for it, and the time allowed for each side. A motion to postpone the argument or to allow longer argument must be filed reasonably in advance of the hearing date.

(c) Order and Contents of Argument. The appellant opens and concludes the argument. Counsel must not read at length from briefs, records, or authorities.

(d) Cross-Appeals and Separate Appeals. If there is a cross-appeal, Rule 28.1(b) determines which party is the appellant and which is the appellee for purposes of oral argument. Unless the court directs otherwise, a cross-appeal or separate appeal must be argued when the initial appeal is argued. Separate parties should avoid duplicative argument.

(e) Non-Appearance of a Party. If the appellee fails to appear for argument, the court must hear appellant's argument. If the appellant fails to appear for argument, the court may hear the appellee's argument. If neither party appears, the case will be decided on the briefs, unless the court orders otherwise.

(f) Submission on Briefs. The parties may agree to submit a case for decision on the briefs, but the court may direct that the case be argued.

(g) Use of Physical Exhibits at Argument; Removal. Counsel intending to use physical exhibits other than documents at the argument must arrange to place them in the courtroom on the day of the argument before the court convenes. After the argument, counsel must remove the exhibits from the courtroom, unless the court directs otherwise. The clerk may destroy or dispose of the exhibits if counsel does not reclaim them within a reasonable time after the clerk gives notice to remove them.

[Amended April 30, 1979, effective August 1, 1979; March 10, 1986, effective July 1, 1986; April 30, 1991, effective December 1, 1991; April 22, 1993, effective December 1, 1993; April 24, 1998, effective December 1, 1998; April 25, 2005, effective December 1, 2005.]

FRAP 35. EN BANC DETERMINATION

(a) When Hearing or Rehearing En Banc May Be Ordered. A majority of the circuit judges who are in regular active service and who are not disqualified may order that an appeal or other proceeding be heard or reheard by the court of appeals en banc. An en banc hearing or rehearing is not favored and ordinarily will not be ordered unless:

(1) en banc consideration is necessary to secure or maintain uniformity of the court's decisions; or

(2) the proceeding involves a question of exceptional importance.

(b) Petition for Hearing or Rehearing En Banc. A party may petition for a hearing or rehearing en banc.

(1) The petition must begin with a statement that either:

(A) the panel decision conflicts with a decision of the United States Supreme Court or of the court to which the petition is addressed (with citation to the conflicting case or cases) and consideration by the full court is therefore necessary to secure and maintain uniformity of the court's decisions; or

(B) the proceeding involves one or more questions of exceptional importance, each of which must be concisely stated; for example, a petition may assert that a proceeding presents a question of exceptional importance if it involves an issue on which the panel decision conflicts with the authoritative decisions of other United States Courts of Appeals that have addressed the issue.

(2) Except by the court's permission, a petition for an en banc hearing or rehearing must not exceed 15 pages, excluding material not counted under Rule 32.

(3) For purposes of the page limit in Rule 35(b)(2), if a party files both a petition for panel rehearing and a petition for rehearing en banc, they are considered a single document even if they are filed separately, unless separate filing is required by local rule.

(c) Time for Petition for Hearing or Rehearing En Banc. A petition that an appeal be heard initially en banc must be filed by the date when the appellee's brief is due. A petition for a rehearing en banc must be filed within the time prescribed by Rule 40 for filing a petition for rehearing.

(d) Number of Copies. The number of copies to be filed must be prescribed by local rule and may be altered by order in a particular case.

(e) Response. No response may be filed to a petition for an en banc consideration unless the court orders a response.

(f) Call for a Vote. A vote need not be taken to determine whether the case will be heard or reheard en banc unless a judge calls for a vote.

[Amended April 30, 1979, effective August 1, 1979; April 29, 1994, effective December 1, 1994; April 24, 1998, effective December 1, 1998; April 1, 2005, effective December 1, 2005.]

FRAP 36. ENTRY OF JUDGMENT; NOTICE

(a) Entry. A judgment is entered when it is noted on the docket. The clerk must prepare, sign, and enter the judgment:

(1) after receiving the court's opinion—but if settlement of the judgment's form is required, after final settlement; or

(2) if a judgment is rendered without an opinion, as the court instructs.

(b) Notice. On the date when judgment is entered, the clerk must serve on all parties a copy of the opinion—or the judgment, if no opinion was written—and a notice of the date when the judgment was entered.

[Amended April 24, 1998, effective December 1, 1998; April 29, 2002, effective December 1, 2002.]

FRAP 37. INTEREST ON JUDGMENT

(a) When the Court Affirms. Unless the law provides otherwise, if a money judgment in a civil case is affirmed, whatever interest is allowed by law is payable from the date when the district court's judgment was entered.

(b) When the Court Reverses. If the court modifies or reverses a judgment with a direction that a money judgment be entered in the district court, the mandate must contain instructions about the allowance of interest.

[Amended April 24, 1998, effective December 1, 1998.]

FRAP 38. FRIVOLOUS APPEAL— DAMAGES AND COSTS

If a court of appeals determines that an appeal is frivolous, it may, after a separately filed motion or notice from the court and reasonable opportunity to respond, award just damages and single or double costs to the appellee.

[Amended April 29, 1994, effective December 1, 1994; April 24, 1998, effective December 1, 1998.]

FRAP 39. COSTS

(a) Against Whom Assessed. The following rules apply unless the law provides or the court orders otherwise:

(1) if an appeal is dismissed, costs are taxed against the appellant, unless the parties agree otherwise;

(2) if a judgment is affirmed, costs are taxed against the appellant;

(3) if a judgment is reversed, costs are taxed against the appellee;

(4) if a judgment is affirmed in part, reversed in part, modified, or vacated, costs are taxed only as the court orders.

(b) Costs For and Against the United States. Costs for or against the United States, its agency, or officer will be assessed under Rule 39(a) only if authorized by law.

(c) Costs of Copies. Each court of appeals must, by local rule, fix the maximum rate for taxing the cost of producing necessary copies of a brief or appendix, or copies of records authorized by Rule 30(f). The rate must not exceed that generally charged for such work in the area where the clerk's office is located and should encourage economical methods of copying.

(d) Bill of Costs: Objections; Insertion in Mandate.

(1) A party who wants costs taxed must—within 14 days after entry of judgment—file with the circuit clerk, with proof of service, an itemized and verified bill of costs.

(2) Objections must be filed within 10 days after service of the bill of costs, unless the court extends the time.

(3) The clerk must prepare and certify an itemized statement of costs for insertion in the mandate, but issuance of the mandate must not be delayed for taxing costs. If the mandate issues before costs are finally determined, the district clerk must—upon the circuit clerk's request—add the statement of costs, or any amendment of it, to the mandate.

(e) Costs on Appeal Taxable in the District Court. The following costs on appeal are taxable in the district court for the benefit of the party entitled to costs under this rule:

(1) the preparation and transmission of the record;

(2) the reporter's transcript, if needed to determine the appeal;

(3) premiums paid for a supersedeas bond or other bond to preserve rights pending appeal; and

(4) the fee for filing the notice of appeal.

[Amended April 30, 1979, effective August 1, 1979; March 10, 1986, effective July 1, 1986; April 24, 1998, effective December 1, 1998.]

FRAP 40. PETITION FOR PANEL REHEARING

(a) Time to File; Contents; Answer; Action by the Court if Granted.

(1) *Time.* Unless the time is shortened or extended by order or local rule, a petition for panel rehearing may be filed within 14 days after entry of judgment. But in a civil case, if the United States or its officer or agency is a party, the time within which any party may seek rehearing is 45 days after entry of judgment, unless an order shortens or extends the time.

(2) *Contents.* The petition must state with particularity each point of law or fact that the petitioner believes the court has overlooked or misapprehended and must argue in support of the petition. Oral argument is not permitted.

(3) *Answer.* Unless the court requests, no answer to a petition for panel rehearing is permitted. But ordinarily rehearing will not be granted in the absence of such a request.

(4) *Action by the Court.* If a petition for panel rehearing is granted, the court may do any of the following:

(A) make a final disposition of the case without reargument;

(B) restore the case to the calendar for reargument or resubmission; or

(C) issue any other appropriate order.

(b) Form of Petition; Length. The petition must comply in form with Rule 32. Copies must be served and filed as Rule 31 prescribes. Unless the court permits or a local rule provides otherwise, a petition for panel rehearing must not exceed 15 pages.

[Amended April 30, 1979, effective August 1, 1979; April 29, 1994, effective December 1, 1994; April 24, 1998, effective December 1, 1998.]

FRAP 41. MANDATE: CONTENTS; ISSUANCE AND EFFECTIVE DATE; STAY

(a) Contents. Unless the court directs that a formal mandate issue, the mandate consists of a certified copy of the judgment, a copy of the court's opinion, if any, and any direction about costs.

(b) When Issued. The court's mandate must issue 7 calendar days after the time to file a petition for rehearing expires, or 7 calendar days after entry of an order denying a timely petition for panel rehearing, petition for rehearing en banc, or motion for stay of mandate, whichever is later. The court may shorten or extend the time.

(c) Effective Date. The mandate is effective when issued.

(d) Staying the Mandate.

(1) *On Petition for Rehearing or Motion.* The timely filing of a petition for panel rehearing, petition for rehearing en banc, or motion for stay of mandate, stays the mandate until disposition of the petition or motion, unless the court orders otherwise.

(2) *Pending Petition for Certiorari.*

(A) A party may move to stay the mandate pending the filing of a petition for a writ of certiorari in the Supreme Court. The motion must be served on all parties and must show that the certiorari petition would present a substantial question and that there is good cause for a stay.

(B) The stay must not exceed 90 days, unless the period is extended for good cause or unless the party who obtained the stay files a petition for the writ and so notifies the circuit clerk in writing within the period of the stay. In that case, the stay continues until the Supreme Court's final disposition.

(C) The court may require a bond or other security as a condition to granting or continuing a stay of the mandate.

(D) The court of appeals must issue the mandate immediately when a copy of a Supreme Court order denying the petition for writ of certiorari is filed.

[Amended April 29, 1994, effective December 1, 1994; April 24, 1998, effective December 1, 1998; April 29, 2002, effective December 1, 2002.]

FRAP 42. VOLUNTARY DISMISSAL

(a) Dismissal in the District Court. Before an appeal has been docketed by the circuit clerk, the district court may dismiss the appeal on the filing of a stipulation signed by all parties or on the appellant's motion with notice to all parties.

(b) Dismissal in the Court of Appeals. The circuit clerk may dismiss a docketed appeal if the parties file a signed dismissal agreement specifying how costs are to be paid and pay any fees that are due. But no mandate or other process may issue without a court order. An appeal may be dismissed on the appellant's motion on terms agreed to by the parties or fixed by the court.

[Amended April 24, 1998, effective December 1, 1998.]

FRAP 43. SUBSTITUTION OF PARTIES

(a) Death of a Party.

(1) *After Notice of Appeal Is Filed.* If a party dies after a notice of appeal has been filed or while a

proceeding is pending in the court of appeals, the decedent's personal representative may be substituted as a party on motion filed with the circuit clerk by the representative or by any party. A party's motion must be served on the representative in accordance with Rule 25. If the decedent has no representative, any party may suggest the death on the record, and the court of appeals may then direct appropriate proceedings.

(2) *Before Notice of Appeal Is Filed—Potential Appellant.* If a party entitled to appeal dies before filing a notice of appeal, the decedent's personal representative—or, if there is no personal representative, the decedent's attorney of record—may file a notice of appeal within the time prescribed by these rules. After the notice of appeal is filed, substitution must be in accordance with Rule 43(a)(1).

(3) *Before Notice of Appeal Is Filed—Potential Appellee.* If a party against whom an appeal may be taken dies after entry of a judgment or order in the district court, but before a notice of appeal is filed, an appellant may proceed as if the death had not occurred. After the notice of appeal is filed, substitution must be in accordance with Rule 43(a)(1).

(b) Substitution for a Reason Other Than Death. If a party needs to be substituted for any reason other than death, the procedure prescribed in Rule 43(a) applies.

(c) Public Officer: Identification; Substitution.

(1) *Identification of Party.* A public officer who is a party to an appeal or other proceeding in an official capacity may be described as a party by the public officer's official title rather than by name. But the court may require the public officer's name to be added.

(2) *Automatic Substitution of Officeholder.* When a public officer who is a party to an appeal or other proceeding in an official capacity dies, resigns, or otherwise ceases to hold office, the action does not abate. The public officer's successor is automatically substituted as a party. Proceedings following the substitution are to be in the name of the substituted party, but any misnomer that does not affect the substantial rights of the parties may be disregarded. An order of substitution may be entered at any time, but failure to enter an order does not affect the substitution.

[Amended March 10, 1986, effective July 1, 1986; April 24, 1998, effective December 1, 1998.]

FRAP 44. CASE INVOLVING A CONSTITUTIONAL QUESTION WHEN THE UNITED STATES OR THE RELEVANT STATE IS NOT A PARTY

(a) Constitutional Challenge to Federal Statute. If a party questions the constitutionality of an Act of

Congress in a proceeding in which the United States or its agency, officer, or employee is not a party in an official capacity, the questioning party must give written notice to the circuit clerk immediately upon the filing of the record or as soon as the question is raised in the court of appeals. The clerk must then certify that fact to the Attorney General.

(b) Constitutional Challenge to State Statute. If a party questions the constitutionality of a statute of a State in a proceeding in which that State or its agency, officer, or employee is not a party in an official capacity, the questioning party must give written notice to the circuit clerk immediately upon the filing of the record or as soon as the question is raised in the court of appeals. The clerk must then certify that fact to the attorney general of the State.

[Amended April 24, 1998, effective December 1, 1998; April 29, 2002, effective December 1, 2002.]

FRAP 45. CLERK'S DUTIES

(a) General Provisions.

(1) *Qualifications.* The circuit clerk must take the oath and post any bond required by law. Neither the clerk nor any deputy clerk may practice as an attorney or counselor in any court while in office.

(2) *When Court Is Open.* The court of appeals is always open for filing any paper, issuing and returning process, making a motion, and entering an order. The clerk's office with the clerk or a deputy in attendance must be open during business hours on all days except Saturdays, Sundays, and legal holidays. A court may provide by local rule or by order that the clerk's office be open for specified hours on Saturdays or on legal holidays other than New Year's Day, Martin Luther King, Jr.'s Birthday, Washington's Birthday, Memorial Day, Independence Day, Labor Day, Columbus Day, Veterans' Day, Thanksgiving Day, and Christmas Day.

(b) Records.

(1) *The Docket.* The circuit clerk must maintain a docket and an index of all docketed cases in the manner prescribed by the Director of the Administrative Office of the United States Courts. The clerk must record all papers filed with the clerk and all process, orders, and judgments.

(2) *Calendar.* Under the court's direction, the clerk must prepare a calendar of cases awaiting argument. In placing cases on the calendar for argument, the clerk must give preference to appeals in criminal cases and to other proceedings and appeals entitled to preference by law.

(3) *Other Records.* The clerk must keep other books and records required by the Director of the Administrative Office of the United States Courts, with the approval of the Judicial Conference of the United States, or by the court.

(c) Notice of an Order or Judgment. Upon the entry of an order or judgment, the circuit clerk must immediately serve a notice of entry on each party, with a copy of any opinion, and must note the date of service on the docket. Service on a party represented by counsel must be made on counsel.

(d) Custody of Records and Papers. The circuit clerk has custody of the court's records and papers. Unless the court orders or instructs otherwise, the clerk must not permit an original record or paper to be taken from the clerk's office. Upon disposition of the case, original papers constituting the record on appeal or review must be returned to the court or agency from which they were received. The clerk must preserve a copy of any brief, appendix, or other paper that has been filed.

[Amended March 1, 1971, effective July 1, 1971; March 10, 1986, effective July 1, 1986; April 24, 1998, effective December 1, 1998; April 29, 2002, effective December 1, 2002; April 25, 2005, effective December 1, 2005.]

FRAP 46. ATTORNEYS

(a) Admission to the Bar.

(1) *Eligibility.* An attorney is eligible for admission to the bar of a court of appeals if that attorney is of good moral and professional character and is admitted to practice before the Supreme Court of the United States, the highest court of a state, another United States court of appeals, or a United States district court (including the district courts for Guam, the Northern Mariana Islands, and the Virgin Islands).

(2) *Application.* An applicant must file an application for admission, on a form approved by the court that contains the applicant's personal statement showing eligibility for membership. The applicant must subscribe to the following oath or affirmation:

"I, _____, do solemnly swear [or affirm] that I will conduct myself as an attorney and counselor of this court, uprightly and according to law; and that I will support the Constitution of the United States."

(3) *Admission Procedures.* On written or oral motion of a member of the court's bar, the court will act on the application. An applicant may be admitted by oral motion in open court. But, unless the court orders otherwise, an applicant need not appear before the court to be admitted. Upon admission, an applicant must pay the clerk the fee prescribed by local rule or court order.

(b) Suspension or Disbarment.

(1) *Standard.* A member of the court's bar is subject to suspension or disbarment by the court if the member:

(A) has been suspended or disbarred from practice in any other court; or

(B) is guilty of conduct unbecoming a member of the court's bar.

(2) *Procedure.* The member must be given an opportunity to show good cause, within the time prescribed by the court, why the member should not be suspended or disbarred.

(3) *Order.* The court must enter an appropriate order after the member responds and a hearing is held, if requested, or after the time prescribed for a response expires, if no response is made.

(c) Discipline. A court of appeals may discipline an attorney who practices before it for conduct unbecoming a member of the bar or for failure to comply with any court rule. First, however, the court must afford the attorney reasonable notice, an opportunity to show cause to the contrary, and, if requested, a hearing.

[Amended March 10, 1986, effective July 1, 1986; April 24, 1998, effective December 1, 1998.]

FRAP 47. LOCAL RULES BY COURTS OF APPEALS

(a) Local Rules.

(1) Each court of appeals acting by a majority of its judges in regular active service may, after giving appropriate public notice and opportunity for comment, make and amend rules governing its practice. A generally applicable direction to parties or lawyers regarding practice before a court must be in a local rule rather than an internal operating procedure or standing order. A local rule must be consistent with—but not duplicative of—Acts of Congress and rules adopted under 28 U.S.C. § 2072 and must conform to any uniform numbering system prescribed by the Judicial Conference of the United States. Each circuit clerk must send the Administrative Office of the United States Courts a copy of each local rule and internal operating procedure when it is promulgated or amended.

(2) A local rule imposing a requirement of form must not be enforced in a manner that causes a party to lose rights because of a nonwillful failure to comply with the requirement.

(b) Procedure When There Is No Controlling Law. A court of appeals may regulate practice in a particular case in any manner consistent with federal law, these rules, and local rules of the circuit. No sanction or other disadvantage may be imposed for noncompliance with any requirement not in federal law, federal rules, or the local circuit rules unless the alleged violator has been furnished in the particular case with actual notice of the requirement.

[Amended April 27, 1995, effective December 1, 1995; April 24, 1998, effective December 1, 1998.]

FRAP 48. MASTERS

(a) Appointment; Powers. A court of appeals may appoint a special master to hold hearings, if necessary, and to recommend factual findings and disposition in matters ancillary to proceedings in the court. Unless the order referring a matter to a master specifies or limits the master's powers, those powers include, but are not limited to, the following:

(1) regulating all aspects of a hearing;

(2) taking all appropriate action for the efficient performance of the master's duties under the order;

(3) requiring the production of evidence on all matters embraced in the reference; and

(4) administering oaths and examining witnesses and parties.

(b) Compensation. If the master is not a judge or court employee, the court must determine the master's compensation and whether the cost is to be charged to any party.

[Former Rule 48 renumbered as Rule 1(c) and new Rule 48 adopted April 29, 1994, effective December 1, 1994; April 24, 1998, effective December 1, 1998.]

APPENDIX OF FORMS

FRAP FORM 1. NOTICE OF APPEAL TO A COURT OF APPEALS FROM A JUDGMENT OR ORDER OF A DISTRICT COURT

United States District Court for the

_____ District of _____

File Number _____

A. B., Plaintiff	)
v.	) Notice of Appeal
C. D., Defendant	)

Notice is hereby given that __(here name all parties taking the appeal)__, (plaintiffs) (defendants) in the above named case,* hereby appeal to the United States Court of Appeals for the _____ Circuit (from the final judgment) (from an order (describing it)) entered in this action on the ___ day of _____, _____.

(s)_____

Attorney for _____

Address:_____

* See Rule 3(c) for permissible ways of identifying appellants.

[Amended April 22, 1993, effective December 1, 1993; amended March 27, 2003, effective December 1, 2003.]

FRAP FORM 2. NOTICE OF APPEAL TO A COURT OF APPEALS FROM A DECISION OF THE UNITED STATES TAX COURT

UNITED STATES TAX COURT
Washington, D.C.

A.B., Petitioner	)
	)
v.	) Docket No. _____
	)
Commissioner of Internal	)
Revenue, Respondent	)

Notice of Appeal

Notice is hereby given that __(here name all parties taking the appeal)* __ hereby appeal to the United States Court of Appeals for the _____ Circuit from (that part of) the decision of this court entered in the above captioned proceeding on the ___ day of _____, _____ (relating to _____).

(s)_____

Counsel for _____

Address:_____

* See Rule 3(c) for permissible ways of identifying appellants.

[Amended April 22, 1993, effective December 1, 1993; amended March 27, 2003, effective December 1, 2003.]

FRAP FORM 3. PETITION FOR REVIEW OF ORDER OF AN AGENCY, BOARD, COMMISSION OR OFFICER

United States Court of Appeals
for the _____ Circuit

A.B., Petitioner)
)
v.) Petition for Review
XYZ Commission,)
Respondent)

___(here name all parties bringing the petition)*___ hereby petition the court for review of the Order of the XYZ Commission (describe the order) entered on _____, 20___.

(s)_____
Attorney for Petitioners
Address:_____

* See Rule 15.

[Amended April 22, 1993, effective December 1, 1993; amended March 27, 2003, effective December 1, 2003.]

FRAP FORM 4. AFFIDAVIT ACCOMPANYING MOTION FOR PERMISSION TO APPEAL IN FORMA PAUPERIS

United States District Court for the _____ District of _____

A.B., Plaintiff
v.   Case No. _____
C.D., Defendant

Affidavit in Support of Motion	**Instructions**
I swear or affirm under penalty of perjury that, because of my poverty, I cannot prepay the docket fees of my appeal or post a bond for them. I believe I am entitled to redress. I swear or affirm under penalty of perjury under United States laws that my answers on this form are true and correct. (28 U.S.C. § 1746; 18 U.S.C. § 1621.)	Complete all questions in this application and then sign it. Do not leave any blanks: if the answer to a question is "0," "none," or "not applicable (N/A)," write in that response. If you need more space to answer a question or to explain your answer, attach a separate sheet of paper identified with your name, your case's docket number, and the question number.
Signed: _____	Date: _____

My issues on appeal are:

1. *For both you and your spouse estimate the average amount of money received from each of the following sources during the past 12 months. Adjust any amount that was received weekly, biweekly, quarterly, semiannually, or annually to show the monthly rate. Use gross amounts, that is, amounts before any deductions for taxes or otherwise.*

Income source	Average monthly amount during the past 12 months		Amount expected next month	
	You	Spouse	You	Spouse
Employment	$_____	$_____	$_____	$_____
Self-employment	$_____	$_____	$_____	$_____
Income from real property (such as rental income)	$_____	$_____	$_____	$_____
Interest and dividends	$_____	$_____	$_____	$_____

Gifts	$____	$____	$____	$____
Alimony	$____	$____	$____	$____
Child support	$____	$____	$____	$____
Retirement (such as Social Security, pensions, annuities, insurance)	$____	$____	$____	$____
Disability (such as Social Security, insurance payments)	$____	$____	$____	$____
Unemployment payments	$____	$____	$____	$____
Public-assistance (such as welfare)	$____	$____	$____	$____
Other (specify): _____	$____	$____	$____	$____
Total monthly income:	$____	$____	$____	$____

2. *List your employment history, most recent employer first. (Gross monthly pay is before taxes or other deductions.)*

Employer	**Address**	**Dates of employment**	**Gross monthly pay**
_____	_____	_____	_____
_____	_____	_____	_____

3. *List your spouse's employment history, most recent employer first. (Gross monthly pay is before taxes or other deductions.)*

Employer	**Address**	**Dates of employment**	**Gross monthly pay**
_____	_____	_____	_____
_____	_____	_____	_____

4. *How much cash do you and your spouse have?* $_____
Below, state any money you or your spouse have in bank accounts or in any other financial institution.

Financial institution	**Type of account**	**Amount you have**	**Amount your spouse has**
_____	_____	$____	$____
_____	_____	$____	$____
_____	_____	$____	$____

If you are a prisoner, seeking to appeal a judgment in a civil action or proceeding, you must attach a statement certified by the appropriate institutional officer showing all receipts, expenditures, and balances during the last six months in your institutional accounts. If you have multiple accounts, perhaps because you have been in multiple institutions, attach one certified statement of each account.

5. *List the assets, and their values, which you own or your spouse owns. Do not list clothing and ordinary household furnishings.*

Home (Value)	**Other real estate** (Value)	**Motor vehicle # 1** (Value)
_____	_____	Make & year: _____
_____	_____	Model: _____
_____	_____	Registration # :_____
Other Assets (Value)	**Other assets** (Value)	**Motor vehicle # 2** (Value)
_____	_____	Make & year: _____
_____	_____	Model: _____
_____	_____	Registration # :_____

6. *State every person, business, or organization owing you or your spouse money, and the amount owed.*

Person owing you or your spouse money	**Amount owed to you**	**Amount owed to your spouse**
_____	_____	_____
_____	_____	_____

7. *State the persons who rely on you or your spouse for support.*

Name	**Relationship**	**Age**
_____	_____	_____
_____	_____	_____

8. *Estimate the average monthly expenses of you and your family. Show separately the amounts paid by your spouse. Adjust any payments that are made weekly, biweekly, quarterly, semiannually, or annually to show the monthly rate.*

	You	Your Spouse
Rent or home-mortgage payment (include lot rented for mobile home)	$_____	$_____
Are real-estate taxes included? ☐ Yes ☐ No		
Is property insurance included? ☐ Yes ☐ No		
Utilities (electricity, heating fuel, water, sewer, and Telephone)	$_____	$_____
Home maintenance (repairs and upkeep)	$_____	$_____
Food	$_____	$_____
Clothing	$_____	$_____
Laundry and dry-cleaning	$_____	$_____
Medical and dental expenses	$_____	$_____
Transportation (not including motor vehicle payments)	$_____	$_____
Recreation, entertainment, newspapers, magazines, etc.	$_____	$_____
Insurance (not deducted from wages or included in Mortgage payments)		
Homeowner's or renter's	$_____	$_____
Life	$_____	$_____
Health	$_____	$_____
Motor Vehicle	$_____	$_____
Other: _____	$_____	$_____
Taxes (not deducted from wages or included in Mortgage payments) (specify): _____	$_____	$_____
Installment payments		
Motor Vehicle	$_____	$_____
Credit card (name): _____	$_____	$_____
Department store (name): _____	$_____	$_____
Other: _____	$_____	$_____
Alimony, maintenance, and support paid to others	$_____	$_____
Regular expenses for operation of business, profession, or farm (attach detailed statement)	$_____	$_____
Other (specify): _____	$_____	$_____
Total monthly expenses:	$_____	$_____

9. *Do you expect any major changes to your monthly income or expenses or in your assets or liabilities during the next 12 months?*
☐ Yes ☐ No   If yes, describe on an attached sheet.

10. *Have you paid—or will you be paying—an attorney any money for services in connection with this case, including the completion of this form?* Yes No
If yes, how much? $_____
If yes, state the attorney's name, address, and telephone number:

_____

_____

11. *Have you paid—or will you be paying—anyone other than an attorney (such as a paralegal or a typist) any money for services in connection with this case, including the completion of this form?*
☐ Yes ☐ No
If yes, how much? $_____
If yes, state the person's name, address, and telephone number:

_____

_____

12. *Provide any other information that will help explain why you cannot pay the docket fees for your appeal.*

13. *State the address of your legal residence.*

_____

_____

Your daytime phone number: (___) _____
Your age: _____ Your years of schooling: _____
Your social-security number: _____

[Amended April 24, 1998, effective December 1, 1998; December 1, 2007.]

FRAP FORM 5. NOTICE OF APPEAL TO A COURT OF APPEALS FROM A JUDGMENT OR ORDER OF A DISTRICT COURT OR A BANKRUPTCY APPELLATE PANEL

United States District Court for the
_____ District of _____

In re   )
_____)
              Debtor   )
_____)   File No. _____
        A.B., Plaintiff   )
              v.   )
_____)
        C.D., Defendant   )

Notice of Appeal to
United States Court of Appeals
for the _____ Circuit

_____, the plaintiff [or defendant or other party] appeals to the United States Court of Appeals for the _____ Circuit from the final judgment [or order or decree] of the district court for the district of _____ [or bankruptcy appellate panel of the _____ circuit], entered in this case on _____, __ [here describe the judgment, order, or decree] _____.

The parties to the judgment [or order or decree] appealed from and the names and addresses of their respective attorneys are as follows:

Dated _____

Signed _____
                Attorney for Appellant

Address: _____

_____

[Adopted April 25, 1989, effective December 1, 1989; amended March 27, 2003, effective December 1, 2003.]

FRAP FORM 6. CERTIFICATE OF COMPLIANCE WITH RULE 32(a)

Certificate of Compliance With Type–Volume Limitation,
Typeface Requirements, and Type Style Requirements

1. This brief complies with the type-volume limitation of Fed. R. App. P. 32(a)(7)(B) because:

☐ this brief contains [*state the number of*] words, excluding the parts of the brief exempted by Fed. R. App. P. 32(a)(7)(B)(iii), *or*

☐ this brief uses a monospaced typeface and contains [*state the number of*] lines of text, excluding the parts of the brief exempted by Fed. R. App. P. 32(a)(7)(B)(iii).

2. This brief complies with the typeface requirements of Fed. R. App. P. 32(a)(5) and the type style requirements of Fed. R. App. P. 32(a)(6) because:

☐ this brief has been prepared in a proportionally spaced typeface using [*state name and version of word processing program*] in [*state font size and name of type style*], *or*

☐ this brief has been prepared in a monospaced typeface using [*state name and version of word processing program*] with [*state number of characters per inch and name of type style*].

(s)_____

Attorney for _____

Dated: _____

[Adopted April 29, 2002, effective December 1, 2002.]

INDEX TO
FEDERAL RULES OF APPELLATE PROCEDURE

Abatement and revival, **FRAP 43**
Administrative law and procedure, **FRAP 15 et seq.**
Administrative Office of the United States Courts, powers
    and duties, **FRAP 45**
Admission to bar, **FRAP 46**
Affidavits,
    Indigent persons, **FRAP 24; FRAP Form 4**
    Injunctions, **FRAP 8**
    Motions, **FRAP 27**
    Stay of proceedings, **FRAP 8**
Agency, definitions, **FRAP 15**
Agreed statement, records and recordation, **FRAP 10**
Amendments,
    Habeas corpus, **FRAP 23**
    Judgments and decrees,
        Interest, **FRAP 37**
        Time, **FRAP 4**
    Records and recordation, **FRAP 10, 16**
Amicus curiae,
    Briefs, **FRAP 21, 29**
    Oral argument, **FRAP 29**
Appeal as of right, **FRAP 3, 4**
Appeals by permission, **FRAP 5**
Appearances,
    Arguments, **FRAP 34**
    Mandamus, **FRAP 21**
    Prohibition, **FRAP 21**
Appellants, definitions, **FRAP 20**
Appellees, definitions, **FRAP 20**
Application of rules, **FRAP 1, 2**
Applications,
    Attorneys, admission to bar, **FRAP 46**
    Extraordinary writs, **FRAP 21**
    Habeas corpus, **FRAP 22**
    Indigent persons, **FRAP 24**
    Mandate, **FRAP 41**
Attorney General, constitutional questions, **FRAP 44**
Attorneys, **FRAP 46**
    Admission to bar, **FRAP 46**
    Books and papers, **FRAP 25**
    Conferences, **FRAP 33**
    Costs, **FRAP 30**
    Crimes and offenses, **FRAP 46**
    Disbarment, **FRAP 46**
    Discipline, **FRAP 46**
    Fees, **FRAP 4**
    Notice, **FRAP 3**
    Statements, **FRAP 12**
    Suspension, **FRAP 46**
Banc, court in banc, **FRAP 35**
Bankruptcy,
    Corporate disclosure statements, **FRAP 26.1**
    Judgments and decrees, **FRAP 6**
    Panels, **FRAP 6; FRAP Form 5**
Bill of costs, **FRAP 39**
Binding, briefs, **FRAP 32**
Bonds (officers and fiduciaries),
    Clerks of courts, **FRAP 45**

Bonds (officers and fiduciaries)—Cont'd
    Costs, **FRAP 5 et seq.**
    Indigent persons, **FRAP 24**
    Mandate, **FRAP 41**
    Permissive appeals, **FRAP 5**
    Supersedeas or stay, **FRAP 7 et seq.**
Books and papers,
    Clerks of courts, **FRAP 45**
    Forms, **FRAP 32**
    Motions, **FRAP 27**
    Signatures, **FRAP 32**
Briefs, **FRAP 28 et seq.**
    Amicus curiae, **FRAP 29**
    Appendices, **FRAP 30**
        Costs, **FRAP 39**
        Filing, **FRAP 25**
        Forms, **FRAP 32**
    Arguments, **FRAP 34**
    Certificates of compliance, **FRAP 32; FRAP Form 6**
    Copies, **FRAP 30 et seq.**
    Corporate disclosure statement, **FRAP 26.1**
    Costs, **FRAP 30, 39**
    Cross appeals, **FRAP 28.1, 30**
    Deferred appendix, **FRAP 30**
    Dismissal and nonsuit, **FRAP 31**
    Exhibits, **FRAP 30**
    Extraordinary writs, **FRAP 21**
    Filing, **FRAP 25**
        Amicus curiae, **FRAP 29**
        Appendices, **FRAP 30**
        Time, **FRAP 31**
    Forms, **FRAP 32; FRAP Form 6**
    Jurisdiction, **FRAP 28**
    Length, **FRAP 32**
    Lists, appendices, **FRAP 30**
    Mandamus, **FRAP 21**
    National Labor Relations Board, **FRAP 15.1**
    Omissions, appendices, **FRAP 30**
    Parties, **FRAP 28**
    Printing, **FRAP 39**
    Prohibition, **FRAP 21**
    References, **FRAP 28, 30**
    Reply briefs, **FRAP 28 et seq.**
        Amicus curiae, **FRAP 29**
        Time, **FRAP 31**
    Service of briefs, **FRAP 31**
    Signatures, **FRAP 32**
    Statutes, **FRAP 28**
    Submission on briefs, **FRAP 34**
    Time,
        Amicus curiae, **FRAP 29**
        Appendices, **FRAP 30**
        Filing, **FRAP 31**
    Typewriting, **FRAP 32**
        Cross appeals, **FRAP 28.1**
Calendars, clerks of courts, **FRAP 45**
Certificates and certification,
    Briefs, **FRAP 32; FRAP Form 6**
    Habeas corpus, **FRAP 22**

Certificates and certification—Cont'd
  Indigent persons, **FRAP 24**
  Lists, filing, **FRAP 17**
Certiorari, **FRAP 41**
Class actions, notice, **FRAP 3**
Clerks of courts, **FRAP 45**
  Attorneys, admission to bar, **FRAP 46**
  Exhibits, **FRAP 34**
  Notice, **FRAP 3**
  Records and recordation, **FRAP 11**
Commercial carriers, process, **FRAP 25**
Compromise and settlement, **FRAP 19**
  Conferences, **FRAP 33**
  Voluntary dismissal, **FRAP 42**
Conferences, **FRAP 33**
Congressional Acts, constitutional questions, **FRAP 44**
Consolidated appeals, **FRAP 3**
Constitutional questions, **FRAP 44**
Contracts, voluntary dismissal, **FRAP 42**
Copies,
  Briefs, **FRAP 30 et seq.**
  Clerks of courts, **FRAP 45**
  Corporate disclosure statements, **FRAP 26.1**
  Costs, **FRAP 39**
  District courts, **FRAP 3, 5**
  Extraordinary writs, **FRAP 21**
  Filing, **FRAP 25**
  Indigent persons, **FRAP 24**
  Judgments and decrees, **FRAP 36**
  Mandamus, **FRAP 21, 41**
  Motions, **FRAP 27**
  Opinions and decisions, **FRAP 32.1, 36**
  Prohibition, **FRAP 21**
  Rehearings, **FRAP 40**
  Tax Court, **FRAP 13**
Corporate disclosure statements, **FRAP 26.1**
Correctional institutions,
  Filing, **FRAP 4, 25**
  Habeas corpus, **FRAP 22, 23**
  Release, **FRAP 9**
Costs, **FRAP 39**
  Appendices, **FRAP 30, 39**
  Attorneys, sanctions, **FRAP 30**
  Bonds (officers and fiduciaries), **FRAP 5 et seq.**
  Dismissal and nonsuit, **FRAP 42**
  Frivolous appeals, **FRAP 38**
  Mandate, **FRAP 39, 41**
  Masters, **FRAP 48**
  Permissive appeals, **FRAP 5**
  United States, **FRAP 39**
Crimes and offenses,
  Attorneys, **FRAP 46**
  Corporate disclosure statements, **FRAP 26.1**
  Notice, **FRAP 3**
  Release, **FRAP 9**
  Supersedeas or stay, **FRAP 8**
  Time, **FRAP 4**
Cross appeals,
  Arguments, **FRAP 34**
  Briefs, **FRAP 28.1, 30**
  Oral arguments, **FRAP 34**
Cross-applications, **FRAP 5, 15**
Damages, frivolous appeals, **FRAP 38**
Death, parties, substitution, **FRAP 3, 43**
Default, **FRAP 15**
Definitions,
  Agency, **FRAP 15**

Definitions—Cont'd
  Appellant, **FRAP 20**
  Appellee, **FRAP 20**
  Legal holidays, **FRAP 26**
  Record on appeal, **FRAP 10**
Destruction, exhibits, **FRAP 34**
Discipline, attorneys, **FRAP 46**
Disclosure, corporations, statements, **FRAP 26.1**
Dismissal and nonsuit, **FRAP 31, 42**
District courts, **FRAP 3 et seq.**
Dockets and docketing, **FRAP 12**
  Clerks of courts, **FRAP 45**
  Entry of judgment, **FRAP 36**
  Tax Court, **FRAP 13**
Electronic filing, **FRAP 25**
En banc, **FRAP 35**
Entry of judgment, **FRAP 36**
Escape, habeas corpus, **FRAP 22, 23**
Evidence, statement of evidence, absence of report or
    transcript, **FRAP 10**
Excusable neglect, **FRAP 4**
Exhibits, **FRAP 34**
  Briefs, **FRAP 30**
Extension of time, **FRAP 4, 11, 26**
Extraordinary writs, **FRAP 2, 21**
Facsimile transmissions, filing, **FRAP 25**
Federal agencies, **FRAP 15 et seq.**
Fees,
  Administrative law and procedure, **FRAP 15**
  Attorneys, admission to bar, **FRAP 46**
  Dismissal and nonsuit, **FRAP 42**
  Permissive appeals, **FRAP 5**
Filing, **FRAP 25**
  Administrative law and procedure, **FRAP 17**
  Amicus curiae, briefs, **FRAP 29**
  Appendix to briefs, **FRAP 30**
  Attorneys, admission to bar, **FRAP 46**
  Clerks of courts, **FRAP 45**
  Electronic filing, **FRAP 25**
  Indigent persons, **FRAP 24**
  Mail and mailing, **FRAP 25**
  Notice, **FRAP 3**
    Tax Court, **FRAP 13**
  Tax Court, **FRAP 13**
Forms, **FRAP 32**
  Administrative law and procedure, **FRAP Form 3**
  Attorneys, admission to bar, **FRAP 46**
  Briefs, **FRAP 32; FRAP Form 6**
  Indigent persons, **FRAP 24; FRAP Form 4**
  Notice,
    District courts, **FRAP Forms 1, 5**
    Tax Court, **FRAP Form 2**
Frivolous appeals, **FRAP 38**
Habeas corpus, **FRAP 2, 22 et seq.**
Hearings,
  En banc, **FRAP 35**
  Oral argument, **FRAP 34**
Holidays,
  Clerks of courts, hours, **FRAP 45**
  Time, **FRAP 26**
Hours, clerks of courts, **FRAP 45**
Indexes, clerks of courts, **FRAP 45**
Indigent persons, **FRAP 24**
  Affidavits, **FRAP Form 4**
  Forms, **FRAP Form 4**
Injunctions, **FRAP 8**
Interest, judgment and decrees, **FRAP 37**

Interlocutory injunctions, **FRAP 8**
Intervention, **FRAP 15**
Joint appeals, **FRAP 3, 15**
Judges or justices,
    En banc, **FRAP 35**
    Habeas corpus, **FRAP 22**
Judgments and decrees,
    Amendments, **FRAP 4**
    Bankruptcy, **FRAP 6**
    Clerks of courts, **FRAP 45**
    Copies, **FRAP 36**
    Crimes and offenses, **FRAP 9**
    En banc, **FRAP 35**
    Entry, **FRAP 4, 36**
    Interest, **FRAP 37**
    Magistrate judges, **FRAP 3**
    Notice, **FRAP 4, 36**
    Rehearings, **FRAP 40**
    Release, **FRAP 9**
    Renewal, **FRAP 4**
Jurisdiction, briefs, **FRAP 28**
Length, briefs, **FRAP 32**
Limitation of actions, **FRAP 4**
Lists,
    Administrative law and procedure, **FRAP 17**
    Briefs, appendices, **FRAP 30**
Local rules, **FRAP 47**
Magistrate judges, **FRAP 3, 5**
Mail and mailing,
    Clerks of courts, **FRAP 45**
    Filing, **FRAP 25**
    Notice, **FRAP 3**
    Opinions, **FRAP 36**
    Time, **FRAP 26**
Mandamus, **FRAP 21, 41**
Mandates, **FRAP 1 et seq.**
Masters, **FRAP 48**
Misstatements, administrative law and procedure, **FRAP 16**
Motions, **FRAP 27**
    Administrative law and procedure, **FRAP 18**
    Amicus curiae, **FRAP 29**
    Appeal as of right, **FRAP 4**
    Arguments, **FRAP 34**
    Clerks of courts, **FRAP 45**
    Corporate disclosure statements, **FRAP 26.1**
    Death, parties, substitution, **FRAP 43**
    Dismissal and nonsuit, **FRAP 42**
    Filing, **FRAP 25**
    Forms,
        Briefs, **FRAP 32**
        Indigent persons, **FRAP Form 4**
    Indigent persons, **FRAP 24; FRAP Form 4**
    Injunctions, **FRAP 8**
    Oral arguments, **FRAP 34**
    Replies, **FRAP 27**
    Statements, **FRAP 27**
    Stay of proceedings,
        Administrative law and procedure, **FRAP 18**
        Mandate, **FRAP 41**
    Substitution, parties, death, **FRAP 43**
    Time, **FRAP 26, 27**
    Typewriting, **FRAP 27**
Multiple parties, **FRAP 28**
National Labor Relations Board, **FRAP 15.1**
New trial, **FRAP 4**
Nonappearance, **FRAP 34**

Notice,
    Administrative law and procedure, **FRAP 17, 18**
    Argument, oral arguments, **FRAP 34**
    Attorneys, discipline, **FRAP 46**
    Clerks of courts, hours, **FRAP 45**
    Constitutional questions, **FRAP 44**
    Death, parties, substitution, **FRAP 43**
    Entry of judgment, **FRAP 36**
    Exhibits, **FRAP 34**
    Filing, **FRAP 3, 13, 17**
    Judgments and decrees, entry of judgment, **FRAP 36**
    Oral arguments, **FRAP 34**
    Partial transcripts, **FRAP 10**
    Tax Court, **FRAP 13; FRAP Form 2**
Oaths and affirmations,
    Attorneys, admission to bar, **FRAP 46**
    Clerks of courts, **FRAP 45**
Officers and employees,
    Attorneys, **FRAP 46**
    Clerks of courts, **FRAP 45**
    Constitutional questions, **FRAP 44**
    Substitution, **FRAP 43**
Offices, clerks of courts, **FRAP 45**
Omissions,
    Administrative law and procedure, **FRAP 16**
    Briefs, appendices, **FRAP 30**
Opinions and decisions, **FRAP 36**
    Copies, **FRAP 32.1**
Oral argument, **FRAP 34**
    Amicus curiae, **FRAP 29**
    Extraordinary writs, **FRAP 21**
    Mandamus, **FRAP 21**
    National Labor Relations Board, **FRAP 15.1**
    Permissive appeals, **FRAP 5**
    Prohibition, **FRAP 21**
    Rehearings, **FRAP 40**
Orders of court, **FRAP 4**
    Attorneys, discipline, **FRAP 46**
    Bankruptcy, **FRAP 6**
    Clerks of courts, **FRAP 45**
    Conferences, **FRAP 33**
    Dismissal and nonsuit, **FRAP 42**
    En banc, **FRAP 35**
    Extraordinary writs, **FRAP 21**
    Mandamus, **FRAP 21**
    Motions, **FRAP 27**
    Prohibition, **FRAP 21**
    Records and recordation, **FRAP 11**
    Rehearings, **FRAP 35**
    Substitution, parties, **FRAP 43**
Partial transcripts, **FRAP 10**
Parties,
    Administrative law and procedure, **FRAP 15, 43 et seq.**
    Arguments, **FRAP 34**
    Briefs, **FRAP 28**
    Conferences, **FRAP 33**
    Constitutional questions, **FRAP 44**
    Costs, **FRAP 39**
    Judgments and decrees, **FRAP 36**
    Opinions, **FRAP 36**
    Representation, statements, **FRAP 12**
    Substitution, **FRAP 43**
Permissive appeals, **FRAP 5**
Personal representatives, substitution, **FRAP 43**

Petitions,
    Administrative law and procedure, **FRAP 15**; **FRAP Form 3**
    Corporate disclosure statements, **FRAP 26.1**
    Extraordinary writs, **FRAP 21**
    Forms, **FRAP 32**
    Mandamus, **FRAP 21**
    Permissive appeals, **FRAP 5**
    Prohibition, **FRAP 21**
    Rehearings, **FRAP 40**
    Writs, extraordinary writs, **FRAP 21**
Plea or answer,
    Administrative law and procedure, **FRAP 15**
    Corporate disclosure statements, **FRAP 26.1**
    Extraordinary writs, **FRAP 21**
    Permissive appeals, **FRAP 5**
    Rehearings, **FRAP 40**
Preliminary hearings, **FRAP 11**
Printing, briefs, **FRAP 32, 39**
Privacy protection, **FRAP 25**
Pro se, **FRAP 3**
Process, **FRAP 25**
    Acknowledgments, **FRAP 25**
    Briefs, **FRAP 27, 31**
    Carriers, **FRAP 25**
    Copies, **FRAP 25**
    Evidence, **FRAP 21, 25**
    Extraordinary writs, **FRAP 21**
    Mandamus, **FRAP 21**
    Notice of appeal, **FRAP 3, 13**
    Prohibition, **FRAP 21**
    Tax Court, **FRAP 13**
    Time, **FRAP 26**
Prohibition, **FRAP 2, 21**
Proposed judgments, administrative law and procedure, **FRAP 19**
Records and recordation, **FRAP 10**
    Administrative law and procedure, **FRAP 16, 17**
    Bankruptcy, **FRAP 6**
    Briefs, **FRAP 28, 30**
    Clerk of courts, **FRAP 45**
    Copies, **FRAP 39**
    Filing,
        Administrative law and procedure, **FRAP 17**
        Tax Court, **FRAP 13**
    Tax Court, **FRAP 13**
Rehearing,
    Bankruptcy, **FRAP 6**
    En banc, **FRAP 35**
    Mandate, **FRAP 41**
Release, habeas corpus, **FRAP 23**
Removal, exhibits, **FRAP 34**
Reports, evidence, **FRAP 10**
Representation, statements, **FRAP 12**
Response,
    Corporate disclosure statements, **FRAP 26.1**
    Motions, **FRAP 27**
Retention, records and recordation, **FRAP 11, 17**
Reversal, judgments and decrees,
    Costs, **FRAP 39**
    Interest, **FRAP 37**
Right to appeal, **FRAP 3, 4**
Saturdays,
    Clerks of courts, **FRAP 45**
    Time, **FRAP 26**
Separate appeals, oral arguments, **FRAP 34**

Signatures, **FRAP 32**
Single judges, motions, **FRAP 27**
Standard of review, briefs, **FRAP 28**
State courts, habeas corpus, **FRAP 22, 23**
State laws, constitutional questions, **FRAP 44**
Statements,
    Agreed statement, records and recordation, **FRAP 10**
    Attorneys, **FRAP 12**
        Misconduct, **FRAP 46**
    Evidence, **FRAP 10**
    Extraordinary writs, **FRAP 21**
Statutes,
    Briefs, **FRAP 28**
    Constitutional questions, **FRAP 44**
    Time, **FRAP 26**
Stay of proceedings,
    Bonds (officers and fiduciaries), **FRAP 7 et seq.**
    Mandate, **FRAP 41**
    Pending appeals, **FRAP 8**
Stipulations,
    Administrative law and procedure, **FRAP 17**
    Records and recordation, **FRAP 11**
    Voluntary dismissal, **FRAP 42**
Substitution, parties, **FRAP 43**
Sundays,
    Clerks of courts, **FRAP 45**
    Time, **FRAP 26**
Suspension,
    Attorneys, **FRAP 46**
    Rules, **FRAP 2**
Taxation of costs, **FRAP 39**
Temporary injunctions, **FRAP 8**
Time, **FRAP 26**
    Administrative law and procedure, **FRAP 17**
    Arguments, **FRAP 34**
    Certiorari, **FRAP 41**
    Clerks of court, hours, **FRAP 45**
    Computation, **FRAP 26**
    En banc, **FRAP 35**
    Legal holidays, **FRAP 26**
    Mandate, **FRAP 41**
    Motions, **FRAP 27**
    Oral arguments, **FRAP 34**
    Process, **FRAP 26**
    Rehearings, **FRAP 35, 40**
    Reply, motions, **FRAP 27**
    Tax Court, notice, **FRAP 13**
Transcripts, **FRAP 10**
    Administrative law and procedure, **FRAP 17**
    Briefs, **FRAP 28**
Typewriting,
    Briefs, **FRAP 32**
        Cross appeals, **FRAP 28.1**
    Motions, **FRAP 27**
United States,
    Constitutional questions, **FRAP 44**
    Costs, **FRAP 39**
    Rehearings, **FRAP 40**
United States Tax Court, **FRAP 2, 14**
    Decisions, **FRAP Form 2**
    Notice, **FRAP 13**; **FRAP Form 2**
Vacating and setting aside, judgments and decrees, **FRAP 39**
Voluntary dismissals, **FRAP 42**
Weather, delays, **FRAP 26**

LOCAL RULES OF THE COURT OF APPEALS FOR THE SECOND CIRCUIT

Including Second Circuit Amendments
Received Through September 15, 2008

Research Note

These rules may be searched electronically on WESTLAW in the US–RULES database; updates to these rules may be found on WESTLAW in US–RULESUP-DATES. For search tips, and a detailed summary of database content, consult the WESTLAW Scope Screen of each database.

Table of Rules

PART 1. LOCAL RULES RELATING TO THE ORGANIZATION OF THE COURT

	Loc.R.
Name	0.11
Seal	0.12
Terms	0.13
Quorum	0.14
Disclosure of Interested Parties [Superseded by FRAP 26.1]	0.15
Clerk	0.16
Clerk's Fees	0.17
Entry of Orders by the Clerk	0.18
Process	0.19
Opinions of the Court	0.20
Library	0.21
Judicial Conference of the Second Circuit	0.22
Dispositions in Open Court or by Summary Order	0.23
Complaints With Respect to Conduct of Judges [Superseded]	0.24
Equal Access to Justice Act Fees	0.25
Permissive Review After Appeal of a Magistrate's Judgment to the District Court	0.26
Certification of Questions of State Law	0.27
Death Penalty Cases	0.28
Non–Argument Calendar (Interim)	0.29

PART 2. FEDERAL RULES OF APPELLATE PROCEDURE AND LOCAL RULES SUPPLEMENTING FEDERAL RULES OF APPELLATE PROCEDURE

TITLE I. APPLICABILITY OF RULES

	FRAP	Loc.R.
SCOPE OF RULES; TITLE	1	
Scope of Rules	1(a)	
[Abrogated]	1(b)	
Title	1(c)	
SUSPENSION OF RULES	2	

	FRAP	Loc.R.
TITLE II. APPEAL FROM A JUDGMENT OR ORDER OF A DISTRICT COURT		
APPEAL AS OF RIGHT—HOW TAKEN	3	
Filing the Notice of Appeal	3(a)	
Joint or Consolidated Appeals	3(b)	
Content of the Notice of Appeal	3(c)	
Serving the Notice of Appeal	3(d)	
Payment of Fees	3(e)	
Mailing of Notice of Appeal by Clerks of District Courts to Clerk of Court of Appeals		3(d)
APPEAL FROM A JUDGMENT ENTERED BY A MAGISTRATE JUDGE IN A CIVIL CASE [Abrogated]	3.1	
APPEAL AS OF RIGHT—WHEN TAKEN	4	
Appeal in a Civil Case	4(a)	
Appeal in a Criminal Case	4(b)	
Appeal by an Inmate Confined in an Institution	4(c)	
Mistaken Filing in the Court of Appeals	4(d)	
Duties of All Retained Attorneys in Criminal Cases and All Criminal Justice Act–Appointed Attorneys; Motions for Leave to Withdraw as Counsel on Appeal Where Retained in a Criminal Case or Appointed Under Criminal Justice Act, Duties of Appellate Counsel in the Event of Affirmance		4(b)
APPEAL BY PERMISSION	5	
Petition for Permission to Appeal	5(a)	
Content of Petition; Answer or Cross-Petition; Oral Argument	5(b)	
Form of Papers; Number of Copies	5(c)	
Grant of Permission; Fees; Cost Bond; Filing the Record	5(d)	
APPEAL BY PERMISSION UNDER 28 U.S.C. § 636(c)(5) [Abrogated]	5.1	
APPEAL IN A BANKRUPTCY CASE FROM A FINAL JUDGMENT, ORDER, OR DECREE OF A DISTRICT COURT OR BANKRUPTCY APPELLATE PANEL	6	
Appeal From a Judgment, Order, or Decree of a District Court Exercising Original Jurisdiction in a Bankruptcy Case	6(a)	
Appeal From a Judgment, Order, or Decree of a District Court or Bankruptcy Appellate Panel Exercising Appellate Jurisdiction in a Bankruptcy Case	6(b)	
BOND FOR COSTS ON APPEAL IN A CIVIL CASE	7	
STAY OR INJUNCTION PENDING APPEAL	8	
Motion for Stay	8(a)	
Proceedings Against a Surety	8(b)	
Stay in a Criminal Case	8(c)	
RELEASE IN A CRIMINAL CASE	9	
Release Before Judgment of Conviction	9(a)	
Release After Judgment of Conviction	9(b)	
Criteria for Release	9(c)	
Release in Criminal Cases		9
THE RECORD ON APPEAL	10	
Composition of the Record on Appeal	10(a)	
The Transcript of Proceedings	10(b)	
Statement of the Evidence When the Proceedings Were Not Recorded or When a Transcript Is Unavailable	10(c)	
Agreed Statement as the Record on Appeal	10(d)	
Correction or Modification of the Record	10(e)	
FORWARDING THE RECORD	11	
Appellant's Duty	11(a)	
Duties of Reporter and District Clerk	11(b)	
Retaining the Record Temporarily in the District Court for Use in Preparing the Appeal	11(c)	
[Abrogated]	11(d)	
Retaining the Record by Court Order	11(e)	
Retaining Parts of the Record in the District Court by Stipulation of the Parties	11(f)	
Record for a Preliminary Motion in the Court of Appeals	11(g)	
Exhibits		11
DOCKETING THE APPEAL; FILING A REPRESENTATION STATEMENT; FILING OF THE RECORD	12	
Docketing the Appeal	12(a)	

	FRAP	Loc.R.
Filing a Representation Statement	12(b)	
Filing the Record, Partial Record, or Certificate	12(c)	

TITLE III.   REVIEW OF A DECISION OF THE
UNITED STATES TAX COURT

	FRAP	Loc.R.
REVIEW OF A DECISION OF THE TAX COURT	13	
How Obtained; Time for Filing Notice of Appeal	13(a)	
Notice of Appeal; How Filed	13(b)	
Content of the Notice of Appeal; Service; Effect of Filing and Service	13(c)	
The Record on Appeal; Forwarding; Filing	13(d)	
APPLICABILITY OF OTHER RULES TO THE REVIEW OF A TAX COURT DECISION	14	

TITLE IV.   REVIEW OR ENFORCEMENT OF AN ORDER
OF AN ADMINISTRATIVE AGENCY,
BOARD, COMMISSION, OR OFFICER

	FRAP	Loc.R.
REVIEW OR ENFORCEMENT OF AN AGENCY ORDER—HOW OBTAINED; INTERVENTION	15	
Petition for Review; Joint Petition	15(a)	
Application or Cross-Application to Enforce a Order; Answer; Default	15(b)	
Service of Petition or Application	15(c)	
Intervention	15(d)	
Payment of Fees	15(e)	
Application by National Labor Relations Board for Enforcement of Order		15
BRIEFS AND ORAL ARGUMENT IN A NATIONAL LABOR RELATIONS BOARD PROCEEDING	15.1	
THE RECORD ON REVIEW OR ENFORCEMENT	16	
Composition of the Record	16(a)	
Omissions From or Misstatements in the Record	16(b)	
FILING THE RECORD	17	
Agency to File; Time for Filing; Notice of Filing	17(a)	
Filing—What Constitutes	17(b)	
STAY PENDING REVIEW	18	
Motion for a Stay	18(a)	
Bond	18(b)	
SETTLEMENT OF A JUDGMENT ENFORCING AN AGENCY ORDER IN PART	19	
APPLICABILITY OF RULES TO THE REVIEW OR ENFORCEMENT OF AN AGENCY ORDERS	20	

TITLE V.   EXTRAORDINARY WRITS

	FRAP	Loc.R.
WRITS OF MANDAMUS AND PROHIBITION, AND OTHER EXTRAORDINARY WRITS	21	
Mandamus or Prohibition to a Court: Petition, Filing, Service, and Docketing	21(a)	
Denial; Order Directing Answer; Briefs; Precedence	21(b)	
Other Extraordinary Writs	21(c)	
Form of Papers; Number of Copies	21(d)	
Petitions for Writs of Mandamus and Prohibition		21

TITLE VI.   HABEAS CORPUS; PROCEEDINGS
IN FORMA PAUPERIS

	FRAP	Loc.R.
HABEAS CORPUS AND SECTION 2255 PROCEEDINGS	22	
Application for the Original Writ	22(a)	
Certificate of Appealability	22(b)	
Certificate of Appealability		22
CUSTODY OR RELEASE OF A PRISONER IN A HABEAS CORPUS PROCEEDING	23	
Transfer of Custody Pending Review	23(a)	
Detention or Release Pending Review of Decision Not to Release	23(b)	
Release Pending Review of Decision Ordering Release	23(c)	
Modification of the Initial Order on Custody	23(d)	
PROCEEDINGS IN FORMA PAUPERIS	24	
Leave to Proceed on Appeal In Forma Pauperis From District Court to Court of Appeals	24(a)	

	FRAP	Loc.R.
Leave to Proceed or Review In Forma Pauperis on Appeal or Review of an Administrative-Agency Proceeding	24(b)	
Leave to Use Original Record	24(c)	

TITLE VII.   GENERAL PROVISIONS

	FRAP	Loc.R.
FILING AND SERVICE	25	
Filing With the Clerk	25(a)	
Service of All Papers Required	25(b)	
Manner of Service	25(c)	
Proof of Service	25(d)	
Number of Copies	25(e)	
Filing and Service		25
COMPUTATION AND EXTENDING TIME	26	
Computing of Time	26(a)	
Extending Time	26(b)	
Additional Time After Service	26(c)	
CORPORATE DISCLOSURE STATEMENT	26.1	
Who Must file	26.1(a)	
Time for Filing; Supplemental Filing	26.1(b)	
Number of Copies	26.1(c)	
MOTIONS	27	
In General	27(a)	
Disposition of Motion for a Procedural Order	27(b)	
Power of a Single Judge to Entertain a Motion	27(c)	
Form of Papers; Page Limits; Number of Copies	27(d)	
Oral Argument	27(e)	
Motions		27
BRIEFS	28	
Appellant's Brief	28(a)	
Appellee's Brief	28(b)	
Reply Brief	28(c)	
References to Parties	28(d)	
References to the Record	28(e)	
Reproduction of Statutes, Rules, Regulations, etc.	28(f)	
[Reserved]	28(g)	
Briefs in a Case Involving a Cross Appeal	28(h)	
[Reserved]	28(h)	
Briefs in a Case Involving Multiple Appellants or Appellees	28(i)	
Citation of Supplemental Authorities	28(j)	
Briefs		28
CROSS–APPEALS	28.1	
Applicability	28.1(a)	
Designation of Appellant	28.1(b)	
Briefs	28.1(c)	
Cover	28.1(d)	
Length	28.1(e)	
Time to Serve and File a Brief	28.1(f)	
BRIEF OF AN AMICUS CURIAE	29	
When Permitted	29(a)	
Motion for Leave to File	29(b)	
Contents and Form	29(c)	
Length	29(d)	
Time for Filing	29(e)	
Reply Brief	29(f)	
Oral Argument	29(g)	
Brief of an Amicus Curiae		29
APPENDIX TO THE BRIEFS	30	
Appellant's Responsibility	30(a)	
All Parties' Responsibilities	30(b)	
Deferred Appendix	30(c)	
Format of the Appendix	30(d)	
Reproduction of Exhibits	30(e)	
Appeal on the Original Record Without an Appendix	30(f)	
Appendix		30
SERVICING AND FILING BRIEFS	31	
Time to Serve and File a Brief	31(a)	

	FRAP	Loc.R.
Number of Copies	31(b)	
Consequence of Failure to File	31(c)	
Number of Copies of Brief to Be Filed with Clerk		31
FORM OF BRIEFS, APPENDICES AND OTHER PAPERS	32	
Form of a Brief	32(a)	
Form of an Appendix	32(b)	
Form of Other Papers	32(c)	
Signature	32(d)	
Local Variation	32(e)	
Briefs and Appendix		32
CITING JUDICIAL DISPOSITIONS	32.1	
Citation Permitted	32.1(a)	
Copies Required	32.1(b)	
APPEAL CONFERENCES	33	
ORAL ARGUMENT	34	
In General	34(a)	
Notice of Argument; Postponement	34(b)	
Order and Content of Argument	34(c)	
Cross-Appeals and Separate Appeals	34(d)	
Nonappearance of Party	34(e)	
Submission on Briefs	34(f)	
Use of Physical Exhibits at Argument; Removal	34(g)	
Oral Argument		34
EN BANC DETERMINATION	35	
When Hearing or Rehearing En Banc May Be Ordered	35(a)	
Petition for Hearing or Rehearing En Banc	35(b)	
Time for Petition for Hearing or Rehearing En Banc	35(c)	
Number of Copies	35(d)	
Response	35(e)	
Call for a Vote	35(f)	
En Banc Procedure		35
ENTRY OF JUDGMENT; NOTICE	36	
Entry	36(a)	
Notice	36(b)	
INTEREST ON JUDGMENT	37	
When the Court Affirms	37(a)	
When the Court Reverses	37(b)	
FRIVOLOUS APPEALS—DAMAGES AND COSTS	38	
Other Sanctions for Delay		38
COSTS	39	
Against Whom Assessed	39(a)	
Costs For and Against the United States	39(b)	
Costs of Copies	39(c)	
Bill of Costs; Objections; Insertion in Mandate	39(d)	
Costs on Appeal Taxable in the District Court	39(e)	
Costs		39
PETITION FOR PANEL REHEARING	40	
Time to Filing; Contents Answer; Action by the Court if Granted	40(a)	
Form of Petition; Length	40(b)	
Panel Rehearing Procedure		40
MANDATE: CONTENTS; ISSUANCE AND EFFECTIVE DATE; STAY	41	
Contents	41(a)	
When Issued	41(b)	
Effective Date	41(c)	
Staying the Mandate	41(d)	
Issuance of Mandate		41
VOLUNTARY DISMISSAL	42	
Dismissal in the District Court	42(a)	
Dismissal in the Court of Appeals	42(b)	
SUBSTITUTION OF PARTIES	43	
Death of a Party	43(a)	
Substitution for a Reason Other Than Death	43(b)	
Public Officer; Identification; Substitution	43(c)	

	FRAP	Loc.R.
CASES INVOLVING A CONSTITUTIONAL QUESTION WHEN THE UNITED STATES OR THE RELEVANT STATE IS NOT A PARTY	44	
Constitutional Challenge to Federal Statute	44(a)	
Constitutional Challenge to State Statute	44(b)	
CLERK'S DUTIES	45	
General Provisions	45(a)	
Records	45(b)	
Notice of an Order or Judgment	45(c)	
Custody of Records and Papers	45(d)	
ATTORNEYS	46	
Admission to the Bar	46(a)	
Suspension or Disbarment	46(b)	
Discipline	46(c)	
Attorneys		46
LOCAL RULES BY COURT OF APPEALS	47	
Local Rules	47(a)	
Procedure When There Is No Controlling Law	47(b)	
MASTERS	48	
Appointment; Powers	48(a)	
Compensation	48(b)	

FORMS

FEDERAL RULES OF APPELLATE PROCEDURE FORMS

Form
1. Notice of Appeal to a Court of Appeals From a Judgment or Order of a District Court.
2. Notice of Appeal to a Court of Appeals From a Decision of the United States Tax Court.
3. Petition for Review of Order of an Agency, Board, Commission or Officer.
4. Affidavit Accompanying Motion for Permission to Appeal In Forma Pauperis.
5. Notice of Appeal to a Court of Appeals From a Judgment or Order of a District Court or a Bankruptcy Appellate Panel.
6. Certificate of Compliance With Rule 32(a).

SECOND CIRCUIT MISCELLANEOUS FORMS

Notice of Appearance Form.
Application for Fees and Other Expenses Under Equal Access to Justice Act (Form AO 291).
Criminal Notice of Appeal Form.
Criminal Case Information Form (Form A).
Civil Appeal Pre-argument Statement (Form C).
Civil Appeal Transcript Information (Form D).
Agency Appeal Pre-argument Statement (Form C–A).
Notice of Motion (Form T 1080).
Instructions for Bill of Costs and Itemized and Verified Bill of Costs Form.
Law Student Practice Forms.
Application for Leave to File a Second or Successive Motion to Vacate, Set Aside or Correct Sentence, 28 U.S.C. § 2255, By Prisoner in Federal Custody.
Application for Leave to File a Second or Successive Habeas Corpus Petition, 28 U.S.C. § 2244(b), By Prisoner in State Custody.
Certificate of Death Penalty Case.
Electronic Notification Agreement.
Anti-Virus Certification Form.
Non-Compliance with Digital Brief Requirement (To Be Completed Only In Counseled Cases).
Local Rule 34(a)(2) Joint Statement.

APPENDIX

PART A. AMENDED PLAN TO IMPLEMENT THE CRIMINAL JUSTICE ACT OF 1964

I. Authority.
II. Statement of Policy..
III. Definitions.
IV. Determination of Need for Appointed Counsel.
V. CJA Attorney Advisory Group.

VI. CJA Panel.
VII. Appointment of Counsel.
VIII. Release of Appointed Counsel.
IX. Duties of Appointed Counsel.
X. Payment of Claims for Compensation and Expenses.
XI. CJA Compensation Guidelines.
XII. Forms.
XIII. Rules and Reports.
XIV. Operation of the Plan.
XV. No Rights Created.
XVI. Amendments.

PART B. REVISED SECOND CIRCUIT PLAN TO EXPEDITE THE
PROCESSING OF CRIMINAL APPEALS

PART C. CIVIL APPEALS MANAGEMENT PLAN

PART D. GUIDELINES FOR CONDUCT OF
PRE–ARGUMENT CONFERENCE UNDER
THE CIVIL APPEALS MANAGEMENT PLAN

PART E. RULES FOR JUDICIAL–CONDUCT AND
JUDICIAL–DISABILITY PROCEEDINGS

PART F. GUIDELINES OF THE COURT OF APPEALS
FOR THE SECOND CIRCUIT CONCERNING
CAMERAS IN THE COURTROOM

SELECTED ORDERS

INDEX

PART 1. LOCAL RULES RELATING TO THE ORGANIZATION OF THE COURT

§ 0.11 Name

The name of the court, as fixed by 28 U.S.C. §§ 41, 43(a), is "United States Court of Appeals for the Second Circuit."

[December 1, 1994.]

§ 0.12 Seal

The seal of the court shall contain the words "United States" on the upper part of the outer edge; and the words "Court of Appeals" on the lower part of the outer edge, running from left to right; and the words "Second Circuit" in two lines, in the center, with a dash beneath.

[December 1, 1994.]

§ 0.13 Terms

One term of this court shall be held annually at the City of New York commencing on such day in August or September as the court may designate. It shall be adjourned to such times and places as the court may from time to time direct.

[December 1, 1994.]

§ 0.14 Quorum

(a) Two judges shall constitute a quorum. If, at any time, a quorum does not attend on any day appointed for holding a session of the court, any judge who does attend or, in the absence of any judge, the clerk may adjourn the court for such time as may be appropriate. Any judge attending when less than a quorum is present or at any time when the court is in recess may make any necessary procedural order touching any suit or proceeding preparatory to hearing or decision of the merits. (See Part 2, Local Rule 27(f).)

(b) (Interim) Unless directed otherwise, a panel of the court shall consist of three judges. If a judge of a panel of the court shall cease to continue with the consideration of any matter by reason of recusal, death, illness, resignation, incapacity, or other reason, the two remaining judges will determine the matter if they reach agreement and neither requests the designation of a third judge. If they do not reach agreement or either requests such a designation, another circuit judge will be designated by the Clerk to sit in place of the judge who has been relieved. The parties shall be advised of such designation, but no additional argument will be had or briefs received unless otherwise ordered.

[December 1, 1994; amendments adopted on an interim basis effective November 16, 2004.]

§ 0.15   Disclosure of Interested Parties [Superseded by FRAP 26.1]

§ 0.16   Clerk

(See generally Federal Rule 45 of the Federal Rules of Appellate Procedure.)

(a) The clerk's office shall be kept at the United States Court House, 40 Foley Square, New York City, and shall be open from 9:00 o'clock A.M. until 5:00 o'clock P.M. daily, except Saturdays, Sundays and legal holidays.

(b) The clerk may permit any original record or paper to be taken from the courtroom or from the office upon such statement of need as the clerk may require, and upon receipt for such record or paper.

(c) When it is required that the record be certified to the Supreme Court of the United States, the clerk if possessed of the original papers, exhibits, and transcript of proceedings of the district court or agency and a copy of the docket entries of that court or agency shall certify and transmit them and the original papers filed in this court.

[December 1, 1994.]

§ 0.17   Clerk's Fees

Following are fees to be charged for services provided by the courts of appeals. No fees are to be charged for services rendered on behalf of the United States, with the exception of those specifically prescribed in items 2, 4 and 5. No fees under this schedule shall be charged to federal agencies or programs which are funded from judiciary appropriations, including, but not limited to, agencies, organizations, and individuals providing services authorized by the Criminal Justice Act, 18 U.S.C. § 3006A, and Bankruptcy Administrator programs.

1. For docketing a case on appeal or review, or docketing any other proceeding, $450. A separate fee shall be paid by each party filing a notice of appeal in the district court, but parties filing a joint notice of appeal in the district court are required to pay only one fee. A docketing fee shall not be charged for the docketing of an application for the allowance of an interlocutory appeal under 28 U.S.C. § 1292(b), unless the appeal is allowed.

2. For every search of the records of the court and certifying the results thereof, $26. This fee shall apply to services rendered on behalf of the United States if the information requested is available through electronic access.

3. For certifying any document or paper, whether the certification is made directly on the document, or by separate instrument, $9.

4. For reproducing any record or paper 50 cents per page. This fee shall apply to paper copies made from either (1) original documents, or (2) microfiche or microfilm reproductions of the original records. This fee shall apply to services rendered on behalf of the United States if the record or paper requested is available through electronic access.

5. For reproduction of recordings of proceedings, regardless of the medium, $26, including the cost of materials. This fee shall apply to services rendered on behalf of the United States if the reproduction of the recording is available electronically.

6. For reproduction of the record in any appeal in which the requirement of an appendix is dispensed with by any court of appeals pursuant to Rule 30(f), F.R.A.P., a flat fee of $71.

7. For each microfiche or microfilm copy of any court record, where available, $5.

8. For retrieval of a record from a Federal Records Center, National Archives, or other storage location removed from the place of business of the court, $45.

9. For a check paid into the court which is returned for a lack of funds, $45.

10. Fees to be charged and collected for copies of opinions shall be fixed, from time to time, by each court, commensurate with the cost of printing.

11. The court may charge and collect fees, commensurate with the cost of printing, for copies of the local rules of court. The court may also distribute copies of the local rules without charge.

12. The clerk shall assess a charge for the handling of registry funds deposited with the court, to be assessed from interest earnings and in accordance with the detailed fee schedule issued by the Director of the Administrative Office of the United States Courts.

13. Upon the filing of any separate or joint notice of appeal or application for appeal from the Bankruptcy Appellate Panel, or notice of the allowance of an appeal from the Bankruptcy Appellate Panel, or of a writ of certiorari, $5 shall be paid by the appellant or petitioner.

14. The court may charge and collect a fee of $200 per remote location for counsel's requested use of video-conferencing equipment in connection with each oral argument.

15. For original admission of attorneys to practice, $190 each, including a certificate of admission. For a duplicate certificate of admission or certificate of good standing, $15.

[December 1, 1994. Amended October 17, 2005.]

§ 0.18 Entry of Orders by the Clerk

The clerk shall prepare, sign and enter the following without submission to the court or a judge unless otherwise directed:

(1) orders for the dismissal of an appeal under Rule 42(b) or pursuant to an order of the court or a judge;

(2) procedural orders on consent;

(3) orders on mandate from the Supreme Court of the United States;

(4) judgments in appeals from the United States Tax Court based on a stipulation of the parties;

(5) orders and judgments on decisions by the court in motions and appeals (See Rule 36 of Federal Rules of Appellate Procedure);

(6) orders scheduling the docketing of the record and filing of briefs and argument, which may include a provision that, in the event of default by the appellant in docketing the record or filing the appellant's brief, the appeal will be dismissed by the clerk;

(7) orders dismissing appeals in all cases where a brief for the appellant has not been filed within nine months of the docketing of the appeal and no stipulation extending the time for such filing has been filed.

(8) orders of dismissal as provided in Interim Local Rule § 0.29(d).

[December 1, 1994; subsection (8) adopted on an interim basis effective August 25, 2005.]

§ 0.19 Process

All process of this court shall be in the name of the President of the United States, and shall be in like form and tested in the same manner as process of the Supreme Court.

[December 1, 1994.]

§ 0.20 Opinions of the Court

(a) **Delivery.** Opinions will be delivered at any time, whether the court is in session or not, and are delivered by handing them to the clerk to be recorded.

(b) **Preservation of Original Opinions.** The original opinions of the court shall be filed with the clerk for preservation.

[December 1, 1994.]

§ 0.21 Library

The library of this court shall be open to members of any court of the United States and their staffs, to law officers of the Government, and to members of the bar of this court. It shall be open during such hours as reasonable needs require and be governed by such regulations as the librarian, with the approval of the court, may prescribe. Books shall not be removed from the building.

[December 1, 1994.]

§ 0.22 Judicial Conference of the Second Circuit

1. Purpose. There shall be held annually, at such time and place as shall be designated by the chief judge of the circuit, a conference of all the circuit, district and bankruptcy judges, and magistrate judges, of the circuit for the purpose of considering the state of business of the courts and ways and means of improving the administration of justice within the circuit. It shall be the duty of each circuit and district judge in the circuit, in active service, and each bankruptcy judge serving for a term pursuant to 28 U.S.C. § 152, to attend the conference unless excused by the chief judge. The circuit justice shall be invited to attend.

2. Sessions. A portion of the conference, to be known as the "executive session," shall be for the judges alone and shall be devoted to a discussion of matters affecting the state of the dockets and the administration of justice throughout the circuit. At other sessions of the conference, members of the bar, to be chosen as set forth in the succeeding paragraph, shall be members of the conference and shall participate in its discussions and deliberations.

3. Members of the Bar. Members of the conference from the bar shall be selected to reflect a cross-section of lawyers who currently practice before federal courts in this circuit; members should be willing and able to contribute actively to conference purposes. In order to assure that fresh views are represented, no judge may invite the same individual more than two years out of any five. The membership shall be composed of the following:

(a) The presidents of the state bar associations of the three states of the circuit and a member from each of such associations to be designated by their respective presidents with a view to giving appropriate representation to various areas of the state.

(b) Each United States Attorney of the circuit or an Assistant United States Attorney designated by the United States Attorney.

(c) The Public Defender (or an assistant designated by the Public Defender) for any district within the circuit, and a representative of a community defender organization, authorized to act generally in any district, designated by the president of such organization.

(d) Such number of invitees by the circuit justice, and the active and senior circuit and district judges, as the judicial council may determine for each conference.

(e) Such additional number of lawyers as shall be selected jointly by the chief judge and the conference chairperson in light of their competence and interest in the subject or subjects to be considered at the conference. These conference members also shall be selected to reflect a cross-section of lawyers who currently practice before federal courts in this circuit, and may include:

(i) Members of county and local bar associations in the circuit, selected in consultation with their respective presidents, reflecting the geography and the relative size and activity in federal litigation of those associations;

(ii) The dean, or other representative of the faculty of law schools within the circuit;

(iii) Members of State/Federal Judicial Councils within the circuit (including especially state court chief judges or chief justices);

(iv) Members of the United States Senate and House of Representatives with a particular interest in the work of the federal courts;

(v) Former presidents of the American Bar Association residing or practicing in the Second Circuit; the current member of the Board of Governors of the American Bar Association from the Second Circuit; the current member of the Standing Committee on the Federal Judiciary of the American Bar Association from the circuit; the chairperson of such committee if residing or practicing in the circuit; and the president, former presidents, and the executive director of the American Law Institute if residing or practicing in the circuit;

(vi) Members of the staff of federal courts within the circuit not enumerated elsewhere in this rule.

(f) Any retired Justice of the Supreme Court of the United States residing within the circuit, any present or former Attorney General of the United States residing or practicing within the circuit, and any circuit or district judge of the circuit who has resigned such office.

(g) The Director (or, if the Director is unable to attend, the Director's designee) of the Administrative Office of the United States Courts, and the Director (or designee) of the Federal Judicial Center.

(h) The circuit and district court executives and clerks of the courts within the circuit.

(i) Members of the committee provided for in paragraph 4 of this Rule, and past chairpersons and executive secretaries of such committee.

4. Committee. To assist in the conduct of the conference (other than the executive session), the chief judge shall appoint annually, subject to the approval of the judicial council, members of a committee to be known as the Planning and Program Committee. The committee, whose members shall be appointed to staggered three-year terms, shall include the presidents of the state bar associations of the three states of the

circuit and such number of judges and members of the bar of the circuit as the chief judge may determine.

5. Chairperson. The chief judge may also appoint a conference chairperson to be selected from among the active judges of the circuit.

6. Representative to the Judicial Conference of the United States.

(a) Three months before the date of the Judicial Conference of the Second Circuit at which the district judge member of the Judicial Conference of the United States from the Second Circuit is to be chosen, the chief judges of the district courts of the circuit, acting together as a nominating committee, shall nominate no more than three active district judges of the circuit (not excluding one of their own number) as candidates for the office of district judge member from the Second Circuit. The names of the nominees will be mailed to all the judges of the circuit and to the Clerk of the Court of Appeals, who is the secretary of the conference, at least thirty days before the date of the executive session of the Circuit Judicial Conference.

(b) Additional active district judges may be put in nomination (i) from the floor at the executive session in replacement of any nominee of the chief judges who is disabled or declines to stand, and (ii) from the floor at the executive session by written nomination signed by at least one-fourth of the judges of the circuit. The one-fourth requirement shall not include vacant judgeships or judgeships for which commissions have been signed but the nominees have not been sworn and have not taken office at the time the nominating petition is signed. No judge may sign more than one such nomination and such nomination may not include more than one judge.

(c) The judge receiving a plurality of the votes of the active judges of the circuit will be the circuit's choice. Voting will be by secret, written ballot. Any judge who expects to be absent from the meeting may send in a judge's ballot unsigned and enclosed in an inner, sealed envelope, to the secretary of the conference provided that the ballot reaches the secretary before the executive meeting is convened.

(d) No judge may succeed himself or herself to a second successive term by election and no judge of any district court may succeed a judge from the same district unless at least three years have elapsed since the expiration of such earlier judge's term; however, in the case of a judge who is a member of the Executive Committee of the Judicial Conference of the United States, such judge may be elected to a second successive term in order to continue eligibility to serve on the Executive Committee.

(e) In the event that it is not convenient to conduct at a Judicial Conference the election referred to herein, such election may be conducted by mail ballot

following action by the nominating committee, according to such procedures as that body may establish.
[December 1, 1994.]

§ 0.24 Complaints With Respect to Conduct of Judges [Superseded]

[Superseded July 1, 1987 by the Rules of Judicial Council of the Second Circuit Governing Complaints against Judicial Officers under 28 U.S.C. § 372(c). See Court's website, Forms Page.]

§ 0.25 Equal Access to Justice Act Fees

Applications authorized by 28 U.S.C. § 2412(d)(1)(B) shall be filed within 30 days of this court's judgment, and petitions for review authorized by 5 U.S.C. § 504(c)(2) shall be filed within 30 days of the agency's fee determination. Applications and petitions shall be filed with the clerk of this court (original and four copies), served on all parties, and submitted on form AO 291. (A T1080 Motion Information Statement is also required.)
[December 1, 1994.]

§ 0.26 Permissive Review After Appeal of a Magistrate's Judgment to the District Court

Petitions for leave to appeal authorized by 28 U.S.C. § 636(c)(5) shall be filed with the clerk of this court (original and four copies) within 30 days of the District Court's judgment and shall be served on all parties.
[December 1, 1994.]

§ 0.27 Certification of Questions of State Law

Where authorized by state law, this Court may certify to the highest court of a state an unsettled and significant question of state law that will control the outcome of a case pending before this Court. Such certification may be made by this Court sua sponte or on motion of a party filed with the clerk of this Court. Certification will be in accordance with the procedures provided by the state's legislature or highest state court rules, e.g., Conn. Public Act No. 85–111; New York Court of Appeals Rule 500.7. Certification may stay the proceedings in this Court pending the state court's decision whether to accept the certification and its decision of the certified question.
[December 1, 1994.]

§ 0.28 Death Penalty Cases

This rule describes the administration of capital cases in this Court. Capital case, as used in this rule, means any application in this Court, to which the person under sentence is a party, that challenges, defends, or otherwise relates to the validity or execution of a death sentence that has been imposed. Capital cases ordinarily will be heard by panels composed

in the manner described herein. The Court, however, may deviate from these procedures; their publication does not give any litigant a right to require that they be followed.

(1) **Certificate of Death Penalty Case.** Upon the filing of any proceeding in a district court of this circuit or in this Court challenging a sentence of death imposed pursuant to a federal or state court judgment, each party in such proceeding must file a Certificate of Death Penalty Case with the Clerk of the Court of Appeals. A Certificate of Death Penalty Case must also be filed by the U.S. Attorney upon the return of a verdict recommending a sentence of death in a district court of this circuit. The Certificate must be in the form provided as annexed to these rules, or in substantially similar form, and must set forth the names, telephone numbers and addresses of the parties and counsel; the proposed date of execution of the sentence, if set; and the emergency nature of the proceedings, if applicable.

A special tracking docket is maintained by the Clerk of this Court for all cases in which a district court of this circuit has imposed a sentence of death, and for all proceedings in a district court of this circuit or in this Court challenging a sentence of death imposed pursuant to a federal or state court judgment.

(2) **Preparation and Transmittal of the Record.** Upon the filing of a notice of appeal from an order under 18 U.S.C. § 3731, 28 U.S.C. § 1291, or 28 U.S.C. § 1292(a)(1) in a death penalty case in the district court, the Clerk of the district court and appellant's counsel must immediately prepare the record for the appeal. The record must be transmitted to this Court within five days of the filing of the notice of appeal unless such order is entered within twenty-one (21) days of the date of a scheduled execution, in which case the record must be transmitted immediately by an expedited means of delivery.

(3) **Monitoring of Cases and Lodging of Relevant Documents.** The Clerk of the Court of Appeals is authorized to monitor the status of scheduled executions and pending litigation in connection with any case within the geographical boundaries of this circuit wherein a warrant or order setting an execution date has been entered, and to establish communications with all parties and relevant state and/or federal courts. The Clerk may direct parties to lodge with this Court five copies of (1) all relevant portions of previous state and/or federal court records, or the entire record, and (2) all pleadings, briefs, and transcripts of any ongoing proceedings. The Clerk may docket such materials in advance of this Court's jurisdiction, under a miscellaneous docket, pending receipt of a notice of appeal or application in such case. This miscellaneous docket case is closed upon the opening of a regularly docketed case in this Court, or upon other final disposition of the case without its reaching this Court (for example, a reversal of the sentence or conviction

which is not appealed, or a carrying out of the execution).

(4) Capital Case Pool and Panels.

(a) *Capital Case Pool.* The capital case pool of judges consists of all active judges of the Court and those senior judges who have filed with the Clerk a statement of willingness to serve on capital case panels.

(b) *Capital Case Panel.* Upon receipt of a notice of appeal from the district court, an application for a certificate of appealability, or other application to this Court for relief in a capital case, the Clerk dockets the case and assigns it to a capital case panel (except as provided in paragraph 5 of this rule). A capital case panel consists of three judges, of whom at least one is an active judge of the Court.

(c) *Selection.* Judges are assigned to capital case panels by random drawing from the capital case pool. If a judge is unable to serve, that judge's name is returned to the pool after a replacement has been drawn. In the event a random drawing results in the names of three senior judges having been selected, the name of the third such senior judge is set aside and the selection process continues until an active judge's name is drawn; after the active judge's name has been drawn, the third senior judge's name is returned to the pool.

(d) *Rotation.* A judge drawn from the capital case pool to serve on a capital case panel is not returned to the pool until the pool is exhausted. When the pool has been exhausted, the Clerk prepares a new capital case pool and selects capital case panels from the pool in like manner.

(e) *Replacement.* If any judge serving on a capital case panel is unable to continue to serve, a replacement is drawn from the capital case pool, and the judge ceasing to serve on the panel is returned to the pool.

(f) *Duties of Capital Case Panel.* A capital case panel assigned to a particular capital case handles all matters pertaining to that case, including but not limited to the merits of a direct appeal and of all petitions for collateral review, motions for stay of execution, motions to vacate a stay of execution, applications for a certificate of appealability, motions for an order authorizing the district court to consider a second or successive application for habeas corpus, appeals from subsequent petitions, and remands from the United States Supreme Court. When practical, a capital case panel hearing a direct appeal from a death sentence imposed in federal court hears together with it the direct appeals of co-defendants, at least to the extent they involve issues in common with the appeal of the person sentenced to death. Non-common issues in the appeals of co-defendants may be severed and assigned to an ordinary panel.

(g) *Applications for Certificate of Appealability.* Applications for a certificate of appealability are referred initially to a single judge of the capital case panel, who has authority to grant the certificate. If the single judge does not grant the certificate, the application is referred to the full panel for disposition by majority vote.

(5) Original Petitions. All original applications for habeas corpus relief filed in the Clerk's office in a capital case are referred to a judge on the capital case panel in accordance with the approved operating procedures of this Court. Such an application ordinarily is transferred to the appropriate district court.

(6) Ruling on Certificate of Appealability. This Court may rule on a certificate of appealability whether or not a formal request is made of this Court, either as a preliminary matter or as part of a merits review of the case.

(7) Stays of Execution and Motions to Vacate Orders Granting Stay of a Federal or State Court Judgment.

(a) *Limits on Stays of Execution.* Notwithstanding any provision of this paragraph 7, stays of execution are not granted, or maintained, except in accordance with law. Thus, the provisions of this paragraph 7 for a stay are ineffective in any case in which such stay would be inconsistent with the limitations of 28 U.S.C. § 2262, or any other governing statute.

(b) *Emergency Motions.* Emergency motions or applications are filed with the Clerk of the Court of Appeals. If time does not permit the filing of a motion or application in person or by mail, counsel may communicate with the Clerk and obtain the Clerk's permission to file the motion by telefacsimile. Counsel are encouraged to communicate with the Clerk by telephone as soon as it becomes evident that emergency relief will be sought from this Court. The motion or application must contain a brief account of the prior actions, if any, of this Court and the name of the judge or judges involved in such prior actions.

(c) *Documents Required for Motions for Stay or to Vacate Stay.* The party moving for a stay of execution of a sentence of death or to vacate a stay must file the original and four (4) copies (a total of five) of the motion and serve all parties. A copy of the documents listed below must be attached to the original and to each copy of the motion. If time does not permit, the motion may be filed without attachments, but the movant must file the necessary copies as soon as possible. (If the respondent (the State or the U.S. Attorney) has indicated to the petitioner that it does not seek to oppose the stay immediately and the petitioner states this fact in the petition, these documents need not be filed with the application but must be filed within ten (10) days after the application is filed.)

(i) The indictment or other accusatory instrument;

(ii) The judgment of conviction containing the sentence of death;

(iii) The petition or complaint filed in the district court;

(iv) The opinion of the district court setting forth the reasons for granting or denying relief;

(v) The district court judgment granting or denying relief;

(vi) The district court order granting or denying a stay, and the statement of reasons for its action;

(vii) The certificate of appealability or order denying a certificate of appealability;

(viii) A copy of each state or federal court opinion or judgment bearing on the issues presented in the motion in cases in which appellant was a party;

(ix) A copy of the docket entries of the district court; and

(x) A copy of the notice of appeal.

(d) *Automatic Stays.* In any case in which a sentence of death has been imposed by a district court of this circuit, or by a state court within the circuit, execution of the sentence of death is automatically stayed upon the filing of a notice of appeal from the judgment of conviction or a notice of appeal from the denial of the first application in federal court seeking relief from the sentence of death. The clerk must promptly enter an order implementing the stay. Unless vacated or modified, the stay provided by this subparagraph remains in effect until the expiration of all proceedings available to the person sentenced to death (including review by the United States Supreme Court) as part of the direct review of the judgment of conviction or of the denial of such first application. The stay may be modified or vacated by the assigned panel at any time.

(e) *Other Stays.* A stay of any duration up to that specified in subparagraph 7(f)(i) may be ordered in any case by the assigned capital case panel, upon the affirmative vote of any judge of that panel.

(f) *Duration of Stays: Terminology.* Use of the following terminology to specify the duration of a stay denotes the durations specified below:

(i) If, in granting a stay of execution of a sentence of death, the Court or judge indicates that the stay shall be in effect "for the standard duration" under this rule, this signifies that, unless vacated or modified, the stay remains in effect until the expiration of all proceedings available to the person sentenced to death (including review by the United States Supreme Court) as part of the direct review of the judgment of the district court, or of the Court of Appeals in the case of an original petition filed there.

(ii) If, in granting a stay of execution of a sentence of death, the Court or judge indicates that the stay shall be in effect "for the duration of the appeal," this signifies that, unless vacated or modified, the stay remains in effect until the Court's mandate issues. Absent an order to the contrary preceded by timely notice to counsel, the mandate does not issue until the time for filing a petition for rehearing has expired, or, if such a petition has been filed, until the petition and any petition for rehearing in banc have been determined.

(g) *Stays in Relation to Petitions for Rehearing.*

(i) Petitions for rehearing accompanied by petitions for rehearing in banc are circulated to all judges of the capital case pool simultaneously with the circulation of the petition for rehearing to the assigned capital case panel. Judges participating in the petition for rehearing in banc may vote on a stay of execution of a sentence of death immediately, without waiting for the action of the assigned panel as to the petition for rehearing.

(ii) A stay of execution of a sentence of death pending disposition of the petition for rehearing and the petition for rehearing in banc is granted upon the affirmative vote of any two judges eligible to participate in a rehearing in banc.

(h) All stay applications must be filed with the Clerk of the Court. In each case in which the Court orders a stay of execution, the Clerk of the Court issues a written order in the name of the Court specifying the duration of the stay.

(i) During non-business hours, emergency stay applications must be directed to an assigned representative of the Clerk (the duty clerk), whose telephone number is left with the courthouse security officers. The duty clerk must immediately advise the members of the assigned panel of the filing of an emergency stay application.

(j) In the event the members of the assigned panel cannot be reached by the duty clerk, the duty clerk advises the judge of the court assigned at that time to hear emergency applications of the filing of an off-hours emergency stay application. Notwithstanding the provisions of subparagraphs 7(e) and 7(g)(ii), the applications judge may stay an execution until such time as the application can be placed before the assigned panel or the Court in banc.

Effective October 13, 1998. Amended effective December 1, 2002.

Interim § 0.29 Non–Argument Calendar

(a) The following appeals or petitions for review, and any motions filed thereon, will be initially placed on the Non-Argument Calendar:

An appeal or petition for review, in which a party seeks review of the denial of—

1. A claim for asylum under the Immigration and Nationality Act ("INA").

2. A claim for withholding of removal under the INA:

3. A claim for withholding or deferral of removal under the Convention Against Torture ("CAT"); or

4. A motion to reopen or reconsider an order involving one of the claims listed above.

Proceedings on the Non-Argument Calendar will be disposed of by a three-judge panel without oral argument unless the Court transfers the proceeding to the Regular Argument Calendar.

(b) To the extent practicable, the Clerk's Office will promptly identify proceedings to be placed on the Non-Argument Calendar and issue scheduling orders for them upon the receipt of the certified record. The scheduling order will inform the parties that the proceeding has been placed on the Non-Argument Calendar. Any party to a proceeding on the Non-Argument Calendar may request to have the proceeding transferred to the Regular Argument Calendar. Such a request shall not be made by motion but must be included in the party's brief, identified by a separate heading, and will be adjudicated in conformity with Federal Rule of Appellate Procedure 34(a)(2) and Local Rule 34(d)(1). In its discretion, the Court may at any time transfer a proceeding from the Non-Argu-ment Calendar to the Regular Argument Calendar. Upon the transfer of a case from the Non-Argument Calendar to the Regular Argument Calendar, no briefs may be filed, other than those specified in the scheduling order, unless leave of Court is obtained. The Court may at any time, sua sponte, with notice to the parties, tentatively transfer a proceeding mistakenly placed on the Regular Argument Calendar to the Non-Argument Calendar.

(c) The Civil Appeals Management Plan shall not apply mandatorily to proceedings on the Non-Argument Calendar. However, any party to a proceeding on the Non-Argument Calendar may request a conference under the Civil Appeals Management Plan, which will be promptly provided. A request for a conference will not alter a scheduling order.

(d) An appeal or petition for review on the Non-Argument Calendar may be dismissed by the Clerk if, 15 days after the due date, the party seeking review has failed to file its brief. The filing of a motion for an extension of time to file a brief does not stay or alter an existing deadline. If the respondent or appellee fails to file its brief by the due date, the Clerk may calendar the proceedings for decision as early as 15 days following the due date.

[Adopted on an interim basis effective August 25, 2005. Amended effective February 23, 2007.]

PART 2. [FEDERAL RULES OF APPELLATE PROCEDURE AND] LOCAL RULES SUPPLEMENTING FEDERAL RULES OF APPELLATE PROCEDURE

TITLE I.   APPLICABILITY OF RULES

FRAP 1.   SCOPE OF RULES; TITLE

[For text of Rule, see the Federal Rules of Appellate Procedure, ante.]

FRAP 2.   SUSPENSION OF RULES

[For text of Rule, see the Federal Rules of Appellate Procedure, ante.]

TITLE II.   APPEAL FROM A JUDGMENT OR ORDER OF A DISTRICT COURT

FRAP 3.   APPEAL AS OF RIGHT— HOW TAKEN

[For text of Rule, see the Federal Rules of Appellate Procedure, ante.]

LOCAL RULE 3(d).   MAILING OF NOTICE OF APPEAL BY CLERKS OF DISTRICT COURTS TO CLERK OF COURT OF AP-PEALS

The clerks of the district courts shall mail to the clerk of the court of appeals copies of notices of appeal in all cases and not simply in those described in FRAP 3(d).

[December 1, 1994.]

FRAP 3.1   APPEAL FROM A JUDGMENT OF A MAGISTRATE JUDGE IN A CIVIL CASE [ABROGATED]

FRAP 4.   APPEAL AS OF RIGHT— WHEN TAKEN

[For text of Rule, see the Federal Rules of Appellate Procedure, ante.]

LOCAL RULE 4(b). DUTIES OF ALL RE-TAINED ATTORNEYS IN CRIMINAL CASES AND ALL CRIMINAL JUSTICE ACT–APPOINTED ATTORNEYS; MOTIONS FOR LEAVE TO WITHDRAW AS COUNSEL ON APPEAL WHERE RETAINED IN A CRIMINAL CASE OR APPOINTED UNDER CRIMINAL JUSTICE ACT, DUTIES OF APPELLATE COUNSEL IN THE EVENT OF AFFIRMANCE

(a) *When a defendant convicted following trial wishes to appeal, trial counsel, whether retained or appointed by the district court, is responsible for representing the defendant until relieved by the Court of Appeals.*

(b) *If trial counsel was appointed under the Criminal Justice Act, 18 U.S.C. § 3006A, and intends to prosecute the appeal, this court may accept the District Court's finding that the defendant is financially unable to employ counsel and no further proof of the defendant's indigency need be submitted unless specifically required.*

(c) *Any counsel wishing to be relieved on appeal shall, before moving to that end, advise the defendant that the defendant must promptly obtain other counsel unless the defendant desires to proceed pro se and that if the defendant is financially unable to obtain counsel, a lawyer may be appointed by this court under the Criminal Justice Act. If the defendant wishes to have a lawyer so appointed on appeal, counsel must see to it that the defendant receives and fills out the appropriate application forms, which are available from the office of the Clerk of this court. If the defendant desires to proceed pro se, counsel must advise the defendant of the requirements concerning the time within which the record must be docketed and the brief filed.*

(d) *A motion to withdraw as counsel on appeal where the attorney is retained in a criminal case or appointed under the Criminal Justice Act must state the reasons for such relief and must be accompanied by one of the following:*

1. A showing that new counsel has been retained or appointed to represent defendant; or

2. The defendant's completed application for appointment of counsel under the Criminal Justice Act or a showing that such application has already been filed in the Court of Appeals; or

3. An affidavit or signed statement from the defendant showing that the defendant may retain new counsel or apply for appointment of counsel and expressly stating that the defendant does not wish to be represented by counsel but elects to appear pro se; or

4. An affidavit or signed statement from the defendant showing that the defendant has been advised of the defendant's rights with regard to the appeal and expressly stating that the defendant elects to withdraw the defendant's appeal; or

5. A showing that exceptional circumstances prevent counsel from meeting any of the requirements stated in subdivisions (1) to (4) above. Such a motion must be accompanied by proof of service on the defendant and the Government and will be determined, without oral argument, by a single judge. See Local Rule 27.

(e) *This Local Rule is supplementary to the Amended Plan to Supplement the Plans Adopted by the Several District Courts Within the Circuit, as required by the Criminal Justice Act of 1964, 18 U.S.C. § 3006A, as amended.*

[December 1, 1994; amended effective March 27, 1996.]

FRAP 5.   APPEAL BY PERMISSION

[For text of Rule, see the Federal Rules
of Appellate Procedure, ante.]

FRAP 5.1   APPEAL BY PERMISSION UNDER 28 U.S.C. § 636(c)(5) [ABROGATED]

FRAP 6.   APPEAL IN A BANKRUPTCY CASE FROM A FINAL JUDGMENT, ORDER, OR DECREE OF A DISTRICT COURT OR BANKRUPTCY APPELLATE PANEL

[For text of Rule, see the Federal Rules
of Appellate Procedure, ante.]

FRAP 7.   BOND FOR COSTS ON APPEAL IN A CIVIL CASE

[For text of Rule, see the Federal Rules
of Appellate Procedure, ante.]

FRAP 8.   STAY OR INJUNCTION PENDING APPEAL

[For text of Rule, see the Federal Rules
of Appellate Procedure, ante.]

FRAP 9.   RELEASE IN A CRIMINAL CASE

[For text of Rule, see the Federal Rules
of Appellate Procedure, ante.]

LOCAL RULE 9.   RELEASE IN CRIMINAL CASES

An application pursuant to Rule 9(b) shall contain in the following order:

1. the name of appellant; the District Court docket number of the case; the offense of which appellant was convicted; the date and terms of sentence; and the place where appellant has been ordered confined;

2. the facts with respect to whether application for bail has been made and denied, and the reasons given for the denial, if known; and the facts and reasons why the action by the District Court on the application does not afford the relief to which the applicant considers himself entitled;

3. a concise statement of the questions involved on the appeal, with sufficient facts to give the essential background and a showing that the questions on appeal are not frivolous;

4. such other matters as may be deemed pertinent;

5. a certificate by counsel, or by applicant if acting pro se, that the appeal is not taken for delay.

[December 1, 1994.]

FRAP 10.   THE RECORD ON APPEAL

[For text of Rule, see the Federal Rules of Appellate Procedure, ante.]

FRAP 11.   FORWARDING THE RECORD

[For text of Rule, see the Federal Rules of Appellate Procedure, ante.]

LOCAL RULE 11.   EXHIBITS

(a) The district court may, by rule or order, direct that any or all exhibits need not be filed with the clerk upon their offer or receipt in evidence but may be retained in the custody of the attorney (or of a party not represented by an attorney) who produced them, unless an appeal is taken, in which event the following provisions of this rule shall apply.

(b) The parties are encouraged to agree with respect to which exhibits are "necessary for the determination of the appeal." See Rule 11(a). In the absence of agreement, the appellant shall, not later than 15 days after the filing of the notice of appeal, serve on the appellee a designation of the exhibits the appellant considers to be necessary. If the appellee considers other exhibits to be necessary, the appellee shall serve a cross-designation upon the appellant within 10 days after service of appellant's designation.

(c) Except as provided in paragraph (d), it shall be the duty of any attorney or party having possession of an exhibit designated pursuant to paragraph (b) of this rule, promptly to make such exhibit or a true copy thereof available at the office of the clerk of the district court. The clerk of the district court shall transmit all such exhibits to the clerk of the court of appeals as part of the record pursuant to Rule 11(b). Exhibits which have not been designated shall be retained by the clerk of the district court or, if the district court has authorized their retention by an attorney or party pursuant to paragraph (a) of this rule, by such attorney or party, but shall be transmitted to the clerk of the court of appeals on the request of that court acting on the motion of any judge thereof or on the motion of a party showing good cause for failure to include any such exhibit in the attorney's designation.

(d) Documents of unusual bulk or weight and physical exhibits other than documents shall remain in the custody of the attorney or party who produced them. The attorney or party retaining custody of the documents shall permit inspection of them by any other party and shall be responsible for having them available at the argument in the court of appeals if they have been designated, and for their later production if subsequently requested by the court of appeals as provided in the last sentence of paragraph (c) of this rule.

(e) This rule does not relieve the parties of their obligation under Rule 30 to reproduce in an appendix to their briefs or in a separate volume, see Rule 30(e), exhibits (other than those described in paragraph (d) of this rule) to which they "wish to direct the particular attention of the court."

[December 1, 1994.]

FRAP 12.   DOCKETING THE APPEAL; FILING A REPRESENTATION STATEMENT; FILING THE RECORD

[For text of Rule, see the Federal Rules of Appellate Procedure, ante.]

TITLE III.   REVIEW OF A DECISION OF THE UNITED STATES TAX COURT

FRAP 13.   REVIEW OF A DECISION OF THE TAX COURT

[For text of Rule, see the Federal Rules of Appellate Procedure, ante.]

FRAP 14. APPLICABILITY OF OTHER RULES TO THE REVIEW OF A TAX COURT DECISION

[For text of Rule, see the Federal Rules of Appellate Procedure, ante.]

TITLE IV. REVIEW OR ENFORCEMENT OF AN ORDER OF AN ADMINISTRATIVE AGENCY, BOARD, COMMISSION, OR OFFICER

FRAP 15. REVIEW OR ENFORCEMENT OF AN AGENCY ORDER—HOW OBTAINED; INTERVENTION

[For text of Rule, see the Federal Rules of Appellate Procedure, ante.]

LOCAL RULE 15. APPLICATION BY NATIONAL LABOR RELATIONS BOARD FOR ENFORCEMENT OF ORDER

In an application for enforcement by the National Labor Relations Board under Rule 15(b), Federal Rules of Appellate Procedure the respondent(s) shall be considered the petitioner(s), and the National Labor Relations Board considered the respondent, for the purposes of briefing and oral argument, unless the court orders otherwise.

[December 1, 1994.]

FRAP 15.1 BRIEFS AND ORAL ARGUMENT IN A NATIONAL LABOR RELATIONS BOARD PROCEEDING

[For text of Rule, see the Federal Rules of Appellate Procedure, ante.]

FRAP 16. THE RECORD ON REVIEW OR ENFORCEMENT

[For text of Rule, see the Federal Rules of Appellate Procedure, ante.]

FRAP 17. FILING THE RECORD

[For text of Rule, see the Federal Rules of Appellate Procedure, ante.]

FRAP 18. STAY PENDING REVIEW

[For text of Rule, see the Federal Rules of Appellate Procedure, ante.]

FRAP 19. SETTLEMENT OF A JUDGMENT ENFORCING AN AGENCY ORDER IN PART

[For text of Rule, see the Federal Rules of Appellate Procedure, ante.]

FRAP 20. APPLICABILITY OF RULES TO THE REVIEW OR ENFORCEMENT OF AN AGENCY ORDER

[For text of Rule, see the Federal Rules of Appellate Procedure, ante.]

TITLE V. EXTRAORDINARY WRITS

FRAP 21. WRITS OF MANDAMUS AND PROHIBITION, AND OTHER EXTRAORDINARY WRITS

[For text of Rule, see the Federal Rules of Appellate Procedure, ante.]

LOCAL RULE 21. PETITIONS FOR WRITS OF MANDAMUS AND PROHIBITION

(a) Caption. *A petition for writ of mandamus or writ of prohibition pursuant to Rule 21 shall not bear the name of the district judge, but shall be entitled simply, "In re _____, Petitioner." To the extent that relief is requested of a particular judge, unless otherwise ordered, the judge shall be represented pro forma by counsel for the party opposing the relief, who shall appear in the name of the party and not that of the judge.*

(b) Number of Copies. *Four copies shall be filed with the original.*

[December 1, 1994.]

TITLE VI.   HABEAS CORPUS; PROCEEDINGS IN FORMA PAUPERIS

FRAP 22.   HABEAS CORPUS AND SECTION 2255 PROCEEDINGS

[For text of Rule, see the Federal Rules of Appellate Procedure, ante.]

LOCAL RULE 22.   CERTIFICATE OF APPEALABILITY

(a) Prompt Application and Contents of Motion. *In cases governed by 28 U.S.C. § 2253 and FRAP Rule 22(b), where an appeal has been taken but no certificate of appealability ("COA") has been issued by the district judge or by this court or a judge thereof, the appellant shall promptly move in this court for such a certificate. Such motion shall identify each issue that the appellant intends to raise on appeal and shall state, with respect to each issue, facts and a brief statement of reasons showing a denial of a constitutional right. When an appeal is filed for which a COA is required and a motion that complies with this rule has not been filed within 30 days after filing the notice of appeal, the clerk shall promptly send the appellant a letter enclosing a copy of this rule and informing the appellant that the required motion for a COA must be filed with the court within 21 days and that failure to file the motion may result in denial of a COA. The motion will be submitted without oral argument. The court* will ordinarily limit its consideration of the motion to the issues identified therein. Such an appeal may not proceed unless and until a certificate is granted.

(b) Time for Filing Appellant's Brief. *In cases governed by 28 U.S.C. § 2253 and FRAP Rule 22(b), the period of time for the filing of appellant's brief and appendix shall not begin to run until a certificate of appealability has issued or, when counsel has been assigned, the date of such assignment, whichever is later.*

[December 1, 1994. Amended effective December 1, 2002; paragraph (a) amended on an interim basis effective May 1, 2003.]

FRAP 23.   CUSTODY OR RELEASE OF A PRISONER IN A HABEAS CORPUS PROCEEDING

[For text of Rule, see the Federal Rules of Appellate Procedure, ante.]

FRAP 24.   PROCEEDING IN FORMA PAUPERIS

[For text of Rule, see the Federal Rules of Appellate Procedure, ante.]

TITLE VII.   GENERAL PROVISIONS

FRAP 25.   FILING AND SERVICE

[For text of Rule, see the Federal Rules of Appellate Procedure, ante.]

INTERIM LOCAL RULE 25. FILING AND SERVICE

(a) Documents in Digital Format.

1. *Document Defined. For the purposes of this rule, document includes every paper submitted to the court, including forms, letters, motions, petitions and briefs but not appendices.*

2. *Submission Requirement. Every document filed by a party represented by counsel must be submitted in a Portable Document Format (PDF), in addition to the required number of paper copies, unless counsel certifies that submission of the paper as a PDF document would constitute hardship. A party not represented by counsel is encouraged, but not required, to submit a PDF version of every document, in addition to filing the required number of paper copies.*

3. Submission of Documents.

(A) The PDF version of a document must be submitted as an e-mail attachment to electronic mailboxes designated according to case type. Case type is determined by the two-letter code found at the end of the docket number assigned to a case. The code, and respective mailboxes, are:

(i) ag, bk, op—agencycases@ca2.uscourts.gov. Cases involving an administrative agency, board, commission or office; tax court; bankruptcy; original proceedings; and, cases in which the United States is a party;

*(ii) cr—<**criminalcases@ca2.uscourts.gov**>. Criminal cases; and*

*(iii) cv—<**civilcases@ca2.uscourts.gov**>. Counseled civil cases.*

(B) Documents in a case that is not yet assigned a docket number must be submitted to <newcases@ca2.uscourts.gov>.

(C) A party who is pro se and a party with counsel in a pro se case may submit documents to

an electronic mail box designated exclusively for pro se filers: <*prosecases@ca2.uscourts.gov*>.

(D) The e-mail in which the document is attached must set forth the following identifying information in the "Subject" or "Re" header box: the docket number; the name of the party on whose behalf the document is filed; that party's designation in the case, i.e., appellant, petitioner; and, the type of document, i.e., form, letter; and the date the document is submitted to the Court. If the document pertains to a case not yet assigned a docket number in this court, the district court docket or agency number should be included in the header box. An example of a subject line: #01–2345–cv, ABC Corp, Appellant, Letter.

4.   Content. *The PDF document must contain the entire paper. Including exhibits and any supplemental material that is bound with the paper copy filed with the court. The exhibits or supplemental material may be attached to the e-mail as a separate, clearly identified, document. A manual signature need not be included on the PDF copy.*

5.   Time for Filing. *The PDF version of a document submitted pursuant to this rule must be e-mailed no later than the time for filing the required copies of the paper with the clerk.*

6.   Virus Protection. *Each party submitting a PDF document must provide a signed certificate which certifies that the PDF document has been scanned for viruses and that no virus has been detected. The signed certificate must be filed along with the paper copies of the document with the clerk. A PDF version of the certificate, which need not include a manual signature, must be attached to the e-mail that includes the PDF document.*

7.   Corrections. *If a document is corrected, a new e-mail attachment with the corrected version must be submitted, and the identifying information in the header box shall identify the document as corrected and include the date the corrected version of the document is submitted to the clerk.*

8.   E-mail Service. *The PDF version of a document must be e-mailed to all parties represented by counsel and to those parties not represented by counsel who elected to submit PDF paper.*

(b) Documents in Other Formats.

1.   Filing Requirement. *Any party, whether represented by counsel or not, who does not provide a document in PDF format, must file one unbound copy (papers not stapled or otherwise attached) of each multi-page document with the clerk. The use of paper clips or rubber bands is permitted. When only the original document is filed, the paper that comprises the document must be unbound.*

[Adopted on an interim basis effective December 1, 2005. Amended effective May 27, 2008.]

FRAP 26.   COMPUTING AND EXTENDING TIME

[For text of Rule, see the Federal Rules of Appellate Procedure, ante.]

FRAP 26.1   CORPORATE DISCLOSURE STATEMENT

[For text of Rule, see the Federal Rules of Appellate Procedure, ante.]

FRAP 27.   MOTIONS

[For text of Rule, see the Federal Rules of Appellate Procedure, ante.]

LOCAL RULE 27.   MOTIONS

(a) Form of Motion and Supporting Papers for Motion and Opposition Statement.

(1) Form of Motion.   A motion must be in writing, unless the court otherwise directs, and must conform to the following requirements:

A.   The front page of the motion must follow the form of the Motion Information Statement approved by the Court (T–1080) and contain all information required by the form.

B.   The Motion Information Statement must be followed by a memorandum which must (i) indicate the relief sought, (ii) set forth the information and legal argument supporting the motion, and (iii) if emergency relief is sought, explain the reasons for the emergency.

C.   Formal Requirements of Motion and Opposition Statement.

(i)   8½ by 11 inch paper;

(ii)   Text double spaced, except for quotations, headings and footnotes;

(iii)   Margins of one inch on all sides;

(iv)   Pages sequentially numbered (page numbers may be placed in the margins);

(v)   Bound or stapled in a secure manner that does not obscure text;

(vi)   Length: no more than 20 pages, not including attachments and the Motion Information Statement;

(vii)   Number of copies: original plus four copies;

(viii)   Required attachments to motion:

a.   An affidavit (containing only statements of fact, not legal argument);

b.   If the motion seeks substantive relief, a copy of lower court opinion or agency decision;

c.   Any exhibits necessary to determine the motion;

    d. *Proof of service.*

    2. Non-Compliance Sanctions. *If the moving party has not complied with this rule, the motion may be dismissed by the clerk without prejudice to renew upon proper papers. If application is promptly made, the action of the clerk may be reviewed by a single judge. The court may impose costs and an appropriate fine against either party for failure to comply with this rule.*

    (b) Motions to Be Heard at Regular Sessions of the Court. *Motions seeking substantive relief will normally be determined by a panel conducting a regular session of the court. These include, without limitation, motions seeking bail pending appeal (see Rule 9(b)); dismissal or summary affirmance, including summary enforcement of an agency order; stay or injunction pending appeal or review (see Rules 8 and 18); certificates of appealability (see Rule 22); leave to proceed in forma pauperis (see Rule 24) except when a certificate of appealability has been granted by the district court or counsel has been assigned under 18 U.S.C. § 3006A; and assignment of counsel in cases not within subsection (e). Except as provided in subdivision (c) of this Rule, such motions will normally be noticed for a Tuesday when the court is in session, and the court will hear oral argument from any party desiring this. Motions to dismiss appeals of incarcerated prisoners not represented by counsel for untimeliness or lack of timely prosecution shall not be noticed for a date earlier than fifteen days after the date when prison officials shall certify the motion was received by the prisoner. Any party requesting an expedited hearing must set forth in writing the facts which justify the urgency. Upon appropriate showing of urgency, the clerk may set any motion for a hearing on any day the court is in session. When the clerk thus sets a hearing for a time not later than 24 hours after application to the clerk during the period Monday to Thursday, or for Tuesday morning during the period after Thursday, the clerk may endorse on the motion papers a direction that the parties will be expected to maintain the status quo and such direction shall have the effect of a stay, unless a judge on application shall otherwise direct. Except as otherwise provided in these rules or by order of the court, all motions noticed for a Tuesday, with supporting papers, must be filed not later than the Monday of the preceding week, with notice by the movant to the adverse party to be served not later than the Thursday preceding the last date for filing, if served in person, and not later than the Monday preceding the last date for filing, if served by mail; any papers in response must be served and filed not later than seven days after service of a motion served in person, or ten days after service of a motion served by mail, but in no event later than 12 noon on the Thursday preceding the Tuesday for which the motion is noticed.*

    (c) Motions to Be Heard by a Panel Which Has Rendered a Decision. *Motions addressed to a previous decision or order of the court or for the stay, recall or modification of any mandate or decision of the court or to withdraw or dismiss an appeal argued but not decided shall be referred by the clerk to the judges who heard the appeal, normally without oral argument.*

    (d) Pro Se Motions by Incarcerated Prisoners Under 28 U.S.C. §§ 2253 and 2255. *Pro se motions by incarcerated prisoners under 28 U.S.C. §§ 2253 and 2255 for certificates of appealability, leave to proceed in forma pauperis, or assignment of counsel shall be made on seven days' notice to the state or the United States, and will be taken on submission, without being calendared, at such time as the material necessary for the court's consideration shall have been assembled by the deputy clerk designated for the purpose.*

    (e) Motions for Leave to Appeal. *Motions for leave to appeal under 28 U.S.C. § 1292(b) or under § 24 of the Bankruptcy Act, 11 U.S.C. § 47 (see Rules 5 and 6), shall be submitted without oral argument.*

    (f) Motions to Be Determined by a Single Judge. *(See Rule 27(b) and (c).) Motions for procedural relief will normally be determined by a single judge without oral argument. Notwithstanding the provision of § 27(a) in regard to dismissals, a single judge may include in an order granting an appellant an extension of time a provision for dismissal of the appeal by the clerk in the event of a default. These include, without limitation, motions for extension of time to file records, briefs, appendices or other papers, or for permission to make late filing in the absence of stipulation; to dispense with printing; for assignment of counsel or transcription of the record at the expense of the United States in cases governed by 18 U.S.C. § 3006A (which action shall be deemed to constitute the grant of leave to proceed in forma pauperis); for allowance of compensation and expenses under 18 U.S.C. § 3006A; for assignment of counsel when a certificate of appealability (see Rule 22) has been granted by the district court and for leave to proceed in forma pauperis in such cases; for leave to file a brief as amicus curiae (see Rule 29); for substitutions (see Rule 43); for consolidation; to intervene or to add or drop parties; for a preference; or for postponement of the argument of an appeal. When the court is not in session, certain of the motions normally returnable before a panel as provided in subdivision (a) may be heard and decided by a single judge. Arrangements for such a hearing shall be made through the clerk.*

    (g) Motions for Permission to File Briefs Exceeding Size Provided by Rule 28(g).

    1. *A motion for permission to file a brief exceeding the size provided by Rule 28(g) shall be accompanied by a statement of reasons therefor and a copy of the page proofs, and will be disposed of by the clerk or*

referred by the clerk to a judge as standing directions of the court provide.

2. Such a motion shall be made not later than seven days before the brief is due in criminal cases and not later than two weeks before the brief is due in all other cases.

(h) Other Motions. Any motion not provided for in this rule or in other rules of this court shall be submitted to the clerk, who will assign it for disposition in accordance with standing directions of the court or, if these are inapplicable, as directed by the judge presiding over the panel of the court in session or assigned for the hearing of motions when the court is not in session. The clerk will notify counsel if and when appearance before the court or a judge is required.

(i) Suggestions for In Banc Consideration of a Motion. A suggestion by a party for in banc consideration in the first instance of a motion shall not be accepted for filing by the clerk unless the motion sought to be considered in banc has previously been ruled on by a panel of this court.

(j) Motions by Pro Se Appellant in Civil Appeals (Including Habeas Corpus). In any civil appeal, including an appeal in a habeas corpus proceeding or other collateral attack on a criminal conviction, a motion filed by a pro se appellant (including, but not limited to, a motion for a certificate of appealability ("COA") from the denial of a writ of habeas corpus, a motion for leave to appeal in forma pauperis, for appointment of counsel, or for a transcript at public expense) shall identify each issue that the appellant intends to raise on appeal and shall state, with respect to each issue, facts and a brief statement of reasons showing that the issue has likely merit. When a motion filed by a pro se appellant does not comply with this rule, the clerk shall promptly send the appellant a letter enclosing a copy of this rule and informing the appellant that (1) the required identification of issues and supporting facts and reasons must be filed with the court within 21 days, and (2) if the appellant fails to file the required statement, or if the court determines on considering the appellant's statement that the appeal is frivolous, the court may dismiss the appeal. The motion will be submitted without oral argument. The court will ordinarily limit its consideration of the motion to the issues identified therein.

This rule was amended on October 31, 1997, to reflect "Certificate of Appealability" rather than Probable Cause.

[December 1, 1994. Amended effective October 31, 1997; July 1, 2002; December 1, 2002; paragraph (j) adopted on an interim basis effective May 1, 2003.]

FRAP 28. BRIEFS

[For text of Rule, see the Federal Rules of Appellate Procedure, ante.]

LOCAL RULE 28. BRIEFS

1. Briefs must be compact, logically arranged with proper headings, concise, and free from burdensome, irrelevant, immaterial, and scandalous matter. Briefs not complying with this rule may be disregarded and stricken by the court.

2. Appellant's brief shall include, as a preliminary statement, the name of the judge or agency member who rendered the decision appealed from and, if the judge's decision or supporting opinion is reported, the citation thereof.

[December 1, 1994.]

FRAP 28.1 CROSS–APPEALS

[For text of Rule, see the Federal Rules of Appellate Procedure, ante.]

FRAP 29. BRIEF OF AN AMICUS CURIAE

[For text of Rule, see the Federal Rules of Appellate Procedure, ante.]

INTERIM LOCAL RULE 29. BRIEF OF AN AMICUS CURIAE

The Court ordinarily will deny leave to file a brief for an amicus curiae where, by reason of a relationship between a judge who would hear the proceeding and the amicus or counsel for the amicus, the filing of the brief would cause the recusal of the judge.

[Adopted on an interim basis, effective February 7, 2005.]

FRAP 30. APPENDIX TO THE BRIEFS

[For text of Rule, see the Federal Rules of Appellate Procedure, ante.]

LOCAL RULE 30. APPENDIX

(a) Deferred Appendix. A deferred appendix as provided in Rule 30(c) may be filed in any case where the parties so stipulate or where, on application, a judge of this court so directs.

(b) Original Record. The procedure described in Rule 30(f) for hearing appeals on the original record without the necessity of an appendix (other than a copy of an opinion rendered by the district court) is authorized in all appeals conducted under the Criminal Justice Act, 18 U.S.C. § 3006A, in all other proceedings conducted in forma pauperis, and in all appeals involving a social security decision of the Secretary of Health and Human Services. In such

cases the appellant shall file along with the appellant's brief five clearly legible copies of the reporter's transcript or of so much thereof as the appellant desires the court to read (or in the case of social security decisions, of the administrative records), and both parties in their briefs shall direct the court's attention to the portions of the transcript or administrative record deemed relevant to each point. If five copies are not available without incurring undue expense, application for leave to proceed with a smaller number of copies may be made.

(c) Index for Exhibits. The index for exhibits required by FRAP 30(e) shall include a description of the exhibit sufficient to inform the court of its nature; designation merely by exhibit number or letter is not a suitable index.

(d) Notice of Appeal. The notice of appeal shall be included in the appendix.

[December 1, 1994.]

FRAP 31. SERVING AND FILING BRIEFS

[For text of Rule, see the Federal Rules of Appellate Procedure, ante.]

LOCAL RULE 31. NUMBER OF COPIES OF BRIEF TO BE FILED WITH CLERK

(b) Notwithstanding FRAP Rule 31(b), the number of copies of each brief that must be filed with the clerk is ten.

[Adopted effective May 24, 2000.]

FRAP 32. FORM OF BRIEFS, APPENDICES, AND OTHER PAPERS

[For text of Rule, see the Federal Rules of Appellate Procedure, ante.]

LOCAL RULE 32. BRIEFS AND APPENDIX

(a) Form of Brief.

(1) Briefs in Digital Format. The digital format of a brief is governed by Interim Local Rule 25.

(2) Briefs in Paper Format. Paper Briefs must conform to FRAP Rule 32(a), with a proviso that, if a litigant prefers to file a printed brief in pamphlet format, it must conform to the following specifications:

Size of Pages: 6⅛ by 9¼ inches.
Sides used: Both.
Margins: At least one inch on all sides.
Font size: 12–point type or larger, for text and footnotes.
Spacing: 2–points or more leading between lines.
　　　　　6–points or more between paragraphs.
Other specifications: Must conform to FRAP Rule 32(a).

(b) Form of Appendix. Appendices must conform to FRAP Rule 32(b).

(1) All appendices must contain:

(A) Sequentially numbered pages beginning with A–1.

(B) A detailed index referring to the sequential page numbers.

(2) Appendices may:

(A) Be printed on both sides of the page.

(B) Employ tabs to identify documents. (Use of tabs does not eliminate the requirements to number pages sequentially.)

(C) Employ the Manuscript form of transcripts.

(c) Covers. The docket number of the case must be printed in type at least one inch high on the cover of each brief and appendix.

(d) Special Appendix.

1. Contents of the Special Appendix. If the application or interpretation of any rule of law, including any constitutional provision, treaty, statute, ordinance, regulation, rule, or sentencing guideline, is significant to the resolution of any issue on appeal, or if the Appendix, exclusive of the orders, opinions, and judgments being appealed, would exceed 300 pages, the parties must provide the court with a Special Appendix, including

(A) the verbatim text, with appropriate citation, of any such rule of law, and

(B) such orders, opinions and judgments being appealed.

The inclusion of such materials in a Special Appendix satisfies the obligations established by FRAP Rules 28(f) and 30(a)(1)(C).

2. Form of the Special Appendix. The Special Appendix may be presented either as an addendum at the end of a brief, or as a separately bound volume (in which case it must be designated "Special Appendix" on its cover). The Special Appendix must conform to the requirements of Local Rule 32(b) relating to the Form of Appendix, with the exception that its pages must be sequentially numbered beginning with SPA–1.

[Former Local Rule 32 rescinded, new Local Rule adopted effective May 24, 2000. Amended effective July 1, 2002; amended on an interim basis effective December 1, 2005; amended effective May 27, 2008.]

FRAP 32.1 CITING JUDICIAL DISPOSITIONS

[For text of Rule, see the Federal Rules of Appellate Procedure, ante.]

LOCAL RULE 32.1 DISPOSITIONS BY SUMMARY ORDER

(a) Use of Summary Orders. The demands of contemporary case loads require the court to be conscious of the need to utilize judicial time effectively. Accordingly, in those cases in which decision is unanimous and each judge of the panel believes that no jurisprudential purpose would be served by an opinion (i.e., a ruling having precedential effect), the ruling may be by summary order instead of by opinion.

(b) Precedential Effect of Summary Orders. Rulings by summary order do not have precedential effect.

(c) Citation of Summary Orders.

(1) Citation to summary orders filed after January 1, 2007, is permitted.

(A) In a brief or other paper in which a litigant cites a summary order, in each paragraph in which a citation appears, at least one citation must either be to the Federal Appendix or be accompanied by the notation: "(summary order)".

(B) Service of Summary Orders on Pro Se Parties. A party citing a summary order must serve a copy of that summary order together with the paper in which the summary order is cited on any party not represented by counsel unless the summary order is available in an electronic database which is publicly accessible without payment of fee (such as the database available at http://www.ca2. uscourts.gov/). If no copy is served by reason of the availability of the order on such a database, the citation must include reference to that database and the docket number of the case in which the order was entered.

(d) Legend. Summary orders filed after January 1, 2007, shall bear the following legend:

SUMMARY ORDER

Rulings by summary order do not have precedential effect. Citation to summary orders filed after January 1, 2007, is permitted and is governed by this court's Local Rule 32.1 and Federal Rule of Appellate Procedure 32.1. In a brief or other paper in which a litigant cites a summary order, in each paragraph in which a citation appears, at least one citation must either be to the Federal Appendix or be accompanied by the notation: "(summary order)". A party citing a summary order must serve a copy of that summary order together with the paper in which the summary order is cited on any party not represented by counsel unless the sum-

mary order is available in an electronic database which is publicly accessible without payment of fee (such as the database available at http://www.ca2. uscourts.gov/). If no copy is served by reason of the availability of the order on such a database, the citation must include reference to that database and the docket number of the case in which the order was entered.

COMMENT

Summary orders are issued in cases in which a precedential opinion would serve no jurisprudential purpose because the result is dictated by pre-existing precedent. Such orders are prepared chiefly for the guidance and information of counsel and parties, and the district court (or other adjudicator) that issued the ruling from which the appeal is taken, all of whom are familiar with the facts, procedural history, and issues presented for review. Summary orders are therefore often abbreviated, and may omit material required to convey a complete, accurate understanding of the disposition and/or the principles of law upon which it rests. Like the great majority of the circuits, the court has chosen to make summary orders non-precedential. Denying summary orders precedential effect does not mean that the court considers itself free to rule differently in similar cases. Non-precedential summary order are used to avoid the risk that abbreviated explanations in summary orders might result in distortions of case law. Resolving some cases by summary order allows the court to devote more time to opinions whose publication will be jurisprudentially valuable.

Effective June 26, 2007.

FRAP 33. APPEAL CONFERENCES

[For text of Rule, see the Federal Rules of Appellate Procedure, ante.]

FRAP 34. ORAL ARGUMENT

[For text of Rule, see the Federal Rules of Appellate Procedure, ante.]

LOCAL RULE 34. ORAL ARGUMENT

(a) Number of Counsel. Only one counsel will be heard for each party on the argument of a case, except by leave of the court.

(b) Time Allotments. The judge scheduled to preside over the panel will set the time allowed for argument by each party after considering the appellant's brief and each party's request for argument time. Normally, ten or fifteen minutes will be allotted to each side. Parties on the same side of an appeal may be obliged to divide the time allotted to their side. Arguments in pro se appeals are normally five minutes per side. The clerk will notify counsel and pro se parties of all such time allotments.

(c) Postponement of Argument. Except in the event of an emergency, such as unforeseen illness of counsel, an application to postpone the date for oral argument will ordinarily not be favorably entertained. Engagement of counsel in courts (other than

the Supreme Court of the United States) or administrative hearings will not be considered good cause for postponement. The date for oral argument may not be postponed by stipulation.

(d) Determination by Court Not to Hear Oral Argument.

1. If the court, acting sua sponte, contemplates deciding an appeal without hearing oral argument, each of the parties will be given an opportunity to file a statement setting forth reasons for hearing oral argument. Oral argument will be allowed in all cases except those in which a panel of three judges, after examination of the briefs and record, shall be of the unanimous view that oral argument is not needed for one of the following reasons:

(i) the appeal is frivolous; or

(ii) the dispositive issue or set of issues has been recently authoritatively decided; or

(iii) the facts and legal arguments are adequately presented in the briefs and record and the decisional process would not be significantly aided by oral argument.

2. To prevent undue delay, incarcerated pro se appellants requesting oral argument shall file the above-mentioned statement of reasons at the time they file their briefs.

[December 1, 1994.]

FRAP 35. EN BANC DETERMINATION

[For text of Rule, see the Federal Rules of Appellate Procedure, ante.]

INTERIM LOCAL RULE 35. EN BANC PROCEDURE

(a) Copy of Opinion or Summary Order Required. *Each petition for rehearing en banc shall include a copy of the opinion or summary order to which the petition relates, unless the opinion or summary order is included in a petition for panel rehearing that has been combined with the petition for rehearing en banc.*

(b) Judges Eligible to Request an En Banc Poll. *Any Judge of the Court in regular active service and any senior judge who is a member of the panel is eligible to request a poll of the judges in regular active service to determine whether a hearing or rehearing en banc should be ordered (see 28 U.S.C. § 46(c)).*

(c) Determination of Majority for Ordering En Banc Consideration. *Neither vacancies nor disqualified judges shall be counted in determining the base on which "a majority of the circuit judges of the circuit who are in regular active service" shall be calculated, pursuant to 28 U.S.C. § 46(c), for purposes of ordering a hearing or rehearing en banc.*

(d) Procedure After Amendment of Court Ruling. *If a panel opinion or summary order is amended, a petition for rehearing en banc, or an amended petition, may be filed within the time specified by F.R.A.P. Rule 35(c), counted from the date of the entry of the amendment. A petition for rehearing en banc filed prior to amendment of the court's ruling will continue to be effective and need not be amended.*

[December 1, 1994; amended rule adopted on an interim basis effective November 16, 2004.]

FRAP 36. ENTRY OF JUDGMENT; NOTICE

[For text of Rule, see the Federal Rules of Appellate Procedure, ante.]

FRAP 37. INTEREST ON JUDGMENT

[For text of Rule, see the Federal Rules of Appellate Procedure, ante.]

FRAP 38. FRIVOLOUS APPEAL— DAMAGES AND COSTS

[For text of Rule, see the Federal Rules of Appellate Procedure, ante.]

LOCAL RULE 38. OTHER SANCTIONS FOR DELAY

In the event of failure by a party to file the record, a brief, or the appendix within the time limited by the Federal Rules of Appellate Procedure, or a rule or order of this court, the court, on motion of a party or on its own motion, may impose other sanctions, including amounts to reimburse an opposing party for the expense of making motions, upon the defaulting party or the defaulting party's attorney.

[December 1, 1994.]

FRAP 39. COSTS

[For text of Rule, see the Federal Rules of Appellate Procedure, ante.]

LOCAL RULE 39. COSTS

The cost of reproducing the necessary copies of appendices or record excerpts shall be taxed at a rate not to exceed $0.20 per page (which figure may be increased from time to time by the clerk of the court to reflect prevailing rates of economical duplicating or copying processes), or at actual cost, whichever shall be less.

[December 1, 1994.]

FRAP 40. PETITION FOR PANEL REHEARING

[For text of Rule, see the Federal Rules of Appellate Procedure, ante.]

INTERIM LOCAL RULE 40. PANEL REHEARING PROCEDURE

(a) Copy of Opinion or Summary Order Required. *Each petition for rehearing shall include a copy of the opinion or summary order to which the petition relates.*

(b) Procedure After Amendment of Court Ruling. *If a panel opinion or summary order is amended, a petition for panel rehearing, or an amended petition, may be filed within the times specified by F.R.A.P. Rule 40(a)(1), counted from the date of the entry of the amendment. A petition for panel rehearing filed prior to amendment of the court's ruling will continue to be effective and need not be amended.*

(c) Sanctions. *If a petition for rehearing is found to be wholly without merit, vexatious and for delay, the court may tax a sum not exceeding $250 against petitioner in favor of the petitioner's adversary, to be collected with the costs in the case.*

[December 1, 1994; amended rule adopted on an interim basis effective November 16, 2004.]

FRAP 41. MANDATE: CONTENTS; ISSUANCE AND EFFECTIVE DATE; STAY

[For text of Rule, see the Federal Rules of Appellate Procedure, ante.]

LOCAL RULE 41. ISSUANCE OF MANDATE

Unless otherwise ordered by the court, the mandate shall issue forthwith in all cases in which (1) an appeal from an order or judgment of a district court or a petition to review or enforce an order of an agency is decided in open court, (2) a petition for a writ of mandamus or other extraordinary writ is adjudicated, or (3) the clerk enters an order dismissing an appeal or a petition to review or enforce an order of an agency for a default in filings, as directed by an order of the court or a judge.

[December 1, 1994.]

FRAP 42. VOLUNTARY DISMISSAL

[For text of Rule, see the Federal Rules of Appellate Procedure, ante.]

FRAP 43. SUBSTITUTION OF PARTIES

[For text of Rule, see the Federal Rules of Appellate Procedure, ante.]

FRAP 44. CASE INVOLVING A CONSTITUTIONAL QUESTION WHEN THE UNITED STATES OR THE RELEVANT STATE IS NOT A PARTY

[For text of Rule, see the Federal Rules of Appellate Procedure, ante.]

FRAP 45. CLERK'S DUTIES

[For text of Rule, see the Federal Rules of Appellate Procedure, ante.]

FRAP 46. ATTORNEYS

[For text of Rule, see the Federal Rules of Appellate Procedure, ante.]

LOCAL RULE 46. ATTORNEYS

(a) (Interim) *An applicant shall file with the clerk of the Court of Appeals, in addition to the material required by F.R.A.P. Rule 46, a certificate in writing on a form approved by the court that the applicant has read and is familiar with the Federal Rules of Appellate Procedure (F.R.A.P.) and the local rules of this court.*

(b) *With the filing required by F.R.A.P. 46 and "(a)" above, a motion for admission may be made in writing, in which event it will be acted upon by a single judge, or orally at the beginning of any session of the Court without presence of the applicant being required. The movant shall represent that the movant has read the certificate filed in accordance with "(a)" above and that it meets the requirements of this Rule.*

(c) *Each applicant upon admission shall pay to the clerk a fee which shall be set by the court, to be held by the court in an appropriate depository and expended upon order of the chief judge for the expenses of the Law Library of the court located in the United States Courthouse, Foley Square, New York City, for out-of-pocket expenses incurred by attorneys or counselors assigned by the court to represent indigent persons not reimbursable under 18 U.S.C. § 3006A or other applicable statute, or for other extraordinary purposes approved by the court.*

(d) *Counsel of record for all parties must be admitted to practice before this court. Oral argument may be presented only by attorneys admitted to practice before this court. Under exceptional circumstances an attorney may be admitted to argue an appeal pro hac vice. Such admission will be extended as a matter of course to a member of the Bar of a District Court within the circuit who has represented a criminal defendant at trial and appears for that defendant*

on an appeal taken pursuant to 18 U.S.C. § 3006A, or who is acting for any party in an appeal taken in forma pauperis.

1. A notice of appearance must be filed in each case by counsel of record and, if different, by counsel who will argue the appeal, not later than the date of filing the appellant's brief on a form to be provided by the clerk.

2. A corporation may not appear pro se. Papers submitted on behalf of a corporation for whom no counsel has entered an appearance will not be filed.

(e) Appearance and Argument by Eligible Law Students.

1. An eligible law student acting under a supervising attorney may appear in this Court on behalf of any indigent person, the United States, or a governmental agency, provided the party on whose behalf the student appears has consented thereto in writing.

2. The supervising attorney shall be a member of the bar of this Court and, with respect to the law student's proposed appearance upon an appeal or other matter before this Court, shall:

(i) file with this Court the attorney's written consent to supervise the student;

(ii) assume personal professional responsibility for the student's work;

(iii) assist the student to the extent necessary;

(iv) appear with the student in all proceedings before this Court and be prepared to supplement any written or oral statement made by the student to this Court or opposing counsel.

3. In order to be eligible to appear, the student shall:

(i) be enrolled in a law school approved by the American Bar Association. The student shall be deemed to continue to meet this requirement as long as, following graduation, the student is preparing to take the first state bar examination, of the state of the student's choice within this circuit, for which the student is eligible or, having taken that examination, the student is awaiting publication of the results or admission to the bar after passing that examination;

(ii) have completed legal studies amounting to at least four semesters, or the equivalent;

(iii) be certified, by either the dean or a faculty member of the student's law school designated by the dean, as qualified to provide the legal representation permitted by this rule. This certification may be withdrawn by mailing a notice of withdrawal to the clerk of this court or it may be terminated, by vote of a majority of the panel sitting on a case in which the student is appearing, at any time without notice or hearing and without any showing of cause. The loss of certification by

action of this court shall not be considered a reflection on the character or ability of the student. The dean or a faculty member designated by the student may recertify such a student for appearances before other panels;

(iv) be introduced to this court by an attorney admitted to practice before this court;

(v) neither ask for nor receive any compensation or remuneration of any kind for the student's services from the party on whose behalf the student renders services, but this shall not prevent an attorney, legal aid bureau, law school, public defender agency, or the United States from paying compensation to the eligible law student, nor shall it prevent any agency from making proper charges for its services;

(vi) certify in writing that the student is familiar and will comply with the Code of Professional Responsibility of the American Bar Association;

(vii) certify in writing that the student is familiar with the Federal Rules of Appellate Procedure, the Rules of this court, and any other federal rules relevant to the appeal in which the student is appearing.

4. Upon filing with the clerk of this court the written consents and certifications required by this rule, an eligible law student supervised in accordance with this rule, may with respect to any appeal or other proceeding for which the student had met the requirements of this rule:

(i) engage in the drafting or preparation of briefs, appendices, motions, or other documents;

(ii) appear before this court and participate in oral argument.

(f) Suspension or Disbarment. Suspension or disbarment shall be governed by Rule 46, Federal Rules of Appellate Procedure.

1. In all cases in which an order disbarring an attorney or suspending the attorney from practice (whether or not on consent) has been entered in any other court of record, federal or state, and a certified copy thereof has been filed in this court, the clerk shall enter an order for the court, to become effective twenty-four days after the date of service upon the attorney unless sooner modified or stayed, disbarring the attorney or suspending the attorney from practice in this court upon terms and conditions comparable to those set forth by the other court of record. A reasonable effort shall be made to locate the attorney's current address, and, if that effort is unsuccessful, mailing a copy of the order to the last-known address shall be deemed proper service. A copy of the order shall also be mailed to the Committee on Admissions and Grievances of the Court of Appeals to be established under subsection (h) hereof (hereafter "Committee").

2. *Within twenty days from the date of service of this court's order, a motion may be filed in this court either by such attorney or the Committee for a modification or revocation of the order of this court. Any such motion shall set forth specifically the facts and principles relied on by applicant as showing cause why a different disposition should be ordered by this court. The timely filing of such a motion will stay the effectiveness of this court's order until further order of this court.*

3. *A motion to modify or revoke an order that has become effective under (1) will not be entertained unless good cause is shown for failure to file a motion timely under (2).*

4. *The court in any matter disputed under (2) or (3) may refer the matter to a special master to be appointed by the court for hearing and report.*

5. *The foregoing paragraphs of this subsection shall apply to any attorney who resigns from the bar of any other court of record, federal or state, while under investigation into allegations of misconduct on the attorney's part. Upon resigning under such conditions the attorney shall promptly inform the clerk of this court of such resignation.*

(g) Attorneys Convicted of Crime.

1. *Upon the filing with the court of a certificate, duly signed by the clerk of the court in which the conviction has occurred, demonstrating that an attorney has been convicted of a serious crime as hereinafter defined, the clerk of this court shall immediately enter an order suspending the attorney, whether the conviction resulted from a plea of guilty or nolo contendere, judgment after trial, or otherwise, and regardless of the pendency of an appeal from the conviction, unless the court orders otherwise. A copy of such order shall be served upon the attorney by mail at the attorney's last known address. Such suspension shall remain in effect pending disposition of a disciplinary proceeding to be commenced upon the filing of the certificate of conviction, unless the court orders otherwise.*

2. *The term "serious crime" shall include any felony, federal or state, and any lesser crime a necessary element of which, as determined by statutory or common law definition of such crime in the jurisdiction where the conviction has occurred, is (a) interference with the administration of justice; (b) false swearing; (c) misrepresentation; (d) fraud; (e) willful failure to file income tax returns; (f) deceit; (g) bribery; (h) extortion; (i) misappropriation; (j) theft; or (k) an attempt, or conspiracy, or solicitation of another to commit a serious crime.*

3. *A certificate of conviction of an attorney for any crime shall be conclusive evidence of the commission of that crime by such attorney in any disciplinary proceeding instituted against the attorney based upon the conviction.*

4. *Upon receipt of a certificate of conviction of an attorney for a serious crime and if no order has been entered under subparagraph (f) above, the court may, in addition to suspending the attorney in accordance with the provisions of (1), supra, also direct the institution of a formal presentment against the attorney, without any probable cause hearing, before the Committee, in which the sole issue to be determined shall be the extent of the final discipline to be imposed. A proceeding under this subparagraph (g)(4) may be terminated if an order is entered under subparagraph (f) above. A disciplinary proceeding so instituted shall not, however, be brought to hearing until all appeals from the conviction are concluded or the time to take such appeal has expired.*

5. *Upon receipt of a certificate of conviction of an attorney for a crime not constituting a serious crime, other than a traffic offense, the court shall refer the matter to the said Committee for whatever action the Committee may deem warranted. The court may, however, in its discretion, make no such reference with respect to convictions for minor offenses.*

6. *An attorney suspended under the provisions of (1), shall be reinstated forthwith upon the filing of a clerk's certificate demonstrating that the underlying conviction for a serious crime has been reversed, but the reinstatement will not terminate any proceeding then pending against the attorney, the disposition of which shall be determined by the court or the Committee on the basis of the available evidence.*

(h) Committee on Admissions and Grievances.

1. Appointment, Members. *The court shall appoint a standing committee of nine members of the bar to be known as the Committee on Admissions and Grievances. Three of those first appointed shall serve for the term of one year; three for two years; and the remainder and all thereafter appointed shall serve for the term of three years. Each member shall serve until a member's successor has been appointed. If a member shall hold over after the expiration of the term for which a member was appointed, the period of the member's hold-over shall be treated as part of the term of the member's successor. The court may vacate any such appointment at any time. In the case of any vacancy caused by death, resignation, or otherwise, any successor appointed shall serve the unexpired term of the successor's predecessor. The court shall designate one of the members to serve as chairman whenever it may for any reason be necessary. Five members of the Committee shall constitute a quorum. The court shall appoint a member of the bar as secretary of the Committee, who shall not be entitled to vote on its proceedings.*

2. Reference on Matters of Misconduct. *The court may refer to the Committee any accusation or evidence of misconduct in respect to any professional matter before this court that allegedly violates the rules of professional conduct or responsibility in ef-*

fect in the state or other jurisdiction where the attorney maintains his or her principal office for such investigation, hearing and report as the court deems advisable. Such matters thus referred may include not only acts of affirmative misconduct but negligent conduct of counsel. The Committee may, in its discretion, refer such matters to an appropriate bar association for preliminary investigation.

3. Committee Action. *In any matter referred to the Committee under the provisions of these Rules it shall provide the attorney with a statement in writing of the charges against him and it shall hold a hearing, on at least ten days' notice to the attorney, making a record of its proceedings; in the event the attorney does not appear, the Committee may take summary action and shall report its recommendation forthwith to the court; in the event that the attorney does appear, the attorney shall be entitled to be represented by counsel, to present witnesses and other evidence on the attorney's behalf, and to confront and cross-examine under oath any witnesses against the attorney. Except as otherwise ordered by the court the Committee shall in its discretion make and be governed by its own rules of procedure.*

4. Committee Recommendation. *The Committee shall file the record of its proceedings, its recommendation and a brief statement of the reasons therefor with the Clerk who shall retain them in camera after furnishing the court with copies thereof, and the Clerk*

shall mail a copy of the Committee's recommendation and statement of its reasons to the affected attorney and make the record of the Committee's proceedings available to the attorney. Within twenty days after filing of the record, report and recommendation the attorney may file with the Clerk a statement, not to exceed ten typewritten pages in length, in opposition to or mitigation of the Committee's recommendation. The court, consisting of the active judges thereof, shall act within a reasonable time thereafter by majority vote.

5. Committee Expense. *The Committee may be reimbursed for its reasonable expenses in the discretion of the court from such sources as may be available to the court for such purposes.*

[December 1, 1994; amended April 26, 1996; amendments adopted on an interim basis effective November 16, 2004. Amended effective February 23, 2007.]

FRAP 47.   LOCAL RULES BY COURTS OF APPEALS

[For text of Rule, see the Federal Rules of Appellate Procedure, ante.]

FRAP 48.   MASTERS

[For text of Rule, see the Federal Rules of Appellate Procedure, ante.]

FORMS

FEDERAL RULES OF APPELLATE PROCEDURE FORMS

FRAP FORM 1.   NOTICE OF APPEAL TO A COURT OF APPEALS FROM A JUDGMENT OR ORDER OF A DISTRICT COURT

[For text of Form, see the Federal Rules
of Appellate Procedure, ante.]

FRAP FORM 2.   NOTICE OF APPEAL TO A COURT OF APPEALS FROM A DECISION OF THE UNITED STATES TAX COURT

[For text of Form, see the Federal Rules
of Appellate Procedure, ante.]

FRAP FORM 3.   PETITION FOR REVIEW OF ORDER OF AN AGENCY, BOARD, COMMISSION OR OFFICER

[For text of Form, see the Federal Rules
of Appellate Procedure, ante.]

FRAP FORM 4.   AFFIDAVIT ACCOMPANYING MOTION FOR PERMISSION TO APPEAL IN FORMA PAUPERIS

[For text of Form, see the Federal Rules
of Appellate Procedure, ante.]

FRAP FORM 5.   NOTICE OF APPEAL TO A COURT OF APPEALS FROM A JUDGMENT OR ORDER OF A DISTRICT COURT OR A BANKRUPTCY APPELLATE PANEL

[For text of Form, see the Federal Rules
of Appellate Procedure, ante.]

FRAP FORM 6.   CERTIFICATE OF COMPLIANCE WITH RULE 32(a)

[For text of Form, see the Federal Rules
of Appellate Procedure, ante.]

SECOND CIRCUIT MISCELLANEOUS FORMS

LOCAL FORM FOR NOTICE OF APPEARANCE

Short Title: Docket No.

_____

NOTICE OF APPEARANCE

Appearance for (provide name of party): _____
Status of Party:
( ) Appellant/Petitioner   ( ) Cross–Appellee/Cross–Respondent
( ) Appellee/Respondent   ( ) Intervenor
( ) Cross–Appellant/Cross–Petitioner   ( ) Amicus Curiae
( ) Other (Specify):

( ) An attorney will argue this appeal.
   • Name of attorney who will argue appeal, if other than counsel of record: _____
   • Date of arguing attorney's admission to this Court (month, day, year): _____
   • Other Federal/State Bar admissions: (month, day, year): _____
( ) I am a pro se litigant who is not an attorney.
( ) I am an incarcerated pro se litigant.

TIME REQUEST

( ) Oral argument is not desired.
( ) Oral argument is desired. Party requests _____ minutes or multi-co-parties request a
   total of _____ minutes to be apportioned as follows:

   If more than 20 minutes per side is requested, set forth reasons: _____

AVAILABILITY OF COUNSEL/PRO SE LITIGANT

I understand that the person who will argue the appeal must be ready at any time during or
after the week of argument which appears on the scheduling order.

( ) I know of no dates which would be inconvenient.
( ) I request that the argument of this appeal not be calendared for the following dates,
   which are inconvenient. I have included religious holidays.

   _____

COUNSEL OR PRO SE LITIGANT MUST ADVISE THE COURT IN WRITING OF ANY
CHANGE IN AVAILABILITY. FAILURE TO DO SO MAY BE CONSIDERED BY THE
COURT IN DECIDING MOTIONS FOR ADJOURNMENT BASED ON UNAVAILABILI-
TY.

RELATED CASES

( ) This case has not been before this Court previously.
( ) This case has been before this Court previously. The short title, docket number and
   citation are: _____
( ) Matters related to this appeal or involving the same issue have been or presently are
   before this Court. The short titles, docket numbers and citations are:

   _____

Signature of counsel of record or pro se   Signature of counsel who will argue the ap-
litigant: peal, if different:

_____   _____
Type or Print Name   Type or Print Name
Name of Firm:
Address:
Telephone: Date: Telephone: Date:
_____

9/98

UNITED STATES COURT OF APPEALS

FOR THE

SECOND CIRCUIT

NOTICE OF APPEARANCE INFORMATION AND FORM

The form on the reverse side containing appearance, time request, availability, and related case information must be completed by all parties and returned to this office when appellant's brief is due.

FAILURE TO SUBMIT THIS FORM ON TIME WILL BE CONSIDERED IN DECIDING ANY MOTIONS FOR ADJOURNMENT BASED ON UNAVAILABILITY.

Each counsel of record or individual appearing pro se must complete this form. If an attorney other than counsel of record will argue the appeal, counsel of record must provide that attorney's name and date of admission to the bar of this Court in the space provided and indicate the dates, if any, when that attorney will be unavailable to argue the appeal.

Counsel of record and counsel who will argue the appeal must be admitted to the bar of this Court or be otherwise eligible to argue an appeal. The Court encourages and prefers *written* pro hac vice motions, filed as early as possible. Admission pro hac vice will be extended as a matter of course to a member of the bar of a district court within the circuit who has represented a criminal defendant at trial and continues representation on an appeal taken pursuant to the Criminal Justice Act. See Local Rule 46. However, counsel are encouraged to apply for general admission to this Court as soon as they meet the qualifications

For information concerning admissions and admission applications, contact the Clerk's Office at 212–857–8603.

APPLICATION FOR FEES AND OTHER EXPENSES UNDER EQUAL ACCESS TO JUSTICE ACT (FORM AO 291)

AO291
(10/81)

APPLICATION
FOR FEES AND OTHER EXPENSES UNDER THE EQUAL ACCESS TO JUSTICE ACT

1. COURT A. ☐ SUPREME COURT E. ☐ COURT OF APPEALS B. ☐ CUSTOMS AND PATENT APPEALS F. ☐ DISTRICT COURT C. ☐ COURT OF CLAIMS G. ☐ BANKRUPTCY COURT D. ☐ COURT OF INTERNATIONAL TRADE	2. DATE FILED 3. DOCKET NO.

4. NAME OF APPLICANT (One per form)

5. GOVERNMENT AGENCY INVOLVED IN CLAIM
(Use agency code on reverse side)

6. NATURE OF APPLICATION

  A. ☐ Original application under 28 USC 2412(d)(1)(A) after judgment in civil action against U.S.

  B. ☐ Appeal of fees and expenses awarded by Lower Court. (If Item 6B is checked go to Item 7.)

  C. ☐ Original application under 28 USC 2412(d)(3) after review of agency decision.

  D. ☐ Petition for leave to appeal an administrative agency fee determination under 5 USC 504(c)(2).

7. APPEAL FROM:

☐ DISTRICT COURT   ☐ BANKRUPTCY COURT

☐ OTHER: _____

7A. DATE FILED IN LOWER COURT   7B. DOCKET NO.

8. ADMINISTRATIVE AGENCY DOCKET NO.

9. DATE FILED IN ADMINISTRATIVE AGENCY

10. SHOWING OF "PREVAILING PARTY" STATUS (28 U.S.C. § 2412(d)(1)(B)):

IS AGENCY ORDER, COURT ORDER, OR OTHER RELEVANT DOCUMENT ATTACHED?   ☐ YES   ☐ NO

11. SHOWING OF ELIGIBILITY (28 U.S.C. § 2412(d)(2)(B)):

IS NET WORTH INFORMATION ATTACHED?   ☐ YES   ☐ NO

12. ENTER ALLEGATION THAT GOVERNMENT POSITION WAS NOT SUBSTANTIALLY JUSTIFIED (28 U.S.C. § 2412(d)(1)(B)):

13. FOR EACH AMOUNT CLAIMED, PLEASE ATTACH ITEMIZATION INFORMATION INDICATING SERVICE PROVIDED, DATE, HOURS, AND RATE (28 U.S.C. § 2412(d)(2)(A)):

AMOUNT CLAIMED

A. ATTORNEY FEES .... $ _____

B. STUDY .... _____

C. ANALYSIS .... _____

D. ENGINEERING REPORT .... _____

E. TEST .... _____

F. PROJECT .... _____

G. EXPERT WITNESS FEES .... _____

H. OTHER FEES AND EXPENSES—SPECIFY

    (1)_____ .... _____

    (2)_____ .... _____

    (3)_____ .... _____

I. TOTAL FEES AND EXPENSES .... $ _____

14. SIGNATURE   15. DATE

NOTE: THIS FORM SHOULD ACCOMPANY YOUR CLAIM WHEN FILED WITH THE CLERK OF COURT.

ADMINISTRATIVE AGENCY CODES

Use the following abbreviations for the U.S. Government Agency involved in claim in Item 5.

BENEFITS REVIEW BOARD	BRB
CIVIL AERONAUTICS BOARD	CAB
CIVIL SERVICE COMMISSION (U.S.)	CSC
CONSUMER PRODUCTS SAFETY COMMISSION	CPSC
COPYRIGHT ROYALTY TRIBUNAL	CRT
DEPARTMENT OF AGRICULTURE	AGRI
DEPARTMENT OF COMMERCE	COMM
DEPARTMENT OF DEFENSE	DOD
DEPARTMENT OF EDUCATION	EDUC
DEPARTMENT OF ENERGY	DOE
DEPARTMENT OF HEALTH, EDUCATION & WELFARE	HEW
DEPARTMENT OF HEALTH & HUMAN SERVICES	HHS
DEPARTMENT OF HOUSING & URBAN DEVELOPMENT	HUD
DEPARTMENT OF INTERIOR	DOI
DEPARTMENT OF JUSTICE	DOJ
DEPARTMENT OF LABOR (Except OSHA)	LABR
DEPARTMENT OF TRANSPORTATION, NATIONAL TRANSPORTATION SAFETY BOARD	TRAN
DEPARTMENT OF THE TREASURY (Except IRS)	TREA
DRUG ENFORCEMENT AGENCY	DEA
ENVIRONMENTAL PROTECTION AGENCY	EPA
EQUAL EMPLOYMENT OPPORTUNITY COMMISSION	EEOC
FEDERAL AVIATION AGENCY	FAA
FEDERAL COAL MINE SAFETY BOARD	FCMS
FEDERAL COMMUNICATIONS COMMISSION	FCC
FEDERAL DEPOSIT INSURANCE CORPORATION	FDIC
FEDERAL ELECTION COMMISSION	FEC
FEDERAL ENERGY AGENCY	FEA
FEDERAL ENERGY REGULATORY COMMISSION	FERC
FEDERAL HOME LOAN BANK BOARD	FHLB
FEDERAL LABOR RELATIONS AUTHORITY	FLRA
FEDERAL MARITIME BOARD	FMBD
FEDERAL MARITIME COMMISSION	FMC
FEDERAL MINE SAFETY & HEALTH ADMINISTRATION	MSHA
FEDERAL MINE SAFETY & HEALTH REVIEW COMMISSION	MSHR
FEDERAL RESERVE SYSTEM	FRS
FEDERAL TRADE COMMISSION	FTC
FOOD & DRUG ADMINISTRATION	FDA
GENERAL SERVICES ADMINISTRATION	GSA
IMMIGRATION & NATURALIZATION SERVICE	INS
INTERNAL REVENUE SERVICE (Except TAX COURT)	IRS
INTERSTATE COMMERCE COMMISSION	ICC
MERIT SYSTEMS PROTECTION BOARD	MSPB
NATIONAL LABOR RELATIONS BOARD	NLRB
NUCLEAR REGULATORY COMMISSION	NRC
OCCUPATIONAL SAFETY & HEALTH ADMINISTRATION	OSHA
OCCUPATIONAL SAFETY & HEALTH REVIEW COMMISSION	OSHC
OFFICE OF MANAGEMENT & BUDGET	OMB
OFFICE OF PERSONNEL MANAGEMENT	OPM
OFFICE OF WORKERS COMPENSATION PROGRAM	OWCP
PATENT OFFICE	PATO
POSTAL RATE COMMISSION (U.S.)	PRC
POSTAL SERVICE (U.S.)	USPS
RR RETIREMENT BOARD	RRRB
SECURITIES & EXCHANGE COMMISSION	SEC
SMALL BUSINESS ADMINISTRATION	SBA
TAX COURT, INTERNAL REVENUE SERVICE	TXC

LOCAL CRIMINAL NOTICE OF APPEAL FORM

NOTICE OF APPEAL
UNITED STATES DISTRICT COURT
_____ District of _____

_____   Docket No.:_____

_____
(District Court Judge)

Notice is hereby given that _____
appeals to the United States Court of Appeals for the Second Circuit from the judgment [_____], other [_____],

(specify)

entered in this action on _____.
(date)
Offense occurred after November 1, 1987   Yes [_____]   No [_____]

The appeal concerns: Conviction only [_____] Sentence only [_____] Conviction and Sentence [_____].

_____
(Counsel for Appellant)

Date _____   Address _____
TO

_____

_____

Telephone Number

ADD ADDITIONAL PAGE (IF NECESSARY)

TO BE COMPLETED BY ATTORNEY	TRANSCRIPT INFORMATION—FORM B
> QUESTIONNAIRE	**> TRANSCRIPT ORDER** > DESCRIPTION OF PROCEEDINGS FOR WHICH TRANSCRIPT IS REQUIRED (INCLUDE DATE).

Dates

[_____] I am ordering a transcript
[_____] I am not ordering a transcript
   Reason:
     [_____] Daily copy is available
     [_____] U.S. Attorney has placed or-
der
     [_____] Other. Attach explanation

Prepare transcript of
[_____] Pre-trial proceedings _____
[_____] Trial _____
[_____] Sentencing _____
[_____] Post-trial proceedings _____

The attorney certifies that he/she will make satisfactory arrangements with the court reporter for payment of the cost of the transcript. (FRAP 10(b)) > Method of payment [___] Funds [___]   CJA Form 24 [___]

ATTORNEY'S SIGNATURE   DATE

>COURT REPORTER ACKNOWLEDGEMENT   To be completed by Court Reporter and forwarded to Court of Appeals.

Date order received   Estimated completion date   Estimated number of pages.

Date _____   Signature _____
(Court Reporter)

DISTRIBUTE COPIES TO THE FOLLOWING:
1. Original to U.S. District Court (Appeals Clerk)
2. Copy U.S. Attorney's Office
3. Copy to Defendant's Attorney
4. U.S. Court of Appeals
5. Court Reporter (District Court)

Revised October, 2002; August 1, 2005.

CRIMINAL CASE INFORMATION FORM
(FORM A)

FORM A—FOR APPEALS IN CRIMINAL CASES

CASE AND SENTENCING INFORMATION   To be completed by courtroom deputy.

CASE TITLE:

DISTRICT   DOCKET NO.   JUDGE

Affidavit of Financial Status (CJA 23)
☐ Filed ☐ Unfiled

DEFENDANT: Name and Address

Leave to Appeal in Forma Pauperis
☐ Granted ☐ Denied ☐ Not Sought

DEFENDANT'S ATTORNEY:
Name and Address

SOCIAL SECURITY NO.

ASSISTANT U.S. ATTORNEY:
Name and Telephone

Phone:

☐ Appointed
☐ Retained

Date of Sentence   Bail/Jail disposition
☐ Committed ☐ Not Committed

Defendant found guilty by
☐ Plea ☐ Trial

Number of other co-defendants found guilty: _____

TRANSCRIPT INFORMATION   To be completed by courtroom deputy.

Court Reporter in Charge: (Name, Telephone)

Was daily copy prepared?   YES   NO

Did Assistant U.S. Attorney order trial minutes?   YES   NO

Did attorney for the defendant order trial minutes?   YES   NO

COUNSEL AND TRANSCRIPT INFORMATION ON APPEAL   To be completed by sentencing judge

1. Does defendant's financial status warrant appointment of   YES   NO
    counsel on appeal?

3. Should trial minutes be transcribed at the expense of the   YES   NO
    United States pursuant to CJA?

2. If so, should trial counsel be appointed on appeal?   YES   NO

SIGNATURE OF JUDGE   DATE

NAME OF COURTROOM DEPUTY   DATE NOTICE OF APPEAL FILED

DISTRIBUTE COPIES TO THE FOLLOWING:
1. Original to U.S. District Court (Appeals Clerk).
2. Copy to U.S. Court of Appeals.
3. Copy to U.S. Attorney's Office.
4. Copy to Probation Office.

USCA–2
FORM A Rev. 10–02

CIVIL APPEAL PRE–ARGUMENT STATEMENT
(FORM C)

UNITED STATES COURT OF APPEALS FOR THE SECOND CIRCUIT
CIVIL APPEAL PRE-ARGUMENT STATEMENT (FORM C)

1. SEE NOTICE ON REVERSE.   **2. PLEASE TYPE OR PRINT.**   **3. STAPLE ALL ADDITIONAL PAGES**

Case Caption:	District Court or Agency:	Judge:
	Date the Order or Judgment Appealed from was Entered on the Docket:	District Court Docket No.:
	Date the Notice of Appeal was Filed:	Is this a Cross Appeal? ☐ Yes ☐ No

Attorney(s) for Appellant(s): ☐ Plaintiff ☐ Defendant	Counsel's Name: Address: Telephone No.: Fax No.: E-mail:
Attorney(s) for Appellee(s): ☐ Plaintiff ☐ Defendant	Counsel's Name: Address: Telephone No.: Fax No.: E-mail:

Has Transcript Been Prepared?	Approx. Number of Transcript Pages:	Number of Exhibits Appended to Transcript:	Has this matter been before this Circuit previously? ☐ Yes ☐ No If Yes, provide the following: Case Name: 2d Cir. Docket No.: Reporter Citation: (i.e., F.3d or Fed. App.)

ADDENDUM "A": COUNSEL MUST ATTACH TO THIS FORM: (1) A BRIEF, BUT NOT PERFUNCTORY, DESCRIPTION OF THE NATURE OF THE ACTION; (2) THE RESULT BELOW; (3) A COPY OF THE NOTICE OF APPEAL AND A CURRENT COPY OF THE LOWER COURT DOCKET SHEET; AND (4) A COPY OF ALL RELEVANT OPINIONS/ORDERS FORMING THE BASIS FOR THIS APPEAL, INCLUDING TRANSCRIPTS OF ORDERS ISSUED FROM THE BENCH OR IN CHAMBERS.

ADDENDUM "B": COUNSEL MUST ATTACH TO THIS FORM A LIST OF THE ISSUES PROPOSED TO BE RAISED ON APPEAL, AS WELL AS THE APPLICABLE APPELLATE STANDARD OF REVIEW FOR EACH PROPOSED ISSUE.

PART A: JURISDICTION

1. Federal Jurisdiction	2. Appellate Jurisdiction
☐ U.S. a party ☐ Diversity	☐ Final Decision ☐ Order Certified by District Judge (i.e., Fed. R. Civ. P. 54(b))
☐ Federal question (U.S. not a party) ☐ Other (specify): _____	☐ Interlocutory Decision Appealable As of Right ☐ Other (specify): _____

IMPORTANT. COMPLETE AND SIGN REVERSE SIDE OF THIS FORM.

FORM C (Rev. April 2006)

PART B: DISTRICT COURT DISPOSITION (Check as many as apply)

1. Stage of Proceedings	2. Type of Judgment/Order Appealed	3. Relief
☐ Pre-trial ☐ During trial ☐ After trial	☐ Default judgment ☐ Judgment / Decision ☐ Dismissal/jurisdiction of the Court ☐ Dismissal/merit ☐ Jury verdict ☐ Summary judgment ☐ Judgment NOV ☐ Declaratory judgment ☐ Directed verdict ☐ Other (specify):	☐ Damages: ☐ Injunctions: ___ Sought: $ ___ ☐ Preliminary ___ Granted: $ ___ ☐ Permanent ___ Denied: $ ___ ☐ Denied

PART C: NATURE OF SUIT (Check as many as apply)

1. Federal Statutes			2. Torts	3. Contracts	4. Prisoner Petitions

☐ Antitrust
☐ Bankruptcy
☐ Banks/Banking
☐ Civil Rights
☐ Commerce,
☐ Energy
☐ Commodities
☐ Other (specify): ___
	☐ Communications
	☐ Consumer Protection
	☐ Copyright ☐ Patent
	☐ Trademark
	☐ Election
	☐ Soc. Security
	☐ Environmental
		☐ Freedom of Information Act
		☐ Immigration
		☐ Labor
		☐ OSHA
		☐ Securities
		☐ Tax
			☐ Admiralty/
			   Maritime
			☐ Assault /
			   Defamation
			☐ FELA
			☐ Products Liability
			☐ Other (Specify):
				☐ Admiralty/
				   Maritime
				☐ Arbitration
				☐ Commercial
				☐ Employment
				☐ Insurance
				☐ Negotiable
				   Instruments
				☐ Other Specify
					☐ Civil Rights
					   Habeas Corpus
					☐ Mandamus
					☐ Parole
					☐ Vacate Sentence
					☐ Other

5. Other	6. General	7. Will appeal raise constitutional issue(s)?
☐ Forfeiture/Penalty ☐ Real Property ☐ Treaty (specify): ___ ☐ Other (specify): ___	☐ Arbitration ☐ Attorney Disqualification ☐ Class Action ☐ Counsel Fees ☐ Shareholder Derivative ☐ Transfer	☐ Yes ☐ No Will appeal raise a matter of first impression? ☐ Yes ☐ No

1. Is any matter relative to this appeal still pending below? ☐ Yes, specify: _____ ☐ No

2. To your knowledge, is there any case presently pending or about to be brought before this Court or another court or administrative agency which:

     (A)   Arises from substantially the same case or controversy as this appeal?   ☐ Yes   ☐ No

     (B)   Involves an issue that is substantially similar or related to an issue in this appeal?   ☐ Yes   ☐ No

If yes, state whether ☐ "A," or ☐ "B," or ☐ both are applicable, and provide in the spaces below the following information on the *other* action(s):

Case Name:	Docket No.	Citation:	Court or Agency:
Name of Appellant:			

Date:	Signature of Counsel of Record:

NOTICE TO COUNSEL

Once you have filed your Notice of Appeal with the District Court or the Tax Court, you have only ten (10) calendar days in which to complete the following important steps:

1. Complete this Civil Appeal Pre-Argument Statement (Form C); serve it upon all parties, and file two copies with the Clerk of the Second Circuit.
2. File **two** copies of the Court of Appeals Transcript Information/Civil Appeal Form (Form D) with the Clerk of the Second Circuit.
3. Pay the $455 docketing fee to the Clerk of the United States District Court, unless you are authorized to prosecute the appeal without payment.

     PLEASE NOTE: IF YOU DO NOT COMPLY WITH THESE REQUIREMENTS WITHIN TEN (10) CALENDAR DAYS, YOUR APPEAL WILL BE DISMISSED. *SEE* THE CIVIL APPEALS MANAGEMENT PLAN OF THE UNITED STATES COURT OF APPEALS FOR THE SECOND CIRCUIT.

FORM C (Rev. April 2006)

[Revised March, 2005; April, 2006.]

AGENCY APPEAL PRE–ARGUMENT STATEMENT
(FORM C–A)

UNITED STATES COURT OF APPEALS FOR THE SECOND CIRCUIT
AGENCY APPEAL PRE-ARGUMENT STATEMENT (FORM C-A)

☐ APPLICATION FOR ENFORCEMENT   ☐ PETITION FOR REVIEW

1. SEE NOTICE ON REVERSE.   2. PLEASE TYPE OR PRINT.   3. STAPLE ALL ADDITIONAL PAGES

CAPTION:	AGENCY NAME:	AGENCY NO.:
	DATE THE ORDER UPON WHICH REVIEW OR ENFORCEMENT IS SOUGHT WAS ENTERED BELOW:	ALIEN NO : (Immigration Only)
	DATE THE PETITION OR APPLICATION WAS FILED:	Is this a cross-petition for review / cross-application for enforcement? ☐ YES ☐ NO

Contact Information for Petitioner(s) Attorney:	Counsel's Name: Address:	Telephone No.: Fax No.: E-mail:
Contact Information for Respondent(s) Attorney:	Counsel's Name: Address:	Telephone No.: Fax No.: E-mail:

JURISDICTION OF THE COURT OF APPEALS (provide U.S.C. title and section):	APPROX. NUMBER OF PAGES IN THE RECORD:	APPROX. NUMBER OF EXHIBITS IN THE RECORD:	Has this matter been before this Circuit previously? ☐ Yes ☐ No If Yes, provide the following: Case Name: 2d Cir. Docket No.: Reporter Citation: (*i.e.*, F.3d or Fed. App.)

ADDENDUM "A": COUNSEL MUST ATTACH TO THIS FORM: (1) A BRIEF, BUT NOT PERFUNCTORY, DESCRIPTION OF THE NATURE OF THE ACTION; (2) THE RESULT BELOW; AND (3) A COPY OF ALL RELEVANT OPINIONS/ORDERS FORMING THE BASIS FOR THIS PETITION FOR REVIEW OR APPLICATION FOR ENFORCEMENT.

ADDENDUM "B": COUNSEL MUST ATTACH TO THIS FORM: (1) THE RELIEF REQUESTED; (2) A LIST OF THE PROPOSED ISSUES; AND (3) THE APPLICABLE APPELLATE STANDARD OF REVIEW FOR EACH PROPOSED ISSUE.

PART A: STANDING AND VENUE

STANDING	**VENUE**
PETITIONER / APPLICANT IS: ☐ AGENCY ☐ OTHER PARTY ☐ NON-PARTY (SPECIFY STANDING):	COUNSEL MUST PROVIDE IN THE SPACE BELOW THE FACTS OR CIRCUMSTANCES UPON WHICH VENUE IS BASED:

IMPORTANT. COMPLETE AND SIGN REVERSE SIDE OF THIS FORM.

FORM C-A (Rev. April 2006)

Page 1 of 2

PART B: NATURE OF ORDER UPON WHICH REVIEW OR ENFORCEMENT IS SOUGHT
(Check as many as apply)

TYPE OF CASE:

_____ADMINISTRATIVE REGULATION/ RULEMAKING	_____ IMMIGRATION-includes denial of an asylum claim
_____BENEFITS REVIEW	_____ IMMIGRATION-does NOT include denial of an asylum claim
_____ UNFAIR LABOR	_____ TARIFFS
_____ HEALTH & SAFETY	_____ OTHER:
_____ COMMERCE	(SPECIFY)
_____ ENERGY	

1. Is any matter relative to this petition or application still pending below? ☐ Yes, specify: _____ ☐ No

2. To your knowledge, is there any case presently pending or about to be brought before this Court or another court or administrative agency which:

    (A)   Arises from substantially the same case or controversy as this petition or application ?   ☐ Yes   ☐ No

    (B)   Involves an issue that is substantially similar or related to an issue in this petition or application ?   ☐ Yes   ☐ No

If yes, state whether ☐ "A," or ☐ "B," or ☐ both are applicable, and provide in the spaces below the following information on the *other* action(s):

Case Name:	Docket No.	Citation:	Court or Agency:
Name of Petitioner or Applicant:			

Date:	Signature of Counsel of Record:

NOTICE TO COUNSEL

Once you have filed your Petition for Review or Application for Enforcement, you have only ten (10) calendar days in which to complete the following important steps:

1. Complete this Agency Appeal Pre-Argument Statement (Form C-A); serve it upon your adversary, and file an original and one copy with the Clerk of the Second Circuit.
2. Pay the $450 docketing fee to the Clerk of the Second Circuit, unless you are authorized to prosecute the appeal without payment.

    PLEASE NOTE: IF YOU DO NOT COMPLY WITH THESE REQUIREMENTS WITHIN TEN (10) CALENDAR DAYS, YOUR PETITION FOR REVIEW OR APPLICATION FOR ENFORCEMENT WILL BE DISMISSED. *SEE* THE CIVIL APPEALS MANAGEMENT PLAN OF THE UNITED STATES COURT OF APPEALS FOR THE SECOND CIRCUIT.

FORM C-A (Rev. April 2006)   Page 2 of 2

[Revised August, 2005; April, 2006.]

CIVIL APPEAL TRANSCRIPT INFORMATION
(FORM D)

UNITED STATES COURT OF APPEALS
FOR THE SECOND CIRCUIT

CIVIL APPEAL TRANSCRIPT INFORMATION (FORM D)

NOTICE TO COUNSEL: COUNSEL FOR THE APPELLANT MUST FILE AN ORIGINAL AND ONE COPY OF THIS FORM WITH THE CLERK OF THE SECOND CIRCUIT IN ALL CIVIL APPEALS WITHIN TEN (10) CALENDAR DAYS AFTER FILING A NOTICE OF APPEAL.

THIS SECTION MUST BE COMPLETED BY COUNSEL FOR APPELLANT		
CASE TITLE	**DISTRICT**	**DOCKET NUMBER**
	JUDGE	**APPELLANT**
	COURT REPORTER	**COUNSEL FOR APPELLANT**

Check the applicable provision:	PROVIDE A DESCRIPTION, INCLUDING DATES, OF THE PROCEEDINGS FOR WHICH A TRANSCRIPT IS REQUIRED (*i.e.*, oral argument, order from the bench, etc.)
☐ I am ordering a transcript.	
☐ I am not ordering a transcript	
Reason for not ordering a transcript:	
☐ Copy is already available	
☐ No transcribed proceedings	
☐ Other (Specify in the space below):	**METHOD OF PAYMENT** ☐ Funds ☐ CJA Voucher (CJA 21)
INSTRUCTIONS TO COURT REPORTER:	**DELIVER TRANSCRIPT TO: (COUNSEL'S NAME, ADDRESS, TELEPHONE)**
☐ **PREPARE TRANSCRIPT OF PRE-TRIAL PROCEEDINGS**	
☐ **PREPARE TRANSCRIPT OF TRIAL**	
☐ **PREPARE TRANSCRIPT OF OTHER POST-TRIAL PROCEEDINGS**	
☐ **OTHER (Specify in the space below):**	

I certify that I have made satisfactory arrangements with the court reporter for payment of the cost of the transcript. *See* Fed. R. App. P. 10(b). I understand that unless I have already ordered the transcript, I shall order its preparation at the time required by the Civil Appeals Management Plan, the Fed. R. App. P., and the local rules.

COUNSEL'S SIGNATURE	DATE

COURT REPORTER ACKNOWLEDGMENT: This section is to be completed by the court reporter. Return one copy to the Clerk of the Second Circuit.

DATE ORDER RECEIVED	ESTIMATED COMPLETION DATE	ESTIMATED NUMBER OF PAGES
SIGNATURE OF COURT REPORTED		DATE

FORM D (Rev. April 2005)

[Revised April, 2005.]

T–1080. MOTION INFORMATION STATEMENT

**UNITED STATES COURT OF APPEALS
FOR THE SECOND CIRCUIT
MOTION INFORMATION STATEMENT**
Thurgood Marshall U.S. Courthouse at Foley Square
40 Centre Street, New York, NY 10007
Telephone: 212–857–8500

Caption [use short title]

Docket Number(s): _____

Motion for: _____

Set forth below precise, complete statement of relief sought:

_____

_____

_____

_____

MOVING PARTY: _____   **OPPOSING PARTY:** _____

☐ Plaintiff ☐ Defendant
☐ Appellant/Petitioner ☐ Appellee/Respondent

MOVING ATTORNEY: _____   **OPPOSING ATTORNEY:** _____
[name of attorney, with firm, address, phone number, and e-mail]   [name of attorney, with firm, address, phone number, and e-mail]

_____   _____

_____   _____

_____   _____

Court–Judge/Agency appealed from: _____

Please check appropriate boxes:

Has **consent** of opposing counsel:
A. been sought?   ☐ Yes ☐ No
B. been obtained?   ☐ Yes ☐ No

Is **oral argument** requested?   ☐ Yes ☐ No
(requests for oral argument will not necessarily be granted)

Has **argument** date of appeal been **set:**   ☐ Yes ☐ No
If yes, enter date _____

Signature of Moving Attorney:

_____   **Date:** _____

**FOR EMERGENCY MOTIONS, MOTIONS
FOR STAYS AND INJUNCTIONS
PENDING APPEAL:**
Has request for relief been made **below**? ☐ Yes ☐ No

Has this relief been previously sought in
this Court?   ☐ Yes ☐ No

Requested return date and explanation of emergency:
_____

_____

Has **service** been effected?   ☐ Yes ☐ No
[Attach proof of service]

_____

ORDER

IT IS HEREBY ORDERED THAT the motion is GRANTED DENIED.

FOR THE COURT:
CATHERINE O'HAGAN WOLFE,
Clerk of Court
By: _____

Date:_____

Revised July 1, 2002; October 31, 2002; November 1, 2006.

LOCAL INSTRUCTIONS FOR BILL OF COSTS

Docket No. _____   Short Title: _____

Dear Counsel or Pro Se Litigant:

If you desire to file a bill of costs, enclosed is a form which you should use. Your bill of costs must be:

1. Served.

2. Filed within fourteen (14) days after entry of judgment with proof of service.

3. Verified.

4. Clear as to the number of copies which comprise the printer's unit.

5. Accompanied by printer's bills, which must include minimum charge for printer's unit

   a. of a page

   b. of a cover

   c. of footlines by the line

   d. of an index and table of cases by the page

6. Only for the number of necessary copies inserted in enclosed form.

7. For actual costs at rates not higher than those generally charged such work in the area where the Clerk's Office is located, otherwise subject to reduction.

8. Devoid of such items as postage, delivery charges, service charge, overtime and author's alterations.

9. One copy shall be filed with the original.

Very truly yours,

CATHERINE O'HAGAN WOLFE
Clerk of Court

By: _____
          Deputy Clerk

ITEMIZED AND VERIFIED BILL OF COSTS

United States Court of Appeals
For the Second Circuit
_____

Docket No. _____

_____

Counsel for _____
respectfully submits, pursuant to Rule 39(c) of the Federal Rules of Appellate
Procedure the within bill of costs and requests the Clerk to prepare an itemized
statement of costs taxed against the _____ and in favor of
_____ for insertion in the mandate.

Docketing Action   _____

Costs of printing appendix (necessary copies _____)   _____
Costs of printing brief (necessary copies _____)   _____
Costs of printing reply brief (necessary copies _____)   _____

(VERIFICATION HERE)

_____
                                              (signature)

LAW STUDENT PRACTICE FORM

UNITED STATES COURT OF APPEALS
FOR THE SECOND CIRCUIT
Thurgood Marshall United States Courthouse
40 Centre Street
New York, NY 10007
(212)857–8500

Case Docket No.: _____

Form to Be Completed by the Party for Whom the Law Student is Rendering Services (if the services are rendered for the Government, by the United States Attorney or an Authorized Representative of the Government Agency Represented).

I authorize _____, a law student, to appear in court or other proceedings on my behalf, and to prepare documents on my behalf.

_____   _____
(Date)   (Signature of Client)

(If more than one client is involved, approvals from each shall be attached.)

To Be Completed by the Law Student's Supervising Attorney:

I will carefully supervise all of this student's work. I authorize this student to appear in court or at other proceedings, and to prepare documents. I will accompany the student at such appearances, sign all documents prepared by the student, assume personal responsibility for the student's work and be prepared to supplement, if necessary, any statements made by the student to the Court or opposing counsel.

_____   _____
(Date)   (Signature of Attorney)

Form for Designating Compliance With Student Practice Rule
(LR 46(a)) of the Court of Appeals for the Second Circuit

_____   _____
(Name of Student)   (Name of Supervising Attorney)
Address & Telephone of Above: Address and Telephone of Above:
_____   _____
_____   _____
Name of Law School Student is Attending:
_____
_____
_____

To Be Completed by Law Student:

I certify that I have completed at least four (4) semesters of law school; that I am familiar and will comply with the Code of Professional Responsibility of the American Bar Association, the Federal Rules of Appellate Procedure, the Rules of this Court, and any other federal rules relevant to this appeal in which I am appearing; and that I am rendering services.

_____   _____
(Date)   (Student's Signature)

To Be Completed by the Dean or a Designated Faculty Member of the Law School Attended by the Student:

I certify that this student has completed at least four (4) semesters of law school work and is, to the best of my knowledge, of good character and competent legal ability.

_____   _____
(Date)   (Signature of Dean or Faculty Member)

                                _____
                                (Position of Above)

APPLICATION FOR LEAVE TO FILE A SECOND OR SUCCESSIVE MOTION TO VACATE, SET ASIDE OR CORRECT SENTENCE 28 U.S.C. § 2255 BY A PRISONER IN FEDERAL CUSTODY

UNITED STATES COURT OF APPEALS
FOR THE SECOND CIRCUIT

Name

_____

Place of Confinement   Prisoner Number

_____   _____

INSTRUCTIONS—READ CAREFULLY

(1) This application must be legibly handwritten or typewritten and signed by the applicant under penalty of perjury. Any false statement of a material fact may serve as the basis for prosecution and conviction for perjury.

(2) All questions must be answered concisely in the proper space on the form.

(3) The Judicial Conference of the United States has adopted the 8½ x 11 inch paper size for use throughout the federal judiciary and directed the elimination of the use of legal size paper. All pleadings must be on 8½ x 11 inch paper, otherwise we cannot accept them.

(4) All applicants seeking leave to file a second or successive petition are required to use this form, except in capital cases. In capital cases only, the use of this form is optional.

(5) Additional pages are not permitted except with respect to additional grounds for relief and facts which you rely upon to support those grounds. Do not submit separate petitions, motions, briefs, arguments, etc., except in capital cases.

(6) In accordance with the "Antiterrorism and Effective Death Penalty Act of 1996," as codified at 28 U.S.C. § 2255, effective April 24, 1996, before leave to file a second or successive motion can be granted by the United States Court of Appeals, *it is the applicant's burden* to make a prima facie showing that he satisfies either of the two conditions stated below.

A second or successive motion must be certified as provided in [28 U.S.C.] section 2255 by a panel of the appropriate court of appeals to contain—

(1) newly discovered evidence that, if proven and viewed in light of the evidence as a whole, would be sufficient to establish by clear and convincing evidence that no reasonable factfinder would have found the movant guilty of the offense; or

(2) a new rule of constitutional law, made retroactive to cases on collateral review by the Supreme Court, that was previously unavailable.

(7) When this application is fully completed, the original and four copies must be mailed to:

Clerk of Court
United States Court of Appeals for the Second Circuit
United States Courthouse
40 Foley Square
New York, New York 10007

APPLICATION

1. (a) State and division of the United States District Court which entered the judgment of conviction under attack _____

   (b) Case number _____

2. Date of judgment of conviction _____

3. Length of sentence _____ Sentencing Judge _____

4. Nature of offense or offenses for which you were convicted: _____
   _____
   _____
   _____

5. Have you taken a direct appeal relating to this conviction and sentence in the federal court?
   Yes ( ) No ( ) If "yes", please note below:
   (a) Name of court _____
   (b) Case number _____
   (c) Grounds raised (list all grounds; use extra pages if necessary) _____
   _____
   _____
   _____
   _____

   (d) Result _____
   (e) Date of result _____

6. Related to this conviction and sentence, have you ever filed a motion to vacate in any federal court?
   Yes ( ) No ( ) If "yes", how many times? _____ (if more than one, complete 6 and 7 below as necessary)
   (a) Name of court _____
   (b) Case number _____
   (c) Nature of proceeding _____
   _____

   (d) Grounds raised (list all grounds; use extra pages if necessary) _____
   _____
   _____
   _____
   _____

   (e) Did you receive an evidentiary hearing on your motion? Yes ( ) No ( )
   (f) Result _____

   (g) Date of result _____

7. As to any second federal motion, give the same information:
   (a) Name of court _____
   (b) Case number _____
   (c) Nature of proceeding _____
   _____

   (d) Grounds raised (list all grounds; use extra pages if necessary) _____
   _____
   _____
   _____
   _____

   (e) Did you receive an evidentiary hearing on your motion? Yes ( ) No ( )
   (f) Result _____
   _____

(g) Date of result _____

8. As to any third federal motion, give the same information:
    (a) Name of court _____
    (b) Case number _____
    (c) Nature of proceeding _____

    _____

    _____

    (d) Grounds raised (list all grounds; use extra pages if necessary) _____

    _____

    _____

    _____

    (e) Did you receive an evidentiary hearing on your motion? Yes ( ) No ( )
    (f) Result _____

    (g) Date of result _____

9. Did you appeal the result of any action taken on your federal motions? (Use extra pages to reflect additional federal motions if necessary)
    (1) First motion   No ( ) Yes ( ) Appeal No. _____
    (2) Second motion   No ( ) Yes ( ) Appeal No. _____
    (3) Third motion   No ( ) Yes ( ) Appeal No. _____

10. If you did not appeal from the adverse action on any motion, explain briefly why you did not: _____

    _____

    _____

11. State concisely every ground on which you now claim that you are being held unlawfully. Summarize briefly the facts supporting each ground.
    A. Ground one: _____

    Supporting FACTS (tell your story briefly without citing cases or law):

    _____

    _____

    _____

    _____

    Was this claim raised in a prior motion? Yes ( ) No ( )
    Does this claim rely on a "new rule of law?" Yes ( ) No ( )
    If "yes," state the new rule of law (give case name and citation):

    _____

    Does this claim rely on "newly discovered evidence?" Yes ( ) No ( )
    If "yes," briefly state the newly discovered evidence, when it was discovered, and why it was not previously available to you _____

    _____

    _____

    _____

    _____

    B. Ground two: _____

    Supporting FACTS (tell your story briefly without citing cases or law):

    _____

_____

_____

_____

_____

_____

_____

Was this claim raised in a prior motion? Yes ( ) No ( )

Does this claim rely on a "new rule of law?" Yes ( ) No ( )

If "yes," state the new rule of law (give case name and citation):

_____

Does this claim rely on "newly discovered evidence?" Yes ( ) No ( )

If "yes," briefly state the newly discovered evidence, when it was discovered, and why it was not previously available to you _____

_____

_____

_____

_____

[Additional grounds may be asserted on additional pages if necessary]

12. Do you have any motion or appeal now pending in any court as to the judgment now under attack? Yes ( ) No ( )

If "yes," name of court _____ Case number _____

Wherefore, applicant prays that the United States Court of Appeals for the Second Circuit grant an Order Authorizing the District Court to Consider Applicant's Second or Successive Motion to Vacate under 28 U.S.C. § 2255.

_____
Applicant's Signature

I declare under Penalty of Perjury that my answers to all the questions in this Application are true and correct.

Executed on _____

       [date]

_____
Applicant's Signature

PROOF OF SERVICE

Applicant must send a copy of this application and all attachments to the United States Attorney's office in the district in which you were convicted.

I certify that on _____[date], I mailed a copy of this Application * and all attachments to _____

at the following address:

_____

_____

_____
Applicant's Signature

* Pursuant to Fed.R.App.P.25(a), "Papers filed by an inmate confined in an institution are timely filed if deposited in the institution's internal mail system on or before the last day of filing. Timely filing of papers by an inmate confined in an institution may be shown by a notarized statement or declaration (in compliance with 28 U.S.C. § 1746) setting forth the date of deposit and stating that first-class postage has been prepaid."

APPLICATION FOR LEAVE TO FILE A SECOND OR SUCCESSIVE HABEAS CORPUS PETITION 28 U.S.C. § 2244(b) BY A PRISONER IN STATE CUSTODY

UNITED STATES COURT OF APPEALS
FOR THE SECOND CIRCUIT

Name

Place of Confinement   Prisoner Number

INSTRUCTIONS—READ CAREFULLY

(1) This application must be legibly handwritten or typewritten and signed by the applicant under penalty of perjury. Any false statement of a material fact may serve as the basis for prosecution and conviction for perjury.

(2) All questions must be answered concisely in the proper space on the form.

(3) The Judicial Conference of the United States has adopted the 8½ x 11 inch paper size for use throughout the federal judiciary and directed the elimination of the use of legal size paper. All pleadings must be on 8½ x 11 inch paper, otherwise we cannot accept them.

(4) All applicants seeking leave to file a second or successive petition are required to use this form, except in capital cases. In capital cases only, the use of this form is optional.

(5) Additional pages are not permitted except with respect to additional grounds for relief and facts which you rely upon to support those grounds. Do not submit separate petitions, motions, briefs, arguments, etc., except in capital cases.

(6) In accordance with the "Anti-Terrorism and Effective Death Penalty Act of 1996," as codified at 28 U.S.C. § 2244(b), effective April 24, 1996, before leave to file a second or successive petition can be granted by the United States Court of Appeals, *it is the applicant's burden* to make a prima facie showing that he satisfies either of the two conditions stated below and in 28 U.S.C. § 2244(b).

(b)(1) a claim presented in a second or successive habeas corpus application under [28 U.S.C.] section 2254 that was presented in a prior application shall be dismissed.

(b)(2) a claim presented in a second or successive habeas corpus application under [28 U.S.C.] section 2254 that was not presented in a prior application shall be dismissed unless—

(A) the applicant shows that the claim relies on a new rule of constitutional law, made retroactive to cases on collateral review by the Supreme Court, that was previously unavailable; or

(B)(i) the factual predicate for the claim could not have been discovered previously through the exercise of due diligence; and

(B)(ii) the facts underlying the claim, if proven and viewed in light of the evidence as a whole, would be sufficient to establish by clear and convincing evidence that, but for constitutional error, no reasonable factfinder would have found the applicant guilty of the underlying offense.

(7) When this application is fully completed, the original and four copies must be mailed to:

Clerk of Court
United States Court of Appeals for the Second Circuit
United States Courthouse
40 Foley Square
New York, New York 10007

APPLICATION

1. (a) Name and location of court which entered the judgment of conviction under attack _____

    (b) Case number _____

2. Date of judgment of conviction _____

3. Length of sentence _____ Sentencing Judge _____

4. Nature of offense or offenses for which you were convicted: _____
_____
_____
_____

5. Have you ever filed a post-conviction petition, application, or motion for collateral relief in any federal court related to this conviction and sentence? Yes ( ) No ( ) If "Yes", how many times? _____ (if more than one, complete 6 and 7 below as necessary)

    (a) Name of court _____

    (b) Case number _____

    (c) Nature of proceeding _____
_____
_____

    (d) Grounds raised (list all grounds; use extra pages if necessary) _____
_____
_____
_____
_____
_____

    (e) Did you receive an evidentiary hearing on your petition, application, or motion? Yes ( ) No ( )

    (f) Result _____
_____

    (g) Date of result _____

6. As to any second federal petition, application, or motion, give the same information:

    (a) Name of court _____

    (b) Case number _____

    (c) Nature of proceeding _____
_____

    (d) Grounds raised (list all grounds; use extra pages if necessary) _____
_____
_____
_____
_____
_____
_____

    (e) Did you receive an evidentiary hearing on your petition, application, or motion? Yes ( ) No ( )

(f) Result _____

(g) Date of result _____

7. As to any third federal petition, application, or motion, give the same information:
   (a) Name of court _____
   (b) Case number _____
   (c) Nature of proceeding _____
   _____

   (d) Grounds raised (list <u>all</u> grounds; use extra pages if necessary) _____
   _____
   _____
   _____

   (e) Did you receive an evidentiary hearing on your petition, application, or motion?
   Yes ( ) No ( )
   (f) Result _____
   _____

   (g) Date of result _____

8. Did you appeal the result of any action taken on your federal petition, application, or motion? (Use extra pages to reflect additional petitions if necessary)
   (1) First petition, etc.   No ( ) Yes ( ) Appeal No. _____
   (2) Second petition, etc.   No ( ) Yes ( ) Appeal No. _____
   (3) Third petition, etc.   No ( ) Yes ( ) Appeal No. _____

9. If you did <u>not</u> appeal from the adverse action on any petition, application, or motion, explain briefly why you did not: _____
   _____
   _____
   _____

10. State <u>concisely</u> every ground on which you <u>now</u> claim that you are being held unlawfully. Summarize <u>briefly</u> the <u>facts</u> supporting each ground.
    A. Ground one: _____

       Supporting FACTS (tell your story briefly without citing cases or law):
       _____
       _____
       _____
       _____
       _____

       Was this claim raised in a prior federal petition, application, or motion?
       Yes ( ) No ( )

       Does this claim rely on a "new rule of law?" Yes ( ) No ( )
       If "yes," state the new rule of law (give case name and citation): _____
       _____
       _____

       Does this claim rely on "newly discovered evidence?" Yes ( ) No ( )
       If "yes," briefly state the newly discovered evidence, and why it was not previously available to you _____
       _____
       _____

_____

_____

_____

_____

B. Ground two: _____

Supporting FACTS (tell your story briefly without citing cases or law):

_____

_____

_____

_____

_____

Was this claim raised in a prior federal petition, application, or motion?
Yes ( ) No ( )

Does this claim rely on a "new rule of law?" Yes ( ) No ( )
If "yes," state the new rule of law (give case name and citation): _____

_____

_____

Does this claim rely on "newly discovered evidence?" Yes ( ) No ( )
If "yes," briefly state the newly discovered evidence, and why it was not
previously available to you _____

_____

_____

_____

_____

[Additional grounds may be asserted on extra pages if necessary]

11. Do you have any motion or appeal now pending in any court as to the judgment
now under attack? Yes ( ) No ( )
If yes, name of court _____ Case number _____

Wherefore, applicant prays that the United States Court of Appeals for the
Second Circuit grant an Order Authorizing the District Court to Consider Applicant's Second or Successive Petition for a Writ of Habeas Corpus under 28 U.S.C.
§ 2254.

_____
Applicant's Signature

I declare under Penalty of Perjury that my answers to all the questions in this
Application are true and correct.

Executed on _____
[date]

_____
Applicant's Signature

PROOF OF SERVICE

Applicant must send a copy of this application and all attachments to the attorney general of the state in which applicant was convicted.

I certify that on _____[date], I mailed a copy of this Application * and all attachments to _____
at the following address:

_____

_____

_____
Applicant's Signature

* Pursuant to Fed.R.App.P. 25(a), "Papers filed by an inmate confined in an institution are timely filed if deposited in the institution's internal mail system on or before the last day of filing. Timely filing of papers by an inmate confined in an institution may be shown by a notarized statement or declaration (in compliance with 28 U.S.C. § 1746) setting forth the date of deposit and stating that first-class postage has been prepaid."

CERTIFICATE OF DEATH PENALTY CASE

UNITED STATES COURT OF APPEALS for the SECOND CIRCUIT
CERTIFICATE OF DEATH PENALTY CASE

U.S.D.C. DOCKET NUMBER | DISTRICT COURT | LOCATION (CITY)

DATE PETITION FILED

[CASE CAPTION],

Petitioner,

Fee Status

-v.-

Paid _____ IFP _____

Respondent.

IFP Pending _____

COUNSEL FOR PETITIONER
(Name, Address & Telephone Number)

COUNSEL FOR RESPONDENT
(Name, Address & Telephone Number)

PETITIONER?S NAME, PRISONER I.D. #, INSTITUTION OF INCARCERATION, ADDRESS & TELEPHONE NUMBER

THIS CASE ARISES FROM: State Court Judgment _____.   Federal Court Judgment _____.

Complete each of the following statements applicable to this case:

1. EXECUTION HAS BEEN SCHEDULED FOR _____.
                                              (Date)

2. A verdict recommending a sentence of death was rendered on _____.
                                                                    (Date)

EXPLANATION OF EMERGENCY NATURE OF PROCEEDINGS (attach pages, as necessary).

HAS PETITIONER PREVIOUSLY FILED CASES IN FEDERAL COURT?   _____ YES   _____ NO

(If yes, give the Court, caption, docket number, filing date, disposition, and disposition date).

DOES PETITIONER HAVE CASES PENDING IN OTHER COURTS?   _____ YES   _____ NO

(If yes, give the Court, caption, docket number, filing date, and status.)

I HEREBY CERTIFY UNDER PENALTY OF PERJURY THAT THE FOREGOING IS TRUE AND CORRECT.

Signature

Type or Print Name

NOTE: THE COURT OF APPEALS PERIODICALLY WILL REQUEST CASE STATUS REPORTS. PARTIES ARE UNDER A CONTINUING AFFIRMATIVE OBLIGATION TO IMMEDIATELY NOTIFY THE UNITED STATES COURT OF APPEALS FOR THE SECOND CIRCUIT OF ANY CHANGES OR ADDITIONS TO THE INFORMATION CONTAINED ON THIS FORM.

[Effective December 1, 2002.]

ELECTRONIC NOTIFICATION AGREEMENT

United States Court of Appeals for the Second Circuit
Thurgood Marshall United States Courthouse
40 Foley Square
New York, NY 10007

To Those Who Practice in the Second Circuit:

Beginning December 1, 2002, you may elect to receive electronic notification of all summary orders and opinions issued by the court in any case in which you are the attorney of record or a pro se litigant. If you wish to be served electronically, please complete the form below and return it to the Clerk's Office at your earliest convenience. **Please complete a separate form for each case in which you elect to receive electronic notification.**

—————

ELECTRONIC NOTIFICATION AGREEMENT

I hereby elect and agree to receive electronic notification of all summary orders and opinions produced by or filed in the Office of the Clerk in the appeal listed below. I agree that electronic notice will be the only notice I receive from the Office of the Clerk and, in the event the automated system that produces these documents is not available, the Clerk may deposit copies of these documents in the United States Mail for first class delivery.

Short Caption: _____

Docket Number: _____

_____   _____
Attorney Name (print)   Attorney Signature

Firm Name and _____
Address: _____
                 _____
                 _____

Voice Number: _____

Fax Number: _____

E-mail Address: _____

I prefer to receive notice by: ___ Fax   ___ E-mail (pdf (Adobe) format)

Special Instructions: _____
(if any)   _____

NOTE: Documents longer than fifteen (15) pages will not be faxed.

ANTI–VIRUS CERTIFICATION FORM

See Second Circuit Interim Local Rule 25(a)(6)

CASE NAME: _____

DOCKET NUMBER: _____

I, (please print your name) _____, certify that I have scanned for viruses the PDF version of the attached document that was submitted in this case as an e-mail attachment to:

☐ <agencycases@ca2.uscourts.gov>.
☐ <criminalcases@ca2.uscourts.gov>.
☐ <civilcases@ca2.uscourts.gov>.
☐ <newcases@ca2.uscourts.gov>.
☐ <prosecases@ca2.uscourts.gov>.

and that no viruses were detected.

Please print the **name** and the **version** of the anti-virus detector that you used

_____

_____

If you know, please print the version of revision and/or the anti-virus signature files _____

_____

(Your Signature) _____

Date: _____

Effective December 1, 2005.

NON–COMPLIANCE WITH DIGITAL DOCUMENT REQUIREMENT
(TO BE COMPLETED ONLY IN COUNSELED CASES)

See Second Circuit Interim Local Rule 32(a)(2)

CASE NAME: _____

DOCKET NUMBER: _____

I, (please print your name) _____, certify that I did not submit a digital copy of the following document(s) in this case:

_____
_____
_____
_____

because (explain why submission of a digital document constituted undue hardship

_____
_____
_____
_____
_____
_____

(Your signature) _____

Date: _____

Phone number: _____

E–mail: _____

Effective December 1, 2005.

LOCAL RULE 34(a)(2) JOINT STATEMENT

UNITED STATES COURT OF APPEALS
FOR THE SECOND CIRCUIT
40 Foley Square, New York, NY 10007

****

Case Name:

Docket Number:

****

Pursuant to Local Rule 34(a)(2), counsel for all parties in the above case have conferred, and have determined that:

☐ All parties seek oral argument.

☐ Only the following parties seek oral argument:

☐ All parties agree to submit the case for decision on the briefs.

Filed by:

Print Name: _____

Counsel for: _____

Signature: _____

Date: _____

APPENDIX

PART A.   AMENDED PLAN TO IMPLEMENT
THE CRIMINAL JUSTICE ACT OF 1964

I.   AUTHORITY

The United States Court of Appeals for the Second Circuit, in accordance with the Criminal Justice Act of 1964, 18 U.S.C. § 3006A, 21 U.S.C. § 848(q), the guidelines for the Administration of the Criminal Justice Act, Vol. VII, Guide to Judiciary Policies and Procedures, and the Federal Rules of Appellate Procedure, hereby adopts this Plan for furnishing representation in the Court of Appeals for eligible persons financially unable to obtain adequate representation in accordance with the Act.

II.   STATEMENT OF POLICY

The Plan shall be administered so that those accused of criminal conduct and who are financially unable to pay for legal representation will be provided with legal representation before this Court.

The Judicial Council, in promulgating the amended Plan set forth below, recognizes that while the Criminal Justice Act provides for limited compensation, attorneys chosen pursuant to the Plan to represent indigents are rendering a public and social service of the greatest importance. The Bar has traditionally represented with high dedication persons unable to pay any compensation for such representation. Services performed for eligible persons qualifying under the Plan will continue to be rendered by members of the Bar, essentially in their capacity as officers of the Courts and in keeping with the high traditions of the legal profession and its vital role in society. We also recognize that despite the nominal compensation provided by the Act, such services will be performed with devotion and vigor so that the lofty ideal—equality before the law for all persons—will be achieved. With this recognition of the importance of representation for indigents, we are confident that all segments of the Bar will accept as part of their professional obligations the need to render the most competent services in each and every phase of criminal and habeas corpus proceedings and that the organized Bar will be encouraged into increased activity with respect to the administration of criminal justice.

III.   DEFINITIONS

A.   **CJA**—the Criminal Justice Act, 18 USC § 3006A.

B.   **CJA client**—a person for whom counsel has been appointed under the CJA.

C.   **CJA attorney**—an attorney who is appointed to represent an eligible person under the CJA.

D.   **CJA Panel member**—an attorney appointed to the CJA Panel of the Second Circuit Court of Appeals.

E.   **CJA applicant**—a person applying for representation under the CJA.

F.   **The or This Court**—the United States Court of Appeals for the Second Circuit.

G.   **The CJA Committee**—the Court's CJA and Pro Bono Committee.

IV.   DETERMINATION OF NEED FOR APPOINTED COUNSEL

A.   **Notice to Defendant.** Whenever in forma pauperis status is ordered by the District Court of this Court in either a criminal appeal in which a defendant appears pro se or in a § 2255 habeas appeal in which the petitioner appears pro se, the Clerk of the Court shall forthwith notify the defendant or petitioner that he or she has the right to be represented and that counsel may be appointed for the defendant or petitioner. The foregoing notice shall also be given in all such appeals taken by the United States.

B.   Request for Attorney on Appeal. In cases where a request for the appointment of an attorney under the Act is made for the first time on appeal, the Chief Judge or the Chief Judge's designee, before making the appointment, shall inquire into and make a finding as to whether the CJA applicant is financially able to employ counsel. In making the determination, such forms as may be prepared and furnished by the Administrative Office of the United States Courts shall be utilized for the purpose of eliciting permanent information.

In cases where the CJA applicant is found by the district court to be financially unable to employ counsel, the Court of Appeals may accept this finding and appoint or continue an attorney without further proof. But see Fed. R. App. P. 24(a).

C.   Partial Payment. If a CJA applicant's net financial resources are insufficient to pay fully for retained counsel, counsel may be appointed under the Act, and the CJA applicant may be directed to make partial payment of attorney's fees to the Clerk of Court under the guidelines as established by the Judicial Conference.

D.   Re-examination of Financial Status. The Court may at any time after appointment of counsel, re-examine the financial status of a CJA client. If the Court finds that a CJA client is financially able to obtain counsel or make partial payment for the CJA client's representation, the appointment should be terminated or partial payment required to be made. If a CJA attorney learns any information indicating that a CJA client or someone on the CJA client's behalf can make payment in whole or in part for legal services, it shall be the CJA attorney's duty to report such information promptly to the Court so that appropriate action may be taken.

V.   CJA ATTORNEY ADVISORY GROUP

A.   Authority and Composition. A CJA Attorney Advisory Group will be appointed by the Court to assist the Court and the CJA Committee in reviewing applications for membership on the CJA Panel and to otherwise promote the furnishing of representation pursuant to this Plan. The CJA Attorney Advisory Group shall consist of the Attorney-in-Charge of the Appeals Bureau of Federal Defenders of New York, Inc. and 12 other attorneys selected by the Court for terms not to exceed three years who will collectively represent all of the districts in the Circuit. The members of the CJA Attorney Advisory Group must be admitted to practice in this Court and may not be members of the CJA Panel. Appointments to the Panel shall be made so that the terms of approximately one-third of the Panel members expire at the conclusion of each Term of Court.

B.   Meetings, Terms and Duties. The Attorney Advisory Group shall review applications filed by attorneys seeking to fill vacancies on the CJA Panel. The Advisory Group shall consider the qualifications and experience of the applicants and recommend to the CJA Committee those applicants it deems qualified to fill the vacancies.

C.   Death Penalty Cases. A CJA Death Penalty Attorney Advisory Group will be appointed by the Court to assist the Court and the CJA Committee in reviewing applications for membership on the Death Penalty CJA Panel.

VI.   CJA PANEL

A.   Maintaining the CJA Panel List. The Clerk of Court, under the direction and supervision of the Chief Judge or the Chief Judge's designee, shall maintain the list of the CJA Panel members that will supplement the services of the Federal Public Defender and Community Defender Offices within this Circuit. The list of

CJA Panel members shall include the name of each attorney and the current business address and telephone number of the attorney. Attorneys accepted for service on the CJA Panel must notify the Clerk of Court, in writing, within 48 hours of any changes in business address, business telephone number, e-mail address, or employment.

B. Appointments. Appointments to the CJA Panel shall be made by the Court upon appropriate recommendation from the CJA Committee after consultation with the Attorney Advisory Group.

C. Applications.

1. *Submission Requirements.* All private attorneys seeking to be included on the CJA Panel must submit to the Clerk of Court an application and a resume. Applications for membership shall be submitted on the Court's form for Application for Appointment to the CJA Panel, available in the Clerk's Office. The Attorney Advisory Group will review these materials. Applicants must be members in good standing of the Bar of this Court, must maintain an office within the Circuit, and must have demonstrated experience in and knowledge of Title 18 and the habeas corpus provisions of Title 28 of the United States Code, the Federal Rules of Appellate Procedure, the Federal Rules of Criminal Procedure, the Federal Rules of Evidence, the Local Rules and the United States Sentencing Guidelines.

The Court will set and publicize an annual application period for appointment to the CJA Panel.

2. *Term of Appointment.* CJA Panel members shall serve for a term not to exceed three years but may be removed by the Court prior to the expiration of their term. See Section D, Removal; see also Section VII, Release of Appointed Counsel. Upon expiration of the term of a CJA Panel member, the CJA Panel member must reapply for membership if he or she wishes to continue as a member of the CJA Panel. Application for renewal shall be made on the Court's form for Application for Renewal of Membership on the CJA Panel, available in the Clerk's Office. Panel members will be selected on the basis of demonstrated qualification, skill and dedication. Because of the limited size of the CJA Panel, the Court will not be able to appoint every qualified applicant to the Panel, but the Court will make an effort to rotate membership on the CJA Panel in order to ensure that new applicants are given an opportunity to serve.

D. Removal.

1. *Court's Discretion.* A CJA Panel member may be removed from the CJA Panel whenever the Court, in its discretion, determines that the member has failed to fulfill satisfactorily the obligations of Panel membership, including the duty to afford competent counsel, or has engaged in other conduct that renders inappropriate his or her continued service on the CJA Panel.

2. *Refusal of Assignments.* The Court may remove a CJA Panel member for refusing three times to accept an appointment during the membership term.

3. *Automatic Removal or Suspension.* A CJA Panel member will be suspended automatically if the member is disbarred or suspended by any state or federal bar or arrested for, charged with, or convicted of a crime. A CJA Panel member is obligated to notify the Clerk of Court, in writing, within 24 hours of any such suspension, disbarment, arrest, filing of criminal charges or conviction (See also Local Rule 46(f)–(h)).

Disbarment or suspension by any state or federal bar or conviction of a crime are grounds for automatic removal from the CJA Panel.

4. *Complaints.* All complaints concerning the conduct of a CJA Panel member shall be forwarded to the Clerk of Court. If the CJA Committee determines that a complaint alleges facts that, if true, would warrant consideration of removal of the CJA Panel member, or that other facts exist potentially warranting removal of a Panel member, the Committee may direct the Attorney Advisory Group to review the complaint, or brief, make such inquiry as it deems appropriate, and issue a report of its findings and recommendations to the Court. The Court has the

authority at any time to remove an attorney from the CJA Panel or to take such other action as it deems appropriate.

VII. APPOINTMENT OF COUNSEL

A. General. In all cases on appeal in which the appointment of an attorney by the Court of Appeals under the Act is required, the Court shall appoint a CJA Panel member to represent a CJA client. The appointment of counsel shall be made within a reasonable time after the appeal is docketed.

The selection of counsel shall be the sole and exclusive responsibility of the Court, and no CJA applicant or CJA client will be permitted to select his or her own attorney from the Panel or otherwise; and no attorney or CJA Panel member shall have the right to be selected to represent a CJA applicant or CJA client.

B. Non–Panel Member Appointments. When the Court determines that the appointment of an attorney who is not a member of the CJA Panel is appropriate in the interest of justice, judicial economy, or some other compelling circumstance warranting such appointment, the attorney may be admitted to the CJA Panel pro hac vice and appointed to represent the CJA client.

C. Retained Counsel. Retained counsel, whether or not a member of the Panel, may seek to be appointed under the Act. Such application must be supported by financial documentation as specified in Section IV herein.

D. Multiple CJA Clients. In appeals involving more than one CJA client, separate counsel may be appointed to represent each client. Where circumstances warrant, one attorney may be appointed to represent multiple CJA clients.

E. Substitution of Counsel. The Court may, at any point in the appellate proceedings, substitute one appointed counsel for another. Total compensation to all counsel is subject to the maximum permitted by the Act. Appointed counsel replaced by such substitution shall, absent the Court's approval of interim payment, await the final disposition of the appeal before submitting a claim for compensation. See Section X(B), infra.

VIII. RELEASE OF APPOINTED COUNSEL

A. Appointed CJA Attorneys. Counsel appointed under the Act to represent a CJA client in the district court shall continue such representation on appeal unless or until relieved by order of the Court of Appeals.

B. Relief of Trial Counsel. If CJA counsel who acted in the district court wishes to be relieved from representing a CJA client on appeal, he or she shall file with the Clerk of the Court of Appeals, and serve upon a CJA client and all other counsel in the case, a motion seeking to be relieved and stating the grounds in support of the motion. Counsel seeking to be relieved nevertheless shall continue to represent the CJA client on appeal unless or until relieved by the Court of Appeals (See Local Rule 4(b)). The district court may also relieve counsel appointed under the Act provided the district court substitutes counsel as provided in the Act. Once the notice of appeal is filed however, only the Court of Appeals may assign or relieve counsel on appeal.

C. CJA Client Seeking to Relieve Counsel. A CJA client seeking to have a CJA attorney relieved and/or the appointment of a substitute CJA attorney must file a typed or legibly handwritten motion, including a sworn affidavit (under penalties of perjury), setting forth compelling reasons for the substitution and giving a detailed account of the facts justifying the request. Such motion shall not be granted absent compelling circumstances.

IX. DUTIES OF APPOINTED COUNSEL

A. General. CJA Panel members must be reasonably available, see also § VI(D)(2) supra, to accept assignments. Upon assignment to represent a CJA client, a CJA attorney shall provide representation in accordance with the Canons of Professional Responsibility and the provisions of this Plan.

B. Advice of Rights and Filing of Transcript. In all cases where trial counsel has acted in the district court under the CJA, such trial counsel shall advise the CJA client of the right to appeal to the United States Court of Appeals and of the obligation to file a timely notice of appeal, and shall file such notice of appeal if requested to do so, unless the CJA client states that the notice of appeal should not be filed. Where appropriate, trial counsel shall also file with the district court the CJA Form 24 for the furnishing of the reporter's transcript at the expense of the United States.

C. Writ of Certiorari. In the event of a decision adverse to the CJA client in this Court, the CJA attorney shall promptly transmit to the CJA client a copy of the Court's decision, advise the CJA client in writing of the right to file a petition for writ of certiorari with the United States Supreme Court, inform the CJA client of the CJA attorney's opinion as to the merit and likelihood of success in obtaining such a writ, and if requested to do so, petition the Supreme Court for certiorari. Despite a CJA client's directive to file a writ, if a CJA attorney has reasonable grounds to believe that a petition for certiorari would have no likelihood of success, the CJA attorney may file with this Court a motion to be relieved and serve a copy on the CJA client and other counsel within ten days of the filing of an adverse decision of this Court. If the Court relieves the CJA attorney, he or she shall, within 48 hours after such motion is granted, so advise the CJA client in writing and inform the CJA client concerning the procedures for filing a petition for a writ of certiorari pro se.

If an adverse party petitions for a writ of certiorari to review a judgment of this Court, the CJA attorney shall take all necessary steps to oppose the petition.

D. Furnishing Documents. A CJA attorney must furnish the client with copies of all papers filed in the matter with the Court that relate to the CJA client's appeal, including all opinions and orders of the Court.

E. Oral Argument. It is expected that the CJA attorney shall appear for oral argument. The CJA attorney shall consult with the attorney for the Government and comply with the provisions of Local Rule 34(a). Presentation of oral argument by an associate attorney not appointed under the Act will be allowed only with permission of the Court.

F. No Delegation of Authority. CJA counsel shall not delegate any non-ministerial tasks in connection with representation of a CJA client to any person other than a partner, associate, paralegal, student or regular employee of the law firm or clinical program of which the Panel member is a partner, associate or affiliate without the written consent of the CJA client and the Court.

G. Representation Upon Remand. The CJA attorney must continue to represent a CJA client in the district court upon remand unless relieved. The fact that a CJA attorney limits his or her practice to appellate work, or that proceedings in the district court on remand will be distant from the CJA attorney's office, will ordinarily be adequate grounds justifying the relief of the CJA attorney upon remand.

H. Anders. If a CJA attorney seeks to be relieved on the grounds that there is no nonfrivolous issue to be raised on the appeal, the CJA attorney must follow the procedures of *Anders v California*, 386 U.S. 738 (1967).

I. No Other Reimbursement. No CJA attorney shall accept a payment from or on behalf of the CJA client in this Court without prior authorization by a United States Circuit Judge on the form provided for such purpose. All such authorized payments shall be received subject to the terms contained in such order and pursuant to the provisions of subsection (f) of the Act.

X. PAYMENT OF CLAIMS FOR COMPENSATION AND EXPENSES

A. What to Submit. No CJA attorney shall be compensated for the representation of a CJA client in this Court except upon the submission of the attorney's voucher in accordance with the rules, regulations and forms promulgated by the Administrative Office of the United States Courts. Unless another means for compensation was specifically approved, such voucher must be accompanied by a written statement specifying the time expended, services rendered, and exact expenses for which reimbursement is sought while the case was pending in this Court.

B. Time to Submit. Unless a judge of the court so orders, a claim for attorney's fees, expenses, and services must be submitted no later than 45 days after a mandate has issued. If the appeal is from an interlocutory order or results in remand to the district court, the claim shall be timely if submitted within 45 days of the termination of the case in the district court or in the Court of Appeals. In the event of termination of the representation prior to the issuance of the mandate or the termination of the case, a motion for interim payment shall be timely if submitted within 45 days of the termination of the representation. See Section VII(E), supra.

C. Maximum Hourly Rates. The maximum hourly rates currently shall be $92.00 for in-court work and out-of-court work.

D. Maximum Compensation. For representation of a party on a direct appeal from a judgment of conviction in a felony, misdemeanor or habeas corpus case, **the total compensation allowed, excluding approved expenses, shall not exceed $5,200, except on appeals taken from the Eastern District and Southern District of New York for which the maximum compensation shall not exceed $7,000** except as described in Section E below. Different limits apply to death penalty federal habeas corpus petitions and federal capital prosecutions.

E. Excess Payments. Payments for representation on appeal in excess of the above limitations may be made for extended or complex representation whenever a judge of the Court certifies that the amount of such excess payment is necessary to provide fair compensation and such excess payment is also approved by the Chief Judge of the Second Circuit or the Chief Judge's designee.

F. Interim Payment. A judge of this Court may authorize interim payment where the judge determines it is appropriate upon the filing of a motion by a CJA attorney. The Chief Judge or the designee of the Chief Judge may arrange for interim payments.

G. Payment. The Clerk of Court shall forthwith forward all approved statements to the Administrative Office of the United States Courts for payment.

XI. CJA COMPENSATION GUIDELINES

A. Writ of Certiorari. Where time and expense for preparation of a Petition for a Writ of Certiorari to the United States Supreme Court has been claimed, a copy of the Petition must accompany the voucher. Vouchers for the CJA attorney's time and expenses involved in the preparation of a Petition are subject to separate compensation limits in the same amounts as listed in Section X(D) supra.

B. Compensation of Associate Attorneys. Compensation may be provided under the CJA for services furnished by a partner, associate or affiliate of the appointed CJA attorney, but the total compensation provided for the representation of the CJA client shall be within the limits described in Section X(D) supra. Such services shall not be compensated unless the participation of such partner, associate or affiliate has been approved in advance by a judge of this court.

C. Excess Voucher. A CJA attorney submitting a voucher in excess of the maximum allowable compensation is required to submit along with a CJA voucher a memorandum detailing how time was spent and why excess payment is warranted.

D. Maximum Compensation. The maximum allowable compensation rates are detailed in Section X of this Plan.

A judge of the court who heard the case shall forward a CJA attorney's application for excess compensation to the Chief Judge or Chief Judge's designee, with a recommendation for approval or denial. Excess compensation will not be paid unless it is approved by the Chief Judge or the Chief Judge's designee.

E.   Reimbursement of Expenses.

1.   *Travel and Transportation.* Reimbursement for travel and transportation expenses shall be consistent with section 2.26 of chapter II, volume VII of the Guide to Judiciary Policies and Procedures. See also chapter VI, volume I, part C of the Guide to Judiciary Policies and Procedures (employee travel regulations). Reimbursement shall be limited to the most economical means of travel and transportation reasonably available. Reimbursement may be claimed only for expenses actually incurred. In all cases, a copy of the ticket used or the bill or receipt must be attached to the voucher for compensation. Travel time to and from court (or the place where the service is rendered) may not be claimed if the round trip is less than one hour.

a.   Commercial Carrier. Reimbursement for transportation by commercial carrier will be limited to economy class accommodations unless unavailable in an emergency. If compensation is claimed at a rate exceeding the economy rates, a detailed explanation in writing must be provided.

b.   Automobile Transportation. If travel is by automobile, the total mileage shall not exceed the fare authorized for travel by economy air travel, except in an emergency, or for other unusual circumstances. Travel reimbursement for a privately owned automobile shall not exceed the current government authorized rate for official travel per mile on a straight mileage basis, plus parking fees, ferry, bridge, road, tolls and tunnel fares.

c.   Meals and Lodging. CJA attorneys will be reimbursed for reasonable actual expenses incurred for meals and lodging within allowable limits. CJA attorneys will not be given a fixed per diem sum. Counsel should be guided by prevailing limitations for travel and subsistence expenses of federal employees. The Clerk of Court can advise attorneys of these limitations. A copy of the hotel or motel bill must be attached to the voucher. Attorneys traveling to attend oral argument will be reimbursed for no more than one and one half days of lodging and meals, absent an order of the Court in compelling circumstances.

d.   Photocopying. Actual costs for reasonable printing services for appendices will be paid if a copy of the bill is submitted. For in-house printing or copying, a maximum of $0.20 per page will be paid. The maximum per page limit is subject to periodic change by directive of the Judicial Conference of the United States. Actual costs for printing of briefs and brief covers will be paid for reasonable printing services if a copy of the bill is submitted. The costs of other forms of reproduction will not be reimbursable including typeset printing.

e.   Courier Service. For delivery of items that could be mailed, expenses will be reimbursed only if a satisfactory explanation is given why normal mail service was not utilized. In non-emergency cases, routine documents such as briefs and motions should be prepared early enough to permit use of the regular mail.

f.   Miscellaneous. CJA Panel members will be permitted to incur only the most reasonable rates for postage, telephone calls, and brief supplies. Supporting documentation is required for single item expenses of $50 or more.

XII.   FORMS

The forms prepared and furnished by the Administrative Office shall be used, where applicable, in all proceedings under this Plan.

XIII. RULES AND REPORTS

The Court shall submit a report on the appointment of counsel under the Act to the Administrative Office of the United States Courts in such form and at such times as the Judicial Conference may specify. This Plan shall be subject to such rules and regulations of the Judicial Conference of the United States governing the operation of such plans under the Act as may be issued from time to time.

XIV. OPERATION OF THE PLAN

This Plan incorporates the Guidelines for the Administration of the Criminal Justice Act of 1964 (18 U.S.C. § 3006A) by reference.

XV. NO RIGHTS CREATED

This Plan is intended only as a description of the procedures this Court will follow; it does not create any rights as against any individual or institution.

XVI. AMENDMENTS

Amendments to this Plan may be made from time to time by the Court, subject to the approval of the Judicial Council of the Second Circuit. As amended December 12, 2007.

Effective January 29, 2002. Amended effective January 1, 2006; January 29, 2007; December 12, 2007.

PART B.   REVISED SECOND CIRCUIT PLAN TO EXPEDITE THE PROCESSING OF CRIMINAL APPEALS

The United States Court of Appeals for the Second Circuit has adopted the following revision of its plan to expedite the processing of criminal appeals, said revision to supersede the plan promulgated December 7, 1971 and to have the force and effect of a local rule adopted pursuant to Rule 47 of the Federal Rules of Appellate Procedure.

1. At the time of the sentencing hearing of any defendant found guilty after trial, the courtroom deputy shall provide attorneys with appropriate forms and instruction sheets regarding the rules of the Court of Appeals for processing appeals. The district judge shall:

(a) advise the defendant of the defendant's right to appeal and other rights in that connection as set forth in and required by Rule 32(a)(2), F.R.Crim.P.;

(b) complete and transmit to the Clerk of the District Court a form (in the form attached hereto as Form A, with such changes as the Chief Judge of this Court may from time to time direct) listing information needed for the prompt disposition of an appeal;

(c) make a finding to be shown in the appropriate place on Form A:

   1. whether defendant is eligible for appointment of counsel on appeal pursuant to the Criminal Justice Act, and

   2. whether there is any reason trial counsel should not be continued on appeal;

(d) make a finding, to be shown in the appropriate place on Form A, whether the minutes of the trial and of any proceedings preliminary thereto or such portions thereof as may be needed for the proper disposition of the appeal should be transcribed at the expense of the United States pursuant to the Criminal Justice Act, and if so, enter an appropriate order to that effect. In any case where a full transcript is not already available, the district judge shall encourage counsel to agree to dispense with the transcription of material not necessary for proper disposition of an appeal.

2. The Clerk of the District Court shall transmit forthwith the notice of appeal, together with the required forms, to the Clerk of the Court of Appeals, who shall promptly enter the appeal upon the appropriate records of this Court.

The Clerk of the District Court shall appoint an appeals clerk to coordinate appeals matters in the district court and serve as the contact between the Clerks of the District Courts and the Court of Appeals.

3. At the time of filing the notice of appeal, counsel for appellant shall complete and transmit to the Clerk of the District Court a form (in the form attached hereto as Form B, with such changes as the Chief Judge of the Court may from time to time direct) certifying that, if trial minutes are necessary, they have been ordered and that satisfactory arrangements for payment of the cost of the transcript have been made with the court reporter.

If the district judge directs the Clerk to file the notice of appeal, the district judge shall order counsel for the appellant to file Form B with the Clerk of the Court of Appeals within 7 days after sentencing.

If retained counsel is to be substituted on appeal by other retained counsel, Form B shall be transmitted within seven days after filing the notice of appeal, together with the substitution of counsel notice.

4. Whenever transcription of the minutes (or a portion thereof) has been ordered in a criminal case, the court reporter shall immediately notify the Clerk of the Court of Appeals on the appropriate form of the estimated length of the transcript and the estimated completion date. The number of days shall not exceed thirty (30) days from the order date except under unusual circumstances which first must be approved by the Court of Appeals upon a showing of need.

5. As soon as practicable after the filing of a notice of appeal in a criminal case, a judge of this Court or a judge's delegate shall issue an order (scheduling order) setting forth as hereafter described, the dates on or before which the record on appeal shall be filed, the brief and appendix of the appellant shall be filed, and the brief of the United States shall be filed, designating the week during which argument of the appeal shall be heard, and making such other provisions as justice may require.

(a) *Docketing of the Record.* The scheduling order shall provide that the record on appeal be docketed within twenty days after filing of the notice of appeal. If, at that time, the transcript is still incomplete a partial record shall be docketed which shall be supplemented when the transcript is complete. This Court will not ordinarily grant motions to extend time to docket the record.

(b) *Appellant's Brief and Appendix.* The scheduling order shall provide that the brief and appendix of appellant be filed not later than thirty days after the date on which the transcription of the trial minutes is scheduled to be completed unless for good cause shown it appears a longer or shorter period should be set. This provision does not affect appellant's right to file a deferred appendix as provided by FRAP 30(c) and § 30(*l*)* of the Rules of this Court.

(c) *Appellee's Brief.* The scheduling order shall provide that the appellee's brief shall be filed not later than 30 days after the date on which appellant's brief and appendix is to be filed, unless for good cause shown it appears a longer or shorter period should be set.

6. At the time a scheduling order is entered, or at any other time the judge or the judge's delegate who signed such order or, if the judge or the judge's delegate is unavailable, any other judge of this Court may enter any other orders desirable to assure the prompt disposition of the appeal. Such orders may include, but are not limited to, orders appointing counsel on appeal pursuant to the Criminal Justice Act, setting deadlines for filing the transcription of the trial minutes, requiring attorneys for co-appellants to share a copy of the transcript, and instructing the Clerk to permit counsel to remove and examine the official copy of the record for such periods as are necessary.

7. Under Rule 4(b)(a) of this Court, when a defendant convicted following trial wishes to appeal, trial counsel, whether retained or appointed by the district court or during the course of the appeal, is responsible for representing the defendant until relieved by the Court of Appeals. Furthermore, it is the policy of this Circuit that, in the absence of good cause shown, counsel appointed under the Criminal Justice Act for the trial shall be continued on appeal.

8. When new counsel is retained on appeal, whether trial counsel was retained or appointed in the district court or during the course of the appeal, new counsel must promptly file a substitution of counsel form endorsed by the defendant and the previous counsel of record. The substitution form must include a statement affirming that the trial minutes have been ordered.

In all cases when trial counsel, whether retained or appointed, wishes to be relieved as counsel on appeal, trial counsel must move pursuant to Rule 4(b) to be relieved. A motion to be relieved as counsel must be made within seven days after filing of a notice of appeal unless exceptional circumstances excusing a delay are shown.

In the event that it is impossible or impractical to obtain the signature of previous counsel of record, counsel on appeal may file the substitution of counsel form signed by the defendant, accompanied by coun-

sel's signed affidavit detailing efforts made to obtain the previous counsel's signature.

9. Motions for leave to file oversized briefs, to postpone the date on which briefs are required to be filed, or to alter the date on which argument is to be heard, shall be accompanied by an affidavit or other statement and shall be made not less than seven days before the brief is due, or the argument is scheduled, unless exceptional circumstances exist. Motions not conforming to this requirement will be denied. Motions to postpone the dates set for filing briefs or for argument are not viewed with favor and will be granted only under extraordinary circumstances.

10. In the event the district court grants an extension for filing a notice of appeal pursuant to FRAP 4(a)(b) the Clerk of the District Court shall promptly transmit a copy of the order to the Clerk of the Court of Appeals.

11. The Clerk shall, without further notice, dismiss an appeal for failure by the appellant to docket the record or file an appellant's brief within the time limited by a scheduling order or, if the time has been extended as provided by paragraph 9, within the time so extended; or in the event of default in any action required by these rules or any order resulting from these rules.

12. In cases where the Chief Judge may deem this desirable the Chief Judge or a person designated by the Chief Judge may direct attorneys to attend a pre-argument conference to be held as soon as practicable before the Chief Judge or a person designated by the Chief Judge, to establish a schedule for the filing of briefs and to consider such other matters as may aid in the prompt disposition of the appeal. At the conclusion of the conference an order shall issue which shall control the subsequent course of the proceeding.

13. When an appeal from a criminal conviction is affirmed in open court, the mandate shall issue forthwith unless the Court shall otherwise direct. In all other criminal appeals, the panel shall consider the desirability of providing for issuance of the mandate at a date earlier than provided by FRAP 41(a).

14. The foregoing Revised Plan to Expedite the Processing of Criminal Appeals shall be applicable to all criminal appeals in which notice of appeal is filed on or after November 18, 1974.

[December 1, 1994.]

* Publisher's Note: So in original. See Local Rule 30(a).

PART C.   CIVIL APPEALS MANAGEMENT PLAN

1.   Notice of Appeal, Transmission of Copy and Entry by Court of Appeals. Upon the filing of a notice of appeal in a civil case, the Clerk of the District Court shall forthwith transmit a copy of the notice of appeal to the Clerk of the Court of Appeals, who shall promptly enter the appeal upon the appropriate records of the Court of Appeals.

2.   Appointment of Counsel for Indigent, Advice by District Court Judge. If the appeal is in an action in which the appellant may be entitled to the discretionary appointment of counsel under 18 U.S.C. § 3006A(g) but has not had such counsel in the district court and there has been an indication that the appellant may be indigent, the judge who heard the case shall advise the Clerk of the Court of Appeals whether in the judge's judgment such appointment would be in the interests of justice.

3.   Docketing the Appeal; Filing Pre–Argument Statement; Ordering Transcript. Within ten calendar days (see FRAP 26(a)) after filing the notice of appeal, the appellant shall cause the appeal to be docketed by taking the following actions:

(a) filing with the Clerk of the Court of Appeals an original and one copy of, and serving on other parties a pre-argument statement (Form C or Form C–A, in the case of a petition for review or enforcement of an agency decision, with such changes as the Chief Judge of this Court may from time to time direct) detailing information needed for the prompt disposition of an appeal;

(b) ordering from the court reporter on a form to be provided by the Clerk of the Court of Appeals (Form D), a transcript of the proceedings pursuant to FRAP 10(b). If desirable the transcript production schedule and the portions of the proceedings to be transcribed shall be subject to determination at the preargument conference, if one should be held, unless the appellant directs the court reporter to begin transcribing the proceedings immediately;

(c) certifying that satisfactory arrangements have been or will be made with the court reporter for payment of the cost of the transcript;

(d) paying the docket fee fixed by the Judicial Conference of the United States pursuant to 28 U.S.C. § 1913 (except when the appellant is authorized to prosecute the appeal without payment of fees).

(e) at the time of filing Form C or Form C–A in the case of a petition for review or enforcement of an agency decision and Form D, the appellant shall also file:

(i) a copy of each of the judgments, orders and/or decisions of the U.S. District Court or agency from which review is sought,

(ii) a copy of each written or transcribed oral opinion rendered in the proceeding from which the review is sought addressing the issues raised on appeal,

(iii) in those cases where a decision is initially reviewed in the U.S. District Court, e.g., bankruptcy, social security, etc., a copy of all judgments, decisions, orders and opinions reviewed by the U.S. District Court which address the issues raised on appeal.

4.   Scheduling Order; Contents.

(a) In all civil appeals the staff counsel of the Court of Appeals shall issue a scheduling order as soon as practicable after the pre-argument statement has been filed unless a pre-argument conference has been directed in which event the scheduling order may be deferred until the time of the conference in which case the scheduling order may be entered as part of the pre-argument conference order.

(b) The scheduling order shall set forth the dates on or before which the record on appeal, the brief and appendix of the appellant, and the brief of the appellee shall be filed and also shall designate the week during which argument of the appeal shall be ready to be heard.

5. Pre–Argument Conference; Pre–Argument Conference Order.

(a) In cases where staff counsel may deem this desirable, the staff counsel may direct the attorneys to attend a pre-argument conference to be held as soon as practicable before staff counsel or a judge designated by the Chief Judge to consider the possibility of settlement, the simplification of the issues, and any other matters which the staff counsel determines may aid in the handling or the disposition of the proceeding.

(b) At the conclusion of the conference the staff counsel shall enter a pre-argument conference order which shall control the subsequent course of the proceeding.

6. Non–Compliance Sanctions.

(a) If the appellant has not taken each of the actions set forth in paragraphs 3(a), (b), (c), and (d) of this Plan within the time therein specified, the appeal may be dismissed by the Clerk without further notice.

(b) With respect to docketed appeals in which a scheduling order has been entered, the Clerk shall dismiss the appeal upon default of the appellant regarding any provision of the schedule calling for action on the appellant's part, unless extended by the Court. An appellee who fails to file an appellee's brief within the time limited by a scheduling order or, if the time has been extended as provided by paragraphs 6 or 8, within the time as so extended, will be subjected to such sanctions as the Court may deem appropriate, including those provided in FRAP 31(c) or FRAP 39(a) or Rule 38 of the Local Rules of this Court supplementing FRAP or the imposition of a fine.

(c) In the event of default in any action required by a pre-argument conference order not the subject of the scheduling order, the Clerk shall issue a notice to the appellant that the appeal will be dismissed unless, within ten days thereafter, the appellant shall file an affidavit showing good cause for the default and indicating when the required action will be taken. The staff counsel shall thereupon prepare a recommendation on the basis of which the Chief Judge or any other judge of this Court designated by the Chief Judge shall take appropriate action.

7. Motions. Motions for leave to file oversized briefs, to postpone the date on which briefs are required to be filed, or to alter the date on which argument is to be heard, shall be accompanied by an affidavit or other statement and shall be made not later than two weeks before the brief is due or the argument is scheduled unless exceptional circumstances exist. Motions not conforming to this requirement will be denied.

Motions to alter the date of arguments placed on the calendar are not viewed with favor and will be granted only under extraordinary circumstances.

8. Submission on Briefs; Assignment to Panel. When the parties agree to submit the appeal on briefs, they shall promptly notify the Clerk, who will cause the appeal to be assigned to the first panel available after the time fixed for the filing of all briefs.

9. Other Proceedings.

(a) *Review of Administrative Agency Orders; Applications for Enforcement.* In a review of an order of an administrative agency, board, commission or officer, or an application for enforcement of an order of an agency,

(i) The Staff Counsel of the Court of Appeals shall issue a scheduling order as soon as practicable setting forth the dates on or before which the record or authorized substitute, the petitioner's brief and the appendix and the brief of the respondent shall be filed and also shall designate the week during which argument of the proceeding shall be ready to be heard;

(ii) Paragraph 5 of this Plan, pertaining to Pre–Argument Conferences, and Pre–Argument Conference Orders, and Paragraphs 7(b) and 7(c) of this Plan, pertaining to noncompliance sanctions, shall be applicable to this subparagraph.

(b) *Appeals from the Tax Court.* In a review of a decision of the Tax Court,

(i) Paragraphs 3(a) and 3(d) of this Plan, pertaining to filing pre-argument statements and payment of the docket fee, shall be applicable to this subparagraph. If the appellant has not taken each of the actions set forth in those paragraphs within the time specified in Paragraph 3, the appeal from the tax court may be dismissed by the Clerk of the Court without further notice.

(ii) Paragraph 4 of this Plan, pertaining to scheduling orders, shall also be applicable hereto.

(iii) Paragraph 5 of this Plan, pertaining to Pre–Argument Conferences and Pre–Argument Conference Orders, and Paragraphs 7(b) and 7(c) of this Plan, pertaining to noncompliance sanctions, shall be applicable to this subparagraph.

PART D. GUIDELINES FOR CONDUCT OF
PRE–ARGUMENT CONFERENCE
UNDER THE CIVIL APPEALS MANAGEMENT PLAN

Pre-argument conferences are conducted by Staff Counsel in counseled civil appeals under Federal Rules of Appellate Procedure 33 and Rule of the Civil Appeals Management Plan (C.A.M.P.), Rules of the Second Circuit, Appendix, Part C. All fully counseled appeals except prisoner and habeas corpus cases are included in the CAMP program. Participation in pre-argument conferences is mandatory.

I. Purpose. The purpose is to explore the possibility for settlement of the dispute, to prevent unnecessary motions or delay—by attempting to resolve any procedural problems in the appeal, and to identify, clarify and simplify the issues submitted for review.

In an effort to enable the parties to resolve issues, Staff Counsel, who are full-time employees of the Second Circuit with extensive experience in appellate mediation, are ordinarily expected to give them the benefit of their views of the merits or other aspects of the appeal. The Staff Counsel typically conducts the conference in a series of joint and sometimes separate caucuses to discuss settlement.

II. Authority and Attendance. The success of the conference depends on the attorneys treating it as a serious and effective procedure which can not only save time and expense for the parties, but also provide an outcome better suited to their needs. All sides should be thoroughly prepared to discuss **in depth** the legal, factual and procedural issues. Prior to the conference, attorneys should discuss the matter with their clients and ascertain their goals in resolving the litigation. They should be prepared to negotiate in good faith and express their views on the merits of their case as well as their client's interests. Attorneys who attend the mediation should be those who have the broadest authority from and the greatest influence with the client.   Attorneys should obtain advance authority from their clients to make such commitments as may reasonably be anticipated.

III. Client Participation. If feasible, counsel should have their clients available by telephone at the time of the mediation. The Court strongly encourages the parties to participate at every stage of the mediation process. Ordinarily, attorneys are expected to attend the conference without their clients. However, with the permission of Staff Counsel, or when appropriate—as required by Staff Counsel, clients may attend with their attorneys. Staff Counsel does NOT talk with clients outside of the presence of their attorneys.

IV.   Conference Location. Conferences are usually in person at the offices of Staff Counsel located in the Woolworth Building, 233 Broadway 6th Floor, New York, NY. However, where considerable distances or other significant reasons warrant, Staff Counsel will, in their discretion, arrange to conduct the conference over the telephone or by video if available.

V. Good Faith Participation. The parties are obligated to participate in the mediation process in good faith with a view to resolving differences as to the merits and other issues in the case. This process requires each attorney, regardless of how strong his or her views are, to exercise a degree of objectivity, patience, cooperation and self-control that will permit the attorney to negotiate based upon reason. The conference provides a neutral forum for appraisal of the case and examination of means to expedite the matter. Staff Counsel may offer their own views and are entitled to the attorney's respect and careful consideration of those views. They are, of course, the individual views of the mediator and are not those of the court.No attorney or party is obligated to agree with the mediator or under any compulsion to reach an agreement to which they believe in good conscience they cannot agree to.

Mediation is not productive when counsel are not adequately prepared, present extreme positions, maintain fixed positions, and engage in hard, bottom-line bargaining. Counsel should be realistic in approaching the mediation. Mediation is most productive when counsel are conversant with the law and the facts in an appeal and are fully aware of their client's interests, goals and needs. Moreover, they should strive to understand, but not necessarily agree with, the views of opposing counsel on the law and facts and the goals, interests and needs of their clients.

VI. Mandatory Participation. Although the mediation sessions are relatively informal, they are official proceedings of the Court. Sanctions may be imposed against any party who fails to appear for the mediation or otherwise participate fully.

VII. Confidentiality. All matters discussed at a pre-argument conference, including the views of Staff Counsel as to the merits, are completely confidential and are not communicated to any member of the Court. Nothing said by any participant to the session is to be disclosed to the judges of the court or judges of any other court that might address the appeal's merits. The mediator's notes do not become part of the Court's file nor anything submitted by the attorneys or parties to Staff Counsel pertaining to the merits. Any ex parte communications are also confidential except to the extent disclosure is authorized. The Court strictly enforces this rule. Likewise, parties are also prohibited from advising members of the Court or any unauthorized third parties of discussions or actions taken at the conference (*Calka v. Kucker Kraus & Bruh,* 167 F.3d 144, 145 (2d Cir. 1999). Thus, the Court never knows what transpired at a conference.

VIII. Grievances. Any grievances regarding the handling of any case in the C.A.M.P. program should be addressed to Elizabeth Cronin, Director of Legal Affairs and Senior Staff Attorney, 40 Foley Square, New York, New York 10007.

Revised effective September 27, 1996.

PART E. RULES FOR JUDICIAL–CONDUCT AND JUDICIAL–DISABILITY PROCEEDINGS

PREFACE

These Rules were promulgated by the Judicial Conference of the United States, after public comment, pursuant to 28 U.S.C. §§ 331 and 358, to establish standards and procedures for addressing complaints filed by complainants or identified by chief judges, under the Judicial Conduct and Disability Act, 28 U.S.C. §§ 351–364.

ARTICLE I. GENERAL PROVISIONS

Rule 1. Scope

These Rules govern proceedings under the Judicial Conduct and Disability Act, 28 U.S.C. §§ 351–364 (the Act), to determine whether a covered judge has engaged in conduct prejudicial to the effective and expeditious administration of the business of the courts or is unable to discharge the duties of office because of mental or physical disability.

(Adopted Mar. 11, 2008, eff. Apr. 10, 2008.)

Commentary on Rule 1

In September 2006, the Judicial Conduct and Disability Act Study Committee, appointed in 2004 by Chief Justice Rehnquist and known as the "Breyer Committee," presented a report, known as the "Breyer Committee Report," 239 F.R.D. 116 (Sept. 2006), to Chief Justice Roberts that evaluated implementation of the Judicial Conduct and Disability Act of 1980, 28 U.S.C. §§ 351–364. The Breyer Committee had been formed in response to criticism from the public and the Congress regarding the effectiveness of the Act's implementation. The Executive Committee of the Judicial Conference directed the Judicial Conference Committee on Judicial Conduct and Disability to consider the recommendations made by the Breyer Committee and to report on their implementation to the Conference.

The Breyer Committee found that it could not evaluate implementation of the Act without establishing interpretive standards, Breyer Committee Report, 239 F.R.D. at 132, and that a major problem faced by chief judges in implementing the Act was the lack of authoritative interpretive standards. Id. at 212–15. The Breyer Committee then established standards to guide its evaluation, some of which were new formulations and some of which were taken from the "Illustrative Rules Governing Complaints of Judicial Misconduct and Disability," discussed below. The principal standards used by the Breyer Committee are in Appendix E of its Report. Id. at 238.

Based on the findings of the Breyer Committee, the Judicial Conference Committee on Judicial Conduct and Disability concluded that there was a need for the Judicial Conference to exercise its power under Section 358 of the Act to fashion standards guiding the various officers and bodies who must exercise responsibility under the Act. To that end, the Judicial Conference Committee proposed rules that were based largely on Appendix E of the Breyer Committee Report and the Illustrative Rules.

The Illustrative Rules were originally prepared in 1986 by the Special Committee of the Conference of Chief Judges of the United States Courts of Appeals, and were subsequently revised and amended, most recently in 2000, by the predecessor to the Committee on Judicial Conduct and Disability. The Illustrative Rules were adopted, with minor variations, by circuit judicial councils, to govern complaints under the Judicial Conduct and Disability Act.

After being submitted for public comment pursuant to 28 U.S.C. § 358(c), the present Rules were promulgated by the Judicial Conference on March 11, 2008.

Rule 2. Effect and Construction

(a) **Generally.** These Rules are mandatory; they supersede any conflicting judicial-council rules. Judicial councils may promulgate additional rules to implement the Act as long as those rules do not conflict with these Rules.

(b) **Exception.** A Rule will not apply if, when performing duties authorized by the Act, a chief judge, a special committee, a judicial council, the Judicial Conference Committee on Judicial Conduct and Disability, or the Judicial Conference of the United States expressly finds that exceptional circumstances render application of that Rule in a particular proceeding manifestly unjust or contrary to the purposes of the Act or these Rules.

(Adopted Mar. 11, 2008, eff. Apr. 10, 2008.)

Commentary on Rule 2

Unlike the Illustrative Rules, these Rules provide mandatory and nationally uniform provisions governing the substantive and procedural aspects of misconduct and disability proceedings under the Act. The mandatory nature of these Rules is authorized by 28 U.S.C. § 358(a) and (c). Judicial councils retain the power to promulgate rules consistent with these Rules. For example, a local rule may authorize electronic distribution of materials pursuant to Rule 8(b).

Rule 2(b) recognizes that unforeseen and exceptional circumstances may call for a different approach in particular cases.

Rule 3. Definitions

(a) **Chief Judge.** "Chief judge" means the chief judge of a United States Court of Appeals, of the United States Court of International Trade, or of the United States Court of Federal Claims.

(b) **Circuit Clerk.** "Circuit clerk" means a clerk of a United States court of appeals, the clerk of the

United States Court of International Trade, the clerk of the United States Court of Federal Claims, or the circuit executive of the United States Court of Appeals for the Federal Circuit.

(c) Complaint. A complaint is:

(1) a document that, in accordance with Rule 6, is filed by any person in his or her individual capacity or on behalf of a professional organization; or

(2) information from any source, other than a document described in (c) (1), that gives a chief judge probable cause to believe that a covered judge, as defined in Rule 4, has engaged in misconduct or may have a disability, whether or not the information is framed as or is intended to be an allegation of misconduct or disability.

(d) Court of Appeals, District Court, and District Judge. "Courts of appeals," "district court," and "district judge," where appropriate, include the United States Court of Federal Claims, the United States Court of International Trade, and the judges thereof.

(e) Disability. "Disability" is a temporary or permanent condition rendering a judge unable to discharge the duties of the particular judicial office. Examples of disability include substance abuse, the inability to stay awake during court proceedings, or a severe impairment of cognitive abilities.

(f) Judicial Council and Circuit. "Judicial council" and "circuit,' ' where appropriate, include any courts designated in 28 U.S.C. § 363.

(g) Magistrate Judge. "Magistrate judge," where appropriate, includes a special master appointed by the Court of Federal Claims under 42 U.S.C. § 300aa–12(c).

(h) Misconduct. Cognizable misconduct:

(1) is conduct prejudicial to the effective and expeditious administration of the business of the courts. Misconduct includes, but is not limited to:

(A) using the judge's office to obtain special treatment for friends or relatives;

(B) accepting bribes, gifts, or other personal favors related to the judicial office;

(C) having improper discussions with parties or counsel for one side in a case;

(D) treating litigants or attorneys in a demonstrably egregious and hostile manner;

(E) engaging in partisan political activity or making inappropriately partisan statements;

(F) soliciting funds for organizations; or

(G) violating other specific, mandatory standards of judicial conduct, such as those pertaining to restrictions on outside income and requirements for financial disclosure.

(2) is conduct occurring outside the performance of official duties if the conduct might have a prejudi-

cial effect on the administration of the business of the courts, including a substantial and widespread lowering of public confidence in the courts among reasonable people.

(3) does not include:

(A) an allegation that is directly related to the merits of a decision or procedural ruling. An allegation that calls into question the correctness of a judge's ruling, including a failure to recuse, without more, is merits-related. If the decision or ruling is alleged to be the result of an improper motive, e.g., a bribe, ex parte contact, racial or ethnic bias, or improper conduct in rendering a decision or ruling, such as personally derogatory remarks irrelevant to the issues, the complaint is not cognizable to the extent that it attacks the merits.

(B) an allegation about delay in rendering a decision or ruling, unless the allegation concerns an improper motive in delaying a particular decision or habitual delay in a significant number of unrelated cases.

(i) Subject Judge. "Subject judge" means any judge described in Rule 4 who is the subject of a complaint.

(Adopted Mar. 11, 2008, eff. Apr. 10, 2008.)

Commentary on Rule 3

Rule 3 is derived and adapted from the Breyer Committee Report and the Illustrative Rules.

Unless otherwise specified or the context otherwise indicates, the term "complaint" is used in these Rules to refer both to complaints identified by a chief judge under Rule 5 and to complaints filed by complainants under Rule 6.

Under the Act, a "complaint" may be filed by "any person" or "identified" by a chief judge. See 28 U.S.C. § 351(a) and (b). Under Rule 3(c)(1), complaints may be submitted by a person, in his or her individual capacity, or by a professional organization. Generally, the word "complaint" brings to mind the commencement of an adversary proceeding in which the contending parties are left to present the evidence and legal arguments, and judges play the role of an essentially passive arbiter. The Act, however, establishes an administrative, inquisitorial process. For example, even absent a complaint under Rule 6, chief judges are expected in some circumstances to trigger the process—"identify a complaint," see 28 U.S.C. § 351(b) and Rule 5—and conduct an investigation without becoming a party. See 28 U.S.C. § 352(a); Breyer Committee Report, 239 F.R.D. at 214; Illustrative Rule 2(j). Even when a complaint is filed by someone other than the chief judge, the complainant lacks many rights that a litigant would have, and the chief judge, instead of being limited to the "four corners of the complaint," must, under Rule 11, proceed as though misconduct or disability has been alleged where the complainant reveals information of misconduct or disability but does not claim it as such. See Breyer Committee Report, 239 F.R.D. at 183–84.

An allegation of misconduct or disability filed under Rule 6 is a "complaint," and the Rule so provides in subsection (c)(1). However, both the nature of the process and the use of the term "identify" suggest that the word "complaint" covers more than a document formally triggering the process. The process relies on chief judges considering known information and triggering the process when appropriate. "Identifying" a "complaint," therefore, is best understood as the chief judge's concluding that information known to the judge constitutes probable cause to believe that misconduct occurred or a disability exists, whether or not the information is framed as, or intended to be an accusation. This definition is codified in (c)(2).

Rule 3(e) relates to disability and provides only the most general definition, recognizing that a fact-specific approach is the only one available.

The phrase "prejudicial to the effective and expeditious administration of the business of the courts" is not subject to precise definition, and subsection (h)(1) therefore provides some specific examples. Although the Code of Conduct for United States Judges may be informative, its main precepts are highly general; the Code is in many potential applications aspirational rather than a set of disciplinary rules. Ultimately, the responsibility for determining what constitutes misconduct under the statute is the province of the judicial council of the circuit subject to such review and limitations as are ordained by the statute and by these Rules.

Even where specific, mandatory rules exist—for example, governing the receipt of gifts by judges, outside earned income, and financial disclosure obligations—the distinction between the misconduct statute and the specific, mandatory rules must be borne in mind. For example, an inadvertent, minor violation of any one of these Rules, promptly remedied when called to the attention of the judge, might still be a violation but might not rise to the level of misconduct under the statute. By contrast, a pattern of such violations of the Code might well rise to the level of misconduct.

An allegation can meet the statutory standard even though the judge's alleged conduct did not occur in the course of the performance of official duties. The Code of Conduct for United States Judges expressly covers a wide range of extra-official activities, and some of these activities may constitute misconduct. For example, allegations that a judge solicited funds for a charity or participated in a partisan political event are cognizable under the Act.

On the other hand, judges are entitled to some leeway in extra-official activities. For example, misconduct may not include a judge being repeatedly and publicly discourteous to a spouse (not including physical abuse) even though this might cause some reasonable people to have diminished confidence in the courts. Rule 3(h)(2) states that conduct of this sort is covered, for example, when it might lead to a "substantial and widespread" lowering of such confidence.

Rule 3(h)(3)(A) tracks the Act, 28 U.S.C. § 352(b)(1)(A)(ii), in excluding from the definition of misconduct allegations "[d]irectly related to the merits of a decision or procedural ruling." This exclusion preserves the independence of judges in the exercise of judicial power by ensuring that the complaint procedure is not used to collaterally attack the substance of a judge's ruling. Any allegation that calls into question the correctness of an official action of a judge—without more—is merits-related. The phrase "decision or procedural ruling" is not limited to rulings issued in deciding Article III cases or controversies. Thus, a complaint challenging the correctness of a chief judge's determination to dismiss a prior misconduct complaint would be properly dismissed as merits-related—in other words, as challenging the substance of the judge's administrative determination to dismiss the complaint—even though it does not concern the

judge's rulings in Article III litigation. Similarly, an allegation that a judge had incorrectly declined to approve a Criminal Justice Act voucher is merits-related under this standard.

Conversely, an allegation—however unsupported—that a judge conspired with a prosecutor to make a particular ruling is not merits-related, even though it "relates" to a ruling in a colloquial sense. Such an allegation attacks the propriety of conspiring with the prosecutor and goes beyond a challenge to the correctness—"the merits"—of the ruling itself. An allegation that a judge ruled against the complainant because the complainant is a member of a particular racial or ethnic group, or because the judge dislikes the complainant personally, is also not merits-related. Such an allegation attacks the propriety of arriving at rulings with an illicit or improper motive. Similarly, an allegation that a judge used an inappropriate term to refer to a class of people is not merits-related even if the judge used it on the bench or in an opinion; the correctness of the judge's rulings is not at stake. An allegation that a judge treated litigants or attorneys in a demonstrably egregious and hostile manner while on the bench is also not merits-related.

The existence of an appellate remedy is usually irrelevant to whether an allegation is merits-related. The merits-related ground for dismissal exists to protect judges' independence in making rulings, not to protect or promote the appellate process. A complaint alleging an incorrect ruling is merits-related even though the complainant has no recourse from that ruling. By the same token, an allegation that is otherwise cognizable under the Act should not be dismissed merely because an appellate remedy appears to exist (for example, vacating a ruling that resulted from an improper ex parte communication). However, there may be occasions when appellate and misconduct proceedings overlap, and consideration and disposition of a complaint under these Rules may be properly deferred by a chief judge until the appellate proceedings are concluded in order to avoid, inter alia, inconsistent decisions.

Because of the special need to protect judges' independence in deciding what to say in an opinion or ruling, a somewhat different standard applies to determine the merits-relatedness of a non-frivolous allegation that a judge's language in a ruling reflected an improper motive. If the judge's language was relevant to the case at hand—for example a statement that a claim is legally or factually "frivolous"—then the judge's choice of language is presumptively merits-related and excluded, absent evidence apart from the ruling itself suggesting an improper motive. If, on the other hand, the challenged language does not seem relevant on its face, then an additional inquiry under Rule 11 is necessary.

With regard to Rule 3(h)(3)(B), a complaint of delay in a single case is excluded as merits-related. Such an allegation may be said to challenge the correctness of an official action of the judge—in other words, assigning a low priority to deciding the particular case. But, by the same token, an allegation of a habitual pattern of delay in a significant number of unrelated cases, or an allegation of deliberate delay in a single case arising out of an illicit motive, is not merits-related.

The remaining subsections of Rule 3 provide technical definitions clarifying the application of the Rules to the various kinds of courts covered.

Rule 4. Covered Judges

A complaint under these Rules may concern the actions or capacity only of judges of United States courts of appeals, judges of United States district courts, judges of United States bankruptcy courts, United States magistrate judges, and judges of the courts specified in 28 U.S.C. § 363.

(Adopted Mar. 11, 2008, eff. Apr. 10, 2008.)

Commentary on Rule 4

This Rule tracks the Act. Rule 8(c) and (d) contain provisions as to the handling of complaints against persons not covered by the Act, such as other court personnel, or against both covered judges and noncovered persons.

ARTICLE II. INITIATION OF A COMPLAINT

Rule 5. Identification of a Complaint

(a) Identification. When a chief judge has information constituting reasonable grounds for inquiry into whether a covered judge has engaged in misconduct or has a disability, the chief judge may conduct an inquiry, as he or she deems appropriate, into the accuracy of the information even if no related complaint has been filed. A chief judge who finds probable cause to believe that misconduct has occurred or that a disability exists may seek an informal resolution that he or she finds satisfactory. If no informal resolution is achieved or is feasible, the chief judge may identify a complaint and, by written order stating the reasons, begin the review provided in Rule 11. If the evidence of misconduct is clear and convincing and no informal resolution is achieved or is feasible, the chief judge must identify a complaint. A chief judge must not decline to identify a complaint merely because the person making the allegation has not filed a complaint under Rule 6. This Rule is subject to Rule 7.

(b) Noncompliance with Rule 6(d). Rule 6 complaints that do not comply with the requirements of Rule 6(d) must be considered under this Rule.

(Adopted Mar. 11, 2008, eff. Apr. 10, 2008.)

Commentary on Rule 5

This Rule is adapted from the Breyer Committee Report, 239 F.R.D. at 245–46.

The Act authorizes the chief judge, by written order stating reasons, to identify a complaint and thereby dispense with the filing of a written complaint. See 28 U.S.C. § 351(b). Under Rule 5, when a chief judge becomes aware of information constituting reasonable grounds to inquire into possible misconduct or disability on the part of a covered judge, and no formal complaint has been filed, the chief judge has the power in his or her discretion to begin an appropriate inquiry. A chief judge's decision whether to informally seek a resolution and/or to identify a complaint is guided by the results of that inquiry. If the chief judge concludes that there is probable cause to believe that misconduct has occurred or a disability exists, the chief judge may seek an informal resolution, if feasible, and if failing in that, may identify a complaint. Discretion is accorded largely for the reasons police officers and prosecutors have discretion in making arrests or bringing charges. The matter may be trivial and isolated, based on marginal evidence, or otherwise highly unlikely to lead to a misconduct or disability finding.

On the other hand, if the inquiry leads the chief judge to conclude that there is clear and convincing evidence of misconduct or a disability, and no satisfactory informal resolution has been achieved or is feasible, the chief judge is required to identify a complaint.

An informal resolution is one agreed to by the subject judge and found satisfactory by the chief judge. Because an informal resolution under Rule 5 reached before a complaint is filed under Rule 6 will generally cause a subsequent Rule 6 complaint alleging the identical matter to be concluded, see Rule 11(d), the chief judge must be sure that the resolution is fully appropriate before endorsing it. In doing so, the chief judge must balance the seriousness of the matter against the particular judge's alacrity in addressing the issue. The availability of this procedure should encourage attempts at swift remedial action before a formal complaint is filed.

When a complaint is identified, a written order stating the reasons for the identification must be provided; this begins the process articulated in Rule 11. Rule 11 provides that once the chief judge has identified a complaint, the chief judge, subject to the disqualification provisions of Rule 25, will perform, with respect to that complaint, all functions assigned to the chief judge for the determination of complaints filed by a complainant.

In high-visibility situations, it may be desirable for the chief judge to identify a complaint without first seeking an informal resolution (and then, if the circumstances warrant, dismiss or conclude the identified complaint without appointment of a special committee) in order to assure the public that the allegations have not been ignored.

A chief judge's decision not to identify a complaint under Rule 5 is not appealable and is subject to Rule 3(h)(3)(A), which excludes merits-related complaints from the definition of misconduct.

A chief judge may not decline to identify a complaint solely on the basis that the unfiled allegations could be raised by one or more persons in a filed complaint, but none of these persons has opted to do so.

Subsection (a) concludes by stating that this Rule is "subject to Rule 7. " This is intended to establish that only: (i) the chief judge of the home circuit of a potential subject judge, or (ii) the chief judge of a circuit in which misconduct is alleged to have occurred in the course of official business while the potential subject judge was sitting by designation, shall have the power or a duty under this Rule to identify a complaint.

Subsection (b) provides that complaints filed under Rule 6 that do not comply with the requirements of Rule 6(d), must be considered under this Rule. For instance, if a complaint has been filed but the form submitted is unsigned, or the truth of the statements therein are not verified in writing under penalty of perjury, then a chief judge must nevertheless consider the allegations as known information, and proceed to follow the process described in Rule 5(a).

Rule 6.   Filing a Complaint

(a) **Form.** A complainant may use the form reproduced in the appendix to these Rules or a form designated by the rules of the judicial council in the circuit in which the complaint is filed. A complaint form is also available on each court of appeals' website or may be obtained from the circuit clerk or any district court or bankruptcy court within the circuit. A form is not necessary to file a complaint, but the complaint must be written and must include the information described in (b).

(b) **Brief Statement of Facts.** A complaint must contain a concise statement that details the specific facts on which the claim of misconduct or disability is based. The statement of facts should include a description of:

(1) what happened;

(2) when and where the relevant events happened;

(3) any information that would help an investigator check the facts; and

(4) for an allegation of disability, any additional facts that form the basis of that allegation.

(c) **Legibility.** A complaint should be typewritten if possible. If not typewritten, it must be legible. An illegible complaint will be returned to the complainant with a request to resubmit it in legible form. If a resubmitted complaint is still illegible, it will not be accepted for filing.

(d) **Complainant's Address and Signature; Verification.** The complainant must provide a contact address and sign the complaint. The truth of the statements made in the complaint must be verified in writing under penalty of perjury. If any of these requirements are not met, the complaint will be accepted for filing, but it will be reviewed under only Rule 5(b).

(e) **Number of Copies; Envelope Marking.** The complainant shall provide the number of copies of the complaint required by local rule. Each copy should be in an envelope marked "Complaint of Misconduct" or "Complaint of Disability." The envelope must not show the name of any subject judge.

(Adopted Mar. 11, 2008, eff. Apr. 10, 2008.)

Commentary on Rule 6

The Rule is adapted from the Illustrative Rules and is self-explanatory.

Rule 7.   Where to Initiate Complaints

(a) **Where to File.** Except as provided in (b),

(1) a complaint against a judge of a United States court of appeals, a United States district court, a United States bankruptcy court, or a United States magistrate judge must be filed with the circuit clerk in the jurisdiction in which the subject judge holds office.

(2) a complaint against a judge of the United States Court of International Trade or the United States Court of Federal Claims must be filed with the respective clerk of that court.

(3) a complaint against a judge of the United States Court of Appeals for the Federal Circuit must be filed with the circuit executive of that court.

(b) **Misconduct in Another Circuit; Transfer.** If a complaint alleges misconduct in the course of official business while the subject judge was sitting on a court by designation under 28 U.S.C. §§ 291–293 and 294(d), the complaint may be filed or identified with the circuit clerk of that circuit or of the subject judge's home circuit. The proceeding will continue in the circuit of the first-filed or first-identified complaint. The judicial council of the circuit where the complaint was first filed or first identified may transfer the complaint to the subject judge's home circuit or to the circuit where the alleged misconduct occurred, as the case may be.

(Adopted Mar. 11, 2008, eff. Apr. 10, 2008.)

Commentary on Rule 7

Title 28 U.S.C. § 351 states that complaints are to be filed with "the clerk of the court of appeals for the circuit." However, in many circuits, this role is filled by circuit executives. Accordingly, the term "circuit clerk," as defined in Rule 3(b) and used throughout these Rules, applies to circuit executives.

Section 351 uses the term "the circuit" in a way that suggests that either the home circuit of the subject judge or the circuit in which misconduct is alleged to have occurred is the proper venue for complaints. With an exception for judges sitting by designation, the Rule requires the identifying or filing of a misconduct or disability complaint in the circuit in which the judge holds office, largely based on the administrative perspective of the Act. Given the Act's emphasis on the future conduct of the business of the courts, the circuit in which the judge holds office is the appropriate forum because that circuit is likely best able to influence a judge's future behavior in constructive ways.

However, when judges sit by designation, the non-home circuit has a strong interest in redressing misconduct in the course of official business, and where allegations also involve a member of the bar—ex parte contact between an attorney and a judge, for example—it may often be desirable to have the judicial and bar misconduct proceedings take place in the same venue. Rule 7(b), therefore, allows transfer to, or filing or identification of a complaint in, the non-home circuit. The proceeding may be transferred by the judicial council of the filing or identified circuit to the other circuit.

Rule 8.   Action by Clerk

(a) **Receipt of Complaint.** Upon receiving a complaint against a judge filed under Rule 5 or 6, the circuit clerk must open a file, assign a docket number according to a uniform numbering scheme promulgated by the Judicial Conference Committee on Judicial Conduct and Disability, and acknowledge the complaint's receipt.

(b) **Distribution of Copies.** The clerk must promptly send copies of a complaint filed under Rule 6 to the chief judge or the judge authorized to act as chief judge under Rule 25(f), and copies of complaints filed under Rule 5 or 6 to each subject judge. The clerk must retain the original complaint. Any further distribution should be as provided by local rule.

(c) **Complaints Against Noncovered Persons.** If the clerk receives a complaint about a person not holding an office described in Rule 4, the clerk must not accept the complaint for filing under these Rules.

(d) **Receipt of Complaint about a Judge and Another Noncovered Person.** If a complaint is received about a judge described in Rule 4 and a person not holding an office described in Rule 4, the clerk must accept the complaint for filing under these Rules only with regard to the judge and must inform the complainant of the limitation.

(Adopted Mar. 11, 2008, eff. Apr. 10, 2008.)

Commentary on Rule 8

This Rule is adapted from the Illustrative Rules and is largely self-explanatory.

The uniform docketing scheme described in subsection (a) should take into account potential problems associated with a complaint that names multiple judges. One solution may be to provide separate docket numbers for each subject judge. Separate docket numbers would help avoid difficulties in tracking cases, particularly if a complaint is dismissed with respect to some, but not all of the named judges.

Complaints against noncovered persons are not to be accepted for processing under these Rules but may, of course, be accepted under other circuit rules or procedures for grievances.

Rule 9.   Time for Filing or Identifying a Complaint

A complaint may be filed or identified at any time. If the passage of time has made an accurate and fair investigation of a complaint impractical, the complaint must be dismissed under Rule 11(c)(1)(E).

(Adopted Mar. 11, 2008, eff. Apr. 10, 2008.)

Commentary on Rule 9

This Rule is adapted from the Act, 28 U.S.C. §§ 351, 352(b)(1)(A)(iii), and the Illustrative Rules.

Rule 10.   Abuse of the Complaint Procedure

(a) **Abusive Complaints.** A complainant who has filed repetitive, harassing, or frivolous complaints, or has otherwise abused the complaint procedure, may be restricted from filing further complaints. After giving the complainant an opportunity to show cause in writing why his or her right to file further complaints should not be limited, a judicial council may prohibit, restrict, or impose conditions on the complainant's use of the complaint procedure. Upon written request of the complainant, the judicial council may revise or withdraw any prohibition, restriction, or condition previously imposed.

(b) **Orchestrated Complaints.** When many essentially identical complaints from different complainants are received and appear to be part of an orchestrated campaign, the chief judge may recommend that the judicial council issue a written order instructing the circuit clerk to accept only a certain number of such complaints for filing and to refuse to accept further ones. The clerk must send a copy of any such order to anyone whose complaint was not accepted.

(Adopted Mar. 11, 2008, eff. Apr. 10, 2008.)

Commentary on Rule 10

This Rule is adapted from the Illustrative Rules.

Rule 10(a) provides a mechanism for a judicial council to restrict the filing of further complaints by a single complainant who has abused the complaint procedure. In some instances, however, the complaint procedure may be abused in a manner for which the remedy provided in Rule 10(a) may not be appropriate. For example, some circuits have been inundated with submissions of dozens or hundreds of essentially identical complaints against the same judge or judges, all submitted by different complainants. In many of these instances, persons with grievances against a particular judge or judges used the Internet or other technology to orchestrate mass complaint-filing campaigns against them. If each complaint submitted as part of such a campaign were accepted for filing and processed according to these Rules, there would be a serious drain on court resources without any benefit to the adjudication of the underlying merits.

A judicial council may, therefore, respond to such mass filings under Rule 10(b) by declining to accept repetitive complaints for filing, regardless of the fact that the complaints are nominally submitted by different complainants. When the first complaint or complaints have been dismissed on the merits, and when further, essentially identical submissions follow, the judicial council may issue a second order noting that these are identical or repetitive complaints, directing the circuit clerk not to accept these complaints or any further such complaints for filing, and directing the clerk to send each putative complainant copies of both orders.

ARTICLE III.   REVIEW OF A COMPLAINT
BY THE CHIEF JUDGE

Rule 11.   Review by the Chief Judge

(a) Purpose of Chief Judge's Review. When a complaint is identified by the chief judge or is filed, the chief judge must review it unless the chief judge is disqualified under Rule 25. If the complaint contains information constituting evidence of misconduct or disability, but the complainant does not claim it as such, the chief judge must treat the complaint as if it did allege misconduct or disability and give notice to the subject judge. After reviewing the complaint, the chief judge must determine whether it should be:

(1) dismissed;

(2) concluded on the ground that voluntary corrective action has been taken;

(3) concluded because intervening events have made action on the complaint no longer necessary; or

(4) referred to a special committee.

(b) Inquiry by Chief Judge. In determining what action to take under Rule 11(a), the chief judge may conduct a limited inquiry. The chief judge, or a designee, may communicate orally or in writing with the complainant, the subject judge, and any others who may have knowledge of the matter, and may review transcripts or other relevant documents. In conducting the inquiry, the chief judge must not determine any reasonably disputed issue.

(c) Dismissal.

(1) **Allowable grounds.** A complaint must be dismissed in whole or in part to the extent that the chief judge concludes that the complaint:

(A) alleges conduct that, even if true, is not prejudicial to the effective and expeditious administration of the business of the courts and does not indicate a mental or physical disability resulting in inability to discharge the duties of judicial office;

(B) is directly related to the merits of a decision or procedural ruling;

(C) is frivolous;

(D) is based on allegations lacking sufficient evidence to raise an inference that misconduct has occurred or that a disability exists;

(E) is based on allegations which are incapable of being established through investigation;

(F) has been filed in the wrong circuit under Rule 7; or

(G) is otherwise not appropriate for consideration under the Act.

(2) **Disallowed grounds.** A complaint must not be dismissed solely because it repeats allegations of a previously dismissed complaint if it also contains material information not previously considered and does not constitute harassment of the subject judge.

(d) Corrective Action. The chief judge may conclude the complaint proceeding in whole or in part if:

(1) an informal resolution under Rule 5 satisfactory to the chief judge was reached before the complaint was filed under Rule 6, or

(2) the chief judge determines that the subject judge has taken appropriate voluntary corrective action that acknowledges and remedies the problems raised by the complaint.

(e) Intervening Events. The chief judge may conclude the complaint proceeding in whole or in part upon determining that intervening events render some or all of the allegations moot or make remedial action impossible.

(f) Appointment of Special Committee. If some or all of the complaint is not dismissed or concluded, the chief judge must promptly appoint a special committee to investigate the complaint or any relevant portion of it and to make recommendations to the judicial council. Before appointing a special committee, the chief judge must invite the subject judge to respond to the complaint either orally or in writing if the judge was not given an opportunity during the limited inquiry. In the chief judge's discretion, separate complaints may be joined and assigned to a single special committee. Similarly, a single complaint about more than one judge may be severed and more than one special committee appointed.

(g) Notice of Chief Judge's Action; Petitions for Review.

(1) **When special committee is appointed.** If a special committee is appointed, the chief judge must notify the complainant and the subject judge that the matter has been referred to a special committee and identify the members of the committee. A copy of the order appointing the special committee must be sent to the Judicial Conference Committee on Judicial Conduct and Disability.

(2) **When chief judge disposes of complaint without appointing special committee.** If the chief judge disposes of the complaint under Rule 11(c), (d), or (e), the chief judge must prepare a supporting memorandum that sets forth the reasons for the disposition. Except as authorized by 28 U.S.C. § 360, the memorandum must not include the name of the complainant or of the subject judge. The order and the supporting memorandum, which may be one document, must be provided to the complainant, the subject judge, and the Judicial

Conference Committee on Judicial Conduct and Disability.

(3) Right of petition for review. If the chief judge disposes of a complaint under Rule 11(c), (d), or (e), the complainant and subject judge must be notified of the right to petition the judicial council for review of the disposition, as provided in Rule 18. If a petition for review is filed, the chief judge must promptly transmit all materials obtained in connection with the inquiry under Rule 11(b) to the circuit clerk for transmittal to the judicial council.

(h) Public Availability of Chief Judge's Decision. The chief judge's decision must be made public to the extent, at the time, and in the manner provided in Rule 24.

(Adopted Mar. 11, 2008, eff. Apr. 10, 2008.)

Commentary on Rule 11

Subsection (a) lists the actions available to a chief judge in reviewing a complaint. This subsection provides that where a complaint has been filed under Rule 6, the ordinary doctrines of waiver do not apply. A chief judge must identify as a complaint any misconduct or disability issues raised by the factual allegations of the complaint even if the complainant makes no such claim with regard to those issues. For example, an allegation limited to misconduct in fact-finding that mentions periods during a trial when the judge was asleep must be treated as a complaint regarding disability. Some formal order giving notice of the expanded scope of the proceeding must be given to the subject judge.

Subsection (b) describes the nature of the chief judge's inquiry. It is based largely on the Breyer Committee Report, 239 F.R.D. at 243–45. The Act states that dismissal is appropriate "when a limited inquiry . . . demonstrates that the allegations in the complaint lack any factual foundation or are conclusively refuted by objective evidence." 28 U.S.C. § 352(b)(1)(B). At the same time, however, Section 352(a) states that "[t]he chief judge shall not undertake to make findings of fact about any matter that is reasonably in dispute." These two statutory standards should be read together, so that a matter is not "reasonably" in dispute if a limited inquiry shows that the allegations do not constitute misconduct or disability, that they lack any reliable factual foundation, or that they are conclusively refuted by objective evidence.

In conducting a limited inquiry under subsection (b), the chief judge must avoid determinations of reasonably disputed issues, including reasonably disputed issues as to whether the facts alleged constitute misconduct or disability, which are ordinarily left to a special committee and the judicial council. An allegation of fact is ordinarily not "refuted" simply because the subject judge denies it. The limited inquiry must reveal something more in the way of refutation before it is appropriate to dismiss a complaint that is otherwise cognizable. If it is the complainant's word against the subject judge's—in other words, there is simply no other significant evidence of what happened or of the complainant's unreliability—then there must be a special-committee investigation. Such a credibility issue is a matter "reasonably in dispute" within the meaning of the Act.

However, dismissal following a limited inquiry may occur when the complaint refers to transcripts or to witnesses and the chief judge determines that the transcripts and witnesses all support the subject judge. Breyer Committee Report, 239 F.R.D. at 243. For example, consider a complaint alleging that the subject judge said X, and the complaint mentions, or it is independently clear, that five people may have heard what the judge said. Id. The chief judge is told by the subject judge and one witness that the judge did not say X, and the chief judge dismisses the complaint without questioning the other four possible witnesses. Id. In this example, the matter remains reasonably in dispute. If all five witnesses say the judge did not say X, dismissal is appropriate, but if potential witnesses who are reasonably accessible have not been questioned, then the matter remains reasonably in dispute. Id.

Similarly, under (c)(1)(A), if it is clear that the conduct or disability alleged, even if true, is not cognizable under these Rules, the complaint should be dismissed. If that issue is reasonably in dispute, however, dismissal under (c)(1)(A) is inappropriate.

Essentially, the standard articulated in subsection (b) is that used to decide motions for summary judgment pursuant to Fed. R. Civ. P. 56. Genuine issues of material fact are not resolved at the summary judgment stage. A material fact is one that "might affect the outcome of the suit under the governing law," and a dispute is "genuine" if "the evidence is such that a reasonable jury could return a verdict for the nonmoving party." *Anderson v. Liberty Lobby*, 477 U.S. 242, 248 (1986). Similarly, the chief judge may not resolve a genuine issue concerning a material fact or the existence of misconduct or a disability when conducting a limited inquiry pursuant to subsection (b).

Subsection (c) describes the grounds on which a complaint may be dismissed. These are adapted from the Act, 28 U.S.C. § 352(b), and the Breyer Committee Report, 239 F.R.D. at 239–45. Subsection (c)(1)(A) permits dismissal of an allegation that, even if true, does not constitute misconduct or disability under the statutory standard. The proper standards are set out in Rule 3 and discussed in the Commentary on that Rule. Subsection (c)(1)(B) permits dismissal of complaints related to the merits of a decision by a subject judge; this standard is also governed by Rule 3 and its accompanying Commentary.

Subsections (c)(1)(C)–(E) implement the statute by allowing dismissal of complaints that are "frivolous, lacking sufficient evidence to raise an inference that misconduct has occurred, or containing allegations which are incapable of being established through investigation." 28 U.S.C. § 352(b)(1)(A)(iii).

Dismissal of a complaint as "frivolous," under Rule 11(c)(1)(C), will generally occur without any inquiry beyond the face of the complaint. For instance, when the allegations are facially incredible or so lacking in indicia of reliability that no further inquiry is warranted, dismissal under this subsection is appropriate.

A complaint warranting dismissal under Rule 11(c)(1)(D) is illustrated by the following example. Consider a complainant who alleges an impropriety and asserts that he knows of it because it was observed and reported to him by a person who is identified. The judge denies that the event occurred. When contacted, the source also denies it. In such a case, the chief judge's proper course of action may turn on whether the source had any role in the allegedly improper conduct. If the complaint was based on a lawyer's statement that he or she had an improper ex parte contact with a judge, the lawyer's denial of the impropriety might not be taken as

251

wholly persuasive, and it would be appropriate to conclude that a real factual issue is raised. On the other hand, if the complaint quoted a disinterested third party and that disinterested party denied that the statement had been made, there would be no value in opening a formal investigation. In such a case, it would be appropriate to dismiss the complaint under Rule 11(c)(1)(D).

Rule 11(c)(1)(E) is intended, among other things, to cover situations when no evidence is offered or identified, or when the only identified source is unavailable. Breyer Committee Report, 239 F.R.D. at 243. For example, a complaint alleges that an unnamed attorney told the complainant that the judge did X. Id. The subject judge denies it. The chief judge requests that the complainant (who does not purport to have observed the judge do X) identify the unnamed witness, or that the unnamed witness come forward so that the chief judge can learn the unnamed witness's account. Id. The complainant responds that he has spoken with the unnamed witness, that the unnamed witness is an attorney who practices in federal court, and that the unnamed witness is unwilling to be identified or to come forward. Id. at 243–44. The allegation is then properly dismissed as containing allegations that are incapable of being established through investigation. Id.

If, however, the situation involves a reasonable dispute over credibility, the matter should proceed. For example, the complainant alleges an impropriety and alleges that he or she observed it and that there were no other witnesses; the subject judge denies that the event occurred. Unless the complainant's allegations are facially incredible or so lacking indicia of reliability warranting dismissal under Rule 11(c)(1)(C), a special committee must be appointed because there is a material factual question that is reasonably in dispute.

Dismissal is also appropriate when a complaint is filed so long after an alleged event that memory loss, death, or changes to unknown residences prevent a proper investigation.

Subsection (c)(2) indicates that the investigative nature of the process prevents the application of claim preclusion principles where new and material evidence becomes available. However, it also recognizes that at some point a renewed investigation may constitute harassment of the subject judge and should be foregone, depending of course on the seriousness of the issues and the weight of the new evidence.

Rule 11(d) implements the Act's provision for dismissal if voluntary appropriate corrective action has been taken. It is largely adapted from the Breyer Committee Report, 239 F.R.D. 244–45. The Act authorizes the chief judge to conclude the proceedings if "appropriate corrective action has been taken." 28 U.S.C. § 352(b)(2). Under the Rule, action taken after the complaint is filed is "appropriate" when it acknowledges and remedies the problem raised by the complaint. Breyer Committee Report, 239 F.R.D. at 244. Because the Act deals with the conduct of judges, the emphasis is on correction of the judicial conduct that was the subject of the complaint. Id. Terminating a complaint based on corrective action is premised on the implicit understanding that voluntary self-correction or redress of misconduct or a disability is preferable to sanctions. Id. The chief judge may facilitate this process by giving the subject judge an objective view of the appearance of the judicial conduct in question and by suggesting appropriate corrective measures. Id. Moreover, when corrective action is taken under Rule 5 satisfacto-

ry to the chief judge before a complaint is filed, that informal resolution will be sufficient to conclude a subsequent complaint based on the identical conduct.

"Corrective action" must be voluntary action taken by the subject judge. Breyer Committee Report, 239 F.R.D. at 244. A remedial action directed by the chief judge or by an appellate court without the participation of the subject judge in formulating the directive or without the subject judge's subsequent agreement to such action does not constitute the requisite voluntary corrective action. Id. Neither the chief judge nor an appellate court has authority under the Act to impose a formal remedy or sanction; only the judicial council can impose a formal remedy or sanction under 28 U.S.C. § 354(a)(2). Id. Compliance with a previous council order may serve as corrective action allowing conclusion of a later complaint about the same behavior. Id.

Where a judge's conduct has resulted in identifiable, particularized harm to the complainant or another individual, appropriate corrective action should include steps taken by that judge to acknowledge and redress the harm, if possible, such as by an apology, recusal from a case, or a pledge to refrain from similar conduct in the future. Id. While the Act is generally forward-looking, any corrective action should, to the extent possible, serve to correct a specific harm to an individual, if such harm can reasonably be remedied. Id. In some cases, corrective action may not be "appropriate" to justify conclusion of a complaint unless the complainant or other individual harmed is meaningfully apprised of the nature of the corrective action in the chief judge's order, in a direct communication from the subject judge, or otherwise. Id.

Voluntary corrective action should be proportionate to any plausible allegations of misconduct in the complaint. The form of corrective action should also be proportionate to any sanctions that a judicial council might impose under Rule 20(b), such as a private or public reprimand or a change in case assignments. Breyer Committee Report, 239 F.R.D at 244–45. In other words, minor corrective action will not suffice to dispose of a serious matter. Id.

Rule 11(e) implements Section 352(b)(2) of the Act, which permits the chief judge to "conclude the proceeding," if "action on the complaint is no longer necessary because of intervening events," such as a resignation from judicial office. Ordinarily, however, stepping down from an administrative post such as chief judge, judicial-council member, or court-committee chair does not constitute an event rendering unnecessary any further action on a complaint alleging judicial misconduct. Breyer Committee Report, 239 F.R.D. at 245. As long as the subject of the complaint performs judicial duties, a complaint alleging judicial misconduct must be addressed. Id.

If a complaint is not disposed of pursuant to Rule 11(c), (d), or (e), a special committee must be appointed. Rule 11(f) states that a subject judge must be invited to respond to the complaint before a special committee is appointed, if no earlier response was invited.

Subject judges, of course, receive copies of complaints at the same time that they are referred to the chief judge, and they are free to volunteer responses to them. Under Rule 11(b), the chief judge may request a response if it is thought necessary. However, many complaints are clear candidates for dismissal even if their allegations are accepted as true, and there is no need for the subject judge to devote time to a defense.

The Act requires that the order dismissing a complaint or concluding the proceeding contain a statement of reasons and that a copy of the order be sent to the complainant. 28 U.S.C. § 352(b). Rule 24, dealing with availability of information to the public, contemplates that the order will be made public, usually without disclosing the names of the complainant or the subject judge. If desired for administrative purposes, more identifying information can be included in a non-public version of the order.

When complaints are disposed of by chief judges, the statutory purposes are best served by providing the complainant with a full, particularized, but concise explanation, giving reasons for the conclusions reached. See also Commentary on Rule 24, dealing with public availability.

Rule 11(g) provides that the complainant and subject judge must be notified, in the case of a disposition by the chief judge, of the right to petition the judicial council for review. A copy of a chief judge's order and memorandum, which may be one document, disposing of a complaint must be sent by the circuit clerk to the Judicial Conference Committee on Judicial Conduct and Disability.

ARTICLE IV.   INVESTIGATION AND REPORT BY SPECIAL COMMITTEE

Rule 12.   Composition of Special Committee

(a) **Membership.** Except as provided in (e), a special committee appointed under Rule 11(f) must consist of the chief judge and equal numbers of circuit and district judges. If the complaint is about a district judge, bankruptcy judge, or magistrate judge, then, when possible, the district-judge members of the committee must be from districts other than the district of the subject judge. For the courts named in 28 U.S.C. § 363, the committee must be selected from the judges serving on the subject judge's court.

(b) **Presiding Officer.** When appointing the committee, the chief judge may serve as the presiding officer or else must designate a committee member as the presiding officer.

(c) **Bankruptcy Judge or Magistrate Judge as Adviser.** If the subject judge is a bankruptcy judge or magistrate judge, he or she may, within 14 days after being notified of the committee's appointment, ask the chief judge to designate as a committee adviser another bankruptcy judge or magistrate judge, as the case may be. The chief judge must grant such a request but may otherwise use discretion in naming the adviser. Unless the adviser is a Court of Federal Claims special master appointed under 42 U.S.C. § 300aa–12(c), the adviser must be from a district other than the district of the subject bankruptcy judge or subject magistrate judge. The adviser cannot vote but has the other privileges of a committee member.

(d) **Provision of Documents.** The chief judge must certify to each other member of the committee and to any adviser copies of the complaint and statement of facts in whole or relevant part, and any other relevant documents on file.

(e) **Continuing Qualification of Committee Members.** A member of a special committee who was qualified to serve when appointed may continue to serve on the committee even though the member relinquishes the position of chief judge, active circuit judge, or active district judge, as the case may be, but only if the member continues to hold office under Article III, Section 1, of the Constitution of the United States, or under 28 U.S.C. § 171.

(f) **Inability of Committee Member to Complete Service.** If a member of a special committee can no longer serve because of death, disability, disqualification, resignation, retirement from office, or other reason, the chief judge must decide whether to appoint a replacement member, either a circuit or district judge as needed under (a). No special committee appointed under these Rules may function with only a single member, and the votes of a two-member committee must be unanimous.

(g) **Voting.** All actions by a committee must be by vote of a majority of all members of the committee.

(Adopted Mar. 11, 2008, eff. Apr. 10, 2008.)

Commentary on Rule 12

This Rule is adapted from the Act and the Illustrative Rules.

Rule 12 leaves the size of a special committee flexible, to be determined on a case-by-case basis. The question of committee size is one that should be weighed with care in view of the potential for consuming the members' time; a large committee should be appointed only if there is a special reason to do so.

Although the Act requires that the chief judge be a member of each special committee, 28 U.S.C. § 353(a)(1), it does not require that the chief judge preside. Accordingly, Rule 12(b) provides that if the chief judge does not preside, he or she must designate another committee member as presiding officer.

Rule 12(c) provides that the chief judge must appoint a bankruptcy judge or magistrate judge as an adviser to a special committee at the request of a bankruptcy or magistrate subject judge.

Subsection (c) also provides that the adviser will have all the privileges of a committee member except a vote. The adviser, therefore, may participate in all deliberations of the committee, question witnesses at hearings, and write a separate statement to accompany the special committee's report to the judicial council.

Rule 12(e) provides that a member of a special committee who remains an Article III judge may continue to serve on the committee even though the member's status otherwise changes. Thus, a committee that originally consisted of the chief judge and an equal number of circuit and district judges, as required by the law, may continue to function even though changes of status alter that composition. This provision reflects the belief that stability of membership will contribute to the quality of the work of such committees.

Stability of membership is also the principal concern animating Rule 12(f), which deals with the case in which a special committee loses a member before its work is complete. The Rule permits the chief judge to determine whether a replacement member should be appointed. Generally, appointment of a replacement member is desirable in these situations unless the committee has conducted evidentiary hearings before the vacancy occurs. However, cases may arise in which a committee is in the late stages of its work, and in which it would be difficult for a new member to play a meaningful role. The Rule also preserves the collegial character of the committee process by prohibiting a single surviving member from serving as a committee and by providing that a committee of two surviving members will, in essence, operate under a unanimity rule.

Rule 12(g) provides that actions of a special committee must be by vote of a majority of all the members. All the members of a committee should participate in committee decisions. In that circumstance, it seems reasonable to require that committee decisions be made by a majority of the membership, rather than a majority of some smaller quorum.

Rule 13.   Conduct of an Investigation

(a) Extent and Methods of Special–Committee Investigation. Each special committee must determine the appropriate extent and methods of the investigation in light of the allegations of the complaint. If, in the course of the investigation, the committee has cause to believe that the subject judge may have engaged in misconduct or has a disability that is beyond the scope of the complaint, the committee must refer the new matter to the chief judge for action under Rule 5 or Rule 11.

(b) Criminal Conduct. If the committee's investigation concerns conduct that may be a crime, the committee must consult with the appropriate prosecutorial authorities to the extent permitted by the Act to avoid compromising any criminal investigation. The committee has final authority over the timing and extent of its investigation and the formulation of its recommendations.

(c) Staff. The committee may arrange for staff assistance to conduct the investigation. It may use existing staff of the judicial branch or may hire special staff through the Director of the Administrative Office of the United States Courts.

(d) Delegation of Subpoena Power; Contempt. The chief judge may delegate the authority to exercise the committee's subpoena powers. The judicial council or special committee may institute a contempt proceeding under 28 U.S.C. § 332(d) against anyone who fails to comply with a subpoena.

(Adopted Mar. 11, 2008, eff. Apr. 10, 2008.)

Commentary on Rule 13

This Rule is adapted from the Illustrative Rules.

Rule 13, as well as Rules 14, 15, and 16, are concerned with the way in which a special committee carries out its mission. They reflect the view that a special committee has two roles that are separated in ordinary litigation. First, the committee has an investigative role of the kind that is characteristically left to executive branch agencies or discovery by civil litigants. 28 U.S.C. § 353(c). Second, it has a formalized fact-finding and recommendation-of-disposition role that is characteristically left to juries, judges, or arbitrators. Id. Rule 13 generally governs the investigative stage. Even though the same body has responsibility for both roles under the Act, it is important to distinguish between them in order to ensure that appropriate rights are afforded at appropriate times to the subject judge.

One of the difficult questions that can arise is the relationship between proceedings under the Act and criminal investigations. Rule 13(b) assigns responsibility for coordination to the special committee in cases in which criminal conduct is suspected, but gives the committee the authority to determine the appropriate pace of its activity in light of any criminal investigation.

Title 28 U.S.C. § 356(a) provides that a special committee will have full subpoena powers as provided in 28 U.S.C. § 332(d). Section 332(d)(1) provides that subpoenas will be issued on behalf of judicial councils by the circuit clerk "at the direction of the chief judge of the circuit or his designee." Rule 13(d) contemplates that, where the chief judge designates someone else as presiding officer of a special committee, the presiding officer also be delegated the authority to direct the circuit clerk to issue subpoenas related to committee proceedings. That is not intended to imply, however, that the decision to use the subpoena power is exercisable by the presiding officer alone. See Rule 12(g).

Rule 14.   Conduct of Hearings by Special Committee

(a) Purpose of Hearings. The committee may hold hearings to take testimony and receive other evidence, to hear argument, or both. If the committee is investigating allegations against more than one judge, it may hold joint or separate hearings.

(b) Committee Evidence. Subject to Rule 15, the committee must obtain material, nonredundant evidence in the form it considers appropriate. In the committee's discretion, evidence may be obtained by committee members, staff, or both. Witnesses offering testimonial evidence may include the complainant and the subject judge.

(c) Counsel for Witnesses. The subject judge has the right to counsel. The special committee has discretion to decide whether other witnesses may have counsel present when they testify.

(d) Witness Fees. Witness fees must be paid as provided in 28 U.S.C. § 1821.

(e) Oath. All testimony taken at a hearing must be given under oath or affirmation.

(f) Rules of Evidence. The Federal Rules of Evidence do not apply to special-committee hearings.

(g) Record and Transcript. A record and transcript must be made of all hearings.

(Adopted Mar. 11, 2008, eff. Apr. 10, 2008.)

Commentary on Rule 14

This Rule is adapted from Section 353 of the Act and the Illustrative Rules.

Rule 14 is concerned with the conduct of fact-finding hearings. Special-committee hearings will normally be held only after the investigative work has been completed and the committee has concluded that there is sufficient evidence to warrant a formal fact-finding proceeding. Special-committee proceedings are primarily inquisitorial rather than adversarial. Accordingly, the Federal Rules of Evidence do not apply to such hearings. Inevitably, a hearing will have something of an adversary character. Nevertheless, that tendency should be moderated to the extent possible. Even though a proceeding will commonly have investigative and hearing stages, committee members should not regard themselves as prosecutors one day and judges the next. Their duty—and that of their staff—is at all times to be impartial seekers of the truth.

Rule 14(b) contemplates that material evidence will be obtained by the committee and presented in the form of affidavits, live testimony, etc. Staff or others who are organizing the hearings should regard it as their role to present evidence representing the entire picture. With respect to testimonial evidence, the subject judge should normally be called as a committee witness. Cases may arise in which the judge will not testify voluntarily. In such cases, subpoena powers are available, subject to the normal testimonial privileges. Although Rule 15(c) recognizes the subject judge's statutory right to call witnesses on his or her own behalf, exercise of this right should not usually be necessary.

Rule 15. Rights of Subject Judge

(a) Notice.

(1) Generally. The subject judge must receive written notice of:

    (A) the appointment of a special committee under Rule 11(f);

    (B) the expansion of the scope of an investigation under Rule 13(a);

    (C) any hearing under Rule 14, including its purposes, the names of any witnesses the committee intends to call, and the text of any statements that have been taken from those witnesses.

(2) Suggestion of additional witnesses. The subject judge may suggest additional witnesses to the committee.

(b) Report of the Special Committee. The subject judge must be sent a copy of the special committee's report when it is filed with the judicial council.

(c) Presentation of Evidence. At any hearing held under Rule 14, the subject judge has the right to present evidence, to compel the attendance of witnesses, and to compel the production of documents. At the request of the subject judge, the chief judge or the judge's designee must direct the circuit clerk to issue a subpoena to a witness under 28 U.S.C. § 332(d)(1). The subject judge must be given the opportunity to cross-examine committee witnesses, in person or by counsel.

(d) Presentation of Argument. The subject judge may submit written argument to the special committee and must be given a reasonable opportunity to present oral argument at an appropriate stage of the investigation.

(e) Attendance at Hearings. The subject judge has the right to attend any hearing held under Rule 14 and to receive copies of the transcript, of any documents introduced, and of any written arguments submitted by the complainant to the committee.

(f) Representation by Counsel. The subject judge may choose to be represented by counsel in the exercise of any right enumerated in this Rule. As provided in Rule 20(e), the United States may bear the costs of the representation.

(Adopted Mar. 11, 2008, eff. Apr. 10, 2008.)

Commentary on Rule 15

This Rule is adapted from the Act and the Illustrative Rules.

The Act states that these Rules must contain provisions requiring that "the judge whose conduct is the subject of a complaint . . . be afforded an opportunity to appear (in person or by counsel) at proceedings conducted by the investigating panel, to present oral and documentary evidence, to compel the attendance of witnesses or the production of documents, to cross-examine witnesses, and to present argument orally or in writing." 28 U.S.C. § 358(b)(2). To implement this provision, Rule 15(e) gives the judge the right to attend any hearing held for the purpose of receiving evidence of record or hearing argument under Rule 14.

The Act does not require that the subject judge be permitted to attend all proceedings of the special committee. Accordingly, the Rules do not give a right to attend other proceedings—for example, meetings at which the committee is engaged in investigative activity, such as interviewing persons to learn whether they ought to be called as witnesses or examining for relevance purposes documents delivered pursuant to a subpoena duces tecum, or meetings in which the committee is deliberating on the evidence or its recommendations.

Rule 16. Rights of Complainant in Investigation

(a) Notice. The complainant must receive written notice of the investigation as provided in Rule 11(g)(1). When the special committee's report to the judicial council is filed, the complainant must be notified of the filing. The judicial council may, in its discretion, provide a copy of the report of a special committee to the complainant.

(b) Opportunity to Provide Evidence. If the committee determines that the complainant may have evidence that does not already exist in writing, a representative of the committee must interview the complainant.

(c) Presentation of Argument. The complainant may submit written argument to the special committee. In its discretion, the special committee may permit the complainant to offer oral argument.

(d) Representation by Counsel. A complainant may submit written argument through counsel and, if permitted to offer oral argument, may do so through counsel.

(e) Cooperation. In exercising its discretion under this Rule, a special committee may take into account the degree of the complainant's cooperation in preserving the confidentiality of the proceedings, including the identity of the subject judge.

(Adopted Mar. 11, 2008, eff. Apr. 10, 2008.)

Commentary on Rule 16

This Rule is adapted from the Act and the Illustrative Rules.

In accordance with the view of the process as fundamentally administrative and inquisitorial, these Rules do not give the complainant the rights of a party to litigation, and leave the complainant's role largely to the discretion of the special committee. However, Rule 16(b) provides that, where a special committee has been appointed and it determines that the complainant may have additional evidence, the complainant must be interviewed by a representative of the committee. Such an interview may be in person or by telephone, and the representative of the committee may be either a member or staff.

Rule 16 does not contemplate that the complainant will ordinarily be permitted to attend proceedings of the special committee except when testifying or presenting oral argument. A special committee may exercise its discretion to permit the complainant to be present at its proceedings, or to permit the complainant, individually or through counsel, to participate in the examination or cross-examination of witnesses.

The Act authorizes an exception to the normal confidentiality provisions where the judicial council in its discretion provides a copy of the report of the special committee to the complainant and to the subject judge. 28 U.S.C. § 360(a)(1). However, the Rules do not entitle the complainant to a copy of the special committee's report.

In exercising their discretion regarding the role of the complainant, the special committee and the judicial council should protect the confidentiality of the complaint process. As a consequence, subsection (e) provides that a special committee may consider the degree to which a complainant has cooperated in preserving the confidentiality of the proceedings in determining what role beyond the minimum required by these Rules should be given to that complainant.

Rule 17. Special–Committee Report

The committee must file with the judicial council a comprehensive report of its investigation, including findings and recommendations for council action. The report must be accompanied by a statement of the vote by which it was adopted, any separate or dissenting statements of committee members, and the record of any hearings held under Rule 14. A copy of the report and accompanying statement must be sent to the Judicial Conference Committee on Judicial Conduct and Disability.

(Adopted Mar. 11, 2008, eff. Apr. 10, 2008.)

Commentary on Rule 17

This Rule is adapted from the Illustrative Rules and is self-explanatory. The provision for sending a copy of the special-committee report and accompanying statement to the Judicial Conference Committee is new.

ARTICLE V. JUDICIAL–COUNCIL REVIEW

Rule 18. Petitions for Review of Chief Judge Dispositions Under Rule 11(c), (d), or (e)

(a) Petitions for Review. After the chief judge issues an order under Rule 11(c), (d), or (e), a complainant or subject judge may petition the judicial council of the circuit to review the order. By rules promulgated under 28 U.S.C. § 358, the judicial council may refer a petition for review filed under this Rule to a panel of no fewer than five members of the council, at least two of whom must be district judges.

(b) When to File; Form; Where to File. A petition for review must be filed in the office of the circuit clerk within 35 days of the date on the clerk's letter informing the parties of the chief judge's order. The petition should be in letter form, addressed to the circuit clerk, and in an envelope marked "Misconduct Petition" or "Disability Petition." The name of the subject judge must not be shown on the envelope. The letter should be typewritten or otherwise legible. It should begin with "I hereby petition the judicial council for review of . . ." and state the reasons why the petition should be granted. It must be signed.

(c) Receipt and Distribution of Petition. A circuit clerk who receives a petition for review filed within the time allowed and in proper form must:

(1) acknowledge its receipt and send a copy to the complainant or subject judge, as the case may be;

(2) promptly distribute to each member of the judicial council, or its relevant panel, except for any member disqualified under Rule 25, or make available in the manner provided by local rule, the following materials:

(A) copies of the complaint;

(B) all materials obtained by the chief judge in connection with the inquiry;

(C) the chief judge's order disposing of the complaint;

(D) any memorandum in support of the chief judge's order;

(E) the petition for review; and

(F) an appropriate ballot;

(3) send the petition for review to the Judicial Conference Committee on Judicial Conduct and Disability. Unless the Judicial Conference Committee requests them, the clerk will not send copies of the materials obtained by the chief judge.

(d) Untimely Petition. The clerk must refuse to accept a petition that is received after the deadline in (b).

(e) Timely Petition Not in Proper Form. When the clerk receives a petition filed within the time allowed but in a form that is improper to a degree that would substantially impair its consideration by the judicial council—such as a document that is ambiguous about whether it is intended to be a petition for review—the clerk must acknowledge its receipt, call the filer's attention to the deficiencies, and give the filer the opportunity to correct the deficiencies within 21 days of the date of the clerk's letter about the deficiencies or within the original deadline for filing the petition, whichever is later. If the deficiencies are corrected within the time allowed, the clerk will proceed according to paragraphs (a) and (c) of this Rule. If the deficiencies are not corrected, the clerk must reject the petition.

(Adopted Mar. 11, 2008, eff. Apr. 10, 2008.)

Commentary on Rule 18

Rule 18 is adapted largely from the Illustrative Rules.

Subsection (a) permits a subject judge, as well as the complainant, to petition for review of a chief judge's order dismissing a complaint under Rule 11(c), or concluding that appropriate corrective action or intervening events have remedied or mooted the problems raised by the complaint pursuant to Rule 11(d) or (e). Although the subject judge may ostensibly be vindicated by the dismissal or conclusion of a complaint, a chief judge's order may include language disagreeable to the subject judge. For example, an order may dismiss a complaint, but state that the subject judge did in fact engage in misconduct. Accordingly, a subject judge may wish to object to the content of the order and is given the opportunity to petition the judicial council of the circuit for review.

Subsection (b) contains a time limit of thirty-five days to file a petition for review. It is important to establish a time limit on petitions for review of chief judges' dispositions in order to provide finality to the process. If the complaint requires an investigation, the investigation should proceed; if it does not, the subject judge should know that the matter is closed.

The standards for timely filing under the Federal Rules of Appellate Procedure should be applied to petitions for review. See Fed. R. App. P. 25(a)(2)(A) and (C).

Rule 18(e) provides for an automatic extension of the time limit imposed under subsection (b) if a person files a petition that is rejected for failure to comply with formal requirements.

Rule 19. Judicial–Council Disposition of Petitions for Review

(a) Rights of Subject Judge. At any time after a complainant files a petition for review, the subject judge may file a written response with the circuit clerk. The clerk must promptly distribute copies of the response to each member of the judicial council or of the relevant panel, unless that member is disqualified under Rule 25. Copies must also be distributed to the chief judge, to the complainant, and to the Judicial Conference Committee on Judicial Conduct and Disability. The subject judge must not otherwise communicate with individual council members about the matter. The subject judge must be given copies of any communications to the judicial council from the complainant.

(b) Judicial–Council Action. After considering a petition for review and the materials before it, a judicial council may:

(1) affirm the chief judge's disposition by denying the petition;

(2) return the matter to the chief judge with directions to conduct a further inquiry under Rule 11(b) or to identify a complaint under Rule 5;

(3) return the matter to the chief judge with directions to appoint a special committee under Rule 11(f); or

(4) in exceptional circumstances, take other appropriate action.

(c) Notice of Council Decision. Copies of the judicial council's order, together with any accompanying memorandum in support of the order or separate concurring or dissenting statements, must be given to the complainant, the subject judge, and the Judicial Conference Committee on Judicial Conduct and Disability.

(d) Memorandum of Council Decision. If the council's order affirms the chief judge's disposition, a supporting memorandum must be prepared only if the judicial council concludes that there is a need to supplement the chief judge's explanation. A memorandum supporting a council order must not include the name of the complainant or the subject judge.

(e) Review of Judicial–Council Decision. If the judicial council's decision is adverse to the petitioner, and if no member of the council dissented on the ground that a special committee should be appointed under Rule 11(f), the complainant must be notified that he or she has no right to seek review of the decision. If there was a dissent, the petitioner must be informed that he or she can file a petition for review under Rule 21(b) solely on the issue of whether a special committee should be appointed.

(f) Public Availability of Judicial–Council Decision. Materials related to the council's decision must be made public to the extent, at the time, and in the manner set forth in Rule 24.

(Adopted Mar. 11, 2008, eff. Apr. 10, 2008.)

Commentary on Rule 19

This Rule is largely adapted from the Act and is self-explanatory.

The council should ordinarily review the decision of the chief judge on the merits, treating the petition for review for all practical purposes as an appeal. The judicial council may respond to a petition by affirming the chief judge's order, remanding the matter, or, in exceptional cases, taking other appropriate action.

Rule 20. Judicial–Council Consideration of Reports and Recommendations of Special Committees

(a) Rights of Subject Judge. Within 21 days after the filing of the report of a special committee, the subject judge may send a written response to the members of the judicial council. The judge must also be given an opportunity to present argument through counsel, written or oral, as determined by the council. The judge must not otherwise communicate with council members about the matter.

(b) Judicial–Council Action.

(1) Discretionary actions. Subject to the judge's rights set forth in subsection (a), the judicial council may:

(A) dismiss the complaint because:

(i) even if the claim is true, the claimed conduct is not conduct prejudicial to the effective and expeditious administration of the business of the courts and does not indicate a mental or physical disability resulting in inability to discharge the duties of office;

(ii) the complaint is directly related to the merits of a decision or procedural ruling;

(iii) the facts on which the complaint is based have not been established; or

(iv) the complaint is otherwise not appropriate for consideration under 28 U.S.C. §§ 351–364.

(B) conclude the proceeding because appropriate corrective action has been taken or intervening events have made the proceeding unnecessary.

(C) refer the complaint to the Judicial Conference of the United States with the council's recommendations for action.

(D) take remedial action to ensure the effective and expeditious administration of the business of the courts, including:

(i) censuring or reprimanding the subject judge, either by private communication or by public announcement;

(ii) ordering that no new cases be assigned to the subject judge for a limited, fixed period;

(iii) in the case of a magistrate judge, ordering the chief judge of the district court to take action specified by the council, including the initiation of removal proceedings under 28 U.S.C. § 631(i) or 42 U.S.C. § 300aa–12(c)(2);

(iv) in the case of a bankruptcy judge, removing the judge from office under 28 U.S.C. § 152(e);

(v) in the case of a circuit or district judge, requesting the judge to retire voluntarily with the provision (if necessary) that ordinary length-of-service requirements will be waived; and

(vi) in the case of a circuit or district judge who is eligible to retire but does not do so, certifying the disability of the judge under 28 U.S.C. § 372(b) so that an additional judge may be appointed.

(E) take any combination of actions described in (b)(1)(A)–(D) of this Rule that is within its power.

(2) Mandatory actions. A judicial council must refer a complaint to the Judicial Conference if the council determines that a circuit judge or district judge may have engaged in conduct that:

(A) might constitute ground for impeachment; or

(B) in the interest of justice, is not amenable to resolution by the judicial council.

(c) Inadequate Basis for Decision. If the judicial council finds that a special committee's report, recommendations, and record provide an inadequate basis for decision, it may return the matter to the committee for further investigation and a new report, or it may conduct further investigation. If the judicial council decides to conduct further investigation, the subject judge must be given adequate prior notice in writing of that decision and of the general scope and purpose of the additional investigation. The judicial council's conduct of the additional investigation must generally accord with the procedures and powers set forth in Rules 13 through 16 for the conduct of an investigation by a special committee.

(d) Council Vote. Council action must be taken by a majority of those members of the council who are not disqualified. A decision to remove a bankruptcy judge from office requires a majority vote of all the members of the council.

(e) Recommendation for Fee Reimbursement. If the complaint has been finally dismissed or concluded under (b)(1)(A) or (B) of this Rule, and if the subject judge so requests, the judicial council may recommend that the Director of the Administrative Office of the United States Courts use funds appropriated to the Judiciary to reimburse the judge for reasonable expenses incurred during the investigation, when those expenses would not have been incurred but for the requirements of the Act and these Rules. Reasonable expenses include attorneys' fees and expenses related to a successful defense or prosecution of a proceeding under Rule 21(a) or (b).

(f) Council Action. Council action must be by written order. Unless the council finds that extraordinary reasons would make it contrary to the interests of justice, the order must be accompanied by a memorandum setting forth the factual determinations on which it is based and the reasons for the council action. The order and the supporting memorandum must be provided to the complainant, the subject judge, and the Judicial Conference Committee on Judicial Conduct and Disability. The complainant and the subject judge must be notified of any right to review of the judicial council's decision as provided in Rule 21(b).

(Adopted Mar. 11, 2008, eff. Apr. 10, 2008.)

Commentary on Rule 20

This Rule is largely adapted from the Illustrative Rules.

Rule 20(a) provides that within twenty-one days after the filing of the report of a special committee, the subject judge may address a written response to all of the members of the judicial council. The subject judge must also be given an opportunity to present oral argument to the council, personally or through counsel. The subject judge may not otherwise communicate with council members about the matter.

Rule 20(c) provides that if the judicial council decides to conduct an additional investigation, the subject judge must be given adequate prior notice in writing of that decision and of the general scope and purpose of the additional investigation. The conduct of the investigation will be generally in accordance with the procedures set forth in Rules 13 through 16 for the conduct of an investigation by a special committee. However, if hearings are held, the council may limit testimony or the presentation of evidence to avoid unnecessary repetition of testimony and evidence before the special committee.

Rule 20(d) provides that council action must be taken by a majority of those members of the council who are not disqualified, except that a decision to remove a bankruptcy judge from office requires a majority of all the members of the council as required by 28 U.S.C. § 152(e). However, it is inappropriate to apply a similar rule to the less severe actions that a judicial council may take under the Act. If some members of the council are disqualified in the matter, their disqualification should not be given the effect of a vote against council action.

With regard to Rule 20(e), the judicial council, on the request of the subject judge, may recommend to the Director of the Administrative Office of the United States Courts that the subject judge be reimbursed for reasonable expenses, including attorneys' fees, incurred. The judicial council has the authority to recommend such reimbursement where, after investigation by a special committee, the complaint has been finally dismissed or concluded under subsection (b)(1)(A) or (B) of this Rule. It is contemplated that such reimbursement may be provided for the successful prosecution or defense of a proceeding under Rule 21(a) or (b), in other words, one that results in a Rule 20(b)(1)(A) or (B) dismissal or conclusion.

Rule 20(f) requires that council action normally be supported with a memorandum of factual determinations and reasons and that notice of the action be given to the complainant and the subject judge. Rule 20(f) also requires that the notification to the complainant and the subject judge include notice of any right to petition for review of the council's decision under Rule 21(b).

ARTICLE VI. REVIEW BY JUDICIAL CONFERENCE COMMITTEE ON CONDUCT AND DISABILITY

Rule 21. Committee on Judicial Conduct and Disability

(a) Review by Committee. The Committee on Judicial Conduct and Disability, consisting of seven members, considers and disposes of all petitions for review under (b) of this Rule, in conformity with the Committee's jurisdictional statement. Its disposition of petitions for review is ordinarily final. The Judicial Conference of the United States may, in its sole discretion, review any such Committee decision, but a complainant or subject judge does not have a right to this review.

(b) Reviewable Matters.

(1) **Upon petition.** A complainant or subject judge may petition the Committee for review of a judicial-council order entered in accordance with:

(A) Rule 20(b)(1)(A), (B), (D), or (E); or

(B) Rule 19(b)(1) or (4) if one or more members of the judicial council dissented from the order on the ground that a special committee should be appointed under Rule 11(f); in that event, the Committee's review will be limited to the issue of whether a special committee should be appointed.

(2) **Upon Committee's initiative.** At its initiative and in its sole discretion, the Committee may review any judicial-council order entered under Rule 19(b)(1) or (4), but only to determine whether a special committee should be appointed. Before undertaking the review, the Committee must invite that judicial council to explain why it believes the appointment of a special committee is unnecessary,

unless the reasons are clearly stated in the judicial council's order denying the petition for review. If the Committee believes that it would benefit from a submission by the subject judge, it may issue an appropriate request. If the Committee determines that a special committee should be appointed, the Committee must issue a written decision giving its reasons.

(c) Committee Vote. Any member of the Committee from the same circuit as the subject judge is disqualified from considering or voting on a petition for review. Committee decisions under (b) of this Rule must be by majority vote of the qualified Committee members. If only six members are qualified to vote on a petition for review, the decision must be made by a majority of a panel of five members drawn from a randomly selected list that rotates after each decision by a panel drawn from the list. The members who will determine the petition must be selected based on committee membership as of the date on which the petition is received. Those members selected to hear the petition should serve in that capacity until final disposition of the petition, whether or not their term of committee membership has ended. If only four members are qualified to vote, the Chief Justice must appoint, if available, an ex-member of the Committee or, if not, another United States judge to consider the petition.

(d) Additional Investigation. Except in extraordinary circumstances, the Committee will not conduct an additional investigation. The Committee may return the matter to the judicial council with directions to undertake an additional investigation. If the Committee conducts an additional investigation, it will exercise the powers of the Judicial Conference under 28 U.S.C. § 331.

(e) Oral Argument; Personal Appearance. There is ordinarily no oral argument or personal appearance before the Committee. In its discretion, the Committee may permit written submissions from the complainant or subject judge.

(f) Committee Decisions. Committee decisions under this Rule must be transmitted promptly to the Judicial Conference of the United States. Other distribution will be by the Administrative Office at the direction of the Committee chair.

(g) Finality. All orders of the Judicial Conference or of the Committee (when the Conference does not exercise its power of review) are final.

(Adopted Mar. 11, 2008, eff. Apr. 10, 2008.)

Commentary on Rule 21

This Rule is largely self-explanatory.

Rule 21(a) is intended to clarify that the delegation of power to the Judicial Conference Committee on Judicial Conduct and Disability to dispose of petitions does not preclude review of such dispositions by the Conference. However, there is no right to such review in any party.

Rules 21(b)(1)(B) and (b)(2) are intended to fill a jurisdictional gap as to review of dismissals or conclusions of complaints under Rule 19(b)(1) or (4). Where one or more members of a judicial council reviewing a petition have dissented on the ground that a special committee should have been appointed, the complainant or subject judge has the right to petition for review by the Committee but only as to that issue. Under Rule 21(b)(2), the Judicial Conference Committee on Judicial Conduct and Disability may review such a dismissal or conclusion in its sole discretion, whether or not such a dissent occurred, and only as to the appointment of a special committee. No party has a right to such review, and such review will be rare.

Rule 21(c) provides for review only by Committee members from circuits other than that of the subject judge. To avoid tie votes, the Committee will decide petitions for review by rotating panels of five when only six members are qualified. If only four members are qualified, the Chief Justice must appoint an additional judge to consider that petition for review.

Under this Rule, all Committee decisions are final in that they are unreviewable unless the Judicial Conference, in its discretion, decides to review a decision. Committee decisions, however, do not necessarily constitute final action on a complaint for purposes of Rule 24.

Rule 22. Procedures for Review

(a) Filing a Petition for Review. A petition for review of a judicial-council decision may be filed by sending a brief written statement to the Judicial Conference Committee on Judicial Conduct and Disability, addressed to:

> Judicial Conference Committee on Judicial Conduct and Disability
> Attn: Office of General Counsel
> Administrative Office of the United States Courts
> One Columbus Circle, NE
> Washington, D.C. 20544

The Administrative Office will send a copy of the petition to the complainant or subject judge, as the case may be.

(b) Form and Contents of Petition for Review. No particular form is required. The petition must contain a short statement of the basic facts underlying the complaint, the history of its consideration before the appropriate judicial council, a copy of the judicial council's decision, and the grounds on which the petitioner seeks review. The petition for review must specify the date and docket number of the judicial-council order for which review is sought. The petitioner may attach any documents or correspondence arising in the course of the proceeding before the judicial council or its special committee. A petition should not normally exceed 20 pages plus necessary attachments.

(c) Time. A petition must be submitted within 63 days of the date of the order for which review is sought.

(d) Copies. Seven copies of the petition for review must be submitted, at least one of which must be signed by the petitioner or his or her attorney. If the petitioner submits a signed declaration of inability to pay the expense of duplicating the petition, the Administrative Office must accept the original petition and must reproduce copies at its expense.

(e) Action on Receipt of Petition for Review. The Administrative Office must acknowledge receipt of a petition for review submitted under this Rule, notify the chair of the Judicial Conference Committee on Judicial Conduct and Disability, and distribute the petition to the members of the Committee for their deliberation.

(Adopted Mar. 11, 2008, eff. Apr. 10, 2008.)

Commentary on Rule 22

Rule 22 is self-explanatory.

ARTICLE VII. MISCELLANEOUS RULES

Rule 23. Confidentiality

(a) General Rule. The consideration of a complaint by the chief judge, a special committee, the judicial council, or the Judicial Conference Committee on Judicial Conduct and Disability is confidential. Information about this consideration must not be disclosed by any judge or employee of the judicial branch or by any person who records or transcribes testimony except as allowed by these Rules. In extraordinary circumstances, a chief judge may disclose the existence of a proceeding under these Rules when necessary to maintain public confidence in the federal judiciary's ability to redress misconduct or disability.

(b) Files. All files related to complaints must be separately maintained with appropriate security precautions to ensure confidentiality.

(c) Disclosure in Decisions. Except as otherwise provided in Rule 24, written decisions of the chief judge, the judicial council, or the Judicial Conference Committee on Judicial Conduct and Disability, and dissenting opinions or separate statements of members of the council or Committee may contain information and exhibits that the authors consider appropriate for inclusion, and the information and exhibits may be made public.

(d) Availability to Judicial Conference. On request of the Judicial Conference or its Committee on Judicial Conduct and Disability, the circuit clerk must furnish any requested records related to a complaint. For auditing purposes, the circuit clerk must provide access to the Committee to records of proceedings under the Act at the site where the records are kept.

(e) Availability to District Court. If the judicial council directs the initiation of proceedings for removal of a magistrate judge under Rule 20(b)(1)(D)(iii), the circuit clerk must provide to the chief judge of the district court copies of the report of the special committee and any other documents and records that were before the judicial council at the time of its decision. On request of the chief judge of the district court, the judicial council may authorize release to that chief judge of any other records relating to the investigation.

(f) Impeachment Proceedings. If the Judicial Conference determines that consideration of impeachment may be warranted, it must transmit the record of all relevant proceedings to the Speaker of the House of Representatives.

(g) Subject Judge's Consent. If both the subject judge and the chief judge consent in writing, any materials from the files may be disclosed to any person. In any such disclosure, the chief judge may require that the identity of the complainant, or of witnesses in an investigation conducted by a chief judge, a special committee, or the judicial council, not be revealed.

(h) Disclosure in Special Circumstances. The Judicial Conference, its Committee on Judicial Conduct and Disability, or a judicial council may authorize disclosure of information about the consideration of a complaint, including the papers, documents, and transcripts relating to the investigation, to the extent that disclosure is justified by special circumstances and is not prohibited by the Act. Disclosure may be made to judicial researchers engaged in the study or evaluation of experience under the Act and related modes of judicial discipline, but only where the study or evaluation has been specifically approved by the Judicial Conference or by the Judicial Conference Committee on Judicial Conduct and Disability. Appropriate steps must be taken to protect the identities of the subject judge, the complainant, and witnesses from public disclosure. Other appropriate safeguards to protect against the dissemination of confidential information may be imposed.

(i) Disclosure of Identity by Subject Judge. Nothing in this Rule precludes the subject judge from acknowledging that he or she is the judge referred to in documents made public under Rule 24.

(j) Assistance and Consultation. Nothing in this Rule precludes the chief judge or judicial council acting on a complaint filed under the Act from seeking the help of qualified staff or from consulting other judges who may be helpful in the disposition of the complaint.

(Adopted Mar. 11, 2008, eff. Apr. 10, 2008.)

Commentary on Rule 23

Rule 23 was adapted from the Illustrative Rules.

The Act applies a rule of confidentiality to "papers, documents, and records of proceedings related to investigations conducted under this chapter" and states that they may not be disclosed "by any person in any proceeding," with enumerated exceptions. 28 U.S.C. § 360(a). Three questions arise: Who is bound by the confidentiality rule, what proceedings are subject to the rule, and who is within the circle of people who may have access to information without breaching the rule?

With regard to the first question, Rule 23(a) provides that judges, employees of the judicial branch, and those persons involved in recording proceedings and preparing transcripts are obliged to respect the confidentiality requirement. This of course includes subject judges who do not consent to identification under Rule 23(i).

With regard to the second question, Rule 23(a) applies the rule of confidentiality broadly to consideration of a complaint at any stage.

With regard to the third question, there is no barrier of confidentiality among a chief judge, judicial council, the Judicial Conference, and the Judicial Conference Committee on Judicial Conduct and Disability. Each may have access to any of the confidential records for use in their consideration of a referred matter, a petition for review, or monitoring the administration of the Act. A district court may have similar access if the judicial council orders the district court to initiate proceedings to remove a magistrate judge from office, and Rule 23(e) so provides.

In extraordinary circumstances, a chief judge may disclose the existence of a proceeding under these Rules. The disclosure of such information in high-visibility or controversial cases is to reassure the public that the federal judiciary is capable of redressing judicial misconduct or disability. Moreover, the confidentiality requirement does not prevent the chief judge from "communicat[ing] orally or in writing with . . . [persons] who may have knowledge of the matter," as part of a limited inquiry conducted by the chief judge under Rule 11(b).

Rule 23 recognizes that there must be some exceptions to the Act's confidentiality requirement. For example, the Act requires that certain orders and the reasons for them must be made public. 28 U.S.C. § 360(b). Rule 23(c) makes it explicit that memoranda supporting chief judge and council orders, as well as dissenting opinions and separate statements, may contain references to information that would otherwise be confidential and that such information may be made public. However, subsection (c) is subject to Rule 24(a) which provides the general rule regarding the public availability of decisions. For example, the name of a subject judge cannot be made public in a decision if disclosure of the name is prohibited by that Rule.

The Act makes clear that there is a barrier of confidentiality between the judicial branch and the legislative. It provides that material may be disclosed to Congress only if it is believed necessary to an impeachment investigation or trial of a judge. 28 U.S.C. § 360(a)(2). Accordingly, Section 355(b) of the Act requires the Judicial Conference to transmit the record of the proceeding to the House of Representatives if the Conference believes that impeachment of a subject judge may be appropriate. Rule 23(f) implements this requirement.

The Act provides that confidential materials may be disclosed if authorized in writing by the subject judge and by the chief judge. 28 U.S.C. § 360(a)(3). Rule 23(g) implements this requirement. Once the subject judge has consented to the disclosure of confidential materials related to a complaint, the chief judge ordinarily will refuse consent only to the extent necessary to protect the confidentiality interests of the complainant or of witnesses who have testified in investigatory proceedings or who have provided information in response to a limited inquiry undertaken pursuant to Rule 11. It will generally be necessary, therefore, for the chief judge to require that the identities of the complainant or of such witnesses, as well as any identifying information, be shielded in any materials disclosed, except insofar as the chief judge has secured the consent of the complainant or of a particular witness to disclosure, or there is a demonstrated need for disclosure of the information that, in the judgment of the chief judge, outweighs the confidentiality interest of the complainant or of a particular witness (as may be the case where the complainant is delusional or where the complainant or a particular witness has already demonstrated a lack of concern about maintaining the confidentiality of the proceedings).

Rule 23(h) permits disclosure of additional information in circumstances not enumerated. For example, disclosure may be appropriate to permit a prosecution for perjury based on testimony given before a special committee. Another example might involve evidence of criminal conduct by a judge discovered by a special committee.

Subsection (h) also permits the authorization of disclosure of information about the consideration of a complaint, including the papers, documents, and transcripts relating to the investigation, to judicial researchers engaged in the study or evaluation of experience under the Act and related modes of judicial discipline. The Rule envisions disclosure of information from the official record of complaint proceedings to a limited category of persons for appropriately authorized research purposes only, and with appropriate safeguards to protect individual identities in any published research results that ensue. In authorizing disclosure, the judicial council may refuse to release particular materials when such release would be contrary to the interests of justice, or that constitute purely internal communications. The Rule does not envision disclosure of purely internal communications between judges and their colleagues and staff.

Under Rule 23(j), chief judges and judicial councils may seek staff assistance or consult with other judges who may be helpful in the process of complaint disposition; the confidentiality requirement does not preclude this. The chief judge, for example, may properly seek the advice and assistance of another judge who the chief judge deems to be in the best position to communicate with the subject judge in an attempt to bring about corrective action. As another example, a new chief judge may wish to confer with a predecessor to learn how similar complaints have been handled. In consulting with other judges, of course, the chief judge should disclose information regarding the complaint only to the extent the chief judge deems necessary under the circumstances.

Rule 24. Public Availability of Decisions

(a) General Rule; Specific Cases. When final action has been taken on a complaint and it is no longer subject to review, all orders entered by the chief judge and judicial council, including any supporting memoranda and any dissenting opinions or separate statements by members of the judicial council, must be made public, with the following exceptions:

(1) if the complaint is finally dismissed under Rule 11(c) without the appointment of a special committee, or if it is concluded under Rule 11(d) because of voluntary corrective action, the publicly available materials must not disclose the name of the subject judge without his or her consent.

(2) if the complaint is concluded because of intervening events, or dismissed at any time after a special committee is appointed, the judicial council must determine whether the name of the subject judge should be disclosed.

(3) if the complaint is finally disposed of by a privately communicated censure or reprimand, the publicly available materials must not disclose either the name of the subject judge or the text of the reprimand.

(4) if the complaint is finally disposed of under Rule 20(b)(1)(D) by any action other than private censure or reprimand, the text of the dispositive order must be included in the materials made public, and the name of the subject judge must be disclosed.

(5) the name of the complainant must not be disclosed in materials made public under this Rule unless the chief judge orders disclosure.

(b) Manner of Making Public. The orders described in (a) must be made public by placing them in a publicly accessible file in the office of the circuit clerk or by placing the orders on the court's public website. If the orders appear to have precedential value, the chief judge may cause them to be published. In addition, the Judicial Conference Committee on Judicial Conduct and Disability will make available on the Federal Judiciary's website, www.uscourts.gov, selected illustrative orders described in paragraph (a), appropriately redacted, to provide additional information to the public on how complaints are addressed under the Act.

(c) Orders of Judicial Conference Committee. Orders of this Committee constituting final action in a complaint proceeding arising from a particular circuit will be made available to the public in the office of the clerk of the relevant court of appeals. The Committee will also make such orders available on the Federal Judiciary's website, www.uscourts.gov. When authorized by the Committee, other orders related to complaint proceedings will similarly be made available.

(d) Complaints Referred to the Judicial Conference of the United States. If a complaint is referred to the Judicial Conference under Rule 20(b)(1)(C) or 20(b)(2), materials relating to the complaint will be made public only if ordered by the Judicial Conference.

(Adopted Mar. 11, 2008, eff. Apr. 10, 2008.)

Commentary on Rule 24

Rule 24 is adapted from the Illustrative Rules and the recommendations of the Breyer Committee.

The Act requires the circuits to make available only written orders of a judicial council or the Judicial Conference imposing some form of sanction. 28 U.S.C. § 360(b). The Judicial Conference, however, has long recognized the desirability of public availability of a broader range of orders and other materials. In 1994, the Judicial Conference "urge[d] all circuits and courts covered by the Act to submit to the West Publishing Company, for publication in Federal Reporter 3d, and to Lexis all orders issued pursuant to [the Act] that are deemed by the issuing circuit or court to have significant precedential value to other circuits and courts covered by the Act." Report of the Proceedings of the Judicial Conference of the United States, Mar. 1994, at 28. Following this recommendation, the 2000 revision of the Illustrative Rules contained a public availability provision very similar to Rule 24. In 2002, the Judicial Conference again voted to encourage the circuits "to submit non-routine public orders disposing of complaints of judicial misconduct or disability for publication by on-line and print services." Report of the Proceedings of the Judicial Conference of the United States, Sept. 2002, at 58. The Breyer Committee Report further emphasized that "[p]osting such orders on the judicial branch's public website would not only benefit judges directly, it would also encourage scholarly commentary and analysis of the orders." Breyer Committee Report, 239 F.R.D. at 216. With these considerations in mind, Rule 24 provides for public availability of a wide range of materials.

Rule 24 provides for public availability of orders of the chief judge, the judicial council, and the Judicial Conference Committee on Judicial Conduct and Disability and the texts of any memoranda supporting their orders, together with any dissenting opinions or separate statements by members of the judicial council. However, these orders and memoranda are to be made public only when final action on the complaint has been taken and any right of review has been exhausted. The provision that decisions will be made public only after final action has been taken is designed in part to avoid public disclosure of the existence of pending proceedings. Whether the name of the subject judge is disclosed will then depend on the nature of the final action. If the final action is an order predicated on a finding of misconduct or disability (other than a privately communicated censure or reprimand) the name of the judge must be made public. If the final action is dismissal of the complaint, the name of the subject judge must not be disclosed. Rule 24(a)(1) provides that where a proceeding is concluded under Rule 11(d) by the chief judge on the basis of voluntary corrective action, the name of the subject judge must not be disclosed. Shielding the name of the subject judge in this circumstance should encourage informal disposition.

If a complaint is dismissed as moot, or because intervening events have made action on the complaint unnecessary, after appointment of a special committee, Rule 24(a)(2) allows the judicial council to determine whether the subject judge will be identified. In such a case, no final decision has been rendered on the merits, but it may be in the public interest— particularly if a judicial officer resigns in the course of an investigation—to make the identity of the judge known.

Once a special committee has been appointed, and a proceeding is concluded by the full council on the basis of a remedial order of the council, Rule 24(a)(4) provides for disclosure of the name of the subject judge.

Finally, Rule 24(a)(5) provides that the identity of the complainant will be disclosed only if the chief judge so orders. Identifying the complainant when the subject judge is not identified would increase the likelihood that the identity of the subject judge would become publicly known, thus circumventing the policy of nondisclosure. It may not always be practicable to shield the complainant's identity while making public disclosure of the judicial council's order and supporting memoranda; in some circumstances, moreover, the complainant may consent to public identification.

Rule 25.   Disqualification

(a) General Rule. Any judge is disqualified from participating in any proceeding under these Rules if the judge, in his or her discretion, concludes that circumstances warrant disqualification. If the complaint is filed by a judge, that judge is disqualified from participating in any consideration of the complaint except to the extent that these Rules provide for a complainant's participation. A chief judge who has identified a complaint under Rule 5 is not automatically disqualified from considering the complaint.

(b) Subject Judge. A subject judge is disqualified from considering the complaint except to the extent that these Rules provide for participation by a subject judge.

(c) Chief Judge Not Disqualified from Considering a Petition for Review of a Chief Judge's Order. If a petition for review of a chief judge's order entered under Rule 11(c), (d), or (e) is filed with the judicial council in accordance with Rule 18, the chief judge is not disqualified from participating in the council's consideration of the petition.

(d) Member of Special Committee Not Disqualified. A member of the judicial council who serves on a special committee, including the chief judge, is not disqualified from participating in council consideration of the committee's report.

(e) Subject Judge's Disqualification After Appointment of a Special Committee. Upon appointment of a special committee, the subject judge is automatically disqualified from participating in any proceeding arising under the Act or these Rules as a member of any special committee, the judicial council of the circuit, the Judicial Conference of the United States, and the Judicial Conference Committee on Judicial Conduct and Disability. The disqualification continues until all proceedings on the complaint against the subject judge are finally terminated with no further right of review.

(f) Substitute for Disqualified Chief Judge. If the chief judge is disqualified from participating in consideration of the complaint, the duties and responsibilities of the chief judge under these Rules must be assigned to the most-senior active circuit judge not disqualified. If all circuit judges in regular active service are disqualified, the judicial council may determine whether to request a transfer under Rule 26, or, in the interest of sound judicial administration, to permit the chief judge to dispose of the complaint on the merits. Members of the judicial council who are named in the complaint may participate in this determination if necessary to obtain a quorum of the judicial council.

(g) Judicial–Council Action When Multiple Judges Are Disqualified. Notwithstanding any other provision in these Rules to the contrary,

(1) a member of the judicial council who is a subject judge may participate in its disposition if:

(A) participation by one or more subject judges is necessary to obtain a quorum of the judicial council;

(B) the judicial council finds that the lack of a quorum is due to the naming of one or more judges in the complaint for the purpose of disqualifying that judge or judges, or to the naming of one or more judges based on their participation in a decision excluded from the definition of misconduct under Rule 3(h)(3); and

(C) the judicial council votes that it is necessary, appropriate, and in the interest of sound judicial administration that one or more subject judges be eligible to act.

(2) otherwise disqualified members may participate in votes taken under (g)(1)(B) and (g)(1)(C).

(h) Disqualification of Members of the Judicial Conference Committee. No member of the Judicial Conference Committee on Judicial Conduct and Disability is disqualified from participating in any proceeding under the Act or these Rules because of consultations with a chief judge, a member of a special committee, or a member of a judicial council about the interpretation or application of the Act or these Rules, unless the member believes that the consultation would prevent fair-minded participation.

(Adopted Mar. 11, 2008, eff. Apr. 10, 2008.)

Commentary on Rule 25

Rule 25 is adapted from the Illustrative Rules.

Subsection (a) provides the general rule for disqualification. Of course, a judge is not disqualified simply because the subject judge is on the same court. However, this subsection recognizes that there may be cases in which an appearance of bias or prejudice is created by circumstances other than an association with the subject judge as a colleague. For example, a judge may have a familial relationship with a complainant or subject judge. When such circumstances exist, a judge may, in his or her discretion, conclude that disqualification is warranted.

Subsection (e) makes it clear that the disqualification of the subject judge relates only to the subject judge's participation in any proceeding arising under the Act or these

Rules as a member of a special committee, judicial council, Judicial Conference, or the Judicial Conference Committee. The Illustrative Rule, based on Section 359(a) of the Act, is ambiguous and could be read to disqualify a subject judge from service of any kind on each of the bodies mentioned. This is undoubtedly not the intent of the Act; such a disqualification would be anomalous in light of the Act's allowing a subject judge to continue to decide cases and to continue to exercise the powers of chief circuit or district judge. It would also create a substantial deterrence to the appointment of special committees, particularly where a special committee is needed solely because the chief judge may not decide matters of credibility in his or her review under Rule 11.

While a subject judge is barred by Rule 25(b) from participating in the disposition of the complaint in which he or she is named, Rule 25(e) recognizes that participation in proceedings arising under the Act or these Rules by a judge who is the subject of a special committee investigation may lead to an appearance of self-interest in creating substantive and procedural precedents governing such proceedings; Rule 25(e) bars such participation.

Under the Act, a complaint against the chief judge is to be handled by "that circuit judge in regular active service next senior in date of commission." 28 U.S.C. § 351(c). Rule 25(f) provides that seniority among judges other than the chief judge is to be determined by date of commission, with the result that complaints against the chief judge may be routed to a former chief judge or other judge who was appointed earlier than the chief judge. The Rules do not purport to prescribe who is to preside over meetings of the judicial council. Consequently, where the presiding member of the judicial council is disqualified from participating under these Rules, the order of precedence prescribed by Rule 25(f) for performing "the duties and responsibilities of the chief circuit judge under these Rules" does not apply to determine the acting presiding member of the judicial council. That is a matter left to the internal rules or operating practices of each judicial council. In most cases the most senior active circuit judge who is a member of the judicial council and who is not disqualified will preside.

Sometimes a single complaint is filed against a large group of judges. If the normal disqualification rules are observed in such a case, no court of appeals judge can serve as acting chief judge of the circuit, and the judicial council will be without appellate members. Where the complaint is against all circuit and district judges, under normal rules no member of the judicial council can perform the duties assigned to the council under the statute.

A similar problem is created by successive complaints arising out of the same underlying grievance. For example, a complainant files a complaint against a district judge based on alleged misconduct, and the complaint is dismissed by the chief judge under the statute. The complainant may then file a complaint against the chief judge for dismissing the first complaint, and when that complaint is dismissed by the next senior judge, still a third complaint may be filed. The threat is that the complainant will bump down the seniority ladder until, once again, there is no member of the court of appeals who can serve as acting chief judge for the purpose of the next complaint. Similarly, complaints involving the merits of litigation may involve a series of decisions in which many judges participated or in which a rehearing en banc was denied by the court of appeals, and the complaint may name a majority of the judicial council as subject judges.

In recognition that these multiple-judge complaints are virtually always meritless, the judicial council is given discretion to determine: (1) whether it is necessary, appropriate, and in the interest of sound judicial administration to permit the chief judge to dispose of a complaint where it would otherwise be impossible for any active circuit judge in the circuit to act, and (2) whether it is necessary, appropriate, and in the interest of sound judicial administration, after appropriate findings as to need and justification are made, to permit subject judges of the judicial council to participate in the disposition of a petition for review where it would otherwise be impossible to obtain a quorum.

Applying a rule of necessity in these situations is consistent with the appearance of justice. *See, e.g., In re Complaint of Doe*, 2 F.3d 308 (8th Cir. Jud. Council 1993) (invoking the rule of necessity); *In re Complaint of Judicial Misconduct*, No. 91–80464 (9th Cir. Jud. Council 1992) (same). There is no unfairness in permitting the chief judge to dispose of a patently insubstantial complaint that names all active circuit judges in the circuit.

Similarly, there is no unfairness in permitting subject judges, in these circumstances, to participate in the review of a chief judge's dismissal of an insubstantial complaint. The remaining option is to assign the matter to another body. Among other alternatives, the council may request a transfer of the petition under Rule 26. Given the administrative inconvenience and delay involved in these alternatives, it is desirable to request a transfer only if the judicial council determines that the petition is substantial enough to warrant such action.

In the unlikely event that a quorum of the judicial council cannot be obtained to consider the report of a special committee, it would normally be necessary to request a transfer under Rule 26.

Rule 25(h) recognizes that the jurisdictional statement of the Judicial Conference Committee contemplates consultation between members of the Committee and judicial participants in proceedings under the Act and these Rules. Such consultation should not automatically preclude participation by a member in that proceeding.

Rule 26. Transfer to Another Judicial Council

In exceptional circumstances, a chief judge or a judicial council may ask the Chief Justice to transfer a proceeding based on a complaint identified under Rule 5 or filed under Rule 6 to the judicial council of another circuit. The request for a transfer may be made at any stage of the proceeding before a reference to the Judicial Conference under Rule 20(b)(1)(C) or 20(b)(2) or a petition for review is filed under Rule 22. Upon receiving such a request, the Chief Justice may refuse the request or select the transferee judicial council, which may then exercise the powers of a judicial council under these Rules.

(Adopted Mar. 11, 2008, eff. Apr. 10, 2008.)

Commentary on Rule 26

Rule 26 is new; it implements the Breyer Committee's recommended use of transfers. Breyer Committee Report, 239 F.R.D. at 214–15.

Rule 26 authorizes the transfer of a complaint proceeding to another judicial council selected by the Chief Justice. Such transfers may be appropriate, for example, in the case of a serious complaint where there are multiple disqualifications among the original council, where the issues are highly visible and a local disposition may weaken public confidence in the process, where internal tensions arising in the council as a result of the complaint render disposition by a less involved council appropriate, or where a complaint calls into question policies or governance of the home court of appeals. The power to effect a transfer is lodged in the Chief Justice to avoid disputes in a council over where to transfer a sensitive matter and to ensure that the transferee council accepts the matter.

Upon receipt of a transferred proceeding, the transferee council shall determine the proper stage at which to begin consideration of the complaint—for example, reference to the transferee chief judge, appointment of a special committee, etc.

Rule 27. Withdrawal of Complaints and Petitions for Review

(a) Complaint Pending Before Chief Judge. With the chief judge's consent, a complainant may withdraw a complaint that is before the chief judge for a decision under Rule 11. The withdrawal of a complaint will not prevent a chief judge from identifying or having to identify a complaint under Rule 5 based on the withdrawn complaint.

(b) Complaint Pending before Special Committee or Judicial Council. After a complaint has been referred to a special committee for investigation and before the committee files its report, the complainant may withdraw the complaint only with the consent of both the subject judge and either the special committee or the judicial council.

(c) Petition for Review. A petition for review addressed to a judicial council under Rule 18, or the Judicial Conference Committee on Judicial Conduct and Disability under Rule 22 may be withdrawn if no action on the petition has been taken.

(Adopted Mar. 11, 2008, eff. Apr. 10, 2008.)

Commentary on Rule 27

Rule 27 is adapted from the Illustrative Rules and treats the complaint proceeding, once begun, as a matter of public business rather than as the property of the complainant.

Accordingly, the chief judge or the judicial council remains responsible for addressing any complaint under the Act, even a complaint that has been formally withdrawn by the complainant.

Under subsection 27(a), a complaint pending before the chief judge may be withdrawn if the chief judge consents. Where the complaint clearly lacked merit, the chief judge may accordingly be saved the burden of preparing a formal order and supporting memorandum. However, the chief judge may, or be obligated under Rule 5, to identify a complaint based on allegations in a withdrawn complaint.

If the chief judge appoints a special committee, Rule 27(b) provides that the complaint may be withdrawn only with the consent of both the body before which it is pending (the special committee or the judicial council) and the subject judge. Once a complaint has reached the stage of appointment of a special committee, a resolution of the issues may be necessary to preserve public confidence. Moreover, the subject judge is given the right to insist that the matter be resolved on the merits, thereby eliminating any ambiguity that might remain if the proceeding were terminated by withdrawal of the complaint.

With regard to all petitions for review, Rule 27(c) grants the petitioner unrestricted authority to withdraw the petition. It is thought that the public's interest in the proceeding is adequately protected, because there will necessarily have been a decision by the chief judge and often by the judicial council as well in such a case.

Rule 28. Availability of Rules and Forms

These Rules and copies of the complaint form as provided in Rule 6(a) must be available without charge in the office of the clerk of each court of appeals, district court, bankruptcy court, or other federal court whose judges are subject to the Act. Each court must also make these Rules and the complaint form available on the court's website, or provide an Internet link to the Rules and complaint form that are available on the appropriate court of appeals' website.

(Adopted Mar. 11, 2008, eff. Apr. 10, 2008.)

Rule 29. Effective Date

These Rules will become effective 30 days after promulgation by the Judicial Conference of the United States.

(Adopted Mar. 11, 2008, eff. Apr. 10, 2008.)

APPENDIX

COMPLAINT FORM

Judicial Council of the _____ Circuit

COMPLAINT OF JUDICIAL MISCONDUCT OR DISABILITY

To begin the complaint process, complete this form and prepare the brief statement of facts described in item 5 (below). The RULES FOR JUDICIAL-CONDUCT AND JUDICIAL-DISABILITY PROCEEDINGS, adopted by the Judicial Conference of the United States, contain information on what to include in a complaint (Rule 6), where to file a complaint (Rule 7), and other important matters. The rules are available in federal court clerks' offices, on individual federal courts' Web sites, and on www.uscourts. gov.

Your complaint (this form and the statement of facts) should be typewritten and must be legible. For the number of copies to file, consult the local rules or clerk's office of the court in which your complaint is required to be filed. Enclose each copy of the complaint in an envelope marked "COMPLAINT OF MISCONDUCT" or "COMPLAINT OF DISABILITY" and submit it to the appropriate clerk of court. **Do not put the name of any judge on the envelope.**

1. Name of Complainant: _____
   Contact Address: _____
   _____

   Daytime telephone: (____) _____

2. Name(s) of Judge(s): _____
   Court: _____

3. Does this complaint concern the behavior of the judge(s) in a particular lawsuit or lawsuits?
         [ ] Yes   [ ] No
   If "yes," give the following information about each lawsuit:
   Court: _____
   Case Number: _____
   Docket number of any appeal to the ____ Circuit: _____
   Are (were) you a party or lawyer in the lawsuit?
   [ ] Party   [ ] Lawyer   [ ] Neither

   If you are (were) a party and have (had) a lawyer, give the lawyer's name, address, and telephone number:
   _____
   _____
   _____

4. Have you filed any lawsuits against the judge?
         [ ] Yes   [ ] No
   If "yes," give the following information about each such lawsuit:
   Court: _____
   Case Number: _____
   Present status of lawsuit: _____
   Name, address, and telephone number of your lawyer for the lawsuit against the judge:
   _____
   _____
   _____

   Court to which any appeal has been taken in the lawsuit against the judge:
   _____

   Docket number of the appeal: _____
   Present status of the appeal: _____

5. **Brief Statement of Facts.** Attach a brief statement of the specific facts on which the claim of judicial misconduct or disability is based. Include what happened, when and where it happened, and any information that would help an investigator check the facts. If the complaint alleges judicial disability, also include any additional facts that form the basis of that allegation.

6. **Declaration and signature:**

I declare under penalty of perjury that the statements made in this complaint are true and correct to the best of my knowledge.

(Signature)_____ (Date)_____

(Adopted Mar. 11, 2008, eff. Apr. 10, 2008.)

PART F. GUIDELINES OF THE COURT OF APPEALS FOR THE SECOND CIRCUIT CONCERNING CAMERAS IN THE COURTROOM

Pursuant to a resolution of the Judicial Conference of the United States adopted on March 12, 1996, authorizing each court of appeals to "decide for itself whether to permit the taking of photographs and radio and television coverage of appellate arguments, subject to any restrictions in statutes, national and local rules, and such guidelines as the Judicial Conference may adopt," the Court hereby adopts the following Guidelines:

1. Exercise of Local Option. From the date of these Guidelines until further order of this Court, proceedings of the Court conducted in open court may be covered by the media using a television camera, sound recording equipment, and a still camera (hereafter referred to as "camera coverage"), subject to these Guidelines.

2. Applicable Guidelines. Camera coverage must be conducted in conformity with applicable statutes, national rules, any guidelines that may be issued by the U.S. Judicial Conference, and these Guidelines of the Second Circuit Court of Appeals.

3. Eligible Proceedings. Camera coverage is allowed for all proceedings conducted in open court, except for criminal matters. *See* Fed.R.Crim.P. 53, 54(a). For purposes of these Guidelines, "criminal matters" include not only direct appeals of criminal convictions but also any appeal, motion, or petition challenging a ruling made in connection with a criminal case (such as bail motions or appeals from the dismissal of an indictment) and any appeal from a ruling concerning a post-conviction remedy (such as a habeas corpus petition). Camera coverage is not permitted for pro se matters, whether criminal or civil. On any day when camera coverage is to occur, the Clerk's Office will endeavor to schedule civil and non-pro se matters ahead of criminal and pro se matters. Camera coverage operators will remain seated, away from their equipment, and their equipment will be turned off, during criminal and pro se proceedings.

4. News Media Pooling. Camera coverage will be permitted by any person or entity regularly engaged in the gathering and dissemination of news (hereinafter "news media"). If coverage is sought by more than one person or entity, a pool system must be used (one for still photography and one for radio and television). It will be the responsibility of the news media to resolve any disputes among them as to which personnel will operate equipment in the courtroom. In the absence of an agreement, camera coverage will not be permitted for that day's proceedings. The television pictures, audio signals, and still photographs of court proceedings made by pool personnel must be made available to any news media requesting them upon payment of a reasonable fee to the employer of the pool personnel to share the costs of the pool personnel.

5. Educational Institutions. The Court may also authorize the coverage of court proceedings and access to pooled coverage by educational institutions.

6. Prior Notification Requirement. News media interested in camera coverage of any court proceeding must notify the Court's calendar clerk no later than noon two days preceding the day of the proceeding to be covered (*i.e.*, notification must be made by noon on Tuesday to cover a proceeding on Thursday, or by noon Friday for the following Monday). A calendar of the following week's cases is made public by the Court each Thursday. For good cause shown, relief from this notification requirement may be granted by the presiding judge of a panel.

7. Discretion of Panel. The panel assigned to hear oral argument will retain the authority, in its sole discretion, to prohibit camera coverage of any proceeding, and will normally exercise this authority upon the request of any member of the panel.

8. Technical Restrictions. Only two television cameras and one still camera will be permitted in the courtroom. The television cameras and the still camera must each be mounted on a tripod and remain at a fixed location along a side wall of the courtroom throughout the proceeding. The still camera must either be capable of silent operation (shutter and film advance) or be enclosed in a sound-muffling device (so-called "blimp"). No artificial lighting is permitted. An unobtrusive microphone may be mounted at the attorney's lectern and in front of each judge. A sound technician may be present in the courtroom with unobtrusive sound-mixing equipment. The Clerk's Office will designate a location for a device outside the courtroom to enable news media to obtain "feeds" of video and audio signals. All camera coverage equipment must be set up prior to the opening of a day's proceedings and may not be removed until after the conclusion of the day's proceedings. If done unobtrusively, film used by the still camera operator and film or tape used by the video camera operator may be removed from the courtroom at the conclusion of the oral argument of a particular case. Operators of camera coverage equipment in the courtroom will wear business attire.

When operational, the Court's video-conferencing equipment may be used for purposes of camera coverage.

9. Authority of Presiding Judge. The presiding judge of the panel may direct the cessation of camera coverage or the removal of camera coverage personnel from the courtroom in the event of noncompliance with these Guidelines.

10. Personnel to Contact. The calendar clerk is Chandella Gaillard (or an alternate designated in her absence). She can be reached at (212) 791–1067. [Adopted effective March 27, 1996.]

SELECTED ORDERS

ORDER. IN THE MATTER OF THE TERMINATION OF THE BANKRUPTCY APPELLATE PANEL SERVICE OF THE SECOND JUDICIAL CIRCUIT

Pursuant to 28 U.S.C. § 158(b)(1)(C) as amended by the Bankruptcy Reform Act of 1994, the Judicial Council of the Second Circuit has determined there are insufficient judicial resources available in the Second Circuit justifying the continuation of the Bankruptcy Appellate Panel Service in the Second Circuit; it is hereby

ORDERED that the Bankruptcy Appellate Panel Service of the Second Circuit is terminated and that appeals of final judgments, orders and decrees and of interlocutory orders and decrees of bankruptcy judges entered in cases and proceedings previously referred to the Bankruptcy Appellate Panel and its appointed judges shall henceforth be referred to and heard by the respective United States District Courts in the Second Circuit; and it is hereby

ORDERED that the Bankruptcy Appellate Panel Service of the Second Circuit and its authority to hear and determine appeals from judgments, orders and decrees entered by bankruptcy judges from districts within the Second Circuit shall be terminated effective Friday, June 30, 2000.

Dated: June 30, 2000.

SELECTED NOTICES

PRIVACY NOTICE

In compliance with the policy of the Judicial Conference of the United States, and the E–Government Act of 2002, and in order to promote electronic access to case files while also protecting personal privacy and other legitimate interests, parties shall refrain from including, or shall partially redact where inclusion is necessary, the following personal data identifiers from all pleadings filed with the court, including exhibits thereto, whether filed electronically or in paper, unless otherwise ordered by the Court.

a. Social Security Numbers. If an individual's Social Security number must be included in a pleading, only the last four digits of that number should be used.

b. Names of Minor Children. If the involvement of a minor child must be mentioned, only the initials of that child should be used.

c. Dates of Birth. If an individual's date of birth must be included in a pleading, only the year should be used.

d. Financial Account Numbers. If financial account numbers are relevant, only the last four digits of these numbers should be used.

In compliance with the E–Government Act of 2002, a party wishing to file a document containing the personal data identifiers listed above may

a. file an unredacted version of the document under seal, or

b. file a reference list under seal. The reference list shall contain the complete personal data identifier(s) and the redacted identifier(s) used in its(their) place in the filing. All references in the case to the redacted identifiers included in the reference list will be construed to refer to the corresponding complete personal data identifier. The reference list must be filed under seal, and may be amended as of right.

The unredacted version of the document or the reference list document shall be retained by the court as part of the record. The court may, however, still require the party to file a redacted copy for the public file.

The responsibility for redacting these personal identifiers rests solely with counsel and the parties. The Clerk will not review each pleading for compliance with this rule.

INDEX TO
THE SECOND CIRCUIT RULES

Administrative law and procedure, **C2R 15 et seq.**

Admissions, attorneys, **C2R 46**

Appointments, attorneys, indigent persons, **C2R App. Part A et seq.**

Attorneys, **C2R 46**
  Admissions, **C2R 46**
  Appointments, indigent persons, **C2R App. Part A et seq.**
  Certificates and certification, rules of court, familiarity, **C2R 46**
  Committees, admissions and grievances committee, **C2R 46**
  Conviction of crime, **C2R 46**
  Crimes and offenses, **C2R 4(b)**
    Appointments, **C2R App. Parts A, B**
    Conviction of crime, **C2R 46**
    Substitution, **C2R App. Part B**
  Discipline, **C2R 46**
  Fees,
    Delay, sanctions, **C2R 38**
    Equal Access to Justice Act, **C2R § 0.25**
  Forms, **C2R App. Parts A, B**
  Indigent persons, appointments, **C2R App. Part A et seq.**
  Law students, **C2R 46**
  Oral argument, numbers and numbering, **C2R 34**
  Revocation or suspension, **C2R 46**
  Substitution, crimes and offenses, **C2R App. Part B**
  Withdrawal, **C2R 4(b)**

Bias or prejudice, judges or justices, complaints, **C2R App. Part E Rule 1 et seq.**

Briefs, **C2R 28 et seq.**
  Appendix, **C2R 30 et seq.**
  Civil appeals management plan, **C2R App. Part C**
  Copies, **C2R 31**
  Crimes and offenses, **C2R App. Part B**
  Electronic filing, **C2R 25**
  Filing, time, **C2R 22**
  Forms, **C2R 32**

Calendars, nonargument calendar, **C2R § 0.29**

Cameras, **C2R App. Part F**

Capital punishment, **C2R § 0.28**

Certificates and certification,
  Attorneys, rules of court, familiarity, **C2R 46**
  Death penalty, **C2R § 0.28**
  Habeas corpus, **C2R 22**
  State law, **C2R § 0.27**

Civil appeals management plan, **C2R App. Part C**

Clerks of courts, **C2R § 0.16 et seq.**

Committees, attorneys, admissions and grievances committee, **C2R 46**

Complaints, judges or justices, **C2R App. Part E Rule 1 et seq.**

Conferences,
  Civil appeals management plan, **C2R App. Parts C, D**
  Judges or justices, **C2R § 0.22**

Confidential or privileged information, preargument conferences, civil appeals management plan, **C2R App. Part D**

Continuances, oral argument, **C2R 34**

Copies,
  Briefs, **C2R 31**
  Costs, **C2R 39**
  En banc, **C2R 35**
  Fees, **C2R § 0.17**
  Notice, mail and mailing, **C2R 3(d)**

Corrections, electronic filing, **C2R 25**

Costs, **C2R 39**

Crimes and offenses,
  Briefs, **C2R App. Part B**
  Correctional institutions, pro se, motions, **C2R 27**
  Death penalty, **C2R § 0.28**
  Dockets and docketing, **C2R App. Part B**
  Release, **C2R 9**
  Time, **C2R App. Part B**

Criminal Justice Act, attorneys, **C2R 4(b)**

Death penalty, **C2R § 0.28**

Delay, sanctions, **C2R 38**

Disability, judges or justices, complaints, **C2R App. Part E Rule 1 et seq.**

Disbarment, attorneys, **C2R 46**

Discipline, attorneys, **C2R 46**

Dockets and docketing,
  Civil appeals management plan, **C2R App. Part C**
  Crimes and offenses, **C2R App. Part B**
  Death penalty, **C2R § 0.28**
  Fees, **C2R § 0.17**

Electronic filing, **C2R 25**

Emergencies,
  Death penalty, motions, **C2R § 0.28**
  Motions, death penalty, **C2R § 0.28**

En banc, **C2R 35**

Entry, orders, **C2R § 0.18**

Equal Access to Justice Act, attorneys, fees, **C2R § 0.25**

Exhibits, **C2R 11**
  Indexes, **C2R 30**

Extraordinary writs, **C2R 21**
  Judges or justices, conferences, **C2R § 0.22**

Fees, **C2R § 0.17**

Filing,
  Briefs, time, **C2R 22**
  Electronic filing, **C2R 25**

Fines and penalties, death penalty, **C2R § 0.28**

Forms, **C2R Form A et seq.**
  Attorneys, crimes and offenses, **C2R App. Parts A, B**
  Briefs, **C2R 32**
  Motions, **C2R 27**

Good faith, preargument conferences, civil appeals management plan, **C2R App. Part D**

Grievances, preargument conferences, civil appeals management plan, **C2R App. Part D**

Guidelines, cameras, **C2R App. Part F**

Habeas corpus,
  Certificates and certification, **C2R 22**
  Death penalty, **C2R § 0.28**

Handicapped persons, judges or justices, complaints, **C2R App. Part E Rule 1 et seq.**

Incompetency, judges or justices, complaints, **C2R App. Part E Rule 1 et seq.**

Indexes, exhibits, **C2R 30**

Indigent persons, attorneys, appointments, **C2R App. Part A et seq.**

Inspection and inspectors, exhibits, **C2R 11**

Investigations, judges or justices, complaints, **C2R App. Part E Rule 1 et seq.**

Judges or justices,
    Complaints, **C2R App. Part E Rule 1 et seq.**
    Conferences, **C2R § 0.22**
    Death penalty, panels, **C2R § 0.28**
    Magistrate judges, **C2R § 0.26**

Law students, **C2R 46**

Libraries, **C2R § 0.21**

Magistrate judges, **C2R § 0.26**

Mail and mailing, notice, **C2R 3(d)**

Mandamus, **C2R 21**

Mandate, **C2R 41**

Motions, **C2R 27**
    Civil appeals management plan, **C2R App. Part C**
    Death penalty, emergencies, **C2R § 0.28**

Names, **C2R § 0.11**

National Labor Relations Board, orders of court, enforcement, **C2R 15**

Nonargument calendar, **C2R § 0.29**

Notice,
    Appendix, **C2R 30**
    Civil appeals management plan, **C2R App. Part C**
    Mail and mailing, **C2R 3(d)**
    Motions, **C2R 27**
    Television and radio, **C2R App. Part F**

Numbers and numbering,
    Attorneys, oral argument, **C2R 34**
    Briefs, copies, **C2R 31**

Opinions and decisions, **C2R § 0.20**
    En banc, copies, **C2R 35**

Oral argument, **C2R 34**

Orders of court,
    Entry, **C2R § 0.18**
    Summary orders, **C2R § 0.23**

Panels, death penalty, **C2R § 0.28**

Petitions, **C2R § 0.26**
    Death penalty, **C2R § 0.28**

Petitions—Cont'd
    Rehearing, **C2R 40**

Photographs and pictures, **C2R App. Part F**

Plans and specifications, **C2R App. Part A et seq.**

Preargument conferences, civil appeals management plan, **C2R App. Parts C, D**

Prejudice or bias, judges or justices, complaints, **C2R App. Part E Rule 1 et seq.**

Process, **C2R § 0.19**
    Petitions, **C2R § 0.26**

Prohibition, extraordinary writs, **C2R 21**

Quorum, **C2R § 0.14**

Records and recordation,
    Death penalty, **C2R § 0.28**
    Fees, **C2R § 0.17; C2R 39**

Rehearing,
    Death penalty, **C2R § 0.28**
    Petitions, **C2R 40**

Release, **C2R 9**

Revocation or suspension, attorneys, **C2R 46**

Sanctions,
    Civil appeals management plan, **C2R App. Part C**
    Delay, **C2R 38**

Schedules, civil appeals management plan, **C2R App. Parts C, D**

Sealing, **C2R § 0.12**

State law, questions of law or fact, certificates and certification, **C2R § 0.27**

Stay of proceedings, death penalty, motions, **C2R § 0.28**

Substitution, attorneys, crimes and offenses, **C2R App. Part B**

Summary orders, **C2R § 0.23**

Supersedeas or stay, death penalty, motions, **C2R § 0.28**

Tax Court, civil appeals management plan, **C2R App. Part C**

Television and radio, **C2R App. Part F**

Terms of court, **C2R § 0.13**

Time,
    Briefs, filing, **C2R 22**
    Crimes and offenses, **C2R App. Part B**
    Electronic filing, **C2R 25**
    Exhibits, transmission, **C2R 11**
    Oral argument, **C2R 34**
    Television and radio, notice, **C2R App. Part F**

Vacating or setting aside, death penalty, motions, **C2R § 0.28**

Withdrawal, attorneys, **C2R 4(b)**

RULES OF THE BANKRUPTCY APPELLATE PANEL SERVICE OF THE SECOND CIRCUIT

Adopted June 14, 1996

Terminated Effective June 30, 2000

Research Note

These rules may be searched electronically on WESTLAW in the US–RULES database; updates to these rules may be found on WESTLAW in US–RULESUP-DATES. For search tips, and a detailed summary of database content, consult the WESTLAW Scope Screen of each database.

ORDER. IN THE MATTER OF THE TERMINATION OF THE BANKRUPTCY APPELLATE PANEL SERVICE OF THE SECOND JUDICIAL CIRCUIT

Pursuant to 28 U.S.C. § 158(b)(1)(C) as amended by the Bankruptcy Reform Act of 1994, the Judicial Council of the Second Circuit has determined there are insufficient judicial resources available in the Second Circuit justifying the continuation of the Bankruptcy Appellate Panel Service in the Second Circuit; it is hereby

ORDERED that the Bankruptcy Appellate Panel Service of the Second Circuit is terminated and that appeals of final judgments, orders and decrees and of interlocutory orders and decrees of bankruptcy judges entered in cases and proceedings previously referred to the Bankruptcy Appellate Panel and its appointed judges shall henceforth be referred to and heard by the respective United States District Courts in the Second Circuit; and it is hereby

ORDERED that the Bankruptcy Appellate Panel Service of the Second Circuit and its authority to hear and determine appeals from judgments, orders and decrees entered by bankruptcy judges from districts within the Second Circuit shall be terminated effective Friday, June 30, 2000.

Dated: June 30, 2000.

*

LOCAL RULES OF THE UNITED STATES DISTRICT COURTS FOR THE SOUTHERN AND EASTERN DISTRICTS OF NEW YORK

Effective April 15, 1997

Including Amendments Received Through September 15, 2008

Research Note

These rules may be searched electronically on Westlaw in the NY-RULES database; updates to these rules may be found on Westlaw in NY-RULESUPDATES. For search tips, and a detailed summary of database content, consult the Westlaw Scope Screen of each database.

LOCAL CIVIL RULES

Rule
1.1. Application of Rules.
1.2. Clerk's Office.
1.3. Admission to the Bar.
1.4. Withdrawal or Displacement of Attorney of Record.
1.5. Discipline of Attorneys.
1.6. Duty of Attorneys in Related Cases.
1.7. Fees of Clerks and Reporters.
1.8. Photographs, Radio, Recordings, Television.
1.9. Disclosure of Interested Parties [Repealed].
1.10. Acceptable Substitutes for Affidavits.
5.1. Filing of Discovery Materials.
5.2. Electronic Service and Filing of Documents.
5.3. Service by Overnight Delivery and Fax.
6.1. Service and Filing of Motion Papers.
6.2. Orders on Motions.
6.3. Motions for Reconsideration or Re-argument.
6.4. Computation of Time.
7.1. Memoranda of Law.
7.1.1. Disclosure Statement.
7.2. Specification of Statutes or Rules.
11.1. Form of Pleadings, Motions, and Other Papers.
12.1. Notice to Pro Se Litigant Who Opposes a Rule 12 Motion Supported by Matters Outside the Pleadings.
16.1. Exemptions From Mandatory Scheduling Order.
16.2. Entry and Modification of Mandatory Scheduling Orders by Magistrate Judges.
23.1. Fees in Stockholder and Class Actions.
23.1.1. Fees in Shareholder Derivative Actions.
24.1. Notice of Claim of Unconstitutionality.
26.1. Address of Party and Original Owner of Claim to Be Furnished.
26.2. Assertion of Claim of Privilege.
26.3. Uniform Definitions in Discovery Requests.

Rule
26.4. Opt–Out From Certain Provisions of Federal Rule of Civil Procedure 26 (Southern District Only)—Repealed December 1, 2000.
26.5. Cooperation Among Counsel in Discovery (Eastern District Only).
26.6. Form Discovery Requests (Eastern District Only).
26.7. Discovery Requests to Be Read Reasonably (Eastern District Only).
30.1. Counsel Fees on Taking Depositions More Than 100 Miles From Courthouse.
30.2. Opt–Out From Certain Provisions of Federal Rule of Civil Procedure 30 (Southern District Only)—Repealed December 1, 2000.
30.3. Telephonic Depositions (Eastern District Only).
30.4. Persons Attending Depositions (Eastern District Only).
30.5. Depositions of Witnesses Who Have No Knowledge of the Facts (Eastern District Only).
30.6. Conferences Between Deponent and Defending Attorney (Eastern District Only).
30.7. Document Production at Depositions (Eastern District Only).
31.1. Opt–Out From Certain Provisions of Federal Rule of Civil Procedure 31 (Southern District Only)—Repealed December 1, 2000.
33.1. Answering Interrogatory by Reference to Records.
33.2. Standard Discovery in Prisoner Pro Se Actions.
33.3. Interrogatories (Southern District Only).
33.4. Opt–Out From Certain Provisions of Federal Rule of Civil Procedure 33 (Southern District Only)—Repealed December 1, 2000.
34.1. Opt–Out From Certain Provisions of Federal Rule of Civil Procedure 34 (Southern District Only)—Repealed December 1, 2000.

Rule

36.1. Opt–Out From Certain Provisions of Federal Rule of Civil Procedure 36 (Southern District Only)—Repealed December 1, 2000.

37.1. Verbatim Quotation of Discovery Materials.

37.2. Mode of Raising Discovery Disputes With the Court (Southern District Only).

37.3. Mode of Raising Discovery and Other Non-dispositive Pretrial Disputes With the Court (Eastern District Only).

39.1. Custody of Exhibits.

39.2. Order of Summation.

47.1. Assessment of Jury Costs.

53.1. Masters.

54.1. Taxable Costs.

54.2. Security for Costs.

54.3. Entering Satisfaction of Money Judgment.

55.1. Certificate of Default.

55.2. Default Judgment.

56.1. Statements of Material Facts on Motion for Summary Judgment.

56.2. Notice to Pro Se Litigant Who Opposes a Summary Judgment.

58.1. Remand by an Appellate Court.

65.1.1. Sureties.

67.1. Order for Deposit in Interest–Bearing Account.

72.1. Powers of Magistrate Judges.

72.2. Reference to Magistrate Judge (Eastern District Only).

73.1. Consent Jurisdiction Procedure.

77.1. Submission of Orders, Judgments and Decrees.

81.1. Removal of Cases From State Courts.

83.1. Transfer of Cases to Another District.

83.2. Settlement of Actions by or on Behalf of Infants or Incompetents, Wrongful Death Actions[, and Conscious Pain and Suffering Actions (EDNY only)].

83.3. Habeas Corpus.

83.4. Proceedings to Stay the Deportation of Aliens in Deportation and Exclusion Cases.

83.5. Three–Judge Court.

83.6. Publication of Advertisements.

83.7. Notice of Sale.

83.8. Filing of Notice of Appeal.

83.9. Contempt Proceedings in Civil Cases.

83.10. Court-Annexed Arbitration (Eastern District Only).

83.11. Court-Annexed Mediation (Eastern District Only).

83.12. Alternative Dispute Resolution (Southern District Only).

LOCAL ADMIRALTY AND MARITIME RULES

Rule

A.1. Application of Rules.

B.1. Affidavit That Defendant Is Not Found Within the District.

B.2. Notice of Attachment.

C.1. Intangible Property.

C.2. Publication of Notice of Action and Arrest; Sale.

C.3. Notice Required for Default Judgment in Action In Rem.

D.1. Return Date in Possessory, Petitory, and Partition Actions.

E.1. Adversary Hearing Following Arrest, Attachment or Garnishment.

E.2. Intervenors' Claims.

E.3. Claims by Suppliers for Payment of Charges.

Rule

E.4. Preservation of Property.

LOCAL CRIMINAL RULES

Rule

1.1. Application of Rules.

1.2. Applications for Ex Parte Orders.

12.1. Service and Filing of Motion Papers.

12.4. Disclosure Statement.

16.1. Conference of Counsel.

23.1. Free Press–Fair Trial Directives.

34.1. Post-trial Motions.

44.1. Notice of Appearance.

45.1. Computation of Time.

58.1. Powers of Magistrate Judges.

58.2. Petty Offenses—Collateral and Appearance.

SOUTHERN DISTRICT SUPPLEMENTAL MATERIALS

Fee Schedules

Procedures Governing Appointment of Attorneys in Pro se Civil Actions

Plan for Achieving Prompt Disposition of Criminal Cases

Revised Plan for Furnishing Representation Pursuant to the Criminal Justice Act of 1964 (18 U.S.C. § 3006A)

Electronic Filing Procedures

EASTERN DISTRICT SUPPLEMENTAL MATERIALS

Fee Schedules

Jury Selection Plan

Procedures Governing Appointment of Attorneys in Pro Se Actions

Plan for Achieving Prompt Disposition of Criminal Cases

Criminal Justice Act Plan

Electronic Filing Procedures

ADMINISTRATIVE ORDERS—EASTERN DISTRICT

Order

2004–05. Requests to Seal Documents.

2004–08. Electronic Case Filing.

2004–09. The August 2, 2004 Amendment to the E–Government Act of 2002.

2007–10. Electronic Devices.

2008–04. Assignment of Criminal Cases.

2008–5. Scheduling in Social Security Cases [Eastern District].

Judicial Conference Policy with Regard to the Availability of Transcripts of Court Proceedings.

RULES FOR THE DIVISION OF BUSINESS AMONG DISTRICT JUDGES

SOUTHERN DISTRICT

Introduction.

Rule

1. Individual Assignment System.

2. Assignment Committee.

3. Part I.

4. Civil Actions or Proceedings (Filing and Assignment).

5. Civil Proceedings in Part I.

Rule

  6. Criminal Actions or Proceedings (Filing and Assignment).
  7. Criminal Proceedings.
  8. Arraignments and Assignments in Criminal Cases.
  9. Cases Certified for Prompt Trial or Disposition.
 10. Motions.
 11. Amendments of Pro Se Petitions for Collateral Relief From Convictions.
 12. Assignments to New Judges.
 13. Assignments to Senior Judges.
 14. Assignments to Visiting Judges.
 15. Transfer of Related Cases.
 16. Transfer of Cases by Consent.
 17. Transfers From Senior Judges.
 18. Transfer Because of Disqualification, etc.
 19. Transfer of Cases Because of Death, Resignation, Prolonged Illness, Disability, Unavoidable Absence, or Excessive Backlog of a Judge.
 20. Transfer of Cases to the Suspense Docket.
 21. Designation of White Plains Cases.
 22. Reassignment of Cases.
 23. Removed Actions and Bankruptcy Matters.
 24. Caseload of White Plains Judge(s).
 25. Prisoner Civil Rights Actions and Habeas Corpus Petitioners.
 26. Filing at Either Courthouse.
 27. Related Cases.
 28. High-Security Criminal Cases.
 29. Part I.
 30. Naturalization.
 31. Jury Assignments.

Rule

 32. Court Hours.
 33. Emergency Matters.

    Appendix. General Calendar Practice—Southern District

General Calendar Practice—Southern District.

EASTERN DISTRICT

Introduction.
Rule
 50.1. Categories and Classification of Cases; Information on Cases and Parties.
 50.2. Assignment of Cases[1].
 50.3. Related Cases; Motion for Consolidation of Cases.
 50.4. Reassignment of Cases.
 50.5. Miscellaneous Judge.
 50.6. Calendars.
 50.7. Conference.

CHAPTER 12 BANKRUPTCY RULES SUPPLEMENT

Rule
 12–1. General Applicability of Bankruptcy Rules.
 12–2. Adaptations of Certain Bankruptcy Rules.
 12–3. Schedules and Statements Required.
 12–4. Filing and Confirmation of Plan.

FORMS

Form
 No. 12–A. Chapter 12 Statement of Individual Debtor.
 No. 12–B. Chapter 12 Statement of Partnership or Corporate Debtor.

LOCAL CIVIL RULES

RULE 1.1 APPLICATION OF RULES

These Local Civil Rules apply in civil actions as defined in Federal Rules of Civil Procedure 1 and 2.

RULE 1.2 CLERK'S OFFICE

The offices of the clerk are open from 8:30 a.m. to 5:00 p.m. Monday through Friday and closed on Saturdays, Sundays, and legal holidays. A night depository with an automatic time and date stamp shall be maintained by the clerk of the Southern District in the Pearl Street Courthouse and by the clerk of the Eastern District in the Brooklyn Courthouse. After regular business hours, papers for the district court only may be deposited in the night depository. Such papers will be considered as having been filed in the district court as of the time and date stamped thereon, which shall be deemed presumptively correct.

[Source: Former Local General Rule 1.]

RULE 1.3 ADMISSION TO THE BAR

(a) A member in good standing of the bar of the state of New York, or a member in good standing of the bar of the United States District Court in Connecticut or Vermont and of the bar of the State in which such district court is located, provided such district court by its rule extends a corresponding privilege to members of the bar of this court, may be admitted to practice in this court on compliance with the following provisions:

In the first instance, each applicant for admission is required to file an application for admission in electronic form on the Court's Web site (www.nysd.uscourts.gov or www.nyed.uscourts.gov). This one application will be utilized both to admit and then to provide the applicant to the bar of this Court with a password and login for use on the court's Electronic Case Filing (ECF) system. The applicant shall adhere to all applicable rules of admission.

The applicant shall (a) complete the application online, (b) submit the application electronically, (c) print and sign a copy of the application, and (d) file the printed application and fee with the clerk, together with a certificate(s) of good standing and a supporting affidavit(s).

After submitting the application in electronic form, each applicant for admission shall file with the clerk, at least ten (10) days prior to hearing (unless, for good cause shown, the judge shall shorten the time), the signed paper copy of the verified written petition for admission stating: (1) applicant's residence and office address; (2) the time when, and courts where, admitted; (3) applicant's legal training and experience; (4) whether applicant has ever been held in contempt of court, and, if so, the nature of the contempt and the final disposition thereof; (5) whether applicant has ever been censured, suspended, disbarred or denied admission or readmission by any court, and, if so, the facts and circumstances connected therewith; (6) that applicant has read and is familiar with (a) the provisions of the Judicial Code (Title 28, U.S.C.) which pertain to the jurisdiction of, and practice in, the United States District Courts; (b) the Federal Rules of Civil Procedure; (c) the Federal Rules of Criminal Procedure; (d) the Federal Rules of Evidence; (e) the Local Rules of the United States District Court for the Southern and Eastern Districts of New York; and (f) the New York State Lawyer's Code of Professional Responsibility as adopted from time to time by the Appellate Divisions of the State of New York; and (7) that applicant will faithfully adhere to all rules applicable to applicant's conduct in connection with any activities in this court.

The petition shall be accompanied by a certificate of the clerk of the court for each of the states in which the applicant is a member of the bar, which has been issued within thirty (30) days and states that the applicant is a member in good standing of the bar of that state court. The petition shall also be accompanied by an affidavit of an attorney of this court who has known the applicant for at least one year, stating when the affiant was admitted to practice in this court, how long and under what circumstances the attorney has known the applicant, and what the attorney knows of the applicant's character and experience at the bar. Such petition shall be placed at the head of the calendar and, on the call thereof, the attorney whose affidavit accompanied the petition shall personally move the admission of the applicant. If the petition is granted, the applicant shall take the oath of office and sign the roll of attorneys.

A member of the bar of the state of New York, Connecticut, or Vermont who has been admitted to the bar of this court pursuant to this subsection and who thereafter voluntarily resigns from membership in the bar of the state pursuant to which he was admitted to the bar of this court, and who does not within 30 days of that voluntary resignation file an affidavit with the clerk of this court indicating that such person remains eligible to be admitted to the bar of this court pursuant to other provisions of this subsection (as because he is still a member of the bar of another eligible state and, where applicable, a corresponding district court), shall be deemed to have voluntarily resigned from the bar of this court as of the same date the member resigned from the bar of the underlying state, provided that such resignation shall not be deemed to deprive this court of jurisdiction to impose discipline on this person, pursuant to Rule 1.5 infra, for conduct preceding the date of such resignation.

(b) A member in good standing of the bar of either the Southern or Eastern District of New York may be admitted to the bar of the other district without formal application (1) upon filing in that district a certificate of the Clerk of the United States District Court for the district in which the applicant is a member of the bar, which has been issued within thirty (30) days and states that the applicant is a member in good standing of the bar of that court and (2) upon taking the oath of office, signing the roll of attorneys of that district, and paying the fee required in that district.

(c) A member in good standing of the bar of any state or of any United States District Court may be permitted to argue or try a particular case in whole or in part as counsel or advocate, upon motion and upon filing with the Clerk of the District Court a certificate of the court for each of the states in which the applicant is a member of the bar, which has been issued within thirty (30) days and states that the applicant is a member in good standing of the bar of that state court. Only an attorney who has been so admitted or who is a member of the bar of this court may enter appearances for parties, sign stipulations or receive payments upon judgments, decrees or orders.

(d) If an attorney who is a member of the bar of this court, or who has been authorized to appear in a case in this court, changes his or her residence or office address, the attorney shall immediately notify the clerk of the court, in addition to serving and filing a notice of change of address in each pending case in which the attorney has appeared.

[Source: Former Local General Rule 2.]

Amended effective April 15, 2005; May 18, 2007.

RULE 1.4   WITHDRAWAL OR DISPLACEMENT OF ATTORNEY OF RECORD

An attorney who has appeared as attorney of record for a party may be relieved or displaced only by order of the court and may not withdraw from a case without leave of the court granted by order. Such an order may be granted only upon a showing by affidavit or otherwise of satisfactory reasons for withdrawal or displacement and the posture of the case, including its position, if any, on the calendar.

[Source: Former Local General Rule 3(c).]

RULE 1.5 DISCIPLINE OF ATTORNEYS

(a) **Committee on Grievances.** The chief judge shall appoint a committee of the board of judges known as the Committee on Grievances, which under the direction of the chief judge shall have charge of all matters relating to the discipline of attorneys. The chief judge shall appoint a panel of attorneys who are members of the bar of this court to advise or assist the Committee on Grievances. At the direction of the Committee on Grievances or its chair, members of this panel of attorneys may investigate complaints, may prepare and support statements of charges, or may serve as members of hearing panels.

(b) **Grounds for Discipline or Other Relief.** Discipline or other relief, of the types set forth in paragraph (c) below, may be imposed, by the Committee on Grievances, after notice and opportunity to respond as set forth in paragraph (d) below, if any of the following grounds is found by clear and convincing evidence:

(1) Any member of the bar of this court has been convicted of a felony or misdemeanor in any federal court, or in a court of any state or territory.

(2) Any member of the bar of this court has been disciplined by any federal court or by a court of any state or territory.

(3) Any member of the bar of this court has resigned from the bar of any federal court or of a court of any state or territory while an investigation into allegations of misconduct by the attorney was pending.

(4) Any member of the bar of this court has an infirmity which prevents the attorney from engaging in the practice of law.

(5) In connection with activities in this court, any attorney is found to have engaged in conduct violative of the New York State Lawyer's Code of Professional Responsibility as adopted from time to time by the Appellate Divisions of the State of New York, and as interpreted and applied by the United States Supreme Court, the United States Court of Appeals for the Second Circuit, and this court.

(6) Any attorney not a member of the bar of this court has appeared at the bar of this court without permission to do so.

(c) **Types of Discipline or Other Relief.**

(1) In the case of an attorney admitted to the bar of this court, discipline imposed pursuant to paragraph (b)(1), (b)(2), (b)(3), or (b)(5) above may consist of a letter of reprimand or admonition, censure, suspen-

sion, or an order striking the name of the attorney from the roll of attorneys admitted to the bar of this court.

(2) In the case of an attorney not admitted to the bar of this court, discipline imposed pursuant to paragraph (b)(5) or (b)(6) above may consist of a letter of reprimand or admonition, censure, or an order precluding the attorney from again appearing at the bar of this court.

(3) Relief required pursuant to paragraph (b)(4) above shall consist of suspending the attorney from practice before this court.

(d) **Procedure.**

(1) If it appears that there exists a ground for discipline set forth in paragraph (b)(1), (b)(2), or (b)(3), notice thereof shall be served by the Committee on Grievances upon the attorney concerned by first class mail, directed to the address of the attorney as shown on the rolls of this court and to the last known address of the attorney (if any) as shown in the complaint and any materials submitted therewith. Service shall be deemed complete upon mailing in accordance with the provisions of this paragraph.

In all cases in which any federal court or a court of any state or territory has entered an order disbarring or censuring an attorney or suspending the attorney from practice, whether or not on consent, the notice shall be served together with an order by the clerk of this court, to become effective twenty-four days after the date of service upon the attorney, disbarring or censuring the attorney or suspending the attorney from practice in this court upon terms and conditions comparable to those set forth by the other court of record. In all cases in which an attorney has resigned from the bar of any federal court or of a court of any state or territory while an investigation into allegations of misconduct by the attorney was pending, even if the attorney remains admitted to the bar of any other court, the notice shall be served together with an order entered by the clerk for this court, to become effective twenty-four days after the date of service upon the attorney, deeming the attorney to have resigned from the bar of this court. Within twenty days of the date of service of either order, the attorney may file a motion for modification or revocation of the order. Any such motion shall set forth with specificity the facts and principles relied upon by the attorney as showing cause why a different disposition should be ordered by this court. The timely filing of such a motion will stay the effectiveness of the order until further order by this court. If good cause is shown to hold an evidentiary hearing, the Committee on Grievances may proceed to impose discipline or to take such other action as justice and this rule may require.

In all other cases, the notice shall be served together with an order by the Committee on Grievances directing the attorney to show cause in writing why discipline should not be imposed. If the attorney fails to respond in writing to the order to show cause, or if the response fails to show good cause to hold an evidentiary hearing, the Committee on Grievances may proceed to impose discipline or to take such other action as justice and this rule may require. If good cause is shown to hold an evidentiary hearing, the Committee on Grievances may direct such a hearing pursuant to paragraph (d)(4) below.

(2) In the case of a ground for discipline set forth in paragraph (b)(2) or (b)(3) above, discipline may be imposed unless the attorney concerned establishes by clear and convincing evidence (i) that there was such an infirmity of proof of misconduct by the attorney as to give rise to the clear conviction that this court could not consistent with its duty accept as final the conclusion of the other court, or (ii) that the procedure resulting in the investigation or discipline of the attorney by the other court was so lacking in notice or opportunity to be heard as to constitute a deprivation of due process, or (iii) that the imposition of discipline by this court would result in grave injustice.

(3) Complaints in writing alleging any ground for discipline or other relief set forth in paragraph (b) above shall be directed to the chief judge, who shall refer such complaints to the Committee on Grievances. The Committee on Grievances, by its chair, may designate an attorney, who may be selected from the panel of attorneys established pursuant to paragraph (a) above, to investigate the complaint, if it deems investigation necessary or warranted, and to prepare a statement of charges, if the Committee deems that necessary or warranted. Complaints, and any files based on them, shall be treated as confidential unless otherwise ordered by the chief judge for good cause shown.

(4) A statement of charges alleging a ground for discipline or other relief set forth in paragraph (b)(4), (b)(5), or (b)(6) shall be served upon the attorney concerned by certified mail, return receipt requested, directed to the address of the attorney as shown on the rolls of this court and to the last known address of the attorney (if any) as shown in the complaint and any materials submitted therewith, together with an order by the Committee on Grievances directing the attorney to show cause in writing why discipline or other relief should not be imposed. Upon the respondent attorney's answer to the charges the matter will be designated by the Committee on Grievances for a prompt evidentiary hearing before a magistrate judge of the court or before a panel of three attorneys, who may be selected from the panel of attorneys established pursuant to paragraph (a) above. The magistrate judge or panel of attorneys conducting the hearing may grant such pre-hearing discovery as they determine to be necessary, shall hear witnesses called by the attorney supporting the charges and by the respondent attorney, and may consider such other evidence included in the record of the hearing as they deem relevant and material. The magistrate judge or panel of attorneys conducting the hearing shall report their findings and recommendations in writing to the Committee on Grievances and shall serve them upon the respondent attorney and the attorney supporting the charges. After affording the respondent attorney and the attorney supporting the charges an opportunity to respond in writing to such report, or if no timely answer is made by the respondent attorney, or if the Committee on Grievances determines that the answer raises no issue requiring a hearing, the Committee on Grievances may proceed to impose discipline or to take such action as justice and this rule may require.

(e) **Reinstatement.** Any attorney who has been suspended or precluded from appearing in this court or whose name has been struck from the roll of the members of the bar of this court may apply in writing to the chief judge, for good cause shown, for the lifting of the suspension or preclusion or for reinstatement to the rolls. The chief judge shall refer such application to the Committee on Grievances. The Committee on Grievances may refer the application to a magistrate judge or hearing panel of attorneys (who may be the same magistrate judge or panel of attorneys who previously heard the matter) for findings and recommendations, or may act upon the application without making such a referral. Absent extraordinary circumstances, no such application will be granted unless the attorney seeking reinstatement meets the requirements for admission set forth in Local Civil Rule 1.3(a).

(f) **Remedies for Misconduct.** The remedies provided by this rule are in addition to the remedies available to individual judges and magistrate judges under applicable law with respect to lawyers appearing before them. Individual judges and magistrate judges may also refer any matter to the chief judge for referral to the Committee on Grievances to consider the imposition of discipline or other relief pursuant to this rule.

(g) **Notice to Other Courts.** When an attorney is known to be admitted to practice in the court of any state or territory, or in any other federal court, and has been convicted of any crime or disbarred, precluded from appearing, suspended or censured in this court, the clerk shall send to such other court or courts a certified copy of the judgment of conviction or order of disbarment, preclusion, suspension or censure, a certified copy of the court's opinion, if any, and a statement of the attorney's last known office and residence address.

[Source: Former Local General Rule 4.]

Amended effective May 2, 2001; April 15, 2005; May 18, 2007.

RULE 1.6 DUTY OF ATTORNEYS IN RELATED CASES

(a) It shall be the continuing duty of each attorney appearing in any civil or criminal case to bring promptly to the attention of the clerk all facts which said attorney believes are relevant to a determination that said case and one or more pending civil or criminal cases should be heard by the same judge, in order to avoid unnecessary duplication of judicial effort. As soon as the attorney becomes aware of such relationship, said attorney shall notify the clerk in writing, who shall transmit that notification to the judges to whom the cases have been assigned.

(b) If counsel fails to comply with Local Civil Rule 1.6(a), the court may assess reasonable costs directly against counsel whose action has obstructed the effective administration of the court's business.

[Source: Former Local General Rule 5.]

RULE 1.7 FEES OF CLERKS AND REPORTERS

(a) The clerk shall not be required to render any service for which a fee is prescribed by statute or by the Judicial Conference of the United States unless the fee for the particular service is paid to the clerk in advance or the court orders otherwise.

(b) Every attorney appearing in any proceeding who orders a transcript of any trial, hearing, or any other proceeding, is obligated to pay the cost thereof to the court reporters of the court upon rendition of the invoice unless at the time of such order, the attorney, in writing, advises the court reporter that only the client is obligated to pay.

[Source: Former Local General Rule 6.]

RULE 1.8 PHOTOGRAPHS, RADIO, RECORDINGS, TELEVISION

No one other than court officials engaged in the conduct of court business shall bring any camera, transmitter, receiver, portable telephone or recording device into any courthouse or its environs without written permission of a judge of that court.

Environs as used in this rule shall include the entire United States Courthouse property, including all entrances to and exits from the buildings.

[Source: Former Local General Rule 7.]

RULE 1.9 DISCLOSURE OF INTERESTED PARTIES [REPEALED]

See Rule 7.1 of the Federal Rules of Civil Procedure.

Adopted effective December 1, 2000. Repealed effective March 3, 2003.

RULE 1.10 ACCEPTABLE SUBSTITUTES FOR AFFIDAVITS

In situations in which any local rule provides for an affidavit or a verified statement, the following are acceptable substitutes: (a) a statement subscribed under penalty of perjury as prescribed in 28 U.S.C. § 1746; or (b) if accepted by the court as a substitute for an affidavit or a verified statement, (1) a statement signed by an attorney or by a party not represented by an attorney pursuant to Federal Rule of Civil Procedure 11, or (2) an oral representation on the record in open court.

RULE 5.1 FILING OF DISCOVERY MATERIALS

A party seeking relief under Rules 26 through 37 inclusive of the Federal Rules of Civil Procedure, or making any other motion or application, shall quote or attach only those portions of the depositions, interrogatories, requests for documents, requests for admissions, or other discovery or disclosure materials, together with the responses and objections thereto, that are the subject of the discovery motion or application, or are cited in papers submitted in connection with any other motion or application. *See also* Local Rule 37.1.

[Source: Former Local Civil Rule 18.]

Amended effective February 22, 2007.

RULE 5.2 ELECTRONIC SERVICE AND FILING OF DOCUMENTS

A paper served and filed by electronic means in accordance with procedures promulgated by the Court is, for purposes of Federal Rule of Civil Procedure 5, served and filed in compliance with the local civil rules of the Southern and Eastern Districts of New York.

Adopted effective March 19, 2003.

RULE 5.3 SERVICE BY OVERNIGHT DELIVERY AND FAX

(a) Service upon an attorney of all papers other than a subpoena or a summons and complaint or any other paper required by statute or rule to be served in the same manner as a summons and complaint shall be permitted by dispatching the paper to the attorney by overnight delivery service at the address designated by the attorney for that purpose, or if none is designated, at the attorney's last known address. Service by overnight delivery service shall be complete upon deposit of the paper enclosed in a properly addressed wrapper into the custody of the overnight delivery service for overnight delivery, prior to the latest time designated by the overnight delivery service for overnight delivery. Overnight service shall be deemed service by mail for purposes of Fed.R.Civ.P. 6(e). "Overnight delivery service" means any delivery service which regularly accepts items for overnight delivery.

(b) No papers shall be served by facsimile unless the parties agree in writing in advance to accept service by this means or it is ordered by the assigned judge. Without such prior agreement or order, such attempted service shall be considered void. Service by electronic means other than facsimile shall be governed by the Standing Order relating to Procedures for Electronic Case Filing, and in the Eastern District Court of New York by that Court's Administrative Order 97–12, In re: Electronic Filing Procedures.

Adopted March 19, 2003.

RULE 6.1   SERVICE AND FILING OF MOTION PAPERS

Unless otherwise provided by statute or rule, or unless otherwise ordered by the court in an individual rule or in a direction in a particular case, upon any motion, the notice of motion, supporting affidavits, and memoranda shall be served and filed as follows:

(a) On all motions and exceptions under Rules 26 through 37 inclusive and Rule 45(c)(3) of the Federal Rules of Civil Procedure, (1) the notice of motion, supporting affidavits, and memoranda of law shall be served by the moving party on all other parties that have appeared in the action, (2) any opposing affidavits and answering memoranda of law shall be served within four business days after service of the moving papers, and (3) any reply affidavits and reply memoranda of law shall be served within one business day after service of the answering papers.

(b) On all civil motions, petitions, applications, and exceptions other than those described in Rule 6.1(a), and other than petitions for writs of habeas corpus, (1) the notice of motion, supporting affidavits, and memoranda of law shall be served by the moving party on all other parties that have appeared in the action, (2) any opposing affidavits and answering memoranda shall be served within ten business days after service of the moving papers, and (3) any reply affidavits and memoranda of law shall be served within five business days after service of the answering papers.

(c) The parties and their attorneys shall only appear to argue the motion if so directed by the court by order or by individual rule or upon application.

(d) No ex parte order, or order to show cause to bring on a motion, will be granted except upon a clear and specific showing by affidavit of good and sufficient reasons why a procedure other than by notice of motion is necessary, and stating whether a previous application for similar relief has been made.

[Source: Former Local Civil Rules 3(c)(1), (2), and (4) and 6(b).]

RULE 6.2   ORDERS ON MOTIONS

A memorandum signed by the court of the decision on a motion that does not finally determine all claims for relief, or an oral decision on such a motion, shall constitute the order unless the memorandum or oral decision directs the submission or settlement of an order in more extended form. The notation in the docket of a memorandum or oral decision that does not direct the submission or settlement of an order in more extended form shall constitute the entry of the order. Where an order in more extended form is required to be submitted or settled, the notation in the docket of such order shall constitute the entry of the order.

[Source: Former Local Civil Rule 6(a).]

RULE 6.3   MOTIONS FOR RECONSIDERATION OR RE-ARGUMENT

A notice of motion for reconsideration or re-argument of a court order determining a motion shall be served within ten (10) days after the entry of the court's determination of the original motion, or, in the case of a court order resulting in a judgment, within ten (10) days after the entry of the judgment. There shall be served with the notice of motion a memorandum setting forth concisely the matters or controlling decisions which counsel believes the court has overlooked. The time periods for the service of answering and reply memoranda, if any, shall be governed by Local Civil Rule 6.1(a) or (b), as in the case of the original motion. No oral argument shall be heard unless the court directs that the matter shall be reargued orally. No affidavits shall be filed by any party unless directed by the court.

[Source: Former Local Civil Rule 3(j).]

Adopted March 25, 2004.

RULE 6.4   COMPUTATION OF TIME

In computing any period of time prescribed or allowed by the Local Civil Rules or the Local Admiralty and Maritime Rules, the provisions of Federal Rule of Civil Procedure 6(a) and 6(e) shall apply unless otherwise stated.

RULE 7.1   MEMORANDA OF LAW

(a) Memoranda of Law Required. Except as otherwise permitted by the court, all motions and all oppositions thereto shall be supported by a memorandum of law, setting forth the points and authorities relied upon in support of or in opposition to the motion, and divided, under appropriate headings, into as many parts as there are points to be determined. Willful failure to comply with this rule may be deemed sufficient cause for the denial of a motion or for the granting of a motion by default.

(b) Length of Briefs on Appeals from Bankruptcy Court. Unless otherwise ordered by the district judge to whom the appeal is assigned, appellate briefs on bankruptcy appeals shall not exceed 25 pages and reply briefs shall not exceed 10 pages.

(c) Service on Pro Se Litigants of Unpublished Opinions Cited. In cases involving a pro se litigant, counsel shall, when serving a memorandum of law (or other submissions to the Court), provide the pro se litigant (but not other counsel or the Court) with printed copies of decisions cited therein that are unreported or reported exclusively on computerized databases.

[Source: Former Local Civil Rule 3(b).]

Amended effective April 11, 2008.

RULE 7.1.1 DISCLOSURE STATEMENT

For purposes of Fed. R. Civ. P. 7.1(b)(2), "promptly" shall mean "within ten business days," that is, parties are required to file supplemental disclosure statement within ten business days of the time there is any change in the information required in a disclosure statement filed pursuant to those rules.

Effective February 22, 2007.

RULE 7.2 SPECIFICATION OF STATUTES OR RULES

Upon any motion based upon rules or statutes, the notice of motion or order to show cause shall specify the rules or statutes upon which the motion is predicated.

[Source: Former Local Civil Rule 3(d).]

RULE 11.1 FORM OF PLEADINGS, MOTIONS, AND OTHER PAPERS

(a) Every pleading, written motion, and other paper must (1) be plainly written, typed, printed, or copied without erasures or interlineations which materially deface it, (2) bear the docket number and the initials of the judge and any magistrate judge before whom the action or proceeding is pending, and (3) have the name of each person signing it clearly printed or typed directly below the signature.

(b) [Deleted eff. May 18, 2007.].

[Source: Former Local Civil Rule 1.]

Amended effective May 18, 2007.

RULE 12.1 NOTICE TO PRO SE LITIGANT WHO OPPOSES A RULE 12 MOTION SUPPORTED BY MATTERS OUTSIDE THE PLEADINGS

A represented party moving to dismiss or for judgment on the pleadings against a party proceeding pro se, who refers in support of the motion to matters outside the pleadings as described in Federal Rule of Civil Procedure 12(b) or 12(c), shall serve and file the following notice at the time the motion is served. If the court rules that a motion to dismiss or for judgment on the pleadings will be treated as one for summary judgment pursuant to Federal Rule of Civil Procedure 12(b) or 12(c), and the movant has not previously served and filed the notice required by this rule, the notice must be served and filed within ten days of the court's ruling.

Notice to Pro Se Litigant Who Opposes
a Rule 12 Motion Supported by
Matters Outside the Pleadings

The defendant in this case has moved to dismiss or for judgment on the pleadings pursuant to Rule 12(b) or 12(c) of the Federal Rules of Civil Procedure, and has submitted additional written materials. This means that the defendant has asked the court to decide this case without a trial, based on these written materials. You are warned that the Court may treat this motion as a motion for summary judgment under Rule 56 of the Federal Rules of Civil Procedure. For this reason, THE CLAIMS YOU ASSERT IN YOUR COMPLAINT MAY BE DISMISSED WITHOUT A TRIAL IF YOU DO NOT RESPOND TO THIS MOTION by filing sworn affidavits or other papers as required by Rule 56(e). An affidavit is a sworn statement of fact based on personal knowledge that would be admissible in evidence at trial. The full text of Rule 56 of the Federal Rules of Civil Procedure is attached.

In short, Rule 56 provides that you may NOT oppose the defendant's motion simply by relying upon the allegations in your complaint. Rather, you must submit evidence, such as witness statements or documents, countering the facts asserted by the defendant and raising issues of fact for trial. Any witness statements must be in the form of affidavits. You may submit your own affidavit and/or the affidavits of others. You may submit affidavits that were prepared specifically in response to defendant's motion.

If you do not respond to the motion on time with affidavits or documentary evidence contradicting the facts asserted by the defendant, the court may accept defendant's factual assertions as true. Judgment may then be entered in defendant's favor without a trial.

If you have any questions, you may direct them to the Pro Se Office.

Adopted March 19, 2003. Amended effective May 18, 2007.

RULE 16.1 EXEMPTIONS FROM MANDATORY SCHEDULING ORDER

Matters involving habeas corpus petitions, social security disability cases, motions to vacate sentences, forfeitures, and reviews from administrative agencies are exempted from the mandatory scheduling order required by Federal Rule of Civil Procedure 16(b).

[Source: Former Local Civil Rule 45 (Eastern District Only).]

RULE 16.2 ENTRY AND MODIFICATION OF MANDATORY SCHEDULING ORDERS BY MAGISTRATE JUDGES

In any case referred to a magistrate judge by a district judge, the magistrate judge may make scheduling orders pursuant to Federal Rule of Civil Procedure 16(b), and may modify for good cause shown scheduling orders previously entered.

[Source: Former Local Magistrate Judge Rule 15 (Eastern District Only and Southern District Only Versions).]

RULE 23.1 FEES IN STOCKHOLDER AND CLASS ACTIONS

Fees for attorneys or others shall not be paid upon recovery or compromise in a derivative or class action on behalf of a corporation or class except as allowed by the court after a hearing upon such notice as the court may direct. The notice shall include a statement of the names and addresses of the applicants for such fees and the amounts requested respectively and shall disclose any fee sharing agreements with anyone. Where the court directs notice of a hearing upon a proposed voluntary dismissal or settlement of a derivative or class action, the above information as to the applications shall be included in the notice.

[Source: Former Local Civil Rule 5(a).]

Amended effective February 22, 2007.

RULE 23.1.1 FEES IN SHAREHOLDER DERIVATIVE ACTIONS

Fees for attorneys or others shall not be paid upon recovery or compromise in a derivative action on behalf of a corporation except as allowed by the court after a hearing upon such notice as the court may direct. The notice shall include a statement of the names and addresses of the applicants for such fees and the amounts requested respectively and shall disclose any fee sharing agreements with anyone.

Where the court directs notice of a hearing upon a proposed voluntary dismissal or settlement of a derivative action, the above information as to the applications shall be included in the notice.

[Source: Former Local Civil Rule 5(a).]

[Amended effective February 22, 2007.]

RULE 24.1 NOTICE OF CLAIM OF UNCONSTITUTIONALITY

(a) If, in any action to which neither the United States nor any agency, officer or employee thereof is a party, a party draws in question the constitutionality of an act of Congress affecting the public interest, such party shall notify the court in writing of the existence of such question so as to enable the court to comply with 28 U.S.C. § 2403(a).

(b) If, in any action to which neither a State nor any agency, officer or employee thereof is a party, a party draws in question the constitutionality of a statute of such State affecting the public interest, such party shall notify the court in writing of the existence of such question so as to enable the court to comply with 28 U.S.C. § 2403(b).

RULE 26.1 ADDRESS OF PARTY AND ORIGINAL OWNER OF CLAIM TO BE FURNISHED

A party shall furnish to any other party, within five (5) days after a demand, a verified statement setting forth that party's post office address and residence, and like information as to partners if a partnership is involved and, if a corporation or an unincorporated association, the name, post office addresses and residences of its principal officers. In the case of an assigned claim, the statement shall include the post office address and residence of the original owner of the claim and of any assignee.

[Source: Former Local Civil Rule 2.]

RULE 26.2 ASSERTION OF CLAIM OF PRIVILEGE

(a) Where a claim of privilege is asserted in objecting to any means of discovery or disclosure, including but not limited to a deposition, and an answer is not provided on the basis of such assertion,

(1) The attorney asserting the privilege shall identify the nature of the privilege (including work product) which is being claimed and, if the privilege is governed by state law, indicate the state's privilege rule being invoked; and

(2) The following information shall be provided in the objection, unless divulgence of such information would cause disclosure of the allegedly privileged information:

(A) For documents: (i) the type of document, e.g., letter or memorandum; (ii) the general subject matter of the document; (iii) the date of the document; and (iv) such other information as is sufficient to identify the document for a subpoena duces tecum, including, where appropriate, the author of the document, the addressees of the document, and any other recipients shown in the document, and, where not apparent, the relationship of the author, addressees, and recipients to each other;

(B) For oral communications: (i) the name of the person making the communication and the names of persons present while the communication was made and, where not apparent, the relationship of the persons present to the person making the communication; (ii) the date and place of communication; and (iii) the general subject matter of the communication.

(b) Where a claim of privilege is asserted during a deposition, and information is not provided on the basis of such assertion, the information set forth in paragraph (a) above shall be furnished (1) at the deposition, to the extent it is readily available from the witness being deposed or otherwise, and (2) to the extent the information is not readily available at the deposition, in writing within ten business days after the deposition session at which the privilege is asserted, unless otherwise ordered by the court.

(c) Where a claim of privilege is asserted in response to discovery or disclosure other than a deposition, and information is not provided on the basis of such assertion, the information set forth in paragraph (a) above shall be furnished in writing at the time of the response to such discovery or disclosure, unless otherwise ordered by the court.

[Source: Former Local Civil Rule 46(e)(2) (Southern District Only); Eastern District Standing Order 21.]

RULE 26.3   UNIFORM DEFINITIONS IN DISCOVERY REQUESTS

(a) The full text of the definitions and rules of construction set forth in paragraphs (c) and (d) is deemed incorporated by reference into all discovery requests. No discovery request shall use broader definitions or rules of construction than those set forth in paragraphs (c) and (d). This rule shall not preclude (1) the definition of other terms specific to the particular litigation, (2) the use of abbreviations, or (3) a more narrow definition of a term defined in paragraph (c).

(b) This rule is not intended to broaden or narrow the scope of discovery permitted by the Federal Rules of Civil Procedure.

(c) The following definitions apply to all discovery requests:

(1) *Communication.* The term "communication" means the transmittal of information (in the form of facts, ideas, inquiries or otherwise).

(2) *Document.* The term "document" is defined to be synonymous in meaning and equal in scope to the usage of this term in Federal Rule of Civil Procedure 34(a), including, without limitation, electronic or computerized data compilations. A draft or non-identical copy is a separate document within the meaning of this term.

(3) *Identify (with respect to persons).* When referring to a person, "to identify" means to give, to the extent known, the person's full name, present or last known address, and when referring to a natural person, additionally, the present or last known place of employment. Once a person has been identified in accordance with this subparagraph, only the name of that person need be listed in response to subsequent discovery requesting the identification of that person.

(4) *Identify (with respect to documents).* When referring to documents, "to identify" means to give, to the extent known, the (i) type of document; (ii) general subject matter; (iii) date of the document; and (iv) author(s), addressee(s) and recipient(s).

(5) *Parties.* The terms "plaintiff" and "defendant" as well as a party's full or abbreviated name or a pronoun referring to a party mean the party and, where applicable, its officers, directors, employees, partners, corporate parent, subsidiaries or affiliates. This definition is not intended to impose a discovery obligation on any person who is not a party to the litigation.

(6) *Person.* The term "person" is defined as any natural person or any business, legal or governmental entity or association.

(7) *Concerning.* The term "concerning" means relating to, referring to, describing, evidencing or constituting.

(d) The following rules of construction apply to all discovery requests:

(1) *All/Each.* The terms "all" and "each" shall be construed as all and each.

(2) *And/Or.* The connectives "and" and "or" shall be construed either disjunctively or conjunctively as necessary to bring within the scope of the discovery request all responses that might otherwise be construed to be outside of its scope.

(3) *Number.* The use of the singular form of any word includes the plural and vice versa.

[Source: Former Local Civil Rule 47.]

RULE 26.4 OPT–OUT FROM CERTAIN PROVISIONS OF FEDERAL RULE OF CIVIL PROCEDURE 26 (SOUTHERN DISTRICT ONLY)—REPEALED DECEMBER 1, 2000

RULE 26.5 COOPERATION AMONG COUNSEL IN DISCOVERY (EASTERN DISTRICT ONLY)

Counsel are expected to cooperate with each other, consistent with the interests of their clients, in all phases of the discovery process and to be courteous in their dealings with each other, including in matters relating to scheduling and timing of various discovery procedures.

[Source: Eastern District Standing Order 1.]

RULE 26.6 FORM DISCOVERY REQUESTS (EASTERN DISTRICT ONLY)

Attorneys using form discovery requests shall review them to ascertain that they are relevant to the subject matter involved in the particular case. Discovery requests which are not relevant to the subject matter involved in the particular case shall not be used.

[Source: Eastern District Standing Orders 15, 18.]

RULE 26.7 DISCOVERY REQUESTS TO BE READ REASONABLY (EASTERN DISTRICT ONLY)

Discovery requests shall be read reasonably in the recognition that the attorney serving them generally does not have the information being sought and the attorney receiving them generally does have such information or can obtain it from the client.

[Source: Eastern District Standing Orders 16(b), 19(b).]

RULE 30.1 COUNSEL FEES ON TAKING DEPOSITIONS MORE THAN 100 MILES FROM COURTHOUSE

When a proposed deposition upon oral examination, including a deposition before action or pending appeal, is sought to be taken at a place more than one hundred (100) miles from the courthouse, the court may by order provide that prior to the examination, the applicant pay the expense (including a reasonable counsel fee) of the attendance of one attorney for each adversary party at the place where the deposition is to be taken. The amounts so paid, unless otherwise directed by the court, shall be a taxable cost in the event that the applicant recovers costs of the action or proceeding.

[Source: Former Local Civil Rule 15(a).]

RULE 30.2 OPT–OUT FROM CERTAIN PROVISIONS OF FEDERAL RULE OF CIVIL PROCEDURE 30 (SOUTHERN DISTRICT ONLY)—REPEALED DECEMBER 1, 2000

RULE 30.3 TELEPHONIC DEPOSITIONS (EASTERN DISTRICT ONLY)

The motion of a party to take the deposition of an adverse party by telephone will presumptively be granted. Where the opposing party is a corporation, the term "adverse party" means an officer, director, managing agent or corporate designee pursuant to Federal Rule of Civil Procedure 30(b)(6).

[Source: Eastern District Standing Order 8.]

RULE 30.4 PERSONS ATTENDING DEPOSITIONS (EASTERN DISTRICT ONLY)

A person who is a party in the action may attend the deposition of a party or witness. A witness or potential witness in the action may attend the deposition of a party or witness unless otherwise ordered by the court.

[Source: Eastern District Standing Order 9.]

RULE 30.5 DEPOSITIONS OF WITNESSES WHO HAVE NO KNOWLEDGE OF THE FACTS (EASTERN DISTRICT ONLY)

(a) Where an officer, director or managing agent of a corporation or a government official is served with a notice of deposition or subpoena regarding a matter about which he or she has no knowledge, he or she may submit reasonably before the date noticed for the deposition an affidavit to the noticing party so stating and identifying a person within the corporation or government entity having knowledge of the subject matter involved in the pending action.

(b) The noticing party may, notwithstanding such affidavit of the noticed witness, proceed with the deposition, subject to the witness's right to seek a protective order.

[Source: Eastern District Standing Order 10.]

RULE 30.6 CONFERENCES BETWEEN DEPONENT AND DEFENDING ATTORNEY (EASTERN DISTRICT ONLY)

An attorney for a deponent shall not initiate a private conference with the deponent during the actual taking of a deposition, except for the purpose of determining whether a privilege should be asserted.

[Source: Eastern District Standing Order 13.]

RULE 30.7 DOCUMENT PRODUCTION AT DEPOSITIONS (EASTERN DISTRICT ONLY)

Consistent with the requirements of Federal Rules of Civil Procedure 30 and 34, a party seeking production of documents of another party in connection with a deposition should schedule the deposition to allow for the production of the documents in advance of the deposition. If documents which have been so requested are not produced prior to the deposition, the party noticing the deposition may either adjourn the deposition until after such documents are produced or, without waiving the right to have access to the documents, may proceed with the deposition.

[Source: Eastern District Standing Order 14.]

RULE 31.1 OPT–OUT FROM CERTAIN PROVISIONS OF FEDERAL RULE OF CIVIL PROCEDURE 31 (SOUTHERN DISTRICT ONLY)—REPEALED DECEMBER 1, 2000

RULE 33.1 ANSWERING INTERROGATORY BY REFERENCE TO RECORDS

Whenever a party answers any interrogatory by reference to records from which the answer may be derived or ascertained, as permitted in Federal Rule of Civil Procedure 33(d):

(a) The specifications of documents to be produced shall be in sufficient detail to permit the interrogating party to locate and identify the records and to ascertain the answer as readily as could the party from whom discovery is sought.

(b) The producing party shall also make available any computerized information or summaries thereof that it either has, or can adduce by a relatively simple procedure, unless these materials are privileged or otherwise immune from discovery.

(c) The producing party shall also provide any relevant compilations, abstracts or summaries in its custody or readily obtainable by it, unless these materials are privileged or otherwise immune from discovery.

(d) Unless otherwise ordered by the court, the documents shall be made available for inspection and copying within ten days after service of the answers to interrogatories or at a date agreed upon by the parties.

[Source: Former Local Civil Rule 46(f) (Southern District Only).]

RULE 33.2 STANDARD DISCOVERY IN PRISONER PRO SE ACTIONS

(a) This rule shall apply in any action commenced pro se in which the plaintiff's complaint includes any claim described in paragraph (b) of this rule and in which any named defendant, including one or more current or former employees of New York State or New York City, is represented by the Office of the Attorney General or the Office of the Corporation Counsel and is sued in matters arising out of events alleged to have occurred while the plaintiff was in the custody of either the Department of Corrections of the City of New York or the New York State Department of Correctional Services. In each such action in the Southern District of New York, such defendants shall, except as otherwise set forth herein, respond to the standing discovery requests adopted by the court, in accordance with the instructions and definitions set forth in the standing requests, unless otherwise ordered by the court. In each such action in the Eastern District of New York, such defendants shall respond to the standing discovery requests if so ordered by the court.

(b) The claims to which the standard discovery requests shall apply are Use of Force Cases, Inmate Against Inmate Assault Cases and Disciplinary Due Process Cases, as defined below, in which the events alleged in the complaint have occurred while the plaintiff was in the custody of either the Department of Corrections of the City of New York or the New York State Department of Correctional Services.

(1) "Use of Force Case" refers to an action in which the complaint alleges that any employee of the Department used physical force against the plaintiff in violation of the plaintiff's rights.

(2) "Inmate against Inmate Assault Case" refers to an action in which the complaint alleges that any defendant was responsible for the plaintiff's injury resulting from physical contact with another inmate.

(3) "Disciplinary Due Process Case" refers to an action in which (i) the complaint alleges that a defendant violated or permitted the violation of a right or rights in a disciplinary proceeding against plaintiff, and (ii) the punishment imposed upon plaintiff as a result of that proceeding was placement in a special housing unit for more than 100 days.

(c) If a response to the requests is required to be made on behalf of an individual defendant, represented by the Office of the Corporation Counsel or the Office of the Attorney General, it shall be made on the basis of information and documents within the possession, custody or control of the New York City Department of Corrections or New York State Department of Correctional Services in accordance with the instructions contained in the requests. If no defendant is represented by the Office of Corporation Counsel of the City of New York or the Office of the Attorney General, responses based upon such information need not be made pursuant to this local rule, without prejudice to such other discovery procedures as the plaintiff shall initiate.

(d) The requests, denominated Plaintiff's Interrogatories and Requests for Production of Documents, shall be answered within 120 days of service of the complaint on any named defendant except (i) as otherwise ordered by the court, for good cause shown, which shall be based upon the facts and procedural status of the particular case and not upon a generalized claim of burden, expense or relevance or (ii) as otherwise provided in the instructions to the requests. The responses to the requests shall be served upon the plaintiff and shall be filed with the Pro Se Office of the court. Copies of the requests are available through the Pro Se Office of the court.

(e) Except upon permission of the court, for good cause shown, the requests shall constitute the sole form of discovery available to plaintiff during the 120-day period as designated above.

(f) If the Pro Se Office determines that this rule applies, it shall provide copies of the standard requests to those pro se plaintiffs for service upon defendants together with the summons and complaint.

[Source: Former Local Civil Rule 48 (Southern District Only).]

Amended effective July 1, 2002; September 24, 2002; April 15, 2005.

RULE 33.3 INTERROGATORIES (SOUTHERN DISTRICT ONLY)

(a) Unless otherwise ordered by the court, at the commencement of discovery, interrogatories will be restricted to those seeking names of witnesses with knowledge of information relevant to the subject matter of the action, the computation of each category of damage alleged, and the existence, custodian, location and general description of relevant documents, including pertinent insurance agreements, and other physical evidence, or information of a similar nature.

(b) During discovery, interrogatories other than those seeking information described in paragraph (a) above may only be served (1) if they are a more practical method of obtaining the information sought than a request for production or a deposition, or (2) if ordered by the court.

(c) At the conclusion of other discovery, and at least 30 days prior to the discovery cut-off date, interrogatories seeking the claims and contentions of the opposing party may be served unless the court has ordered otherwise.

[Source: Former Local Civil Rule 46 (Southern District Only).]

RULE 33.4 OPT–OUT FROM CERTAIN PROVISIONS OF FEDERAL RULE OF CIVIL PROCEDURE 33 (SOUTHERN DISTRICT ONLY)—REPEALED DECEMBER 1, 2000

RULE 34.1 OPT–OUT FROM CERTAIN PROVISIONS OF FEDERAL RULE OF CIVIL PROCEDURE 34 (SOUTHERN DISTRICT ONLY)—REPEALED DECEMBER 1, 2000

RULE 36.1 OPT–OUT FROM CERTAIN PROVISIONS OF FEDERAL RULE OF CIVIL PROCEDURE 36 (SOUTHERN DISTRICT ONLY)—REPEALED DECEMBER 1, 2000

RULE 37.1 VERBATIM QUOTATION OF DISCOVERY MATERIALS

Upon any motion or application involving discovery or disclosure requests or responses under Rule 37 of the Federal Rules of Civil Procedure, the moving party shall specify and quote or set forth verbatim in the motion papers each discovery request and response to which the motion or application is addressed. The motion or application shall also set forth the grounds upon which the moving party is entitled to prevail as to each request or response. Local Civil Rule 5.1 also applies to the motion or application.

[Source: Former Local Civil Rule 3(c).]

Amended effective February 22, 2007.

RULE 37.2 MODE OF RAISING DISCOVERY DISPUTES WITH THE COURT (SOUTHERN DISTRICT ONLY)

No motion under Rules 26 through 37 inclusive of the Federal Rules of Civil Procedure shall be heard unless counsel for the moving party has first requested an informal conference with the court and such request has either been denied or the discovery dispute has not been resolved as a consequence of such a conference.

[Source: Former Local Civil Rule 3(*l*) (Southern District Only).]

RULE 37.3 MODE OF RAISING DISCOVERY AND OTHER NON-DISPOSITIVE PRETRIAL DISPUTES WITH THE COURT (EASTERN DISTRICT ONLY)

(a) Premotion Conference. Prior to seeking judicial resolution of a discovery or non-dispositive pretrial dispute, the attorneys for the affected parties or non-party witness shall attempt to confer in good faith in person or by telephone in an effort to resolve the dispute.

(b) Disputes Arising During Depositions. Where the attorneys for the affected parties or a non-party witness cannot agree on a resolution of a discovery dispute that arises during a deposition, they shall, to the extent practicable, notify the court by telephone and seek a ruling while the deposition is in progress. If a prompt ruling cannot be obtained, and the dispute involves an instruction to the witness not to answer a question, the instruction not to answer may stand and the deposition shall continue until a ruling is obtained pursuant to the procedure set forth in paragraph (c) below.

(c) Other Discovery and Non-dispositive Pretrial Disputes. Where the attorneys for the affected parties or non-party witness cannot agree on a resolution of any other discovery dispute or non-dispositive pretrial dispute, or if they are unable to obtain a telephonic ruling on a discovery dispute that arises during a deposition as provided in paragraph (b) above, they shall notify the court, at the option of the attorney for any affected party or non-party witness, either by telephone conference with all affected parties on the line or by letter not exceeding three pages in length outlining the nature of the dispute and attaching relevant materials. Within three days of receiving such a letter, any opposing affected party or non-party witness may submit a responsive letter not exceeding three pages attaching relevant materials. Except for the letters and attachments authorized herein, or where a ruling which was made exclusively as a result of a telephone conference is the subject of de novo review pursuant to paragraph (d) hereof, papers shall not be submitted with respect to a dispute governed by this rule unless the court has so directed.

(d) Motion for Reconsideration. A ruling made exclusively as a result of a telephone conference may be the subject of de novo reconsideration by a letter not exceeding five pages in length attaching relevant materials submitted by any affected party or non-party witness. Within three days of receiving such a letter, any other affected party or non-party witness may submit a responsive letter not exceeding five pages in length attaching relevant materials.

(e) Decision of the Court. The court shall record or arrange for the recording of the court's decision in writing. Such written order may take the form of an oral order read into the record of a deposition or other proceeding, a handwritten memorandum, a handwritten marginal notation on a letter or other document, or any other form the court deems appropriate.

[Source: Eastern District Standing Orders 6, 11(c).]

Amended effective April 15, 2005.

RULE 39.1   CUSTODY OF EXHIBITS

(a) Except in proceedings before a master or commissioner, and unless the court orders otherwise, exhibits shall not be filed with the clerk, but shall be retained in the custody of the respective attorneys who produced them in court.

(b) Exhibits which have been filed with the clerk shall be removed by the party responsible for them (1) if no appeal is taken, within ninety (90) days after a final decision is rendered, or (2) if an appeal has been taken, within thirty (30) days after the final disposition of the appeal. Parties failing to comply with this rule shall be notified by the clerk to remove their exhibits and upon their failure to do so within thirty (30) days, the clerk may dispose of them as the clerk may see fit.

[Source: Former Local Civil Rule 24(a), (d).]

RULE 39.2   ORDER OF SUMMATION

After the close of evidence in civil trials, the order of summation shall be determined in the discretion of the court.

[Source: Former Local Civil Rule 44.]

RULE 47.1   ASSESSMENT OF JURY COSTS

All counsel in civil cases shall seriously discuss the possibility of settlement a reasonable time prior to trial. The court may, in its discretion, assess the parties or counsel with the cost of one day's attendance of the jurors if a case is settled after the jury has been summoned or during trial, the amount to be paid to the clerk of the court. For purposes of this rule, a civil jury is considered summoned for a trial as of Noon of the business day prior to the designated date of the trial.

[Source: Former Local Civil Rule 22.]

RULE 53.1   MASTERS

(a) Oath. Every person appointed pursuant to Rule 53 shall, before entering upon his or her duties, take and subscribe an oath, which, except as otherwise prescribed by statute or rule, shall be the same as the oath prescribed for judges pursuant to 28 U.S.C. § 453, with the addition of the words "in conformance with the order of appointment" after the words "administer justice." Such an oath may be taken before any federal or state officer authorized by federal law to administer oaths, and shall be filed in the office of the clerk.

(b) May Sit Outside District. A person appointed pursuant to Rule 53 may sit within or outside the district. When the person appointed is requested to sit outside the district for the convenience of a party and there is opposition by another party, he or she may make an order for the holding of the hearing, or a part thereof, outside the district, upon such terms and conditions as shall be just. Such order may be reviewed by the court upon motion of any party, served within ten (10) days after service on all parties by the master of the order.

[Source: Former Local Civil Rules 19(a) and (b) and 20.]

[Amended effective February 22, 2007.]

RULE 54.1 TAXABLE COSTS

(a) Request to Tax Costs. Within thirty (30) days after the entry of final judgment, or, in the case of an appeal by any party, within thirty (30) days after the final disposition of the appeal, unless this period is extended by the court for good cause shown, any party seeking to recover costs shall file with the clerk a request to tax costs annexing a bill of costs and indicating the date and time of taxation. Costs will not be taxed during the pendency of any appeal. Any party failing to file a request to tax costs within this thirty (30) day period will be deemed to have waived costs. The request to tax costs shall be served upon each other party not less than three (3) days (if service is made by hand delivery) or six (6) days (if service is made by any means other than hand delivery) before the date and time fixed for taxation. The bill of costs shall include an affidavit that the costs claimed are allowable by law, are correctly stated and were necessarily incurred. Bills for the costs claimed shall be attached as exhibits.

(b) Objections to Bill of Costs. A party objecting to any cost item shall serve objections in writing prior to or at the time for taxation. The clerk will proceed to tax costs at the time noticed and allow such items as are properly taxable. In the absence of written objection, any item listed may be taxed within the discretion of the clerk.

(c) Items Taxable as Costs.

(1) *Transcripts.* The cost of any part of the original trial transcript that was necessarily obtained for use in this court or on appeal is taxable. The cost of a transcript of court proceedings prior to or subsequent to trial is taxable only when authorized in advance or ordered by the court.

(2) *Depositions.* Unless otherwise ordered by the court, the original transcript of a deposition, plus one copy, is taxable if the deposition was used or received in evidence at the trial, whether or not it was read in its entirety. Costs for depositions are also taxable if they were used by the court in ruling on a motion for summary judgment or other dispositive substantive motion. Costs for depositions taken solely for discovery are not taxable. Counsel's fees and expenses in attending the taking of a deposition are not taxable except as provided by statute, rule (including Local Civil Rule 30.1), or order of the court. Fees, mileage,

and subsistence for the witness at the deposition are taxable at the same rates as for attendance at trial if the deposition taken was used or received in evidence at the trial.

(3) *Witness Fees, Mileage and Subsistence.* Witness fees and mileage pursuant to 28 U.S.C. § 1821 are taxable if the witness testifies. Subsistence pursuant to 28 U.S.C. § 1821 is taxable if the witness testifies and it is not practical for the witness to return to his or her residence from day to day. No party to the action may receive witness fees, mileage, or subsistence. Fees for expert witnesses are taxable only to the extent of fees for ordinary witnesses unless prior court approval was obtained.

(4) *Interpreting Costs.* The reasonable fee of a competent interpreter, and the reasonable cost of special interpretation services pursuant to 28 U.S.C. § 1828, are taxable if the fee of the witness involved is taxable. The reasonable fee of a translator is also taxable if the document translated is used or received in evidence.

(5) *Exemplifications and Copies of Papers.* A copy of an exhibit is taxable if the original was not available and the copy was used or received in evidence. The cost of copies used for the convenience of counsel or the court are not taxable. The fees for a search and certification or proof of the non-existence of a document in a public office is taxable.

(6) *Maps, Charts, Models, Photographs and Summaries.* The cost of photographs, 8″ × 10″ in size or less, is taxable if used or received in evidence. Enlargements greater than 8″ × 10″ are not taxable except by order of court. Costs of maps, charts, and models, including computer generated models, are not taxable except by order of court. The cost of compiling summaries, statistical comparisons and reports is not taxable.

(7) *Attorney Fees and Related Costs.* Attorney fees and disbursements and other related fees and paralegal expenses are not taxable except by order of the court.

(8) *Fees of Masters, Receivers, Commissioners and Court Appointed Experts.* Fees of masters, receivers, commissioners, and court appointed experts are taxable as costs, unless otherwise ordered by the court.

(9) *Costs for Title Searches.* A party is entitled to tax necessary disbursements for the expenses of searches made by title insurance, abstract or searching companies, or by any public officer authorized to make official searches and certify to the same, taxable at rates not exceeding the cost of similar official searches.

(10) *Docket and Miscellaneous Fees.* Docket fees, and the reasonable and actual fees of the clerk and of a marshal, sheriff, and process server, are taxable unless otherwise ordered by the court.

[Source: Former Local Civil Rules 11, 12.]

RULE 54.2 SECURITY FOR COSTS

The court, on motion or on its own initiative, may order any party to file an original bond for costs or additional security for costs in such an amount and so conditioned as it may designate. For failure to comply with the order the court may make such orders in regard to non-compliance as are just, and among others the following: an order striking out pleadings or staying further proceedings until the bond is filed or dismissing the action or rendering a judgment by default against the non-complying party.

[Source: Former Local Civil Rule 39.]

RULE 54.3 ENTERING SATISFACTION OF MONEY JUDGMENT

Satisfaction of a money judgment recovered or registered in this district shall be entered by the clerk as follows:

(a) Upon the payment into the court of the amount thereof, plus interest, and the payment of the clerk's and marshal's fees, if any;

(b) Upon the filing of a satisfaction executed and acknowledged by: (1) the judgment creditor; or (2) the judgment creditor's legal representatives or assigns, with evidence of their authority; or (3) the judgment creditor's attorney if within ten (10) years of the entry of the judgment or decree;

(c) If the judgment creditor is the United States, upon the filing of a satisfaction executed by the United States Attorney;

(d) Pursuant to an order of satisfaction entered by the court; or

(e) Upon the registration of a certified copy of a satisfaction entered in another district.

[Source: Former Local Civil Rule 13.]

RULE 55.1 CERTIFICATE OF DEFAULT

A party applying for a certificate of default by the clerk pursuant to Federal Rule of Civil Procedure 55(a) shall submit an affidavit showing (1) that the party against whom a notation of default is sought is not an infant, in the military, or an incompetent person; (2) that the party has failed to plead or otherwise defend the action; and (3) that the pleading to which no response has been made was properly served.

[Source: Former Local Civil Rule 10(a).]

RULE 55.2 DEFAULT JUDGMENT

(a) By the Clerk. Upon issuance of a clerk's certificate of default, if the claim to which no response has been made only sought payment of a sum certain, and does not include a request for attorney's fees or other substantive relief, and if a default judgment is sought against all remaining parties to the action, the moving party may request the clerk to enter a default judgment, by submitting an affidavit showing the principal amount due and owing, not exceeding the amount sought in the claim to which no response has been made, plus interest, if any, computed by the party, with credit for all payments received to date clearly set forth, and costs, if any, pursuant to 28 U.S.C. § 1920.

(b) By the Court. In all other cases the party seeking a judgment by default shall apply to the court as described in Federal Rule of Civil Procedure 55(b)(2), and shall append to the application (1) the clerk's certificate of default, (2) a copy of the claim to which no response has been made, and (3) a proposed form of default judgment.

[Source: Former Local Civil Rule 10.]

RULE 56.1 STATEMENTS OF MATERIAL FACTS ON MOTION FOR SUMMARY JUDGMENT

(a) Upon any motion for summary judgment pursuant to Rule 56 of the Federal Rules of Civil Procedure, there shall be annexed to the notice of motion a separate, short and concise statement, in numbered paragraphs, of the material facts as to which the moving party contends there is no genuine issue to be tried. Failure to submit such a statement may constitute grounds for denial of the motion.

(b) The papers opposing a motion for summary judgment shall include a correspondingly numbered paragraph responding to each numbered paragraph in the statement of the moving party, and if necessary, additional paragraphs containing a separate, short and concise statement of additional material facts as to which it is contended that there exists a genuine issue to be tried.

(c) Each numbered paragraph in the statement of material facts set forth in the statement required to be served by the moving party will be deemed to be admitted for purposes of the motion unless specifically controverted by a correspondingly numbered paragraph in the statement required to be served by the opposing party.

(d) Each statement by the movant or opponent pursuant to Rule 56.1(a) and (b), including each statement controverting any statement of material fact, must be followed by citation to evidence which would be admissible, set forth as required by Federal Rule of Civil Procedure 56(e).

[Source: Former Local Civil Rule 3(g).]

Adopted March 25, 2004.

RULE 56.2 NOTICE TO PRO SE LITIGANT WHO OPPOSES A SUMMARY JUDGMENT

Any represented party moving for summary judgment against a party proceeding *pro se* shall serve and file as a separate document, together with the papers in support of the motion, a "Notice To Pro Se Litigant Who Opposes a Motion For Summary Judgment" in the form indicated below. Where the pro se party is not the plaintiff, the movant shall amend the form notice as necessary to reflect that fact.

Notice To Pro Se Litigant Who Opposes a Motion For Summary Judgment

The defendant in this case has moved for summary judgment pursuant to Rule 56 of the Federal Rules of Civil Procedure. This means that the defendant has asked the court to decide this case without a trial, based on written materials, including affidavits, submitted in support of the motion. THE CLAIMS YOU ASSERT IN YOUR COMPLAINT MAY BE DISMISSED WITHOUT A TRIAL IF YOU DO NOT RESPOND TO THIS MOTION by filing sworn affidavits and other papers as required by Rule 56(e) of the Federal Rules of Civil Procedure and by Local Civil Rule 56.1. An affidavit is a sworn statement of fact based on personal knowledge that would be admissible in evidence at trial. The full text of Rule 56 of the Federal Rules of Civil Procedure and Local Civil Rule 56.1 is attached.

In short, Rule 56 provides that you may NOT oppose summary judgment simply by relying upon the allegations in your complaint. Rather, you must submit evidence, such as witness statements or documents, countering the facts asserted by the defendant and raising material issues of fact for trial. Any witness statements must be in the form of affidavits. You may submit your own affidavit and/or the affidavits of others. You may submit affidavits that were prepared specifically in response to defendant's motion for summary judgment.

If you do not respond to the motion for summary judgment on time with affidavits or documentary evidence contradicting the material facts asserted by the defendant, the court may accept defendant's factual assertions as true. Judgment may then be entered in defendant's favor without a trial.

If you have any questions you may direct them to the Pro Se Office.

Effective September 23, 1999. Amended effective May 18, 2007.

RULE 58.1 REMAND BY AN APPELLATE COURT

Any order or judgment of an appellate court, when filed in the office of the clerk of the district court, shall automatically become the order or judgment of the district court and be entered as such by the clerk without further order, except if such order or judgment of the appellate court requires further proceedings in the district court other than a new trial, an order shall be entered making the order or judgment of the appellate court the order or judgment of the district court.

[Source: Former Local Civil Rule 42.]

RULE 65.1.1 SURETIES

(a) Whenever a bond, undertaking or stipulation is required, it shall be sufficient, except as otherwise prescribed by law, if the instrument is executed by the surety or sureties only.

(b) Except as otherwise provided by law, every bond, undertaking or stipulation must be secured by: (1) the deposit of cash or government bonds in the amount of the bond, undertaking or stipulation; or (2) the undertaking or guaranty of a corporate surety holding a certificate of authority from the Secretary of the Treasury; or (3) the undertaking or guaranty of two individual residents of the district in which the case is pending, each of whom owns real or personal property within the district worth double the amount of the bond, undertaking or stipulation, over all his or her debts and liabilities, and over all obligations assumed by said surety on other bonds, undertakings or stipulations, and exclusive of all legal exemptions.

(c) Except as otherwise provided by law, all bonds, undertakings and stipulations of corporate sureties holding certificates of authority from the Secretary of the Treasury, where the amount of such bonds or undertakings has been fixed by a judge or by court rule or statute, may be approved by the clerk.

(d) In the case of a bond, or undertaking, or stipulation executed by individual sureties, each surety shall attach the surety's affidavit of justification, giving the surety's full name, occupation, residence and business addresses, and showing that the surety is qualified as an individual surety under paragraph (b) of this rule.

(e) Members of the bar who have appeared in the case, administrative officers and employees of the court, the marshal, and the marshal's deputies and assistants, shall not act as a surety in any suit, action or proceeding pending in this court.

(f) Whenever a notice of motion to enforce the liability of a surety upon an appeal or a supersedeas bond is served upon the clerk pursuant to Federal Rule of Appellate Procedure 8(b), the party making such motion shall deposit with the clerk the original, three copies, and one additional copy for each surety to be served.

[Source: Former Local Civil Rules 37, 38, 40(b).]

RULE 67.1 ORDER FOR DEPOSIT IN INTEREST–BEARING ACCOUNT

(a) Whenever a party seeks a court order for money to be deposited by the clerk in an interest-bearing account, the party shall personally deliver the order to the clerk or financial deputy who will inspect the proposed order for proper form and content and compliance with this rule prior to signature by the judge for whom the order is prepared. After the judge has signed the order, the person who obtained the order shall serve the clerk and the financial deputy with a copy of the order signed by the judge.

(b) Proposed orders directing the clerk to invest such funds in an interest-bearing account or other instrument shall include the following:

(1) The exact United States dollar amount of the principal sum to be invested; and

(2) Wording which directs the clerk to deduct from the income on the investment a fee equal to ten per cent (10%) of the income earned, but not exceeding the fee authorized by the Judicial Conference of the United States and set by the Director of the Administrative Office.

[Source: Former Local Civil Rule 8(c).]

RULE 72.1 POWERS OF MAGISTRATE JUDGES

In addition to other powers of magistrate judges:

(a) Full-time magistrate judges are hereby specially designated to exercise the jurisdiction set forth in 28 U.S.C. § 636(c).

(b) Magistrate judges are authorized to entertain ex parte applications by appropriate representatives of the United States government for the issuance of administrative inspection orders or warrants.

(c) Magistrate judges may issue subpoenas, writs of habeas corpus ad testificandum or ad prosequendum or other orders necessary to obtain the presence of parties or witnesses or evidence needed for court proceedings, and may sign in forma pauperis orders.

(d) Matters arising under 28 U.S.C. §§ 2254 and 2255 or challenging the conditions of the confinement of prisoners may be referred to a magistrate judge by the judge to whom the case has been assigned. A magistrate judge may perform any or all of the duties imposed upon a judge by the rules governing such proceedings in the United States district courts. In so doing, a magistrate judge may issue any preliminary orders and conduct any necessary evidentiary hearing or other appropriate proceeding and shall submit to a judge a report containing proposed findings of fact and recommendations for disposition of the matter by the judge. Any order disposing of the petition may only be made by a judge.

[Source: Former Local Magistrate Judge Rules 1, 4, 6, and 10.]

RULE 72.2 REFERENCE TO MAGISTRATE JUDGE (EASTERN DISTRICT ONLY)

(a) Selection of Magistrate Judge. A magistrate judge shall be assigned to each case upon the commencement of the action, except in those categories of actions set forth in Local Civil Rule 16.1. In any courthouse in this District in which there is more than one magistrate judge such assignment shall be at random on a rotating basis. Except in multi-district cases and antitrust cases, a magistrate judge so assigned is empowered to act with respect to all non-dispositive pretrial matters unless the assigned district judge orders otherwise.

(b) Orders Affecting Reference. The attorneys for the parties shall be provided with copies of all orders affecting the scope of the reference to the magistrate judge.

[Source: Eastern District Standing Order 4(a), (c).]

RULE 73.1 CONSENT JURISDICTION PROCEDURE

(a) When a civil action is filed with the clerk, the clerk shall give the filing party notice of the magistrate judge's consent jurisdiction in a form approved by the court, with sufficient copies to be served with the complaint on adversary parties. A copy of such notice shall be attached to any third-party complaint served by a defendant.

(b) When a completed consent form has been filed, the clerk shall forward the form for final approval to the district judge to whom the case was originally assigned. Once the district judge has approved the transfer and returned the consent form to the clerk for filing, the clerk shall reassign the case for all purposes to the magistrate judge previously designated to receive any referrals or to whom the case has previously been referred for any purpose. If no designation or referral has been made, or in the Eastern District upon application of the parties, the clerk shall select a new magistrate judge at random.

[Source: Former Local Magistrate Judge Rule 8(a) and (c).]

RULE 77.1 SUBMISSION OF ORDERS, JUDGMENTS AND DECREES

(a) Proposed orders, judgments and decrees shall be presented to the clerk, and not presented directly to the judge. Unless the form of order, judgment or decree is consented to in writing, or unless the court otherwise directs, three (3) days' notice of settlement is required. One (1) day's notice is required of all counter-proposals. Unless adopted by the court or submitted for docketing by a party in connection with an anticipated appeal, such proposed orders, judgments or decrees shall not form any part of the record of this action.

(b) The party who obtains entry of an order or judgment shall append to or endorse upon it a list of the names of the parties entitled to be notified of the entry thereof and the names and addresses of their respective attorneys.

[Source: Former Local Civil Rule 8.]

RULE 81.1 REMOVAL OF CASES FROM STATE COURTS

(a) If the court's jurisdiction is based upon diversity of citizenship, and regardless of whether or not service of process has been effected on all parties, the notice of removal shall set forth (1) in the case of each individual named as a party, the states of citizenship and residence and the address of that party, (2) in the case of each corporation named as a party, the state of incorporation and of its principal place of business, and (3) the date on which each party that has been served was served. If such information or a designated part is unknown to the removing party, the removing party may so state, and in that case plaintiff within twenty (20) days after removal shall file in the office of the clerk a statement of the omitted information.

(b) Unless otherwise ordered by the court, within twenty (20) days after filing the notice of removal, the removing party shall file with the clerk a copy of all records and proceedings in the state court.

[Source: Former Local Civil Rule 25(b), (c).]

RULE 83.1 TRANSFER OF CASES TO ANOTHER DISTRICT

In a case ordered transferred from this district, the clerk, unless otherwise ordered, shall upon the expiration of five (5) days mail to the clerk of the court to which the case is transferred (1) certified copies of the court's opinion ordering the transfer, of its order, and of the docket entries in the case, and (2) the originals of all other papers on file in the case.

[Source: Former Local Civil Rule 26.]

RULE 83.2 SETTLEMENT OF ACTIONS BY OR ON BEHALF OF INFANTS OR INCOMPETENTS, WRONGFUL DEATH ACTIONS[, *AND CONSCIOUS PAIN AND SUFFERING ACTIONS (EDNY ONLY)*]

(a) Settlement of Actions by or on Behalf of Infants or Incompetents.

(1) An action by or on behalf of an infant or incompetent shall not be settled or compromised, or volun-

tarily discontinued, dismissed or terminated, without leave of the court embodied in an order, judgment or decree. The proceeding upon an application to settle or compromise such an action shall conform, as nearly as may be, to the New York State statutes and rules, but the court, for cause shown, may dispense with any New York State requirement.

(2) The court shall authorize payment to counsel for the infant or incompetent of a reasonable attorney's fee and proper disbursements from the amount recovered in such an action, whether realized by settlement, execution or otherwise and shall determine the said fee and disbursements, after due inquiry as to all charges against the fund.

(3) The court shall order the balance of the proceeds of the recovery or settlement to be distributed as it deems may best protect the interest of the infant or incompetent.

(b) Settlement of Wrongful Death Actions [*and Actions for Conscious Pain and Suffering (EDNY only)*]. In an action for wrongful death [*or conscious pain and suffering (EDNY only)*]:

(1) Where required by statute or otherwise, the court shall apportion the avails of the action, and shall approve the terms of any settlement.

(2) The court shall approve an attorney's fee only upon application in accordance with the provisions of the New York State statutes and rules.

[Source: Former Local Civil Rules 28, 29.]

[Amended effective February 1, 1999; December 1, 2000.]

RULE 83.3 HABEAS CORPUS

Unless otherwise provided by statute, applications for a writ of habeas corpus made by persons under the judgment and sentence of a court of the State of New York shall be filed, heard and determined in the district court for the district within which they were convicted and sentenced; provided, however, that if the convenience of the parties and witnesses requires a hearing in a different district, such application may be transferred to any district which is found by the assigned judge to be more convenient. The clerks of the Southern and Eastern District Courts are authorized and directed to transfer such applications to the District herein designated for filing, hearing and determination.

[Source: Former Local Civil Rule 32(d).]

RULE 83.4 PROCEEDINGS TO STAY THE DEPORTATION OF ALIENS IN DEPORTATION AND EXCLUSION CASES

(a) The Petition or Complaint.

(1) Any application to stay an alien's deportation must be verified and, if made by someone other than

the alien, must show either that the applicant has been authorized by the alien to make the application, or that the applicant is the parent, child, spouse, brother, sister, attorney or next friend of the alien.

(2) The application must state in detail why the alien's deportation is invalid. This shall include a statement setting forth the reasons why a stay is warranted, including a description of the irreparable harm that the alien will suffer if the application is not granted. The application shall also state in what manner the applicable administrative remedies have been exhausted or why such exhaustion is not required and whether any prior application to the court for the same or similar relief has been made.

(3) The application shall recite the source of the factual allegations it contains. If the Immigration and Naturalization Service has been requested to grant the alien, the alien's attorney or the alien's representative access to the alien's records and access has been refused, the application shall state who made the request to review the records, when and to whom it was made, and by whom access was refused. In the event it is claimed that insufficient time was available to examine the alien's records, the application shall state when the alien was informed of his deportation and why he has been unable to examine the records since that time.

(4) Every application to stay the alien's deportation shall contain the alien's immigration file number or other identifying information supplied to the applicant, and the decision, if any, the alien seeks the court to review. In the event this decision was oral, the application shall state the nature of the relief requested, who denied the request, the reasons for the denial and the date the request was denied.

(5) The application shall also state the basis upon which the applicant believes that this court has jurisdiction over the custodian of the alien.

(b) **Commencement of the Proceeding.** In any proceeding to stay the deportation of an alien, the original verified petition or complaint shall be filed with the clerk. In addition to service pursuant to Federal Rule of Civil Procedure 4, a copy of the petition or complaint, and application for a writ of habeas corpus or order to show cause shall be delivered to the United States attorney prior to the issuance of any writ or order staying the deportation; if the United States attorney's office is closed, delivery shall be made before 10:00 a.m. the following business day, unless the court otherwise directs.

(c) **Procedure for Issuance of an Order or Writ.**

(1) In the event the court determines to stay temporarily an alien's deportation, it shall briefly set forth why the order or writ was issued, endorse upon the

order or writ the date and time it was issued, and set the matter for prompt hearing on the merits.

(2) All orders or writs temporarily enjoining an alien's expulsion shall expire by their terms within such time after entry, not to exceed ten (10) days, as the court fixes, unless within the time so fixed the order, for good cause shown, is extended for a like period or unless the government consents to an extension for a longer period.

(d) Service of the writ or order upon the United States attorney's office within the time specified by the court shall be sufficient service to stay an alien's deportation.

(e) After delivery of an alien for deportation to the master of a ship or the commanding officer of an airplane, the writ or order staying the alien's deportation shall be addressed to and served upon only such master or commanding officer. Notice to the respondent, or the United States attorney's office, of the allowance of the writ or issuance of the order shall not operate to stay an alien's deportation if the alien is no longer in the government's custody. Service of the writ or order may not be made upon a master after the ship has left on her voyage or upon a commanding officer once the airplane has closed its doors and left the terminal.

[Source: Former Local Civil Rules 30, 31.]

RULE 83.5 THREE–JUDGE COURT

Whenever upon an application for injunctive relief counsel is of opinion that the relief is such as may be granted only by a three-judge court, the petition shall so state, and the proposed order to show cause (whether or not containing a stay), or the notice of motion, shall include a request for a hearing before a three-judge court. Upon the convening of a three-judge court, in addition to the original papers on file, there shall be submitted three additional copies of all papers filed with the court.

[Source: Former Local Civil Rule 34.]

RULE 83.6 PUBLICATION OF ADVERTISEMENTS

(a) All advertisements except notices of sale of real estate or of any interest in land shall be published in a newspaper which has a general circulation in this district or a circulation reasonably calculated to give public notice of a legal publication. The court may direct the publication of such additional advertisement as it may deem advisable.

(b) Unless otherwise ordered, notices for the sale of real estate or of any interest in land shall be published in a newspaper of general circulation in the county in which the real estate or the land in question is located.

[Source: Former Local Civil Rule 35.]

RULE 83.7   NOTICE OF SALE

In any civil action, the notice of any proposed sale of property directed to be made by any order or judgment of the court, unless otherwise ordered by the court, need not set out the terms of sale specified in the order or judgment, and the notice will be sufficient if in substantially the following form:

UNITED STATES DISTRICT COURT

_____ DISTRICT OF NEW YORK

[CAPTION]   [Docket No. and Judge's Initials]

NOTICE OF SALE

Pursuant to ___(Order or Judgment)___ of the United States Court for the _____ District of New York, filed in the office of the clerk on ___(Date)___ in the case entitled ___(Name and Docket Number)___ the undersigned will sell at ___(Place of Sale)___ on ___(Date and Hour of Sale)___ the property in said ___ (Order or Judgment)___ described and therein directed to be sold, to which ___(Order or Judgment)___ reference is made for the terms of sale and for a description of the property which may be briefly described as follows:

DATED:

_____

Signature and Official Title

The notice need not describe the property by metes and bounds or otherwise in detail and will be sufficient if in general terms it identifies the property by specifying its nature and location. However, it shall state: the approximate acreage of any real estate outside the limits of any town or city; the street, lot and block number of any real estate within any town or city; and a general statement of the character of any improvements upon the property.

[Source: Former Local Civil Rule 36.]

RULE 83.8   FILING OF NOTICE OF APPEAL

A notice of appeal shall state the names of the several parties to the judgment, and the names and addresses of their respective attorneys of record. Upon the filing of the notice of appeal the appellant shall furnish the clerk with three additional copies thereof, as well as a sufficient number of further copies thereof to enable the clerk to comply with the provisions of Federal Rule of Appellate Procedure 3(a).

[Source: Former Local Civil Rule 40(a).]

RULE 83.9   CONTEMPT PROCEEDINGS IN CIVIL CASES

(a) A proceeding to adjudicate a person in civil contempt, including a case provided for in Federal Rules of Civil Procedure 37(b)(1) and 37(b)(2)(D), shall be commenced by the service of a notice of motion or order to show cause. The affidavit upon which such notice of motion or order to show cause is based shall set out with particularity the misconduct complained of, the claim, if any, for damages occasioned thereby and such evidence as to the amount of damages as may be available to the moving party. A reasonable counsel fee, necessitated by the contempt proceedings, may be included as an item of damage. Where the alleged contemnor has appeared in the action by an attorney, the notice of motion or order to show cause and the papers upon which it is based may be served upon said attorney; otherwise service shall be made personally, in the manner provided for by the Federal Rules of Civil Procedure for the service of a summons. If an order to show cause is sought, such order may, upon necessity shown, embody a direction to the United States marshal to arrest the alleged contemnor and hold such person unless bail is posted in an amount fixed by the order, conditioned on the appearance of such person in all further proceedings on the motion, and further conditioned that the alleged contemnor will hold himself or herself amenable to all orders of the court for surrender.

(b) If the alleged contemnor puts in issue his or her alleged misconduct or the damages thereby occasioned, said person shall upon demand be entitled to have oral evidence taken, either before the court or before a master appointed by the court. When by law such alleged contemnor is entitled to a trial by jury, said person shall make written demand before the beginning of the hearing on the application; otherwise the alleged contemnor will be deemed to have waived a trial by jury.

(c) If the alleged contemnor is found to be in contempt of court, an order shall be entered (1) reciting or referring to the verdict or findings of fact upon which the adjudication is based; (2) setting forth the amount of damages, if any, to which the complainant is entitled; (3) fixing the fine, if any, imposed by the court, which fine shall include the damages found and naming the person to whom such fine shall be payable; (4) stating any other conditions, the performance of which will operate to purge the contempt; and (5) directing, where appropriate, the arrest of the contemnor by the United States marshal and confinement until the performance of the condition fixed in the order and the payment of the fine, or until the contemnor be otherwise discharged pursuant to law. Upon such an order, no person shall be detained in prison by reason of the non-payment of the fine for a period exceeding six months. A certified copy of the order committing the contemnor shall be sufficient warrant to the marshal for the arrest and confinement of the contemnor. The complainant shall also have the same remedies against the property of the contemnor as if the order awarding the fine were a final judgment.

(d) If the alleged contemnor is found not guilty of the charges, said person shall be discharged from the proceedings and, in the discretion of the court, may have judgment against the complainant for costs and disbursements and a reasonable counsel fee.

[Source: Former Local Civil Rule 43.]

RULE 83.10 COURT-ANNEXED ARBITRATION (EASTERN DISTRICT ONLY)

(a) Certification of Arbitrators.

(1) The Chief Judge or a judge or judges authorized by the Chief Judge to act (hereafter referred to as the certifying judge) shall certify as many arbitrators as may be determined to be necessary under this rule.

(2) An individual may be certified to serve as an arbitrator if he or she: (A) has been for at least five years a member of the bar of the highest court of a state or a District of Columbia, (B) is admitted to practice before this court, and (C) is determined by the certifying judge to be competent to perform the duties of an arbitrator.

(3) Each individual certified as an arbitrator shall take the oath or affirmation required by Title 28, U.S.C. § 453 before serving as an arbitrator.

(4) A list of all persons certified as arbitrators shall be maintained in the Office of the Clerk.

(b) Compensation and Expenses of Arbitrators. An arbitrator shall be compensated $250 for services in each case. If an arbitration hearing is protracted, the certifying judge may entertain a petition for additional compensation. If a party requests three arbitrators then each arbitrator shall be compensated $100 for service. The fees shall be paid by or pursuant to the order of the Court subject to the limits set by the Judicial Conference of the United States.

(c) Immunity of Arbitrators. Arbitrators shall be immune from liability or suit with respect to their conduct as such to the maximum extent permitted by applicable law.

(d) Civil Cases Eligible for Compulsory Arbitration.

(1) The Clerk of Court shall, as to all cases filed after January 1, 1986, designate and process for compulsory arbitration all civil cases (excluding social security cases, tax matters, prisoners' civil rights cases and any action based on an alleged violation of a right secured by the Constitution of the United States or if jurisdiction is based in whole or in part on Title 28, U.S.C. § 1343) wherein money damages only are being sought in an amount not in excess of $150,000.00 exclusive of interest and costs.

(2) The parties may by written stipulation agree that the Clerk of Court shall designate and process for court-annexed arbitration any civil case that is not subject to compulsory arbitration hereunder.

(3) For purposes of this Rule only, in all civil cases damages shall be presumed to be not in excess of $150,000.00 exclusive of interest and costs, unless:

(A) Counsel for plaintiff, at the time of filing the complaint, or in the event of the removal of a case from state court or transfer of a case from another district to this court, within thirty (30) days of the docketing of the case in this district, files a certification with the court that the damages sought exceed $150,000.00, exclusive of interest and costs; or

(B) Counsel for a defendant, at the time of filing a counterclaim or cross-claim files a certification with the court that the damages sought by the counter-claim or cross-claim exceed $150,000.00 exclusive of interest and costs.

(e) Referral to Arbitration.

(1) After an answer is filed in a case determined eligible for arbitration, the arbitration clerk shall send a notice to counsel setting for the date and time for the arbitration hearing. The date of the arbitration hearing set forth in the notice shall be approximately four months but in no event later than 120 days from the date the answer was filed, except that the arbitration proceeding shall not, in the absence of the consent of the parties, commence until 30 days after the disposition by the district court of any motion to dismiss the complaint, motion for judgment on the pleadings, motion to join necessary parties, or motion for summary judgment, if the motion was filed during a time period specified by the district court. The 120–day and 30–day periods specified in the preceding sentence may be modified by the court for good cause shown. The notice shall also advise counsel that they may agree to an earlier date for the arbitration hearing provided the arbitration clerk is notified with 30 days of the date of the notice. The notice shall also advise counsel that they have 90 days to complete discovery unless the judge to whom the case has been assigned orders a shorter or longer period for discovery. The judge may refer the case to a magistrate for purposes of discovery. In the event a third party has been brought into the action, this notice shall not be sent until an answer has been filed by the third party.

(2) The court shall, sua sponte, or on motion of a party, exempt any case from arbitration in which the objectives of arbitration would not be realized

(A) because the case involves complex or novel issues,

(B) because legal issues predominate over factual issues, or

(C) for other good cause.

Application by a party for an exemption from compulsory arbitration shall be made by written letter to the court not exceeding three pages in length, outlining the basis for the request and attaching relevant materials, which shall be submitted no later than 20 days after receipt of the notice to counsel setting forth the date and time for the arbitration hearing. Within three days of receiving such a letter, any opposing affected party may submit a responsive letter not exceeding three pages attaching relevant materials.

(3) Cases not originally designated as eligible for compulsory arbitration, but which in the discretion of the assigned judge, are later found to qualify, may be referred to arbitration. A U.S. District Judge or a U.S. Magistrate Judge, in cases that exceed the arbitration ceiling of $150,000 exclusive of interest and costs, in their discretion, may suggest that the parties should consider arbitration. If the parties are agreeable, an appropriate consent form signed by all parties or their representatives may be entered and filed in the case prior to scheduling an arbitration hearing.

(4) The arbitration shall be held before one arbitrator unless a panel of three arbitrators is requested by a party, in which case one of whom shall be designated as chairperson of the panel. If the amount of controversy, exclusive of interest and costs, if $5,000 or less, the arbitration shall be held before a single arbitrator. The arbitration panel shall be chosen at random by the Clerk of the Court from the lawyers who have been duly certified as arbitrators. The arbitration panel shall be scheduled to hear not more than three cases.

(5) The judge to whom the case has been assigned shall, 30 days prior to the date scheduled for the arbitration hearing, sign an order setting forth the date and time of the arbitration hearing and the names of the arbitrators designated to hear the case. If a party has filed a motion for judgment on the pleadings, summary judgment or similar relief, the judge shall not sign the order before ruling on the motion, but the filing of such a motion on or after the date of the order shall not stay the arbitration unless the judge so orders.

(6) Upon entry of the order designating the arbitrators, the arbitration clerk shall send to each arbitrator a copy of all pleadings, including the order designating the arbitrators, and the guidelines for arbitrators.

(7) Persons selected to be arbitrators shall be disqualified for bias or prejudice as provided in Title 28, U.S.C. § 144, and shall disqualify themselves in any action which they would be required under Title 28,

U.S.C. § 455 to disqualify themselves if they were a justice, judge, or magistrate.

(f) Arbitration Hearing.

(1) The arbitration hearing shall take place in the United States Courthouse in a courtroom assigned by the arbitration clerk on the date and at the time set forth in the order of the Court. The arbitrators are authorized to change the date and time of the hearing provided the hearing is commenced within 30 days of the hearing date set forth in the order of the Court. Any continuance beyond this 30 day period must be approved by the judge to whom the case has been assigned. The arbitration clerk must be notified immediately of any continuance.

(2) Counsel for the parties shall report settlement of the case to the arbitration clerk and all members of the arbitration panel assigned to the case.

(3) The arbitration hearing may proceed in the absence of any party who, after notice, fails to be present. In the event, however, that a party fails to participate in the arbitration process in a meaningful manner, the Court may impose appropriate sanctions, including, but no limited to, the striking of any demand for a trial de novo filed by that party.

(4) Rule 45 of the Federal Rules of Civil Procedure shall apply to subpoenas for attendance of witnesses and the production of documentary evidence at an arbitration hearing under this Rule. Testimony at an arbitration hearing shall be under oath or affirmation.

(5) The Federal Rules of Evidence shall be used as guides to the admissibility of evidence. Copies or photographs of all exhibits, except those intended solely for impeachment, must be marked for identification and delivered to adverse parties at least ten (10) days prior to the hearing. The arbitrators shall receive exhibits in evidence without formal proof unless counsel has been notified at least five (5) days prior to the hearing that the adverse party intends to raise an issue concerning the authenticity of the exhibit. The arbitrators may refuse to receive in evidence any exhibit, a copy or photograph of which has not been delivered to the adverse party as provided herein.

(6) A party may have a recording and transcript made of the arbitration hearing, but that party shall make all necessary arrangements and bear all expenses thereof.

(g) Arbitration Award and Judgment.

(1) The arbitration award shall be filed with the court promptly after the hearing is concluded and shall be entered as the judgment of the court after the 30 day period for requesting a trial de novo pursuant to section (g) has expired, unless a party has demanded a trial de novo. The judgment so entered shall be subject to the same provisions of law and shall have

the same force and effect as a judgment of the court in a civil action, except that it shall not be appealable. In a case involving multiple claims and parties, any segregable part of an arbitration award as to which an aggrieved party has not timely demanded a trial de novo shall become part of the final judgment with the same force and effect as a judgment of the court in a civil action, except that it shall not be appealable.

(2) The contents of any arbitration award shall not be made known to any judge who might be assigned the case,

    (A) except as necessary for the court to determine whether to assess costs or attorneys fees,

    (B) until the district court has entered final judgment in the action or the action has been otherwise terminated, or

    (C) except for purposes of preparing the report required by section 903(b) of the Judicial Improvement and Access to Justice Act.

(3) Costs may be taxed as part of any arbitration award pursuant to Title 28, U.S.C. § 1920.

(h) Trial De Novo.

(1) Within 30 days after the arbitration award is entered on the docket, any party may demand in writing a trial de novo in the district court. Such demand shall be filed with the arbitration clerk, and served by the moving party upon all counsel of record or other parties. Withdrawal of a demand for a trial de novo shall not reinstate the arbitrators' award and the case shall proceed as if it had not been arbitrated.

(2) Upon demand for a trial de novo and the payment to the clerk required by paragraph (4) of this section, the action shall be placed on the calendar of the court and treated for all purposes as if it had not been referred to arbitration, and any right of trial by jury that a party would otherwise have shall be preserved inviolate.

(3) At the trial de novo, the court shall not admit evidence that there had been an arbitration proceeding, the nature or amount of the award, or any other matter concerning the conduct of the arbitration proceeding.

(4) Upon making a demand for trial de novo the moving party shall, unless permitted to proceed in forma pauperis, deposit with the clerk of the court an amount equal to the arbitration fees of the arbitrators as provided in Section (b). The sum so deposited shall be returned to the party demanding a trial de novo in the event that party obtains a final judgment, exclusive of interest and costs, more favorable than the arbitration award. If the party demanding a trial de novo does not obtain a more favorable result after trial or if the court determines that the party's conduct in seeking a trial de novo was in bad faith, the

sum so deposited shall be paid by the Clerk to the Treasury of the United States.

RULE 83.11 COURT-ANNEXED MEDIATION (EASTERN DISTRICT ONLY)

(a) Description. Mediation is a process in which parties and counsel agree to meet with a neutral mediator trained to assist them in settling disputes. The mediator improves communication across party lines, helps parties articulate their interests and understand those of the other party, probes the strengths and weaknesses of each party's legal positions, and identifies areas of agreement and helps generate options for a mutually agreeable resolution to the dispute. In all cases, mediation provides an opportunity to explore a wide range of potential solutions and to address interests that may be outside the scope of the stated controversy or which could not be addressed by judicial action. A hallmark of mediation is its capacity to expand traditional settlement discussions and broaden resolution options, often by exploring litigant needs and interests that may be formally independent of the legal issues in controversy.

(b) Mediation Procedures.

(1) *Eligible Cases.* Judges and Magistrate Judges may designate civil cases for inclusion in the mediation program, and when doing so shall prepare an order to that effect. Alternatively, and subject to the availability of qualified mediators, the parties may consent to participation in the mediation program by preparing and executing a stipulation signed by all parties to the action and so-ordered by the Court.

    (A) Mediation Deadline. Any court order designating a case for inclusion in the mediation program, however arrived at, may contain a deadline not to exceed six months from the date of entry on the docket of that order. This deadline may be extended upon motion to the Court for good cause shown.

(2) *Mediators.* Parties whose case has been designated for inclusion in the mediation program shall be offered the options of (a) using a mediator from the Court's panel, a listing of which is available in the Clerk's Office; (b) selecting a mediator on their own; or (c) seeking the assistance of a reputable neutral ADR organization in the selection of a mediator.

    (A) Court's Panel of Mediators. When the parties opt to use a mediator from the Court's panel, the Clerk's Office will appoint a mediator to handle the case who (i) has been for at least five years a member of the bar of a state or the District of Columbia; (ii) is admitted to practice before this Court; and (iii) has completed the Court's requirements for mediator training and mediator expertise. If any party so requests, the appointed mediator also shall have expertise in the area of law in the case. The Clerk's Office will provide notice of their appointment to all counsel.

(B) Disqualification. Any party may submit a written request to the Clerk's Office within ten days from the date of the notification of the mediator for the disqualification of the mediator for bias or prejudice as provided in 28 U.S.C. § 144. A denial of such a request by the Clerk's Office is subject to review by the assigned Judge upon motion filed within ten days of the date of the Clerk's Office denial.

(3) *Scheduling the Mediation.* The mediator, however chosen, will contact all attorneys to fix the date and place of the first mediation session, which shall be held within thirty days of the date the mediator was appointed or at such other time as the Court may establish.

(A) The Clerk's Office will provide counsel with copies of the Judge's order referring the case to the mediation program, the Clerk's Office notice of appointment of mediator (if applicable), and a copy of the program procedures.

(4) *Written Mediation Statements.* No less than seven days prior to the first mediation session, each party shall submit directly to the mediator a mediation statement not to exceed ten pages double-spaced, not including exhibits, outlining the key facts and legal issues in the case. The statement will also include a description of motions filed and their status, and any other information that will advance settlement prospects or make the mediation more productive. Mediation statements are not briefs and are not filed with the Court, nor shall the assigned Judge or Magistrate Judge have access to them.

(5) *Mediation Session(s).* The mediator meets initially with all parties to the dispute and their counsel in a joint session. The mediator may hold mediation sessions in his/her office, or at the Court, or at such other place as the parties and the mediator shall agree. At this meeting, the mediator explains the mediation process and gives each party an opportunity to explain his or her views about the matters in dispute. There is then likely to be discussion and questioning among the parties as well as between the mediator and the parties.

(A) Separate Caucuses. At the conclusion of the joint session, the mediator will typically caucus individually with each party. Caucuses permit the mediator and the parties to explore more fully the needs and interests underlying the stated positions. In caucuses the mediator strives to facilitate settlement on matters in dispute and the possibilities for settlement. In some cases the mediator may offer specific suggestions for settlement; in other cases the mediator may help the parties generate creative settlement proposals.

(B) Additional Sessions. The mediator may conduct additional joint sessions to promote further direct discussion between the parties, or she/he may continue to work with the parties in private caucuses.

(C) Conclusion. The mediation concludes when the parties reach a mutually acceptable resolution, when the parties fail to reach an agreement, on the date the Judge or Magistrate Judge specified as the mediation deadline in their designation order, or in the event no such date has been specified by the Court, at such other time as the parties and/or the mediator may determine. The mediator has no power to impose settlement and the mediation process is confidential, whether or not a settlement is reached.

(6) *Settlement.* If settlement is reached, in whole or in part, the agreement, which shall be binding upon all parties, will be put into writing and counsel will file a stipulation of dismissal or such other document as may be appropriate. If the case does not settle, the mediator will immediately notify the Clerk's Office, and the case or the portion of the case that has not settled will continue in the litigation process.

(c) Attendance at Mediation Sessions.

(1) In all civil cases designated by the Court for inclusion in the mediation program, attendance at one mediation session shall be mandatory: thereafter, attendance shall be voluntary. The Court requires of each party that the attorney who has primary responsibility for handling the trial of the matter attend the mediation sessions.

(2) In addition, the Court may require, and if it does not, the mediator may require the attendance at the mediation session of a party or its representative in the case of a business or governmental entity or a minor, with authority to settle the matter and to bind the party. This requirement reflects the Court's view that the principal values of mediation include affording litigants with an opportunity to articulate their positions and interests directly to the other parties and to a mediator and to hear, first hand, the other party's version of the matters in dispute. Mediation also enables parties to search directly with the other party for mutually agreeable solutions.

(d) Confidentiality.

(1) The parties will be asked to sign an agreement of confidentiality at the beginning of the first mediation session to the following effect:

(A) Unless the parties otherwise agree, all written and oral communications made by the parties and the mediator in connection with or during any mediation session are confidential and may not be disclosed or used for any purpose unrelated to the mediation,

(B) The mediator shall not be called by any party as a witness in any court proceeding related to the subject matter of the mediation unless related to the alleged misconduct of the mediator.

(2) Mediators will maintain the confidentiality of all information provided to, or discussed with, them. The Clerk of Court and the ADR Administrator are responsible for program administration, evaluation, and liaison between the mediators and the Court and will maintain strict confidentiality.

(3) No papers generated by the mediation process will be included in Court files, nor shall the Judge or Magistrate Judge assigned to the case have access to them. Information about what transpires during mediation sessions will not at any time be made known to the Court, except to the extent required to resolve issues of noncompliance with the mediation procedures. However, communications made in connection with or during a mediation may be disclosed if all parties and, if appropriate as determined by the mediator, the mediator so agree. Nothing in this section shall be construed to prohibit parties from entering into written agreements resolving some or all of the case or entering and filing with the Court procedural or factual stipulations based on suggestions or agreements made in connection with a mediation.

(e) Oath and Disqualification of Mediator.

(1) Each individual certified as a mediator shall take the oath or affirmation prescribed by 28 U.S.C. § 453 before serving as a mediator.

(2) No mediator may serve in any matter in violation of the standards set forth in Section 455 of Title 28 of the United States Code. If a mediator is concerned that a circumstance covered by subparagraph (a) of that section might exist, e.g., if the mediator's law firm has represented one or more of the parties, or if one of the lawyers who would appear before the mediator at the mediation session is involved in a case on which an attorney in the mediator's firm is working, the mediator shall promptly disclose that circumstance to all counsel in writing. A party who believes that the assigned mediator has a conflict of interest shall bring this concern to the attention of the Clerk's Office in writing, within ten calendar days of learning the source of the potential conflict or the objection to such a potential conflict shall be deemed to have been waived. Any objections that cannot be resolved by the parties in consultation with the Clerk's Office shall be referred to the Judge or Magistrate Judge who has designated the case for inclusion in the mediation program.

(3) A party who believes that the assigned mediator has engaged in misconduct in such capacity shall bring this concern to the attention of the Clerk's Office in writing, within ten calendar days of learning of the alleged misconduct or the objection to such alleged misconduct shall be deemed to have been waived. Any objections that cannot be resolved by the parties in consultation with the Clerk's Office shall be referred to the Judge who has designated the case for inclusion in the mediation program.

(f) Services of the Mediators.

(1) Participation by mediators in the program is on a voluntary basis, without compensation. Attorneys serving on the Court's panel will be given credit for pro bono work.

(2) Appointment to the Court's panel is for a three year term, subject to renewal. A panelist will not be expected to serve on more than two cases during any twelve month period and will not be required to accept each assignment offered. Repeated rejection of assignments will result in the attorney being dropped from the panel.

(g) Immunity of the Mediators. Mediators shall be immune from liability or suit with respect to their conduct as such to the maximum extent permitted by applicable law.

RULE 83.12   ALTERNATIVE DISPUTE RESOLUTION (SOUTHERN DISTRICT ONLY)

Introduction

The Court's existing alternative dispute resolution ("ADR") program of mediation shall continue as set forth below.

(a) Definition. Mediation is a confidential ADR process in which a disinterested third party directs settlement discussions but does not evaluate the merits of either side's position or render any judgments. By holding meetings, defining issues, diffusing emotions and suggesting possibilities of resolution, the mediator assists the parties in reaching their own negotiated settlement. The main benefit of mediation is that it can produce creative solutions to complex disputes often unavailable in traditional litigation.

(b) Administration. Staff Counsel, appointed by the Clerk of the Court, shall administer the Court's mediation program. The Chief Judge shall appoint one or more judicial officers to oversee the program.

(c) Service as a Mediator. An individual may serve as a mediator if he or she: 1) has been a member of the Bar of any state or the District of Columbia for at least five years; 2) is admitted to practice in this Court; and 3) is certified by the Chief Judge or the Judicial Officer appointed by the Chief Judge pursuant to paragraph (b) above to be competent to perform the duties of a mediator. Each individual certified as a mediator shall take the oath or affirmation prescribed by 28 U.S.C. § 453 and complete the training program provided by the Court before serving as a mediator.

(d) Consideration of Mediation. In all civil cases eligible for mediation pursuant to paragraph (e), each party shall consider the use of mediation and shall report to the assigned Judge at the initial case management conference whether the party believes mediation may facilitate the resolution of the lawsuit.

(e) Entry Into the Program. All civil cases other than social security, tax, prisoner civil rights and pro se matters are eligible for mediation, whether assigned to Foley Square or White Plains.

The assigned Judge or Magistrate Judge may determine that a case is appropriate for mediation and may order that case to mediation with or without the consent of the parties. Alternatively, the parties may notify the assigned Judge and Staff Counsel at any time of their desire to mediate by filing a stipulation to that effect signed by all parties. Notification of the date, time and place will be forwarded by Staff Counsel to the parties.

(f) Scheduling Orders. In no event is the scheduling of mediation to interfere with any scheduling order of the Court.

(g) Assignment of the Mediator. Staff Counsel shall assign a mediator from the individuals certified as mediators and notify the mediator and the parties of the assignment.

(h) Disqualification. The mediator shall disqualify himself or herself in any action in which he or she would be required under 28 U.S.C. § 455 to be disqualified if a Justice, Judge or Magistrate Judge. Any party may submit a written request to Staff Counsel within ten days from the date of the notification of the name of the mediator for the disqualification of the mediator for bias or prejudice as provided in 28 U.S.C. § 144. A denial of such a request by Staff Counsel is subject to review by the assigned Judge upon motion filed within ten days of the date of Staff Counsel's denial.

(i) Submission. Unless otherwise agreed, upon notification of the scheduled date of the mediation session but in no event less than seven days before the mediation, each party shall prepare and forward to the mediator (but not to the adversary) a memorandum presenting in concise form, not exceeding ten double-spaced pages, the party's contentions as to both liability and damages and the status of any settlement negotiations.

(j) Mediation Sessions. The attorney primarily responsible for each party's case shall personally attend the first mediation session and shall be fully authorized to resolve the matter and prepared to discuss all liability issues, damage issues, and the party's settlement position in detail and in good faith. At the discretion of the mediator, the party, if an individual, or a representative of the party, if a corporation, partnership or governmental entity, with knowledge of the facts and full settlement authority, may be required to attend.

The mediation will conclude when the parties reach a resolution of some or all issues in the case or where the mediator concludes that resolution (or further resolution) is impossible. If resolution is reached, a binding agreement shall be signed by all the parties, and a stipulation of discontinuance or other appropriate document filed promptly. Where resolution is not reached, the assigned judge shall be notified promptly.

(k) Confidentiality. The entire mediation process shall be confidential. The parties and the mediator shall not disclose information regarding the process, including settlement terms, to the Court or to third persons unless all parties agree. The identity of the mediator shall not be disclosed, including to the Court. However, persons authorized by the Court to administer or evaluate the program shall have access to information and documents necessary to do so, and the parties, counsel and mediators may respond to confidential inquiries or surveys by such persons.

The mediation process shall be treated as a compromise negotiation for purposes of the Federal Rules of Evidence and state rules of evidence. The mediator is disqualified as a witness, consultant, attorney, or expert in any pending or future action relating to the dispute, including actions between persons not parties to the mediation process.

(*l*) Compensation of Mediators and Locations of Sessions. All mediators shall serve without compensation and be eligible for credit for pro bono service. All ADR sessions will take place at the "ADR Center" in the Federal Courthouses in Manhattan or White Plains, as designated.

Effective September 30, 1999.

LOCAL ADMIRALTY AND MARITIME RULES

RULE A.1 APPLICATION OF RULES

(a) These Local Admiralty and Maritime Rules apply to the procedure in the claims and proceedings governed by the Supplemental Rules for Certain Admiralty and Maritime Claims of the Federal Rules of Civil Procedure.

(b) The Local Civil Rules also apply to the procedure in such claims and proceedings, except to the extent that they are inconsistent with the Supplemental Rules or with these Local Admiralty and Maritime Rules.

[Source: Former Local Admiralty Rule 1 and Supplemental Rule 1.]

RULE B.1 AFFIDAVIT THAT DEFENDANT IS NOT FOUND WITHIN THE DISTRICT

The affidavit required by Supplemental Rule B(1) to accompany the complaint, and the affidavit required by Supplemental Rule B(2)(c), shall list the efforts made by and on behalf of the plaintiff to find and serve the defendant within the district.

[Source: Maritime Law Association Model Rule (b)(1).]

RULE B.2 NOTICE OF ATTACHMENT

In an action where any property of a defendant is attached, the plaintiff shall give prompt notice to the defendant of the attachment. Such notice shall be in writing, and may be given by telex, telegram, cable, fax, or other verifiable electronic means.

[Source: Former Local Admiralty Rule 10(b).]

RULE C.1 INTANGIBLE PROPERTY

The summons issued pursuant to Supplemental Rule C(3) shall direct the person having control of freight or proceeds of property sold or other intangible property to show cause at a date which shall be at least ten (10) days after service (unless the court, for good cause shown, shortens the period) why the intangible property should not be delivered to the court to abide the judgment. The person who is served may deliver or pay over to the marshal the intangible property proceeded against to the extent sufficient to satisfy the plaintiff's claim. If such delivery or payment is made, the person served is excused from the duty to show cause.

[Source: Former Local Admiralty Rule 2.]

RULE C.2 PUBLICATION OF NOTICE OF ACTION AND ARREST; SALE

(a) The notice required by Supplemental Rule C(4) shall be published at least once and shall contain (1) the fact and date of the arrest, (2) the caption of the case, (3) the nature of the action, (4) the amount demanded, (5) the name of the marshal, (6) the name, address, and telephone number of the attorney for the plaintiff, and (7) a statement that claimants must file their claims with the clerk of this court within ten (10) days after notice or first publication (whichever is earlier) or within such additional time as may be allowed by the court and must serve their answers within twenty (20) days after the filing of their claims. The notice shall also state that all interested persons should file claims and answers within the times so

fixed otherwise default will be noted and condemnation ordered.

(b) Except in the event of private sale pursuant to 28 U.S.C. §§ 2001 and 2004, or unless otherwise ordered as provided by law, notice of sale of the property after condemnation in suits in rem shall be published daily for at least six (6) days before sale.

[Source: Former Local Admiralty Rule 3(a), (c).]

RULE C.3 NOTICE REQUIRED FOR DEFAULT JUDGMENT IN ACTION IN REM

(a) Notice Required in General. A party seeking a default judgment in an action in rem must satisfy the court that due notice of the action and arrest of the property has been given:

(1) By publication as required in Supplemental Rule C(4) and Local Admiralty Rule C.2;

(2) By service upon the master or other person having custody of the property; and

(3) By service under Federal Rule of Civil Procedure 5(b) upon every other person who has not appeared in the action and is known to have an interest in the property.

(b) Notice Required to Persons With Recorded Interests.

(1) If the defendant property is a vessel documented under the laws of the United States, plaintiff must attempt to notify all persons named in the certificate of ownership issued by the United States Coast Guard, or other designated agency of the United States, as holding an ownership interest in or as holding a lien in or as having filed a notice of claim of lien with respect to the vessel.

(2) If the defendant property is a vessel numbered as provided in 46 U.S.C. § 12301(a), plaintiff must attempt to notify the persons named in the records of the issuing authority.

(3) If the defendant property is of such character that there exists a governmental registry of recorded property interests or security interests in the property, the plaintiff must attempt to notify all persons named in the records of each such registry.

[Source: Maritime Law Association Model Rule (c)(3).]

RULE D.1 RETURN DATE IN POSSESSORY, PETITORY, AND PARTITION ACTIONS

In an action under Supplemental Rule D, the court may order that the claim and answer be filed on a date earlier than twenty (20) days after arrest, and may by order set a date for expedited hearing of the action.

[Source: Maritime Law Association Model Rule (d)(1).]

RULE E.1　ADVERSARY HEARING FOLLOWING ARREST, ATTACHMENT OR GARNISHMENT

The adversary hearing following arrest or attachment or garnishment that is called for in Supplemental Rule E(4)(f) shall be conducted by a judicial officer within three court days, unless otherwise ordered.

[Source: Maritime Law Association Model Rule (e)(8).]

RULE E.2　INTERVENORS' CLAIMS

(a) Presentation of Claim. When a vessel or other property has been arrested, attached, or garnished, and is in the hands of the marshal or custodian substituted therefor, anyone having a claim against the vessel or property is required to present the claim by filing an intervening complaint, and not by filing an original complaint, unless otherwise ordered by a judicial officer. Upon the satisfaction of the requirements of Federal Rule of Civil Procedure 24, the clerk shall forthwith deliver a conformed copy of the complaint to the marshal, who shall deliver the copy to the vessel or custodian of the property. Intervenors shall thereafter be subject to the rights and obligations of parties, and the vessel or property shall stand arrested, attached, or garnished by the intervenor.

(b) Sharing Marshal's Fees and Expenses. An intervenor shall have a responsibility to the first plaintiff, enforceable on motion, consisting of the intervenor's share of the marshal's fees and expenses in the proportion that the intervenor's claim bears to the sum of all the claims. If a party plaintiff permits vacation of an arrest, attachment, or garnishment, remaining plaintiffs share the responsibility to the

marshal for the fees and expenses in proportion to the remaining claims and for the duration of the marshal's custody because of each claim.

[Source: Maritime Law Association Model Rule (e)(11).]

RULE E.3　CLAIMS BY SUPPLIERS FOR PAYMENT OF CHARGES

A person who furnishes supplies or services to a vessel, cargo, or other property in custody of the court who has not been paid and claims the right to payment as an expense of administration shall submit an invoice to the clerk in the form of a verified claim at any time before the vessel, cargo or other property is released or sold. The supplier must serve copies of the claim on the marshal, substitute custodian if one has been appointed, and all parties of record. The court may consider the claims individually or schedule a single hearing for all claims.

[Source: Maritime Law Association Model Rule (e)(12)(d).]

RULE E.4　PRESERVATION OF PROPERTY

Whenever property is attached or arrested pursuant to the provisions of Supplemental Rule E(4)(b) that permit the marshal or other person having the warrant to execute the process without taking actual possession of the property, and the owner or occupant of the property is thereby permitted to remain in possession, the court, on motion of any party or on its own motion, may enter any order necessary to preserve the value of the property, its contents, and any income derived therefrom, and to prevent the destruction, removal or diminution in value of such property, contents and income.

LOCAL CRIMINAL RULES

RULE 1.1　APPLICATION OF RULES

(a) These Local Criminal Rules apply in criminal proceedings.

(b) In addition to these Local Criminal Rules, Local Civil Rules 1.2 through 1.10, 39.1, 58.1, and 67.1 apply in criminal proceedings.

RULE 1.2　APPLICATIONS FOR EX PARTE ORDERS

Any application for an ex parte order shall state whether a previous application for similar relief has been made and, if so, shall state (a) the nature of the previous application, (b) the judicial officer to whom such application was presented, and (c) the disposition of such application.

RULE 12.1　SERVICE AND FILING OF MOTION PAPERS

Unless otherwise provided by statute or rule, or unless otherwise ordered by the court in an individual rule or in a direction in a particular case, upon any motion, the papers shall be served and filed as follows:

(a) All papers in support of the motion shall be served by the moving party on all other parties that have appeared in the action.

(b) Any opposing papers shall be served within ten business days after service of the motion papers.

(c) Any reply papers shall be served within five business days after service of the opposing papers.

(d) All papers in support of or in opposition to a motion shall be filed, with proof of service specifying the means of service, within a reasonable time after service. The parties and their attorneys shall only appear to argue the motion if so directed by the court by order or by individual rule or upon application.

[Source: Former Local Criminal Rule 3(a).]

RULE 12.4. DISCLOSURE STATEMENT

For purposes of Fed. R. Crim. P. 12.4(b)(2), "promptly" shall mean "within ten business days," that is, parties are required to file supplemental disclosure statements within ten business days of the time there is any change in the information required in a disclosure statement filed pursuant to those rules.

[Effective February 22, 2007.]

RULE 16.1. CONFERENCE OF COUNSEL

No motion addressed to a bill of particulars or answers or to discovery and inspection shall be heard unless counsel for the moving party files with the court simultaneously with the filing of the moving papers an affidavit certifying that said counsel has conferred with counsel for the opposing party in an effort in good faith to resolve by agreement the issues raised by the motion without the intervention of the court and has been unable to reach such an agreement. If some of the issues raised by the motion have been resolved by agreement, the affidavit shall specify the issues remaining unresolved.

[Source: Former Local Criminal Rule 3(d).]

RULE 23.1 FREE PRESS–FAIR TRIAL DIRECTIVES

(a) It is the duty of the lawyer or law firm, and of non-lawyer personnel employed by a lawyer's office or subject to a lawyer's supervision, private investigators acting under the supervision of a criminal defense lawyer, and government agents and police officers, not to release or authorize the release of non-public information or opinion which a reasonable person would expect to be disseminated by means of public communication, in connection with pending or imminent criminal litigation with which they are associated, if there is a substantial likelihood that such dissemination will interfere with a fair trial or otherwise prejudice the due administration of justice.

(b) With respect to a grand jury or other pending investigation of any criminal matter, a lawyer participating in or associated with the investigation (including government lawyers and lawyers for targets, subjects, and witnesses in the investigation) shall refrain from making any extrajudicial statement which a reasonable person would expect to be disseminated by means of public communication that goes beyond the public record or that is not necessary to inform the public that the investigation is underway, to describe the general scope of the investigation, to obtain assistance in the apprehension of a suspect, to warn the public of any dangers or otherwise to aid in the investigation, if there is a substantial likelihood that such dissemination will interfere with a fair trial or otherwise prejudice the administration of justice.

(c) During a jury trial of any criminal matter, including the period of selection of the jury, no lawyer or law firm associated with the prosecution or defense shall give or authorize any extrajudicial statement or interview relating to the trial or the parties or issues in the trial which a reasonable person would expect to be disseminated by means of public communication if there is a substantial likelihood that such dissemination will interfere with a fair trial; except that the lawyer or the law firm may quote from or refer without comment to public records of the court in the case.

(d) Statements concerning the following subject matters presumptively involve a substantial likelihood that their public dissemination will interfere with a fair trial or otherwise prejudice the due administration of justice within the meaning of this rule:

(1) The prior criminal record (including arrests, indictments or other charges of crime), or the character or reputation of the accused, except that the lawyer or law firm may make a factual statement of the accused's name, age, residence, occupation and family status; and if the accused has not been apprehended, a lawyer associated with the prosecution may release any information necessary to aid in the accused's apprehension or to warn the public of any dangers the accused may present;

(2) The existence or contents of any confession, admission or statement given by the accused, or the refusal or failure of the accused to make any statement;

(3) The performance of any examinations or tests or the accused's refusal or failure to submit to an examination or test;

(4) The identity, testimony or credibility of prospective witnesses, except that the lawyer or law firm may announce the identity of the victim if the announcement is not otherwise prohibited by law;

(5) The possibility of a plea of guilty to the offense charged or a lesser offense;

(6) Information the lawyer or law firm knows is likely to be inadmissible at trial and would if disclosed create a substantial likelihood of prejudicing an impartial trial; and

(7) Any opinion as to the accused's guilt or innocence or as to the merits of the case or the evidence in the case.

(e) Statements concerning the following subject matters presumptively do not involve a substantial likelihood that their public dissemination will interfere with a fair trial or otherwise prejudice the due administration of justice within the meaning of this rule:

(1) An announcement, at the time of arrest, of the fact and circumstances of arrest (including time and place of arrest, resistance, pursuit and use of weapons), the identity of the investigating and arresting officer or agency and the length of investigation;

(2) An announcement, at the time of seizure, stating whether any items of physical evidence were seized and, if so, a description of the items seized (but not including any confession, admission or statement);

(3) The nature, substance or text of the charge, including a brief description of the offense charged;

(4) Quoting or referring without comment to public records of the court in the case;

(5) An announcement of the scheduling or result of any stage in the judicial process, or an announcement that a matter is no longer under investigation;

(6) A request for assistance in obtaining evidence; and

(7) An announcement, without further comment, that the accused denies the charges, and a brief description of the nature of the defense.

(**f**) Nothing in this rule is intended to preclude the formulation or application of more restrictive rules relating to the release of information about juvenile or other offenders, to preclude the holding of hearings or the lawful issuance of reports by legislative, administrative or investigative bodies, or to preclude any lawyer from replying to charges of misconduct that are publicly made against said lawyer.

(**g**) All court supporting personnel, including, among others, marshals, deputy marshals, court clerks, bailiffs and court reporters and employees or sub-contractors retained by the court-appointed official reporters, are prohibited from disclosing to any person, without authorization by the court, information relating to a pending grand jury proceeding or criminal case that is not part of the public records of the court. The divulgence by such court supporting personnel of information concerning grand jury proceedings, *in camera* arguments and hearings held in chambers or otherwise outside the presence of the public is also forbidden.

(**h**) The court, on motion of either party or on its own motion, may issue a special order governing such matters as extrajudicial statements by parties and witnesses likely to interfere with the rights of the accused to a fair trial by an impartial jury, the seating and conduct in the courtroom of spectators and news media representatives, the management and sequestration of jurors and witnesses and any other matters which the court may deem appropriate for inclusion in such order. In determining whether to impose such a special order, the court shall consider whether such an order will be necessary to ensure an impartial jury and must find that other, less extreme available remedies, singly or collectively, are not feasible or would not effectively mitigate the pretrial publicity and bring about a fair trial. Among the alternative remedies to be considered are: change of venue, postponing the trial, a searching voir dire, emphatic jury instructions, and sequestration of jurors.

(**i**) Any lawyer who violates the terms of this rule may be disciplined pursuant to Local Civil Rule 1.5.

[Source: Former Local Criminal Rule 7.]

RULE 34.1   POST-TRIAL MOTIONS

Post-trial motions in criminal cases, including motions for correction or reduction of sentence under Federal Rule of Criminal Procedure 35, or to suspend execution of sentence, or in arrest of judgment under Federal Rule of Criminal Procedure 34, shall be referred to the trial judge. If the trial judge served by designation and assignment under 28 U.S.C. §§ 291–296, and is absent from the district, such motions may be referred to said judge for consideration and disposition.

[Source: Former Local Criminal Rule 3(c).]

RULE 44.1   NOTICE OF APPEARANCE

(**a**) Attorneys representing defendants in criminal cases shall file a notice of appearance in the clerk's office and serve a copy on the United States attorney. Once such a notice of appearance has been filed, the attorney may not withdraw except upon prior order of the court pursuant to Local Civil Rule 1.4.

(**b**) Within twenty (20) days after an attorney files and serves a notice of appearance in a criminal case, said attorney shall submit to the Clerk of the District Court a certificate of the court for at least one of the states in which the attorney is a member of the bar, which has been issued within thirty (30) days and states that the attorney is a member in good standing of the bar of that state court. If the Clerk is satisfied that the submitted certificate shows the attorney to be a member in good standing of the bar of a state described in Local Civil Rule 1.3(a), said attorney need not file and serve any further certification to the Clerk pursuant to this rule in connection with any subsequent appearances in this court.

[Source: Former Local Criminal Rule 1.]

RULE 45.1   COMPUTATION OF TIME

In computing any period of time prescribed or allowed by the Local Criminal Rules, the provisions of Federal Rule of Criminal Procedure 45(a) and 45(e) shall apply unless otherwise stated.

RULE 58.1 POWERS OF MAGISTRATE JUDGES

In addition to other powers of magistrate judges:

(a) Full-time magistrate judges are hereby specially designated to exercise the jurisdiction set forth in 18 U.S.C. § 3401. Unless there is a pending related indictment before a district judge, the clerk shall automatically refer misdemeanor cases initiated by information or indictment or transferred to the district under Federal Rule of Criminal Procedure 20 to a magistrate judge for arraignment. A petition by the government that the trial of a misdemeanor proceed before a district judge pursuant to 18 U.S.C. § 3401(f) shall be filed prior to arraignment of the defendant.

(b) Magistrate judges are hereby authorized to exercise the jurisdiction set forth in 18 U.S.C. § 3184.

(c) Magistrate judges may issue subpoenas, writs of *habeas corpus ad testificandum* or *ad prosequendum* or other orders necessary to obtain the presence of parties or witnesses or evidence needed for court proceedings, and may sign in forma pauperis orders.

[Source: Former Local Magistrate Judge Rules 2, 5, 6, and 9.]

RULE 58.2 PETTY OFFENSES— COLLATERAL AND APPEARANCE

(a) A person who is charged with a petty offense as defined in 18 U.S.C. § 19, or with violating any regulation promulgated by any department or agency of the United States government, may, in lieu of appearance, post collateral in the amount indicated in the summons or other accusatory instrument, waive appearance before a United States magistrate judge, and consent to forfeiture of collateral.

(b) For all other petty offenses the person charged must appear before a magistrate judge.

[Source: Former Local Magistrate Judge Rule 11.]

SOUTHERN DISTRICT SUPPLEMENTAL MATERIALS

FEE SCHEDULES

Following are fees to be charged for services to be performed by clerks of the district courts. No fees are to be charged for services rendered on behalf of the United States, with the exception of those specifically prescribed in items 2, 4, and 5. (more full text, *see, post*)

Fees may be paid in *cash, by certified check, money order or credit card*. All major credit cards are accepted. Personal checks will be accepted from attorneys admitted to practice in the Southern District of New York. Please make your check or money order payable to the *"Clerk of Court–SDNY"*.

New Action	
(Complaint, Notice of Removal, Petition, etc.)	$ 350.00
Atty. Admission	$ 185.00
Atty. Admission/Waiver EDNY	$ 170.00
Certificate of Good Standing	$ 15.00
Pro Hac Vice Motion	
(per attorney—due at the time of filing motion)	$ 25.00/ atty
Notice of Appeal	$ 455.00
Certified Copy	$ 9.00
Certificate of Disposition	$ 9.00
Exemplification	$ 18.00
Apostile	$ 2.00
Search	$ 26.00
Docket Sheet	$ .50/ page
Pro Se Manual	$ 15.00
Transcript of Judgment	$ 9.00
Registration of Judgment	$ 39.00
Miscellaneous Filing Fees	$ 39.00/ doc
Returned Check Fee	$ 45.00
Microfiche of Court Record	$ 5.00
Retrieval of Archived Record	$ 45.00
Appeal to District Judge from a Conviction by a Magistrate in a Misdemeanor Case	$ 32.00
Tape Duplication	$ 26.00
Cuban Liberation Civil Filing Fee	$5431.00

District Court Fee Schedule and Related Information
Issued in accordance with 28 U.S.C. § 1914(b)

Following are fees to be charged for services to be performed by clerks of the district courts. No fees are to be charged for services rendered on behalf of the United States, with the exception of those specifically prescribed in items 2, 4, and 5. No fees under this schedule shall be charged to federal agencies or programs which are funded from judiciary appropriations, including, but not limited to, agencies, organizations, and individuals providing services authorized by the Criminal Justice Act, 18 U.S.C. § 3006A, and Bankruptcy Administrator programs.

(1) for filing or indexing any document not in a case or proceeding for which a case filing fee has been paid, $ 39.

(2) For every search of the records of the district court conducted by the clerk of the district court or a deputy clerk, $ 26 per name or item searched. This fee shall apply to services rendered on behalf of the United States if the information requested is available through electronic access.

(3) For certification of any document or paper, whether the certification is made directly on the document or by separate instrument, $ 9. For exemplification of any document or paper, twice the amount of the fee for certification.

(4) For reproducing any record or paper, $ .50 per page. This fee shall apply to paper copies made from either: (1) original documents; or (2) microfiche or micro-film reproductions of the original records. This fee shall apply to services rendered on behalf of the United States if the record or paper requested is available through electronic access.

(5) For reproduction of recordings of proceedings, regardless of the medium, $ 26 including the cost of materials. This fee shall apply to services rendered on behalf of the United States, if the reproduction of the recording is available.

(6) For each microfiche sheet of film or microfilm jacket copy of any court record, where available, $ 5.

(7) For retrieval of a record from a Federal Records Center, National Archives, or other storage location removed from the place of business of the court, $ 45.

(8) For a check paid into the court which is returned for lack of funds, $ 45.

(9) For an appeal to a district judge from a judgment of conviction by a magistrate in a misdemeanor case, $ 32.

(10) For original admission of attorneys to practice, $ 185 each, including a certificate of admission. For a duplicate certificate of admission or certificate of good standing, $ 15. [Local Pro Hac Vice Admission Fee]

(11) The court may charge and collect fees commensurate with the cost of providing copies of the local rules of court. The court may also distribute copies of the local rules without charge.

(12) The clerk shall assess a charge for the handling of registry funds deposited with the court, to be assessed from interest earnings and in accordance with the detailed fee schedule issued by the Director of the Administrative Office of the United States Courts.

(13) For filing an action brought under Title III of the Cuban Liberty and Democratic Solidarity (LIBERTAD) Act of 1996, P.L. 104–114, 110 Stat. § 785 (1996), $ 5431. (This fee is in addition to the filing fee prescribed in 28 U.S.C. § 1914(a) for instituting any civil action other than a writ of habeas corpus.)

Effective June 1, 2004; amended effective February 7, 2005; April 9, 2006.

PROCEDURES GOVERNING APPOINTMENT OF
ATTORNEYS IN PRO SE CIVIL ACTIONS

1. Civil Pro Bono Panel. There shall be a panel of attorneys who are willing to accept appointment to represent pro se parties in civil actions when such parties lack the resources to retain counsel. Appointment shall be administered by the Pro Se Office in accordance with the written procedures on file there.

2. Committee on Pro Se Litigation. The Chief Judge shall appoint a committee on pro se litigation to oversee the operation of the Pro Bono Panel.

3. Composition of the Civil Pro Bono Panel. The Civil Pro Bono Panel will consist of the following:

a. *Law Firms.* Law firms, including public interest law firms, may apply to participate in the panel as firms by completing an application available from the Pro Se Office and providing, among other things:

1. the ability of participating attorneys to represent non-English-speaking clients;

2. the firm's preference for appointment among various types of actions; (e.g., social security appeals, employment discrimination actions, civil rights, and miscellaneous [other than the above]);

3. the name of the firm's attorney designated as the panel liaison, along with the attorney's electronic mail address and facsimile number, as well as the firm's website address.

Appearance in an action may be entered by either the firm or the assigned attorney, at the firm's option. If a firm is a member of the panel, individual attorneys in that firm need not apply to become individual members of the panel.

b. *Individual Attorneys.* Attorneys may apply to participate in the panel by completing an application available from the Pro Se Office and providing, among other things:

1. that the attorney is in good standing in the Southern District;

2. the attorney's prior civil trial experience, including the number of trials and areas of trial experience;

3. the ability of the attorney to represent non-English-speaking clients;

4. the attorney's preference for appointment among various types of actions (e.g., social security appeals, employment discrimination actions, civil rights, and miscellaneous [other than the above]);

5. the attorney's electronic mail address, and facsimile number along with the attorney's website address, if any.

c. *Attorney Instructors in Law School Clinical Programs.* An attorney working with a clinical program from a law school accredited by the American Bar Association and located in the Southern or Eastern District may apply to participate in the panel by completing an application available from the Pro Se Office and providing, among other things:

1. that the attorney is in good standing in the Southern District;

2. the number of students involved in the clinical program;

3. the ability of the attorney and the clinical program to represent non-English-speaking clients;

4. the preference for appointment among the types of actions (e.g. social security appeals, employment discrimination actions, civil rights, and miscellaneous [other than the above]);

5. the name of the supervisor of the clinical program;

6. the attorney instructor's electronic mail address, and facsimile number along with the law school's Web site address.

d. *Review of Applications.* The Committee on Pro Se Litigation will review the applications received and appoint attorneys to the panel. The Committee may remove an attorney or firm from the panel at any time.

e. *Amendment or Withdrawal.* It is the responsibility of the panel member to advise the Court of any changes in contact information. See, Local Civil Rule 1.3(d). Information on an application may be amended at any time by letter. An attorney or firm may by letter withdraw from the panel at any time, subject to paragraph 7 (Relief from Appointment).

4. Appointment Procedure.

a. The Pro Se Office shall advise any party appearing Pro Se of the opportunity to request that the judge assigned to the case appoint counsel.

b. The district judge or magistrate judge (hereinafter "judge") assigned to the action shall determine if an application for the appointment of counsel should be granted pursuant to 28 U.S.C. § 1915(e)(1) or other applicable statute, or where the Court determines that such appointment would serve the interests of justice.

c. Whenever the assigned judge concludes that appointment of counsel is warranted, the judge shall either appoint counsel directly or refer the case to the Pro Se Office for appointment of an attorney from the Civil Pro Bono Panel. If the judge appoints counsel directly, notice of the appointment shall be forwarded to the Pro Se Office. The judge's staff shall forward to the attorney a copy of the docket sheet, of the pleadings filed to date, and of relevant correspondence and other documents. If the judge refers the case to the Pro Se Office for appointment of an attorney from the Pro Bono Panel, the judge's staff shall forward a copy of the order granting the application for appointment of counsel, the pleadings, and a copy of relevant correspondence and other documents. If the file is unusually voluminous, upon appointment, counsel will be asked to designate the papers needed for copying. The copying shall be arranged by the judge's staff. The judge may also direct the applicant to a bar association referral service in any case where it appears that substantial counsel fees may be awarded as provided by statute.

d. Before referring a case to a law firm, an individual attorney, or a law school clinical program, the Pro Se Office shall determine if the litigant has any other case pending before the court and if an attorney has been appointed in such case. Where an appointed attorney is already representing the litigant in another action, such attorney is encouraged but not required to represent the litigant in the new action.

e. Each case referred to the Pro Se Office for appointment of counsel shall be summarized by extracting the essential allegations made by the pro se party. The summary shall also include the status of the case, if there are motions pending, if the case is trial ready, and the names of any counsel appearing in the case. The summary shall be added to the list of cases seeking Pro Bono attorneys and electronically mailed to the members of the panel on a monthly basis.

f. Attorneys shall review the list of summaries to determine if they are interested in a case. Attorneys may contact the Pro Se Office by electronic mail or telephone to request case files that interest them. The Pro Se Office will send the attorney copies of the file, which may be kept by the attorney for up to one month while the attorney decides whether or not to take the case. The attorney may contact the litigant for further information or a preliminary interview, but must advise the litigant that s/he has not yet decided to represent the litigant. If, after thirty days, the attorney reviewing the case file has not yet made a decision, the Pro Se Office will contact the attorney. The Pro Se Office may grant attorneys additional time to review case files on a case-by-case basis. Attorneys may also contact the Pro Se Office to set up appointments to view case files at the Pro Se Office.

g. If several attorneys are interested in the same case, a wait list will be established. Generally, cases will be made available for review by attorneys on a first-come, first-served basis. When a wait list is established for a particular case, the Pro Se Office will keep strict account of the time the case has been out for review, and contact the attorneys prior to the thirty-day grace period in order to prompt expedited decisions.

h. As soon as the attorney decides to accept an appointment, the attorney shall serve and file a notice of appearance in the action. A copy of the notice of appearance shall also be sent to the litigant, the Pro Se Office, and the judge. If the attorney determines that s/he cannot accept an appointment, the attorney will promptly return the complete file to the Pro Se Office.

i. The Court has adopted standards of service for law firms to retain their membership on the Pro Bono Panel. Under these standards:

   * A firm with less than 50 attorneys is required to take one new case every other year;

   * A firm with more than 50 attorneys but less than 100 attorneys is required to take one new case every year;

   * A firm with over 100 attorneys is required to take two cases every year.

Panel member participation will be reviewed on an annual basis. If a member fails to participate in the program, the Pro Se Committee may upon notice and opportunity to respond, remove them from the panel.

5. Responsibilities of the Appointed Attorney.

a. Upon receiving an appointment, the attorney shall promptly communicate with the newly represented party concerning the action.

b. The appointed attorney, should discuss fully the merits of the dispute with the party and explore with the party the possibilities of resolving the dispute by other means, including but not limited to administrative forum.

c. If, after consultation with the appointed attorney, the party decides to prosecute or defend the action, the appointed attorney shall proceed to represent the party in the action, unless or until the attorney-client relationship is terminated as provided herein.

6. Duration of Representation.

a. An appointed attorney shall represent the party in the action in the trial court from the date the attorney enters an appearance until the attorney has been relieved from appointment by the Court or until a final judgment is entered in the action and reasonable efforts are made to enforce the judgment. The attorney shall, if it is appropriate in his or her judgment or requested by the litigant, file a notice of appeal from the final judgment.

b. If the party wishes to take an appeal from a final judgment or appealable interlocutory order, or if such judgment or order is appealed by another party, or if the matter is remanded to an administrative forum, the appointed attorney is encouraged but not required to represent the party on the appeal and in any proceeding, judicial or administrative, that may ensue upon an order of remand.

7. Relief From Appointment.

a. Subsequent to filing a notice of appearance, an appointed attorney should apply to be relieved from appointment only on the following grounds:

(i) a conflict of interest precludes the attorney from accepting the responsibilities of representing the party in the action;

(ii) the attorney believes that he or she is not competent to represent the party in the particular type of action assigned;

(iii) a personal incompatibility exists between the attorney and the party, or a substantial disagreement exists between the attorney and the party on litigation strategy;

(iv) the attorney believes that the party is proceeding for purposes of harassment or malicious injury, or that the party's claims or defenses are not supported by fact or are not warranted under existing law and cannot be supported by good faith argument for extension, modification, or reversal of existing law; or

(v) other good case is shown.

b. An application by an appointed attorney for relief from an appointment on any of the grounds set forth above must be made to the judge promptly upon knowledge of the facts leading to the application.

c. If an attorney wishes for any reason other than those stated in 7(a)(i), (ii) and (iii) to be relieved from an appointment, the attorney will send a request to that effect stating the grounds for relief to the client. If the client does not object to the request, the attorney shall so advise the judge and the request will be granted. If the client objects to the request for relief, the attorney shall submit the request and the grounds therefore to the judge. The substance of any such request shall not be available to the parties in discovery or otherwise.

Any application for the appointment of counsel shall contain the following language: "I hereby waive my privilege of attorney-client confidentiality to the extent necessary for my appointed attorney to make an application to be relieved as provided in the Procedures Regarding Appointment of Attorneys in Pro Se Civil Actions."

d. If an application for relief from appointment is granted, the judge may appoint or direct the appointment of another attorney to represent the party.

8. Discharge.
A party for whom an attorney has been appointed shall be permitted to relieve the attorney from the representation. The party may ask the judge to discharge the attorney. Upon showing affidavit of satisfactory reasons, the judge may appoint a new attorney.

9. Expenses.

a. The Court has established the Pro Bono Fund ("Fund") for the reimbursement of expenses incurred in the preparation and presentation of a case. The Rules governing the Fund are available at the Pro Se Office. An attorney may seek reimbursement for the following expenses: fees for service of papers and appearances of witnesses (including those associated with experts or medical personnel), costs of transcripts of court proceedings and depositions, interpreter services, travel, photocopies, photographs, telephone toll calls, and telegrams. Attorneys should consult the Rules governing the Fund for further guidance.

b. The judge to whom the case is assigned may authorize reimbursements totaling $1,000.00. If the reimbursement requested, as well as those already allowed, exceeds $1,000.00, the request shall be forwarded to the Chief Judge. In no instance will more than $2,000.00 in such expenses be paid to a party in any proceeding. Where two or more parties in the same proceeding are represented by the same counsel, these limits apply to each party, but in no event shall the total amount paid from the Fund for the case exceed $6,000.00. Where a fee award is awarded to an attorney, the attorney shall waive any and all rights to reimbursement and shall surrender any amounts paid on the case previously.

c. An attorney may seek reimbursement by completing the appropriate form available from the Pro Se Office. The attorney must include sufficient documentation to support the application in order to permit the Court to determine that the expenses have been incurred and that the application is appropriate and reasonable. The application shall be submitted to the Pro Se Office. The Senior Staff Attorney of the Pro Se Office shall process the application, determine if the amount indicated is within the limits set by the Fund's Rules and forward the application to the assigned judge and the Chief Judge, where appropriate. If the application is approved, the Clerk of Court shall promptly issue payment. If the assigned judge or Chief Judge disallows any or all of the amounts requested, the Senior Staff Attorney shall promptly transmit a copy of the application showing the decision to the attorney.

10. Compensation for Services.

a. The action may be one for which compensation for legal services may become available to the appointed attorney by statute and be deductible from any recovery

b. Pro Se litigants in social security disability cases shall be specifically advised by the Pro Bono attorney that a statutory attorney's fee may be awarded to be paid from the award, if any, of retroactive disability benefits.

c. Upon appropriate application by the appointed attorney, the judge may award attorney's fees to the appointed attorney or legal clinic for services rendered in the action, as authorized by applicable statute, regulation, rule or other provisions of law, and as the judge deems just and proper.

PLAN FOR ACHIEVING PROMPT DISPOSITION OF CRIMINAL CASES

Pursuant to the requirement of Rule 50(b) of the Federal Rules of Criminal Procedure, the Speedy Trial Act of 1974, 18 U.S.C. chapter 208 [18 U.S.C.A. 3161 et seq.], the Speedy Trial Act Amendments Act of 1979, Pub.L.No. 96–43, 93 Stat. 327, and the Federal Juvenile Delinquency Act, 18 U.S.C. sections 5036, 5037, the judges of the United States District Court for the Southern District of New York have adopted the following time limits and procedures to minimize undue delay and to further the prompt disposition of criminal cases and certain juvenile proceedings:

1. Applicability.

(a) *Offenses.* The time limits set forth herein are applicable to all criminal offenses triable in this court, including cases triable by United States magistrates, except for petty offenses as defined in 18 U.S.C. section 1(3). Except as specifically provided, they are not applicable to proceedings under the Federal Juvenile Delinquency Act.

(b) *Persons.* The time limits set forth herein are applicable to persons accused who have not been indicted or informed against, as well as those who have, and the word "defendant" includes such persons unless the context indicates otherwise.

2. Priorities in Scheduling Criminal Cases. Preference shall be given to criminal proceedings as far as practicable as required by Rule 50(a) of the Federal Rules of Criminal Procedure. The trial of defendants in custody solely because they are awaiting trial and the trial of "high-risk" defendants as defined in section 5(b), infra, should be given preference over other criminal cases. When a preference is given criminal proceedings, the court shall seek to avoid prejudice to the prompt disposition of civil litigation.

3. Time Within Which an Indictment or Information Must Be Filed.

(a) *Time Limits.* If an individual is arrested or served with a summons and the complaint charges an offense to be prosecuted in this district, any indictment or information subsequently filed in connection with such charge shall be filed within 30 days of arrest or service.

(b) *Measurement of Time Periods.* If a person has not been arrested or served with a summons on a federal charge, an arrest will be deemed to have been made at such time as the person (i) is held in custody solely for the purpose of responding to a federal charge; (ii) is delivered to the custody of a federal official in connection with a federal charge; or (iii) appears before a judicial officer in connection with a federal charge.

(c) *Related Procedures.*

(1) At the time of the earliest appearance before a judicial officer of a person who has been arrested for an offense not charged in an indictment or information, the judicial officer shall establish for the record the date on which the arrest took place.

(2) In the absence of a showing to the contrary, a summons shall be considered to have been served on the date of service shown on the return thereof.

4. Time Within Which Trial Must Commence.

(a) *Time Limits.* The trial of a defendant shall commence not later than 70 days after the last to occur of the following dates:

(1) the date on which an indictment or information is filed in this district;

(2) the date on which a sealed indictment or information is unsealed; or

(3) the date of the defendant's first appearance before a judicial officer of this district.

(b) *Retrial; Trial After Reinstatement of an Indictment or Information.* The retrial of a defendant shall commence within 70 days from the date the order occasioning the retrial becomes final, as shall the trial of a defendant upon an indictment or information dismissed by a trial court and reinstated following an appeal. If the retrial or trial follows an appeal or collateral attack, the court may extend the period if unavailability of witnesses or other factors resulting from passage of time make trial within 70 days impractical. The extended period shall not exceed 180 days.

(c) *Withdrawal of Plea.* If a defendant enters a plea of guilty or nolo contendere to any or all charges in an indictment or information and is subsequently permitted to withdraw it, the time limit shall be determined for all counts as if the indictment or information were filed on the day the order permitting withdrawal of the plea became final.

(d) *Superseding Charges.* If, after a complaint, indictment or information has been filed, a complaint, indictment or information is filed which charges the defendant with the same offense or with an offense required to be joined with that offense, the time limit applicable to the subsequent charge will be determined as follows:

(1) If the original indictment or information was dismissed upon motion of the defendant, or any charge contained in a complaint was dismissed or otherwise dropped, before the filing of the subsequent charge, the time limit shall be determined without regard to the existence of the original charge.

(2) If the original indictment or information was pending at the time the subsequent charge is filed, the trial shall commence within the time limit for commencement of trial on the original indictment or information.

(3) If the original indictment or information was dismissed on motion of the United States Attorney before the filing of the subsequent charge, the trial shall commence within the time limit for commencement of trial on the original indictment or information but the period during which the defendant was not under charges shall be excluded from the computations. Such period is the period between the dismissal of the original indictment or information and the date the time would have commenced to run on the subsequent charge had there been no previous charge. (Under the rule of this paragraph, if an indictment was dismissed on motion of the government on May 1, with 20 days remaining within which trial must be commenced, and the defendant was arrested on a new complaint on June 1, the time remaining for trial would be 20 days from June 1. This time limit would be based on the original indictment, but the period from the dismissal to the new arrest would not be counted. Although the 30-day arrest-to-indictment time limit would apply to the new arrest as a formal matter, 18 U.S.C. section 3161(b), the short deadline for trial, would necessitate earlier grand jury action.)

If the subsequent charge is contained in a complaint, the formal time limit within which an indictment or information must be obtained on the charge shall be determined without regard to the existence of the original indictment or information. However, earlier action may in fact be required if the time limit for commencement of trial is to be satisfied under (d)(2) and (d)(3), supra. (See example in parentheses immediately above.)

(e) *Measurement of Time Periods.* For the purposes of this section (Subsections (3) and (4) have no applicability to double jeopardy determinations.):

(1) If a defendant signs a written consent to be tried before a magistrate and no indictment or information charging the offense has been filed, the time limit shall run from the date of such consent.

(2) In the event of a transfer to this district under Rule 20 of the Federal Rules of Criminal Procedure, the indictment or information shall be deemed filed in this district when the papers in the proceeding or certified copies thereof are received by the clerk.

(3) A trial in a jury case shall be deemed to commence at the beginning of voir dire.

(4) A trial in a non-jury case shall be deemed to commence on the day the case is called, provided that some step in the trial procedure immediately follows on that day.

(f) *Related Procedures.*

(1) At the time of the defendant's earliest appearance before a judicial officer of this district, the officer will take appropriate steps to assure that the defendant is represented by counsel and shall appoint counsel where appropriate under the Criminal Justice Act and Rule 44 of the Federal Rules of Criminal Procedure.

(2) The court shall have sole responsibility for setting cases for trial after consultation with counsel. The court shall, as soon as practical, after consultation with counsel, set each case for trial on a day certain or list it for trial on a weekly or other short-term calendar.

(3) Individual calendars shall be managed so that it will be reasonably anticipated that every criminal case set for trial will be reached at the time scheduled by the court. Neither a conflict in scheduling of defense counsel nor in the schedules of Assistant United States Attorneys will be grounds for a continuance or delayed setting except under circumstances approved by the court and called to the court's attention at the earliest practicable time.

(4) At the time of the filing of a complaint, indictment or information against a defendant charged in a pending indictment or information, the United States Attorney shall give written notice to the court if the new charge is not for the same offense charged in the original indictment or information or an offense required to be joined therewith.

(5) All pretrial hearings shall be conducted as soon after the arraignment as possible, consistent with the priorities of other matters on the court's criminal docket.

5. Defendants in Custody and High-Risk Defendants.

(a) *Time Limits.* (If a defendant's presence has been obtained through the filing of a detainer with state authorities, the Interstate Agreement on Detainers, 18 U.S.C., Appendix, may require that trial commence before the deadline established by the Speedy Trial Act. (See United States v. Mauro, 436 U.S. 340, 356–57 n. 24; 1978)). Notwithstanding any longer time periods that may be permitted under sections 3 and 4, supra, the following time limits are applicable to defendants in custody and high-risk defendants as herein defined:

(1) The trial of a defendant in custody solely for the purpose of trial on a federal charge shall commence within 90 days following the beginning of continuous custody.

(2) The trial of a high-risk defendant shall commence within 90 days of the designation as high-risk.

(b) *Definition of "High-Risk Defendant"*. A high-risk defendant is one reasonably designated by the United States Attorney as posing a danger to himself or any other person or to the community.

(c) *Measurement of Time Periods*. For the purposes of this section:

(1) a defendant is deemed to be in detention awaiting trial when he is arrested on a federal charge or otherwise held for the purpose of responding to a federal charge. Detention is deemed to be solely because the defendant is awaiting trial unless the person exercising custodial authority has an independent basis (not including a detainer) for continuing to hold the defendant.

(2) if a case is transferred pursuant to Rule 20 of the Federal Rules of Criminal Procedure and the defendant subsequently rejects disposition under Rule 20 or the court declines to accept the plea, a new period of continuous detention awaiting trial will begin at that time.

(3) a trial shall be deemed to commence as provided in sections 4(e)(3) and 4(e)(4), supra.

(d) *Related Procedures*.

(1) If a defendant is being held in custody solely for the purpose of awaiting trial, the United States Attorney shall advise the court at the earliest practicable time of the date of the beginning of such custody.

(2) The United States Attorney shall advise the court at the earliest practicable time (usually at the hearing with respect to bail) if he intends to designate the defendant as being of high-risk.

(3) If the court finds that the filing of a "high-risk" designation as a public record may result in prejudice to the defendant, it may order the designation sealed for such period as is necessary to protect the defendant's right to a fair trial, but not beyond the time that the court's judgment in the case becomes final. During the time the designation is under seal, it shall be made known to the defendant and his counsel but shall not be made known to other persons without the permission of the court.

6. Exclusion of Time From Computations.

(a) *Applicability*. In computing any time limit under section 3, 4 or 5, the periods of delay set forth in U.S.C. section 3161(h) [18 U.S.C.A. 3161(h)] shall be excluded. Such periods of delay shall not be excluded

in computing the minimum period for commencement of trial under section 7. The time limits for sections 3, 4, and 5 cannot be waived, except as provided in 18 U.S.C. section 3162(a)(2). Periods of delay are excludable only as provided in the Speedy Trial Act of 1974, as amended.

(b) *Records of Excludable Time*. The clerk of the court shall enter on the docket, in the form prescribed by the Administrative Office of the United States Courts, information with respect to excludable periods of time for each criminal defendant. With respect to proceedings prior to the filing of an indictment or information, excludable time shall be reported to the clerk by the United States Attorney.

(c) *Stipulations*.

(1) The attorney for the government and the attorney for the defendant may at any time enter into stipulations with respect to the accuracy of the docket entries recording excludable time.

(2) To the extent that the amount of time stipulated by the parties does not exceed the amount recorded on the docket for any excludable period of delay, the stipulation shall be conclusive as between the parties unless it has no basis in fact or law. It shall similarly be conclusive as to a co-defendant for the limited purpose of determining, under 18 U.S.C. section 3161(h)(7), whether time has run against the defendant entering into the stipulation.

(3) To the extent that the amount of time stipulated exceeds the amount recorded on the docket, the stipulation shall have no effect unless approved by the court.

(d) *Pre-indictment Procedures*.

(1) The court may at any time recompute the time limit set forth in section 3 to exclude time pursuant to 18 U.S.C. section 3161(h).

(2) In the event that the United States Attorney anticipates that an indictment or information will not be filed within the time limit set forth in section 3, he may move for a determination of excludable time. In the event that the United States Attorney seeks a continuance under 18 U.S.C. section 3161(h)(8), he shall move for such a continuance.

(3) The motion of the United States Attorney shall state (i) the period of time proposed for exclusion, and (ii) the basis of the proposed exclusion. If the motion is for a continuance under 18 U.S.C. section 3161(h)(8), it shall also state whether or not the defendant is being held in custody on the basis of the complaint.

(4) The court may grant a continuance under 18 U.S.C. section 3161(h)(8) for either a specific period of time or a period to be determined by reference to an event (such as recovery from illness) not within the control of the government. If the continuance is to a date not certain, the court shall require one

or both parties to inform the court promptly when and if the circumstances that justify the continuance no longer exist. In addition, the court may require one or both parties to file periodic reports bearing on the continued existence of such circumstances, and may determine the frequency of such reports in the light of the facts of the particular case.

(e) *Post-indictment Procedure.*

(1) The court may at any time recompute the time limit set forth in section 4 or 5 to exclude time pursuant to 18 U.S.C. section 3161(h).

(2) Counsel shall bring to the court's immediate attention any claim that the clerk's record of excludable time is in any way incorrect.

(3) If it is determined that a continuance is justified, the court shall set forth its findings in the record, either orally or in writing. If the continuance is granted under 18 U.S.C. section 3161(h)(8), the court shall also set forth its reasons for finding that the ends of justice served by granting the continuance outweigh the best interests of the public and the defendant in a speedy trial. If the continuance is to a date not certain, the court shall require one or both parties to inform the court promptly when and if the circumstances that justify the continuance no longer exist. In addition, the court may require one or both parties to file periodic reports bearing on the continued existence of such circumstances, and may determine the frequency of such reports in the light of the facts of a particular case.

(f) *Continuance When Trial Cannot Begin as Scheduled.*

(1) In the event the judge to whom the case is assigned for trial is actually engaged in another proceeding on the day set for such trial, the judge may grant a continuance pursuant to 18 U.S.C. section 3161(h)(8) until after the conclusion of the other proceeding, upon the findings required by that section and upon a finding that it is likely the other proceeding will not be concluded in due course prior to the expiration of the time limit specified in section 4 for the commencement of such trial. In no event shall such continuance be in excess of thirty days.

(2) As used in this subsection, "other proceeding" shall mean a trial or an evidentiary hearing, and "day set for such trial" shall mean either the day set for trial or the last day of the week or other short-term calendar period set for the commencement of the trial.

7. Minimum Period for Defense Preparation.
Unless the defendant consents in writing to the contrary, the trial shall not commence earlier than 30 days from the date on which the indictment or information is filed or, if later, from the date on which

counsel first enters an appearance or on which the defendant expressly waives counsel and elects to proceed pro se. In circumstances in which the 70-day time limit for commencing trial on a charge in an indictment or information is determined by reference to an earlier indictment or information pursuant to section 4(d), the 30-day minimum period shall be determined by reference to the earlier indictment or information. When prosecution is resumed on an original indictment or information following a mistrial, appeal or withdrawal of a guilty plea, a new 30-day minimum period will not begin to run. The court will in all cases schedule trials so as to permit defense counsel adequate preparation time in light of all the circumstances.

8. Time Within Which Defendant Should Be Sentenced.
Time Limit. A defendant shall ordinarily be sentenced within a reasonable time of his conviction or plea of guilty or nolo contendere.

9. Juvenile Proceedings.

(a) *Time Within Which Trial Must Commence.* An alleged delinquent who is in detention pending trial shall be brought to trial within 30 days of the date on which such detention was begun, as provided in 18 U.S.C. section 5036.

(b) *Time of Dispositional Hearing.* If a juvenile is adjudicated delinquent, a separate dispositional hearing shall be held no later than 20 court days after trial, unless the court has ordered further study of the juvenile in accordance with 18 U.S.C. section 5037(c).

10. Sanctions.

(a) *Dismissal or Release From Custody.* Failure to comply with the requirements of Title I of the Speedy Trial Act may entitle the defendant to dismissal of the charges against him or to release from pretrial custody. Nothing in this plan shall be construed to require that a case be dismissed or defendant released from custody in circumstances in which such action would not be required by 18 U.S.C. sections 3162 and 3164.

(b) *High-Risk Defendants.* A high-risk defendant whose trial has not commenced within the time limit set forth in 18 U.S.C. section 3164(b) shall, if the failure to commence trial was through no fault of the attorney for the government, have his release conditions automatically reviewed. A high-risk defendant who is found by the court to have intentionally delayed the trial of his case shall be subject to an order of the court modifying his nonfinancial conditions of release under chapter 207 of title 18, U.S.C. [18 U.S.C.A. 3141 et seq.], to ensure that he shall appear at trial as required.

(c) *Discipline of Attorneys.* In a case in which counsel (1) knowingly allows the case to be set for trial without disclosing the fact that a necessary witness would be unavailable for trial, (2) files a motion solely for the purpose of delay which he knows is frivolous and without merit, (3) makes a statement for the purpose of obtaining a continuance which he knows to be false and which is material to the granting of the continuance, or (4) otherwise willfully fails to proceed to trial without justification consistent with 18 U.S.C. section 3161, the court may act as provided in 18 U.S.C. sections 3162(b) and (c).

(d) *Alleged Juvenile Delinquents.* An alleged delinquent in custody whose trial has not commenced within the time limit set forth in 18 U.S.C. section 5036 shall be entitled to dismissal of his case pursuant to that section unless the Attorney General shows that the delay was consented to or caused by the juvenile or his counsel, or would be in the interest of justice in the particular case.

11. Persons Serving Terms of Imprisonment. If the United States Attorney knows that a person charged with an offense is serving a term of imprisonment in any penal institution, he shall promptly seek to obtain the presence of the prisoner for trial, or cause a detainer to be filed, in accordance with the provisions of 18 U.S.C. section 3161(j).

12. Effective Dates.

(a) The amendments to the Speedy Trial Act made by Public Law 96–43 became effective August 2, 1979. To the extent that this revision of the district's plan does more than merely reflect the amendments, the revised plan shall take effect upon approval of the reviewing panel designated in accordance with 18 U.S.C. section 3165(c).

(b) The dismissal sanction and the sanction against attorneys authorized by 18 U.S.C. section 3162 and reflected in sections 10(a) and (c) of this plan shall apply to only cases which are commenced by arrest or summons on or after July 1, 1980, and to indictments and information filed on or after that date.

(c) If a defendant was arrested or served with a summons before July 1, 1979, the time within which an information or indictment must be filed shall be determined under the plan that was in effect at the time of such arrest or service.

(d) If a defendant was arraigned before August 2, 1979, the time within which the trial must commence shall be determined under the plan that was in effect at the time of such arraignment.

(e) If a defendant was in custody on August 2, 1979, solely because he was awaiting trial, the 90-day period under section 5 shall be computed from that date.

REVISED PLAN FOR FURNISHING REPRESENTATION PURSUANT TO THE CRIMINAL JUSTICE ACT OF 1964 (18 U.S.C. § 3006A)

Adopted by the Board of Judges
of the Southern District of New York
on December 16, 2004

Approved by the Judicial Council
of the Second Circuit
on October 10, 2007

I. INTRODUCTION

The Judges of the United States District Court for the Southern District of New York have adopted the following revised Plan for furnishing representation pursuant to the Criminal Justice Act of 1964, as amended (18 U.S.C. § 3006A).

Representation under this Plan shall include the appointment of counsel and the furnishing of investigative, expert and other services necessary for an adequate defense, and shall be provided by the staff of a community defender organization and by private attorneys serving on a panel selected by the Judges of the Court, as set forth herein.

II. COMMUNITY DEFENDER ORGANIZATION

The Federal Defenders of New York, Inc., a non-profit defense counsel service, (hereinafter "FDNY"), is authorized by this Plan to provide representation as a Community Defender Organization, and shall be eligible to furnish attorneys and receive payments pursuant to 18 U.S.C. § 3006(g)(2)(B). The by-laws of the Federal Defenders of New York, Inc. incorporated as part of the Plan, and a copy of said by-laws shall be maintained by the Clerk of the Court and attached to the original of this Plan.

III. PANEL OF PRIVATE ATTORNEYS
(CJA Panel)

A. Membership Qualifications. Private attorneys who are members in good standing of the bar of this Court, and have demonstrated experience in, and knowledge of, the Federal Rules of Criminal Procedure, the Federal Rules of Evidence and the United States Sentencing Guidelines shall be eligible to serve as members of the Court's Criminal Justice Act Panel of Private Attorneys (hereinafter "CJA Panel") and, upon selection to the Panel as provided in ¶ III(C) herein, shall be authorized to serve as appointed counsel pursuant to this Plan.

B. Composition and Size of the Panel. The CJA Panel shall consist of four lists. The first shall include attorneys to whom appointments as counsel shall be made in cases heard at the courthouses at Foley Square in New York City. The second list shall include attorneys to whom appointments as counsel shall be made in cases heard at the courthouse at White Plains, New York. When special circumstances exist and the interests of justice would be served, however, an attorney who is a member of the CJA Panel may be appointed, with his or her consent, to provide representation at any of the courthouses without regard to the list on which he or she appears. The third list shall consist of those attorneys eligible for appointment in death eligible cases. The fourth list shall consist of those attorneys willing and able to represent defendants in non-trial matters, particularly extraordinary habeas cases where the Court determined that counsel should be appointed.

The Board of Judges shall periodically fix the size of the CJA Panel, and of each list which comprises the Panel, so as to insure that, at all times, the number of private attorneys on the Panel and on each list is sufficient to handle the volume of cases assigned to Panel members at each courthouse.

A copy of each list shall be maintained by the Clerk of the Court and furnished to each district judge and magistrate judge of the Court.

C. Application for Approval as Panel Member. Application forms for membership on the CJA Panel shall be made available, upon request, by the Clerk of the Court. The application form shall indicate to which list or lists the applicant is applying, and shall require information regarding the applicant's educational background, professional qualifications, previous experience, prior service as a member of an assigned counsel panel, and such other factors as the Committee on Defender Services of the Board of Judges deems relevant. Completed applications shall be submitted to the Chairperson of the Committee on Defender Services. At least once each year, the Chairperson shall forward all applications received, and not previously passed upon, to the CJA Panel Review Committee established pursuant to ¶ IV herein for its review and recommendations. Private attorneys who have filed applications shall be appointed to the CJA Panel only upon 1) the recommendation by the Panel Review Committee, 2) approval by the

Committee on Defender Services of the Board of Judges, and 3) approval by the Board of Judges.

All qualified attorneys shall be encouraged to participate in the furnishing of representation in CJA cases, without regard to race, color, religion, sex, age, national origin, disabling condition, or sexual orientation.

D. Membership Term. Private attorneys appointed as members of the CJA Panel shall serve for a term of three years but may be removed by the Board of Judges as provided in ¶ III(F) herein. Whenever the term of a CJA Panel member expires, he or she may apply for a new term and said application shall be considered along with all other applications as set forth in ¶ III(C) above.

Appointments to the CJA Panel shall be made so that the terms of approximately one-third of the Panel members expire at the conclusion of each year.

E. Obligations of CJA Panel Members. Private attorneys who are accepted as members of the CJA Panel shall be available on call to appear at arraignments and presentments, and to otherwise accept assignments as counsel on designated "intake duty" days as arranged by the Clerk of the Court. In addition, Panel members shall accept assignments on such other occasions as it is found necessary by the Clerk of the Court so as to insure an equitable distribution of assignments among CJA Panel members.

Upon assignment to represent a person pursuant to this Plan, a CJA Panel member shall provide representation in accordance with the Code of Professional Responsibility and the provisions of ¶ VIII herein.

F. Removal of CJA Panel Members. A member of the CJA Panel may be removed from the Panel prior to the expiration of his or her term whenever the Board of Judges determines that the member has failed to fulfill the obligations of Panel membership or has engaged in other conduct which renders it inappropriate that he or she be continued as a Panel member.

All complaints concerning the conduct of Panel members shall be forwarded to the Chairperson of the Committee on Defender Services of the Board of Judges. If the Chairperson determines that the complaint alleges facts which, if true, would warrant consideration of removal of the Panel member, the Chairperson shall direct the CJA Panel Review Committee to review the complaint, make such inquiry as it deems appropriate, and issue a report of its findings and recommendation to the Committee on Defender Services. The report and recommendations of the Committee shall be presented to the Board of Judges which shall have authority to remove the attorney from the Panel or to take such other action as it deems appropriate.

IV. CJA PANEL REVIEW COMMITTEE

A. Membership. A CJA Panel Review Committee is hereby established to assist the Court in reviewing applications for membership on the CJA Panel and otherwise to promote the furnishing of quality representation pursuant to this Plan. The CJA Panel Review Committee shall consist of the head of the FDNY, who shall be chairperson, and six attorneys chosen annually by him or her with the approval of the Chairperson of the Committee on Defender Services. The members of the CJA Panel Review Committee must be admitted to practice in this Court and may be members of the CJA Panel.

B. Duties of the Committee.

1. The Committee shall meet at least once each year to consider applications filed by attorneys seeking to fill vacancies on the CJA Panel created by the expiration of Panel members' terms or a decision by the Board of Judges to increase the size of the Panel. The Committee shall review the qualifications of the applicants and recommend for approval by the Committee on Defender Services of the Board of Judges and the Board of Judges those applicants deemed best qualified to fill the vacancies.

2. If, at any time during the course of a year, the number of vacancies due to resignation, removal or death significantly decreases the size of the CJA Panel, the Committee shall, upon request by the Chairperson of the Committee on Defender Services of the Board of Judges, convene to review any previously filed applications and/or solicit and review new applications for membership on the CJA Panel for the purpose of recommending applicants to fill the vacancies to the Committee on Defender Services of the Board of Judges and the Board of Judges. Applicants who are appointed to fill these mid-term vacancies shall serve until the expiration of the term which was vacated, and may re-apply for membership on the Panel as set forth in ¶ III(D) above.

3. The Committee shall also, in cooperation with the Office of the District Executive, organize and sponsor continuing legal education programs relating to federal criminal defense practice for the benefit of private attorneys who are members or potential members of the CJA Panel.

V. PROCEEDINGS IN WHICH REPRESENTATION SHALL BE FURNISHED

Representation pursuant to this Plan shall be furnished to any person financially unable to obtain adequate representation (as defined in ¶ VI herein) in the circumstances set forth in 18 U.S.C. § 3006A and in the guidelines promulgated by the Administrative Office of the United States Courts, both of which are incorporated by reference.

VI. FINANCIAL ELIGIBILITY FOR REPRESENTATION

A. Standard of Eligibility. A person shall be furnished representation pursuant to this Plan if he or she is financially unable to obtain adequate representation; that is, if his or her net financial resources and income are insufficient to enable the person to obtain qualified counsel. In determining whether such an insufficiency exists, consideration should be given to: 1) the cost of providing the person and his or her dependents with the necessities of life; and 2) the cost of a defendant's bail bond or the amount of cash deposit a defendant is required to make to secure his or her release on bond.

B. Partial Eligibility. A person whose net financial resources and income are found to be in excess of the amount needed to provide him or her and any dependents with the necessities of life, and to secure the person's release on bond, but are insufficient to pay fully for retained counsel, shall be eligible for appointment of counsel pursuant to this Plan on the condition that he or she pay the available funds to the Clerk of the Court as directed by the judicial officer appointing counsel.

C. Determination of Eligibility. The determination of whether a person is financially eligible for the appointment of counsel pursuant to this Plan shall be made by a judicial officer as soon as feasible after the necessity for counsel arises. The information upon which the determination shall be made shall be provided by the person seeking the appointment of counsel either: 1) by affidavit sworn to before a district judge, magistrate judge, court clerk, deputy clerk, or notary public; or 2) under oath in open court before a district judge or magistrate judge. Whenever possible, the standard forms provided by the Administrative Office of the United States Courts shall be utilized in such inquiry. At the time of determining financial eligibility, the judicial officer shall inform the person seeking appointment of counsel of the penalties for making a false statement, and of the obligation to inform the Court of any changes in his or her financial status.

D. Redetermination of Eligibility.

1. If, at any time after the appointment of counsel pursuant to this Plan, the Court finds that the person to whom counsel was assigned is, in fact, financially able to obtain adequate representation or to make partial payment for representation as contemplated by ¶ VI(B) above, the Court may, as the interests of justice dictate, a) terminate the appointment of counsel; or b) permit the assigned counsel to continue to represent the person upon the condition that the person make such payments to the Clerk of the Court as the Court deems appropriate.

2. If, at any time after appointment by the Court pursuant to this Plan, assigned counsel obtains infor-

mation that a client is financially able to make payment, in whole or in part, for legal services in connection with his or her representation, and the source of the attorney's information is not protected as a privileged communication, counsel shall advise the Court. Upon receiving such information, the Court shall take action as provided in ¶ VI(D)(1) above.

3. If, at any time during the course of a proceeding described in ¶ V above, the presiding judicial officer shall find that a person for whom counsel has not previously been appointed under this Plan is, in fact, financially unable to retain counsel or to pay counsel whom he or she has retained, the Court may appoint counsel as provided in ¶ VII(C) or ¶ VII(D) herein.

E. Use of Financial Information. The Government may not use as part of its direct case, other than a prosecution for perjury or false statements, any information provided by a defendant in connection with his or her request for the appointment of counsel pursuant to this Plan.

VII. PROCEDURES FOR APPOINTMENT OF COUNSEL

A. Necessity of Prompt Provision of Counsel. Counsel should be provided to eligible persons pursuant to this Plan as soon as feasible after they are taken into custody, when they appear before a committing magistrate judge or district judge, when they are formally charged, or when they otherwise become entitled to counsel under the Criminal Justice Act, whichever occurs earliest.

To effectuate this objective, federal law enforcement and prosecutorial agencies in this district, and those acting on their behalf, shall promptly inquire of any person in custody, or who is otherwise entitled to counsel under the Criminal Justice Act, whether he or she is financially able to secure representation, and shall, in such cases in which the person indicates that he or she is not, promptly present said person before a magistrate judge or district judge of this Court for the assignment of counsel.

B. Duty of Magistrate Judges and District Judges. Upon the appearance of a person before a magistrate judge or district judge as provided in ¶ VII(A) above, or at any proceeding in which a person is entitled to representation under this Plan and appears without counsel, it shall be the duty of the presiding magistrate judge or district judge to advise the person of his or her right to counsel, and to promptly appoint counsel if it is determined, pursuant to ¶ VI above, that the person is financially unable to secure adequate representation, unless the person waives his or her right to counsel.

C. Distribution of Appointments.

1. Unless a special circumstance is found to exist pursuant to ¶ VII(D) herein, the FDNY or, if such Unit determines it has a conflict of interest, a private attorney who is a member of the CJA Panel shall be selected to serve as appointed counsel pursuant to this Plan.

2. The Clerk of the Court shall maintain a record of all appointments of counsel and shall advise the Chairperson of the Committee on Defender Services if, during any year, appointments to the FDNY exceed 75% of all appointments. The Chairperson of the Committee on Defender Services shall then take such steps as may be necessary to assure that, as far as possible, CJA Panel members are appointed in at least 25% of cases in which appointment is required. The Clerk of the Court shall assure that assignments among CJA Panel members are distributed equitably, with due consideration given to the nature and complexity of the cases assigned. No person shall have the right to select the counsel appointed to provide representation pursuant to this Plan.

3. Separate counsel shall be appointed for persons having interests that cannot properly be represented by the same counsel. Whenever counsel who has been appointed pursuant to this Plan discovers that a conflict of interest exists, an application to be relieved from said appointment shall be made promptly to the Court, and the Court shall, if satisfied that such a conflict does exist, appoint substitute counsel.

4. In an extremely difficult case, where the Court finds it in the interest of justice and so states, a district judge may appoint two attorneys to represent one defendant, and each attorney shall be paid for his or her services, not to exceed as to each, the limits provided in ¶ IX herein.

D. Appointments in Special Circumstances. Whenever a judge makes a written finding, in a proceeding in which counsel must be assigned pursuant to this Plan, that there is good cause shown which renders it in the interests of justice that counsel who is not employed by the FDNY or a member of the CJA Panel be assigned, the district judge or magistrate judge may appoint that counsel with the consent of the person to be so represented and the approval of the Chief Judge of the District. Such appointment shall constitute a temporary appointment to the CJA Panel for the purpose of that proceeding only. If the magistrate judge makes such an appointment and the case is transferred to a district judge, the district judge will review the matter and either confirm the appointment or assign a new attorney from the CJA Panel.

E. Substitution of Counsel. A district judge or magistrate judge may, in the interest of justice, substitute one appointed counsel for another. Such a substitution should not be made when it would unreasonably impinge upon a person's interest in continuity of representation.

VIII. OBLIGATIONS OF APPOINTED COUNSEL

A. Counsel appointed by a magistrate judge or district judge shall, unless excused by order of the Court, continue to act for the party throughout the proceedings for which he or she was assigned. An appointed attorney shall not delegate any substantive tasks in connection with representation of a defendant to any person other than a partner or associate of the law firm of which the appointed attorney is a partner or associate, without the written consent of the defendant and the Court.

B. If, at any stage of the proceedings, counsel appointed by a district judge or magistrate judge wishes to be relieved, he or she shall inform the district judge or magistrate judge before whom the case is pending. Relief of counsel shall be at the Court's discretion.

C. In the event that a criminal defendant enters a plea of guilty or is convicted following trial, appointed counsel shall advise the defendant of the right of appeal and of the right to counsel on appeal. If requested by the defendant, or upon the Court's own application, counsel must file a timely Notice of Appeal. When an appeal is taken, counsel shall continue to represent the appellant unless or until he or she has been notified by the Court of Appeals that other counsel has been appointed or that his or her services are no longer required.

D. Assigned counsel shall also provide representation for a person to whom he or she has been assigned in connection with any post-trial motions which he or she, in the exercise of professional judgment, deems non-frivolous.

In any case in which a person to whom counsel has been assigned requests that a post-sentence motion be filed which the assigned counsel, in the exercise of his or her professional judgment, deems frivolous, counsel shall so inform the client and advise the client of the right to file such a motion pro se.

E. Counsel appointed pursuant to this Plan shall at no time seek or accept any fee or other things of value from, or on behalf of, the person represented, for representing the person to whom he or she was assigned. Nor shall counsel appointed pursuant to this Plan agree to be privately retained by the person to whom he or she was assigned or by persons acting on that person's behalf, without advising and securing the approval of the Court.

IX. COMPENSATION FOR APPOINTED COUNSEL

A. Maximum Fees. Counsel appointed to provide representation pursuant to this Plan (other than mem-

bers of the staff of the FDNY) shall receive compensation for their services in accordance with the following schedules:

1. *Maximum Hourly Rate.* The maximum hourly rate for appointed counsel shall not exceed the amount provided by statute and Judicial Conference policy. In addition, appointed counsel may be reimbursed for expenses reasonably incurred, including the cost of any necessary transcripts authorized by the Court and the costs of defending actions alleging malpractice of counsel in furnishing representational services under this section. Expenses reasonably incurred are limited to out-of-pocket expenses and shall not include any allocations for general office overhead, such as rent, telephone services or secretarial help. No reimbursement for expenses in defending against malpractice claims shall be made if a judgment of malpractice is rendered against the counsel furnishing representational services under this section. The magistrate judge or district judge shall make determinations relating to reimbursement of expenses under this paragraph.

2. *Maximum Payment for Counsel Per Case.* For representation of a defendant before a magistrate judge or a district judge, or both, provided on or after December 8, 2004, the maximum compensation for the entire representation to be paid assigned counsel shall not exceed $7,000 for each attorney in a case in which one or more felonies are charged, and $2,000 for each attorney in a case in which only misdemeanors are charged. Representation of a defendant in a new trial shall be considered a separate case and fees shall be paid on the same basis as the original trial.

For any other representation required or authorized by this Plan, the compensation shall not exceed $1,500 for each attorney in each proceeding.

For representation of a defendant before a magistrate judge or a district judge, or both, in which all services were performed before December 8, 2004, the maximum compensation for the entire representation to be paid appointed counsel shall not exceed $5,200.00 for each attorney in a case in which a felony is charged, $1,500 for each attorney in a case in which only misdemeanors are charged, and $1,200 for each attorney for any other proceeding authorized under this Plan. Representation of a defendant in a new trial shall be considered a separate case and fees shall be paid on the same basis as the original trial, unless that representation was provided on or after December 8, 2004, in which case the maximums provided in the preceding paragraphs shall apply.

The maximum fee schedules set forth above shall be interpreted and applied in accordance with the provisions of the Guidelines for the Administration of the Criminal Justice Act ("Guidelines"). The maximum fee schedules for federal death penalty cases and federal capital habeas corpus proceedings shall be consistent with the rates provided by 21 U.S.C. § 848(q)(10) as interpreted and applied by the Guidelines.

B. Waiver of Maximum Limits on Counsel Fees. Payment in excess of the maximum limits on counsel fees, set forth in ¶ IX(A) above, may be made in cases involving extended or complex representation whenever the district judge before whom representation was rendered, or the magistrate judge (if the representation was furnished exclusively before the magistrate judge) certifies that the amount of the excess payment is necessary to provide fair compensation and the payment is approved by the Chief Judge of the Second Circuit or such active Circuit Judge to whom the Chief Judge has delegated such approval authority. Counsel claiming payment in excess of the statutory maximum shall submit a detailed memorandum supporting and justifying counsel's claim that the representation given was in an extended or complex case, and that the excess payment is necessary to provide fair compensation.

C. Applications for Payment. Applications for payment of counsel fees pursuant to this Plan shall be filed on voucher forms provided by the Administrative Office of the United States Courts. Vouchers shall be submitted no later than 45 days after the final disposition of the case, unless good cause is shown. If the Court determines, for any reason, that the amount of an attorney's voucher should be reduced, it shall notify the attorney before submitting the voucher for payment, and permit a response by the attorney.

D. Interim Compensation. In non-death penalty cases, where it is considered necessary and appropriate, the presiding trial judge may arrange for periodic or interim payments to counsel. In death penalty cases, the presiding trial judge may permit interim payments.

X. SERVICES OTHER THAN COUNSEL

A. Upon Request. Counsel (whether or not appointed pursuant to this Plan) who represents a party who is financially unable to obtain investigative, expert or other services necessary for an adequate defense may request such services in an ex parte application before a district judge or magistrate judge (if the services are required in connection with a matter over which the magistrate judge has jurisdiction or if the district judge otherwise refers such application to a magistrate judge for findings and report). Any such ex parte application for investigative, expert or other services necessary for an adequate defense shall be heard in camera and shall not be revealed without the consent of the defendant. The statements made in support of the application shall be made under oath or by sworn affidavit. If, after appropriate inquiry, the Court shall find that the services are necessary, and that the person is finan-

cially unable to obtain them, it shall issue an order authorizing the counsel to obtain the services. The order shall specify the type, purpose, and limitation of the services to be obtained, including the maximum amount to be expended for such services. In no instance shall the amount authorized to be expended exceed $1,600 per individual or corporation providing the services (exclusive of expenses reasonably incurred) unless payment in excess of that limit is certified by the district judge or magistrate judge as necessary to provide fair compensation for services of an unusual character or duration and the amount of the excess payment is approved by the Chief Judge of the Circuit or such active Circuit Judge to whom the Chief Judge has delegated such approval authority.

B. Without Prior Request. Counsel appointed pursuant to this Plan may obtain—subject to later review—investigative, expert or other services without prior judicial authorization if it is necessary for an adequate defense. The total cost of services obtained without prior authorization may not exceed a maximum of $500 per individual or corporation providing the services (exclusive of expenses reasonably incurred). However, a district judge or magistrate judge (if the services were rendered in a case disposed of entirely by a magistrate judge) may, in the interests of justice, and upon finding that timely procurement of necessary services could not await prior authorization, approve payment for such services after they have been obtained, even if the cost of such services exceeds $500.

XI. AUTHORITY OF ADMINISTRATIVE OFFICE OF THE UNITED STATES COURTS

The Judicial Conference has authorized the Director of the Administrative Office to employ a central disbursement system for payment of all CJA claims. In addition, the Judicial Conference has authorized the Director, under the supervision and direction of its Committee on Defender Services, to request reports from district courts and judicial councils, in such form and at such time as he deems necessary or desirable, for statistical information or other purposes under the Act.

XII. FORMS

The forms prepared and furnished by the Administrative Office shall be used, where applicable, in all proceedings under this Plan. Any revisions of said forms or any additional forms that may be prescribed by the Administrative Office under the authority of the Judicial Conference of the United States or of the Committee of that Conference designated to implement the Criminal Justice Act shall likewise be used where applicable, in all proceedings under this Plan.

XIII. RULES AND REPORTS

The Chief Judge, on behalf of the Court, may promulgate such rules as may from time to time be adopted by the Court, and the Chief Judge, on behalf of the Court, shall make such reports as may be prescribed from time to time, by the Judicial Conference of the United States or by the Committee on Defender Services.

XIV. AMENDMENTS

Amendments to this Plan may be made from time to time by the District Judges of the Southern District of New York with the approval of the Judicial Council of the Circuit. Notice of all amendments to this Plan shall be given to the Administrative Office.

XV. EFFECTIVE DATE

The revised Plan, as amended, shall become effective on October 10, 2007.

Adopted by the Board of Judges of the Southern District of New York on December 16, 2004; approved by the Judicial Council of the Second Circuit on January 7, 2005. Amended effective October 1, 2005, subject to approval of the Judicial Council. The revised Plan, as amended, shall become effective on October 10, 2007.

ELECTRONIC FILING PROCEDURES

ELECTRONIC CASE FILING RULES & INSTRUCTIONS

IMPORTANT INFORMATION FOR NEW CASES

A party filing a new civil case assigned to the Electronic Case Filing (ECF) system must do the following after obtaining a civil case number:

(1) E-mail a pdf copy of the case initiating documents to the Clerk's Office within 24 hours of delivering the paper documents to the Court; and

(2) Serve each party to the action with the initiating documents and a copy of:

(a) SDNY Electronic Case Filing Rules & Instructions (attached); and

(b) The assigned Judge's Individual Practices.

For complete instructions and e-mail addresses see Section 14—Opening a Civil Action.

Introduction

The United States District Court for the Southern District of New York implemented an Electronic Case Filing (ECF) system in December 2003. Electronic versions of documents filed by attorneys over the Internet have largely replaced paper documents in the Court's files. Almost all new civil and criminal cases filed in this Court after December 2, 2003 are Electronic Case Filing (ECF) cases. Cases filed before December 2, 2003, Pro se cases (unless the pro se litigant is a member of the bar), Social Security cases and habeas corpus cases however are not ECF cases and must be filed on paper. The information in this document applies only to cases assigned to the ECF system.

Electronic Case Filing has several advantages for both the attorney and the Court:

- Twenty-four hour concurrent access to case files from any location over the Internet
- Remote document filing from any Internet connection worldwide
- Secure access to the ECF system via unique user password
- Immediate e-mail notification of case activity to parties and the Court
- Storage of documents in a reliable and secure electronic format

In addition to the Federal Rules of Civil and Criminal Procedure, the following govern Electronic Case Filing in this District (available at www.nysd.uscourts.gov):

- **SDNY Electronic Case Filing Rules & Instructions (this document):**

  Part I. Electronic Case Filing Rules (ECF Rules), approved by the Board of Judges of this Court, provide the broad outline of the rules of Electronic Case Filing.

  Part II. Electronic Case Filing Instructions (ECF Instructions), written by the Clerk of Court under the authority of the ECF Rules, provide step by step instructions for Electronic Case Filing.

- **The Judge's Individual Practices**

  Each Judge's Individual Practices outline their own specific filing requirements.

The Court is prepared to assist you in filing electronically in several ways:

- The SDNY Electronic Case Filing Rules & Instructions will answer many of your ECF questions.

- Training in Electronic Case Filing (ECF) is available both in person at the courthouse and on-line at www.nysd.uscourts.gov (*See section 24—ECF Help Desk and Training*).

- ECF Help Desk operators are available by telephone to answer your electronic filing questions (*See section 24—ECF Help Desk and Training*).

Part I.　Electronic Case Filing Rules

The Court will accept for filing documents submitted, signed or verified by electronic means that comply with the following rules.

Section 1.　Scope of Electronic Filing

1.1 The Court will designate which cases will be assigned to the Electronic Case Filing (ECF) system. Except as expressly provided and in exceptional circumstances preventing a Filing User from filing electronically, all petitions, motions, memoranda of law, or other pleadings and documents required to be filed with the Court in a case assigned to the ECF system must be filed electronically. A paper may be filed electronically (a) from a remote location, (b) by bringing it to the Clerk's office during regular business hours, in a form or electronic format prescribed by the Clerk, for input into the system, or (c) by bringing the paper and the Filing User's SDNY ECF password and log-in to the Clerk's Office during regular business hours to be scanned into the system by the Filing User.

1.2 Unless limited by their terms to civil cases, the provisions of these procedures relating to electronic filing apply in criminal cases that are initiated by the filing of an indictment or information. Electronic filing procedures shall not apply to applications for arrest, search or electronic surveillance warrants; for other orders in aid of or ancillary to a criminal investigation; or to proceedings relating to the grand jury.

1.3 Electronic filing procedures shall not apply to Social Security cases, Pro Se cases (unless the pro se litigant is a member of the bar), Habeas Corpus cases or cases initiated before December 2, 2003.

(*See section 13—ECF Basics*).

1.4 The filing and service of the initial papers in a civil case, including the complaint, the issuance of the summons and the proof of service of the summons and complaint, as well as service of non-party subpoenas, will be accomplished in the traditional manner on paper in accordance with the Federal Rules of Civil Procedure and applicable Local Rules governing service, rather than electronically. In a criminal case, the indictment or information, including any superseders, shall also be filed and given to the defendant in the traditional manner on paper in accordance with the Federal Rules of Criminal Procedure and applicable Local Rules rather than electronically; in addition, service of subpoenas shall be made in the traditional manner on paper in accordance with the Federal Rules of Criminal Procedure and applicable Local Rules. In a case assigned to the ECF system after it has been opened, parties must promptly provide the Clerk with electronic copies of all documents previously provided in paper form. All subsequent documents must be filed electronically except as provided in these Rules & Instructions or as ordered by the Court.

(*See section 14—Opening a Civil Action*).

1.5 The Clerk shall write and revise as necessary Instructions to guide Filing Users and maximize the efficiency of the Electronic Case Filing system.

(*See Part II—Electronic Case Filing Instructions*).

Section 2.   Eligibility, Registration, Passwords

2.1 Attorneys admitted to the bar of this Court, including those admitted pro hac vice and attorneys authorized to represent the United States, may register and may be required to register as Filing Users of the Court's ECF system. Unless excused by the Court, attorneys not already Filing Users appearing in cases assigned to the ECF system must register as Filing Users forthwith upon the case being so designated. Registration is in a form prescribed by the Clerk and requires the Filing User's name, address, telephone number, Internet e-mail address, and a declaration that the attorney is admitted to the bar of this Court or authorized to represent the United States.

2.2 If the Court permits or requires, a party to a pending civil action who is not represented by an attorney may register as a Filing User in the ECF system solely for purposes of the action. Registration is in a form prescribed by the Clerk and requires identification of the action as well as the name, address, telephone number and Internet e-mail address of the party. The Court may require the party to attend in-person training for Electronic Case Filing as a condition of registering as a Filing User. If, during the course of the proceeding, the party retains an attorney who appears on the party's behalf, the attorney must advise the Clerk to terminate the party's registration as a Filing User upon the attorney's appearance.

2.3 Once registration is completed, the Filing User will receive notification of the user log-in and password. Filing Users agree to protect the security of their passwords and immediately notify the Clerk if they learn that their password has been compromised. Users may be subject to sanctions for failure to comply with this provision.

2.4 In a civil action, the Clerk will enter, as Filing Users to whom Notices of Electronic Filing will be transmitted, (a) each attorney identified on the Civil Cover Sheet, as well as (b) each additional attorney who subsequently appears in the action and files a Notice of Appearance (which must be filed electronically). In a criminal case, the Clerk will enter, as Filing Users to whom Notices of Electronic Filing will be transmitted and who will be granted access to electronically file and retrieve documents in the case, the attorney(s) for the United States identified on the Criminal Designation Form or subsequently identified as representing the United States in the case and each attorney filing a Notice of Appearance on behalf of a defendant. Notices of Appearance on behalf of a criminal defendant will be filed in the traditional manner on paper.

2.5 An attorney of record may, by written or electronic request to the Clerk, have transmission of Notices of Electronic Filing to another attorney in his or her firm terminated.

(*See section 22—ECF Passwords*).

Section 3.   Consequences of Electronic Filing

3.1 Except as otherwise provided in Rule 4 herein, electronic filing of a document in the ECF system consistent with these procedures, together with the transmission of a Notice of Electronic Filing from the Court, constitutes filing of the document for all purposes of the Federal Rules of Civil Procedure, the Federal Rules of Criminal Procedure, and the Local Rules of this Court and constitutes entry of the document on the docket kept by the Clerk under Fed. R. Civ. P. 58 and 79 and Fed. R. Crim. P. 49 and 55.

3.2 When a document has been filed electronically, the official record is the electronic recording of the document as stored by the Court (subject to the exception set out in Rule 4 below), and the filing party is bound by the document as filed. Except in the case of documents first filed in paper form and subsequently submitted electronically under Rule 1, a document filed electronically is deemed filed on the date and time stated on the Notice of Electronic Filing from the Court.

3.3 Electronic filing must be completed before midnight local time where the Court is located in order to be considered timely filed that day.

3.4 Individual Judges' Practices should continue to be followed with respect to delivery of courtesy copies.

(*See section 19—Service of Electronically Filed Documents*).

Section 4.   Entry of Court Orders

4.1 All orders, decrees, judgments and proceedings of the Court will be filed in accordance with these procedures and entered on the docket kept by the Clerk under Fed. R. Civ. P. 58 and 79 and Fed. R. Crim. P. 49 and 55. Each document signed by a judge shall be scanned so as to contain an image of the judge's signature and shall be filed electronically by the Court, and the manually signed original shall be filed by the Clerk. In the event of a discrepancy between the electronically filed copy and the manually signed original, the manually signed original shall control.

4.2 A Filing User submitting a document electronically that requires a judge's signature must promptly deliver the document in such other form as the Court requires, if any.

Section 5.   Attachments and Exhibits

5.1 Filing Users must submit in electronic form all documents referenced as exhibits or attachments, unless the Court permits paper filing.

5.2 A Filing User must submit as exhibits or attachments only those excerpts of the referenced documents that are relevant to the matter under consideration by the Court. Excerpted material must be clearly and prominently identified as such. Filing Users who file excerpts of documents as exhibits or attachments under this procedure do so without prejudice to their right to file timely additional excerpts or the complete document. Responding parties may file timely additional excerpts that they believe are relevant or the complete document. A party may move for permission to serve and file in hard copy documents that cannot reasonably be scanned.

5.3 In cases where the record of an administrative or other prior proceeding must be filed with the Court, such record may be served and filed in hard copy without prior motion and order of the Court.

(*See section 15—Motions*).

Section 6.   Sealed Documents

6.1 Documents ordered to be placed under seal may not be filed electronically.

6.2 A motion to file documents under seal should be filed electronically unless prohibited by law, in redacted form if necessary; however, a motion to file under seal that includes a statement of why the filing should not be made electronically may be made in paper copy. The order of the Court authorizing the filing of documents under seal may be filed electronically unless prohibited by law.

6.3 A paper copy of the sealing order must be attached to the outside of the envelope containing the documents under seal and be delivered to the Clerk's Office.

(See section 18—Non–Electronic Documents).

Section 7. Retention Requirements

Documents that are electronically filed and require original signatures other than that of the Filing User must be maintained in paper form by the Filing User until one year after all time periods for appeals expire, except that affidavits, declarations and proofs of service must be maintained in paper form by the Filing User until five years after all time periods for appeals expire. On request of the Court, the Filing User must provide original documents for review.

(See section 13—ECF Basics).

Section 8. Signatures

8.1 The user log-in and password required to submit documents to the ECF system serve as the Filing User's signature on all electronic documents filed with the Court. They also serve as a signature for purposes of the Federal Rules of Civil Procedure, including Rule 11, the Federal Rules of Criminal Procedure, the Local Rules of this Court, and any other purpose for which a signature is required in connection with proceedings before the Court. Each document filed electronically must indicate that it has been electronically filed.

8.2 Electronically filed documents must include a signature block and must set forth the name, address, telephone number and e-mail address all in compliance with the Federal Rules of Civil Procedure and Local Civil Rule 11.1. In addition, the name of the Filing User under whose log-in and password the document is submitted must be preceded by an "s/" typed in the space where the signature would otherwise appear.

8.3 No Filing User or other person may knowingly permit or cause to permit a Filing User's password to be used by anyone other than an authorized agent of the Filing User.

8.4 A document requiring the signature of a defendant in a criminal case may be electronically filed only in a scanned format that contains an image of the defendant's signature.

8.5 Documents requiring signatures of more than one party must be electronically filed either by: (a) submitting a scanned document containing all necessary signatures; (b) representing the consent of the other parties on the document; (c) identifying on the document the parties whose signatures are required and by the submission of a notice of endorsement by the other parties no later than three business days after filing; or (d) in any other manner approved by the Court.

(See section 13—ECF Basics).

Section 9. Service of Documents by Electronic Means

Transmission of the Clerk's Notice of Electronic Filing of a document shall constitute service of such document upon any Filing User in that case. It remains the duty of the attorney for a party to review regularly the docket sheet of the case.

Attorneys and pro se parties who are not Filing Users shall be served with a paper copy of any electronically filed pleading or other document. Service of such paper copy must be made according to the Federal Rules of Civil Procedure, the Federal Rules of Criminal Procedure and the Local Rules.

(*See section 19—Service of Electronically Filed Documents*).

Section 10.   Notice of Court Orders and Judgments

Immediately upon the entry of an order or judgment in a proceeding assigned to the ECF system, the Clerk will transmit to all Filing Users in the case, in electronic form, a Notice of Electronic Filing. Electronic transmission of the Notice of Electronic Filing constitutes the notice required by Fed.R.Crim.P. 49(c) and Fed. R.Civ.P. 77(d). It remains the duty of the attorney for a party to review regularly the docket sheet of the case. The Clerk must give notice in paper form to a person who is not a Filing User in accordance with the Federal Rules of Civil Procedure or the Federal Rules of Criminal Procedure.

(*See section 19—Service of Electronically Filed Documents*).

Section 11.   Technical Failures

A Filing User whose filing is made untimely as the result of a technical failure may seek appropriate relief from the Court.

(*See section 23—ECF Computer System Information*).

Section 12.   Public Access

A person may review at the Clerk's Office filings that have not been sealed by the Court. A person also may access the ECF system at the Court's Internet site www. nysd.uscourts.gov by obtaining a PACER log-in and password. A person who has PACER access may retrieve docket sheets in civil and criminal cases, documents in a civil case assigned to the ECF System, and documents in a criminal case filed after November 1, 2004. Only counsel for the government and for a defendant may retrieve documents in a criminal case filed prior to November 1, 2004. Only a Filing User under Rule 2 herein may file documents.

(*See section 13—ECF Basics*).

Part II.   Electronic Case Filing Instructions

Section 13.   ECF Basics

13.1 May letters be filed electronically?

No. Letters are submitted in the traditional manner on paper. An attorney should not file a letter electronically on the ECF system. The Judge may direct the Clerk to place a letter on the docket if it is deemed appropriate.

13.2 In brief, how do I file a document electronically?

(a) Use your secure SDNY ECF password (*see section 22—ECF Passwords*) to log-in to the ECF system from any Internet connection.

(b) Select the appropriate category, CIVIL or CRIMINAL.

(c) Find the appropriate ECF Filing Event, or title, for your document. (*See below*).

(d) Indicate the party filing the document (hold down the control key to designate more than one party).

(e) Upload a PDF copy (*see section 23—ECF Computer System Information*) of your document. Include any exhibits as attachments to the main document. File supporting documents separately.

(f) Print the final screen, the Notice of Electronic Filing (NEF), for your records.

(g) Service is complete provided all parties receive electronic notice of the filing (via the NEF email sent automatically by the Court—see the NEF for a list of who was/was not served electronically). If a party will not receive electronic notice via the NEF email, you must serve him/her in the traditional manner, on paper, then electronically file an affidavit of service (*see section 19—Service of Electronically Filed Documents*).

(h) Submit a paper courtesy copy to the Judge if required (*see the Judge's Individual Practices at www.nysd.uscourts.gov*).

13.3 What is the secure website for electronic filing on the SDNY ECF system?

To file electronically go to **https://ecf.nysd.uscourts.gov**, or link to the filing website via the Court's public website (see below). You will need your SDNY ECF log-in and password to file electronically.

13.4 What is the public website for information about the Court?

For publicly available information go to **www.nysd.uscourts.gov** (no password required). From the homepage click on ECF for information on Electronic Case Filing.

13.5 What are the mailing addresses for the Court?

United States District Court, 500 Pearl Street, New York, NY 10007; or United States District Court, 300 Quarropas Street, White Plains, NY 10601.

13.6 Is an electronically filed document filed in accordance with the Federal Rules of Civil Procedure?

Yes. Local Civil Rule 5.2 provides:

> A paper filed by electronic means in accordance with procedures promulgated by the Court is, for purposes of Federal Rule of Civil Procedure 5(e), filed in compliance with the local civil rules of the Southern and Eastern Districts of New York.

(*See section 3—Consequences of Electronic Case Filing*).

13.7 Which cases are ECF cases?

Civil and criminal cases filed after December 2, 2003, are subject to electronic filing. Cases filed before that date, Social Security cases, habeas corpus cases and pro se cases will not be assigned to the ECF system and must be filed on paper.

(*See section 1—Scope of Electronic Filing*).

13.8 Which Judges entertain ECF cases?

All of the Court's District Judges and Magistrate Judges are able to entertain ECF cases.

13.9 How can I tell if my case is an ECF case?

The docket sheet will include the letters "ECF" in the upper right corner and an entry titled "CASE DESIGNATED ECF". If you are not sure if you are required to file electronically, call the ECF Help Desk at (212) 805–0800.

13.10 If a case is deemed an ECF case, am I required to file documents electronically?

Yes. In an ECF case the attorney is responsible for electronically filing documents over the Internet using a secure SDNY log-in and password. With certain exceptions outlined below the Clerk's Office will not accept paper filings in an ECF case.

(*See section 1—Scope of Electronic Case Filing* and *section 18 —Non–Electronic Documents*).

13.11 May I file documents electronically in a non-ECF (paper) case?

No. Do not file documents electronically in non-ECF (paper) case. Only those cases filed after December 2, 2003 are subject to electronic filing. Pro Se cases, Social Security cases, habeas corpus cases and cases filed before December 2, 2003, will not be assigned to the ECF system and must be filed on paper.

(See section 1—Scope of Electronic Case Filing).

13.12 Will the Court file documents electronically in a non-ECF (paper) case?

Yes, the Court may file Orders and Opinions in electronic format (pdf) in a non-ECF (paper) case. This will not convert a non-ECF case to an ECF case, and parties should continue to file documents on paper.

13.13 Can I file electronically at any time?

Yes. You can file electronically 24 hours a day, 7 days a week, 365 days a year from any Internet connection worldwide. Filing must be completed before midnight local time where the Court is located in order to be considered timely filed that day.

(See section 3—Consequences of Electronic Case Filing).

13.14 When is an electronically filed document deemed filed?

An electronically filed document is deemed filed on the date and time stated on the Notice of Electronic Filing (also referred to herein as the "filing receipt") from the Court.

(See section 3—Consequences of Electronic Case Filing).

13.15 What is a docket sheet, and how can I view one?

The docket sheet is the official record of all filings in a case. You can view the docket sheet, including images of electronically filed documents, via the PACER public access system (for details go to http://pacer.psc.uscourts.gov or call 800–676–6856). Or you can use one of the public access computers available in the Clerk's Office.

(See section 12—Public Access).

13.16 Should I routinely view the docket sheet in my case?

Yes. In ECF cases, service is accomplished by an e-mail sent by the Court. However e-mail is not foolproof, and you may miss an e-mail message. Therefore it remains the duty of the attorney for a party to review regularly the docket sheet of the case in order not to miss a filing.

(See section 9—Service of Documents by Electronic Means).

13.17 How do I view an electronically filed document in an ECF case?

Click on Query, enter the case number, go to Docket Report, find the document and click on the blue number (hyperlink) next to that entry. A pdf copy of the complete document will then appear. If there is no blue hyperlink, then there is no electronic version of that document. In non-ECF (paper) cases you will not be able to view documents, only document summaries.

13.18 How will I know if it's appropriate to electronically file my document?

First, determine if your case is an ECF case—not all cases are ECF cases. When filing in an ECF case if you can find an ECF Filing Event that directly matches your document then it should be electronically filed. If you cannot find a matching ECF Filing Event it probably should not be electronically filed. The ECF Event Dictionary (a PDF document available on our public website at www.nysd.uscourts.gov) is very useful for finding your event and the category in which it is listed. See the list of non-ECF documents below or call the ECF Help Desk at (212) 805–0800.

(See section 24—ECF Help Desk and Training).

13.19 Must the caption indicate the case is an electronic (ECF) case?

Yes. The case number must be followed by the judge's initials in parenthesis, and "ECF CASE" below the case number. For example:

06 cv 1234 (ABC)
ECF Case

(See section 8—Signatures).

13.20 How do I sign an electronically filed document?

The ECF log-in and password of the filing attorney serve as his/her electronic signature. The filing attorney may place an S/ in place of his/her signature. The attorney's name and contact information, including e-mail address, must appear below the signature line. Signatures for all other persons (clients, witnesses etc.) must be scanned in order to capture the actual ink signature.

(See section 8—Signatures).

13.21 When filing must I choose a name for my document on the ECF Docket Sheet?

Yes. When filing electronically you will be asked to name your document by selecting the appropriate ECF Filing Event. The ECF Filing Event is essentially the title of the document on the docket sheet, such as Motion for Summary Judgment or Affidavit in Support of Motion.

13.22 How do I find the correct ECF Filing Event for my document?

ECF Filing Events are listed by category on the ECF system. Within each category is an alphabetical listing of available ECF Filing Events. You may use the search function to find your Filing Event. The ECF Event Dictionary (a pdf document available on our public website at www.nysd.uscourts.gov) is also very useful for finding your event and the category in which it's listed. Print the dictionary for future reference. If you cannot find the appropriate event for your document do not file it using the wrong event. Call the ECF Help Desk at (212) 805–0800 for assistance if necessary.

(See section 24—ECF Help Desk and Training).

13.23 Must I retain paper originals of documents I electronically file?

Yes. Filing Users must retain original versions of electronically filed documents for a period of time after filing. On request of the Court, the Filing User must provide original documents for review.

(See section 7—Retention Requirements).

13.24 Should I continue to submit courtesy copies?

Yes, continue your current practice. In the past if you would have submitted a paper courtesy copy of a document, you should now submit a paper courtesy copy of the document in an ECF case. For example, most Judges require courtesy copies of motion papers. Read the Judge's Individual Practices for specific practices.

(See section 3—Consequences of Electronic Case Filing).

13.25 Are Administrative Records filed electronically?

Yes, if possible. However, if the administrative record is too large to be scanned it may be served and filed in hard copy without prior motion and order of the Court.

(See section 5—Attachments and Exhibits).

13.26 In Consolidated and MDL cases can I file simultaneously in member cases?

Yes. When filing in Consolidated and Multi–District Litigation (MDL) cases you can save time by electronically filing a document simultaneously in the member case(s) using the computer function titled "Spread Text and Effects" (not available in related cases). Please observe the following MDL filing rules:

- In consolidated and MDL cases you must file all documents first under the Lead or MDL case number.

- You may then precisely designate the member case(s) in which you wish to simultaneously file.

- Do not file in all cases unless it is appropriate. Your document may not relate to all member cases.

- The case caption must include all the case numbers in which your document will be filed.

- Instructions for Spread Text and Effects and information on in-person training are available on-line at www.nysd.uscourts.gov.

13.27 What if I make a mistake in electronic filing?

Call the ECF Help Desk immediately at (212) 805–0800.

(*See section 24—ECF Help Desk and Training*).

Section 14.   Opening a Civil Action

14.1 Electronically filed (ECF) cases are opened and service of the initiating documents (complaint, notice of removal, etc.) is accomplished in the traditional manner, on paper.

14.2 In order to alert your adversary(s) to the requirements of Electronic Case Filing and the Judge's Individual Practices you are required to deliver paper copies of the following documents to all parties (available at the courthouse, and www.nysd. uscourts.gov):

● **Electronic Case Filing Rules & Instructions** (this document)

● **The Individual Practices** of the assigned Judge

14.3 Then within 24 hours of the assignment of a case number, you are required to e-mail to the Clerk's Office (e-mail is not ECF filing) the initiating documents in PDF format only (such as Adobe Acrobat PDF, see section 21). Include a F.R.C.P. Rule 7.1 Statement (if applicable) and all exhibits. The case number followed by the Judge's initials and "ECF CASE" must appear in the case caption. Failure to do so within 24 hours will delay adding your PDF documents to the computerized ECF docket.

Each document must be in a separate PDF file no larger than 2.5 megabytes (separate large computer files into smaller parts if necessary, and label accordingly). The subject line of the e-mail and the name of the PDF file should list the case number followed by a brief document description (ex. "Re: 01cv1234 KMW–complaint").

Send a PDF copy of the initiating documents by e-mail (do not file on the ECF system) to:

● For new civil cases assigned to a Manhattan Judge e-mail to:

caseopenings@nysd.uscourts.gov
or **case_openings@nysd.uscourts.gov**

● For new civil cases assigned to a White Plains Judge e-mail to:

wpclerk@nysd.uscourts.gov

14.4 File the Affidavit of Service (or the Acknowledgment of Service, Certificate of Service, Request for Waiver of Service, Summons Returned Executed/Unexecuted, Waiver of Service Executed/Unexecuted) for the initiating document (complaint, notice of removal, etc.) in the following manner:

(a) Electronically file the Affidavit of Service for the initiating document on the ECF system (do not e-mail), and

(b) Deliver the original paper Affidavit of Service, with summons attached, to the Clerk's Office. Include a copy of the ECF Notice of Electronic Filing for this document (the filing receipt).

(*See section 19—Service of Electronically Filed Documents*).

14.5 Subsequent documents, including the Defendant's Answer, <u>must be filed electronically</u> on the ECF system at **https://ecf.nysd.uscourts.gov**. With certain exceptions outlined below, the Clerk's Office will not accept a paper document for filing in an ECF case.

(*See section 1—Scope of Electronic Filing* and *section 18—Non-electronic Documents*).

Section 15. Motions

15.1 What ECF Filing Event should be used to file a motion?

A motion must be filed using an ECF Filing Event beginning with the word "Motion". The ECF system contains over 160 separate motion Filing Events for your use, all beginning with the word "Motion" (eg. "Motion for Summary Judgment", etc.). See the ECF Events Dictionary at www.nysd.uscourts.gov for a complete list of motions and supporting documents. Do not use the "Notice" filing event to file a motion.

15.2 Should I file supporting papers as attachments to the motion?

No. File supporting or response documents separately under the appropriate ECF Filing Event found in the category "Replies, Opposition and Supporting Documents". For example, a motion, an affidavit in support and a memorandum of law in support must be filed separately.

15.3 What ECF Filing Event should be used to file supporting papers?

Use the appropriate ECF Filing Events for supporting papers found in the category "Replies, Opposition and Supporting Documents" (e.g., Affidavit in Support of Motion, Memorandum of Law in Support of Motion, etc.). Never use the ECF Filing Event for Motion to file supporting papers. For example, filing a motion, an affidavit in support and a memorandum of law in support, and labeling each one "Motion" would make it appear incorrectly that three motions were filed instead of one.

15.4 How do I file exhibits?

Exhibits shall be filed only as attachments to a document, such as a motion or an affidavit. Do not use the ECF Filing Event for "Motion" to file exhibits separately. Exhibits are the only items that should be attached to electronically filed documents. You are limited to electronically filing only relevant excerpts of exhibits. Excerpts must be clearly identified as such. If the exhibit is too large to be scanned and electronically filed call the ECF Help Desk at (212) 805–0800.

(*See section 5—Attachments and Exhibits; see also section 24—ECF Help Desk and Training*).

Section 16.   Default Judgments

16.1 How do I file a Default Judgment?

In one of the three ways outlined below. Consult the Individual Practices of the Judge to determine the appropriate method (at www.nysd.uscourts.gov). If the Judge's Individual Practices contain no specific rules regarding Default Judgments you should follow section 16.4 below.

If you wish to electronically file a Request to Enter Default Judgment before submitting a Default Judgment, you must file an unsigned Clerk's Certificate as an attachment to the Request. Then submit a paper copy of the proposed Clerk's Certificate to the Orders, Appeals & Judgments Clerk. The clerk will sign and return the Clerk's Certificate, and you may then move for a Default Judgment using the appropriate method outlined below.

When necessary, submit paper documents to the Orders, Appeals & Judgments Clerk in Manhattan (212–805–0143) or White Plains (914–390–4000) depending upon where the Judge sits. If sending documents by mail, enclose a return envelope with postage. For mailing addresses *see section 13—ECF Basics.*

16.2 Default Judgment brought by Motion:

(a) Submit to the Orders, Appeals & Judgment Clerk two paper Clerk's Certificates. The clerk will sign and return both Certificates to the filing party.

(b) Electronically file the Motion for Default Judgment on the ECF system. The following items should be filed as attachments to the Motion: the signed Clerk's Certificate; and a copy of the Summons and Complaint with proof of service. The following supporting documents should be filed as separate ECF Filing Events: Affidavit in Support; and Statement of Damages (unless requesting an inquest).

(c) Electronically file an Affidavit of Service for the Motion for Default Judgment.

(d) Submit a courtesy copy of the Motion to the Judge, including the original signed Clerk's Certificate and a copy of the Affidavit of Service.

16.3 Default Judgment brought by Order to Show Cause (OSC):

(a) Submit to the Orders, Appeals & Judgments Clerk a paper original of the OSC. Include as exhibits to the Affidavit in Support a Clerk's Certificate and a proposed Default Judgment. Include courtesy copies of all documents.

(b) If signed by the Court, the Clerk's Office will electronically file only the Order. After the Order appears on the docket sheet, the attorney must electronically file all supporting papers.

(c) Electronically file an Affidavit of Service for the Order to Show Cause.

16.4 Default Judgment brought on by Default Judgment and Order:

(a) Submit to the Orders, Appeals & Judgments Clerk: a paper original of the proposed Default Judgment and Order; the Affidavit in Support; a Statement of Damages (unless requesting an inquest); a copy of the Summons and Complaint with proof of service; and a Clerk's Certificate. The papers will be forwarded to the Judge for signature.

(b) If signed by the Court, the Clerk's Office will electronically file only the Order. After the Order appears on the docket sheet, the attorney must electronically file all supporting papers.

Section 17.   Appeals

17.1 Are appeals filed electronically?

No. Appeals in ECF and non-ECF cases must be filed in the traditional manner, on paper.

17.2 How do I file an appeal in an ECF case?

File the appeal in the traditional manner, on paper either at the courthouse or by mail. Include the filing fee if necessary. Then within 24 hours of filing the paper copy of your Appeal, you are required to e-mail to the Clerk's Office an electronic copy of the Appeal in PDF format. Include any exhibits. Each document must be in a separate PDF file no larger than 2.5 megabytes. The District Court case number followed by the Judge's initials and "ECF CASE" must appear in the document's case caption. When sending e-mail, the subject line of the e-mail should always list the case number followed by a document description (ex. "Re: 01cv1234–appeal"). Questions may be directed to the Orders, Appeals & Judgments Clerk in Manhattan at (212) 805–0636, or in White Plains at (914) 390–4000. Send the e-mail (do not file on the ECF system) to:

- For appeals from an ECF case assigned to a <u>Manhattan Judge</u> e-mail to:

appeals@nysd.uscourts.gov

- For appeals from an ECF case assigned to a <u>White Plains Judge</u> e-mail to:

wpclerk@nysd.uscourts.gov

Section 18.   Non–Electronic Documents

18.1 In an ECF case are there documents that I should not file electronically?

Yes, including:

- Letters, see instruction 18.2 below.
- Case initiating documents (complaint, notice of removal, etc.), see section 14;
- All types of complaints (3rd party, Interpleader etc.), see instruction 18.3 below;
- Proposed orders; proposed judgments, stipulations; consents, see instruction 18.4 below;
- Orders to show cause (with or without a temporary restraining order), see instruction 18.6 below;
- Motions for Admission pro hac vice, see instruction 18.7 below;
- Miscellaneous cases, see instruction 18.8 below;
- Sealed documents, see instruction 18.9 below;
- Surety bonds, see instruction 18.10 below;
- Bill of Costs, see instruction 18.11 below;
- Notices of Appeal, see section 17;

18.2 May letters be filed electronically?

No. Letters are submitted in the traditional manner on paper. An attorney should not file a letter electronically on the ECF system. The Judge may direct the Clerk to place a letter on the docket if it is deemed appropriate.

18.3 Are Amended Complaints, Third Party Complaints, Interpleader Complaints, etc. filed electronically?

No. All complaints, no matter what type, are filed the same way:

(a) Deliver the paper original to the appropriate Clerk's Office (Manhattan or White Plains), and

(b) E-mail a PDF copy of the document within 24 hours, including exhibits and Rule 7.1 Disclosure Statement (if required) to the Clerk's Office. Send the e-mail to:

- For cases assigned to a Manhattan Judge e-mail to:

caseopenings@nysd.uscourts.gov

or **case_openings@nysd.uscourts.gov**

• For cases assigned to a White Plains Judge e-mail to:

wpclerk@nysd.uscourts.gov

18.4 Are Proposed Orders, Proposed Judgments, Stipulations or Consents filed electronically?

No. Any document that requires the signature of a Judge should not be electronically filed. Proposed orders, judgments, stipulations, and consents should not be submitted through the ECF system. Instead they should be sent by e-mail to the Clerk. Proposed orders should be submitted in word processing format (WordPerfect or Word) rather than as a pdf document. Stipulations should be submitted in PDF format. Stipulations must contain ink signatures (faxed signatures are acceptable, the last person to sign may e-mail it to the clerk). [Please note, effective August 1, 2008, Stipulations of Voluntary Dismissal pursuant to F.R.C.P. Rule 41(a)(1)(A)(ii) do not require the signature of a Judge, and should be electronically filed in ECF cases.] Questions may be directed to the Orders, Appeals & Judgments Clerk in Manhattan at (212)805–0143 or in White Plains at (914)390–4000. E-mail the proposed order, judgment or stipulation to:

• For cases assigned to a Manhattan Judge e-mail to:

judgments@nysd.uscourts.gov

• For cases assigned to a White Plains Judge e-mail to:

wpclerk@nysd.uscourts.gov

18.5 Must a Stipulation or Consent include a traditional ink signature?

Yes. You cannot substitute s/ for a traditional ink signature for these documents. Faxed signatures are acceptable.

(*See section 8—Signatures*).

18.6 Are Orders to Show Cause filed electronically?

No. An Order to Show Cause (with or without a Temporary Restraining Order) must be submitted in the traditional manner, on paper, to the Orders, Appeals & Judgments clerk. If signed by the Court, the Clerk's Office will electronically file only the Order. <u>After</u> the Order appears on the docket sheet, the attorney must electronically file all supporting papers.

18.7 Are Motions for Admission pro hac vice filed electronically?

No. A Motion for Admission pro hac vice is filed in the traditional manner, on paper. See the Attorney Admissions page at www.nysd.uscourts.gov for details and sample forms.

18.8 Are Miscellaneous cases filed electronically?

No. Miscellaneous cases are filed in the traditional manner, in paper form. Miscellaneous cases are those that use an "M" docket number (eg. "M 8–85") instead of a traditional case number, and require payment of a Miscellaneous filing fee for each document.

18.9 Are sealed documents filed electronically?

No. Sealed documents are filed in the traditional manner, in paper form. The sealed envelope must contain the paper document and a CD–ROM containing a pdf copy of the document. A copy of the Judge's sealing order must be attached to the outside of the envelope.

(*See section 6—Sealed Documents*).

18.10 Are surety bonds filed electronically?

No. Surety bonds are filed in the traditional manner, on paper. Include a copy of the Court's Order regarding the bond.

18.11 Is a Bill of Costs filed electronically?

No. A Bill of Costs should be filed in the traditional manner, in paper form. See Local Civil Rule 54.1 for details. See also the required Bill of Costs form at www.nysd.uscourts.gov.

Section 19.   Service of Electronically Filed Documents

19.1 How is service accomplished for electronically filed documents?

After you register for an ECF password (*see section 22—ECF Passwords*) you will receive a Notice of Electronic Filing (NEF) by e-mail whenever there is activity in your case, including court orders and filings by your adversary. That e-mail from the Court constitutes service. A hyperlink to a PDF image of any electronically filed document will be included (not all activity includes a PDF document). Print a copy of the document and the NEF for your records. The Clerk's Office will no longer mail paper copies of electronically filed documents.

(*See section 9—Service of Documents by Electronic Means*).

19.2 Am I required to serve a paper copy of an electronically filed document?

Maybe. If all parties will receive electronic notification of the filing, then service is complete upon transmission by the Court of the Notice of Electronic Filing email (NEF) and you are not required to serve a paper copy.

If any party will not receive a NEF, you are required to accomplish service on that party in the traditional manner, on paper. Then you must electronically file an Affidavit of Service (see below).

The Notice of Electronic Filing receipt will inform you who will receive notice of the filing "electronically" (by e-mail from the Court) and who will receive notice "by other means" (traditional service on paper).

(*See section 9—Service of Documents by Electronic Means*).

19.3 Am I required to electronically file an Affidavit of Service in an ECF case?

Only two circumstances require the electronic filing of an Affidavit of Service in an ECF case:

(a) The Affidavit of Service for the initiating document (complaint, notice of removal, etc.) must be filed as follows:

(1) Electronically file the Affidavit of Service for the initiating document on the ECF system (do not send by e-mail), and

(2) Deliver the original paper Affidavit of Service with summons attached to the Clerk's Office. Attach a copy of the ECF filing receipt for this document. And

(b) An Affidavit of Service must be electronically filed anytime a party is served with a paper document. This usually occurs when a party will not receive electronic notice of the filing (via email) from the Court. See the Notice of Electronic Filing (NEF) for a list of who was or was not served electronically.

(*See section 9—Service of Documents by Electronic Means*).

19.4 Is a filing timely if it is completed before midnight?

Yes. Filing must be completed before midnight local time where the Court is located in order to be considered timely filed that day.

(*See section 3—Consequences of Electronic Case Filing*).

19.5 Do I receive a receipt (Notice of Electronic Filing) when I file electronically?

Yes. When you successfully complete an electronic filing the final screen will display a NOTICE OF ELECTRONIC FILING (NEF), or filing receipt. Print a copy for your records. The NEF receipt will tell you what was filed, by whom, when it was filed and if a document number was assigned on the docket sheet (not all case activity merits a document number). If you do not see the NEF screen your filing may not have been successful and you are advised to check the docket sheet.

19.6 Should I routinely view the docket sheet in my case?

Yes. Although service is accomplished in ECF cases by an e-mail sent by the Court, e-mail is not foolproof and you risk missing an e-mail message. Therefore it remains the duty of the attorney for a party to review regularly the docket sheet of the case in order not to miss a filing.

(*See section 9—Service of Documents by Electronic Means*).

Section 20.   Attorney Appearances

20.1 How does an attorney's name appear on the docket sheet?

The attorney who signs the initiating document will be added to the docket sheet when the Clerk's Office opens the case on the ECF system. The attorney responding to that filing must add his or her own name to the docket sheet the first time he or she appears in the case. When electronically filing the first document, the responding attorney must: (a) click to create an "Association" with the client (i.e. represent the client); (b) click the "Notice" box to receive electronic notice of case activity; and (c) click the "Lead" attorney box if applicable. If the responding attorney is not offered the opportunity to create an "association" with the client on his/her first electronic filing, he/she must electronically file a Notice of Appearance in order to appear on the docket.

20.2 If the attorney's name is on the docket sheet why doesn't he/she receive e-mail notification of filings?

It could be because his or her name was added to the docket sheet before the attorney obtained an ECF password. In that case the attorney's name and firm address will appear at the top of the docket sheet, but the e-mail address will be missing. If this is the case the solution is to obtain an ECF password. Or it could be because the attorney filed a Notice of Appearance but failed to check the "Notice" box when creating an association with the client to indicate that he or she would like to receive e-mail notification of activity in the case. In this case, call the ECF Help Desk at (212)805–0800.

(*See section 24—ECF Help Desk and Training*).

20.3 How do I electronically file a Notice of Appearance in an ECF case?

If an attorney joins a case already in progress he or she must electronically file a Notice of Appearance. When electronically filing the Notice of Appearance, the attorney must: (a) click to create an "Association" with the client (i.e. represent the client); (b) click the "Notice" box to receive electronic notice of case activity; and (c) click the "Lead" attorney box if applicable. Please note the ECF system will not allow an attorney to electronically file a Notice of Appearance on behalf of another attorney. The Notice of Appearance and the ECF password must belong to the same attorney.

(*See section 2—Eligibility, Registration, Passwords*).

20.4 How do I file a Motion for Admission pro hac vice in an ECF case?

In the traditional manner, on paper. After the Order of Admission pro hac vice is signed, the attorney must apply for an ECF password. See the Attorney Admissions page at www.nysd.uscourts.gov for details and sample forms.

20.5 Am I required to notify the Court when my contact information changes?

Yes. Local Civil Rule 1.3 requires an attorney to notify the court when his/her contact information changes. For information go to www.nysd.uscourts.gov or call the Attorney Admissions Clerk at (212) 805–0645. Follow the steps below to change your contact information:

(a) If you have a pending case provide notice to the Court and your adversary(s) by electronically filing a NOTICE OF CHANGE OF ADDRESS in each open case where you remain the attorney of record, or

(b) If you do not have a pending case mail written notice of the change to: Attorney Admissions Clerk, United States District Court, 500 Pearl Street, NY, NY 10007.

20.6 What if only my e-mail address has changed?

You can make a simple change of your e-mail address yourself on the ECF system. To update your primary e-mail address click on Maintain Your Account and E-mail Information. However, if your other contact information has changed you must follow the directions above to update your full contact information.

20.7 Can I specify additional e-mail addresses to receive notification of activity in my cases?

Yes. You can add an alternate e-mail address for yourself, or add a colleague's e-mail address. On the ECF system click on Utilities, Maintain Your Account, and E-mail Information.

20.8 Can I receive electronic notification of activity in cases where I do not represent a party?

Yes. You can add cases to your e-mail notification list on the SDNY ECF system even if you don't represent a party to the case. Click on Utilities, Maintain Your Account, and E-mail Information.

Section 21. Privacy and Public Access to ECF Cases

21.1 Has electronic filing expanded public access to documents?

Yes, documents filed electronically on the ECF system are more widely available than ever before. Electronic documents can now be viewed over the Internet via a PACER account. In order to protect people's privacy and reduce the threat of identity theft, parties should be cautious when filing sensitive information.

21.2 Who is responsible for redacting sensitive information from filed documents?

It is the sole responsibility of counsel and the parties to be sure that all documents comply with the rules of this Court requiring redaction of personal identifiers. Neither the judge nor the Clerk of Court will review documents for compliance with this rule.

21.3 Am I required to redact certain sensitive information in a document?

Yes. Amendments to Federal Rule of Civil Procedure 5.2 and Criminal Procedure 49.1 require that personal identification information be redacted from documents filed with the court. You should not include sensitive information in any document filed with the Court unless such inclusion is necessary and relevant to the case. This applies to both ECF cases and non-ECF (paper) cases. In compliance with the E–Government Act of 2002, a party wishing to file a document containing the personal data identifiers listed below must file a redacted version in the public file:

- Social Security Numbers: include only the last four digits of the number.
- Names of Minor Children: include only the initials of the child.
- Dates of Birth: include only the year.
- Financial Account #'s: include only the last four digits of these numbers.
- Home Addresses: include only the City and State.

21.4 Is there other sensitive information that I should consider redacting?

Yes. Caution should be exercised when filing documents that contain the following:

- Personal identifying numbers (PIN #'s), such as a driver's license number
- Medical records, treatment and diagnosis
- Employment history
- Individual financial information
- Proprietary or trade secret information
- Information regarding an individual's cooperation with the government

21.5 Am I required to file sensitive information under seal?

No. In addition to the redacted public filing a party may file, but is not required to file, the personal data identifiers listed above by filing under seal.

You may file under seal either: (a) a reference list, or (b) an original, unredacted version of the document.

If you find it necessary to file sensitive information, the Court prefers a reference list to the filing of a complete document. The reference list shall contain the complete personal data identifier(s) and the redacted identifier(s) used in its (their) place in the filing. The reference list may be amended as of right.

21.6 Are sealed documents filed electronically?

No. Sealed documents are filed in the traditional manner, in paper form. The sealed envelope must contain the paper document and a CD–ROM containing a pdf copy of the document. A copy of the Judge's sealing order must be attached to the outside of the envelope.

(*See section 6—Sealed Documents*).

21.7 Who should maintain custody of original unredacted documents?

Parties are responsible for maintaining possession of original, unredacted documents, and information redacted from publicly filed documents. The Court may later require counsel to furnish the unredacted information.

21.8 What if I mistakenly file sensitive or confidential information?

(a) Immediately contact the ECF Help Desk at (212)805–0800. The filing will be temporarily sealed and made invisible to the public.

(b) After notifying the ECF Help Desk, the filing party must ask the Judge, in writing, for the entry to be formally sealed by the Court.

(c) Electronically file a redacted version of the mistaken filing.

Section 22.　ECF Passwords

22.1 To file electronically in this Court, do I need an ECF password from the United States District Court for the Southern District of New York?

Yes. To file electronically in this District Court you must have an ECF log-in and password issued by this Court. This password is unique, and is not the same as a password from another District or Bankruptcy Court, or a PACER password. Protect the security of your password by reporting a lost or stolen password immediately to the ECF Help Desk at (212)805–0800.

(*See section 2—Eligibility, Registration, Passwords*).

22.2 Is my SDNY ECF password the same as my PACER password?

No. Your SDNY ECF password is unique and is not the same as your password for the PACER public access system. For information on PACER go to http://pacer.psc.uscourts.gov or call 800–676–6856.

22.3 Must I be an attorney admitted to this Court to obtain an ECF password?

Yes. ECF passwords are available only to attorneys in good standing with this Court.

22.4 How do I obtain an ECF password if I am already admitted to practice in this Court?

An attorney admitted to practice in this court may register for an ECF password on-line at www.nysd.uscourts.gov. From the homepage click on CM/ECF, then Attorney Registration. You will need your SDNY bar code (your first and last initials followed by four numbers of your own choosing), and the exact date you were admitted to practice in this Court (the date is printed on your Certificate of Good Standing). Contact the Attorney Admissions Office at (212) 805–0645 if you have forgotten any of this information. Click to submit your application on-line, and wait for your ECF password to arrive by e-mail.

22.5 How do I obtain an ECF password if I am not yet admitted to practice in this Court?

The application to be fully admitted to the bar of this court includes a request for an ECF password. Go to www.nysd.uscourts.gov and from the homepage click on Attorney Admission. The application to the bar of this Court requires you to: (a) submit your application on-line, and (b) deliver a paper copy of that application and the appropriate fee to the Clerk's Office. Your ECF password will be sent by e-mail after you are sworn-in. If you wish to practice in one case only, you should move for admission Pro Hac Vice (see instructions below).

22.6 How do I obtain an ECF password if I am admitted to practice pro hac vice?

An attorney may be admitted to practice in one case by moving for admission pro hac vice. For complete pro hac vice motion instructions go to www.nysd.uscourts. gov, then click on Attorney Admission. Immediately after a motion to be admitted pro hac vice is granted, the attorney is required to register on-line for an ECF password at www.nysd.uscourts.gov. Enter the date the order was signed and enter XXXXXX for the bar code. Click to submit your application on-line, and wait for your ECF password to arrive by e-mail.

22.7 Do I need a new ECF password if I change law firms?

No. Your ECF password will remain the same even if you change your contact information. Local Civil Rule 1.3 requires an attorney to notify the court when his/her contact information changes. For information go to www.nysd.uscourts.gov or call the Attorney Admissions Clerk at (212) 805–0645. Follow the steps below to change your contact information:

(a) If you have a pending case provide notice to the Court and your adversary(s) by electronically filing a NOTICE OF CHANGE OF ADDRESS in each open case where you remain the attorney of record, or

(b) If you do not have a pending case mail written notice of the change to: Attorney Admissions Clerk, United States District Court, 500 Pearl Street, NY, NY 10007.

22.8 How will I know if my ECF password application was submitted successfully on-line?

When you are ready click the "Submit" button on the bottom of the form. The screen will turn red and you will be asked to review your answers for accuracy. After review click "Proceed". If the screen turns green your application was successfully submitted.

22.9 How long does it take to obtain an ECF password?

Your ECF password will be sent to you by e-mail, within 48 hours of your on-line request. Print a copy for your records.

Section 23.   ECF Computer System Information

23.1 What Internet browser should I use to file electronically on the ECF system?

Each new version of ECF is tested with specific Internet browsers before release. Check the ECF log-in page for a list of approved Internet browsers.

23.2 What is a PDF file and how do I create one?

All documents filed on the ECF system must be PDF computer files (portable document format). A PDF file is created by scanning a printed document using PDF writer software such as Adobe Acrobat (go to Adobe.com for details). PDF files cannot be altered, providing security to the filer and the Court.

23.3 Can I file electronically at the courthouse?

Yes, you may scan and electronically file documents using the document scanners and computers available at the ECF Help Desk in the Clerk's Office. Bring your paper documents and your SDNY ECF log-in and password.

23.4 Is there a limit to the size of a document that can be filed on ECF?

Yes. No single PDF computer file may be larger than 2.5 megabytes (2.5 mb). No single filing event including attachments (e.g., Affidavit in Support with exhibits attached) may be larger than 15 megabytes. If the filing is too large, the ECF system will not allow it to be filed, and you will not see a Notice of Electronic Filing (filing receipt) screen. To determine the size of an Adobe Acrobat PDF file click on File, Document Properties, Summary.

23.5 What if my document exceeds the file size limit?

Scan your documents at low resolution. Within the Adobe Acrobat program, on the "Scan Manager" screen, adjust the settings for black and white and 200 dpi (dots per inch). This creates a good quality picture and allows you to fit more pages into a single PDF file. If that doesn't work, separate an oversized file into 2 or more parts. Simply label each file 1a, 1b, 1c, etc. Only relevant excerpts of exhibits should be electronically filed (see below). Finally, if you still experience problems call the ECF Help Desk at (212)805–0800.

(*See section 24—ECF Help Desk and Training*).

23.6 Do I need the Court's permission to file on paper in an ECF case?

Yes. If your document is too large to file electronically after following the directions above, you may seek permission from the Judge to file on paper. Call the ECF Help Desk first for guidance at (212)805–0800.

(*See section 5—Attachments and Exhibits*).

23.7 Must I file only relevant excerpts of exhibits?

Yes. You are limited to electronically filing only relevant excerpts of exhibits. Excerpts must be clearly identified as such.

(*See section 5—Attachments and Exhibits*).

23.8 What if a technical failure prevents me from filing electronically?

If a technical failure prevents you from filing electronically, follow the steps below:

(a) Do not attempt to file paper documents in ECF cases except for emergency filings (eg. Temporary Restraining Order).

(b) If the problem concerns the Filing User's equipment or Internet Service Provider (ISP), and the Court's ECF system remains in service, the Filing User may use the document scanners at the ECF Help Desk in the Clerk's Office to file electronically. Bring your paper documents and your SDNY ECF password.

(c) If the Court's ECF system is out of order you should electronically file your document as soon as the system is restored.

(d) If you missed a filing deadline when the ECF system was out of order, attach a statement to your filing explaining how the interruption in service prevented you from filing in a timely fashion.

(*See section 11—Technical Failures*)

Section 24.   ECF Help Desk & Training

24.1 How can I learn how to file electronically?

The Court offers several options for ECF training. Details are available on the CM/ECF page at www.nysd.uscourts.gov

(a) In-person training classes are offered weekly for attorneys and support staff (approx. 2 hours).

(b) Step by step filing instructions can be found on-line in the course materials for our in-person training. From the CM/ECF page click on Training. Then click on Instructor Led Training, and click on the course title.

(c) "ECF 101" is a short interactive web-based introduction to electronic filing available on-line.

24.2 How do I sign up for free e-mail alerts concerning ECF news?

Sign up for free e-mail alerts from the Court at www.nysd.uscourts.gov. From the homepage click on CM/ECF, then POC. You will receive periodic e-mails alerting you to planned ECF service interruptions for maintenance, and unplanned interruptions due to technical difficulties. You will also receive periodic ECF Newsletter e-mails containing news and helpful filing hints. You do not need to be an attorney to sign up for free e-mail alerts.

24.3 How do I contact the ECF Help Desk?

The ECF telephone Help Desk is available from 8:30 AM to 7:00 PM Monday through Friday at (212) 805–0800. Or you can e-mail your ECF questions to **helpdesk@nysd.uscourts.gov**

The preceding Rules for Electronic Case Filing were approved by the Board of Judges of the Southern District of New York on May 28, 2008.

The preceding Electronic Case Filing Instructions were written by the Clerk of Court under the authority of the ECF Rules and were last revised on August 1, 2008.

Effective March 6, 2003. Revised effective May 28, 2008; August 1, 2008.

EASTERN DISTRICT SUPPLEMENTAL MATERIALS
FEE SCHEDULES

Attorney Admission	$170.00
Certificate of Good Standing	$ 15.00
Civil Pro Bono Fund	$ 10.00
Civil Purpose Fund	$ 10.00
Document Certification	$ 9.00
Exemplification	$ 18.00
Filing Fee for Civil Case*	$350.00
Habeas Corpus	$ 5.00
Misdemeanor Appeal	$ 32.00
Miscellaneous Case	$ 39.00
Notice of Appeal	$455.00
Notice of Appeal (Appeal to a District Judge from a judgment of conviction by a Magistrate Judge in a misdemeanor case)	$ 32.00
Photocopy (per page)	$ .50
Pro Hac Vice Application	$ 25.00
Record Retrieval (FRC)	$ 45.00
Record Search (per name)	$ 26.00
Registration of Foreign Judgment	$ 20.00
Returned Check	$ 45.00
Statutory Fee	$ 50.00
Tape Duplication	$ 26.00
Title III of the Cuban Liberty and Democratic Solidarity (LIBERTAD) Act of 1996, P.L. 104-114, 110 Stat. § 785 (1996), $ 5431 (This fee is in addition to the filing fee prescribed by 28 U.S.C. § 1914(a) for instituting any civil action other than a writ of habeas corpus)	$5431.00

[Last modified July 15, 2005; February 8, 2006.]

* **Deficit Reduction Act of 2005 (Pub.L. 109–171.** This law was enacted on February 8, 2006 and includes several changes to the filing fees. These fee increases will take effect for all new cases filed 60 days from enactment of the bill. Thus, the increases will apply to all new cases filed on or after Sunday April 9, 2006. **District Court: civil action filing fee will increase from $250 to $350 and Appeal Filing Fees— increased from $250 to $455.**

JURY SELECTION PLAN

**[Adopted March 21, 1995; Approved June 14, 1996,
by the Second Circuit Judicial Council]**

**[Amended December 19, 1995; Approved January 22,
1996, by the Second Circuit Judicial Council]**

**[Amended September 12, 2006; Approved September 25,
2006, by the Second Circuit Judicial Council]**

§ 1. APPLICABILITY OF PLAN

This plan is applicable to the Eastern District of New York, which consists of the counties of: Kings, Nassau, Queens, Richmond and Suffolk. There are no statutory divisions in the Eastern District of New York. Places where court shall be held for the Eastern District of New York are designated in 28 U.S.C. § 112(c), and include Brooklyn and Long Island courthouse locations.

Amended May 18, 1999.

§ 2. POLICY

All litigants in federal courts entitled to trial by jury shall have the right to grand and petit juries selected at random from a fair cross section of the community. All citizens shall have the opportunity to be considered for service on grand and petit jurors and shall have an obligation to serve as jurors when summoned for that purpose. No citizens shall be excluded from service as a grand or petit juror on account of race, color, religion, sex, national origin, or economic status.

§ 3. MANAGEMENT AND SUPERVISION OF JURY SELECTION

The clerk of the court shall manage the jury selection process, under the supervision and control of the Chief Judge.

§ 4. RANDOM SELECTION FROM VOTER LISTS

While voter registration lists of the component counties represent a fair cross section of the community in the Eastern District of New York an even greater number of citizens will be eligible for jury service if supplemental source lists are used. Accordingly, names of grand and petit jurors serving on or after the effective date of this plan shall be selected at random from the voter registration lists of all the counties within the Eastern District of New York supplemented by lists for these counties from the New York State Department of Motor Vehicles.

For the Eastern District as a whole, at the clerk's option, and after consultation with the court, the selection of names from complete source list databases in electronic media for the master jury wheel may be accomplished by a purely randomized process through a properly programmed electronic data processing system. Similarly, at the option of the clerk and after consultation with the court, a properly programmed electronic data processing system for pure randomized selection may be used to select names from the master wheel for the purpose of determining qualification for jury service, and from the qualified wheel for summoning persons to serve as grand and petit jurors. Such random selections of names from the source lists for inclusion in the master wheel by data computer personnel must insure that each county within the district is substantially proportionally represented in the master jury wheel in accordance with 28 U.S.C. § 1863(b)(3). The selections of names from the source lists, the master wheel, and the qualified wheel must also insure that the mathematical odds of any single name being picked are substantially equal.

Amended May 18, 1999.

§ 5. MASTER JURY WHEEL

A master jury wheel shall consist of the combined source lists with names selected under § 4 marked, or, in the discretion of the clerk in consultation with the Chief Judge a properly programmed electronic data processing system, devices similar in purpose and function to a wheel.

The clerk shall establish a master jury wheel for the Eastern District as a whole. The Eastern District's master jury wheel shall include the names of all persons randomly selected from the combined source lists of all the counties of the Eastern District. The

minimum number of names to be placed initially in the master jury wheel shall be five thousand.

The Chief Judge may order additional names to be placed in a master jury wheel using the same system described in section 4 from time to time as necessary. A master jury wheel shall be emptied and refilled from the combined source lists on or before September 1 following each presidential election and every two years thereafter.

Amended May 18, 1999.

§ 6. COMPLETION OF JUROR QUALIFICATION FORM

From time to time as directed by the Chief Judge, the clerk shall publicly draw at random from a master jury wheel the names of as many persons as may be required for jury service. The clerk shall prepare an alphabetical list of the names drawn.

If mailing of the juror qualification forms can be accomplished within two months, the clerk may, with the consent of the Chief Judge, draw the entire list on a master jury wheel at one time.

The clerk, at such time as shall be practicable and consistent with his other duties and those of this staff, shall mail to every person whose name is drawn from a master wheel a juror qualification form accompanied by instructions to fill out and return the form, duly signed and sworn, to the clerk by mail within ten days.

In any case in which it appears that there is an omission, ambiguity, or error in a form, the clerk shall return the form with instructions to the person to make such additions or corrections as may be necessary and to return the form to the clerk within ten days. Any person who fails to return a completed juror qualification form as instructed may be summoned by the clerk forthwith to appear before the clerk to fill out a juror qualification form.

A person summoned to appear because of failure to return a juror qualification form as instructed who personally appears and executes a juror qualification form before the clerk, may, in the discretion of the court, except where his prior failure to execute and mail such form was willful, be entitled to receive for such appearance the same fees and travel allowances paid to jurors. At the time of his appearance for jury service, any person may be required to fill out another juror qualification form in the presence of the clerk or the court at which time, in such cases as it appears warranted, the person may be questioned, but only with regard to his responses to questions contained on the form. Any information thus acquired by the clerk or a judge of the court may be noted on the juror qualification form and transmitted to the Chief Judge.

§ 7. EXCUSES ON INDIVIDUAL REQUEST

The court hereby finds that jury service by members of the following occupational classes or groups of persons would entail undue hardship or extreme inconvenience, and the excuse of such members is not inconsistent with the Federal Jury Act, 28 U.S.C. §§ 1861–1878, and shall be granted upon individual request:

(1) Persons over 70 years of age.

(2) Actively engaged members of the clergy.

(3) Persons having active care and custody of a child or children under 10 years of age whose health and/or safety would be jeopardized by their absence for jury service; or a person who is essential to the care of aged or infirm persons.

(4) Actively practicing attorneys, physicians, dentists, and registered nurses.

(5) Persons who have served as a grand or petit juror in a state or federal court within the preceding two years.

(6) Any person whose services are so essential to the operation of a business, commercial, or agricultural enterprise that it must close if the person were required to perform jury duty.

§ 8. EXEMPTION FROM JURY SERVICE

The district court hereby finds that exemption of the following groups of persons or occupational classes is in the public interest and would not be inconsistent with the act and accordingly members of such groups are exempt from jury service:

(1) Members in active service in the Armed Forces of the United States.

(2) Active full-time paid members of a fire or police department.

(3) Public officers in the executive, legislative, or judicial branches of the Government of the United States, or any State, district, territory, or possession or subdivision thereof, who are actively engaged in the performance of official duties. Public officer shall mean a person who is either elected to public office or who is directly appointed by a person elected to public office.

§ 9. DETERMINATION OF QUALIFICATIONS, EXCUSES, AND EXEMPTIONS

The Chief Judge, on his initiative or upon recommendation of the clerk, shall determine solely on the basis of information provided on the juror qualification form and other competent evidence whether a person is qualified for, or exempt, or to be excused from jury service. The clerk shall enter such determination in the space provided on the juror qualification form and the list of names drawn from the master jury wheel. If a person did not appear in response to a summons, this fact shall be noted on the list.

In making the determination the Chief Judge shall deem any citizen qualified to serve on grand and petit juries in the district court unless he, or she—

(1) is under 18 years of age;

(2) has not resided within the district for one year;

(3) is unable to read, write, and understand the English language well enough to fill out satisfactorily the juror qualification form;

(4) is unable to speak the English language;

(5) is incapable, by reason of mental or physical infirmity, to render satisfactory jury service; or

(6) has a charge pending against him for the commission of, or has been convicted in a State or Federal court of record of a crime punishable by imprisonment for more than one year and his civil rights have not been restored by pardon or amnesty.

§ 10. LIMITATION OR DISQUALIFICATIONS, EXCLUSIONS, EXCUSES OR EXEMPTIONS

Except as provided by law or this plan, no person or class of persons shall be disqualified, excluded, excused, or exempt from service as jurors: Provided, that any person summoned for jury service may be (1) excused by the court, upon a showing of undue hardship or extreme inconvenience, for such period as the court deems necessary, at the conclusion of which such person shall be summoned again for jury service, or (2) excluded by the court on the ground that such person may be unable to render impartial jury service or that his service as a juror would be likely to disrupt the proceedings, or (3) excluded upon peremptory challenge as provided by law, or (4) excluded pursuant to the procedure specified by law upon a challenge by any part for good cause shown, or (5) excluded upon determination by the court that his service as a juror would be likely to threaten the secrecy of the proceedings, or otherwise adversely affect the integrity of jury deliberations. No person shall be excluded under clause (5) of this section unless a judge, in open court, determines that exclusion is warranted and that exclusion of the person will not be inconsistent with the law.

The number of persons excluded under clause (5) of this section shall not exceed one per centum of the number of persons who return executed jury qualification forms during the period, specified in this plan, between two consecutive fillings of a master jury wheel. The names of persons excluded under clause (5) of this section together with detailed explanations for the exclusions, shall be forwarded immediately to the judicial council of the second circuit, which shall have the power to make any appropriate order, prospective or retroactive, to redress any misapplication of clause (5) of this section but otherwise exclusions effectuated under such clause shall not be subject to challenge under the provisions of the Act. Any person excluded from a particular jury under clause (2), (3), or (4) of this section shall be eligible to sit on another jury if the basis for his initial exclusion would not be relevant to his ability to serve on such other jury.

Whenever a person is disqualified, excused, exempt, or excluded from jury service, the clerk shall note the specific reason therefor.

§ 11. QUALIFIED JURY WHEELS

The clerk shall maintain a qualified jury wheel for the Eastern District in the form of an electronic data processing system or some equivalent. The clerk shall place in such wheel the names of persons drawn from the master jury wheel who are determined to be qualified as jurors and not exempt or excused pursuant to this plan.

§ 12. PUBLICATION OF NAMES DRAWN FROM QUALIFIED JUROR WHEELS

Names drawn from a qualified jury wheel shall not be made available to the public until the jurors have been summoned and have appeared at the courthouse, provided that the Chief Judge or the trial judge for whom a panel is drawn may order the names to be kept confidential in a case or cases when the interests of justice so require.

§ 13. ASSIGNMENT TO PANELS

From time to time, the clerk shall publicly draw at random from the Eastern District's qualified jury wheel such number of names of persons as may be required for assignment to grand and petit jury panels to sit in Brooklyn, and in Long Island. The clerk shall prepare a separate list of names of persons assigned to each grand and petit jury panel.

The clerk shall assign persons whose names have been drawn from the qualified jury wheel to grand and petit panels by random selection. No separate group drawn from the Eastern District's qualified jury wheel shall be assigned in advance to grand jury or petit jury duties but jurors shall be drawn from that qualified jury wheel for these duties as required from month to month.

§ 14. SUMMONING OF JURY PANELS

When the court orders a grand or petit jury to be drawn, the clerk shall issue summonses for the re-quired number of jurors. Each person drawn for jury service may be served personally or by registered or certified or first class mail addressed to such person at his usual residence or business address.

§ 15. LIMITATION OF SERVICE IN TWO-YEAR PERIOD

In any two-year period, no person shall be required to (1) serve or attend court for prospective service as a petit juror for a total of more than thirty days, except when necessary to complete service in a particular case, or (2) serve on more than one grand jury, or (3) serve as both a grand and petit juror.

§ 16. UNANTICIPATED SHORTAGE OF JURORS

When there is an unanticipated shortage of available petit or grand jurors drawn from a qualified jury wheel, the court may require the clerk to summon a sufficient number of jurors selected at random from the appropriate voter registration lists and New York State Department of Motor Vehicle lists, in a manner ordered by the court consistent with 28 U.S.C. § 1866(f).

§ 17. LETTERS OF TRANSMITTAL, QUESTIONNAIRES AND SCHEDULE OF EXCUSES

Any juror qualification form, letters of transmittal, questionnaires, notices or other forms used by the clerk in carrying out this plan shall be in the form prescribed by the Administrative Office of the United States Courts and approved by the Judicial Conference of the United States.

§ 18. MAINTENANCE AND INSPECTION OF RECORDS

After a master jury wheel is emptied and refilled, and after all persons selected to serve as jurors before that master wheel was emptied have completed such service, all records and papers compiled and maintained by the clerk before that master wheel was emptied shall be preserved in the custody of the clerk for four years or for such longer period as may be ordered by a court, and shall be available for public inspection for the purpose of determining the validity of the selection of any jury.

§ 19. MODIFICATION OF THE PLAN

This plan may be modified at any time and shall be modified when this Court is so directed by the Judicial Council of the Second Circuit.

Modifications of this plan, made at the instance of this Court, shall become effective after approval by the Second Circuit Panel, in accordance with 28 U.S.C. § 1863(a).

§ 20. FILING COPIES OF THE PLAN

Copies of the plan as initially adopted and of future modifications shall be filed with the Judicial Council of the Second Circuit, the Administrative Office of the United States Courts and the Attorney General of the United States.

§ 21. EFFECTIVE DATE OF THE PLAN

This plan shall be placed into operation after it has been approved by a Reviewing Panel consisting of the members of the Judicial Council of the Second Circuit and the Chief Judge of this district, in accordance with 28 U.S.C. § 1863.

PROCEDURES GOVERNING APPOINTMENT OF ATTORNEYS IN PRO SE ACTIONS

The following procedures shall govern the appointment of attorneys from the Eastern District Civil Pro Bono Panel to represent pro se parties in civil actions who lack the resources to retain counsel by any other means. For each civil action duly commenced in the Eastern District of New York, by or against such a pro se party, the District Judge to whom the action is assigned may issue an order of appointment and other orders relating to representation by the appointed attorney in accordance with these Rules. In civil cases assigned to a Magistrate Judge for all purposes, the term Judge in these Rules shall include a Magistrate Judge.

Rule 1. Civil Pro Bono Panel.

(A) Attorneys who are willing to accept appointment to represent pro se parties in civil actions when such parties lack the resources to retain counsel shall apply for designation to the Civil Pro Bono Panel on appropriate forms available from the Clerk of Court. Each application shall set forth, among other things:

(i) the attorney's prior civil trial experience, including the number of trials and areas of trial experience;

(ii) the attorney's ability to consult and advise in languages other than English;

(iii) the attorney's preference for appointment among various types of actions (e.g., Social Security Appeals, Employment Discrimination Actions, Civil Rights Actions; and,

(iv) the attorney's preference for appointment between the Brooklyn and Long Island courthouses.

Application may be filed in the Office of the Clerk in either courthouse.

(B) A law firm may apply to participate in the Panel as a firm by completing the appropriate form available from the Clerk. In its application, the law firm shall set forth, among other things:

(i) the number of appointed cases per calendar year the firm is willing to accept;

(ii) the ability of participating firm attorneys to consult and advise in languages other than English;

(iii) the firm's specialty, if any, and preference for appointment among various types of actions (e.g., Social Security Appeals, Employment Discrimination Actions, Civil Rights Actions);

(iv) the name of the firm's managing partner or a senior member of the firm designated as Panel Liaison; and,

(v) preference, if any, for appointment between the Brooklyn and Long Island courthouses.

Applications may be filed in the Office of the Clerk in either courthouse. Where an action is assigned to a participating firm, the order of appointment may be directed to the firm and the assignment of a firm attorney to the action may be made by the managing partner or Panel Liaison.

(C) Information on an application may be amended at any time by letter. An attorney or firm may, by letter, withdraw from the Panel at any time.

Rule 2. Appointment Procedure.

(A) The Clerk shall advise and assist any party appearing pro se in filing an in forma pauperis affidavit in circumstances where the party lacks the resources to retain counsel. At the time the pro se party files such an affidavit, the Clerk shall also inform the party of the opportunity to apply in writing to the assigned Judge for appointment of counsel, and shall provide the party with an application form and necessary assistance for this purpose.

(B) Where a pro se litigant who was ineligible for appointed counsel at the outset of the litigation subsequently becomes eligible by reason of changed circumstances, the pro se litigant may apply to the Judge for appointment of counsel within a reasonable time after the change in circumstances has occurred.

(C) The Judge assigned the action shall determine whether a Panel Attorney is to be appointed to represent the pro se party pursuant to 28 U.S.C. § 1915(d). Such a determination should be made as soon as practicable after the action is assigned. The factors to be taken into account in making this determination are:

(i) the nature and complexity of the action;

(ii) the potential merit of the claims as set forth in the pleadings;

(iii) the inability of the pro se party to retain counsel by other means;

(iv) the degree to which the interests of justice will be served by appointment of counsel, including the benefit the Court may derive from the assistance of the appointed counsel; and,

(v) any other factors deemed appropriate by the Judge.

Failure of the pro se party to make a written application for appointed counsel shall not preclude appointment with the consent of the pro se party.

(D) Whenever the assigned Judge concludes that appointment of counsel is warranted, the Judge shall issue an order pursuant to 28 U.S.C. § 1915(d), directing appointment of an attorney from the Civil Pro Bono Panel to represent the pro se party. The Judge may, if he or she deems it desirable, direct appointment of an attorney not on the Panel or a specific attorney on the Panel who is especially qualified by interest or otherwise to undertake the representation. This order shall be transmitted forthwith to the office of the Clerk at the courthouse where the action is pending. If service of the summons and complaint has not yet been made, an order directing service by the Marshall for the District or by other appropriate method of service shall accompany the appointment order.

(E) When the action involves a petition for habeas corpus filed by a pro se party, the appointment, if any, shall be made from the Criminal Justice Act Panel of Attorneys.

(F) Once the Clerk has received the appointment order from the Judge, he shall select an attorney from the Panel to represent the pro se party in the action, unless the order directs appointment of a specific attorney. Selection by the Clerk shall be made on a random basis from the lists of attorneys on the Panel, which shall be grouped according to the courthouse and types of actions entered as preferences or specialties on the attorney's application forms filed in the Office of the Clerk.

(G) Before selecting an attorney to represent a pro se litigant, the Clerk shall determine whether the litigant has any other case pending before the Court and whether an attorney has been appointed in such case. Where an appointed attorney is already representing the litigant in prior action, such attorney is encouraged, but not required, to represent the litigant in the new action. The Clerk shall inquire of the appointed counsel whether he or she will accept appointment in the new action. If the appointed counsel declines, the Clerk shall appoint an attorney, at random, in accordance with this Rule.

(H) The Clerk shall immediately send written notice of the appointment to the selected attorney. Copies of the order of appointment, these rules governing procedures for appointment, the pleadings filed to date, relevant correspondence and other documents shall accompany such notice. Upon receiving such notice, the appointed attorney shall forthwith enter an appearance in the action.

(I) The Clerk shall maintain a record of all appointments. If a notice of appearance is not entered within thirty (30) days of receipt of the notice of appointment the Clerk shall contact the attorney to clarify the status of the appointment and to reiterate the attorney's obligation to file an appearance or to file an application for relief from appointment within thirty (30) days of receipt of the notice of appointment.

Rule 3. Responsibilities of the Appointed Attorney.

(A) Upon receiving a notice of appointment and entering an appearance in the action, the appointed attorney shall promptly communicate with the newly represented party concerning the action.

(B) If the appointed attorney after reviewing the file reasonably anticipates a need to request relief from appointment on any of the grounds enumerated in subparagraph (v) of Rule 4(a), the attorney shall, before discussing the merits of the case with the client, advise the client that a procedure for such relief exists. Where the attorney did not reasonably anticipate the need for such relief prior to discussing the merits of the case with the client, the attorney may request the waiver at any time the need for such relief becomes apparent. The attorney should then request the client to execute a limited waiver of the attorney-client privilege permitting the attorney to disclose under seal to the Court the attorney's reasons for seeking to be relieved of the appointment. The waiver should indicate that the application for relief will be a privileged court document and may not be used in the litigation. The client's refusal to execute a waiver shall not preclude the attorney from applying for relief.

(C) The appointed attorney should discuss fully the merits of the dispute with the party, and explore with the party the possibilities of resolving the dispute in other forums, including but not limited to administrative forums.

(D) If the party decides to prosecute or defend the action after consultation with the appointed attorney, the appointed attorney shall proceed to represent the party in the action, unless or until the attorney-client relationship is terminated as provided in these Rules.

(E) Once the appointed attorney accepts the case and the client, the attorney shall be free in the exercise of his or her professional judgment, but not required, to represent the client in or out of court in any other matter that would be appropriate in the case of a retained attorney and a fee-paying client.

Rule 4. Relief from Appointment.

(A) An appointed attorney may apply to be relieved of an order of appointment only on the following grounds:

(i) a conflict of interest precludes the attorney from accepting the responsibilities of representing the party in the action;

(ii) the attorney believes that he or she is not competent to represent the party in the particular type of action assigned;

(iii) a personal incompatibility exists between the attorney and the party, or a substantial disagreement exists between the attorney and the party on litigation strategy;

(iv) the attorney lacks the time necessary to represent the plaintiff in the action because of the temporary burden of other professional commitments involved in the practice of law; or,

(v) the attorney believes that the party is proceeding for purposes of harassment or malicious injury, or that the party's claims or defenses are not warranted under existing law and cannot be supported by good faith argument for extension, modification or reversal of existing law.

(B) Where an order of appointment has been directed to a participating law firm the action shall remain the responsibility of the firm notwithstanding the firm's assignment of the case to one of its attorneys. Accordingly, a firm attorney ordinarily shall not seek relief from appointment from the Court on any of the grounds enumerated in subparagraph (ii) through subparagraph (iv) of Rule 4(a).

(C) An application by an appointed attorney for relief from an order of appointment on any of the grounds set forth in subparagraphs (i) through (iv) of Rule 4(a) must be made to the Judge within thirty (30) days after the attorney's receipt of the order of appointment, or within such additional period permitted by the Judge for good cause shown.

(D) If an application for relief from an order of appointment is granted, the Judge may issue an order directing appointment of another attorney to represent the party. The Judge shall have the discretion not to issue a further order of appointment, in which case the party shall be permitted to prosecute or defend the action pro se.

(E) Whenever an attorney seeks to be relieved of an order of appointment on any of the grounds set forth in subparagraph (v) of Rule 4(a), he or she shall file an application for relief with the Clerk within thirty (30) days after receiving an order of appointment or within a reasonable period of time not to exceed thirty (30) days after learning of the facts warranting such relief. The application shall set forth in full, the factual and legal basis for the request for relief. The application shall be a privileged court document kept under seal and shall not be available in discovery or otherwise used in the litigation. The Clerk shall thereupon submit the application for relief of the appointed attorney to the assigned Judge for review. The Judge shall either (i) deny the application of the attorney and direct that attorney to proceed with the representation, or (ii) grant the application and permit the party to prosecute or defend the action pro se. In the latter case, the Clerk shall inform the party that no further appointments shall be made and upon request of the pro se party the Judge shall recuse himself.

Rule 5. Discharge.

(A) A party for whom an attorney has been appointed shall be permitted to request the Judge to discharge the attorney from the representation and to appoint another attorney. Such a request must be made within thirty (30) days after the party's initial consultation with the appointed attorney, or within such additional period permitted by the Judge.

(B) When such a request is supported by good cause (e.g., substantial disagreement between the party and the appointed attorney on litigation strategy), the Judge shall forthwith issue an order discharging the appointed attorney from further representation of the party in the action. In such cases, the Judge may issue a further order directing appointment of another attorney to undertake the representation, in accordance with the provisions of Rule 2(C) through Rule 2(I). The Judge shall have the discretion not to issue a further order of appointment in such cases. Where a party requests discharge of a second appointed attorney, no additional appointments shall be made.

(C) In actions where (i) the party's request for discharge is not supported by good cause, or (ii) the party seeks discharge of a second appointed attorney, the party shall be permitted to prosecute or defend the action pro se. In either case, the appointed attorney shall be discharged from the representation.

Rule 6. Expenses.

(A) The appointed attorney or the firm with which he or she is affiliated shall bear the cost of any expenses of the litigation (e.g., discovery expenses, subpoena fees, transcript expenses), except as specified in Rule 6(b).

(B) If the appointed attorney or the firm with which he or she is affiliated is unable to conveniently bear the cost of expenses of the litigation, or believes that bearing them would contravene the Code of Professional Responsibility or other ethical standards, the attorney may apply for reimbursement of expenses of up to $200.00 to the Eastern District Civil Litigation Fund, Inc., a nonprofit corporation formed for the purpose, inter alia, of providing monies for this purpose. Where the attorney anticipates expenses in excess of $200.00 and will seek reimbursement for such expenses, he or she shall make an application to the Judge specifying the need for particular expenses in the prosecution or defense of the action and the reasons for the application. The Judge shall then determine whether the expenses are necessary in the interest of justice to the party's case. Where such expenses are found necessary, the attorney may then apply for reimbursement thereof in accordance with Rule 6(c).

(C) Upon appropriate application by the appointed attorney, the Clerk shall certify those expenses for which the appointed attorney may be reimbursed, in accordance with the procedures utilized in In Forma Pauperis proceedings under the Criminal Justice Act or other guidelines issued by the court. Thereafter, the assigned Judge may order reimbursement of the expenses of the litigation, as authorized by applicable statute, regulation, rule or other provision of law. In the absence of such an order and upon appropriate application by the appointed attorney, reimbursement of such expenses may be paid from funds of the Eastern District Civil Litigation Fund, Inc. to the extent available and authorized by that corporation.

Rule 7. Compensation for Services.

(A) If the action is one for which compensation for legal services may become available to the appointed attorney by statute, the Clerk shall so inform the pro se party at the time the application for appointed counsel is made and at the time the order of appointment is issued. The Clerk shall also inform the party at those times that any statutory fee award may be made only by the Judge at the conclusion of the case.

(B) Pro Se litigants in Social Security Disability cases shall be specifically advised by the Clerk that a statutory attorney's fee may be awarded to be paid from the award, if any, of retroactive disability benefits.

(C) Upon appropriate application by the appointed attorney, the Judge may award attorney's fees to the appointed attorney for services rendered in the action, as authorized by applicable statute, regulation, rule or other provision of law, and as the Judge deems just and proper. In deciding whether to award attorney's fees the Judge shall consider:

(i) the relevant statutes and provisions of law;

(ii) the source of the fee award;

(iii) the services rendered; and,

(iv) any other factors he or she deems appropriate.

(D) If, after appointment, the appointed attorney discovers that the party is able to pay for legal services, the attorney shall bring this information to the attention of the assigned Judge unless precluded from doing so by the attorney-client privilege. The Judge may thereupon (i) approve a fee arrangement between the party and the attorney, or (ii) relieve the attorney from the responsibilities of the order of appointment and permit the party to retain another attorney or to proceed pro se.

Rule 8. Duration of Representation.

(A) An appointed attorney shall represent the party in the action in the trial court from the date he or she enters an appearance until he or she has been relieved from appointment by the Court according to the provisions of Rules 4 or 5 or until a final judgment is entered in the action.

(B) If the party desires to take an appeal from a final judgment or appealable interlocutory order, or if such judgment or order is appealed by another party, or if the matter is remanded to an administrative forum, the appointed attorney is encouraged but not required to represent the party on the appeal, and in any proceeding, judicial or administrative, which may ensue upon an order of remand.

(C) Where the appointed attorney elects not to represent the party on an appeal or in a proceeding upon remand, the attorney shall advise the party of all required steps to be taken in perfecting the appeal or appearing in the proceeding on remand. Upon request of the pro se party the attorney shall file the Notice of Appeal. Such advice shall include available sources of appointed counsel, including, but not limited to the panel for appellate representation of indigent parties before the United States Court of Appeal for the Second Circuit.

Rule 9. Educational Panels.

(A) The Court shall authorize the establishment of panels of attorneys and others experienced in the preparation and trial of the most common types of civil actions involving pro se parties brought before the Court (e.g., Social Security Appeals, Employment Discrimination Actions, Civil Rights Actions, Habeas Corpus Actions).

(B) The Educational Panels are authorized to conduct educational programs for attorneys on the Civil Pro Bono Panel to train and assist said attorneys in the preparation and trial of the most common types of civil actions involving pro se parties brought before the Court.

(C) The Clerk is authorized to maintain a list of attorneys experienced in the preparation and trial of the most common types of civil actions involving pro se parties brought before the Court, whether or not such attorneys serve on an educational panel or the Pro Bono Panel. The Clerk shall obtain the prior consent of the attorneys to their inclusion on such lists. Such attorneys may be consulted by attorneys on the Civil Pro Bono Panel as necessary and appropriate.

Effective February 3, 1997.

PLAN FOR ACHIEVING PROMPT DISPOSITION OF CRIMINAL CASES

Pursuant to the requirements of Rule 50(b) of the Federal Rules of Criminal Procedure, the Speedy Trial Act of 1974 (18 U.S.C. Chapter 208), the Speedy Trial Act Amendments Act of 1979 (Pub.L. No. 96–43, 93 Stat. 327), and the Federal Juvenile Delinquency Act (18 U.S.C. §§ 5036, 5037), the judges of the United States District Court for the Eastern District of New York have adopted the following Plan to minimize undue delay and to further the prompt disposition of criminal cases and certain juvenile proceedings and have incorporated therein the time limits and procedures required by law.

1. Applicability.

(a) *Offenses.* The time limits set forth herein are applicable to all criminal offenses triable in this court, including cases triable by United States magistrates, except for petty offenses as defined in 18 U.S.C. § 1(3). Except as specifically provided, they are not applicable to proceedings under the Federal Juvenile Delinquency Act.

(b) *Persons.* The time limits are applicable to persons accused who have not been indicted or informed against as well as those who have, and the word "defendant" includes such persons unless the context indicates otherwise.

2. Priorities in Scheduling Criminal Cases.
Preference shall be given to criminal proceedings as far as practicable as required by Rule 50(a) of the Federal Rules of Criminal Procedure. The trial of defendants in custody solely because they are awaiting trial and of high risk defendants as defined in section 5 should be given preference over other criminal cases. The preference to be given to the prompt disposition of criminal cases shall not be unduly prejudicial to the prompt disposition of civil litigation.

3. Time Within Which an Indictment or Information Must Be Filed.

(a) *Time Limits.* If an individual is arrested or served with a summons and the complaint charges an offense to be prosecuted in this district, any indictment or information subsequently filed in connection with such charge shall be filed within 30 days of arrest or service.

(b) *Measurement of Time Periods.* If a person has not been arrested or served with a summons on a Federal charge, an arrest will be deemed to have been made at such time as the person (i) is held in custody

solely for the purpose of responding to a Federal charge; (ii) is delivered to the custody of a Federal official in connection with a Federal charge; or (iii) appears before a judicial officer in connection with a Federal charge.

(c) *Related Procedures.*

(1) At the time of the earliest appearance before a judicial officer of a person who has been arrested for an offense not charged in an indictment or information, the judicial officer shall establish for the record the date on which the arrest took place.

(2) In the absence of a showing to the contrary, a summons shall be considered to have been served on the date of service shown on the return thereof.

4. Time Within Which Trial Must Commence.

(a) *Time Limits.* The trial of a defendant shall commence not later than 70 days after the last to occur of the following dates:

(1) The date on which an indictment or information is filed in this district;

(2) The date on which a sealed indictment or information is unsealed; or

(3) The date of the defendant's first appearance before a judicial officer of this district.

(b) *Retrial; Trial After Reinstatement of an Indictment or Information.* The retrial of a defendant shall commence within 70 days from the date the order occasioning the retrial becomes final, as shall the trial of a defendant upon an indictment or information dismissed by a trial court and reinstated following an appeal. If the retrial or trial follows an appeal or collateral attack, the court may extend the period if unavailability of witnesses or other factors resulting from passage of time make trial within 70 days impractical. The extended period shall not exceed 180 days.

(c) *Withdrawal of Plea.* If a defendant enters a plea of guilty or nolo contendere to any or all charges in an indictment or information and is subsequently permitted to withdraw it, the time limit shall be determined for all counts as if the indictment or information were filed on the day the order permitting withdrawal of the plea became final.

(d) *Superseding Charges.* If, after an indictment or information has been filed, a complaint, indictment, or information is filed which charges the defendant with the same offense or with an offense required to be joined with that offense, the time limit applicable to the subsequent charge will be determined as follows:

(1) If the original indictment or information was dismissed on motion of the defendant before the filing of the subsequent charge, the time limit shall be determined without regard to the existence of the original charge.

(2) If the original indictment or information is pending at the time the subsequent charge is filed, the trial shall commence within the time limit for commencement of trial on the original indictment or information.

(3) If the original indictment or information was dismissed on motion of the United States Attorney before the filing of the subsequent charge, the trial shall commence within the time limit for commencement of trial on the original indictment or information, but the period during which the defendant was not under charges shall be excluded from the computations. Such period is the period between the dismissal of the original indictment or information and the date the time would have commenced to run on the subsequent charge had there been no previous charge.

If the subsequent charge is contained in a complaint, the formal time limit within which an indictment or information must be obtained on the charge shall be determined without regard to the existence of the original indictment or information, but earlier action may in fact be required if the time limit for commencement of trial is to be satisfied.

(e) *Measurement of Time Periods.* For the purposes of this section:

(1) If a defendant signs a written consent to be tried before a magistrate and no indictment or information charging the offense has been filed, the time limit shall run from the date of such consent.

(2) In the event of a transfer to this district under Rule 20 of the Federal Rules of Criminal Procedure, the indictment or information shall be deemed filed in this district when the papers in the proceeding or certified copies thereof are received by the clerk.

(3) A trial in a jury case shall be deemed to commence at the beginning of voir dire for the purposes of this Plan.

(4) A trial in a non-jury case shall be deemed to commence on the day the case is called, provided that some step in the trial procedure immediately follows.

(f) *Related Procedures.*

(1) At the time of the defendant's earliest appearance before a judicial officer of this district, the officer will take appropriate steps to assure that the defendant is represented by counsel and shall appoint counsel where appropriate under the Criminal Justice Act and Rule 44 of the Federal Rules of Criminal Procedure.

(2) The court shall have sole responsibility for setting cases for trial after consultation with counsel. At the time of the pre-trial conference or as soon thereafter as is practicable, each case will be set for trial on a day certain or listed for trial on a weekly or other short-term calendar consistent with section 7 of this plan.

(3) Individual calendars shall be managed so that it will be reasonably anticipated that every criminal case set for trial will be reached on the day or during the week or other short-term calendar period set for trial. A conflict in schedules of Assistant United States Attorneys or defense counsel will be grounds for a continuance or delayed setting only if approved by the court and called to the court's attention at the earliest practicable time. The United States Attorney will familiarize himself with the scheduling procedures of each judge and will assign or reassign cases in such a manner that the government will be ready for trial.

(4) In the event that a complaint, indictment, or information is filed against a defendant charged in a pending indictment or information or in an indictment or information dismissed on motion of the United States Attorney, the trial on the new charge shall commence within the time limit for commencement of trial on the original indictment or information unless the court finds that the new charge is not for the same offense charged in the original indictment or information or an offense required to be joined therewith.

(5) At the time of the filing of a complaint, indictment, or information described in paragraph (4), the United States Attorney shall give notice to the court in writing or in court on the record if the new charge is not for the same offense charged in the original indictment or information or an offense required to be joined therewith.

(6) Pre-trial conferences pursuant to Rule 17.1 of the Federal Rules of Criminal Procedure shall be conducted as soon after arraignment as possible consistent with the priorities of other matters on the court's criminal docket.

(7)(A) In the event the judge to whom a case is assigned for trial is actually engaged in another proceeding on the day set for such trial, he may grant a continuance pursuant to section 18 U.S.C. § 3161(h)(8) until after the conclusion of the other proceedings, upon the findings required by that section and upon a finding that it is likely the other proceeding will not be concluded in due course prior to the expiration of the time limit specified in section 5 for the commencement of such trial. In no event shall such continuance be for a period in excess of 30 days.

(B)(1) As used in paragraph 7(A) "other proceeding" shall mean a trial or an evidentiary hearing.

(2) As used in paragraph 7(A) "day set for such trial" shall mean either the day set for trial or the last day of the week or other short-term calendar period set for the commencement of the trial.

5. Defendants in Custody and High-Risk Defendants.

(a) *Time Limits.* Notwithstanding any longer time periods that may be permitted under sections 3 and 4, the following time limits will also be applicable to defendants in custody and high-risk defendants as herein defined:

(1) The trial of a defendant held in custody solely for the purpose of trial on a Federal charge shall commence within 90 days following the beginning of continuous custody.

(2) The trial of a high-risk defendant shall commence within 90 days of the designation as high-risk.

(b) *Definition of "High-Risk Defendant."* A high-risk defendant is one reasonably designated by the United States Attorney as posing a danger to himself or any other person or to the community.

(c) *Measurement of Time Periods.* For the purposes of this section:

(1) A defendant is deemed to be in detention awaiting trial when he is arrested on a Federal charge or otherwise held for the purpose of responding to a Federal charge. Detention is deemed to be solely because the defendant is awaiting trial unless the person exercising custodial authority has an independent basis (not including a detainer) for continuing to hold the defendant.

(2) If a case is transferred pursuant to Rule 20 of the Federal Rules of Criminal Procedure and the defendant subsequently rejects disposition under Rule 20 or the court declines to accept the plea, a new period of continuous detention awaiting trial will begin at that time.

(3) A trial shall be deemed to commence as provided in sections 4(e)(3) and 4(e)(4).

(d) *Related Procedures.*

(1) If a defendant is being held in custody solely for the purpose of awaiting trial, the United States Attorney shall advise the court at the earliest practicable time of the date of the beginning of such custody.

(2) The United States Attorney shall advise the court at the earliest practicable time (usually at the hearing with respect to bail) if the defendant is considered by him to be high-risk.

(3) If the court finds that the filing of a "high-risk" designation as a public record may result in prejudice to the defendant, it may order the designation sealed for such period as is necessary to protect the defendant's right to a fair trial, but not beyond the time that the court's judgment in the case becomes final. During the time the designation is under seal, it shall be made known to the defendant and his counsel but shall not be made known to other persons without the permission of the court.

6. Exclusion of Time From Computations.

(a) *Applicability.* In computing any time limit under section 3, 4, or 5, the following periods of delay shall be excluded. Such periods of delay shall not be excluded in computing the minimum period for commencement of trial under section 7.

(1) Any period of delay resulting from other proceedings concerning the defendant, including but not limited to—

(A) delay resulting from any proceeding, including any examinations, to determine the mental competency or physical capacity of the defendant;

(B) delay resulting from any proceeding, including any examination of the defendant, pursuant to Section 2902 of Title 28, United States Code;

(C) delay resulting from deferral of prosecution pursuant to Section 2902 of Title 28, United States Code;

(D) delay resulting from trial with respect to other charges against the defendant;

(E) delay resulting from any interlocutory appeal;

(F) delay resulting from any pretrial motion, from the filing of the motion through the conclusion of the hearing on, or other prompt disposition of, such motion;

(G) delay resulting from any proceeding relating to the transfer of a case or the removal of any defendant from another district under the Federal Rules of Criminal Procedure;

(H) delay resulting from transportation of any defendant from another district, or to and from places of examination or hospitalization, except that any time consumed in excess of ten days from the date an order of removal or an order directing such transportation, and the defendant's arrival at the destination shall be presumed to be unreasonable;

(I) delay resulting from consideration by the court of a proposed plea agreement to be entered into by the defendant and the attorney for the Government; and

(J) delay reasonably attributable to any period, not to exceed thirty days, during which any proceeding concerning the defendant is actually under advisement by the court.

(2) Any period of delay during which prosecution is deferred by the attorney for the Government pursuant to written agreement with the defendant, with the approval of the court, for the purpose of allowing the defendant to demonstrate his good conduct.

(3)(A) Any period of delay resulting from the absence or unavailability of the defendant or essential witness.

(B) For purposes of subparagraph (A) of this paragraph, a defendant or an essential witness shall be considered absent when his whereabouts are unknown and, in addition, he is attempting to avoid apprehension or prosecution or his whereabouts cannot be determined by due diligence. For purposes of such subparagraph, a defendant or an essential witness shall be considered unavailable whenever his whereabouts are known but his presence for trial cannot be obtained by due diligence or he resists appearing at or being returned for trial.

(4) Any period of delay resulting from the fact that the defendant is mentally incompetent or physically unable to stand trial.

(5) Any period of delay resulting from the treatment of the defendant pursuant to Section 2902 of Title 28, United States Code.

(6) If the information or indictment is dismissed upon motion of the attorney for the Government and thereafter a charge is filed against the defendant for the same offense, or any offense required to be joined with that offense, any period of delay from the date the charge was dismissed to the date the time limitation would commence to run as to the subsequent charge had there been no previous charge.

(7) A reasonable period of delay when the defendant is joined for trial with a codefendant as to whom the time for trial has not run and no motion for severance has been granted.

(8)(A) Any period of delay resulting from a continuance granted by any judge on his own motion or at the request of the defendant or his counsel or at the request of the attorney for the Government, if the judge granted such continuance on the basis of his findings that the ends of justice served by taking such action outweigh the best interests of the public and the defendant in a speedy trial. No such period of delay resulting from a continuance granted by the court in accordance with this paragraph shall be excludable under this subsection unless the court sets forth, in the record of the case, either orally or in writing, its reasons for finding that the ends of justice served by the granting of such continuance outweigh the best interest of the public and the defendant in a speedy trial.

(B) The factors among others, which a judge shall consider in determining whether to grant a continuance under subparagraph (A) of this paragraph in any case are as follows:

(i) Whether the failure to grant such a continuance in the proceeding would be likely to make a continuation of such proceeding impossible, or result in a miscarriage of justice.

(ii) Whether the case is so unusual or so complex, due to the number of defendants, the nature of the prosecution, or the existence of novel questions of fact or law, that it is unreasonable to expect adequate preparation for pre-trial proceedings or for the trial itself within the time limits established by sections 3, 4 and 5.

(iii) Whether, in a case in which arrest precedes indictment, delay in the filing of the indictment is caused because the arrest occurs at a time such that it is unreasonable to expect return and filing of the indictment within the period specified in section 3, or because the facts upon which the grand jury must base its determination are unusual or complex.

(iv) Whether the failure to grant such a continuance in a case which, taken as a whole, is not so unusual or so complex as to fall within clause (ii), would deny the defendant reasonable time to obtain counsel, would unreasonably deny the defendant or the Government continuity of counsel, or would deny counsel for the defendant or the attorney for the Government the reasonable time necessary for effective preparation, taking into account the exercise of due diligence.

(C) No continuance under paragraph (8)(A) of this subsection shall be granted because of general congestion of the court's calendar, or lack of diligent preparation or failure to obtain available witnesses on the part of the attorney for the Government.

(9)(A) Any period of delay resulting from a request by the defendant or his counsel for a continuance and a waiver by the defendant of the time limits contained in sections 3, 4 or 5, provided the court first grants such a continuance or approves such a waiver in accordance with the provisions of Section 3161(h)(8) of the Speedy Trial Act.

(B) Any such waiver shall be in writing; provided, however, that no such waiver shall be accepted without the court first determining, by addressing the defendant personally in open court (or in camera where appropriate), that the waiver is voluntary.

(b) *Records of Excludable Time.* The clerk of the court shall enter on the docket, in the form prescribed by the Administrative Office of the United States Courts, information with respect to excludable periods of time for each criminal defendant. With respect to proceedings prior to the filing of an indictment or information, excludable time shall be reported to the clerk by the United States Attorney.

(c) *Stipulations.*

(1) The attorney for the Government and the attorney for the defendant may at any time enter into stipulations with respect to the accuracy of the docket entries recording excludable time. Such stipulations must be promptly filed with the clerk.

(2) To the extent that the amount of time stipulated by the parties does not exceed the amount recorded on the docket for any excludable period of delay, the stipulation shall be conclusive as between the parties unless it has no basis in fact or law. It shall similarly be conclusive as to a codefendant for the limited purpose of determining, under 18 U.S.C. § 3161(h)(7), whether time has run against the defendant entering into the stipulation.

(3) To the extent that the amount of time stipulated exceeds the amount recorded on the docket, the stipulation shall have no effect unless approved by the court.

(d) *Pre-indictment Procedures.*

(1) In the event that the United States Attorney anticipates that an indictment or information will not be filed within the time limit set forth in section 3, he may file a written motion with the court for a determination of excludable time. In the event that the United States Attorney seeks a continuance under 18 U.S.C. § 3161(h)(8), he shall file a written motion with the court requesting such a continuance.

(2) The motion of the United States Attorney shall state (i) the period of time proposed for exclusion, and (ii) the basis of the proposed exclusion. If the motion is for a continuance under 18 U.S.C. § 3161(h)(8), it shall also state whether or not the defendant is being held in custody on the basis of the complaint. In appropriate circumstances, the motion may include a request that some or all of the supporting material be considered ex parte and in camera.

(3) The court may grant a continuance under 18 U.S.C. § 3161(h)(8) for either a specific period of time or a period to be determined by reference to

an event (such as recovery from illness) not within the control of the government. If the continuance is to a date not certain, the court shall require one or both parties to inform the court promptly when and if the circumstances that justify the continuance no longer exist. In addition, the court shall require one or both parties to file periodic reports bearing on the continued existence of such circumstances. The court shall determine the frequency of such reports in the light of the facts of the particular case.

(e) *Post-indictment Procedures.*

(1) Counsel shall be responsible for examining the clerk's records of excludable time for completeness and accuracy and shall bring to the court's immediate attention any claim that the clerk's record is in any way incorrect.

(2) In the event that the court continues a trial beyond the time limit set forth in section 4 or 5, the court shall determine whether the limit may be recomputed by excluding time pursuant to 18 U.S.C. § 3161(h).

(3) If it is determined that a continuance is justified, the court shall set forth its findings in the record, either orally or in writing. If the continuance is granted under 18 U.S.C. § 3161(h)(8), the court shall also set forth its reasons for finding that the ends of justice served by granting the continuance outweigh the best interests of the public and the defendant in a speedy trial. If the continuance is to a date not certain, the court shall require one or both parties to inform the court promptly when and if the circumstances that justify the continuance no longer exist. In addition, the court shall require one or both parties to file periodic reports bearing on the continued existence of such circumstances. The court shall determine the frequency of such reports in the light of the facts of the particular case.

7. **Minimum Period for Defense Preparation.** Unless the defendant consents in writing to the contrary, the trial shall not commence earlier than 30 days from the date on which the indictment or information is filed or, if later, from the date on which counsel first enters an appearance or on which the defendant expressly waives counsel and elects to proceed pro se. In circumstances in which the 70-day time limit for commencing trial on a charge in an indictment or information is determined by reference to an earlier indictment or information pursuant to section 4(d), the 30-day minimum period shall also be determined by reference to the earlier indictment or information. When prosecution is resumed on an original indictment or information following a mistrial, appeal, or withdrawal of a guilty plea, a new 30-day minimum period will not begin to run. The court will in all cases schedule trials so as to permit defense

counsel adequate preparation time in the light of all the circumstances.

8. Time Within Which Defendant Should Be Sentenced.

(a) *Time Limit.* A defendant shall ordinarily be sentenced within 45 court days of the date of his conviction or plea of guilty or nolo contendere. This specific period, however, may be varied in accordance with the presentence report practices and procedures in this district.

(b) *Related Procedures.* If the defendant and his counsel consent thereto, a presentence investigation may be commenced prior to a plea of guilty or nolo contendere or a conviction.

9. Juvenile Proceedings.

(a) *Time Within Which Trial Must Commence.* An alleged delinquent who is in detention pending trial shall be brought to trial within 30 days of the date on which such detention was begun, as provided in 18 U.S.C. § 5036.

(b) *Time of Dispositional Hearing.* If a juvenile is adjudicated delinquent, a separate dispositional hearing shall be held no later than 20 court days after trial, unless the court has ordered further study of the juvenile in accordance with 18 U.S.C. § 5037(c).

10. Sanctions.

(a) *Dismissal or Release From Custody.* Failure to comply with the requirements of Title I of the Speedy Trial Act may entitle the defendant to a dismissal of the charges against him or to release from pretrial custody. Nothing in this plan shall be construed to require that a case be dismissed or a defendant released from custody in circumstances in which such action would not be required by 18 U.S.C. §§ 3162 and 3164.

(b) *High-Risk Defendants.* A high-risk defendant whose trial has not commenced within the time limit set forth in 18 U.S.C. § 3164(b) shall, if the failure to commence trial was through no fault of the attorney for the government, have his release conditions automatically reviewed. A high-risk defendant who is found by the court to have intentionally delayed the trial of his case shall be subject to an order of the court modifying his nonfinancial conditions of release under Chapter 207 of Title 18, U.S.C., to ensure that he shall appear at trial as required.

(c) *Discipline of Attorneys.* In a case in which counsel (1) knowingly allows the case to be set for trial without disclosing the fact that a necessary witness would be unavailable for trial, (2) files a motion solely for the purpose of delay which he knows is frivolous and without merit, (3) makes a statement for the purpose of obtaining a continuance which he

knows to be false and which is material to the granting of the continuance, or (4) otherwise willfully fails to proceed to trial without justification consistent with 18 U.S.C. § 3161, the court may punish such counsel as provided in 18 U.S.C. §§ 3162(b) and (c).

(d) *Alleged Juvenile Delinquents.* An alleged delinquent in custody whose trial has not commenced within the time limit set forth in 18 U.S.C. § 5036 shall be entitled to dismissal of his case pursuant to that section unless the Attorney General shows that the delay was consented to or caused by the juvenile or his counsel, or would be in the interest of justice in the particular case.

11. Persons Serving Terms of Imprisonment.

If the United States Attorney knows that a person charged with a criminal offense is serving a term of imprisonment in a federal, state, or other institution or that of another jurisdiction, it is his duty promptly:

(i) to undertake to obtain the presence of the prisoner for plea and trial; or

(ii) when the Government is unable to obtain the presence of the defendant, to cause a detainer in compliance with the Interstate Agreement on Detainers to be filed with the official having custody of the prisoner and request him to advise the prisoner of the detainer.

12. Effective Dates.

(a) The amendments to the Speedy Trial Act made by Public Law 96–43 became effective August 2, 1979. To the extent that this revision of the district's Plan does more than merely reflect the amendments, the revised Plan shall take effect upon approval of the reviewing panel designated in accordance with 18 U.S.C. § 3165(c). However, the dismissal sanction and the sanctions against attorneys authorized by 18 U.S.C. § 3162 and reflected in sections 10(a) and (c) of this Plan shall apply only to defendants whose cases are commenced by arrest or summons on or after July 1, 1980, and to indictments and informations filed on or after that date.

(b) If a defendant was arrested or served with a summons before July 1, 1979, the time within which an information or indictment must be filed shall be determined under the Plan that was in effect at the time of such arrest or service.

(c) If a defendant was arraigned before August 2, 1979, the time within which the trial must commence shall be determined under the Plan that was in effect at the time of such arraignment.

(d) If a defendant was in custody on August 2, 1979, solely because he was awaiting trial, the 90-day period under section 5 shall be computed from that date.

CRIMINAL JUSTICE ACT PLAN

Introduction. The judges of the United States District Court for the Eastern District of New York, pursuant to the Criminal Justice Act of 1964 (18 U.S.C. § 3006A), as amended, ("the Act"), have adopted the following Plan for furnishing representation for persons financially unable to obtain adequate representation.

Representation under the Plan shall include the appointment of counsel and the furnishing of investigative, expert, and other services necessary for an adequate defense.

I. Provision for Furnishing Counsel.

A. *Legal Services.* This Plan provides for the furnishing of legal services by a Community Defender Organization as provided in 18 U.S.C. § 3006(h)(2)(B) and for the continued appointment and compensation of private counsel from a list maintained by the Clerk of Court in a substantial proportion of cases. The attorneys whose names appear on the list shall be selected by the Court in accordance with procedures in this Plan.

B. *Court's Discretion.* The Court, in its discretion, will determine whether any party entitled to representation will be represented by the Community Defender Organization or by a private attorney.

Insofar as practicable, private attorney appointments will be made in at least 25 percent of the case. A "case" shall be any proceeding actually docketed in the court or a "new trial" as defined in 18 U.S.C. § 3006A(d)(5).

C. *Community Defender Organization.* The Federal Defenders of New York, Inc., a non-profit defense counsel service, is authorized by this Plan to serve as a Community Defender Organization and is eligible to furnish attorneys and to receive payments under 18 U.S.C. § 3006A(g)(2)(B). The by-laws of the Federal Defenders of New York, Inc., are incorporated by reference in this Plan, with the same force and effect as though fully set forth therein, and a copy of said by-laws shall be maintained by the Clerk of Court and attached to the original of this Plan.

II. Composition of Panel of Private Attorneys.

A. *CJA Panel.*

1. Approval. The Court shall establish a panel of private attorneys ("the CJA Panel") who are eligible and willing to be appointed to provide representation under the Act. The Panel Selection Committee established under section II B below shall approve attorneys for membership on the panel. A copy of the panel list shall be maintained by the clerk and be furnished to each judge and magistrate judge. Members of the CJA Panel shall serve at the pleasure of the Court.

2. Size of Panel. The panel shall be large enough to provide sufficient experienced attorneys to handle the caseload under the Act, but small enough to provide panel members with adequate appointments to maintain a high proficiency in Federal criminal defense work. The size of the CJA Panel shall be set by the Court on an annual basis.

3. Eligibility. Attorneys who serve on the CJA Panel must be members in good standing of the bar of this Court and have demonstrated experience in and knowledge of the Federal Rules of Criminal Procedure and the Federal Rules of Evidence. Experience with and knowledge of, the United States Sentencing Guidelines is a qualification for membership on the district CJA Panel.

4. Terms. Attorneys appointed to the CJA Panel shall serve a term of three years. Membership in the CJA Panel is a privilege, not a right, which may be terminated at any time by the Board of Judges or by the Panel Selection Committee, as they, in their sole discretion, may determine.

5. Retention of Appointed Counsel. Counsel appointed pursuant to this Plan shall report to the judicial officer presiding any attempt to retain him or her as counsel for a fee. If such counsel is subsequently retained by or on behalf of the person he or she was assigned to represent, without permission of the assigned magistrate judge or the district judge, he or she shall immediately notify the magistrate judge or the district judge of that fact. The magistrate judge or district judge may thereupon recommend to the Board of Judges or the Panel Selection Committee that membership of that counsel in the CJA Panel be terminated and that his or her name be stricken from the Panel list.

6. Reappointment. A member of the CJA Panel who wishes to be considered for reappointment must apply for appointment for an additional three year term within four months of the expiration of his or her current term. Applications for reappointment will be reviewed on an annual basis along with all other applications for appointment to the panel.

7. Application. Application forms for membership on the CJA Panel shall be made available on request by the Clerk of the Court. Completed applications shall be submitted to the clerk, who will transmit them to the chair of the Panel

Selection committee. Applications and reappointment applications will be reviewed at regular intervals as scheduled by the Court or the Panel Selection Committee. All qualified attorneys shall be encouraged to participate in the furnishing of representation in CJA cases, without regard to race, color, religion, sex, age, national origin or disabling condition.

B. *Panel Selection Committee.*

1. Membership. A Panel Selection Committee, consisting of one district judge, one magistrate judge, the head of the Federal Defenders of New York, Inc., one criminal defense attorney, the Clerk of the Court, and other attorneys as appointed by the district judge in charge of the Selection Committee, is hereby established. A district judge shall chair the Committee.

2. Duties of Committee.

a. The Panel Selection Committee will meet annually, if necessary, to consider Panel applications. The Committee shall review the qualifications of the applicants and make appointment recommendations to the Court of those best qualified.

b. The Committee shall also continually review the operation and administration of the panel and recommend to the Court any changes deemed necessary regarding the appointment process or panel management.

c. Whenever the size of the panel is significantly reduced by vacancies, the Committee may solicit applications to fill the vacancies, convene a special meeting to review the applicants, and recommend new members to the Court.

d. The Committee shall furnish information to the Court regarding recruitment efforts undertaken by the Committee in furtherance of the Equal Opportunity statement herein at Section II.A.7.

III. Selection for Appointment.

A. *Maintenance of List and Distribution of Appointments.* The Clerk of the Court shall maintain a current list of all attorneys on the CJA Panel, with current office addresses and telephone numbers, as well as a statement of qualifications and experience. The Clerk shall furnish a copy of this list to each judge and magistrate judge. The Clerk shall also maintain a public record of assignments to private counsel and statistical data reflecting the proration of appointments between attorneys from the Community Defender Organization and private attorneys, according to section I.B.

B. *Method of Selection.* Appointments from the list of private attorneys should be made on a rotating basis, subject to the Court's discretion to make

exceptions due to the nature and complexity of the case, the attorney's experience, and geographical considerations. This procedure should result in a balanced distribution of appointments and compensation among the members of the CJA Panel, and quality representation for each CJA defendant.

When a judicial officer decides to appoint an attorney from the panel, the Clerk's Office shall notify a panel member who is on duty on that date who is available for appointment, and shall provide the name to the appointing district judge or magistrate judge. If there is no panel member on duty a panel member who is available for assignment maybe appointed.

During weekends, holidays, or other non-working hours, or at any other time necessary, the presiding district judge or magistrate judge may appoint any attorney from the list. When members of the CJA Panel are appointed directly by the Court the appointing district judge or magistrate judge shall notify the Clerk of Court of the name of the attorney appointed and the date of the appointment.

C. *Panel Attorneys.* A panel attorney who is unable to serve on his or her assigned duty day shall arrange for a replacement attorney from the existing CJA Panel member list to cover the assigned date. That replacement attorney shall continue to serve as counsel to the defendants assigned to him or her on that date, unless otherwise ordered by the Court. Absent an order from the Court, attorneys who are not currently Panel members may not appear as replacement counsel, even if they are members of, or associated with, the same firm, or share office space with a panel attorney. The Magistrate Clericals shall be informed whenever a panel member agrees to switch duty dates with another panel member.

IV. Determination of Need for Counsel.

A. *Appearing before a Magistrate Judge or a District Judge in a Criminal Case.* If any person is charged with a felony or misdemeanor (other than a petty offense for which he or she does not face imprisonment); or with juvenile delinquency (see 18 U.S.C. § 5034); or with a violation of probation; or who is entitled to appointment of counsel in parole proceedings, pursuant to Chapter 311 of Title 18 U.S.C.; or for whom the Sixth Amendment to the Constitution requires the appointment of counsel; or for whom in a case in which he faces loss of liberty, any federal law requires the appointment of counsel, and such defendant appears without counsel, the magistrate judge or district judge shall advise the defendant of his or her right to counsel.

Whenever such a person states that he or she is financially unable to obtain counsel, and applies for the appointment of counsel, it shall be the duty of the judge or magistrate judge to inquire whether such person is financially able to obtain counsel.

All statements made by such person in such inquiry shall be either (a) by affidavit sworn to before a district judge, magistrate judge, Court Clerk, or deputy clerk, or notary public, or (b) under oath in open court before a judge or magistrate judge.

If on the basis of such inquiry, the district judge or magistrate judge finds that such person is financially unable to obtain counsel, he shall appoint counsel for such person. The district judge or the magistrate judge shall appoint separate counsel for defendants having interests that cannot properly be represented by the same counsel, or when a conflict of interest exists in having one attorney represent more than one defendant, or when other good cause is shown.

B. *Representation Required by Law.* When a person arrested has been represented by counsel under circumstances where representation is required by law prior to appearing before a judicial officer, such counsel, if appointed by a judge or magistrate judge, may subsequently apply to the Court for approval or compensation. If the Court finds the person has been and is financially unable to obtain an adequate defense, and that representation was required by law, compensation will be made retroactive to cover out-of-court time expended by the attorney during the arrest period. In addition, the services rendered from the time of the initial presentation before a district judge or magistrate judge will be compensated.

The Court may make retroactive appointment of counsel where an attorney will continue to represent the party in criminal proceedings in this Court. If the person represented is unavailable at the time counsel applies to the Court for approval of compensation, the attorney may nevertheless submit his or her claim to the Court for approval based upon the client's financial condition and upon showing that such representation was required by law.

C. *Discretionary Appointments.* Any person in custody as a material witness, or seeking relief under 28 U.S.C. §§ 2241, 2254, or 2255 of Title 28 or 18 U.S.C. § 4245 may apply to the Court or a magistrate judge for representation based on a showing (1) that the interests of justice so require and (2) that such person is financially unable to obtain representation. The application must be verified and in the form prescribed by the Judicial Conference of the United States. If the party is not before the Court, the judicial officer may, without requiring personal appearance of the party, act on the basis of the form alone supplemented by any information made available by an officer, custodian or other responsible person. This information must

be made available to the party. The Court may approve the representation if in the interest of justice or if the person is financially unable to obtain representation.

V. Appointment of Counsel.

A. *Judicial Officer Appointments.* In every criminal case in which a party may be entitled to representation under the Act and that party appears without counsel before a magistrate judge or district judge, it is the duty of the magistrate judge or district judge not only to advise the party of his or her right to counsel throughout the case, but also promptly to appoint counsel to represent the party if the magistrate judge or district judge finds that the party is financially unable to obtain an attorney, unless the party waives his or her right to be represented by counsel.

If a judicial officer, the United States Attorney, or other law enforcement officer, a Parole Board representative, an appointed attorney, or a representative of a Bar association challenges the claimed financial inability of a party to employ a lawyer, the determination of the defendant's right to have appointed counsel shall be made by a judge of this Court or by a the magistrate judge assigned to the case.

The judicial officer shall, in appointing counsel use the Federal Defenders of New York, Inc. or select a private attorney from the panel as approved by the Court, except in extraordinary circumstances where it becomes necessary to make another selection of a member of the Bar of this Court. The party shall not have the right to select appointed counsel from the Federal Defenders of New York, Inc. or from the panel of attorneys, or otherwise.

Counsel appointed by a judicial officer shall, unless excused by order of court, continue to act for the party throughout the proceedings in this Court. An appointed attorney shall not delegate any substantive tasks in connection with representation of a defendant to any person other than a partner, associate, or regular employee of the law firm of which the appointed attorney is a partner or associate, without the written consent of the defendant and the Court.

If a criminal defendant enters a plea of guilty or is convicted following trial, appointed counsel shall advise the defendant of the right of appeal and of the right to counsel on appeal. If requested by the defendant, or upon the Court's own application, counsel must file a timely Notice of Appeal. When an appeal is taken, appointed trial court counsel shall continue to represent the appellant unless or until he or she has been appointed as appellate counsel or has been notified that his or her services are not longer required.

If at any stage of the proceedings, counsel appointed by a judicial officer in any proceedings wishes to be relieved, he or she shall inform the magistrate judge or district judge before whom the case is pending.

The judicial officer may, in the interests of justice, substitute one appointed counsel for another.

B. *Special Circumstances.* If the judicial officer shall find that a defendant could be more adequately represented by counsel other than a member of the Federal Defenders of New York, Inc. or the panel of attorneys, he or she may request the Chief Judge to add such counsel to the panel, stating briefly the reason therefor, and upon the granting of the request the district judge or magistrate judge may appoint such counsel for such limited purpose.

If after appointment counsel learns that a client is financially able to pay all or part of the fee for legal representation and the source of the attorney's information is not a privileged communication, counsel shall so advise the Court. The Court will take appropriate action, including but not limited to: permitting assigned counsel to continue to represent the defendant with all or part of the cost defrayed by the defendant; terminating the appointment of counsel; or ordering any funds available to the party to be paid as provided in 18 U.S.C. § 3006A(f) as the interests of justice may dictate. Any amount paid by the party will be considered by the court in determining the total compensation allowed to the attorney.

C. *The Clerk.* The Clerk of the Court shall provide defendants the appropriate forms and affidavits pertaining to financial liability. If no affidavit of financial inability to employ counsel has been filed with the clerk, he shall promptly send the party a form affidavit to complete and return.

As soon as the clerk receives an affidavit of financial inability to employ counsel, whether with the notice or subsequently, he shall promptly arrange for the appointment of counsel. If the clerk becomes aware that a party wishes to apply for discretionary appointment of counsel, he shall promptly send such party the appropriate CJA forms to be executed and filed.

The clerk shall screen each claim for compensation and reimbursement of expenses for accuracy and compliance with all relevant guidelines.

D. *Redetermination of Need.* If at any stage of the proceedings, a judicial officer finds that a party for whom counsel has not previously been appointed but who had retained his or her own attorney is financially unable to provide for continued representation, the magistrate judge or district judge may appoint counsel for the party. The Court will not ordinarily appoint the same attorney.

No appointed counsel may request or accept any payment or promise of payment for assisting in the representation of a defendant, unless such payment is approved by an order of the Court.

VI. Investigative, Expert and Other Services.

A. *Upon Request.* Counsel for a party who is financially unable to obtain investigative, expert or other services necessary for an adequate defense may request such services ex parte before a judicial officer having jurisdiction over the case. Such application shall be heard in camera and shall not be revealed without the consent of the defendant. On finding that the services are necessary and that the person is financially unable to afford them, the judicial officer shall authorize counsel to obtain them. An order setting forth the type, purpose, and limitations of such services will be issued by the Court. The district judge or magistrate judge may establish a limit on the amount that may be expended or committed for such services within the maximum prescribed by 18 U.S.C. § 3006A(e)(3).

B. *Without Prior Request.* Counsel appointed pursuant to this Plan may obtain, subject to later review, investigative, expert, or other services without prior judicial authorization if they are necessary for an adequate defense. The total cost of services so obtained may not exceed $500 per individual or corporation providing the services (exclusive of reasonable expenses). However, in the interests of justice and upon finding that timely procurement of necessary services could not await prior authorization a district judge or magistrate judge (in a case disposed entirely by the magistrate judge) may approve payment for such services after they have been obtained, even if the cost of the services exceeds $500.

C. *Necessity of Affidavit.* Statements made by or on behalf of the party in support of requests under ¶¶ A and B supra shall be made or supported by affidavit.

VII. Compensation.

A. *Payments to Counsel Appointed Under Plan.* Payment of fees and expenses to counsel under this plan and payment for investigative, expert, and other services authorized pursuant to Section V shall be made in accordance with the United States Judicial Conference Guidelines for the Administration of the Criminal Justice Act and with the fiscal policies of the Administrative Office of the United States Courts.

B. *Schedule of Maximum Fees for Counsel and Other Services.* The following fees are hereby prescribed for the Eastern District:

1. Maximum Hourly Rate for Counsel. The maximum hourly rate of attorneys shall not exceed the amount provided by statute and Judicial

Conference policy. In addition, such attorney or the organization furnishing the attorney shall be reimbursed for expenses reasonably incurred, including the cost of any necessary transcripts authorized by the district judge or magistrate judge.

2. Maximum Amounts for Counsel.

a. For representation of a defendant before a judicial officer of this Court, provided on or after December 8, 2004, the compensation paid any attorney shall not exceed $7,000 for each attorney in a felony case or $2,000 for each attorney in a misdemeanor case. Representation of a defendant in a new trial shall be considered a separate case for fee purposes.

b. A maximum of $1,500 per attorney is provided for any other representation required or authorized by this Plan.

For representation of a defendant before a magistrate judge or a district judge, or both, in which all services were performed before December 8, 2004, the maximum compensation for the entire representation to be paid appointed counsel shall not exceed $5,200 for each attorney in a case in which a felony is charged, $1,500 for each attorney in a case in which only misdemeanors are charged, and $1,200 for each attorney for any other proceeding authorized under this Plan. Representation of a defendant in a new trial shall be considered a separate case and fees shall be paid on the same basis as the original trial, unless that representation was provided on or after December 8, 2004, in which case the maximums provided in the preceding paragraphs shall apply.

Any request for compensation in excess of $1,500 shall be accompanied by an affidavit of counsel detailing in both narrative and statistical form the services provided. Reasonable out-of-pocket expenses may be claimed if itemized and suitably documented. Expenses for investigative, expert and other services under section VI shall not be considered out-of-pocket expenses.

When warranted counsel claiming less than $1,200 may be required by the presiding judicial officer to submit a memorandum justifying the compensation claimed.

3. Waiver of Limits on Counsel Fees. Payment in excess of any maximum provided above for counsel fees or for other services may be made for extended or complex representation whenever the district judge or magistrate judge (if the representation was entirely before the magistrate judge) certifies that the amount sought is necessary to provide fair compensation and the payment is approved by the Chief Judge of the Second Circuit or such active Circuit Judge to whom the Chief Judge has delegated approval authority. Counsel claiming such excess payment shall submit a detailed memorandum justifying counsel's claim that the representation was in an extended or complex case and that the excess payment is necessary to provide fair compensation.

VIII. Forms. Where standard forms have been approved by the Judicial Conference of the United States or an appropriate committee, such forms shall be used by the Court, the Clerk of Court and counsel.

IX. Rules and Reports. The Chief Judge on behalf of the Court may promulgate such rules as the Board of Judges of this Court adopts in furtherance of this Plan. The Chief Judge shall similarly make such reports on the implementation of the Act to the Judicial Conference of the United States or a committee thereof as are required or requested.

X. Amendments. Amendments to this Plan may be made from time to time by the Board of Judges of this Court, subject to the approval of the Judicial Council of the Second Circuit.

XI. Effective Date. This Plan as amended this 8th day of July, 2005, shall take effect when the amendment is approved by the Judicial Council of the Second Circuit.

The CJA Plan as amended was approved by the Judicial Council of the Second Circuit on July 27, 2005.

ELECTRONIC FILING PROCEDURES

ADMINISTRATIVE ORDER 97-12. IN RE ELECTRONIC FILING PROCEDURES

WHEREAS the Eastern District of New York was selected by the Administrative Office of the United States Courts as one of the four federal district courts to engage in a prototype program of electronic filing, and

WHEREAS the Court appointed a Rules Committee including members of the bench and bar in May, 1997 to draft a comprehensive proposed Order, and

WHEREAS a proposed Administrative Order was prepared and circulated for public comment on August 1, 1997, and

WHEREAS revisions to the proposed Administrative Order were recommended to the Court following the close of the comment period on September 2, 1997,

NOW THEREFORE, following review the Board of Judges of the Eastern District of New York at a meeting held on October 21, 1997 adopted the at-tached Electronic Filing Procedures subject to revi-sion from time to time as necessary.

SO ORDERED.

Dated: Brooklyn, New York
       October 22, 1997

WHEREAS, Rules 5 and 83 of the Federal Rules of Civil Procedure and 28 U.S.C. §§ 132, 136, 451, 452 and 1651 authorize this Court to enter all appropriate orders respecting practices and procedures for the filing, signing, verifying and providing public access to Court documents, including establishing such prac-tices and procedures making use of the Internet; and

WHEREAS, this Administrative Order is intended to be applied and interpreted in connection with a proposed Electronic filing Procedures Users' Manual (the "Users' Manual") which, together with this Ad-ministrative Order, shall be termed the "Electronic Filing Procedures" or "EFP"; and

WHEREAS, the Court has solicited and considered the views of the bar and the public in formulating the EFP for civil actions, inter alia by establishing a Rules Committee and a Users Committee to assist in the formulation of the EFP; by publishing in August, 1997 a draft version of this Administrative Order for public comment; and by reviewing and considering the comments submitted to the Court in response to such publication; and

WHEREAS, consistent with the EFP, the Court has established a World Wide Web site ("E.D.N.Y. Public Web Site") connected to the Internet with the technological capacity to provide public access to all contents of that Web Site, including all electronically-filed papers, and to permit direct electronic filing of Court papers on that Web Site via the Internet; and

WHEREAS, the EFP make adequate provision for filing, service and notice of all papers and proceedings in civil actions, consistent with the requirements of the Federal Rules of Civil Procedure; and

WHEREAS, the EFP provide a means for counsel of record and unrepresented parties to sign papers electronically through use of a unique password and other identifying information; and

WHEREAS, the EFP require the Clerk's Office to provide adequate procedures for electronic filing of papers by persons who are not able to access the E.D.N.Y. Public Web Site via the Internet from a remote location; and

WHEREAS, the EFP require the Clerk's Office to provide adequate public access to the records and dockets of this Court, including access for persons who are not able to access the E.D.N.Y. Public Web Site via the Internet from a remote location; and

WHEREAS, the EFP do not impose fees inconsis-tent with the present fee structure adopted by the Judicial Conference of the United States Courts pur-suant to 28 U.S.C. § 1914;

NOW, THEREFORE, IT IS ORDERED as fol-lows:

1. Summons and Complaint. Nothing in the EFP shall affect the manner of filing and service of com-plaints (including third-party complaints) and the issu-ance and service of summonses, which in all civil actions shall continue to be filed, issued and served in paper form and in conformance with the Federal Rules of Civil Procedure and the Local Rules of this Court.

2. Actions Subject to EFP.

(a) The Clerk shall maintain and post on the E.D.N.Y. Public Web Site a list of the Judges of this Court who permit use of EFP in actions assigned to them ("Participating Judicial Officers"). A magistrate judge assigned to an action in which the assigned judge is a Participating Judicial Officer shall be deemed a Participating Judicial Officer for the pur-poses of that action. Upon the filing of the complaint in any action in which the Judge initially assigned is a Participating Judicial Officer, the Clerk shall provide the plaintiff(s) with a copy of a Notice Regarding Availability of Electronic Filing in a form approved by the Chief Judge. Such Notice shall be served upon the defendant(s) in the action together with the summons and complaint. At the initial scheduling conference in the action, if the assigned judicial officer consents to use of EFP, and if all parties appearing also consent to use of EFP, then the parties shall sign at the initial conference a Joint Consent to EFP satisfying the requirements of paragraph 3; otherwise the assigned judicial officer shall note on the initial Scheduling Order that the action shall not be subject to EFP. If an initial scheduling conference is not to be held in the action, within 120 days after the first appearance of any defendant, either (i) all parties appearing shall jointly apply for an order designating the action as subject to EFP by submitting a Joint Consent to EFP, which the assigned judicial officer in his or her absolute discretion may grant or deny, or (ii) one or more parties shall file a Notice Declining EFP, in which case the action shall not be subject to EFP.

(b) In addition to the means set forth in subpara-graph (a) for designating an action as subject to EFP, in any civil action in which the assigned Judge is or becomes a Participating Judicial Officer, the parties may apply at any time for an order designating the action as subject to EFP by submitting a Joint Consent to EFP, which the assigned Judge in his or her absolute discretion may grant or deny.

(c) Within ten days after an action becomes subject to EFP, each party shall refile electronically pursuant to subparagraphs (a) or (b) every paper in the action that the party previously filed.

(d) In any action subject to EFP, upon application of any party or sua sponte, the assigned Judge may terminate or modify application of EFP to the action.

3. Consents to EFP and E–Mail Addresses of Record.

(a) Any Consent to EFP shall clearly state that the submitting parties consent to the use of EFP in the action and shall set forth the Internet e-mail address of each attorney of record and each unrepresented party for the purposes of service and giving notice of each filing (the "E–Mail Addresses of Record"). Any Consent to EFP shall further state that the consenting persons have exchanged test e-mail messages successfully with each other and with all persons previously or concurrently consenting to EFP at the E-mail Addresses of Record.

(b) Each attorney of record and each unrepresented party shall provide one Internet e-mail address as the E–Mail Address of Record for that person. Parties may have multiple attorneys of record for the purpose of receiving additional e-mail notifications, and the E-mail Address of Record for an attorney of record or for an unrepresented party need not be that person's personal e-mail address.

(c) The E.D.N.Y. Public Web Site shall include for each action subject to EFP a current list of the E–Mail Addresses of Record maintained by the Clerk. Each attorney of record and each unrepresented party shall promptly serve notice upon all parties of any change in such person's E–Mail Addresses of Record for the purposes of the action, and shall promptly notify the Clerk of such change, including identifying to the Clerk each action subject to EFP in which such e-mail address must be updated and confirming that such person has received test e-mail messages successfully from all persons who have consented to EFP in each such action.

4. Electronic Filing of Papers.

(a) In any case designated as subject to EFP, all papers required to be filed with the Clerk shall be filed electronically on the E.D.N.Y. Public Web Site pursuant to EFP, except as expressly provided herein. Electronic filing may only be conducted by a Filing User, as that term is defined in paragraph 12.

(b) Every paper filed electronically shall be signed for the purposes of Rule 11 of the Federal Rules of Civil Procedure and Rule 11.1 of the Local Civil Rules of this Court by one or more counsel of record or unrepresented parties (each, a "Rule 11 Signatory")

pursuant to paragraph 5. For each Rule 11 Signatory, the paper shall provide such Signatory's name, address, telephone number, and E-mail Address of Record; shall provide the information required pursuant to Rule 11.1 of the Local Civil Rules of this Court; and shall identify the Rule 11 Signatory as such.

(c) Electronic transmission of a paper to the E.D.N.Y. Public Web Site consistent with EFP, together with the receipt of a Notice of Electronic Filing from the Court in the form shown in the Users' Manual, shall constitute filing of the paper for all purposes of the Federal Rules of Civil Procedure and the Local Rules of this Court, and shall constitute entry of that paper on the docket kept by the Clerk pursuant to Rules 58 and 79 of the Federal Rules of Civil Procedure. Only upon receipt of such Notice of Electronic Filing from the Court will the paper be deemed filed and entered.

(d) When a paper has been filed electronically, the official paper of record is the electronic recording of the paper as stored by the Court, and the filing party shall be bound by the paper as filed.

(e) Except in the case of papers first filed in paper form and subsequently submitted electronically, a paper filed electronically shall be deemed filed at the date and time stated on the Notice of Electronic Filing from the Court.

(f) Any Filing User filing a paper electronically shall make and keep copies of the paper in both paper and electronic form for subsequent production to the Court if so ordered or for inspection upon request by a party until one year after final resolution of the action (including appeal, if any) in the case of the copy in paper form, and until ten years after final resolution of the action (including appeal, if any) in the case of the copy in electronic form. In the case of electronic copies, this paragraph shall not be construed to require the Filing User to duplicate the copy periodically or otherwise to prevent loss of the copy through normal degradation of the storage medium under reasonably prudent storage conditions, or to retain software or hardware sufficient to permit the viewing or interpretation of the electronic copy.

(g) Papers or sets of papers that are too bulky to permit electronic filing conveniently via the Filing User's Internet connection may be filed by bringing EFP-compliant copies on electronic media approved by the Clerk and filed electronically by the Filing User using a high-bandwidth Internet connection and equipment to be provided by the Clerk in the Clerk's Office pursuant to subparagraph 16(a).

(h) A Filing User filing any paper electronically that requires a judicial officer's signature shall also promptly deliver such document in paper form to the judicial officer by U.S. mail or other means.

(i) Nothing in the EFP shall be interpreted to permit material prohibited by order from filing except under seal to be filed by any means except under physical seal.

(j) Individual rules of a Participating Judicial Officer requiring delivery of courtesy copies of any paper filed shall remain in force until rescinded by the Participating Judicial Officer, but the provisions of any such rule requiring equivalent service of the paper upon all parties shall be satisfied by compliance with the electronic filing and service provisions of the EFP.

5. Signatures. A paper filed with the Court electronically shall be deemed to be signed by a person (the "Signatory") when the paper identifies the person as a Signatory and the filing complies with either subparagraph (a), (b) or (c). When the paper is filed with the Court in accordance any with these methods, the filing shall bind the Signatory as if the paper (or the paper to which the filing refers, in the case of a Notice of Endorsement filed pursuant to subparagraph (c)) were physically signed and filed, and shall function as the Signatory's signature, whether for purposes of Rule 11 of the Federal Rules of Civil Procedure, to attest to the truthfulness of an affidavit or declaration, or for any other purpose.

(a) In the case of a Signatory who is a Filing User (as that term is defined in paragraph 12), such paper shall be deemed signed, regardless of the existence of a physical signature on the paper, provided that such paper is filed using the User ID and Password of the Signatory. The page on which the physical signature would appear if filed in paper form must be filed electronically, but need not be filed in an optically scanned format displaying the signature of the Signatory.

(b) In the case of a Signatory who is not a Filing User, or who is a Filing User but whose User ID and Password will not be utilized in the electronic filing of the paper, such paper shall be deemed signed and filed when the paper is physically signed by the Signatory, the paper is filed electronically, and the signature page is filed in optically scanned form pursuant to and consistent with the EFP. The Filing User who files such paper shall retain the executed original of the paper as the copy in paper form required pursuant to paragraph 4(f).

(c) In the case of a paper that has already been filed electronically with the Court, the paper shall be deemed signed and filed by the Signatory when a Notice of Endorsement of the paper is signed and filed by the Signatory pursuant to either subparagraph (a) or (b). Such Notice must provide the title, electronic docket number, and date and time filed of the paper being so signed.

(d) In the case of a stipulation or other paper to be signed by two or more persons, the paper may be filed and signatures may be provided in a single electronic filing in which all signatures are authorized either (i) pursuant to subparagraph (b) alone, or (ii) pursuant to subparagraph (a) in the case of one Signatory who is a Filing User and pursuant to subparagraph (b) in the case of all other Signatories.

(e) In the case of a stipulation or other paper to be filed and signed by two or more persons, the paper may be filed and signatures may be provided in two or more electronic filings as follows: One Filing User shall initially confirm that the content of the paper is acceptable to all persons due to sign the paper and shall obtain the physical signatures on the paper of the Signatories who do not intend independently to transmit their signatures electronically to the Court. Such Filing User shall then file the paper and submit all such signatures electronically in a single electronic filing in which the signatures are authorized by subparagraphs (a) or (b) or both. The paper shall also list all persons whose signatures are due to be transmitted independently to the Court. Not later than the first business day after such filing, all other persons due to sign the paper shall file one or more Notices of Endorsement of the paper pursuant to subparagraph (c). The paper shall be deemed fully executed upon the filing of all Notices of Endorsement that are due.

6. Service on Parties or Other Persons Who Have Consented to EFP.

(a) An attorney or unrepresented party filing a paper pursuant to EFP shall, within one hour following filing, send by e-mail a Notice of Filing of the paper to all E–Mail Addresses of Record. Such Notice shall provide, at a minimum, the electronic docket number and the title of the paper filed, and shall provide the date and time filed, as set forth in the Notice of Electronic Filing received from the Court. Such e-mail transmission(s) shall constitute service on the attorney or unrepresented party or other persons who have consented to EFP. Proof of such service shall be filed with the Court pursuant to the EFP, but such proof of service need not itself be served.

(b) Whenever a person has the right or is required to do some act or take some proceedings within a prescribed period after the service of a notice or other paper upon the person, and such paper is filed and served electronically pursuant to EFP, one day shall be added to the prescribed period. Service pursuant to subparagraph (a) shall not constitute service by mail to which Rule 6(e) of the Federal Rule of Civil Procedure applies. Service shall be deemed complete on the date of e-mail transmission pursuant to subparagraph (a).

(c) The filing of a Consent to EFP constitutes consent to service of all papers as provided herein as a full, adequate and timely substitute for service pursuant to Federal Rules of Civil Procedure.

7. Service on Persons Who Have Not Consented to EFP.

(a) Upon the filing of a third-party complaint pursuant to paragraph 1 in an action which is subject to EFP, the third-party plaintiff(s) shall serve notice that the action is subject to EFP upon the third-party defendant together with the third-party complaint. Concurrent with the filing of the third-party answer or other papers responsive to the third-party complaint, the third-party defendant shall either (i) file a Consent to EFP for purposes of the action, or (ii) move for exemption from EFP pursuant to subparagraph 2(d).

(b) In an action subject to EFP, when service of a paper other than a third-party complaint is required to be made upon a person who has not filed a Consent to EFP, a paper copy of the document shall be served on the person as otherwise required by the Federal Rules of Civil Procedure or the Local Rules of this Court. If the person so served is permitted or required to respond to the paper, such time to respond shall be computed without regard to the EFP. Such person may file a Consent to EFP conforming to the requirements of paragraph 3 and thereby become subject to the EFP for the purposes of the action.

8. Docket. The E.D.N.Y. Public Web Site shall denote in a separate electronic document for each action subject to EFP the filing of any paper by or on behalf of a party and the entry of any order or judgment by the Court, regardless of whether such paper was filed electronically. The record of those filings and entries for each case shall be consistent with Rule 79(a) of the Federal Rules of Civil Procedure and shall constitute the docket for purposes of that Rule. The Clerk shall make such technical accommodations as may be necessary to permit the Court's existing PACER system to access electronic dockets for actions subject to EFP.

9. Notice and Entry of Orders and Judgments. The Clerk shall file electronically all orders, decrees, judgments, and proceedings of the Court in accordance with the EFP, which shall constitute entry of the order, decree, judgment or proceeding on the docket kept by the Clerk pursuant to Rules 58 and 79 of the Federal Rules of Civil Procedure. Immediately upon the entry of an order or judgment in an action subject to EFP, the Clerk shall transmit by e-mail to the E-Mail Addresses of Record a notice of the entry of the order or judgment and shall make a note in the docket of the transmission. Transmission of the notice of entry shall constitute notice as required by Rule 77(d) of the Federal Rules of Civil Procedure. When notice of the order or judgment is due to be provided to a person who has not consented to EFP, the Clerk shall give such notice in paper form pursuant to the Federal Rules of Civil Procedure.

10. Technical Failures.

(a) The Clerk shall deem the E.D.N.Y. Public Web Site to be subject to a technical failure on a given day if the Site is unable to accept filings continuously or intermittently over the course of any period of time greater than one hour after 12:00 noon that day, in which case filings due that day which were not filed due solely to such technical failures shall become due the next business day. Such delayed filings shall be rejected unless accompanied by a declaration or affidavit attesting to the filing person's failed attempts to file electronically at least two times after 12:00 p.m. separated by at least one hour on each day of delay due to such technical failure. The Clerk shall provide notice of all such technical failures on the E.D.N.Y. Public Web Site, and by means of an E.D.N.Y. Public Web Site status line which persons may telephone in order to learn the current status of the Site.

(b) If a Notice of Electronic Filing is not received from the Court following transmission of a paper for filing, the paper will not be deemed filed. The filing person must attempt to re-file the document electronically until such a Notice is received, consistent with the provisions of subparagraph (a) permitting delayed filings.

(c) If, within 24 hours after filing a paper electronically, the filing party discovers that the version of the paper available for viewing on the E.D.N.Y. Public Web site does not conform to the paper as transmitted upon filing, the filing party may file of right a Retransmitted copy of the paper. This provision (and the designation "Retransmitted") shall not be used for the filing of corrections of typographical errors or other changes or variations from the paper as transmitted upon filing.

11. Voluntary Electronic Filing of Papers Not Otherwise Permitted to Be Filed. Notwithstanding the provisions of Local Civil Rule 5.1(a), in any action subject to EFP, the assigned Judge may enter an order authorizing the filing of discovery requests, discovery responses, discovery materials or other matter subject to Local Civil Rule 5.1(a), but only to the degree and upon terms and conditions to which all of the parties (or non-parties producing such materials) have previously agreed in a stipulation submitted to the Court. In the absence of such an order, no party shall file any such materials except in the form of excerpts, quotations, or selected exhibits from such materials as part of motion papers, pleading or other filings with the Court which must refer to such excerpts, quotations, etc.

12. Passwords and Other Attorney Information.

(a) Any attorney admitted to the Bar of this Court may register as a Filing User of the E.D.N.Y. Public Web Site. Registration shall be by paper on a form prescribed by the Clerk which shall require identification of the action as well as the name, address, telephone number and Internet e-mail address of the attorney, together with a declaration that the attorney is admitted to the Bar of this Court.

(b) Any party to a pending civil action who is not represented by an attorney may register as a Filing User of the E.D.N.Y. Public Web Site solely for purposes of the action. Registration shall be by paper on a form prescribed by the Clerk which shall require identification of the action as well as the name, address, telephone number and Internet e-mail address of the party. If, during the course of the action, the party retains an attorney who appears on the party's behalf, the appearing attorney shall advise the Clerk to terminate the party's registration as a Filing User upon the attorney's appearance.

(c) Each attorney of record and each unrepresented party is obligated to become a Filing User immediately upon designation of the action as being subject to EFP.

(d) Every Filing User shall notify the Clerk immediately of any change in the information provided in the Filing User's registration and such notice shall be separate and apart from the notice given pursuant to paragraph 3 or Local Civil Rule 1.3(d).

(e) Each Filing User shall, upon registration, be issued a User Identification Designation ("User ID") and a Password by the Clerk. The Clerk shall maintain a confidential record of issued User IDs and Passwords.

(f) Each Filing User shall maintain as confidential, except as expressly provided in subparagraph (h), the User ID and Password issued by the Clerk. Upon learning of the compromise of the confidentiality of either the User ID or the Password, the Filing User shall immediately notify the Clerk, who will issue the User a new User ID or Password, as appropriate.

(g) The Clerk may at any time issue and transmit by e-mail a new User ID or Password to any Filing User. A Filing User may at any time obtain a new User ID or Password upon request to the Clerk by following secure procedures to be prescribed by the Clerk.

(h) A Filing User may authorize another person to file a paper using the User ID and Password of the Filing User, and the Filing User shall retain full responsibility for any paper so filed.

13. Copyright And Other Proprietary Rights.

(a) The E.D.N.Y. Public Web Site shall bear a prominent notice as follows: "The contents of each filing in the electronic case files on the E.D.N.Y. Public Web Site are subject to copyright and other proprietary rights (with the exception of the opinions, memoranda and orders of this Court). Unless additional rights are expressly granted by the holder of the copyright or other proprietary right, the following terms of use shall apply: (i) Any person accessing this Web Site may view any filing, may print one copy of any filing for personal use, and may allow his or her browsing software, acting automatically, to cache locally any filing. (ii) Any other use inconsistent with such proprietary rights is prohibited, including but not limited to reproduction, adaptation, and public distribution, display and performance; and, in particular, the reproduction or other representation of such filings in an electronic database is prohibited. (iii) This notice does not purport to limit any fair use pursuant to applicable law."

(b) By consenting to EFP, each party or other person and their counsel shall be deemed to consent to all uses of the filed materials consistent with the notice set forth in subparagraph (a).

(c) Materials filed electronically may bear copyright notices or other claims of proprietary rights for the purpose of such filing, but no such notice shall expressly claim to prohibit any of the uses permitted according to the notice set forth in subparagraph (a).

(d) By producing discovery materials in an action subject to electronic filing, or by filing any material in the action electronically or otherwise, each party or subpoenaed non-party or other non-party so producing or filing, and all of the counsel to such persons, shall be deemed to consent to all uses of such materials by all parties to the action solely in connection with and for the purposes of the action, including the electronic filing in the action (by a party who did not originally file or produce such materials) of portions of such excerpts, quotations, or selected exhibits from such discovery materials or other filed materials as part of motion papers, pleading or other filings with the Court which must refer to such excerpts, quotations, etc.

14. Protective Order Respecting Proprietary Rights. In connection with discovery or the filing of any material in an action subject to EFP, any person may apply by motion for an order prohibiting the electronic filing in the action of certain specifically-identified materials on the grounds that such materials are subject to copyright or other proprietary rights and that, notwithstanding the existence of such rights and the notice for which subparagraph 13(a) provides, electronic filing in the action is likely to result in substantial prejudice to those proprietary rights. A motion for such an order shall be filed not less than five days before the materials to which the motion pertains are due to be produced or filed with the Court. Any material not filed electronically pursuant to such an order shall be filed with the Clerk and served as if the action were not subject to EFP. Nothing in this paragraph shall be construed to change the standard for the issuance of a protective order respecting confidentiality in an action subject to EFP.

15. Protective Order Respecting Privacy Interests. In connection with discovery or the filing of any material in an action subject to EFP, any person may apply by motion for an order prohibiting the electronic filing in the action of certain specifically-identified materials on the grounds that the electronic filing of such materials is subject to privacy interests and that electronic filing in the action is likely to prejudice those privacy interests. A motion for such an order shall be filed not less than five days before the materials to which the motion pertains are due to be produced or filed with the Court. Any material not filed electronically pursuant to such an order shall be filed with the Clerk and served as if the action were not subject to EFP. Nothing in this paragraph shall be construed to change the standard for the issuance of a protective order respecting confidentiality in an action subject to EFP.

16. Miscellaneous Provisions.

(a) The Clerk's Office shall provide sufficient equipment and facilities, including high-bandwidth Internet access, to allow for public electronic filing of papers and for public access to all Court records. The use of such facilities and equipment for any purpose other than accessing the E.D.N.Y. Public Web Site is prohibited.

(b) Until such time as the United States Court of Appeals for the Second Circuit provides notice to the Chief Judge that public access to the E.D.N.Y. Public Web Site obviates or modifies any need for transmittal of the record on appeal of any action subject to EFP as to which a notice of appeal to that Court of Appeals has been filed, when required, the Clerk shall deliver to the Court of Appeals, at that Court's election, either a complete paper copy of the record on appeal or an electronic reproduction of that record on appeal as such record is reflected in the E.D.N.Y. Public Web Site.

(c) This Administrative Order and the Users' Manual shall be posted on the E.D.N.Y. Public Web Site in a location which may be reached from the home page of that Site via one or more highly visible and easily found hyperlinks; shall be published periodically in the New York Law Journal; and shall be posted prominently in each of the Courthouses of this District. Any amendments to the EFP shall be similarly posted and published.

(d) This Administrative Order and the Users' Manual shall be effective when this Order is signed and may be amended by the Court from time to time on the Court's own initiative.

Dated: Brooklyn, New York
　　　　September ＿＿, 1997

ADMINISTRATIVE ORDERS—EASTERN DISTRICT

ADMINISTRATIVE ORDER 2004–05.
REQUESTS TO SEAL
DOCUMENTS

WHEREAS the Court intends to establish a uniform procedure for the submission of requests by litigants or counsel who wish to file a document under seal; and

WHEREAS no civil case document submitted for filing, except for documents not served on defendants pursuant to provisions of the False Claims Act, 31 U.S.C. § 3730(b), will be sealed absent the express authorization of the assigned district judge or magistrate judge; and

WHEREAS in criminal cases, except for an indictment or an information sealed by the grand jury, no documents submitted by either the government or defense counsel after the public filing of an indictment or information will be sealed absent the express authorization of the assigned district judge or magistrate judge; it is

ORDERED as follows:

1.) The moving litigant or counsel who wishes to file a document under seal must provide to the Clerk's Office, on the form annexed, either a.) the case caption, docket number, assigned judge, and date of the order that authorized filing under seal; or, b.) if there is no such preexisting order, the statute, regulation, or other legal basis that authorizes filing under seal.

2.) The United States Attorney's Office may continue to follow existing procedures for sealing criminal case documents of all kinds pre-indictment; this Administrative Order and form will apply only to requests to seal documents made by either the government or defense counsel after the public filing of an indictment or information.

3.) Nothing in this Administrative Order is intended to preclude the right of any party to bring a formal motion before the assigned judicial officer for leave to file a particular document or documents under seal and/or ex parte.

4.) Any party or person who believes that a filing should not have been made under seal, may raise that question with the Court by letter, with copies served on all parties.

SO ORDERED.

Dated: April 20, 2004.

ADMINISTRATIVE ORDER 2004–08.
ELECTRONIC CASE FILING

The Board of Judges of the Eastern District of New York, at a meeting held on June 22, 2004, resolved to complete the electronic case filing project begun in 1997.

Beginning on August 2, 2004, electronic case filing will be mandatory for all civil cases other than pro se cases and for all criminal cases.

Requests by attorneys for an exemption to the mandatory policy will be considered for good cause hardship reasons only, and will be reviewed on an individual basis by the assigned United States Magistrate Judge. The Clerk's Office provides an electronic filing training program to assist attorneys filing electronically. Before seeking a hardship exemption, attorneys are advised to participate in the training program or otherwise seek the assistance of the Clerk's Office.

SO ORDERED.

Dated: Brooklyn, New York
June, 2004.

ADMINISTRATIVE ORDER 2004–09. THE AUGUST 2, 2004 AMENDMENT TO THE E–GOVERNMENT ACT OF 2002

WHEREAS the Eastern District of New York requires mandatory electronic case filing for all civil cases other than pro se cases and for all criminal cases; and

WHEREAS in compliance with the E–Government Act of 2002, Pub. L. No. 107–347 (as amended August 2, 2004) and the policy of the Judicial Conference of the United States, and to promote electronic access to case files while also protecting personal privacy and other legitimate interests, parties must refrain from including, or shall partially redact where inclusion is necessary, certain personal data identifiers from all pleadings filed with the Court, including exhibits thereto, whether filed electronically or in paper, unless otherwise ordered by the Court, it is

ORDERED that, effective immediately, the attached Guidelines for compliance with the E–Government Act of 2002, as amended, are issued as an Administrative Order of the Eastern District of New York, and compliance will be mandatory by any party wishing to file a document containing the personal data identifiers listed in the attachment; and that compliance will be strictly enforced, unless otherwise specifically ordered to the contrary by the Court in an individual civil or criminal action. The Court may strike an unredacted document from the record, or deny the relief sought.

SO ORDERED.

Dated: October ___, 2004.

GUIDELINES FOR COMPLIANCE WITH THE AUGUST 2, 2004 AMENDMENTS TO THE E–GOVERNMENT ACT OF 2002

In compliance with the policy of the Judicial Conference of the United States, and the E-Government Act of 2002, and in order to promote electronic access to case files while also protecting personal privacy and other legitimate interests, parties shall refrain from including, or shall partially redact where inclusion is necessary, the following personal data identifiers from all pleadings filed with the court, including exhibits thereto, whether filed electronically or in paper, unless otherwise ordered by the Court.

a. **Social Security numbers.** If an individual's Social Security number must be included in a pleading, only the last four digits of that number should be used.

b. **Names of minor children.** If the involvement of a minor child must be mentioned, only the initials of that child should be used.

c. **Dates of birth.** If an individual's date of birth must be included in a pleading, only the year should be used.

d. **Financial account numbers.** If financial account numbers are relevant, only the last four digits of these numbers should be used.

In compliance with the E–Government Act of 2002, a party wishing to file a document containing the personal data identifiers listed above may:

a. file an unredacted version of the document under seal, or

b. file a reference under seal. The reference list shall contain the complete personal data identifier(s) and the redacted identifier(s) used in its (their) place in the filing. All references in the case to the redacted identifiers included in the reference list will be construed to refer to the corresponding complete personal data identifier. The reference list must be filed under seal, and may be amended as of right.

The unredacted version of the document or the reference list shall be retained by the court as part of the record. The court may, however, still require the party to file a redacted copy for the public file.

The responsibility for redacting these personal identifiers rests solely with counsel and the parties. The Clerk will not review each pleading for compliance with this rule.

The court may, however, still require the party to file a redacted copy for the public file.

In addition, exercise caution when filing documents that contain the following:

1) Personal identifying number, such as driver's license number;

2) medical records, treatment and diagnosis;

3) employment history;

4) individual financial information; and

5) proprietary or trade secret information.

Counsel is strongly urged to share this notice with all clients so that an informed decision about the inclusion of certain materials may be made. **If a redacted document is filed, it is the sole responsibility of counsel and the parties to be sure that all pleadings comply with the rules of this court requiring redaction of personal data identifiers. The clerk will not review each pleading for redaction.**

SO ORDERED.

Dated: October, 2004.

ADMINISTRATIVE ORDER 2007–10.
ELECTRONIC DEVICES

By vote of the Board of Judges of the United States District Court for the Eastern District of New York, effective January 2, 2008, attorneys presenting appropriate verification of bar membership will be permitted to enter the courthouses of the Eastern District of New York in possession of Personal Digital Assistants ("PDAs"), laptop computers and cellular telephones. In all courtrooms cellular telephones must be in the off position and PDAs and computers must be off or rendered "silent." This administrative order does not limit in any way the authority of a district judge or magistrate judge to curtail the presence or use of such devices as circumstances may warrant. In accordance with the Local and General Rules of the Court, photographs, video and audio recordings in the courthouse at any time are strictly forbidden. Violations of this order may result in court imposed sanctions, including but not limited to fines and forfeiture of the privileges hereby extended.

SO ORDERED.

Dated: Brooklyn, New York,
    December 17, 2007.

ADMINISTRATIVE ORDER 2008–04.
ASSIGNMENT OF CRIMINAL
CASES

Effective March 3, 2008 and pending further order of the Court or action by the Board of Judges, and notwithstanding any provision of Rule 50.3 of the Rules for the Division of Business Among District Judges, the Clerk of the Court is directed to assign all criminal cases randomly, unless the United States Attorney certifies in writing at the time of filing that a case to be assigned satisfies one of the three conditions in Rule 50.3 (c), or involves the same specific conduct that is a subject of a pending case.

The foregoing is without prejudice to an application by any party seeking to relate a criminal case to a previously filed indictment or information on the grounds that a substantial saving of judicial resources will result or that the ends of justice and fair administration so require. Any such application shall be made on ten days notice to the judge to whom the case was randomly assigned, and granted only upon a clear showing of the grounds for relief.

SO ORDERED.

Dated: Brooklyn, New York, February 27, 2008.

ADMINISTRATIVE ORDER 2008–5.
SCHEDULING IN SOCIAL SECURITY
CASES [EASTERN DISTRICT]

Effective April 1, 2008, the revised policy of the Board of Judges for docketing and calendaring Social Security cases and expediting their disposition expects the parties to adhere to the following schedule: (i) that defendant will obtain and serve upon plaintiff the administrative record of the proceedings, along with its answer, within 90 days of commencement of the action; (ii) that, unless otherwise directed by a district judge or magistrate judge, defendant will move for judgment on the pleadings within the next sixty (60) days by service of motion papers upon plaintiff; (iii) that plaintiff's response papers will be served upon defendant within thirty days thereafter; and (iv) that upon receipt of plaintiff's papers, defendant will then file the entire set of motion papers and the administrative record with the Court.

This administrative order does not limit in any way the authority of a district judge or magistrate judge to enter such orders and directives that sound administration may require.

SO ORDERED.

Dated: Brooklyn, New York
    March 20, 2008.

JUDICIAL CONFERENCE POLICY WITH REGARD
TO THE AVAILABILITY OF TRANSCRIPTS
OF COURT PROCEEDINGS

Effective May 15, 2008, the Eastern District of New York, in accordance with Judicial Conference Policy and Federal Rule of Civil Procedure 5.2 and Federal Rule of Criminal Procedure 49.1, will implement the following policy regarding official court transcripts:

1. A transcript provided to the Court by a court reporter or transcriber will be available at the Clerk's Office, for inspection only, for a period of 90 days after it is filed.

2. During the 90–day period, a copy of the transcript may be obtained from the court reporter or transcriber at the rate established by the Judicial Conference. The transcript will be available at the public terminal at the courthouse, and remotely electronically available to any attorneys of record who have purchased a copy from the court reporter.

3. After the 90–day period has ended, the transcript will be available for copying in the Clerk's Office and for download through PACER.

Note: The policy applies to transcripts of events taking place in the court's courtrooms, not depositions taken outside of court or proceedings of state courts or other jurisdictions. This policy establishes a procedure for counsel to request the redaction from the transcript of specific personal data identifiers before the transcript is made electronically available to the general public.

Counsel are strongly urged to share this notice with their clients so that an informed decision about the inclusion of certain materials may be made. **The responsibility for redacting personal identifiers rests solely with counsel and the parties**. Neither the Clerk nor the court reporter will review transcripts for compliance with this policy.

Notice of Intent to Redact. The Eastern District will not be using this document.

Redaction Request. If a redaction is requested, counsel must e-file their Redaction Request as well as submit a hard copy of the Redaction Request to the court reporter **within 21 days** from the filing of the transcript, indicating where the personal identifiers appear in the transcript by page and line and how they are to be redacted. (A Redaction Request form is available on our website: http://www.nyed. uscourts.gov/).

Filing of Redacted Transcript. Once a court reporter/transcriber receives the list of redactions, the court reporter/transcriber has ten (10) days after the deadline for receipt of the attorney's redaction request to file a redacted transcript with the Clerk of Court.

Note: This procedure is limited to the redaction of the specific personal data identifiers listed below:

- Social Security numbers to the last four digits;
- financial account numbers to the last four digits
- dates of birth to the year;
- names of minor children to the initials; and
- home addresses to the city and state.

If an attorney fails to timely file a Redaction Request or motion to extend time, no redactions will be made and the original transcript will be remotely publicly available after 90 days.

Request for Additional Redactions. If counsel would like to request further redactions, in addition to these personal identifiers listed above, counsel must move the Court by filing a separate motion for redaction of electronic transcript. Until the Court has ruled on any such motion, the transcript will not be electronically available, even if the 90–day restriction period has ended.

Remote Public Access to Transcripts. If a redacted transcript is filed with the Court, that redacted transcript will be remotely electronically available through PACER after 90 calendar days from the date of filing of the original transcript and the original transcript will never be made publicly available. If the original transcript is filed without redaction, that original transcript will be remotely electronically available through PACER after 90 calendar days.

CJA Panel Attorneys. An attorney who is serving as appointed "standby" counsel for a pro se litigant must review the transcript as if the pro se party were his/her client. If an attorney represents a client pursuant to the Criminal Justice Act (CJA), including serving as standby counsel, the attorney conducting the review of the transcript is entitled to compensation under the CJA for functions reasonably performed to fulfill the obligation and for reimbursement of related reasonable expenses.

PACER Fees. PACER fees will be applied both during and after the 90–day restriction period. Charges will not be capped at 30 pages as they are for other court documents, but will rather accrue for the entire transcript. The user will incur PACER charges for each time the transcript is accessed even though he/she may have purchased it from the court reporter and obtained remote access through CM/ECF. There is no "free look" for transcripts.

Note to court reporters: If the portion of the transcript being ordered includes voir dire, or other jury information that does not fall within the responsibilities of either party, the court reporter should ask the court whether that part of the transcript should be restricted from remote electronic access, or whether the attorneys should be ordered to review it and offer redactions.

UNITED STATES DISTRICT COURT
EASTERN DISTRICT OF NEW YORK
--x

_____

_____
                    Plaintiff(s),   _____
Vs. _____   Case Number: _____

_____
                    Defendant(s).
--x

TRANSCRIPT REDACTION REQUEST

Comes now _____, by counsel, and gives this Transcript Redaction Request. The Redaction Policy requires redaction of the following personal identifiers from the transcripts made electronically available:

- Social Security numbers to the last four digits

- Financial Account numbers to the last four digits

- Dates of Birth to the year

- Names of Minor Children to the initials, and

- Home Address to the city and state.

It is requested that consistent with the Policy, the following information be redacted prior to the transcript being made remotely electronically available:

Document Number of the Transcript	Page Number	Line Number	Identifier [Example: SSN 009–99–9999	Redaction Requested [Example: SSN 9999]

The undersigned understands that redactions other than the personal identifiers listed in the Policy requires a separate Motion for Additional Redactions to be filed within 21 days of the filing of the transcript, and requires court approval.

_____
                                        Attorney

Dated: _____

NOTE: This Redaction Request should be filed directly with the Court Reporter and <u>NOT</u> with the Court.

Effective May 15, 2008.

RULES FOR THE DIVISION OF BUSINESS AMONG DISTRICT JUDGES

SOUTHERN DISTRICT

INTRODUCTION

These rules are adopted for the internal management of the case load of the court and shall not be deemed to vest any rights in litigants or their attorneys and shall be subject to such amendments from time to time as shall be approved by the court.

RULE 1. INDIVIDUAL ASSIGNMENT SYSTEM

This court shall operate under an individual assignment system to assure continuous and close judicial supervision of every case. Each civil and criminal action and proceeding, except as otherwise provided, shall be assigned by lot to one judge for all purposes. The system shall be administered by an assignment committee in such a manner that all active judges, except the chief judge, shall be assigned substantially an equal share and kind of the work of the court over a period of time. There shall be assigned or transferred to the chief judge such matters as the chief judge is willing and able to undertake, consistent with the chief judge's administrative duties.

RULE 2. ASSIGNMENT COMMITTEE

An assignment committee is established for the administration of the assignment system. The committee shall consist of the chief judge and two other active judges selected by the chief judge, each to serve for one year. The chief judge shall also select two other active judges, each to serve for a period of one year, as alternate members of the committee.

The assignment committee shall supervise and rule upon all problems relating to assignments under this system, in accordance with these rules, as amended from time to time by the board of judges.

RULE 3. PART I

Part I is established for hearing and determining certain emergency and miscellaneous matters in civil and criminal cases and for processing criminal actions and proceedings through the pleading stage.

Judges shall choose assignment to Part I from an appropriate schedule, in order of their seniority, for periods not to exceed three weeks in each year. The assignment committee may, on consent of the judges

affected, change such assignments, if necessary, to meet the needs of the court.

Part I shall be open from 10:00 a.m. to 5:00 p.m. Monday through Friday except on holidays and a magistrate judge shall be available at the courthouse on Saturdays up to 12:00 p.m. The judge presiding in Part I shall be available for emergency matters.

The judge presiding in Part I may fix such other times for any proceeding as necessary.

RULE 4. CIVIL ACTIONS OR PROCEEDINGS (FILING AND ASSIGNMENT)

(a) **Filing With the Clerk.** All civil actions and proceedings shall be numbered consecutively by year upon the filing of the first document in the case.

When a complaint or the first document is filed in a civil action or proceeding, counsel shall complete and file an information and designation form, in triplicate, indicating: (1) the title of the action; (2) the residence address and county of each plaintiff and defendant; (3) the basis of federal jurisdiction; (4) whether the action is a class action; (5) a brief statement of the nature of the action and amount involved; (6) whether the action is claimed to be a related case within the meaning of Rule 15, and if so, the docket number and name of the judge assigned to the earlier filed related action; (7) the category of the case; (8) the name of the sentencing judge, if brought under 28 U.S.C. Sec. 2255; and (9) the name, address and telephone number of the attorney of record and of the attorney's firm, if any. Forms for this purpose will be on file in the office of the clerk of the court and shall be furnished to counsel.

(b) **Assignment by the Clerk by Lot.** All civil actions and proceedings, except applications for leave to proceed in forma pauperis, upon being filed and all appeals from the bankruptcy court upon being docketed in this court shall be assigned by lot within each designated category to one judge for all purposes.

An action, case or proceeding may not be dismissed and thereafter refiled for the purpose of obtaining a different judge. If an action, case or proceeding, or one essentially the same, is dismissed and refiled, it shall be assigned to the same judge. It is the duty of every attorney appearing to bring the facts of the refiling to the attention of the clerk.

RULE 5. CIVIL PROCEEDINGS IN PART I

Admissions to the bar and civil matters other than emergencies shall be heard on Tuesdays commencing at 11:00 a.m. Naturalization proceedings shall be conducted on Fridays, commencing at 11:00 a.m.

(a) Miscellaneous Civil Matters. The judge presiding in Part I shall hear and determine all miscellaneous proceedings in civil matters, such as application for naturalization, for admission to the bar, for relief relating to orders and subpoenas of administrative agencies and shall purge jurors in the central jury part as and when required. When a modification or further action on such determination is sought, it shall be referred to the judge who made the original determination even though said judge is no longer sitting in Part I.

(b) Civil Emergency Matters. The Part I judge shall hear and determine all emergency matters in civil cases which have been assigned to a judge when the assigned judge is absent or has expressly referred the matter to Part I because said judge is unavailable due to extraordinary circumstances. Depending on which procedures the Part I judge deems the more efficient, the Part I judge may either dispose of an emergency matter only to the extent necessary to meet the emergency, or, on consent of the assigned judge and notice to the clerk, transfer the action to himself or herself for all further proceedings.

(c) Subsequent Emergency Proceedings. If a civil emergency matter is brought before the Part I judge and the judge concludes that for lack of emergency or otherwise the proceeding should not be determined in Part I the party who brought the proceeding shall not present the same matter again to any other Part I judge unless relevant circumstances have changed in the interim in which case the party shall advise the judge of the prior proceedings and changed circumstances.

Revised effective January 25, 2005.

RULE 6. CRIMINAL ACTIONS OR PROCEEDINGS (FILING AND ASSIGNMENT)

(a) Filing With the Clerk. Criminal actions shall be numbered consecutively by year upon the filing of the indictment or information. The number of a superseding indictment or information shall be preceded by the letter "S".

When an indictment or information is filed, the United States attorney shall simultaneously file the original and two copies of the indictment or informa-

tion. The United States attorney shall also supply an information and designation form, in triplicate, indicating: (1) the category of crime charged and the number of counts; (2) the maximum penalty for each count; (3) a statement as to whether the defendant is in custody and, if so where; (4) the name and telephone extension of the assistant United States attorney in charge of the case; and (5) all other data required by the information and designation form.

RULE 7. CRIMINAL PROCEEDINGS

Indictments designated for Foley Square may be returned by the grand jury to the magistrate judge presiding in the criminal part, in open court. Indictments designated for White Plains may be returned by the grand jury to the magistrate judge presiding in the White Plains Courthouse, or in his or her absence, before any available judge.

The judge presiding in Part I shall:

(a) Conduct all preliminary criminal proceedings, such as empaneling the grand jury.

(b) Hear and determine, except for matters referable to a magistrate judge and so referred, all proceedings in criminal actions before the entry of a plea, except as provided in Rule 8(c), 8(d) and 8(e).

(c) Hear and determine all emergency matters in criminal cases which have been assigned to a judge when the assigned judge is absent or has expressly referred the matter to Part I because said judge is unavailable due to extraordinary circumstances.

(d) Hear and determine all matters relating to proceedings before the grand jury. When a modification or further action on such determination is sought, however, it shall be referred to the judge who made the original determination even though said judge is no longer sitting in Part I.

RULE 8. ARRAIGNMENTS AND ASSIGNMENTS IN CRIMINAL CASES

(a) Assignments. In a criminal case, after an indictment has been returned by the Grand Jury or a notice has been filed by the United States Attorney's Office of an intention to file an information upon the defendant's waiver of indictment, the magistrate judge on duty will randomly draw the name of a judge in open court from the criminal wheel, and assign the case to said judge for all purposes thereafter. Said notice to file an information upon the defendant's waiver of indictment shall be signed by the United States Attorney's Office and by the defendant's attorney. Waiver of indictment cases will not be assigned a criminal docket number until the waiver has been accepted by the assigned judge. Sealed indictments will be assigned a criminal docket number upon filing, but a judge will not be selected until such time that the indictment is unsealed.

(b) Arraignments. The United States Attorney's Office will promptly contact the judge to whom the case is assigned and request the scheduling of a pretrial conference at which the defendant will be arraigned.

(c) Waiver of Indictments. If any person offers to waive indictment, the judge to whom the case has been assigned will conduct such proceedings as may be required by law to establish that the waiver is both knowing and voluntary before an information is filed. The judge shall then arraign the defendant and call on the defendant to enter a plea. If the defendant fails to waive indictment and is subsequently indicted on the same or similar charges, the case shall be assigned by the clerk to the same judge to whom the original information was assigned.

(d) Assignment of Superseding Indictments and Informations. A superseding indictment or information will be assigned directly and immediately for the entry of a plea and all further proceedings to the same judge to whom the original indictment or information was assigned.

(e) This rules applies to Foley Square. The judges in the White Plains Courthouse will continue to follow such procedures as they find convenient.

Amended effective December 1, 2000.

RULE 9. CASES CERTIFIED FOR PROMPT TRIAL OR DISPOSITION

Immediately after assignment to a judge, civil and criminal actions shall be screened by the assignment committee for the purpose of identifying cases which are likely to be subject to delays and which, because of exceptional and special circumstances, demand extraordinary priority, prompt disposition, and immediate judicial supervision in the public interest.

When a case has been so identified by the assignment committee, the committee shall certify that the case requires extraordinary priority and a prompt trial or other disposition within sixty (60) days and shall so advise the judge to whom the case has been assigned. The judge so assigned shall advise the assignment committee whether said judge can accord the case the required priority. In the event the judge so assigned advises the assignment committee that he or she cannot accord the required priority, the case shall immediately be assigned to another judge by lot and the same procedure followed until the case is assigned to a judge able to accord it the required priority. The name of the judge to be so assigned shall be drawn by lot in the same manner as other civil and criminal actions are initially assigned.

Cross References
Speedy Trial Act, see 18 U.S.C.A.

RULE 10. MOTIONS

(a) Civil Motions. Civil motions shall be made within the time required by the Federal Rules of Civil Procedure and the Civil Rules of this court. Motions shall be made returnable before the assigned judge.

(b) Criminal Motions. Motions in criminal actions shall be made returnable before the assigned judge at such time as said judge directs. Criminal motions must be made within the time required by the Federal Rules of Criminal Procedure and the Criminal Rules of this court, except that the time for motions otherwise required by such rules to be made before the entry of a plea shall be made within ten (10) days after the entry of a plea, or at such other time as the assigned judge directs.

Cross References
Federal Rules of Criminal Procedure, see 18 U.S.C.A.
Federal Rules of Civil Procedure, see 28 U.S.C.A.

RULE 11. AMENDMENTS OF PRO SE PETITIONS FOR COLLATERAL RELIEF FROM CONVICTIONS

(a) Federal Convictions. When a pro se motion for collateral relief under 28 U.S.C. § 2255 is filed, the pro se clerk shall first ascertain whether the petition is in proper form and, if not, take appropriate steps to have it corrected. The petition shall be submitted for all further proceedings to the judge who accepted the plea or sentenced the defendant, whichever is applicable. The judge may either act on the application without responsive papers or advise the United States attorney of the date when answering or reply papers are due.

If the judge concerned is deceased; is a visiting judge who declines to entertain the application within a reasonable time because of illness, disqualification, disability or prolonged absence; or a senior judge who elects not to entertain the application, the application shall be assigned by lot.

(b) State Convictions. When a pro se petition for collateral relief from a state conviction is filed, the pro se clerk shall first ascertain whether the petition is in proper form and if not take proper steps to have it corrected. If the petitioner seeks leave to proceed in forma pauperis, the petition shall be first submitted to the pro se law clerk for study and, where appropriate, a recommendation shall be submitted to a magistrate judge designated by the chief judge for intermediate review and ultimate submission to the chief judge for disposition.

If the petition is not dismissed by the chief judge, the papers shall be sent to the pro se clerk for further processing. The pro se clerk shall ascertain if the petition is related to any prior application and, if so, advise the clerk, who shall assign the case directly to the judge who last acted upon the related application. If the related application was before a deceased or a retired judge, or if the application is unrelated to any prior application, the clerk shall assign the case by lot.

RULE 12. ASSIGNMENTS TO NEW JUDGES

When a new judge is inducted, the assignment committee shall transfer to the new judge an equal share of all cases then pending (including cases on the suspense docket). The cases shall be taken equally, by lot, from the dockets of each of the judges' most recent chronological list of cases which have been designated by the transferor as eligible for transfer. No case shall be transferred without the consent of the transferor judge. The assignment committee shall also direct the clerk to add the name of the new judge to the random selection system for assigning new cases to active judges.

RULE 13. ASSIGNMENTS TO SENIOR JUDGES

If a senior judge is willing and able to undertake assignment of new cases for all purposes, said judge shall advise the assignment committee of the number and categories of new cases which said judge is willing and able to undertake. New cases in the requested number in each category shall then be assigned to said judge in the same manner as new cases are assigned to active judges.

If a senior judge is willing and able to undertake assignment of pending cases from other judges, said judge may (1) accept assignment of all or any part of any case from any judge on mutual consent, or (2) advise the assignment committee of the number, status and categories of pending cases which said judge is willing to undertake. Such cases will be drawn by lot from current lists provided to the assignment committee by the judges wishing to transfer cases under this rule. If a senior judge does not terminate any action so transferred, it shall be reassigned to the transferor judge.

RULE 14. ASSIGNMENTS TO VISITING JUDGES

When a visiting judge is assigned to this district, said judge shall advise the assignment committee of the number and categories of pending cases which said judge is required or willing to accept. The assignment committee shall then transfer to said judge the required number of cases in each category by drawing them equally and by lot from each judge's list of cases ready for trial, but no case shall be so

transferred without the consent of the transferor judge. If the visiting judge does not terminate the action, it shall be reassigned to the transferor judge.

RULE 15. TRANSFER OF RELATED CASES

(a) Subject to the limitations set forth below, a civil case will be deemed related to one or more other civil cases and will be transferred for consolidation or coordinated pretrial proceedings when the interests of justice and efficiency will be served. In determining relatedness, a judge will consider whether (i) a substantial saving of judicial resources would result; or (ii) the just efficient and economical conduct of the litigations would be advanced; or (iii) the convenience of the parties or witnesses would be served. Without intending to limit the criteria considered by the judges of this Court in determining relatedness, a congruence of parties or witnesses or the likelihood of a consolidated or joint trial or joint pre-trial discovery may be deemed relevant.

(b) Criminal cases are not treated as related to civil cases or vice versa. Criminal cases are not treated as related unless a motion is granted for a joint trial. Bankruptcy appeals are not considered related merely because they arise from the same bankruptcy proceeding.

(c) When a civil case is being filed or removed, the person filing or removing shall disclose on an appropriate form, to be furnished by the Clerk's Office, any contention of relatedness. A copy of such form shall be served with the complaint or notice of removal. A case filed or removed and designated as related shall be forwarded to the judge before whom the earlier filed case is then pending who shall accept or reject the case in his or her sole discretion. Cases rejected by the judge as being not related shall be assigned by random selection. Any party believing its case to be related to another may apply on notice in writing to the judge assigned in its case for transfer to the judge having the related case with the lowest docket number. If the assigned judge believes the case should be transferred, he or she shall refer the question to the judge who would receive the transfer. In the event of disagreement among the assigned judges, a judge (but not a party) may refer the question to the Assignment Committee. Litigants will not be heard by the Assignment Committee.

(d) Motions in civil and criminal cases to consolidate, or for a joint trial, are regulated by the Federal Rules. A defendant in a criminal case may move on notice to have all of his or her sentences in this district imposed by a single judge. All such motions shall be noticed for hearing before the judge having the lowest docket number, with courtesy copies to be provided to the judge or judges having the cases with higher docket numbers.

(e) Nothing contained in this rule limits the use of Rule 1, infra, for reassignment of all or part of any case from the docket of one judge to that of another by agreement of the respective judges.

RULE 16. TRANSFER OF CASES BY CONSENT

Any active or senior judge, upon written advice to the assignment committee, may transfer directly any case or any part of any case on said judge's docket to any consenting active or senior judge except where Rule 18 applies.

RULE 17. TRANSFERS FROM SENIOR JUDGES

When an active judge becomes a senior judge, or later as the judge chooses, the judge may keep as much of his or her existing docket as said judge desires and furnish the assignment committee with a list of all cases which the judge desires to have transferred. The assignment committee will distribute these cases as equally as is feasible, by lot, to each active judge.

RULE 18. TRANSFER BECAUSE OF DISQUALIFICATION, ETC.

In case the assigned judge is disqualified or upon request, if said judge has presided at a mistrial or former trial of the case, upon written notice to it, the assignment committee shall transfer the case by lot.

RULE 19. TRANSFER OF CASES BE-CAUSE OF DEATH, RESIGNATION, PROLONGED ILLNESS, DISABILITY, UNAVOIDABLE ABSENCE, OR EX-CESSIVE BACKLOG OF A JUDGE

The assignment committee shall, in the case of death or resignation, and may, in the event of prolonged illness, disability, unavoidable absence of an assigned judge, or the buildup of an excessive backlog, transfer any case or cases pending on the docket of such judge by distributing them as equally as is feasible by lot, to all remaining active judges and to such senior judges who are willing and able to undertake them.

RULE 20. TRANSFER OF CASES TO THE SUSPENSE DOCKET

A civil case which, for reasons beyond the control of the court, can neither be tried nor otherwise terminated shall be transferred to the suspense docket. In the event the case becomes activated, it shall be restored to the docket of the transferor judge if available, otherwise it shall be reassigned by lot.

Historical and Statutory Notes

Note: The following provisions of the Plan of Operation for the White Plains Courthouse, as amended, are reprinted here, for information, since they affect the Division of the Business of the Court.

RULE 21. DESIGNATION OF WHITE PLAINS CASES

(a) Civil. At the time of filing, the plaintiff's attorney shall designate on the civil cover sheet whether the case should be assigned to White Plains or Foley Square.

A civil case shall be designated for assignment to White Plains if:

(i) The claim arose in whole or in major part in the Counties of Dutchess, Orange, Putnam, Rockland, Sullivan and Westchester (the "Northern Counties") and at least one of the parties resides in the Northern Counties; or

(ii) The claim arose in whole or in major part in the Northern Counties and none of the parties resides in this District.

A civil case may also be designated for assignment to White Plains if:

(iii) The claim arose outside this district and at least some of the parties reside in the Northern Counties; or

(iv) At least half of the parties reside in the Northern Counties.

All civil cases other than those specified in the foregoing paragraphs (i), (ii), (iii), and (iv) shall be designated for assignment to Foley Square.

(b) Criminal. The U.S. Attorney designates on the criminal cover sheet that the case is to be assigned to White Plains if the crime was allegedly committed in whole or predominant part in the Northern Counties.

Defendants in any [criminal] case designated for White Plains may be arraigned at the White Plains Courthouse before a district judge if one is present and available, at any hour on any business day by prior arrangement with the United States Attorney or the Court. If no district judge is available in the White Plains Courthouse, such arraignment may be conducted before a magistrate judge at White Plains. If neither a judge nor a magistrate judge [at White Plains] is available and likely to remain unavailable until the next date of arraignment in Foley Square, such defendants shall be arraigned in Part I.

Bail applications in any case designated for White Plains may be heard before the magistrate judge at White Plains, or, if he/she is unavailable, before a judge in White Plains, or in Part I if no magistrate judge or judge is available.

RULE 22. REASSIGNMENT OF CASES

The judge to whom the case is assigned may reassign it in the interest of justice or sound judicial administration. If the Judge to whom the case is assigned determines that it should be reassigned, it is sent to the clerk for reassignment. If upon reassignment there is a dispute as to the proper place of holding court, it will be referred to the Assignment Committee for final determination. If the case is reassigned, it will be reassigned as if it were a new filing, but will retain its original case number.

RULE 23. REMOVED ACTIONS AND BANKRUPTCY MATTERS

Actions removed from a state court in New York County or Bronx County will be assigned to Foley Square. Actions removed from a state court in any of the other counties within the district will be assigned to White Plains. In either case, the attorney for the defendant may move for reassignment as provided in the section entitled Reassignment of Cases.

Bankruptcy appeals from the White Plains and Poughkeepsie bankruptcy courts are also assigned to said judge(s).

RULE 24. CASELOAD OF WHITE PLAINS JUDGE(S)

Any judge reassigned to White Plains retains his or her existing caseload.

RULE 25. PRISONER CIVIL RIGHTS ACTIONS AND HABEAS CORPUS PETITIONERS

Cases from the prisoner petitions wheel (wheel 5), including prisoner civil rights cases, are assigned proportionately to all judges of the court, whether sitting at White Plains or Foley Square. Non-prisoner civil rights cases (wheel 4) are assigned in accordance with the designation by the plaintiff's attorney unless reassigned as provided herein.

District judges assigned to White Plains will receive writs of habeas corpus arising out of state convictions obtained in the counties of Westchester, Rockland, Putnam, Dutchess, Orange and Sullivan; and those arising out of state convictions in the counties of Bronx and New York will be assigned to Judges in the Foley Square Courthouse.

RULE 26. FILING AT EITHER COURTHOUSE

Complaints and all subsequent papers are accepted at either the Foley Square or the White Plains Courthouse, regardless of the place for which the case is designated, and summons is issued from either place of holding court.

RULE 27. RELATED CASES

Related cases are heard at the place of holding court where the earliest case was filed.

RULE 28. HIGH-SECURITY CRIMINAL CASES

If the White Plains judge(s) determine(s) that the White Plains facility is inadequate for a particular case, the case is tried at Foley Square or returned for reassignment.

RULE 29. PART I

The judge(s) assigned full-time to White Plains do not sit in Part I in Foley Square.

RULE 30. NATURALIZATION

The court does not hold naturalization proceedings in White Plains.

RULE 31. JURY ASSIGNMENTS

Jury panels are assigned to White Plains on an as-needed basis from the master jury wheel. Jury panels for White Plains are drawn from the following counties: Dutchess, Orange, Putnam, Rockland, Sullivan and Westchester.

RULE 32. COURT HOURS

The offices of the clerk are open from 8:30 a.m. to 5:00 p.m., Monday through Friday. The offices of the clerk are closed Saturdays, Sundays and legal holidays. After hours, papers may be submitted for filing in a night depository located at 500 Pearl Street, New York, New York, at the Worth Street (north) entrance. These papers will be considered filed at 8:30 a.m. the following business day.

Amended effective December 1, 2000.

RULE 33. EMERGENCY MATTERS

In the absence of a judge at the White Plains Courthouse, emergency matters are heard in Part I at the Foley Square Courthouse.

APPENDIX. GENERAL CALENDAR PRACTICE—
SOUTHERN DISTRICT

GENERAL CALENDAR PRACTICE—
SOUTHERN DISTRICT

Effective immediately all papers, including complaints, motions, and briefs, must be signed by an attorney of record in his/her own name. Pursuant to authority delegated by the Court, the Clerk's office will not accept for filing any unsigned paper.

1. Applications for orders to show cause, provisional remedies, emergency relief or to proceed in forma pauperis, and orders and notice of settlement of judgments, shall be presented to the Orders and Appeals Clerk (Room 14). Judgments shall be presented to the Judgment Clerk (Room 14A). These documents will be examined as to form and thereafter transmitted to the assigned Judge.

2. Motions and responses thereto, with proof of service thereof, should be submitted to the Clerk (Room 10) for docketing.

(a) Any party wishing to make a motion should arrange for a pre-motion conference prior to preparation and submission of any papers in cases assigned to Judges Broderick, Cannella, Conner, Edelstein, Griesa, Keenan, Knapp (as to summary judgment only), Kram, Leisure, Leval, Pollack, Sprizzo, Stanton and Stewart (as to discovery only).

(b) Judges require that copies of all motion papers be delivered to their chambers on the same date as delivered to the Clerk. Judge Owen does not require courtesy copies except for papers filed later than 10 days prior to the return date. All papers in summary judgment motions before Judge Knapp must be received in chambers by the Friday prior to the return date. Papers on other motions before Judge Knapp must be received in chambers by noon on the Wednesday before the return date.

3. All motions, except those of an emergency nature or requiring provisional relief, may be made returnable for docketing purposes on any business day at 9:30 A.M. The notice and responses to be given shall conform to the times specified in Civil Rule 3 of this Court. The motion on five day motions and the motion and responsive papers on ten day motions shall be lodged not less than two business days before the return day with the Clerk (Room 10) for docketing and transmittal to the assigned Judge. The responsive papers on five days motions shall be lodged with the Clerk before noon of the business day preceding the return day.

No motion of the type described in subparagraph (1) of paragraph (c) of Rule 3 of the Civil Rules of this Court shall be heard unless counsel for the moving party has first requested an informal conference with the court or the magistrate assigned by the Court and such request has either been denied or the discovery dispute has not been resolved as a consequence of such a conference.

Oral argument is required on all motions in cases assigned to Judges Bonsal, Brieant, Cedarbaum, Goettel, Knapp (except discovery), Lasker (by letter request only attached to courtesy copy of motion), Owen, Pollack, Sand, Sweet and Weinfeld. The return dates for motions are as follows: Judge Bonsal—Wednesday at 10 A.M; Judge Brieant—any business day at 9 A.M.; Judge Cedarbaum—Fridays at 9:30 A.M.; Judge Goettel—Fridays at 10 A.M.; Judge Knapp— Fridays at 2 P.M.; Judge Lasker (counsel will be notified); Judge Owen—Fridays at 2:15 P.M.; Judge Pollack—any business day at 2 P.M.; Judge Sand— Thursdays at 2:15 P.M.; Judge Sweet—Fridays at 12 noon; and Judge Weinfeld—Tuesdays at 2:15 P.M.

Argument is generally not required in pro se matters, motions to reargue, appeals from magistrates' rulings, applications for attorneys' fees and motions for reductions of sentence. All motions before Judge Owen must be fully briefed no later than one week prior to the return date. Chambers will notify counsel of the time and place of the argument. Parties wishing to make discovery or summary judgment motions before Judge Knapp should arrange for a conference. For motions before Judge Cedarbaum moving papers must be served and filed by 12 noon on the Monday of the week before the week of the return date. Answering papers must be served and filed by 12 noon on the Monday before the return date. Reply paper, if any, must be served and filed by 12 noon on the Wednesday before the return date.

As to the other Judges, Counsel will be notified by telephone of the time and place for oral argument, if desired by the Court. In the absence of such notification Counsel should not appear on the return date.

4. In cases assigned to Judges Cedarbaum, Cooper, Goettel, Griesa, Haight, Lasker, Lowe, Motley, Sand, Stanton, Sweet, Walker, and Ward, communication with chambers on requests and inquiries shall be made by letter other than on urgent matters requiring the Court's immediate attention. Their telephone numbers are given in the calendar notices and may be used at the times indicated for an urgency. In cases assigned to the other Judges, those not named above in this paragraph, letters are not required and phone calls will be received during business hours.

5. Calls to chambers except those of an emergency nature should be made before 10 A.M. or after 4 P.M. for Judges Broderick, Cannella, Conner, Keenan, Sand and Walker, Judge Haight's deputy clerk re-

ceives calls between 9:30 A.M. and 4:30 P.M. Judge Kram receives calls before 11 A.M. or after 4 P.M. Judge Sprizzo's chambers receives calls before 10 A.M. Judge Stewart's deputy clerk receives calls 9:30 A.M. to noon and 2 P.M. to 4:30 P.M. Judge Owen's chambers receives calls before noon.

6. All requests for extensions of time or adjournments of motions, pre-trial conferences and other matters to Judges Broderick, Cedarbaum, Goettel, Keenan, Leisure, Sand, Stanton, Stewart, Walker and Ward must be made in writing with copies sent to all counsel for their consent and received in chambers not later than 48 hours before the scheduled time. The above procedures must be followed for Judge Sweet in communications regarding conferences or pre-trial scheduling, but not for the adjournment of motions. Requests regarding the adjournment of motions require the consent of all parties and receipt of written notice by 5 P.M. of the Wednesday before the scheduled return date. Applications to adjourn pre-trial conferences and pre-motion conferences to Judge Sprizzo must be made by 12 noon the day before the scheduled conference. Where adjournment is by consent before Judge Sprizzo a stipulation and order must be submitted to the court by 12 noon the day before the scheduled conference. Judge Haight requires that requests for adjournment be made at least three days before the date on which oral argument is scheduled. Judge Knapp requires that a stipulation of adjournment be received in the Judge's chambers by Wednesday noon for a motion noticed for a Friday. Judge Kram requires that all requests for adjournments or extensions be made at least one week before the scheduled proceeding or deadline. All such requests, to the judges named in this paragraph, must include the original return date, the number and disposition of any prior extensions or adjournments, and the reasons for the request.

7. Stipulation of adjournment or extensions of time for cases assigned to Judge Stewart are limited to three adjournments or extensions. In cases assigned to Judge Sprizzo, pre-sentence memoranda will not be accepted and parties will be heard at the time of sentencing. Pre-trial Conferences before Judge Owen will be scheduled on the request of any party or by the court.

EASTERN DISTRICT

INTRODUCTION

These rules are adopted for the internal management of the case load of the court and shall not be deemed to vest any rights in litigants or their attorneys and shall be subject to such amendments from time to time as shall be approved by the court.

RULE 50.1 CATEGORIES AND CLASSIFICATION OF CASES; INFORMATION ON CASES AND PARTIES

(a) **Categories of Cases.** Cases shall be divided into the following main categories:

(1) *Civil.*

(A) Regular.

(B) Multidistrict litigation.

(2) *Criminal.*

(3) *Miscellaneous.*

(b) **Information Sheet.** The party filing the initial paper in a civil or criminal case shall complete and attach an information sheet. The information sheet shall be placed in the case file.

Where it appears to the Court that the filing party's reasons for joinder of parties are not apparent from the face of the complaint, the Clerk of Court is authorized to request a written explanation consistent with Federal Rule of Civil Procedure 19 and any other appropriate Federal Rule. The response of the filing party will be docketed and a copy forwarded to the assigned judicial officer.

(c) **Disclosure of Interested Parties.** To enable judges and magistrates to evaluate possible disqualification or recusal, counsel for a private (nongovernmental) party shall submit at the time of initial pleading a certificate identifying any corporate parent, subsidiaries, or affiliates of that party.

(d) **Long Island Cases.**

(1) A criminal case shall be designated a "Long Island case" if the crime was allegedly committed wholly or in substantial part in Nassau or Suffolk County.

(2) A civil case shall be designated a Long Island case if the cause arose wholly or in substantial part in Nassau or Suffolk County.

(3) As provided in 50.2(f) a party may move to designate a case as a Long Island case or to cancel such designation on the grounds that such action will serve the convenience of the parties and witnesses or is otherwise in the interests of justice.

(e) **Miscellaneous Cases.** All matters that do not receive a civil or criminal docket number shall be given a miscellaneous docket number and assigned to the miscellaneous judge. The matter will continue to be assigned to that judge after he or she ceases to be miscellaneous judge.

[Amended effective June 1, 2000.]

RULE 50.2   ASSIGNMENT OF CASES[1]

(a) Time of Assignment. The clerk shall assign a civil case upon the filing of the initial pleading. In a criminal case after an indictment is returned or after an information (including a juvenile information under 18 U.S.C. § 5032) or a motion to transfer under 18 U.S.C. § 5032 has been filed, the United States Attorney shall refer the case to the clerk who shall then assign the case. The United States Attorney shall arrange with the judge to whom the case is assigned, or if that judge is absent or unavailable as provided in Rule 50.5, with the miscellaneous judge, to have the defendant arraigned and a plea entered as promptly as practicable.

(b) Random Selection Procedure. All cases shall be randomly assigned by the clerk or his designee in public view in one of the clerk's offices in such a manner that each active judge shall receive as nearly as possible the same number of cases, except as provided in paragraph (h). Where a party or his counsel requests prior to selection that he or she be present at the selection, the clerk shall make reasonable efforts to comply with the request. In Brooklyn civil cases a magistrate judge shall be drawn at the same time and in the same manner as a judge. All Long Island civil cases shall be assigned to the Long Island magistrate judge. The parties to any Long Island case assigned to a Brooklyn judge may stipulate that the case be assigned to the Long Island magistrate judge for pretrial purposes.

(c) Assignment of Civil Cases. There shall be separate Brooklyn, Uniondale and Hauppauge civil assignment wheels. At least quarterly the Chief Judge shall fix the proportion of cases to be assigned to the Long Island courthouses so as to distribute the civil cases relatively equally among all the active judges.

(d) Assignment of Criminal Cases.

(1) There shall be a Brooklyn criminal and a Long Island criminal assignment wheel.

(2) There shall be a Brooklyn and Long Island criminal misdemeanor assignment wheels for the random assignment of these matters to a magistrate.

(e) Place of Trial. Except in emergencies a case shall be tried at the place to which it has been assigned.

(f) Objection. Any objection by a party to a designation of a judge or to place of trial shall be made by letter or motion to the judge assigned

(1) in a criminal case, within ten days from arraignment or from initial notice of appearance, whichever is earlier; or

(2) in a civil case, within the time allowed to respond to the complaint.

(g) Special Cases.

(1) The miscellaneous judge shall send all narcotics addict commitment cases involving "eligible individuals" as defined by 28 U.S.C. § 2901(g) to the clerk for assignment as provided in paragraph (b).

(2) Pro se applications or claims by persons in custody shall be filed without prepayment of fees upon receipt, prior to decision on their in forma pauperis petitions.

(3) Multidistrict litigation is to be assigned to the judge selected by the multidistrict litigation panel; subject to reassignment by the Chief Judge of the Eastern District of New York, according to the usual reassignment rules of the district, to adjust caseload distribution in the interests of justice.

(h) Chief Judge; Senior Judges; Temporarily Overloaded Judges; Notice of Removal From Wheel. The chief judge and each senior judge shall indicate from time to time to the clerk the percentage of a full caseload that he or she elects to have assigned. The chief judge, with the consent of a judge, may remove that judge from any wheel temporarily to reduce the number of pending cases and prevent delay in the disposition of cases by a judge who is then overburdened by cases or due to ill health. The chief judge shall return that judge to the wheel only on consent of the judge. The clerk shall upon request inform any attorney or party of the identity of judges whose names have been removed from a wheel.

(i) Visiting Judge. The chief judge shall approve the assignment or transfer of cases to a visiting judge.

(j) Proceedings After Assignment. All proceedings in a case after assignment shall be conducted by the assigned judge, except as provided by these guidelines.

(k) Recusal. A judge or magistrate judge may recuse himself or herself at any time in accordance with U.S.C. § 455. This guideline takes precedence over any other guideline.

(*l*) Appeals—Assignment on Reversal or Remand.

(1) In a criminal case upon reversal of a judgment and a direction for retrial or resentence, on receipt of the mandate of the appellate court the clerk shall randomly select a different judge to preside over the case. Notwithstanding this provision the chief judge may order the case assigned to the original presiding judge to avoid placing an excessive burden on another judge.

(2) In a civil case upon reversal the case shall remain assigned to the judge who was previously assigned, unless the chief judge or his designee orders otherwise.

Amended effective December 1, 2000.

1 Weighted Criminal Assignment Wheel

Please take notice that effective July 1, 1993, the Eastern District of New York will establish a new weighted criminal assignment wheel for matters with an estimated trial duration of six weeks or longer. There will be separate Brooklyn and Long Island weighted criminal wheels. The Long Island wheel will include district judges from the Uniondale and Hauppauge courthouses, including Judge Denis R. Hurley, who will move his place of holding court to Hauppauge by late summer.

Please also take notice that most miscellaneous case matters will be assigned to a specific judge through separate Brooklyn and Long Island wheels. In forma pauperis requests to file a new civil action without pre-payment of fees, and grand jury matters will be excluded from the new miscellaneous assignment wheel. These matters will continue to be referred to the appropriate miscellaneous duty judge. If a judge assigned to a miscellaneous matter is unavailable on a given day, urgent matters will be handled by the miscellaneous duty judge, on a day to day basis, until the assigned judge is available.

The Clerk's Office plans to automate the assignment of cases to district judges and magistrate judges for all matters—criminal, civil and miscellaneous—by July 1, 1993 or shortly thereafter.

The attention of the Bar is called to the preamble to the "Guidelines for the Division of Business Among District Judges" in the Eastern District Court which states that: These rules are adopted for the internal management of the case load of the court and shall not be deemed to vest any rights in litigants or their attorneys and shall be subject to such amendments from time to time as shall be approved by the Court.

RULE 50.3 RELATED CASES; MOTION FOR CONSOLIDATION OF CASES

(a) "Related" Case Defined. A case is "related" to another for purposes of this guideline when, because of the similarity of facts and legal issues or because the cases arise from the same transactions or events, a substantial saving of judicial resources is likely to result from assigning both cases to the same judge and magistrate judge.

(b) Civil Cases. By way of illustration and not limitation, a civil case may be deemed "related" to an earlier case when the civil case: (A) relates to property involved in an earlier case, or (B) involves the same factual issue or grows out of the same transaction as does an earlier case, or (C) involves the validity or infringement of a patent already in suit in a prior case.

(c) Criminal Cases. Criminal cases are "related" only when (A) a superseding indictment is filed, or (B) more than one indictment or information is filed against the same defendant or defendants, or (C) when an application is filed by a person in custody that relates to a prior action. Other cases will be deemed "related" only upon written application by a party, upon not less than ten days' notice to each other party, to the judge presiding over the earlier assigned case. The application will be granted only if a substantial saving of judicial resources is likely to result from assigning both cases to the same judge, or is otherwise in the interest of justice.

(d) Designation of Related Case; Service of Civil Information Sheet. If the party filing a case believes it to be related to a prior case, whether pending or closed, the party shall so indicate on the information sheet, specifying for each such case the title and the docket number, if any. A copy of the information sheet shall be served with the summons and complaint or petition for removal of the action. A case designated by the filing party as related shall be forwarded by the Clerk's Office to the judge before whom the earlier filed case is or was pending, together with a memorandum stating that the case has been assigned as a related case and identifying the prior case to which it is asserted to be related. The memorandum shall be filed in the record and noted in the docket. Cases determined by the judge not to be related shall be reassigned by random selection. Each attorney in a case has an ongoing duty to advise the clerk in writing upon learning of any facts indicating that his or her case may be related to any other pending case.

(e) Assignment of Related Cases. Related cases shall be assigned by the clerk to the judge to whom was assigned the case with the lowest docket number in the series of cases. The clerk shall advise the judge of such assignment of a "related case." In the interest of judicial economy, all habeas corpus petitions filed by the same petitioner shall be deemed related. Likewise, all pro se civil actions filed by the same individual shall be deemed related.

(f) Case Erroneously Assigned as Related. The designation of cases as related may be corrected sua sponte by the judge to whom they are assigned, by returning to the clerk for reassignment cases erroneously so assigned. The failure to assign related cases appropriately shall be corrected only by agreement of all the judges to whom the related cases are assigned; if they agree, they may transfer the later-filed cases as provided in paragraph (e), and notify the clerk of that action.

(g) Credit for Related Cases. A related case transferred or assigned to a judge shall be counted as would a newly-filed case regularly assigned. A judge shall be assigned an additional case for each case transferred from him or her under this guideline.

[Amended effective May 1, 1998; April 15, 2005.]

RULE 50.4 REASSIGNMENT OF CASES

No case shall be reassigned except in the interest of justice and the efficient disposition of the business of the court. The chief judge may at any time, with the consent of the judges involved, reassign individual cases. Reassignment of cases to accommodate changes in the complement of judges shall be made in accordance with the order of the Board of Judges.

RULE 50.5 MISCELLANEOUS JUDGE

(a) Duties and Functions.

(1) Hear and determine:

(A) Matters requiring immediate action in cases already assigned to any judge of the court, if that judge is unavailable or otherwise unable to hear the matter only for such immediate emergency action; the case to remain with the assigned judge.

(B) Special proceedings which cannot be assigned in the ordinary course, including motions under Fed.R.Crim.Proc. 41 [1] made prior to indictment;

(C) Any other proceeding not part of or related to a case, including admissions to the bar and naturalization proceedings;

(D) Requests to be excused from service on the grand and petit juries; and

(E) All matters relating to proceedings before the grand jury;

(2) Impanel the grand jury, receive indictments, and refer criminal cases to the clerk for assignment pursuant to 50.2.

(b) Emergency Matters. The miscellaneous judge shall dispose of matters under paragraph (a)(1) only to the extent necessary and shall continue the case before the assigned judge. All applications for emergency action or relief shall disclose any prior application to a judge for the same or related relief and the outcome thereof.

[1] Fed.Rules Cr.Proc. Rule 1 et seq., 18 U.S.C.A.

RULE 50.6   CALENDARS

(a) Numbers; Order of Cases. The docket number of each case shall be the calendar number. No note of issue shall be required to place the case on the calendar. Each judge shall dispose of cases assigned to him or her as required by law and the efficient administration of justice.

(b) Preferences. Each judge shall schedule cases appearing on his or her docket in such order as seems just and appropriate, giving preference to the processing and disposition of the following:

(1) Habeas corpus petitions and motions attacking a federal sentence;

(2) Proceedings involving recalcitrant witnesses before federal courts or grand juries, under 28 U.S.C. § 1846;

(3) Actions for temporary or preliminary injunctive relief; and

(4) Any other action if good cause is shown.

(c) Publication of Calendars. Each court day the clerk shall post on bulletin boards throughout the courthouse and provide to legal newspapers for publication copies of the judges' calendars.

RULE 50.7   CONFERENCE

The judge assigned to any case may direct the attorneys to appear to discuss the case informally, to entertain oral motions, to discuss settlement, or to set a schedule for the events in the case, including completion of discovery, pretrial and trial.

CHAPTER 12 BANKRUPTCY RULES SUPPLEMENT

RULE 12–1. GENERAL APPLICABILITY OF BANKRUPTCY RULES

The Bankruptcy Rules and Forms,[1] now in effect or as later amended, as supplemented by these rules govern procedure in cases under chapter 12 of title 11 of the United States Code.[2]

[1] Federal Bankruptcy Rules 1 et seq. and the Official Bankruptcy Forms are set out in 11 U.S.C.A.

[2] 11 U.S.C.A. § 1201 et seq.

Historical and Statutory Notes

Note: Section 305(b) of the Bankruptcy Judges, United States Trustees, and Family Farmer Bankruptcy Act of 1986, Pub.L. No. 99–554, 100 Stat. 3088, provides that the Bankruptcy Rules in effect on the day of enactment shall apply to chapter 12 family farmer's debt adjustment cases "to the extent practicable and not inconsistent" with chapter 12. Amendments to the Bankruptcy Rules are currently under consideration by the Supreme Court. This rule provides that if the proposed amendments become effective, the rules as amended will apply to chapter 12 cases.

RULE 12–2. ADAPTATIONS OF CERTAIN BANKRUPTCY RULES

(1) The reference in Rule 1002(b)(1) to chapter 13 shall be read also as a reference to chapter 12.

(2) The reference in Rule 1007(a)(1) to a Chapter 13 Statement shall be read also as a reference to a Chapter 12 Statement, and the references in Rule 1007(c) and (h) to a chapter 13 case and a chapter 13 individual's debt adjustment case shall be read also as references to a chapter 12 case and a chapter 12 family farmer's debt adjustment case.

(3) The reference in Rule 1008 to Chapter 13 Statements shall be read also as a reference to Chapter 12 Statements.

(4) The references in Rule 1009 to a Chapter 13 Statement shall be read also as references to a Chapter 12 Statement.

(5) The references in Rule 1016 to an individual's debt adjustment case under chapter 13 shall be read also as references to a family farmer's debt adjustment case under chapter 12.

(6) The reference in Rule 1017(a) to § 1307(b) of the Code shall be read also as a reference to § 1208(b) of the Code.

(7) The references in Rule 1019 to a chapter 13 case shall be read also as references to a chapter 12 case.

(8) The reference in Rule 2004(b) to an individual's debt adjustment case under chapter 13 shall be read also as a reference to a family farmer's debt adjustment case under chapter 12.

(9) The references in Rule 2009(c)(3) to chapter 13 individual's debt adjustment cases and chapter 13 cases shall be read also as references to chapter 12 family farmer's debt adjustment cases and chapter 12 cases.

(10) The references in Rule 2015(b)(1) to chapter 13 trustee and debtor and chapter 13 individual's debt adjustment case shall be read also as references to chapter 12 trustee and debtor and chapter 12 individual's debt adjustment case.

(11) The reference in Rule 2018(b) to a chapter 13 case shall be read also as a reference to a chapter 12 case.

(12) The reference in Rule 3002(c) to a chapter 13 individual's debt adjustment case shall be read also as a reference to a chapter 12 family farmer's debt adjustment case.

(13) The references in the captions of Rule 3010 and Rule 3010(b) to chapter 13 individual's debt adjustment cases and chapter 13 cases shall be read also as references to chapter 12 family farmer's debt adjustment cases and chapter 12 cases.

(14) The reference in the caption to Rule 3011 to chapter 13 individual's debt adjustment cases shall be read also as a reference to chapter 12 family farmer's debt adjustment cases.

(15) The reference in Rule 3013 to § 1322(b)(1) of the Code shall be read also as a reference to § 1222(b)(1) of the Code.

(16) The reference in the caption of Rule 4007(c) to chapter 11 reorganization cases shall be read also as a reference to chapter 12 family farmer's debt adjustment cases.

(17) The reference in Rule 6006(b) to a chapter 13 individual's debt adjustment case shall be read also as a reference to a chapter 12 family farmer's debt adjustment case.

(18) The references in Rule 7001(5) and (8) to a chapter 13 plan shall be read also as references to a chapter 12 plan.

(19) The reference in Rule 7062 to § 1301 of the Code shall be read also as a reference to § 1201 of the Code.

(20) The reference in Rule 9011(a) to a Chapter 13 Statement shall be read also as a reference to a Chapter 12 Statement.

(21) The reference in Rule 9024 to § 1330 of the Code shall be read also as a reference to § 1230 of the Code.

(22) The reference in Rule X–1002(a)(1) to a Chapter 13 Statement shall be read also as a reference to a Chapter 12 Statement.

(23) The references in Rule X–1005(a)(3) to chapter 13 individual's debt adjustment cases and chapter 13 cases shall be read also as references to chapter 12 family farmer's debt adjustment cases and chapter 12 cases.

(24) The reference in Rule X–1007(b) to a chapter 13 individual's debt adjustment case shall be read also as a reference to a chapter 12 family farmer's debt adjustment case.

(25) Rule X–1008(a)(1) shall be read to include a reference to Rule 12–4.

Historical and Statutory Notes

Note: Many of the Bankruptcy Rules apply to cases under all chapters of the Code. Others apply only to specified chapters. Since the procedural aspects of chapters 12 and 13 are almost identical, the Bankruptcy Rules applicable to chapter 13 cases are appropriate for use in chapter 12 cases, and pursuant to § 305(b) of the 1986 Act, these rules are applicable to chapter 12 cases.

This rule provides that references in certain Bankruptcy Rules to chapter 13 or an aspect of a chapter 13 case shall be read to include a comparable reference to chapter 12 or an aspect of a chapter 12 case. Rule 1007(b) is omitted because Rule 12–3 covers the subject of filing schedules and statements.

Paragraph (16) makes Rule 4007(c), which fixes the time for filing a complaint under § 523(c) to determine the dischargeability of certain debts at 60 days from the first date set for the meeting of creditors, applicable in chapter 12 cases. Rule 4007(c) does not apply to chapter 13 cases because the § 523(c) debts are discharged pursuant to § 1328(a). Under § 1228(a) the chapter 12 discharge does not discharge the § 523(c) debts.

Rule 12–4 governs the filing and confirmation of a chapter 12 plan. Rule X–1008(a) requires that the United States trustee receive notice of and pleadings relating to important aspects of the case. Paragraph (25), in effect, expands Rule X–1008(a) to include the chapter 12 plan and confirmation matters.

RULE 12–3. SCHEDULES AND STATEMENTS REQUIRED

Unless the court orders otherwise, the debtor shall file with the court a Chapter 12 Statement conforming to Form No. 12–A or 12–B, whichever is appropriate, and a statement of financial affairs prepared as prescribed by Official Form No. 8. The budget included in the Chapter 12 Statement shall constitute the schedule of current income and expenditures.

Historical and Statutory Notes

Note: This rule is derived from Bankruptcy Rule 1007(b). Under § 109(f) of the Code, a chapter 12 debtor must have regular annual income. A plan may be confirmed over an objection only if the plan commits the debtor's projected disposable income for three years to payments under the plan. § 1225(b)(1)(B). The Chapter 12 Statement (Form No. 12–A or 12–B) required by this rule contains essential information for determining eligibility for commencing a chapter 12 case and the amount of the debtor's disposable income.

The time for the filing of the Chapter 12 Statement is prescribed by Bankruptcy Rule 1007(c). Rule 12–2(2).

RULE 12–4. FILING AND CONFIRMATION OF PLAN

(a) Time for Filing. The debtor may file a chapter 12 plan with the petition. If a plan is not filed with the petition, it shall be filed within 90 days thereafter unless the court pursuant to § 1221 of the Code extends the time for filing the plan. If required by the court, the debtor shall furnish a sufficient number of copies of the plan, or any court approved summary of the plan, to enable the clerk to include a copy of the plan or summary with the notice of the hearing on confirmation of the plan.

(b) Objections. Objections to confirmation of the plan shall be filed with the court and served on the debtor, the trustee, and on any other entity designated by the court, within a time fixed by the court. An objection to confirmation is governed by Bankruptcy Rule 9014.

(c) Hearing. After notice as provided in subdivision (d) of this rule, the court shall conduct and conclude a hearing within the time prescribed by § 1224 of the Code and rule on confirmation of the plan. If no objection is timely filed, the court may determine that the plan has been proposed in good faith and not by any means forbidden by law without receiving evidence on those issues.

(d) Notice. The clerk, or some other person as the court may direct, shall give the debtor, the trustee, all creditors, and all equity security holders notice by mail of the time fixed for filing objections to and the hearing to consider confirmation of the plan. Unless the court fixes a shorter period, notice of the hearing shall be given not less than 15 days before the hearing. A copy of the plan or a court approved summary of the plan shall accompany the notice.

(e) Order of Confirmation. The order of confirmation shall conform to Official Form No. 31 and notice of entry thereof shall be mailed promptly by the clerk, or some other person as the court may direct, to the debtor, the trustee, all creditors, all equity security holders, and other parties in interest.

(f) Retained Power. Notwithstanding the entry of the order of confirmation, the court may enter all orders necessary to administer the estate.

Historical and Statutory Notes

Note: Section 1221 of the Code requires that the plan be filed within 90 days of the order for relief. The date of the order for relief is the date of the filing of the chapter 12 petition. See § 301 of the Code. Involuntary petitions are not permitted under chapter 12. Section 1224 requires that the confirmation hearing be held after "expedited notice." The confirmation hearing must be concluded within 45 days after the plan is filed unless the court extends the period for cause. This rule is derived from Bankruptcy Rules 3015 and 3020 and supplements the statutory requirements.

Subdivision (a) is derived from Bankruptcy Rule 3015. An extension of the time for the filing of a plan may be granted pursuant to § 1221 if the court finds "an extension is substantially justified." A summary of the plan may not be distributed unless approved by the court.

Subdivision (b) is derived from Bankruptcy Rule 3020(b)(1). Notice of the time for filing objections shall be included in the notice given pursuant to subdivision (d) of this rule.

Subdivision (c) is derived from Bankruptcy Rule 3020(b)(2). Section 1224 requires that the confirmation hearing be concluded within 45 days unless the court grants an extension for cause.

Subdivision (d). Section 1224 requires that there be "expedited notice" of the confirmation hearing. This rule establishes 15 days as the notice period. The court may shorten this time on its own motion or on motion of a party in interest. The coordination of the hearing date and the date for filing objections is determined by the court. The notice should include both dates and be accompanied by a copy of the plan or a court approved summary of the plan.

Subdivisions (e) and (f) are derived from Bankruptcy Rule 3020(c) and (d).

FORMS
FORM NO. 12–A. CHAPTER 12 STATEMENT
OF INDIVIDUAL DEBTOR

[Caption as in Official Form No. 1]

Chapter 12 Statement of Individual Debtor

[Each applicable question shall be answered or the failure to answer explained. If the answer is "none" or "not applicable," so state. If additional space is needed for the answer to any question, a separate sheet, properly identified and made a part hereof, should be used and attached.

The term "original petition," used in the following questions, shall mean the original petition filed under § 301 of the Code or, if the chapter 12 case was converted from another chapter of the Code, shall mean the petition by or against you which originated the first case.

Individual debtors must complete all questions. This form should be completed whether a married individual or a married individual and a spouse filed the petition. For convenience, the word "debtors" is used to refer to a married individual and spouse who have filed a chapter 12 petition. If such debtors' answers to any question are different, their respective answer shall be separately designated as the answer of the husband and the answer of the wife.]

1. Filing Status. (Check appropriate status.)
    Unmarried individual
    Married individual and spouse are debtors   _____
    Married individual is the sole debtor   _____
2. Name and residence.
    a. Full name
        Debtor or debtors. . . . .
        . . . .
        Spouse who is not a debtor . . . .
        . . . .
    b. Residence of the debtor or debtors
        (1) Mailing address of debtor or debtors . . . .
        . . . .
        City or town, state and zip code.
        (2) Mailing address of spouse who is not a debtor
        . . . .
        City or town, state and zip code.
        (3) Telephone number including area code
        Debtor or debtors . . . .
        . . . .
        Spouse who is not a debtor . . . .
        . . . .
3. Summary of debt.
    Give amounts as of the date of the filing of the petition.
    a. Noncontingent, liquidated debt.
        (1) Amount of noncontingent, liquidated debt from farming operations. $. . . . .
        (2) Amount of noncontingent, liquidated non-farm debt $. . . . .
        (3) Total noncontingent, liquidated debt $. . . . .
    b. Contingent or unliquidated debt.
        (1) Amount of contingent or unliquidated debt from farming operations $. . . . .
        (2) Amount of contingent or unliquidated non-farm debt $. . . . .
        (3) Total contingent or unliquidated debt $. . . . .

   c.   <u>Principal Residence.</u>
Amount of non-farm debt that is secured by the principal residence of the debtor or debtors $....

4.   <u>Summary of income from last tax year.</u>
   a.   Debtor or debtors' last tax year before the current tax year was calendar year 19____.
   b.   Debtor or debtors' gross income for the last tax year before the current tax year $....
   c.   Amount of debtor or debtors' gross income for last tax year before the current tax year from farming operations $....

5.   <u>Nature of farming operations.</u> (Place an "X" on the appropriate line to identify each type of farming operation in which the debtor or debtors are engaged and supply the other information requested below.)
   a.   Crops   _____
        Kind(s)...................................
        Acres owned..............leased ....
   b.   Dairy operations   _____
        Acres owned..............leased ....
   c.   Ranching   _____
        Kind(s)...................................
        Acres owned..............leased ....
   d.   Poultry   _____
        Kind(s)...................................
        Acres owned..............leased ....
   e.   Livestock   _____
        Kind(s)...................................
        Acres owned..............leased ....
   f.   Production of poultry products   _____
        Kind(s)...................................
   g.   Production of livestock products   _____
        Kind(s)...................................

6.   <u>Non-farming activities.</u>
   a.   If a debtor or debtors are self employed in other than farming operations, state the nature thereof

        ....
        ....
   b.   If a debtor or debtors are employed by others in either farming operations or non-farming activity, state the nature thereof

        ....
        ....
   c.   If a spouse who is not a debtor is either self employed in other than farming operations or employed by others in either farming operations or non-farming activity, state the nature thereof.

        ....
        ....
   d.   Give the name, address, and telephone number of each present employer of the debtor or debtors.

        ....
        ....
   e.   Give the name, address, and telephone number of each present employer of a spouse who is not a debtor.

        ....
   f.   State how long the debtor or debtors have been employed by each present employer.

        ....

    g. How long has the spouse who is not a debtor been employed by each present employer?

. . . .

7. <u>Budget.</u>

    a. <u>Current income.</u>

      (1) Estimated gross income from farming operations for the next twelve months. (Include all government program payments.) $. . . . .

      (2) Income from non-farming activities:

        Give estimated average monthly income of debtor and spouse, consisting of:

	Debtor	Spouse
(A) Gross pay from employer (wages, salary, or commissions)	$.	$. . . . .
(B) Take-home pay from employer (Gross pay less all deductions)	$.	$. . . . .
(C) Regular income available from self employment not included in item 7a(1)	$.	$. . . . .
(D) Other income:		
Interest and dividends	$.	$. . . . .
From real estate or personal property	$.	$. . . . .
Social security	$.	$. . . . .
Pension or other retirement income	$.	$. . . . .
Other (specify)		
. . . .	$.	$. . . . .
(E) Alimony, maintenance, or support payments:		
Payable to the debtor for the debtor's use	$.	$. . . . .
Payable to the debtor for support of another (Attach additional sheet listing the name, age, and relationship to the debtor of persons for whose benefit payments are made)	$.	$. . . . .
(F) Total estimated average monthly income from non-farming activities	$.	$. . . . .

If you anticipate receiving additional income on other than a monthly basis in the next year (such as an income tax refund) attach an additional sheet of paper and explain.

If you anticipate a substantial change in your income in the immediate future, attach an additional sheet of paper and explain.

      (4)[1] Total estimated income for next twelve months (twelve times total estimated average monthly income from non-farming activities (item 7a(2)(F)) with any adjustment for a substantial change in such income plus income from farming operations (item 7a(1)). $. . . . .

    b. <u>Current expenses related to farming operations.</u>

      (1) Real Property expenses. (Include expenses of the home of the debtor if the home is located on the debtor's property used in farming operations.)

        Give estimated current monthly expenditures consisting of:

        (A) Mortgage payment(s) $. . . . .

        (B) Rental or lease payment(s) $. . . . .

        (C) Real estate taxes $. . . . .

        (D) Repairs & upkeep $. . . . .

          Total real property expenses $. . . . .

    (2) Other expenses.
        Give estimated current monthly expenditures for
          the debtor or debtors consisting of:
        (A) Installment or lease payments on equipment
            Specify .... $.....
                          .... $.....
                          .... $.....
                          .... $.....
            Total Monthly installment or lease payments
              on equipment .... $.....
        (B) Maintenance of equipment
            Service contracts .... $.....
            Other (specify)
                          .... $.....
                          .... $.....
            Total maintenance of equipment .... $.....
        (C) Utilities:
                Electricity .... $.....
                Fuel .... $.....
                Water .... $.....
                Telephone (business use) .... $.....
            Total utilities .... $.....
        (D) Production expenses:
                Labor (gross) .... $.....
                Seed .... $.....
                Fertilizer .... $.....
                Feed .... $.....
                Pesticides .... $.....
                Veterinary, etc. .... $.....
                Other (specify)
                          .... $.....
                          .... $.....
                          .... $.....
            Total production expenses .... $.....
        (E) Miscellaneous expenses
            Give any expenses of farming operation not
              reflected above.
              (i) .... $.....
              (ii) .... $.....
              (iii) .... $.....
            Total miscellaneous expenses .... $.....
    (3) Total estimated monthly expenses. .... $.....
    (4) Total current yearly expenses related to farming
        operations (twelve times total estimated monthly
        expenses (item 7c(3))). .... $.....
  c. Current expenses not related to farming operations.
  Give estimated average current monthly expenditures for the individual debtor or
debtors, consisting of:
        (1) Home expenses. (Complete this item c(1) only if
            the home is located on property not used in
            farming operations)
          (A) Rent or home loan payment (including any
             assessment or maintenance fee) ...... $.....
          (B) Real estate taxes .... $.....
          (C) Utilities:
                Electricity .... $.....
                Gas .... $.....
                Water .... $.....
                Telephone (personal use) .... $.....
                Other (specify) .... $.....
            Total utilities .... $.....

      (D) Home maintenance (repairs and upkeep) $.....

      (E) Total of all home expenses $....

  (2) Other expenses not related to farming activities.

      (A) Taxes (not deducted from wages or included in home loan payment or included in real estate taxes) $.....

      (B) Alimony, maintenance, or support payments (attach additional sheet listing name, age, and relationship of beneficiaries) $.....

      (C) Insurance (not deducted from wages)

          Life $.....

          Health $.....

          Auto $.....

          Homeowner's or Renter's $.....

          Other (specify)

          .... $.....

          Total insurance expenses $....

      (D) Installment payments:

          Auto $.....

          Other (specify)

          .... $.....

          .... $.....

          Total installment payments $....

      (E) Transportation (not including auto payments) $....

      (F) Education (including tuition and school books) $....

      (G) Food $....

      (H) Clothing $....

      (I) Medical, dental, and medicines $....

      (J) Telephone $....

      (K) Laundry and cleaning $....

      (L) Newspapers, periodicals and books $....

      (M) Recreation, clubs and entertainment $....

      (N) Charitable contributions $....

      (O) Other expenses (specify)

          .... $....

          .... $....

      (P) Total of other expenses related to non-farming activities $....

1 Pub. Note: There is no subdivision (3) in original.

If you anticipate a substantial change in your expenses in the immediate future, attach additional sheet of paper and explain.

  (3) Total expenses for next twelve months related to the debtor's non-farming activities (twelve times the total estimated current monthly expenses (item 7c(1)(E) plus item 7c(2)(P)) with an adjustment for any substantial change) $....

  d. Summary of budget information.

      (A) Total income for next twelve months (item 7a(4)) $....

      (B) Total estimated expenses for next twelve months (item 7b(4) plus 7c(3)).   ($....)

          Available income ((A) minus (B)) $.....

8. Dependents.

The debtor supports the following dependents (other than the debtor's spouse):

Name	Age	Relationship to Debtor
....	......	....
....	......	....
....	......	....
....	......	....

9. Payment of Attorney.
    a. How much have you agreed to pay or what property
       have you agreed to transfer to your attorney in
       connection with the case? $. . . . .
    b. How much have you paid or what have you transferred
       to the attorney? $. . . . .

10. Tax refunds and government program payments. (To be answered by debtor
    or debtors and, unless spouses are separated, by a spouse who is not a
    debtor.)
    To what tax refunds (income or other) and government program payments, if
      any, is either of you, or may either of you be, entitled? (Give particulars,
      including information as to any refunds payable jointly to you and any other
      person. All such refunds should also be listed in Item 18(b).)
    . . . .
    . . . .

11. Financial accounts, certificates of deposit and safe deposit boxes. (To be
    answered by debtor or debtors and, unless spouses are separated, by a
    spouse who is not a debtor.)
    a. Does either of you currently have any accounts or certificates of deposit or
       shares in banks, savings and loan, thrift, building and loan and homestead
       associations, credit unions, brokerage houses, pension funds and the like?
       (If so, give name and address of each institution, number and nature of
       account, current balance, and name and address of every other person
       authorized to make withdrawals from the account. Such accounts should
       also be listed in Item 18(b).)
       . . . .
       . . . .

    b. Does either of you currently keep any safe deposit boxes or other
       depositories? (If so, give name and address of bank or other depository,
       name and address of every other person who has a right of access thereto,
       and a brief description of the contents thereof, which should also be listed
       in Item 18(b).)
       . . . .
       . . . .

12. Prior Bankruptcy.
    What cases under the Bankruptcy Act or Bankruptcy Code have previously
      been brought by or against you or either spouse filing a petition? (State the
      location of the bankruptcy court, the nature and number of each case, the
      date when it was filed, and whether a discharge was granted or denied, the
      case was dismissed, or a composition, arrangement, or plan was confirmed.)
    . . . .
    . . . .

13. Foreclosures, executions, and attachments. (To be answered by debtor or
    debtors and, unless spouses are separated, by a spouse who is not a debtor.)
    a. Is any of the property of either of you, including real estate, involved in a
       foreclosure proceeding, in or out of court? (If so, identify the property and
       the person foreclosing.)
       . . . .
       . . . .

    b. Has any property or income of either of you been attached, garnished, or
       seized under any legal or equitable process within the 90 days immediately
       preceding the filing of the original petition herein? (If so, describe the
       property seized, or person garnished, and who filed the law suit.)
       . . . .
       . . . .

14. Repossessions and returns. (To be answered by debtor or debtors and, unless
    spouses are separated, by a spouse who is not a debtor.)
    Has any property of either of you been returned to, repossessed, or seized by
      the seller or by any other party, including a landlord, during the 90 days

immediately preceding the filing of the original petition herein? (If so, give particulars, including the name and address of the party taking the property and its description and value.)

....

....

15. Transfers of Property. (To be answered by debtor or debtors and, unless spouses are separated, by a spouse who is not a debtor.)
    a. Has either of you made any gifts, other than ordinary and usual presents to family members and charitable donations, during the year immediately preceding the filing of the original petition herein? (If so, give names and addresses of donees and dates, description and value of gifts.)

....

....

    b. Has either of you made any other transfer, absolute or for the purpose of security, or any other disposition, of real or personal property during the year immediately preceding the filing of the original petition herein? (Give a description of the property, the date of the transfer or disposition, to whom transferred or how disposed of, and, if the transferee is a relative or insider, the relationship, the consideration, if any, received therefor, and the disposition of such consideration.)

....

....

16. Debts. (To be answered by debtor or debtors and by a spouse who is not a debtor.)
    a. Debts Having Priority.

(1) Nature of claim	(2) Name of creditor and complete mailing address including zip code	(3) Specify when claim was incurred and the consideration therefor: whether claim is subject to setoff, evidenced by a judgment, negotiable instrument, or other writing	(4) Indicate if claim is contingent, unliquidated, or disputed	(5) Amount of claim
....	....	....	....	....
....	....	....	....	....
....	....	....	....	....
....	....	....	....	....
....	....	....	....	....

1. Wages, salary, and commissions, including vacation, severance and sick leave pay owing to employees not exceeding $2,000 to each, earned within 90 days before filing of petition or cessation of business (if earlier specify date). $.....
2. Contributions to employee benefit plans for services rendered within 180 days before filing of petition or cessation of business (if earlier specify date). $.....
3. Deposits by individuals, not exceeding $900 for each purchase, lease, or rental of property or services for personal, family, or household use that were not delivered or provided. $.....
4. Taxes owing [itemize by type of tax and taxing authority]
    (A) To the United States $.....
    (B) To any state $.....
    (C) To any other taxing authority $.....

                                             Total $.....

    b. Secured Debts. List all debts which are or may be secured by real or personal property. (Indicate in the next to last column, if debt payable in installments, the amount of each installment, the installment period (monthly, weekly, or otherwise) and number of installments in arrears, if any. Indicate in last column whether husband or wife solely liable, or whether you are jointly liable.)

Creditor's name, account number and complete mailing address including zip code	Consideration or basis for debt	Amount claimed by creditor	If disputed, amount admitted by debtor	Description of collateral [include year and make of automobile]	Installment amount, period, and number of installments in arrears	Husband or wife solely liable, or jointly liable
....	....	....	....	....	....	....
....	....	....	....	....	....	....
....	....	....	....	....	....	....
....	....	....	....	....	....	....
....	....	....	....	....	....	....
....	....	....	....	....	....	....
					Total secured debts	....

c. <u>Unsecured Debts</u>. List all other debts, liquidated and unliquidated, including taxes, attorney fees, and tort claims.

Creditor's name, account number and complete mailing address including zip code	Consideration or basis for debt	Amount claimed by creditor	If disputed, amount admitted by debtor	Husband or wife solely liable, or jointly liable
....	....	....	....	....
....	....	....	....	....
....	....	....	....	....
....	....	....	....	....
....	....	....	....	....
		Total unsecured debts	....	

17. <u>Codebtors</u>. (To be answered by debtor or debtors and by a spouse who is not a debtor.)

    a. Are any other persons liable, as cosigners, guarantors, or in any other manner, on any of the debts of either of you or is either of you so liable on the debts of others? (If so, give particulars, indicating which spouse is liable and including names of creditors, nature of debt, names and addresses of codebtors, and their relationship, if any, to you.)

       ....

       ....

    b. If so, have the codebtors made any payments on the debts? (Give name of each codebtor and amount paid by codebtor.)

       ....

       ....

    c. Has either of you made any payments on the debts? (If so, specify total amount paid to each creditor, whether paid by husband or wife, and name of codebtor.)

       ....

       ....

       ....

18. <u>Property and Exemptions</u>. (To be answered by debtor or debtors and a spouse who is not a debtor.)

    a. <u>Real Property</u>. List all real property owned at date of filing of original petition herein. (Indicate in next to last column whether an exemption is claimed and in last column whether owned solely by husband or wife, or jointly.)

Description and location of property	Name of any co-owner other than spouse	Present market value (without deduction for mortgage or other security interest)	Amount of mortgage or other security interest on this property	Name of mortgagee or other secured creditor	Value claimed exempt (specify federal or state statute creating the exemption)	Owned solely by husband or by wife, or jointly
....	....	....	....	....	....	....
....	....	....	....	....	....	....
....	....	....	....	....	....	....
....	....	....	....	....	....	....
....	....	....	....	....	....	....

   b. <u>Personal Property</u>. List all other property owned by debtor or debtors and spouse who is not a debtor at date of filing of original petition herein. (Indicate in the next to last column whether an exemption is claimed and in last column whether owned solely by husband or wife, or jointly.)

Description	Location of property if not at debtor's residence	Name of any coowner other than spouse	Present market value (without deduction for mortgage or other security interest)	Amount of mortgage or other security interest on this property	Name of mortgagee or other secured creditor	Value claimed exempt (specify federal or state statute creating the exemption)	Owned solely by husband or wife or jointly
Autos [give year and make]							
....	....						
Farming equipment [give type & make]							
....	....	....	....	....	....	....	....
Household goods							
....	....	....	....	....	....	....	....
Personal effects							
....	....	....	....	....	....	....	....
Cash or financial account							
....	....	....	....	....	....	....	....
Other [specify]							
....	....	....	....	....	....	....	....

Unsworn Declaration under Penalty of Perjury of Individual to Chapter 12 Statement

[To be signed by debtor or debtors]

I, ..., [an unmarried individual] [*or* a married individual] [*if both husband and wife are debtors* and I, ..., the spouse], declare under penalty of perjury that I have read the answers contained in the foregoing statement, consisting of ... sheets, and that they are true and complete to the best of my knowledge, information, and belief.

Executed on ....

....
Debtor

....
Debtor

Historical and Statutory Notes

  Note: A Chapter 12 debtor must also prepare and file a statement of affairs as prescribed by Official Form No. 8. Rule 12.3.

FORM NO. 12–B. CHAPTER 12 STATEMENT OF PARTNERSHIP OR CORPORATE DEBTOR

[Caption as in Official Form No. 1]

Chapter 12 Statement
of Partnership or Corporate Debtor

[Each applicable question shall be answered or the failure to answer explained. If the answer is "none" or "not applicable," so state. If additional space is needed for the answer to any question, a separate sheet, properly identified and made a part hereof, should be used and attached.

The term "original petition," used in the following questions, shall mean the original petition filed under § 301 of the Code or, if the chapter 12 case was converted from another chapter of the Code, shall mean the petition by or against you which originated the first case.

The questions are to be addressed to, and shall be answered on behalf of, the corporation or partnership, and the statement shall be certified by a duly authorized officer of the corporation or by a member of the partnership.]

1. Filing Status. (Place an "X" on the appropriate line.)
    Corporation   _____
    Partnership   _____
    Limited Partnership   _____
2. Name, and other information.
    a. Full name . . . .
    b. Principal place of business of the debtor
        (1) Mailing address . . . .
             . . . .
             City or town, state and zip code.
        (2) Telephone number including area code
             . . . .
        (3) Date and the state of incorporation of the corporate debtor
             . . . .
        (4) Date and the state law under which the partnership debtor was formed
             . . . .
             . . . .
        (5) Name of the family or name of the family and relatives that conduct farming operations and own more than 50% of the stock or equity of the corporate or partnership debtor
             . . . .
             . . . .

3. Summary of debt.
    Give amounts as of the date of the filing of the petition.
    a. Noncontingent, liquidated debt.
        (1) Amount of noncontingent, liquidated debt from farming operations $. . . . .
        (2) Amount of noncontingent, liquidated non-farm debt $. . . . .
        (3) Total noncontingent, liquidated debt $. . . . .
    b. Contingent or unliquidated debt.
        (1) Amount of contingent or unliquidated debt from farming operations $. . . . .
        (2) Amount of contingent or unliquidated non-farm debt $. . . . .
        (3) Total contingent or unliquidated debt $. . . . .

    c.   <u>Principal Residence.</u>

        Amount of non-farm debt that is secured by a dwelling owned by the corporate or partnership debtor and used as a principal residence by a shareholder or partner of the debtor $.....

4. <u>Assets.</u>

    a.   Total value of assets $.....

    b.   Value of assets related to farming operations $.....

5. <u>Summary of income from last tax year.</u>

    a.   Debtor's last tax year before the current tax year was calendar year 19___ [or fiscal year _____ _____, 19___ to _____ _____, 19___]

    b.   Debtor's gross income for the last tax year before the current tax year $.....

    c.   Amount of debtor's gross income for last tax year before the current tax year from farming operations $.....

6. <u>Nature of farming operations.</u> (Place an "X" on the appropriate line to identify each type of farming operation in which the debtor is engaged and supply the other information requested below.)

    a.   Crops   _____

        Kind(s)..

        Acres owned...............leased...............

    b.   Dairy operations   _____

        Acres owned...............leased...............

    c.   Ranching   _____

        Kind(s)..

        Acres owned...............leased...............

    d.   Poultry   _____

        Kind(s)..

        Acres owned...............leased...............

    e.   Livestock   _____

        Kind(s)..

        Acres owned...............leased...............

    f.   Production of poultry products   _____

        Kind(s)..

    g.   Production of livestock products   _____

        Kind(s)..

7. <u>Non-farming activities.</u>

    If the debtor is engaged in business other than farming operations, state the nature thereof

    ....

    ....

8. <u>Budget.</u>

    a.   <u>Current income.</u>

        (1) Estimated gross income from farming operations for the next twelve months. (Include all government program payments.) $.....

        (2) Estimated gross income from non-farming activities for the next twelve months. $.....

        (3) Total income $.....

    b.   <u>Current expenses related to farming operations.</u>

        (1) Real Property expenses. <u>(Include expenses of a home of a shareholder or partner of the debtor if the home is located on the debtor's property used in farming operations.)</u>

        Give estimated current monthly expenditures consisting of:

        (A) Mortgage payment(s) $.....

        (B) Rental or lease payment(s) $.....

    (C) Real estate taxes $.....

    (D) Repairs & upkeep $.....

          Total real property expenses $.....

(2) Other expenses.

    Give estimated current average monthly expenditures consisting of:

    (A) Installment or lease payments on equipment

        Specify .... $.....

                .... $.....

                .... $.....

                .... $.....

        Total Monthly installment or lease payments on equipment $.....

    (B) Maintenance of equipment

        Service contracts $.....

        Other (specify)

        .... $.....

        .... $.....

        Total maintenance of equipment $.....

    (C) Utilities

        Electricity $.....

        Fuel $.....

        Water $.....

        Telephone (business use) $.....

        Total utilities $.....

    (D) Production expenses:

        Labor (gross) $.....

        Seed $.....

        Fertilizer $.....

        Feed $.....

        Pesticides $.....

        Veterinary, etc. $.....

        Other (specify)

        .... $.....

        .... $.....

        .... $.....

        Total production expenses $.....

    (E) Miscellaneous expenses

        Give any expenses of farming operation not reflected above

        (i) .... $.....

        (ii) .... $.....

        (iii) .... $.....

        Total miscellaneous expenses $.....

(3) Total estimated monthly expenses $.....

(4) Total current expenses related to farming operations

    (twelve times total estimated monthly expenses (item 8c(3)) $.....

c. Current expenses related to non-farming activities.

    Estimated expenses of the debtor's non-farming activities for the next twelve months $.....

d. Summary of budget information.

    (A) Debtor's total estimated income for next twelve months (item 8a(3)). $.....

    (B) Debtor's total estimated expenses for next twelve months (item 8b(4) plus item 8c). ($....)

        Available Income ((A) minus (B)) $.....

9. <u>Payment of Attorney</u>.
   a. How much has the debtor agreed to pay or what property has the debtor agreed to transfer to its attorney in connection with the case? $.....
   b. How much has the debtor paid or what has the debtor transferred to its attorney? $.....

10. <u>Tax refunds and government program payments</u>.
    To what tax refunds (income or other) and government program payments, if any, is the debtor entitled? (Give particulars, including information as to any refunds payable jointly to the debtor and any other person. All such refunds should also be listed in Item 18(b)).
    ....

11. <u>Financial accounts, certificates of deposit and safe deposit boxes</u>.
    a. Does the debtor currently have any accounts or certificates of deposit or shares in banks, savings and loan, thrift, building and loan and homestead associations, credit unions, brokerage houses, pension funds and the like? (If so, give name and address of each institution, number and nature of account, current balance, and name and address of every person authorized to make withdrawals from the account. Such accounts should also be listed in Item 18(b).)
    ....

    b. Does the debtor currently have any safe deposit boxes or other depositories? (If so, give name and address of bank or other depository, name and address of every person who has a right of access thereto, and a brief description of the contents thereof, which should also be listed in Item 18(b).)
    ....

12. <u>Prior Bankruptcy</u>.
    What cases under the Bankruptcy Act or Bankruptcy Code have previously been brought by or against the debtor? (State the location of the bankruptcy court, the nature and number of each case, the date when it was filed, and whether a discharge was granted or denied, whether the case was dismissed, or whether an arrangement or plan was confirmed.)
    ....

13. <u>Foreclosures, executions, and attachments</u>.
    a. Is any of the property of debtor, including real estate, involved in a foreclosure proceeding, in or out of court? (If so, identify the property and the person foreclosing.)
    ....

    b. Has any property or income of debtor been attached, garnished, or seized under any legal or equitable process within the 90 days immediately preceding the filing of the original petition herein? (If so, describe the property seized, or person garnished, and who filed the law suit.)
    ....

14. <u>Repossessions and returns</u>.
    Has any property of debtor been returned to or been repossessed or seized by the seller or by any other party, including a landlord, during the 90 days immediately preceding the filing of the original petition herein? (If so, give

particulars, including the name and address of the party obtaining the property and its description and value.)

....

15. Transfers of Property.
   a. Has the debtor made any gifts, during the year immediately preceding the filing of the original petition herein? (If so, give names and addresses of donees and dates, description and value of gifts.)

....

   b. Has the debtor made any other transfer, absolute or for the purpose of security, or any other disposition, of real or personal property during the year immediately preceding the filing of the original petition herein? (Give a description of the property, the date of the transfer or disposition, to whom transferred or how disposed of, and, if the transferee is an insider, the relationship, the consideration, if any, received therefor, and the disposition of such consideration.)

....
....

16. Debts.
   a. Debts Having Priority.

(1) Nature of claim	(2) Name of creditor and complete mailing address including zip code	(3) Specify when claim was incurred and the consideration therefor: whether claim is subject to setoff, evidenced by a judgment, negotiable instrument, or other writing	(4) Indicate if claim is contingent, unliquidated, or disputed	(5) Amount of claim
....	....	....	....	....
....	....	....	....	....
....	....	....	....	....
....	....	....	....	....
....	....	....	....	....

1. Wages, salary, and commissions, including vacation, severance and sick leave pay owing to employees not exceeding $2,000 to each earned within 90 days before filing of petition or cessation of business (if earlier specify date). $.....

2. Contributions to employee benefit plans for services rendered within 180 days before filing of petition or cessation of business (if earlier specify date). $.....

3. Deposits by individuals, not exceeding $900 for each purchase, lease, or rental of property or services for personal, family, or household use that were not delivered or provided. $.....

4. Taxes owing [itemize by type of tax and taxing authority]
   (A) To the United States $.....
   (B) To any state $.....
   (C) To any other taxing authority $.....

   Total $.....

b. Secured Debts. List all debts which are or may be secured by real or personal property. (Indicate in the last column, if debt payable in installments, the amount of each installment, the installment period (monthly, weekly, or otherwise) and number of installments in arrears, if any.)

Creditor's name, account number and complete mailing address including zip code	Consideration or basis for debt	Amount claimed by creditor	If disputed, amount admitted by debtor	Description of collateral [include year and make of vehicles]	Installment amount, period, and number of installments in arrears
....	....	....	....	....	....
....	....	....	....	....	....
....	....	....	....	....	....
....	....	....	....	....	....
....	....	....	....	....	....
			Total secured debts	....	

c. Unsecured Debts. List all other debts, liquidated and unliquidated, including taxes, attorney fees, and tort claims.

Creditor's name, account number and complete mailing address including zip code	Consideration or basis for debt	Amount claimed by creditor	If disputed, amount admitted by debtor
....	....	....	....
....	....	....	....
....	....	....	....
....	....	....	....
....	....	....	....
		Total unsecured debts	....

17. Codebtors.

a. Are any other persons liable, as cosigners, guarantors, or in any other manner, on any of the debts of the debtor or is the debtor so liable on the debts of others? (If so, give particulars including names of creditors, nature of debt, names and addresses of codebtors, and their relationship, if any, to the debtor.)

....

....

b. If so, have the codebtors made any payments on the debts? (Give name of each codebtor and amount paid by codebtor.)

....

....

c. Has the debtor made any payments on the debts? (If so, specify total amount paid to each creditor and name of codebtor.)

....

....

18. Property.

a. Real Property. List all real property owned at date of filing of original petition herein.

Description and location of property	Name of any co-owner	Present market value (without deduction for mortgage or other security interest)	Amount of mortgage or other security interest on this property	Name of mortgagee or other secured creditor
....	....	....	....	....
....	....	....	....	....
....	....	....	....	....

. . . .	. . . .	. . . .	. . . .	. . . .
. . . .	. . . .	. . . .	. . . .	. . . .
. . . .	. . . .	. . . .	. . . .	. . . .

b. <u>Personal Property</u>. List all other property owned by debtor at date of filing of original petition herein.

Description	Location of property if not at debtor's farm	Name of any co-owner	Present market value (without deduction for mortgage or other security interest)	Amount of mortgage or other security interest on this property	Name of mortgagee or other secured creditor
Autos [give year and make]					
. . . .	. . . .	. . . .	. . . .	. . . .	. . . .
. . . .	. . . .	. . . .	. . . .	. . . .	. . . .
Farming equipment [give type and make]					
. . . .	. . . .	. . . .	. . . .	. . . .	. . . .
. . . .	. . . .	. . . .	. . . .	. . . .	. . . .
Other equipment and office furnishings					
. . . .	. . . .	. . . .	. . . .	. . . .	. . . .
. . . .	. . . .	. . . .	. . . .	. . . .	. . . .
Cash or financial account					
. . . .	. . . .	. . . .	. . . .	. . . .	. . . .
. . . .	. . . .	. . . .	. . . .	. . . .	. . . .
Other [specify]					
. . . .	. . . .	. . . .	. . . .	. . . .	. . . .
. . . .	. . . .	. . . .	. . . .	. . . .	. . . .

Unsworn Declaration under Penalty of Perjury on Behalf of Corporation or Partnership to Chapter 12 Statement

I, ..., [the president or other officer or an authorized agent of the corporation] [or a member <u>or</u> an authorized agent of the partnership] named as debtor in this case, declare under penalty of perjury that I have read the answers contained in the foregoing statement, consisting of . . . sheets, and that they are true and correct to the best of my knowledge, information, and belief.

Executed on . . . .

Signature: . . . .

Historical and Statutory Notes

Note: A chapter 12 debtor must also prepare and file a statement of affairs as prescribed by Official Form No. 8. Rule 12.3.

*

UNITED STATES BANKRUPTCY COURT
FOR THE SOUTHERN DISTRICT OF NEW YORK

Effective April 15, 1997

Including Amendments Received Through
September 15, 2008

Research Note

These rules may be searched electronically on Westlaw in the NY-RULES database; updates to these rules may be found on Westlaw in NY-RULESUPDATES. For search tips, and a detailed summary of database content, consult the Westlaw Scope Screen of each database.

PART I. COMMENCEMENT OF CASE; PROCEEDINGS RELATING TO PETITION AND ORDER FOR RELIEF

Rule
1001–1. Short Title; Applicability.
1002–1. Filing of Petition.
1005–1. Debtor's Address in Petition.
1007–1. List of Creditors and Equity Security Holders.
1007–2. Debtor's Affidavit and Proposed Case Conference Order to be Filed in Chapter 11 Cases.
1007–3. Debtor's Corporate Ownership Statement.
1009–1. Notice of Amendment of Schedules in Chapter 11 Cases.
1014–1. Transfer of Cases.
1020–1. Small Business Election [Repealed].
1073–1. Assignment of Cases and Proceedings.
1074–1. Corporate Resolution; Partnership Statement.

PART II. OFFICERS AND ADMINISTRATION; NOTICES; MEETINGS; EXAMINATIONS; ELECTIONS; ATTORNEYS AND ACCOUNTANTS

2002–1. Notice to United States Trustee.
2002–2. Notice of Proposed Action or Order When Not Proceeding by Motion.
2007.1–1. Election of Trustee in Chapter 11 Cases.
2014–1. Employment of Professional Persons.
2015–1. Storage of Books and Records.
2016–1. Compensation of Professionals.
2016–2. Compensation or Reimbursement of Expenses in Chapter 7 Cases.
2090–1. Admission to Practice; Withdrawal As Attorney of Record.

PART III. CLAIMS AND DISTRIBUTION TO CREDITORS AND EQUITY INTEREST HOLDERS; PLANS

3003–1. Requests for Orders Establishing Deadlines for Filing Claims in Chapter 11 Cases.
3008–1. Reconsideration of Claims.

Rule
3015–1. Chapter 13 Plans: Payments Exceeding Three Years; Treatment of Debtor's Attorney's Fees As Administrative Expense; Service.
3015–2. Modification of Chapter 13 Plan Before Confirmation.
3015–3. Hearing on Confirmation of Chapter 13 Plan.
3017–1. Proposed Disclosure Statements in Chapter 9 and Chapter 11 Cases: Transmittal and Disclaimer.
3018–1. Certification of Acceptance or Rejection of Plans in Chapter 9 and Chapter 11 Cases.
3018–2. Acceptances or Rejections of Plan Obtained Before Petition in Chapter 11 Cases.
3019–1. Modification of Chapter 11 Plan Before Close of Voting.
3020–1. Time for Objecting to Confirmation in Chapter 9 and Chapter 11 Cases; Withdrawal of Objections.
3021–1. Postconfirmation Requirements in Chapter 11 Cases.
3022–1. Closing Reports in Chapter 11 Cases.

PART IV. THE DEBTOR: DUTIES AND BENEFITS

4001–1. Relief From Automatic Stay.
4001–2. Requests for Use of Cash Collateral or to Obtain Credit.
4001–3. Requests for Use of Cash Collateral or to Obtain Credit—Repealed.
4003–1. Exemptions.
4004–1. Automatic Extension of Time to File Complaint Objecting to Discharge in Event of Amendment.
4007–1. Automatic Extension of Time to File Complaint to Determine Dischargeability of a Debt in Event of Amendment.
4007–2. Withdrawal or Settlement of Proceedings to Determine Discharge and Dischargeability.

PART V. COURTS AND CLERKS

5001–1. Clerk's Office: Hours; After Hours Filing.
5005–1. Filing Papers.

Rule

5005–2. Filing by Electronic Means.
5009–1. Final Report and Account and Closing Report in a Chapter 7 Case.
5010–1. Reopening Cases.
5011–1. Withdrawal of Reference.
5070–1. Obtaining Return Date.
5073–1. Photographing, Broadcasting, and Televising in Courtrooms and Environs.
5075–1. Clerk's Use of Outside Services and Agents.
5076–1. Deposit for Court Reporting Expenses.
5078–1. Payment of Fees.

PART VI. COLLECTION AND LIQUIDATION OF THE ESTATE

6004–1. Sales of Property, Appraisals, and Auctions.
6005–1. Auctioneers.
6006–1. Executory Contracts and Unexpired Leases.
6007–1. Abandonment or Disposition of Property.

PART VII. ADVERSARY PROCEEDINGS

7005–1. Filing of Discovery–Related Documents.
7007–1. Discovery–Related Motion Practice.
7007.1–1. Corporate Ownership Statement.
7016–1. Submission of Marked Pleadings.
7024–1. Notice of Claim of Unconstitutionality—Repealed.
7026–1. Uniform Definitions in Discovery Requests.
7026–2. Opt–Out from Certain Provisions of Rule 26 of the Federal Rules of Civil Procedure—Repealed.
7027–1. Depositions Prior to Commencement of Adversary Proceeding or Pending Appeal when Deposition is More than 100 Miles from Courthouse.
7030–1. Depositions upon Oral Examination.
7030–2. Opt–Out from Certain Provisions of Rule 30 of the Federal Rules of Civil Procedure—Repealed.
7031–1. Opt–Out from Certain Provisions of Rule 31 of the Federal Rules of Civil Procedure—Repealed.
7033–1. Interrogatories.
7033–2. Opt–Out from Certain Provisions of Rule 33 of the Federal Rules of Civil Procedure—Repealed.
7034–1. Objections to, and Requests for Relief with Respect to Production of Documents.
7034–2. Opt–Out From Certain Provisions of Rule 34 of the Federal Rules of Civil Procedure—Repealed.
7036–1. Requests for Admission.
7036–2. Opt–Out from Certain Provisions of Rule 36 of the Federal Rules of Civil Procedure—Repealed.
7052–1. Proposed Findings of Fact and Conclusions of Law.
7055–1. Certificate of Default.
7055–2. Default Judgment.
7056–1. Summary Judgment.
7087–1. Transfer of Adversary Proceedings—Repealed.

PART VIII. APPEALS

8004–1. Copies of Notice of Appeal.
8005–1. Supersedeas Bond.

Rule

8007–1. Record on Appeal.
8016–1. Order, Judgment, or Remand by Appellate Court.

PART IX. GENERAL PROVISIONS

9001–1. Definitions.
9004–1. Form of Papers.
9004–2. Caption.
9006–1. Time for Service and Filing of Motions and Answering Papers.
9011–1. Signing of Papers.
9013–1. Motion Practice.
9014–1. Contested Matters.
9014–2. First Scheduled Hearing.
9015–1. Jury Trials.
9019–1. Alternative Dispute Resolution.
9020–1. Default Sanctions; Imposition of Costs.
9021–1. Entry of Orders, Judgments, and Decrees.
9023–1. Motions for Reargument.
9025–1. Sureties.
9028–1. Action in Absence of Assigned Judge.
9070–1. Copies of Filed Papers.
9072–1. Custody of Exhibits.
9074–1. Settlement or Presentment of Order, Judgment, or Decree.
9075–1. Request for Hearing.
9076–1. Status Conferences.
9077–1. Orders to Show Cause; Ex Parte Orders.
9078–1. Certificate of Service.

GENERAL ORDERS OF THE BANKRUPTCY COURT FOR THE SOUTHERN DISTRICT OF NEW YORK

Order

M–68. Rules Governing Procedures for Appointment of Pro Bono Counsel in Bankruptcy Proceedings—Southern District [See General Order M–320, post].
M–104. Original Guidelines for Fees and Disbursements for Professionals in Southern District of New York Bankruptcy Cases.
M–117. Adoption of Procedures Governing Mediation of Matters in Bankruptcy Cases and Advisory Proceedings.
M–118. Time for Motions for Assumption/Rejection/Assignment under Federal Rule of Bankruptcy Procedure 6006, Debtor.
M–138. Filing a List of Creditors in a Bankruptcy Case.
M–143. Court Annexed Mediation Program: Adoption of Procedures Governing Mediation of Matters in Bankruptcy Cases and Adversary Proceedings.
M–151. Amended Guidelines for Fees and Disbursements for Professionals in Southern District of New York Bankruptcy Cases.
M–182. Electronic Means for Filing, General Order Signing, and Verification of (Electronic Filing Procedures) Documents.
M–192. Filing a List of Creditors in a Bankruptcy Case.
M–193. Electronic Means for Filing, Signing, and Verification of Documents.

Order

M–201. Adoption of Prepackaged Chapter 11 Case Guidelines.

M–203. Amending General Order 201.

M–206. Second Amendment to General Order M–182 Electronic Means for Filing, Signing, and Verification of Documents.

M–219 (M–348). In the Matter of: Order Establishing Procedures for Monthly Compensation and Reimbursement of Expenses of Professionals.

M–242. Revised Electronic Means for Filing, Signing, and Verification of Documents.

M–269. First Amendment to ECF General Order M–242.

M–274. Adoption of Guidelines for Financing Requests.

M–279. In the Matter of: Adoption of Amended Procedural Guidelines for Filing Requests for Bar Orders [M–350].

M–289. Order Limiting FED.R.CIV.P. 26 in Contested Matters.

M–290. Order Regarding Personal Data Identifiers [Vacated. See, now, General Order M–353].

M–293. Order Imposing Sanctions on Attorneys Disciplined by the Committee on Grievances.

M–295. Amended General Order M–292—Order Regarding Attorney Bar Identification Numbers [Vacated, See, now, General Order M–349].

Order

M–302. Claims Bar Date Pursuant to Rule 3002(C)(5), Federal Rules of Bankruptcy Procedure.

M–306. Order Regarding the Reassignment of Certain Chapter 7 Cases.

M–308. Adoption of Interim Bankruptcy Rules and Forms*.

M–311. In re: Procedures for Payment and Cure of Pre–Petition Judgment of Possession Involving Residential Property [M–352].

M–313. Criminal Referrals of Certain Bankruptcy Crimes.

M–315. Procedures Relating to the Implementation of 11 U.S.C. § 521.

M–320. Rules Governing Procedures for Appointment of Pro Bono Counsel in Bankruptcy Proceedings from a Bankruptcy Pro Bono Panel.

M–323. Procedures Relating to the Notice of the Commencement of a Chapter 15 Case.

M–331. Adoption of Guidelines for the Conduct of Asset Sales.

M–346. In re: Adoption of Relief from Stay/ Worksheet for Real Estate and Cooperative Apartments [M–347].

M–349. In Re: Order Vacating General Order # M–295 Regarding Attorney Bar Identification Numbers.

M–353. In re: Order Vacating General Order #M–290 Regarding Personal Data Identifiers.

PART I. COMMENCEMENT OF CASE; PROCEEDINGS RELATING TO PETITION AND ORDER FOR RELIEF

RULE 1001–1. SHORT TITLE; APPLICABILITY

(a) Short Title. These rules shall be known and cited as the "Local Bankruptcy Rules."

(b) Applicability.

(1) The Local Bankruptcy Rules shall apply to all cases in this district governed by the Bankruptcy Code.

(2) Rules 1 through 35 and 63 through 82 of the Former Local Bankruptcy Rules shall apply to all cases in this district governed by the Bankruptcy Act.

[Adopted April 15, 1997.]

Comment

This rule is derived from Former Local Bankruptcy Rule 1.

Pursuant to Bankruptcy Rule 9029, "[e]ach district court . . . may make and amend rules governing practice and procedure . . . which are not inconsistent with" the Bankruptcy Rules and "[i]n all cases not provided for by rule, the court may regulate its practice in any manner not inconsistent with" the Bankruptcy Rules. The Judges of this district have been authorized to make and amend rules of practice and procedure pursuant to an order of the District Court (Griesa, C.J.), dated December 1, 1994.

Pursuant to the Memorandum of the Administrative Office of the United States Courts, dated November 22, 1994, the appropriate citation form for a local bankruptcy rule, using the uniform numbers, is "LBR _____." For example, this rule would be cited as "LBR 1001–1." In a brief or other document in which the district prescribing the rule must be identified, this rule would be cited as "S.D.N.Y. LBR 1001–1."

Except with respect to cases under the Bankruptcy Act, these Local Bankruptcy Rules supersede the Former Local Bankruptcy Rules.

From time to time, the Court may issue standing orders to supplement these Local Bankruptcy Rules, copies of which may be obtained from the Clerk and are available on the Court's website at www.nysb.uscourts.gov.

Capitalized terms used in these Local Bankruptcy Rules are defined in Local Bankruptcy Rule 9001–1.

[Comment amended effective July 28, 1998; August 2, 2004.]

RULE 1002–1. FILING OF PETITION

A petition commencing a case under the Bankruptcy Code may be filed in any office of the Clerk or by electronic means established by the Court.

[Adopted April 15, 1997.]

Comment

This rule is derived from Former Local Bankruptcy Rule 9(a).

Local Bankruptcy Rule 5005–2 permits filing by electronic means to the extent permitted by any standing orders issued by the Court. Procedures for filing by electronic means are governed by General Order M–242 and any amendments or supplemental standing orders of the Court. Copies of General Order M–242, as well as any amendments or subsequent standing orders on this subject, may be obtained from the Clerk and are available on the Court's website at www.nysb.uscourts.gov.

[Comment amended effective July 28, 1998; August 2, 2004.]

RULE 1005–1. DEBTOR'S ADDRESS IN PETITION

If not included in the debtor's post office address, the petition also shall state the debtor's residence and place of business, including the street number, street, apartment or suite number, and zip code.

[Adopted April 15, 1997.]

Comment

This rule is derived from Former Local Bankruptcy Rule 50(a).

RULE 1007–1. LIST OF CREDITORS AND EQUITY SECURITY HOLDERS

A person filing any lists, schedules, or statements pursuant to Bankruptcy Rule 1007 shall comply with such filing requirements as are contained in any standing order issued by the Court.

[Adopted April 15, 1997; amended effective July 28, 1998.]

Comment

Filing requirements with respect to lists, statements, and schedules are governed by General Order M–192 and any amendments or supplemental standing orders of the Court. Copies of General Order M–192, as well as any amendments or subsequent standing orders on this subject, may be obtained from the Clerk and are available on the Court's website at www.nysb.uscourts.gov.

[Comment amended effective August 2, 2004.]

RULE 1007–2. DEBTOR'S AFFIDAVIT AND PROPOSED CASE CONFERENCE ORDER TO BE FILED IN CHAPTER 11 CASES

(a) Contents of Affidavit. A debtor in a chapter 11 case shall file an affidavit setting forth:

(1) the nature of the debtor's business and a concise statement of the circumstances leading to the debtor's filing under chapter 11;

(2) if the case originally was commenced under chapter 7 or chapter 13, the name and address of any trustee appointed in the case and, in a case originally commenced under chapter 7, the names and addresses of the members of any creditors' committee;

(3) the names and addresses of the members of, and attorneys for, any committee organized prior to the order for relief in the chapter 11 case, and a brief description of the circumstances surrounding the formation of the committee and the date of its formation;

(4) the following information with respect to each of the holders of the 20 largest unsecured claims, excluding insiders: the name, the address (including the number, street, apartment or suite number, and zip code, if not included in the post office address), the telephone number, the name(s) of person(s) familiar with the debtor's account, the amount of the claim, and an indication of whether the claim is contingent, unliquidated, disputed, or partially secured;

(5) the following information with respect to each of the holders of the five largest secured claims: the name, the address (including the number, street, apartment or suite number, and zip code, if not included in the post office address), the amount of the claim, a brief description and an estimate of the value of the collateral securing the claim, and whether the claim or lien is disputed;

(6) a summary of the debtor's assets and liabilities;

(7) the number and classes of shares of stock, debentures, or other securities of the debtor that are publicly held, and the number of holders thereof, listing separately those held by each of the debtor's officers and directors and the amounts so held;

(8) a list of all of the debtor's property in the possession or custody of any custodian, public officer, mortgagee, pledgee, assignee of rents, or secured creditor, or agent for any such entity, giving the name, address, and telephone number of each such entity and the court in which any proceeding relating thereto is pending;

(9) a list of the premises owned, leased, or held under other arrangement from which the debtor operates its business;

(10) the location of the debtor's substantial assets, the location of its books and records, and the nature,

location, and value of any assets held by the debtor outside the territorial limits of the United States;

(11) the nature and present status of each action or proceeding, pending or threatened, against the debtor or its property where a judgment against the debtor or a seizure of its property may be imminent; and

(12) the names of the individuals who comprise the debtor's existing senior management, their tenure with the debtor, and a brief summary of their relevant responsibilities and experience.

(b) Additional Information if Business Is to Continue. If the debtor intends to continue to operate its business, the affidavit shall so state and set forth:

(1) the estimated amount of the weekly payroll to employees (exclusive of officers, directors, stockholders, and partners) for the 30 day period following the filing of the chapter 11 petition;

(2) the amount paid and proposed to be paid for services for the 30 day period following the filing of the chapter 11 petition—

(A) if the debtor is a corporation, to officers, stockholders, and directors;

(B) if the debtor is an individual or a partnership, to the individual or the members of the partnership; and

(C) if a financial or business consultant has been retained by the debtor, to the consultant; and

(3) a schedule, for the 30 day period following the filing of the chapter 11 petition, of estimated cash receipts and disbursements, net cash gain or loss, obligations and receivables expected to accrue but remain unpaid, other than professional fees, and any other information relevant to an understanding of the foregoing.

(c) When to File. In a voluntary chapter 11 case, the affidavit shall accompany the petition. In an involuntary chapter 11 case, the affidavit shall be filed within 15 days after the date on which (i) the order for relief is entered, or (ii) a consent to the petition is filed.

(d) Waiver of Requirements. Upon motion of the debtor on notice to the United States Trustee showing that it is impracticable or impossible to furnish any of the foregoing information, the Court may dispense with any of the foregoing provisions, with the exception of those contained in paragraphs (1), (2), (3), and (4) of subdivision (a) of this rule.

(e) Proposed Case Conference Order. There shall be submitted to the Court with the chapter 11 petition a proposed case conference order in the following form. Any initial conference shall be conducted

approximately 30 days after the filing of the petition or at such other time as the Court may direct.

UNITED STATES BANKRUPTCY COURT
SOUTHERN DISTRICT OF NEW YORK

	:	
	:	
	:	
[Caption of Case]	:	Chapter 11 Case No. _____
	:	
	:	
	:	

ORDER SCHEDULING INITIAL
CASE CONFERENCE

[INSERT NAME OF DEBTOR] (the "Debtor ") having filed a petition for reorganization under chapter 11 of the Bankruptcy Code on [date], and the Court having determined that a case management conference will aid in the efficient conduct of the case, it is

ORDERED, pursuant to 11 U.S.C. § 105(d), that an initial case management conference will be conducted by the undersigned Bankruptcy Judge in Room ____, United States Bankruptcy Court, [One Bowling Green, New York, New York 10004] [176 Church Street, Poughkeepsie, New York, 12601] [300 Quarropas Street, White Plains, New York, 10601] on _____, ____, at ____: ____ .m., or as soon thereafter as counsel may be heard, to consider the efficient administration of the case, which may include, inter alia, such topics as retention of professionals, creation of a committee to review budget and fee requests, use of alternative dispute resolution, timetables, and scheduling of additional case management conferences; and it is further

ORDERED, that the Debtor shall give notice by mail of this order at least seven days prior to the scheduled conference to each committee appointed to serve in the case pursuant to 11 U.S.C. § 1102 (or, if no committee has been appointed, to the holders of the 10 largest unsecured claims), the holders of the five largest secured claims, any postpetition lender to the Debtor, and the United States Trustee, and shall promptly file proof of service of such notice with the Clerk of the Court.

Dated: _____, New York

_____ —, ____

UNITED STATES BANKRUPTCY JUDGE

[Adopted April 15, 1997; amended effective July 28, 1998; August 2, 2004.]

Comment

This rule is derived from Former Local Bankruptcy Rule 52, with the exception of subdivisions (a)(5) and (a)(11), which are derived from former Standing Order M–147.

Subdivision (e) of this rule, added in 1996, is intended to aid in the implementation of Local Bankruptcy Rule 9076–1.

[Comment amended effective July 28, 1998.]

RULE 1007–3. DEBTOR'S CORPORATE OWNERSHIP STATEMENT

The Corporate Ownership Statement required to be filed by the debtor with the petition under Bankruptcy Rule 1007(a)(1) shall also be filed by any debtor that is a general or limited partnership or joint venture. In addition to the information required under Bankruptcy Rule 7007.1, the statement shall include the name and address of any corporation whose securities are publicly traded in which the debtor directly or indirectly owns 10% or more of any class of the corporation's equity interests, and any general or limited partnership or joint venture in which the debtor owns an interest.

[Adopted effective August 2, 2004.]

COMMENT

Bankruptcy Rule 1007(a), as amended effective December 1, 2003, requires a Corporate Ownership Statement containing the information described in Bankruptcy Rule 7007.1 to be filed by the debtor with the petition. Bankruptcy Rule 1007(a), however, only refers to a debtor that is a corporation. "Corporation" is broadly defined under § 101(9) of the Bankruptcy Code (and includes, among other entities, limited liability companies and other unincorporated companies or associations), but it does not cover general or limited partnerships. The reasons for which this rule was enacted—to give the Judges of this Court information by which they can determine whether or not they need to recuse themselves in a particular case—apply equally with respect to debtors that are general and limited partnerships, and joint ventures. This local rule requires a similar disclosure with respect to business organizations of that character.

[Comment adopted effective August 2, 2004.]

RULE 1009–1. NOTICE OF AMENDMENT OF SCHEDULES IN CHAPTER 11 CASES

Whenever the debtor or trustee in a chapter 11 case amends the debtor's schedules to change the amount, nature, classification, or characterization of a debt owing to a creditor, the debtor or trustee promptly shall transmit notice of the amendment to the creditor.

[Adopted April 15, 1997.]

Comment

This rule is derived from Former Local Bankruptcy Rule 53.

The term "characterization," as used in this rule, includes a description of whether the debt is disputed or undisputed, fixed or contingent, and liquidated or unliquidated.

RULE 1014–1. TRANSFER OF CASES

Unless the Court orders otherwise, whenever a case is ordered transferred from this district, the Clerk, promptly after entry of the order, shall transmit to the court to which the case is transferred (i) certified copies of the opinion ordering the transfer, the order thereon, and the case docket, and (ii) the originals of all other papers on file in the case.

[Adopted April 15, 1997.]

Comment

This rule is derived from Former Local Bankruptcy Rule 7 and is an adaptation of Civil Rule 83.1 of the Local District Rules.

Although not expressly stated, this rule contemplates that whenever transfer of a case under the Bankruptcy Code is ordered by a District Judge, the District Clerk will transmit the order and related documents to the Clerk of the Bankruptcy Court.

Transfers of adversary proceedings are governed by Local Bankruptcy Rule 7087–1.

[Comment amended effective July 28, 1998.]

RULE 1020–1. SMALL BUSINESS ELECTION [REPEALED]

[Adopted effective July 28, 1998. Repealed effective October 17, 2005.]

RULE 1073–1. ASSIGNMENT OF CASES AND PROCEEDINGS

(a) **Cases.** Where the street address of the debtor set forth on the petition is in (i) New York County or Bronx County, the Clerk shall assign the case to a Judge sitting in New York County; (ii) Rockland County or Westchester County, the Clerk shall assign the case to a Judge sitting in Westchester County; or (iii) Dutchess County, Orange County, Putnam County, or Sullivan County, the Clerk shall assign the case to a Judge sitting in Dutchess County. No case assignment will be based upon a post office box address. Where more than one Judge is sitting in a county, cases, other than chapter 13 cases, shall be assigned by random selection so that each Judge shall be assigned approximately the same number of cases. The Judges may direct that chapter 13 cases be referred to the same Judge or Judges. The Clerk shall have no discretion in determining the Judge to whom any case is assigned; the action shall be solely ministerial.

(b) **Cases Involving Affiliates.** Cases involving debtors that are affiliates shall be assigned to the same Judge.

(c) Proceedings. Except as otherwise provided in the Bankruptcy Code or Bankruptcy Rules, the assignment of a case to a Judge includes the assignment of all proceedings arising under title 11 or arising in, or related to, a case under title 11.

(d) Removed Actions. A removed action that does not arise out of a case pending in this Court shall be deemed to have venue in the county in which the court from which it was removed is situated and be assigned to a Judge in the manner provided in subdivision (a) of this rule.

(e) Adversary Proceedings or Contested Matters in Cases Pending Outside of this Court. An adversary proceeding or contested matter that does not arise out of a case pending in this Court shall be designated by the Clerk to an office of the Clerk in New York County, Westchester County, or Dutchess County. In making the designation, the Clerk shall take into consideration the residence of the defendant, the convenience of litigants, counsel, and witnesses, and the place where the cause of action arose. Unless the Court orders otherwise, the county designated by the Clerk shall be the place of trial and all other proceedings. The designation shall be made at the time of commencement or transfer of the adversary proceeding or contested matter, and the Clerk shall give prompt notice thereof to the parties or their counsel. After the designation, the adversary proceeding or contested matter shall be assigned to a Judge in the manner provided in subdivision (a) of this rule. Objections, if any, to the designation shall be made, on notice to opposing counsel, before the Judge to whom the adversary proceeding or contested matter has been assigned.

(f) Assignments and Reassignments. The Chief Judge shall supervise and rule upon all assignments and reassignments of cases, adversary proceedings, contested matters, and actions.

[Adopted April 15, 1997; amended effective July 28, 1998; August 2, 2004.]

Comment

This rule is derived from Former Local Bankruptcy Rule 5. This rule was amended in 2004 to eliminate the use of a post office box address as the basis for case assignment.

[Comment amended effective August 2, 2004.]

RULE 1074–1. CORPORATE RESOLUTION; PARTNERSHIP STATEMENT

(a) Corporate Resolution. A voluntary petition or consent to an involuntary petition filed by a corporation shall be accompanied by a copy of the duly attested corporate resolution authorizing, or other appropriate authorization for, the filing.

(b) Partnership Statement. A voluntary petition filed by, or consent to an involuntary petition filed on behalf of, a partnership shall be accompanied by a duly attested statement that all partners whose consent is required for the filing have consented.

[Adopted April 15, 1997.]

Comment

Subdivision (a) of this rule is derived from Former Local Bankruptcy Rule 51. Subdivision (b) of this rule was added in 1996.

[Comment amended effective July 28, 1998.]

PART II. OFFICERS AND ADMINISTRATION; NOTICES; MEETINGS; EXAMINATIONS; ELECTIONS; ATTORNEYS AND ACCOUNTANTS

RULE 2002–1. NOTICE TO UNITED STATES TRUSTEE

Unless the case is a chapter 9 case or the United States Trustee requests otherwise, any notice required to be given to creditors under Bankruptcy Rule 2002 also shall be given to the United States Trustee.

[Adopted April 15, 1997.]

Comment

This rule is derived from Former Local Bankruptcy Rule 36.

RULE 2002–2. NOTICE OF PROPOSED ACTION OR ORDER WHEN NOT PROCEEDING BY MOTION

(a) Contents of Notice. Unless the Court orders otherwise, whenever "notice and a hearing" are specified in the Bankruptcy Code or Bankruptcy Rules but a motion is not mandatory, the entity proposing to act or obtain an order, in lieu of proceeding by motion, may give written notice, which, together with proof of service, shall be filed with the Clerk with a copy delivered to the Judge's chambers, setting forth:

(1) a statement of the action proposed to be taken or the order to be presented, including a concise statement of the terms and conditions of, and the reasons for, the proposed action or order;

(2) the date by which objections or responses to the proposed action or order shall be served and filed;

(3) the date and time when the action will be taken or the proposed order will be presented for signature if there is no objection, and a statement that the action will be taken or the order may be entered without a hearing unless a timely objection is made; and

(4) the date on which a hearing will be held if a timely objection is made, which date shall be obtained in the manner provided by Local Bankruptcy Rule 5070–1.

(b) Time for Notice. Unless the Court orders otherwise, if notice is to be given to all creditors under subdivision (a) of this rule, the notice shall be given at least 20 days prior to the date on which the proposed action is to be taken or the proposed order is to be presented. If the Court issues an order requiring that notice be given to fewer than all creditors, the notice shall be given at least seven days prior to such date.

(c) Entities to Receive Notice. Unless the Court orders otherwise, in addition to the requirements of Bankruptcy Rule 2002 and Local Bankruptcy Rule 2002–1, notice under subdivision (a) of this rule shall be given to any entity having or claiming an interest in the subject matter of the proposed action or order or who otherwise would be affected by the proposed action or order.

(d) Objection. Unless the Court orders otherwise, any objection to the proposed action or order shall be in writing, state with particularity the reasons for the objection, and be served on the party proposing the action or order so as to be received (i) at least three days prior to the date set for the hearing if at least 20 days' notice has been given and (ii) at least one day prior to the date set for the hearing if at least 7 (but less than 20) days' notice has been given. The objection, together with proof of service, shall be filed with the Clerk and a copy thereof shall be delivered to the Judge's chambers prior to the date set for the hearing.

[Adopted April 15, 1997; amended effective July 28, 1998.]

Comment

This rule is derived from Former Local Bankruptcy Rule 45.

This rule provides a standard procedure that may be used whenever the Bankruptcy Code requires "notice and a hearing," including, without limitation, §§ 363, 364, 554, and 725 of the Bankruptcy Code, where the entity proposing to act or obtain an order is not required, and does not intend, to proceed by motion.

The "notice and a hearing" requirements concerning the use, sale, or lease of property and the abandonment or other disposition of property are governed by Bankruptcy Rules 6004 and 6007, respectively. To the extent not inconsistent with those Bankruptcy Rules, this rule shall apply.

Other procedures for the submission of orders are provided for by Local Bankruptcy Rule 9074–1.

Local Bankruptcy Rule 9078–1 governs the filing of proofs of service of notices.

[Comment amended effective July 28, 1998.]

RULE 2007.1–1   ELECTION OF TRUSTEE IN CHAPTER 11 CASES

A meeting of creditors convened for the purpose of electing a chapter 11 trustee pursuant to § 1104(b) of the Bankruptcy Code shall be deemed a meeting of creditors under § 341   of the Bankruptcy Code.

[Adopted April 15, 1997.]

Comment

This rule clarifies that a meeting convened for the purpose of electing a chapter 11 trustee pursuant to § 1104(b) of the Bankruptcy Code satisfies the requirement of § 702(b) of the Bankruptcy Code that a trustee be elected at a meeting of creditors held under § 341 of the Bankruptcy Code.

RULE 2014–1.   EMPLOYMENT OF PROFESSIONAL PERSONS

An application for the employment of a professional person pursuant to §§ 327 and 328 of the Bankruptcy Code shall state the specific facts showing the reasonableness of the terms and conditions of the employment, including the terms of any retainer, hourly fee, or contingent fee arrangement.

[Adopted April 15, 1997.]

Comment

This rule is derived from Former Local Bankruptcy Rule 39.

The information required by Bankruptcy Rule 2014(a) and this rule may be contained in the same application.

RULE 2015–1.   STORAGE OF BOOKS AND RECORDS

The trustee or debtor in possession may place in storage, at the expense of the estate, the debtor's books, records, and papers.

[Adopted April 15, 1997.]

Comment

This rule is derived from Former Local Bankruptcy Rule 43.

This rule sets no time limit on the storage of books and records. On request, the Court may issue an appropriate order limiting storage of the debtor's books, records, and papers. Disposal of the debtor's books, records, and papers is governed by §§ 363 and 554 of the Bankruptcy Code.

RULE 2016–1. COMPENSATION OF PROFESSIONALS

A person seeking an award of compensation or reimbursement of expenses shall comply with the requirements contained in any guidelines for fees and disbursements promulgated by the Court.

[Adopted April 15, 1997; amended effective July 28, 1998.]

Comment

Guidelines for fees and disbursements are governed by General Order M–151 and any amendments or supplemental standing orders of the Court. Copies of General Order M–151, as well as any amendments or subsequent standing orders on this subject, may be obtained from the Clerk and are available on the Court's website at www.nysb.uscourts.gov.

[Comment adopted effective July 28, 1998; amended effective August 2, 2004.]

RULE 2016–2. COMPENSATION OR REIMBURSEMENT OF EXPENSES IN CHAPTER 7 CASES

Unless the Court orders otherwise, a person seeking an award of compensation or reimbursement of expenses in a chapter 7 case shall file an application with the Clerk and serve a copy on the trustee and the United States Trustee not later than 20 days prior to the date of the hearing on the trustee's final account. Failure to file and serve an application within the time prescribed by this rule may result in its disallowance. Unless the Court orders otherwise, the United States Trustee shall file any objection to such application at least two business days prior to the date of the hearing.

[Adopted April 15, 1997.]

Comment

This rule is derived from former Standing Order M–90.

This rule supplements Local Bankruptcy Rule 2016–1 and facilitates the expeditious closing of chapter 7 cases. Pursuant to Local Bankruptcy Rule 5009–1, the trustee is obligated to set forth the language contained in this rule, or words of similar import, on the notice of filing of a final account.

[Comment amended effective July 28, 1998.]

RULE 2090–1. ADMISSION TO PRACTICE; WITHDRAWAL AS ATTORNEY OF RECORD

(a) General. An attorney who may practice in the District Court pursuant to Civil Rule 1.3(a) and (b) of the Local District Rules may practice in this Court.

(b) Pro Hac Vice. Upon motion to the Court, a member in good standing of the bar of any state or of any United States District Court may be permitted to practice in this Court in a particular case, adversary proceeding, or contested matter.

(c) Repealed.

(d) Pro Se Designation of Address. An individual appearing pro se shall include the individual's residence address and telephone number in the individual's initial notice or pleading.

(e) Withdrawal as Attorney of Record. An attorney who has appeared as attorney of record may withdraw or be replaced only by order of the Court for cause shown.

(f) Exceptions. Rule 2090–1 shall not apply to (i) the filing of a proof of claim or interest, or (ii) an appearance by a child support creditor or such creditor's representative.

[Adopted April 15, 1997; amended effective July 28, 1998; August 2, 2004.]

Comment

Subdivisions (a) and (b) of this rule are derived from Former Local Bankruptcy Rule 3. Subdivisions (c), (d), (e), and (f)(i) of this rule are derived from Former Local Bankruptcy Rule 4 and are an adaptation of Civil Rules 1.3(c), (d), and 1.4 of the Local District Rules. Subdivision (f)(ii) of this rule, added in 1996, is derived from § 304(g) of the Bankruptcy Reform Act of 1994, which permits child support creditors or their representatives to appear and intervene without charge and without meeting any special local court rule requirements for attorney appearances.

Subdivision (c) of this rule, requiring a local address for service, was repealed in 2004 because it could have been construed to require retention of local counsel when the attorney for the debtor or for a petitioning creditor does not have an office located in the district.

[Comment amended effective July 28, 1998; August 2, 2004.]

PART III. CLAIMS AND DISTRIBUTION TO CREDITORS AND EQUITY INTEREST HOLDERS; PLANS

RULE 3003–1. REQUESTS FOR ORDERS ESTABLISHING DEADLINES FOR FILING CLAIMS IN CHAPTER 11 CASES

A request for an order establishing a deadline for filing proofs of claim in a chapter 11 case shall conform to procedural guidelines for requests for bar orders contained in any applicable standing order issued by the Court.

[Adopted effective August 2, 2004.]

Comment

Procedures for requesting deadlines for filing claims, traditionally known as "bar dates," are governed by General

Order M–279 and any amendments or supplemental standing orders of the Court. Copies of General Order M–279, as well as any amendments or subsequent standing orders on this subject, may be obtained from the Clerk and are available on the Court's website at www.nysb.uscourts.gov.

[Comment adopted effective August 2, 2004.]

RULE 3008–1. RECONSIDERATION OF CLAIMS

No oral argument shall be heard on a motion to reconsider an order of allowance or disallowance of a claim unless the Court grants the motion and specifically orders that the matter be reconsidered upon oral argument. If a motion to reconsider is granted, notice and a hearing shall be afforded to parties in interest before the previous action taken with respect to the claim may be vacated or modified.

[Adopted April 15, 1997.]

Comment

This rule, added in 1996, is derived from the Advisory Committee Note to Bankruptcy Rule 3008 and Former Local Bankruptcy Rule 13(i).

[Comment amended effective July 28, 1998.]

RULE 3015–1. CHAPTER 13 PLANS: PAYMENTS EXCEEDING THREE YEARS; TREATMENT OF DEBTOR'S ATTORNEY'S FEES AS ADMINISTRATIVE EXPENSE; SERVICE

(a) [Repealed effective October 17, 2005].

(b) **Notice and Hearing for Attorney's Fees to be Treated as Administrative Expense.** If the compensation, or any portion thereof, of the attorney for a chapter 13 debtor is to be treated as an administrative expense under the plan, the attorney shall provide adequate notice of that fact to the trustee, the United States Trustee, and all creditors. The notice shall be deemed adequate if the plan, or a summary of the plan, is transmitted timely to all parties in interest and states with particularity the timing and amount of any payments to be made to the attorney.

(c) **Service of Plan.** If the notice of commencement of a chapter 13 case is served without a copy of the plan or a summary of the plan, the debtor shall serve the plan or a summary of the plan on the chapter 13 trustee and all creditors.

[Adopted April 15, 1997; amended effective July 28, 1998.]

RULE 3015–2. MODIFICATION OF CHAPTER 13 PLAN BEFORE CONFIRMATION

If the debtor seeks to modify a chapter 13 plan prior to confirmation, the debtor shall serve a copy of the modified plan on the chapter 13 trustee, the United States Trustee, and such creditors as the Court may direct.

[Adopted April 15, 1997.]

Comment

This rule is derived from Former Local Bankruptcy Rule 60 and supplements § 1323 of the Bankruptcy Code.

RULE 3015–3. HEARING ON CONFIRMATION OF CHAPTER 13 PLAN

The debtor shall attend the hearing on confirmation of the chapter 13 plan, unless the Court, upon application of the debtor on such notice as the Court directs, and for cause shown, orders otherwise.

[Adopted April 15, 1997.]

Comment

This rule is derived from Former Local Bankruptcy Rule 59.

RULE 3017–1. PROPOSED DISCLOSURE STATEMENTS IN CHAPTER 9 AND CHAPTER 11 CASES: TRANSMITTAL AND DISCLAIMER

(a) **Transmittal.** Unless the Court orders otherwise, the proponent of a plan shall transmit all notices and documents required to be transmitted by Bankruptcy Rule 3017(a). Upon request, the Clerk shall supply the proponent, at a reasonable cost, with any available matrix of creditors for the purpose of preparing address labels.

(b) **Disclaimer Other Than in Small Business Cases.** Except in a case where the debtor is a small business, before a proposed disclosure statement has been approved by the Court, the proposed disclosure statement shall have on its cover, in boldface type, the following language, or words of similar import:

THIS IS NOT A SOLICITATION OF ACCEPTANCE OR REJECTION OF THE PLAN. ACCEPTANCES OR REJECTIONS MAY NOT BE SOLICITED UNTIL A DISCLOSURE STATEMENT HAS BEEN APPROVED BY THE BANKRUPTCY COURT. THIS DISCLOSURE STATEMENT IS BEING SUBMITTED FOR APPROVAL BUT HAS NOT BEEN APPROVED BY THE COURT.

(c) **Disclaimer in Small Business Cases.** In a case where the debtor is a small business, after conditional approval but before final approval of a proposed disclosure statement has been given, the proposed disclosure statement shall have on its cover, in boldface type, the following language, or words of similar import:

THE DEBTOR IN THIS CASE IS A SMALL BUSINESS. AS A RESULT, THE DEBTOR IS PERMITTED TO DISTRIBUTE AND HAS DISTRIBUTED THIS DISCLOSURE STATEMENT BEFORE ITS FINAL APPROVAL BY THE COURT. IF AN OBJECTION TO THIS DISCLOSURE STATEMENT IS FILED BY A PARTY IN INTEREST, FINAL APPROVAL OF THIS DISCLOSURE STATEMENT WILL BE CONSIDERED AT OR BEFORE THE HEARING ON CONFIRMATION OF THE PLAN.

[Adopted April 15, 1997; amended effective July 28, 1998; October 17, 2005.]

Comment

Subdivisions (a) and (b) of this rule are derived from Former Local Bankruptcy Rule 55. Subdivision (c) of this rule, added in 1996, is derived from § 217 of the Bankruptcy Reform Act of 1994.

Bankruptcy Rule 3017(a) provides that the plan and the disclosure statement shall be mailed with the notice of the hearing to the debtor, the trustee, each committee, the Securities and Exchange Commission, the United States Trustee, and any party in interest who requests in writing a copy of the disclosure statement or plan.

Bankruptcy Rule 2002(b) permits the Court to require a party other than the Clerk to bear the responsibility for transmitting the notices and documents specified in this rule.

The reasonable cost, if any, provided for in subdivision (a) of this rule is the fee prescribed by the Judicial Conference of the United States pursuant to 28 U.S.C. § 1930(b).

[Comment amended effective July 28, 1998.]

RULE 3018–1. CERTIFICATION OF ACCEPTANCE OR REJECTION OF PLANS IN CHAPTER 9 AND CHAPTER 11 CASES

(a) **Certification of Vote.** At least five days prior to the hearing on confirmation of a chapter 9 or chapter 11 plan, the proponent of a plan or the party authorized to receive the acceptances and rejections of the plan shall certify to the Court in writing the amount and number of allowed claims or allowed interests of each class accepting or rejecting the plan. A copy of the certification shall be served upon the debtor, the trustee, each committee, and the United States Trustee. The Court may find that the plan has been accepted or rejected on the basis of the certification.

(b) **Notice of Ineffective Election.** If a plan in a chapter 9 or chapter 11 case permits the holder of a claim or interest to make an election with respect to the treatment of the claim or interest, and for any reason the holder's election is deemed ineffective or otherwise is not counted by the person authorized to tabulate ballots, that person shall give notice of that fact to the holder at least five days prior to the hearing on confirmation.

[Adopted April 15, 1997; amended effective July 28, 1998.]

Comment

Subdivision (a) of this rule is derived from Former Local Bankruptcy Rule 54 and is intended to permit the Court to rely on a certification in determining whether a plan has been accepted or rejected under § 1126 of the Bankruptcy Code. If an issue has been raised with respect to the acceptance or rejection of a plan, the Court may hold an evidentiary hearing. Where acceptances or rejections of a plan of reorganization have been solicited prior to the commencement of the case, the certification may be filed together with the petition.

Subdivision (b) of this rule, added in 1996, is intended to enable a creditor or interest holder who has the right to elect the treatment of its claim or interest on a ballot to be notified if its ballot was not counted or was rejected, and therefore that its election may not be effective.

[Comment amended effective July 28, 1998.]

RULE 3018–2. ACCEPTANCES OR REJECTIONS OF PLAN OBTAINED BEFORE PETITION IN CHAPTER 11 CASES

A party seeking to obtain confirmation of any plan proposed and accepted before the commencement of a chapter 11 case shall comply with procedural guidelines for prepackaged chapter 11 cases contained in any applicable standing order issued by the Court.

[Adopted effective July 28, 1998. Amended effective August 2, 2004.]

Comment

Procedures with respect to prepackaged chapter 11 plans are governed by General Order M–201, as amended by General Order M–203, and any further amendments or supplemental standing orders of the Court, Copies of General Orders M–201 and M–203, as well as any amendments or subsequent standing orders on this subject, may be obtained from the Clerk and are available on the Court's website at www.nysb.uscourts.gov. This rule was amended in 2004 to delete the reference to chapter 9 because there are no General Orders governing prepackaged chapter 9 cases.

[Comment amended effective August 2, 2004.]

RULE 3019–1. MODIFICATION OF CHAPTER 11 PLAN BEFORE CLOSE OF VOTING

If the proponent of a chapter 11 plan files a modification of the plan after transmission of the approved disclosure statement and before the close of voting on the plan, the proponent shall serve a copy of the plan, as modified, upon the debtor, the trustee, each committee, the United States Trustee, all entities directly affected by the proposed modification, and such other entities as the Court may direct. On notice to such entities, the Court shall determine whether the modification adversely affects the treatment of the claim of any creditor or the interest of any equity security holder who has not accepted the modification in writing. If the Court determines that the modification is not adverse, the plan, as modified, shall be deemed accepted by all creditors and equity security holders who accepted the plan prior to modification. If the modification is adverse, the requirements of Bankruptcy Rule 3017 shall apply to the modified plan and any amendment of the disclosure statement necessitated by the modification.

[Adopted April 15, 1997.]

Comment

This rule is derived from Former Local Bankruptcy Rule 56.

Pursuant to § 1127(a) of the Bankruptcy Code, the proponent of a chapter 11 plan may modify the plan at any time before confirmation. While Bankruptcy Rule 3019 governs modification of a plan after acceptance and before confirmation, this rule governs modification subsequent to the transmission of an approved disclosure statement and before the close of voting.

RULE 3020–1. TIME FOR OBJECTING TO CONFIRMATION IN CHAPTER 9 AND CHAPTER 11 CASES; WITHDRAWAL OF OBJECTIONS

(a) Objections to Confirmation. Unless the Court orders otherwise, objections to confirmation of a plan shall be filed not later than three days prior to the first date set for the hearing to consider confirmation of the plan.

(b) Withdrawal of Objections. In the event of the withdrawal of an objection to confirmation of a plan or the failure to prosecute an objection, the plan shall not be confirmed unless the proponent has disclosed to the Court the terms of any agreement reached between the proponent and the objecting party resulting in the withdrawal or failure to prosecute.

[Adopted April 15, 1997.]

Comment

This rule is derived from Former Local Bankruptcy Rule 57.

Subdivision (a) of this rule designates a fixed time for objecting to confirmation as permitted by Bankruptcy Rule 3020(b)(1).

Subdivision (b) of this rule requires disclosure of the circumstances surrounding the withdrawal of, or failure to prosecute, any objections to confirmation. The purpose of this rule is to allow the Court to determine the propriety of any agreement between the proponent and an objecting party that results in the withdrawal of, or failure to prosecute, an objection.

RULE 3021–1. POSTCONFIRMATION REQUIREMENTS IN CHAPTER 11 CASES

(a) Notice of Postconfirmation Filing Requirements. Upon confirmation of a chapter 11 plan, the plan proponent shall obtain from the Clerk a notice of postconfirmation filing requirements.

(b) Repealed.

(c) Postconfirmation Order and Notice. At the time a proposed confirmation order is submitted to the Court, the plan proponent shall submit to the Court a proposed order and notice substantially in the following form:

UNITED STATES BANKRUPTCY COURT
SOUTHERN DISTRICT OF NEW YORK

	:	
	:	
[Caption of Case]	:	Chapter 11 Case No. _____
	:	
	:	

POSTCONFIRMATION ORDER AND NOTICE

WHEREAS, a confirmation order has been issued on [insert date], and whereas it is the responsibility of [insert Name of Debtor] (the "Debtor") to inform the Court of the progress made toward (i) consummation of the plan under 11 U.S.C. § 1101(2), (ii) entry of a final decree under Rule 3022 of the Federal Rules of Bankruptcy Procedure, and (iii) case closing under 11 U.S.C. § 350; it is therefore

ORDERED, that the Debtor or such other party as the Court may direct (the "Responsible Party"), shall comply with the following, except to the extent the Court orders otherwise:

(1) Periodic Status Reports. Subject to the requirements set forth in paragraph 5 of this Order and 11 U.S.C. § 1106(a)(7), the Responsible Party shall file, within 45 days after the date of this Order, a status report detailing the actions taken by the Responsible Party and the progress made toward the consummation of the plan. Reports shall be filed thereafter every January 15th, April 15th, July 15th, and October 15th until a final decree has been entered.

(2) Notices. The Responsible Party shall mail a copy of the confirmation order and this Order to the Debtor, the attorney for the Debtor, all committees, the attorney for each committee, and all parties who filed a notice of appearance.

(3) Closing Report and Final Decree. Within 15 days following the distribution of any deposit required by the plan or, if no deposit was required, upon the payment of the first distribution required by the plan, the Responsible Party shall file a closing report in accordance with Local Bankruptcy Rule 3022–1 and an application for a final decree.

(4) Case Closing. The Responsible Party shall submit the information described in paragraph 3 herein, including a final decree closing the case, within six calendar months from the date of the order confirming the plan. If the Responsible Party fails to comply with this Order, the Clerk shall so advise the Judge and an order to show cause may be issued.

Dated: _____, New York
_____ __, ___

_____

UNITED STATES BANKRUPTCY
JUDGE

[Adopted April 15, 1997; amended effective July 28, 1998; August 2, 2004.]

Comment

This rule is derived from former Standing Order M–111. Where the circumstances warrant, the Court has the discretion to alter the time periods prescribed herein. This rule was amended in 2004 to repeal subdivision (b) and delete paragraph (3) of the form Postconfirmation Order and Notice contained in subdivision (c), each of which related to the postconfirmation requirement to pay to the Clerk any special charges that may be assessed by the Court. The Court no longer assesses such charges.

[Comment amended effective July 28, 1998; August 2, 2004.]

RULE 3022–1. CLOSING REPORTS IN CHAPTER 11 CASES

Unless the Court orders otherwise, within 15 days following substantial consummation of a chapter 11 plan, the debtor or trustee shall file and serve upon the United States Trustee a closing report substantially in the following form:

UNITED STATES BANKRUPTCY COURT
SOUTHERN DISTRICT OF NEW YORK

_____

                 :
                 :
[Caption of Case]   : Chapter 11 Case No. _____
                 :
                 :

_____

CLOSING REPORT IN CHAPTER 11 CASE

To the best of my knowledge and belief, the following is a breakdown in this case:

FEES AND EXPENSES (from case inception):

_____ FEE for ATTORNEY for DEBTOR

_____ OTHER PROFESSIONAL FEES and ALL EXPENSES

_____ TRUSTEE FEE (if applicable)

_____ FEE FOR ATTORNEY for TRUSTEE (if applicable)

____% DIVIDEND PAID/TO BE PAID

____ FUTURE DIVIDENDS (check if % of future dividend under plan not yet determinable)

STEPS TAKEN TO CONSUMMATE PLAN:

_____ Initial distribution under the plan completed

_____ Other: (explain)

DATE: APPLICANT
                      BY

[Adopted April 15, 1997; amended effective July 28, 1998.]

PART IV. THE DEBTOR: DUTIES AND BENEFITS
RULE 4001–1. RELIEF FROM AUTOMATIC STAY

(a) A party moving for relief from the automatic stay under § 362 of the Bankruptcy Code shall obtain a return date for the motion that is not more than 30 days after the date on which the motion will be filed.

(b) If the debtor is an individual, the motion shall be supported by an affidavit, based on personal knowledge, attesting to the circumstances of any default with respect to an obligation related to the motion.

(c) If the debtor is an individual, a party moving for relief from the automatic stay under § 362 of the Bankruptcy Code relating to a mortgage on real property or a security interest in a cooperative apartment shall file, as an exhibit to the motion, a completed copy of the following form. Compliance with this subdivision shall constitute compliance with subdivision (b) of this rule.

UNITED STATES BANKRUPTCY COURT SOUTHERN DISTRICT OF NEW YORK

```
------------------------------------------- X
<CASE CAPTION>                                  CASE NO. ___–____ ( ____ )


------------------------------------------- X
```

RELIEF FROM STAY—REAL ESTATE AND COOPERATIVE APARTMENTS

I, _____ <NAME AND TITLE> OF _____ <NAME OF ORGANIZA-TION/CORPORATION/MOVING PARTY> (HEREINAFTER, "Movant"), HEREBY DECLARE (OR CERTIFY, VERIFY, OR STATE):

BACKGROUND INFORMATION

1. REAL PROPERTY OR COOPERATIVE APARTMENT ADDRESS WHICH IS THE SUBJECT OF THIS MOTION: _____

_____

2. LENDER NAME: _____

3. DATE OF MORTGAGE <MM/DD/YYYY>: _____

_____

4. POST-PETITION PAYMENT ADDRESS:

_____

_____

DEBT/VALUE REPRESENTATIONS

5. TOTAL PRE-PETITION AND POST-PETITION INDEBTEDNESS OF DEBTOR(S) TO MOVANT AT THE TIME OF FILING THE MOTION: $ _____

(Note: this amount may not be relied on as a "payoff" quotation.)

6. MOVANT'S ESTIMATED MARKET VALUE OF THE REAL PROPERTY OR COOPERATIVE APART-MENT: $ _____

7. SOURCE OF ESTIMATED VALUATION: _____

STATUS OF DEBT AS OF THE PETITION DATE

8. TOTAL PRE-PETITION INDEBTEDNESS OF DEBTOR(S) TO MOVANT AS OF PETITION FILING DATE: $ _____
     A. AMOUNT OF PRINCIPAL: $ _____
     B. AMOUNT OF INTEREST: $ _____
     C. AMOUNT OF ESCROW (TAXES AND INSURANCE): $ _____
     D. AMOUNT OF FORCED PLACED INSURANCE EXPENDED BY MOVANT: $ _____

E.   AMOUNT OF ATTORNEYS' FEES BILLED TO DEBTOR(S) PRE-PETITION: $ _____

F.   AMOUNT OF PRE-PETITION LATE FEES, IF ANY, BILLED TO DEBTOR(S): $ _____

9.   CONTRACTUAL INTEREST RATE: _____ (If interest rate is (or was) adjustable, please list the rate(s) and date(s) the rate(s) was/were in effect on a separate sheet and attach the sheet as an exhibit to this form; please list the exhibit number here: ___.)

10. PLEASE EXPLAIN ANY ADDITIONAL PRE-PETITION FEES, CHARGES OR AMOUNTS CHARGED TO DEBTOR'S/DEBTORS' ACCOUNT AND NOT LISTED ABOVE:

_____

(If additional space is needed, please list the amounts on a separate sheet and attach the sheet as an exhibit to this form; please list the exhibit number here: ___.)

AMOUNT OF ALLEGED POST–PETITION DEFAULT

(AS OF _____ <MM/DD/YYYY>)

11. DATE LAST PAYMENT WAS RECEIVED: _____ <MM/DD/YYYY>

12. ALLEGED TOTAL NUMBER OF PAYMENTS DUE POST-PETITION FROM FILING OF PETITION THROUGH PAYMENT DUE ON _____ <MM/DD/YYYY>: _____.

13. PLEASE LIST ALL POST-PETITION PAYMENTS ALLEGED TO BE IN DEFAULT:

ALLEGED PAYMENT DUE DATE	ALLEGED AMOUNT DUE	AMOUNT RECEIVED	AMOUNT APPLIED TO PRINCIPAL	AMOUNT APPLIED TO INTEREST	AMOUNT APPLIED TO ESCROW	LATE FEE CHARGED (IF ANY)
TOTALS:	$	$	$	$	$	$

14. AMOUNT OF MOVANT'S ATTORNEYS' FEES BILLED TO DEBTOR FOR THE PREPARATION, FILING AND PROSECUTION OF THIS MOTION: $ _____

15. AMOUNT OF MOVANT'S FILING FEE FOR THIS MOTION: $ _____

16. OTHER ATTORNEYS' FEES BILLED TO DEBTOR POST-PETITION: $ _____

17. AMOUNT OF MOVANT'S POST-PETITION INSPECTION FEES: $ _____

18. AMOUNT OF MOVANT'S POST-PETITION APPRAISAL/BROKER'S PRICE OPINION: $ _____

19. AMOUNT OF FORCED PLACED INSURANCE OR INSURANCE PROVIDED BY THE MOVANT POST-PETITION: $ _____

20. SUM HELD IN SUSPENSE BY MOVANT IN CONNECTION WITH THIS CONTRACT, IF APPLICABLE: $ _____

21. AMOUNT OF OTHER POST-PETITION ADVANCES OR CHARGES, FOR EXAMPLE, TAXES, INSURANCE INCURRED BY DEBTOR, ETC.: $ _____

REQUIRED ATTACHMENTS TO MOTION

Please attach the following documents to this motion and indicate the exhibit number associated with the documents.

   (1) Copies of documents that indicate Movant's interest in the subject property. For purposes of example only, a complete and legible copy of the promissory

note or other debt instrument together with a complete and legible copy of the mortgage and any assignments in the chain from the original mortgagee to the current moving party. (Exhibit ___.)

(2) Copies of documents establishing proof of standing to bring this Motion. (Exhibit ___.)

(3) Copies of documents establishing that Movant's interest in the real property or cooperative apartment was perfected. For the purposes of example only, a complete and legible copy of the Financing Statement (UCC–1) filed with either the Clerk's Office or the Register of the county the property or cooperative apartment is located in. (Exhibit ___.)

CERTIFICATION FOR BUSINESS RECORDS

I CERTIFY THAT THE INFORMATION PROVIDED IN THIS FORM AND/OR ANY EXHIBITS ATTACHED TO THIS FORM (OTHER THAN THE TRANSACTIONAL DOCUMENTS ATTACHED AS REQUIRED BY PARAGRAPHS 1, 2 AND 3, IMMEDIATELY ABOVE) IS DERIVED FROM RECORDS THAT WERE MADE AT OR NEAR THE TIME OF THE OCCURRENCE OF THE MATTERS SET FORTH BY, OR FROM INFORMATION TRANSMITTED BY, A PERSON WITH KNOWLEDGE OF THOSE MATTERS, WERE KEPT IN THE COURSE OF THE REGULARLY CONDUCTED ACTIVITY; AND WERE MADE BY THE REGULARLY CONDUCTED ACTIVITY AS A REGULAR PRACTICE.

I FURTHER CERTIFY THAT COPIES OF ANY TRANSACTIONAL DOCUMENTS ATTACHED TO THIS FORM AS REQUIRED BY PARAGRAPHS 1, 2 AND 3, IMMEDIATELY ABOVE, ARE TRUE AND ACCURATE COPIES OF THE ORIGINAL DOCUMENTS. I FURTHER CERTIFY THAT THE ORIGINAL DOCUMENTS ARE IN MOVANT'S POSSESSION, EXCEPT AS FOLLOWS: _____.

DECLARATION

I, _____ <NAME AND TITLE> OF _____ <NAME OF MOVANT>, HEREBY DECLARE (OR CERTIFY, VERIFY, OR STATE) PURSUANT TO 28 U.S.C. SECTION 1746 UNDER PENALTY OF PERJURY THAT THE FOREGOING IS TRUE AND CORRECT BASED ON PERSONAL KNOWLEDGE OF THE MOVANT'S BOOKS AND BUSINESS RECORDS.

EXECUTED AT _____ <CITY/TOWN>, ___ <STATE> ON THIS ___ DAY OF <MONTH>, 20 ___ <YEAR>.

<Print Name>
<Title>
<Movant>
<Street Address>
<City, State and Zip Code>

[Adopted April 15, 1997. Amended effective August 2, 2004; August 4, 2008.]

Comment

This rule is derived from Former Local Bankruptcy Rule 44(a).

Bankruptcy Rule 4001(a) provides that a request for relief from the automatic stay shall be made by motion. Section 362(e) of the Bankruptcy Code contemplates that a hearing will commence within 30 days from the date of the request for relief from the automatic stay. Local Bankruptcy Rule 9006–1 governs the time within which responsive papers may be served.

Subdivision (a) of this rule was amended in 2004 to put the burden of obtaining a timely return date on the movant. It does not attempt to deal with the ramifications of the movant's failure to comply with the rule.

Subdivision (b) of this rule was added in 2004 to assure the Court of the accuracy of allegations of default in cases concerning an individual debtor.

Subdivision (c) of this rule, which derives from General Order M–346 as amended by General Order M–347, was added in 2008 to assure the Court of the accuracy of allegations of default in proceedings relating to a mortgage on real property or a security interest in a cooperative apartment of an individual debtor. The Court may direct the submission of the form set forth in subdivision (c) of this rule in connection with other motions, including motions for adequate protection.

[Comment amended effective August 2, 2004; August 4, 2008.]

RULE 4001–2. REQUESTS FOR USE OF CASH COLLATERAL OR TO OBTAIN CREDIT

(a) Contents of Motion. The following provisions, to the extent applicable, are added to the enumerated lists of material provisions set forth in Bankruptcy Rule 4001(b)(1)(B), (c)(1)(B), and (d)(1)(B):

(1) the amount of cash collateral the party seeks permission to use or the amount of credit the party seeks to obtain, including any committed amount or the existence of a borrowing base formula and the estimated availability under the formula;

(2) material conditions to closing and borrowing, including budget provisions;

(3) pricing and economic terms, including letter of credit fees, commitment fees, any other fees, and the treatment of costs and expenses of the lender, any agent for the lender, and their respective professionals;

(4) any effect on existing liens of the granting of collateral or adequate protection provided to the lender and any priority or superpriority provisions;

(5) any carve-outs from liens or superpriorities;

(6) any cross-collateralization provision that elevates prepetition debt to administrative expense (or higher) status or that secures prepetition debt with liens on postpetition assets (which liens the creditor would not otherwise have by virtue of the prepetition security agreement or applicable law);

(7) any roll-up provision which applies the proceeds of postpetition financing to pay, in whole or in part, prepetition debt or which otherwise has the effect of converting prepetition debt to postpetition debt;

(8) any provision that would limit the Court's power or discretion in a material way, or would interfere with the exercise of the fiduciary duties, or restrict the rights and powers, of the trustee, debtor in possession, or a committee appointed under § 1102 or § 1114 of the Bankruptcy Code, or any other fiduciary of the estate, in connection with the operation, financ-

ing, use or sale of the business or property of the estate, but excluding any agreement to repay postpetition financing in connection with a plan or to waive any right to incur liens that prime or are pari passu with liens granted under § 364;

(9) any limitation on the lender's obligation to fund certain activities of the trustee, debtor in possession, or a committee appointed under § 1102 or § 1114 of the Bankruptcy Code;

(10) termination or default provisions, including events of default, any effect of termination or default on the automatic stay or the lender's ability to enforce remedies, any cross-default provision, and any terms that provide that the use of cash collateral or the availability of credit will cease on (i) the filing of a challenge to the lender's prepetition lien or the lender's prepetition claim based on the lender's prepetition conduct; (ii) entry of an order granting relief from the automatic stay other than an order granting relief from the stay with respect to material assets; (iii) the grant of a change of venue with respect to the case or any adversary proceeding; (iv) management changes or the departure, from the debtor, of any identified employees; (v) the expiration of a specified time for filing a plan; or (vi) the making of a motion by a party in interest seeking any relief (as distinct from an order granting such relief);

(11) any change-of-control provisions;

(12) any provision establishing a deadline for, or otherwise requiring, the sale of property of the estate;

(13) any provision that affects the debtor's right or ability to repay the financing in full during the course of the chapter 11 reorganization case;

(14) in jointly administered cases, terms that govern the joint liability of debtors including any provision described in subdivision (e) of this rule; and

(15) any provision for the funding of non-debtor affiliates with cash collateral or proceeds of the loan, as applicable, and the approximate amount of such funding.

(b) Disclosure of Efforts to Obtain Financing and Good Faith. A motion for authority to obtain credit shall describe in general terms the efforts of the trustee or debtor in possession to obtain financing, the basis on which the debtor determined that the proposed financing is on the best terms available, and material facts bearing on the issue of whether the extension of credit is being extended in good faith.

(c) Inadequacy of Notice After Event of Default.

(1) If the proposed order contains a provision that modifies or terminates the automatic stay or permits the lender to enforce remedies after an event of default, either the proposed order shall require at least five business days' notice to the trustee or debtor in possession, the United States Trustee and each

committee appointed under § 1102 or § 1114 of the Bankruptcy Code (or the 20 largest creditors if no committee has been appointed under § 1102 of the Bankruptcy Code), before the modification or termination of the automatic stay or the enforcement of the lender's remedies, or the motion shall explain why such notice provision is not contained in the proposed order.

(2) If the proposed order contains a provision that terminates the use of cash collateral, either the proposed order shall require at least three business days' notice before the use of cash collateral ceases (provided that the use of cash collateral conforms to any budget in effect) or the motion shall explain why such notice provision is not contained in the proposed order.

(d) Carve–Outs. Any provision in a motion or proposed order relating to a carve-out from liens or superpriorities shall disclose when a carve-out takes effect, whether it remains unaltered after payment of interim fees made before an event of default, and any effect of the carve-out on any borrowing base or borrowing availability under the postpetition loan. If a provision relating to a carve-out provides disparate treatment for the professionals retained by a committee appointed under § 1102 or § 1114 of the Bankruptcy Code, when compared with the treatment for professionals retained by the trustee or debtor in possession, or if the carve-out does not include fees payable to either the Bankruptcy Court or the United States Trustee, reasonable expenses of committee members (excluding fees and expenses of professionals employed by such committee members individually), and reasonable post-conversion fees and expenses of a chapter 7 trustee, or if a carve-out does not include the costs of investigating whether any claims or causes of action against the lender exist, there shall be disclosure thereof under subdivision (a) of this Local Rule and the motion shall contain a detailed explanation of the reasons therefor.

(e) Joint Obligations. In jointly-administered cases, if one or more debtors will be liable for the repayment of indebtedness for funds advanced to or for the benefit of another debtor, the motion and the proposed order shall describe, with specificity, any provisions of the agreement or proposed order that would affect the nature and priority, if any, of any interdebtor claims that would result if a debtor were to repay debt incurred by or for the benefit of another debtor.

(f) Investigation Period Relating to Waivers and Concessions as to Prepetition Debt. If a motion seeks entry of an order in which the debtor stipulates, acknowledges or otherwise admits to the validity, enforceability, priority, or amount of a claim that arose before the commencement of the case, or of any lien securing the claim, either the proposed order shall

include a provision that permits a committee appointed under § 1102 of the Bankruptcy Code and other parties in interest to undertake an investigation of the facts relating thereto, and proceedings relating to such determination, or the motion shall explain why the proposed order does not contain such a provision. The minimum time period for such committee or other party in interest to commence, or to file a motion to obtain authority to commence, any related proceedings as representative of the estate shall ordinarily be 60 days from the date of entry of the final order authorizing the use of cash collateral or the obtaining of credit, or such longer period as the Court orders for cause shown prior to the expiration of such period.

(g) Content of Interim Orders. A motion that seeks entry of an emergency or interim order before a final hearing under Bankruptcy Rule 4001(b)(2) or (c)(2) shall describe the amount and purpose of funds sought to be used or borrowed on an emergency or interim basis and shall set forth facts to support a finding that immediate or irreparable harm will be caused to the estate if immediate relief is not granted before the final hearing.

(h) Adequacy of Budget. If the debtor in possession or trustee will be subject to a budget under a proposed cash collateral or financing order or agreement, the motion filed under Bankruptcy Rule 4001(b), (c), or (d) shall include a statement by the trustee or debtor in possession as to whether it has reason to believe that the budget will be adequate, considering all available assets, to pay all administrative expenses due or accruing during the period covered by the financing or the budget.

(i) Notice. Notice of a preliminary or final hearing shall be given to the persons required by Bankruptcy Rules 4001(b)(3) and 4001(c)(3), as the case may be, the United States Trustee, and any other persons whose interests may be directly affected by the outcome of the motion or any provision of the proposed order.

(j) Presence at Hearing. Unless the court directs otherwise,

(1) counsel for each proposed lender, or for an agent representing such lender, shall be present at all preliminary and final hearings on the authority to obtain credit from such lender, and counsel for each entity, or for an agent of such entity, with an interest in cash collateral to be used with the entity's consent shall be present at all preliminary and final hearings on the authority to use such cash collateral; and

(2) a business representative of the trustee or debtor in possession, the proposed lender or an agent representing such lender, and any party objecting to the motion for authority to obtain credit, each with appropriate authority, must be present at, or reasonably available by telephone for, all preliminary and

final hearings for the purpose of making necessary decisions with respect to the proposed financing.

(k) Provisions of the Proposed Order.

(1) *Findings of Fact.*

(A) A proposed order approving the use of cash collateral under § 363(c) of the Bankruptcy Code, or granting authority to obtain credit under § 364 of the Bankruptcy Code, shall limit the recitation of findings to essential facts, including the facts required under § 364 of the Bankruptcy Code regarding efforts to obtain financing on a less onerous basis and (where required) facts sufficient to support a finding of good faith under § 364(e) of the Bankruptcy Code, and shall not include any findings extraneous to the use of cash collateral or to the financing.

(B) A proposed emergency or interim order shall include a finding that immediate and irreparable loss or damage will be caused to the estate if immediate financing is not obtained and should state with respect to notice only that the hearing was held pursuant to Bankruptcy Rule 4001(b)(2) or (c)(2), that notice was given to certain parties in the manner described, and that the notice was, in the debtor's belief, the best available under the circumstances.

(C) A proposed final order may include factual findings as to notice and the adequacy thereof.

(D) To the extent that a proposed order incorporates by reference to, or refers to a specific section of, a prepetition or postpetition loan agreement or other document, the proposed order shall also include a statement of such section's import.

(2) *Mandatory Provisions.* The proposed order shall contain all applicable provisions included in the enumerated lists of material provisions set forth in Bankruptcy Rule 4001(b)(1)(B), (c)(1)(B), and (d)(1)(B), as supplemented by subsection (a) of this Local Rule.

(3) *Cross–Collateralization and Rollups.* A proposed order approving cross-collateralization or a rollup shall include language that reserves the right of the Court to unwind, after notice and hearing, the postpetition protection provided to the prepetition lender or the paydown of the prepetition debt, whichever is applicable, in the event that there is a timely and successful challenge to the validity, enforceability, extent, perfection, or priority of the prepetition lender's claims or liens, or a determination that the prepetition debt was undersecured as of the petition date, and the cross-collateralization or rollup unduly advantaged the lender.

(4) *Waivers, Consents or Amendments with Respect to the Loan Agreement.* A proposed order may permit the parties to enter into waivers or consents with respect to the loan agreement or amendments thereof without the need for further court approval provided that (i) the agreement as so modified is not materially different from that approved, (ii) notice of all amendments is filed with the Court, and (iii) notice of all amendments (other than those that are ministerial or technical and do not adversely affect the debtor) are provided in advance to counsel for any committee appointed under § 1102 or § 1114 of the Bankruptcy Code, all parties requesting notice, and the United States Trustee.

(5) *Conclusions of Law.* A proposed interim order may provide that the debtor is authorized to enter into the loan or other agreement, but it shall not state that the Court has examined and approved the loan or other agreement.

(6) *Order to Control.* The proposed order shall state that to the extent that a loan or other agreement differs from the order, the order shall control.

(7) *Statutory Provisions Affected.* The proposed order shall specify those provisions of the Bankruptcy Code, Bankruptcy Rules and Local Rules relied upon as authority for granting relief, and shall identify those sections that are, to the extent permitted by law, being limited or abridged.

(8) *Conclusions of Law Regarding Notice.* A proposed final order may contain conclusions of law with respect to the adequacy of notice under § 364 of the Bankruptcy Code and Rule 4001.

[Adopted April 15, 1997. Amended effective August 4, 2008.]

Comment

This rule was amended in its entirety in 2008 to conform to the 2007 amendments to Bankruptcy Rule 4001 and to replace the procedures for requests for the use of cash collateral or to obtain credit that were governed by former General Order M–274. Thus, this rule should be read in conjunction with Bankruptcy Rule 4001 as the requirements contained in this rule are meant to supplement, but not duplicate, Bankruptcy Rule 4001. This rule is not intended to fundamentally change practice under former General Order M–274, except as expressly provided.

As provided in former General Order M–274, a single motion may be filed seeking entry of an interim order and a final order, which orders would be normally entered at the conclusion of the preliminary hearing and the final hearing, respectively, as those terms are used in Bankruptcy Rules 4001(b)(2) and (c)(2). In addition, where circumstances warrant, the debtor may seek emergency relief for financing limited to the amount necessary to avoid immediate and irreparable harm to the estate pending the preliminary hearing, but in the usual case, only a preliminary and a final hearing will be required.

Notwithstanding the provisions of subsection (i), emergency and interim relief may be entered after the best notice available under the circumstances; however, emergency and interim relief will ordinarily not be considered unless the United States Trustee and the Court have had a reasonable opportunity to review the motion, the financing agreement, and the proposed interim order, and the Court normally will not approve provisions that directly affect the interests of landlords, taxing and environmental authorities and other third-parties without notice to them.

As suggested in former General Order M–274, prospective debtors may provide substantially complete drafts of the motion, interim order, and related financing documents to the United States Trustee in advance of a filing, on a confidential basis. Debtors are encouraged to provide drafts of financing requests, including proposed orders, to the United States Trustee as early as possible in advance of filing to provide that office with the opportunity to comment.

The hearing on a final order for use of cash collateral under § 363(c) of the Bankruptcy Code, or for authority to obtain credit under § 364 of the Bankruptcy Code will ordinarily not commence until there has been a reasonable opportunity for the formation of a creditors committee under § 1102 of the Bankruptcy Code and either the creditors committee's appointment of counsel or reasonable opportunity to do so.

Reasonable allocations in a carve-out provision may be proposed among (i) expenses of professionals retained by committees appointed in the case, (ii) expenses of professionals retained by the debtor, (iii) fees payable to either the Bankruptcy Court or the United States Trustee, (iv) the reasonable expenses of committee members, and (v) reasonable post-conversion fees and expenses of a chapter 7 trustee, and the lender may refuse to include in a carve-out the costs of litigation or other assertions of claims against it.

As provided in former General Order M–274, non-essential facts regarding prepetition dealings and agreements may be included in an order approving the use of cash collateral or granting authority to obtain credit under a heading entitled "stipulations between the debtor and the lender" or "background."

As provided in former General Order M–274, an interim order will not ordinarily bind the Court with respect to the provisions of the final order provided that (i) the lender will be afforded all the benefits and protections of the interim order, including a lender's § 364(e) and § 363(m) protection with respect to funds advanced during the interim period, and (ii) the interim order will not bind the lender to advance funds pursuant to a final order that contains provisions contrary to or inconsistent with the interim order.

RULE 4001–3. REQUESTS FOR USE OF CASH COLLATERAL OR TO OBTAIN CREDIT—REPEALED

[Adopted effective August 2, 2004. Repealed effective August 4, 2008.]

Comment

This rule was repealed in 2008 because of the amendments to Local Bankruptcy Rule 4001–2 made in 2008, which govern cash collateral and financing motions.

RULE 4003–1. EXEMPTIONS

(a) **Amendment to Claim of Exemptions.** An amendment to a claim of exemptions pursuant to Bankruptcy Rules 1009 and 4003 shall be filed and served by the debtor or dependent of the debtor on

the trustee, the United States Trustee, and all creditors.

(b) **Automatic Extension of Time to File Objections to Claim of Exemptions in Event of Amendment to Schedules to Add a Creditor.** Unless the Court orders otherwise, if the schedules are amended to add a creditor, and the amendment is filed and served either (i) fewer than 30 days prior to the expiration of the time set forth in Bankruptcy Rule 4003(b) for the filing of objections to the list of property claimed as exempt, or (ii) at any time after such filing deadline, the added creditor shall have 30 days from the date of service of the amendment to file an objection to the list of property claimed as exempt.

[Adopted April 15, 1997; amended effective July 28, 1998; August 2, 2004.]

Comment

Subdivision (a) of this rule is derived from Former Local Bankruptcy Rule 37. See Bankruptcy Rule 4003(b), which permits the trustee or any creditor to object to the list of property claimed as exempt within 30 days following the conclusion of the meeting of creditors held pursuant to Bankruptcy Rule 2003(a), or the filing of any amendment to the list or supplemental schedules unless, within such period, the Court grants additional time.

[Comment amended effective July 28, 1998; August 2, 2004.]

RULE 4004–1. AUTOMATIC EXTENSION OF TIME TO FILE COMPLAINT OBJECTING TO DISCHARGE IN EVENT OF AMENDMENT

Unless the Court orders otherwise, if the schedules are amended to add a creditor, and the amendment is filed and served either (i) less than 60 days prior to the expiration of the time set forth in Bankruptcy Rule 4004(a) for the filing of a complaint objecting to discharge, or (ii) at any time after such filing deadline, the added creditor shall have 60 days from the date of service of the amendment to file the complaint objecting to discharge.

[Adopted April 15, 1997.]

RULE 4007–1. AUTOMATIC EXTENSION OF TIME TO FILE COMPLAINT TO DETERMINE DISCHARGEABILITY OF A DEBT IN EVENT OF AMENDMENT

Unless the Court orders otherwise, if the schedules are amended to add a creditor, and the amendment is filed and served either (i) less than 60 days prior to the expiration of the time set forth in Bankruptcy Rule 4007 for the filing of a complaint to obtain a determination of the dischargeability of any debt, or (ii) at any time after such filing deadline, the deadline for the filing of a complaint with respect to a claim of such creditor shall be 60 days from the date of service of the amendment upon such creditor.

[Adopted April 15, 1997.]

RULE 4007–2. WITHDRAWAL OR SETTLEMENT OF PROCEEDINGS TO DETERMINE DISCHARGE AND DISCHARGEABILITY

(a) Withdrawal of Complaint. In the event of the withdrawal of a complaint objecting to discharge or failure to prosecute an adversary proceeding objecting to discharge, no discharge shall be granted unless the debtor shall make and file an affidavit and the debtor's attorney shall make and file a certification that no consideration has been promised or given, directly or indirectly, for the withdrawal or failure to prosecute.

(b) Settlement of Proceedings. In all instances not governed by § 524(d) of the Bankruptcy Code, no adversary proceeding to determine the dischargeability of a debt shall be settled except pursuant to an order of the Court after due inquiry into the circumstances of any settlement, including the terms of any agreement entered into between the debtor and creditor relating to the payment of the debt, in whole or in part.

[Adopted April 15, 1997.]

Comment

This rule is derived from Former Local Bankruptcy Rule 48.

PART V. COURTS AND CLERKS

RULE 5001–1. CLERK'S OFFICE: HOURS; AFTER HOURS FILING

The offices of the Clerk shall be open Monday through Friday, from 8:30 a.m. to 5:00 p.m., except on legal and Court holidays, and shall be closed on Saturdays and Sundays. When the Clerk's office is closed, papers not filed electronically may be filed with the Court by depositing them in the night depository maintained by the District Clerk and are deemed filed as of the date and time stamped thereon. Any required fees for such filings shall be delivered to the Clerk's office no later than noon on the next business day.

[Adopted April 15, 1997; amended effective July 28, 1998; August 2, 2004.]

Comment

This rule is derived from Former Local Bankruptcy Rule 8 as modified to conform to Civil Rule 1.2 of the Local District Rules.

Bankruptcy Rule 5001(c) permits the adoption of a local rule setting forth the business hours of the Clerk.

The District Clerk maintains a night depository at the United States Courthouse located at 500 Pearl Street, New York, New York. The filing of papers in the District Court's night depository is intended to be used where exigent circumstances exist and is not intended as a regular alternative for filing papers with the Court during normal business hours or electronically at any time.

Under Former Local Bankruptcy Rule 8, papers filed in the District Court's night depository were deemed filed in the Court as of 8:30 a.m. the following business day. In accordance with Civil Rule 1.2 of the Local District Rules and *Greenwood v. New York*, 842 F.2d 636 (2d Cir. 1988), this rule deems papers deposited in the District Court's night depository to have been filed as of the date and time stamped thereon.

[Comment amended effective July 28, 1998; August 2, 2004.]

RULE 5005–1. FILING PAPERS

Except as provided in Local Bankruptcy Rule 1002–1, unless submitted by electronic means, all papers may be submitted for filing in the Clerk's office located in any of the three divisions of the Court identified in Rule 1073–1(a). However, all chambers copies required by Rule 9070–1(b) shall be submitted in the Clerk's office located where the Judge assigned to the case or proceeding sits.

[Adopted April 15, 1997; amended effective July 28, 1998; August 2, 2004.]

Comment

This rule is derived from Former Local Bankruptcy Rule 9(a).

[Comment amended effective July 28, 1998.]

RULE 5005–2. FILING BY ELECTRONIC MEANS

In cases in which electronic filing is required by applicable standing orders issued by the Court, documents shall be filed, signed, or verified by means that are consistent with such standing orders.

[Adopted effective July 28, 1998. Amended effective August 2, 2004.]

Comment

This rule implements the authority contained in Bankruptcy Rule 5005(a). Procedures for filing by electronic means are governed by General Order M–242 and any amendments or supplemental standing orders of the Court. Copies of General Order M–242, as well as any amendments or subsequent standing orders on this subject, may be obtained from the Clerk and are available on the Court's website at www.nysb.uscourts.gov.

[Comment amended effective August 2, 2004.]

RULE 5009–1. FINAL REPORT AND ACCOUNT AND CLOSING REPORT IN A CHAPTER 7 CASE

(a) Final Report and Account. Unless the Court orders otherwise, the notice given by the trustee of the filing of a final report and account in the form prescribed by the United States Trustee in a chapter 7 case shall have on its face in bold type the following language, or words of similar import:

A PERSON SEEKING AN AWARD OF COMPENSATION OR REIMBURSEMENT OF EXPENSES SHALL FILE AN APPLICATION WITH THE CLERK AND SERVE A COPY ON THE TRUSTEE AND THE UNITED STATES TRUSTEE NOT LATER THAN 20 DAYS PRIOR TO THE DATE OF THE HEARING ON THE TRUSTEE'S FINAL ACCOUNT. FAILURE TO FILE AND SERVE SUCH AN APPLICATION WITHIN THAT TIME MAY RESULT IN THE DISALLOWANCE OF FEES AND EXPENSES.

(b) Closing Report in an Asset Case. Unless the Court orders otherwise, in a chapter 7 asset case, the trustee shall file and serve upon the United States Trustee, together with the affidavit of final distribution, a closing report substantially in the following form:

TRUSTEE REPORT
TO THE CLERK'S OFFICE

CHAPTER 7 CLOSING REPORT
IN AN ASSET CASE

UNITED STATES BANKRUPTCY COURT
SOUTHERN DISTRICT OF NEW YORK

CHAPTER 7

DEBTOR NAME: CASE NO.

GROSS CASH RECEIPTS: $_____

FEES AND EXPENSES (From case inception):

TRUSTEE COMPENSATION

FEE for ATTORNEY FOR TRUSTEE

OTHER PROFESSIONAL FEES
and ALL EXPENSES

(including fee for debtor's attorney)

DISTRIBUTIONS (From case inception):

SECURED CREDITORS

PRIORITY CREDITORS

UNSECURED CREDITORS

EQUITY SECURITY HOLDERS

OTHER DISTRIBUTIONS (including payments to debtor, bond premiums, court reporters, storage, lien searches)

TOTAL

DATED: FOR THE TRUSTEE:

BY _____

(c) Closing Report in a No Asset Case. Unless the Court orders otherwise, in a chapter 7 no asset case, the trustee shall file and serve upon the United States Trustee a closing report substantially in the following form:

UNITED STATES BANKRUPTCY COURT
SOUTHERN DISTRICT OF NEW YORK

[Caption of Case]   : Chapter 7 Case No. ____

TRUSTEE'S REPORT OF NO DISTRIBUTION

I, ____, having been appointed trustee of the estate of the above-named debtor, report that I neither received any property nor paid any money on account of this estate except exempt property; that I have made a diligent inquiry into the financial affairs of the debtor(s) and the location of property belonging to the estate; and that there is no property available for distribution from the estate over and above that exempted by law.

Pursuant to Bankruptcy Rule 5009, I hereby certify that the estate of the above-named debtor has been fully administered.

I request that this report be approved and that I be discharged from any further duties as trustee.

DATED: _____, ____

_____
Trustee

[Adopted April 15, 1997; amended effective July 28, 1998.]

Comment

Subdivision (a) of this rule is derived from former Standing Order M–90.

Subdivisions (b) and (c) of this rule, added in 1996, complement § 704(9) of the Bankruptcy Code. Although not specifying a particular time period, subdivision (b) of this rule contemplates that the trustee will file the closing report as soon as practicable after the filing of a final account and the final allowance of fees. Thereafter, the Clerk may close the case upon the entry of a final decree.

[Comment amended effective July 28, 1998.]

RULE 5010–1. REOPENING CASES

(a) **Contents of Motion.** A motion to reopen a case pursuant to Bankruptcy Rule 5010 shall be in writing and state the name of the Judge to whom the case was assigned at the time it was closed.

(b) **Reference.** A motion to reopen a case shall be filed with the Clerk. The Clerk shall refer the motion to the Judge to whom the case was assigned at the time it was closed. If that Judge is no longer sitting, the motion shall be assigned in accordance with Local Bankruptcy Rule 1073–1.

[Adopted April 15, 1997; amended effective July 28, 1998.]

Comment

This rule is derived from Former Local Bankruptcy Rule 11.

[Comment amended effective July 28, 1998.]

RULE 5011–1. WITHDRAWAL OF REFERENCE

A motion for withdrawal of the reference shall be filed with the Clerk of the Bankruptcy Court. The movant is then required to file with the Clerk of the District Court a copy of the motion, the receipt for payment of the filing fee, three copies of the District Court Civil Cover Sheet, and a copy of any corporate ownership statement previously filed pursuant to Bankruptcy Rule 1007(a) or 7007.1. The movant shall then file with the Clerk of the Bankruptcy Court a statement indicating the Civil Case Number and District Court Judge assigned to the matter. All subsequent papers relating to the motion shall be filed with the Clerk of the District Court.

[Adopted April 15, 1997.]

Comment

This rule was amended in 2004 to specify the procedural requirements imposed on the party moving for withdrawal of the reference under 28 U.S.C. § 157(d).

[Comment adopted effective August 2, 2004.]

RULE 5070–1. OBTAINING RETURN DATE

Unless the Court orders otherwise, prior to serving a motion, cross-motion, or application, the moving party or applicant shall obtain a return date from the assigned Judge's chambers.

[Adopted April 15, 1997. Amended effective August 2, 2004.]

Comment

This rule is derived from former Standing Order M–99.

Pursuant to Local Bankruptcy Rule 9004–2(b), the return date obtained under this rule shall be included in the upper right-hand corner of the caption of the motion or application.

RULE 5073–1. PHOTOGRAPHING, BROADCASTING, AND TELEVISING IN COURTROOMS AND ENVIRONS

The taking of photographs and the use of recording devices in a courtroom or its environs, except by officials of the Court in the conduct of the Court's business, and radio or television broadcasting from a courtroom or its environs, during the progress of, or in connection with, judicial proceedings or otherwise, whether or not the Court is actually in session, are prohibited.

[Adopted April 15, 1997.]

Comment

This rule is derived from Former Local Bankruptcy Rule 35 and is an adaptation of Civil Rule 1.8 of the Local District Rules.

This rule extends the District Court's restrictions to all bankruptcy courtrooms in this district, including those located in White Plains and Poughkeepsie.

[Comment amended effective July 28, 1998.]

RULE 5075–1. CLERK'S USE OF OUTSIDE SERVICES AND AGENTS

(a) The Court may direct, subject to the supervision of the Clerk, the use of agents either on or off the Court's premises to file Court records, either by paper or electronic means, to issue notices, to maintain case dockets, to maintain Judges' calendars, and to maintain and disseminate other administrative information where the costs of such facilities or services are paid for by the estate.

(b) The Clerk shall maintain a duplicate of all electronic records maintained by agents appointed by the Court.

[Adopted April 15, 1997.]

Comment

This rule complements 28 U.S.C. § 156(c). Pursuant to the guidelines of the Judicial Conference of the United States, the Clerk is responsible for the security and integrity of all Court records.

RULE 5076–1. DEPOSIT FOR COURT REPORTING EXPENSES

The Court may enter an order directing a party who commences an adversary proceeding or contested matter to deposit with the court reporter such sums as the Judge may determine are necessary to pay the court reporting expense. The order also may state that the adversary proceeding or contested matter may be dismissed without prejudice if the deposit is not made.

[Adopted April 15, 1997.]

Comment

This rule is derived from Former Local Bankruptcy Rule 12.

Local Bankruptcy Rule 9023–1(b) governs the taxing of costs of court reporting services.

RULE 5078–1. PAYMENT OF FEES

Unless the Court orders otherwise, the Clerk shall not be required to render any service for which a fee is prescribed by statute or the Judicial Conference of the United States unless the fee is paid in advance.

[Adopted April 15, 1997.]

Comment

This rule is derived from Former Local Bankruptcy Rule 10 and is an adaptation of Civil Rule 1.7 of the Local District Rules.

An application for permission to make installment payments may be filed pursuant to Bankruptcy Rule 1006(b).

[Comment amended effective July 28, 1998.]

PART VI. COLLECTION AND LIQUIDATION OF THE ESTATE

RULE 6004–1. SALES OF PROPERTY, APPRAISALS, AND AUCTIONS

(a) Notice. The trustee may sell property of the estate that the trustee reasonably believes has an aggregate gross value of no more than $10,000 by public or private sale on five days' written notice to any party with an interest in such property, the landlord of the premises on which the property is located, and such other parties as the Court may direct. The notice of any proposed sale of property of the estate having an aggregate gross value of at least $2,500 shall include the time and place of the proposed sale, whether the sale will be public or private, and the terms and conditions of the proposed sale.

(b) Appraisals. Unless the Court orders otherwise, if an appraiser has been employed, the property to be appraised shall not be sold until after the appraisal has been filed.

(1) *Caption.* All appraisals filed with the Court shall have a cover sheet bearing the caption of the case in compliance with Local Bankruptcy Rule 9004–2 and the date, if any, of the proposed sale.

(2) *Filing and Access.* Unless the Court orders otherwise, any appraiser employed pursuant to § 327(a) of the Bankruptcy Code shall file with the Court and the United States Trustee each appraisal made of property of the estate not later than 12:00 noon on the business day prior to the scheduled sale of the property. Each appraisal shall be kept under seal upon filing and treated as confidential by the Court and the United States Trustee. Access to the appraisal may be had only by the Court, the United States Trustee, and such other parties as the Court may direct, and neither they nor the appraiser shall disclose any of the contents thereof until after the conclusion of the bidding at any sale of the appraised property, at which time the Court may order the appraisal to be unsealed. Unless the Court orders

otherwise, the appraisal shall be unsealed six months from the date on which the appraisal is filed.

(3) *Conformity With Auctioneer's Catalogue of Sale.* If property is to be appraised and sold at auction, upon request, the auctioneer promptly shall deliver the catalogue of sale to the appraiser. The appraisal shall conform to the catalogue to the greatest extent possible.

(c) Manner of Display and Conduct of Auction. Unless the Court orders otherwise, the auction shall be conducted in the following manner:

(1) the property shall be on public display for a reasonable period of time prior to the sale;

(2) prior to receiving bids, the auctioneer shall announce the terms of sale;

(3) where practicable, the property shall be offered for sale first in bulk and then in lots; and

(4) any property that is not to be included in the sale shall be set apart and conspicuously marked "not included in the sale," and such fact shall be announced by the auctioneer before the sale.

(d) Joint Sales.

(1) If the trustee and a secured party, or other third party having an interest in the property, desire to conduct a joint auction sale, or if the joint sale of property in more than one bankruptcy estate is anticipated to be more cost effective or beneficial for all the bankruptcy estates, the Court shall enter an order prior to the sale fixing the method of allocating the commissions and expenses of sale.

(2) The commissions and expenses incurred on behalf of one bankruptcy estate in a joint auction sale shall not be charged to any other estate unless the motion requesting the joint auction reveals the identity and number of any other estate participants in the

joint auction sale, and how such commissions and expenses shall be apportioned among them.

(3) Nothing in this rule shall prevent the trustee from participating in a joint sale with a non-debtor, provided it is in the best interest of the debtor's estate and its creditors.

(e) Proceeds of Sale. Upon receipt of the proceeds of sale, the auctioneer immediately shall deposit the proceeds in a separate account that the auctioneer maintains for each estate in accordance with the requirements of § 345(a) of the Bankruptcy Code. Unless the Court orders otherwise, payment of the gross proceeds of the sale, less the auctioneer's reimbursable expenses, shall be made promptly by the auctioneer to the trustee or debtor in possession, but in no event later than 10 days after the date on which the proceeds are received with respect to each item or lot sold.

(f) Report of Sale. Unless the Court orders otherwise, (i) within 20 days after the last date of the auction, the auctioneer shall file a report with the Court and transmit a copy of the report to the United States Trustee, and (ii) if all proceeds of the auction have not been received by such date, the auctioneer shall file a supplemental report within 10 days after all proceeds have been received. The report shall set forth:

(1) the time, date, and place of the sale;

(2) the gross dollar amount of the sale;

(3) if property was sold in lots, a description of the items in each lot, the quantity in each lot, the dollar amount received for each lot, and any bulk bid(s) received;

(4) an itemized statement of expenditures, disbursements, and commissions allowable under Local Bankruptcy Rule 6005–1, including the name and address of the payee, together with the original receipts or canceled checks, or true copies thereof, for the expenditures or disbursements. Where labor charges are included, the report shall specify the days worked and the number of hours worked each day by each person and the last four digits of the person's social security number. If the canceled checks are not available at the time the report is filed, the report shall so state, and the canceled checks shall be filed as soon as they become available;

(5) where the auctioneer has a blanket insurance policy covering all sales conducted by the auctioneer, for which original receipts and canceled checks are not available, an explanation of how the insurance expense charged to the estate was computed;

(6) if any articles were withdrawn from the sale because of a third party claim of an interest therein, a separate itemized statement of the articles reflecting the names of such third parties;

(7) the names and addresses of all purchasers;

(8) the sign-in sheet, if any; otherwise, the approximate number of people attending the sale;

(9) the items for which there were no bids and the disposition of those items;

(10) the terms and conditions of sale that were read to the audience immediately prior to the commencement of the sale;

(11) a statement of the manner and extent of advertising of the sale;

(12) a statement of the manner and extent of the availability of the items for inspection; and

(13) any other information that the United States Trustee may request.

(g) Affidavit to Accompany Report of Sale. The auctioneer shall submit with the report of sale an affidavit stating: (i) that the auctioneer is a duly licensed auctioneer; (ii) the auctioneer's license number and place of business; (iii) the authority pursuant to which the auctioneer conducted the auction; (iv) the date and place of the auction; (v) that the labor and other expenses incurred on behalf of the estate as listed in the report of sale were reasonable and necessary; and (vi) that the gross proceeds of sale, exclusive of expenses, were remitted to the trustee or debtor in possession and the date of the remittance.

(h) Advertisement and Publication of Notice of Sale. An advertisement or publication of notice of a sale by auction or otherwise may be made without Court approval if it is sufficient to provide adequate notice of the sale and is advertised or published at least once in a newspaper of general circulation in the city or county in which the property is located. The advertisement or publication shall include: (i) the date, time, and place of the sale; (ii) a description of the property to be sold including, with respect to real property, the approximate acreage of any real estate outside the limits of any town or city, the street, lot, and block number of any real estate within any town or city, and a general statement of the character of any improvements upon the property; (iii) the terms and conditions of the sale; and (iv) the name, address, and telephone number of the trustee or debtor in possession. The Court may fix the manner and extent of advertising and publication at any time.

(i) No Order Needed to Confirm Sale. Unless a timely objection is made, no order of the Court shall be required to confirm a sale of property pursuant to this rule. The trustee, debtor, or debtor in possession may execute any documents and instruments that are necessary to complete the sale and shall file with the Court and transmit to the United States Trustee a report of the sale as required by Local Bankruptcy Rule 6004–1(f) when the sale is completed. On request, the Clerk shall issue a certificate stating that a notice of a proposed action, with proof of service, has been filed with the Court pursuant to Local Bankruptcy Rule 2002–2 and that no timely objection has been filed.

(j) Compliance With United States Trustee's Guidelines. In addition to the foregoing requirements, parties conducting a sale of property of the estate, including trustees and auctioneers, shall comply with the requirements contained in any guidelines promulgated by the United States Trustee.

[Adopted April 15, 1997; amended effective July 28, 1998; August 2, 2004.]

Comment

Subdivision (a) of this rule was added in 1996. Subdivision (b) of this rule is derived from Former Local Bankruptcy Rule 40. Subdivisions (c), (d), (e), (f), and (g) of this rule are derived from Former Local Bankruptcy Rule 41. Subdivision (h) of this rule is derived from Former Local Bankruptcy Rule 42. Subdivision (i) of this rule is derived from Former Local Bankruptcy Rule 45(g).

Subdivision (d) of this rule was amended in 2004 to provide for joint sales of property from more than one estate. Subdivision (e) makes clear that the proceeds of an auction shall be turned over within 10 days of their receipt, even if the auction has not yet concluded. Unlike subdivision (e), which requires the turnover of proceeds with respect to each lot or item of property, subdivision (f) contemplates the filing of a report within 20 days after the auction has been concluded and the supplementing of such report when the proceeds are received thereafter. Due to privacy concerns, subdivision (f) of this rule was amended in 2004 to delete the requirement that an auctioneer include in its report the social security numbers of people being paid labor charges.

The contents of a notice of a proposed sale are governed by Bankruptcy Rule 2002(c)(1).

[Comment amended effective July 28, 1998; August 2, 2004.]

RULE 6005–1. AUCTIONEERS

(a) No Official Auctioneer. There shall be no official auctioneer.

(b) Compensation. Unless the Court orders otherwise for cause, compensation and reimbursement of expenses shall be allowed to an auctioneer for sales of property as follows:

(1) commissions on each sale conducted by the auctioneer at the following rates:

(A) 10% of any gross proceeds of sale up to $50,000;

(B) 8% of any gross proceeds of sale in excess of $50,000 but not more than $75,000;

(C) 6% of any gross proceeds of sale in excess of $75,000 but not more than $100,000;

(D) 4% of any gross proceeds of sale in excess of $100,000 but not more than $150,000; and

(E) 2% of any gross proceeds of sale in excess of $150,000; and

(2) reimbursement for reasonable and necessary expenses directly related to the sale, including labor, printing, advertising, and insurance, but excluding workers' compensation, social security, unemployment insurance, and other payroll taxes. When directed by the trustee or debtor in possession to transport goods, the auctioneer shall be reimbursed for expenditures related thereto. No travel expenses shall be allowed, except as ordered by the Court.

(c) Purchase Prohibited. An auctioneer, or officer, director, stockholder, agent, or employee of an auctioneer, shall not purchase directly or indirectly, or have a financial interest in the purchase of, any property of the estate that the auctioneer has been employed to sell.

(d) Bond. An auctioneer employed pursuant to § 327 of the Bankruptcy Code shall not act until the auctioneer files with respect to each estate, at the auctioneer's expense, a surety bond in favor of the United States, to be approved, and in such sum as may be fixed, by the United States Trustee, which is conditioned upon:

(1) the faithful and prompt accounting for all monies and property that may come into the auctioneer's possession;

(2) compliance with all rules, orders, and decrees of the Court; and

(3) the faithful performance of the auctioneer's duties.

(e) Blanket Bond. In lieu of a bond in each case, an auctioneer may be permitted to file, at the auctioneer's own expense, a blanket bond covering all cases in which the auctioneer may act. The blanket bond shall be in favor of the United States in such sum as the United States Trustee shall fix and shall be conditioned for each estate on the same terms as bonds in separate estates.

(f) Application for Commissions. An auctioneer shall file an application with the Court for approval of commissions on not less than five days' notice to the debtor, the trustee, the United States Trustee, and each committee. No application shall be granted unless the report of sale referred to in Local Bankruptcy Rule 6004–1(f) has been filed.

(g) Compliance With United States Trustee's Guidelines. In addition to the foregoing requirements, an auctioneer shall comply with the requirements contained in any guidelines promulgated by the United States Trustee.

[Adopted April 15, 1997; amended effective July 28, 1998.]

Comment

This rule is derived from Former Local Bankruptcy Rule 41.

Subdivision (g) of this rule is new. Advertisements of auction sales are governed by Local Bankruptcy Rule 6004–1(h).

[Comment amended effective July 28, 1998.]

RULE 6006–1. EXECUTORY CONTRACTS AND UNEXPIRED LEASES

(a) Motion to Assume, Reject, or Assign Executory Contract or Unexpired Lease. A motion to assume, reject, or assign an executory contract or unexpired lease shall be served in accordance with the time limits set forth in Local Bankruptcy Rule 9006–1(b), which may be waived or modified upon the written consent of all parties entitled to notice of the motion. In the event that a nonconsensual order is sought on less than 10 days' notice, Local Bankruptcy Rule 9077–1 shall govern and an actual hearing shall be held.

(b) Motion to Assume Executory Contract or Unexpired Lease in Chapter 7 Case. Unless the Court orders otherwise, in a chapter 7 case, a trustee moving to assume an executory contract or unexpired lease of residential real property or personal property of the debtor shall seek to obtain a return date for the hearing on the motion that is within 60 days after the order for relief or, if the time to assume has been extended, before the expiration of such extended period. If the trustee files a motion to assume or to extend the time to assume or reject an executory contract or unexpired lease of residential real property or personal property, and the motion is filed not later than 60 days after the order for relief (or, if the time to assume or reject the executory contract or unexpired lease has been extended previously by order of the Court, before the expiration of the extended time) with a return date no later than 14 days from the date of such filing, the time to assume or reject the executory contract or unexpired lease shall be extended automatically and without court order until the entry of the order resolving the motion.

(c) Motion to Assume Unexpired Lease of Nonresidential Real Property. Unless the Court orders otherwise, in a case under any chapter, a debtor, debtor in possession, or trustee moving to assume an unexpired lease of nonresidential real property under which the debtor is the lessee shall seek to obtain a return date for the hearing on the motion that is within 120 days after the order for relief or, if the time to assume has been extended, before the expiration of such extended period. If the debtor, debtor in possession, or the trustee files a motion to assume or to extend the time to assume or reject an unexpired lease of nonresidential real property, and the motion is filed not later than 120 days after the order for relief (or, if the time to assume or reject the unexpired lease has been extended previously by order of the Court, before the expiration of the extended time)

with a return date no later than 14 days from the date of such filing, the time to assume or reject the unexpired lease will be extended automatically and without court order until the entry of the order resolving the motion, except that the time for the debtor, debtor in possession, or trustee to assume or reject such unexpired lease shall not be extended beyond the date that is 210 days after the entry of the order for relief without the prior written consent of the landlord.

(d) Aircraft Equipment and Vessels. Unless the Court orders otherwise, a debtor in possession or trustee moving for approval of an agreement to perform all obligations of the debtor pursuant to § 1110(a)(1)(A) of the Bankruptcy Code shall seek to obtain a return date for the hearing on the motion that is within 60 days after the order for relief or, if the time to assume has been extended by order of the Court, before the expiration of such extended period.

(e) Rolling Stock Equipment. Unless the Court orders otherwise, a trustee moving for approval of an agreement to perform all obligations of the debtor pursuant to § 1168(a)(1)(A) of the Bankruptcy Code shall seek to obtain a return date for the hearing on the motion that is within 60 days after the date of commencement of the case or, if the time to assume has been extended by order of the Court, before the expiration of such extended period.

[Adopted April 15, 1997. Amended effective August 2, 2004.]

Comment

Subdivision (a) of this rule is derived from former Standing Order M–118. Subdivisions (b) and (c) of this rule are derived from Former Local Bankruptcy Rule 44(b) and (c). Subdivisions (d) and (e) of this rule, added in 1996, are derived from §§ 1110 and 1168 of the Bankruptcy Code.

Section 365(d)(1) of the Bankruptcy Code contemplates that a hearing on a motion by a chapter 7 trustee to assume an executory contract or unexpired lease of residential real property or personal property of the debtor ordinarily will take place within 60 days from the date of the order for relief. Likewise, § 365(d)(4) of the Bankruptcy Code contemplates that a final hearing on a motion by a debtor, debtor in possession, or trustee to assume an unexpired lease of nonresidential real property of the debtor ordinarily will take place within 60 days from the date of the order for relief.

Under § 365(d)(1) of the Bankruptcy Code, in a chapter 7 case, the Court may, for cause, extend the 60-day time period for assuming or rejecting an executory contract or unexpired lease of residential real property or personal property. Similarly, under § 365(d)(4), the Court may, for cause, extend the 60-day time period for assuming or rejecting an unexpired lease of nonresidential real property. In 2004, subdivisions (b) and (c) of this rule were amended to avoid the necessity of obtaining a "bridge order" extending these time periods in the event that a timely motion to assume or a timely motion to extend the time was filed but not resolved by the Court before the expiration of the time to assume or reject the contract or lease. Adequate cause for an extension of time to assume or reject the executory contract or unexpired lease until the Court rules on the motion exists by virtue of the fact that a motion to assume or to extend the time was filed in a timely manner. Any party in interest objecting to the extension of time may request a hearing on an expedited basis. To prevent abuse of the automatic extension, the return date of the motion must be no later than 14 days after the motion is filed.

[Comment amended effective July 28, 1998; August 2, 2004; October 17, 2005.]

RULE 6007–1. ABANDONMENT OR DISPOSITION OF PROPERTY

(a) Unless the Court orders otherwise, the notice of a proposed abandonment or disposition of property pursuant to Bankruptcy Rule 6007(a) shall describe the property to be abandoned or disposed of, state concisely the reason for the proposed abandonment or disposition, and, in the case of abandonment, identify the entity to whom the property is proposed to be abandoned.

(b) If the trustee files a notice of abandonment of a residential real property lease, other than a proprietary lease for a cooperative residence, the notice need only be served on the debtor and the landlord.

[Adopted April 15, 1997.]

Comment

This rule, added in 1996, simplifies the procedure for abandonment of an individual debtor's leased residence that is of no value to the estate so that the debtor may remain in such premises.

[Comment amended effective July 28, 1998.]

PART VII. ADVERSARY PROCEEDINGS

RULE 7005–1. FILING OF DISCOVERY–RELATED DOCUMENTS

(a) Except as provided in subdivision (b) of this rule, unless the Court orders otherwise, transcripts of depositions, exhibits to depositions, interrogatories, answers to interrogatories, document requests, responses to document requests, requests for admissions, and responses to requests for admissions shall not be filed with the Court.

(b) When discovery or disclosure material not on file with the Court is needed for an appeal, the necessary portion of that material may be filed with the Clerk.

[Adopted April 15, 1997; amended effective July 28, 1998.]

Comment

This rule is derived from Civil Rule 5.1 of the Local District Rules.

[Comment amended effective July 28, 1998.]

RULE 7007–1. DISCOVERY–RELATED MOTION PRACTICE

(a) **Attorney's Affidavit.** No discovery-related motion under Bankruptcy Rules 7026 through 7037 shall be heard unless counsel for the moving party files with the Court, at or prior to the hearing, an affidavit certifying that such counsel has conferred with counsel for the opposing party in a good faith effort to resolve by agreement the issues raised by the motion without the intervention of the Court and has been unable to reach an agreement. If any of the issues raised by motion have been resolved by agreement, the affidavit shall specify the issues so resolved and the issues remaining unresolved.

(b) **Request for Informal Conference.** No discovery-related motion under Bankruptcy Rules 7026 through 7037 shall be heard unless counsel for the moving party first requests an informal conference with the Court and either the request has been denied or the discovery dispute has not been resolved as a consequence of the conference.

[Adopted April 15, 1997.]

Comment

This rule is derived from Former Local Bankruptcy Rule 13.

Subdivision (a) of this rule is an adaptation of Civil Rule 3(f) of the Former District Rules. Subdivision (b) of this rule is an adaptation of Civil Rule 37.2 of the Local District Rules.

[Comment amended effective July 28, 1998.]

RULE 7007.1–1 CORPORATE OWNERSHIP STATEMENT

The Corporate Ownership Statement required under Bankruptcy Rule 7007.1 shall also be filed by any party to an adversary proceeding, other than the debtor or a governmental entity, that is a general or limited partnership or joint venture.

[Adopted effective August 2, 2004.]

Comment

Bankruptcy Rule 7007.1, effective December 1, 2003, requires a Corporate Ownership Statement to be filed for any corporation that is a party to an adversary proceeding other than the debtor or a governmental entity. "Corporation" is broadly defined under § 101(9) of the Bankruptcy Code (and includes, for instance, limited liability companies and other unincorporated companies or associations), but it does not cover general or limited partnerships. The reasons for which this rule was enacted—to give the Judges of this Court information by which they can determine whether or not they need to recuse themselves—apply equally to general and limited partnerships, and joint ventures. This local rule requires a similar disclosure with respect to business organizations of that character.

[Comment adopted effective August 2, 2004.]

RULE 7016–1. SUBMISSION OF MARKED PLEADINGS

Unless the Court orders otherwise, marked pleadings are not required.

[Adopted April 15, 1997. Amended effective August 2, 2004.]

Comment

The Judges of the Court have determined that the benefits derived from the submission of marked pleadings normally do not justify the burdens on the plaintiff in submitting them, particularly in light of the information contained in pre-trial orders.

[Comment amended effective July 28, 1998; August 2, 2004.]

RULE 7024–1. NOTICE OF CLAIM OF UNCONSTITUTIONALITY— REPEALED

[Adopted April 15, 1997; amended effective July 28, 1998; repealed effective August 4, 2008.]

Comment

This rule was repealed in 2008 as unnecessary because of the adoption in 2008 of Bankruptcy Rule 9005.1, which makes Rule 5.1 of the Federal Rules of Civil Procedure applicable to cases under the Bankruptcy Code. Rule 5.1 accomplishes the same objective as former Local Bankruptcy Rule 7024–1.

RULE 7026–1. UNIFORM DEFINITIONS IN DISCOVERY REQUESTS

Civil Rule 26.3 of the Local District Rules shall apply to discovery requests made in cases and proceedings commenced under the Bankruptcy Code.

[Adopted April 15, 1997; amended effective July 28, 1998.]

Comment

This rule contains a technical change to reflect a renumbering of the applicable Local District Rule.

[Comment adopted effective July 28, 1998.]

RULE 7026–2. OPT–OUT FROM CERTAIN PROVISIONS OF RULE 26 OF THE FEDERAL RULES OF CIVIL PROCEDURE—REPEALED

[Adopted effective July 28, 1998. Repealed effective August 2, 2004.]

RULE 7027–1. DEPOSITIONS PRIOR TO COMMENCEMENT OF ADVERSARY PROCEEDING OR PENDING APPEAL WHEN DEPOSITION IS MORE THAN 100 MILES FROM COURTHOUSE

If, prior to the commencement of an adversary proceeding or pending appeal, a proposed deposition pursuant to Bankruptcy Rule 7027 is sought to be taken at a location more than 100 miles from the courthouse, the Court may provide in the order therefor that, prior to the examination, the party seeking to take the deposition shall pay the expense of the attendance of one attorney for each adverse party, or expected adverse party, including reasonable attorney's fees. Unless the Court orders otherwise, any amounts paid pursuant to this subdivision shall be a taxable cost in the event the party taking the deposition is awarded costs of the adversary proceeding.

[Adopted April 15, 1997; amended effective July 28, 1998.]

Comment

This rule is derived from Former Local Bankruptcy Rule 24 and is an adaptation of Civil Rule 30.1 of the Local District Rules.

[Comment amended effective July 28, 1998.]

RULE 7030–1. DEPOSITIONS UPON ORAL EXAMINATION

If a proposed deposition upon oral examination is sought to be taken at a location more than 100 miles from the courthouse, the Court may provide in any order entered pursuant to Bankruptcy Rule 7030 that, prior to the examination, the party seeking to take the deposition shall pay the expense of the attendance of one attorney for each adverse party, or expected adverse party, including reasonable attorneys' fees. Unless the Court orders otherwise, any amounts paid pursuant to this subdivision shall be a taxable cost in the event that the party taking the deposition is awarded costs of the adversary proceeding.

[Adopted April 15, 1997.]

Comment

This rule is derived from Former Local Bankruptcy Rule 24 and is an adaptation of Civil Rule 30.1 of the Local District Rules.

[Comment amended effective July 28, 1998.]

RULE 7030–2. OPT–OUT FROM CERTAIN PROVISIONS OF RULE 30 OF THE FEDERAL RULES OF CIVIL PROCEDURE—REPEALED

[Adopted effective July 28, 1998. Repealed effective August 2, 2004.]

RULE 7031–1. OPT–OUT FROM CERTAIN PROVISIONS OF RULE 31 OF THE FEDERAL RULES OF CIVIL PROCEDURE—REPEALED

[Adopted effective July 28, 1998. Repealed effective August 2, 2004.]

RULE 7033–1. INTERROGATORIES

(a) Restrictions. At the commencement of discovery, interrogatories will be restricted to those questions seeking names of witnesses with knowledge or information relevant to the subject matter of the action, the computation of each category of damage alleged, and the existence, custodian, location, and general description of relevant documents, including pertinent insurance agreements, and other physical evidence, and information of a similar nature, to the extent such information has not already been provided under Fed.R.Civ.P. 26(a)(1).

(b) Method of Obtaining Information. During discovery, interrogatories, other than those seeking information described in subdivision (a) of this rule, may be served only if (i) they are a more practical method of obtaining the information sought than a request for production or a deposition or (ii) ordered by the Court.

(c) What May Be Served. Unless the Court orders otherwise, at the conclusion of each party's discovery, and prior to the discovery cut-off date, interrogatories seeking the claims and contentions of the opposing party may be served. Questions seeking the names of expert witnesses and the substance of their opinions also may be served if such information has not yet been supplied.

(d) No Interrogatories to Be Unanswered. No part of an interrogatory shall be left unanswered merely because an objection is interposed to another part of the interrogatory.

(e) Objections or Requests for Relief.

(1) In connection with any objection or request for relief with respect to interrogatories or answers to interrogatories, the party making the objection or request for relief shall (i) simultaneously file a copy of the interrogatories or answers to interrogatories and (ii) specify and quote verbatim each relevant interrogatory or answer and, immediately following each specification, set forth the basis of the objection or relief requested.

(2) If an objection or request for relief is made to any interrogatory or portion thereof, the objection shall state all grounds with specificity. Any ground not stated in the objection or request for relief within the time provided by the Bankruptcy Rules, or any extensions thereof, shall be deemed waived.

(3) If a claim of privilege is asserted in an objection or request for relief with respect to any interrogatory or portion thereof, and an answer is not provided on the basis of the assertion, the objection or request for relief shall identify:

(A) the nature of the privilege being claimed and, if the privilege is being asserted in connection with a claim or defense governed by state law, the state's privilege rule being invoked; and

(B) unless divulgence of such information would cause disclosure of the allegedly privileged information:

1. for documents: (i) the type of document; (ii) the general subject matter of the document; (iii) the date of the document; and (iv) such other information as is sufficient to identify the document for a subpoena duces tecum, including, where appropriate, the author of the document, the addressee of the document, and, where not apparent, the relationship of the author to the addressee and the names of all entities that received a copy of the document.

2. for oral communications: (i) the name of the person making the communication, the names of any persons present while the communication was made, and, where not apparent, the relationship of the persons present to the person making the communication; (ii) the date and place of the communication; and (iii) the general subject matter of the communication.

(f) Reference to Records. If a party answers an interrogatory by reference to records from which the answer may be derived or ascertained, as permitted by Bankruptcy Rule 7033:

(1) the specification of documents to be produced shall be in sufficient detail to permit the interrogating party to locate and identify the records and ascertain the answer as readily as could the party from whom discovery is sought;

(2) the producing party shall also make available any computerized information or summaries thereof that it has, or can adduce by a relatively simple procedure, unless these materials are privileged or otherwise immune from discovery;

(3) the producing party shall also provide any relevant compilations, abstracts, or summaries in its custody or readily obtainable by it, unless these materials are privileged or otherwise immune from discovery; and

(4) unless the Court orders otherwise, the documents shall be made available for inspection and copying within 10 days after service of the answers to

interrogatories or on a date agreed upon by the parties.

[Adopted April 15, 1997; amended effective July 28, 1998; August 2, 2004.]

Comment

This rule is derived from Former Local Bankruptcy Rule 14 and is an adaptation of Civil Rules 5.1, 33.1, 33.3, and 37.1 of the Local District Rules, with the exception of subdivision (e)(1) of this rule, which is derived from Former Local Bankruptcy Rule 13.

The initial disclosures required under Fed.R.Civ.P. 26(a)(1) must be made in adversary proceedings. Because information previously sought by interrogatories will frequently have been obtained by those initial disclosures, this rule has been amended accordingly.

[Comment amended effective July 28, 1998; August 2, 2004.]

RULE 7033–2. OPT–OUT FROM CERTAIN PROVISIONS OF RULE 33 OF THE FEDERAL RULES OF CIVIL PROCEDURE—REPEALED

[Adopted effective July 28, 1998. Repealed effective August 2, 2004.]

RULE 7034–1. OBJECTIONS TO, AND REQUESTS FOR RELIEF WITH RESPECT TO PRODUCTION OF DOCUMENTS

(a) In connection with any objection or request for relief with respect to document requests or answers thereto, the party making the objection or request for relief shall (i) simultaneously file a copy of the document request or answer and (ii) specify and quote verbatim each relevant document request or answer and, immediately following each specification, set forth the basis of the objection or relief requested.

(b) If an objection or request for relief is made with respect to any document request or portion thereof, the objection or request for relief shall state all grounds with specificity. Any ground not stated in the objection or request for relief within the time provided by the Bankruptcy Rules, or any extensions thereof, shall be deemed waived.

(c) If a claim of privilege is asserted in an objection or request for relief with respect to any document request or portion thereof, and an answer is not provided on the basis of the assertion, the objection or request for relief shall identify:

(1) the nature of the privilege being claimed and, if the privilege is being asserted in connection with a claim or defense governed by state law, the state's privilege rule being invoked; and

(2) unless divulgence of such information would cause disclosure of the allegedly privileged information: (i) the type of document; (ii) the general subject matter of the document; (iii) the date of the document; and (iv) such other information as is sufficient to identify the document for a subpoena duces tecum, including, where appropriate, the author of the document, the addressee of the document, and, where not apparent, the relationship of the author to the addressee, and the names of all entities that received a copy of the document.

[Adopted April 15, 1997; amended effective July 28, 1998.]

Comment

This rule is derived from Former Local Bankruptcy Rule 14(e). Subdivision (a) of this rule is new and has been added to conform to subdivision (e)(1) of Local Bankruptcy Rule 7033–1.

Subdivision (c)(2) of this rule has been modified to conform to subdivision (e)(3)(B)(1) of Local Bankruptcy Rule 7033–1.

[Comment amended effective July 28, 1998.]

RULE 7034–2. OPT–OUT FROM CERTAIN PROVISIONS OF RULE 34 OF THE FEDERAL RULES OF CIVIL PROCEDURE—REPEALED

[Adopted effective July 28, 1998. Repealed effective August 2, 2004.]

RULE 7036–1. REQUESTS FOR ADMISSION

In connection with any objection to a request for admission, the objecting party shall (i) file a copy of the request for admission simultaneously with the filing of the objection, (ii) specify and quote verbatim in the objection each request to which the objection is made, and (iii) immediately following each specification, set forth the basis of the objection.

[Adopted April 15, 1997; amended effective July 28, 1998.]

Comment

This rule is derived from Former Local Bankruptcy Rule 13(f) and is an adaptation of Civil Rule 37.1 of the Local District Rules.

[Comment amended effective July 28, 1998.]

RULE 7036–2. OPT–OUT FROM CERTAIN PROVISIONS OF RULE 36 OF THE FEDERAL RULES OF CIVIL PROCEDURE—REPEALED

[Adopted effective July 28, 1998. Repealed effective August 2, 2004.]

RULE 7052–1. PROPOSED FINDINGS OF FACT AND CONCLUSIONS OF LAW

Before or after the announcement of its decision, the Court, on notice to all parties, may require one or more parties to submit proposed findings of fact and conclusions of law. Any party submitting proposed findings of fact and conclusions of law shall serve them on all other parties within the time fixed by the Court. Unless the Court orders simultaneous submissions, any party may submit counter-findings and conclusions and shall serve them on all other parties within the time fixed by the Court. Unless adopted or otherwise ordered by the Court, proposed findings of fact and conclusions of law shall not form any part of the record on appeal.

[Adopted April 15, 1997. Amended effective August 2, 2004.]

Comment

This rule is derived from Former Local Bankruptcy Rule 18 and is an adaptation of Civil Rule 23 of the Former District Rules.

[Comment amended effective July 28, 1998.]

RULE 7055–1. CERTIFICATE OF DEFAULT

A party applying for a certificate of default from the Clerk pursuant to Bankruptcy Rule 7055 shall submit an affidavit, together with proof of service, showing that (i) the party against whom a default is sought is not an infant, in the military, or an incompetent person, (ii) the party has failed to plead or otherwise defend the action, and (iii) the pleading to which no response has been made was properly served.

[Adopted effective July 28, 1998.]

Comment

This rule is new and is derived from Civil Rule 55.1 of the Local District Rules.

RULE 7055–2. DEFAULT JUDGMENT

(a) By the Clerk. Upon issuance by the Clerk of a certificate of default, if the claim to which no response has been made only seeks payment of a sum certain and does not include a request for attorney's fees or other substantive relief, and if a default judgment is sought against all remaining parties to the action, the moving party may request that the Clerk enter a default judgment by submitting an affidavit, together with proof of service, showing the principal amount due and owing, not exceeding the amount sought in the claim to which no response has been made, plus interest, if any, computed by the party, with credit for all payments received to date clearly set forth, and costs, if any, pursuant to 28 U.S.C. § 1920.

(b) By the Court. In all other cases, the party seeking a judgment by default shall apply to the Court as described in Bankruptcy Rule 7055, and shall append to the application (i) the Clerk's certificate of default, (ii) a copy of the claim to which no response

has been made, (iii) a proposed form of default judgment, and (iv) proof of service of the application.

[Adopted effective July 28, 1998.]

Comment

This rule is new and is derived from Civil Rule 55.2 of the Local District Rules.

RULE 7056–1. SUMMARY JUDGMENT

(a) Unless the Court orders otherwise, no party shall file a motion for summary judgment without first seeking a pre-motion conference. The request for a pre-motion conference shall be made by letter, filed on the CM/ECF system, setting forth the issues to be presented in the motion and the grounds for relief.

(b) Upon any motion for summary judgment pursuant to Bankruptcy Rule 7056, there shall be annexed to the motion a separate, short, and concise statement, in numbered paragraphs, of the material facts as to which the moving party contends there is no genuine issue to be tried. Failure to submit the statement shall constitute grounds for denial of the motion.

(c) Papers opposing a motion for summary judgment shall include a correspondingly numbered paragraph responding to each numbered paragraph in the statement of the moving party, and if necessary, additional paragraphs containing a separate, short, and concise statement of additional material facts as to which it is contended that there is a genuine issue to be tried.

(d) Each numbered paragraph in the statement of material facts required to be served by the moving party shall be deemed admitted for purposes of the motion unless specifically controverted by a correspondingly numbered paragraph in the statement required to be served by the opposing party.

(e) Each statement by the movant or opponent pursuant to subdivisions (b) or (c) of this rule, including each statement controverting any statements of material fact by a movant or opponent, shall be followed by citation to evidence which would be admissible.

[Adopted April 15, 1997; amended effective July 28, 1998; August 2, 2004.]

Comment

Subdivision (a) of this rule was added in 2004 because motions for summary judgment are frequently burdensome, in time and expense, for the Court and the parties. Parties frequently file motions for summary judgment when an objective examination would reveal triable issues of fact or when the Court might conclude that it would be more cost-effective to resolve all issues at trial, given that most trials in bankruptcy court are bench trials. Subdivision (a) provides the Court with opportunity to notify the parties of its observations at a pre-motion conference. The rule does not limit a party's right to file a motion for summary judgment after the pre-motion conference.

Subdivisions (b) through (e) of this rule are derived from Former Local Bankruptcy Rule 13(h) and are an adaptation of Civil Rule 56.1 of the Local District Rules. The statement of material facts shall be sufficiently complete to permit the Court to render judgment on the claim or defense. These subdivisions were amended in 2004 to conform with the 2004 amendments to Local District Rule 56.1.

PART VIII.   APPEALS

RULE 8004–1.   COPIES OF NOTICE OF APPEAL

Upon the filing of a notice of appeal, the appellant shall provide the Clerk with sufficient copies of the notice and address labels for all parties to be served to permit the Clerk to comply with Bankruptcy Rule 8004.

[Adopted April 15, 1997.]

Comment

This rule is derived from Former Local Bankruptcy Rule 32.

Bankruptcy Rule 8004 requires the Clerk to mail a copy of a notice of appeal to "counsel of record of each party other than the appellant or, if a party is not represented by counsel, to the party's last known address." Although the appellant is required to provide address labels, envelopes should not be provided.

RULE 8005–1.   SUPERSEDEAS BOND

(a) A supersedeas bond, where the judgment is for a sum of money only, shall be in the amount of the judgment plus 11% to cover interest and such damages for delay as may be awarded, plus $250 to cover costs.

(b) When the stay may be effected as of right solely by the giving of the supersedeas bond, but the judgment or order is not solely for a sum of money, the Court, on notice, shall fix the amount of the bond. In all other cases, the Court may, on notice, grant a stay on such terms as to security and otherwise as it may deem proper.

(c) On approval, a supersedeas bond shall be filed with the Clerk, and a copy thereof, with notice of filing, promptly served on all parties affected thereby. If the appellee raises objections to the form of the bond or to the sufficiency of the surety, the Court shall hold a hearing on notice to all parties.

[Adopted April 15, 1997; amended effective July 28, 1998.]

Comment

This rule is derived from Former Local Bankruptcy Rule 30 and is an adaptation of Civil Rule 41 of the Former District Rules.

Compare Local Bankruptcy Rule 7052–1 (Proposed Findings of Fact and Conclusions of Law).

[Comment amended effective July 28, 1998; August 2, 2004.]

RULE 7087–1.   TRANSFER OF ADVERSARY PROCEED- INGS—REPEALED

[Adopted April 15, 1997. Repealed effective August 2, 2004.]

[Comment amended effective July 28, 1998.]

RULE 8007–1.   RECORD ON APPEAL

(a) Furnishing and Transmitting Record on Appeal. Except as provided in subdivision (b) of this rule, a party filing a designation of items to be included in a record on appeal shall cause to be filed on the CM/ECF system, unless previously filed, a copy of each item designated and attached to the designation.

(b) Documents of Unusual Bulk or Weight and Physical Exhibits. Documents of unusual bulk or weight and physical exhibits shall remain in the custody of the attorney producing them, who shall permit their inspection by any party for the purpose of preparing the record on appeal and who shall be charged with the responsibility for their safekeeping and transportation to the appellate court.

[Adopted April 15, 1997; amended effective July 28, 1998; August 2, 2004.]

Comment

Subdivision (a) of this rule is derived from former Standing Order M–93. Subdivision (b) of this rule is derived from Civil Rule 24(c) of the Former District Rules.

This rule was amended in 2004 to take into account new procedures for electronic filing.

[Comment amended effective July 28, 1998; August 2, 2004.]

RULE 8016–1.   ORDER, JUDGMENT, OR REMAND BY APPELLATE COURT

An order or judgment of an appellate court, when filed in the office of the Clerk, shall automatically become the order or judgment of the Court and be entered as such by the Clerk without further order. If the order or judgment of the appellate court remands for further proceedings, a motion for such further proceedings shall be referred to the Judge who heard the proceeding below unless the appellate court orders otherwise.

[Adopted April 15, 1997.]

If a proceeding has been remanded by the appellate court, it is the responsibility of the parties to file a motion for further proceedings in the court to which it was remanded.

[Comment amended effective July 28, 1998.]

PART IX.   GENERAL PROVISIONS

RULE 9001–1.   DEFINITIONS

(a) **Definitions.**   Unless inconsistent with the context, in these Local Bankruptcy Rules—

(1) "Bankruptcy Act" means the Bankruptcy Act of 1898, ch. 541, 30 Stat. 544 (repealed 1978);

(2) "Bankruptcy Code" means title 11 of the United States Code, as amended from time to time;

(3) "Bankruptcy Rules" means the Federal Rules of Bankruptcy Procedure and Official Bankruptcy Forms promulgated pursuant to 28 U.S.C. § 2075, as amended from time to time;

(4) "Chief Judge" means the Chief Judge of the Court;

(5) "Clerk" means the clerk or deputy clerk of the Court;

(6) "CM/ECF" means the Case Management/Electronic Case File System implemented in this Court, sometimes referred to herein as "ECF";

(7) "Court" means the United States Bankruptcy Court for the Southern District of New York;

(8) "District Clerk" means the clerk or deputy clerk of the District Court;

(9) "District Court" means the United States District Court for the Southern District of New York;

(10) "District Judge" means a United States District Judge appointed to, or sitting by designation in, the District Court;

(11) "Former District Rules" means the Rules for General, Civil, Criminal, Admiralty and Magistrate Judge Proceedings for the United States District Court for the Southern District of New York, effective from October 26, 1983 through April 15, 1997;

(12) "Former Local Bankruptcy Rules" means the United States Bankruptcy Court Southern District of New York Local Bankruptcy Rules, effective from April 21, 1986 through April 10, 1996;

(13) "Judge" means a bankruptcy judge appointed to or sitting by designation in the Court (or, with respect to a proceeding that has not been referred or which has been withdrawn, the District Judge);

(14) "Local District Rules" means the Local Rules for the United States District Court for the Southern and Eastern Districts of New York, as amended from time to time; and

(15) "United States Trustee" means the United States trustee or an assistant United States trustee for the Southern District of New York.

(b) **Construction.**   Unless inconsistent with the context, the meanings of other words and phrases used in these Local Bankruptcy Rules shall be construed in accordance with the Bankruptcy Code and Bankruptcy Rules.

(c) Use of Terms "Documents" and "Papers." The terms "documents" and "papers" as used in these Local Bankruptcy Rules include those filed or transmitted by electronic means.

[Adopted April 15, 1997; amended effective July 28, 1998; August 2, 2004.]

Comment

Subdivisions (a) and (b) of this rule are derived from Former Local Bankruptcy Rule 2. Subdivision (c) of this rule was added in 1996.

[Comment amended effective July 28, 1998.]

RULE 9004–1.   FORM OF PAPERS

(a) **Papers Submitted for Filing.**   Papers submitted for filing shall

(1) be plainly typed or printed;

(2) not be bound or stapled;

(3) have no erasures or interlineations which materially deface them; and

(4) state on the face of the document:

(A) the name of the attorney for the filing party;

(B) the attorney's office and post office addresses; and

(C) the attorney's telephone number.

(b) Chambers copies and copies for the United States Trustee shall be bound or stapled and submitted in accordance with Local Bankruptcy Rule 9070–1.

[Adopted April 15, 1997; amended effective July 28, 1998; August 2, 2004; August 4, 2008.]

Comment

This rule is derived from Former Local Bankruptcy Rule 9(b) and is an adaptation of Civil Rule 11.1 of the Local District Rules.

The general rules for form of papers are set forth in Bankruptcy Rule 9004 and Official Bankruptcy Forms 16A, 16B, 16C, and 16D.

This rule was amended in 2004 to conform to Civil Rule 11.1(b) of the Local District Rules to allow attorneys to use an identification number issued by the District Court instead of the last four digits of the attorney's social security number.

This rule was also amended in 2004 to clarify that pleadings no longer require litigation backs or covers.

This rule was amended in 2008 to conform to the repeal of Civil Rule 11.1(b) of the Local District Rules, which previously required that every pleading, written motion and other paper signed by an attorney include the attorney's initials and the last four digits of the attorney's social security number or any other four digit number registered by the attorney with the clerk of the court.

[Comment amended effective July 28, 1998; August 2, 2004; August 4, 2008.]

RULE 9004–2. CAPTION

(a) Papers submitted for filing shall bear the title of the case, the initials of the Judge to whom the case has been assigned, the docket number assigned to the case, and, if applicable, the adversary proceeding number.

(b) The return date and time of a motion shall be included in the upper right-hand corner of the caption of the motion and all related pleadings.

[Adopted April 15, 1997.]

Comment

Subdivision (a) of this rule is derived from Former Local Bankruptcy Rule 9. Subdivision (b) of this rule is derived from former Standing Order M–99.

The return date for a motion is obtained pursuant to Local Bankruptcy Rule 5070–1.

RULE 9006–1. TIME FOR SERVICE AND FILING OF MOTIONS AND ANSWERING PAPERS

(a) Discovery-Related Motions. Unless the Court orders otherwise, all motion papers under Bankruptcy Rules 7026 through 7037 shall be served at least five days before the return date. Where such service is made, any answering papers shall be served so as to ensure actual receipt not later than the day preceding the return date.

(b) All Other Motions. Unless the Court orders otherwise, all other motion papers shall be served at least 10 days before the return date. Where such service is made, any answering papers shall be served so as to ensure actual receipt not later than three days before the return date.

(c) Time for Filing with Court. Unless the Court orders otherwise, all motions and answering papers shall be filed with the Clerk not later than one business day following the date of service.

[Adopted April 15, 1997.]

Comment

This rule is derived from Former Local Bankruptcy Rule 13(c) and is an adaptation of Civil Rule 6.1 of the Local District Rules. Subdivision (b) of this rule is an exercise of the Court's authority contained in Bankruptcy Rule 9006(d) to enlarge the time for service of motion papers.

[Comment amended effective July 28, 1998.]

RULE 9011–1. SIGNING OF PAPERS

(a) All pleadings, motions, and other papers that are submitted for filing, except a list, schedule, or statement, or amendments thereto, shall be signed by an attorney of record in the attorney's own name or, if there is no attorney, all papers submitted for filing shall by signed by the party. The name of the attorney or party shall be clearly printed or typed below the signature, together with the attorney's or party's address and telephone number.

(b) The signing of documents filed electronically shall be governed by the applicable standing order on electronically filed cases issued by the Court. An original signed copy of the filing shall be maintained in the attorney's files.

(c) Any password required for electronic filing shall be used only by the attorney to whom the password is assigned and authorized members and employees of such attorney's firm.

[Adopted April 15, 1997. Amended effective August 2, 2004; August 4, 2008.]

Comment

This rule is an adaptation of Civil Rule 11.1 of the Local District Rules.

This rule was amended in 2004 to conform to Civil Rule 11.1(b) of the Local District Rules to allow attorneys to use an identification number issued by the District Court instead of the last four digits of the attorney's social security number.

This rule was amended in 2008 to conform to the repeal of Civil Rule 11.1(b) of the Local District Rules, which previously required that every pleading, written motion and other paper signed by an attorney include the attorney's initials and the last four digits of the attorney's social security number or any other four digit number registered by the attorney with the clerk of the court.

Subdivision (a) was also amended in 2008 to conform to Rule 9011(a), which does not require an attorney's signature on lists, schedules, and statements.

Subdivision (b) was also amended in 2008 to provide that signing electronically filed documents is governed by the Court's standing order on electronically filed cases, which is General Order M–242, and any amendments or supplemental standing orders of the Court. Such standing orders may be obtained from the Clerk and are available on the Court's website at www.nysb.uscourts.gov.

[Comment amended effective July 28, 1998; August 2, 2004; August 4, 2008.]

RULE 9013–1. MOTION PRACTICE

(a) Rule or Statutory Basis. Each motion shall specify the rules and statutory provisions upon which it is predicated and the legal authorities that support the requested relief, either in the motion or in a separate memorandum of law. If such specification has not been made, the Court may strike the motion from the calendar.

(b) Entities to Receive Notice. In addition to all entities otherwise entitled to receive notice, notice of a motion shall be given to any entity believed to have or be claiming an interest in the subject matter of the proposed order or who, it is believed, otherwise would be affected by the proposed order.

[Adopted April 15, 1997; amended effective July 28, 1998; August 4, 2008.]

Comment

This rule is derived from Former Local Bankruptcy Rule 13.

Local Bankruptcy Rule 7007–1 provides additional requirements for discovery-related motion practice.

This rule was amended in 2008 to delete the requirement that a separate memorandum of law be filed with every motion. A discussion of the law must be included in the motion or responsive pleading if a separate memorandum of law is not filed.

RULE 9014–1. CONTESTED MATTERS

Unless the Court orders otherwise, Rules 7(b) and 24 of the Federal Rules of Civil Procedure, as incorporated in Bankruptcy Rules 7007 and 7024, respectively, and Local Bankruptcy Rules 7005–1, 7007–1, 7016–1, 7024–1, 7026–1, 7027–1, 7030–1, 7033–1, 7034–1, 7036–1, 7052–1, 7055–1, 7055–2, and 7056–1, shall apply in contested matters.

[Adopted April 15, 1997; amended effective July 28, 1998; August 2, 2004.]

Comment

This rule is an exercise of the Court's discretion under Bankruptcy Rule 9014 to make any rule in Part VII of the Bankruptcy Rules applicable to contested matters.

RULE 9014–2. FIRST SCHEDULED HEARING

The first scheduled hearing in a contested matter will not be an evidentiary hearing at which witnesses may testify, unless:

(a) the Court gives prior notice to the parties that such hearing will be an evidentiary hearing;

(b) the motion requests emergency relief and is made at the commencement of the case;

(c) the motion requests interim or final relief under § 363(c)(2)(B) or § 364 of the Bankruptcy Code;

(d) the motion requests the Court's approval of rejection of an unexpired lease of real property under § 365(a) of the Bankruptcy Code, and a timely objection thereto is filed;

(e) the hearing is on confirmation of a plan in a case under chapter 9, chapter 11, chapter 12, or chapter 13 of the Bankruptcy Code; or

(f) the Court, by general order, has directed that the first scheduled hearing with respect to the type of relief requested in the motion shall be an evidentiary hearing at which witnesses may testify.

[Adopted effective August 2, 2004.]

Comment

Bankruptcy Rule 9014(e), added in 2002, requires that the Court provide procedures that enable parties to ascertain at a reasonable time before any scheduled hearing whether the hearing will be an evidentiary hearing at which witnesses may testify. Local Rule 9014–2 was added in 2004 to provide such a procedure. Nothing in Local Rule 9014–2 precludes a party from requesting an evidentiary hearing at the first scheduled hearing and asking the Court to provide for notice thereof under paragraph (a).

[Comment adopted effective August 2, 2004.]

RULE 9015–1. JURY TRIALS

A statement of consent to have a jury trial conducted by a Bankruptcy Judge under 28 U.S.C. § 157(e) shall be filed not later than 10 days after the service of the last pleading directed to the issue for which the demand was made.

[Adopted effective July 28, 1998. Amended effective August 2, 2004.]

Comment

Section 157(e) of title 28 provides that a Bankruptcy Judge may conduct a jury trial on proper demand with the consent of the parties to the proceeding if the District Court has specifically designated the Bankruptcy Court to exercise such jurisdiction. The District Court, by order dated December 7, 1994, has specifically designated the Bankruptcy Court to conduct jury trials pursuant to § 157(e). Bankruptcy Rule 9015(b) provides that the time for filing a statement of consent to a jury trial shall be specified by local rule.

This rule provides a 10-day period for filing the statement of consent, which runs from the service of the last pleading, as specified in Bankruptcy Rule 7007.

[Comment amended August 2, 2004.]

RULE 9019–1. ALTERNATIVE DISPUTE RESOLUTION

Alternative dispute resolution shall be conducted in the manner required by any applicable standing order of the Court.

[Adopted April 15, 1997. Amended effective January 26, 1999.]

Comment

Procedures governing mediation programs in bankruptcy cases and adversary proceedings are governed by General Order M–143 and any amendments or supplemental standing orders of the Court. Copies of General Order M–143, as well as, any amendments or subsequent standing orders on this subject, may be obtained from the Clerk and are available on the Court's website at www.nysb.uscourts.gov.

[Comment amended effective August 2, 2004.]

RULE 9020–1. DEFAULT SANCTIONS; IMPOSITION OF COSTS

(a) Default Sanctions. Failure of a party or counsel for a party to appear before the Court at a conference, complete the necessary preparations, or be prepared to proceed at the time set for trial or hearing may be considered an abandonment of the adversary proceeding or contested matter or a failure to prosecute or defend diligently, and an appropriate order of the Court may be entered against the defaulting party with respect to either a specific issue or the entire adversary proceeding or contested matter.

(b) Imposition of Costs. If the Judge finds that the sanctions in subdivision (a) of this rule are either inadequate or unjust to the parties, the Judge may assess reasonable costs directly against the party or counsel whose action has obstructed the effective administration of the Court's business.

[Adopted April 15, 1997.]

Comment

This rule is derived from Former Local Bankruptcy Rule 21 and is an adaptation of General Rule 5(b) and (c) of the Former District Rules.

[Comment amended effective July 28, 1998.]

RULE 9021–1. ENTRY OF ORDERS, JUDGMENTS, AND DECREES

The Clerk shall enter all orders, decrees, and judgments of the Court in the electronic filing system, which shall constitute docketing of the order, decree, or judgment for all purposes. The Clerk's notation on the appropriate docket of an order, judgment, or decree shall constitute the entry of the order, judgment, or decree.

[Adopted April 15, 1997; amended effective July 28, 1998.]

Comment

This rule is derived from Former Local Bankruptcy Rule 19(a) and is an adaptation of Civil Rule 6.2 of the Local District Rules.

This rule supplements Bankruptcy Rule 9021, which requires that a judgment in an adversary proceeding or contested matter be set forth on a separate document and entered on the docket.

[Comment amended effective July 28, 1998.]

RULE 9023–1. MOTIONS FOR REARGUMENT

(a) A motion for reargument of a court order determining a motion shall be served within 10 days after the entry of the Court's order determining the original motion, or in the case of a court order resulting in a judgment, within 10 days after the entry of the judgment, and, unless the Court orders otherwise, shall be made returnable within the same amount of time as required for the original motion. The motion shall set forth concisely the matters or controlling decisions which counsel believes the Court has not considered. No oral argument shall be heard unless the Court grants the motion and specifically orders that the matter be re-argued orally.

(b) The expense of any party in obtaining all or any part of a transcript for purposes of a new trial or for amended findings may be a cost taxable against the losing party.

[Adopted April 15, 1997. Amended effective August 2, 2004.]

Comment

Subdivision (a) of this rule is derived from Former Local Bankruptcy Rule 13(j) and is an adaptation of Civil Rule 6.3 of the Local District Rules. Subdivision (b) of this rule is derived from Former Local Bankruptcy Rule 33 and is an adaptation of Civil Rule 12 of the Former District Rules.

This rule does not apply to motions made under Bankruptcy Rule 3008 or 9024.

Subdivision (a) of this rule was amended in 2004 to conform with the 2004 amendments to Local District Rule 6.3.

[Comment amended effective August 2, 2004.]

RULE 9025–1. SURETIES

(a) Execution by Surety Only. If a bond, undertaking, or stipulation is required, an instrument executed only by the surety shall be sufficient.

(b) Security for Bond. Except as otherwise provided by law, every bond, undertaking, or stipulation shall be secured by (i) the deposit of cash or government bonds in the amount of the bond, undertaking, or stipulation, (ii) the undertaking or guaranty of a corporate surety holding a certificate of authority from the Secretary of the Treasury, or (iii) the undertaking or guaranty of two individual residents of the Southern District or Eastern District of New York, each of whom owns real or personal property within such district with a value of twice the amount of the bond in excess of the surety's debts, liabilities, legal exemptions, and obligations on other bonds, guaranties, undertakings, or stipulations.

(c) Affidavit by Individual Surety. In the case of a bond, undertaking, or stipulation executed by individual sureties, each surety shall attach an affidavit of justification, giving the surety's full name, occupation, and residence and business addresses, and showing that the surety is not disqualified from acting as an individual surety under subdivision (d) of this rule.

(d) Persons Who May Not Act as Sureties. Members of the bar, administrative officers and employees of the Court, the marshal, and the marshal's deputies and assistants may not act as sureties in any pending case, adversary proceeding, or contested matter.

(e) Approval of Bonds of Corporate Sureties. Except as otherwise provided by §§ 303 and 322(b) of the Bankruptcy Code, Bankruptcy Rule 2010, and Local Bankruptcy Rule 8005–1, all bonds, undertakings, and stipulations of corporate sureties holding certificates of authority from the Secretary of the Treasury, where the amount of such bonds or undertakings has been fixed by a Judge, an order of the Court, a statute, or Local Bankruptcy Rule 8005–1, may be approved by the Clerk.

[Adopted April 15, 1997; amended effective July 28, 1998.]

Comment

Subdivisions (a), (b), (c), and (d) of this rule are derived from Former Local Bankruptcy Rule 28 and are an adaptation of Civil Rule 65.1.1(a), (b), (d), and (e) of the Local District Rules. Subdivision (b) of this rule has been modified to conform to Civil Rule 65.1.1(b) of the Local District Rules. Subdivision (e) of this rule is derived from Former Local Bankruptcy Rule 29 and is an adaptation of Civil Rule 65.1.1(f) of the Local District Rules.

[Comment amended effective July 28, 1998.]

RULE 9028–1. ACTION IN ABSENCE OF ASSIGNED JUDGE

In the absence of an assigned Judge, any other Judge who is available may act temporarily in the absent Judge's place. To obtain the assistance of an available Judge, the parties shall communicate first with the chambers staff of the assigned Judge and, if chambers staff is unavailable, then with the Clerk.

[Adopted April 15, 1997; amended effective July 28, 1998.]

Comment

This rule is derived from Former Local Bankruptcy Rule 6.

This rule is intended to assure that the business of the Court will not be impeded by the absence of an assigned Judge.

[Comment amended effective July 28, 1998.]

RULE 9070–1. COPIES OF FILED PAPERS

(a) Copy for United States Trustee. A hard copy of all papers filed with the Court, including those filed electronically, other than proofs of claim, shall be submitted to the Clerk for transmittal to the United States Trustee.

(b) Chambers Copy. A copy of all papers filed with the Court, other than proofs of claim, shall be marked "Chambers Copy" and delivered in an unsealed envelope to the Clerk's office located in the division in which the assigned Judge sits on the same day as the papers are filed with the Clerk or, if filed electronically, not later than the next business day.

[Adopted April 15, 1997; amended effective July 28, 1998; August 2, 2004.]

Comment

This rule is derived from Former Local Bankruptcy Rule 9(d) and (e).

RULE 9072–1. CUSTODY OF EXHIBITS

(a) Retention by Attorney. Unless the Court orders otherwise, exhibits shall not be filed with the Clerk, but shall be retained in the custody of the attorney who produced them in Court.

(b) Removal of Exhibits from Court. Exhibits that have been filed with the Clerk shall be removed by the party responsible for the exhibits (i) if no appeal has been taken, at the expiration of the time for taking an appeal, or (ii) if an appeal has been taken, within 30 days after the record on appeal has been returned to the Clerk. Parties failing to comply with this rule shall be notified by the Clerk to remove their exhibits, and, upon their failure to do so within 30 days of such notification, the Clerk may dispose of the exhibits.

[Adopted April 15, 1997; amended effective July 28, 1998.]

Comment

This rule is derived from Former Local Bankruptcy Rule 27 and is an adaptation of Civil Rule 39.1 of the Local District Rules.

Former subdivision (c) of this rule has been included, as modified, in Local Bankruptcy Rule 8007–1(b).

As used in this rule, "exhibits" includes trial exhibits admitted into evidence, in a case, adversary proceeding, or contested matter.

[Comment amended effective July 28, 1998.]

RULE 9074–1. SETTLEMENT OR PRESENTMENT OF ORDER, JUDGMENT, OR DECREE

(a) Settlement of Order, Judgment, or Decree. Unless the Court orders otherwise, if, following a hearing or decision, the Court directs a party to settle an order, judgment, or decree, the party, within 15 days of the issuance of the Court's ruling, shall deliver the proposed order, judgment, or decree directly to the Judge's chambers upon not less than two days' notice to all parties to the adversary proceeding or contested matter, except that such notice period shall not apply if all parties to the adversary proceeding or contested matter have consented in writing to the proposed order, judgment, or decree. Failure to settle an order, judgment, or decree within the 15 day period may result in the imposition of sanctions, including, without limitation, (i) dismissal for failure to prosecute or (ii) an award of attorney's fees. One day's notice is required of all counterproposals. Unless the Court orders otherwise, no proposed or counterproposed order, judgment, or decree settled pursuant to this rule shall form a part of the record of the case, adversary proceeding, or contested matter.

(b) Notice of Presentment of Order in Lieu of Hearing Where Notice and a Hearing Are Not Required.

(1) *Use.* If notice and a hearing are not required, and a motion is not mandatory, the form set forth in subdivision (b)(3) of this rule may be used for the submission of orders to the Court.

(2) *Notice.* Unless the Court orders otherwise, notice of the presentment of an order pursuant to this subdivision shall be filed with the Clerk, and a copy shall be delivered to the Judge's chambers and served upon the debtor, the trustee, each committee, the United States Trustee, all parties who have filed a notice of appearance and request for service of documents, and all other parties in interest on not less than three days' notice.

(3) *Form.* A notice of presentment of a proposed order shall be substantially in the following form.

Presentment Date and Time:

UNITED STATES BANK-RUPTCY COURT SOUTHERN DISTRICT OF NEW YORK	[Insert date] at 12:00 noon

	:	
	:	
	:	
Caption of Case	:	Chapter 11 Case No.
	:	
	:	

NOTICE OF PRESENTMENT OF [INSERT TITLE OF ORDER]

PLEASE TAKE NOTICE that upon the annexed [application or motion] of [insert name of applicant or movant], the undersigned will present the attached proposed order to the Honorable [insert name], United States Bankruptcy Judge, for signature on [insert date] at 12:00 noon.

PLEASE TAKE FURTHER NOTICE that objections, if any, to the proposed order must be made in writing and received in the Bankruptcy Judge's chambers and by the undersigned not later than 11:30 a.m. [on that date.] Unless objections are received by that time, the order may be signed.

Dated: [place]
     [date]

                    [insert signature block]

To: [insert names and addresses
     of entities to receive notice]

(c) Notice of Motion upon Presentment and Opportunity for Hearing with Respect to Certain Motions, Applications, and Objections.

(1) *Use.* Where it is anticipated that a motion, application, or objection of a type set forth below will be uncontested, the motion, application, or objection may be made upon notice of presentment using the form set forth in subdivision (c)(4) of this rule:

(A) Application to confirm a sale pursuant to Local Bankruptcy Rule 6004–1;

(B) Motion to extend the time to assume or reject a lease pursuant to § 365(d)(4) of the Bankruptcy Code;

(C) Motion for entry of a default judgment in an adversary proceeding pursuant to Bankruptcy Rule 7055 and Local Bankruptcy Rule 7055–2;

(D) Motion to extend the time to object to discharge or dischargeability pursuant to Bankruptcy Rule 4004 or 4007;

(E) Application to avoid a judicial lien that impairs an exemption pursuant to § 522(f) of the Bankruptcy Code;

(F) Application for an examination pursuant to Bankruptcy Rule 2004 to the extent that the application is not granted ex parte;

(G) Objection to a claim of exemption pursuant to Bankruptcy Rule 4003(b).

(2) *Notice.* Unless the Court orders otherwise, notice of the presentment of an order pursuant to this subdivision shall be filed with the Clerk and a copy shall be delivered to the Judge's chambers and served upon the debtor, the trustee, each committee, the United States Trustee, all parties who have filed a notice of appearance and request for service of documents, and all other parties in interest. The notice shall comport with the notice requirements under the applicable provisions of the Bankruptcy Code, Bankruptcy Rules, and Local Bankruptcy Rules.

(3) *Objection; Opportunity for a Hearing.* A written objection, if any, to the proposed order, together with proof of service, shall be filed with the Clerk and a courtesy copy shall be delivered to the Judge's chambers at least three days before the date of presentment. Unless the Court orders otherwise, no hearing will be held absent the timely filing of an objection. If an objection has been timely filed, the Court will notify the moving and objecting parties of the date and time of any hearing.

(4) *Form.* A notice of presentment of a proposed order shall be substantially in the following form.

	Presentment Date and Time:
	[Insert date]
UNITED STATES BANK- RUPTCY COURT SOUTHERN DISTRICT OF NEW YORK	at 12:00 noon

Caption of Case   : Chapter 11 Case No.

NOTICE OF PRESENTMENT OF
[INSERT TITLE OF ORDER]
AND
OPPORTUNITY FOR HEARING

PLEASE TAKE NOTICE that upon the annexed [application, motion, or objection] of [insert name of applicant, movant, or objectant], the undersigned will present the attached proposed order to the Honorable [insert name], United States Bankruptcy Judge, for signature on [insert a date conforming to the notice requirements under applicable rules for the particular type of application, motion, or objection] at 12:00 noon.

PLEASE TAKE FURTHER NOTICE that unless a written objection to the proposed order, with proof of service, is filed with the Clerk of the Court and a courtesy copy is delivered to the Bankruptcy Judge's chambers at least three days before the date of presentment, there will not be a hearing and the order may be signed.

PLEASE TAKE FURTHER NOTICE that if a written objection is timely filed, the Court will notify the moving and objecting parties of the date and time of the hearing and of the moving party's obligation to notify all other parties entitled to receive notice. The moving and objecting parties are required to attend the hearing, and failure to attend in person or by counsel may result in relief being granted or denied upon default.

Dated: [place]
       [date]

                   [insert signature block]

To: [insert names and addresses
        of entities to receive notice]

[Adopted April 15, 1997; amended effective July 28, 1998; August 4, 2008.]

Comment

Subdivision (a) of this rule, which is derived from Former Local Bankruptcy Rule 17 and is an adaptation of Civil Rule 77.1 of the Local District Rules, applies to the settlement of orders, judgments, and decrees following a hearing or decision. Subdivision (b) of this rule, which is derived from Former Local Bankruptcy Rule 46, applies in situations in which "notice and a hearing" are not required by the Bankruptcy Code. Subdivision (c) of this rule, which is new and is an adaptation of former Standing Order 186, applies only to the types of proceedings specified therein and where it is anticipated that the relief requested will be uncontested.

Subdivision (c)(1) of this rule was amended in 2008 to delete from the list of motions that may be made on presentment a motion to terminate the automatic stay pursuant to § 362 of the Bankruptcy Code in a chapter 13 case. The purpose of this amendment is to assure that the Court will properly hear, and consider the accuracy of, allegations of default in cases concerning an individual debtor.

A motion is mandatory if required by the Bankruptcy Rules, the Local Bankruptcy Rules, or an order of the Court.

Times for the presentment of and objections to proposed orders are specified in this rule to promote uniformity in practice. If notice of presentment is given by mail, three additional days must be added in accordance with Bankruptcy Rule 9006(f).

[Comment amended effective July 28, 1998; August 4, 2008.]

RULE 9075–1. REQUEST FOR HEARING

An objection to a proposed action or order shall constitute a request for a hearing.

[Adopted April 15, 1997; amended effective July 28, 1998.]

Comment

This rule is derived from Former Local Bankruptcy Rules 13(i) and 45.

RULE 9076–1. STATUS CONFERENCES

(a) **In General.** Subject to the notice provisions of subdivision (c) of this rule, the Court, on its own motion or on request of a party in interest, may hold a conference, with or without a court reporter present, at any time during a case or proceeding, for any purpose consistent with the Bankruptcy Code, including:

(1) to address the posture and efficient administration of the case or proceeding; and

(2) to establish a case management or scheduling order.

(b) Request for Conference. A request for a conference may be made either in writing or orally at a hearing. Any request, whether written or oral, shall (i) specify the matters proposed to be addressed at the conference, (ii) identify the parties who have a direct interest in such matters, and (iii) include such further information as may assist the Court in evaluating whether a conference should be held and in conducting the conference. If a conference is requested for a date prior to the appointment of a creditors' committee and the retention of its counsel, the requesting party shall state why the conference should not be delayed until after the appointment and retention. If made in writing, the request shall be directed to the chambers of the Judge presiding over the case or proceeding and served, together with a copy of any papers submitted with the request, upon the following parties:

(1) in an adversary proceeding, to the parties to the adversary proceeding; or

(2) in a case or proceeding other than an adversary proceeding, to the debtor, the trustee, the United States Trustee, each official committee appointed to serve in the case (or, if no official committee has been appointed, the holders of the 10 largest unsecured claims), the holders of the five largest secured claims, and each unofficial committee which previously has requested the opportunity to participate in conferences.

(c) Notice of Conference. If all necessary parties are present before the Court, the Judge may direct that a conference be held immediately without further notice. In the event that a conference is called under any other circumstances, unless the Court orders otherwise, as soon as practicable, the requesting party (or, if the conference is to be held on the Court's own motion, the debtor, the trustee, or such other party as the Court may direct) shall provide notice of the time, date, place, and purpose of the conference, to the parties required to be served under subdivision (b) of this rule.

(d) Submission of Proposed Case Management and Scheduling Orders. If one of the purposes of the conference is to establish a case management or scheduling order, unless the Court orders otherwise, the party requesting the conference (or, if the conference is to be held on the Court's own motion, the debtor, the trustee, or such other party as the Court may direct) shall submit to the Court prior to the conference, on notice to all necessary parties (as identified in subdivision (b) of this rule), a proposed case management or scheduling order. The submitting party in good faith shall attempt to obtain the consent of all necessary parties (as identified in subdivision (b) of this rule) with respect to the form of the order and indicate to the Court whether such consent has been obtained.

[Adopted April 15, 1997; amended effective July 28, 1998.]

Comment

This rule is an exercise of the Court's authority under § 105(d) of the Bankruptcy Code.

RULE 9077–1. ORDERS TO SHOW CAUSE; EX PARTE ORDERS

(a) Orders to Show Cause. No order to show cause shall be granted except upon a clear and specific showing by affidavit of good and sufficient reasons why proceeding other than by notice of motion is necessary. The affidavit also shall state whether a previous application for similar relief has been made.

(b) Ex Parte Orders. No ex parte order in an adversary proceeding or contested matter shall be granted unless it is based upon an affidavit or motion showing cause for ex parte action as well as cause for the relief requested, and states whether a previous application for similar relief has been made.

[Adopted April 15, 1997; amended effective July 28, 1998.]

Comment

Subdivision (a) of this rule is derived from Former Local Bankruptcy Rule 13(d) and is an adaptation of Civil Rule 6.1(d) of the Local District Rules. Subdivision (b) of this rule is derived from Former Local Bankruptcy Rule 19(b).

[Comment amended effective July 28, 1998.]

RULE 9078–1. CERTIFICATE OF SERVICE

Unless the Court orders otherwise, any party serving a pleading or other document shall file proof of service by the earlier of (i) three days following the date of service, and (ii) the hearing date.

[Adopted April 15, 1997; amended effective July 28, 1998.]

Comment

This rule is derived from Former Local Bankruptcy Rule 45(d).

Although Former Local Bankruptcy Rule 45(d) applied only to proofs of service of notices, this rule applies to proofs of service of all pleadings and documents. The general requirements for service of notices are contained in Local Bankruptcy Rule 2002–1.

GENERAL ORDERS OF THE BANKRUPTCY COURT FOR THE SOUTHERN DISTRICT OF NEW YORK

GENERAL ORDER M-68. RULES GOVERNING PROCEDURES FOR APPOINTMENT OF PRO BONO COUNSEL IN BANKRUPTCY PROCEEDINGS—SOUTHERN DISTRICT

[*SEE* GENERAL ORDER M-320, POST]

GENERAL ORDER M-104. ORIGINAL GUIDELINES FOR FEES AND DISBURSEMENTS FOR PROFESSIONALS IN SOUTHERN DISTRICT OF NEW YORK BANKRUPTCY CASES [1]

See, also, General Order M-151, post.

The following guidelines apply in all bankruptcy cases in the Southern District of New York. They delineate information that each interim and final application for professional fees and expenses must contain, and guidelines for reimbursement of disbursements. Those provisions preceded by an asterisk are mandatory guidelines to which an applicant must certify the application adheres. No deviation from those guidelines marked with an asterisk is permissible, regardless of circumstances. Fee applications must comply with the remainder of these guidelines, provided that if the fee application departs therefrom (a) the certification shall specifically so state, and (b) the application must explain why the applicant believes departure from the guidelines is justified in the circumstances. The presumption is that the Court will follow the guidelines set forth herein. Any application departing from these guidelines shall include, in the paragraph proffering the justification for departing from the guidelines, the amount that the applicant would be entitled to receive under the guidelines.

A. Certification.

1. Each application for fees and disbursements must contain a certification by the professional designated by the applicant with the responsibility in the particular case for compliance with these guidelines (the Certifying Professional), that (a) the Certifying Professional has read the application; (b) to the best of the Certifying Professional's knowledge, information and belief formed after reasonable inquiry, the application complies with the mandatory guidelines set forth herein; (c) to the best of the Certifying Professional's knowledge, information and belief formed after reasonable inquiry, the fees and disbursements sought fall within these guidelines, except as specifically noted in the certification and described in the fee application; and (d) except to the extent that fees or disbursements are prohibited by these guidelines, the fees and disbursements sought are billed at rates and in accordance with practices customarily employed by the applicant and generally accepted by applicant's clients.

2. Each application for fees and disbursements must contain a certification by either the Certifying Professional or by the trustee, the debtor, or the chair of each official committee represented by the applicant that the trustee, the debtor, or the chair of each official committee (as to each respective committee's professionals) has reviewed the fee application and has approved it. If the Certifying Professional is unable to certify that the trustee, debtor or committee chair, as the case may be, has approved the application, then the application must so state.

3. Each application for fees and disbursements must contain a certification by the Certifying Professional that the trustee, the chair of each official committee and the debtor have all been provided no later than 20 days after the end of each month with a statement of fees and disbursements accrued during such month. The statement must contain a list of professionals and paraprofessionals providing services, their respective billing rates, the aggregate hours spent by each professional and paraprofessional, a general description of services rendered, a reasonably detailed breakdown of the disbursements incurred and an explanation of billing practices.

4. Each application for fees and disbursements must contain a certification by the Certifying Professional that the trustee, the chair of each official committee and the debtor have all been provided with a copy of the relevant fee application at least 10 days before the date set by the Court or any applicable rules for filing fee applications.

5. The Certifying Professional and, where applicable, the trustee, the debtor, or the chair of each official committee providing a certification should be present at the hearing unless previously excused by the Court.

B. Time Records Required to Support Fee Applications.

1. Each professional and paraprofessional must record time in increments of tenths of an hour, and must keep contemporaneous time records on a daily basis.

2. Time records must set forth in reasonable detail an appropriate narrative description of the services rendered. Without limiting the foregoing, the description should include indications of the participants in, as well as the scope, identification and purpose of

the activity that is reasonable in the circumstances, especially in relation to the hours sought to be charged to the estate for that particular activity.[2]

3. In recording time, each professional and paraprofessional may describe in one entry the nature of the services rendered during that day and the aggregate time expended for that day without delineating the actual time spent on each discrete activity, *provided, however,* that if the professional or paraprofessional expends more than 1 hour on a particular activity the time record for that day must include, internally in the description of services for that day, the amount of time spent on that activity. A hypothetical time record complying with this guideline is included in the margin.[3]

4. To the extent a professional is engaged in rendering services in a discrete activity within the case (a) that can reasonably be expected to continue over a period of at least three months, and (b) that can reasonably be expected to constitute approximately 10–20 percent or more of the fees to be sought for an interim period, the professional shall establish a separate record entry for that matter, and record time therein separate from any other services in the case. Within that separate entry the professional shall comply with section 8(3), including the proviso thereof. Examples of such discrete services within a case where such separate recording may be appropriate, in a particular case, include: an extended program of Rule 2004 examinations; sale of a significant asset or subsidiary; a significant adversary proceeding or contested matter; negotiating a plan; drafting and commenting on plan documents (plan, disclosure statement, related corporate documents, etc.) . . .

Paraprofessionals working on such a discrete activity shall similarly account separately for their services and time.

5. The Court may direct, in the order scheduling the hearing on fees or otherwise, the fee applicant to make available to parties in interest, or to file with the Clerk of the Court, a copy of the contemporaneous time records required to be kept by Sections B(1)–(4). If the Court so directs, the Court shall provide that time record entries referring to or disclosing privileged material and confidential material may be excised from such records: provided, however, that if the excised material is sufficiently extensive to infringe upon the Court's ability to judge reasonableness of the services, the Court may request submission of in camera, unredacted time records.

C. Description of Services Rendered.

1. *Content of the Application.* In addition to the description of services rendered to the trustee, the debtor or an official committee, as the case may be, each fee application must include:

(a) A statement at the outset thereof of

(i) the amount of fees and disbursements sought;

(ii) the time period covered by the application; and

(iii) unless the order authorizing retention dispenses with this subparagraph, the total professional hours expended, as well as the total paraprofessional hours expended.

(b) Unless the order authorizing retention upon application therefor dispenses with this paragraph, a schedule showing the name of each professional, with his or her position in the firm, the name of each paraprofessional who worked on the case during the fee period, the year that the professional was licensed to practice, the hours worked by each professional and paraprofessional, and the hourly rate for each professional and paraprofessional. Any change in hourly rates or billing practices from those utilized in the prior application period must be noted on the schedule.

2. To the extent an applicant is required by Section B(4) hereof to maintain a separate time record, the fee application shall describe in reasonable detail the nature of that discrete activity as well as the results of the applicant's efforts. The description shall include an approximation of the percentage of the total fee requested in the application attributable to such activity.

3. Any request for an enhancement of fees over the fee which would be consistent with Section A(1)(d) hereof or which would be derived solely from applicable hourly rates must be specifically identified in the application, and the justification for the requested enhancement must be set forth in detail.

D. Reimbursement for Expenses and Services.

1. *Certification.* Each application requesting reimbursement for services and expenses must contain a certification by the Certifying Professional that:

a. in providing a reimbursable service, the applicant does not make a profit on that service.

b. in charging for a particular service, the applicant does not include in the amount for which reimbursement is sought the amortization of the cost of any investment, equipment, or capital outlay.

c. in seeking reimbursement for a service which the applicant justifiably purchased or contracted for from a third party (such as temporary paralegal or secretary services, or messenger service), the applicant requests reimbursement only for the amount billed to the applicant by the third-party vendor and paid by the applicant to such vendor.

2. *Presentation of Disbursements and Expenses in Fee Application.*

a. In requesting reimbursement for expenses and services, applicants are specifically reminded of other certifications required by these guidelines, and in particular the certification under Section A(1)(c) hereof. Excessive charges shall not be reimbursed. To the extent that an applicant seeks reimbursement for expenses and services, the application shall categorize them (if applicable) in the following manner:

(i) Photocopying

a. Internal (see D(3))

b. External (see D(1)(c))

(ii) Telecommunications

a. Toll charges (see D(6))

b. Facsimile (see D(1)(c))

(iii) Courier and freight (see D(6))

(iv) Printing (see D(1)(a))

(v) Court reporter and transcripts

(vi) Messenger service (see D(1)(c))

(vii) Computerized research (see D(4))

(viii) Out of town travel expenses (see D(7))

a. Transportation

b. Lodging

c. Meals

(ix) Word Processing, Secretarial and other Staff Services (see D(1)(b) and D(11))

(x) Overtime expense (see D(9))

a. Non-professional

b. Professional

(xi) Local Meals (see D(10))

(xii) Local Transportation (see D(12))

Expenses and disbursements which do not fall within any of the foregoing categories and which exceed $500 in the aggregate should be listed separately and adequately described.

b. Support for each item for which reimbursements is sought must be kept. Such support shall be provided on request to the Court and the United States Trustee, and in appropriate circumstances to any party in interest provided that, where applicable, privilege or confidentiality can be preserved.

3. *Photocopying.* Photocopying shall be reimbursable at the lesser of $.20 per page or cost.

4. *Computerized Research.* Computerized legal services such as Lexis and WESTLAW are reimbursable to the extent of the invoiced cost from the vendor.

5. *Facsimile Transmission.* A charge for outgoing facsimile transmission to long distance telephone numbers is reimbursable at the lower of (a) toll charges or (b) if such amount is not readily determinable, $1.25 per page for domestic and $2.50 per page

for international transmissions. Charges for in-coming facsimiles are not reimbursable.

6. *Postage, Telephone, Courier and Freight.* The cost of postage, freight, overnight delivery, courier services, and telephone toll charges are reimbursable, if reasonably incurred. Thus, charges should be minimized whenever possible. For example, messengers and overnight mail should be used only when first-class mail is impracticable. Delivery of papers to professionals at their homes or similar locales by radio car or taxi is not reimbursable. Charges for local telephone exchange service are not reimbursable.

7. *Travel Charges.* First class air fare, luxury accommodations and deluxe meals are not reimbursable, nor are personal, incidental charges such as telephone and laundry unless necessary as a result of an unforeseen extended stay. Mileage charges for out-of-town travel with one's own car are reimbursable at the lesser of the amount charged clients in the non-bankruptcy context or the amount allowed by the Internal Revenue Service for per mile deductions.

8. *Proofreading.* Charges for proofreading for typographical or similar errors are not reimbursable whether the services are performed by a paralegal, secretary or temporary staff.

9. *Overtime Expense.* Overtime for non-professional and paraprofessional staff is not reimbursable unless justified under the first paragraph of these guidelines. Any such justification must indicate, at a minimum, that (i) services after normal closing hours are absolutely necessary for the case, and (ii) the charges are for overtime expenses paid. The reasonable expenses of a professional required to work on the case after 8:00 p.m. are reimbursable provided that, if the professional dines before 8:00 p.m., the expense is reimbursable only if the professional returns to the office to work for at least 1½ hours. In any event, the expense for an individual's meal may not exceed $20.00.

10. *Daytime Meals.* Daytime meals are not reimbursable unless the individual is participating, during the meal, in a necessary meeting respecting the case.

11. *Word Processing, Secretarial and Other Services.* Daytime, ordinary business hour charges for secretarial, library, word processing and other staff services (exclusive of paraprofessional services) are not reimbursable unless such charges are not included in the firm's overhead for the purpose of setting billing rates, in which case the application shall so state. Special office charges, such as the temporary employment of additional staff: a) necessitated by the case and b) not incurred in replacement of permanent staff or to shift otherwise nonreimbursable charges, will be reimbursed if reasonable and justified in each instance.

12. *Local Transportation.* Local taxi and limousine charges should be minimized and justified. Because of the proximity of mass transit to the court, mass transit should be used whenever practicable.

---

1 These guidelines shall apply to all professionals seeking compensation pursuant to 11 U.S.C. §§ 327, 328, 330 and 331, including investment bankers and real estate advisors, unless the Court, in the order of retention, provides otherwise.

2 By way of illustration only, and not by way of limitation, the following descriptions are inadequate or incomplete:

(i) J. SMITH—1/10/91—legal research re fraudulent transfers—10.0

(ii) J. SMITH—1/11/91—lengthy telephone call with J. Doe re status—.7

(iii) J. SMITH—1/12/91—drafting motion papers—5.0

(iv) J. SMITH—1/13/91—interoffice conferences w/J. Doe and P. Jones re direction of case—2.0

(v) J. SMITH—1/14/91—meeting with creditors—8.0

(vi) J. SMITH—1/14/91—document organization—3.0

(vii) J. SMITH—1/15/91—various correspondence—1.0.

3 A complying time entry would be:

["Conf. W/X re 362 hearing; revising draft motion re ordinary course (1.1); numerous TCs re adeq. protection; conf. call W/Y, Z re taxes (1.4); review court filings . . . Total Time 3.8"].

Additional Filing and Administrative Fees. [Southern District] Effective December 1, 1992, the Judicial Conference has authorized the collection of a miscellaneous administrative fee of $30 in all Chapter 7 and Chapter 13 cases. This is to be collected in lieu of the noticing fees currently charged by the clerks of court under the Fee Schedule issued in accordance with 28 U.S.C. § 1930(b). However, the $50 fee for all notices generated will continue to be billed for all pending Chapter 7 and Chapter 13 cases.

This fee is due in its entirety at the time of filing and cannot be paid in installments. It is not subject to Federal Rule of Bankruptcy Procedure 1006(b), which applies to filing fees.

The approval of this new fee by the Judicial Conference does not preclude trustees from seeking reimbursement for noticing they perform.

GENERAL ORDER M–117. ADOPTION OF PROCEDURES GOVERNING MEDIATION OF MATTERS IN BANKRUPTCY CASES AND ADVISORY PROCEEDINGS

IT IS ORDERED that a court mediation program for matters not involving a governmental unit is established under the following Rules:

1.0 Assignment of Matters to Mediation.

1.1 By Court Order. The court may order assignment of a matter to mediation upon its own motion, or upon a motion by any party in interest or the U.S. Trustee. The motion by a party in interest must be filed promptly after filing the initial document in the matter. Notwithstanding assignment of a matter or proceeding to mediation, it shall be set for the next appropriate hearing on the court docket in the normal course of setting required for such a matter.

1.2 Stipulation of Counsel. Any matter may be referred to mediation upon stipulated order submitted by counsel of record or by a party appearing pro se.

1.3 Types of Matters Subject to Mediation. Unless otherwise ordered by the presiding judge, any adversary proceeding, contested matter or other dispute may be referred by the court to mediation.

1.4 Mediation Procedures. Upon assignment of a matter to mediation, this General Order shall become binding on all parties subject to such mediation.

2.0 The Mediator.

2.1 Mediation Register. The Clerk of the U.S. Bankruptcy Court for the Southern District of N.Y. shall establish and maintain a Register of persons qualifying under paragraph 2.1.A.

A. *Application and Qualification Procedures for Mediation Register.* To qualify for the Mediation Register of this court, a person must apply and meet the following minimum qualifications:

(1) For General Services as a Mediator. A person must have been a member of the Bar in any state or the District of Columbia for at least five years; currently be a member of the Bar in good standing of any state or the District of Columbia; be admitted to practice in the Southern District of N.Y.; and be certified by the Chief Judge to be competent to perform the duties of a mediator. Each person certified as a mediator should take the oath or affirmation prescribed by 28 U.S.C. § 453 before serving as a mediator.

(2) For Services as a Mediator Where the Court Has Determined the Need for Special Skills.

(a) A person must have been authorized to practice for at least four years under the laws of the State of New York as a professional, including but not limited to, an accountant, real estate broker, appraiser, engineer or other professional. Notwithstanding the requirement for authorization to practice under the laws of the State of N.Y., an investment banker professional who has been practicing for a period of at least four years shall be eligible to serve as a mediator; and

(b) Be an active member in good standing, or if retired, have been a member in good standing, of any applicable professional organization; and

(c) Not have:

(1) Been suspended, or have had a professional license revoked, or have pending any proceeding to suspend or revoke such license; or

(2) Resigned from applicable professional organization while an investigation into allegations of misconduct which would warrant suspension, disbarment or professional license revocation was pending; or

(3) Have been convicted of a felony.

B. *Removal From Mediation Register.* A person shall be removed from the Mediation Register either at the person's request or by court order. If removed from the Register by court order, the person shall not be returned to the Register absent a court order obtained upon motion to the Chief Judge and affidavit sufficiently explaining the circumstances of such removal and reasons justifying the return of the person to the Register.

2.2 Appointment of the Mediator.

A. The parties will choose a mediator from the Register. If the parties cannot agree upon a mediator within seven (7) days of assignment to mediation, the court shall appoint a mediator and alternate mediator.

B. If the mediator is unable to serve, the mediator shall file, within seven (7) days after receipt of the notice of appointment, a notice of inability to accept appointment and immediately serve a copy upon the appointed alternate mediator. The alternate mediator shall become the mediator for the matter if such person fails to file a notice of inability to accept appointment within seven (7) days after filing of the original mediator's notice of inability. If neither can serve, the court will appoint another mediator and alternate mediator.

2.3 Disqualification of a Mediator.

Any person selected as a mediator may be disqualified for bias or prejudice as provided in 28 U.S.C. § 144 or if not, disinterested under 11 U.S.C. § 101. Any party selected as a mediator shall be disqualified in any matter where 28 U.S.C. § 455 would require disqualification if that person were a justice, judge or magistrate.

3.0 The Mediation.

3.1 Time and Place of Mediation.

Upon consultation with all attorneys and pro se parties subject to the mediation, the mediator shall fix a reasonable time and place for the initial mediation conference of the parties with the mediator and promptly shall give the attorneys and pro se parties advance written notice of the conference. The conference shall be set as soon after the entry of the mediation order and as long in advance of the court's final evidentiary hearing as practicable. To ensure prompt dispute resolution, the mediator shall have the duty and authority to establish the time for all mediation activities, including private meetings between the mediator and parties and the submission of relevant documents. The mediator shall have the authority to establish a deadline for the parties to act upon a proposed settlement or upon a settlement recommendation from the mediator.

3.2 Mediation Conference.

A representative of each party shall attend the mediation conference, and must have complete authority to negotiate all disputed amounts and issues. The mediator shall control all procedural aspects of the mediation. The mediator shall also have the discretion to require that the party representative or a non-attorney principal of the party with settlement authority be present at any conference. The mediator shall also determine when the parties are to be present in the conference room. The mediator shall report any willful failure to attend or participate in good faith in the mediation process or conference. Such failure may result in the imposition of sanctions by the court.

3.3 Recommendations of the Mediator.

The mediator shall have no obligation to make written comments or recommendations; provided, however, that the mediator may furnish the attorneys for the parties and any pro se party with a written settlement recommendation. Any such recommendation shall not be filed with the court.

3.4 Post-mediation Procedures.

Promptly upon conclusion of the mediation conference, and in any event no later than 3 P.M. two (2) business days prior to the date fixed for hearing referred to in paragraph 1.1, the mediator shall file a final report showing compliance or non-compliance with the requirements of this General Order by the parties and the mediation results. If in the mediation the parties reach an agreement regarding the disposition of the matter, they shall determine who shall prepare and submit to the court a stipulated order or judgment, or joint motion for approval of compromise of controversy (as appropriate), within twenty (20) days of the conference. Failure to timely file such a stipulated order or judgment or motion when agreement is reached shall be a basis for the court to impose appropriate sanctions. Absent such a stipulated order or judgment or motion, no party shall be bound by any statement made or action taken during the mediation process. If the mediation ends in an impasse, the matter will be heard or tried as scheduled.

3.5 Termination of Mediation.

Upon receipt of the mediator's final report, the mediation will be deemed terminated, and the mediator excused, and relieved from further responsibilities in the matter without further court order.

3.6 Withdrawal From Mediation.

Any matter referred pursuant to this General Order may be withdrawn from mediation by the judge assigned to the matter at any time upon determination for any reason the matter is not suitable for mediation. Nothing in this General Order shall prohibit or prevent any party in interest, the U.S. Trustee or the mediator from filing a motion to withdraw a matter from mediation for cause.

4.0 Compensation of Mediators. The mediator's compensation shall be on such terms as are satisfactory to the mediator and the parties, and subject to court approval if the estate is to be charged with such expense.

5.0 Confidentiality.

5.1 Confidentiality as to the Court and Third Parties. Any statements made by the mediator, by the parties or by others during the mediation process shall not be divulged by any of the participants in the mediation (or their agents) or by the mediator to the court or to any third party. All records, reports, or other documents received or made by a mediator while serving in such capacity shall be confidential and shall not be provided to the court, unless they would be otherwise admissible. The mediator shall not be compelled to divulge such records or to testify in regard to the mediation in connection with any arbitral, judicial or other proceeding, including any hearing held by the court in connection with the referred matter. Nothing in this section, however, precludes the mediator from reporting the status (though not content) of the mediation effort to the court orally or in writing, or from complying with the obligation set forth in 3.2 to report failures to attend or to participate in good faith.

5.2 Confidentiality of Mediation Effort. Rule 408 of the Federal Rules of Evidence shall apply to mediation proceedings. Except as permitted by Rule 408, no person may rely on or introduce as evidence in connection with any arbitral, judicial or other proceeding, including any hearing held by this court in connection with the referred matter, any aspect of the mediation effort, including, but not limited to:

A. Views expressed or suggestions made by any party with respect to a possible settlement of the dispute;

B. Admissions made by the other party in the course of the mediation proceedings;

C. Proposals made or views expressed by the mediator.

6.0 Consensual Modification of Mediation Procedures. Additional rules and procedures for the mediation may be negotiated and agreed upon by the mediator and the parties at any time during the mediation process.

7.0 Compliance With the U.S. Code, Federal Rules of Bankruptcy Procedure, and Court Rules and Orders. Nothing in this General Order shall relieve any debtor, party in interest, or the U.S. Trustee from complying with any other court orders, U.S. Code, the Federal Rules of Bankruptcy Procedure, or this court's Local Rules, including times fixed for discovery or preparation for any court hearing pending on the matter.

Dated: Nov. 10, 1993,
New York, N.Y.

GENERAL ORDER M–118. TIME FOR MOTIONS FOR ASSUMPTION/REJECTION/ASSIGNMENT UNDER FEDERAL RULE OF BANKRUPTCY PROCEDURE 6006, DEBTOR

WHEREAS, effective Aug. 1, 1993, Federal Rule of Bankruptcy Procedure 6006, dealing with motions for the assumption, rejection and assignment of executory contracts and unexpired leases, was amended to delete the requirement for a hearing; and

WHEREAS, the judges of this court desire to advise the Bar of their adoption of a uniform interpretation of the Local Bankruptcy Rules, as they apply to motions requesting an order for the assumption, rejection or assignment of an executory contract or unexpired lease; and

WHEREAS, Federal Rule of Bankruptcy Procedure 6006 requires that such relief be requested by motion and motions are governed by Federal Rule of Bankruptcy Procedure 9013; and

WHEREAS, Local Bankruptcy Rule 13 deals with motions and Local Bankruptcy Rule 13(c)(2) requires that motions are to be served at least ten (10) days before the return date; and

WHEREAS, the return date of a motion under Federal Rule of Bankruptcy Procedure 6006, requesting relief without a hearing should be determined to be the day it is requested that an order be signed granting the relief; and

WHEREAS, the judges of this court are in agreement that the time limits governing the presentation of a motion under Federal Rule of Bankruptcy Procedure 6006 are those set forth in Local Bankruptcy Rule 13, rather than those set forth in Local Bankruptcy Rule 46(c); and good and sufficient cause appearing therefor.

IT IS NOW ORDERED that any motion requesting an order under Federal Rule of Procedure 6006 for the assumption, rejection or assignment of an executory contract or unexpired lease should be noticed on not less than the time limits set forth in Local Bankruptcy Rule 13(c)(2); and

IT IS FURTHER ORDERED the application of the time limits may be waived in an appropriate case in the event that an order is sought upon the written consent of all parties entitled to notice of the motion; and

IT IS FURTHER ORDERED that in the event that a nonconsensual order is sought on shortened time, Local Bankruptcy Rule 13(d) shall govern and an actual hearing shall be required.

Dated: Nov. 10, 1993,
     New York, N.Y.

GENERAL ORDER M–138. FILING A LIST OF CREDITORS IN A BANKRUPTCY CASE

See, also, Order M—192, post.

* * * * *

EXHIBIT "B"

Floppy disk: Multiple Cases (lists of creditors with more than 10 creditors per case but no more than 1000 creditors for all cases entered on the disk)

The disk must be tiled in a sealed 8½" x 11" envelope. The debtors' names and addresses, social security/taxpayer identification numbers, chapter filed under and the attorney name, address and telephone number shall appear on the envelope. The floppy disk shall be segmented by individual debtor and shall conform to the following format and specifications:

1. Must be 3.5" or 5.25";
2. Must be formatted for use on an IBM or compatible PC;
3. Contain one ASCII file;
4. One file per disk;
5. File must be named "creditor.scn";
6. The first line for each case on the tile must be the name of the debtor. If the disk is not tiled with the petitions, then the case numbers must be substituted for the debtors' names (***9412345***); use three asterisks before and after each case number.
7. The second line must be blank;
8. Start the list of creditors on the third line;
9. The address must be 4 lines or less;
10. Each line of the address must not contain more than 30 characters;
11. Each address must be separated by two blank lines;
12. State name can be either two characters or written out fully, however the state name cannot contain periods (i.e. "N.Y." is invalid but "NY" and "New York" are valid);
13. There should be no trailing blanks after the zip code;
14. No more than 1000 creditors should be listed;
15. After the last creditor for each case, there should be five blank lines before listing the name (or case number) of the next debtor., and
16. Follow instructions B.6–12.

FOR FURTHER INFORMATION ON FORMATTING OR DISK PREPARATION, CONTACT PAT-

RICK DELL'ARENA AT (212) 668–2870 EXT.3522 OR VITO GENNA AT (212) 668–2870 EXT.3521.

GENERAL ORDER M–143. COURT ANNEXED MEDIATION PROGRAM: ADOPTION OF PROCEDURES GOVERNING MEDIATION OF MATTERS IN BANKRUPTCY CASES AND ADVERSARY PROCEEDINGS

IT IS ORDERED that a court mediation program for matters not involving a governmental unit is established under the following Rules:

1.0   Assignment of Matters to Mediation

1.1 By Court Order. The court may a matter to mediation upon its own motion, or order assignment of upon a motion by any party in interest or the U.S. Trustee. The motion by a party in interest must be filed promptly after filing the initial document in the matter. Notwithstanding assignment of a matter or proceeding to mediation, it shall be set for the next appropriate hearing on the court docket in the normal course of setting required for such a matter.

1.2 Stipulation of Counsel. Any matter may be referred to mediation upon stipulated order submitted by counsel of record or by a party appearing pro se.

1.3 Types of Matters Subject to Mediation. Unless otherwise ordered by the presiding judge, any adversary proceeding, contested matter or other dispute may be referred by the court to mediation.

1.4 Mediation Procedures. Upon assignment of a matter to mediation, this General Order shall become binding on all parties subject to such mediation.

2.0   The Mediator

2.1 Mediation Register. The Clerk of the United States Bankruptcy Court for the Southern District of New York shall establish and maintain a Register of persons qualifying under paragraph 2.1.A.

A. *Application and Qualification Procedures for Mediation Register.* To qualify for the Mediation Register of this court, a person must apply and meet the following minimum qualifications:

(1) For General Services as a Mediator. A person must have been a member of the bar in any state or the District of Columbia for at least five years; currently a member of the bar in good standing of any state or the District of Columbia; be admitted to practice in the Southern District of New York; and be certified by the Chief Judge to be competent to perform the duties of a mediator. Each person certified as a mediator should take the oath or affirmation prescribed by 28 U.S.C. § 453 before serving as a mediator.

(2) For Services as a Mediator where the Court Has Determined the Need for Special Skills.

(a) A person must have been authorized to practice for at least four years under the laws of the State of New York as a professional, including but not limited to, an accountant, real estate broker, appraiser, engineer or other professional. Notwithstanding the requirement for authorization to practice under the laws of the State of New York, an investment banker professional who has been practicing for a period of at least four years shall be eligible to serve as a mediator; and

(b) Be an active member in good standing, or if retired, have been a member in good standing, of any applicable professional organization;

(c) Not have:

(1) Been suspended, or have had a professional license revoked, or have pending any proceeding to suspend or revoke such license; or

(2) Resigned from applicable professional organization while an investigation into allegations of misconduct which would warrant suspension, disbarment or professional license revocation was pending; or

(3) Have been convicted of a felony.

B. *Removal From Mediation Register.* A person shall be removed from the Mediation Register either at the person's request or by court order. If removed from the Register by court order, the person shall not be returned to the Register absent a court order obtained upon motion to the Chief Judge and affidavit sufficiently explaining the circumstances of such removal and reasons justifying the return of the person to the Register.

2.2 Appointment of the Mediator.

A. The parties will ordinarily choose a mediator from the Register for appointment by the Court. If the parties cannot agree upon a mediator within seven (7) days of assignment to mediation, the court shall appoint a mediator and alternate mediator.

B. In the event of a determination by the court that there are special issues presented which suggest reference to an appropriately experienced mediator other than the mediator chosen by the parties, then the court shall appoint a mediator and an alternate mediator.

C. If the mediator is unable to serve, the mediator shall file within seven (7) days after receipt of the notice of appointment, a notice of inability to accept appointment and immediately serve a copy upon the appointed alternate mediator. The alternate mediator shall become the mediator for the matter if such person fails to file a notice of inability to accept appointment within seven (7) days after filing of the

original mediator's notice of inability. If neither can serve, the court will appoint another mediator and alternate mediator.

2.3 Disqualification of a Mediator. Any person selected as a mediator may be disqualified for bias or prejudice as provided in 28 U.S.C. § 144 or if not, disinterested under 11 U.S.C. § 101. Any party selected as a mediator shall be disqualified in any matter where 28 U.S.C. § 455 would require disqualification if that person were a justice, judge or magistrate.

3.0 The Mediation

3.1 Time and Place of Mediation. Upon consultation with all attorneys and pro se parties subject to the mediation, the mediator shall fix a reasonable time and place for the initial mediation conference of the parties with the mediator and promptly shall give the attorneys and pro se parties advance written notice of the conference. The conference shall be set as soon after the entry of the mediation order and as long in advance of the court's final evidentiary hearing as practicable. To ensure prompt dispute resolution, the mediator shall have the duty and authority to establish the time for all mediation activities, including private meetings between the mediator and parties and the submission of relevant documents. The mediator shall have the authority to establish a deadline for the parties to act upon a proposed settlement or upon a settlement recommendation from the mediator.

3.2 Mediation Conference. A representative of each party shall attend the mediation conference, and must have complete authority to negotiate all disputed amounts and issues. The mediator shall control all procedural aspects of the mediation. The mediator shall also have the discretion to require that the party representative or a non-attorney principal of the party with settlement authority be present at any conference. The mediator shall also determine when the parties are to be present in the conference room. The mediator shall report any willful failure to attend or participate in good faith in the mediation process or conference. Such failure may result in the imposition of sanctions by the court.

3.3 Recommendations of the Mediator. The mediator shall have no obligation to make written comments or recommendations; provided, however, that the mediator may furnish the attorneys for the parties and any pro se party with a written settlement recommendation. Any such recommendation shall not be filed with the court.

3.4 Post–Mediation Procedures. Promptly upon conclusion of the mediation conference, and in any event no later than 3:00 P.M. two (2) business days prior to the date fixed for hearing referred to in paragraph 1.1, the mediator shall file a final report showing compliance or noncompliance with the requirements of this General Order by the parties and the mediation results. If in the mediation the parties reach an agreement regarding the disposition of the matter, they shall determine who shall prepare and submit to the court a stipulated order or judgment, or joint motion for approval of compromise of controversy (as appropriate), within twenty (20) days of the conference. Failure to timely file such a stipulated order or judgment or motion when agreement is reached shall be a basis for the court to impose appropriate sanctions. Absent such a stipulated order or judgment or motion, no party shall be bound by any statement made or action taken during the mediation process. If the mediation ends in an impasse, the matter will be heard or tried as scheduled.

3.5 Termination of Mediation. Upon receipt of the mediator's final report, the mediation will be deemed terminated, and the mediator excused and relieved from further responsibilities in the matter without further court order.

3.6 Withdrawal From Mediation. Any matter referred pursuant to this General Order may be withdrawn from mediation by the judge assigned to the matter at any time upon determination for any reason the matter is not suitable for mediation. Nothing in this General Order shall prohibit or prevent any party in interest, the U.S. Trustee or the mediator from filing a motion to withdraw a matter from mediation for cause.

4.0 Compensation of Mediators

The mediator's compensation shall be on such terms as are satisfactory to the mediator and the parties, and subject to court approval if the estate is to be charged with such expense. In the event that the mediator and the parties cannot agree on terms of compensation, then the court shall fix such terms as are reasonable and just.

5.0 Confidentiality

5.1 Confidentiality as to the Court and Third Parties. Any statements made by the mediator, by the parties or by others during the mediation process shall not be divulged by any of the participants in the mediation (or their agents) or by the mediator to the court or to any third party. All records, reports, or other documents received or made by a mediator while serving in such capacity shall be confidential and shall not be provided to the court, unless they would be otherwise admissable. The mediator shall not be compelled to divulge such records or to testify in regard to the mediation in connection with any arbitral, judicial or other proceeding, including any hearing held by the court in connection with the referred matter. Nothing in this section, however, precludes the mediator from reporting the status (though not content) of the mediation effort to the court orally or in writing, or from complying with the obligation set forth in 3.2 to report failures to attend or to participate in good faith.

5.2 Confidentiality of Mediation Effort. Rule 408 of the Federal Rules of Evidence shall apply to mediation proceedings. Except as permitted by Rule 408, no person may rely on or introduce as evidence in connection with any arbitral, judicial or other proceeding, including any hearing held by this court in connection with the referred matter, any aspect of the mediation effort, including, but not limited to:

A. Views expressed or suggestions made by any party with respect to a possible settlement of the dispute;

B. Admissions made by the other party in the course of the mediation proceedings;

C. Proposals made or views expressed by the mediator.

6.0 Immunity

The Mediators shall be immune from claims arising out of acts or omissions incident to their service as court appointees in this Mediation Program. See Wagshal v. Foster, 28 F.3d 1249, D.C.Cir.1994.

7.0 Consensual Modification of Mediation Procedures

Additional rules and procedures for the mediation may be negotiated and agreed upon by the mediator and the parties at any time during the mediation process.

8.0 Compliance With the U.S. Code, Federal Rules of Bankruptcy Procedure, and Court Rules and Orders

Nothing in this General Order shall relieve any debtor, party in interest, or the U.S. Trustee from complying with any other court orders, U.S. Code, the Federal Rules of Bankruptcy Procedure, or this court's Local Rules, including times fixed for discovery or preparation for any court hearing pending on the matter.

Dated: New York, New York
January 17, 1995.

GENERAL ORDER M–151. AMENDED GUIDELINES FOR FEES AND DISBURSEMENTS FOR PROFESSIONALS IN SOUTHERN DISTRICT OF NEW YORK BANKRUPTCY CASES

See, also, Order M–104, ante.

Pursuant to the Bankruptcy Reform Act of 1994, the Executive Office for the United States Trustees has promulgated guidelines (the "UST Guidelines") to be applied by all United States Trustee personnel unless the United States Trustee determines that circumstances warrant different treatment. These UST Guidelines are patterned in large measure after the existing guidelines promulgated pursuant to the order of Chief Judge Lifland dated June 24, 1991 (the

"Original Guidelines"). The UST Guidelines state that they are not intended to affect local rules and they leave for determination by local rule or otherwise a variety of procedural matters including the fixing of appropriate ceilings on certain types of reimbursements. These Amended Guidelines are consistent with and supplemental to the requirements contained in those guidelines.

A. Effective Date and Applicability of Amended Guidelines. The following Amended Guidelines apply to all applications for compensation and reimbursement of expenses under sections 330 and 331 of the Bankruptcy Code filed on or after May 1, 1995 in all cases commenced on or after October 22, 1994. Cases filed earlier than October 22, 1994 and fee applications filed earlier than May 1, 1995, the effective dates of the UST Guidelines, will continue to be governed by the Original Guidelines. Unless the court otherwise orders, all applications for compensation and reimbursement covered by the UST Guidelines must be prepared in accordance with these Amended Guidelines as well.

B. Certification.

1. Each application for fees and disbursements must contain a certification by the professional designated by the applicant with the responsibility in the particular case for compliance with these Amended Guidelines (the "Certifying Professional"), that (a) the Certifying Professional has read the application; (b) to the best of the Certifying Professional's knowledge, information and belief formed after reasonable inquiry, the fees and disbursements sought fall within these Amended Guidelines and the UST Guidelines, except as specifically noted in the certification and described in the fee application; (c) except to the extent that fees or disbursements are prohibited by these Amended Guidelines or the UST Guidelines, the fees and disbursements sought are billed at rates and in accordance with practices customarily employed by the applicant and generally accepted by the applicant's clients; and (d) in providing a reimbursable service, the applicant does not make a profit on that service, whether the service is performed by the applicant in-house or through a third party.

2. Each application for fees and disbursements must contain a certification by the Certifying Professional that the trustee, and, in chapter 11 cases, the chair of each official committee and the debtor have all been provided not later than 20 days after the end of each month with a statement of fees and disbursements accrued during such month. The statement must contain a list of professionals and paraprofessionals providing services, their respective billing rates, the aggregate hours spent by each professional and paraprofessional, a general description of services rendered, a reasonably detailed breakdown of the disbursements incurred and an explanation of billing practices.

3. Each application for fees and disbursements must contain a certification by the Certifying Professional that the trustee, and, in a chapter 11 case, the chair of each official committee and the debtor have all been provided with a copy of the relevant fee application at least 10 days before the date set by the court or any applicable rules for filing fee applications.

C. Confidentiality Requests. If there is a need to omit any information or description of services as privileged or confidential, the applicant may make such a request of the court; provided, however, that if such a request is granted, the court may request that it be furnished with a set of unredacted time records for in camera inspection.

D. Fee Enhancement.

1. Any request for an enhancement of fees over the fee which would be derived from the applicable hourly rates multiplied by the hours expended or from the court order authorizing retention must be specifically identified in the application, including as to amount, and the justification for the requested enhancement must be set forth in detail.

2. Any request for such an enhancement of fees must be set forth in the summary sheet required by the UST Guidelines.

E. Voluntary Reduction of Fees or Disbursements. If an applicant is not requesting all of the fees or disbursements to which it might be entitled based on the applicable hourly rates multiplied by the hours expended or based on the court order authorizing retention, the voluntary reduction must be identified in the application, including as to amount. If the voluntary reduction pertains to services which continue to appear in the detailed description of services rendered or to disbursements which continue to be listed, the entries for which no compensation or reimbursement is sought must be identified.

F. Provisions Regarding Disbursements.

1. *No Enhanced Charges for Disbursements.* Except to the extent that disbursements are prohibited by these Amended Guidelines or the UST Guidelines, the disbursements sought must be billed at rates and in accordance with practices customarily employed by the applicant and generally accepted by the applicant's clients.

2. *Photocopies.* Photocopies shall be reimbursable at the lesser of $.20 per page or cost.

3. *Facsimile Transmission.* A charge for outgoing facsimile transmission to long distance telephone numbers is reimbursable at the lower of (a) toll charges or (b) if such amount is not readily determinable, $1.25 per page for domestic and $2.50 per page

for international transmissions. Charges for in-coming facsimiles are not reimbursable.

4. *Cellular Telephone.* Cellular telephone charges shall be reimbursable if reasonably incurred and if the calls cannot be timely made from a conventional telephone. Routine use of cellular telephones is not acceptable.

5. *Overtime Expense.* No overtime expense for non-professional and paraprofessional staff shall be reimbursable unless fully explained and justified. Any such justification must indicate, at a minimum, that (i) services after normal closing hours are absolutely necessary for the case and (ii) the charges are for overtime expenses paid. The reasonable expenses of a professional required to work on the case after 8:00 p.m. are reimbursable *provided* that, if the professional dines before 8:00 p.m., the expense is reimbursable only if the professional returns to the office to work for at least one and one-half hours. In any event, the expense for an individual's meal may not exceed $20.00.

6. *Daytime Meals.* Daytime meals are not reimbursable unless the individual is participating, during the meal, in a necessary meeting respecting the case.

The foregoing Guidelines have been approved by the Board of Judges on April 19, 1995 and shall be subject to annual review as to adjustments to disbursement reimbursement amounts set forth hereinabove in Provision F.

Dated: New York, New York
      April 19, 1995.

GENERAL ORDER M–182. ELECTRONIC MEANS FOR FILING, GENERAL ORDER SIGNING, AND VERIFICATION OF (ELECTRONIC FILING PROCEDURES) DOCUMENTS

See, now, General Order M–242, post.

GENERAL ORDER M–192. FILING A LIST OF CREDITORS IN A BANKRUPTCY CASE

See, also, General Order M–138, ante.

This order amends General Order M–138, dated December 12, 1994. If you are filing a petition for a debtor with fewer than one thousand (1000) creditors and equity security holders, you must also file a separate, additional creditor list on a floppy disk (3.5" only), in addition to the list or schedules included in the petition. The disk should be filed in a sealed 8½" × 11" envelope or disk mailer and contain names and post office address, including zip codes, of the debtor's creditors. If a debt is owed to a United States agency,

you must list the particular agency or department and address to which such debt is owing. The floppy disk should be filed using the format and specifications annexed as Exhibit "A". You should include a certification in your petition that the information entered on the floppy disk is true, complete and correct. If you file the floppy disk separately, you should include a single page certification in the same envelope or disk mailer as the disk. The debtor's name as well as the case number, if it is known, should be on the envelope or disk mailer.

If an attorney or petition preparer is filing several petitions simultaneously, including one or more petitions with fewer than one thousand (1000) creditors and equity security holders, an individual disk for each petition is required. The disk should be submitted in a sealed 8½" × 11" envelope or disk mailer with the names of each of the debtors listed on the envelope or disk mailer at the time of filing. When schedules are amended for the purpose of adding creditors, you must file a disk listing the additional creditors only.

The requirements for filing a disk cannot be waived, except for a pro se debtor who has not used an outside service to prepare the petition. If a service is used, the service must provide a floppy disk listing creditors.

Moreover, the court will assist attorneys and pro se debtors in preparing creditor listings by providing training and access to a personal computer. Vendors can also be used to prepare a creditor disk.

If you are filing a petition with one thousand (1000) or more creditors and equity security holders, immediately contact the Clerk of Court to determine if 28 U.S.C. § 156(c) is applicable. Pursuant to this section, an outside agent may be used to process claims and noticing.

Dated: March 16, 1998
      New York, New York.

EXHIBIT "A"
Floppy Disk: Single Case (less than 1000 Creditors)

The additional list of creditors on floppy disk shall be tiled in a sealed 8½" × 11" envelope. The debtor's name and address, social security/taxpayer's identification number, chapter tiled under and attorney name, address and telephone number shall appear on the envelope. The disk should be in the following format:

1. Must be 3.5" disk ONLY.
2. Must be formatted for use on an IBM or compatible PC.
3. Contain one ASCII format; Save ASCII (DOS) TXT.
4. One case per tile.
5. One file per disk.

6. File must be named "Creditor.scn".

7. The first line of the file must be the name of the debtor. If the disk is not tiled with the petition, then the case number must be substituted for the debtor name using three asterisks before and after the case number (i.e. ***9412345***).

8. The second line must be blank.

9. Start the list of creditors on the third line; ALL CAPS.

10. The address must be 4 lines or less; do not include account numbers.

11. Each line of the address must contain no more than 30 characters.

12. Each CREDITOR must be separated by two blank lines.

13. "Attention" or "c/o" cannot be entered as either the first or last line of the address.

14. The state name can be either two characters or written out fully, however the state name cannot contain periods (i.e. "N.Y."). NY or New York are valid.

15. Use only one space between the state and the zip code.

16. Use a hyphen between the first five and second four digits in the zip code (ie. 99999–9999).

17. There should be no trailing blanks after the zip code.

18. No more than 1000 creditors should be listed on one disk.

GENERAL ORDER M–193. ELECTRONIC MEANS FOR FILING, SIGNING, AND VERIFICATION OF DOCUMENTS

See, now, General Order M–242, post.

GENERAL ORDER M–201. ADOPTION OF PREPACKAGED CHAPTER 11 CASE GUIDELINES

By resolution of the Board of Judges for the Southern District of New York; it is resolved that in an attempt to provide bankruptcy practitioners with guidelines in dealing with practical matters when filing a prepackaged Chapter 11 case, including filing all documents via the Internet by means of the Court's Electronic Case Filing System; Prepackaged Chapter 11 Case Guidelines, annexed hereto, to be revised from time to time as new features are added to the Court's Electronic Case Filing System, be and the same hereby are adopted and are to take effect as of the date of this order.

Dated February 2, 1999.

GENERAL ORDER M–203. AMENDING GENERAL ORDER 201

By resolution of the Board of Judges for the Southern District of New York; it is resolved that in an attempt to provide bankruptcy practitioners with guidelines in dealing with practical matters when filing a prepackaged Chapter 11 case, including filing all documents via the Internet by means of the Court's Electronic Case Filing System, Prepackaged Chapter 11 Case Guidelines, as amended and annexed hereto, to be revised from time to time as new features are added to the Court's Electronic Case Filing System, be and the same hereby are adopted and are in effect as of the date of General Order 201, dated February 2, 1999.

PROCEDURAL GUIDELINES FOR PREPACKAGED CHAPTER 11 CASES IN THE UNITED STATES BANKRUPTCY COURT FOR THE SOUTHERN DISTRICT OF NEW YORK

I. GOALS.

The purpose of this document is to establish uniform guidelines for commencing and administering "prepackaged Chapter 11 cases" in the United States Bankruptcy Court for the Southern District of New York (the "Court"). Specifically, this document defines "prepackaged Chapter 11 case" and attempts to provide bankruptcy practitioners with help in dealing with practical matters which either are not addressed at all by statute or rules or are addressed indirectly in a piecemeal fashion by statutes, general rules, and/or local rules that were not enacted specifically with prepackaged Chapter 11 cases in mind. Although each case is different, many issues are common to all prepackaged cases. Judicial economy, as well as procedural predictability for debtors and creditors, will be enhanced by promulgation of uniform guidelines to deal with these common issues. The guidelines are advisory only; the Court retains the power to depart from them.

In order to ease the burden on practitioners and the Court, Chief Judge Tina L. Brozman convened a committee of judges, attorneys, clerk's office staff and the United States Trustee to assist in developing a uniform set of procedures applicable to prepackaged Chapter 11 cases filed in the Southern District of New York. Those meetings resulted in a general order adopted by the Court on February 2, 1999, after a vote of the Board of Judges, which established the following procedural guidelines for prepackaged Chapter 11 cases.

II. DEFINITION OF PREPACKAGED CHAPTER 11 CASE.

For purposes of these guidelines, a "prepackaged Chapter 11 case" is one in which the Debtor, substantially contemporaneously with the filing of its Chapter 11 petition, files a Confirmation Hearing Scheduling Motion For Prepackaged Plan in substantially the form annexed hereto as Exhibit A and satisfying the criteria set forth in Part III.A. below ("Prepack Scheduling Motion"), plan, disclosure statement (or other solicitation document), and voting certification.

III. CRITERIA FOR PREPACKAGED CHAPTER 11 CASE; CONTENTS OF PREPACK SCHEDULING MOTION.

A. *Content of Prepack Scheduling Motion.*

The Prepack Scheduling Motion shall:

(i) represent that (x) the solicitation of all votes to accept or reject the Debtor's plan required for confirmation of that plan was completed prior to commencement of the Debtor's Chapter 11 case or in accordance with § 1125(g), and that no additional solicitation of votes on that plan is contemplated by the Debtor, or (y) the solicitation of all votes to accept or reject the Debtor's plan required for confirmation of that plan has been deemed adequate by the Court pursuant to Part III.C.(ii) below such that no additional solicitation will be required;

(ii) represent that the requisite acceptances of such plan have been obtained from each class of claims or interests as to which solicitation is required except as provided in Part III.A.(iii) below; and

(iii) with respect to any class of interests that has not accepted the plan whether or not it is deemed not to have accepted the plan under § 1126(g), represent that the Debtor is requesting confirmation under § 1129(b); and

(iv) request entry of an order scheduling the hearing (x) on confirmation of the plan and (y) to determine whether the Debtor has satisfied the requirements of either 11 U.S.C. § 1126(b)(1) or 11 U.S.C. § 1126(b)(2), for a date that is not more than ninety (90) days following the petition date.

B. *Confirmation Pursuant to 11 U.S.C. § 1129(b)(2)(C).*

A Chapter 11 case may constitute a "prepackaged Chapter 11 case" for purposes of these guidelines notwithstanding the fact that the Debtor proposes to confirm the Plan pursuant to 11 U.S.C. § 1129(b)(2)(C) as to a class of interests.

C. *Filing of Petition After Solicitation Has Commenced But Before Expiration of Voting Deadline.*

Unless the Court orders otherwise, if a Chapter 11 case is commenced by or against the Debtor, or if a Chapter 7 case is commenced against the Debtor and

converted to a Chapter 11 case by the Debtor pursuant to 11 U.S.C. § 706(a), after the Debtor has transmitted all solicitation materials to holders of claims and interests whose vote is sought but before the deadline for casting acceptances or rejections of the Debtor's plan (the "Voting Deadline"),

(i) the Debtor and other parties in interest shall be permitted to accept but not solicit ballots until the Voting Deadline; and

(ii) After notice and a hearing the Court shall determine the effect of any and all such votes.

D. *Applicability of Guidelines To Cases Involving Cramdown of Classes of Claims and Interests and "Partial Prepackaged Chapter 11 Cases."*

The Court may, upon request of the Debtor or other party in interest in an appropriate case, apply some or all of these guidelines to

(i) cases in which the Debtor has satisfied the requirements of Part III.A.(i) above but intends to seek confirmation of the plan pursuant to 11 U.S.C. § 1129(b) as to a class of (a) claims which is deemed not to have accepted the plan under 11 U.S.C. § 1126(g); (b) claims or interests which is receiving or retaining property under or pursuant to the plan but whose members' votes were not solicited prepetition and whose rejection of the plan has been assumed by the Debtor for purposes of confirming the plan; or (c) claims or interests which is receiving or retaining property under or pursuant to the plan and which voted prepetition to reject the plan, as long as no class junior to such rejecting class is receiving or retaining any property under or pursuant to the plan; and

(ii) "partial prepackaged Chapter 11 cases"—*i.e.,* cases in which acceptances of the Debtor's plan were solicited prior to the commencement of the case from some, but not all, classes of claims or interests whose solicitation is required to confirm the Debtor's plan.

IV. PREFILING NOTIFICATION TO UNITED STATES TRUSTEE AND CLERK OF THE COURT.

A. *Notice of Proposed Filing to United States Trustee.*

At least two (2) business days prior to the anticipated filing date of the prepackaged Chapter 11 case, the Debtor should (i) notify the United States Trustee of the Debtor's intention to file a prepackaged Chapter 11 case and (ii) supply the United States Trustee with two (2) copies of the Debtor's plan and disclosure statement (or other solicitation document).

B. *Notice of Proposed "First Day Orders" to United States Trustee.*

If possible, drafts of all First Day Motions (as defined in Part VI.A. below), with the proposed orders attached as exhibits, should be furnished to the United States Trustee at least one (1) and preferably two (2) business days in advance of the filing of the petition or as soon as practicable after the filing of an involuntary petition.

C. *Notice of Proposed Filing to Clerk of Court.*

At least two (2) business days prior to the anticipated filing date of the prepackaged Chapter 11 case, counsel for the Debtor, without disclosing the name of the Debtor, should contact the Clerk of the Court to discuss the anticipated filing, the amount of the Debtor's assets, number and type of creditors, procedures for handling public inquiries (*i.e.*, the names, addresses and telephone numbers of the persons to whom such inquiries should be directed), procedures for handling claims and proofs of claim or interest, whether the Debtor will request the Court to set a last date to file proofs of claim or interest, and related matters. On request, the Clerk of the Court will reserve a last date to file proofs of claim or interest for the Debtor. The Clerk of the Court will not assign the case to or discuss the case with a judge until the petition is filed.

V. FILING OF PREPACKAGED CHAPTER 11 CASE.

A. *Electronic Case Filing Via the Internet.*

The Court has established and requires electronic filing of all Chapter 11 cases on the Internet. Information on electronic filing procedures, including a user's manual (copy annexed as Exhibit "E") and registration form, is available at the Court's world wide web site at: http://www.nysb.uscourts.gov. In electronically filing a prepackaged Chapter 11 case, the Debtor should file the petition(s) first, followed by the affidavit pursuant to Local Rule 1007–2 and the motions and proposed orders, and should file lengthy documents, such as the disclosure statement (or other solicitation materials) and plan, last. Electronically filing lengthy documents last will expedite the filing process. (See electronic filing instructions).

B. *Proposed Orders as Exhibits to Electronically Filed Motions.*

All "First Day Motions" (as defined in Part VI.A. below) shall have attached as an exhibit a copy of the proposed order sought to be signed.

C. *Paper Copies Furnished to Assigned Judge.*

As soon as practicable following filing of a prepackaged Chapter 11 case, the Debtor shall furnish to the judge assigned to the case a paper copy of the plan, the disclosure statement (or other solicitation document), "First Day Motions" (with proposed orders attached as exhibits), any other filed motion and any Order To Show Cause on which the Court's signature is requested. Proposed Orders should be presented on a 3.5 inch disk in WordPerfect or other Windows-based format. (See electronic filing instructions). To

the extent that documents filed by the Debtor at or following the commencement of the Debtor's Chapter 11 case differ in substance from the versions supplied to the United States Trustee under Parts VI.A. and IV.B. above, the Debtor shall furnish to the United States Trustee two (2) paper copies of any such documents that have been modified, preferably blacklined to show changes.

D. *Abeyance of Local Rule 1007–2(e).*

Notwithstanding Local Rule 1007–2(e), a proposed case conference order need not be submitted to the Court unless the confirmation hearing is delayed until a date that is more than ninety (90) days following the petition date.

VI. FIRST DAY ORDERS.

A. *Motions for Request for Entry of Immediate Orders.*

"First Day Orders" are orders which the Debtor seeks to have entered by the Court on or shortly after the filing of the petition. The request for a First Day Order should be made by motion (a "First Day Motion"), and a copy of the proposed First Day Order should be filed with and attached as an exhibit to the First Day Motion. First Day Motions may request a waiver of the requirement under Local Rule 9013–1 to file a separate memorandum of law only if the legal authority for the relief being sought is set forth in the First Day Motions.

B. *Purpose of First Day Orders.*

Generally, the purpose of First Day Orders is to deal with administrative matters ("Administrative Orders") and to ensure that the Debtor's business and operations are stabilized and conducted in a manner consistent with past practice and the proposed plan, pending consideration of confirmation of that plan ("Operational Orders"). While the Court recognizes the necessity and desirability of entertaining appropriate First Day Motions, the terms and conditions of First Day Orders (particularly Operational Orders) necessarily will depend upon the facts and circumstances of the case, the terms of the plan, the notice given, and related factors, and will take into account the needs of the Debtor and the rights of other parties in interest.

C. *Typical First Day Motions and Orders.*

First Day Orders typically entertained by the Court on or within one (1) business day of the later of the petition date or the date of filing of the First Day Motions include (but are not limited to) the following:

1. Prepack Scheduling Motion, setting forth the information required in Part III above.[1]

---

[1] In the event solicitation has not been completed prior to the petition date, an alternative first day motion should be submitted consistent with sections III.A.(i) and III.C.

2. Motion for order directing joint administration of Debtors' cases if more than one case is commenced.

3. Motion for order authorizing Debtor to mail initial notices, including the notice of meeting of creditors under 11 U.S.C. § 341(a).

4. Motion for order (i) dispensing with the requirement of filing any or all schedules and statement of financial affairs in the event the Debtor is not seeking to bar and subsequently discharge all or certain categories of debt or (ii) extending Debtor's time for filing schedules and statement of financial affairs to a specified date.

5. Motion for an order setting the last date for filing proofs of claim or interest if the Debtor has determined that a deadline should be set.

6. Applications to employ appropriate professionals, which may include:

- attorneys
- accountants
- financial advisors.

If accountants, investment advisors, vote tabulators, solicitation agents or similar non-legal professionals were retained prepetition and are not seeking any payment in connection with the plan or the case in addition to payments that they received prior to the filing of the petition ("Additional Post–Petition Payments"), such professionals need not be retained pursuant to 11 U.S.C. § 327 and may continue to provide services to the Debtor with respect to the plan and the case (e.g., testifying at the confirmation/disclosure adequacy hearing); provided, however, that the postpetition services provided by accountants and financial advisors who have not been retained pursuant to 11 U.S.C. § 327 shall not include any work of a substantive nature, such as, for example, the preparation of new financial data, even if such accountants and financial advisors are not seeking any Additional Post–Petition Payments.

7. Motion for order authorizing employment and payment without fee applications of professionals used in ordinary course of business, not to exceed a specified individual and aggregate amount.

8. Motion for order establishing procedures for compensation and reimbursement of expenses of professionals.

9. Motion for order authorizing Debtor to maintain existing bank accounts and cash management system, and to continue using existing business forms (including checks) without "debtor-in-possession" designation. Any motion should describe the proposed cash management system and, in cases where money will be transferred between Debtors or from a Debtor to a non-debtor affiliate, represent why such transfers are desirable from the Debtor's perspective, that the Debtor(s) will maintain records of all postpetition intercompany transfers of funds and describe what repayment terms exist.

10. Motion under 11 U.S.C. § 363 for interim order authorizing Debtor's use of cash collateral on an emergency basis, pending a hearing, and providing adequate protection.

11. Motion under 11 U.S.C. § 364 for interim order authorizing Debtor to obtain postpetition financing on an emergency basis, pending a hearing.

12. Motion under 11 U.S.C. § 345(b) for order authorizing Debtor to deviate from enumerated permitted investments set forth in 11 U.S.C. § 345. Motion should disclose the amount of funds which the Debtor proposes to invest outside the statute's enumerated permitted investments and the proposed types of investments to be made. If the Debtor proposes to invest or deposit money in or with an entity that has not satisfied the requirement of 11 U.S.C. § 345(b) (a "Non–Qualified Entity") the First Day Motion should demonstrate and explain why such an investment or deposit is necessary and, to the extent known, why the Non–Qualified Entity cannot or has not satisfied the requirements of 11 U.S.C. § 345(b).

13. Motion for order authorizing Debtor to pay (i) prepetition wages, salaries and commissions (including vacation, severance and sick leave pay) earned by an individual in an amount not to exceed specified per employee and aggregate amounts, which amounts shall be set forth in the Motion. If the Motion requests authority to pay amounts in excess of $4,300 (or such higher amount as is subsequently determined in accordance with 11 U.S.C. § 104(b)) per employee, then a list of the names and position/job titles of all employees as to whom those payments will be made shall be attached. However, the propriety of those requests shall be considered on a case by case basis. The Motion also shall state whether, and the extent to which, the claims proposed to be paid constitute priority claims under 11 U.S.C. § 507 ("Priority Claims") and, if such claims are not Priority Claims, the Motion should explain why those claims should be afforded the treatment requested in the Motion. The Motion may also ask the Court to direct banks to honor prepetition checks for such amounts and authorize the Debtor to replace prepetition checks that have been dishonored.

14. Motion for order authorizing Debtor to pay claims for contribution to employee benefit plans in an amount not to exceed a specified amount, which amount shall be set forth in the Motion. If the Motion requests authority to pay amounts in excess of the amounts set forth in 11 U.S.C. § 507(a)(4) (as modified by 11 U.S.C. § 104(b)) then a list of the names and position/job titles of all employees as to

whom those payments will be made shall be attached. However, the propriety of those requests shall be considered on a case by case basis. The Motion also shall state whether, and the extent to which, the claims proposed to be paid constitute Priority Claims and, if such claims are not Priority Claims, the Motion should explain why those claims should be afforded the treatment requested in the Motion.

15. Motion for an order authorizing Debtor to reimburse employee business expenses in an amount not to exceed a specified amount per employee and not to exceed a specified aggregate amount, which amounts shall be set forth in the Motion. The Motion also shall state whether, and the extent to which, the claims proposed to be paid constitute Priority Claims and, if such claims are not Priority Claims, the Motion should explain why those claims should be afforded the treatment requested in the Motion.

16. Motion for an order authorizing Debtor to pay creditors whose prepetition claims will be paid in full in cash on consummation under the Debtor's plan, not to exceed a specified aggregate amount, which amount shall be set forth in the Motion. The Motion should disclose the types of claims that the Debtor proposes to pay (e.g., trade creditors supplying goods; trade creditors supplying services; professionals involved in the routine, day-to-day operations and business of the Debtor). The Motion also shall state whether, and the extent to which, the claims proposed to be paid constitute Priority Claims and, if such claims are not Priority Claims, the Motion should explain why those claims should be afforded the treatment requested in the Motion.

17. Motion for an order authorizing Debtor to honor prepetition customer claims (e.g., refund of deposits, lay-a-way plans) and warranties, not to exceed specified aggregate and per claimant amounts, which amounts shall be set forth in the Motion. The Motion also shall state whether, and the extent to which, the claims proposed to be paid constitute Priority Claims and, if such claims are not Priority Claims, the Motion should explain why those claims should be afforded the treatment requested in the Motion.

18. Motion for an order authorizing continued performance without assumption under key executory contracts, including payment of prepetition amounts due and owing thereunder in an amount not to exceed specified aggregate and per claimant amounts. The Motion shall list and state all contracts subject to the motion and whether, and the extent to which, the claims proposed to be paid are believed to be Priority Claims and, if such claims are not Priority Claims, the Motion should explain why those claims should be afforded the treatment requested in the Motion.

19. Motion for interim order prohibiting utilities from altering, refusing or discontinuing service on account of prepetition claims and establishing procedures for determining requests for additional adequate assurance.

20. In a case involving a sale of any or all of the Debtor's assets, Motion for order authorizing and scheduling auction at which the Debtor may sell its assets free and clear of claims and interests and approving auction procedures and related matters.

D. *Request for Related Relief Need Not be Filed in Separate Motions.*

Motions for related relief under First Day Orders referred to above need not be filed as separate motions. For example, in a given case it may be appropriate to combine cash collateral and financing motions, or deal with all employee-related matters in a single motion.

VII. VOTING PERIOD; BALLOT; MULTIPLE VOTES; NOTICE PRESUMPTIONS.

A. *Voting Period Guidelines.*

Fed.R.Bankr.P. 3018(b) requires the Court to consider whether "an unreasonably short" time was prescribed for creditors and equity security holders to accept or reject the plan. Under ordinary circumstances, in determining whether the time allowed for casting acceptances and rejections on the Debtor's plan satisfied Fed.R. Bankr. P. 3018(b), the Court will approve as reasonable:

1. For securities listed or admitted to trading on the New York Stock Exchange or American Stock Exchange or any international exchanges quoted on NASDAQ, and for securities publicly traded on any other national securities exchange ("Publicly Traded Securities"), a twenty (20) business day voting period, measured from the date of commencement of mailing.

2. For securities which are not Publicly Traded Securities and for debt for borrowed money which is not evidenced by a Publicly Traded Security, a ten (10) business day voting period, measured from the date of commencement of mailing.

3. For all other claims and interests, a twenty (20) business day voting period, measured from the date of commencement of mailing.

B. *Shorter or Longer Voting Period.*

Nothing herein is intended to preclude (i) a shorter voting period if it is justified in a particular case, or (ii) any party in interest from demonstrating that the presumptions set forth above were not reasonable in a particular case.

C. *Ballot.*

1. The Debtor may, but shall not be required to, use a ballot substantially in the form of the Official

Form of Ballot For Accepting or Rejecting A Plan (the "Prepackaged Chapter 11 Case Ballot Form attached as Exhibit 'B' ") in connection with a pre-packaged plan solicitation.

2. Prepackaged Chapter 11 Master Ballot Form attached as Exhibit "C" may be used to report voting by beneficial owners of claims and interests.

3. The ballot may include information in addition to that set forth on the Official Ballot Form, and may request and provide space for the holder of a claim or interest to vote on matters in addition to the plan. By way of example, the ballot may seek and record (i) votes relating to an exchange offer, (ii) consents to or votes with respect to benefits plans, and (iii) elections provided for in the plan (or exchange offer).

D. *Multiple Votes.*

If the holder of a claim or interest changes its vote during the prepetition voting period, only the last timely ballot cast by such holder shall be counted in determining whether the plan has been accepted or rejected unless the disclosure statement (or other solicitation document) clearly provides for some other procedure for determining votes on the prepackaged plan. If a holder of a claim or interest wants to change a vote post-petition, Rule 3018(a) requires a showing of cause and Court approval.

E. *Notice Guidelines.*

Fed.R.Bankr. P. 3018(b) requires the Court to consider whether the plan was transmitted to substantially all creditors and equity security holders of the same class. In making that determination, the Court will take into account (i) whether the Debtor transmitted the plan and disclosure statement (or other solicitation document) in substantial compliance with applicable nonbankruptcy law, rules, or regulations and (ii) the fact that creditors and equity security holders who are not record holders of the securities upon which their claims or interests are based generally assume the risk associated with their decision to hold their securities in "street name."

VIII. ORGANIZATIONAL MEETING; CREDITORS' COMMITTEE.

A. Unless the Court finds that a meeting of creditors need not be convened pursuant to § 341(e), after the filing of the Chapter 11 petition, the Debtor shall notify creditors of the date, time and place of the meeting of creditors pursuant to 11 U.S.C. § 341(a), as well as the other information set forth in Part X.B.2 below. The date set for the § 341(a) meeting should be no more than forty (40) days after the filing of the petition.

B. If a meeting of creditors pursuant to 11 U.S.C. § 341(a) has not yet been convened prior to the date upon which the plan is confirmed, no such meeting will be convened if the order confirming the plan or order

entered substantially contemporaneously therewith contains a provision waiving the convening of such a meeting.

C. Typically, no creditors' committee will be appointed in a prepackaged Chapter 11 case where the unsecured creditors are unimpaired. However, where members of a pre-petition committee seek to serve as a member of an official creditors' committee, they shall demonstrate to the United States Trustee their compliance with Fed.R.Bankr.P. 2007(b).

IX. LAST DATE FOR FILING PROOFS OF CLAIM OR INTEREST.

A. A last date of file proofs of claim or interest will not be set unless the Debtor seeks an order fixing such a deadline for filing proofs of claim or proofs of interest.

B. As provided in Part IV.C. above, the Debtor should consult with the Clerk of the Court in advance of the filing of the case to discuss whether a last date to file proofs of claim or interest will be sought, the need for appointment of a claims' agent for the Court (at the Debtor's expense), and related matters.

C. If a claims' agent is appointed, such agent shall docket all proofs of claim and proofs of interest and deliver to the Debtor complete copies of the proofs of claim and interest, along with a complete claims and interest docket, not later than five (5) business days after the last date to file proofs of claim or interest.

D. Fed.R.Bankr.P. 2002(a)(7) requires at least twenty (20) days' notice by mail of the last day to file proofs of claim or interest. If the notice is being directed to creditors whose mailing addresses are outside the United States, the Court may extend the period beyond twenty days.

E. Paper copies of the notice of the last date to file proofs of claim or interest must be mailed as required under Fed.R.Bankr.P. 2002(a)(7).

X. NOTICE.

A. *In General.*

Notice of the filing of the plan and disclosure statement (or other solicitation document) and of the hearing to consider compliance with disclosure requirements and confirmation of the plan must be given to all parties-in-interest. Paper copy of a notice must be mailed; service of a notice of electronic filing will not suffice. No further distribution of the plan and disclosure statement (or other solicitation document) beyond that which occurred prepetition is required unless requested by a party-in-interest. Parties are advised to check General Order M–182 because paper copies of other notices may be required.

B. *Hearing Notice.*

1. Where the disclosure statement has not been approved by the Court prior to confirmation, the Debtor shall prepare and mail paper copies to all parties-in-interest of a Notice of Confirmation Hearing and Approval of Disclosure Statement (or other solicitation documents) in substantially the form annexed hereto as Exhibit "D" (the "Hearing Notice"). The Hearing Notice must:

- set forth (i) the date, time and place of the hearing to consider compliance with disclosure requirements and confirmation of the plan, and (ii) the date and time by which objections to the foregoing must be filed and served;
- include a chart summarizing plan distributions;
- set forth the name, address and telephone number of the person from whom copies of the plan and disclosure statement (or other solicitation document) can be obtained (at the Debtor's expense); and
- state that the plan and disclosure statement (or other solicitation document) can be viewed electronically and explain briefly how electronic access to these documents may be obtained.

2. Either the Hearing Notice or a separate notice must:

- set forth the date, time and place of the § 341(a) meeting and state that such meeting will not be convened if (i) the plan is confirmed prior to the date set for the § 341(a) meeting and (ii) the order confirming the plan (or order entered substantially contemporaneously therewith) contains a provision waiving the convening of such a meeting.

C. *Service.*

1. The Hearing Notice shall be served upon (i) record (registered) holders of debt and equity securities (determined as of the record date established in the disclosure statement or other solicitation document) that were entitled to vote on the plan, (ii) record (registered) holders of all *other* claims and interests of any class (determined as of a record date that is not more than ten (10) days prior to the date of the filing of the petition), (iii) all other creditors listed in the Debtor's schedules, unless Debtor is not seeking to bar and subsequently discharge claims, in which case schedules may not be required to be filed, (iv) the United States Trustee, (v) all indenture trustees, (vi) any committee(s) that may have been appointed in the case, and (vii) the United States in accordance with Fed. R.Bankr.P. 2002(j).

2. The Debtor shall inform the Court of the proposed procedures for transmitting the Hearing Notice to beneficial holders of stock, bonds, debentures, notes, and other securities, and the Court shall determine the adequacy of those procedures and enter such orders as it deems appropriate.

D. *Time Period.*

The Official Notice shall be mailed at least twenty (20) days prior to the scheduled hearing date on confirmation of the plan and adequacy of disclosure unless the Court shortens such notice period.

XI. COMBINED HEARINGS.

The hearings on the Debtor's compliance with either 11 U.S.C. § 1126(b)(1) or 11 U.S.C. § 1126(b)(2), as applicable, and on confirmation of the plan in a prepackaged Chapter 11 case shall be combined whenever practicable.

[Amended effective October 1, 2005.]

EXHIBIT "A"

UNITED STATES BANKRUPTCY COURT
SOUTHERN DISTRICT OF NEW YORK

In re:	) Chapter 11 Case No.
	)
[NAME],	) _____(__)
	)
Debtor.	) Tax ID No._____

SCHEDULING MOTION FOR PREPACKAGED CHAPTER 11 CASE

TO THE HONORABLE UNITED STATES BANKRUPTCY JUDGE:

The [NAME OF DEBTOR], as debtor and debtor in possession (the "Debtor"), respectfully represents:

Background

1.   [Brief background of the Debtor].

Jurisdiction and Venue

2.   This Court has jurisdiction to consider this application pursuant to 28 U.S.C. §§ 157 and 1334. Consideration of this application is a core proceeding pursuant to 28 U.S.C. § 157(b). Venue of this proceeding is proper in this district pursuant to 28 U.S.C. §§ 1408 and 1409.

The Debtor's Business

3.   [Brief Description of the Debtor's business].

The Proposed Plan of Reorganization

4.   [Brief description of the proposed plan of reorganization].

This Court Should Schedule A Hearing
To Consider Confirmation Of The Proposed Plan

5.   Pursuant to section 1128(a) of the Bankruptcy Code, the Debtor requests that the Court set a hearing to consider confirmation of the Plan. Section 1128(a) of the Bankruptcy Code provides that "[a]fter notice, the court shall hold a hearing on confirmation of a plan."

6.   [Summarize results of pre-petition solicitation].

7.   [Indicate whether Debtor requests that confirmation hearing and disclosure hearing be combined]. [Indicate proposed date and time for confirmation/disclosure hearings].

8.   The Debtor proposes to publish notice of the Confirmation and Disclosure Compliance Hearing (the "Hearing Notice") [insert where notice will be published]. [Indicate whether the proposed notice schedule complies with the minimum twenty-five (25) days' notice required under Rules 2002(b) and 3017(a) of the Federal Rules of Bankruptcy Procedure (the "Bankruptcy Rules".][1]

9.   In addition to the Hearing Notice, the Debtor will transmit, in accordance with Bankruptcy Rule 3017(d), via first class mail, postage prepaid, a copy of the Disclosure Statement and the Plan to all holders of claims against, or equity interests in, the Debtor other than [insert parties who received such materials pursuant to the prepetition solicitation], which are the parties to whom the Disclosure Statement and Plan have already been transmitted pursuant to the prepetition solicitation.

Notice

10.   Notice of this application has been given to [insert names of persons to whom notice has been given] which shall include the U.S. Trustee, [others?].

11.   No previous application for the relief sought herein has been made to this or any other court.

WHEREFORE the Debtor respectfully requests entry of an order granting the relief requested herein and granting the Debtor such other and further relief as is just.

Dated: _____, ____

By: _____

[signing attorney]

Attorneys for Debtor

1 A form of Hearing Notice, which includes a summary of the Plan, also is appended to the Guidelines.

EXHIBIT "B"

NO PERSON HAS BEEN AUTHORIZED TO GIVE ANY INFORMATION OR ADVICE, OR TO MAKE ANY REPRESENTATION, OTHER THAN WHAT IS INCLUDED IN THE MATERIALS MAILED WITH THIS BALLOT.

[NAME OF DEBTOR],	)
	)
Debtor.	)
	)
[DEBTOR'S ADDRESS]	)
	)
Tax ID No. _____	)
	)

BALLOT FOR ACCEPTING OR REJECTING PREPACKAGED PLAN OF REORGANIZATION OF [NAME OF DEBTOR] UNDER CHAPTER 11 OF THE BANKRUPTCY CODE BALLOT FOR VOTING __% NOTES (Class __: __% NOTE CLAIMS) [Insert Exact Name of Notes/Bonds, If Applicable]* [Insert CUSIP #, If Applicable]

If you are a beneficial owner of [NAME OF SECURITIES] (the "__% Notes") issued by [NAME OF DEBTOR], please use this Ballot to cast your vote to accept or reject the chapter 11 plan of reorganization (the "Plan") which is being proposed by [DEBTOR]. The Plan is Exhibit [ ] to the Disclosure Statement, dated _____, ____, (the "Disclosure Statement"), which accompanies this Ballot. The Plan can be confirmed by the Bankruptcy Court and thereby made binding upon you if it is accepted by the holders of two-thirds in amount and more than one-half in number of claims in each class that vote on the Plan, and by the holders of two-thirds in amount of equity security interests in each class that vote on the Plan, and if it otherwise satisfies the requirements of section 1129(a) of the Bankruptcy Code. [If the requisite acceptances are not obtained, the Bankruptcy Court may nonetheless confirm the Plan if it finds that the Plan provides fair and equitable treatment to, and does not discriminate unfairly against, the class or classes rejecting it, and otherwise satisfies the requirements of section 1129(b) of the Bankruptcy Code.]

IMPORTANT

VOTING DEADLINE: __:__ __.M., EASTERN TIME ON ____ __, ____.
REVIEW THE ACCOMPANYING DISCLOSURE STATEMENT FOR THE PLAN.
[BALLOTS WILL NOT BE ACCEPTED BY FACSIMILE TRANSMISSION.]
DO NOT RETURN ANY SECURITIES WITH THIS BALLOT. This ballot is *not* a letter of transmittal and may *not* be used for any purpose other than to cast votes to accept or reject the Plan.

[Ballot Code]

HOW TO VOTE

1. COMPLETE ITEM 1 (if not already filled out by your nominee) AND ITEM 2 AND COMPLETE ITEM 3 (if applicable).
2. REVIEW THE CERTIFICATIONS CONTAINED IN ITEM 4.
3. **SIGN THE BALLOT** (unless your Ballot has already been signed or "prevalidated" by your nominee).
4. RETURN THE BALLOT IN THE PRE-ADDRESSED POSTAGE-PAID ENVELOPE(if the enclosed envelope is addressed to your nominee, make sure your nominee receives your Ballot in time to submit it before the Voting Deadline).
5. YOU WILL RECEIVE A SEPARATE BALLOT FOR EACH ISSUE OF SECURITIES YOU OWN WHICH IS ENTITLED TO BE VOTED UNDER THE PLAN.
6. YOU MUST VOTE *ALL YOUR* __% NOTES *EITHER* TO ACCEPT *OR* TO REJECT THE PLAN AND MAY NOT SPLIT YOUR VOTE.

Item 1. Principal Amount of __% Notes Voted. The undersigned certifies that as of [the record date] the undersigned was either the beneficial owner, or the nominee of a beneficial owner, of __% Notes in the following aggregate unpaid principal amount (insert amount in the box below). If your __% Notes are held by a nominee on your behalf and you do not know the amount, please contact your nominee immediately.

$

Item 2. Vote. The beneficial owner of the __% Notes identified in Item I votes as follows (check one box only-if you do not check a box your vote will not be counted):

☐ to Accept the Plan. ☐ to Reject the Plan.

Item 3. Identify All Other __% Notes Voted. By returning this Ballot, the beneficial owner of the __% Notes identified in Item 1 certifies that (a) this Ballot is the only Ballot submitted for the __% Notes owned by such beneficial owner, except for the __% Notes identified in the following table, and (b) *all* Ballots for __% Notes submitted by the beneficial owner indicate the same vote to accept or reject the Plan that the beneficial owner has indicated in Item 2 of this Ballot (please use additional sheets of paper if necessary):

ONLY COMPLETE ITEM 3 IF YOU HAVE SUBMITTED OTHER BALLOTS

Account Number	Name of Holder *	Principal Amount of Other __% Notes Voted
		$
		$

* Insert your name if the notes are held by you in record name or, if held in street name, insert the name of your broker or bank.

Item 4. Authorization. By returning this Ballot, the beneficial owner of the __% Notes identified in Item 1 certifies that it (a) has full power and authority to vote to accept or reject the Plan with respect to the __% Notes listed in Item 1, (b) was the beneficial owner of the __% Notes described in Item 1 on _____, ____, and (c) has received a copy of the Disclosure Statement (including the exhibits thereto) and understands that the solicitation of votes for the Plan is subject to all the terms and conditions set forth in the Disclosure Statement.

Name: _____
        (Print or Type)

Social Security or Federal Tax I.D. No.: _____
                (Optional)

Signature: _____

By: _____
      (If Appropriate)

Title: _____
      (If Appropriate)

Street Address: _____

City, State, Zip Code: _____

Telephone Number: (____)_____

Date Completed: _____

No fees, commissions, or other remuneration will be payable to any broker, dealer, or other person for soliciting votes on the Plan. This Ballot shall not constitute or be deemed a proof of claim or equity interest or an assertion of a claim or equity interest.

YOUR VOTE MUST BE FORWARDED IN AMPLE TIME FOR YOUR VOTE TO BE RECEIVED BY [DEBTOR or DEBTOR'S AGENT], BY ____:____ ____.M. EASTERN TIME, ON ____ ____, ____, OR YOUR VOTE WILL NOT BE COUNTED. IF THE ENCLOSED ENVELOPE IS ADDRESSED TO YOUR NOMINEE, MAKE SURE YOUR NOMINEE RECEIVES YOUR BALLOT IN TIME TO SUBMIT IT BEFORE THE VOTING DEADLINE.

IF YOU HAVE ANY QUESTIONS REGARDING THIS BALLOT OR THE VOTING PROCEDURES, OR IF YOU NEED A BALLOT OR ADDITIONAL COPIES OF THE DISCLOSURE STATEMENT OR OTHER ENCLOSED MATERIALS, PLEASE CALL [DEBTOR or DEBTOR'S AGENT], AT _____.

3 This form ballot does not contemplate multiple securities within the same class.

EXHIBIT "C"

NO PERSON HAS BEEN AUTHORIZED TO GIVE ANY INFORMATION OR ADVICE, OR TO MAKE ANY REPRESENTATION, OTHER THAN WHAT IS INCLUDED IN THE MATERIALS MAILED WITH THIS BALLOT.

```
                                    )
[NAME OF DEBTOR],                   )
                 Debtor.            )
[DEBTOR'S ADDRESS]                  )
                                    )
Tax ID No. _____                   )
                                    )
```

**MASTER BALLOT FOR ACCEPTING
OR REJECTING
PREPACKAGED PLAN OF
REORGANIZATION OF
[NAME OF DEBTOR]
TO BE FILED UNDER CHAPTER 11
OF THE BANKRUPTCY CODE**

MASTER BALLOT FOR VOTING __% NOTES

(Class __: __% NOTE CLAIMS)

[Insert exact name of Notes/Bonds][3]

[3] This form ballot does not contemplate multiple securities within the same class.

[Insert CUSIP #If Applicable]

THE **VOTING DEADLINE** BY WHICH YOUR MASTER BALLOT MUST BE **RECEIVED** BY [DEBTOR or DEBTOR'S AGENT] IS ____:____ ___.M. EASTERN TIME ON ____ ___, ____. IF YOUR MASTER BALLOT IS NOT RECEIVED ON OR BEFORE THE VOTING DEADLINE, THE VOTES REPRESENTED BY YOUR MASTER BALLOT WILL NOT BE COUNTED.

This Master Ballot is to be used by you, as a broker, bank, or other nominee (or as their proxy holder or agent) (each of the foregoing, a "Nominee"), for beneficial owners of [NAME OF SECURITIES] (the "__% Notes") issued by [NAME OF DEBTOR], to transmit the votes of such holders in respect of their __% Notes to accept or reject the chapter 11 plan of reorganization (the "Plan") described in, and attached as Exhibit "__" to the Disclosure Statement, dated ____ ___, ____(the "Disclosure Statement") provided to you. Before you transmit such votes, please review the Disclosure Statement carefully, including the voting procedures explained in Section __.

The Plan can be confirmed by the Bankruptcy Court and thereby made binding upon you and the beneficial owners of __% Notes for which you are the Nominee if it is accepted by the holders of two-thirds in amount and more than one-half in number of claims in each class that vote on the Plan, and by the holders of two-thirds in amount of equity security interests in each class that vote on the Plan, and if it otherwise satisfies the requirements of section 1129(a) of the Bankruptcy Code. [If the requisite acceptances are not obtained, the Bankruptcy Court may nonetheless confirm the Plan if it finds that the Plan provides fair and equitable treatment to, and does not discriminate unfairly against, the class or classes rejecting it, and otherwise satisfies the requirements of section 1129(b) of the Bankruptcy Code.]

PLEASE READ AND FOLLOW THE ATTACHED INSTRUCTIONS CAREFULLY. COMPLETE, SIGN, AND DATE THIS MASTER BALLOT, AND

RETURN IT SO THAT IT IS RECEIVED BY [DEBTOR or DEBTOR'S AGENT] ON OR BEFORE THE VOTING DEADLINE OF __:__ __.M., EASTERN TIME, ON ____ _, ____. IF THIS MASTER BALLOT IS NOT COMPLETED, SIGNED, AND TIMELY RECEIVED, THE VOTES TRANSMITTED BY THIS MASTER BALLOT WILL NOT BE COUNTED.

[Master Ballot Code]

Item 1. Certification of Authority to Vote. The undersigned certifies that as of the ____ _, ____ record date, the undersigned (please check the applicable box):

☐ Is a broker, bank, or other nominee for the beneficial owners of the aggregate principal amount of _% Notes listed in Item 2 below, and is the registered holder of such securities, or

☐ Is acting under a power of attorney and/or agency (a copy of which will be provided upon request) granted by a broker, bank, or other nominee that is the registered holder of the aggregate principal amount of _% Notes listed in Item 2 below, or

☐ Has been granted a proxy (an original of which is attached hereto) from a broker, bank, or other nominee, or a beneficial owner, that is the registered holder of the aggregate principal amount of _% Notes listed in Item 2 below.

and, accordingly, has full power and authority to vote to accept or reject the Plan on behalf of the beneficial owners of the _% Notes described in Item 2 below.

Item 2. Class __ (_% Note Claims) Vote. The undersigned transmits the following votes of beneficial owners in respect of their _% Notes, and certifies that the following beneficial owners of _% Notes, as identified by their respective customer account numbers set forth below, are beneficial owners of such securities as of the ____ _, ____ record date and have delivered to the undersigned, as Nominee, Ballots casting such votes (Indicate in the appropriate column the aggregate principal amount voted for each account, or attach such information to this Master Ballot in the form of the following table. Please note: Each beneficial owner must vote *all* his, her, or its Class __ claims (_% Notes) *either* to accept or reject the Plan, and may *not* split such vote.):

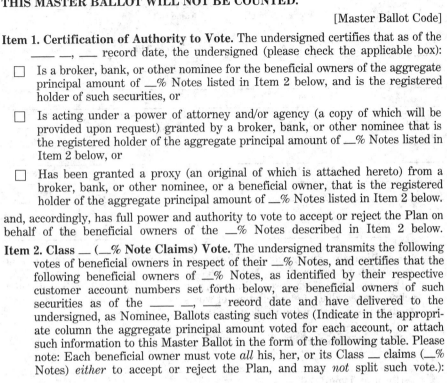

Your Customer Account Number for Each Beneficial Owner of _% Notes	Principal Amount of _% Notes Voted to ACCEPT the Plan		Principal Amount of _% Notes Voted to REJECT the Plan
1.	$	OR	
2.	$	OR	
3.	$	OR	
4.	$	OR	
5.	$	OR	
6.	$	OR	
7.	$	OR	
8.	$	OR	
9.	$	OR	
10.	$	OR	
TOTALS	$		$

Item 3. Certification As to Transcription of Information From Item 3 As to Other _% Notes Voted by Beneficial Owners. The undersigned certifies that the undersigned has transcribed in the following table the information, if any, provided by beneficial owners in Item 3 of the _% Note Ballots, identifying any other _% Notes for which such beneficial owners have submitted other Ballots:

YOUR customer account number for each beneficial owner who completed Item 3 of the __% Note Ballot	TRANSCRIBE FROM ITEM 3 OF [ ] NOTES BALLOT:		
	Account Number	Name Holder	Principal Amount of Other __% Notes Voted
	(Transcribe from Item 3 of __% Note Ballot)	*(Transcribe from Item 3 of __% Note Ballot)*	*(Transcribe from Item 3 of __% Note Ballot)*
1.			$
2.			$
3.			$
4.			$
5.			$
6.			$
7.			$
8.			$
9.			$
10.			$

Item 4. Certification. By signing this Master Ballot, the undersigned certifies that each beneficial owner of __% Notes listed in Item 2, above, has been provided with a copy of the Disclosure Statement, including the exhibits thereto, and acknowledges that the solicitation of votes is subject to all the terms and conditions set forth in the Disclosure Statement.

Name of Broker, Bank, or Other Nominee:

_____
(Print or Type)

Name of Proxy Holder or Agent for Broker,
Bank, or Other Nominee (if applicable):

_____
(Print or Type)

Social Security or Federal Tax I.D. No.: _____
                                  (If Applicable)

Signature: _____

By: _____
                  (If Appropriate)

Title: _____
                  (If Appropriate)

Street Address: _____

City, State, Zip Code: _____

Telephone Number: (___)_____

Date Completed: _____

THIS MASTER BALLOT MUST BE RECEIVED BY [DEBTOR or DEBT-OR'S AGENT], BEFORE ____:____ __.M., EASTERN TIME ON ____ __, ____ OR THE VOTES TRANSMITTED HEREBY WILL NOT BE COUNTED.

[PLEASE NOTE: BALLOTS AND MASTER BALLOTS WILL *NOT* BE ACCEPTED BY FACSIMILE TRANSMISSION.]

IF YOU HAVE ANY QUESTIONS REGARDING THIS MASTER BALLOT OR THE VOTING PROCEDURES, OR IF YOU NEED ADDITIONAL COPIES OF THE MASTER BALLOT, BALLOTS, DISCLOSURE STATE-MENT, OR OTHER RELATED MATERIALS, PLEASE CALL [DEBTOR or DEBTOR'S AGENT], AT _____.

INSTRUCTIONS FOR COMPLETING THE MASTER BALLOT

VOTING DEADLINE:

The Voting Deadline is ____:____ __.m., Eastern Time, on ____ __, __, unless extended by the Debtor. To have the vote of your customers count, you must complete, sign, and return this Master Ballot so that it is received by [DEBTOR or DEBTOR'S AGENT], [ADDRESS], *on or before* the Voting Deadline.

HOW TO VOTE:

If you are both the registered owner *and* beneficial owner of any principal amount of __% Notes and you wish to vote such __% Notes, you may complete, execute, and return to [DEBTOR or DEBTOR'S AGENT] *either* a __% Note Ballot or a __% Note Master Ballot.

If you are transmitting the votes of any beneficial owners of __% Notes other than yourself,

you may *either*:

1. Complete and execute the __% Note Ballot (other than Items 2 and 3) and deliver to the beneficial owner such "prevalidated" __% Note Ballot, along with the Disclosure Statement and other materials requested to be forwarded. The beneficial owner should complete Items 2 and 3 of that Ballot and return the completed Ballot to [DEBTOR or DEBTOR'S AGENT] so as to be received before the Voting Deadline:

OR

2. *For any __% Note Ballots you do not "prevalidate":*

Deliver the __% Note Ballot to the beneficial owner, along with the Disclosure Statement and other materials requested to be forwarded, and take the necessary actions to enable such beneficial owner to (i) complete and execute such Ballot voting to accept or reject the Plan, and (ii) return the complete, executed Ballot to you in sufficient time to enable you to complete the Master Ballot and deliver it to [DEBTOR or DEBTOR'S AGENT] before the Voting Deadline; and

With respect to all __% Note Ballots returned to you, you must properly complete the Master Ballot, as follows:

a. Check the appropriate box in Item 1 on the Master Ballot;

b. Indicate the votes to accept or reject the Plan in Item 2 of this Master Ballot, as transmitted to you by the beneficial owners of __% Notes. To identify such beneficial owners without disclosing their names, please use the customer account number assigned by you to each such beneficial owner, or if no such customer account number exists, please assign a number to each account (making sure to retain a separate list of each beneficial owner and the assigned number). **IMPORTANT: BENEFICIAL OWNERS MAY *NOT* SPLIT THEIR VOTES. EACH BENEFICIAL OWNER MUST VOTE *ALL* HIS, HER, OR ITS __% NOTES *EITHER* TO ACCEPT OR REJECT THE PLAN. IF ANY BENEFICIAL OWNER HAS ATTEMPTED TO SPLIT SUCH VOTE, PLEASE CONTACT [DEBTOR or DEBTOR'S AGENT] IMMEDIATELY.** Any Ballot or Master Ballot which is validly executed but which does not indicate acceptance or rejection of the Plan by the indicated beneficial owner or which impermissibly attempts to split a vote will not be counted;

c. Please note that Item 3 of this Master Ballot requests that you transcribe the information provided by each beneficial owner from Item 3 of each completed __% Note Ballot relating to other __% Notes voted;

d. Review the certification in Item 4 of the Master Ballot;

e. Sign and date the Master Ballot, and provide the remaining information requested;

f. If additional space is required to respond to any item on the Master Ballot, please use additional sheets of paper clearly marked to indicate the applicable Item of the Master Ballot to which you are responding;

g. Contact [DEBTOR or DEBTOR'S AGENT] to arrange for delivery of the completed Master Ballot to its offices; and

h. Deliver the completed, executed Master Ballot so that it is actually *received* by [DEBTOR or DEBTOR'S AGENT] on or before the Voting Deadline. For each completed, executed __% Note Ballot returned to you by a beneficial owner, either forward such Ballot (along with your Master Ballot) to [DEBTOR or DEBTOR'S AGENT] or retain such __% Note Ballot in your files for one year from the Voting Deadline.

PLEASE NOTE:

This Master Ballot is *not* a letter of transmittal and may *not* be used for any purpose other than to cast votes to accept or reject the Plan. Holders should not surrender, at this time, certificates representing their securities. [DEBTOR or DEBTOR'S AGENT] will not accept delivery of any such certificates surrendered together with this Master Ballot. Surrender of securities for exchange may only be made by you, and will only be accepted pursuant to a letter of transmittal which will be furnished to you by the Debtor following confirmation of the Plan by the United States Bankruptcy Court.

No Ballot or Master Ballot shall constitute or be deemed a proof of claim or equity interest or an assertion of a claim or equity interest.

No fees or commissions or other remuneration will be payable to any broker, dealer, or other person for soliciting votes on the Plan. [We will, however, upon request, reimburse you for customary mailing and handling expenses incurred by you in forwarding the Ballots and other enclosed materials to the beneficial owners of __% Notes held by you as a nominee or in a fiduciary capacity. We will also pay all transfer taxes, if any, applicable to the transfer and exchange of your securities pursuant to and following confirmation of the Plan.]

NOTHING CONTAINED HEREIN OR IN THE ENCLOSED DOCUMENTS SHALL RENDER YOU OR ANY OTHER PERSON THE AGENT OF THE DEBTOR [OR THE DEBTOR'S AGENT], OR AUTHORIZE YOU OR ANY OTHER PERSON TO USE ANY DOCUMENT OR MAKE ANY STATEMENTS ON BEHALF OF THEM WITH RESPECT TO THE PLAN, EXCEPT FOR THE STATEMENTS CONTAINED IN THE ENCLOSED DOCUMENTS.

IF YOU HAVE ANY QUESTIONS REGARDING THIS MASTER BALLOT OR THE VOTING PROCEDURES, OR IF YOU NEED ADDITIONAL COPIES IF THE MASTER BALLOT, BALLOTS, DISCLOSURE STATEMENT, OR OTHER RELATED MATERIALS, PLEASE CALL [DEBTOR or DEBTOR'S AGENT], AT _____.

EXHIBIT "D"

UNITED STATES BANKRUPTCY COURT
SOUTHERN DISTRICT OF NEW YORK

In re	)
	)
	) Chapter 11 Case No.
[NAME],	) __-_____ (__)
	)
Debtor.	)
	)
[DEBTOR'S ADDRESS]	) Tax ID No. _____
	)

SUMMARY OF PLAN OF REORGANIZATION AND NOTICE OF HEARING TO CONSIDER (i) DEBTOR'S COMPLIANCE WITH DISCLOSURE REQUIREMENTS AND (ii) CONFIRMATION OF PLAN OF REORGANIZATION

NOTICE IS HEREBY GIVEN as follows:

1.   On _____ __, _____ (the "Petition Date"), [NAME OF DEBTOR], the above-captioned debtor (the "Debtor"), filed with the United States Bankruptcy Court for the Southern District of New York (the "Bankruptcy Court") a proposed plan of reorganization (the "Plan") and a proposed disclosure statement (the "Disclosure Statement") pursuant to §§ 1125 and 1126(b) of title 11 of the United States Code (the "Bankruptcy Code"). Copies of the Plan and the Disclosure Statement may be obtained upon request of Debtor's counsel at the address specified below and are on file with the Clerk of the Bankruptcy Court, [ADDRESS], where they are available for review between the hours of 9:00 a.m.–4:30 p.m. The Plan and Disclosure Statement also are available for inspection on the Bankruptcy Court's internet site at www.nysb.uscourts.gov.

Summary of Plan of Reorganization

2.   [Provide one-paragraph general description of salient Plan provisions, including whether proponent requests confirmation pursuant to 11 U.S.C. § 1129(b).] Votes on the Plan were solicited prior to the Petition Date. The following chart summarizes the treatment provided by the Plan to each class of claims and interests and indicates the acceptance or rejection of the Plan by each class entitled to vote.

CLASS	CLASS DESCRIPTION	IMPAIRMENT/TREATMENT	ACCEPT/ REJECT

Hearing to Consider Compliance with Disclosure Requirements

3. A hearing to consider compliance with the disclosure requirements, any objections to the Disclosure Statement, and any other matter that may properly come before the Bankruptcy Court will be held before the Honorable _____, United States Bankruptcy Judge, in Room __ of the United States Bankruptcy Court, [ADDRESS], on _____ at _:_ _.m. or as soon thereafter as counsel may be heard (the "Disclosure Compliance Hearing"). The Disclosure Compliance Hearing may be adjourned from time to time without further notice other than an announcement of the adjourned date or dates at the Disclosure Compliance Hearing or at an adjourned Disclosure Compliance Hearing and will be available on the electronic case filing docket.

4. Any objections to the Disclosure Statement shall be in writing, shall conform to the Federal Rules of Bankruptcy Procedure and the Local Rules of the Bankruptcy Court, shall set forth the name of the objector, the nature and amount of any claims or interests held or asserted by the objector against the estate or property of the Debtor, the basis for the objection, and the specific grounds therefor, and shall be filed with the Bankruptcy Court at the address specified in the previous paragraph, with a copy delivered directly to Chambers, together with proof of service thereof, and served upon the following persons so as to be received on or before _____ __, _____, at 5:00 p.m. (Eastern Time):

(i)   [NAME AND ADDRESS OF DEBTOR'S COUNSEL]

(ii) [NAME AND ADDRESS OF COMMITTEE COUNSEL]

(iii) [NAME AND ADDRESS OF BANK COUNSEL]

(iv) [NAME AND ADDRESS OF INDENTURE TRUSTEE]

(v)   OFFICE OF THE UNITED STATES TRUSTEE
33 Whitehall Street, 21st Floor
New York, NY 10004
Attn: Carolyn S. Schwartz, Esq.

[AND IF APPLICABLE:]

(vi) OFFICE OF THE UNITED STATES ATTORNEY FOR THE SOUTHERN DISTRICT OF NEW YORK
One St. Andrew's Plaza
New York, NY 10007
Attn: Mary Jo White, Esq.

(vii) SECURITIES AND EXCHANGE COMMISSION

7 World Trade Center
New York, NY 10048
Attn: Nathan M. Fuchs, Esq.

UNLESS AN OBJECTION IS TIMELY SERVED AND FILED IN ACCORDANCE WITH THIS NOTICE, IT MAY NOT BE CONSIDERED BY THE BANKRUPTCY COURT.

Hearing on Confirmation of the Plan

5. A hearing to consider confirmation of the Plan, any objections thereto, and any other matter that may properly come before the Bankruptcy Court shall be held before the Honorable _____, United States Bankruptcy Judge, in Room __ of the United States Bankruptcy Court, [ADDRESS], immediately following the Disclosure Compliance Hearing referred to above or at such later time as determined by the Bankruptcy Court at the conclusion of the Disclosure Compliance Hearing (the "Confirmation Hearing"). The Confirmation Hearing may be adjourned from time to

time without further notice other than an announcement of the adjourned date or dates at the Confirmation Hearing or at an adjourned Confirmation Hearing.

6. Objections to the Plan, if any, shall be in writing, shall conform to the Federal Rules of Bankruptcy Procedure and the Local Rules of the Bankruptcy Court, shall set forth the name of the objector, the nature and amount of any claims or interests held or asserted by the objector against the estate or property of the Debtor, the basis for the objection, and the specific grounds therefor, and shall be filed with the Bankruptcy Court at the address specified in the previous paragraph, with a copy delivered directly to Chambers, together with proof of service thereof, and served upon the persons set forth in paragraph 4 above so as to be received on or before _____ __, _____, at 5:00 p.m. (Eastern Time). **UNLESS AN OBJECTION IS TIMELY SERVED AND FILED IN ACCORDANCE WITH THIS NOTICE, IT MAY NOT BE CONSIDERED BY THE BANKRUPTCY COURT.**

7. The times fixed for the Confirmation Hearing and objections to confirmation of the Plan may be rescheduled by the Bankruptcy Court in the event that the Bankruptcy Court does not find compliance with the disclosure requirements on _____ __, _____. Notice of the rescheduled date or dates, if any, will be provided by an announcement at the Disclosure Compliance Hearing or at an adjourned Disclosure Compliance Hearing and will be available on the electronic case filing docket.

Section 341(a) Meeting

8. A meeting pursuant to section 341(a) of the Bankruptcy Code (the "Section 341(a) Meeting") shall be held at the United States Bankruptcy Court, in room ___, [ADDRESS], on _____ __, _____ at __: __ __.m. Such meeting will not be convened if (i) the Plan is confirmed prior to the date set forth above for the Section 341(a) Meeting and (ii) the order confirming the Plan (or order entered substantially contemporaneously therewith) contains a provision waiving the convening of a Section 341(a) Meeting.

Dated: New York, New York

_____ __, _____

BY ORDER OF THE COURT

_____
United States Bankruptcy Judge

[NAME, ADDRESS, AND
TELEPHONE NUMBER OF
DEBTOR'S COUNSEL]

EXHIBIT "E"

INSTRUCTIONS FOR FILING A PREPACKAGED CHAPTER 11 PETITION

[Publisher's Note: Due to the volume of unpublishable, Internet Screen Captures imbedded within Exhibit "E", the publisher requests that you contact the Clerk of Court for full text.]

Dated: New York, New York
      February 24, 1999.

GENERAL ORDER M–206. SECOND AMENDMENT TO GENERAL ORDER M–182 ELECTRONIC MEANS FOR FILING, SIGNING, AND VERIFICATION OF DOCUMENTS

See, also, General Orders M–182 and M–193, ante, and General Order M–242, post.

UNITED STATES BANKRUPTCY COURT
SOUTHERN DISTRICT OF NEW YORK

WHEREAS, by General Order #M–182, entered nunc pro tunc to November 25, 1996 and dated June 26, 1997, the Court adopted Electronic Case Filing Procedures for filing, signing and verifying documents by electronic means;

WHEREAS the Court has reviewed the operation of the Electronic Case Filing Procedures since its implementation and has considered refinements suggested by the Judges of the Court, the Clerk and staff of the Clerk's Office, the Administrative Office of the United States Courts and members of the Bar;

WHEREAS, the Court has considered how best to ensure the smooth operation of the Electronic Case Filing System while simultaneously safeguarding the right of parties in interest to put before the Court all information relevant to cases and controversies;

NOW, THEREFORE, IT IS ORDERED that:

General Order #M–182 is hereby amended by adding the following clarifying paragraph:

16. Nothing contained in General Order #M–182, in cases wherein service of documents filed electronically is required to be made on the United States and its agencies, corporations or officers, shall be read to excuse full compliance with Rules 2002 (j) and 7004 (b)(4), (5) and (6) of the Federal Rules of Bankruptcy Procedure and Rule 4 (i) and (j) of the Federal Rules of Civil Procedure.

The Clerk of Court shall promulgate Administrative Procedures consistent with the Order.

This Order amending General Order #M–182, dated June 26, 1997, but entered nunc pro tunc to November 25, 1996 shall be filed in accordance with the Electronic Case Filing Procedures.

This Order shall be immediately effective.

Dated: July 13, 1999.

AMENDED GENERAL ORDER M–219 (M–348). IN THE MATTER OF: ORDER ESTABLISHING PROCEDURES FOR MONTHLY COMPENSATION AND REIMBURSEMENT OF EXPENSES OF PROFESSIONALS

By resolution of the Board of Judges for the Southern District of New York, it is resolved that in order to provide professionals with clear and concise procedures for monthly compensation and reimbursement of expenses in chapter 11 cases (the "Monthly Fee Order"), and as amended to address the issue of foreign currency conversion to U.S. dollars, all Monthly Fee Orders filed in the bankruptcy court for the Southern District of New York shall conform substantially to the official Monthly Fee Order form annexed hereto.

NOW, THEREFORE, IT IS ORDERED that the annexed official Monthly Fee Order be, and the same is adopted, effective immediately.

Dated: New York, New York,
    March 21, 2008.

UNITED STATES BANKRUPTCY COURT
SOUTHERN DISTRICT OF NEW YORK

In re:	)	
	)	Chapter 11
	)	Case Nos.: ___–B–___ (___)
Debtors.	)	through ___–B–___ (___)
	)	(Jointly Administered)
	)	

ORDER PURSUANT TO 11 U.S.C. §§ 105(a) AND 331
ESTABLISHING PROCEDURES FOR MONTHLY COMPENSATION
AND REIMBURSEMENT OF EXPENSES OF PROFESSIONALS

[NAMES OF DEBTORS], debtors and debtors-in-possession (collectively, the "Debtors"), move, by a motion dated _____ ___, 20___ (the "Motion"), for an order, pursuant to §§ 105(a) and 331 of the United States Bankruptcy Code (the "Code"), establishing procedures for monthly compensation and reimbursement of expenses of professionals retained by order of this Court, and this Court having determined that the relief requested in the Motion is in the best interests of the Debtors, their estates, and creditors; and it appearing that proper and adequate notice has been given by service of the Motion on the Office of the United States Trustee, counsel to each official committee (If no committee is appointed, the 20 largest unsecured creditors.), counsel to all post-petition lenders (or counsel to their agent(s)), and all parties who filed a notice of appearance; and that no other or further notice is necessary; and upon the record of the hearing herein; and upon the representation of the Debtors that this estate is administratively solvent; and after due deliberation thereon; and good and sufficient cause appearing therefor, it is hereby

ORDERED, that except as may otherwise be provided in Court orders authorizing the retention of specific professionals, all professionals in these cases may seek monthly compensation in accordance with the following procedure:

(a) On or before the twentieth (20th) day of each month following the month for which compensation is sought, each professional seeking compensation under this Order will serve a monthly statement, by hand or overnight delivery on (i) _____, the officer designated by the Debtors to be responsible for such matters; (ii) counsel to the Debtors; (iii) counsel to all official committees; (iv) counsel for the Office of the United States Trustee, 33 Whitehall Street, 21st Floor, New York, New York 10004 (Attn: _____, Esq.); (vi) counsel to all post-petition lenders or their agent(s); and (v) _____ (anyone else the Court may designate);

(b) The monthly statement need not be filed with the Court and a courtesy copy need not be delivered to the presiding judge's chambers since this Order is not intended to alter the fee application requirements outlined in §§ 330 and 331 of the Code and since professionals are still required to serve and file interim and final applications for approval of fees and expenses in accordance with the relevant provisions of the Code, the Federal Rules of Bankruptcy Procedure and the Local Rules for the United States Bankruptcy Court, Southern District of New York;

(c) Each monthly fee statement must contain a list of the individuals and their respective titles (e.g. attorney, accountant, or paralegal) who provided services during the statement period, their respective billing rates, the aggregate hours spent by each individual, a reasonably detailed breakdown of the disbursements incurred

(No professional should seek reimbursement of an expense which would otherwise not be allowed pursuant to the Court's Administrative Orders dated June 24, 1991 and April 21, 1995 or the United States Trustee Guidelines for Reviewing Applications for Compensation and Reimbursement of Expenses Filed under 11 U.S.C. § 330 dated January 30, 1996.), and contemporaneously maintained time entries for each individual in increments of tenths (1/10) of an hour;

(d) Each person receiving a statement will have at least fifteen (15) days after its receipt to review it and, in the event that he or she has an objection to the compensation or reimbursement sought in a particular statement, he or she shall, by no later than the thirty-fifth (35th) day following the month for which compensation is sought, serve upon the professional whose statement is objected to, and the other persons designated to receive statements in paragraph (a), a written "Notice Of Objection To Fee Statement," setting forth the nature of the objection and the amount of fees or expenses at issue;

(e) At the expiration of the thirty-five (35) day period, the Debtors shall promptly pay eighty percent (80%) of the fees and one hundred percent (100%) of the expenses identified in each monthly statement to which no objection has been served in accordance with paragraph (d);

(f) If the Debtors receive an objection to a particular fee statement, they shall withhold payment of that portion of the fee statement to which the objection is directed and promptly pay the remainder of the fees and disbursements in the percentages set forth in paragraph (e);

(g) Similarly, if the parties to an objection are able to resolve their dispute following the service of a Notice Of Objection To Fee Statement and if the party whose statement was objected to serves on all of the parties listed in paragraph (a) a statement indicating that the objection is withdrawn and describing in detail the terms of the resolution, then the debtor shall promptly pay, in accordance with paragraph (e), that portion of the fee statement which is no longer subject to an objection;

(h) All objections that are not resolved by the parties, shall be preserved and presented to the Court at the next interim or final fee application hearing to be heard by the Court. See paragraph (j), below;

(i) The service of an objection in accordance with paragraph (d) shall not prejudice the objecting party's right to object to any fee application made to the Court in accordance with the Code on any ground whether raised in the objection or not. Furthermore, the decision by any party not to object to a fee statement shall not be a waiver of any kind or prejudice that party's right to object to any fee application subsequently made to the Court in accordance with the Code;

(j) Approximately every 120 days, but no more than every 150 days, each of the professionals shall serve and file with the Court an application for interim or final Court approval and allowance, pursuant to sections 330 and 331 of the Bankruptcy Code (as the case may be), of the compensation and reimbursement of expenses requested;

(k) Any professional who fails to file an application seeking approval of compensation and expenses previously paid under this Order when due shall (1) be ineligible to receive further monthly payments of fees or expenses as provided herein until further order of the Court and (2) may be required to disgorge any fees paid since retention or the last fee application, whichever is later;

(*l*) The pendency of an application or a Court order that payment of compensation or reimbursement of expenses was improper as to a particular statement shall not disqualify a professional from the future payment of compensation or reimbursement of expenses as set forth above, unless otherwise ordered by the Court;

(m) Neither the payment of, nor the failure to pay, in whole or in part, monthly compensation and reimbursement as provided herein shall have any effect on this

Court's interim or final allowance of compensation and reimbursement of expenses of any professionals;

(n) Counsel for each official committee may, in accordance with the foregoing procedure for monthly compensation and reimbursement of professionals, collect and submit statements of expenses, with supporting vouchers, from members of the committee he or she represents; provided, however, that such committee counsel ensures that these reimbursement requests comply with this Court's Administrative Orders dated June 24, 1991 and April 21, 1995;

and it is further

ORDERED, that each professional may seek, in its first request for compensation and reimbursement of expenses pursuant to this Order, compensation for work performed and reimbursement for expenses incurred during the period beginning on the date of the professional's retention and ending on _____ ___, 20___; and it is further

ORDERED, that the amount of fees and disbursements sought be set out in U.S. dollars; [if the fees and disbursements are to be paid in foreign currency, the amount shall be set out in U.S. dollars and the conversion amount in the foreign currency, calculated at the time of the submission of the application;] and it is further

ORDERED, that the Debtors shall include all payments to professionals on their monthly operating reports, detailed so as to state the amount paid to each of the professionals; and it is further

ORDERED, that any party may object to requests for payments made pursuant to this Order on the grounds that the Debtors have not timely filed monthly operating reports, remained current with their administrative expenses and 28 U.S.C. § 1930 fees, or a manifest exigency exists by seeking a further order of this Court, otherwise, this Order shall continue and shall remain in effect during the pendency of this case; and it is further

ORDERED, that all time periods set forth in this Order shall be calculated in accordance with Federal Rule of Bankruptcy Procedure 9006(a); and it is further

ORDERED, that any and all other and further notice of the relief requested in the Motion shall be, and hereby is, dispensed with and waived; provided, however, that the Debtors must serve a copy of this Order on all entities specified in paragraph (a) hereof.

Dated: New York, New York

_____ ___, 20___

UNITED STATES BANKRUPTCY
JUDGE

GENERAL ORDER M–242. REVISED ELECTRONIC MEANS FOR FILING, SIGNING, AND VERIFICATION OF DOCUMENTS

See, also, General Order M–269.

UNITED STATES BANKRUPTCY COURT
SOUTHERN DISTRICT OF NEW YORK

WHEREAS, Federal Rule of Civil Procedure ("FRCP") 83 and Federal Rules of Bankruptcy Procedure ("FRBP") 5005(a)(2) and 9029 authorize this Court to establish practices and procedures for the filing, signing and verification of documents by electronic means; and

WHEREAS, by General Order #M–182, dated June 26, 1997, as amended by the First Amendment to General Order #M–182, dated May 1, 1998, and the Second

Amendment to General Order #M–182, dated July 13, 1999, the Court established such practices and procedures; and

WHEREAS, a proposal for Revised Administrative Procedures for Filing, Signing and Verifying Documents by Electronic Means and Revised Electronic Filing System User's Manual (collectively, the "Revised Electronic Filing Procedures") have been reviewed by the Court; and

WHEREAS, the Revised Electronic Filing Procedures are consistent with and further the responsibility of the Clerk of the Court for the control of the Court's docket under FRBP 5003 and 5005, including safeguarding the integrity of the Court's docket; and

WHEREAS, the Revised Electronic Filing Procedures do not impose fees inconsistent with the present fee structure adopted by the Judicial Conference of the United States pursuant to 28 U.S.C. §§ 1913, 1914, 1926 and 1930; and

WHEREAS, the Revised Electronic Filing Procedures provide a means for the signature on documents through the mechanism of a password, in compliance with the Local Rules of Bankruptcy Procedure ("LRBP") 9011–1(b) and 9011–1(c), and a secure mechanism for the creation and distribution of passwords; and

WHEREAS, the Revised Electronic Filing Procedures provide adequate procedures for the filing, review and retrieval of documents by parties who are not able to access the Electronic Filing System (the "System") from a remote location; and

WHEREAS, the Revised Electronic Filing Procedures do not impair the ability of the Clerk of the Court to perform statistical reporting responsibilities both to the Court and the Administrative Office of the United States Courts; and

WHEREAS, the Revised Electronic Filing Procedures are consistent with the notice requirements of FRBP 2002:

NOW, THEREFORE, IT IS ORDERED that:

1. The Revised Electronic Filing Procedures, attached as Exhibits 1 and 2[1] to this order, are approved by the Court.

2. Electronic files, consisting of the images of documents filed in cases or proceedings and documents filed by electronic means, are designated as and shall constitute the official record of the Court together with the other records kept by the Court.

3. No attorney or other person shall knowingly permit or cause to permit the attorney's password to be utilized by anyone other than an authorized member or employee of the attorney's law firm.

4. The use of an attorney's password to file a document electronically shall constitute the signature of that attorney for purposes of FRBP 9011 and LRBP 9011–1.

5. The electronic filing of a document in accordance with the Revised Electronic Filing Procedures shall constitute entry of that document on the docket kept by the clerk under FRBP 5003, and shall be deemed accepted for filing by the clerk's office.

6. The Office of the Clerk shall enter all orders, decrees, judgments and proceedings of the Court in accordance with the Revised Electronic Filing Procedures, which shall constitute entry of the order, decree, judgment or proceeding on the docket kept by the Clerk under FRBP 5003 and for purposes of FRBP 9021.

7. The request for and receipt of a System password from the Court shall constitute a request for electronic service pursuant to FRBP 9036, and except as otherwise provided in the Revised Electronic Filing Procedures, a waiver of the right to receive notice and service conventionally.

8. The original of this order shall be filed in accordance with the Revised Electronic Filing Procedures.

9.   Amendments to this order or the Revised Electronic Filing Procedures may be entered from time to time in keeping with the needs of the Court.

10.   This order shall become effective on January 22, 2001, shall apply to all cases and proceedings pending on the effective date, and shall supersede General Order #M–182, as amended.

Dated: January 19, 2001.

1 Publisher's Note: For the most current text of "Exhibit 1. Revised Administrative Procedures for Electronically Filed Case," and "Exhibit 2. Electronic Filing System Attorney User's Manual," contact the Office of the Clerk of Court.

GENERAL ORDER M–269.   FIRST AMENDMENT TO ECF GENERAL ORDER M–242

Supplement to General Order #M–242

Federal Rule of Civil Procedure ("FRCP") 83 and Federal Rules of Bankruptcy Procedure ("FRBP") 5005(a)(2) and 9029 authorize this Court to establish practices and procedures for the filing, signing and verification of documents by electronic means.

By General Order M–242, dated January 19, 2001, the Court revised such practices and procedures[1]—as contained in the Revised Administrative Procedures for Electronically Filed Cases and the Electronic Filing System Attorney's User Manual ("Revised Electronic Filing Procedures")—pertaining to the Court's Case Management/Electronic Case Filing ("CM/ECF") System.

The practice under the Revised Electronic Filing Procedures limited eligibility for obtaining a CM/ECF password to attorneys admitted to practice law.

The Court will now provide CM/ECF passwords to non-attorneys for the limited purpose of electronically filing certain documents relating to claims. To obtain a password, an individual must apply to the court and, where possible, attend a court training session in New York City, Poughkeepsie or White Plains.

The provisions set forth in the Revised Electronic Filing Procedures apply to those issued a limited-access password. Thus, the use of a limited-access password shall constitute the signature of the password holder, and those holding such passwords bear the responsibility of keeping the password secure. Additionally, each password holder has a duty to notify the Court at the earliest opportunity in the event that the holder accidentally obtains greater access than the limited-access password permits or if the holder of the password believes the security of the password has been compromised. The Clerk of the Court, in her discretion, may cancel the password of any individual who does not comply with this General Order and the provisions contained in the Revised Electronic Filing Procedures.

Dated: June 3, 2002.

1   General Order M–242 superseded General Order M–182, which had been amended by General Orders M–193 and M–206.

AMENDED GENERAL ORDER M–279.   IN THE MATTER OF: ADOPTION OF AMENDED PROCEDURAL GUIDELINES FOR FILING REQUESTS FOR BAR ORDERS [M–350]

By resolution of the Board of Judges for the Southern District of New York, it is resolved that in order to expedite the review and entry of orders to establish deadlines for filing proofs of claim in Chapter 11 cases and to provide a standard form of order and notice, the Amended Guidelines for Filing Requests for Bar Orders (the "Guidelines"), annexed hereto, are adopted.   All requests for bar orders filed in the United States Bankruptcy Court for the Southern District of New York shall conform substantially to the standard order and notice set forth in the amended Guidelines.

NOW, THEREFORE, IT IS ORDERED that the annexed amended Guidelines are adopted, effective immediately.

Dated: New York, New York, March 27, 2008.

AMENDED PROCEDURAL GUIDELINES FOR FILING
REQUESTS FOR BAR ORDERS IN THE UNITED STATES
BANKRUPTCY COURT FOR THE SOUTHERN DISTRICT OF
NEW YORK

The purpose of these guidelines is to provide a standard form for orders to establish deadlines for the filing of proofs of claim ("Bar Order") in chapter 11 cases and thereby expedite court review and entry of such orders.

The court will expect that all proposed Bar Orders will conform to the following guidelines and use the standard form of order and notice, with only such revisions as are necessary under the circumstances of the individual case or cases. **If a proposed Bar Order and accompanying notice do not comply with these guidelines, counsel must identify and explain, in the application for approval of the Bar Order, the reason for each deviation.** These forms and the guidelines apply only in chapter 11 cases and do not apply to deadlines for filing administrative claims.

Guidelines

1. An application for entry of a Bar Order must ordinarily be filed within 30 days after the later of (i) the initial case conference and (ii) the filing of the debtor's Schedules of Assets and Liabilities and Schedules of Executory Contracts and Unexpired Leases. If counsel believes that entry of a Bar Order should be further delayed for any reason, counsel is urged to take up the matter at the initial case conference.

2. Assuming these guidelines are followed, the application and accompanying papers may be submitted to the court without further notice as long as the application represents that the order has been approved in form and substance by any official creditors committee, by any debtor in possession lender and by any secured creditor with a lien on a substantial portion of the debtor's assets. Otherwise, the proposed Bar Order may be submitted by notice of presentment or by notice of motion on notice to any official committee, any debtor in possession lender, any party requesting notice, and the United States trustee.

3. The application may contain suggested dates for the last date to file claims (the "Bar Date"), for mailing the notice and, where appropriate, for publication, provided that, in most cases the suggested Bar Date should be at least 35 days after the mailing date and at least 25 days after the publication date, and provided further, if possible, the dates proposed by counsel provide the court with at least five business days after the application is submitted to process the order. If applicable, the application should take into account the new procedural provisions pertaining to creditors with foreign addresses [see Interim Federal Rule of Bankruptcy Procedure 2002(p)]. For cause shown the court can reduce the notice period to 20 days after mailing in accordance with Federal Rules of Bankruptcy Procedure ("Bankruptcy Rules") 2002(a)(7) and 9006(c)(2).

4. The attached form of order and the accompanying form of notice to creditors assume that there are multiple debtors in jointly administered cases. In such cases the debtors must list each of the debtors and their related case numbers as part of, or as an addendum to, the notice to creditors. In single-debtor cases, the attached forms should be modified to reflect that only one debtor has filed.

5. The attached form of order contains a paragraph in brackets providing for publication of notice of the Bar Date. These guidelines do not take any position as to whether publication notice of the Bar Date is required in a particular case. Counsel should state in the application for a Bar Date whether they believe publication is required and, if so, the time and place of publication, and in

appropriate cases should raise the issue at the initial case conference. The published notice should be substantially similar to the written notice to creditors, although it may omit certain provisions (such as the definition of the term "claim") in order to reduce costs.

6. The attached form of order and notice contain instructions for proofs of claim to be mailed to the court or to be hand delivered or delivered by overnight courier directly to the division of the court where the case is being administered. In cases where it is anticipated that more than 1,000 proofs of claim will be filed, counsel must arrange with a claims/noticing agent ("Claims Agent") appointed by court order provide an address to receive of mailed proofs of claim. In such cases counsel must also provide creditors with individualized proof of claim forms, and the order has a suggested paragraph for use in such situations. In smaller cases it is not necessary to utilize a claims agent, and all claims may be filed directly with the division of the court where the case is being administered. Furthermore, in cases *without* claims agents, attorneys (with full access accounts) and employees of institutional creditors (with limited access accounts) should file proofs of claim electronically on the Court's Case Management/Electronic Case File ("CM/ECF") system.

7. If a Claims Agent is used in connection with the administration of the mailing of the notice of the Bar Date and related matters, such agent should be retained pursuant to court order. A form of order that lists the services the firm should provide is available from the Office of the Clerk of the Court and on the Court's web site.

8. The attached form of order is intended for use only in connection with the filing of proofs of claim. If a deadline is required for the filing of proofs of equity interest, a substantially similar motion may be filed, or counsel may submit an order and accompanying notice that combines a Bar Date for the filing of proofs of claim and proofs of interest. Notice of a deadline for the filing of administrative claims should **not** ordinarily be combined with a notice of any other Bar Date.

9. The attached forms of order and notice contain a list of persons and entities that are exempted from the requirement to file a proof of claim. It is anticipated that the persons and entities listed in the forms provided will not be required to file proofs of claim in most chapter 11 cases, although there will of course be variations in specific situations and the list is not intended to be exhaustive. Some of the subparagraphs are bracketed, reflecting the fact that the exemption may often have no application or that the debtor may choose not to exempt the particular category from the filing requirement. In addition to those creditors who are included in the attached form of notice and order, a debtor may wish to consider (i) exempting claims of its officers, directors, and employees for indemnification, contribution or reimbursement; (ii) exempting claims of persons or entities against any of the debtors' non-debtor affiliates; and (iii) exempting claims for principal, interest and applicable fees and charges on a bond, note or debenture, provided that any indenture trustee for such instrument would not be exempted from the requirement of filing a proof of claim, and provided further that each holder would be required to file a proof of claim for damages in connection with respect to its ownership of, or purchase or sale of, the applicable instrument.

10. The notice to creditors should contain the name and telephone number of an individual at the law firm representing the debtor or at a bankruptcy services firm retained by the debtor to whom questions may be addressed. The notice should not contain the name of the bankruptcy judge but may provide that the notice is "By Order of the Court."

11. The computer disk submitted to the court with the order should contain not only the form of Bar Order but also the text of the notice to creditors, in the event that the notice needs to be revised before entry.

[FORM OF BAR ORDER]

UNITED STATES BANKRUPTCY COURT
SOUTHERN DISTRICT OF NEW YORK
---x

In re:

                              Chapter 11

                              Case Nos.: ___-_____ (___)
                              Through ___-___ (___)

            Debtors.

                              (Jointly Administered)

---x

ORDER ESTABLISHING DEADLINE FOR FILING PROOFS OF CLAIM AND APPROVING THE FORM AND MANNER OF NOTICE THEREOF

Upon the application of the above-captioned Debtors and Debtors in Possession (collectively, the "Debtors"), for an order, pursuant to Federal Rule of Bankruptcy Procedure ("Bankruptcy Rule") 3003(c)(3), fixing a deadline (the "Bar Date") and establishing procedures for filing proofs of claim and approving the form and manner of service thereof, and it appearing that the relief requested is in the best interests of the Debtors, their estates, and creditors and that adequate notice has been given and that no further notice is necessary; and after due deliberation and good and sufficient cause appearing therefor, it is hereby

ORDERED, that except as otherwise provided herein, all persons and entities, (including, without limitation, individuals, partnerships, corporations, joint ventures, trusts and governmental units) that assert a claim, as defined in § 101(5) of the Bankruptcy Code, against the Debtors which arose on or prior to the filing of the Chapter 11 petitions on _____ (the "Filing Date"), shall file a proof of such claim in writing so that it is received on or before _____ ___, 20__; and it is further

[ORDERED, that notwithstanding any other provision hereof, proofs of claim filed by governmental units must be filed on or before _____ (the date that is 180 days after the date of the order for relief); and it is further][1]

ORDERED, that the following procedures for the filing of proofs of claim shall apply:

(a) Proofs of claim must conform substantially to Official Bankruptcy Form No. 10;

(b) [(1) *Cases with Claims Agents—Insert this Subparagraph:*] Proofs of claim must be filed either by U.S. Postal Service mail or overnight delivery [the original proof of claim to the United States Bankruptcy Court, Southern District of New York, c/o [address provided by Claims Agent] or by delivering the original proof of claim by hand to the United States Bankruptcy Court, Southern District of New York [insert the address of the division of the court where the case is being administered];

[(2) *Cases Without Claims Agents—Insert this Subparagraph:*] Attorneys (with full access accounts) and employees of institutional creditors (with limited access accounts) should file proofs of claim electronically on the Court's Case Management/Electronic Case File ("CM/ECF") system. Those without accounts to the CM/ECF system must file their proofs of claim by mailing or delivering the original proof of claim by hand to the United States Bankruptcy Court, Southern District of New York, [insert the address of the division of the court where the case is being administered];

(c) Proofs of claim will be deemed filed only when <u>received</u> by the Clerk of the Bankruptcy Court on or before the Bar Date;

(d) Proofs of claim must (i) be signed; (ii) include supporting documentation (if voluminous, attach a summary) or an explanation as to why documentation is not available; (iii) be in the English language; and (iv) be denominated in United States currency;

(e) [In multiple debtor cases] Proofs of claim must specify by name and case number the Debtor against which the claim is filed; if the holder asserts a claim against more than one Debtor or has claims against different Debtors, a separate proof of claim form must be filed with respect to each Debtor; and it is further

ORDERED, that the following persons or entities need not file a proof of claim on or prior to the Bar Date:

(a) Any person or entity that has already filed a proof of claim against the Debtors with the Clerk of the Bankruptcy Court for the Southern District of New York in a form substantially similar to Official Bankruptcy Form No. 10;

(b) Any person or entity whose claim is listed on the Schedules filed by the Debtors, provided that (i) the claim is not scheduled as "disputed," "contingent" or "unliquidated"; and (ii) the claimant does not disagree with the amount, nature and priority of the claim as set forth in the Schedules; [and (iii) the claimant does not dispute that the claim is an obligation of the specific Debtor against which the claim is listed in the Schedules];

(c) Any holder of a claim that heretofore has been allowed by order of this Court;

(d) Any person or entity whose claim has been paid in full by any of the Debtors;

(e) Any holder of a claim for which specific deadlines have previously been fixed by this Court;

(f) [Any Debtor having a claim against another Debtor or any of the non-debtor subsidiaries of [name of parent corporation] having a claim against any of the Debtors;]

(g) Any holder of a claim allowable under § 503(b) and § 507(a)(2) of the Bankruptcy Code as an expense of administration;

(h) [Others;] and it is further

ORDERED, that any person or entity that holds a claim that arises from the rejection of an executory contract or unexpired lease, as to which the order authorizing such rejection is dated on or before the date of entry of this Order, must file a proof of claim based on such rejection on or before the Bar Date, and any person or entity that holds a claim that arises from the rejection of an executory contract or unexpired lease, as to which an order authorizing such rejection is dated after the date of entry of this Order, must file a proof of claim on or before such date as the Court may fix in the applicable order authorizing such rejection; and it is further

ORDERED, that holders of equity security interests in the Debtors need not file proofs of interest with respect to the ownership of such equity interests, provided, however, that if any such holder asserts a claim against the Debtors (including a claim relating to an equity interest or the purchase or sale of such equity interest), a proof of such claim must be filed on or prior to the Bar Date pursuant to the procedures set forth in this Order; and it is further

ORDERED, that if the Debtors amend or supplement the Schedules subsequent to the date hereof, the Debtors shall give notice of any amendment or supplement to the holders of claims affected thereby, and such holders shall be afforded 30 days from the date of such notice to file proofs of claim in respect of their claims or be barred from doing so, and shall be given notice of such deadline; and it is further

ORDERED, that nothing in this Order shall prejudice the right of the Debtors or any other party in interest to dispute or assert offsets or defenses to any claim reflected in the Schedules; and it is further

ORDERED, that pursuant to Bankruptcy Rule 3003(c)(2), all holders of claims that fail to comply with this Order by timely filing a proof of claim in appropriate form shall not be treated as a creditor with respect to such claim for the purposes of voting and distribution; and it is further

ORDERED, that a copy of the notice substantially in the form annexed hereto is approved and shall be deemed adequate and sufficient if served by first-class mail at least 35 days prior to the Bar Date on:

(a) the United States trustee;

(b) counsel to each official committee;

(c) all persons or entities that have requested notice of the proceedings in the chapter 11 cases;

(d) all persons or entities that have filed claims;

(e) all creditors and other known holders of claims as of the date of this Order, including all persons or entities listed in the Schedules as holding claims;

(f) all parties to executory contracts and unexpired leases of the Debtors;

(g) all parties to litigation with the Debtors;

(h) the Internal Revenue Service for the district in which the case is pending and, if required by Bankruptcy Rule 2002(j), the Securities and Exchange Commission and any other required governmental units (a list of such agencies is available from the Office of the Clerk of the Court); and

(i) such additional persons and entities as deemed appropriate by the Debtors; and it is further

[ORDERED, that with regard to those holders of claims listed on the Schedules, the Debtors shall mail one or more proof of claim forms (as appropriate) substantially similar to the Proof of Claim form annexed to the application as Exhibit ___, indicating on the form how the Debtors have scheduled such creditor's claim in the Schedules (including the identity of the Debtor, the amount of the claim and whether the claim has been scheduled as contingent, unliquidated or disputed);[2] and it is further]

[ORDERED, that with regard to its current employees, the Debtors shall distribute notice of the Bar Date to such employees using a notice substantially similar to the form of notice annexed to the application as Exhibit ___, which notice is approved;[3] and it is further]

[ORDERED, that pursuant to Bankruptcy Rule 2002(f), the Debtors shall publish notice of the Bar Date in substantially the form hereto as Exhibit ___ (the "Publication Notice") once, in the _____ [and the _____] at least 25 days prior to the Bar Date, which publication is hereby approved and shall be deemed good, adequate and sufficient publication notice of the Bar Date;[4] and it is further]

[ORDERED, that any person or entity who desires to rely on the Schedules will have the responsibility for determining that the claim is accurately listed in the Schedules;[5] and it is further]

ORDERED, that the Debtors [and their Claims Agent] are authorized and empowered to take such steps and perform such acts as may be necessary to implement and effectuate the terms of this Order; and it is further

ORDERED, that entry of this Order is without prejudice to the right of the Debtors to seek a further order of this Court fixing a date by which holders of claims or interests not subject to the Bar Date established herein must file such proofs of claim or interest or be barred from doing so.

Dated: _____, New York

_____ __, 20___

UNITED STATES BANKRUPTCY
JUDGE

[FORM OF NOTICE OF BAR DATE]

UNITED STATES BANKRUPTCY COURT
SOUTHERN DISTRICT OF NEW YORK
--x

In re: Chapter 11

                                                    Case Nos.: ___-_____ (___)
                                                    Through ___-_____ (___)
                              Debtors.
                                                    (Jointly Administered)

--x

Notice of Deadline Requiring Filing of Proofs of Claim on or Before _____

TO ALL PERSONS AND ENTITIES WITH CLAIMS AGAINST [NAME DEBT-ORS] [ANY OF THE DEBTOR ENTITIES LISTED [ABOVE] [ON PAGE ___ OF THIS NOTICE]]

The United States Bankruptcy Court for the Southern District of New York has entered an Order establishing [**set forth date in bold**](the "Bar Date") as the last date for each person or entity (including individuals, partnerships, corporations, joint ventures, trusts and governmental units) to file a proof of claim against any of the Debtors listed [above] [on page ___ of this Notice] (the "Debtors").

The Bar Date and the procedures set forth below for filing proofs of claim apply to all claims against the Debtors that arose prior to _____, the date on which the Debtors commenced cases under chapter 11 of the United States Bankruptcy Code, except for those holders of the claims listed in Section 4 below that are specifically excluded from the Bar Date filing requirement.

1. WHO MUST FILE A PROOF OF CLAIM.

You MUST file a proof of claim to vote on a Chapter 11 plan filed by the Debtors or to share in distributions from the Debtors' bankruptcy estates if you have a claim that arose prior to _____ (the "Filing Date"), and it is not one of the types of claim described in Section 4 below. Claims based on acts or omissions of the Debtors that occurred before the Filing Date must be filed on or prior to the Bar Date, even if such claims are not now fixed, liquidated or certain or did not mature or become fixed, liquidated or certain before the Filing Date.

Under section 101(5) of the Bankruptcy Code and as used in this Notice, the word "claim" means: (a) a right to payment, whether or not such right is reduced to judgment, liquidated, unliquidated, fixed, contingent, matured, unmatured, disputed, undisputed, legal, equitable, secured, or unsecured; or (b) a right to an equitable remedy for breach of performance if such breach gives rise to a right to payment, whether or not such right to an equitable remedy is reduced to judgment, fixed, contingent, matured, unmatured, disputed, undisputed, secured or unsecured.

2. WHAT TO FILE.

[Your filed proof of claim must conform substantially to Official Form No. 10; a case-specific proof of claim form accompanies this notice.] [The Debtors are enclosing a proof of claim form for use in these cases; if your claim is scheduled by the Debtors, the form also sets forth the amount of your claim as scheduled by the Debtors, the specific Debtor against which the claim is scheduled and whether the claim is scheduled as disputed, contingent or unliquidated. You will receive a different proof of claim form for each claim scheduled in your name by the Debtors. You may utilize the proof of claim form(s) provided by the Debtors to file your claim.][6] [Additional proof of claim forms may be obtained at www.uscourts.gov/bkforms.]

All proof of claim forms must be **signed** by the claimant or, if the claimant is not an individual, by an authorized agent of the claimant. It must be written in English and be denominated in United States currency. You should attach to your completed proof of claim any documents on which the claim is based (if voluminous, attach a summary) or an explanation as to why the documents are not available.

Any holder of a claim against more than one Debtor must file a separate proof of claim with respect to each such Debtor and all holders of claims must identify on their proof of claim the specific Debtor against which their claim is asserted and the case number of that Debtor's bankruptcy case. A list of the names of the Debtors and their case numbers is [set forth in the case caption above] [attached to this Notice].

3. WHEN AND WHERE TO FILE

[(A) *Cases with Claims Agents—Insert the following as Paragraph 3:*]

Except as provided for herein, all proofs of claim must be filed so as to be received **on or before** _____ at the following address:

[Insert address provided by claims agent]	IF DELIVERED BY HAND:
	United States Bankruptcy Court Southern District of New York One Bowling Green, Room 534 New York, NY 10004–1408 **[or the address of the division where the case is being administered.]**

Proofs of claim will be deemed filed only when <u>received</u> by the Bankruptcy Court or at the addresses listed herein on or before the Bar Date. Proofs of claim may not be delivered by facsimile, telecopy or electronic mail transmission.

[Governmental units may have until _____, the date that is 180 days after the order for relief, to file proofs of claim.] [7]

[(B) *Cases Without Claims Agents—Insert the following as Paragraph 3:*]

Except as provided for herein, all proofs of claim must be filed so as to be received **on or before** _____.

Attorneys (with full access accounts) and employees of institutional creditors (with limited access accounts) should file proofs of claim electronically on the Court's Case Management/Electronic Case File ("CM/ECF") system.

Those without accounts to the CM/ECF system must file their proofs of claim by mailing or delivering the original proof of claim by hand or overnight courier to the Court at the address provided below:

United States Bankruptcy Court
Southern District of New York
One Bowling Green, Room 534
New York, New York 10004–1408
[or the address of the division where the case is being administered.]

Proofs of claim will be deemed filed only when <u>received</u> by the Bankruptcy Court on or before the Bar Date. Proofs of claim may not be delivered by facsimile, telecopy or electronic mail transmission.

[Governmental units may have until _____, the date that is 180 days after the order for relief, to file proofs of claim.] [8]

4. WHO NEED NOT FILE A PROOF OF CLAIM.

You do **not** need to file a proof of claim on or prior to the Bar Date if you are:

(a) A person or entity that has already filed a proof of claim against the Debtors with the Clerk of the Bankruptcy Court for the Southern District of New York in a form substantially similar to Official Bankruptcy Form No. 10;

(b) A person or entity whose claim is listed on the Schedules if (i) the claim is <u>not</u> scheduled as "disputed," "contingent," or "unliquidated" <u>and</u> (ii) you do <u>not</u> disagree with the amount, nature and priority of the claim as set forth in the Schedules [<u>and</u> (iii) you do not dispute that your claim is an obligation only of the specific Debtor against which the claim is listed in the Schedules];

(b) A holder of a claim that has previously been allowed by order of the Court;

(c) A holder of a claim that has been paid in full by any of the Debtors;

(d) A holder of a claim for which a specific deadline has previously been fixed by this Court;

(e) [Any Debtor having a claim against another Debtor or any of the non-debtor subsidiaries of [Parent Corporation] having a claim against any of the Debtors;]

(f) A holder of a claim allowable under § 503(b) and § 507(a)(2) of the Bankruptcy Code as an expense of administration of the Debtors' estates;

(g) [Others.]

If you are a holder of an equity interest in the Debtors, you need not file a proof of interest with respect to the ownership of such equity interest at this time. However, if you assert a claim against the Debtors, including a claim relating to such equity interest or the purchase or sale of such interest, a proof of such claim must be filed on or prior to the Bar Date pursuant to procedures set forth in this Notice.

This Notice is being sent to many persons and entities that have had some relationship with or have done business with the Debtors but may not have an unpaid claim against the Debtors. The fact that you have received this Notice does not mean that you have a claim or that the Debtors or the Court believe that you have a claim against the Debtors.

5.   EXECUTORY CONTRACTS AND UNEXPIRED LEASES.

If you have a claim arising out of the rejection of an executory contract or unexpired lease as to which the order authorizing such rejection is dated on or before _____, the date of entry of the Bar Order, you must file a proof of claim by the Bar Date. Any person or entity that has a claim arising from the rejection of an executory contract or unexpired lease, as to which the order is dated after the date of entry of the Bar Order, you must file a proof of claim with respect to such claim by the date fixed by the Court in the applicable order authorizing rejection of such contract or lease.

6.   CONSEQUENCES OF FAILURE TO FILE A PROOF OF CLAIM BY THE BAR DATE.

ANY HOLDER OF A CLAIM THAT IS NOT EXCEPTED FROM THE REQUIREMENTS OF THIS ORDER, AS SET FORTH IN SECTION 4 ABOVE, AND THAT FAILS TO TIMELY FILE A PROOF OF CLAIM IN THE APPRO-PRIATE FORM WILL BE BARRED FROM ASSERTING SUCH CLAIM AGAINST THE DEBTORS AND THEIR CHAPTER 11 ESTATES, FROM VOTING ON ANY PLAN OF REORGANIZATION FILED IN THESE CASES, AND FROM PARTICIPATING IN ANY DISTRIBUTION IN THE DEBTORS' CASES ON ACCOUNT OF SUCH CLAIM.

7.   THE DEBTORS' SCHEDULES AND ACCESS THERETO.

You may be listed as the holder of a claim against one or more of the Debtors in the Debtors' Schedules of Assets and Liabilities and/or Schedules of Executory Contracts and Unexpired Leases (collectively, the "Schedules").

[To determine if and how you are listed on the Schedules, please refer to the descriptions set forth on the enclosed proof of claim forms regarding the nature, amount, and status of your claim(s). If you received postpetition payments from the Debtors (as authorized by the Court) on account of your claim, the enclosed proof of claim form will reflect the net amount of your claims. If the Debtors believe that you hold claims against more than one Debtor, you will receive multiple proof of claim forms, each of which will reflect the nature and amount of your claim against one Debtor, as listed in the Schedules.] [9]

[If you rely on the Debtors' Schedules, it is your responsibility to determine that the claim is accurately listed in the Schedules][however, you may rely on the enclosed form, which lists your claim as scheduled, identifies the Debtor against which it is scheduled, and specifies whether the claim is disputed, contingent or unliquidated.] [10]

As set forth above, if you agree with the nature, amount and status of your claim as listed in the Debtors' Schedules, and if you do not dispute that your claim is only against the Debtor specified by the Debtors, and if your claim is not described as "disputed," "contingent," or "unliquidated," you need not file a proof of claim. Otherwise, or if you decide to file a proof of claim, you must do so before the Bar Date in accordance with the procedures set forth in this Notice.

Copies of the Debtors' Schedules are available for inspection on the Court's Internet Website at http://www.nysb.uscourts.gov. A login and password to the Court's Public Access to Electronic Court Records ("PACER") are required to access this information and can be obtained through the PACER Service Center at http://www.pacer.psc.uscourts.gov. Copies of the Schedules may also be examined between the hours of 9:00 a.m. and 4:30 p.m., Monday through Friday at the Office of the Clerk of the Bankruptcy Court, One Bowling Green, Room 511, New York, New York 10004–1408 [or 300 Quarropas Street, Room 248, White Plains, New York 10601 or 355 Main Street, Poughkeepsie, New York 12601]. Copies of the Debtors' Schedules may also be obtained by written request to Debtors' [counsel at the address and telephone number set forth below] [Claims Agent at the following address and telephone number]:

A holder of a possible claim against the Debtors should consult an attorney regarding any matters not covered by this notice, such as whether the holder should file a proof of claim.

Dated: _____, New York

_____ __, 20__

BY ORDER OF THE COURT

COUNSEL FOR THE DEBTORS AND DEBTORS IN POSSESSION

FIRM NAME

ADDRESS

PHONE NUMBER

1 For use only when the general Bar Date is less than 180 days after the Filing Date. Section 502(b)(9) of the Bankruptcy Code requires that governmental units have at least 180 days after the order for relief to file a proof of claim (however, a different deadline may apply for certain tax-related claims in a chapter 13 case).

2 For use only by Debtors that provide individualized proof of claim forms;

3 For use only by Debtors that provide a special notice to current employees; the form of notice may state in substance that the Debtors have filed under chapter 11 and believe they have, by court order or otherwise, paid all prepetition employee obligations, but that if the employee believes that he or she has an unpaid claim for prepetition wages, salaries or commissions, including vacation, severance and sick leave pay, or contributions to employee benefit plans or other benefits, the employee must file such claims on or before the Bar Date. The notice must also provide information as to the form and manner of filing a claim or provide the employee with reasonable access to such information.

4 For Debtors that propose to publish notice of the Bar Date. See Guideline 5.

5 For use only by Debtors that do not provide individualized proof of claim forms. See footnote 3, above.

6 One of these two bracketed statements will ordinarily be appropriate depending on whether individualized proof of claim forms are provided to creditors.

7 See footnote 1, above.

8 See footnote 1, above.

9 For use only by Debtors that provide individualized proof of claim forms.

10 A variant of this paragraph may be used depending on whether the Debtors provide individualized proof of claim forms.

GENERAL ORDER M–289. ORDER LIMITING Fed.R.Civ.P. 26 IN CONTESTED MATTERS

By resolution of the Board of Judges for the Southern District of New York, it is resolved that the following subdivisions of Fed. R. Civ. P. 26, as incorporated by Fed. R. Bankr. P. 7026, shall not apply in a contested matter unless the court directs otherwise: 26(a)(1)(mandatory disclosure), 26(a)(2)(disclosures regarding expert testimony) and 26(a)(3)(additional pretrial disclosure), and 26(f)(mandatory meeting before scheduling conference/discovery plan).

Dated: November 19, 2003.

GENERAL ORDER M–290. ORDER REGARDING PERSONAL DATA IDENTIFIERS [VACATED. SEE, NOW, GENERAL ORDER M–353]

Dated: November 20, 2003. Vacated July 11, 2008.

GENERAL ORDER M–293. ORDER IMPOSING SANCTIONS ON ATTORNEYS DISCIPLINED BY THE COMMITTEE ON GRIEVANCES

WHEREAS, Southern District of New York Local Civil Rule 1.5(a) states that the Committee on Grievances appointed by the board of judges of the District Court, and under the direction of the chief judge, shall have charge of all matters relating to the discipline of attorneys and pursuant to Local Civil Rule 1.5(d)(4), the Committee on Grievances may impose discipline or take other actions as justice may require, including disbarment and suspension.

WHEREAS, Southern District of New York Local Rule of Bankruptcy Procedure 2090–1(a), states that an attorney who may practice in the District Court pursuant to Civil Rule 1.3(a) and (b) of the Local District Rules may practice in this Court, and Local Rule of Bankruptcy Procedure 2090–1(b), further states that an attorney in good standing of the bar of any state or of any United States District Court may be admitted pro hac vice to practice in this Court in a particular case, adversary proceeding or contested matter; and

WHEREAS, the rules governing the Court's Electronic Case Filing System restrict the issuance of general System passwords that authorize the filing of documents on the Court's Electronic Filing System to attorneys admitted to practice in this Court; it is hereby

ORDERED that the Clerk of the Court is directed to revoke the general System password issued to any attorney who has been disbarred or suspended by the District Court pursuant to Local Civil Rule 1.5, or whose right to practice pro hac vice in this Court has been revoked, without prejudice, however, to that person's right to apply for a limited-access password that the Court makes available to non-attorneys.

Dated: New York, New York
      December 19, 2003.

GENERAL ORDER M–295. AMENDED GENERAL ORDER M–292—ORDER REGARDING ATTORNEY BAR IDENTIFICATION NUMBERS [VACATED, SEE, NOW, GENERAL ORDER M–349]

Dated: New York, New York
      February 9, 2004.
Vacated: March 21, 2008.

GENERAL ORDER M–302. CLAIMS BAR DATE PURSUANT TO RULE 3002(c)(5), FEDERAL RULES OF BANKRUPTCY PROCEDURE

Rule 3002(c)(5) of the Federal Rules of Bankruptcy Procedure provides:

> If notice of insufficient assets to pay a dividend was given to creditors pursuant to Rule 2002(e), and subsequently the trustee notifies the court that payment of a dividend appears possible, the clerk shall notify the creditors of that fact and that they may file proofs of claim within 90 days after the mailing of the notice.

In this District notices sent pursuant to Rule 3002(c)(5) are mailed by a notice provider and the Bankruptcy Clerk, who prepares the notice that includes the date certain by which the proofs of claim are to be filed, and who is unable to know when the notice will be mailed. Consequently, for purposes of Rule 3002(c)(5) the date of mailing shall be deemed to be four days after transmission by the Bankruptcy Clerk to the notice provider, and the Bankruptcy Clerk shall use 94 days after transmission to the notice provider to calculate the bar date for filing claims under Rule 3002(c)(5).

The Bankruptcy Judges of this District having considered this clarification to Rule 3002(c)(5) and agreeing this practice should be adopted.

NOW, it is

ORDERED, that, effective immediately, any notices transmitted to a notice provider by the Bankruptcy Clerk shall use 94 days after transmission to calculate the bar date for filing claims under Rule 3002(c)(5).

Dated: New York, New York
      February 17, 2005.

GENERAL ORDER M-306. ORDER RE-GARDING THE REASSIGNMENT OF CERTAIN CHAPTER 7 CASES

WHEREAS, a feature of the Court's CM/ECF System automatically assigns a judge to a chapter 7 case soon after filing on CM/ECF, but does not automatically assign affiliated cases to the same judge in accordance with Local Bankruptcy Rule 1073–1(b); and

WHEREAS, the incorrect automatic assignment, which is most likely to occur in the Manhattan divisional office, presently requires approval of the Chief Judge each time the Clerk must reassign a chapter 7 case to the judge already presiding over the affiliated debtor's case, it is hereby

ORDERED that the Clerk is directed to reassign any chapter 7 case filed in the Manhattan divisional office where, after the automatic assignment of a judge, it becomes necessary to reassign the chapter 7 case to the judge who is assigned to a pending case of the same debtor or an affiliate of the debtor.

Dated: New York, New York
August 4, 2005.

GENERAL ORDER M-308. ADOPTION OF INTERIM BANKRUPTCY RULES AND FORMS*

WHEREAS, the Bankruptcy Abuse Prevention and Consumer Protection Act of 2005 (the "Act") was enacted into law on April 20, 2005, and becomes fully effective on October 17, 2005;

WHEREAS, the Advisory Committee on Bankruptcy Rules of the Judicial Conference of the United States has prepared Interim Rules and Official Forms** (collectively, the "Interim Rules") designed to implement the Act; and

WHEREAS, the Committee on Rules of Practice and Procedure of the Judicial Conference of the United States has also approved these Interim Rules and recommends the adoption of the Interim Rules to provide uniform procedures for implementing the Act; and

WHEREAS, the general effective date of the Act has not provided sufficient time to promulgate rules after appropriate public notice and an opportunity for comment;

NOW THEREFORE, pursuant to 28 U.S.C. § 2075, Rule 83 of the Federal Rules of Civil Procedure, and Rule 9029 of the Federal Rules of Bankruptcy Procedure, the Interim Rules referenced herein, as may be amended from time to time, are adopted in their entirety and shall apply to cases governed by the Act, unless otherwise ordered by the Court.

Dated: New York, New York, October 11, 2005.

* The Interim Bankruptcy Rules follow the Administrative Orders of the United States Bankruptcy Court for the Northern District of New York.

** The Official Forms are not published in this pamphlet.

AMENDED GENERAL ORDER M-311. IN RE: PROCEDURES FOR PAYMENT AND CURE OF PRE-PETITION JUDGMENT OF POSSESSION INVOLVING RESIDENTIAL PROPERTY [M-352]

WHEREAS, the Bankruptcy Abuse Prevention and Consumer Protection Act of 2005, as codified in 11 U.S.C. §§ 362(b)(22) and 362(l), creates certain rights and obligations with respect to the cure of a monetary default giving rise to a pre-petition judgment of possession regarding residential property in which the debtor resides as a tenant under a lease or rental agreement, it is hereby

ORDERED, that the debtor shall be deemed to have complied with 11 U.S.C. § 362(l)(1) by:

1. Making the required certification by completing the four check boxes, **including the landlord's name and address**, listed in the voluntary petition under the section entitled "Statement by a Debtor who Resides as a Tenant of Residential Property"; and

2. Delivering to the Clerk, together with the petition (or within one business day of the filing, if the petition is filed electronically) (a) a certified or cashier's check or money order, made payable to the lessor, in the amount of any rent that would become due during the 30 day period after the filing of the petition, and (b) a copy of the judgment of possession; and it is further

ORDERED, that if the debtor complies with the preceding paragraph, the Clerk of the Court shall, within one business day, send notice of compliance to the lessor who shall then have the option, exercisable within ten days of the date of the notice,

(1) to consent to receive the check in which event the lessor shall provide payment instructions, or (2) object to the debtor's certification, which objection shall constitute a request for a hearing; and it is further

ORDERED, that if the lessor does not respond within the 10 day deadline, the lessor shall be deemed to have consented to receive the check, and the Clerk shall send the check to the lessor at the address set forth in the debtor's certification.

Dated: New York, New York
    October 14, 2005; April 28, 2008.

GENERAL ORDER M-313. CRIMINAL REFERRALS OF CERTAIN BANKRUPTCY CRIMES

WHEREAS, the Bankruptcy Abuse and Prevention and Consumer Protection Act of 2005 enacted section 158 of title 28 regarding, inter alia, the designation of certain individuals within the Department of Justice with primary responsibility for carrying out enforcement activities in addressing violations of 18 U.S.C. §§ 152 and 157 relating to abusive reaffirmations of debt or materially fraudulent statements in bankruptcy schedules that are intentionally false or intentionally misleading; and

WHEREAS, 18 U.S.C. § 158(d) directs the bankruptcy courts to establish procedures for referring any case that may contain a materially fraudulent statement in a bankruptcy schedule to the individuals designated under 18 U.S.C. § 158; it is hereby

ORDERED, that in addition to the obligations imposed under 18 U.S.C. § 3057, any person having reasonable grounds to believe that a bankruptcy schedule contains a materially fraudulent statement in violation of 18 U.S.C. §§ 152 or 157 shall report such violation to one or more of the individuals designated under 18 U.S.C. § 158 by completing the attached referral form or otherwise providing the same information in writing.

Dated: New York, New York
November 30, 2005.

United States Bankruptcy Court for the Southern District of New York

NOTIFICATION STATEMENT REGARDING POTENTIAL VIOLATION OF 18 U.S.C. § 152 OR 157

TO: _____ POSITION:_____

FROM: _____ TITLE (if any): _____

DATE: _____ SIGNATURE _____

1. Background Information

a. Name of Debtor _____

  i. Case number _____

  ii. Debtor's Address _____

  iii. Debtor's Telephone no. _____

b. Debtor's Attorney _____

  i. Address _____

  ii. Telephone no. _____

c. Name of Trustee (if any) _____

  i. Address _____

  ii. Telephone no. _____

2. Case Chapter

a. Under what chapter was the case originally filed: 7 ( ); 11( ); 12 ( ); 13 ( )

b. Under what chapter is the case now pending: 7 ( ); 11( ); 12 ( ); 13 ( )

c. Type of Case: Voluntary ( ); Involuntary ( )

3. Report all facts and circumstances of the offense or offenses believed to have been committed (provide as complete a description as possible), including the following:

a. Identify the schedule that contains the materially fraudulent statement.

b. Explain why the statement is materially fraudulent.

c. Provide the names, addresses, and telephone numbers of persons with knowledge of an information relating to the suspected offense.

d. Disclose any other pertinent information regarding the suspected offense.

GENERAL ORDER M-315. PROCEDURES RELATING TO THE IMPLEMENTATION OF 11 U.S.C. § 521

WHEREAS, on April 20, 2005, the Bankruptcy Abuse Prevention and Consumer Protection Act of 2005 (the "Act") was enacted into law, and became fully effective on October 17, 2005; and

WHEREAS, 11 U.S.C. § 521(a)(1)(B), as amended by the Act, requires a debtor to file certain information "unless the court orders otherwise," and 11 U.S.C. § 521(i) requires the dismissal of the case if this information is not filed within forty-five (45) days after the commencement of the case, it is hereby

ORDERED that effective as to cases filed on or after October 17, 2005, and unless the Court orders otherwise:

1. Copies of all payment advices or other evidence of payment received by an individual debtor within 60 days before the date of the filing of the petition from any employer of the debtor (a) shall not be filed with the Court, and (b) shall be provided to the chapter 7 or 13 case trustee no later than the time of the meeting of creditors conducted pursuant to 11 U.S.C. § 341(a).

2. If a party in interest requests an order of dismissal under 11 U.S.C. § 521(i) (2), the following procedures shall apply:

a) The party in interest will serve a copy of the request on the debtor's attorney and the debtor at the same time that the party in interest sends the request to the Court.

b) If the debtor objects to the request within five days of service, the debtor's objection will be treated as a request for a hearing, which the Court shall schedule promptly.

c) No order of dismissal will be entered until the debtor's objection has been resolved, except that nothing herein shall affect the right of any party in interest to seek dismissal, or the authority of the Court to dismiss the case, pursuant to any other provision of applicable bankruptcy law.

Dated: New York, New York
    December 8, 2005.

GENERAL ORDER M–320. RULES GOVERNING PROCEDURES FOR APPOINTMENT OF PRO BONO COUNSEL IN BANKRUPTCY PROCEEDINGS FROM A BANKRUPTCY PRO BONO PANEL

The Court having issued General Order M–68, dated May 8, 1985, adopting the "Rules Governing Appointment of Pro Bono Counsel" (the "Old Rules"); and the Bankruptcy Judges of this District having subsequently adopted the annexed "Rules Governing Procedures for Appointment of Pro Bono Counsel in Bankruptcy Proceedings From a Bankruptcy Pro Bono Panel" (the "New Rules") to replace the Old Rules; it is hereby

ORDERED, that General Order M–68 is vacated; and it is further

ORDERED, that the New Rules are adopted.

Dated: New York, New York
    February 15, 2006.

UNITED STATES BANKRUPTCY COURTS FOR THE SOUTHERN AND EASTERN DISTRICTS OF NEW YORK

RULES GOVERNING PROCEDURES FOR APPOINTMENT OF PRO BONO COUNSEL IN BANKRUPTCY PROCEEDINGS FROM A BANKRUPTCY PRO BONO PANEL

The following procedures shall govern the appointment of pro bono counsel from a bankruptcy pro bono panel to represent pro se parties in bankruptcy proceedings when such parties lack the resources to retain counsel by any other means.

1. **Bankruptcy Pro Bono Panel.** There shall be a bankruptcy pro bono panel (the "Panel") of attorneys and law firms who are willing to accept appointment to represent pro se parties in bankruptcy proceedings when such parties lack the resources to retain counsel. Registration forms to participate in the Panel shall be available at the Clerk's office in the Southern and Eastern District Bankruptcy Courts, on each court's respective website (Southern District: www.nysb.uscourts.gov; Eastern District: www.nyeb.uscourts.gov) and through the Panel Administrator (as defined in Rule 3).

2. **Composition of Bankruptcy Pro Bono Panel.** The Panel will consist of the following:

(a) *Law Firms.* Law firms, including public interest law firms, may register to participate on the Panel as firms by completing a registration form setting forth, among other things: (i) the firm's mailing and website addresses; (ii) the name of the attorney or pro bono coordinator with the firm designated as Panel liaison, along with such individual's electronic mail address, phone number and facsimile number; (iii) the number of attorneys employed by the firm; (iv) the ability of participating attorneys to represent non-English speaking clients, and the languages that can be accommodated; and (v) preference, if any, for appointment between courthouses. Where a firm is appointed to an action, the appointment will be directed to the Panel liaison and appearance in the action may be entered by the firm or the assigned attorney, at the firm's option.

(b) *Individual Attorneys.* Attorneys who are willing to accept appointment to represent pro se parties may register to participate on the Panel by completing a registration form setting forth, among other things: (i) the name, mailing address and website address, if any, of the attorney, along with the attorney's electronic mail address, phone number and facsimile number; (ii) the firm or organization, if any, with which the attorney is affiliated; (iii) the number of years the attorney has been admitted to practice; (iv) the attorney's principal practice areas; (v) the attorney's experience in bankruptcy and/or litigation matters; (vi) the ability of the attorney to represent non-English speaking clients; (vii) the courts in which the attorney is admitted to practice; and

(viii) the attorney's preference, if any, for appointment between the courthouses.

(c) *Attorney Instructors in Law School Clinical Programs.* The Southern and Eastern District Bankruptcy Courts may authorize a clinical program, under the auspices of one or more law schools accredited by the American Bar Association and located in the Southern or Eastern District, through which students, appropriately supervised by an attorney instructor, may appear in matters referred to the Panel. An attorney instructor may apply to participate on the Panel by completing a registration form setting forth, among other things: (i) the name, mailing address and website address of the law school administering the clinical program; (ii) the number of students involved in the clinical program; (iii) the practices of the clinical program in supervising participating students; (iv) the name, mailing address and website address, if any, of the attorney instructor, along with the attorney instructor's electronic mail address, phone number and facsimile number; (v) the firm or organization, if any, with which the attorney instructor is affiliated; (vi) the name and mailing address of the supervisor of the clinical program, along with the supervisor's electronic mail address, phone number and facsimile number; (vii) the number of years the attorney instructor has been admitted to practice; (viii) the attorney instructor's principal practice areas; (ix) the attorney instructor's experience in bankruptcy and/or litigation matters; (x) the ability of the attorney instructor and the clinical program to represent non-English speaking clients; (xi) the courts in which the attorney instructor is admitted to practice; and (xii) preference, if any, for appointment between the courthouses.

(d) Information on a registration form may be amended at any time by letter. An attorney or firm may by letter withdraw from the Panel at any time subject to Rule 6 (Relief From Appointment).

(e) Nothing in these rules shall restrict the authority of a bankruptcy judge to appoint pro bono counsel by other means, including direct appointment or appointment through organizations other than the pro bono panel established by these rules, whether or not the counsel appointed is a member of such panel.

3. Panel Administrator. A list of law firms, individual attorneys and attorney instructors who have registered to participate on the Panel shall be maintained by a representative of the City Bar Justice Center (hereinafter, the "Panel Administrator"). The Panel Administrator may receive assistance in administering the Panel from members of the Association of the Bar of the City of New York's Committee on Bankruptcy and Corporate Reorganization, from New York City Bankruptcy Assistance Project and from other qualified organizations. The Panel Administrator may remove an attorney or firm from the Panel at any time. It is not intended that the Panel Administrator shall be responsible for supervising attorneys appointed to represent clients. The Southern and Eastern District Bankruptcy Courts may appoint additional Panel Administrators. Attorneys and law firms participating in the Panel are not required to be members of any bar association.

4. Appointment Procedure.

(a) Whenever a bankruptcy judge concludes that appointment of counsel from the Panel may be warranted and the client consents, the judge may request, on the record or in writing, that the Panel Administrator select counsel from the Panel. The judge's chambers shall inform the Panel Administrator of the appointment and any scheduled court dates and provide the Panel Administrator with a copy of the docket sheet and any necessary pleadings. The Panel Administrator may, in its discretion, if deemed desirable in specific cases, select counsel not on the Panel or select a specific attorney on the Panel who is especially qualified to undertake the representation. The Panel Administrator may direct the applicant to a bar association referral service in any case where it appears that adequate counsel fees may be awarded as provided by statute. The provisions of the Bankruptcy Code relating to the appointment of counsel by the court shall be complied with.

(b) Pro bono counsel will be appointed only for individuals who have appeared pro se and are unable to afford counsel, or who had counsel but were unable to pay for litigated matters. Such persons may be requested to file with the court an in forma pauperis affidavit affirming they lack the resources to retain counsel. In determining whether to request that the Panel Administrator select counsel from the Panel for appointment, the judge may take the following factors into account: (i) the nature and complexity of the matter in which the pro bono counsel is to represent the client; (ii) the apparent potential merit of the claim or issue involved; (iii) the inability of the client to retain counsel by other means; (iv) the degree to which the interests of justice will be served by the appointment of counsel, including the benefit the court may derive from the assistance of the appointed counsel; and (v) any other factors deemed appropriate. It is not intended that counsel will be appointed for any party prior to the filing of a petition under Title 11 of the U.S. Code. These rules are not intended to provide any party with a right to have counsel appointed.

(c) It is intended that counsel will be appointed to represent debtors only on a specific contested matter or adversary proceeding rather than generally with respect to the bankruptcy case, and counsel's responsibilities shall be limited only to such matter or proceeding. Counsel also may be appointed to represent non-debtors in connection with specific contested matters, adversary proceedings or other litigated matters arising in or relating to a bankruptcy case.

(d) Upon receiving a request, as set forth in Rule 4(a), to select counsel from the Panel, it is expected that the Panel Administrator shall forward a request for pro bono counsel to members of the Panel via electronic mail or otherwise. Panel members may contact the Panel Administrator to indicate their interest in accepting a case. Appointments of counsel generally shall be on a first-come first-served basis; provided, however, that the Panel Administrator may select counsel on other bases where appropriate. If several Panel members are interested in the same case, a wait list may be established. The Panel Administrator shall forward a notice of appointment, along with the client's name and contact information, to the selected Panel member. In the event no Panel member accepts the assignment, the Panel Administrator shall so inform the client and the judge's chambers and no further attempts at assignment shall be required.

5. Responsibilities of the Appointed Attorney.

(a) Upon receiving a notice of appointment, counsel shall obtain, either through the applicable Case Management/Electronic Case Files System or otherwise, and review the case file and, if deemed appropriate, communicate with the client, but must advise the client that s/he has not yet decided whether to accept the appointment. Counsel shall determine as soon as practicable, and within such time prior to the matter's next scheduled hearing date so as to permit another appointment to be made, whether to accept the representation. Upon accepting the representation, and upon the client's consent, counsel shall file a notice of appearance and inform other counsel as appropriate. The notice of appearance shall, if appropriate, specify the discrete matter or matters upon which pro bono counsel is to represent the client and further state that all pleadings and other papers shall continue to be served upon the client as well as upon pro bono counsel. Pro bono counsel shall send a copy of the notice of appearance to the client, the judge's chambers and the Panel Administrator. The Panel Administrator shall maintain a record of all assigned matters.

(b) Upon accepting an appointment and filing a notice of appearance, counsel shall fully discuss the merits of the matter with the client. Counsel may, if appropriate, explore with the client the possibility of resolving the dispute by other means, including but not limited to seeking a negotiated settlement or proceeding to mediation. If, after consultation with counsel, the client decides to prosecute or defend the action, counsel shall represent the party until the attorney-client relationship is terminated in the ordinary course in connection with the matter as to which counsel was appointed or until terminated as provided for herein.

(c) If the appointed attorney after reviewing the file reasonably anticipates a need to request relief from appointment, the attorney shall, before discussing the merits of the case with the client, advise the client that a procedure for such relief exists. Where the

attorney did not reasonably anticipate the need for such relief prior to discussing the merits of the case with the client, the attorney may request the waiver at any time the need for such relief becomes apparent. The attorney should then request the client to execute a limited waiver of the attorney client privilege permitting the attorney to disclose under seal to the Court the attorney's reasons for seeking to be relieved of the appointment. The waiver should indicate that the application for relief will be a privileged court document and may not be used in the litigation. The client's refusal to execute a waiver shall not preclude the attorney from applying for relief.

6. Relief From Appointment.

(a) Prior to filing a notice of appearance and within the time period set forth in Rule 5(a), if counsel does not wish to accept an appointment due to lack of time, personal preference or any other ground set forth below, or upon the client's request, counsel shall promptly inform the Panel Administrator, who will attempt to reassign the case to another Panel member. In the event no Panel member accepts the assignment, the Panel Administrator shall so inform the client and the judge's chambers and no further attempts at assignment shall be required.

(b) Subsequent to filing a notice of appearance, pro bono counsel may apply pursuant to the Court's Local Rules to be relieved of an appointment on any grounds available to an attorney-of record except for the non-payment of fees or expenses.

(c) An application by counsel for relief from an appointment on any of the grounds set forth above must be made promptly upon counsel acquiring knowledge of the facts leading to the application.

(d) If counsel wishes to be relieved from an appointment on any of the grounds set forth in Rule 6(b) or similar grounds, counsel shall send a request to that effect to the client, stating the grounds for relief. If the client does not object to the request for relief, counsel shall so advise the Panel Administrator and submit a proposed order, endorsed by the Panel Administrator, to the court. If the client objects to the request for relief, counsel shall submit the request and the grounds therefor to the judge's chambers for consideration, along with a proposed order, in a document to be kept under seal and not to be available in discovery or otherwise used in connection with the matter or any other litigation. Counsel shall provide a copy of the request and proposed order to the client and the Panel Administrator.

(e) If an order for relief from appointment is entered, the judge may request, on the record or in writing, that the Panel Administrator attempt to reassign the case to another Panel member. In the event no Panel member accepts the assignment, the Panel Administrator shall so inform the client and the judge's chambers and no further attempts at reassignment shall be required.

7. Discharge. A party for whom counsel has been appointed may request the judge, on the record or in writing, to discharge such counsel from the representation. The client shall provide a copy of any written request to the appointed counsel. When such a request is supported by good cause (e.g., substantial disagreement between the party and counsel on strategy), the order of discharge shall be granted and the appointed counsel shall duly inform the Panel Administrator and the client. The judge may request, on the record or in writing, that the Panel Administrator attempt to reassign the case to another Panel member. In the event no Panel member accepts the assignment, the Panel Administrator shall so inform the client and the judge's chambers and no further attempts at reassignment shall be required.

8. Expenses. There being no public funds available for the purpose, appointed counsel or the firm may advance the expenses of the matter.

9. Compensation for Services.

(a) No payment of money or other valuable consideration shall be demanded or accepted in connection with the services rendered by pro bono counsel.

(b) Notwithstanding paragraph (a), the matter may be one for which compensation for legal services may become available to the appointed counsel under the Bankruptcy Code or other authority. Upon appropriate application by appointed counsel, and taking into consideration counsel's initial agreement to take the matter without compensation, the judge may award fees to the appointed counsel or law firm for services rendered, as permitted by applicable law.

(c) If, after appointment, the appointed counsel discovers that the party is able to pay for legal services, counsel shall bring this information to the attention of the Panel Administrator. Upon appropriate motion, the court may relieve counsel from the representation and permit the party to retain other counsel or proceed pro se.

10. Duration of Representation.

(a) Subject to the provisions of Rules 10(b) and (c), appointed counsel shall represent the party in connection with the matter on which counsel was appointed from the date counsel enters an appearance until a final order or judgment is entered in the matter and reasonable efforts have been made to enforce the order or judgment, or until counsel has been relieved from appointment by the court. If the bankruptcy case is continuing after the matter is concluded, counsel shall inform the client in writing with a copy to the Panel Administrator that counsel's responsibilities have concluded and that the party is again proceeding pro se.

(b) If an appealable order or judgment is entered in connection with the matter, counsel shall inform the client of the possibility of appeal and, if the client requests, file a notice of appeal, a designation of the items to be included in the record on appeal and a statement of the issues to be presented, or assist the party in filing such papers.

(c) In the event the party desires to take an appeal from an appealable order or judgment, or if such order or judgment is appealed by another party, counsel is encouraged but not required to represent the party on the appeal and in any proceeding that may ensue upon an order of remand. If counsel elects not to represent the client on the appeal or remand, counsel shall give prompt notice of such election to the Panel Administrator who may attempt to reassign the matter to another Panel member or refer the client to the pro se panel of the court to which the appeal is taken.

(d) Nothing in these rules shall be read to affect: (i) an attorney's responsibilities under the Code of Professional Responsibility or applicable law; or (ii) the manner in which and to whom a notice of appearance or notice of withdrawal must be given under the Federal Rules of Bankruptcy Procedure, the Local Bankruptcy Rules, or any order of the court in the particular bankruptcy case.

GENERAL ORDER M–323. PROCEDURES RELATING TO THE NOTICE OF THE COMMENCEMENT OF A CHAPTER 15 CASE

WHEREAS, on April 20, 2005, the Bankruptcy Abuse Prevention and Consumer Protection Act of 2005 (the "Act") was enacted into law, and became fully effective on October 17, 2005;

WHEREAS, Interim Federal Bankruptcy Rule 2002(q)(1), as adopted by the Judicial Conference of the United States and implemented by this Court's General Order M–308, dated October 11, 2005, directs the clerk, "or some other person as the court may direct," to provide certain notice in connection with a petition filed under Chapter 15 of the Bankruptcy Code; it is hereby

ORDERED that a foreign representative commencing a chapter 15 case in this district is directed to provide without delay the notice mandated by Interim Federal Bankruptcy Rule 2002(q)(1) in lieu of the clerk, and to promptly file an affidavit of service with the Court.

Dated: New York, New York

April 5, 2006.

GENERAL ORDER M-331. ADOPTION OF GUIDELINES FOR THE CONDUCT OF ASSET SALES

By resolution of the Board of Judges of the Southern District of New York, it is resolved that in order to expedite the review and determination of applications to conduct asset sales, it is hereby

ORDERED that the Guidelines for the Conduct of Asset Sales (the "Guidelines"), annexed hereto, are adopted and shall be effective immediately; and it is further

ORDERED that all sales applications filed in the United States Bankruptcy Court for the Southern District of New York, and all proceedings and orders relating to such applications, shall conform substantially to these Guidelines.

Dated: New York, New York
September 5, 2006.

GUIDELINES FOR THE CONDUCT OF ASSET SALES

The United States Bankruptcy Court for the Southern District of New York (the "Court") has established the following guidelines (the "Guidelines") for the conduct of asset sales under section 363(b) of 11 U.S.C. § 101, et seq. (the "Bankruptcy Code"). The Guidelines are designed to help practitioners identify issues that typically are of concern to parties and the Court, so that, among other things, determinations can be made, if necessary, on an expedited basis.

By offering the Guidelines, this Court does not address the circumstances under which an asset sale or asset sale process is appropriate or express a preference for asset sales under section 363(b) of the Bankruptcy Code as opposed to those conducted in the context of confirming a chapter 11 plan, address other substantive legal issues, or establish any substantive rules. However, the Guidelines do require disclosure of the "Extraordinary Provisions," discussed below, pertaining to the conduct of asset sales, which ordinarily will not be approved without good cause shown for such Extraordinary Provisions, or compelling circumstances, and reasonable notice.

The Guidelines are intended to supplement the requirements of section 363(b) and 365 of the Bankruptcy Code, Rules 2002 and 6004 of the Federal Rules of Bankruptcy Procedure (the "Bankruptcy Rules"), and Rules 6004-1 and 6005-1 of the Court's Local Rules.

I. MOTIONS

A. Motion Content. When an auction is contemplated, the debtor [1] should file a single motion seeking the entry of two orders to be considered at two separate hearings. The first order (the "Sale Procedures Order") will approve procedures for the sale process, including any protections for an initial bidder, or stalking horse buyer, and the second order (the "Sale Order") will approve the sale to the successful bidder at the auction. If no auction procedures or stalking horse buyer protection provisions are contemplated, only one order (the Sale Order) and one hearing is required. If no auction is contemplated or the debtor has not actively solicited or will not actively solicit higher and better offers, the motion seeking approval of the sale should explain why the debtor proposes to structure the sale in such manner. [2]

1. The proposed purchase agreement, or a form of proposed agreement acceptable to the debtor if the debtor has not yet entered into an agreement with a proposed buyer, should be attached to the motion.

2. The motion also should include a copy of the proposed order(s), particularly if the order(s) include any Extraordinary Provisions.

3. The motion must comply in form with the Local Rules.

4. If a hearing is required under section 363(b) of the Bankruptcy Code in connection with the sale of personally identifiable information subject to a privacy policy of the debtor, the motion should request appointment of a consumer privacy ombudsman under section 332 of the Bankruptcy Code.

B. Bidding Procedures. Generally, the Court will entertain a motion for approval, in a Sale Procedures Order, of proposed bidding procedures if such procedures are, as a matter of reasonable business judgment, likely to maximize the sale price. Such procedures must not chill the receipt of higher and better offers and must be consistent with the seller's fiduciary duties. It is recommended that such procedures include the following:[3]

1. *Qualification of Bidders.* An entity that is seeking to become a qualified bidder will deliver financial information by a stated deadline to the debtor and other key parties (ordinarily excluding other bidders) [4] reasonably demonstrating such bidder's ability to consummate a sale on the terms proposed. Such financial information, which may be provided confidentially, if appropriate, may include current audited or verified financial statements of, or verified financial commitments obtained by, the potential bidder (or, if the potential bidder is an entity formed for the purpose of acquiring the property to be sold, the party that will bear liability for a breach). To be qualified, a prospective bidder also may be required by a stated deadline to make a non-binding expression of interest and execute a reasonable form of non-disclosure agreement before being provided due diligence access to non-public information.

2. *Qualification of Bids Prior to Auction.*

(a) The bidding procedures should state the criteria for a qualifying bid and any deadlines for (i) submitting such a bid and (ii) notification whether the bid constitutes a qualifying bid.

(b) The bidding procedures may require each qualified bid to be marked against the form of a stalking horse agreement or a template of the debtor's preferred sale terms, showing amendments and other modifications (including price and other terms) proposed by the qualified bidder. The proposed bidding procedures may, but are not required to, limit bidding to the terms of a stalking horse agreement or preferred form of agreement; for example, bidding on less than all of the assets proposed to be acquired by an initial, or stalking horse, bidder normally should be permitted, unless such bidding is inconsistent with the purpose of the sale.

(c) A qualified bid should clearly identify all conditions to the qualified bidder's obligation to consummate the purchase.

(d) A qualified bid should include a good faith deposit, which will be non-refundable if the bidder is selected as the successful bidder and fails to consummate the purchase (other than as a result of a breach by the seller) and refundable if it is not selected as the successful bidder (other than as a result of its own breach). The amount of, and precise rules governing, the good faith deposit will be determined on a case-by-case basis, but generally each qualified bidder, including any initial, or stalking horse, bidder, should be required to make the same form of deposit.

3. *Backup Buyer.* The Sale Procedures Order may provide that the debtor in the reasonable exercise of its judgment may accept and close on the second highest qualified bid received if the winning bidder fails to close the transaction within a specified period. In such case, the debtor would retain the second highest bidder's good faith deposit until such bidder was relieved of its obligation to be a back-up buyer.

4. *Stalking Horse or Initial Bidder Protections/Bidding Increments.*

(a) **No-Shop or No-Solicitation Provisions.** Limited no-shop or no-solicitation provisions may be permissible, in unusual circumstances, if they are necessary to obtain a sale, they are consistent with the debtor's fiduciary duties and they do not chill the receipt of higher or better offers. Such provisions must be prominently disclosed in the motion, with particularity. If the relevant documents do not include a "fiduciary out" provision, the debtor must disclose the fact of and the reason for the exclusion of the provision.

(b) **Break-Up/Topping Fees and Expense Reimbursement.** The propriety of any break-up or topping fees and other bidding protections (such as the estate's proposed payment of out-of-pocket expenses incurred by a bidder in connection with the proposed transaction or the compensation of a bidder for lost opportunity costs) will be determined on a case-by-case basis. Generally such obligations should be payable only from the proceeds of a higher or better transaction entered into with a third party within a reasonable time of the closing of the sale. Such provisions must be set forth with particularity, and conspicuously disclosed in the motion.

(c) **Bidding Increments.** If a proposed sale contemplates the granting of a break-up or topping fee or expense reimbursement, the initial bidding increment must be more than sufficient to pay the maximum amount payable thereunder. Additional bidding increments should not be so high that they chill further bids, or so low that they provide insubstantial consideration to the estate.

(d) **Rebidding.** If a break-up or topping fee is requested, the Sale Procedures Order should state whether the stalking horse will be deemed to waive the break-up or topping fee by rebidding. In the absence of a waiver, the Sales Procedure Order should state whether the stalking horse will receive a "credit" equal to the break-up or topping fee when bidding at the auction.

5. *Auction Procedures.*

(a) If an auction is proposed, the Sale Procedures Order generally should provide that the auction will be conducted openly, and that each bidder will be informed of the terms of the previous bid. The motion should explain the rationale for proposing a different auction format in the Sale Procedures Order.

(b) If a professional auctioneer will conduct the auction, the parties should refer to the statutory provisions and rules governing the conduct of professional auctioneers. See Bankruptcy Rule 6004 and Rules 6004-1 and 6005-1 of the Local Bankruptcy Rules for the Southern District of New York (the "Local Rules").

(c) If the auction is sufficiently complex or disputes can reasonably be expected to arise, it is advisable at the sale procedures hearing to ask the Court whether it will consider conducting the auction in open court, or otherwise be available to resolve disputes. If the debtor proposes to conduct the auction outside the presence of the judge, the actual bidding should be transcribed or videotaped to ensure a record, or the motion should explain why this is not advisable.

(d) Each bidder is expected to confirm at the auction that it has not engaged in any collusion with respect to the bidding or the sale.

(e) The Sale Procedures Order should provide that, absent irregularities in the conduct of the auction, or reasonable and material confusion during the bidding, the Court will not consider bids made after the auction has been closed, or the motion should explain why this is not advisable.

C. Sale Motion. With regard to the proposed sale, the motion and the evidence presented or proffered at any sale hearing should be sufficient to enable the Court to make the following findings: (1) a sound business reason exists for the transaction; (2) the property has been adequately marketed, the purchase price constitutes the highest or otherwise best offer and provides fair and reasonable consideration; (3) the proposed transaction is in the best interests of the debtor's estate, its creditors, and where relevant, its interest holders; (4) the transaction has been proposed and negotiated in good faith; (5) adequate and reasonable notice has been provided; (6) the 'free and clear' requirements of section 363(f) of the Bankruptcy Code, if applicable, have been met; (7) if applicable, the sale is consistent with the debtor's privacy policy concerning personally identifiable information, or, after appointment of a consumer ombudsman in accordance with section 332 of the Bankruptcy Code and notice and a hearing, no showing was made that such sale would violate applicable nonbankruptcy law; (8) the requirements of section 365 of the Bankruptcy Code have been met in respect of the proposed assumption and assignment or rejection of any executory contracts and unexpired leases; (9) where necessary, the debtor's board of directors or other governing body has authorized the proposed transaction; and (10) the debtor and the purchaser have entered into the transaction without collusion, in good faith, and from arm's-length bargaining positions, and neither party has engaged in any conduct that would cause or permit the agreement to be avoided under section 363(n) of the Bankruptcy Code.

1. *Sound Business Purpose.* A debtor must demonstrate the facts that support a finding that a sound business reason exists for the sale.

2. *Marketing Efforts.* A debtor must demonstrate facts that support a finding that the property to be sold has been marketed adequately.

3. *Purchase Price.* A debtor must demonstrate that fair and reasonable value will be received and that the proffered purchase price is the highest or best under the circumstances. If a bid includes deferred payments or any equity component, a debtor should discuss its assessment of the credit worthiness of competing bidders, if any, and the proposed buyer's ability to realize the projected earnings upon which future payments or other forms of consideration to the estate are based. Any material purchase price adjustment provisions should be identified.

4. *Assumption and Assignment of Contracts and Leases.* A debtor must demonstrate at a minimum: (a) that it or the assignee/acquiror has cured or will promptly cure all existing defaults under the agreement(s), and (b) that the assignee/acquiror can provide adequate assurance that it will perform under the terms of the agreement(s) to be assumed and assigned under section 365 of the Bankruptcy Code. Additional notice and opportunity for a hearing may be required, if the offer sought to be approved at the sale hearing is submitted by a different entity than the initial, stalking horse bidder or the winning bid identifies different contracts or leases for assumption and assignment, or rejection, than the initial bid that was noticed for approval. If this possibility exists, the sale motion should acknowledge the debtor will provide such additional notice and opportunity to object under such circumstances.

D. Extraordinary Provisions. The following provisions must be disclosed conspicuously in a separate section of the sale motion and, where applicable, in the related proposed Sale Procedures Order or Sale Order, and the motion must provide substantial justification therefor: [5]

1. *Sale to Insider.* If the motion proposes a sale to an insider, as defined in the Bankruptcy Code, the motion must disclose what measures have been taken to ensure the fairness of the sale process and the proposed transaction.

2. *Agreements with Management.* The sale motion must disclose whether the proposed buyer has discussed or entered into any agreements with management or key employees regarding compensation or future employment, the material terms of any such agreements, and what measures have been taken to ensure the fairness of the sale and the proposed transaction in the light of any such agreements.

3. *Private Sale/No Competitive Bidding.* If no auction is contemplated, the debtor has agreed to a limited no-shop or no-solicitation provision, or the debtor has otherwise not sought or is not actively seeking higher or better offers, the sale motion must so state and explain why such sale is likely to maximize the sale price.

4. *Deadlines that Effectively Limit Notice.* If the proposed transaction includes deadlines for the closing or Court approval of the Sale Procedures Order or the Sale Order that have the effect of limiting notice to less than that discussed in II, below, the sale motion must provide an explanation.

5. *No Good Faith Deposit.* If any qualified bidder, including a stalking horse, is excused from submitting a good faith deposit, the sale motion must provide an explanation.

6. *Interim Arrangements with Proposed Buyer.* If a debtor is entering into any interim agreements or arrangements with the proposed purchaser, such as interim management arrangements (which, if out of the ordinary course, also must be subject to notice and

a hearing under section 363(b) of the Bankruptcy Code), the sale motion must disclose the terms of such agreements.

7. *Use of Proceeds.* If a debtor proposes to release sale proceeds on or after the closing without further Court order, or to provide for a definitive allocation of sale proceeds between or among various sellers or collateral, the sale motion must describe the intended disposition of such amounts and the rationale therefor.

8. *Tax Exemption.* If the debtor is seeking to have the sale declared exempt from taxes under section 1146(a) of the Bankruptcy Code, the sale motion must prominently disclose the type of tax (e.g., recording tax, stamp tax, use tax, capital gains tax) for which the exemption is sought. It is not sufficient to refer simply to "transfer" taxes. In addition, the debtor must identify the state or states in which the affected property is located.

9. *Record Retention.* If the debtor proposes to sell substantially all of its assets, the sale motion must confirm that the debtor will retain, or have reasonable access to, its books and records to enable it to administer its bankruptcy case.

[10. No "10." in original copy received from court.]

11. *Sale of Avoidance Actions.* If the debtor seeks to sell its rights to pursue avoidance claims under chapter 5 of the Bankruptcy Code, the sale motion must so state and provide an explanation of the basis therefor.

12. *Requested Findings as to Successor Liability.* If the debtor seeks findings limiting the purchaser's successor liability, the sale motion must disclose the adequacy of the debtor's proposed notice of such requested relief and the basis for such relief. Generally, the proposed Sale Order should not contain voluminous findings with respect to successor liability, or injunctive provisions except as provided in III, below.

13. *Future Conduct.* If the debtor seeks a determination regarding the effect of conduct or actions that may or will be taken after the date of the Sale Order, the sale motion must set forth the legal authority for such a determination.

14. *Requested Findings as to Fraudulent Conveyance.* If debtor seeks a finding to the effect that the sale does not constitute a fraudulent conveyance, it must explain why a finding that the purchase price is fair and reasonable is not sufficient.

15. *Sale Free and Clear of Unexpired Leases.* If the debtor seeks to sell property free and clear of a possessory leasehold interest, license or other right, the debtor must identify the non-debtor parties whose interests will be affected, and explain what adequate protection will be provided for those interests.

16. *Relief from Bankruptcy Rule 6004(h).* If the debtor seeks relief from the ten-day stay imposed by Bankruptcy Rule 6004(h), the sale motion must disclose the business or other basis for such request.

II. NOTICE

A. General. Notice is always required under section 363(b); however, a hearing is required only if there are timely objections or the Court otherwise schedules a hearing.

B. Notice of Proposed Sale Procedures.

1. *Notice Parties.* Notice should be limited to those parties-in-interest best situated to articulate an objection to the limited relief sought at this stage, including:

(a) counsel for official and informal committees of creditors, equity holders, retirees, etc.;

(b) office of the United States Trustee;

(c) postpetition lenders;

(d) indenture trustees;

(e) agent for prepetition lenders;

(f) entities who have requested notice under Bankruptcy Rule 2002;

(g) all entities known or reasonably believed to have asserted a lien, encumbrance, claim or other interest in any of the assets offered for sale; and

(h) parties to executory contracts and unexpired leases proposed to be assumed and assigned, or rejected as part of the proposed transaction.

To provide additional marketing of the assets, the debtor also should send a copy of the motion to entities known or reasonably believed to have expressed an interest in acquiring any of the assets offered for sale. Nothing herein is meant to imply that prospective bidders have standing to be heard with respect to the Sales Procedures.

2. *Notice Period.* As a general matter, the minimum 20-day notice period set forth in Bankruptcy Rule 2002(a) can be shortened with respect to the request for approval of a proposed Sale Procedures Order, that does not involve Extraordinary Provisions and complies with these Guidelines, without compromising the finality of the proposed transaction. The 10-day notice period provided for in Local Rule 9006-1(b) should provide sufficient time, under most circumstances, to enable any parties-in-interest to file an objection to proposed sale procedures.

3. *Contents of Notice.* Notice should comport with Bankruptcy Rules 2002 and 6004.

C. Notice of Sale.

1. *Notice Parties.* Generally the proposed sale requires more expansive notice than proposed sale procedures. (But see footnote 2, above, regarding omnibus procedures for de minimis sales.) Notice should ordinarily be given to: [6]

(a) counsel for official and informal committees of creditors, equity holders, retirees, etc.;

(b) office of the United States Trustee;

(c) entities who have requested notice under Bankruptcy Rule 2002 [7] (and, if the proposed sale is of substantially all of the debtor's assets, all known creditors of the debtor);

(d) postpetition lenders;

(e) indenture trustees;

(f) agent for prepetition lenders;

(g) all entities known or reasonably believed to have asserted a lien, encumbrance, claim or other interest in any of the assets offered for sale;

(h) all parties to executory contracts or unexpired leases to be assumed and assigned, or rejected as part of the transaction;

(i) all affected federal, state and local regulatory (including, for example, environmental agencies) and taxing authorities, [8] including the Internal Revenue Service;

(j) if applicable, a consumer privacy ombudsman appointed under section 332 of the Bankruptcy Code; and

(k) the Securities and Exchange Commission (if appropriate).

If the contemplated sale implicates the anti-trust laws of the United States, or a debt (other than for taxes) is owed by the debtor to the United States government, notice also should be given to:

(*l*) the Federal Trade Commission;

(m) the Assistant Attorney General in charge of the Antitrust Division of the Department of Justice; and

(n) the United States Attorney's Office.

To provide additional marketing of the assets, notice also should be sent to any entities known or reasonably believed to have expressed an interest in acquiring any of the assets.

See I.C.4, above for circumstances in which it may be required, based on changes in the proposed transaction that had originally been noticed, to give additional notice to parties to executory contracts and unexpired leases proposed to be assumed and assigned or rejected under section 365 of the Bankruptcy Code.

2. *Notice Period.* The statutory 20-day notice period should not be shortened for notice of the actual sale without a showing of good cause. The service of a prior notice or order, that discloses an intention to conduct a sale but does not state a specific sale date, does not affect the 20-day notice period.

3. *Contents of Notice.* Proper notice should comport with Bankruptcy Rules 2002 and 6004 and should include:

(a) the Sale Procedures Order (including the date, time and place of any auction, the bidding procedures related thereto, the objection deadline for the sale motion and the date and time of the sale hearing);

(b) reasonably specific identification of the assets to be sold;

(c) the proposed form of asset purchase agreement, or instructions for promptly obtaining a copy;

(d) if appropriate, representations describing the sale as being free and clear of liens, claims, interests and other encumbrances (other than any claims and defenses of a consumer under any consumer credit transaction that is subject to the Truth in Lending Act or a consumer credit contract (as defined in 16 C.F.R. § 433.1, as amended), with all such liens, claims, interests and other encumbrances attaching with the same validity and priority to the sale proceeds;

(e) any commitment by the buyer to assume liabilities of the debtor; and

(f) notice of proposed cure amounts and the right and deadline to object thereto and otherwise to object to the proposed assumption and assignment, or rejection of executory contracts and unexpired leases (see I.C.4, above for additional notice that debtor may need to acknowledge may be required). [9]

III. SALE ORDER.

The Court discourages unduly long sale orders that contain unnecessary and redundant provisions. In the typical case, the findings should be limited to those set out in I.C, supra, tailored to the particular case. The decretal paragraphs should also be limited, and if more than one decretal paragraph deals with the same subject matter or form of relief, the proponent of the Sale Order should explain the reason in a separate pleading. Finally, if the order contains a decretal paragraph that approves the purchase agreement or authorizes the debtor to execute the purchase agreement, it should not also contain separate decretal paragraphs that approve specific provisions of the purchase agreement or declare their legal effect.

With these admonitions, the Court may enter a Sale Order containing the following, if substantiated through evidence presented or proffered in the motion or at the sale hearing:

A. Approval of Sale and Purchase Agreement. The order should authorize the debtor to (1) execute the purchase agreement, along with any additional instruments or documents that may be necessary to implement the purchase agreement, provided that such additional documents do not materially change its terms; (2) consummate the sale in accordance with the terms and conditions of the purchase agreement and the instruments and agreements contemplated thereby; and (3) take all further actions as may reasonably be requested by the purchaser for the purpose of transferring the assets. [10]

B. Transfer of Assets. The assets will be transferred free and clear of all liens, claims, encumbrances and interests in such property, other than any claims and defenses of a consumer under any consumer credit transaction subject to the Truth in Lending Act or a consumer credit contract, as defined in 16 C.F.R. § 433.1 (and as may be amended), with all such interests attaching to the sale proceeds with the same validity and priority, and the same defenses, as existed immediately prior to the sale, [11] and persons and entities holding any such interests will be enjoined from asserting such interests against the purchaser, its successors or assigns, or the purchased assets, unless the purchaser has otherwise agreed.

C. Assumption and Assignment of Executory Contracts and Leases to Purchaser. The debtor will be authorized and directed to assume and assign to the purchaser executory contracts and leases free and clear of all liens, claims, encumbrances and interests, with all such interests attaching to the sale proceeds with the same validity and priority as they had in the assets being sold (provided, however, that in certain circumstances additional notice may be required before assumption and assignment or rejection of executory contracts and leases can be granted. See I.C.4, above.)

D. Statutory Provisions. The proposed order should specify those sections of the Bankruptcy Code and Bankruptcy Rules that are being relied on, and identify those sections, such as Bankruptcy Rule 6004(h), that are, to the extent permitted by law, proposed to be limited or abridged.

E. Good Faith/No Collusion. The transaction has been proposed and entered into by the debtors and the purchaser without collusion, in good faith, and from arm's-length bargaining positions. The proposed Sale Order should also specify that neither the debtor nor the purchaser have engaged in any conduct that would cause or permit the transaction to be avoided under Bankruptcy Code section 363(n).

[1] The term "debtor" includes "debtor in possession" and "trustee," as appropriate under the particular circumstances.

[2] With the exception of providing for such disclosure, these Guidelines do not express a preference for public over private sales as a means to maximize the sale price.

[3] When multiple asset sales over time are expected, a debtor should consider seeking Court approval of global bidding procedures to avoid the need to obtain Court approval of procedures for each sale. Similarly, the debtor should consider seeking Court approval of global notice and other appropriate procedures to facilitate sales of assets of limited value or de minimis sales that do not warrant an auction or a

separate motion for each sale. What constitutes a de minimis sale will depend on the facts of each case. See Local Rule 6004-1.

[4] It is expected that the debtor will also share its evaluation of bids with key parties-in-interest, such as representatives of official committees, and that it will in its reasonable judgment identify the winning bidder only after consultation with such parties.

[5] The fact that a similar provision was included in an order entered in a different case does not constitute a justification.

[6] In larger cases, a sale of significant assets may also require notice of the proposed sale in publications of national circulation or other appropriate publications.

[7] In the case of publicly traded debt securities, notice to indenture trustees and record holders may be sufficient to the extent that the identity of beneficial holders is not known.

[8] Notice must be given to applicable taxing authorities, including the state attorney general or other appropriate legal officer, affected by the relief requested under section 1146(a) of the Bankruptcy Code.

[9] This notice may be provided in a separate schedule sent only to the parties to such agreements.

[10] Each and every federal, state and local government agency or department may be directed to accept any and all documents and instruments necessary and appropriate to consummate the transactions contemplated by the purchase agreement.

[11] If any person or entity that has filed financing statements, mortgages, mechanic's liens, lis pendens, or other documents evidencing interests in the assets has not delivered to the debtor prior to the closing date termination statements, instruments of satisfaction, and/or releases of all such interests, the debtor may be authorized and directed to execute and file such statements, instruments, releases and other documents on behalf of such person or entity. The debtor should try to anticipate whether there are any complex allocation issues presented by the proposed 'free and clear' relief.

GENERAL ORDER M–349. IN RE: ORDER VACATING GENERAL ORDER # M–295 REGARDING ATTORNEY BAR IDENTIFICATION NUMBERS

WHEREAS, General Order M–295, dated February 9, 2004, requires, inter alia, an attorney to endorse papers submitted for filing with the Court using either the last four digits of the attorney's social security number or the four-digit number that the attorney has duly registered with the Clerk of the United States District Court for the Southern District of New York pursuant to Local Civil Rule 11.1.(b) of the Rules of the United States District Courts for the Southern and Eastern Districts of New York; and

WHEREAS, Civil Rule 11.1(b) of the Local District Rules has been repealed; it is hereby

ORDERED, that General Order M–295 is vacated, effective as of the date of this Order.

Dated: New York, New York,
    March 21, 2008.

GENERAL ORDER M–353. IN RE: ORDER VACATING GENERAL ORDER #M–290 REGARDING PERSONAL DATA IDENTIFIERS

WHEREAS, General Order M–290, dated November 20, 2003, requires, inter alia, debtors or debtors' attorneys to submit redacted personal data identifiers on required official bankruptcy forms in order to protect personal privacy; and

WHEREAS, Federal Rule of Bankruptcy Procedure 9037, which became effective on December 1, 2007, supersedes General Order M–290; it is hereby

ORDERED, that General Order M–290 is vacated nunc pro tunc to December 1, 2007.

Dated: New York, New York
        July 11, 2008.

UNITED STATES BANKRUPTCY COURT FOR THE EASTERN DISTRICT OF NEW YORK

Effective July 1, 1997

Including Amendments Received Through
September 15, 2008

Research Note

These rules may be searched electronically on Westlaw in the NY-RULES database; updates to these rules may be found on Westlaw in NY-RULESUPDATES. For search tips, and a detailed summary of database content, consult the Westlaw Scope Screen of each database.

Rule
1001–1.   Short Title; Applicability.

PART I.   COMMENCEMENT OF CASE; PROCEEDINGS RELATING TO PETITION AND ORDER FOR RELIEF

1002–1.   Filing of Petition.
1005–1.   Debtor's Address in Petition.
1005–2.   Amending Caption to Correct Debtor's Name.
1007–1.   List of Creditors.
1007–2.   Exemptions and Waivers Regarding Credit Counseling Requirement; Waiver of Personal Financial Management Course.
1007–3.   Mailing Matrix.
1007–4.   Debtor's Affidavit to Be Filed in Chapter 11 Cases.
1009–1.   Amendments of Voluntary Petitions, Lists, Schedules and Statements.
1013–1.   Involuntary Petitions.
1017–1.   Dismissal of Case After Conversion.
1073–1.   Assignment of Cases and Proceedings.
1073–2.   Disclosure of Related Cases.
1073–3.   Corporate Disclosure.
1074–1.   Corporate Resolution; Partnership Statement.

PART II.   OFFICERS AND ADMINISTRATION; NOTICES; MEETINGS; EXAMINATIONS; ELECTIONS; ATTORNEYS AND ACCOUNTANTS

2002–1.   Notices of Presentment.
2002–2.   Notice to Governmental Agencies.
2003–1.   Mandatory Disclosures in Chapter 13 Cases.
2014–1.   Employment of Professional Persons.
2015–1.   Monthly Reports in All Chapter 11, 12 and Business Chapter 13 Cases.
2016–1.   Compensation of Professionals.
2016–2.   Final Compensation or Reimbursement of Expenses in Chapter 7 Cases.
2017–1.   Description of Pre–Petition Services of Debtor's Counsel in Chapter 7 or 13 Cases.
2090–1.   Practice Before the Court; Withdrawal as Attorney of Record; Suspension.

Rule
2090–2.   Appearance by Debtor's Counsel in Adversary Proceedings, Contested Matters, Etc.

PART III.   CLAIMS AND DISTRIBUTION TO CREDITORS AND EQUITY INTEREST HOLDERS; PLANS

3007–1.   Objections to Claims.
3007–2.   Modification of Schedules of Claims.
3015–1.   Chapter 13 Plan.
3015–2.   Chapter 13 Plan Modification.
3015–3.   Hearing on Confirmation of Chapter 13 Plan.
3016–1.   Omission of Separate Disclosure Statement in Chapter 11 Small Business Cases: Disclaimer.
3017–1.   Proposed Disclosure Statements in Chapter 9 and 11 Cases: Transmittal and Disclaimer.
3018–1.   Summary and Certification of Acceptance or Rejection of Plans in Chapter 9 and 11 Cases.
3020–1.   Time for Objecting to Confirmation in Chapter 9 and 11 Cases; Withdrawal of Objections.
3020–2.   Confirmation Orders in Chapter 9 and 11 Cases.
3021–1.   Confirmation Requirements in Chapter 9 and 11 Cases [Abrogated].
3022–1.   Final Decree.

PART IV.   THE DEBTOR: DUTIES AND BENEFITS

4001–1.   Relief From Automatic Stay.
4001–2.   Orders Confirming the Inapplicability of the Automatic Stay.
4001–3.   Orders Continuing or Imposing the Automatic Stay.
4001–4.   Payment and Cure of Pre–Petition Judgment of Possession Involving Residential Property.
4001–5.   Cash Collateral and Obtaining Credit.
4002–1.   Personal Identifiers and Tax Information of the Debtor.
4003–1.   Amendment to Claim of Exemptions.
4003–2.   Objection to a Claim of Exemption.
4004–1.   Settlement or Dismissal of Proceedings Objecting to Discharge.

Rule
4007–1. Settlement or Dismissal of Proceedings Objecting to Dischargeability.

PART V. COURTS AND CLERKS

5001–1. Clerk's Office: Contact Information.
5001–2. Clerk's Office: Hours; After Hours Filing.
5005–1. Filing and Transmittal of Papers in Non–Electronic Cases.
5005–2. Filing by Electronic Means.
5010–1. Reopening Cases.
5011–1. Withdrawal of Reference.
5070–1. Calendars and Scheduling.
5073–1. Cameras, Radio, Recorders and Other Electronic Devices [Abrogated].
5075–1. Use of Services and Agents.
5080–1. Fees—General.

PART VI. COLLECTION AND LIQUIDATION OF THE ESTATE

6004–1. Sale of Property, Appraisals and Auctions.
6005–1. Auctioneers.
6007–1. Abandonment or Disposition of Property.

PART VII. ADVERSARY PROCEEDINGS

7005–1. Filing of Discovery–Related Documents.
7007–1. Discovery Related Motions.
7024–1. Notice of Claim of Unconstitutionality [Abrogated].
7054–1. Taxable Costs.
7055–1. Default Judgment.
7056–1. Summary Judgment.

PART VIII. APPEALS

8004–1. Copies of Notice of Appeal and Certification for Direct Appeal to Circuit Court.
8006–1. Record on Appeal.
8016–1. Order, Judgment or Remand by Appellate Court.

PART IX. GENERAL PROVISIONS

9001–1. Definitions.
9004–1. Papers—Requirements of Form.
9004–2. Caption—Papers, General.
9005.1–1. Notice of Claim of Unconstitutionality.
9006–1. Time for Service and Filing of Motions and Answering Papers.
9011–1. Signing of Papers.
9013–1. Motion Practice.
9014–1. Contested Matters.

Rule
9018–1. Documents Filed Under Seal in Electronic Cases.
9019–1. Alternative Dispute Resolution—Mediation.
9021–1. Entry of Orders, Judgments and Decrees.
9023–1. Costs; New Trials; Motions for Reconsideration.
9025–1. Sureties.
9028–1. Unavailability of a Judge.
9036–1. Consent to Notice by Electronic Transmission.
9036–2. Consent to Service by Electronic Transmission.
9070–1. Custody of Exhibits.
9072–1. Settlement or Submission of Order, Judgment or Decree.
9077–1. Orders to Show Cause; Ex Parte Orders; Orders Shortening Time.

APPENDIX

Local Rules of the United States District Courts for the Southern and Eastern Districts of New York (Effective April 15, 1997) Referred to in these Rules.

SELECTED ORDERS

Order
473. Electronic Means for Filing, Signing, and Verification of Documents.
476. Mandatory Filing of Documents by Electronic Means.
487. Transfer of Cases in which Petition was Inadvertently Filed in this District.
488. Dismissal of Duplicate Petition Filed in Error.
489. Dismissal of Cases Exhibiting Certain Defects.
490. Dismissal of Cases for which Filing Fee has not been Paid.
497. In the Matter of Adoption of Interim Bankruptcy Rules[1].
501. Rules Governing Procedures for Appointment of Pro Bono Counsel in Bankruptcy Proceedings From a Bankruptcy Pro Bono Panel.
502. Procedures for Payment and Cure of Pre–Petition Judgment of Possession Involving Residential Property.
504. Revised Procedural Form B 240, Reaffirmation Agreement [Abrogated].
506. Adoption of Interim Bankruptcy Rule 1007.
512. Limited Access Filing of Documents by Electronic Means.
517. Revised and Reformatted Reaffirmation Agreement and Order (Procedural Forms B 240A and B 240B).
533. In re: Adoption of Form for Motions for Relief from Stay to Foreclose a Mortgage on Real Property or a Security Interest in a Cooperative Apartment.

RULE 1001–1. SHORT TITLE; APPLICABILITY

(a) **Short Title.** These rules shall be known as the "E.D.N.Y. Local Bankruptcy Rules."

(b) **Applicability.**

(i) The E.D.N.Y. Local Bankruptcy Rules, as amended as of May 28, 2008, shall supersede the Former Local Bankruptcy Rules and shall apply to all cases and proceedings in this Court.

(ii) The appropriate citation form for an E.D.N.Y. Local Bankruptcy Rule is "E.D.N.Y. LBR _____." For example, this rule shall be cited as "E.D.N.Y. LBR 1001–1."

(c) **Modification or Suspension.** In the interest of justice or for cause, the Court may modify or suspend the requirements set forth in these rules.

REFERENCE: Individual chambers rules of Judges, when applicable.

[Effective July 1, 1997. Amended July 1, 1999; May 28, 2008.]

PART I. COMMENCEMENT OF CASE; PROCEEDINGS RELATING TO PETITION AND ORDER FOR RELIEF

RULE 1002–1. FILING OF PETITION

(a) Petition.

(i) A petition commencing a case under any chapter of the Bankruptcy Code in which the debtor's address is located in Kings, Richmond, or Queens County shall be filed in the office of the Clerk in the Brooklyn courthouse or designated as a Brooklyn case if filed electronically.

(ii) A petition commencing a case under any chapter of the Bankruptcy Code in which the debtor's address is located in Nassau or Suffolk County shall be filed in the office of the Clerk in the Central Islip courthouse or designated as a Central Islip case if filed electronically.

(b) Electronic Filing. Notwithstanding subdivision (a) of this rule, a petition commencing a case under any chapter of the Bankruptcy Code shall be filed by electronic means in the manner specified by the General Order on Electronic Filing Procedures and these rules.

(c) Incomplete Filing. In the event that a petition is submitted without full compliance with all requirements, the Clerk shall accept the same for filing and shall provide the debtor, debtor's counsel and the trustee, if any, with a notice of the deficiencies.

[Effective July 1, 1997; amended effective July 1, 1998; July 1, 1999; May 28, 2008.]

CROSS REFERENCE: E.D.N.Y. LBR 1073–1, 9011–1.

REFERENCES: Bankruptcy Code § 521; Court's Website; General Order on Electronic Filing Procedures

RULE 1005–1. DEBTOR'S ADDRESS IN PETITION

If the debtor's post office address is not the debtor's residence or place of business, the petition shall also state the debtor's residence or place of business, including the street number, street, apartment or suite number and zip code.

[Effective July 1, 1997.]

RULE 1005–2. AMENDING CAPTION TO CORRECT DEBTOR'S NAME

If the debtor's name is incorrect in the caption of the petition, the debtor shall file an application and proposed order amending the caption to correct the debtor's name.

[Effective May 28, 2008.]

REFERENCE: Court's Website

Committee Note: A form of order is located at the intake counter of the Clerk's Office and at the Court's Website.

RULE 1007–1. LIST OF CREDITORS

(a) Creditor List. In addition to the schedules, a list shall be filed which sets forth the names of all creditors in alphabetical order (the "Creditor List"). The Creditor List shall also set forth the post office address, zip code, and the specific amount of debt, if known, owed to each listed creditor. The provider of the Creditor List shall certify that it is accurate.

(b) Schedules and Lists Filed After Filing of Petition. Schedules D, E, and F which were not submitted at the time of filing of the petition but are filed thereafter shall be accompanied by (i) Local Form No. USBC–64 entitled "Affidavit Pursuant to Local Rule 1007–1(b)" and (ii) the applicable filing fee.

[Effective July 1, 1997; amended effective July 1, 1999; May 28, 2008.]

CROSS–REFERENCE: E.D.N.Y. LBR 1009–1

REFERENCE: Court's Website

Committee Note: Local Form No. USBC–64 is available at the intake counter of the Clerk's office and at the Court's Website.

RULE 1007–2. EXEMPTIONS AND WAIVERS REGARDING CREDIT COUNSELING REQUIREMENT; WAIVER OF PERSONAL FINANCIAL MANAGEMENT COURSE

(a) A motion pursuant to Bankruptcy Code § 109(h)(3)(B) for a further exemption from the credit counseling requirement imposed by Bankruptcy Code § 109(h)(1) shall be made on notice to the trustee and the United States trustee, and shall explain the circumstances which warrant the relief requested.

(b) A motion pursuant to Bankruptcy Code § 109(h)(4) for a waiver of the credit counseling requirement imposed by Bankruptcy Code § 109(h)(1) or a waiver of the requirement to file a statement regarding completion of an instructional course concerning personal financial management imposed by Bankruptcy Code § 727(a)(11) shall be on notice to the trustee and the United States trustee and should be supported by documentary evidence of the debtor's entitlement to the relief requested.

[Effective July 1, 1997; amended effective May 28, 2008.]

REFERENCES: Bankruptcy Code §§ 109(h)(1), (3) and (4), 727(a)(11)

RULE 1007–3. MAILING MATRIX

(a) General Requirements.

(i) At the time of filing a voluntary petition or within 15 days following the entry of an order for relief on an involuntary petition, the debtor shall file a mailing matrix which shall include, in alphabetical order, the name and last known mailing address (including zip codes) for every scheduled creditor. The mailing matrix shall also include those agencies and officers of the United States entitled to receive notice under Bankruptcy Rule 2002(j).

(ii) If the debtor is a partnership, the mailing matrix shall contain the names and current mailing addresses of each general and limited partner.

(iii) If the debtor is a corporation, the mailing matrix shall contain: (1) the names and current mailing addresses of the present officers and directors and the position held by each, or if none, the immediate past officers and past directors; and (2) the name and address of any person who may be served pursuant to Bankruptcy Rule 7004(b)(3). In addition, the debtor shall file with its list of equity security holders a separate mailing matrix containing the name and last known address or place of business of each equity security holder.

(b) Accuracy of Information Provided and Amendment of Mailing Matrix. The debtor and debtor's attorney are responsible for the preparation of the mailing matrix and any amendments thereto. Upon the need for any amendment to a mailing matrix, the debtor shall file an amended creditor mailing matrix together with a list of all creditors who were added or deleted. The debtor shall file Local Form No. USBC–44 entitled "Verification of Mailing Matrix/List of Creditors."

[Effective July 1, 1997; amended effective May 28, 2008.]

REFERENCES: Court's Website; General Order on Electronic Filing Procedures

Committee Note: Specifications for preparation of the mailing matrix are available at the intake counter of the Clerk's office and at the Court's Website. Local Form No. USBC–44 is available at the intake counter of the Clerk's office and at the Court's Website.

RULE 1007–4. DEBTOR'S AFFIDAVIT TO BE FILED IN CHAPTER 11 CASES

(a) Contents of Affidavit. In addition to the requirements set forth in Bankruptcy Rule 1007, a debtor in a chapter 11 case shall file an affidavit setting forth:

(i) whether the debtor is a small business debtor within the meaning of Bankruptcy Code § 101(51D);

(ii) the nature of the debtor's business and a statement of the circumstances leading to the debtor's filing under chapter 11;

(iii) in a case originally commenced under chapter 7, 12 or 13, the name and address of any trustee appointed in the case and, in a case originally commenced under chapter 7, the names and addresses of the members of any creditors' committee elected under Bankruptcy Code § 705;

(iv) the names and addresses of the members of, and professionals employed by, any committee organized prior to the order for relief in the chapter 11 case, and a description of the circumstances surrounding the formation of the committee and the date of its formation;

(v) with respect to each of the holders of the 20 largest general unsecured claims, excluding insiders: name, address (including the number, street, apartment or suite number, and zip code, if not included in the post office address), telephone number, name(s) of person(s) familiar with the debtor's account, amount of the claim, and whether the claim is contingent, unliquidated, disputed, or partially secured;

(vi) with respect to each of the holders of the 5 largest secured claims: name, address (including the number, street, apartment or suite number, and zip code, if not included in the post office address), amount of the claim, a description and an estimate of the value of the collateral securing the claim, and whether the claim or lien is disputed;

(vii) a summary of the debtor's assets and liabilities;

(viii) the number and classes of shares of stock, debentures, or other securities of the debtor that are publicly held, and the number of record holders thereof, listing separately those held by each of the debtor's officers and directors and the amounts so held;

(ix) a list of all of the debtor's property in the possession or custody of any custodian, public officer, mortgagee, pledgee, assignee of rents, or secured creditor, or agent for any such entity, giving the name, address, and telephone number of each such entity, the title of any proceeding relating thereto, and the court in which it is pending;

(x) a list of the premises owned, leased, or held under any other arrangement from which the debtor operates its business;

(xi) the location of the debtor's significant assets, the location of its books and records, and the nature, location, and value of any assets held by the debtor outside the territorial limits of the United States;

(xii) the nature and present status of each action or proceeding, pending or threatened, against the debtor or its property where a judgment against the debtor or a seizure of its property may be imminent;

(xiii) the names of the debtor's existing senior management, their tenure with the debtor, and a summary of their relevant responsibilities and experience;

(xiv) the estimated amount of the weekly payroll to employees (exclusive of officers, directors, stockholders, partners and members) for the 30–day period following the filing of the chapter 11 petition;

(xv) the amount paid and proposed to be paid for services for the 30–day period following the filing of the chapter 11 petition—

(A) if the debtor is a corporation, to officers and directors;

(B) if the debtor is an individual or a partnership, to the individual or the members of the partnership; and

(C) if a financial or business consultant has been retained by the debtor, to the consultant;

(xvi) a schedule, for the 30–day period following the filing of the chapter 11 petition, of estimated cash receipts and disbursements, net cash gain or loss, obligations and receivables expected to accrue but remaining unpaid, other than professional fees, and any other information relevant to an understanding of the foregoing; and

(xvii) such additional information as may be necessary to fully inform the Court of the debtor's rehabilitation prospects.

(b) When to File. In a chapter 11 case, upon the entry of an order for relief, the affidavit shall be filed forthwith, but no later than 15 days after the date on which the order for relief is entered.

(c) Waiver of Requirements. Upon motion of the debtor on notice to the United States trustee showing that it is impracticable or impossible to furnish any of the foregoing information, the Court may waive any of the foregoing provisions, with the exception of those

contained in paragraphs (i) through (vii) of subdivision (a) of this rule.

[Effective May 28, 2008.]

REFERENCES: Bankruptcy Code §§ 101(51D), 705

RULE 1009–1. AMENDMENTS OF VOLUNTARY PETITIONS, LISTS, SCHEDULES AND STATEMENTS

(a) Effectuation of Amendment. An order is not required to file an amended voluntary petition, list, schedule, or statement by the debtor. Amendments to Schedules D, E, or F shall be accompanied by (i) Local Form No. USBC–63 entitled "Affidavit Pursuant to Local Rule 1009–1(a)" and (ii) the applicable filing fee. An amendment shall not be effective until proof of service in accordance with subdivision (b) of this rule has been filed. If a creditor is added or deleted, an amended mailing matrix shall also be filed.

(b) Notice of Amendment. A complete copy of the voluntary petition, list, schedule, or statement, as amended, together with Local Form No. USBC–63, shall be served by the amending party upon:

(i) the United States trustee;

(ii) the trustee;

(iii) all creditors who were added or deleted; and

(iv) any other party affected thereby.

If the amendment affects claimed exemptions, the amending party must also serve all creditors. If the amendment adds a creditor, the papers to be served on such creditor shall consist of the amendment, together with copies of all notices previously sent to creditors that appear in the Court's docket, including without limitation the notice informing creditors of the date by which all proofs of claim must be filed. If the amendment modifies an existing creditor's claim, service on such creditor shall include any notices informing creditors of the date by which proofs of claim must be filed.

(c) Number of Copies.

(i) Filing in connection with Non-electronic Cases: whenever amendments are made to a debtor's voluntary petition, lists, schedules, or statements, the amending party shall file with the Clerk:

(A) in a chapter 7, 12, or 13 case, an original and 3 copies of the document as amended; or

(B) in a chapter 11 case, an original and 6 copies of the document as amended.

(ii) Filing in connection with ECF cases: copies of the voluntary petition, lists, schedules or documents, as amended, are not required.

[Effective July 1, 1997; amended effective July 1, 1999; May 28, 2008.]

CROSS–REFERENCES: E.D.N.Y. LBR 3007–3, 4003–1, 9004–1

REFERENCES: Court's Website; General Order on Electronic Filing Procedures

Committee Note: Local Form No. USBC–63 is available at the intake counter of the Clerk's office and at the Court's Website.

RULE 1013–1. INVOLUNTARY PETITIONS

(a) Entry of Order for Relief Upon Default of Alleged Debtor. An order for relief shall be entered if proof of service of the summons and involuntary petition has been filed and the alleged debtor has not timely responded.

(b) Notice of Entry. Upon entry of an order for relief in an involuntary case, the Clerk shall forthwith serve a copy of the order with notice of entry upon the petitioners, the debtor, the debtor's attorney of record, if any, and the United States trustee.

(c) Dismissal. The Court may dismiss the case if proof of service of the summons and involuntary petition pursuant to Bankruptcy Rule 7004 is not timely filed.

[Effective July 1, 1997; amended effective May 28, 2008.]

REFERENCE: Bankruptcy Rule 7004

RULE 1017–1. DISMISSAL OF CASE AFTER CONVERSION

If a case has been converted from chapter 11 to chapter 7, and the trustee is seeking to dismiss the case for failure of the debtor to attend the meeting of creditors under Bankruptcy Code § 341, the trustee must file an affidavit setting forth what efforts, if any, have been made to locate and serve the debtor.

[Effective July 1, 1997; amended effective May 28, 2008.]

RULE 1073–1. ASSIGNMENT OF CASES AND PROCEEDINGS

(a) Assignment of Cases. The Clerk shall randomly assign cases to the Judges. Notwithstanding the foregoing, the Court may adopt internal procedures whereby cases are assigned to Judges sitting in Brooklyn or Central Islip depending upon the location of the debtor's address.

(b) Petitions of Affiliates or Related Cases. Notwithstanding subdivision (a) of this rule, cases involving affiliated or related debtors shall be assigned to the Judge to whom the first such case was assigned, and any case subsequently filed by a debtor who has previously filed a petition shall be assigned to the Judge to whom the last such case was assigned.

(c) Assignments and Reassignments. Notwithstanding the provisions of this rule, the Chief Judge may, in the interests of justice or the proper administration of the Court, assign or re-assign cases or proceedings.

[Effective July 1, 1997; amended effective March 1, 1998; July 1, 1999; May 28, 2008.]

CROSS–REFERENCE: E.D.N.Y. LBR 1002–1

RULE 1073–2. DISCLOSURE OF RELATED CASES

(a) Definition of Related Cases. Cases shall be deemed "Related Cases" for purposes of this rule and E.D.N.Y. LBR 1073–1 if the earlier case was pending at any time within 8 years before the filing of the current petition, and the debtors in such cases:

(i) are the same;

(ii) are spouses or ex-spouses;

(iii) are affiliates, as defined in Bankruptcy Code § 101(2);

(iv) are general partners in the same partnership;

(v) are a partnership and one or more of its general partners;

(vi) are partnerships which share one or more common general partners; or

(vii) have, or within 180 days of the commencement of either of the Related Cases had, an interest in property that was or is included in the property of the other debtor's estate under Bankruptcy Code § 541(a).

(b) Disclosure of Related Cases.

(i) A petition commencing a case shall be accompanied by Local Form No. USBC–2 entitled "E.D.N.Y. LBR 1073–2 Statement."

(ii) The E.D.N.Y. LBR 1073–2 Statement shall be executed by the debtor or any other petitioner under penalty of perjury and shall disclose, to the petitioner's best knowledge, information, and belief:

(A) whether any Related Case is pending or has been pending at any time;

(B) the name of the debtor in such Related Case;

(C) the case number of such Related Case;

(D) the district and division in which such Related Case is or was pending;

(E) the Judge to whom such Related Case was assigned;

(F) the current status of such Related Case;

(G) the manner in which the cases are related; and

(H) any real property listed in a debtor's Schedule A which was also listed in a Schedule A filed in a Related case.

(c) Sanctions. The failure to fully and truthfully provide all information required by the E.D.N.Y. LBR 1073–2 Statement may subject the debtor or any other petitioner and their attorney to appropriate sanctions, including without limitation, conversion, the appointment of a trustee, or the dismissal of the case with prejudice.

[Adopted effective July 1, 1999; amended effective May 28, 2008.]

CROSS–REFERENCE: E.D.N.Y. LBR 1073–1

REFERENCES: Bankruptcy Code §§ 101(2), 541(a); Court's Website

Committee Note: Local Form No. USBC–2 is available at the Court's Website and at the intake counter of the Clerk's office.

RULE 1073–3. CORPORATE DISCLOSURE

(a) Who Must File. Any corporation that is a debtor shall file a statement that identifies any corporation that directly or indirectly owns 10% or more of any class of the debtor's equity interests, or states that there are no entities to report under this subdivision (the "E.D.N.Y. LBR 1073–3 Statement").

(b) Time for Filing.

(i) In a voluntary case, the debtor shall file the E.D.N.Y. LBR 1073–3 Statement with the petition.

(ii) In an involuntary case, the debtor shall file the E.D.N.Y. LBR 1073–3 Statement within 15 days after the entry of the order for relief.

(iii) Upon any change in the information required under this rule, the debtor shall promptly file an amended E.D.N.Y. LBR 1073–3 Statement.

[Effective May 28, 2008.]

REFERENCE: Bankruptcy Rule 7007.1; Federal Rule of Civil Procedure 7.1

RULE 1074–1. CORPORATE RESOLUTION; PARTNERSHIP STATEMENT

(a) Corporate Resolution. A voluntary petition or consent to an involuntary petition filed by a corporation shall be accompanied by a duly attested copy of the corporate resolution authorizing, or other appropriate authorization for, the filing.

(b) Partnership or Limited Liability Partnership Statements. A voluntary petition filed by, or consent to an involuntary petition filed on behalf of, a partnership or limited liability partnership shall be accompanied by a duly attested statement that all partners whose consent is required for the filing have consented.

(c) Limited Liability Company Statements. A voluntary petition filed by, or consent to an involuntary petition filed on behalf of a limited liability company shall be accompanied by a duly attested statement by the managing member, or by at least one member if there is no managing member, that the filing is duly authorized.

[Effective July 1, 1997; amended effective May 28, 2008.]

PART II. OFFICERS AND ADMINISTRATION; NOTICES; MEETINGS; EXAMINATIONS; ELECTIONS; ATTORNEYS AND ACCOUNTANTS

RULE 2002–1. NOTICES OF PRESENTMENT

(a) Contents of Notice of Presentment. Whenever "notice and a hearing" (as defined in Bankruptcy Code § 102(1)) are specified in the Bankruptcy Code or Bankruptcy Rules but a hearing is not mandatory, the entity proposing to act or obtain an order, in lieu of proceeding by notice of hearing, may proceed by filing a motion or application with the Clerk, together with proof of service and a notice of presentment. The notice of presentment shall set forth:

(i) the date by which objections or responses to the proposed action or order shall be served and filed;

(ii) the date and time when the action will be taken or the proposed order will be presented for signature if there is no objection, and a statement that the action will be taken or the order may be entered without a hearing unless a timely objection is made; and

(iii) the date on which a hearing will be held if a timely objection is made.

(b) Proposed Order. A copy of the proposed order shall be filed and served along with the notice of presentment.

(c) Time for Notice. A notice of presentment under subdivision (a) of this rule shall provide at least 20 days' notice of the date set for the proposed action or the presentment of the proposed order. If papers are served by first-class mail, an additional 3 days shall be added to the minimum service requirement. If papers are served by overnight mail or courier, an additional day shall be added to the minimum service requirement.

(d) Entities to Receive Notice. In addition to the requirements of Bankruptcy Rule 2002 and E.D.N.Y. LBR 2002–2, a notice of presentment under subdivision (a) of this rule shall be served upon any entity having or claiming an interest in the subject matter of the proposed action or order or who otherwise would be affected by the proposed action or order.

(e) Objection. Any objection to the proposed action or order shall be in writing, set forth the nature of the objector's interest in the estate, state the reasons and legal basis for the objection, and be served on the proponent and filed at least 3 Business Days prior to the date set for the proposed action or the presentment of the proposed order. The objection and proof of service shall be filed and a courtesy copy shall be provided to chambers.

[Effective July 1, 1997; amended effective July 1, 1999; May 28, 2008.]

CROSS–REFERENCES: E.D.N.Y. LBR 2002–2, 3015–2, 4001–1, 5070–1
Committee Note: Each Judge's chambers should also be consulted regarding the relief that may be sought by notice of presentment.

RULE 2002–2. NOTICE TO GOVERNMENTAL AGENCIES

(a) United States Trustee. Unless the case is a chapter 9 case or the United States trustee requests otherwise, any notice required to be given to creditors also shall be given to the United States trustee. Notices to the United States trustee shall be sent to the address specified at the Court's Website.

(b) Internal Revenue Service. Except as otherwise requested by it, any notices required to be given to the Internal Revenue Service shall also be given to the United States Attorney for the Eastern District of New York and the Tax Division of the U.S. Department of Justice. Notices to these entities shall be sent to the addresses specified at the Court's Website.

(c) New York State Department of Taxation and Finance. Except as otherwise requested by it, any notices required to be given to the New York State Department of Taxation and Finance shall also be given to the New York State Attorney General. Notices to these entities shall be sent to the addresses specified at the Court's Website.

[Effective July 1, 1997; amended effective July 1, 1999; May 28, 2008.]

REFERENCE: Court's Website
Committee Note: The addresses referred to in this local rule are available at the intake counter of the Clerk's office and at the Court's Website.

RULE 2003–1. MANDATORY DISCLOSURES IN CHAPTER 13 CASES

(a) In all chapter 13 cases, the debtor shall provide the following documents to the trustee no later than 7 Business Days before the first date set for the meeting of creditors pursuant to Bankruptcy Code § 341(a):

(i) copies of all payment advices or other evidence of payment received within 60 days before the date of the filing of the petition, by the debtor from any employer of the debtor, or a written statement that such proof of income does not exist;

(ii) copies of affidavits of contribution and copies of all payment advices or other evidence of payment received within 60 days before the date of the filing of the petition, by each person contributing to the proposed plan or to payment of expenses of the debtor's household;

(iii) except in cases where the debtor proposes to pay 100% to unsecured creditors, documentation (other than tax assessments) of the current value of all real property, condominiums, cooperative apartments, vacant land, cemetery plots and/or timeshares in which the debtor has an ownership interest. If a valuation is prepared by a real estate broker, then the broker shall (A) have personally inspected the premises, (B) maintain an office in the vicinity of the premises, and (C) provide information on 4 recent comparable sales. All valuations must be less than 90 days old prior to filing;

(iv) copies of leases for all real property for which the debtor is lessor;

(v) in a case where the debtor had a prior chapter 13 case pending within a year of the filing date, a copy of a detailed affidavit of changed circumstances, describing the disposition of each prior case and explaining how the debtor's circumstances have changed; and

(vi) copies of canceled checks, receipts, money orders, or other documentation of payment of all mortgage installments, real property lease payments, auto loan payments, and co-op or condo maintenance and management fees that have come due since the petition was filed.

(b) A debtor shall provide the following documents to the trustee no later than 7 days before the first date set for confirmation of the chapter 13 plan:

(i) copies of canceled checks, receipts, money orders or other documentation of payment of all mortgage installments and real property lease payments that have come due since the disclosure was made under subdivision (a)(vi) of this rule;

(ii) a copy of an affidavit by the debtor stating:

(A) whether the debtor has paid all amounts that are required to be paid under a domestic support obligation and that first became payable after the date of the filing of the petition if the debtor is required by a judicial or administrative order or by statute to pay such domestic support obligation; or

(B) that the debtor has no domestic support obligations; and

(iii) a copy of an affidavit by the debtor stating whether the debtor has filed all applicable federal, state, and local tax returns as required by Bankruptcy Code § 1308.

(c) A debtor shall file the original affidavits required under subdivisions (a)(ii) and (v), and (b)(ii) and (iii) of this rule.

(d) A debtor shall promptly provide to the trustee any other documents within the scope of Bankruptcy Rule 2004(b) that the trustee may request from time to time.

[Adopted effective July 1, 1999; amended effective May 28, 2008.]

CROSS–REFERENCE: E.D.N.Y. LBR 4002–1
REFERENCES: Bankruptcy Code §§ 1308, 1325(a)(8), (9); Bankruptcy Rule 2004(b)
Committee Note: Subdivision (a)(1) of former E.D.N.Y. LBR 2003–1 was abrogated because it was inconsistent with Bankruptcy Code § 521(e)(2)(A)(i).

RULE 2014–1. EMPLOYMENT OF PROFESSIONAL PERSONS

(a) In addition to the requirements set forth in Bankruptcy Rule 2014(a), an application for the employment of a professional person pursuant to Bankruptcy Code §§ 327, 1103 or 1114 shall state:

(i) the terms and conditions of the employment, including the terms of any retainer, hourly fee, or contingent fee arrangement;

(ii) all compensation already paid or promised to the professional person in contemplation of or in connection with the services to be performed, and the specific source of such compensation; and

(iii) whether the professional person has previously rendered any professional services to the trustee, debtor, debtor in possession, the extent thereof and the status of the compensation therefor.

(b) In addition to the requirements set forth in Bankruptcy Rule 2014(a), the application referred to in subdivision (a) shall be accompanied by a verified statement of the person to be employed stating that such person does not hold or represent an interest adverse to the estate except as specifically disclosed therein, and where employment is sought pursuant to Bankruptcy Code § 327(a), that the professional is disinterested.

(c) In addition to the requirements set forth in subdivisions (a) and (b), and Bankruptcy Rule 2014(a), an application seeking authorization to employ an accountant shall include a verified statement by an authorized representative of the accounting firm that sets forth:

(i) whether or not the accountant is a certified public accountant; and

(ii) the estimated cost of the accountant's proposed services, the basis of such estimate and the extent to which the accountant is familiar with the books or accounts of the debtor.

(d) All ex parte proposed orders and supporting documentation for employment of any professional must be submitted to the United States trustee for review prior to filing.

[Effective July 1, 1997; amended effective May 28, 2008.]

CROSS–REFERENCE: E.D.N.Y. LBR 6005–1
REFERENCES: Bankruptcy Code §§ 327, 1103

RULE 2015–1. MONTHLY REPORTS IN ALL CHAPTER 11, 12 AND BUSINESS CHAPTER 13 CASES

The debtor in possession or trustee in all chapter 11 and 12 cases, or a chapter 13 debtor engaged in business within the meaning of Bankruptcy Code § 1304(a), shall file and serve upon the United States trustee and counsel for the creditors' committee (if any) in a chapter 11 or 12 case, or the trustee in a chapter 13 case, and provide to chambers, a verified monthly report no later than the 20th day of each month, which shall be completed in the manner prescribed by the United States trustee Guidelines, and in the case of a small business chapter 11 debtor, in accordance with Bankruptcy Code § 308 when such provisions shall become effective. Failure to file required reports may constitute cause for dismissal or conversion of the case.

[Effective July 1, 1997; amended effective May 28, 2008.]

REFERENCES: Bankruptcy Code §§ 308, 1304(a)

RULE 2016–1. COMPENSATION OF PROFESSIONALS

A person seeking an award of compensation or reimbursement of expenses shall comply with the requirements contained in any fee guidelines promulgated by the United States trustee. A copy of the order authorizing the retention of the professional shall accompany all such applications.

[Effective July 1, 1997; amended effective July 1, 1999; May 28, 2008.]

RULE 2016–2. FINAL COMPENSATION OR REIMBURSEMENT OF EXPENSES IN CHAPTER 7 CASES

A person seeking a final award of compensation or reimbursement of expenses in a chapter 7 case shall file and serve an application on the trustee and the United States trustee no later than 20 days prior to the date of the hearing on the trustee's final account. Failure to file and serve an application within the time prescribed by this rule may result in its disallowance. Objections, if any, to such application shall be filed at least 5 Business Days prior to the date of the hearing.

[Effective July 1, 1997; amended effective May 28, 2008.]

RULE 2017–1. DESCRIPTION OF PRE–PETITION SERVICES OF DEBTOR'S COUNSEL IN CHAPTER 7 OR 13 CASES

Upon the filing of a chapter 7 or 13 case, the attorney for the debtor shall submit a statement, together with and in addition to the statement required by Bankruptcy Rule 2016(b), containing:

(i) a description of pre-petition services performed for and on behalf of the debtor in contemplation of the petition;

(ii) an itemization of the services performed by each member, associate, or paraprofessional of the firm;

(iii) the time spent in the performance thereof, including the dates upon which the services were rendered and the time spent on each date;

(iv) an itemization of expenses incurred by the debtor's attorney; and

(v) the firm's billing rates for comparable services for each member, associate or paraprofessional.

[Effective July 1, 1997; amended effective May 28, 2008.]

REFERENCE: Bankruptcy Rule 2016(b)

RULE 2090–1. PRACTICE BEFORE THE COURT; WITHDRAWAL AS ATTORNEY OF RECORD; SUSPENSION

(a) **General.** An attorney who may practice in the District Court pursuant to District Rule 1.3 may practice in this Court.

(b) **Pro Hac Vice.** Upon motion made in accordance with District Rule 1.3(c), a member in good standing of the bar of any state or of any United States District Court may be permitted to practice in this Court in a particular case, adversary proceeding, or contested matter.

A member in good standing of the bar of any state or of any United States District Court whose involvement in the case is limited to filing a notice of appearance under Bankruptcy Rule 2002, filing a proof of claim or interest, or representing a child support creditor, may appear for those purposes without obtaining authorization to appear pro hac vice.

(c) **Pro Se.** An individual may appear pro se. Such an individual shall include his or her residence or place of business address and telephone number on every paper filed with the court.

(d) **Withdrawal or Substitution of Attorneys of Record.** An attorney who has been authorized to be retained or has appeared as the attorney of record for any party in any case or adversary proceeding may not withdraw or be relieved or displaced except by order after notice to the party represented, any adversaries (if applicable), the United States trustee and the trustee. An application for such an order shall include a showing by affidavit of satisfactory reasons for withdrawal or displacement and the posture of the case, including the status of any pending matters.

(e) **Suspension.**

(i) Any attorney admitted to practice before this Court may, for good cause shown, after notice and a hearing, be suspended from practice before the Court for an indefinite period, pending the outcome of disciplinary proceedings in the District Court.

(ii) Grounds for suspension include conviction in another court of a serious crime; disbarment, suspension or reprimand by another court, with or without the attorney's consent; or resignation from the bar of another court while an investigation into allegations of misconduct is pending.

(iii) In all pending cases in which a suspended attorney has made an appearance, the Clerk shall issue notice of the suspension to any party affected thereby.

(iv) The Court may order a suspended attorney to return any fees received in cases currently before the Court, pending the outcome of disciplinary proceedings in the District Court.

[Effective July 1, 1997; amended effective May 28, 2008.]

REFERENCES: District Rules 1.3, 1.4 and 1.5; Bankruptcy Rule 9014; Court's Website

Committee Note: Forms to request authorization to appear pro hac vice, and a proposed order are available at the intake counter of the Clerk's office and at the Court's Website.

RULE 2090-2. APPEARANCE BY DEBTOR'S COUNSEL IN ADVERSARY PROCEEDINGS, CONTESTED MATTERS, ETC.

(a) In General. The attorney of record for a debtor, or an attorney acting of counsel to such attorney and who is knowledgeable in all aspects of the case, shall appear on behalf of the debtor in every aspect of the case, including but not limited to appearing at the Bankruptcy Code § 341 meeting and any adjournments thereof, and defending an adversary proceeding, contested matter, motion, or application filed against the debtor during the pendency of the bankruptcy case. Except as provided in subdivisions (b) and (c) of this rule, an attorney of record for a debtor shall not exclude from the attorney's representation of the debtor any aspect of the case, including but not limited to, appearing at the Bankruptcy Code § 341 meeting and any adjournment thereof, and defending an adversary proceeding, contested matter, motion, or application filed against the debtor during the pendency of the bankruptcy case.

(b) Exclusion of Adversary Proceeding Defense from Scope of Representation. If the debtor's prepetition written retainer agreement with the attorney of record excludes the defense of an adversary proceeding from the agreed scope of representation, and if the attorney will not for that reason appear on the debtor's behalf in the adversary proceeding, and unless the debtor has obtained new counsel for the defense of such adversary proceeding and that counsel has appeared in the adversary proceeding, the attorney shall, within 15 days of service of the summons and complaint, file and serve on the debtor and counsel for the plaintiff a signed copy of the relevant portions of the retainer agreement (which may be redacted, subject to further disclosure upon direction by the Court, to the extent required to protect privileged or proprietary information, but which must include the signature page) and an affirmation setting forth:

(i) that such attorney has not been retained to represent the debtor in the adversary proceeding and for that reason will not undertake the representation;

(ii) the applicable provisions of the attorney's written retainer agreement with the debtor;

(iii) that such attorney, following the commencement of the adversary proceeding, has advised the debtor of:

(A) the nature of the adversary proceeding and the claims asserted therein;

(B) the debtor's obligation to file and serve an appropriate response to the initial pleading and the consequences of failing timely to answer or move with respect to the pleading;

(C) the requirements of form and time limits applicable to the preparation, filing and service of a responsive pleading; and

(D) how to serve and file a responsive pleading;

and

(iv) if the attorney is, despite best efforts, unable to contact the debtor to communicate the information described in subdivision (b)(iii) of this rule, the affirmation shall also set forth the nature of the attorney's efforts to contact the debtor.

(c) Relief from Representation of Chapter 11 or Chapter 13 Debtor Upon Conversion to Chapter 7. Notwithstanding the requirements of subdivision (a) of this rule, upon conversion of a chapter 11 or chapter 13 case to a case under chapter 7, counsel for the debtor or chapter 11 trustee, if one was appointed, is relieved from any further obligation to represent the debtor or the chapter 11 trustee in the bankruptcy case, except that such counsel shall assist the debtor or chapter 11 trustee in the performance of their duties upon conversion under any applicable statute or rule.

(d) Relief from Representation of the Debtor Under Other Circumstances. Applications for relief from representation of a debtor under circumstances other than those described in subdivision (b) of this rule shall be made pursuant to E.D.N.Y. LBR 2090-1. The filing of a withdrawal application pursuant to E.D.N.Y. LBR 2090-1 does not suspend the requirements of subdivision (a) of this rule or toll the running of the time limitations applicable to the interposition of responses to papers initiating adversary proceedings, contested matters, motions, or any other application against the debtor.

(e) Sanctions. An attorney of record for a debtor who fails or refuses without reasonable excuse to represent the debtor in any aspect of the case, including but not limited to appearing at the Bankruptcy Code § 341 meeting and any adjournments thereof, and defending an adversary proceeding, contested matter, motion, or application filed against the debtor during the pendency of the bankruptcy case (other than any attorney who excludes the defense of adversary proceedings from the attorney's representation of the debtor in accordance with subdivision (b) of this rule and who complies with all of the requirements of subdivision (b) of this rule) may, after notice and a hearing, be sanctioned pursuant to this rule and may be ordered to disgorge fees paid in connection with the case pursuant to Bankruptcy Rule 2017.

[Adopted effective July 1, 1999; amended effective May 28, 2008.]

CROSS–REFERENCE: E.D.N.Y. LBR 2090–1

REFERENCE: Bankruptcy Rule 2017

PART III. CLAIMS AND DISTRIBUTION TO CREDITORS AND EQUITY INTEREST HOLDERS; PLANS

RULE 3007–1. OBJECTIONS TO CLAIMS

A motion to reduce, expunge, or reclassify a claim shall have attached thereto a copy of the proof of claim as filed (without exhibits) which identifies the claimant by name and the claim number. Each reference to a filed claim in the moving papers and any proposed order to be entered thereon shall refer to the claim both by name of the claimant and claim number. The title of the motion shall refer to the claim by claim number.

[Effective July 1, 1997; amended effective July 1, 1999.]

Committee Note: Each Judge's chambers should be consulted regarding procedures for filing omnibus objections to claims.

RULE 3007–2. MODIFICATION OF SCHEDULES OF CLAIMS

If a claim is scheduled by the debtor and is not listed as disputed, contingent, or unliquidated, and a proof of claim has not been filed under Bankruptcy Rules 3003, 3004 and/or 3005, the debtor may not object to the claim. The debtor may amend the debtor's schedules under Bankruptcy Rule 1009 and provide notice as required by E.D.N.Y. LBR 1009–1(b). If the amendment modifies a creditor's scheduled claim or adds a creditor to the schedules of claims and if the deadline by which proofs of claim must be filed has expired or will expire in less than 30 days, the creditor shall have 30 days from the effective date of amendment to file a proof of claim.

[Effective May 28, 2008.]

CROSS–REFERENCE: E.D.N.Y. LBR 1009–1

REFERENCES: Bankruptcy Rules 1009, 3003, 3004, 3005

RULE 3015–1. CHAPTER 13 PLAN

(a) Service of Plan. If a chapter 13 petition is filed without a plan, or if a case is converted to one under chapter 13, the debtor shall:

(i) file the plan within 15 days, unless an extension is requested and granted by the Court; and

(ii) serve the plan on the trustee and all creditors within 10 days of filing the plan and file proof of service thereof.

(b) Notice and Hearing for Attorney's Fees To Be Treated as Administrative Expense. If the compensation, or any portion thereof, of the attorney for a chapter 13 debtor is to be treated as an administrative expense under the plan, the attorney shall provide notice of that fact to the debtor, the trustee, the United States trustee, and all creditors. Separate notices shall not be required if the plan, or a summary of the plan, states the date(s) and amount of any payments to be made to the attorney, and is served upon all parties in interest at least 15 days prior to the confirmation hearing.

[Effective July 1, 1997; amended effective May 28, 2008.]

RULE 3015–2. CHAPTER 13 PLAN MODIFICATION

(a) Modification of Chapter 13 Plan Before Confirmation. If a debtor in a chapter 13 case proposes to modify his or her chapter 13 plan before confirmation, and the modification of the chapter 13 plan adversely affects the treatment of the claim of any creditor, the debtor shall serve a copy of the modified plan on the trustee and on all creditors not later than 10 days prior to the hearing on confirmation or any adjournment thereof.

(b) Modification of Chapter 13 Plan After Confirmation. If a debtor in a chapter 13 case proposes to modify his or her chapter 13 plan after confirmation, the debtor shall proceed by motion or on presentment in accordance with E.D.N.Y. LBR 2002–1, if there is compliance with Bankruptcy Rule 3015(g). A copy of the proposed modified plan shall be attached to the motion or notice of presentment.

[Effective July 1, 1997; amended effective May 28, 2008.]

CROSS–REFERENCE: E.D.N.Y. LBR 2002–1

RULE 3015–3. HEARING ON CONFIRMATION OF CHAPTER 13 PLAN

Unless excused, the debtor and debtor's attorney shall attend the hearing on confirmation of the chapter 13 plan.

[Effective July 1, 1997.]

RULE 3016–1. OMISSION OF SEPARATE DISCLOSURE STATEMENT IN CHAPTER 11 SMALL BUSINESS CASES: DISCLAIMER

When a chapter 11 case is a small business case as defined in Bankruptcy Code § 101(51C), and the Court finds that the plan provides adequate information under Bankruptcy Code § 1125(f)(1) and a separate disclosure statement is unnecessary, such plan shall have on its cover, in boldface type, the following language or words of similar import:

THE DEBTOR IN THIS CASE IS A SMALL BUSINESS. THE COURT HAS CONDITIONALLY FOUND THAT THIS PLAN PROVIDES ADEQUATE INFORMATION AS REQUIRED UNDER 11 U.S.C. § 1125(a)(1). AS A RESULT, THE DEBTOR MAY DISTRIBUTE THIS PLAN WITHOUT FILING A DISCLOSURE STATEMENT. IF A PARTY IN INTEREST FILES AN OBJECTION TO THIS PLAN BASED ON LACK OF ADEQUATE INFORMATION, THE COURT SHALL MAKE A FINDING REGARDING COMPLIANCE WITH 11 U.S.C. § 1125(a)(1) AT OR BEFORE THE HEARING ON CONFIRMATION OF THE PLAN.

[Effective May 28, 2008.]

REFERENCES: Bankruptcy Code §§ 101(51C), 1125(f)(1); Bankruptcy Rule 3017.1

RULE 3017–1. PROPOSED DISCLOSURE STATEMENTS IN CHAPTER 9 AND 11 CASES: TRANSMITTAL AND DISCLAIMER

(a) Transmittal. The proponent of a plan shall transmit all notices and documents required to be transmitted by Bankruptcy Rule 3017(a).

(b) Disclaimer. Before a proposed disclosure statement has been approved, it shall have on its cover, in boldface type, the following language or words of similar import:

THIS IS NOT A SOLICITATION OF ACCEPTANCE OR REJECTION OF THE PLAN. ACCEPTANCES OR REJECTIONS MAY NOT BE SOLICITED UNTIL A DISCLOSURE STATEMENT HAS BEEN APPROVED BY THE BANKRUPTCY COURT. THIS DISCLOSURE STATEMENT IS BEING SUBMITTED FOR APPROVAL BUT HAS NOT BEEN APPROVED BY THE COURT.

(c) Disclosure Statement Disclaimer in Small Business Cases. When a chapter 11 case is a small business case as defined in Bankruptcy Code § 101(51C), after conditional approval, but before final

approval of a proposed disclosure statement has been given, such statement shall have on its cover, in boldface type, the following language or words of similar import:

THE DEBTOR IN THIS CASE IS A SMALL BUSINESS. AS A RESULT, THE DEBTOR MAY DISTRIBUTE THIS DISCLOSURE STATEMENT BEFORE ITS FINAL APPROVAL BY THE COURT. IF AN OBJECTION TO THIS DISCLOSURE STATEMENT IS FILED BY A PARTY IN INTEREST, FINAL APPROVAL OF THIS DISCLOSURE STATEMENT WILL BE CONSIDERED AT OR BEFORE THE HEARING ON CONFIRMATION OF THE PLAN.

[Effective July 1, 1997; amended effective May 28, 2008.]

REFERENCE: Bankruptcy Code § 101(51C)

RULE 3018–1. SUMMARY AND CERTIFICATION OF ACCEPTANCE OR REJECTION OF PLANS IN CHAPTER 9 AND 11 CASES

(a) Summary of Ballots and Notice of Cramdown. At least 5 business days prior to the hearing on confirmation of a chapter 9 or 11 plan, the proponent of the plan shall file, and serve upon the United States trustee and counsel to any committee appointed in the case, a one-page statement setting forth the following information:

(i) a summary of the ballots received;

(ii) whether the proponent proposes to confirm the plan over the objection of one or more impaired classes; and

(iii) whether any witnesses other than the proponent's witness in favor of the plan are expected to testify as to any facts relevant to confirmation (testimony by the proponent on behalf of the plan is required).

(b) Certification of Vote. Prior to the hearing on confirmation of a chapter 9 or 11 plan, the proponent of a plan or the party authorized to receive the acceptances and rejections of the plan shall file a certification setting forth the amount and number of allowed claims or allowed interests of each class accepting or rejecting the plan. A copy of the certification shall be served upon the debtor, the trustee, each committee, and the United States trustee. The Court may find that the plan has been accepted or rejected on the basis of the certification.

(c) Notice of Ineffective Election. If a plan in a chapter 9 or 11 case permits the holder of a claim or interest to make an election with respect to the treatment of the claim or interest, and if the holder's

election is deemed ineffective or otherwise is not counted by the person authorized to tabulate ballots, that person shall give notice of that fact to the holder at least 5 days prior to the hearing on confirmation.
[Effective July 1, 1997; amended effective July 1, 1999; May 28, 2008.]

RULE 3020–1. TIME FOR OBJECTING TO CONFIRMATION IN CHAPTER 9 AND 11 CASES; WITHDRAWAL OF OBJECTIONS

(a) Objections to Confirmation. Objections to confirmation of a plan shall be filed at least 5 Business Days prior to the hearing to consider confirmation of the plan.

(b) Withdrawal of Objections. If an objection to confirmation of a plan is withdrawn, the proponent shall disclose to the Court the reasons for the withdrawal, including the terms of any agreement precipitating the withdrawal of the objection.
[Effective July 1, 1997; amended effective May 28, 2008.]

RULE 3020–2. CONFIRMATION ORDERS IN CHAPTER 9 AND 11 CASES

A proposed order confirming a chapter 9 or 11 plan shall have annexed a copy of the plan to be confirmed.
[Effective May 28, 2008.]

PART IV. THE DEBTOR:

RULE 4001–1. RELIEF FROM AUTOMATIC STAY

(a) By Motion. A motion for relief from the automatic stay under Bankruptcy Code § 362 shall be made returnable within 30 days of the date filed.

(b) By Presentment. If a motion for relief from the automatic stay under Bankruptcy Code § 362 is made by presentment as set forth in E.D.N.Y. LBR 2002–1, and a hearing is scheduled, the time limitation set forth in Bankruptcy Code § 362(e) is deemed waived.
[Effective July 1, 1997; amended effective May 28, 2008.]

CROSS–REFERENCES: E.D.N.Y. LBR 2002–1, 5070–1
REFERENCE: Bankruptcy Code § 362

RULE 4001–2. ORDERS CONFIRMING THE INAPPLICABILITY OF THE AUTOMATIC STAY

A request for an order pursuant to Bankruptcy Code §§ 362(c)(4)(A)(ii) or (j) shall be on notice to the debtor, the debtor's attorney, if any, and the trustee and shall include evidence of entitlement to the order.
[Effective May 28, 2008.]

Committee Note: This rule is derived from former E.D.N.Y. LBR 3021–1(a), which was omitted from these rules.

RULE 3021–1. CONFIRMATION REQUIREMENTS IN CHAPTER 9 AND 11 CASES [ABROGATED]

[Effective July 1, 1997. Abrogated effective May 28, 2008]

Committee Note: Subdivision (a) of Former E.D.N.Y. 3021–1 was redesignated E.D.N.Y. LBR 3020–2. Subdivision (b) of Former E.D.N.Y. 3021–1 was abrogated because it is no longer applicable. Subdivision (c) of Former E.D.N.Y. 3021–1 was redesignated E.D.N.Y. LBR 3022–1.

RULE 3022–1. FINAL DECREE

Within 90 days after confirmation, the plan proponent shall file, on notice to the United States trustee, an application and a proposed order for a final decree pursuant to Bankruptcy Rule 3022. Upon request, the Court may reduce or extend the time to file such application.

[Effective May 28, 2008.]

DUTIES AND BENEFITS

REFERENCES: Bankruptcy Code § 362(c)(4)(A)(ii), (j).

RULE 4001–3. ORDERS CONTINUING OR IMPOSING THE AUTOMATIC STAY

A motion for an order pursuant to Bankruptcy Code § 362(c)(3)(B) continuing the automatic stay or an order pursuant to Bankruptcy Code § 362(c)(4)(B) imposing the automatic stay shall be on notice to all parties in interest, including but not limited to, all creditors and the trustee.

[Effective July 1, 1997; amended effective May 28, 2008.]

REFERENCES: Bankruptcy Code § 362(c)(3)(B), (c)(4)(B)

RULE 4001–4. PAYMENT AND CURE OF PRE–PETITION JUDGMENT OF POSSESSION INVOLVING RESIDENTIAL PROPERTY

(a) A debtor seeking to obtain a 30–day stay of eviction pursuant to Bankruptcy Code § 362(b)(22) and (l) shall:

(i) provide the landlord's name and address in the certification required under Bankruptcy Code § 362(*l*)(1);

(ii) deliver to the Clerk, together with the petition (or, if the petition is filed electronically, within 1 Business Day of the filing), a certified or cashier's check or money order, made payable to the lessor, in the amount of any rent that would become due during the 30–day period after the filing of the petition;

(iii) serve the landlord with a copy of the debtor's petition;

(iv) file a copy of the judgment for possession, if available; and

(v) if the landlord objects to the debtor's certification, attend the hearing on such objection.

(b) A debtor who obtained a 30–day stay pursuant to Bankruptcy Code § 362(b)(22) and (*l*) and who wishes to extend the stay beyond the 30–day period shall comply with subdivision (a) of this rule and, within the 30–day period after the filing of the petition, shall:

(i) cure the entire monetary default that gave rise to the judgment of possession;

(ii) if the landlord objects to the debtor's certification under Bankruptcy Code § 362(*l*)(2) that the entire monetary default that gave rise to the judgment of possession has been cured, attend the hearing on such objection.

[Effective May 28, 2008.]

REFERENCE: Bankruptcy Code § 362(b)(22), (*l*).

RULE 4001–5.   CASH COLLATERAL AND OBTAINING CREDIT

(a) Motions. In addition to the requirements set forth in Bankruptcy Rule 4001, all motions to use cash collateral and to obtain credit pursuant to Bankruptcy Code §§ 363 and 364 ("Financing Motions") shall recite whether the proposed form of order and/or underlying cash collateral stipulation or loan agreement contains any provision of the type indicated below, identify the location of any such provision in the proposed form of order, cash collateral stipulation and/or loan agreement, and state the justification for the inclusion of such provision:

(i) the absence of any carve-out for professional fees, or provisions that provide treatment for the professionals retained by the debtor that is different than that provided for the professionals retained by a creditors' committee with respect to a professional fee carve-out;

(ii) provisions that require the debtor to pay the secured creditor's expenses and attorneys' fees in connection with the proposed financing or use of cash collateral, without any notice or review by the Office of the United States trustee, creditors' committee (if formed), or the Court; or

(iii) provisions that exclude from a carve-out any request for professional fees related to the investigation of whether the secured creditor's lien is valid and/or properly perfected.

(b) Interim Relief. When Financing Motions are filed with the Court on or shortly after the date of entry of the order for relief, the Court may grant interim relief on shortened notice. Such interim relief is intended to avoid immediate and irreparable harm to the estate pending a final hearing. In the absence of extraordinary circumstances, the Court will not approve ex parte interim financing orders that include any of the provisions listed in Bankruptcy Rule 4001 and in subdivision (a)(i)–(iii), inclusive, of this rule.

[Effective May 28, 2008.]

REFERENCES: Bankruptcy Code §§ 363 and 364
Committee Note: The proposed amendments to Bankruptcy Rule 4001, which took effect on December 1, 2007, contain provisions governing the form of cash collateral and financing motions. This rule is not intended to supersede or duplicate Bankruptcy Rule 4001, but imposes additional requirements on proponents of cash collateral and financing motions.

RULE 4002–1.   PERSONAL IDENTIFIERS AND TAX INFORMATION OF THE DEBTOR

(a) Debtor's Duty to Redact Personal Identifiers. An individual debtor providing information to the trustee or a creditor pursuant to Bankruptcy Code § 521(e) shall redact personal identifiers as follows:

(i) if an individual's social security number, alien registration number, or tax identification number is included, only the last four digits of that number shall appear;

(ii) if minor children are identified by name, only the children's initials shall appear;

(iii) if an individual's date of birth is included, only the year shall appear; and

(iv) if financial account numbers are provided, only the last four digits of these numbers shall appear.

(b) Electronic Filing of Debtor's Tax Information. All tax information electronically filed shall be entered under the event titled "Tax Documents" (Category–Other) in the CM/ECF event list.

(c) Procedure for Requesting Tax Information Filed With the Court Pursuant to Bankruptcy Code § 521(f). Any party in interest seeking access to a debtor's tax information that is filed with the Court pursuant to Bankruptcy Code § 521(f) shall file a motion with the Court on notice to the debtor and the debtor's attorney, if any. A motion requesting access to such information shall include:

(i) a description of the movant's status in the case;

(ii) a description of the specific tax information sought;

(iii) a statement indicating that the information cannot be obtained by the movant from any other sources; and

(iv) an explanation of the movant's need for the tax information.

(d) Procedure for Obtaining Access to Tax Information Filed With the Court Pursuant to Bankruptcy Code § 521(f) After Access to the Tax Information Is Granted. Any party in interest whose motion seeking to obtain access to a debtor's tax information filed pursuant to Bankruptcy Code § 521(f) was granted by the Court shall present to the Clerk a copy of the Court's order granting such movant access to the tax information and a valid, government issued picture identification card in order to obtain such tax information.

(e) Confidentiality of Personal Identifiers. Any party in interest who obtains the personal identifiers listed in subdivision (a) of this rule shall keep such information confidential and shall disclose it only to an employee or financial or legal advisor with a need to know such information in connection with the bankruptcy case. Any person or entity who uses, discloses, or disseminates personal identifiers in a manner inconsistent with this rule may be found in contempt of court and may be subject to penalties therefor.

(f) Confidentiality of Tax Information. Any party in interest who obtains tax information of the debtor shall keep such information confidential and shall disclose only to the extent necessary in connection with the case or related adversary proceeding. Any party in interest who seeks to disclose tax information of the debtor for any other purpose shall seek authority to do so by motion on notice to the debtor and the debtor's attorney, if any. Any person or entity who discloses a debtor's tax information in a manner inconsistent with this rule may be found in contempt of court and may be subject to penalties therefor.

(g) Waiver of Protection of Personal Identifiers. An individual debtor waives the protection of subdivisions (e) of this rule as to personal identifiers provided to the trustee or a creditor pursuant to Bankruptcy Code § 521(e) to the extent such personal identifiers are not redacted in accordance with subdivision (a) of this rule.

[Effective May 28, 2008.]

REFERENCES: Bankruptcy Code § 521(e); Bankruptcy Rule 9037; Director of the Administrative Office of the United States Courts' Interim Guidance Regarding Tax Information under 11 U.S.C. § 521 dated Sept. 20, 2005.

RULE 4003–1. AMENDMENT TO CLAIM OF EXEMPTIONS

An amendment to a claim of exemptions pursuant to Bankruptcy Rules 1009 and 4003 and these rules shall be filed and served on the trustee, the United States trustee, all creditors, and other parties in interest. An amendment shall not be effective until proof of service is filed, which shall be done within 10 days of service.

[Effective July 1, 1997; amended effective May 28, 2008.]

CROSS–REFERENCE: E.D.N.Y. LBR 1009–1
REFERENCE: Bankruptcy Rule 1009

RULE 4003–2. OBJECTION TO A CLAIM OF EXEMPTION

An objection to a claim of exemption shall be served on the debtor in addition to the parties specified in Bankruptcy Rule 4003(b)(3).

[Effective May 28, 2008.]

Committee Note: This rule shall be deemed abrogated to the extent it becomes duplicative of Bankruptcy Rule 4003.

RULE 4004–1. SETTLEMENT OR DISMISSAL OF PROCEEDINGS OBJECTING TO DISCHARGE

A complaint objecting to discharge may be settled or dismissed only if the debtor or representative of the objecting party files an affidavit or affirmation setting forth what consideration, if any, has been paid or promised to the objecting party. The affidavit or affirmation must be served upon the trustee, all creditors, and other parties in interest.

[Formerly Rule 4004–2. Redesignated effective May 28, 2008.]

RULE 4007–1. SETTLEMENT OR DISMISSAL OF PROCEEDINGS OBJECTING TO DISCHARGEABILITY

In all instances not governed by Bankruptcy Code § 524(d), an adversary proceeding objecting to dischargeability of a debt may be settled or dismissed only if a proponent of the settlement or dismissal files an affidavit or affirmation setting forth the terms of any agreement entered into between the debtor and creditor relating to the payment of the debt in whole or in part.

[Effective July 1, 1997. Formerly Rule 4007–2, redesignated effective May 28, 2008.]

REFERENCE: Bankruptcy Code § 524(d)

PART V.   COURTS AND CLERKS

RULE 5001–1.   CLERK'S OFFICE: CONTACT INFORMATION

(a) Mailing Addresses.

Brooklyn Cases:
United States Bankruptcy Court
Eastern District of New York
271 Cadman Plaza East
Suite 1595
Brooklyn, New York 11201–1800

Central Islip Cases:
United States Bankruptcy Court
Eastern District of New York
290 Federal Plaza
P.O. Box 9013
Central Islip, New York 11722–9013

(b) Physical Addresses and Phone Numbers.

Brooklyn Office:
United States Bankruptcy Court
271 Cadman Plaza East

Brooklyn, New York 11201
Phone No. (347) 394–1700

Central Islip Office:
United States Bankruptcy Court
Alphonse M. D'Amato Federal Courthouse
290 Federal Plaza
Central Islip, New York 11722
Phone No. (631) 712–6200

(c) Website Address. The Court's Website is located at www.nyeb.uscourts.gov.

[Effective July 1, 1997; amended effective July 1, 1999; May 28, 2008.]

RULE 5001–2.   CLERK'S OFFICE: HOURS; AFTER HOURS FILING

The offices of the Clerk shall be open on Monday through Friday between the hours of 9:00 a.m. and 4:30 p.m., except on legal or court holidays, and shall be closed on Saturdays and Sundays. When the Clerk's office is closed, papers relating to cases pending in Brooklyn may be submitted in a night depository located in the courthouse lobby of the United States District Court, 225 Cadman Plaza East, Brooklyn, New York 11201; papers relating to cases pending in Central Islip may be submitted in a night depository located in the courthouse lobby of the Alfonse M. D'Amato Federal Courthouse, 290 Federal Plaza, Central Islip, New York 11722. If the papers are deposited in a night depository, they will be deemed filed as of the exact time and date stamped on the papers.

Persons may review records, request files for review, review dockets, request dockets for review, or make a public inquiry at the Clerk's office between the hours of 9:00 a.m. and 4:00 p.m. Telephone inquiries to the Clerk's office may be made between the hours of 9:00 a.m. and 4:00 p.m.

Committee Note: Parties shall consult the Court's Website for the hours of accessibility to the night depositories in each Court location.

RULE 5005–1.   FILING AND TRANSMITTAL OF PAPERS IN NON–ELECTRONIC CASES

All papers in any Non-electronic Case shall be filed in the office of the Clerk located where the Judge who is assigned to the matter regularly sits.

[Effective July 1, 1997; amended effective May 28, 2008.]

RULE 5005–2.   FILING BY ELECTRONIC MEANS

(a) Password and Registration.

(i) *Attorneys.* An attorney admitted to practice before the Court may obtain a password to permit the attorney to file documents electronically. An attorney may register to use the electronic filing system by filing a password application.

(ii) *Limited Creditors.* Creditors may register for limited use of the electronic filing system by filing a password application.

(b) Filing Requirements.

(i) All motions, pleadings, memoranda of law, exhibits, and other documents required to be filed with the Court in connection with a case and documents filed under seal in accordance with E.D.N.Y. LBR 9018, shall be electronically filed over the Internet. Within 1 Business Day of the electronic filing, a chambers copy shall be filed with the Clerk to the attention of the appropriate Judge's chambers, which copy is to be marked "Chambers Copy." The date and time of the electronic filing shall be the official date and time of the filing of the document.

(ii) Proofs of claim may be filed electronically. A "Chambers Copy" shall not be filed with the Clerk.

(iii) All documents that form part of a motion or pleading, and which are being filed at the same time and by the same party, except for a memorandum of law, may be electronically filed together under one docket number. A memorandum of law shall be filed separately and shall indicate the motion or pleading to which it relates.

(iv) Relevant excerpts of exhibits that are not in electronic form shall be scanned and electronically filed. Such document excerpts shall be identified as excerpts, shall not exceed 20 pages, and shall state that the entire document is in the possession of the filing party and is available upon request. The complete exhibit shall be made available forthwith to counsel on request, and shall be available in the courtroom at any hearing on the matter. Persons filing excerpts of exhibits pursuant to these procedures do so without prejudice to their right to file additional excerpts or the entire exhibit with the Court at any time. Opposing parties may file any additional excerpts that they believe to be germane. Chambers copies of complete exhibits shall be provided to the Court on request.

[Effective May 28, 2008.]

CROSS–REFERENCE: E.D.N.Y. LBR 9018–1
REFERENCE: General Order on Electronic Filing Procedures
Committee Note: Attorney and Limited Creditor ECF password applications are available at the intake counter of the Clerk's office and at the Court's Website.

RULE 5010–1. REOPENING CASES

(a) **Contents of Motion.** A motion to reopen a case pursuant to Bankruptcy Code § 350(b) and Bankruptcy Rule 5010 shall state the name of the Judge to whom the case had been assigned and the date on which the case was closed.

(b) **Assignment of Matter.** The Clerk shall assign the motion to the Judge to whom the case had been assigned at the time it was closed. If that Judge is no longer sitting, the motion shall be assigned in accordance with E.D.N.Y. LBR 1073–1.

(c) **Filing Fee.** A filing fee shall be due at the time of making a motion to reopen a case (including a motion to reopen for the purpose of filing a personal financial management certificate) in the same amount as the filing fee prescribed by 28 U.S.C. § 1930(a) for commencing a new case on the date of reopening, except that no filing fee shall be due if the reopening is requested to correct an administrative error, or for actions related to the debtor's discharge. The Court may defer or waive the filing fee under appropriate circumstances.

[Effective July 1, 1997; amended effective July 1, 1999; May 28, 2008.]

CROSS–REFERENCE: E.D.N.Y. LBR 1073–1
REFERENCES: Bankruptcy Code §§ 111, 350(b), 727; Bankruptcy Rule 4006; 28 U.S.C. § 1930(a)

RULE 5011–1. WITHDRAWAL OF REFERENCE

A motion for withdrawal of the reference shall be filed with the Court, and the Clerk shall transmit the motion to the District Clerk promptly and so notify the movant. The movant shall be responsible for notifying all other parties. Following the transmittal of the motion, all further papers with respect to the motion shall be filed in the District Court.

[Effective July 1, 1997; amended effective May 28, 2008.]

RULE 5070–1. CALENDARS AND SCHEDULING

(a) **Obtaining Return Date.** Prior to serving a motion or application, the moving party or applicant shall obtain a return date from the Court's Website, if appropriate, or from the Judge's courtroom deputy or chambers.

(b) **Adjournments Without Date.** Any matter adjourned without date and not restored to the calendar within 60 days may be deemed withdrawn without prejudice.

[Effective July 1, 1997; amended effective May 28, 2008.]

CROSS–REFERENCES: E.D.N.Y. LBR 2002–1, 4001–1
Committee Note: Parties shall consult the Court's Website for each Judge's procedures with respect to the designation of return and adjournment dates.

RULE 5073–1. CAMERAS, RADIO, RECORDERS AND OTHER ELECTRONIC DEVICES [ABROGATED]

[Effective July 1, 1997; abrogated effective May 28, 2008.]

Committee Note: Parties are directed to the Court's Website for the Court's policy on cameras, radio, recorders, and other electronic devices.

RULE 5075–1. USE OF SERVICES AND AGENTS

The Court may permit, subject to the supervision of the Clerk, the use of services and agents to maintain Court records, issue notices, file certain documents, and maintain and disseminate other administrative information when the costs of such services and agents are paid for by the estate.

[Effective July 1, 1997; amended effective May 28, 2008.]

CROSS–REFERENCES: E.D.N.Y. LBR 3007–1, 3007–2

RULE 5080–1.   FEES—GENERAL

Except as otherwise authorized by statute, rule, or order, the Clerk shall not render any service for which a fee is prescribed by statute or by the Judicial Conference of the United States unless the fee has been paid or waived, or an application for waiver of the filing fee under applicable law is pending.

[Effective July 1, 1997; amended effective July 1, 1999; May 28, 2008.]

REFERENCES: 28 U.S.C. § 1930, Bankruptcy Rule 1006

PART VI.   COLLECTION AND LIQUIDATION OF THE ESTATE

RULE 6004–1.   SALE OF PROPERTY, APPRAISALS AND AUCTIONS

(a) **Conflict of Interest.** An appraiser, auctioneer, or officer, director, stockholder, agent, employee, or insider of an appraiser or auctioneer, or any relative of any of the foregoing, shall not purchase, directly or indirectly, or have a financial interest in the purchase of, any property of the estate that the appraiser or auctioneer has been employed to appraise or sell.

(b) **Notice of Sale of Estate Property by Private Sale.** A party seeking to sell property of the estate outside the ordinary course of business shall give the notice required by Bankruptcy Rule 2002(a)(2) and, if applicable, Bankruptcy Rule 6004(g). Such notice shall contain:

(i) a general description of the property;

(ii) a statement explaining where a complete description or inventory of the property may be obtained or examined;

(iii) the terms of sale, including the upset price, if any, the procedures for bidding on the property to be sold, and the terms of any pending offer proposed to be accepted;

(iv) the place, date, and time of the sale;

(v) the place, date, and time the property may be examined prior to the sale;

(vi) the date by which objections to the sale must be filed with the Court;

(vii) the date of the hearing to consider any objections to the sale; and

(viii) the name and address of the trustee, if any.

(c) **Manner of Display and Conduct of Auction.** The auction shall be conducted in the following manner:

(i) the property shall be on public display for a reasonable period of time prior to the auction;

(ii) prior to receiving bids, the auctioneer shall announce the terms of sale;

(iii) when practicable, the property shall be offered for sale first in bulk and then in lots; and

(iv) any property that is not to be included in the auction shall be set apart and conspicuously marked "not included in the sale," and such fact shall be announced by the auctioneer before the auction.

(d) **Joint Auctions.** Whenever the trustee and a secured party, or other third party having an interest in the property, desire to conduct a joint auction, the Court may enter an order fixing the method of allocating the commissions and expenses of sale.

(e) **Proceeds of Auction.** Upon receipt of the proceeds of sale, the auctioneer shall immediately deposit the proceeds in a separate account that the auctioneer maintains for the estate in accordance with Bankruptcy Code § 345(a). Payment of the gross proceeds of the sale shall be made promptly by the auctioneer to the trustee or debtor in possession, but in no event later than 10 days after the proceeds are received.

(f) **Report of Auction.** Within 20 days after the last date of the auction, the auctioneer shall file a verified report and provide the report to the trustee and the United States trustee. If all proceeds of the auction have not been received by such date, the auctioneer shall file a supplemental report within 10 days after all proceeds have been received. The report shall set forth:

(i) the time, date, and place of the auction;

(ii) the gross dollar amount received at the auction;

(iii) if property was sold in lots, a description of the items in each lot, the quantity in each lot, the dollar amount received for each lot, and any bulk bid(s) received;

(iv) an itemized statement of expenditures, disbursements, and commissions allowable under E.D.N.Y. LBR 6005–1, including the name and address of the payee and receipts or canceled checks for the expenditures or disbursements. When labor charges are included, the report shall specify the days worked and the number of hours worked each day by each person supported, by an affidavit from every person receiving compensation which also sets forth all amounts received. If the canceled checks are not available at the time the report is filed, the report shall so state, and the canceled checks shall be filed as soon as they become available;

(v) when the auctioneer has a blanket insurance policy covering all sales conducted by the auctioneer, a statement of how any insurance expense charged to the estate was computed;

(vi) if any articles were withdrawn from the auction because of a third party claim of an interest therein, a statement of the articles and the names of the third parties;

(vii) the names and addresses of all purchasers;

(viii) the sign-in sheet, or, if none, the approximate number of people attending the auction;

(ix) the items for which there were no bids and the disposition of those items;

(x) the terms of sale that were announced prior to receiving bids;

(xi) a statement of the manner and extent of advertising of the auction, including a copy of the published advertisement and a certificate of publication;

(xii) a statement of the manner and extent of the availability of the items for inspection;

(xiii) a copy of the order retaining the auctioneer; and

(xiv) any other information that the trustee, the United States trustee, or the Court may request.

(g) Affidavit to Accompany Report of Auction. The auctioneer shall submit with the report of auction an affidavit stating:

(i) whether the auctioneer is duly licensed;

(ii) the auctioneer's license number and place of business;

(iii) the authority pursuant to which the auctioneer conducted the auction;

(iv) the date and place of the auction;

(v) that the labor and other expenses incurred on behalf of the estate as listed in the report of auction were reasonable and necessary; and

(vi) that the gross proceeds were remitted to the trustee or debtor in possession and the date of the remittance.

(h) Notice of Sale by Auction; Advertisement and Publication. An advertisement or publication of notice of a sale by auction or otherwise may be made without Court approval if it is sufficient to provide adequate notice of the sale and is advertised or published at least once in a newspaper of general circulation in the city or county in which the property is located. The advertisement or publication shall include:

(i) the date, time, and place of the sale;

(ii) a description of the property to be sold;

(iii) the terms and conditions of the sale; and

(iv) the name, address, and telephone number of the auctioneer.

The Judge may fix the manner and extent of advertising and publication at any time.

(i) No Order Needed to Confirm Sale. Unless a timely objection is made, an order of the Court shall not be required to confirm a sale of property otherwise authorized by the Bankruptcy Code, the Bankruptcy Rules, or Court order. The trustee, debtor, or debtor in possession may execute any documents and instruments that are necessary to complete the sale, and shall file with the Clerk and transmit to the United States trustee a report of the sale as required by Bankruptcy Rule 6004(f) when the sale is completed. On request, the Clerk shall issue a certificate stating that a notice of a proposed auction, with proof of service, has been filed pursuant to E.D.N.Y. LBR 2002–1 and that no timely objection has been filed.

[Effective July 1, 1997; amended effective July 1, 1999; May 28, 2008.]

CROSS–REFERENCES: E.D.N.Y. LBR 2002–1, 2014–1, 6005–1, 9018–1

REFERENCES: Bankruptcy Code § 245(a); Bankruptcy Rules 2002, 6004, General Order on Electronic Filing Procedures

Committee Note: Subdivisions (c) and (d) of former E.D.N.Y. LBR 6004–1 were abrogated.

RULE 6005–1. AUCTIONEERS

(a) Retention of Auctioneer. A debtor in possession or trustee may retain the services of an auctioneer, subject to prior Court approval.

(b) Compensation. An auctioneer may be allowed to receive commissions and reimbursement of expenses for sales of property, subject to Court approval, in an amount not to exceed:

(i) commissions on each sale conducted by the auctioneer at the following rates:

(A) 10% of any gross proceeds of sale up to $50,000;

(B) 8% of any gross proceeds of sale in excess of $50,000 but not more than $75,000;

(C) 6% of any gross proceeds of sale in excess of $75,000 but not more than $100,000;

(D) 4% of any gross proceeds of sale in excess of $100,000 but not more than $150,000; and

(E) 2% of any gross proceeds of sale in excess of $150,000; and

(ii) reimbursement for reasonable and necessary expenses directly related to the sale, including labor, printing, advertising, and insurance, but excluding workers' compensation, social security, unemployment insurance, and other payroll taxes. When directed by the trustee or debtor in possession to transport goods, the auctioneer may be reimbursed for expenditures related thereto. No travel expenses shall be allowed, except as ordered by the Court.

(c) Bond. An auctioneer employed pursuant to Bankruptcy Code § 327 shall not act until the auctioneer files and provides to the United States trustee, with respect to each estate, at the auctioneer's expense, a surety bond in favor of the United States, to be approved, and in such sum as may be fixed, by the United States trustee, conditioned upon:

(i) the faithful and prompt accounting for all monies and property that may come into the auctioneer's possession;

(ii) compliance with all rules, orders, and decrees of the Court; and

(iii) the faithful performance of the auctioneer's duties.

(d) Blanket Bond. In lieu of a bond in each case, an auctioneer may file, at the auctioneer's own expense, a blanket bond covering all cases in which the auctioneer may act. The blanket bond shall be in favor of the United States in such sum as the United States trustee shall fix and shall be conditioned for each estate on the same terms as bonds in separate estates.

(e) Application for Commissions and Reimbursement of Expenses. An auctioneer shall file an application with the Clerk for approval of commissions and reimbursement of expenses and give notice in accordance with Bankruptcy Rule 2002(a). An application may not be granted if the report of sale and accompanying affidavit described in E.D.N.Y. LBR 6004–1(f) and (g) have not been filed. The application shall state whether the debtor or the trustee has any objection to such application.

[Effective July 1, 1997; amended effective May 28, 2008.]

CROSS–REFERENCES: E.D.N.Y. LBR 2014–1, 6004–1, 9025–1

REFERENCE: Bankruptcy Code § 327; Bankruptcy Rule 2002

RULE 6007–1. ABANDONMENT OR DISPOSITION OF PROPERTY

Notice of a proposed abandonment or disposition of property pursuant to Bankruptcy Rule 6007(a) shall describe the property to be abandoned or disposed of and state the reason for the proposed abandonment or disposition.

[Effective July 1, 1997; amended effective May 28, 2008.]

PART VII. ADVERSARY PROCEEDINGS

RULE 7005–1. FILING OF DISCOVERY–RELATED DOCUMENTS

Transcripts of depositions, exhibits to depositions, interrogatories, responses to interrogatories, document requests, responses to document requests, requests for admissions, and responses to requests for admissions are not required to be filed, but may be filed when necessary for the consideration of a matter by the Court.

[Effective July 1, 1997; amended effective July 1, 1999; May 28, 2008.]

CROSS–REFERENCE: E.D.N.Y. LBR 8007–1.
Committee Note: Former E.D.N.Y. LBR 7005–1(b) was abrogated.

RULE 7007–1. DISCOVERY RELATED MOTIONS

A discovery motion under Bankruptcy Rules 7026 through 7037 shall be supported by an affidavit or affirmation certifying that the moving party has made a good faith effort to confer with the opposing party to resolve the issues raised by the motion by agreement and without judicial intervention, but has been unable to reach an agreement. The affidavit or affirmation shall describe the efforts to resolve the discovery dispute without judicial intervention. The affidavit or affirmation shall specify any issues so resolved and the issues remaining unresolved. The affidavit or affirmation shall be filed and served together with the motion.

[Effective July 1, 1997; amended effective May 28, 2008.]

CROSS–REFERENCES: E.D.N.Y. LBR 9006–1, 9013–1
REFERENCES: Bankruptcy Rules 7026, 7037

RULE 7024–1. NOTICE OF CLAIM OF UNCONSTITUTIONALITY [ABROGATED]

[Effective July 1, 1997. Abrogated effective May 28, 2008.]

Committee Note: Former E.D.N.Y. LBR 7024–1 was redesignated E.D.N.Y. LBR 9005–1.

RULE 7054–1. TAXABLE COSTS

District Rule 54.1 applies in cases and adversary proceedings.

[Effective July 1, 1997; amended effective May 28, 2008.]

REFERENCE: District Rule 54.1

RULE 7055–1. DEFAULT JUDGMENT

A motion seeking a default judgment may be sought only by motion, which shall be served on the defaulting party, the defaulting party's attorney, if any, and, except in an adversary proceeding to determine dischargeability, the trustee.

[Effective July 1, 1997; amended effective May 28, 2008.]

PART VIII. APPEALS

RULE 8004–1. COPIES OF NOTICE OF APPEAL AND CERTIFICATION FOR DIRECT APPEAL TO CIRCUIT COURT

No later than 1 Business Day after the filing of a notice of appeal, the appellant shall provide the Clerk with sufficient copies of the notice of appeal or certification for direct appeal and address labels for all parties to be served to permit the Clerk to comply with Bankruptcy Rule 8004.

[Effective July 1, 1997; amended effective May 28, 2008.]

RULE 8006–1. RECORD ON APPEAL

(a) **Designation of Items.**

(i) *Non-electronic Cases.* A party filing a designation of items to be included in a record on appeal pursuant to Bankruptcy Rule 8006 in a Non-electronic Case shall provide the Clerk with a copy of each item designated. The Clerk shall transmit to the District Clerk, as the record on appeal, copies of the designated items.

(ii) *Electronic Cases.* When a party files a designation of items to be included in a record on appeal pursuant to Bankruptcy Rule 8006 and only an excerpted version of an item is on the docket, that party shall provide the Clerk with a full copy of such designated item. The Clerk shall transmit to the District Clerk, as the record on appeal, the full copies of such excerpted items. A party shall electronically file in the bankruptcy case any item that party has

RULE 7056–1. SUMMARY JUDGMENT

A motion for summary judgment pursuant to Bankruptcy Rule 7056 shall include a separate statement of the material facts as to which the moving party contends there is no genuine issue to be tried. Failure to submit such a statement may be grounds for denial of the motion. The opposition to a motion for summary judgment shall include a separate statement of the material facts as to which it is contended that there exists a genuine issue to be tried. All material facts set forth in the statement required to be served by the moving party will be deemed to be admitted by the opposing party unless controverted by the statement required to be served by the opposing party. Each statement of material fact by a movant or opponent must be followed by citation to evidence which would be admissible, set forth as required by Federal Rule of Civil Procedure 56(e).

[Effective July 1, 1997; amended effective May 28, 2008.]

REFERENCE: Federal Rule of Civil Procedure 56(e)

designated that does not already appear on the docket.

(b) **Exhibits Not Designated.** Exhibits not designated to be included in a record on appeal shall remain in the custody of the attorney who has possession of such exhibits, who shall have the responsibility of promptly forwarding them to the clerk of the appellate court upon that clerk's request.

(c) **Filing Papers Relating to the Appeal.** Upon the docketing of the notice of appeal in the District Court, all papers relating to the appeal shall be filed electronically with the District Clerk, whether the case is an Electronic Case or Non-electronic Case, except for a request for a stay pending appeal, which must be filed in accordance with Bankruptcy Rule 8005.

[Redesignated and amended effective May 28, 2008.]

REFERENCE: Bankruptcy Rules 8005 and 8007
Committee Note: This is former E.D.N.Y. LBR 8007–1.

RULE 8016–1. ORDER, JUDGMENT OR REMAND BY APPELLATE COURT

An order or judgment of an appellate court, when filed in the office of the Clerk, shall become the order or judgment of the Court and be entered as such by the Clerk without further order. If the order or judgment of the appellate court remands for further proceedings, a motion for such further proceedings shall be made by the appropriate party within 20 days of the remand and referred to the Judge who heard the proceeding below, unless the appellate court orders otherwise.

[Effective July 1, 1997; amended effective May 28, 2008.]

PART IX. GENERAL PROVISIONS

RULE 9001-1. DEFINITIONS

(a) **Definitions.** Unless inconsistent with the context, in these rules—

(i) *"Bankruptcy Code"* or *"Code"* means title 11 of the United States Code, as amended from time to time;

(ii) *"Bankruptcy Rules"* means the Federal Rules of Bankruptcy Procedure and Official Bankruptcy Forms promulgated pursuant to 28 U.S.C. § 2075, as amended from time to time;

(iii) *"Business Day"* means any day that is not a Saturday, Sunday, or "legal holiday" as that term is defined in Bankruptcy Rule 9006(a).

(iv) *"Chief Judge"* means the Chief Judge of the Court;

(v) *"Clerk"* means the clerk or a deputy clerk of the Court;

(vi) *"Court"* means the United States Bankruptcy Court for the Eastern District of New York and any Judge;

(vii) *"Court's Website"* means www.nyeb.uscourts. gov;

(viii) *"District Clerk"* means the clerk or a deputy clerk of the District Court;

(ix) *"District Court"* means the United States District Court for the Eastern District of New York;

(x) *"District Judge"* means a United States District Judge or a judge appointed to, or sitting by designation in, the District Court;

(xi) *"District Rules"* means the Local Rules of the United States District Courts for the Southern and Eastern Districts of New York;

(xii) *"Electronic Case Filing"* or *"ECF"* means the Electronic Case File System implemented in this Court;

(xiii) *"Electronic Case"* means any case (except chapter 11) or adversary proceeding filed after January 1, 2003, or any chapter 11 case and any associated adversary proceeding filed after April 1, 2002;

(xiv) *"Former Local Bankruptcy Rules"* means the United States Bankruptcy Court Eastern District of New York Local Bankruptcy Rules, effective July 1, 1999, as revised;

(xv) *"General Order on Electronic Filing Procedures"* means the Revised General Order on Electronic Filing Procedures, dated December 26, 2002, as amended from time to time;

(xvi) *"Judge"* means a bankruptcy judge appointed to or sitting by designation in the United States Bankruptcy Court for the Eastern District of New York (or, with respect to a proceeding that has not been referred or which has been withdrawn, the District Judge);

(xvii) *"Non-electronic Case"* means any case (except chapter 11) or adversary proceeding filed before January 1, 2003, or any chapter 11 case and any associated adversary proceeding filed before April 1, 2002; and

(xviii) *"United States trustee"* means the Office of the United States trustee for Region 2 or its authorized representative for the Eastern District of New York.

(b) **Construction.**

(i) Unless inconsistent with the context or stated otherwise above, words and phrases used in these rules shall be construed in accordance with the definitions and rules of construction set forth in the Bankruptcy Code and Bankruptcy Rules.

(ii) Unless inconsistent with the context or stated otherwise, the singular shall be construed to include the plural, and the plural shall be construed to include the singular.

(c) **Use of Terms "Documents" and "Papers."** The terms "documents" and "papers" as used in these rules include those filed or transmitted by electronic means.

[Effective July 1, 1997; amended effective May 28, 2008.]

RULE 9004-1. PAPERS— REQUIREMENTS OF FORM

(a) **Papers Submitted for Filing.**

(i) Papers filed shall:

(A) be plainly typed, printed, or copied;

(B) have no erasures or interlineations which materially deface them; and

(C) be signed in accordance with Bankruptcy Rule 9011.

(ii) Papers filed shall be on 8 ½″ × 11″ paper and shall not be stapled or otherwise bound on the side.

(b) Amendments. An amendment filed as a matter of right or allowed by order shall be filed in a form that is complete, including exhibits, and shall not incorporate by reference any prior paper.

(c) Chambers Copy. A paper copy of each document filed electronically or otherwise, other than petitions, schedules, and proofs of claim, shall be marked "Chambers Copy" and delivered to the Clerk within 1 Business Day of filing.

[Effective July 1, 1997; amended effective May 28, 2008.]

CROSS–REFERENCES: E.D.N.Y. LBR 5005–1, 5005–2

RULE 9004–2. CAPTION— PAPERS, GENERAL

(a) All papers submitted for filing shall have a caption stating "United States Bankruptcy Court, Eastern District of New York" and shall include the title and chapter of the case. Subsequent to the filing of the petition for relief, all papers shall also include the case number and the Judge code. All papers filed in an adversary proceeding shall also contain the full title of the lawsuit and the adversary proceeding case number. Except for involuntary petitions, all petitions for relief shall also set forth the last four digits of the debtor's social security number and/or any other federal tax identification number of the debtor.

(b) In consolidated cases, the docket number for the lead case shall be listed first and shall be followed by the docket numbers of all cases contained in the consolidation in ascending order.

(c) The return date and time of a motion shall be included in the upper right hand corner of the caption of the motion and all related papers.

[Effective July 1, 1997; amended effective May 28, 2008.]

CROSS–REFERENCE: E.D.N.Y. LBR 5070–1

RULE 9005.1–1. NOTICE OF CLAIM OF UNCONSTITUTIONALITY

If a party raises a question concerning the constitutionality of an act of Congress or a state legislative body, that party shall notify the Court of the existence of the question, the title of the case and proceeding, the statute in question, and the grounds upon which it is claimed to be unconstitutional.

[Effective May 28, 2008.]

CROSS–REFERENCE: E.D.N.Y. LBR 9014–1
REFERENCE: 28 U.S.C. § 2403
This is former E.D.N.Y. LBR 7024–1.

RULE 9006–1. TIME FOR SERVICE AND FILING OF MOTIONS AND ANSWERING PAPERS

(a) Motions. Unless otherwise provided by these rules, the Bankruptcy Rules, or by Court order:

(i) all motion papers shall be served at least 10 days before the hearing date;

(ii) any answering papers shall be served so as to be received not later than 3 Business Days before the hearing date;

(iii) any reply papers shall be served and filed, and a paper copy shall be delivered to the Clerk's office, at least 1 Business Day prior to the hearing date.

Any party filing papers with the Court within 2 Business Days prior to a hearing date shall contact chambers to advise that such papers have been filed.

(b) Time for Filing with Clerk. All motions and answering papers (except reply papers as provided in subdivision (a) of this rule) shall be filed no later than 1 Business Day following the date of service.

(c) Extra Time for Service. If papers are served by first-class mail, an additional 3 days shall be added to the minimum service requirement. If papers are served by overnight mail or courier, an additional day shall be added to the minimum service requirement.

[Effective July 1, 1997; amended effective July 1, 1999; May 28, 2008.]

CROSS–REFERENCES: E.D.N.Y. LBR 5005–1, 7007–1, 9013–1

REFERENCE: Bankruptcy Rule 2002

RULE 9011–1. SIGNING OF PAPERS

(a) Whenever Bankruptcy Rule 9011(a) requires a paper to be signed by an attorney or by a party acting pro se, the name of the attorney or party pro se shall be printed or typed below the signature.

(b) Electronic Signatures. Whenever any applicable statute, rule, or order requires a document to be signed and the document is filed in an Electronic Case, the document shall contain an electronic signature or a scanned copy of the original signature. An electronic signature shall consist of "s/" followed by the first and last name of the person signing. The original executed document and any original exhibits, shall be maintained by the filer for two years after the entry of a final order closing the case or proceeding. On request of the Court, the filer shall provide an original document for review.

(c) An electronic filing password shall be used only by the attorney to whom the password is assigned and authorized members and employees of such attorney's firm.

[Effective July 1, 1997; amended effective May 28, 2008.]

CROSS–REFERENCES: E.D.N.Y. LBR 1002–1(c) and (d), 5005–2

REFERENCE: 28 U.S.C. § 1746; Bankruptcy Rule 1008

RULE 9013–1. MOTION PRACTICE

(a) Rule or Statutory Basis. A motion shall be in writing, unless made during a hearing, and shall specify the rules and statutory provisions upon which it is based and the legal authorities that support the requested relief, either in the motion or in a separate memorandum of law, and the factual grounds for relief. Failure to provide this information may be grounds to strike the motion from the calendar or deny the motion.

(b) Responsive Papers. A response to a written motion shall be in writing and shall state the factual grounds upon which relief is opposed, and the legal authorities that support the respondent's position, either in the response or in a separate memorandum of law. Failure to provide this information may be grounds to strike the response or to grant the motion by default.

(c) Proposed Order. Whenever possible, a motion shall be accompanied by a proposed order.

(d) Entities to Receive Notice. In addition to the notice required by any applicable Bankruptcy Rule or local rule, notice of a motion shall be given to any entity having or claiming an interest in the subject matter of the proposed action or order or who otherwise would be affected by the proposed action or order.

(e) Proof of Service. Unless the movant is proceeding by order to show cause or has otherwise requested that the Court issue an order scheduling a hearing under E.D.N.Y. LBR 9077–1, all motions, documents, or proposed orders shall be filed with proof of service on all relevant parties.

(f) Hearing and Oral Argument Required. Except as provided in E.D.N.Y. LBR 2002–1, a hearing and oral argument is required on all calendar matters unless the Court directs that no hearing is required.

(g) Motions to Avoid Liens. Motions seeking relief pursuant to Bankruptcy Code § 522(f) shall be supported by an affidavit or affirmation stating:

(i) the date of filing of the bankruptcy petition;

(ii) a description of the judgments to be avoided (*e.g.*, name of judgment holder, date and place of docketing of the judgment, amount of judgment);

(iii) the amount of each lien on the property (including all mortgages); and

(iv) the amount of the exemption claimed by the debtor.

Such motion shall also be supported by evidence showing the fair market value of the property as of the date of the filing of the bankruptcy petition; copies of tax assessments or a statement by a debtor or counsel regarding the value of the property are not sufficient. Copies of relevant documents must also be annexed as exhibits, including, *e.g.*, the lien search from the County Clerk's office and pay-off statements from the mortgage holders.

[Effective July 1, 1997; amended effective July 1, 1999; May 28, 2008.]

CROSS REFERENCES: E.D.N.Y. LBR 1002–1, 2002–2, 5005–1, 7007–1, 9006–1, 9023–1, 9077–1

REFERENCES: Bankruptcy Code § 522(f); Bankruptcy Rule 2002

RULE 9014–1. CONTESTED MATTERS

E.D.N.Y. LBR 7005–1, 7007–1, 7054–1, and 7056–1 shall apply in contested matters. Any reference to adversary proceedings in such rules shall be deemed for this purpose a reference to contested matters.

[Effective July 1, 1997; amended effective May 28, 2008.]

CROSS–REFERENCES: E.D.N.Y. LBR 7005–1, 7007–1, 7054–1, 7056–1

RULE 9018–1. DOCUMENTS FILED UNDER SEAL IN ELECTRONIC CASES

(a) Motion. A motion to file a document under seal (but not the document itself) shall be filed electronically. If the motion itself contains confidential information, the movant shall serve and file electronically a redacted version clearly marked as such, and submit an unredacted version for *in camera* review.

(b) Delivery of Sealed Documents. If the Court grants a motion to file a document under seal, in whole or in part, the movant shall deliver to the Clerk:

(i) the documents to be filed under seal (the "sealed documents") and the proposed sealing order in an envelope clearly marked "Under Seal"; and

(ii) an electronically stored document submitted in physical form containing the sealed documents in "pdf" format and the proposed sealing order in a word processing format.

(c) Destruction of Documents Filed Under Seal. Sealed documents shall be destroyed when the bankruptcy case is closed.

[Effective May 28, 2008.]

REFERENCE: General Order on Electronic Case Filing

RULE 9019–1. ALTERNATIVE DISPUTE RESOLUTION—MEDIATION

(a) Assignment of a Matter to Mediation. The Court may direct any dispute arising in any case or proceeding (collectively, "Matter") to mediation sua sponte or upon the request of one or more party in interest. The Court may determine which parties in interest shall participate in the mediation. If a Matter is assigned to mediation, the parties shall comply with all applicable pleading, discovery, and other deadlines and scheduling requirements.

(b) Appointment of a Mediator. The mediation participants shall select a mediator and at least one alternate from the Mediation Register of approved mediators kept by the Clerk within 10 days of the entry of the order assigning the matter to mediation. If the mediation participants cannot agree within that time, or if the Court determines that selection of a mediator by the Court is appropriate, then the Court shall appoint a mediator. Within 10 days of the selection of a mediator, the mediation participants and the mediator shall submit a proposed consent order appointing the mediator and describing the mediation procedures, including the terms of the mediator's compensation and expense reimbursement (the "Mediation Order"). Procedures that are not set forth in the Mediation Order shall be governed by agreement of the parties, by this rule, or by the mediator.

The proposed Mediation Order shall be accompanied by a verified statement by the mediator stating that such person does not hold or represent an interest adverse to the estate, except as specifically disclosed therein, and that such person is disinterested.

(c) Mediation Procedures.

(i) Unless the Court orders otherwise, the mediator and the mediation participants shall agree on the time and location for the initial mediation conference, which shall take place as soon as practicable after the entry of the Mediation Order, but no later than 30 days after the entry of the Mediation Order. The mediator may require the mediation participants to submit or exchange documents or information, including a mediation statement, before the initial mediation conference.

(ii) Each mediation participant that is an individual shall attend the mediation conference in person. Each mediation participant that is a government entity shall attend in person by a representative who has,

to the extent practicable, authority to settle the matter. All other mediation participants shall attend the mediation conference in person through a representative with authority to settle the matter. The mediator may permit telephonic or video participation in the mediation conference in appropriate circumstances.

(iii) The mediator shall determine the time and place for the mediation, including mediation conferences and caucuses between the mediator and a mediation participant, and the submission or exchange of documents or information. The mediator may not require a mediation participant who is represented by counsel to meet with the mediator without counsel present.

(iv) The mediator may set a deadline for the mediation participants to respond to a settlement proposal, including a settlement proposal by the mediator.

(v) Additional mediation procedures for the mediation may be agreed upon by the mediator and the mediation participants during the mediation process.

(d) Settlement Proposals by the Mediator. The mediator may, but shall not be required to, make a settlement proposal to the mediation participants. A settlement proposal by the mediator that is not accepted by the mediation participants shall not be disclosed to the Court.

(e) Failure to Comply with the Mediation Rule. If a mediation participant willfully fails to participate in good faith in the mediation process, then the mediator shall submit to the Clerk and serve on the mediation participants a report of the failure to participate. The report shall not be electronically filed, shall state on the first page at the top right corner that it is being submitted to the attention of the Clerk, and shall state that it is a report of a failure to mediate in good faith that should not be filed or given to the Judge. The report shall not be sent to the Judge presiding over the matter. The Clerk shall deliver the report to the Judge designated by the Chief Judge for mediation, who will take appropriate action, including holding a conference or hearing in person or telephone, and who may, in appropriate circumstances, impose sanctions.

(f) Post–Mediation Procedures.

(i) If the mediation participants reach an agreement, then the mediator shall serve upon the parties and file electronically with the Court a report stating that the matter has been settled.

(ii) If the mediation participants do not reach an agreement, and the mediator concludes that the mediation is at an impasse, then the mediator shall serve upon the parties and file with the Court a report stating that the mediation has reached an impasse and should be concluded.

(iii) Upon the filing of the mediator's report, the mediation will be placed in suspense and the mediator will be excused from undertaking any further actions, unless otherwise requested by the mediation participants or directed by the Court.

(g) Withdrawal from Mediation. At any time, the Court may withdraw a matter from mediation if the Court determines that the mediation referral is no longer appropriate. At any time, a party in interest, the United States trustee, or the mediator may request a conference with the Court or file a motion to withdraw a matter from mediation for cause.

(h) Mediator Compensation. The mediator shall be compensated on terms that are satisfactory to the mediator and the mediation participants. The mediator's compensation shall be subject to Court approval if the estate is to pay any part of the expense. The mediator and the mediation participants shall set forth the terms of the mediator's compensation in the Mediation Order. Absent agreement or order to the contrary, the mediation participants shall pay equal shares of the mediator's compensation. If the mediator and the mediation participants cannot agree on compensation terms, the Court shall fix terms that are reasonable and just. The Court may also request the mediator serve pro bono or on a reduced fee basis.

(i) Qualifications of the Mediator. The Clerk shall maintain a Mediation Register. Appointments to the Mediation Register shall be for 5–year terms. To qualify for appointment to the Mediation Register, a person must:

(i) file an application in the form established by the Clerk;

(ii) not have been suspended from a professional organization or have had a professional license revoked, not have pending any proceeding to suspend or revoke such license, not have resigned from any applicable professional organization while an investigation into allegations of misconduct which would warrant suspension, disbarment, or professional license revocation was pending; and not been convicted of a felony;

(iii) not have been employed by the Court during the 36–month period preceding the date of such person's appointment to the Mediation Register; and

(iv) meet the following minimum qualifications:

(A) For Lawyers Applying to be a Mediator: A lawyer must:

(1) be, or have been, a member in good standing of the New York State bar for at least 5 years;

(2) be admitted to practice in one of the district courts in the Second Circuit;

(3) have completed at least 12 hours of mediation training;

(4) be willing to undertake a minimum of 5 pro bono mediation assignments during the course of the 5–year term;

(5) file with the application original and current certificates of good standing from the department of the Supreme Court of New York Appellate Division in which he or she is admitted and from one of the district courts within the Second Circuit, or if retired, have been a member in good standing in such courts; and

(6) be certified by the Chief Judge.

(B) For Other Professionals Applying to be a Mediator: A person must:

(1) be, or have been, authorized to practice for at least 5 years under the laws of the State of New York as a professional, including but not limited to, an accountant, real estate broker, appraiser, engineer, or other professional occupation;

(2) be an active member in good standing and submit to the Clerk proof of his or her professional status, or if retired, have been a member in good standing, of any applicable professional organization;

(3) have completed a mediation course or courses consisting of at least 12 hours of training;

(4) be willing to undertake a minimum of five pro bono mediation assignments during the course of the 5–year term; and

(5) be certified by the Chief Judge.

The Chief Judge may waive any of the requirements of this subdivision for good cause set forth in the application. Each person certified as a mediator shall take an oath or affirmation before his or her appointment to the Mediation Register.

(j) Removal from the Mediation Register. A person may be removed from the Mediation Register at the person's request or by the Chief Judge.

(k) The Mediation Register. The Clerk shall maintain the Mediation Register at the Court's Website and in the Clerk's office. The Mediation Register shall list the persons appointed to the Mediation Register, together with a brief biography and fee information supplied by the mediator to the Clerk. The Clerk shall also maintain for public inspection the applications filed by persons appointed to the Mediation Register.

(*l*) Confidentiality. Any oral or written statements made by the mediator, the mediation participants, or others during the mediation process shall not be disclosed by any of the mediation participants, their agents, or the mediator, except that such statements may be disclosed to a Judge designated to hear a matter under subdivision (e) of this rule. Matters not to be disclosed include, without limitation:

(i) views expressed or suggestions made by a participant with respect to a possible settlement of the dispute;

(ii) whether a participant indicated a willingness to accept a proposal for settlement made by the mediator;

(iii) proposals made or views expressed by the mediator;

(iv) statements or admissions made by a participant; and

(v) documents prepared for use in the mediation.

Records, reports, or other documents received by a mediator shall be confidential and shall not be provided to the Court except as required by subdivision (e) of this rule. The mediator shall not be compelled to testify or disclose any information concerning the mediation in any forum or proceeding, except as required by subdivision (e) of this rule. Unless the mediation participants and the mediator agree or the Court orders otherwise, 60 days after the mediator files a report under subdivision (f) of this rule, the mediator may discard the submissions made by the mediation participants and any other documents or information relating to the mediation.

Rule 408 of the Federal Rules of Evidence and any applicable federal or state statute, rule, common law, or judicial precedent relating to the privileged nature of settlement discussions, mediation, or other alternative dispute resolution procedure shall apply to statements and information that may not be disclosed pursuant to this rule. Information otherwise discoverable or admissible in evidence shall not be immunized from discovery or inadmissible in evidence because it was disclosed in the mediation.

(m) Immunity. The mediator shall be immune from claims arising out of acts or omissions arising from or relating to his or her service as a Court appointee, to the maximum extent allowed by law.

[Effective May 28, 2008.]

REFERENCE: Federal Rule of Evidence 408

RULE 9021–1. ENTRY OF ORDERS, JUDGMENTS AND DECREES

(a) Entry. The Clerk shall enter all orders, decrees, and judgments of the Court in the Electronic Case Filing system which shall constitute docketing of the order, decree, or judgment for all purposes. The Clerk's notation in the appropriate docket of an order, judgment, or decree shall constitute the entry of the order, judgment, or decree.

(b) Official Location. Each Court maintains a separate index of judgments signed by the Judges located at that site.

[Effective July 1, 1997; amended effective July 1, 1999; May 28, 2008.]

RULE 9023–1. COSTS; NEW TRIALS; MOTIONS FOR RECONSIDERATION

(a) Costs. The expense of any party in obtaining all or any part of a transcript for purposes of a new trial or amended findings may be a cost taxable against the losing party.

(b) Motions for Reconsideration. A motion for reconsideration of an order may be made pursuant to Bankruptcy Rule 9023.

[Effective July 1, 1997; amended effective May 28, 2008.]

RULE 9025–1. SURETIES

(a) Execution by Surety Only. If a bond, undertaking, or stipulation is required, an instrument executed only by the surety shall be sufficient.

(b) Security for Bond. Except as otherwise provided by law, every bond, undertaking, or stipulation referring to a bond shall be secured by:

(i) the deposit of cash or government bonds in the amount of the bond, undertaking, or stipulation;

(ii) the undertaking or guaranty of a corporate surety holding a certificate of authority from the Secretary of the Treasury; or

(iii) the undertaking or guaranty of two individual residents of the Eastern District or Southern District of New York, each of whom owns real or personal property within such district with an unencumbered value of twice the amount of the bond in excess of the surety's debts, liabilities, legal exemptions, and obligations on other bonds, guaranties, undertakings, or stipulations.

(c) Affidavit by Individual Surety. In the case of a bond, undertaking, or stipulation executed by individual sureties, each surety shall attach an affidavit of justification, giving the surety's full name, occupation, and residence and business addresses, and showing that the surety is not disqualified from acting as an individual surety under subdivision (d) of this rule.

(d) Persons Who May Not Act as Sureties. Members of the bar, administrative officers and employees of the Court, the marshal, and the marshal's deputies and assistants may not act as sureties in any pending case, adversary proceeding, or contested matter.

(e) Approval of Bonds of Corporate Sureties. Except as otherwise provided by Bankruptcy Code §§ 303 and 322(b) and Bankruptcy Rule 2010, all bonds, undertakings, and stipulations of corporate sureties holding certificates of authority from the Secretary of the Treasury, may be approved by the Clerk when the amount of such bonds or undertakings has been fixed by Court order or statute.

[Effective July 1, 1997; amended effective July 1, 1999; May 28, 2008.]

CROSS–REFERENCE: E.D.N.Y. LBR 6005–1

REFERENCES: Bankruptcy Code §§ 303, 322(b); Bankruptcy Rule 2010

RULE 9028–1. UNAVAILABILITY OF A JUDGE

In the event of the unavailability of a Judge, any other Judge may act. To obtain the assistance of an available Judge, the parties shall communicate first with the chambers staff of the assigned Judge or, if chambers staff is unavailable, then with the Clerk.

[Effective July 1, 1997; amended effective July 1, 1999.]

RULE 9036–1. CONSENT TO NOTICE BY ELECTRONIC TRANSMISSION

The receipt of an Electronic Case Filing password from the Court shall constitute a consent to electronic notice by the attorney receiving the password pursuant to Bankruptcy Rule 9036, and shall constitute a waiver by such attorney of the right to receive notice by other, non-electronic means.

[Effective May 28, 2008.]

RULE 9036–2. CONSENT TO SERVICE BY ELECTRONIC TRANSMISSION

(a) **Consent to Electronic Service.** The receipt of an Electronic Case Filing password from the Court shall constitute a consent to electronic service by the attorney receiving the password pursuant to Bankruptcy Rule 9036, and except as otherwise provided in subdivision (c) of this rule, constitutes a waiver by such attorney of the right to receive service by other, non-electronic means.

(b) **Service by Electronic Transmission.** Whenever service is required to be made on a person who has consented to, or is deemed to have consented to, electronic service in accordance with Bankruptcy Rule 9036 or subdivision (a) of this rule, service shall be made by serving the "Notice of Electronic Filing" generated by the ECF system either by hand, facsimile, or e-mail, or by overnight mail if service by hand, facsimile, or e-mail is impracticable.

(c) **Exceptions to Electronic Service.** Notwithstanding E.D.N.Y. LBR 9036–1 and subdivisions (a) and (b) of this rule, paper copies of documents or notices shall be served in the following circumstances:

(i) Service made in accordance with Bankruptcy Rules 7004 and 9016; and

(ii) Upon commencement of a case, service by counsel for the debtor of the petition, schedules, and statement of affairs on the United States trustee, all applicable governmental agencies, and the trustee assigned to the case, when applicable.

(d) **Proof of Service.** Proof of service under this rule as required by E.D.N.Y. LBR 9013–1(f), shall include a list of parties electronically served and the e-mail address where service was transmitted.

[Effective May 28, 2008.]

CROSS–REFERENCE: E.D.N.Y. LBR 2002–2, 9013–1

REFERENCE: General Order on Electronic Filing Procedures, Bankruptcy Rules 2002, 7004, 9016; Federal Rules of Civil Procedure 4, 45

RULE 9070–1. CUSTODY OF EXHIBITS

(a) **Retention by Attorney.** In any trial or contested hearing in which exhibits are introduced, exhibits shall not be filed with the Clerk unless the Court orders such filing, but shall be retained by the attorney or party who offered them in Court. That attorney or party shall permit their inspection by any party for the purpose of preparing the record on appeal and shall be charged with the responsibility for their safekeeping and transportation to the appellate court.

(b) **Removal of Exhibits from Court.** Exhibits that have been filed with the Clerk shall be removed by the party responsible for the exhibits:

(i) if no appeal has been taken, at the expiration of the time for taking an appeal; or

(ii) if an appeal has been taken, within 30 days after the record on appeal has been returned to the Clerk.

Parties failing to comply with this rule shall be notified by the Clerk to remove their exhibits, and, upon their failure to do so within 30 days of such notification, the Clerk may dispose of the exhibits at the expense of the party responsible.

[Effective July 1, 1997; amended effective May 28, 2008.]

CROSS–REFERENCE: E.D.N.Y. LBR 8007–1

RULE 9072–1. SETTLEMENT OR SUBMISSION OF ORDER, JUDGMENT OR DECREE

(a) **Settlement of Order, Judgment or Decree.** If, following a trial, hearing, or decision in an adversary proceeding or contested matter, the Court directs a party to settle an order, judgment, or decree, the party shall, within 15 days of the Court's direction, or such other time period as the Court may direct, file its proposed order, judgment, or decree upon at least 5 days' notice to all parties to the adversary proceeding or contested matter, except that such notice period shall not apply if all parties to the adversary proceeding or contested matter have consented in writing to the proposed order, judgment, or decree. Counter-proposals of the proposed order, judgment, or decree shall be filed and served on at least 2 days' notice. If the proposed or counter-proposed order, judgment, or decree is served by first-class mail, an additional 3 days shall be added to the minimum service requirement. If the proposed or counter-proposed order, judgment, or decree is served by overnight mail or courier, an additional day shall be added to the minimum service requirement.

(b) Submission of Order, Judgment or Decree. If, following a trial, hearing or decision in an adversary proceeding or contested matter, the Court directs a party to submit an order, judgment, or decree, the party shall, within 15 days of the Court's direction, file its proposed order, judgment, or decree.

(c) Reference to Hearing Date. The proposed order, judgment, or decree and any counter-proposal shall refer to the hearing date to which the order applies.

(d) Abandonment of Matter. If the order is not timely submitted or settled, the matter may be deemed abandoned.

[Effective July 1, 1997; amended effective May 28, 2008.]

RULE 9077–1. ORDERS TO SHOW CAUSE; EX PARTE ORDERS; ORDERS SHORTENING TIME

(a) Orders to Show Cause. An order to show cause shall be based on an affidavit or an affirmation showing reasons why proceeding other than by notice of motion is necessary. The affidavit or affirmation also shall state whether a previous application for similar relief has been made.

(b) Ex Parte Orders. An ex parte request for an order shall be based on an affidavit or an affirmation showing cause for ex parte relief, and stating whether a previous application for similar relief has been made.

(c) Orders Shortening Time. When expedited relief is thought necessary and the requirements for an order to show cause are not present and ex parte relief is not appropriate, the moving party may proceed by submitting a proposed order shortening time. A request for an order shortening time may be made ex parte and shall be supported by an affidavit or an affirmation showing cause for such expedited relief and stating whether a previous application for similar relief has been made.

[Effective July 1, 1997; amended effective May 28, 2008.]

REFERENCE: Bankruptcy Rule 9006

Committee Note: Former E.D.N.Y. LBR 9078–1 was redesignated E.D.N.Y. LBR 9013–1(f).

APPENDIX

APPENDIX. LOCAL RULES OF THE UNITED STATES DISTRICT COURTS FOR THE SOUTHERN AND EASTERN DISTRICTS OF NEW YORK (EFFECTIVE APRIL 15, 1997) REFERRED TO IN THESE RULES

[For the text of District Court Rules 1.3, 1.8, and 54.1, please see the U.S. District Court Rules for the Southern and Eastern Districts, ante.]

SELECTED ORDERS

ADMINISTRATIVE ORDER 473. ELECTRONIC MEANS FOR FILING, SIGNING, AND VERIFICATION OF DOCUMENTS

WHEREAS, Federal Rule of Civil Procedure ("FRCP") 83 and Federal Rules of Bankruptcy Procedure ("FRBP") 5005(a)(2) and 9029 authorize this court to establish practices and procedures for the filing, signing and verification of documents by electronic means; and

WHEREAS, by General Order #462, dated August 24, 2001, the court established such practices and procedures; and

WHEREAS, a proposal as to the adoption of revised Administrative Procedures for Filing, Signing and Verifying Documents by Electronic Means ("Electronic Filing Procedures") has been reviewed by the court; and

WHEREAS, the Electronic Filing Procedures are consistent with and enhance the responsibility of the Clerk of the Court in the control of the court's docket under FRBP 5003 and 5005, including safeguarding the integrity of the court's docket; and

WHEREAS, the Electronic Filing Procedures do not impose fees inconsistent with the present fee structure adopted by the Judicial Conference of the United States pursuant to 28 U.S.C. §§ 1913, 1914, 1926 and 1930; and

WHEREAS, the Electronic Filing Procedures allow for the obtaining of a password by attorneys, which password identifies the party filing electronically; and

WHEREAS, the Electronic Filing Procedures provide for the signing of electronically filed documents in a manner consistent with terms set forth in Local Rule of Bankruptcy Procedure ("LRBP") 9011–1(b); and

WHEREAS, the Electronic Filing Procedures make adequate provision for the filing, review and retrieval of documents by parties who are not able to access the Electronic Filing System (the "System") from a remote location; and

WHEREAS, the Electronic Filing Procedures do not impair the ability of the Clerk of the Court to discharge statistical reporting responsibilities both to the court and the Administrative Office of the United States Courts; and

WHEREAS, the Electronic Filing Procedures are consistent with the notice requirements of FRBP 2002;

NOW, THEREFORE, IT IS ORDERED that:

1. The Electronic Filing Procedures, attached as Exhibit 1 to this order, are approved by the court.

2. Electronic files, consisting of the images of documents filed in cases or proceedings and documents filed by electronic means, are designated as and shall constitute the official record of the court together with the other records kept by the court.

3. No attorney or other person shall knowingly permit or cause to permit the attorney's password to be utilized by anyone other than an authorized member or employee of the attorney's law firm.

4. The initials of the attorney's first and last names and the last four digits of the social security number of the attorney who is signing an electronically filed document in accordance with Part II(i) of the Electronic Filing Procedures, shall constitute the signature of that attorney for purposes of FRBP 9011 and LRBP 9011–1.

5. The electronic filing of a document in accordance with the Electronic Filing Procedures shall constitute entry of that document on the docket kept by the clerk under FRBP 5003, and shall be deemed accepted for filing by the clerk's office.

6. The Office of the Clerk shall enter all applicable orders, decrees, judgments and proceedings of the court in accordance with the Electronic Filing Procedures, which shall constitute entry of the order, decree, judgment or proceeding on the docket kept by the Clerk under FRBP 5003 and for purposes of FRBP 9021.

7. The request for and receipt of a System password from the court shall constitute a request for electronic service by the attorney receiving the password pursuant to FRBP 9036, and except as otherwise provided in the Electronic Filing Procedures, a waiver by such attorney of the right to receive notice and service conventionally.

8. The original of this order shall be filed in accordance with the Electronic Filing Procedures.

9. Amendments to this order or the Electronic Filing Procedures may be entered from time to time in keeping with the needs of the court.

10. This order shall become effective on January 1, 2003, and shall apply to all bankruptcy cases and adversary proceedings filed on or after such effective date. Only proofs of claim are to be filed in paper form.

Dated: Brooklyn, New York
     December 26, 2002.

EXHIBIT 1. REVISED ADMINISTRATIVE PROCEDURES FOR ELECTRONICALLY FILED CASES

I. REGISTRATION FOR THE ELECTRONIC FILING SYSTEM.

A. *Designation of Cases.* All bankruptcy cases and adversary proceedings filed on or after January 1, 2003 shall be assigned to the Electronic Case Filing System.

B. *Passwords.* Each attorney admitted to practice in this court shall be entitled to one System password to permit the attorney to participate in the electronic retrieval and filing of documents in accordance with the System. Application for a password is governed by paragraphs I.C.1 and 2.

C. *Registration.*

1. To register to use the System, attorneys must submit a password application, in the form attached. A duplicate copy of the attached form may be used.

2. Completed password applications are to be mailed or delivered to the Office of the Clerk, United States Bankruptcy Court, Eastern District of New York, Long Island Federal Courthouse, 290 Federal Plaza, Central Islip, New York 11722, Attn: Electronic Case Filing System Registration.

3. Upon registering, attorneys will receive an envelope from the Office of the Clerk, clearly marked "Personal and Confidential," containing the attorney's assigned System password. Attorneys may request an alternative means of delivery of the password by telephoning the Office of the Clerk.

4. Attorneys may find it desirable to change their court assigned password periodically. This can be done by following instructions in the CM/ECF Attorney Manual, available at the court's Web site at www.nyeb.uscourts.gov. In the event an attorney believes that the security of an existing password has been compromised and a threat to the System exists, the attorney shall give immediate telephonic notice to the Clerk of Court, Chief Deputy Clerk or Systems Department Manager, confirmed by facsimile, to prevent access to the System through use of that password.

II. ELECTRONIC FILING AND SERVICE OF DOCUMENTS.

A. *Filing.*

1. All motions, pleadings, memoranda of law, or other documents required to be filed with the court in connection with a case, other than proofs of claim and certain exceptions specified in paragraph III below, shall be electronically filed on the System. Within 24 hours of the electronic filing, a hard copy shall be provided to chambers, which copy is to be marked "Chambers Copy" in the top center of the title page. The hard copy is to be filed with the Office of the Clerk, to the attention of the appropriate judge's chambers. The date and time of the electronic filing shall be the official date and time of filing of the document.

2. Attorneys who do not file electronically will be required to submit all filings to the court on diskette in PDF format.

3. All documents that form part of a motion or pleading, and which are being filed at the same time and by the same party, may be electronically filed together under one docket number, i.e., the motion and a supporting affidavit or application,

with the exception of a memorandum of law. A memorandum of law must be filed separately and specified as related to the motion or pleading.

4. Persons filing documents that reference exhibits which are not in electronic form shall scan and electronically file excerpts of the exhibits that are directly germane to the matter under consideration by the court. Such filings must be clearly and prominently identified as excerpts, must not exceed twenty (20) pages, and state that the entire document is in the possession of the filing party. The entire exhibit must be made available forthwith to counsel and the court on request, and must be available in the courtroom at any hearing pertaining to the matter. Persons filing excerpts of exhibits pursuant to these Procedures do so without prejudice to their right to file additional excerpts or the entire exhibit with the court at any time. Opposing parties may file additional excerpts if they believe that they are germane.

5. Title of Docket Entries. The person electronically filing a document is responsible for designating a title for the document using one of the main categories provided in the System, i.e., motion, application, etc.

6. Payment of Filing Fees. An application for authorization to pay filing fees by credit card will be made as part of the attorney's password application form.

7. Electronic Filing in Non–Electronic Case. Documents filed electronically in a non-electronic case will be purged from the database, with the associated docket event annotated "Entered in Error." The filer will be required to resubmit the document to the court in paper form. The document will be deemed officially filed as of the date and time of the court's receipt of the filing in paper form.

B. *Service.*

1. General Rule. Except as otherwise provided in paragraph 2 below, all documents required to be served shall be served in paper (i.e., "hard copy") form in the manner mandated by the applicable law and rules.

2. Consent to Electronic Service. Whenever service is required to be made on a person who has requested, or is deemed to have requested, electronic notice in accordance with FRBP 9036 or paragraph 7 of the court's General Order on Electronic Filing Procedures, service may be made by serving the "Notice of Electronic Filing" generated by the System by hand, facsimile or e-mail in the first instance, or by overnight mail if service by hand, facsimile or e-mail is impracticable.

3. Notwithstanding the foregoing, hard copies of documents or notices shall be served in the following circumstances:

(a) Service made in accordance with FRCP 4, FRCP 45, FRBP 7004 or FRBP 9016.

(b) Service made upon an agency of the United States, including the United States Attorney, the United States Trustee, or chambers, in accordance with the FRBP, LRBP or an order of the court.

(c) Notice served pursuant to FRBP 2002(a)(1).

(d) Upon the commencement of a case, service by counsel for the debtor of the petition, schedules and statement of affairs on the United States Trustee, all applicable governmental agencies and the trustee assigned to the case, where applicable.

4. Orders. All signed orders (including, without limitation, orders to show cause) shall be filed electronically by the court. To facilitate the review, execution and filing of a proposed order, the person presenting the proposed order shall provide the presiding judge with a 3.5 inch floppy disk containing the proposed order (in word processing, not PDF format), together with any document to be electronically filed in connection therewith (in PDF format). Simultaneously, the presiding judge shall also be provided with a chambers copy of all such documents.

5. Notice of Electronic Filing Procedure, Adversary Proceedings. Upon issuance by the Office of the Clerk of the Summons and Notice of Pretrial Conference, the attorney for the plaintiff shall serve same along with a Notice of Electronic Filing Procedure upon all parties to the proceeding.

C. *Signatures; Affidavits of Service.*

1. Every petition, pleading, motion and other paper served or filed in accordance with the Electronic Filing Procedures shall include by way of signature the initials of the filing attorney's first and last name followed by the last four digits of the attorney's social security number. Additionally, an "electronic signature" in the form "s/Jane Doe" shall be included in every electronically filed document.

2. Petitions, lists, schedules, statements, amendments, pleadings, affidavits, stipulations and other documents which must contain original signatures, documents requiring verification under FRBP 1008, and unsworn declarations under 28 U.S.C. § 1746, shall be filed electronically and bear "electronic signatures." The hard copy of the originally executed document, and/or original exhibits, shall be maintained by the filer for two years after the entry of a final order terminating the case or proceeding to which the document relates. On request of the court, the filer must provide original documents for review.

3. Every order and judgment signed by the judge shall be filed electronically by the Clerk's Office at the direction of the court and bear an "electronic signature." The hard copy of the manually executed document shall be maintained by the Clerk until the entry of a final order terminating the case or proceeding to which the document relates.

III. DOCUMENTS FILED UNDER SEAL.

A. *Motion.* A motion to file documents under seal (but not the documents themselves) shall be filed electronically. If the motion itself contains confidential information, the movant shall serve and file electronically a redacted version clearly marked as such, and submit an unredacted version in camera. If requested by the court, the movant shall deliver hard copies of the documents proposed to be filed under seal to the presiding judge for in camera review.

B. *Order.* The order of the court determining the motion shall be filed electronically by the court.

C. *Copies.* If the court grants the motion, in whole or in part, the movant shall deliver the following to the Clerk of the Court or Chief Deputy Clerk of the Court:

1. A hard copy of the documents to be filed under seal (the "sealed documents") and

2. A 3.5 inch floppy disk containing the sealed documents and the sealing order. The disk shall be submitted in an envelope or disk mailer, clearly labeled with the case name and number, and if applicable, the document number assigned to the sealed document.

3. Hard copies of the sealing order shall be attached to the hard copy of the sealed documents and to the 3.5 inch disk.

D. *Clerk's Responsibilities.* Unless otherwise ordered by the court, the Clerk of the Court shall file any documents ordered to be filed under seal conventionally and not electronically.

IV. PUBLIC ACCESS TO THE SYSTEM DOCKET.

A. *Internet Access.* Any person or organization may access the System at the court's Internet site at: www.nyeb.uscourts.gov. Access to the System through the Internet site will be available using a password to retrieve the docket sheet and documents in a "read only" format. With the introduction of Electronic Case Filing, "Version 1," a password obtained from the Public Access to Electronic Court Records Center ("PACER") will be required by all users of the System. (See D. below and the court's web site for further information.) Information posted on the

System shall not be downloaded for uses inconsistent with the privacy concerns of debtors and third parties.

B. *Access at the Court.* Documents filed on the System and case dockets are available for viewing in the Office of the Clerk during regular business hours No password is required.

C. *Conventional Copies and Certified Copies.* Conventional copies and certified copies of electronically filed documents may be purchased at the Office of the Clerk, at Long Island Federal Courthouse, 290 Federal Plaza, Central Islip, New York, or the United States Bankruptcy Court, 75 Clinton Street, Brooklyn, New York during regular business hours. Fees for copying and certification shall be in accordance with 28 U.S.C. § 1930.

D. *Access Charges.* At such time as the Court implements charges required by the Judicial Conference of the United States, as set out in 28 U.S.C. § 1930, for the usage of electronic access to the Court's records, users of the System will be charged in accordance with the fees and procedures established by the Administrative Office of the United States Courts.

ELECTRONIC CASE FILING SYSTEM—
ATTORNEY PASSWORD APPLICATION LIVE SYSTEM

I, _____ , swear or affirm that I am a member in good standing of the Bar of the State of _____. By submitting this application and receiving a password, I agree to adhere to the court's order authorizing electronic case filing, any supplements and/or amendments thereto and the rules promulgated for the court's ELECTRONIC CASE FILING (ECF) SYSTEM. I am providing the following information as a condition of receiving my password:

Attorney Code (first & last name initials/last 4 digits of social security #): _____

Attorney Name: _____

Firm Name: _____

Address: _____

Phone #: _____ FAX #: _____

Internet E–Mail Address for Service: _____
☐ I consent to delivery of my assigned System password to the above-mentioned e-mail address.

Class Training Completion Date: _____

I have read and understand the following rules:

1. I will employ the Electronic Case Filing System for cases filed in the United States Bankruptcy Court for the Eastern District of New York.

2. I will meet all hardware and software requirements disseminated by the court for system use. I understand that the current minimum requirements for filing documents are: a personal computer running a standard Windows platform (Windows 98/Me/NT/2000/XP); an Internet provider using Point to Point Protocol (PPP) for dial-up service, or offering DSL or cable service; Netscape Navigator 4.7x or higher or Microsoft Internet Explorer 5.5 or higher; Adobe Acrobat 4.01 or higher [to convert word processor format documents to portable document format (PDF)]; and a document scanner.

3. Each use of my password for filing documents will meet the requirements of Fed. R. Civ. P. 11, Fed. R. Bankr. P. 9011 and Local Bankruptcy Rule 9011–1. I understand that the use of my password together with my electronic signature constitutes my signature on the document being submitted. If I submit a

document for another party, I understand it is my responsibility to maintain a copy of that document bearing the signer's signature in my records.

4. I agree to protect and secure the confidentiality of my password. Therefore, if I have reason to believe that my password has been compromised, it is my responsibility to immediately notify the court in writing. Moreover, it is also my responsibility to immediately inform the court of any change in my firm affiliation, addresses, telephone, fax or E-mail address.

5. I understand that the issuance of a password to me constitutes a waiver of conventional service pursuant to the court's Electronic Filing Procedures General Order. I agree to accept a Notice of Electronic Filing by hand, facsimile, first class mail or authorized e-mail in lieu of conventional service. Moreover, I will use the automatic E-mail notification feature of the Electronic Case Filing System wherever feasible.

6. Notwithstanding No. 5 herein, conventional (paper) service is required in all non-electronic filings as well as on the United States and its agencies, and on foreign, state or local governments, in full compliance with Rules 2002(j) and 7004(b)(4), (5) and (6) of the Federal Rules of Bankruptcy Procedure and Rule 4(i) and (j) of the Federal Rules of Civil Procedure.

7. In compliance with the Electronic Filing Procedures General Order, I understand that if documents being submitted electronically have lengthy exhibits, the filing of relevant excerpts of the exhibits is preferred and permitted without prejudice to my right to file additional excerpts or the complete exhibit with the court at any time.

8. In compliance with the Electronic Filing Procedures General Order, once I receive my password, I will make every reasonable effort to file documents electronically. If I am unable to file electronically, documents will be submitted to the court on diskette in PDF format. Paper filings received at the court will be scanned by the delivering party.

9. I understand that receipt of a password and access to the ECF Filing System is contingent upon my completing the Eastern District Bankruptcy Court Attorney Password Application, and the required training class, unless a waiver is granted.

10. I understand that I will pay for all fee-related Internet filings through the court's Internet credit card payment process (Pay.gov). I understand that I must maintain a valid VISA, MasterCard, Discover, Diners Club or American Express credit or debit card to pay for fee-related filings.

11. I understand that I will be required to pay for all fee-related filings by midnight of the day of filing, and that any failure to pay the fees due may result in revocation of my ECF password.

Date: _____

_____
Attorney Applicant Signature

Please return to:

United States Bankruptcy Court
290 Federal Plaza
P.O. Box 9013
Central Islip, New York 11722–9013

FOR COURT OFFICE USE ONLY:

Date application received: _/_/___ Date access permitted: _/_/___

Date reviewed for compliance: _/_/___ Authorized by: _____

CREDIT CARD BLANKET AUTHORIZATION FORM

I hereby authorize the United States Bankruptcy Court for the Eastern District of New York to charge the main credit card or the alternate credit card listed below for payment of fees, costs, and expenses which are incurred by myself or any member or employee of the law firm, partnership, or professional corporations stated below. I certify that I am authorized to sign this form on behalf of my law firm.

(Please indicate which card is to be the main card and the alternate card)

___MasterCard No. _____ Exp. Date: _____

___Visa Card No. _____ Exp. Date: _____

___Discover Card No. _____ Exp. Date: _____

___American Express No. _____ Exp. Date: _____

___Diners Club No. _____ Exp. Date: _____

Credit Cardholder's Name: _____

NAMES OF INDIVIDUALS AUTHORIZED TO USE ACCOUNT NUMBERS LISTED ABOVE FOR PAYMENT OF FEES, COSTS, AND EXPENSES:

_____ _____

_____ _____

_____ _____

Cardholder's Mailing Address: _____

City: _____ State: _____ Zip Code:____

Law Firm Name:_____ (Or name of sole practitioner)

Address: _____

Phone No: _____ Fax No: _____

This form will be kept on file in the clerk's office and will remain in effect until specifically revoked in writing. It is the responsibility of the law firm/company named above to submit a new form and notify the court of any changes to authorized users, a new expiration date when a credit card has been renewed, or if a card has been revoked, cancelled, or stolen.

Signature: _____ Date: _____

* Note: The card indicated above as the main card will be used for all transactions with this court unless otherwise specified by the authorized user.

ADMINISTRATIVE ORDER 476. MANDATORY FILING OF DOCUMENTS BY ELECTRONIC MEANS

Whereas, the court having established, by General Order dated December 26, 2002, electronic filing procedures applicable to all bankruptcy cases and adversary proceedings filed on or after January 1, 2003, and

Whereas, it being in the court's interest to ensure compliance with such procedures by the practicing bar without any undue delay, it is

ORDERED, that effective October 1, 2003, any document (other than a proof of claim) filed by an attorney in a case which has been assigned to the court's Electronic Case Filing System shall be filed electronically, either over the Internet or on diskette in PDF format, and it is further,

ORDERED, that the Clerk is hereby authorized to reject for filing any document not submitted in accordance with the foregoing specification. Mandatory filing of all documents over the Internet will become effective as of a date to be determined by the court.

Dated: June 4, 2003.

ADMINISTRATIVE ORDER 487. TRANSFER OF CASES IN WHICH PETITION WAS INADVERTENTLY FILED IN THIS DISTRICT

Whereas, Pay.gov financial services are to be implemented in this Court effective May 1, 2005, and

Whereas, the implementation of Pay.gov requires that certain Court procedures be modified, it is

ORDERED, that effective May 1, 2005, in connection with any bankruptcy petition filed over the Internet, the Clerk is authorized and directed, upon being informed by the debtor's counsel that a bankruptcy petition was inadvertently filed in this district, to transfer the bankruptcy case to the appropriate district.

Dated: Brooklyn, New York
      March 31, 2005.

ADMINISTRATIVE ORDER 488. DISMISSAL OF DUPLICATE PETITION FILED IN ERROR

Whereas, Pay.gov financial services are to be implemented in this Court effective May 1, 2005, and

Whereas, the implementation of Pay.gov requires that certain Court Procedures be modified, it is

ORDERED, that effective May 1, 2005, in connection with any bankruptcy petition filed over the Internet, the Clerk is authorized and directed, upon being informed by the debtor's counsel that a duplicate bankruptcy petition was inadvertently filed, to dismiss the duplicate bankruptcy case; and it is further

ORDERED, that the Clerk is authorized and directed to refund any filing fee which may have been paid in connection with such duplicate filing; and it is further

ORDERED, that the entry on the case docket of the order of dismissal shall be deemed sufficient notice of the dismissal of the case.

Dated: Brooklyn, New York
      March 31, 2005.

ADMINISTRATIVE ORDER 489. DISMISSAL OF CASES EXHIBITING CERTAIN DEFECTS

Whereas, Pay.gov financial services are to be implemented in this Court effective May 1, 2005, and

Whereas, the implementation of Pay.gov requires that certain Court Procedures be modified, it is

ORDERED, that effective May 1, 2005, in connection with any bankruptcy petition filed over the Internet, the Clerk is authorized and directed to send an electronic notice to the debtor's counsel (substantially in the form annexed hereto) that identifies one or more deficiency(ies) that, if not cured within two (2) business days of transmission of such notice (the "Cure Period"), will result in dismissal of the bankruptcy case without further notice; and it is further

ORDERED, that the Clerk is authorized and directed to dismiss such bankruptcy case when the debtor's counsel fails to respond within the Cure Period; and it is further

ORDERED, that the entry on the case docket of the order of dismissal shall be deemed sufficient notice of the dismissal of the case.

Dated: Brooklyn, New York
      March 31, 2005.

NOTICE TO CURE DEFICIENCIES IN CONNECTION WITH ELECTRONICALLY FILED BANKRUPTCY PETITION

Bankruptcy Case No.: _____

Date of Filing: _____

Name(s) of Debtor(s): _____

Date of Notice: _____

The above-referenced bankruptcy filing has the following deficiency(ies) (indicated by an "X"):

_____ 1.   the bankruptcy petition was not attached at the time of filing;

_____ 2.   the bankruptcy petition for a different debtor was attached at the time of filing;

_____ 3.   the bankruptcy petition was not signed by the debtor; and/or

_____ 4.   the bankruptcy petition was not signed by the debtor's attorney;

The deficiencies identified in this Notice must be cured within two (2) business days of the transmission of this Notice. If the deficiencies are not cured within this time period, the above-referenced bankruptcy filing will be dismissed without further notice.

      Joseph P. Hurley
      Clerk, U.S. Bankruptcy Court
      Eastern District of New York

ADMINISTRATIVE ORDER 490. DISMISSAL OF CASES FOR WHICH FILING FEE HAS NOT BEEN PAID

Whereas, Pay.gov financial services are to be implemented in this Court effective May 1, 2005, and

Whereas, the implementation of Pay.gov requires that certain Court Procedures be modified, it is

ORDERED, that effective May 1, 2005, where a bankruptcy petition is filed electronically over the Internet and the filing fee has not been paid in full, the Clerk is authorized and directed to send a notice (substantially in the form annexed hereto) to the debtor and the debtor's counsel informing them that the filing fee must be paid in full within five (5) business days of the date of the Notice (the "Cure Period"), failing which the bankruptcy case will be dismissed without further notice; and it is further

ORDERED, that the Clerk is authorized and directed to dismiss such bankruptcy case if the filing fee is not paid in full by the expiration of the Cure Period; and it is further

ORDERED, that the entry on the case docket of the order of dismissal shall be deemed sufficient notice of the dismissal of the case.

Dated: Brooklyn, New York
March 31, 2005.

ADMINISTRATIVE ORDER 497. IN THE MATTER OF ADOPTION OF INTERIM BANKRUPTCY RULES[1]

Whereas, on April 20, 2005 the Bankruptcy Abuse Prevention and Consumer Protection Act (the Act) was enacted into law; and

Whereas, most provisions of the Act are effective on October 17, 2005; and

Whereas, the Advisory Committee on Bankruptcy Rules has prepared Interim Rules designed to implement the substantive and procedural changes mandated by the Act; and

Whereas, the Committee on Rules of Practice and Procedure of the Judicial Conference of the United States has also approved these Interim Rules and recommends the adoption of the Interim Rules to provide uniform procedures for implementing the Act; and

Whereas, the general effective date of the Act has not provided sufficient time to promulgate rules after appropriate public notice and an opportunity for comment;

NOW THEREFORE, pursuant to 28 U.S.C. section 2071, Rule 83 of the Federal Rules of Civil Procedure, and Rule 9029 of the Federal Rules of Bankruptcy Procedure, the attached Interim Rules are adopted in their entirety without change by a majority of the judges of this Court to be effective October 17, 2005 to conform with the Act. For cases and proceedings not governed by the Act, the Federal Rules of Bankruptcy Procedure and the Local Rules of this Court, other than the Interim Rules, shall apply. The Interim

Rules shall remain in effect until further order of the court.

Dated: Brooklyn, New York,
September 27, 2005.

[1] The Interim Bankruptcy Rules follow the Administrative Orders of the United States Bankruptcy Court for the Northern District of New York.

ADMINISTRATIVE ORDER 501. RULES GOVERNING PROCEDURES FOR APPOINTMENT OF PRO BONO COUNSEL IN BANKRUPTCY PROCEEDINGS FROM A BANKRUPTCY PRO BONO PANEL

The Court having adopted in May of 1985 the "Rules Governing Appointment of Pro Bono Counsel" (the "Old Rules"); and the Bankruptcy Judges of this District having subsequently adopted the annexed "Rules Governing Procedures for Appointment of Pro Bono Counsel in Bankruptcy Proceedings from a Bankruptcy Pro Bono Panel" (the "New Rules") to replace the Old Rules; it is hereby

ORDERED, that the New Rules* are adopted.

Dated: Brooklyn, New York
February 21, 2006.

* For the text of the New Rules, see General Order 320 of the United States Bankruptcy Court for the Southern District of New York, ante.

ADMINISTRATIVE ORDER 502. PROCEDURES FOR PAYMENT AND CURE OF PRE–PETITION JUDGMENT OF POSSESSION INVOLVING RESIDENTIAL PROPERTY

WHEREAS, the Bankruptcy Abuse Prevention and Consumer Protection Act of 2005, as codified in 11 U.S.C. § 362(b)(22) and 362(l), creates certain rights and obligations with respect to the cure of a monetary default giving rise to a pre-petition judgment for possession regarding residential property in which the debtor resides as a tenant under a lease or rental agreement, it is hereby

ORDERED, that a debtor shall be deemed to have complied with 11 U.S.C. § 362(l)(1) by:

1. Making the required certification by completing the three check boxes, **including the landlord's name and address,** listed in the voluntary petition under the section entitled "Statement by a Debtor who Resides as a Tenant of Residential Property"; and

2. Delivering to the Clerk of the Court ("Clerk"), together with the petition (or within one business day of the filing, if the petition is filed electronically), a certified or cashier's check or money order, made payable to the lessor, in the amount of any rent that

would become due during the 30–day period after the filing of the petition ("Rent Check"); and it is further

ORDERED, that if a debtor complies with the preceding paragraph, the Clerk shall, within two business days, send notice of the debtor's compliance ("Notice of Compliance") to the lessor which notice shall also request that the lessor inform the Clerk whether it consents or declines to receive the Rent Check. If a lessor consents to receive the Rent Check, the notice will further request that the lessor provide the Clerk with an address to which the Rent Check should be sent; and it is further

ORDERED, that if a lessor fails, within 10 days of the date of the Notice of Compliance, to notify the Clerk whether it consents to or declines receipt of the Rent Check the lessor shall be deemed to have consented to receive the Rent Check and the Clerk shall send the Rent Check to the lessor at the address set forth in the debtor's certification; and it is further

ORDERED, that a lessor's consent to receive the Rent Check shall not preclude the lessor from objecting to a debtor's certification pursuant to 11 U.S.C. §§ 362(l)(1) and/or (2).

Dated: Central Islip, New York
    March 13, 2006.

ADMINISTRATIVE ORDER 504. REVISED PROCEDURAL FORM B 240, REAFFIR-MATION AGREEMENT [ABROGATED]

[See, now, Administrative Order 517.]

Dated: Brooklyn, New York
    August 1, 2006.
    Abrogated January 1, 2007.

ADMINISTRATIVE ORDER 506. ADOPTION OF INTERIM BANKRUPTCY RULE 1007

Whereas, on September 27, 2005, the court adopted the Amendments to the Federal Rules ("Interim Rules"), prepared by the Advisory Committee on Bankruptcy Rules of the Judicial Conference of the Untied States to implement the substantive and procedural changes mandated by the Bankruptcy Abuse Prevention and Consumer Protection Act of 2005, and

Whereas, the Judicial Conference has approved an amendment to Rule 1007 of the Interim Rules and has recommended its adoption by bankruptcy courts by way of local rule or standing order, to be effective October 1, 2006,

NOW THEREFORE, pursuant to 28 U.S.C. section 2071, Rule 83 of the Federal Rules of Civil Procedure and Rule 9029 of the Federal Rules of Bankruptcy Procedure, amended Rule 1007 of the Interim Rules is adopted by this court to be effective October 1, 2006.[1]

For cases filed on and after October 1, 2006, this rule supplants and supersedes Rule 1007 of the Federal Rules of Bankruptcy Procedure.

Dated: Brooklyn, New York
September 29, 2006.

1 The Interim Bankruptcy Rules follow the Administrative Orders of the United States Bankruptcy Court for the Northern District of New York, post.

ADMINISTRATIVE ORDER 512. LIMITED ACCESS FILING OF DOCUMENTS BY ELECTRONIC MEANS

Whereas, the court having established, by General Order dated December 26, 2002, electronic filing procedures applicable to all bankruptcy cases and adversary proceedings filed on or after January 1, 2003, and

Whereas, it being in the court's interest to enable creditors (limited users) to utilize the court's Electronic Case Filing System to electronically file claims, transfers of claim and notices of appearance, and

Whereas, a creditor (limited user) will utilize the Limited Access Password Application to request access to the Electronic Case Filing system and will follow the rules of the ECF General Order and the Limited Access Password Application, it is

ORDERED, that effective January 3, 2007, all proofs of claim, transfers of claim and notices of appearance may be filed electronically in a case which has been designated as an electronic case in the court's Electronic Case Filing System (Chapter 11 cases filed on or after April 1, 2002 and all cases filed on or after January 1, 2003).

Dated: Central Islip, New York
    December 11, 2006.

ADMINISTRATIVE ORDER 517. REVISED AND REFORMATTED REAFFIRMA-TION AGREEMENT AND ORDER (PROCEDURAL FORMS B 240A AND B 240B)

WHEREAS, by Administrative Order #504, dated August 1, 2006, the Court having designated Procedural Form B 240, as revised effective August 1, 2006, for use in this District in the memorializing of Reaffirmation Agreements; and

WHEREAS, the Director of the Administrative Office of the United States Courts having revised and reformatted the Reaffirmation Agreement and Order as two forms (Form B 240A, Reaffirmation Agreement and Form B 240B, Order on Reaffirmation Agreement), which forms having been made effective January 1, 2007; it is

ORDERED, the Administrative Order #504 be and it is hereby abrogated; and it is further

ORDERED, that effective immediately, the annexed Procedural Forms B 240A, Reaffirmation Agreement and B 240B, Order on Reaffirmation Agreement will be required for use in this District in the memorializing of any agreement between the debtor and a creditor to repay a debt pursuant to 11 U.S.C. § 524(c); and it is further

ORDERED, that the Clerk is directed to make the forms available at the Court's Internet site and at the Clerk's Office at each Court location.

Dated: Central Islip, New York
      February 1, 2007.

GENERAL ORDER 533. IN RE: ADOPTION OF FORM FOR MOTIONS FOR RELIEF FROM STAY TO FORECLOSE A MORTGAGE ON REAL PROPERTY OR A SECURITY INTEREST IN A COOPERATIVE APARTMENT

BY resolution of the Board of Judges of the Bankruptcy Court for the Eastern District of New York, it is hereby

ORDERED, that all motions filed on or after September 1, 2008, in the United States Bankruptcy Court for the Eastern District of New York, in cases filed by individuals, seeking relief from the automatic stay pursuant to 11 U.S.C. § 362 to foreclose a mortgage on real property or a security interest in a cooperative apartment, shall include, as an exhibit to the motion, a completed copy of the annexed **Form for Motions for Relief from Stay to Foreclose a Mortgage on Real Property or a Security Interest in a Cooperative Apartment** (the "Form"); and it is further

ORDERED, that unexcused failure to comply with this order may constitute grounds for adjournment or denial of the motion.

Dated: Brooklyn, NY
      July 18, 2008.

UNITED STATES BANKRUPTCY COURT
EASTERN DISTRICT OF NEW YORK
-- X

              CASE NO. ___–_____ (_____)

              CHAPTER ____

-- x

RELIEF FROM STAY—REAL ESTATE AND COOPERATIVE APARTMENTS

BACKGROUND INFORMATION

1. ADDRESS OF REAL PROPERTY OR COOPERATIVE APARTMENT: _____

    _____

2. LENDER NAME: _____

    _____

3. MORTGAGE DATE: _____

4. POST-PETITION PAYMENT ADDRESS: _____

_____

_____

DEBT AND VALUE REPRESENTATIONS

5. TOTAL PRE-PETITION AND POST-PETITION INDEBTEDNESS OF DEBTOR(S) TO MOVANT AS OF THE MOTION FILING DATE: $ _____

(THIS MAY NOT BE RELIED UPON AS A "PAYOFF" QUOTATION.)

6. MOVANT'S ESTIMATED MARKET VALUE OF THE REAL PROPERTY OR COOPERATIVE APARTMENT AS OF THE MOTION FILING DATE: $ _____

7. SOURCE OF ESTIMATED MARKET VALUE: _____

STATUS OF THE DEBT AS OF THE PETITION DATE

8. DEBTOR(S)'S INDEBTEDNESS TO MOVANT AS OF THE PETITION DATE:

    A. TOTAL: $ _____

    B. PRINCIPAL: $ _____

    C. INTEREST: $ _____

    D. ESCROW (TAXES AND INSURANCE): $ _____

    E. FORCED PLACED INSURANCE EXPENDED BY MOVANT: $ _____

    F. PRE-PETITION ATTORNEYS' FEES CHARGED TO DEBTOR(S): $ _____

    G. PRE-PETITION LATE FEES CHARGED TO DEBTOR(S): $ _____

9. CONTRACT INTEREST RATE: _____

(IF THE INTEREST RATE HAS CHANGED, LIST THE RATE(S) AND DATE(S) THAT EACH RATE WAS IN EFFECT ON A SEPARATE SHEET AND ATTACH THE SHEET AS AN EXHIBIT TO THIS FORM. STATE THE EXHIBIT NUMBER HERE: ____)

10. OTHER PRE-PETITION FEES, CHARGES OR AMOUNTS CHARGED TO DEBTOR(S)'S ACCOUNT AND NOT LISTED ABOVE: _____

_____

_____

(IF ADDITIONAL SPACE IS REQUIRED, LIST THE AMOUNT(S) ON A SEPARATE SHEET AND ATTACH THE SHEET AS AN EXHIBIT TO THIS FORM. STATE THE EXHIBIT NUMBER HERE: ____)

AMOUNT OF POST–PETITION DEFAULT AS OF THE MOTION FILING DATE

11. DATE OF RECEIPT OF LAST PAYMENT: _____

12. NUMBER OF PAYMENTS DUE FROM PETITION DATE TO MOTION FILING DATE: ___ PAYMENTS.

13. POST–PETITION PAYMENTS IN DEFAULT:

PAYMENT DUE DATE	AMOUNT DUE	AMOUNT RECEIVED	AMOUNT APPLIED TO PRINCIPAL	AMOUNT APPLIED TO INTEREST	AMOUNT APPLIED TO ESCROW	LATE FEE CHARGED
TOTAL: $	$	$		$	$	$

14. OTHER POST-PETITION FEES CHARGED TO DEBTOR(S):

  A. TOTAL: $ _____

  B. ATTORNEYS' FEES IN CONNECTION WITH THIS MOTION: $ _____

  C. FILING FEE IN CONNECTION WITH THIS MOTION: $ _____

  D. OTHER POST-PETITION ATTORNEYS' FEES: $ _____

  E. POST-PETITION INSPECTION FEES: $ _____

  F. POST-PETITION APPRAISAL/BROKER'S PRICE OPINION FEES: $ _____

  G. FORCED PLACED INSURANCE EXPENDED BY MOVANT: $ _____

15. AMOUNT HELD IN SUSPENSE BY MOVANT: $ _____

16. OTHER POST-PETITION FEES, CHARGES OR AMOUNTS CHARGED TO DEBTOR(S)'S ACCOUNT AND NOT LISTED ABOVE: _____

_____

_____

(IF ADDITIONAL SPACE IS REQUIRED, LIST THE AMOUNT(S) ON A SEPARATE SHEET AND ATTACH THE SHEET AS AN EXHIBIT TO THIS FORM. STATE THE EXHIBIT NUMBER HERE: ____)

REQUIRED ATTACHMENTS TO MOTION

PLEASE ATTACH THE FOLLOWING DOCUMENTS TO THIS MOTION AND INDICATE THE EXHIBIT NUMBER ASSOCIATED WITH EACH DOCUMENT.

(1) COPIES OF DOCUMENTS THAT ESTABLISH MOVANT'S INTEREST IN THE SUBJECT PROPERTY. FOR PURPOSES OF EXAMPLE ONLY, THIS MAY BE A COMPLETE AND LEGIBLE COPY OF THE PROMISSORY NOTE OR OTHER DEBT INSTRUMENT TOGETHER WITH A COMPLETE AND LEGIBLE COPY OF THE MORTGAGE AND ANY ASSIGNMENTS IN THE CHAIN FROM THE ORIGINAL MORTGAGEE TO THE CURRENT MOVING PARTY. (EXHIBIT ____.)

(2) COPIES OF DOCUMENTS THAT ESTABLISH MOVANT'S STANDING TO BRING THIS MOTION. (EXHIBIT ____.)

(3) COPIES OF DOCUMENTS THAT ESTABLISH THAT MOVANT'S INTEREST IN THE REAL PROPERTY OR COOPERATIVE APARTMENT WAS PERFECTED. FOR THE PURPOSES OF EXAMPLE ONLY, THIS MAY BE A COMPLETE AND LEGIBLE COPY OF THE FINANCING STATEMENT (UCC–1) FILED WITH THE CLERK'S OFFICE OR THE REGISTER OF THE COUNTY IN WHICH THE PROPERTY OR COOPERATIVE APARTMENT IS LOCATED. (EXHIBIT ____.)

DECLARATION AS TO BUSINESS RECORDS

I, _____, THE _____ OF _____, THE MOVANT HEREIN, DECLARE PURSUANT TO 28 U.S.C. SECTION 1746 UNDER PENALTY OF PERJURY THAT THE INFORMATION PROVIDED IN THIS FORM AND ANY EXHIBITS ATTACHED HERETO (OTHER THAN THE TRANSACTIONAL DOCUMENTS ATTACHED AS REQUIRED BY PARAGRAPHS 1, 2, AND 3, ABOVE) IS DERIVED FROM RECORDS THAT WERE MADE AT OR NEAR THE TIME OF THE OCCURRENCE OF THE MATTERS SET FORTH BY, OR FROM INFORMATION TRANSMITTED BY, A PERSON WITH KNOWLEDGE OF THOSE MATTERS; THAT THE RECORDS WERE KEPT IN THE COURSE OF THE REGULARLY CONDUCTED ACTIVITY; AND THAT THE RECORDS WERE MADE IN THE COURSE OF THE REGULARLY CONDUCTED ACTIVITY AS A REGULAR PRACTICE.

I FURTHER DECLARE THAT COPIES OF ANY TRANSACTIONAL DOCUMENTS ATTACHED TO THIS FORM AS REQUIRED BY PARAGRAPHS 1, 2, AND 3, ABOVE, ARE TRUE AND CORRECT COPIES OF THE ORIGINAL DOCUMENTS.

EXECUTED AT _____

on this ___ day of _____, 20___

<NAME>
<TITLE>
<MOVANT>
<STREET ADDRESS>
<CITY, STATE AND ZIP CODE>

DECLARATION

I, _____, THE _____ OF _____, THE MOVANT HEREIN, DECLARE PURSUANT TO 28 U.S.C. SECTION 1746 UNDER PENALTY OF PERJURY THAT THE FOREGOING IS TRUE AND CORRECT BASED ON PERSONAL KNOWLEDGE OF THE MOVANT'S BOOKS AND BUSINESS RECORDS.

EXECUTED AT _____

on this ___ day of _____, 20___

<NAME>
<TITLE>
<MOVANT>
<STREET ADDRESS>
<CITY, STATE AND ZIP CODE>

LOCAL RULES OF PRACTICE OF THE UNITED STATES DISTRICT COURT FOR THE NORTHERN DISTRICT OF NEW YORK

Including Amendments Received Through
September 15, 2008

Research Note

These rules may be searched electronically on Westlaw in the NY-RULES database; updates to these rules may be found on Westlaw in NY-RULESUPDATES. For search tips, and a detailed summary of database content, consult the Westlaw Scope Screen of each database.

Forward.

LOCAL RULES OF PRACTICE
SECTION I. SCOPE OF THE RULES— ONE FORM OF ACTION

Rule
1.1. Scope of the Rules.
1.2. Availability of the Local Rules.
2.1. One Form of Action [Reserved].

SECTION II. COMMENCEMENT OF ACTION; SERVICE OF PROCESS, PLEADINGS, MOTIONS AND ORDERS

3.1.   Civil Cover Sheet.
3.2.   Venue.
3.3.   Complex and Multi–District Litigation.
4.1.   Service of Process.
5.1.   Service and Filing of Papers.
5.1.2. Electronic Case Filing.
5.2.   Prepayment of Fees.
5.3.   Schedule of Fees.
5.4.   Civil Actions Filed in Forma Pauperis; Applications for Leave to Proceed in Forma Pauperis.
5.5.   Filing by Facsimile.
5.6.   Service of the Writ in Exclusion and Deportation Cases.
5.7.   Documents to be Provided to the Clerk.
6.1.   Calculation of Time Periods [Reserved].

SECTION III. PLEADINGS AND MOTIONS

7.1.   Motion Practice.
8.1.   Personal Privacy Protection.
9.1.   Request for Three–Judge Court.
9.2.   Requirement to File a Civil RICO Statement.
9.3.   Requirement of Certain Information to Be Contained in Complaints Filed under Section 205(g) of the Social Security Act [Deleted].
10.1. Form of Papers.

Rule
11.1. Signing of Pleadings, Motions, and Other Papers; Sanctions [Reserved].
12.1. Defenses and Objections—How Presented [Reserved].
13.1. Counterclaims and Cross–Claims [Reserved].
14.1. Impleader.
15.1. Form of a Motion to Amend and its Supporting Documentation.
16.1. Civil Case Management.
16.2. Discovery Cut–Off.

SECTION IV. PARTIES

17.1. Actions by or on Behalf of Infants and/or Incompetents.
18.1. Joinder of Claims and Remedies.
19.1. Joinder of Persons Necessary for Just Adjudication.
20.1. Permissive Joinder of Parties.
21.1. Misjoinder and Nonjoinder of Parties.
22.1. Interpleader [Reserved].
23.1. Designation of "Class Action" in the Caption.
23.2. Certification of a Class Action.
24.1. Intervention [Reserved].
25.1. Substitution of Parties [Reserved].

SECTION V. DEPOSITIONS AND DISCOVERY

26.1. Form of Certain Discovery Documents.
26.2. Filing Discovery.
26.3. Production of Expert Witness Information.
26.4. Timing of Discovery.
27.1. Depositions Before Action or Pending Appeal [Reserved].
28.1. Persons Before Whom Depositions Shall Be Taken [Reserved].
29.1. Discovery Stipulations.
30.1. Depositions.
31.1. Depositions on Written Questions [Reserved].
32.1. Use of Depositions in Court Proceedings [Reserved].
33.1. Interrogatories [Reserved].
34.1. Production of Documents and Things [Reserved].

Rule

35.1. Physical and Mental Examination of Persons [Reserved].
36.1. Requests for Admission [Reserved].
37.1. Form of Discovery Motions.

SECTION VI. TRIALS

38.1. Notation of "Jury Demand" in the Pleading.
39.1. Opening Statements and Closing Arguments.
39.2. Submission of Pretrial Papers.
40.1. Case Assignment System.
40.2. Preferences.
40.3. Trial Calendar.
41.1. Settlements, Apportionments and Allowances in Wrongful Death Actions.
41.2. Dismissal of Actions.
41.3. Actions Dismissed by Stipulation.
42.1. Separation of Issues in Civil Suits [Reserved].
43.1. Examination of Witnesses [Reserved].
44.1. Official Records [Reserved].
45.1. Subpoenas [Reserved].
46.1. Exceptions to Rulings [Reserved].
47.1. Grand and Petit Jurors.
47.2. Jury Selection.
47.3. Assessment of Juror Costs.
47.4. Jury Deliberation.
47.5. Jury Contact Prohibition.
48.1. Number of Jurors.
49.1. Special Verdicts and Interrogatories [Reserved].
50.1. Judgment as a Matter of Law in Actions Tried by Jury; Alternative Motion for New Trial; Conditional Rulings [Reserved].
51.1. Instructions to the Jury.
52.1. Proposed Findings in Civil Cases.
53.1. Masters [Reserved].
53.2. Master's Fees.
53.3. Oath of Master, Commissioner, Etc.

SECTION VII. JUDGMENTS

54.1. Taxation of Costs.
54.2. Jury Cost Assessment.
54.3. Award of Attorney's Fees [Reserved].
54.4. Allowances to Attorneys and Receivers.
55.1. Certificate of Entry of Default.
55.2. Default Judgment.
56.1. Summary Judgment Procedure.
56.2. Notice to Pro Se Litigants of the Consequences of Failing to Respond to a Summary Judgment Motion.
57.1. Declaratory Judgment [Reserved].
58.1. Entry of Judgment.
58.2. Entering Satisfaction of Judgment or Decree.
59.1. New Trial; Amendment of Judgment.
60.1. Relief From Judgment or Order [Reserved].
61.1. Harmless Error [Reserved].
62.1. Stay of Proceedings [Reserved].
62.2. Supersedeas Bond.
63.1. Disability of a Judge [Reserved].

SECTION VIII. PROVISIONAL AND FINAL REMEDIES AND SPECIAL PROCEEDINGS

64.1. Seizure of Person or Property.
65.1. Injunctions.
65.1.1. Sureties.
65.2. Temporary Restraining Orders.

Rule

66.1. Receiverships [Reserved].
67.1. Deposits in Court.
67.2. Withdrawal of a Deposit Pursuant to FED.R.CIV.P. 67.
67.3. Bonds and Other Sureties.
68.1. Settlement Conferences.
68.2. Settlement Procedures.
69.1. Execution [Reserved].
70.1. Judgment for Specific Acts; Vesting Title [Reserved].
71.1. Process in Behalf of and Against Persons Not Parties [Reserved].
71A.1. Condemnation Cases [Reserved].
72.1. Authority of Magistrate Judges.
72.2. Duties of Magistrate Judges.
72.3. Assignment of Duties to Magistrate Judges.
72.4. Habeas Corpus.
72.5. Habeas Corpus Petitions Involving the Death Penalty; Special Requirements.
73.1. Magistrate Judges: Trial by Consent.
74.1. Method of Appeal to District Judge in Consent Cases [Reserved].
75.1. Proceedings on Appeal From Magistrate Judge to District Judge Under Rule 73(d) [Reserved].
76.1. Bankruptcy Cases.
76.2. Bankruptcy Appeals.
76.3. Bankruptcy Record of Transmittal, Certificate of Facts, and Proposed Findings Pursuant to Title 11, Section 110(I).

SECTION IX. DISTRICT COURT AND CLERKS

77.1. Hours of Court [Reserved].
77.2. Orders.
77.3. Sessions of Court.
77.4. Court Library.
77.5. Official Newspapers.
77.6. Release of Information.
77.7. Official Station of the Clerk.
78.1. Motion Days.
79.1. Custody of Exhibits and Transcripts.
79.2. Books and Records of the Clerk [Reserved].
80.1. Stenographic Transcript: Court Reporting Fees.
81.1. Removal Bonds [Reserved].
81.2. Copies of State Court Proceedings in Removed Actions [Reserved].
81.3. Removed Cases, Demand for Jury Trial.
81.4. Actions Removed Pursuant to 28 U.S.C. § 1452.
82.1. Jurisdiction and Venue Unaffected [Reserved].
83.1. Admission to the Bar.
83.2. Appearance and Withdrawal of Attorney.
83.3. Pro Bono Panel.
83.4. Discipline of Attorneys.
83.5. Contempt.
83.6. Transfer of Cases to Another District.

SECTION X. ALTERNATE DISPUTE RESOLUTION AND GENERAL PROVISIONS

Rule 83.7. Arbitration

83.7–1. Scope and Effectiveness of Rule.
83.7–2. Actions Subject to this Rule.
83.7–3. Referral to Arbitration.
83.7–4. Selection and Compensation of Arbitrator.
83.7–5. Arbitration Hearings.
83.7–6. Award and Judgment.

Rule
83.7–7.   Trial De Novo.
83.7–8.   Cases Pending Prior to the Implementation of Arbitration.
83.8.   Number of Experts in Patent Cases.
83.9.   Commission to Take Testimony.
83.10.   Student Practice.
83.11–1.   Mediation.
83.11–2.   Designation and Qualifications of Mediators.
83.11–3.   Actions Subject to Mediation.
83.11–4.   Procedures for Referral, Selecting the Mediator, and Scheduling the Mediation Session.
83.11–5.   The Mediation Session.
83.11–6.   Mediation Report; Notice of Settlement or Trial.
83.12–1.   Early Neutral Evaluation.
83.12–2.   Designation and Qualifications of Evaluators.
83.12–3.   Actions Subject to Early Neutral Evaluation.
83.12–4.   Administrative Procedures and Requirements.
83.12–5.   Evaluation Statements.
83.12–6.   Attendance at ENE Sessions.
83.12–7.   Procedures at ENE Sessions.
83.12–8.   Confidentiality.
83.12–9.   Role of Evaluators.
83.12–10. Early Neutral Evaluation Report.
83.13.   Sealed Matters.
83.14.   Production and Disclosure of Documents and Testimony of Judicial Personnel in Legal Proceedings.
84.1.   Forms [Reserved].
85.1.   Title [Reserved].
86.1.   Effective Date.

SECTION XI.   CRIMINAL PROCEDURE

1.1.   Scope of the Rules.
1.2.   Electronic Case Filing.
1.3.   Personal Privacy Protection.
4.1.   [Reserved].
5.1.   Notice of Arrest.
10.1.   [Reserved].
11.1.   Pleas.
12.1.   Motions and Other Papers.
13.1.   Sealed Matters.
14.1.   Discovery.
16.1.   [Reserved].
17.1.   Subpoenas.

Rule
17.1.1.   Pretrial Conferences.
19.1.   [Reserved].
20.1.   Transfer From a District for Plea and Sentence.
22.1.   [Reserved].
23.1.   Free Press—Fair Trial Directives.
29.1.   [Reserved].
30.1.   Jury Instructions.
31.1.   [Reserved].
32.1.   Presentence Reports.
43.1.   [Reserved].
44.1.   Right to and Assignment of Counsel.
44.2.   Appearance and Withdrawal of Counsel.
45.1.   Excludable Time under the Speedy Trial Act.
46.1.   Pretrial Services and Release on Bail.
47.1.   Motions.
56.1.   [Reserved].
57.1.   Criminal Designation Forms.
57.2.   Release of Bond.
58.1.   Magistrate Judges.
58.2.   Forfeiture of Collateral in Lieu of Appearance.
60.1.   [Reserved].

SECTION XII.   LOCAL RULES OF PROCEDURE FOR ADMIRALTY AND MARITIME CASES

Rule
A. Scope of the Rules.
B. Maritime Attachment and Garnishment.
C. Actions in Rem—Special Provisions.
D. Possessory, Petitory, and Partition Actions.
E. Actions in Rem and Quasi in Rem—General Provisions.
F. Limitation of Liability.
G. Special Rules.

LIST OF GENERAL ORDERS OF THE NORTHERN DISTRICT OF NEW YORK[1]

NOTICES

Notice Regarding Privacy and Public Access to Electronic Civil and Criminal Case Files.
Notice to Members of the Northern District Bar Regarding Electronic Availability of Civil and Criminal Transcripts.

CHAPTER 12 BANKRUPTCY RULES SUPPLEMENT

FORWARD

The Board of Judges for the Northern District of New York have adopted the following time schedule for the approval and amendment of the Local Rules of Practice. The Court will solicit comment on new and amended local rules from the bar and public during the months of May, June and July. Comments should be addressed to:

Lawrence K. Baerman
Clerk of Court
James Hanley Federal Building
P.O. Box 7367
100 South Clinton Street
Syracuse, New York 13261–7367

New and amended rules of practice will be forwarded to the Circuit Council of the Second Circuit for review and approval during the month of October. All new and amended local rules will become effective on

January 1st each year. The Clerk of the Court will then make available to the bar and public the amended local rules.

LOCAL RULES OF PRACTICE

SECTION I. SCOPE OF THE RULES— ONE FORM OF ACTION

RULE 1.1 SCOPE OF THE RULES

(a) Title and Citation. These are the Local Rules of Practice for the United States District Court for the Northern District of New York. They shall be cited as "L.R. . . "

(b) Effective Date; Transitional Provision. These Rules became effective on **January 1, 2008.** Recent amendments are noted with the phrase (Amended January 1, 2008).

(c) Scope of the Rules; Construction. These Rules supplement the Federal Rules of Civil and Criminal Procedure. They shall be construed to be consistent with those Rules and to promote the just, efficient and economical determination of every action and proceeding.

(d) Sanctions and Penalties for Noncompliance. Failure of an attorney or of a party to comply with any provision of these Rules, General Orders of this District, Orders of the Court, or the Federal Rules of Civil or Criminal Procedure shall be a ground for imposition of sanctions.

(e) Definitions.

1. The word "court," except where the context otherwise requires, refers to the United States District Court for the Northern District of New York.

2. The word "judge" refers either to a United States District Judge or to a United States Magistrate Judge.

3. The words "assigned judge," except where the context otherwise requires, refer to the United States District Judge or United States Magistrate Judge

exercising jurisdiction with respect to a particular action or proceeding.

4. The words "Chief Judge" refer to the Chief Judge or a judge temporarily performing the duties of Chief Judge under 28 U.S.C. § 136(e).

5. The word "clerk" refers to the Clerk of the Court or to a deputy clerk whom the Clerk designates to perform services of the general class provided for in Fed. R. Civ. P. 77.

6. The word "marshal" refers to the United States Marshal of this District and includes deputy marshals.

7. The word "party" includes a party's representative.

8. Reference in these Rules to an attorney for a party is in no way intended to preclude a party from appearing pro se, in which case reference to an attorney applies to the pro se litigant.

9. Where appropriate, the "singular" shall include the "plural" and vice versa.

[Amended effective January 1, 1999; January 1, 2004; January 1, 2005; January 1, 2006; January 1, 2007; January 1, 2008.]

RULE 1.2 AVAILABILITY OF THE LOCAL RULES

Copies of these Rules are available from the Clerk's office or at the Court's webpage at "**www.nynd. uscourts.gov.**"

[Amended effective January 1, 2004.]

RULE 2.1 ONE FORM OF ACTION [RESERVED]

SECTION II. COMMENCEMENT OF ACTION; SERVICE OF PROCESS, PLEADINGS, MOTIONS AND ORDERS

RULE 3.1 CIVIL COVER SHEET

A completed civil cover sheet on a form available from the Clerk shall be submitted with every com-

plaint, notice of removal, or other document initiating a civil action. This requirement is solely for administrative purposes, and matters appearing on the civil cover sheet have no legal effect in the action.

RULE 3.2   VENUE

The Court's Civil Case Assignment Plan shall control venue for civil cases filed in the Northern District of New York.

[Amended effective January 1, 1999.]

RULE 3.3   COMPLEX AND MULTI-DISTRICT LITIGATION

(a) If the assigned judge determines, in his or her discretion, that the case is of such a complex nature that it cannot reasonably be trial ready within eighteen months from the date the complaint is filed, the assigned judge may design and issue a particularized case management order that will move the case to trial as quickly as the complexity of the case allows.

(b) The parties shall promptly notify the Court in writing if any action commenced is appropriate for multi-district litigation.

[Amended effective January 1, 1999; January 1, 2008.]

RULE 4.1   SERVICE OF PROCESS

(a) Service shall be made in the manner specified in the Federal Rules of Civil Procedure or as required or permitted by statute. The party seeking service of papers shall be responsible for arranging the service. The Clerk is authorized to sign orders appointing persons to serve process.

(b) Upon the filing of a complaint, the Clerk shall issue to the plaintiff General Order 25 which requires, among other things, service of process upon all defendants within sixty (60) days of the filing of the complaint. This expedited service requirement is necessary to ensure adequate time for pretrial discovery and motion practice. In no event shall service of process be completed after the time specified in Fed. R. Civ. P. 4.

(c) At the time the complaint or notice of removal is served, the party seeking to invoke the jurisdiction of this Court shall also serve on all parties the following materials:

1. Judicial Case Assignment Form;

2. Joint Civil Case Management Plan Containing Notice of Initial Pretrial Conference;

3. Notice and Consent Form to Proceed Before a United States Magistrate Judge; and

4. Notice and Consent Form for the Court Sponsored Alternative Dispute Resolution Procedures.

The Clerk shall furnish these material to the party seeking to invoke the jurisdiction of the Court at the time the complaint or notice of removal is filed.

[Amended effective January 1, 1999.]

RULE 5.1   SERVICE AND FILING OF PAPERS

(a) All pleadings and other papers shall be served and filed in accordance with the Federal Rules of Civil Procedure and shall be in the form prescribed by L.R. 10.1. The party or its designee shall declare, by affidavit or certification, that it has provided all other parties in the action with all documents it has filed with the Court. See also L.R. 26.2 (discovery material).

(b) In civil actions where the Court has directed a party to submit an order or judgment, that party shall file all such orders or judgments in duplicate, and the Clerk's entry of such duplicate in the proper record book shall be deemed in compliance with Fed. R. Civ. P. 79(b). Such party shall also furnish the Clerk with a sufficient number of additional copies for each party to the action, which the Clerk shall mail with notice of entry in accordance with Fed. R. Civ. P. 77(d).

(c) In a civil action, upon filing a notice of appeal, the appellant shall furnish the Clerk with a sufficient number of copies for mailing in accordance with Fed. R. App. P. 3(d).

(d) Upon filing of a motion pursuant to Fed. R. Civ. P. 65.1, the moving party shall furnish the Clerk with a sufficient number of copies of the motion and notice of the motion in compliance with the mailing provision of that rule.

(e) No paper on file in the Clerk's office shall be removed except pursuant to the Court's order.

(f) All civil complaints submitted to the Clerk for filing shall be accompanied by a summons or, if electing to serve by mail, the approved service by mail forms, together with sufficient copies of the complaint for service on each of the named defendants.

(g) A private process server shall serve every summons, except as otherwise required by statute or rule or as the Court directs for good cause shown. A private process server is any person authorized to serve process in an action brought in the New York State Supreme Court or in the court of general jurisdiction of the State in which service is made.

(h) In the case of a prisoner's civil rights action, or any action where a party has been granted leave to proceed in forma pauperis, the Marshal shall serve the summons and complaint by regular mail pursuant to Fed. R. Civ. P. 4(c)(2). The Marshal shall file the return or other acknowledgment of service with the Court. The return shall constitute prima facie evidence of the service of process. If no acknowledgment of service is filed with the Court, the Marshal shall notify the plaintiff; and, if the plaintiff so requests, the Marshal shall make personal service as provided in Fed. R. Civ. P. 4.

RULE 5.1.2   ELECTRONIC CASE FILING

All cases filed in this Court may be assigned to the Electronic Case Files System ("ECF") in accordance with the *Procedural Order on Electronic Case Filing* (**General Order #22***)*, the provisions of which are incorporated herein by reference, and which the Court may amend from time to time. Copies of General Order #22 are available at the Clerk's office or at the Court's webpage at "**www.nynd.uscourts.gov.**"

[Adopted effective January 1, 2004.]

RULE 5.2   PREPAYMENT OF FEES

(a) Filing Fees. A party commencing an action or removing an action from a state court must pay to the Clerk the statutory filing fee before the case will be docketed and process issued. Title 28 U.S.C. § 1915 and L.R. 5.4 govern in forma pauperis proceedings.

(b) Miscellaneous Fees. The Clerk is not required to render any service for which a fee is prescribed by statute or by the Judicial Conference of the United States unless the fee for the service is paid in advance.

RULE 5.3   SCHEDULE OF FEES

Fee schedules are available at the Clerk's office or at the Court's webpage at "**www.nynd.uscourts.gov.**"

[Adopted effective January 1, 2004.]

RULE 5.4   CIVIL ACTIONS FILED IN FORMA PAUPERIS; APPLICATIONS FOR LEAVE TO PROCEED IN FORMA PAUPERIS

(a) On receipt of a complaint or petition and an application to proceed in forma pauperis, and supporting documentation as required for prisoner litigants, the Clerk shall promptly file the complaint or petition without the payment of fees and assign the action in accordance with L.R. 40.1. The Clerk shall then forward the complaint or petition, application and supporting documentation to the assigned judicial officer for a determination of the in forma pauperis application and the sufficiency of the complaint or petition and, if appropriate, to direct service. The granting of an in forma pauperis application shall not relieve a party of the obligation to pay all other fees for which that party is responsible regarding the action, including but not limited to copying and/or witness fees.

(b) Whenever a fee is due for a civil action subject to the Prison Litigation Reform Act ("PLRA"), the prisoner must comply with the following procedure:

1. (A) Submit a signed, fully completed and properly certified in forma pauperis application; and

(B) Submit the authorization form issued by the Clerk's office.

2. (A)(i) If the prisoner **has not** fully complied with the requirements set forth in paragraph 1 above, and the action is not subject to *sua sponte* dismissal, a judicial officer shall, by Court order, inform the prisoner about what he or she must submit in order to proceed with such action in this District ("Order").

(ii) The Order shall afford the prisoner **thirty (30) days** in which to comply with the terms of same. If the prisoner fails to comply fully with the terms of such Order within such period of time, the Court shall dismiss the action.

(B) If the prisoner **has** fully complied with the requirements set forth in paragraph 1 above, and the action is not subject to *sua sponte* dismissal, the judicial officer shall review the in forma pauperis application. The granting of the application shall in no way relieve the prisoner of the obligation to pay the full amount of the filing fee.

3. After being notified of the filing of the civil action, the agency having custody of the prisoner shall comply with the provisions of 28 U.S.C. § 1915(b) regarding the filing fee due for the action.

[Amended effective January 1, 1999; February 7, 2008.]

RULE 5.5   FILING BY FACSIMILE

Neither the Court nor the Clerk's Office will accept for filing any facsimile transmission without prior authorization from the Court. The party using facsimile transmission to file its papers must accompany any such documents with a cover letter stating that the Court authorized such transmission and the date on which the Court provided that authorization. Violations of this Rule subject the offending party to the Court's full disciplinary powers.

RULE 5.6   SERVICE OF THE WRIT IN EXCLUSION AND DEPORTATION CASES

(a) After delivery of an alien for deportation to the master of a ship or the commanding officer of an airplane, the writ shall be addressed to, and served on, the master or commanding officer only. Notice to the respondent of the allowance or issuance of the writ shall not be recognized as binding without proper service. Service shall be made by delivery of the original writ to the respondent while the alien is in custody. Service shall not be made on a master after a ship has cast off her moorings.

(b) In case the writ is served on the master of a ship or on the commanding officer of an airplane, such person may deliver the alien at once to the officer from whom such person received the alien for custody until the return day. In such case, the writ shall be deemed returnable promptly; and the custody of the officer receiving the alien shall be deemed that of the respondent, pending disposition of the writ.

RULE 5.7   DOCUMENTS TO BE PROVIDED TO THE CLERK

All pretrial and settlement conference statements shall be provided to the Clerk but not filed. These documents are not for public view. Forms for preparation of pretrial and settlement conference statements are available from the Clerk's office or at the Court's webpage at "**www.nynd.uscourts.gov.**"

[Amended effective January 1, 2004.]

RULE 6.1   CALCULATION OF TIME PERIODS [RESERVED]

SECTION III.   PLEADINGS AND MOTIONS

RULE 7.1   MOTION PRACTICE

Introduction—Motion Dates and Times. Unless the Court directs otherwise, the moving party shall make its motion returnable at the **next regularly scheduled motion date at least thirty-one days from the date the moving party files and serves its motion.** The moving party shall select a return date in accordance with the procedures set forth in subdivision (b). If the return date the moving party selects is not the next regularly scheduled motion date, or if the moving party selects no return date, the Clerk will set the proper return date and notify the parties.

Information regarding motion dates and times is specified on the case assignment form that the Court provides to the parties at the commencement of the litigation or the parties may obtain this form from the Clerk's office or at the Court's webpage at "**www. nynd.uscourts.gov.**"

(a) Papers Required. Except as otherwise provided in this paragraph, all motions and opposition to motions require a memorandum of law, supporting affidavit, and proof of service on all the parties. See L.R. 5.1(a). Additional requirements for specific types of motions, including cross-motions, see L.R. 7.1(c), are set forth in this rule.

1. *Memorandum of Law.* No party shall file or serve a memorandum of law that exceeds twenty-five (25) pages in length, unless that party obtains leave of the judge hearing the motion prior to filing. All memoranda of law shall contain a table of contents and, wherever possible, parallel citations. Memoranda of law that contain citations to decisions exclusively reported on computerized databases, e.g., Westlaw, Lexis, Juris, shall include copies of those decisions.

When a moving party makes a motion based upon a rule or statute, the moving party must specify in its moving papers the rule or statute upon which it bases its motion.

A memorandum of law is required for all motions except the following:

(A) a motion pursuant to Fed. R. Civ. P. 12(e) for a more definite statement;

(B) a motion pursuant to Fed. R. Civ. P. 15 to amend or supplement a pleading;

(C) a motion pursuant to Fed. R. Civ. P. 17 to appoint next friend or guardian ad litem;

(D) a motion pursuant to Fed. R. Civ. P. 25 for substitution of parties;

(E) a motion pursuant to Fed. R. Civ. P. 37 to compel discovery; and

(F) a motion pursuant to Fed. R. Civ. P. 55 for default.

2. *Affidavit.* An affidavit must not contain legal arguments but must contain factual and procedural background that is relevant to the motion the affidavit supports.

An affidavit is required for all motions except the following:

(A) a motion pursuant to Fed. R. Civ. P. 12(b)(6) for failure to state a claim upon which relief can be granted;

(B) a motion pursuant to Fed. R. Civ. P. 12(c) for judgment on the pleadings; and

(C) a motion pursuant to Fed. R. Civ. P. 12(f) to strike a portion of a pleading.

3. *Summary Judgment Motions.* Any motion for summary judgment shall contain a Statement of Material Facts. The Statement of Material Facts shall set forth, in numbered paragraphs, each material fact about which the moving party contends there exists no genuine issue. Each fact listed shall set forth a specific citation to the record where the fact is established. The record for purposes of the Statement of Material Facts includes the pleadings, depositions, answers to interrogatories, admissions and affidavits. It does not, however, include attorney's affidavits. Failure of the moving party to submit an accurate and complete Statement of Material Facts shall result in a denial of the motion.

The moving party shall also advise pro se litigants about the consequences of their failure to respond to a motion for summary judgment. See L.R. 56.2. The opposing party shall file a response to the Statement of Material Facts. The non-movant's response shall mirror the movant's Statement of Material Facts by admitting and/or denying each of the movant's assertions in matching numbered paragraphs. Each denial shall set forth a specific citation to the record where the factual issue arises. The non-movant's response may also set forth any additional material facts that the non-movant contends are in dispute in separately numbered paragraphs. The Court shall deem admitted any facts set forth in the Statement of Material Facts that the opposing party does not specifically controvert.

4. *Motions to Amend or Supplement Pleadings or for Joinder or Interpleader.* A party moving to amend a pleading pursuant to Fed. R. Civ. P. 14, 15, 19-22 must attach an unsigned copy of the proposed amended pleading to its motion papers. Except if the Court otherwise orders, the proposed amended pleading must be a complete pleading, which will supersede the original pleading in all respects. A party shall not incorporate any portion of its prior pleading into the proposed amended pleading by reference.

The motion must set forth specifically the proposed amendments and identify the amendments in the proposed pleading, either through the submission of a red-lined version of the original pleading or other equivalent means.

Where a party seeks leave to supplement a pleading pursuant to Fed. R. Civ. P. 15(d), the party must limit the proposed supplemental pleading to transactions or occurrences or events which have occurred since the date of the pleading that the party seeks to supplement. The party must number the paragraphs in the proposed pleading consecutively to the paragraphs contained in the pleading that it seeks to supplement. In addition to the pleading requirements set forth above, the party requesting leave to supplement must set forth specifically the proposed supplements and identify the supplements in the proposed pleading, either through the submission of a red-lined version of the original pleading or other equivalent means.

Caveat: The granting of the motion does not constitute the filing of the amended pleading. After the Court grants leave, unless the Court otherwise orders, the moving party must file and serve the original signed amended pleading within ten (10) days of the Order granting the motion.

(b) Motions.

1. *Dispositive Motions.* The moving party must file all motion papers with the Court and serve them upon the other parties not less than **THIRTY-ONE DAYS** prior to the return date of the motion. The Notice of Motion must state the return date that the moving party has selected.

The party opposing the motion must file its opposition papers with the Court and serve them upon the other parties not less than **SEVENTEEN DAYS** prior to the return date of the motion.

The moving party must file its reply papers, which may not exceed ten (10) pages, with the Court and serve them upon the other parties not less than **ELEVEN DAYS** prior to the return date of the motion.

A surreply is not permitted.

Parties shall file all original motion papers, including memoranda of law and supporting affidavits, if any, in accordance with the *Administrative Procedures for Electronic Case Filing* (General Order #22) and/or the case assignment form provided to the parties at the commencement of the litigation. The parties need not provide a courtesy copy of their motion papers to the assigned judge unless the assigned judge requests a copy.

2. *Non-Dispositive Motions.* Prior to making any non-dispositive motion before the assigned Magistrate Judge, the parties must make **good faith efforts among themselves to resolve or reduce all differences relating to the non-dispositive issue**. If, after conferring, the parties are unable to arrive at a mutually satisfactory resolution, the party seeking relief must then request a court conference with the assigned Magistrate Judge.

A court conference is a prerequisite to filing a non-dispositive motion before the assigned Magistrate Judge. In the Notice of Motion, the moving party is required to set forth the date that the court conference with the Magistrate Judge was held regarding the issues being presented in the motion. Failure to include this information in the Notice of Motion may result in the Court rejecting the motion papers.

Actions which involve an incarcerated, pro se party are not subject to the requirement that a court conference be held prior to filing a non-dispositive motion.

Unless the Court orders otherwise, the moving party must file all motion papers with the Court and serve them upon the other parties not less than **THIRTY-ONE DAYS** prior to the return date of the motion.

The party opposing the motion must file its Opposition papers with the Court and serve them upon the other parties not less than **SEVENTEEN DAYS** prior to the return date of the motion.

Reply papers and adjournments are not permitted without the Court's prior permission.

3. *Failure To Timely File or Comply.* The Court shall not consider any papers required under this Rule that are not timely filed or are otherwise not in compliance with this Rule unless good cause is shown. Where a properly filed motion is unopposed and the Court determines that the moving party has met its

burden to demonstrate entitlement to the relief requested therein, the non-moving party's failure to file or serve any papers as this Rule requires shall be deemed as consent to the granting or denial of the motion, as the case may be, unless good cause is shown.

Any party who does not intend to oppose a motion, or a movant who does not intend to pursue a motion, shall promptly notify the Court and the other parties of such intention. They should provide such notice at the earliest practicable date, but in any event no less than **FOURTEEN CALENDAR DAYS** prior to the scheduled return date of the motion, unless for good cause shown. **Failure to comply with this Rule may result in the Court imposing sanctions.**

(c) Cross–Motions. A party may file and serve a cross-motion at the time it files and serves its opposition papers to the original motion, i.e., not less than **SEVENTEEN DAYS** prior to the return date of the motion. If a party makes a cross-motion, it must join its cross-motion brief with its opposition brief, and this combined brief may not exceed twenty-five (25) pages in length, exclusive of exhibits. A separate brief in opposition to the original motion is not permissible.

The original moving party may reply in further support of the original motion and in opposition to the cross-motion with a reply/opposition brief that does not exceed twenty-five (25) pages in length, exclusive of exhibits. The original moving party must file its reply/opposition papers with the Court and serve them on the other parties not less than **ELEVEN DAYS** prior to the return date of the original motion.

The cross-moving party may not reply in further support of its cross-motion without the Court's prior permission.

(d) Discovery Motions. The following steps are required prior to making any discovery motion pursuant to Rules 26 through 37 of the Federal Rules of Civil Procedure.

1. Parties must make good faith efforts among themselves to resolve or reduce all differences relating to discovery prior to seeking court intervention.

2. The moving party must confer in detail with the opposing party concerning the discovery issues between them in a good faith effort to eliminate or reduce the area of controversy and to arrive at a mutually satisfactory resolution. Failure to do so may result in denial of a motion to compel discovery and/or imposition of sanctions.

3. If the parties' conference does not fully resolve the discovery issues, the party seeking relief must then request a court conference with the assigned Magistrate Judge. Incarcerated, pro se parties are not subject to the court conference requirement prior to filing a motion to compel discovery. The assigned Magistrate Judge may direct the party making the

request for a court conference to file an affidavit setting forth the date(s) and mode(s) of the consultation(s) with the opposing party and a letter that concisely sets forth the nature of the dispute and a specific listing of each of the items of discovery sought or opposed. Immediately following each disputed item, the party must set forth the reason why the Court should allow or disallow that item.

4. Following a request for a discovery conference, the Court may schedule a conference and advise all parties of a date and time. The assigned Magistrate Judge may, in his or her discretion, conduct the discovery conference by telephone conference call, initiated by the party making the request for the conference, by video conference, or by personal appearance.

5. Following a discovery conference, the Court may direct the prevailing party to submit a proposed order, on notice to the other parties.

6. If a party fails or refuses to confer in good faith with the requesting party, thus requiring the request for a discovery conference, the Court, at its discretion, may subject the resisting party to the sanction of the imposition of costs, including the attorney's fees of the opposing party in accordance with Fed. R. Civ. P. 37.

7. A party claiming privilege with respect to a communication or other item must specifically identify the privilege and the grounds for the claimed privilege. The parties may not make any generalized claims of privilege.

8. The parties shall file any motion to compel discovery that these Rules authorize no later than **TEN CALENDAR DAYS** after the discovery cut-off date. See L.R. 16.2. A party shall accompany any motion that it files pursuant to Fed.R.Civ.P. 37 with the discovery materials to which the motion relates if the parties have not previously filed those materials with the Court.

(e) Order to Show Cause. All motions that a party brings by Order to Show Cause shall conform to the requirements set forth in L. R. 7.1(a)(1) and (2). **Immediately after filing an Order to Show Cause, the moving party must telephone the Chambers of the presiding judicial officer and inform Chambers staff that it has filed an Order to Show Cause.** Parties may obtain the telephone numbers for all Chambers from the Clerk's office or at the Court's webpage at "www.nynd.uscourts.gov." The Court shall determine the briefing schedule and return date applicable to motions brought by Order to Show Cause.

In addition to the requirements set forth in Local Rule 7.1(a)(1) and (2), a motion brought by Order to Show Cause must include an affidavit clearly and specifically showing good and sufficient cause why the standard Notice of Motion procedure cannot be used.

The moving party must give reasonable advance notice of the application for an Order to Show Cause to the other parties, except in those circumstances where the movant can demonstrate, in a detailed and specific affidavit, good cause and substantial prejudice that would result from the requirement of reasonable notice.

An Order to Show Cause must contain a space for the assigned judge to set forth (a) the deadline for filing and serving supporting papers, (b) the deadline for filing and serving opposing papers, and (c) the date and time for the hearing.

(f) Temporary Restraining Order. A party may seek a temporary restraining order by Notice of Motion or Order to Show Cause, as appropriate. Filing procedures and requirements for supporting documents are the same as set forth in this Rule for other motions. The moving party must serve any application for a temporary restraining order on all other parties unless Fed.R.Civ.P. 65 otherwise permits. L.R. 7.1(b)(2) governs motions for injunctive relief, other than those brought by Order to Show Cause. L.R. 7.1(e) governs motions brought by Order to Show Cause.

(g) Motion for Reconsideration. Unless Fed. R.Civ.P. 60 otherwise governs, a party may file and serve a motion for reconsideration or reargument no later than **TEN CALENDAR DAYS** after the entry of the challenged judgment, order, or decree. All motions for reconsideration shall conform with the requirements set forth in L.R. 7.1(a)(1) and (2). The briefing schedule and return date applicable to motions for reconsideration shall conform to L.R. 7.1(b)(2). A motion for reconsideration of a Magistrate Judge's determination of a non-dispositive matter shall toll the ten (10) day time period to file objections pursuant to L.R. 72.1(b). The Court will decide motions for reconsideration or reargument on submission of the papers, without oral argument, unless the Court directs otherwise.

(h) Oral Argument. The parties shall appear for oral argument on all motions that they make returnable before a district court judge, except motions for reconsideration, on the scheduled return date of the motion. In the district court judge's discretion, or on consideration of a request of any party, the district court judge may dispose of a motion without oral argument. Thus, the parties should be prepared to have their motion papers serve as the sole method of argument on the motion.

The parties shall not appear for oral argument on motions that they make returnable before a magistrate judge on the scheduled return date of the motion unless the Magistrate Judge *sua sponte* directs or grants the request of any party for oral argument.

(i) Sanctions for Vexatious or Frivolous Motions or Failure to Comply with this Rule. A party who presents vexatious or frivolous motion papers or fails to comply with this Rule is subject to discipline as the Court deems appropriate, including sanctions and the imposition of costs and attorney's fees to the opposing party.

(j) Adjournments of Dispositive Motions. After the moving party files and serves its motion papers requesting dispositive relief, but before the time that the opposing party must file and serve its opposing papers, the parties may agree to an adjournment of the return date for the motion. However, any such adjournment may not be for more than **THIRTY-ONE DAYS** from the return date that the moving party selected. In addition, the parties may agree to new dates for the filing and service of opposition and reply papers. However, the parties must file all papers with the Court and serve them upon the other parties not less than **ELEVEN DAYS** prior to the newly selected return date of the motion. If the parties agree to such an adjournment, they must file a letter with the Court stating the following: (1) that they have agreed to an adjournment of the return date for the motion, (2) the new return date, (3) the date on which the opposing party must file and serve its opposition papers, and (4) the date on which the moving party must file and serve its reply papers. The parties may not agree to any further adjournment.

If one of the parties seeks an adjournment of not more than **THIRTY-ONE DAYS** from the return date that the moving party selected, but the other parties will not agree to such an adjournment, the party seeking the adjournment must file a letter request with the Court and serve the same upon the other parties, stating the following: (1) that the parties cannot agree to an adjournment, (2) the reason that the party is seeking the adjournment, and (3) the suggested return date for the motion. Within three days of receiving this letter request, the parties who have not agreed to an adjournment may file a letter with the Court, and serve the same upon the other parties, setting forth the reasons that they do not agree to the requested adjournment. The Court will then take the request under advisement and, as soon as practicable, will enter an order granting or denying the request and, if granting the request, will set forth new dates for the filing and serving of opposition and reply papers.

If any party seeks an adjournment of the return date that is more than **THIRTY-ONE DAYS** from the return date that the moving party selected, that party must file a letter request with the Court stating the following: (1) why the party needs a longer adjournment and (2) a suggested return date for the motion. The Court will grant such an adjournment only upon a showing of exceptional circumstances. In the alternative or if the Court denies the request for an adjournment, the moving party may **withdraw its motion without prejudice** to refile at a later date. The moving party must refile its motion within the time frame set in the Uniform Pretrial Scheduling Order unless either the assigned District Judge or the assigned Magistrate Judge has granted an extension of the motion–filing deadline.

[Amended effective January 1, 1999; amended effective January 1, 2001; January 1, 2003; January 1, 2004; January 1, 2005; January 1, 2007; January 1, 2008.]

RULE 8.1   PERSONAL PRIVACY PROTECTION

Parties shall refrain from including, or shall redact where inclusion is necessary, the following personal identifiers from all pleadings that they file with the Court, including exhibits thereto, whether filed electronically or in paper form, unless the Court orders otherwise.

1. *Social Security Numbers.* If an individual's social security number must be included in a document, use only the last four digits of that number.

2. *Names of Minor Children.* If the involvement of a minor child must be mentioned, use only the initials of that child.

3. *Dates of Birth.* If an individual's date of birth must be included in a document, use only the year.

4. *Financial Account Numbers.* If financial account numbers are relevant, use only the last four digits of those numbers.

5. *Home Addresses.* If a home address must be used, use only the City and State.

In addition, caution shall be exercised when filing documents that contain the following:

1) personal identifying number, such as a driver's license number;

2) medical records, treatment and diagnosis;

3) employment history;

4) individual financial information; and

5) proprietary or trade secret information.

In compliance with the E–Government Act of 2002, a party wishing to file a document containing the personal data identifiers listed above may

1. file an unredacted version of the document under seal, or

2. file a reference list under seal. The reference list shall contain the complete personal data identifier(s) and the redacted identifier(s) used in its(their) place in the filing. All references in the case to the redacted identifiers included in the reference list will be construed to refer to the corresponding complete personal data identifier. The reference list must be filed under seal and may be amended as of right.

Counsel is strongly urged to discuss this issue with all their clients so that they can make an informed decision about the inclusion of certain information. The responsibility for redacting these personal identifiers **rests solely with counsel and the parties.** The Clerk will not review each pleading for compliance with this Rule. Counsel and the parties are cautioned that failure to redact these personal identifiers may subject them to the Court's full disciplinary power.

Exception: Transcripts of the administrative record in social security proceedings and state court records relating to a habeas corpus petitions are exempt from this requirement.

[Adopted effective January 1, 2004; amended effective January 1, 2005.]

RULE 9.1   REQUEST FOR THREE– JUDGE COURT

Whenever a party believes that only a three-judge court may grant the relief requested in a lawsuit, the party shall include the words "Three–Judge Court," or the equivalent, immediately following the title of the first pleading in which the party asserts the cause of action requesting a three-judge court. Unless the basis for the request is apparent from the pleading, the party shall set forth the basis for the request in the pleading or in an attached statement. On the convening of a three-judge court, in addition to the original papers on file, the parties shall make the following documents available to the Clerk for distribution: three copies of the pleadings, three copies of the motion papers, and three copies of all memoranda of law.

RULE 9.2   REQUIREMENT TO FILE A CIVIL RICO STATEMENT

In any action in which a party asserts a claim under the Racketeer Influenced and Corrupt Organizations Act ("RICO"), 18 U.S.C. § 1961 et seq., the party asserting such a claim shall file a RICO statement within thirty (30) days of the filing of the pleading containing such claim. This statement shall conform to the format that the Court has adopted and shall be entitled "RICO Statement." Parties may obtain copies of General Order #14—CIVIL RICO STATEMENT FILING REQUIREMENTS from the Clerk's office or at the Court's webpage at "**www.nynd.uscourts. gov.**" This statement shall state in detail and with specificity the information requested in the RICO Statement. The Court shall construe the RICO Statement as an amendment to the pleadings.

[Amended effective January 1, 2004.]

RULE 9.3 REQUIREMENT OF CERTAIN INFORMATION TO BE CONTAINED IN COMPLAINTS FILED UNDER SECTION 205(g) OF THE SOCIAL SECURITY ACT [DELETED]

[Deleted effective January 1, 2004.]

RULE 10.1 FORM OF PAPERS

(a) Form Generally. All pleadings, motions, and other documents that a party presents for filing, whether in paper form or in electronic form, shall meet the following requirements:

1. All text, whether in the body of the document or in footnotes, must be a minimum of 12-point type;

2. All documents must have one-inch margins on all four sides of the page;

3. All text in the body of the document must be double-spaced;

4. The text in block quotations and footnotes may be single-spaced;

5. Extensive footnotes must not be used to circumvent page limitations;

6. Compacted or other compressed printing features must not be used;

7. Pages must be consecutively numbered.

(b) Additional requirements for all pleadings, motions, and other documents that a party presents for filing in paper form:

1. All documents must be on 8 ½ x 11 inch white paper of good quality;

2. All text must be plainly and legibly written, typewritten, printed or reproduced without erasures or interlineations materially defacing them;

3. All documents must be in black or blue ink;

4. Pages of all documents must be stapled (or in some other way fastened) together;

5. All documents must be single-sided;

6. The Court, at its discretion, may require the electronic submission of any document in a WordPerfect-compatible format.

The Court may reject documents that do not comply with the above-listed requirements.

(c) Information Required. The following information must appear on each document that a party files:

1. A caption, which must include the title of the Court, the title of the action, the civil action number of the case, the initials of the assigned judges, and the name or nature of the paper in sufficient detail for identification. **The parties must separately caption affidavits and declarations and must not physically** attach them to the Notice of Motion or Memorandum of Law.

2. Each document must identify the person filing the document. This identification must include an original signature of the attorney or pro se litigant; the typewritten name of that person; the address of a pro se litigant; and the bar roll number, office address, telephone number, e-mail address and fax number of the attorney. **All attorneys of record and pro se litigants must immediately notify the Court of any change of address.** Parties must file the notice of change of address with the Clerk and serve the same on all other parties to the action. The notice must identify each and every action to which the notice applies.

Attorneys shall also file a new registration statement within ten days of a change of address, firm name, telephone number, e-mail address and fax number. Attorneys may obtain registration forms at the Court's webpage at **"www.nynd.uscourts.gov;"** see also L.R. 41.2(b); L.R. 83.1(e).

(d) The record on hearings, unless ordered printed, shall be plainly typewritten and bound in book form, paged and indexed.

(e) All documents including exhibits must be in the English language or be accompanied by an English translation.

[Amended effective January 1, 1999; January 1, 2004; January 1, 2005; January 1, 2006; January 1, 2007; January 1, 2008.]

RULE 11.1 SIGNING OF PLEADINGS, MOTIONS, AND OTHER PAPERS; SANCTIONS [RESERVED]

RULE 12.1 DEFENSES AND OBJECTIONS—HOW PRESENTED [RESERVED]

RULE 13.1 COUNTERCLAIMS AND CROSS–CLAIMS [RESERVED]

RULE 14.1 IMPLEADER

See L.R. 7.1(a)(4).

[Amended effective January 1, 1999.]

RULE 15.1 FORM OF A MOTION TO AMEND AND ITS SUPPORTING DOCUMENTATION

See L.R. 7.1(a)(4).

[Amended effective January 1, 1999.]

RULE 16.1 CIVIL CASE MANAGEMENT

This Court has found that the interests of justice are most effectively served by adopting a systematic, differential case management system that tailors the level of individualized and case-specific management to such criteria as case complexity, time required to prepare a case for trial, and availability of judicial and other resources.

(a) Filing of Complaint/Service of Process. Upon the filing of a complaint, the Clerk shall issue to the plaintiff General Order 25, which requires, among other things, service of process upon all defendants within sixty (60) days of the filing of the complaint. This expedited service requirement is necessary to ensure adequate time for pretrial discovery and motion practice.

(b) Assignment of District Judge/Magistrate Judge. Immediately upon the filing of a civil action, the Clerk shall assign the action to a District Judge and may also assign the action to a Magistrate Judge pursuant to the Court's assignment plan. When a civil action is assigned to a Magistrate Judge, the Magistrate Judge shall conduct proceedings in accordance with these Rules and 28 U.S.C. § 636 as directed by the District Judge. Once assigned, either judicial officer shall have authority to design and issue a case management order.

(c) Initial Pretrial Conference. Except for cases excluded under section II of General Order 25, an initial pretrial conference pursuant to Fed. R. Civ. P. 16 shall be held within 120 days after the filing of the complaint. The Clerk shall set the date of this conference upon the filing of the complaint. The purpose of this conference is to prepare and adopt a case-specific management plan which will be memorialized in a case management order. See subsection (d) below. In order to facilitate the adoption of such a plan, prior to the scheduled conference, counsel for all parties shall confer among themselves as Fed. R. Civ. P. 26(f) requires and shall use the Civil Case Management Plan form contained in the General Order 25 filing packet. The parties shall file their jointly-proposed plan or, if they cannot reach consensus, each party shall file its own proposed plan with the Clerk at least ten (10) business days prior to the scheduled pretrial conference.

(d) Subject Matter of Initial Pretrial Conference. At the initial pretrial conference, the Court shall consider, and the parties shall be prepared to discuss, the following:

1. Deadlines for joinder of parties, amendment of pleadings, completion of discovery, and filing of dispositive motions;

2. Trial date;

3. Requests for jury trial;

4. Subject matter and personal jurisdiction;

5. Factual and legal bases for claims and defenses;

6. Factual and legal issues in dispute;

7. Factual and legal issues upon which the parties can agree or which they can narrow through motion practice and which will expedite resolution of the dispute;

8. Specific relief requested, including method for computing damages;

9. Intended discovery and proposed methods to limit and/or decrease time and expense thereof;

10. Suitability of case for voluntary arbitration;

11. Measures for reducing length of trial;

12. Related cases pending before this or other U.S. District Courts;

13. Procedures for certifying class actions, if appropriate;

14. Settlement prospects; and

15. If the case is in the ADR track, choice of ADR method and estimated time for completion of ADR.

(e) Uniform Pretrial Scheduling Order. Upon completion of the initial pretrial conference, the presiding judge may issue a Uniform Pretrial Scheduling Order setting forth deadlines for joinder of parties, amendment of pleadings, production of expert reports, completion of discovery, and filing of motions; a trial ready date; the requirements for all trial submissions; and if an ADR track case, the ADR method to be used and the deadline for completion of ADR.

(f) Enforcement of Deadlines. The Court shall strictly enforce any deadlines that it establishes in any case management order, and the Court shall not modify these deadlines, even upon stipulation of the parties, except upon a showing of good cause.

[Amended effective January 1, 1999; January 1, 2008; February 7, 2008.]

RULE 16.2 DISCOVERY CUT–OFF

The "discovery cut-off" is that date by which all responses to written discovery, including requests for admissions, shall be due according to the Federal Rules of Civil Procedure and by which all depositions shall be concluded. Counsel are advised to initiate discovery requests and notice depositions sufficiently in advance of the cut-off date to comply with this Rule. Discovery requests that call for responses or scheduled depositions after the discovery cut-off will not be enforceable except by order of the court for good cause shown. Parties shall file and serve motions to compel discovery no later than ten (10) days after the discovery cut-off. See L.R. 7.1(d)(8).

[Amended effective January 1, 2001; January 1, 2004; January 1, 2007; January 1, 2008.]

SECTION IV. PARTIES

RULE 17.1 ACTIONS BY OR ON BEHALF OF INFANTS AND/OR INCOMPETENTS

(a) An action by or on behalf of an infant or incompetent shall not be settled or compromised, or voluntarily discontinued, dismissed or terminated, without leave of the Court embodied in an order, judgment or decree. The proceedings on an application to settle or compromise such an action shall conform to the New York State statutes and rules; but the Court, for good cause shown, may dispense with any New York State requirement.

(b) The Court shall authorize payment of a reasonable attorneys' fee and proper disbursements from the amount recovered in such an action, whether realized by settlement, execution or otherwise, and shall determine the fee and disbursements, after due inquiry as to all charges against the amount recovered.

(c) The Court shall order the balance of the proceeds of the recovery or settlement to be distributed as it deems will best protect the interest of the infant or incompetent.

RULE 18.1 JOINDER OF CLAIMS AND REMEDIES

See L.R. 7.1(a)(4).

[Amended effective January 1, 1999.]

RULE 19.1 JOINDER OF PERSONS NECESSARY FOR JUST ADJUDICATION

See L.R. 7.1(a)(4).

[Amended effective January 1, 1999.]

RULE 20.1 PERMISSIVE JOINDER OF PARTIES

See L.R. 7.1(a)(4).

[Amended effective January 1, 1999.]

RULE 21.1 MISJOINDER AND NONJOINDER OF PARTIES

See L.R. 7.1(a)(4).

[Amended effective January 1, 1999.]

RULE 22.1 INTERPLEADER [RESERVED]

RULE 23.1 DESIGNATION OF "CLASS ACTION" IN THE CAPTION

(a) If a party seeks to maintain a case as a class action pursuant to Fed. R. Civ. P. 23, the party shall include the words "Class Action" in the complaint or other pleading asserting a class action next to its caption.

(b) The plaintiff also shall check the appropriate box on the Civil Cover Sheet at the time if files the action.

[Amended effective January 1, 2008.]

RULE 23.2 CERTIFICATION OF A CLASS ACTION

As soon as practicable after the commencement of an action designated as a "Class Action," the plaintiff shall file a motion, with the assigned district judge, seeking an order of the court determining that the plaintiff may maintain the action as a class action.

[Effective January 1, 2003.]

RULE 24.1 INTERVENTION [RESERVED]

RULE 25.1 SUBSTITUTION OF PARTIES [RESERVED]

SECTION V. DEPOSITIONS AND DISCOVERY

RULE 26.1 FORM OF CERTAIN DISCOVERY DOCUMENTS

The parties shall number each interrogatory or request sequentially, regardless of the number of sets of interrogatories or requests. In answering or objecting to interrogatories, requests for admission, or requests to produce or inspect, the responding party shall first state verbatim the propounded interrogatory or request and immediately thereafter the answer or objection.

RULE 26.2   FILING DISCOVERY

Parties shall not file notices to take depositions, transcripts of depositions, interrogatories, requests for documents, requests for admissions, disclosures, and answers and responses to these notices and requests unless the Court orders otherwise; provided, however, that a party shall file any discovery material that it expects to use at trial or to support any motion, including a motion to compel or for summary judgment, prior to the trial or motion return date. A party shall include with any motion pursuant to Fed. R. Civ. P. 37 the discovery materials to which the motion relates if the parties have not previously filed those materials with the Court.

[Amended effective January 1, 1999; January 1, 2008.]

RULE 26.3   PRODUCTION OF EXPERT WITNESS INFORMATION

There shall be binding disclosure of the identity of expert witnesses. The parties shall make such disclosure, including a curriculum vitae and, unless waived by the other parties, service of the expert's written report pursuant to Fed. R. Civ. P. 26(a)(2)(B), before the completion of discovery in accordance with the deadlines contained in the Uniform Pretrial Scheduling Order or any other Court order. Failure to comply with these deadlines may result in the imposition of sanctions, including the preclusion of testimony, pursuant to Fed. R. Civ. P. 16(f).

If a party expects to call a treating physician as a witness, the party must identify the treating physician in accordance with the timetable provided in the Uniform Pretrial Scheduling Order or other Court order.

For information on the number of experts allowed in Patent cases see Local Rule 83.8.

[Amended effective January 1, 1999; January 1, 2006; January 1, 2008.]

RULE 26.4   TIMING OF DISCOVERY

Fed. R. Civ. P. 26(d), which prohibits discovery prior to a meeting and conference between the parties, and Fed. R. Civ. P. 26(f), which directs parties to meet and confer with each other relative to the nature

and basis of claims and defenses to a lawsuit, shall not apply to any action in which a party is incarcerated.

[Adopted effective January 1, 1999.]

RULE 27.1   DEPOSITIONS BEFORE ACTION OR PENDING APPEAL [RESERVED]

RULE 28.1   PERSONS BEFORE WHOM DEPOSITIONS SHALL BE TAKEN [RESERVED]

RULE 29.1   DISCOVERY STIPULATIONS

See L.R. 16.1(f); 16.2.

[Amended effective January 1, 1999.]

RULE 30.1   DEPOSITIONS

Unless the Court orders otherwise pursuant to Fed. R. Civ. P. 5(d) and 26(c), transcripts of depositions when received and filed by the Clerk, shall then be opened by the Clerk who shall affix the filing stamp to the cover page of the transcripts. See L.R. 26.2.

[Amended effective January 1, 2004.]

RULE 31.1   DEPOSITIONS ON WRITTEN QUESTIONS [RESERVED]

RULE 32.1   USE OF DEPOSITIONS IN COURT PROCEEDINGS [RESERVED]

RULE 33.1   INTERROGATORIES [RESERVED]

RULE 34.1   PRODUCTION OF DOCUMENTS AND THINGS [RESERVED]

RULE 35.1   PHYSICAL AND MENTAL EXAMINATION OF PERSONS [RESERVED]

RULE 36.1   REQUESTS FOR ADMISSION [RESERVED]

RULE 37.1   FORM OF DISCOVERY MOTIONS

See L.R. 7.1(d).

SECTION VI. TRIALS

RULE 38.1 NOTATION OF "JURY DEMAND" IN THE PLEADING

(a) If a party demands a jury trial as Fed. R. Civ. P. 38(b) permits, the party shall place a notation on the front page of the initial pleading which that party signed, stating "Demand for Jury Trial" or an equivalent statement. This notation shall serve as a sufficient demand under Fed. R. Civ. P. 38(b).

(b) In cases removed from state court, a party may file a "Demand for Jury Trial" that is separate from the initial pleading. See Fed. R. Civ. P. 81.3; L.R. 81.3.

[Amended effective January 1, 1999; January 1, 2008.]

RULE 39.1 OPENING STATEMENTS AND CLOSING ARGUMENTS

The Court will determine the time to be allotted for opening and closing arguments.

RULE 39.2 SUBMISSION OF PRETRIAL PAPERS

The parties shall file all pretrial submissions in accordance with the requirements of the Uniform Pretrial Scheduling Order unless the Court orders otherwise.

[Amended effective January 1, 1999; January 1, 2008.]

RULE 40.1 CASE ASSIGNMENT SYSTEM

Immediately upon the filing of a civil action or proceeding, the Clerk shall assign the action or proceeding to a District Judge and may also assign the action or proceeding to a Magistrate Judge pursuant to the Court's Assignment Plan. When a civil action or proceeding is assigned to a Magistrate Judge, the Magistrate Judge shall conduct proceedings in accordance with these Rules and 28 U.S.C. § 636 as directed by the District Judge. (See General Order #12)

[Amended effective January 1, 1999; February 7, 2008.]

RULE 40.2 PREFERENCES

Only the following causes shall be entitled to preferences:

1. Issues in bankruptcy framed by an answer to a bankruptcy petition which are triable by a jury;

2. Causes entitled to a preference under any statute of the United States;

3. Causes restored to the calendar for a new trial by the setting aside of a former verdict, by reversal of a former judgment, or after a mistrial;

4. Causes to which a receiver appointed by any court or a trustee or debtor-in-possession in a bankruptcy proceeding is a party;

5. Causes which, in the discretion of the assigned judge, are entitled to a preference for meritorious reasons.

Preferences shall be obtained only by order of the Court on two-days notice of the application.

RULE 40.3 TRIAL CALENDAR

The trial calendar number shall be the same as the docket number. No note of issue is required. Each judge shall dispose of cases as the law and the effective administration of justice require.

[Amended effective January 1, 1999.]

RULE 41.1 SETTLEMENTS, APPORTIONMENTS AND ALLOWANCES IN WRONGFUL DEATH ACTIONS

In an action for wrongful death,

1. The Court shall apportion the proceeds of the action only where required by statute;

2. The Court shall approve a settlement only in a case covered by subdivision 1; and

3. The Court shall approve an attorney's fee only upon application in accordance with the provisions of the Judiciary Law of the State of New York.

RULE 41.2 DISMISSAL OF ACTIONS

(a) Each judge shall from time to time notice for hearing on a dismissal calendar such actions or proceedings assigned to that judge which appear not to have been diligently prosecuted. Whenever it appears that the plaintiff has failed to prosecute an action or proceeding diligently, the assigned judge shall order it dismissed. In the absence of an order by the assigned judge or magistrate judge setting any date for any pretrial proceeding or for trial, the plaintiff's failure to take action for four (4) months shall be presumptive evidence of lack of prosecution. Unless the assigned judge or magistrate judge otherwise orders, each party shall, not less than ten (10) days prior to the noticed hearing date, serve and file a certificate setting forth the status of the action or proceeding and whether good cause exists to dismiss it for failure to prosecute. The parties need not appear in person. No explanations communicated in person, over the telephone, or by letter shall be acceptable. If a party fails to respond as this Rule requires, the Court shall issue a written order dismissing the case for failure to prosecute or providing for sanctions or making other directives to the parties as justice requires. Nothing in this Rule shall preclude any party from filing a motion to dismiss an action or proceeding for failure to prosecute under Fed. R. Civ. P. 41(b).

(b) Failure to notify the Court of a change of address in accordance with L.R. 10.1(b) may result in the dismissal of any pending action.

[Amended effective January 1, 1999.]

RULE 41.3 ACTIONS DISMISSED BY STIPULATION

Stipulations of dismissal shall be signed by each attorney and/or pro se litigant appearing in the action. Any action which is submitted for dismissal by stipulation of the parties shall contain the following language, if applicable: "That no party hereto is an infant or incompetent." For actions involving an infant or incompetent, see L.R. 17.1.

RULE 42.1 SEPARATION OF ISSUES IN CIVIL SUITS [RESERVED]

RULE 43.1 EXAMINATION OF WITNESSES [RESERVED]

RULE 44.1 OFFICIAL RECORDS [RESERVED]

RULE 45.1 SUBPOENAS [RESERVED]

See Fed.R.Civ.P. 45.

RULE 46.1 EXCEPTIONS TO RULINGS [RESERVED]

RULE 47.1 GRAND AND PETIT JURORS

Grand and petit jurors to serve at stated and special sessions of the Court shall be summoned pursuant to the Jury Selection and Service Act of 1968, as amended, codified in Sections 1861–1867 of Title 28 of the United States Code, and the Plan adopted and approved by the judges of this Court and approved by the Judicial Council for the Court of Appeals for the Second Circuit. The selection of grand and petit jurors is made by random selection from voter registration lists and supplemented by, if available, lists of licensed drivers from the New York State Department of Motor Vehicles. Court sessions, pursuant to 28 U.S.C. § 112, are designated to be held in the Northern District of New York in the cities of Albany, Auburn, Binghamton, Malone, Syracuse, Utica and Watertown. For jury selection purposes under § 1869(c) of the Act, this District is divided into divisions from which jurors are selected for the particular place where jury sessions are to be held. The divisions are as follows:

1. ALBANY DIVISION: Albany, Columbia, Greene, Rensselaer, Saratoga, Schenectady, Schoharie, Ulster, Warren and Washington Counties.

2. BINGHAMTON DIVISION: Broome, Chenango, Delaware, Otsego and Tioga Counties.

3. SYRACUSE–AUBURN DIVISION: Cayuga, Cortland, Madison, Onondaga, Oswego, and Tompkins Counties.

4. UTICA DIVISION: Fulton, Hamilton, Herkimer, Montgomery and Oneida Counties.

5. WATERTOWN DIVISION: Jefferson, Lewis and St. Lawrence Counties.

6. MALONE DIVISION: Clinton, Essex and Franklin Counties.

A copy of the Plan for the Northern District of New York for Random Selection of Grand and Petit Jurors, is available upon request at the Clerk's office or on the Court's webpage at "www.nynd.uscourts.gov."

[Amended effective January 1, 1999; January 1, 2004; January 1, 2008.]

RULE 47.2 JURY SELECTION

(a) Voir Dire. The Court, the attorneys, or both, shall conduct voir dire examination as the Court shall determine. The Court, in its sound discretion, may limit the attorneys' examination in time and subject matter.

(b) Impanelment of the Jury. In its discretion, the Court shall impanel the jury by use of either the "Strike" or "Jury Box" selection method unless the Court determines otherwise.

(c) Peremptory Challenges. Unless the Court orders otherwise, all parties shall alternately exercise their peremptory challenges.

(d) Waiver of Peremptory Challenges. Except when using the strike method, if a party passes or refuses to exercise a peremptory challenge, such action shall constitute a waiver of the right to exercise the challenge.

[Amended effective January 1, 2008.]

RULE 47.3 ASSESSMENT OF JUROR COSTS

Whenever any civil action scheduled for jury trial is postponed, settled or otherwise disposed of in advance of the actual trial, then, except for good cause shown, all juror costs, including marshal's fees, mileage and per diem, shall be assessed against the parties and/or their attorneys as the Court directs, unless the parties or their attorneys notify the Court and the Clerk's office at least one full business day prior to the day on which the action is scheduled for trial, so that the Clerk has time to advise the jurors that it shall not be necessary for them to attend. The parties may request an advance estimate of costs from the Clerk.

[Amended effective January 1, 2008.]

RULE 47.4   JURY DELIBERATION

Availability of Attorneys During Jury Deliberations. Attorneys shall be available on short notice during jury deliberations in the event of a verdict or a question by the jury. Attorneys shall keep the Clerk informed as to where they will be at all times when the jury is deliberating. Attorneys should not leave the building without the presiding judge's prior approval.

[Amended effective January 1, 2008.]

RULE 47.5   JURY CONTACT PROHIBITION

The following rules apply in connection with contact between attorneys or parties and jurors:

1. At any time after the Court has called a jury panel from which jurors shall be selected to try cases for a term of Court fixed by the presiding judge or otherwise impaneled, no party or attorney, or anyone associated with the party or the attorney, shall have any communication or contact by any means or manner with any juror until such time as the panel of jurors has been excused and the term of court ended.

2. This prohibition is designed to prevent all unauthorized contact between attorneys or parties and jurors and does not apply when authorized by the judge while court is in session or when otherwise authorized by the presiding judge.

RULE 48.1   NUMBER OF JURORS

In civil cases the Court shall determine the number of jurors, which shall not be less than six nor more than twelve.

RULE 49.1   SPECIAL VERDICTS AND INTERROGATORIES [RESERVED]

RULE 50.1   JUDGMENT AS A MATTER OF LAW IN ACTIONS TRIED BY JURY; ALTERNATIVE MOTION FOR NEW TRIAL; CONDITIONAL RULINGS [RESERVED]

RULE 51.1   INSTRUCTIONS TO THE JURY

When Submitted and Served. See Uniform Pretrial Scheduling Order issued by the court following the initial pretrial conference. See L.R. 16.1(e).

[Amended effective January 1, 1999.]

RULE 52.1   PROPOSED FINDINGS IN CIVIL CASES

(a) In civil non-jury trials, each party shall submit proposed findings of fact and conclusions of law sufficiently detailed that, if the Court adopts them, would form an adequate factual basis, supported by anticipated evidence, for the resolution of the case and the entry of judgment.

(b) **When Submitted and Served.** See Uniform Pretrial Scheduling Order issued by the Court following the initial pretrial conference. See L.R. 16.1(e).

[Amended effective January 1, 1999.]

RULE 53.1   MASTERS [RESERVED]

RULE 53.2   MASTER'S FEES

The Court, in its discretion, shall fix the compensation of masters. Factors the Court shall consider include expended hours, disbursements, the relative complexity of the matter, and whether the parties have previously consented to a reasonable rate of compensation. The compensation and disbursements shall be paid and taxed as costs in the manner and amounts that the Court directs unless the parties stipulate otherwise.

RULE 53.3   OATH OF MASTER, COMMISSIONER, ETC.

Every person appointed master, special master, commissioner, special commissioner, referee, assessor or appraiser (collectively referred to as "master") shall take and subscribe an oath, which, except as otherwise prescribed by statute or rule, shall be to the effect that they will faithfully and impartially discharge their duties. The oath shall be taken before any federal or state officer authorized by federal law to administer oaths and shall be filed in the Clerk's office.

[Amended effective January 1, 2008.]

SECTION VII.   JUDGMENTS

RULE 54.1   TAXATION OF COSTS

(a) **Procedure for Taxation in Civil Cases.** The party entitled to recover costs shall file, within thirty (30) days after entry of judgment, a verified bill of costs on the forms that the Clerk provides. The party seeking costs shall accompany its request with receipts indicating that the party actually incurred the costs that it seeks. The verified bill of costs shall include the date on which the party shall appear before the Clerk for taxation of the costs and proof of service of a copy on the party liable for the costs. Post-trial motions shall not serve to extend the time within which a party may file a verified bill of costs as provided in this Rule, except on an order extending the time. Forms for the preparation of a bill of costs are available from the Clerk's office or at the Court's webpage at "**www.nynd.uscourts.gov.**"

(b) **To Whom Payable.** Except in criminal cases, suits for civil penalties for violations of criminal statutes, and government cases that the Department of Justice does not handle, all costs taxed are payable directly to the party entitled thereto and not to the Clerk, unless the Court orders otherwise.

(c) **Waiver of Costs.** Failure to file a bill of costs within the time provided for in this Rule shall constitute a waiver of the taxable costs.

[Amended effective August 12, 2004; January 1, 2005.]

RULE 54.2   JURY COST ASSESSMENT

See L.R. 47.3.

RULE 54.3   AWARD OF ATTORNEY'S FEES [RESERVED]

RULE 54.4   ALLOWANCES TO ATTORNEYS AND RECEIVERS

Every attorney and receiver requesting an allowance for services rendered in a civil action in which the Court has appointed a receiver shall, on filing the receiver's report with the Clerk, file a detailed statement of the services rendered and the amount claimed, with a statement of any partial allowance previously made, together with an affidavit of the applicants, stating that no agreement has been made, directly or indirectly, and that no understanding exists for a division of fees between the attorney and the receiver. The petition shall be heard and allowance made on notice as the Court shall direct.

[Amended effective January 1, 2008.]

RULE 55.1   CERTIFICATE OF ENTRY OF DEFAULT

A party applying to the Clerk for a certificate of entry of default pursuant to Fed. R. Civ. P. 55(a) shall submit an affidavit showing that (1) a party against whom it seeks a judgment for affirmative relief has failed to plead or otherwise defend the action as provided in the Federal Rules of Civil Procedure and

(2) it has properly served the pleading to which the opposing party has not responded.

[Amended effective January 1, 2003; January 1, 2004; January 1, 2008.]

RULE 55.2   DEFAULT JUDGMENT

(a) **By the Clerk.** When a party is entitled to have the Clerk enter a default judgment pursuant to Fed. R. Civ. P. 55(b)(1), the party shall submit, with the form of judgment, **the Clerk's certificate of entry of default**, a statement showing the principal amount due, not to exceed the amount demanded in the complaint, giving credit for any payments, and showing the amounts and dates of payment, a computation of the interest to the day of judgment, a per diem rate of interest, and the costs and taxable disbursements claimed. An affidavit of the party or the party's attorney shall be appended to the statement showing that

1. The party against whom it seeks judgment is not an infant or an incompetent person;

2. The party against whom it seeks judgment is not in the military service, or if unable to set forth this fact, the affidavit shall state that the party against whom the moving party seeks judgment by default is in the military service or that the party seeking a default judgment is not able to determine whether or not the party against whom it seeks judgment by default is in the military service;

3. The party has defaulted in appearance in the action;

4. Service was properly effected under Fed. R. Civ. P. 4;

5. The amount shown in the statement is justly due and owing and that no part has been paid except as set forth in the statement this Rule requires; and

6. The disbursements sought to be taxed have been made in the action or will necessarily be made or incurred.

The Clerk shall then enter judgment for principal, interest and costs. If, however, the Clerk determines, for whatever reason, that it is not proper for a default judgment to be entered, the Clerk shall forward the documents submitted in accordance with **L.R. 55.2(a)** to the assigned district judge for review. The assigned district judge shall then promptly notify the Clerk as to whether the Clerk shall properly enter a default judgment under L.R. 55.2(a).

(b) **By the Court.** A party shall accompany a motion to the Court for the entry of a default judgment, pursuant to Fed. R. Civ. P. 55(b)(2), with a **clerk's certificate of entry of default** in accordance with Fed. R. Civ. P. 55(a), a **proposed form of default judgment**, and a copy of the pleading to which no response has been made. The moving party shall also include in its application an affidavit of the moving party or the moving party's attorney setting forth facts as required by L.R. 55.2(a).

[Adopted effective January 1, 2004; January 1, 2008.]

RULE 56.1   SUMMARY JUDGMENT PROCEDURE

See L.R. 7.1(a)(3).

RULE 56.2   NOTICE TO PRO SE LITIGANTS OF THE CONSEQUENCES OF FAILING TO RESPOND TO A SUMMARY JUDGMENT MOTION

When moving for summary judgment against a pro se litigant, the moving party shall inform the pro se litigant of the consequences of failing to respond to the summary judgment motion. Counsel for the moving party shall send a notice to the pro se litigant that a motion for summary judgment seeks dismissal of some or all of the claims or defenses asserted in their complaint or answer and that the pro se litigant's failure to respond to the motion may result in the Court entering a judgment against the pro se litigant. Parties can obtain a sample notice from the Court's webpage at "www.nynd.uscourts.gov."

[Effective January 1, 2001; January 1, 2008.]

RULE 57.1   DECLARATORY JUDGMENT [RESERVED]

RULE 58.1   ENTRY OF JUDGMENT

(a) Upon the verdict of a jury or the decision of the Court, the Clerk shall sign and enter a separate document which shall constitute the judgment. The judgment shall contain no recitals other than a recital of the verdict or any direction of the Court on which the judgment is entered. Unless the Court specifically directs otherwise, the Clerk shall promptly prepare the judgment. The Clerk shall promptly sign and enter the judgment, except that where Fed.R.Civ.P. 58 requires the Court's approval, the Clerk shall first submit the judgment to the Court, which shall manifest approval by signing it or noting approval on the margin. The notation of the judgment in the appropriate docket shall constitute the entry of judgment.

(b) The attorney causing the entry of an order or judgment shall append to, or endorse on, it a list of the names of the parties entitled to be notified of the entry and the names and addresses of their respective attorneys if known.

RULE 58.2   ENTERING SATISFACTION OF JUDGMENT OR DECREE

The Clerk shall enter satisfaction of a money judgment recovered or registered in the District as follows:

(a) Upon the payment into Court of the amount, plus applicable interest, and the payment of the Marshal's fees, if any;

(b) Upon the filing of a satisfaction-piece executed and acknowledged by:

1. The judgment-creditor; or

2. The judgment-creditor's legal representative or assigns, with evidence of the representative's authority; or

3. The judgment-creditor's attorney or proctor, if within two years of the entry of the judgment or decree.

(c) If the judgment-creditor is the United States, upon the filing of a satisfaction-piece executed by the United States Attorney.

(d) In admiralty, pursuant to an order of satisfaction; but an order shall not be made on the consent of the proctors only, unless consent is given within two years from the entry of the decree to be satisfied.

(e) Upon the registration of a certified copy of a satisfaction entered in another district.

RULE 59.1   NEW TRIAL; AMENDMENT OF JUDGMENT

See L.R. 7.1(g): Motions for Reconsideration.

RULE 60.1   RELIEF FROM JUDGMENT OR ORDER [RESERVED]

RULE 61.1   HARMLESS ERROR [RESERVED]

RULE 62.1   STAY OF PROCEEDINGS [RESERVED]

RULE 62.2   SUPERSEDEAS BOND

See L.R. 67.1.

RULE 63.1   DISABILITY OF A JUDGE [RESERVED]

SECTION VIII. PROVISIONAL AND FINAL REMEDIES AND SPECIAL PROCEEDINGS

RULE 64.1 SEIZURE OF PERSON OR PROPERTY

The Court has adopted a Uniform Procedure for Civil Forfeiture Cases which is available from the Clerk's office or at the Court's webpage at "**www.nynd.uscourts.gov**."

[Amended effective January 1, 2004.]

RULE 65.1 INJUNCTIONS

See L.R. 7.1(f).

RULE 65.1.1 SURETIES

(a) Whenever a bond, undertaking or stipulation is required, it shall be sufficient, except in bankruptcy or criminal cases, or as otherwise prescribed by law, if the instrument is executed by the surety or sureties only.

(b) Except as otherwise provided by law, every bond, undertaking or stipulation shall be secured by the deposit of cash or government bonds in the amount of the bond, undertaking or stipulation; or be secured by the undertaking or guaranty of a corporate surety holding a certificate of authority from the Secretary of the Treasury; or the undertaking or guaranty of two individual residents of the Northern District of New York, each of whom owns real or personal property within the District worth double the amount of the bond, undertaking or stipulation, over all the debts and liabilities of each of the residents, and over all obligations assumed by each of the residents on other bonds, undertakings or stipulations, and exclusive of all legal exemptions.

(c) In the case of a bond or undertaking, or stipulation executed by individual sureties, each surety shall attach an affidavit of justification, giving full name, occupation, residence and business address and showing that the surety is qualified as an individual surety under subdivision (b) of this Rule.

(d) Members of the bar, administrative officers or employees of this Court, the Marshal, or the Marshal's deputies or assistants shall not act as sureties in any suit, action or proceeding pending in this Court. See L.R. 67.3.

RULE 65.2 TEMPORARY RESTRAINING ORDERS

See L.R. 7.1(f).

RULE 66.1 RECEIVERSHIPS [RESERVED]

RULE 67.1 DEPOSITS IN COURT

(a) A supersedeas bond, where the judgment is for a sum of money only, shall be in the amount of the judgment plus 11% to cover interest and any damage for delay as may be awarded, plus $250 to cover costs.

When a stay shall be effected solely by the giving of the supersedeas bond, but the judgment or order is not solely for a sum of money, the Court, on notice, shall fix the amount of the bond. In all other cases, the Court shall, on notice, grant a stay on the terms it deems proper.

On approval, a party shall file the supersedeas bond with the Clerk, and shall promptly serve a copy thereof, with notice of filing, upon all parties affected thereby. If a party raises objections to the form of the bond or to the sufficiency of the surety, the Court shall provide prompt notice of a hearing to consider such objections.

(b) **Order Directing the Investment of Funds.** Any order directing the Clerk to invest funds deposited with the registry account of the Court pursuant to 28 U.S.C. § 2041 shall include the following:

1. The amount to be invested; and

2. The type of interest-bearing account in which the funds are to be invested.

(c) **Time for Investing Funds.** The Clerk shall take all reasonable steps to invest the funds within ten (10) days of the filing date of the order.

(d) **Fee.** Unless the Court orders otherwise, the Clerk, at the time the income becomes available, shall deduct from the income earned on the investment a fee as authorized by the Judicial Conference of the United States and set out by the Director of the Administrative Office.

[Amended effective January 1, 2008.]

RULE 67.2 WITHDRAWAL OF A DEPOSIT PURSUANT TO Fed.R.Civ.P. 67

Any person seeking withdrawal of money deposited in the Court pursuant to Fed. R. Civ. P. 67 and subsequently deposited into an interest-bearing account or instrument as Fed. R. Civ. P. 67 requires shall provide a completed Internal Revenue Service Form W–9 with the motion papers seeking withdrawal of the funds.

RULE 67.3　BONDS AND OTHER SURETIES

(a) General Requirements. Unless the Court expressly directs otherwise pursuant to the provisions of 18 U.S.C. § 3146 in the supervision of a criminal matter, the principal obligor or one or more sureties qualified under this Rule shall execute every bond, recognizance or other undertaking that the law or a court order requires in any proceeding.

(b) Unacceptable Sureties. An attorney or the attorney's employee, a party to an action, or the spouse of a party to an action or of an attorney shall not be accepted as surety on a cost bond, bail bond, appeal bond, or any other bond.

(c) Corporate Surety. A corporate surety on any undertaking in which the United States is the obligee shall be qualified in accordance with the provisions of 6 U.S.C. §§ 6–13, and approved thereunder by the Secretary of the Treasury of the United States. In all other instances, a corporate surety qualified to write bonds in the State of New York shall be an acceptable surety. In all actions, a power of attorney showing authority of the agent signing the bond shall be attached to the bond.

(d) Personal Surety. Persons competent to convey real property who own real property in the State of New York of an unencumbered value of at least the stated penalty of the bond shall obtain consideration for qualification as surety thereon by attaching thereto a duly acknowledged justification showing (1) the legal description of the real property; (2) a complete list of all encumbrances and liens thereon; (3) its market value based upon recent sales of like property; (4) a waiver of inchoate rights of any character and certification that the real property is not exempt from execution; and (5) certification as to the aggregate amount of penalties of all other existing undertakings, if any, assured by the bondsperson as of that date. The Court will review the justifications and certifications for approval or disapproval of the surety.

(e) Cost Bonds. The Court on motion, or upon its own initiative, may order any party to file an original bond for costs or additional security for costs in such an amount and so conditioned as the court by its order shall designate.

(f) Cash Bonds. Cash bonds shall be deposited into the Court's registry only upon execution and filing of a written bond sufficient as to form and setting forth the conditions of the bond. Withdrawal of cash bonds so deposited shall not be made except upon the Court's written order.

(g) Insufficiency—Remedy. An opposing party may raise objections to a bond's form or timeliness or the sufficiency of the surety. If the bond is found to be insufficient, the Court shall order that a party file a sufficient bond within a stated time. If the party does not comply with the order, the Court shall dismiss the case for want of prosecution, or the Court shall take other appropriate action as justice requires.

[Amended effective January 1, 2008.]

RULE 68.1　SETTLEMENT CONFERENCES

See L.R. 16.1.

RULE 68.2　SETTLEMENT PROCEDURES

(a) On notice to the Court or the Clerk that the parties have settled an action, and upon confirmation of all parties of the settlement, the Court may issue a judgment dismissing the action by reason of settlement. The Court shall issue the order without prejudice to the parties' right to secure reinstatement of the case within thirty (30) days after the date of judgment by making a showing that the settlement was not, in fact, consummated.

(b) If the Court decides not to follow the procedures set forth in L.R. 68.2(a), the parties shall file within thirty (30) days of the notification to the Court, unless otherwise directed by written order, such pleadings as are necessary to terminate the action. If the required documents are not filed within the thirty (30) day period, the Clerk shall place the action on the dismissal calendar.

See also L.R. 17.1 (Actions Involving Infants and/or Incompetents).

[Amended effective January 1, 2008.]

RULE 69.1　EXECUTION [RESERVED]

RULE 70.1　JUDGMENT FOR SPECIFIC ACTS;　VESTING TITLE [RESERVED]

RULE 71.1　PROCESS IN BEHALF OF AND AGAINST PERSONS NOT PARTIES [RESERVED]

RULE 71A.1　CONDEMNATION CASES [RESERVED]

RULE 72.1　AUTHORITY OF MAGISTRATE JUDGES

(a) A full-time Magistrate Judge is authorized to exercise all powers and perform all duties permitted by 28 U.S.C. § 636(a), (b), and (c) and any additional duties that are consistent with the Constitution and laws of the United States. Part-time Magistrate Judges are authorized to exercise all of those duties, except that only those Magistrate Judges whom the Court specifically designates are authorized to perform duties allowed under 28 U.S.C. § 636(c) and any additional duties consistent with the Constitution and laws of the United States.

(b) Any party may file objections to a Magistrate Judge's determination of a non-dispositive matter by filing with the Clerk and serving upon all parties their objections. The party must file and serve its objections within ten (10) days after being served with the Magistrate Judge's order, must state a return date in accordance with L.R. 7.1(b)(2) and must specifically designate the order or part of the order from which the party seeks relief and the basis for the objection. The parties shall file all supporting and opposition papers in accordance with L.R. 7.1(b)(2). The supporting papers shall include the following documents:

1. A designation of the contents of the record on appeal, including the documents, exhibits and other materials the Court is to consider; and

2. A memorandum of law.

Opposition papers shall also include a memorandum of law responsive to the appellant's arguments. Unless the Court directs otherwise, it will decide all appeals on submission of the papers without oral argument.

(c) Any party may object to a Magistrate Judge's proposed findings, recommendations, or report issued pursuant to 28 U.S.C. § 636(b)(1)(B) and (C) within ten (10) days after being served with a copy of the Magistrate Judge's recommendation. The party must file with the Clerk and serve upon all parties written objections which specifically identify the portions of the proposed findings, recommendations, or report to which it has an objection and the basis for the objection. The party shall file with the Clerk a transcript of the specific portions of any evidentiary proceedings to which it has an objection. Objections may not exceed twenty-five (25) pages without the Court's prior approval. The opposing party may file and serve its response to the objections within ten (10) days after being served with a copy of the objections. The objecting party may not file a reply. The Court will proceed in accordance with Fed. R. Civ. P. 72(b) or Rule 8(b) of the Rules Governing Section 2254 Petitions, as applicable.

[Amended effective January 1, 1999; January 1, 2001; January 1, 2003; January 1, 2008.]

RULE 72.2 DUTIES OF MAGISTRATE JUDGES

(a) In all civil cases, in accordance with Fed. R. Civ. P. 16, the Magistrate Judge assigned pursuant to L.R. 40.1 is authorized to hold conferences before trial, enter scheduling orders, and modify scheduling orders. The scheduling order may limit the time to join parties, amend pleadings, file and hear motions, and complete discovery. It may also include dates for a final pretrial conference and other conferences, a trial ready date, a trial date, and any other matters appropriate under the circumstances of the case. A schedule cannot be modified except by order of the Court. The Magistrate Judge may explore the possibility of settlement and hold settlement conferences.

(b) The following procedure shall be followed regarding consent of the parties and designation of a Magistrate Judge to exercise civil trial jurisdiction under 28 U.S.C. § 636(c):

1. Upon the filing of a complaint or petition for removal, the Clerk shall promptly provide to the plaintiff, or the plaintiff's attorney, a notice, as approved by the Court, informing the parties of their right to consent to have the full-time Magistrate Judge conduct all proceedings in the case. Proceedings in the case include hearing and determining all pretrial and post-trial motions, including dispositive motions; conducting a jury or non-jury trial; and ordering the entry of a final judgment. The plaintiff shall attach copies of the notice to the copies of the complaint and summons when served. Additional copies of the notice shall be furnished to the parties at later stages of the proceedings and shall be included with pretrial notices and instructions. The consent form will state that any appeal lies directly with the Court of Appeals for the Second Circuit.

2. If the parties agree to consent, the attorney for each party or the party, if pro se, must execute the consent form. The parties shall file the executed consent forms directly with the Clerk. No consent form shall be made available, nor shall its contents be made known, to any District Judge or Magistrate Judge, unless all of the parties have executed the consent form. No judge or other court official shall attempt to persuade or induce any party to consent to the reference of any matter to a Magistrate Judge. A District Judge, Magistrate Judge, or other court official may again inform or remind the parties that they have the option of referring the case to a Magistrate Judge. In reminding the parties about the availability of consent to a Magistrate Judge, the judge or other court official must inform the parties that they are free to withhold consent without adverse substantive consequences. The parties may agree to a Magistrate Judge's exercise of civil jurisdiction at any time prior to trial, subject to the approval of the District Judge.

3. When all of the parties have executed and filed the consent forms, the Clerk shall then transmit those forms along with the file to the assigned District Judge for approval and referral of the case to a Magistrate Judge. If the District Judge assigns the case to a Magistrate Judge on consent, authority vests in the Magistrate Judge to conduct all proceedings and to direct the Clerk to enter a final judgment in the same manner as if a District Judge presided over the case.

4. The Clerk shall notify any parties added to an action after consent and reference to a Magistrate Judge of their right to consent to the exercise of jurisdiction by the Magistrate Judge. If an added party does not consent to the Magistrate Judge's jurisdiction, the action shall be returned to the referring District Judge for further proceedings.

(c) Assignment of Magistrate Judges to Serve as Special Masters. A Magistrate Judge shall serve as a special master subject to the procedures and limitations of 28 U.S.C. § 636(b)(2) and Fed. R. Civ. P. 53. Where the parties consent, a Magistrate Judge shall serve as a special master in any civil case without regard to the provisions of Fed. R. Civ. P. 53(b).

(d) Other Duties in Civil Actions. A Magistrate Judge is also authorized to:

1. Conduct proceedings for the collection of civil penalties of not more than $200 assessed under the Federal Boat Safety Act of 1971, as amended, in accordance with 46 U.S.C. §§ 4311(d), 12309(c);

2. Conduct examinations of judgment debtors in accordance with Fed. R. Civ. P. 69;

3. Review petitions in civil commitment proceedings under Title III of the Narcotic Rehabilitation Act;

4. Supervise proceedings conducted pursuant to letters rogatory in accordance with 28 U.S.C. § 1782;

5. Exercise general supervision of the Court's civil calendar, conduct calendar and status calls, and determine motions to expedite or postpone the trial of cases for the judges; and

6. Administer oaths and affirmations and take acknowledgments, affidavits, and depositions.

[Amended effective January 1, 1999; January 1, 2008.]

RULE 72.3 ASSIGNMENT OF DUTIES TO MAGISTRATE JUDGES

(a) Immediately upon the filing of a civil action or proceeding, the Clerk shall assign the action or proceeding to a District Judge and may also assign the action or proceeding to a Magistrate Judge pursuant to the Court's Assignment Plan. When a civil action or proceeding is assigned to a Magistrate Judge, the Magistrate Judge shall conduct proceedings in accordance with these Rules and 28 U.S.C. § 636 as directed by the District Judge. (See L.R. 40.1)

(b) All civil cases in which the parties have executed and filed consent forms pursuant to 28 U.S.C. § 636(c) and L.R. 72.2(b) shall be transmitted to the assigned District Judge for approval and referral of the case to a Magistrate Judge, who shall then have the authority to conduct all proceedings and to direct the Clerk to enter final a judgment. (See L.R. 72.2(b)(3)

(c) Federal Debt Collection Act Cases.

1. Any action brought pursuant to the Federal Debt Collection Act, 28 U.S.C. § 3001 et seq., shall be handled on an expedited basis and brought before a Magistrate Judge in Syracuse, New York, or to a District Judge if no Magistrate Judge is available, for an initial determination.

2. If appropriate, an order shall be issued directing the clerk to issue the writ being sought, except that an application under 28 U.S.C. § 3203 for a writ of execution in a post-judgment proceeding shall not require an order of the Court.

3. Thereafter, the Clerk is directed to assign geographically a Magistrate Judge if none was previously assigned in accordance with General Order # 12.

4. The assigned Magistrate Judge shall conduct any hearing that may be requested, decide all non-dispositive issues, and issue a report-recommendation on any and all dispositive issues.

5. The parties shall file written objections to the report-recommendation within twenty (20) days of the filing of same. Without oral argument, the assigned judge shall review the report-recommendation along with any objections that the parties have filed.

6. On the request for a hearing, the clerk shall make a good faith effort to schedule the hearing within five (5) days of the receipt of the request or "as soon after that as possible," pursuant to 28 U.S.C. § 3101(d)(1).

[Amended effective January 1, 1999; February 7, 2008.]

RULE 72.4 HABEAS CORPUS

(a) Petitions under 28 U.S.C. §§ 2241, 2254 and 2255 shall be filed pursuant to the Rules Governing § 2254 Cases in the United States District Courts and the Rules Governing § 2255 Proceedings in the United States District Courts. All memoranda of law filed in Habeas Corpus proceedings shall conform to the requirements set forth in Local Rule 7.1(a)(1).

(b) Subject to the requirement of subsection (c), the petitioner shall file the original verified petition with the Clerk at Syracuse, New York. Applications for a writ of habeas corpus made by persons in custody shall be filed, heard and determined in the district court for the district in which they were convicted and sentenced provided, however, that if the convenience of the parties and witnesses requires a hearing in a different district, such application shall be transferred to any district that the assigned judge finds or determines to be more convenient.

(c) Before a second or successive application is filed in this Court, the applicant shall move in the Second Circuit Court of Appeals for an order authorizing the district court to consider the application.

(d) If the respondent submits the state court records with its answer to the petition, the respondent must properly identify the records in the answer and arrange them in chronological order. The respondent must also sequentially number the pages of the state court records so that citations to those records will identify the exact location where the information appears. If documents are separately bound and the citation to the documents is easily identifiable, the respondent does not need to repaginate the documents.

[Amended effective January 1, 2001; January 1, 2006; January 1, 2008.]

RULE 72.5 HABEAS CORPUS PETITIONS INVOLVING THE DEATH PENALTY; SPECIAL REQUIREMENTS

(a) Applicability. This Rule shall govern the procedures for a first petition for a writ of habeas corpus filed pursuant to 28 U.S.C. § 2254 in which a petitioner seeks relief from a judgment imposing the penalty of death. The Court may deem a subsequent filing relating to a particular petition a first petition under this Rule if a court did not dismiss the original filing on the merits. The District Judge or Magistrate Judge to whom the petition is assigned may modify the application of this Rule. This Rule shall supplement the Rules Governing § 2254 Cases and does not in any regard alter or supplant those rules.

(b) Notices From Office of the Attorney General for the State of New York. The Office of the Attorney General for the State of New York ("Attorney General") shall send to the Clerk (1) prompt notice whenever the New York State Court of Appeals affirms a sentence of death; (2) at least once a month, a list of scheduled executions; and (3) at least once a month, a list of the death penalty appeals pending before the New York State Court of Appeals.

(c) Notice From Petitioner's Counsel. Whenever counsel decides to file a petition in this Court, counsel shall promptly file with the Clerk and serve on the Attorney General a written notice of counsel's intention to file a petition. The notice shall state the name of the petitioner, the district in which the petitioner was convicted, the place of the petitioner's incarceration, the status of the petitioner's state court proceedings, and the scheduled date of execution. The notice is for the Court's information only, and the failure to file the notice shall not preclude the filing of the petition.

(d) Counsel.

1. *Appointment of Counsel.* Each indigent petitioner shall be represented by counsel unless petitioner has clearly elected to proceed pro se and the Court is satisfied, after a hearing, that petitioner's election is intelligent, competent, and voluntary. Where the Court is to appoint counsel, such appointment shall be made at the earliest practicable time. The active judges of this District will certify a panel of attorneys qualified for appointment in death penalty cases ("qualified panel").

If state appellate counsel is available to continue representation in the federal courts and the assigned District Judge deems counsel qualified to continue representation, there is a presumption in favor of continued representation except when state appellate counsel was also counsel at trial. In light of this presumption, it is expected that any appointed counsel who is willing to continue representation and whom the assigned District Judge has found qualified to do so, would ordinarily file a motion for appointment of counsel on behalf of his or her client together with the client's federal habeas corpus petition. If, however, counsel for any reason wishes to confirm appointment before preparing the petition, counsel may move for appointment as described above before filing the petition.

If state appellate counsel is not available to represent the petitioner in the federal habeas corpus proceeding or if appointment of state appellate counsel would be inappropriate for any reason, the Court may appoint counsel upon application of the petitioner. The Clerk shall have available forms for such application. The Court may appoint counsel from the qualified panel. The assigned District Judge may suggest one or more counsel for appointment. If a petitioner makes an application for appointed counsel before filing the petition, the Clerk shall assign the application to a District Judge and Magistrate Judge in the same manner that the Clerk would assign a noncapital petition. The District Judge and Magistrate Judge so assigned shall be the District Judge and Magistrate Judge assigned when counsel files a petition for writ of habeas corpus.

2. *Second Counsel.* The Guide to Judiciary Policies and Procedures, Appointment of Counsel in Criminal Cases shall govern the appointment and compensation of second counsel.

(e) Filing.

1. *General Requirement.* Petitioners shall file petitions as to which venue lies in this District in accordance with the applicable Local Rules. Petitioners shall fill in their petitions by printing or typewriting. In the alternative, the petitioner may typewrite or legibly write a petition which contains all of the information that the form requires. All petitions shall (1) state whether the petitioner has previously sought relief arising out of the same matter from this Court or any other federal court, together with the ruling and reasons given for denial of relief; (2) set forth any scheduled execution date; and (3) contain the wording in full caps and underscored "Death Penalty Case" directly under the case number on each pleading.

Counsel for petitioner shall file an original and three (3) copies of the petition. A *pro se* petitioner need file only the original.

The Clerk will immediately notify the Attorney General's office when a petition is filed.

When a petitioner who was convicted outside of this District files a petition, the Court will immediately advise the clerk of the district in which the petitioner was convicted.

2. *Emergency Motions or Applications.* Counsel shall file emergency motions or applications with the Clerk. If time does not permit the filing of a motion or application in person or by mail, counsel may communicate with the Clerk and obtain the Clerk's permission to file the motion by facsimile. Counsel should communicate with the Clerk by telephone as soon as it becomes evident that he or she will seek emergency relief from this Court. The motion or application shall contain a brief account of the prior actions, if any, of this Court and the name of the judge or judges involved in the prior actions.

(f) Assignment to Judges. Notwithstanding the Court's case assignment plan, the Clerk shall assign petitions to judges of the Court as follows: (1) the Clerk shall establish a separate category for these petitions, to be designated with the title "Capital Case"; (2) all active judges of this Court shall participate in the assignments; (3) the Clerk shall assign petitions in the Capital Case category randomly to each of the available active judges of the Court; (4) if a petitioner has previously sought relief in this Court with respect to the same conviction, the petition shall, when practical, be assigned to the judges who were assigned to the prior proceeding; and (5) pursuant to 28 U.S.C. § 636(b)(1)(B), and consistent with law, the Court may designate Magistrate Judges to perform all duties under this Rule, including evidentiary hearings.

(g) Transfer of Venue. Subject to the provisions of 28 U.S.C. § 2241(d), it is the Court's policy that a petition should be heard in the district in which the petitioner was convicted rather than in the district of the petitioner's present confinement. See L.R. 72.4(b). If an order for the transfer of venue is made, the Court will order a stay of execution which shall continue until such time as the transferee court acts upon the petition or the order of stay.

(h) Stays of Execution.

1. *Stay Pending Final Disposition.* Upon the filing of a habeas corpus petition, unless the petition is patently frivolous, the Court shall issue a stay of execution pending final disposition of the matter. Notwithstanding any provision of this paragraph (h), the Court shall not grant or maintain stays of execution, except in accordance with law. Thus, the provisions of this paragraph (h) for a stay shall be ineffective in any case in which the stay would be inconsistent with the

limitations of 28 U.S.C. § 2262 or any other governing statute.

2. *Temporary Stay for Appointment of Counsel.* Where counsel in the state court proceedings withdraws at the conclusion of the state court proceedings or is otherwise not available or qualified to proceed, the Court may designate an attorney who will assist an indigent petitioner in filing *pro se* applications for appointment of counsel and for a temporary stay of execution. Upon the filing of this application, the Court shall issue a temporary stay of execution and appoint counsel. The temporary stay will remain in effect for forty-five (45) days unless the Court extends this time.

3. *Temporary Stay for Preparation of the Petition.* Where the Court appoints new counsel to the case, upon counsel's application for a temporary stay of execution accompanied by a specification of nonfrivolous issues to be raised in the petition, the Court shall issue a temporary stay of execution unless no nonfrivolous issues are presented. The temporary stay will remain in effect for one hundred twenty (120) days to allow newly appointed counsel to prepare and file the petition. The Court may extend the temporary stay upon a subsequent showing of good cause.

4. *Temporary Stay for Transfer of Venue.* See paragraph (g).

5. *Temporary Stay for Unexhausted Claims.* If the petition indicates that there are unexhausted claims for which a state court remedy is still available, the Court shall grant the petitioner a sixty (60) day stay of execution in which to seek a further stay from the state court in order to litigate the unexhausted claims in state court. During the proceedings in state court, the Court will stay the proceedings on the petition. After the state court proceedings have been completed, the petitioner may amend the petition with respect to the newly exhausted claims.

6. *Stay Pending Appeal.* If the Court denies the petition and issues a certificate of appealability, the Court will grant a stay of execution which will continue in effect until the court of appeals acts upon the appeal or the order of stay.

7. *Notice of Stay.* Upon the granting of any stay of execution, the Clerk will immediately notify the appropriate prison superintendent and the Attorney General. The Attorney General shall ensure that the Clerk has a twenty-four (24) hour telephone number for the superintendent.

(i) Procedures for Considering the Petition. Unless the Court summarily dismisses the petition as patently frivolous, the following schedule and procedures shall apply subject to the Court's modification. Requests for enlargement of any time period in this Rule shall comply with these Local Rules.

1. Respondent shall, as soon as practicable, but in any event on or before twenty (20) days from the date of service of the petition, file with the Court the following:

(A) Transcripts of the state trial court proceedings;

(B) Appellant's and respondent's briefs on direct appeal to the Court of Appeals, and the opinion or orders of that Court;

(C) Petitioner's and respondent's briefs in any state court habeas corpus proceedings, and all opinions, orders and transcripts of such proceedings;

(D) Copies of all pleadings, opinions and orders that the petitioner has filed in any previous federal habeas corpus proceeding which arose from the same conviction; and

(E) An index of all materials described in paragraphs (A) through (D) above.

Respondent shall mark and number the materials so that they can be uniformly cited. Respondent shall serve this index upon counsel for petitioner or the petitioner pro se. If time does not permit, the respondent may file the answer without attachments (A) through (D) above, but the respondent shall file the necessary these* attachments as soon as possible. If any items identified in paragraphs (A) through (D) above are not available, respondent shall state when, if at all, such missing material can be filed.

2. If counsel for petitioner claims that respondent has not complied with the requirements of paragraph (1), or if counsel for petitioner does not have copies of all the documents that respondent filed with the Court, counsel for petitioner shall immediately notify the Court in writing, with a copy to respondent. The Court will provide copies of any missing documents to the petitioner's counsel.

3. Respondent shall file an answer to the petition with accompanying points and authorities within thirty (30) days from the date of service of the petition. Respondent shall attach to the answer any other relevant documents that the parties have not already filed.

4. Within thirty (30) days after respondent has filed the answer, petitioner may file a traverse.

5. There shall be no discovery without leave of the Court.

6. Either party shall make any request for an evidentiary hearing within fifteen (15) days from the filing of the traverse or within fifteen (15) days from the expiration of the time for filing the traverse. The request shall include a specification of which factual issues require a hearing and a summary of what evidence petitioner proposes to offer. Any opposition to the request for an evidentiary hearing shall be made within fifteen (15) days from the filing of the

request. The Court will then give due consideration to whether it will hold an evidentiary hearing.

(j) Evidentiary Hearing. If the Court holds an evidentiary hearing, the Court will order the preparation of a transcript of the hearing, which is to be immediately provided to petitioner and respondent for use in briefing and argument. Upon the preparation of the transcript, the Court may establish a reasonable schedule for further briefing and argument about the issues considered at the hearing.

(k) Rulings. The Court's rulings may be in the form of a written opinion, which will be filed, or in the form of an oral opinion on the record in open court, which shall be promptly transcribed and filed. The Clerk will immediately notify the appropriate prison superintendent and the Attorney General whenever relief is granted on a petition. The Clerk will immediately notify the clerk of the United States Court of Appeals for the Second Circuit by telephone of (1) the issuance of a final order denying or dismissing a petition without a certificate of probable cause for appeal or (2) the denial of a stay of execution. If the petitioner files a notice of appeal, the Clerk will transmit the appropriate documents to the United States Court of Appeals for the Second Circuit immediately.

[Adopted effective January 1, 1999; January 1, 2008.]

* Publisher's Note: So in original.

RULE 73.1 MAGISTRATE JUDGES: TRIAL BY CONSENT

Upon the consent of the parties, a Magistrate Judge shall conduct all proceedings in any civil case, including a jury or non-jury trial and shall order the entry of a final judgment, in accordance with 28 U.S.C. § 636(c). See L.R. 72.2(b)(2).

RULE 74.1 METHOD OF APPEAL TO DISTRICT JUDGE IN CONSENT CASES [RESERVED]

RULE 75.1 PROCEEDINGS ON APPEAL FROM MAGISTRATE JUDGE TO DISTRICT JUDGE UNDER RULE 73(d) [RESERVED]

RULE 76.1 BANKRUPTCY CASES

Reference to Bankruptcy Court. All cases under Title 11 of the United States Code, and all proceedings arising under Title 11, or arising in, or related to, a case under Title 11, are referred to the bankruptcy court of this District pursuant to 28 U.S.C. § 157.

RULE 76.2　BANKRUPTCY APPEALS

(a) When a party files a notice of appeal with the bankruptcy court clerk, and the notice is not timely filed in accordance with Fed. R. Bankr. P. 8002(a), and the party did not file a motion for extension of time in accordance with Fed. R. Bankr. P. 8002(c), the bankruptcy court clerk shall forward the notice of appeal together with a "Certification of Noncompliance" to the Clerk without assembling the record as provided for in Fed. R. Bankr. P. 8007(b). The Clerk shall file the notice and certificate, assign a civil action number, and forward the file to a District Judge to determine whether the party timely filed the notice of appeal or whether to dismiss the appeal as untimely. If the District Judge determines that the party timely filed the appeal was timely filed* or that the appeal should otherwise be perfected, the Clerk shall notify the bankruptcy court clerk to complete the record promptly in accordance with Fed. R. Bankr. P. 8007(b).

(b) The Clerk shall issue a standard bankruptcy appeal scheduling order at the time of the filing of the record on appeal, a copy of which the Clerk shall provide to the parties, the bankruptcy judge from whom the appeal was taken, and the bankruptcy court clerk.

(c) Appeals from a decision of the bankruptcy court shall be in accordance with 28 U.S.C. § 158 and applicable bankruptcy rules. Fed. R. Bankr. P. 8009 respecting the filing of briefs shall not be applicable, and the parties shall file their briefs in accordance with this Court's scheduling order.

[Amended effective January 1, 2008.]

　* Publisher's Note: So in original.

RULE 76.3　BANKRUPTCY RECORD OF TRANSMITTAL, CERTIFICATE OF FACTS, AND PROPOSED FINDINGS PURSUANT TO TITLE 11, SECTION 110(i)

(a) Upon direction of the bankruptcy judge, the bankruptcy court clerk shall cause to be filed with the Clerk the designated record of transmittal, which shall consist of certified copies of the Memorandum–Decision, Findings of Fact, Conclusions of Law, bankruptcy docket, and transcript of proceedings which relate to the bankruptcy judge's findings. The bankruptcy court clerk shall also provide the Clerk with a list of those individuals to whom the notice of filing shall be given.

(b) Upon receipt of the above, the Clerk shall assign a civil action number, assign a District Judge and issue a scheduling order for the filing of motions pursuant to 11 U.S.C. § 110(i)(1). The Clerk shall serve copies of the scheduling order upon those individuals whom the bankruptcy court clerk designates.

Upon the filing of any motion(s), the Clerk shall schedule and notice all concerned parties of a hearing date. Failure to file motions within the time ordered will be deemed a waiver of the provisions of 11 U.S.C. § 110(i)(1). The Clerk shall prepare and present to the assigned District Judge a proposed order pursuant to the provisions of L. R. 41.2.

[Amended effective January 1, 2008.]

SECTION IX.　DISTRICT COURT AND CLERKS

RULE 77.1　HOURS OF COURT
[RESERVED]

RULE 77.2　ORDERS

(a) With these exceptions, all orders, whether by consent or otherwise, shall be presented for approval and execution to the assigned judge. The Clerk may sign without submission to the assigned judge the following orders:

1. Orders specifically appointing persons to serve process in accordance with Fed. R. Civ. P. 4;

2. Orders on consent for the substitution of attorneys in civil cases where the trial of the action has not been set. See also L.R. 83.2;

3. Orders restoring an action to the court docket after the filing of a demand for trial de novo pursuant to L.R. 83.7–7 (Consensual Arbitration Program);

4. Orders on consent satisfying decrees and orders on consent canceling stipulations and bonds.

(b) If the assigned judge instructs the prevailing party to do so, that party shall submit a proposed order which the opposing party has approved and which contains the endorsement of the opposing party: "Approved as to form."

When the parties are unable to agree as to the form of the proposed order, the prevailing party shall, on three (3) days notice to all other parties, submit a proposed order and a written explanation for the form of that order. The Court may award costs and attorneys' fees against a party whose unreasonable conduct the Court deemed to have required the bringing of the motion. The provisions of L.R. 7.1 shall not apply to such motion, and the Court shall not hear oral argument.

RULE 77.3　SESSIONS OF COURT

The Court shall be in continuous session in Albany, Binghamton, Syracuse, and Utica. The Court shall from time to time hold sessions in Auburn, Malone and Watertown, or such other place as the Court shall, by order, deem appropriate. Jurors shall serve as the Court directs.

RULE 77.4 COURT LIBRARY

The district court libraries are not open for use by the public.

RULE 77.5 OFFICIAL NEWSPAPERS

All process, notices, and orders required to be published shall be published in the proper county in an official newspaper. The Court shall direct the publication of process, notices, and orders in any other newspaper, upon proper showing, as it shall deem advisable. The following are designated as official newspapers:

County	Newspaper	City
Albany	Times Union (D)	Albany, NY
Broome	Binghamton Press/Sun Bulletin (D)	Binghamton, NY
Cayuga	The Citizen (D)	Auburn, NY
Clinton	Press–Republican (D)	Plattsburgh, NY
Chenango	Evening Sun (D)	Norwich, NY
Columbia	Register Star (D)	Hudson, NY
	The Independent (W)	Hillsdale, NY
Cortland	Cortland Standard (D)	Cortland, NY
Delaware	Walton Reporter (W)	Walton, NY
Essex	Lake Placid News (W)	Lake Placid, NY
Franklin	Adirondack Enterprise (D)	Saranac Lake, NY
Fulton	Leader Herald (D)	Gloversville, NY
Greene	Catskill Daily Mail (D)	Catskill, NY
Hamilton	Post Star (D)	Glen Falls, NY
Herkimer	Telegram (D)	Herkimer, NY
	The Evening Times (D)	Little Falls, NY
Jefferson	Watertown Times (D)	Watertown, NY
	Thousand Island Sun (W)	Alexandria Bay, NY
Lewis	Journal Republican (W)	Lowville, NY
Madison	Oneida Dispatch (D)	Oneida, NY
Montgomery	The Recorder (D)	Amsterdam, NY
Oneida	Utica Observer Dispatch (D)	Utica, NY
	Rome Sentinel (D)	Rome, NY
Onondaga	Post Standard (D)	Syracuse, NY
Oswego	Palladium Times (D)	Oswego, NY
Otsego	The Daily Star	Oneonta, NY
Rensselaer	Times Record (D)	Troy, NY
St. Lawrence	Ogdensburg Journal (D)	Ogdensburg, NY
	Tribune Press (W)	Gouverneur, NY
	Daily Courier Observer (D)	Massena, NY
Saratoga	Saratogian–Tri City News (D)	Saratoga Springs, NY
Schenectady	Schenectady Gazette (D)	Schenectady, NY
Schoharie	Times Journal (W)	Cobleskill, NY
Tioga	Owego Pennysaver (W)	Owego, NY
Tompkins	Ithaca Journal (D)	Ithaca, NY
Ulster	The Daily Freeman (D)	Kingston, NY
Warren	Post Star (D)	Glen Falls, NY
	Times (D)	Glen Falls, NY
Washington	Whitehall Times (W)	Whitehall, NY

(D) Daily
(W) Weekly

[Amended effective January 1, 2004.]

RULE 77.6 RELEASE OF INFORMATION

All court personnel, including but not limited to marshals, deputy clerks, court clerks, bailiffs, court reporters, law clerks, secretaries, and probation officers, shall not disclose to any person, without the Court's authorization, information divulged in arguments and hearings held in chambers or otherwise outside the presence of the public or any information relating to a pending case that is not part of the Court's public records.

RULE 77.7 OFFICIAL STATION OF THE CLERK

The Clerk's official station shall be Syracuse. The Clerk shall appoint deputy clerks in such number as are necessary, and they shall be stationed in Albany, Binghamton, Utica, Syracuse and Watertown.

RULE 78.1 MOTION DAYS

Listings of the regularly scheduled motion days for all judges shall be available at each Clerk's office and are available on the Court's webpage at "www.nynd.uscourts.gov." The Clerk shall provide notice of the regular motion days for all judges to the parties at the time an action is commenced.

[Amended effective January 1, 2004; January 1, 2008.]

RULE 79.1 CUSTODY OF EXHIBITS AND TRANSCRIPTS

(a) Unless the Court orders otherwise, the parties shall not file exhibits and transcripts with the Clerk. Rather, the party that produced them in court shall retain them.

(b) In the case of an appeal or other review by an appellate court, the parties are encouraged to agree with respect to which exhibits and transcripts are necessary for the determination of the appeal. In the absence of agreement and except as provided in this Rule, a party, upon written request of any other party or by Court order, shall make available at the Clerk's office all the original exhibits in the party's possession, or true copies, to enable such other party to prepare the record on appeal. At the same time and place, such other party also shall make available all the original exhibits in that party's possession. All exhibits made available at the Clerk's office, which any party designates as part of the record on appeal, shall be filed with the Clerk, who shall transmit them together with the record on appeal to the clerk of the Second Circuit Court of Appeals. Exhibits and transcripts not so designated shall remain in the custody of the respective attorneys who shall have the responsibility of promptly forwarding them to the clerk of the Second Circuit Court of Appeals on request.

(c) Documents of unusual bulk or weight and physical exhibits, other than documents, shall remain in the custody of the party producing them, who shall permit any party to inspect them for the purpose of preparing the record on appeal and who shall be charged with the responsibility for their safekeeping and transportation to the Second Circuit Court of Appeals.

(d) The party responsible for filing the exhibits and transcripts with the Clerk shall be responsible for removing them (1) if no appeal is taken, within ninety (90) days after a final decision is rendered or (2) if an appeal has been taken, within thirty (30) days after the mandate of the final reviewing court is filed. The Clerk shall notify the parties that fail to comply with this Rule to remove their exhibits. Upon their failure to do so within thirty (30) days, the Clerk shall dispose of these exhibits and transcripts as the Clerk sees fit.

[Amended effective January 1, 2008.]

RULE 79.2   BOOKS AND RECORDS OF THE CLERK [RESERVED]

RULE 80.1   STENOGRAPHIC TRANSCRIPT: COURT REPORTING FEES

Subject to the provisions of Fed. R. Civ. P. 54(d), the expense of any party in obtaining all or any part of a transcript for the Court's use when the Court so orders and the expense of any party in obtaining all or any part of a transcript for the purposes of a new trial or for amended findings or for appeals shall be a taxable cost against the unsuccessful party. A fee schedule of transcript rates is available on the Court's webpage at "www.nynd.uscourts.gov."

[Amended effective January 1, 2004.]

RULE 81.1   REMOVAL BONDS [RESERVED]

RULE 81.2   COPIES OF STATE COURT PROCEEDINGS IN REMOVED ACTIONS [RESERVED]

RULE 81.3   REMOVED CASES, DEMAND FOR JURY TRIAL

In an action removed from a state court, a party entitled to trial by jury under Fed. R. Civ. P. 38 shall be accorded a jury trial if the party files and serves a demand in accordance with the provisions of Fed. R. Civ. P. 81 and L.R. 38.1. The Court will not consider a motion that a party filed in state court unless that party refiles the motion in this Court in accordance with the Local Rules of Practice for the Northern District of New York.

[Amended effective January 1, 2007; January 1, 2008.]

RULE 81.4   ACTIONS REMOVED PURSUANT TO 28 U.S.C. § 1452

If removal is based upon 28 U.S.C. § 1452 (Removal of claims related to bankruptcy cases), the removing party shall specifically identify in its Notice of Removal which claims or causes of action it is removing and which of the parties in the state court action are parties to the removed claims or causes of action.

[Effective January 1, 2003.]

RULE 82.1   JURISDICTION AND VENUE UNAFFECTED [RESERVED]

RULE 83.1   ADMISSION TO THE BAR

(a) Permanent Admission. A member in good standing of the bar of the State of New York or of the bar of any United States District Court, whose professional character is good, may be permanently admitted to practice in this Court on motion of a member of the bar of this Court in compliance with the requirements of this Rule. **An admission packet containing all the required forms is available from the Clerk's office and on the Court's webpage at "www.nynd. uscourts.gov."**

Each applicant for permanent admission must file, at least ten (10) days prior to the scheduled hearing (unless, for good cause shown, the Court shortens the time), documentation for admission as set forth below. Ordinarily, the Court entertains applications for admission only on regularly scheduled motion days. Documentation required for permanent admission includes the following:

1. *A verified petition for admission* stating the following:

- place of residence and office address;

- the date(s) when and court(s) where previously admitted;

- legal training and trial experience;

- whether the applicant has ever been held in contempt of court, censured, suspended or disbarred by any court and, if so, the facts and circumstances connected therewith; and

- that the applicant is familiar with the provisions of the Judicial Code (Title 28 U.S.C.), which pertain to the jurisdiction of, and practice in, the United States District Courts; the Federal Rules of Civil Procedure and the Federal Rules of Evidence for the District Courts; the Federal Rules of Criminal Procedure for the District Courts; the Local Rules of the District Court for the Northern District of New York; and the N.Y.S. Lawyer's Code of Professional Responsibility. The applicant shall further affirm faithful adherence to these Rules and responsibilities.

2. *Affidavit of Sponsor.* The sponsor must be a member in good standing of the bar of the Northern District of New York who has personal knowledge of the petitioner's background and character. A form Affidavit of Sponsor is available from the Clerk's office.

3. *Attorney E-Filing Registration Form.* The E-Filing Registration Form must be in the form the Clerk prescribes and set forth the attorney's current office address(es); telephone and fax number(s), and e-mail address. A copy of the Attorney E-Filing Registration Form is available on the Court's webpage at "www.nynd.uscourts.gov." See subdivision (e) for requirements when information on the Registration Form changes.

4. *Certificate of Good Standing.* The certificate of good standing must be dated within six (6) months of the date of admission.

5. *The Required Fee.* As prescribed by and pursuant to the Judicial Conference of the United States and the Rules of this Court, the fee for admission to the bar is **$150.00**.

In addition to the initial admission fee, there shall be a **$30.00** biennial registration fee. This fee shall be due and owning on **June 1, 2001,** and every two years thereafter unless the Board of Judges directs otherwise. Failure to remit this fee will result in the removal of the non-paying attorney from the Court's bar roll. Should the payment of this biennial fee present a significant financial hardship, an attorney may request, by submitting an application to the Chief Judge, that the biennial registration fee be waived.

The Clerk shall deposit the additional **$30.00** fee required for admission to the bar and the **$30.00** biennial registration fee into the District Court Fund. The Clerk shall be the trustee of the Fund, and the monies deposited in the Fund shall be used only for the benefit of the bench and bar in the administration of justice. All withdrawals from the Fund require the approval of the Chief Judge or a judge designated by the Chief Judge to authorize the withdrawals.

The admission fees and biennial registration fees are waived for all attorneys in the employ of the United States Government.

The biennial registration fees **only** are waived for all attorneys employed by state and local public sector entities.

6. *Oath on Admission.* An applicant must swear or affirm that as an attorney and counselor of this Court the applicant will conduct himself or herself uprightly and according to law and that he or she will support the Constitution of the United States. The applicant signs the Oath on Admission, form AO 153, in court at the time of the admission.

(b) Applicants who are not admitted to another United States District Court in New York State must appear with their sponsor for formal admission unless the Court, in the exercise of its discretion, waives such appearance. If the applicant is admitted to practice in New York State, the Certificate of Good Standing submitted with the application for admission must be from the appropriate New York State Appellate Division. All requirements of subdivision (a) apply.

If the applicant is from outside New York State, the Certificate of Good Standing may be from the highest court of the state or from a United States District Court. All requirements of subdivision (a) apply. An out-of-state applicant must maintain an office in the state in which the applicant is admitted. Upon ceasing to maintain an office in that state, the attorney automatically ceases to be a member of the bar of this Court.

(c) Applicants who are members in good standing of a United States District Court for the Eastern, Western, or Southern District of New York need not appear for formal admission. The applicant must submit a Certificate of Good Standing from the United States District Court where the applicant is a member and a proposed order granting the admission. A sponsor's affidavit is not required. All other requirements of subdivision (a) apply.

(d) Pro Hac Vice Admission. A member in good standing of the bar of any state, or of any United States District Court, may be admitted pro hac vice to argue or try a particular case in whole or in part. In addition to the requirements of L.R. 83.1(a)(1)(3) and (4), an applicant must make a Motion for Pro Hac Vice Admission, which includes the case caption of the particular case for which the applicant seeks admission. See L.R. 10.1(b). In lieu of a written motion for admission, the sponsoring attorney may make an oral motion in open court on the record. In that case, the attorney seeking pro hac vice admission must immediately complete and file the required documents as set forth above.

The pro hac vice admission fee is $30.00. The Clerk deposits all pro hac vice admission fees into the District Court Fund. See L.R. 83.1(a)(5). An attorney admitted pro hac vice must file a written notice of appearance in the case for which the attorney was admitted in accordance with L.R. 83.2.

(e) Registration Form Changes. Every attorney must file a supplemental statement setting forth any change in the information on the Registration Form within ten (10) days of the change. The attorney should make this supplemental statement by filing a new Registration Form which reflects the new information and which identifies which information changed. Failure to timely file a supplemental Registration Form may result in the Court's inability to notify that attorney of developments in the case or other sanctions in the Court's discretion. See L.R. 41.2(b). A copy of the Attorney Registration Form is available on the Court's webpage at "**www.nynd. uscourts.gov.**"

(f) Pro Bono Service. Every member of the bar of this Court shall be available upon the Court's request for appointment to represent or assist in the representation of indigent parties. The Court shall make appointments under this Rule in a manner such that the Court shall not request any attorney to accept more than one appointment during any twelve-month period.

(g) United States Attorney's Office. An attorney appointed by the United States Attorney General as a United States Attorney, an assistant United States attorney, or as a special assistant United States attorney under 28 U.S.C. §§ 541–543, who has been admitted to practice before any United States District Court, shall be admitted to practice in this Court upon motion of a member of the bar of this Court. Thereafter, the attorney may appear before this Court on any matter on behalf of the United States.

[Amended effective January 1, 1999; January 1, 2001; January 1, 2004; January 1, 2005; January 1, 2008.]

RULE 83.2 APPEARANCE AND WITHDRAWAL OF ATTORNEY

(a) Appearance. An attorney appearing for a party in a civil case shall promptly file with the Clerk a written notice of appearance; however, an attorney does not need to file a notice of appearance if the attorney who would be filing the notice of appearance is the same individual who has signed the complaint, notice of removal, pre-answer motion, or answer.

(b) Withdrawal. An attorney who has appeared may withdraw only upon notice to the client and all parties to the case and an order of the Court, upon a finding of good cause, granting leave to withdraw. If the Court grants leave to withdraw, the withdrawing attorney must serve a copy of the order upon the affected party and file an affidavit of service.

Unless the Court orders otherwise, withdrawal of counsel shall not result in the extension of any of the deadlines contained in any case management orders, including the Uniform Pretrial Scheduling Order, see L.R. 16.1(e), or the adjournment of a trial ready or trial date.

[Amended effective January 1, 1999; January 1, 2008.]

RULE 83.3 PRO BONO PANEL

(a) Description of Panel. In recognition of the need for representation of indigent parties in civil actions, this Court has established the Pro Bono Panel ("Panel") of the Northern District of New York.

1. The Panel shall include those members of the Criminal Assigned Counsel Panel in this Court. The court also expects any other attorney admitted to practice in this Court to participate in periodic training that the Court offers and to accept no more than one pro bono assignment per year.

2. The Court shall maintain a list of Panel members, which shall include the information deemed necessary for the effective administration and assignment of Panel attorneys.

3. The Court shall select Panel members for assignment upon its determination that the appointment of an attorney is warranted. The Court shall select from the Panel a member who has not received an appointment from the Court during the past year and (i) has attended a training seminar that this Court sponsors, (ii) has adequate prior experience closely related to the matter assigned, or (iii) has accepted criminal (CJA) assignments from the Court.

4. Where a pro se party has one or more other cases pending before this Court in which the Court has appointed an attorney, the Court may determine that it is appropriate to appoint the same attorney to represent the pro se party in the case before the Court.

5. Where the Court finds that the nature of the case requires specific expertise, and among the Panel members available for appointment there are some with the required expertise, the attorney may be selected from among those included in the group or the Court may designate a specific member of the Panel.

6. Where the Court finds that the nature of the case requires specific expertise and none of the Panel members available for appointment has indicated that expertise, the Court may appoint an attorney with the required expertise who is not a member of the Panel.

(b) Application for Appointment of Attorney.

1. Any application that a party appearing pro se makes for the appointment of an attorney by a party appearing pro se shall include a form of affidavit stating the party's efforts to obtain an attorney by means other than appointment and indicating any prior pro bono appointments of an attorney to represent the party in cases brought in this Court, including both pending and terminated actions.

2. Failure of a party to make a written application for an appointed attorney shall not preclude appointment.

3. Where a pro se litigant, who was ineligible for an appointed attorney at the time of initial or subsequent requests, later becomes eligible by reason of changed circumstances, the Court may entertain a subsequent application, using the procedures specified

above, within a reasonable time after the change in circumstances has occurred.

(c) Factors Used in Determining Whether to Appoint Counsel. Upon receipt of an application for the appointment of an attorney, the Court shall determine whether to appoint an attorney to represent the pro se party. The Court shall make that determination within a reasonable time after the party makes the application. Factors that the Court will take into account in making the determination are as follows:

1. The potential merit of the claims as set forth in the pleading;

2. The nature and complexity of the action, both factual and legal, including the need for factual investigation;

3. The presence of conflicting testimony calling for an attorney's presentation of evidence and cross-examination;

4. The capability of the pro se party to present the case;

5. The inability of the pro se party to retain an attorney by other means;

6. The degree to which the interests of justice shall be served by appointment of an attorney, including the benefit that the Court shall derive from the assistance of an appointed attorney;

7. Any other factors the Court deems appropriate.

(d) Order of Appointment. Whenever the Court concludes that the appointment of an attorney is warranted, the Court shall issue an order directing the appointment of an attorney to represent the pro se party. The Court shall promptly transmit the order to the Clerk. If service of the summons and complaint has not yet been made, the Court shall accompany its appointment order with an order directing service by the United States Marshal or by other appropriate method of service.

(e) Notification of Appointment. After the Court has appointed an attorney, the Clerk shall send the attorney a copy of the order of appointment. Copies of the pleadings filed to date, relevant correspondence, and all other relevant documents shall be forwarded to the Clerk's office nearest to the attorney and made available for immediate review and copying of the necessary papers without charge. In addition to notifying the attorney, the Clerk shall also notify all of the parties to the action of the appointment, together with the name, address and telephone number of the appointed attorney.

(f) Duties and Responsibilities of Appointed Counsel. On receiving notice of the appointment, the attorney shall promptly file an appearance in the action to which the appointment applies unless precluded from acting in the action or appeal, in which event the attorney shall promptly notify the Court and the putative client. Promptly following the filing of an appearance, the attorney shall communicate with the newly-represented party concerning the action. In addition to a full discussion of the merits of the dispute, the attorney shall explore with the party any possibilities of resolving the dispute in other forums, including but not limited to administrative forums. If after consultation with the attorney the party decides to prosecute or defend the action, the attorney shall proceed to represent the party in the action unless or until the attorney-client relationship is terminated as these Rules provide.

In its discretion, the Court may appoint stand-by counsel to act in an advisory capacity. "Stand-by counsel" is not the party's representative; rather, the role of stand-by counsel is to provide assistance to the litigant and the Court where appropriate. The Court may in its discretion appoint counsel for other purposes.

(g) Reimbursement for Expenses. Pro Bono attorneys who are appointed pursuant to this Rule may seek reimbursement for expenses incident to representation of indigent clients by application to the Court. Reimbursement or advances shall be permitted to the extent possible in light of available resources and, absent extraordinary circumstances, shall not exceed **$2,000.00**. Any expenses in excess of **$500.00** should receive the Court's prior approval. If good cause is shown, the Court may approve additional expenses. Request for reimbursement should be submitted on the Pro Bono Fund Voucher and Request for Reimbursement Form and be accompanied by detailed documentation. Counsel are advised that vouchers submitted in excess of **$2,000.00**, absent the Court's prior approval, may be reduced or denied. All reimbursements made by withdrawal from the District Fund shall require the approval of the Chief Judge or a judge designated by the Chief Judge to authorize withdrawals. **To the extent that appointed counsel seeks reimbursement for expenses that are recoverable as costs to a prevailing party under Fed. R.Civ.P. 54, the appointed attorney must submit a verified bill of costs on the form the Clerk provides for reimbursement of such expenses.**

(h) Attorney's Fees. Except as provided in this subsection, an appointed attorney cannot recover attorney's fees from the Pro Bono Fund. However, in its discretion, the Court may award an appointed attorney for a prevailing party attorney's fees from the judgment or settlement to the extent that the applicable law permits. See, e.g., 28 U.S.C. § 2678 (permitting the attorney for a prevailing party under the Federal Tort Claims Act to recover up to 25% of any judgment or settlement): 42 U.S.C. § 1988(b) (authorizing an additional award of attorney's fees to prevailing parties in civil rights actions.

(i) Grounds for Relief from Appointment. After appointment, an attorney may apply to be relieved from an order of appointment only on one or more of the following grounds, or on such other grounds as the appointing judge finds adequate for good cause shown:

1. some conflict of interest precludes the attorney from accepting the responsibilities of representing the party in the action;

2. the attorney does not feel competent to represent the party in the particular type of action assigned;

3. some personal incompatibility exists between the attorney and the party or a substantial disagreement exists between the attorney and the party concerning litigation strategy; or

4. in the attorney's opinion the party is proceeding for purposes of harassment or malicious injury or the party's claims or defenses are not warranted under existing law and cannot be supported by a good faith argument for extension, modification or reversal of existing law.

(j) Application for Relief from Appointment. Any appointed attorney shall make any application for relief from an order of appointment on any of the grounds set forth in this Rule to the Court promptly after the attorney becomes aware of the existence of such grounds or within such additional period as the Court may permit for good cause shown.

(k) Order Granting Relief from Appointment. If the Court grants an application for relief from an order of appointment, the Court shall issue an order directing the appointment of another attorney to represent the party. Where the application for relief from appointment identifies an attorney affiliated with the moving attorney who is able to represent the party, the order shall direct appointment of the affiliated attorney with the consent of the affiliated attorney. Any other appointment shall be made in accordance with the procedures set forth in these Rules. Alternatively, the Court shall have the discretion not to issue a further order of appointment, in which case the party shall be permitted to prosecute or defend the action pro se.

[Amended effective January 1, 1999; January 1, 2005; January 1, 2008; March 20, 2008.]

RULE 83.4 DISCIPLINE OF ATTORNEYS

(a) The Chief Judge shall have charge of all matters relating to discipline of members of the bar of this Court.

(b) Any member of the bar of this Court who is convicted of a felony in any State, Territory, other District, Commonwealth, or Possession shall be suspended from practice before this Court and, upon the judgment of conviction becoming final, shall cease to be a member of the bar of this Court.

1. On the presentation to the Court of a certified or exemplified copy of a judgment of conviction, the attorney shall be suspended from practicing before this Court and, on presentation of proof that judgment of conviction is final, the name of the attorney convicted shall, by order of the Court, be struck from the roll of members of the bar of this Court.

(c) Any member of the bar of the Northern District of New York who shall resign from the bar of any State, Territory, other District, Commonwealth or Possession while an investigation into allegations of misconduct is pending shall cease to be a member of the bar of this Court.

On the presentation to the Court of a certified or exemplified copy of an order accepting resignation, the name of the attorney resigning shall, by order of the Court, be struck from the roll of members of the bar of this Court.

(d) Any member of the bar of the Northern District of New York who shall be disciplined by a court in any State, Territory, other District, Commonwealth, or Possession shall be disciplined to the same extent by this Court unless an examination of the record resulting in the discipline discloses

1. that the procedure was so lacking in notice or opportunity to be heard as to constitute a deprivation of due process;

2. that there was such an infirmity of proof establishing the misconduct as to give rise to the clear conviction that this Court should not accept as final the conclusion on that subject;

3. that this Court's imposition of the same discipline would result in grave injustice; or

4. that this Court has held that the misconduct to warrant substantially different discipline.*

On the filing of a certified or exemplified copy of an order imposing discipline, this Court shall, by order, discipline the attorney to the same extent. It is provided, however, that, within thirty (30) days of service on the attorney of this Court's order of discipline, either the attorney or a bar association that the Chief Judge designated in the order imposing discipline shall apply to the Chief Judge for an order to show cause why the discipline imposed in this District should not be modified on the basis of one or more of the grounds set forth in this Rule. The term "bar association" as used in this Rule shall mean the following: The New York State Bar Association or any city or county bar association.

(e) The Court may disbar, suspend, or censure any member of the bar of this Court who is convicted of a misdemeanor in any State, Territory, other District, Commonwealth, or Possession, upon such conviction.

Upon the filing of a certified or exemplified copy of a judgment of conviction, the Chief Judge may designate a bar association to prosecute a proceeding against the attorney. The bar association shall obtain an order requiring the attorney to show cause within thirty (30) days after service, personally or by mail, why the attorney should not be disciplined. The Chief Judge may, for good cause, temporarily suspend the attorney pending the determination of the proceeding. Upon receiving the attorney's answer to the order to show cause, the Chief Judge may set the matter for prompt hearing before a court of one or more judges or shall appoint a master to hear and to report findings and a recommendation. After a hearing and report, or if the attorney makes no timely answer or the answer raises no issue requiring a hearing, the Court shall take action as justice requires. In all proceedings, a certificate of conviction shall constitute conclusive proof of the attorney's guilt of the conduct for which the attorney was convicted.

(f) Any attorney who has been disbarred from the bar of a state in which the attorney was admitted to practice shall have his or her name stricken from the roll of attorneys of this Court or, if suspended from practice for a period at such bar, shall be suspended automatically for a like period from practice in this Court.

(g)(1) In addition to any other sanctions imposed in any particular case under these Rules, any person admitted to practice in this Court may be prohibited from practicing in this Court or otherwise disciplined for cause.

(2) Complaints alleging any cause for discipline shall be directed to the Chief Judge and must be in writing. If the Chief Judge deems the conduct alleged in the complaint sanctionable, the Chief Judge shall appoint a panel attorney to investigate and, if necessary, support the complaint. At the same time, the Chief Judge shall refer the matter to a Magistrate Judge for all pre-disposition proceedings.

(3) The Chief Judge shall appoint a panel of attorneys who are members of the bar of this Court to investigate complaints and, if the complaint is supported by the evidence, to prepare statements of charges and to support such charges at any hearing. In making appointments to the panel, the Chief Judge may solicit recommendations from the Federal Court Bar Association and other bar associations and groups. The Chief Judge shall appoint attorneys to the panel for terms not to exceed four years without limitation as to the number of terms an attorney may serve. The Court may reimburse an attorney from this panel whom the Chief Judge appoints to investigate and support a complaint in accordance with subsection (3) below ("panel attorney") for expenses incurred in performing such duties from the Pro Bono

Fund to the extent and in the manner provided in L.R. 83.3(g).

(4) If the panel attorney determines after investigation that the evidence fails to establish probable cause to believe that any violation of the Code of Professional Responsibilities has occurred, the panel attorney shall submit a report of such findings and conclusions to the Chief Judge for the consideration of the active district court judges.

(5) If the panel attorney determines after investigation that the evidence establishes probable cause to believe that one or more violations of the Code of Professional Responsibilities has occurred, the panel attorney shall prepare a statement of charges alleging the grounds for discipline. The Clerk shall cause the Statement of Charges to be served upon the attorney concerned ("responding attorney") by certified mail, return receipt requested, directed to the address of the attorney as shown on the rolls of this Court and, if different, to the last known address of the attorney as shown in any other source together with a direction from the Clerk that the responding attorney shall show cause in writing within thirty days why discipline should not be imposed.

(6) If the responding attorney fails to respond to the statement of charges, the charges shall be deemed admitted. If the responding attorney denies any charge, the assigned Magistrate Judge shall schedule a prompt evidentiary hearing. The Magistrate Judge may grant such pre-hearing discovery as deemed necessary, shall hear witnesses called by the panel attorney supporting the charges and by the responding attorney, and may consider such other evidence included in the record of the hearing that the Magistrate Judge deems relevant and material. A disciplinary charge may not be found proven unless supported by clear and convincing evidence. The Magistrate Judge shall report his or her findings and recommendations in writing to the Chief Judge and shall serve them upon the responding attorney and the panel attorney. The responding attorney and the panel attorney may file objections to the Magistrate Judge's report and recommendations within twenty days of the date thereof.

(7) An attorney may not be found guilty of a disciplinary charge except upon a majority vote of the district judges, including senior district judges, that such charge has been proven by clear and convincing evidence. Any discipline imposed shall also be determined by a majority vote of the district judges, including senior district judges, except that in the event of a tie vote, the Chief Judge shall cast a tie-breaking vote. If a district judge submitted the complaint under subsection (2) above giving rise to the disciplinary proceeding, that judge shall be recused from participating in the decisions regarding guilt and discipline.

(8) Unless the Court orders otherwise, all documents, records, and proceedings concerning a disciplinary matter shall be filed and conducted confidentially except that, without further order of the Court, the Clerk may notify other licensing jurisdictions of the imposition of any sanctions.

(h) A visiting attorney permitted to argue or try a particular cause in accordance with L.R. 83.1 who is found guilty of misconduct shall be precluded from again appearing in this Court. On entry of an order of preclusion, the Clerk shall transmit to the court of the State, Territory, District, Commonwealth, or Possession where the attorney was admitted to practice a certified copy of the order and of the Court's opinion.

(i) Unless the Court orders otherwise, no action shall be taken pursuant to L.R. 83.4(e) and (f) in any case in which disciplinary proceedings against the attorney have been instituted in the State.

(j) The Court shall enforce the N.Y.S. Lawyer's Code of Professional Responsibilities, as adopted from time to time by the Appellate Division of the State of New York and as interpreted and applied by the United States Court of Appeals for the Second Circuit.

(k) Nothing in this Rule shall limit the Court's power to punish contempts or to sanction counsel in accordance with the Federal Rules of Civil or Criminal Procedure or the Court's inherent authority to enforce its rules and orders.

[Amended effective January 1, 2001; January 1, 2007; January 1, 2008.]

* Publisher's Note: So in original.

RULE 83.5 CONTEMPT

(a) A proceeding to adjudicate a person in civil contempt of court, including a case provided for in Fed. R. Civ. P. 37(b)(2)(D), shall be commenced by the service of a notice of motion or order to show cause.

The affidavit on which the notice of motion or order to show cause is based shall set out with particularity the misconduct complained of, the claim, if any, for resulting damages, and evidence as to the amount of damages that is available to the moving party. A reasonable attorney's fee, necessitated by the contempt proceeding, may be included as an item of damages. Where the alleged contemnor has appeared in the action by an attorney, the notice of motion or order to show cause and the papers on which it is based shall be served on the contemnor's attorney; otherwise service shall be made personally in the manner provided by the Federal Rules of Civil Procedure for the service of summons. If an order to show cause is sought, the order may, on necessity shown, embody a direction to the United States Marshal to arrest and hold the alleged contemnor on bail in an amount fixed by the order, conditioned upon appearance at the hearing and further conditioned upon the

alleged contemnor's amenability to all orders of the Court for surrender.

(b) If the alleged contemnor puts in issue the alleged misconduct or the resulting damages, the alleged contemnor shall, on demand, be entitled to have oral evidence taken either before the Court or before a master whom the Court appoints. When by law the alleged contemnor is entitled to a trial by jury, the contemnor shall make a written demand on or before the return day or adjourned day of the application; otherwise the Court will deem that the alleged contemnor has waived a trial by jury.

(c) If the Court finds that the alleged contemnor is in contempt of the Court, the Court shall issue and enter an order—

1. Reciting or referring to the verdict or findings of fact on which the adjudication is based;

2. Setting forth the amount of the damages to which the complainant is entitled;

3. Fixing the fine, if any, imposed by the Court, which fine shall include the damages found and naming the person to whom the fine shall be payable;

4. Stating any other conditions, the performance of which shall operate to purge the contempt;

5. Directing, in the Court's discretion, the Marshal to arrest and confine the contemnor until the performance of the condition fixed in the order and payment of the fine or until the contemnor is otherwise discharged pursuant to law. The order shall specify the place of confinement. No party shall be required to pay or to advance to the Marshal any expenses for the upkeep of the prisoner. On an order of contempt, no person shall be detained in prison by reason of the non-payment of the fine for a period exceeding six months. A certified copy of the order committing the contemnor shall be sufficient warrant to the Marshal for the arrest and confinement. The aggrieved party shall also have the same remedies against the property of the contemnor as if the order awarding the fine were a final judgment.

(d) If the alleged contemnor is found not guilty of the charges, the contemnor shall be discharged from the proceeding and, in the discretion of the Court, shall have judgment against the complainant for costs, disbursements and a reasonable attorney's fee.

[Amended effective January 1, 2008.]

RULE 83.6 TRANSFER OF CASES TO ANOTHER DISTRICT

In a case ordered transferred from this District, the Clerk, unless otherwise ordered, shall, upon the expiration of ten (10) days, mail to the court to which the case is transferred

1. Certified copies of the Court's opinion and order compelling the transfer and of the docket entries in the case; and

2. The originals of all papers on file in the case except for the opinion ordering the transfer of the action.

SECTION X. ALTERNATE DISPUTE RESOLUTION AND GENERAL PROVISIONS

RULE 83.7. ARBITRATION

RULE 83.7–1 SCOPE AND EFFECTIVENESS OF RULE

This Rule governs the consensual arbitration program for referral of civil actions to court-annexed arbitration. It may remain in effect until further order of the Court. Its purpose is to establish a less formal procedure for the just, efficient and economical resolution of disputes, while preserving the right to a full trial on demand.

RULE 83.7–2 ACTIONS SUBJECT TO THIS RULE

The Clerk shall notify the parties in all civil cases, except as the Rules otherwise direct, that they may consent to non-binding arbitration under this Rule. The notice shall be furnished to the parties at pre-trial/scheduling conferences or shall be included with pretrial conference notices and instructions. Consent to arbitration under this Rule shall be discussed at the pretrial/scheduling conference. No party or attorney shall be prejudiced for refusing to participate in arbitration. The Court shall allow the referral of any civil action pending before it to the arbitration process if the parties consent. The plaintiff shall be responsible for securing the execution of a consent form by the parties and for filing the form with the Clerk within ten (10) days after the parties receive the form. The parties shall freely and knowingly enter into the consent.

[Amended effective January 1, 2008.]

RULE 83.7–3 REFERRAL TO ARBITRATION

(a) **Time for Referral.** The Clerk shall refer every action subject to this Rule to arbitration in accordance with the procedures under this Rule twenty (20) days after the filing of the last responsive pleading or within twenty (20) days of the filing of a stipulated consent order referring the action to arbitration, whichever event occurs last, except as otherwise provided. If any party notices a motion to dismiss under the provisions of Fed. R. Civ. P. 12(a) and/or (b), or a motion to join necessary parties pursuant to the Federal Rules of Civil Procedure prior to the expiration of

the twenty (20) day period, the assigned judge shall hear the motion and further proceedings under this Rule shall be deferred pending decision on the motion. If the Court does not dismiss the action on the motion, the Court shall refer the action to arbitration twenty (20) days after the filing of the decision.

Motions for summary judgment pursuant to Fed. R. Civ. P. 56 shall be filed and served within twenty (20) days following the close of discovery. The filing of a Rule 56 motion shall defer further proceedings under this Rule pending decision on the motion.

(b) **Authority of Assigned Judge.** Notwithstanding any provision of this Rule, the Clerk shall assign every action subject to this Rule to a judge upon filing in the normal course, in accordance with the Court's Assignment Plan. The assigned judge shall have authority to conduct status and settlement conferences, hear motions and in all other respects supervise the action in accordance with these Rules notwithstanding its referral by consent to arbitration.

(c) **Relief from Referral.** Any party shall request relief from the operation of this Rule by filing with the Court a motion for the relief within twenty (20) days after entry of the initial stipulated consent order which refers the case for arbitration. The assigned judge shall, sua sponte, exempt an action from the application of this Rule where the objectives of arbitration would not be realized because (1) the case involves complex or novel legal issues, (2) legal issues predominate over factual issues, or (3) for other good cause.

[Amended effective January 1, 2008.]

RULE 83.7–4 SELECTION AND COMPENSATION OF ARBITRATOR

(a) **Selection of Arbitrators.** The Clerk shall maintain a roster of arbitrators qualified to hear and determine actions under this Rule. The Court shall select arbitrators from time to time from applications submitted by or on behalf of attorneys willing to serve. To be eligible for selection, an attorney (1) shall have been admitted to practice for not less than five (5) years; (2) shall be a member of the bar of this Court or a member of the New York bar and reside within the Northern District of New York; and (3) shall either (i) for not less than five (5) years have devoted 50% or more of the attorney's professional time to matters involving litigation, or (ii) have substantial experience serving as a "neutral" in dispute resolution proceedings, or (iii) have substantial experience negotiating consensual resolutions to complex problems. Each attorney shall, upon selection, take the oath or affirmation prescribed in 28 U.S.C. § 453 and shall complete any training that the Court requires.

(b) Selection of the Panel. Whenever an action has been referred to arbitration through consent of the parties pursuant to this Rule, the parties shall nominate the arbitrator or arbitrators whom they select to serve as an arbitrator(s) in full compliance with L.R. 83.7–4(a), or the Clerk shall promptly furnish to each party a list of arbitrators whose names shall have been drawn at random from the roster for the division in which the case is pending. If the parties have elected to proceed with a **single** arbitrator, the Clerk shall provide five (5) names for the selection process. If the parties have elected to proceed with a panel of **three** (3) arbitrators, the Clerk shall provide seven (7) names for the selection process.

1. Each side shall be entitled to strike two names from the list. All parties shall sign the list and return it to the Clerk within ten (10) days of receipt. Failure of the parties to timely notify the Clerk of strikes shall result in the Clerk's selection of the panel.

2. The Clerk shall promptly notify the person or persons whom the parties did not strike. If the parties have elected to proceed with a single arbitrator, and the arbitrator they selected is unable or unwilling to serve, the process of selection under this Rule shall begin anew. If the parties have elected to proceed with a panel of arbitrators and any person whom they selected is unable or unwilling to serve, the Clerk shall select an additional individual at random who shall constitute the third member of the panel. If the Clerk is still unable to form a panel of three arbitrators for any reason, the process of selection under this Rule shall begin anew. When a single arbitrator, or when three of the selected arbitrators have agreed to serve, the Clerk shall promptly send written notice of the membership of the panel to each arbitrator and the parties.

(c) Disqualification. No person shall serve as an arbitrator in an action in which any of the circumstances specified in 28 U.S.C. § 455 (conflict of interest) exist or in good faith shall be believed to exist.

(d) Withdrawal by Arbitrator. Any person whose name appears on the roster maintained in the Clerk's office may ask at any time to have his or her name removed or, if selected to serve on a panel, decline to serve but remain on the roster.

(e) Compensation and Reimbursement. Arbitrators shall be paid $250.00 per day or portion of each day of hearing in which they participate serving as a single arbitrator or $100.00 for each day or portion of

a day if serving as a member of a panel of three (3). Compensation for an arbitrator's services outside the hearing shall be supported by an affidavit setting forth in detail the time required for pre-and post-hearing matters. When the arbitrators file their decision, each shall submit a voucher, on the form that the Clerk prescribes, for payment by the Administrative Office of the United States Courts of compensation and out-of-pocket expenses necessarily incurred in the performance of their duties under this Rule. No reimbursement shall be made for the cost of office or other space for the hearing.

[Amended effective January 1, 2008.]

RULE 83.7–5 ARBITRATION HEARINGS

(a) Hearing date. After an answer is filed in a case in which the parties have consented to arbitration and the Court has approved the consent and on completion of the parties' selection of the panel, the arbitration clerk shall send a notice to the attorneys setting forth the date, time and location for the arbitration hearing. The date of the arbitration hearing set forth in the notice shall be approximately five (5) months, but in no event later than 180 days, from the date the answer was filed, except that the arbitration proceeding shall not, in the absence of the parties' consent, commence until thirty (30) days after the Court's disposition of any motion to dismiss the complaint, motion for judgment on the pleadings, or motion to join necessary parties if such a motion was filed and served within twenty (20) days after the filing of the last responsive pleading. Motions for summary judgment pursuant to Fed. R. Civ. P. 56 shall be filed in accordance with L.R. 83.7–3(a). The Court may modify the 180–day and twenty (20) day periods specified in L.R. 83.7 for good cause shown. The notice shall also advise the attorneys that they may agree to an earlier date for the arbitration hearing provided the arbitration clerk is notified within thirty (30) days of the date of the notice.

The notice shall also advise the attorneys that they have 120 days to complete discovery unless the Court orders a shorter or longer period for discovery. If a third party has been brought into the action, this notice shall not be sent until the third party has filed an answer.

(b) Upon entry of the order designating the arbitrator(s), the arbitration clerk shall send to each arbitrator a copy of the order designating the arbitrator, a copy of the court docket sheet and a copy of the guidelines for arbitrators. On receipt of the notice scheduling the case to proceed to arbitration and appointing an arbitrator, the plaintiff's attorney shall promptly forward to the arbitrator copies of all pleadings, including any counterclaim or third party complaint and respective answer. Thereafter, and at least ten (10) days prior to the arbitration hearing, each attorney shall deliver to the arbitrator(s) and to the adverse attorney pre-marked copies of all exhibits, including expert reports and all portions of depositions and interrogatories to which reference shall be made at the hearing (but not including documents intended solely for impeachment).

(c) Default of a Party. The arbitration hearing shall proceed in the absence of any party who, after notice, fails to be present. If a party fails to participate in the arbitration process in a meaningful manner, the arbitrator(s) shall make that determination and shall support it with specific written findings filed with the Clerk. The Court shall then conduct a hearing, on notice to all attorneys and personal notice to any party adversely affected by the arbitrator's determination, and may impose any appropriate sanctions, including, but not limited to, the striking of any demand for a trial de novo which that party has filed.

(d) Conduct of Hearing. The arbitrator is authorized to administer oaths and affirmations and all testimony shall be given under oath or affirmation. Each party shall have the right to cross-examine witnesses, except as otherwise provided. In receiving evidence, the arbitrator shall be guided by the Federal Rules of Evidence. These rules, however, shall not preclude the arbitrator from receiving evidence that the arbitrator considers to be relevant and trustworthy and that is not privileged. A party desiring to offer a document, otherwise subject to hearsay objections, at the hearing shall serve a copy on the adverse party not less than ten (10) days in advance of the hearing, indicating intent to offer it as an exhibit. Unless the adverse party gives written notice in advance of the hearing of intent to cross-examine the author of the document, the arbitrator shall deem that the adverse party has waived any hearsay objection to the document. Attendance of witnesses and production of documents shall be compelled in accordance with Fed. R. Civ. P. 45.

(e) Transcript or Recording. A party may cause a transcript or recording to be made of the proceedings at its expense but shall, at the request of the opposing party, make a copy available to that party at no charge, unless the parties have otherwise agreed. Except as provided in L.R. 83.7–7(c), no transcript of the proceeding shall be admissible in evidence at any subsequent de novo trial of the action.

(f) Place of Hearing. Hearings shall be held at any location within the Northern District of New York that the arbitrator(s) designates. Hearings may be held in any courtroom or other room in any federal courthouse that the Clerk makes available to the arbitrator(s). When no room is available, the hearing shall be held at any suitable location that the arbitrator(s) selects. In selecting a hearing location, the arbitrator shall consider the convenience of the panel, the parties and the witnesses. The date for the hear-

ing shall not be continued except for extreme and unanticipated emergencies.

(g) Time of Hearing. Unless the parties agree otherwise, hearings shall be held during normal business hours.

(h) Authority of Arbitrator. The arbitrator(s) shall be authorized to make reasonable rules and issue orders necessary for the fair and efficient conduct of the hearing before the arbitrator(s). Any two members of a panel shall constitute a quorum; but, unless the parties stipulate otherwise, the concurrence of a majority of the entire panel shall be required for any action or decision.

(i) Ex Parte Communication. There shall be no ex parte communication between the arbitrator(s) and any attorney or party on any matter related to the action except for purposes of scheduling or continuing the hearing.

[Amended effective January 1, 2008.]

RULE 83.7–6   AWARD AND JUDGMENT

(a) Filing of Award. The arbitrator(s) shall file the award with the Clerk promptly following the close of the hearing and in any event not more than ten (10) days following the close of the hearing. As soon as the arbitrator(s) files the award, the Clerk shall serve copies on the parties.

(b) Form of Award. The award shall state clearly and concisely the name or names of the prevailing party or parties, the party or parties against which the award is rendered, and the precise amount of money and other relief, if any, awarded. The award shall be in writing; and, unless the parties stipulate otherwise, the arbitrator or at least two members of a panel must sign the award. No panel member shall participate in the award without having attended the hearing.

(c) Entry of Judgment on Award. Unless a party has filed a demand for a trial de novo (or a notice of appeal which shall be treated as a demand for trial de novo) within thirty (30) days of the filing of the arbitration award, the Clerk shall enter judgment on the arbitration award in accordance with Fed. R. Civ. P. 58. A judgment so entered shall be subject to the same provisions of law and shall have the same force and effect as a judgment of the Court in a civil action, except that the judgment shall not be subject to review in any other court by appeal or otherwise.

(d) Sealing of Arbitration Awards. The contents of any arbitration award made under this Rule shall not be made known to any judicial officer who might be assigned to preside at the trial of the case or to rule on potentially dispositive motions

1. Until the district court has entered final judgment in the action or the action has been otherwise terminated;

2. Except for purposes of preparing the report required by section 903(b) of the Judicial Improvements and Access to Justice Act; or

3. Except as necessary for the Court to determine whether to assess costs or attorneys' fees under 28 U.S.C. § 655.

[Amended effective January 1, 2004; January 1, 2008.]

RULE 83.7–7 TRIAL DE NOVO

(a) Time for Demand. If either party files and serves a written demand for a trial de novo within thirty (30) days of entry of judgment on the award, the Clerk shall immediately vacate the judgment and the action shall proceed in the normal manner before the assigned judge.

(b) Restoration to Court Docket. On a demand for a trial de novo, the Clerk shall restore the action to the Court's docket, trial ready, and the action shall be treated for all purposes as if it had not been referred to arbitration. In such a case, any right of trial by jury that a party otherwise would have had, as well as any place on the Court calendar which is no later than that which a party otherwise would have had, is preserved.

(c) Limitation on Admission of Evidence. At the trial de novo, the Court shall not admit any evidence that an arbitration proceeding has occurred, the nature or amount of any award, or any other matter concerning the conduct of the arbitration proceeding unless

1. The evidence would otherwise be admissible in the Court under the Federal Rules of Evidence; or

2. The parties have stipulated otherwise.

(d) Arbitrator's Costs. The party requesting a trial de novo shall deposit the cost of the arbitrator's services as a prerequisite to the trial. If the requesting party fails to obtain judgment in an amount which, exclusive of interest and costs, is more favorable to that party, the Clerk shall retain those funds. However, if that party is successful in obtaining a more favorable result, the Clerk shall return the prepaid costs to the party who deposited them.

(e) Opposing Party's Costs. If a party has rejected an award and the action proceeds to trial, that party shall pay the opposing party's actual costs unless the verdict is more favorable to the rejecting party than the arbitrator's award on that claim. If the opposing party has also rejected that award, however, a party is entitled to costs only if the verdict is more favorable to that party than the arbitrator's award:

1. Actual costs include those costs and fees taxable in any civil action and attorney's fees for each day of trial not to exceed $500.00.

2. For good cause shown, the Court shall order relief from payment of any or all costs.

3. The provisions of L.R. 83.7–7(d) and (e) shall not apply to claims to which the United States or one of its agencies is a party.

[Amended effective January 1, 2008.]

RULE 83.7–8 CASES PENDING PRIOR TO THE IMPLEMENTATION OF ARBITRATION

Notwithstanding the provisions of the Rules set forth above, each district judge shall select cases from the docket currently in process and notify the attorneys involved of the availability of the consensual arbitration program. A case shall qualify for referral to arbitration if it complies with the provisions of this Rule.

RULE 83.8 NUMBER OF EXPERTS IN PATENT CASES

On the trial of a patent case, whether in open court or by deposition, or partly in each way, only one expert witness shall be allowed to each side, unless the parties have obtained leave for additional experts from the Court on motion made and cause shown.

[Amended effective January 1, 2008.]

RULE 83.9 COMMISSION TO TAKE TESTIMONY

(a) Except as the law otherwise provides, in all actions or proceedings where the taking of depositions of witnesses or of parties is authorized, the procedure for obtaining and using the depositions shall comply with the Federal Rules of Civil Procedure. The party seeking the deposition shall furnish the officer to whom the commission is issued with a copy of the Federal Rules of Civil Procedure pertaining to discovery.

(b) Upon receipt of a deposition, the Clerk, unless otherwise ordered, shall open and file it promptly.

[Amended January 1, 2008.]

RULE 83.10 STUDENT PRACTICE

General Order #13 pertains to the rules regarding student practice in this District. Parties may obtain a copy of General Order #13 from the Clerk's office or on the Court's webpage at "www.nynd.uscourts.gov."

[Amended effective January 1, 2004; January 1, 2008.]

RULE 83.11–1   MEDIATION

(a) **Purpose.** The purpose of this Rule is to provide a supplementary procedure to the Court's existing alternative dispute resolution procedures. This Rule provides for an earlier resolution of civil disputes resulting in savings of time and cost to litigants and the Court without sacrificing the quality of justice rendered or the right of litigants to a full trial on all issues not resolved through mediation.

(b) **Definitions.** Mediation is a process by which an impartial person, the mediator, facilitates communication between disputing parties to promote understanding, reconciliation and settlement. The mediator is an advocate for settlement and uses the mediation process to help the parties fully explore any potential area of agreement. The mediator does not serve as a judge or arbitrator and has no authority to render any decision on any disputed issue or to force a settlement. The parties themselves are responsible for negotiating any resolution(s) to their dispute.

RULE 83.11–2   DESIGNATION AND QUALIFICATIONS OF MEDIATORS

(a) **Designation of Mediators.** The judges of this Court may authorize those persons who are eligible and qualified to serve as mediators under this Rule in such numbers as the Court shall deem appropriate. The Court may withdraw such designation of any mediator at any time. Applications for designation as an ADR panel member are available at the Clerk's office.

(b) **List of Mediators.** The Alternative Dispute Resolution clerk (ADR clerk) shall maintain a list of court-approved mediators and make that list available to counsel and the public upon request.

(c) **Required Qualifications of Mediators.**

1. An individual may be designated as a mediator if he or she (1) has practiced law for at least five (5) years; and (2) is a member in good standing of the bar of this Court or of the New York bar and resides within the Northern District of New York; or (3) is a professional mediator who would otherwise qualify as a special master or is a professional whom the Court has determined to be competent to perform the duties of the mediator and has completed appropriate training in the process of mediation as the Court may from time to time determine and direct; and (4) shall attend and complete a mediation training course that the Court sponsors. Upon Court approval as a mediator, every mediator shall take the oath prescribed by 28 U.S.C. § 453.

2. No person shall serve as a mediator in an action in which any of the circumstances specified in 28 U.S.C. § 455 exists or may in good faith be believed to exist. Additionally, any mediator may be disqualified for bias or prejudice as provided in 28 U.S.C. § 144. Furthermore, the mediator has a continuing obligation to disclose any information that may cause a party or the court to believe, in good faith, that such mediator should be disqualified.

(d) **Removal from the Panel.** Membership in the ADR Panel is a privilege, not a right, which the Board of Judges may terminate at any time as it, in its sole discretion, may determine.

(e) **Service to the Bar and Court Provided by Mediators.** The individuals serving as mediators in the Northern District of New York perform their mediation duties as a pro bono service to the Court, litigants and the bar.

[Amended effective January 1, 2004; January 1, 2008.]

RULE 83.11–3   ACTIONS SUBJECT TO MEDIATION

(a) The Court may refer any civil action (or any portion thereof) to mediation under this Rule

1. By order of referral; or

2. On the motion of any party; or

3. By consent of the parties.

(b) The parties may withdraw from mediation any civil action or claim that the Court refers to mediation pursuant to this Rule by application to the assigned judge at least ten (10) days prior to the scheduled mediation session.

(c) Notwithstanding the provisions of the Rules set forth above, each judge shall select cases from the docket currently pending and notify the attorneys involved of the availability of the mediation program.

[Amended effective January 1, 2008.]

RULE 83.11–4   PROCEDURES FOR REFERRAL, SELECTING THE MEDIATOR, AND SCHEDULING THE MEDIATION SESSION

(a) The parties shall discuss with the Court the possibility and appropriateness of mediation under this Rule at the initial status/scheduling conference of the case that the Court holds in accordance with the provisions of General Order #25.

(b) In every case in which the Court determines that referral to mediation is appropriate pursuant to L.R. 83.11–3, the Court shall enter an order of reference, which shall define the period of time during which the mediation session shall be conducted. The Court intends that mediation under this Rule shall occur at the earliest practical time in an effort to encourage earlier, less costly resolutions of disputes. Referral to mediation under this Rule shall not delay or stay other proceedings, including but not limited to discovery, unless the Court so orders.

(c) Within ten (10) days of the order of reference, parties are to select a mediator of their choice from a list of mediators available from the Court and submit the selection to the ADR clerk in the Clerk's office. If the parties do not select a mediator in a timely manner or if the parties cannot agree upon a mediator, the ADR clerk shall select a mediator for them. The ADR clerk shall work with the selected mediator and counsel of record to set a mutually agreeable date for the mediation within the time prescribed in the order of reference.

(d) Mediation sessions under this Rule may be held in any available court space or in any other suitable location agreeable to the mediator and the parties. Consideration shall be given to the convenience of the parties and to the cost and time of travel involved.

(e) There shall be no continuance of a mediation session beyond the time set in the referral order except by order of the Court upon a showing of good cause. If any rescheduling occurs within the prescribed time, the parties or the mediator must notify the ADR clerk and select the location of the rescheduled hearing.

(f) The parties shall promptly report any settlement that occurs prior to the scheduled mediation to the mediator and to the ADR clerk.

[Amended effective January 1, 2008.]

RULE 83.11–5   THE MEDIATION SESSION

(a) Memorandum for Mediation. At least two days prior to the mediation session, each party shall provide to the mediator and all other such parties a "memorandum for mediation." This memo shall:

1. State the name and role of each person expected to attend;

2. Identify each person with full settlement authority;

3. Include a concise summary of the parties' claims or defenses;

4. Discuss liability and damages; and

5. State the relief sought by such party.

The memorandum for mediation shall not exceed five pages, and the parties shall not file these documents in the case or otherwise make them part of the court file.

(b) Attendance Required. The attorneys who are expected to try the case for the parties shall appear and shall be accompanied by an individual with authority to settle the lawsuit. Those latter individuals shall be the parties (if the parties are natural persons) or representatives of parties that are not natural

persons. These latter individuals may not be counsel (except in-house counsel). Attorneys for the parties shall notify other interested parties such as insurers or indemnitors who shall attend and are subject to the provisions of this Rule. Only the assigned judge may excuse attendance of any attorney, party, or party's representative. Anyone who wants to be excused from attending the mediation must make such request in writing to the presiding judge at least forty-eight (48) hours in advance of the mediation session.

(c) Good Faith Participation in the Process. Parties and counsel shall participate in good faith, without any time constraints, and put forth their best efforts toward settlement. Typically, the mediator will meet initially with all parties to the dispute and their counsel in a joint session and thereafter separately with each party and their representative. This process permits the mediator and the parties to explore the needs and interests underlying their respective positions, generate and evaluate alternative settlement proposals or potential solutions, and consider interests that may be outside the scope of the stated controversy including matters that the Court may not address. The parties will participate in crafting a resolution of the dispute.

(d) Confidentiality. Mediation is regarded as a settlement procedure and is confidential and private. No participant may disclose, without consent of the other parties, any confidential information acquired during mediation. There shall be no stenographic or electronic record, e.g., audio or video, of the mediation process.

1. All written and oral communications made in connection with or during the mediation session are confidential.

2. No communication made in connection with or during any mediation session may be disclosed or used for any purpose in any pending or future proceeding in the U.S. District Court for the Northern District of New York.

3. Privileged and confidential status is afforded all communications made in connection with the mediation session, including matters emanating from parties and counsel as well as mediators' comments, assessments, and recommendations concerning case development, discovery, and motions. Except for communication between the assigned judge and the mediator regarding noncompliance with program procedures (*as set forth in this Rule*), there will be no communications between the Court and the mediator regarding a case that has been designated for mediation. The parties will be asked to sign an agreement of confidentiality at the beginning of the mediation session.

4. Parties, counsel and mediators may respond to inquiries from authorized court staff which are made for the purpose of program evaluation. Such responses will be kept in strict confidence.

5. The mediator may not be required to testify in any proceeding relating to or arising out of the matter in dispute. Nor may the mediator be subject to process requiring disclosure of information or data relating to or arising out of the matter in dispute.

6. *Immunity.* Mediators, as well as the Mediation Administrator (ADR clerk), shall be immune from claims arising out of acts or omissions incident to service as a court appointee in the mediation program. *See, e.g., Wagshal v. Foster,* 28 F.3d 1249 (D.C. Cir. 1994).

7. *Default.* Subject to the mediator's approval, the mediation session may proceed in the absence of a party, who, after due notice, fails to be present. The Court may impose sanctions on any party who, absent good cause shown, fails to attend or participate in the mediation session in good faith in accordance with this Rule.

8. *Conclusion of the Mediation Session.* The mediation shall be concluded:

a. By the parties' resolution and settlement of the dispute;

b. By adjournment for future mediation by agreement of the parties and the mediator; or

c. Upon the mediator's declaration of impasse that future efforts to resolve the dispute are no longer worthwhile.

Unless the Court authorizes otherwise, mediation sessions shall be concluded at least ten (10) days prior to any final pretrial conference that the Court has scheduled.

If the mediation is adjourned by agreement for further mediation, the additional session shall be concluded within the time the Court orders.

[Amended effective January 1, 2008.]

RULE 83.11–6 MEDIATION REPORT; NOTICE OF SETTLEMENT OR TRIAL

(a) Immediately upon conclusion of the mediation, the mediator shall file a mediation report with the ADR clerk, indicating only whether the case settled, settled in part, or did not settle.

(b) In the event the parties reach an agreement to settle the case, the representatives for each party shall promptly notify the ADR clerk and promptly prepare and file the appropriate stipulation of dismissal.

(c) If the parties reach a partial agreement to narrow, withdraw or settle some but not all claims, they shall file a stipulation concisely setting forth the resolved claims with the ADR clerk within five (5) days of the mediation. The stipulation shall bind the parties.

(d) If the mediation session does not conclude in settlement of all the issues in the case, the case will proceed toward trial pursuant to the scheduling orders entered in the case.

RULE 83.12–1 EARLY NEUTRAL EVALUATION

The ENE Process. Early neutral evaluation (ENE) is a process in which parties obtain from an experienced neutral (an "evaluator") a nonbinding, reasoned, oral evaluation of the merits of the case. The first step in the ENE process involves the Court appointing an evaluator who has expertise in the area of law in the case. After the parties exchange essential information and position statements early in the pretrial period (usually within 150 to 200 days after a complaint has been filed), the evaluator convenes an ENE session that typically lasts about two hours. At the ENE meeting, each side briefly presents the factual and legal basis of its position. The evaluator may ask questions of the parties and help them identify the main issues in dispute and the areas of agreement. The evaluator may also help the parties explore options for settlement. If settlement does not occur, the evaluator then offers an opinion as to the settlement value of the case, including the likelihood of liability and the likely range of damages. With the benefit of this assessment, the parties are again encouraged to discuss settlement, with or without the evaluator's assistance. The parties may also explore ways to narrow the issues in dispute, exchange information about the case or otherwise prepare efficiently for trial.

The evaluator has no power to impose a settlement or to dictate any agreement regarding the pretrial management of the case. The ENE process, whether or not it results in settlement, is confidential.

[Amended effective January 1, 2008.]

RULE 83.12–2 DESIGNATION AND QUALIFICATIONS OF EVALUATORS

(a) **Designation of Evaluators.** The judges of this Court may authorize those persons who are eligible and qualified to serve as evaluators under this Rule in such numbers as the Court shall deem appropriate. The Court may withdraw such designation of any evaluator at any time. Applications for designation as an ADR panel member are available at the Clerk's office.

(b) **List of Evaluators.** The ADR clerk shall maintain a list of court-approved evaluators and shall make that list available to counsel and the public upon request.

(c) Required Qualifications of Evaluators.

1. An individual may be designated as an Early Neutral Evaluator if he or she (1) has practiced law for at least fifteen years; and (2) is a member in good standing of the bar of this court or of the New York bar and resides within the Northern District of New York; or (3) is a professional whom this Court determines to be competent to perform the duties of the evaluator and has completed appropriate training in the process of Early Neutral Evaluation as the Court may from time to time determine and direct. Upon Court approval as an evaluator, every evaluator shall take the oath prescribed by 28 U.S.C. § 453.

2. No person shall serve as an evaluator in an action in which any of the circumstances specified in 28 U.S.C. § 455 exist or may in good faith be believed to exist. Additionally, any evaluator may be disqualified for bias or prejudice as provided in 28 U.S.C. § 144. Furthermore, the evaluator has a continuing obligation to disclose any information which may cause a party or the Court to believe in good faith that such evaluator should be disqualified.

(d) Removal from the Panel. Membership in the ADR Panel is a privilege, not a right, which the Board of Judges may terminate at any time as it, in its sole discretion, may determine.

(e) Service to the Bar and Court Provided by Evaluators. The individuals serving as evaluators in the Northern District of New York perform their duties as a pro bono service to the Court, litigants, and the bar.

[Amended effective January 1, 2004; January 1, 2008.]

RULE 83.12–3 ACTIONS SUBJECT TO EARLY NEUTRAL EVALUATION

(a) The Court may refer any civil action (or any portion thereof) to Early Neutral Evaluation under this Rule

1. By order of referral;

2. On the motion of any party; or

3. By consent of the parties.

(b) The parties may withdraw any civil action or claim that the Court has referred to the Early Neutral Evaluation Process pursuant to this Rule by application to the assigned judge at least ten (10) days before the scheduled evaluation session.

(c) Notwithstanding the provisions of the rules set forth above, each judge shall select cases from the docket currently pending and notify the attorneys involved of the availability of the Early Neutral Evaluation Process.

(d) When a case is designated for ENE, the ADR clerk will provide counsel with copies of the judge's designation order, a listing by division of the available

early neutral evaluators, and a copy of the ENE procedure guide.

[Amended effective January 1, 2008.]

RULE 83.12–4 ADMINISTRATIVE PROCEDURES AND REQUIREMENTS

(a) In most cases, the Court will issue the ENE order early enough in the pretrial period to allow the ENE session to be held within 150 to 200 days from the filing of the complaint.

(b) When the ADR clerk receives a copy of a judicial order designating a case for ENE, the ADR clerk will give the parties a date by which they must choose an evaluator from the list provided to counsel. If the parties do not select an evaluator by the designated date, the ADR clerk will assign an evaluator with expertise in the subject matter of the lawsuit and notify counsel.

(c) The evaluator will contact all attorneys and set the date and place of the evaluation session. Whenever possible, the evaluator shall hold the ENE session within 150 to 200 days of the filing of the complaint and within forty-five days of the date that the ADR clerk notifies counsel of the identity of the evaluator.

(d) The ADR clerk and evaluators shall schedule ENE proceedings in a manner that does not interfere in any way with the management of case processing or the actions of the referring judge. No party may avoid or postpone any obligation imposed by the order of reference on any ground related to the ENE process.

[Amended effective January 1, 2008.]

RULE 83.12–5 EVALUATION STATEMENTS

(a) No later than ten (10) calendar days prior to the ENE session, each party shall submit directly to the evaluator, and shall serve on all other parties, a written evaluation statement not to exceed ten (10) pages *excluding exhibits and attachments.*

Such statements must

1. Identify person(s), in addition to counsel, who will attend the ENE session and who have decision-making authority;

2. Address whether the case involves legal or factual issues the early resolution of which might reduce the scope of the dispute or contribute significantly to settlement negotiations; and

3. Identify the discovery that will contribute most to meaningful settlement negotiations.

(b) Parties may also identify persons whose presence at the ENE session might improve significantly the productivity of the session.

(c) Parties shall attach to the evaluation statements, copies of key documents out of which the suit arose (*e.g.*, *contracts*) or materials that might advance the purposes of the ENE session (*e.g.*, *medical reports*).

The parties shall <u>not</u> file written evaluation statements with the Court. Evaluation statements are considered confidential between the parties and the evaluator.

[Amended effective January 1, 2008.]

RULE 83.12–6 ATTENDANCE AT ENE SESSIONS

(a) The Court requires parties to attend evaluation sessions. The main purposes of an ENE session are to give litigants the opportunity (1) to present their positions; (2) to hear their opponents' view of the issues in dispute; and (3) to hear a neutral assessment of the strengths of each side's case.

(b) When a party to a case is not a natural person (*e.g.*, *a corporation*), a person *other than the outside counsel* who has authority to enter stipulations and to bind the party in a settlement must attend.

(c) In cases involving insurance carriers, company representatives with settlement authority shall attend.

(d) When a party is a unit of the federal government, an agency representative and counsel from the U.S. Attorney's Office, must attend the ENE session.

(e) An attorney for each party who has primary responsibility for handling the trial of the matter must attend the ENE session.

(f) A party or attorney may be excused from attending an ENE session only after petitioning the referring judge in writing no fewer than ten (10) calendar days before the scheduled ENE session. Such a petition must show that attendance at the ENE session would impose an extraordinary or unjustifiable hardship.

(g) **Default.** Subject to the evaluator's approval, the evaluation session may proceed in the absence of a party, who, after due notice, fails to be present. The Court may impose sanctions on any party who, absent good cause shown, fails to attend or participate in the evaluation session in good faith in accordance with this Rule.

RULE 83.12–7 PROCEDURES AT ENE SESSIONS

(a) The evaluator has broad discretion to structure the ENE session. The evaluator will determine the time and place of the session and will structure the session and any follow-up sessions. Rules of Evidence shall not apply and there is no formal examination or cross-examination of witnesses.

(b) The evaluator shall:

1. Permit each party, or counsel, to make an oral presentation of its position;

2. Help parties identify areas of agreement and enter stipulations, wherever feasible;

3. Assess the relative strengths and weaknesses of the parties' positions and explain the reasons for the assessments;

4. Help parties explore settlement;

5. Estimate, where possible, the likelihood of liability and the range of damages;

6. Help parties develop an information-sharing or discovery plan to expedite settlement discussions or to position the case for disposition by other means; and

7. Determine what, if any, follow-up measures will contribute to case development or settlement (*e.g.*, *written reports; telephone reports; additional ENE sessions; or other forms of ADR, such as arbitration, mediation, settlement conference, or consent before a Magistrate Judge*).

(c) When an evaluator completes work on a case, the evaluator will, regardless of case outcome, submit an evaluator assessment form to the ADR clerk.

[Amended effective January 1, 2008.]

RULE 83.12–8 CONFIDENTIALITY

Early Neutral Evaluation is regarded as a settlement procedure and is confidential and private. No participant may disclose, without consent of the other parties, any confidential information acquired during the ENE session. There shall be no stenographic or electronic record, e.g., audio or video, of the ENE process.

(a) All written and oral communications made in connection with or during any ENE sessions are confidential.

(b) No communication made in connection with or during any ENE sessions may be disclosed or used for any purpose in any pending or future proceeding in this Court.

(c) Privileged and confidential status is afforded all communications made in connection with ENE sessions, including matters emanating from parties and counsel as well as evaluators' comments, assessments, and recommendations concerning case development, discovery and motions. Except for communication between the assigned judge and the evaluator regarding noncompliance with program procedures *as set forth in this Rule*, there will be no communications between the Court and the evaluator regarding a case that has been designated for evaluation. The parties will be asked to sign an agreement of confidentiality at the beginning of the evaluation session.

(d) Parties, counsel, and evaluators may respond to inquiries from authorized court staff which are made for the purposes of program evaluation. Such responses will be kept in strict confidence.

(e) The evaluator may not be required to testify in any proceeding relating to or arising out of the matter in dispute. Nor may the evaluator be subject to process requiring disclosure of information or data relating to or arising out of the matter in dispute.

RULE 83.12–9 ROLE OF EVALUATORS

(a) Evaluators may not compel parties or counsel to conduct or respond to discovery or to file motions.

(b) Evaluators may not determine the issues in a case or impose limits on pretrial activities.

(c) Evaluators, and any parties who encounter a problem during the ENE session and have discussed such problem with the evaluator without obtaining a satisfactory resolution of the matter, shall report to the assigned judge any instances of noncompliance with ENE procedures that, in their view, may disrupt the evaluation process or threaten the integrity of the ENE program.

(d) **Immunity.** Evaluators, as well as the ADR clerk, shall be immune from claims arising out of acts or omissions incident to service as a court appointee in this Early Neutral Evaluation Program.

RULE 83.12–10 EARLY NEUTRAL EVALUATION REPORT

(a) Immediately upon conclusion of the evaluation session, the evaluator shall file a report with the ADR clerk indicating only whether the case settled, settled in part, or did not settle.

(b) In the event the parties reach an agreement to settle the case, the representatives for each party shall promptly notify the ADR clerk and promptly prepare and file the appropriate stipulation of dismissal.

(c) If the parties reach a partial agreement to narrow, withdraw, or settle some but not all claims, they shall file a stipulation concisely setting forth the resolved claims with the ADR clerk within five (5) days of the evaluation session. The stipulation shall bind the parties.

(d) If the Early Neutral Evaluation Session does not conclude in settlement of all the issues in the case, the case will proceed toward trial pursuant to the scheduling orders entered in the case.

RULE 83.13 SEALED MATTERS

The Court may seal cases in their entirety, or only as to certain parties or documents, when the cases are initiated or at various stages of the proceedings. The Court may on its own motion enter an order directing that a document, party or entire case be sealed. A party seeking to have a document, party or entire case sealed shall submit an application, under seal, setting forth the reason(s) why the Court should seal the document, party or entire case, together with a proposed order for the assigned judge's approval. The proposed order shall include language in the "ORDERED" paragraph stating which document(s) are to be sealed and should include the phrase "including this sealing order." Upon the assigned judge's approval of the sealing order, the Clerk shall seal the document(s) and the sealing order. A complaint presented for filing with a motion to seal and a proposed order shall be treated as a sealed case, pending approval of the order. Once the Court seals a document or case, it shall remain under seal until a subsequent order, upon the Court's own motion or in response to the motion of a party, is entered directing that the document or case be unsealed.

[Adopted effective January 1, 1999; amended effective January 1, 2008.]

RULE 83.14 PRODUCTION AND DISCLOSURE OF DOCUMENTS AND TESTIMONY OF JUDICIAL PERSONNEL IN LEGAL PROCEEDINGS

(A) The purpose of the rule is to implement the policy of the Judicial Conference of the United States with regard

(1) to the production or disclosure of official information or records by the federal judiciary, and

(2) the testimony of present or former judiciary personnel relating to any official information acquired by any such individual as part of the individual's performance of official duties, or by virtue of that individual's official status, in federal, state, or other legal proceedings. Implementation of this Rule is subject to the regulations that the Judicial Conference of the United States has established and which are incorporated herein. Parties can obtain a copy of such regulations from the Clerk's office.)

(B) Requests that this Rule covers include an order, subpoena, or other demand of a court or administrative or other authority, of competent jurisdiction, under color of law, or any other request by whatever method, for the production, disclosure, or release of information or records by the federal judiciary, or for the appearance and testimony of federal judicial personnel as witnesses regarding matters arising out of the performance of their official duties, in legal proceedings. This includes requests for voluntary production or testimony in the absence of any legal process.

(C) This Rule does not apply to requests that members of the public make, when properly made through the procedures that the Court has established for records or documents, such as court files or dockets, routinely made available to members of the public for inspection or copying.

(D) In any request for testimony or production of records, the party shall set forth a written statement explaining the nature of the testimony or records the party seeks, the relevance of that testimony or those records to the legal proceedings, and the reasons why that testimony or those records, or the information contained therein, are not readily available from other sources or by other means. This explanation shall contain sufficient information for the determining officer to decide whether or not federal judicial personnel should be allowed to testify or the records should be produced. Where the request does not contain an explanation sufficient for this purpose, the determining officer may deny the request or may ask the requester to provide additional information. The request for testimony or production of records shall be provided to the federal judicial personnel from whom testimony or production of records is sought at least fifteen (15) working days in advance of the date on which the testimony or production of records is required. Failure to meet this requirement shall provide a sufficient basis for denial of the request.

(E) In the case of a request directed to a district judge or a magistrate judge, or directed to a current or former member of such a judge's personal staff, the determining officer shall be the district judge or the magistrate judge.

(F) Procedures to be followed:

(1) In the case of a request directed to an employee or former employee of the Clerk's office, the determining officer shall be the Clerk. The Clerk shall consult with the Chief Judge for determination of the proper response to a request.

(2) In the case of a request directed to an employee or former employee of the Probation Office, the determining officer will be the Chief Probation Officer or his or her designee. The determining officer shall consult with the Chief Judge or his or her designee regarding the proper response to a request. The Chief Probation Officer's designee(s) will be the officer to whom the request is directed and the officer's supervisor or manager. The Chief Judge's designee will be the judge who sentenced the offender who made the request or whose records are the subject of the request. Requests for disclosure, other than subpoenas, not otherwise covered by memorandum of understanding, statute, rule of procedure, regulation, case law, or court-approved local policy, will be presented to the sentencing judge, or in that judge's absence, the Chief Judge, for approval. All subpoenas will be presented to the court.

[Effective January 1, 2006; amended effective January 1, 2008.]

RULE 84.1   FORMS [RESERVED]

RULE 85.1   TITLE [RESERVED]

RULE 86.1   EFFECTIVE DATE

See L.R. 1.1(b).

SECTION XI.   CRIMINAL PROCEDURE

RULE 1.1   SCOPE OF THE RULES

These are the Local Rules of Practice for Criminal Cases in the United States District Court for the Northern District of New York. They shall be cited as "L.R.Cr.P. ____."

RULE 1.2   ELECTRONIC CASE FILING

All criminal cases filed in this Court may be assigned to the Electronic Case Files System in accordance with the *General Order # 22*, the provisions of which are incorporated herein by reference, and which the Court may amend from time to time.

[Effective January 1, 2004.]

RULE 1.3.   PERSONAL PRIVACY PROTECTION

Effective November 1, 2004, the public will be able to view via the internet all non-sealed documents filed in criminal cases. Parties shall refrain from including, or shall redact where inclusion is necessary, the fol-

lowing personal identifiers from all pleadings they file with the Court, including exhibits thereto, whether filed electronically or in paper form, unless the Court orders otherwise.

1. *Social security numbers.* If an individual's social security number must be included in a document, use only the last four digits of that number.

2. *Names of minor children.* If the involvement of a minor child must be mentioned, use only the initials of that child.

3. *Dates of birth.* If an individual's date of birth must be included in a document, use only the year.

4. *Financial account numbers.* If financial account numbers are relevant, use only the last four digits of those numbers.

5. *Home addresses.* If a home address must be used, use only the City and State.

In addition, caution shall be exercised when filing documents that contain the following: (1) personal identifying number, such as a driver's license number;

(2) medical records, treatment and diagnosis; (3) employment history; (4) individual financial information; and (5) proprietary or trade secret information.

In compliance with the E-Government Act of 2002, a party wishing to file a document containing the personal data identifiers listed above may

a. file an unredacted version of the document under seal, or

b. file a reference list under seal. The reference list shall contain the complete personal data identifier(s) and the redacted identifier(s) used in its(their) place in the filing. The Court will construe all references in the case to the redacted identifiers included in the reference list to refer to the corresponding complete personal data identifier. The party must file the reference list under seal and may amend the reference list as of right.

The Court strongly urges counsel to discuss this issue with all their clients so that they can make an informed decision about the inclusion of certain information. The responsibility for redacting these personal identifiers **rests solely with counsel and the parties**. The Clerk will not review each pleading for compliance with this Rule. The Court cautions counsel and the parties that failure to redact these personal identifiers may subject them to the Court's full disciplinary power.

Exception: Transcripts of the administrative record in social security proceedings and state court records relating to habeas corpus petitions are exempt from this requirement.

[Adopted effective January 1, 2005; January 1, 2008.]

RULES 2.1 TO 4.1. [RESERVED]

RULE 5.1 NOTICE OF ARREST

(a) Notice of Arrest of Parole, Special Parole, Mandatory Release or Military Parole Violators. As soon as practicable after taking into custody any person charged with a violation of parole, special parole, mandatory release, or military parole, the United States Marshal shall give written notice to the Chief Probation Officer of the date of the arrest and the place of confinement of the alleged violator.

(b) Notice of Arrest of Probation or Supervised Release Violators. As soon as practicable after taking into custody any person charged with a violation of probation or supervised release, the United States Marshal shall give written notice to the Chief Probation Officer, the United States Attorney, and the United States Magistrate Judge assigned to the case.

(c) Notice of Arrest by Federal Agencies and Others. It shall be the duty of the United States Marshal to require all federal agencies and others who arrest or hold any person as a federal prisoner in this District, and all jailers who incarcerate any such person in any jail or place of confinement in this District, to give the United States Marshal notice of the arrest or incarceration promptly.

As soon as practicable after receiving notice or other knowledge of any such arrest or incarceration anywhere within the District, the United States Marshal shall give written notice to the United States Magistrate Judge at the office closest to the place of confinement and to the United States Attorney and the pretrial services officer of the date of arrest and the prisoner's place of confinement.

[Amended effective January 1, 2008.]

RULES 5.1.1 TO 10.1. [RESERVED]

RULE 11.1 PLEAS

(a) In all cases in which a presentence report is required, the Court will defer its decision to accept or reject any nonbinding recommendation pursuant to Rule 11(e)(1)(B) and its decision to accept or reject any plea agreement pursuant to Rules 11(e)(1)(A) and (e)(1)(C) until there has been an opportunity to consider the presentence report, unless the Court states otherwise.

(b) An attorney for a defendant indicating a desire to change a previously entered "not guilty" plea shall give notice to the United States Attorney and the assigned judge as soon as practicable and, if possible, at least twenty-four (24) hours prior to the commencement of the trial.

(c) For any plea agreement that is to be sealed, the United States Attorney shall provide the Court with a proposed sealing order.

[Effective January 1, 2004; amended effective January 1, 2005.]

RULE 12.1 MOTIONS AND OTHER PAPERS

(a) The moving party must file all motion papers with the Court and serve them upon the other parties no less than **THIRTY-ONE CALENDAR DAYS** prior to the return date of the motion. The Notice of Motion should state the return date that the moving party selected. The moving party must specifically articulate the relief requested and must set forth a factual basis which, if proven true, would entitle the moving party to the requested relief. The opposing party must file opposing papers with the Court and serve them upon the other parties not less than **SEVENTEEN CALENDAR DAYS** prior to the return date of the motion. The moving party may file reply papers only with leave of the Court, upon a showing of necessity. If the Court grants leave, the moving party must file reply papers with the Court and serve them upon the other parties not less than **ELEVEN CALENDAR DAYS** prior to the return date of the motion.

The parties shall not file, or otherwise provide to the assigned judge, a courtesy copy of the motion papers unless the assigned judge specifically requests that they do so.

In addition, no party shall file or serve a memorandum of law which exceeds twenty-five (25) pages in length, unless the party obtains permission from the Court to do so prior to filing. All memoranda of law exceeding five (5) pages shall contain a table of contents and, wherever possible, parallel citations. A separate memorandum of law is unnecessary when the case law may be concisely cited (i.e. several paragraphs) in the body of the motion.

(b) The Court shall not hear a motion to compel discovery unless the attorney for the moving party files with the Court, simultaneously with the filing of the moving papers, a notice stating that the moving party has conferred and discussed in detail with the opposing party the issues between them in a good faith effort to eliminate or reduce the area of controversy and to arrive at a mutually satisfactory resolution.

(c) All motions and other papers filed in a criminal action or proceeding shall show on the first page beneath the file number which, if any, of the speedy trial exclusions under 18 U.S.C. § 3161 are applicable to the action sought or opposed by the motion or other paper and the amount of resulting excludable time.

(d) Adjournment of motions shall be in the Court's discretion. Any party seeking an adjournment from the Court shall first contact the opposing attorney. A party shall make any application for an adjournment of a motion in writing and shall set forth the reason for requesting the adjournment.

(e) If the parties agree that a suppression hearing is necessary and the papers conform to the requirements of L.R. Cr. P. 12.1(a), the Court will set the matter for a hearing. If the government contests whether the Court should conduct a hearing, the defendant must accompany the motion with an affidavit, based upon personal knowledge, setting forth facts which, if proven true, would entitle the defendant to relief.

(f) An affidavit of counsel is not required when filing motions in criminal cases. A certificate of service is required at the conclusion of the motion.

(g) All papers filed in criminal cases shall comply with the guidelines established in Local Rule 8.1 regarding personal privacy protection.

[Amended effective January 1, 1999; January 1, 2001; January 1, 2004; January 1, 2008.]

RULE 13.1 SEALED MATTERS

The Court may seal cases in their entirety, or only as to certain parties or documents, when the cases are initiated or at various stages of the proceedings. The Court may on its own motion enter an order directing that a document, party or entire case be sealed. A party seeking to have a document, party or entire case sealed shall submit an application, under seal, setting forth the reason(s) why the Court should seal the document, party or entire case, together with a proposed order for the assigned judge's approval. The proposed order shall include language in the "ORDERED" paragraph stating which document(s) are to be sealed and should include the phrase "including this sealing order." Upon the assigned judge's approval of the sealing order, the Clerk shall seal the document(s) and the sealing order. A complaint presented for filing with a motion to seal and a proposed order shall be treated as a sealed case, pending approval of the order. Once the Court orders a document or case sealed, it shall remain under seal until the Court enters a subsequent order, upon its own motion or in response to the motion of a party, directing that the Clerk unseal the document or case.

[Adopted effective January 1, 1999; January 1, 2008.]

RULE 14.1 DISCOVERY

(a) It is the Court's policy to rely on the discovery procedure as set forth in this Rule as the sole means for the exchange of discovery in criminal actions except in extraordinary circumstances. This Rule is intended to promote the efficient exchange of discovery without altering the rights and obligations of the parties, while at the same time eliminating the practice of routinely filing perfunctory and duplicative discovery motions.

(b) Fourteen (14) days after arraignment, or on a date that the Court otherwise sets for good cause shown, the government shall make available for inspection and copying to the defendant the following:

1. *Fed.R.Crim.P. 16(a) & Fed.R.Crim.P. 12(d) Information.* All discoverable information within the scope of Fed. R. Crim. P 16(a), together with a notice pursuant to Fed. R. Crim. P. 12(d) of the government's intent to use this evidence, in order to afford the defendant an opportunity to file motions to suppress evidence.

2. *Brady Material.* All information and material that the government knows that may be favorable to the defendant on the issues of guilt or punishment, within the scope of *Brady v. Maryland*, 373 U.S. 83 (1963).

3. *Federal Rule of Evidence 404(b).* The government shall advise the defendant of its intention to introduce evidence in its case in chief at trial, pursuant to Rule 404(b) of the Federal Rules of Evidence.

This requirement shall replace the defendant's duty to demand such notice.

(c) Unless a defendant, in writing, affirmatively refuses discoverable materials under Fed. R. Crim. P. 16(a)(1)(C), (D), or (E), the defendant shall make available to the government all discoverable information within the scope of Fed. R. Crim. P. 16(b) within twenty-one (21) days of arraignment.

(d) No less than fourteen (14) days prior to the start of jury selection, or on a date the Court sets otherwise for good cause shown, the government shall tender to the defendant the following:

1. *Giglio Material.* The existence and substance of any payments, promises of immunity, leniency, preferential treatment, or other inducements made to prospective witnesses, within the scope of *United States v. Giglio*, 405 U.S. 150 (1972).

2. Testifying Informant's Convictions. A record of prior convictions of any alleged informant who will testify for the government at trial.

(e) The government shall anticipate the need for, and arrange for the transcription of, the grand jury testimony of all witnesses who will testify in the government's case in chief, if subject to Fed. R. Crim. P. 26.2 and 18 U.S.C. § 3500. The Court requests that the government, and where applicable, the defendant, make materials and statements subject to Fed. R. Crim. P. 26.2 and 18 U.S.C. § 3500 available to the other party at a time earlier than rule or law requires, to avoid undue delay at trial or hearings.

(f) It shall be the duty of counsel for all parties immediately to reveal to opposing counsel all newly discovered information, evidence, or other material within the scope of this Rule, and there is a continuing duty upon each attorney to disclose expeditiously. The government shall advise all government agents and officers involved in the action to preserve all rough notes.

(g) No attorney shall file a discovery motion without first conferring with opposing counsel, and the Court will not consider a motion unless it is accompanied by a certification of such conference and a statement of the moving party's good faith efforts to resolve the subject matter of the motion by agreement with opposing counsel. The parties shall not file any discovery motions for information or material within the scope of this Rule unless it is a motion to compel, a motion for protective order or a motion for an order modifying discovery. See Fed. R. Crim. P. 16(d). Discovery requests made pursuant to Fed. R. Crim. P. 16 and this Rule require no action on the part of the Court and should not be filed with the Court unless the party making the request desires to preserve the discovery matter for appeal.

[Effective January 1, 2003; amended effective January 1, 2008.]

RULES 15.1 TO 16.1.   [RESERVED]

RULE 17.1   SUBPOENAS

(a) Production Before Trial. Except on order of a judge, no subpoena for production of documents or objects shall be sought or issued if the subpoena requests production before trial. See Fed. R. Crim. P. 17(c).

(b) Depositions. Except on order of a judge, no subpoena for a deposition shall be sought or issued. See Fed. R. Crim. P. 15; 17(f).

(c) Subpoenas Requested by Attorneys Appointed Under the Criminal Justice Act.

1. The Clerk shall issue subpoenas, signed but otherwise in blank, to an attorney appointed under the Criminal Justice Act. No subpoena so issued shall be served outside the boundaries of this district. Attorneys shall file with the clerk of the court a list of those witnesses whom they have subpoenaed. This filing shall constitute certification that the subpoena(s) is necessary to obtain relevant and material testimony and that the witness' attendance is reasonably necessary to the defense of the charge.

2. If an attorney needs to subpoena a witness outside the boundaries of this District, the attorney shall make an ex parte application for issuance of a subpoena to the appropriate court.

3. The defense attorney shall request that the United States Marshal serve the subpoenas under this Rule. The defense attorney shall obtain an order from the Court directing the Marshal to serve subpoenas. The Marshal shall serve the subpoenas in the same manner as in other cases, except that the name and address of the person served shall not be disclosed without prior authorization of the defense attorney. No fee shall be allowed for private service of any subpoena issued under this Rule unless the attorney obtains express advance authorization by written order of the court.

4. As authorized by Fed. R. Crim. P. 17(b), the Court orders that the costs for service of process and payment of witness fees for each witness subpoenaed under this Rule shall be paid in the same manner in which similar costs and fees are paid in the case of a witness subpoenaed on behalf of the government.

[Amended effective January 1, 2008.]

RULE 17.1.1   PRETRIAL CONFERENCES

At the request of any party or upon the Court's own motion, the assigned judge may hold one or more pretrial conferences in any criminal action or proceeding. The agenda at the pretrial conference shall consist of any of the following items, so far as applicable, and such other matters that the judge designates as may tend to promote the fair and expeditious trial of the action or proceeding:

(a) Production of witness statements under the Jencks Act, 18 U.S.C. § 3500 or Fed. R. Crim. P. 26.2;

(b) Production of grand jury testimony of witnesses that the parties intend to call at trial;

(c) Production of exculpatory or other evidence favorable to the defendant on the issue of guilt or punishment;

(d) Stipulation of facts which may be deemed proved at the trial without further proof by either party, and limitation of witnesses;

(e) Court appointment of interpreters under Fed. R. Crim. P. 28;

(f) Dismissal of certain counts and elimination from the case of certain issues; e.g., insanity, alibi, and statute of limitations;

(g) Severance of trial as to any co-defendant or joinder of any related case;

(h) Identification of informers, use of lineup or other identification evidence, use of evidence of prior convictions of defendant or any witness, etc.;

(i) Pretrial exchange of lists of witnesses whom the parties intend to call in person or by deposition to testify at trial, except those whom they may call only for impeachment or rebuttal;

(j) Pretrial exchange of documents, exhibits, summaries, schedules, models, or diagrams that the parties intend to offer or use at trial;

(k) Pretrial resolution of objections to exhibits or testimony that the parties intend to offer at trial;

(l) Preparation of trial briefs on controversial points of law likely to arise at trial;

(m) Scheduling of the trial and of witnesses;

(n) Settlement of jury instructions, voir dire questions, and challenges to the jury; and

(o) Any other matter which may tend to promote a fair and expeditious trial.

[Amended effective January 1, 2008.]

RULES 18.1 TO 19.1. [RESERVED]

RULE 20.1 TRANSFER FROM A DISTRICT FOR PLEA AND SENTENCE

Upon the transfer under Fed. R. Crim. P. 20 of an information or indictment charging a minor offense, the Court shall refer the case immediately to a Magistrate Judge who shall take the plea and impose sentence in accordance with the rules for the trial of minor offenses if, pursuant to 18 U.S.C. § 3401, the defendant consents in writing to this procedure.

[Amended effective January 1, 2008.]

RULES 21.1 TO 22.1. [RESERVED]

RULE 23.1 FREE PRESS—FAIR TRIAL DIRECTIVES

(a) It is the duty of the lawyer or law firm, and of non-lawyer personnel employed by a lawyer's office or subject to a lawyer's supervision, private investigators acting under the supervision of a criminal defense lawyer, and government agents and police officers, not to release or authorize the release of non-public information or opinion which a reasonable person would expect to be disseminated by means of public communication, in connection with pending or imminent criminal litigation with which they are associated, if there is a substantial likelihood that such dissemination will interfere with a fair trial or otherwise prejudice the due administration of justice.

(b) With regard to a grand jury or other pending investigation of any criminal matter, a lawyer participating in or associated with the investigation (including government lawyers and lawyers for targets, subjects, and witnesses in the investigation) shall refrain from making any extrajudicial statement which a reasonable person would expect to be disseminated by means of public communication that goes beyond the public record or that is not necessary to inform the public that the investigation is underway, to describe the general scope of the investigation, to obtain assistance in the apprehension of a suspect, and to warn the public of any dangers or otherwise to aid in the investigation if there is a substantial likelihood that such dissemination will interfere with a fair trial or otherwise prejudice the administration of justice.

(c) During a jury trial of any criminal matter, including the period of selection of the jury, no lawyer or law firm associated with the prosecution or defense shall give or authorize any extrajudicial statement or interview relating to the trial or the parties or issues in the trial which a reasonable person would expect to be disseminated by means of public communication if there is a substantial likelihood that such dissemination will interfere with a fair trial; except that the lawyer or the law firm may quote from or refer without comment to public records of the Court in the case.

(d) Statements concerning the following subject matters presumptively involve a substantial likelihood that their public dissemination will interfere with a fair trial or otherwise prejudice the due administration of justice within the meaning of this rule:

(1) The prior criminal record (including arrests, indictments or other charges of crime) or the character or reputation of the accused, except that the lawyer or law firm may make a factual statement of the accused's name, age, residence, occupation and family status; and if the accused has not been apprehended, a lawyer associated with the prosecution may release any information necessary to aid in the accused's apprehension or to warn the public of any dangers the accused may present;

(2) The existence or contents of any confession, admission or statement that the accused has given or the refusal or failure of the accused to make any statement;

(3) The performance of any examinations or tests or the accused's refusal or failure to submit to an examination or test;

(4) The identity, testimony or credibility of prospective witnesses, except that the lawyer or law firm may announce the identity of the victim if the announcement is not otherwise prohibited by law;

(5) The possibility of a plea of guilty to the offense charged or a lesser offense;

(6) Information the lawyer or law firm knows is likely to be inadmissible at trial and would, if disclosed, create a substantial likelihood of prejudicing an impartial trial: and

(7) Any opinion as to the accused's guilt or innocence or as to the merits of the case or the evidence in the case.

(e) Statements concerning the following subject matters presumptively do not involve a substantial likelihood that their public dissemination will interfere with a fair trial or otherwise prejudice the due administration of justice within the meaning of this Rule:

(1) An announcement, at the time of arrest, of the fact and circumstances of arrest (including time and place of arrest, resistance, pursuit and use of weapons), the identity of the investigating and arresting officer or agency and the length of the investigation;

(2) An announcement, at the time of seizure, stating whether any items of physical evidence were seized and, if so, a description of the items seized (but not including any confession, admission or statement);

(3) The nature, substance or text of the charge, including a brief description of the offense charges;

(4) Quoting or referring without comment to public records of the Court in the case;

(5) An announcement of the scheduling or result of any state in the judicial process, or an announcement that a matter is no longer under investigation;

(6) A request for assistance in obtaining evidence and the disclosure of information necessary to further such a request for assistance; and

(7) An announcement, without further comment, that the accused denies the charges, and a brief description of the nature of the defense.

(f) Nothing in this Rule is intended to preclude the formulation or application of more restrictive rules relating to the release of information about juvenile or other offenders, to preclude the holding of hearings or the lawful issuance of reports by legislative, administrative or investigative bodies, or to preclude any lawyer from replying to charges of misconduct that are publicly made against said lawyer.

(g) The Court, on motion of either party or on its own motion, may issue a special order governing such matters as extrajudicial statements by parties and witnesses likely to interfere with the rights of the accused to a fair trial by an impartial jury, the seating and conduct in the courtroom of spectators and news media representatives, the management and sequestration of jurors and witnesses and any other matters which the Court may deem appropriate for inclusion in such order. In determining whether to impose such a special order, the Court shall consider whether such an order will be necessary to ensure an impartial jury and must find that other, less extreme available remedies, singly or collectively, are not feasible or would not effectively mitigate the pretrial publicity and bring about a fair trial. Among the alternative remedies the Court must consider are as follows: change of venue, postponing the trial, a searching voir dire, emphatic jury instructions, and sequestration of jurors.

(h) The Court may take disciplinary action against any attorney who violates the terms of this Rule.

[Effective January 1, 2006; amended effective January 1, 2008.]

RULES 24.1 TO 29.1. [RESERVED]

RULE 30.1 JURY INSTRUCTIONS

The parties shall submit proposed jury instructions, accompanied by citations to relevant authorities, to the Court in accordance with the time frames set forth in the Criminal Pretrial Scheduling Order issued at the time of arraignment.

[Amended effective January 1, 2008.]

RULE 31.1 [RESERVED]

RULE 32.1 PRESENTENCE REPORTS

(a) **Order for Presentence Report.** The Court will impose sentences without unnecessary delay following the completion of the presentence investigation and report. This Court adopts the use of a uniform presentence order. The uniform presentence order shall contain: (1) the date by which the presentence report is to be made available; (2) the deadlines for filing objections, if any, to the presentence report; (3) the deadlines for filing presentence memoranda, recommendations and motions; and, (4) a date for sentencing.

(b) Presence of Counsel. On request, the defendant's counsel is entitled to notice and a reasonable opportunity to attend any interview that a probation officer conducts of the defendant in the course of a presentence investigation. It shall be incumbent upon the defendant's counsel to advise the Probation Office within two (2) business days of the date that the presentence report is ordered that counsel wishes to be present at any interview with the defendant.

(c) Disclosure Procedures.

1. The Presentence Report is confidential and should not be disclosed to anyone other than the defendant, the defendant's attorney, the United States Attorney and the Bureau of Prisons without the Court's consent.

2. The Court directs the probation officer not to disclose the probation officer's confidential recommendation to any of the parties.

3. The Court admonishes all counsel that they shall adhere to the time limits set forth in the Uniform Presentence Order in order to allow sufficient time for the Court to read and analyze the material which the Court receives.

4. The Court, on motion of either party or of the probation office, may modify the time requirements set forth in the Uniform Presentence Order subject to the provisions of Title 18 U.S.C. § 3552(d).

(d) Responsibilities of the Clerk and Probation Office.

1. Within three (3) business days after sentencing, the Clerk shall serve a copy of the judgment upon the parties and the United States Marshal.

2. Copies of the Presentence Report that the Clerk provides to the Court of Appeals for the Second Circuit shall include the Court's finding on unresolved objections.

[Amended effective January 1, 2005; amended effective January 1, 2008.]

RULES 33.1 TO 43.1. [RESERVED]

RULE 44.1   RIGHT TO AND ASSIGNMENT OF COUNSEL

If a defendant, appearing without an attorney in a criminal proceeding, desires to obtain an attorney, the Court shall grant a reasonable continuance for arraignment, not to exceed one week at any one time, for that purpose. If the defendant requests that the Court appoint an attorney or fails for an unreasonable time to appear with an attorney, the assigned District Judge or Magistrate Judge shall, subject to the applicable financial eligibility requirements, appoint an attorney unless the defendant, electing to proceed without an attorney, waives the right to an attorney in a manner that the District Judge or the Magistrate Judge approves. In that case, the District Judge or Magistrate Judge shall, nevertheless, designate an attorney to advise and assist the defendant to the extent the defendant might thereafter desire. The Court shall appoint an attorney in accordance with the Court's Plan adopted pursuant to the Criminal Justice Act of 1964 and on file with the Clerk.

[Amended effective January 1, 2008.]

RULE 44.2   APPEARANCE AND WITHDRAWAL OF COUNSEL

(a) An attorney appearing for a defendant in a criminal case, whether retained or appointed, shall promptly file a written appearance with the Clerk. An attorney who has appeared shall thereafter withdraw only upon notice to the defendant and all parties to the case and an order of the Court finding that good cause exists and granting leave to withdraw. Failure of a defendant to pay agreed compensation shall not be deemed good cause unless the Court determines otherwise.

(b) Unless leave is granted, the attorney shall continue to represent the defendant until the case is dismissed, the defendant is acquitted or convicted, or the time for making post-trial motions and for filing a notice of appeal, as specified in Fed. R. App. P. 4(b), has expired. If an appeal is taken, the attorney shall continue to serve until the court having jurisdiction of the case grants leave to withdraw or until that court has appointed another attorney as provided in 18 U.S.C. § 3006A and other applicable provisions of law.

RULE 45.1   EXCLUDABLE TIME UNDER THE SPEEDY TRIAL ACT

The Court shall not grant a continuance or extension under the Speedy Trial Act unless a party submits a motion or stipulation that recites the appropriate exclusionary provision of the Speedy Trial Act, 18 U.S.C. § 3161. In addition, the party shall accompany the motion or stipulation with an affidavit of facts upon which the Court can base a finding that the requested relief is warranted. The attorneys shall also submit a proposed order setting forth the time to be excluded and the basis for its exclusion. If the exclusion affects the trial date of the action, the stipulation or proposed order shall have a space for the Court to enter a new trial date in accordance with the excludable time period. The Court shall disallow all requests for a continuance or extension that do not comply with this Rule.

[Amended effective January 1, 2008.]

RULE 46.1 PRETRIAL SERVICES AND RELEASE ON BAIL

Pursuant to the Pretrial Services Act of 1982, 18 U.S.C. §§ 3152–3155, the Court authorizes the United States Probation Office and/or Pretrial Services Office of the Northern District of New York to perform all services as the Act provides.

(a) Pretrial Service Officers shall conduct an interview and investigate each individual charged with an offense and shall submit a report to the Court as soon as practicable. The judicial officer setting conditions of release or reviewing conditions previously set shall receive and consider all reports that Pretrial Service Officers, the government and defense counsel submit.

(b) Pretrial service reports shall be made available to the attorney for the accused and the attorney for the government and shall be used only for the purpose of fixing conditions of release, including bail determinations. Otherwise, the reports shall remain confidential, as provided in 18 U.S.C. § 3153, subject to the exceptions provided therein.

(c) Pretrial Service Officers shall supervise persons released on bail at the discretion of the judicial officer granting the release or modifications of the release.

RULE 47.1 MOTIONS

See L.R.Cr.P. 12.1.

RULES 48.1 TO 56.1. [RESERVED]

RULE 57.1 CRIMINAL DESIGNATION FORMS

The United States Attorney shall file a criminal designation form with each new indictment or information. On this sheet the United States Attorney shall indicate the name and address of the defendant and the magistrate judge case number, if any. The criminal designation form also shall contain any further information that the Court or the Clerk deems pertinent. The United States Attorney can obtain a copy of the designation form from the Court's webpage at "www.nynd.uscourts.gov."

[Amended effective January 1, 2004; amended effective January 1, 2008.]

RULE 57.2 RELEASE OF BOND

When a defendant has obtained release by depositing a sum of money or other collateral as bond as provided by 18 U.S.C. § 3142, the payee or depositor shall be entitled to a refund or release thereof when the conditions of the bond have been performed and the defendant has been discharged from all obligations thereon. The defendant's attorney shall prepare a motion and proposed order for the release of the bond and submit the motion to the Court for the assigned judge's signature. Unless otherwise specified by court order, or upon such proof as the Court shall require, all bond refunds shall be disbursed to the individual whose name appears on the Court's receipt for payment.

RULE 58.1 MAGISTRATE JUDGES

(a) Powers and Duties.

1. A full-time Magistrate Judge is authorized to exercise all powers and perform all duties permitted by 28 U.S.C. § 636(a), (b), and (c), and any additional duties that are consistent with the Constitution and laws of the United States. A part-time Magistrate Judge is authorized to exercise all of those duties, except those permitted under 28 U.S.C. § 636(c), and any additional duties consistent with the Constitution and laws of the United States.

2. A Magistrate Judge is also authorized to:

(A) Conduct removal proceedings and issue warrants of removal in accordance with Fed. R. Crim. P. 40;

(B) Conduct extradition proceedings in accordance with 18 U.S.C. § 3184;

(C) Impanel and charge a Grand Jury and Special Grand Juries and receive grand jury returns in accordance with Fed. R. Crim. P. 6(f);

(D) Conduct voir dire and select petit juries for the Court;

(E) Conduct necessary proceedings leading to the potential revocation of probation;

(F) Order the exoneration or forfeiture of bonds;

(G) Exercise general supervision of the Court's criminal calendar, conduct calendar and status calls, and determine motions to expedite or postpone the trial of cases for the Court;

(H) Exercise all the powers and duties conferred or imposed upon United States commissioners by law or the Federal Rules of Criminal Procedure;

(I) Administer oaths and affirmations, impose conditions of release under 18 U.S.C. § 3146, and take acknowledgments, affidavits, and depositions;

(J) Determine motions pursuant to 18 U.S.C. § 4241(a) for a hearing to determine the mental competency of the defendant and, if necessary, order that a psychiatric or psychological examination of the defendant be conducted pursuant to 18 U.S.C. § 4241(b); and

(K) Conduct hearings to determine the mental competency of the defendant pursuant to 18 U.S.C. § 4247(d) and issue a report and recommendation to the assigned District Judge pursuant to 28 U.S.C. § 636(b).

(3) A party seeking review of a magistrate judge's release or detention order pursuant to 18 U.S.C. § 3145 shall file the following documents in support of its motions:

(A) Notice of motion;

(B) Memorandum of law;

(C) Attorney affidavit;

(D) Written transcript of all proceedings relating to the defendant's release or detention.

Upon the filing of any such motion, the opposing party shall file its papers in opposition to said motion within ten (10) days of the filing date of said motion.

No reply is permitted.

The Court shall promptly determine the motion based upon the submitted papers without oral argument.

(b) Felonies. On the return of an indictment or the filing of an information, a District Judge shall assign felony matters to a Magistrate Judge for the purpose of arraignment, for the determination and fixing the conditions of pretrial release, and for the assignment of an attorney to the extent authorized by law.

(c) Misdemeanors.

1. A Magistrate Judge is authorized to conduct trials of persons accused of misdemeanors committed within this District in accordance with 18 U.S.C. § 3401, order a presentence investigation report on any such persons who are convicted or plead guilty or nolo contendere, and sentence such persons.

2. Any person charged with a misdemeanor may, however, elect to be tried before a judge of the district court for the district in which the offense was committed. The Magistrate Judge shall carefully advise de-fendants of their right to trial, judgment, and sentencing by a judge of the district court and their right to a trial by jury before a District Judge or Magistrate Judge. The Magistrate Judge shall not proceed to try the case unless the defendant, after such explanation, files a written consent to be tried before the Magistrate Judge. That consent specifically must waive trial, judgment, and sentencing by a judge of the district court.

3. Procedures on appeal to a District Judge in a consent case pursuant to 18 U.S.C. § 3401 shall be as provided in Fed. R. Crim. P. 58(g). Unless otherwise ordered,

(A) The appellant's brief shall be filed within ten (10) days following the filing of the notice of appeal;

(B) The appellee's brief shall be filed within ten (10) days following submission of the appellant's brief;

(C) No oral argument shall be permitted.

[Amended effective January 1, 2004; January 1, 2008.]

RULE 58.2 FORFEITURE OF COLLATERAL IN LIEU OF APPEARANCE

In accordance with Fed. R. Crim. P. 58(d)(1), the U.S. District Court for the Northern District of New York has adopted the schedule for violations as set forth in General Order #4. Parties may obtain copies of General Order #4 from the Clerk's office or on the Court's webpage at **"www.nynd.uscourts.gov."**

[Amended effective January 1, 2004; January 1, 2008.]

RULES 59.1 TO 60.1.   [RESERVED]

SECTION XII.   LOCAL RULES OF PROCEDURE FOR ADMIRALTY AND MARITIME CASES

RULE A. SCOPE OF THE RULES

(a)1. Authority. A majority of the judges have promulgated this Court's local admiralty rules as authorized by and subject to the limitations of the Fed. R. Civ. P. 83.

(a)2. Scope. The local admiralty rules apply only to civil actions that are governed by Supplemental Rule A of the Supplemental Rules for Certain Admiralty and Maritime Claims ("Supplemental Rule or Rules"). All other local rules are applicable in these cases, but to the extent that another local rule is inconsistent with the applicable local admiralty rules, the local admiralty rules shall govern.

(a)3. Citation. The local admiralty rules may be cited by the letter "LAR" and the lowercase letters and numbers in the parentheses that appear at the beginning of each section. The lower case letter is intended to associate the local admiralty rule with the Supplemental Rule that bears the same capital letter.

(a)4. Definitions. As used in the local admiralty rules, "court" refers to United States District Court for the Northern District of New York; "judge" refers to a United States District Judge or to a United States Magistrate Judge; "clerk" refers to the Clerk of the Court and includes deputy clerks of the Court; "marshal" refers to the United States Marshal of this district and includes deputy marshals; "keeper" refers to any person or entity that the Marshal appoints to take physical custody of and maintain the vessel or other property under arrest or attachment; and "substitute custodian" refers to the individual or entity who, upon motion and order of the Court, assumes the duties of the marshal or keeper with respect to the vessel or other property arrested or attached.

[Amended effective January 1, 2001; January 1, 2006.]

RULE B. MARITIME ATTACHMENT AND GARNISHMENT

(b)1. Found within the District. A defendant is not found within the district unless the defendant can be personally served therein by delivering process (i) in the case of an individual, to the individual personally, or by leaving a copy thereof at the individual's dwelling, house or usual place of abode with some person of suitable age and discretion; (ii) in the case of a corporation, trust or association, to an officer, trustee, managing or general agent thereof; (iii) in the case of a partnership, to a general partner thereof; and (iv) in the case of a limited liability company, to a manager thereof.

(b)2. Affidavit that Defendant is Not Found Within the District. The affidavit that Supplemental Rule B(1) requires to accompany the complaint shall specify with particularity the efforts made by and on behalf of the plaintiff to find and serve the defendant within the District.

(b)3. Notice to Defendant. In default applications, the affidavit or other proof that Supplemental Rule B(2) requires from the plaintiff or the garnishee shall specify with particularity the effort made to give notice of the action to the defendant.

(b)4. Service by Marshal. If property to be attached is a vessel or tangible property aboard a vessel, the process shall be delivered to the Marshal for service.

[Amended effective January 1, 2001; January 1, 2006.]

RULE C. ACTIONS IN REM— SPECIAL PROVISIONS

(c)1. Intangible Property. The summons to show cause why property should not be deposited in the Court issued pursuant to Supplemental Rule C(3) shall direct the person having control of intangible property to show cause no later than ten (10) calendar days after service why the intangible property should not be delivered to the Court to abide the judgment. The Court for good cause shown may lengthen or shorten the time. Service of the warrant has the effect of arresting the intangible property and bringing it within the Court's control. Service of the summons to show cause requires a garnishee wishing to retain possession of the property to establish grounds for doing so, including specification of the measures taken to segregate and safeguard the intangible property arrested. The person who is served may, upon order of the Court, deliver or pay over to the person on whose behalf the warrant was served or to the clerk the intangible property proceeded against to the extent sufficient to satisfy the plaintiff's claim. If such delivery or payment is made, the person served is excused from the duty to show cause. The person asserting any ownership interest in the property or a right of possession may show cause as provided in Supplemental Rule C(6) why the property should not be delivered to the Court.

(c)2. Publication of Notice of Action and Arrest. The notice that Supplemental Rule C(4) requires shall be published at least once in a newspaper named in LAR (g)2, and the plaintiff's attorney shall file a copy of the notice as it was published with the Clerk. The notice shall contain:

(a) The court, title, and number of the action;

(b) The date of the arrest;

(c) The identity of the property arrested;

(d) The name, address, and telephone number of the attorney or the plaintiff;

(e) A statement that a person asserting any ownership interest in the property or a right of possession pursuant to Supplemental Rule C(6) must file a statement of such interest with the Clerk and serve it on the plaintiff's attorney within ten (10) calendar days after publication.

(f) A statement that an answer to the complaint must be filed and served within thirty (30) calendar days after publication and that, otherwise, default may be entered and condemnation ordered;

(g) A statement that applications for intervention under Fed. R. Civ. P. 24 by persons asserting maritime liens or other interests shall be filed within the time fixed by the Court; and

(h) The name, address, and telephone number of the Marshal, keeper, or substitute custodian.

(c)3. Default In Action In Rem.

(a) *Notice Required.* A party seeking a default judgment in an action in rem must satisfy the Court that due notice of the action and arrest of property has been given:

(1) by publication as required in LAR (c)(2), and

(2) by service upon the Marshal and keeper, substitute custodian, master, or other person having custody of the property, and

(3) by mailing such notice to every other person who has not appeared in the action and is known to have an interest in the property.

(b) *Persons with Recorded Interests.*

(1) If the defendant property is a vessel documented under the law of the United States, the plaintiff must attempt to notify all persons named in the United States Coast Guard Certificate of ownership.

(2) If the defendant property is a vessel numbered as provided in the Federal Boat Safety Act, the plaintiff must attempt to notify the persons named in the records of the issuing authority.

(3) If the defendant property is of such character that there exists a governmental registry of recorded property interests and/or security interests in the property, the plaintiff must attempt to notify all persons named in the records of each such registry.

(c)4. Entry of Default and Default Judgment. After the time for filing an answer has expired, the plaintiff may move for entry of default under Fed. R. Civ. P. 55(a). Default will be entered upon showing that:

(a) Notice has been given as LAR (c)(3)(a) requires; and

(b) Notice has been attempted as LAR (c)(3)(b) requires, where appropriate; and

(c) The time for claimants of ownership to or possession of the property to answer has expired; and

(d) No answer has been filed or no one has appeared to defend on behalf of the property. The plaintiff may move for judgment under Fed. R. Civ. P. Rule 55(b) at any time after default has been entered.

[Amended effective January 1, 2001; January 1, 2006.]

RULE D. POSSESSORY, PETITORY, AND PARTITION ACTIONS

(d)1. Return Date. In a possessory action under Supplemental Rule D, a judge may order that the statement of interest and answer be filed on a date earlier than twenty (20) calendar days after arrest. The order may also set a date for expedited hearing of the action.

[Amended effective January 1, 2001.]

RULE E. ACTIONS IN REM AND QUASI IN REM—GENERAL PROVISIONS

(e)1. Itemized Demand for Judgment. The demand for judgment in every complaint filed under Supplemental Rule B or C shall allege the dollar amount of the debt or damages for which the action was commenced. The demand for judgment shall also allege the nature of other items of damage. The amount of the special bond posted under Supplemental Rule E(5)(a) may be based upon these allegations.

(e)2. Salvage Action Complaints. In an action for a salvage award, the complaint shall allege the dollar value of the vessel, cargo, freight, and other property salved or other basis for an award and the dollar amount of the award sought.

(e)3. Verification of Pleadings. A party or authorized officer of a corporate party shall verify every complaint in Supplemental Rule B, C, and D actions upon oath or solemn affirmation or in the form provided by 28 U.S.C. § 1746. If no party or authorized corporate officer is present within the District, an agent, attorney in fact, or attorney of record shall verify the complaint and shall state the sources of the knowledge, information and belief contained in the complaint; declare that the document verified is true to the best of that knowledge, information, and belief; state why the party or authorized representative of the party is not making the verification; and state that the affiant or declarant is authorized so to verify. If a party or authorized representative of the party did not make the verification, any interested party may move, with or without requesting a stay, for the personal oath of a party or an authorized representative, which shall be procured by commission or as otherwise ordered.

(e)4. Review by Judicial Officer. Unless the Court requires otherwise, the review of complaints and papers that Supplemental Rules B(1) and C(3) require does not require the affiant or declarant party or attorney to be present. The applicant for review shall include a form of order to the Clerk which, upon the assigned judge's signature, will direct the arrest, attachment or garnishment that the applicant seeks. In exigent circumstances, the certification of the plaintiff or his attorney under Supplemental Rules B and C shall consist of an affidavit or a declaration pursuant to 28 U.S.C. § 1746 describing in detail the facts establishing the exigent circumstances.

(e)5. Instructions to the Marshal. The party who requests a warrant of arrest or process of attachment or garnishment shall provide instructions to the Marshal.

(e)6. Property in Possession of United States Officer. When the property to be attached or arrested is in the custody of an employee or officer of the United States, the Marshal will deliver a copy of the complaint and warrant of arrest or summons and process of attachment or garnishment to that officer or employee, if present, and otherwise to the custodian of the property. The Marshal will instruct the officer or employee or custodian to retain custody of the property unless the Court orders otherwise.

(e)7. Security for Costs. In an action under the Supplemental Rules, a party may move upon notice to all parties for an order to compel an adverse party to post security for costs with the Clerk pursuant to Supplemental Rule E(2)(b). Unless otherwise ordered, the amount of security shall be $500.00. The party so ordered shall post the security within five (5) days after the order is entered. A party who fails to post security when due may not participate further in the proceedings, except by order of the Court. A party may move for an order increasing the amount of security for costs.

(e)8. Adversary Hearing. The Court shall conduct the adversary hearing following arrest or attachment or garnishment provided for in Supplemental Rule E(4)(f) within three business days, unless otherwise ordered. The person(s) requesting the hearing shall notify all persons known to have an interest in the property of the time and place of the hearing.

(e)9. Appraisal. The Clerk will enter an order for appraisal of property so that security may be given or altered at the request of any interested party. If the parties do not agree in writing upon an appraiser, a judge will appoint the appraiser. The appraiser shall be sworn to the faithful and impartial discharge of the appraiser's duties before any federal or state officer authorized by law to administer oaths. The appraiser shall promptly file the appraisal with the Clerk and serve it upon counsel of record. The moving party shall pay the appraiser's fee in the first instance, but this fee is taxable as an administrative cost of the action.

(e)10. Security Deposit for Seizure of Vessels. The first party who seeks arrest or attachment of a vessel or property aboard a vessel shall deposit $1,000 with the Marshal to cover the Marshal's expenses, including, but not limited to, dockage, keepers, maintenance and insurance. The Marshal is not required to execute process until the deposit is made. The Marshal may also require the party to arrange, in advance of the seizure, for a private security company to maintain security over the vessel or property after attachment. Parties requesting the attachment of a vessel or property are advised to contact the local Marshal's office for further information regarding this requirement. The party shall advance additional sums from time to time as requested to cover the Marshal's estimated expenses until the property is released or disposed of as provided in Supplemental Rule E. Any party who fails to advance such additional costs that the Marshal requires may not participate further in the proceedings, except by order of the Court. The Marshal may, upon notice to all parties, petition the Court for an order to be issued forthwith releasing the vessel if additional sums are not advanced within three business days of the initial request for additional sums.

(e)11. Intervenors' Claims.

(a) *Presentation of Claims.* When a vessel or property has been arrested, attached, or garnished, and is in the hands of the Marshal or custodian substituted therefor, anyone having a claim against the vessel or property is required to present that claim by filing an intervening complaint and obtaining a warrant of arrest, and not by filing an original complaint, unless the Court orders otherwise. No formal motion is required. The intervening party shall serve a copy of the intervening complaint and warrant of arrest upon all parties to the action and shall forthwith deliver a con-formed copy of the complaint and warrant of arrest to the Marshal, who shall deliver the copies to the vessel or custodian of the property. Intervenors shall thereafter be subject to the rights and obligations of parties, and the vessel or property shall stand arrested, attached, or garnished by the intervenor. An intervenor shall not be required to advance a security deposit to the Marshal for the intervenor's seizure of a vessel as LAR (e)(10) requires.

(b) *Sharing Marshal's Fees and Expenses.* An intervenor shall owe a debt to the preceding plaintiffs and intervenors, enforceable on motion, consisting of the intervenor's share of the Marshal's fees and expenses in the proportion that the intervenor's claim against the property bears to the sum of all the claims asserted against the property. If any plaintiff permits vacation of an arrest, attachment, or garnishment, the remaining plaintiffs shall share the responsibility to the Marshal for fees and expenses in proportion to the remaining claims asserted against the property and for the duration of the Marshal's custody because of each such claim.

(e)12. Custody of Property.

(a) *Safekeeping of Property.* When a vessel or other property is brought into the Marshal's custody by arrest or attachment, the Marshal shall arrange for the adequate safekeeping, which may include the placing of keepers on or near the vessel. A substitute custodian in place of the Marshal may be appointed by order of the Court. An application seeking appointment of a substitute custodian shall be on notice to all parties and the Marshal and must show the name of the proposed substitute custodian, the location of the vessel during the period of such custody, and that adequate insurance coverage is in place.

(b) *Insurance.* The Marshal may order insurance to protect the Marshal, his deputies, keepers, and substitute custodians from liabilities assumed in arresting and holding the vessel, cargo, or other property, and in performing whatever services may be undertaken to protect the vessel, cargo, or other property and in maintaining the Court's custody. The arresting or attaching party shall reimburse the Marshal for premiums paid for the insurance and, where possible, shall be named as an additional insured on the policy. A party who applies for removal of the vessel, cargo, or other property to another location, for designation of a substitute custodian, or for other relief that will require an additional premium, shall reimburse the Marshal therefor. The initial party obtaining the arrest and holding of the property shall pay the premiums charged for the liability insurance in the first instance, but these premiums are taxable as administrative costs of the action while the vessel, cargo, or other property is in the custody of the Court.

(c)(1) Cargo Handling, Repairs, and Movement of the Vessel. Following arrest or attachment of a vessel, cargo handling shall be permitted to commence or continue unless the Court orders otherwise. No movement of or repairs to the vessel shall take place without order of the Court. The applicant for an order under this Rule shall give notice to the Marshal and to all parties of record.

(c)(2) Insurance. Upon any application under (c)(1) above, the moving party shall obtain and provide proof of adequate insurance coverage of the moving party to indemnify the Marshal for any liability arising out of such activity, and any such activity shall be at the cost and expense of the moving party and shall not be taxable as an administrative cost of the action, unless the Court orders otherwise. Before or after the Marshal has taken custody of a vessel, cargo, or other property, any party of record may move for an order to dispense with keepers or to remove or place the vessel, cargo, or other property at a specified facility, to designate a substitute custodian, or for similar relief. The moving party shall give notice of the motion to the Marshal and to all parties of record. The Court will require that the successor to the Marshal will maintain adequate insurances on the property before issuing the order to change arrangements.

(d) *Claims by Suppliers for Payment of Charges.* A person who furnishes supplies or services to a vessel, cargo, or other property in custody of the Court, who has not been paid and claims the right to payment as an expense of administration, shall submit an invoice to the Clerk in the form of a verified claim at any time before the vessel, cargo, or other property is released or sold. The supplier must serve copies of the claim on the Marshal, substitute custodian if one has been appointed, and all parties of record. The Court may consider the claims individually or schedule a single hearing for all claims.

(e)(13) Sale of Property.

(a) *Notice.* Unless otherwise ordered upon good cause shown or as provided by law, notice of sale of property in an action in rem shall be published as provided in LAR (g)(2) at least three (3) times during the period of time consisting of thirty (30) days prior to the day of the sale.

(b) *Payment of Bid.* These provisions apply unless otherwise ordered in the order of sale; the person whose bid is accepted shall immediately pay the Marshal the full purchase price if the bid is $1,000 or less. If the bid exceeds $1,000, the bidder shall immediately pay a deposit of at least $1,000 or 10% of the bid, whichever is greater, and shall pay the balance within three business days after the day on which the bid was accepted. If an objection to the sale or any upset bid permitted by the order of sale is filed within that period, the bidder is excused from paying the balance of the purchase price until three business days after the sale is approved. Payment shall be made in cash, by certified check, or by cashier's check drawn on

banks insured by the Federal Deposit Insurance Corporation or the Federal Savings and Loan Insurance Corporation.

(c) *Late Payment.* If the successful bidder does not pay the balance of the purchase price within the time allowed, the bidder shall pay the Marshal the cost of keeping the property from the due date until the balance is paid, and the Marshal may refuse to release the property until this charge is paid.

(d) *Default.* If the successful bidder does not pay the balance of the purchase price within the time allowed, the bidder shall be in default. In such a case, the Court may accept the second highest bid or arrange a new sale. The defaulting bidder's deposit shall be forfeited and applied to any additional costs that the Marshal incurs because of the default, the balance being retained in the registry of the Court awaiting further order of the Court.

(e) *Report of Sale by Marshal.* At the conclusion of the sale, the Marshal shall forthwith file a written report with the Court of the fact of sale, the date, the names and addresses, and bid amounts of the bidders, and any other pertinent information.

(f) *Time and Procedure for Objection to Sale.* An interested person may object to the sale by filing a written objection with the Clerk within three (3) business days following the sale, serving the objection on all parties of record, the successful bidder, and the Marshal, and depositing a sum with the Marshal that is sufficient to pay the expense of keeping the property for at least seven calendar days. If additional custodial expenses are required, the objector must furnish same forthwith, failing which, the objection shall be immediately dismissed. Payment to the Marshal shall be in cash, certified check, or cashier's check drawn on banks insured by the Federal Deposit Insurance Corporation or the Federal Savings and Loan Insurance Corporation.

(g) *Confirmation of Sale.* Unless an objection to the sale is filed, or any upset bid permitted by and conforming to the terms provided in the order of sale is filed, within three (3) business days of the sale, the sale shall be deemed confirmed without further order of the Court. The Clerk shall prepare and deliver to the Marshal a certificate of confirmation, and the Marshal shall transfer title to the confirmed purchaser only upon further order of the Court.

(h) *Disposition of Deposits.*

(1) Objection Sustained. If an objection is sustained, sums that the successful bidder deposited will be returned to the bidder forthwith. The sum that the objector deposited will be applied to pay the fees and expenses that the Marshal incurred in keeping the property until it is resold, and any balance remaining shall be returned to the objector. The objector will be

reimbursed from the proceeds of a subsequent sale for any expense of keeping the property.

(2) Objection Overruled. If the objection is overruled, the sum that the objector deposited will be applied to pay the expenses of keeping the property from the day the objection was filed until the day the sale is confirmed. Any balance remaining will be returned to the objector forthwith.

[Amended effective January 1, 2001; January 1, 2006; January 1, 2008.]

RULE F.   LIMITATION OF LIABILITY

(f)1.   Security for Costs. The amount of security for costs under Supplemental Rule F(1) shall be $1,000, and it may be combined with the security for value and interest, unless otherwise ordered.

(f)2.   Order of Proof at Trial. Where the vessel interests seeking statutory limitation of liability have raised the statutory defense by way of answer or complaint, the plaintiff in the former or the party asserting a claim against the vessel or owner in the latter shall proceed with its proof first, as is normal at civil trials.

[Amended effective January 1, 2001.]

RULE G.   SPECIAL RULES

(g)1.   Newspapers for Publishing Notices Unless the Court orders otherwise, every notice required to be published under the Local Admiralty Rules or any rules or statutes applying to admiralty and maritime proceedings shall be published in the following newspapers of general circulation in accordance with the L. R. 77.5.

(g)2.   Use of State Procedures. When the plaintiff invokes a state procedure in order to attach or garnish as the Federal Rules of Civil Procedure or the Supplemental Rules for Certain Admiralty and Maritime Claims permit, the process for attachment or garnishment shall identify the state law upon which the attachment or garnishment is based.

[Effective January 1, 2001; January 1, 2006.]

ELECTRONIC CASE FILING
ADMINISTRATIVE PROCEDURES FOR ELECTRONIC CASE FILING (GENERAL ORDER #22)
DATED: December 20, 2006

1. Definitions.

1.1. "All documents" means all documents traditionally filed with the Court excluding the hearing record in social security appeals and state court records submitted with a respondent's answer to a habeas corpus petition.

1.2. "Traditionally Filed Document" means a document or pleading presented to the Court for filing in paper or other non-electronic, tangible format.

1.3. "Electronic Filing" means uploading a pleading or document directly from the Filing User's computer using the Court's Internet-based Electronic Filing System (the "System") to file that pleading or document in the Court's case file.

1.4. "Filing User" is an individual who has a court-issued login and password to file documents electronically.

1.5. "Notice of Electronic Filing" means the notice that the System generates that establishes the electronic receipt of a document filed electronically with the System.

1.6. "Portable Document Format" or ".pdf format" means a type of document formatting that can be created with almost any word processing program. Scanned documents can also be converted to .pdf format. For information on converting word processing documents into .pdf text documents, users should visit the Court's web page at www.nynd.uscourts.gov or the websites of .pdf vendors such as http://www.adobe.com/products/acrobat or http://www.fineprint.com/.

1.7. ".pdf scanned document" means a document converted into .pdf format by means of a document scanner. ".pdf scanned documents" differ from ".pdf text documents" in that ".pdf scanned documents" are essentially pictures of the original documents and do not allow for text searches within those documents.

1.8. ".pdf text document" means a document converted from a word processing program (e.g., WordPerfect, Microsoft Word) directly into .pdf format without the use of a scanner. A ".pdf text document" is the preferred format for filing documents with the Court because a ".pdf text document" is considerably smaller in size and allows for text searches within that document.

2. Scope of Electronic Filing. After January 1, 2004, all documents that attorneys admitted to practice in the Northern District of New York submit for filing shall be filed electronically using the System or shall be scanned and uploaded to the System, no matter when a case was originally filed, unless these Administrative Procedures otherwise permit or unless the assigned judge otherwise authorizes. An attorney who is not a Filing User by January 1, 2004, must show good cause to the assigned judge to file and serve pleadings and other papers in the traditional manner. If the Court grants permission to file a document traditionally, the attorney must submit the documents for filing to the Clerk's Office on a 3.5″ disk or CD/ROM in .pdf format.

2.1. *Exceptions and/or Waivers from Mandatory Electronic Filing.* The following types of cases and/or documents are not required to be filed electronically:

1. If you are seeking to have your complaint filed under seal, please file your complaint and proposed sealing order traditionally at the Clerk's Office.

2. Any document that a party proceeding pro se files. (See Section 12.1 for procedural details).

3. Sealed documents, sealed cases, documents for in camera review, documents lodged with the Court, ex parte documents, confidential agreements, Qui Tam

actions and Grand Jury material and warrants must be filed traditionally. (See Section 12.2 for further information the filing of the above-referenced documents).

4. Social security transcripts. (See Section 11 for procedural details regarding filing papers in social security cases).

5. State court records submitted with a respondent's answer to a habeas corpus petition.

6. Discovery: In accordance with Local Rule 26.2, parties shall not file discovery, provided, however, that discovery material to be used at trial or in support of any motion, including a motion to compel or for summary judgment, shall be filed electronically with the Court prior to the trial or with the motion. Any motion pursuant to Rule 37 of the Federal Rules of Civil Procedure shall be accompanied by the electronically filed discovery materials to which the motion relates if those materials have not previously been filed with the Court.

7. Transport Orders: All orders requesting that an incarcerated individual be transported that a judicial officer of the Northern District of New York signs shall be filed traditionally. These Orders will not be filed with the case or uploaded to the docket but rather will be processed in accordance with the procedures that the Clerk of Court promulgates.

The Court may deviate from these Administrative Procedures in specific cases, without prior notice, if deemed appropriate in the exercise of discretion, considering the need for the just, speedy, and inexpensive determination of matters pending before the Court. The Court may require that courtesy copies of electronically filed documents be submitted for its review and may amend these Administrative Procedures at any time without prior notice. Updates to these Administrative Procedures will be immediately posted to the Court's web page at www.nynd. uscourts.gov.

3. Eligibility, Registration and Passwords.

3.1. *Eligibility.* An attorney admitted to practice and in good standing in the Northern District of New York must register as a Filing User unless these Administrative Procedures or the assigned judge otherwise authorizes. (See Section 2 for further information). To be in good standing, an attorney must meet the requirements of Local Rule 83.1, including timely payment of the biennial assessment imposed in Local Rule 83.1(a)(5).[1]

3.2. *Registration.* Attorneys meeting the requirements of section 3.1 of this Order and who were admitted to the Northern District of New York prior to December 1, 2003, may register for electronic filing via the Court's web page at www.nynd. uscourts.gov/cmecf/. Attorneys who meet the requirements of section 3.1 of this Order but who were admitted to the Northern District of New York after December 1, 2003, will need to complete and conventionally mail an E-filing Registration Form to the Clerk, U.S. District Court, c/o E-filing Registration, James Hanley Federal Building, P.O. Box 7367, 100 South Clinton Street, Syracuse, NY 13261. Copies of the E-Filing Registration Form are available at the Court's web page at www.nynd. uscourts.gov/cmecf/.

To ensure that the Clerk's Office has correctly entered a registering attorney's Internet e-mail address in the System, the Clerk's Office will send the attorney an Internet email message after receiving his or her E-filing Registration Form. Upon confirmation that the e-mail address is valid, the Clerk's Office will transmit the attorney's password to that address. Upon receipt of a password, attorneys have 10 days to activate their CM–ECF account with the Northern District. Detailed instructions on how to activate your CM–ECF account can be found on the District's web page at www.nynd.uscourt.gov/cmecf/ under the "Registration" section. Failure to comply with this requirement may result in the removal from the Northern District Bar. If a Filing User's e-mail address, mailing address, telephone or fax number change, they shall immediately update this information within their CM–

ECF user account. Detailed instructions are available in the Northern District of New York's CM/ECF Users Manual.

3.3. *Passwords.* Upon receiving their initial court-generated password, attorneys are encouraged to select a new password of their own choosing. Please consult the Court's CM/ECF Users Manual for detailed instructions on changing passwords. (See www.nynd.uscourts.gov/cmecf/).

The password permits the attorney to participate in the electronic retrieval and filing of pleadings and other papers. Once registered, the attorney shall be responsible for all documents filed with his or her password. Documents filed under an attorney's login and password shall constitute that attorney's signature for purposes of the Local and Federal Rules of Civil and Criminal Procedure, including but not limited to Rule 11 of the Federal Rules of Civil Procedure.

No attorney shall knowingly permit or cause to permit anyone other than an authorized employee of his or her office to use his or her password. If, at any time, an attorney believes that the security of an existing password has been compromised, the attorney must change his or her password immediately. In addition, the attorney shall immediately notify the Court via e-mail at the following address www. nynd.uscourts.gov of his or her belief that the password has been compromised.

4. Electronic Filing and Service of Documents.

4.1. *Filing Defined.* Electronic transmission of a document to the System in accordance with these Administrative Procedures, together with the transmission of a Notice of Electronic Filing from the Court, constitutes filing of the document for all purposes of the Federal Rules of Civil Procedure, the Federal Rules of Criminal Procedure and the Local Rules of this Court and constitutes entry of the document on the docket that the Clerk's Office keeps under Rules 58 and 79 of the Federal Rules of Civil Procedure and Rules 49 and 55 of the Federal Rules of Criminal Procedure. E-mailing a document to the Clerk's Office or to the assigned judge shall not constitute "filing" of the document.

4.2. *Complaints.* Effective January 1, 2007, all civil actions commenced by members of the Bar must be filed electronically in CM/ECF. The payment of the filing fee will be made through a secure United States Treasury Internet Credit Card site known as (Pay.Gov2). The attorney will log into CM/ECF and submit all initiating documents in .pdf format to a universal shell case "5:00-at-99999." The Clerk will transfer your case from the shell file, and assign a case number, district court judge and magistrate judge. Once the new case is opened by the Clerk you will receive a Notice of Electronic Filing (NEF).

Please note—the action will be filed as of the date that you paid the filing fee and uploaded the complaint into the shell case. In a case removed to this Court, parties are required to provide electronic copies of all documents previously filed in the underlying state court action. If you are seeking to have the filing fee waived, an In Forma Pauperis application should be filed as an attachment to the electronically filed civil complaint and you would answer "yes" at the IFP screen. If your initial complaint includes a motion for a TRO, please file the complaint with summons and civil cover sheet, motion for TRO and supporting documents as attachments, and call the Clerk's Office to notify of the filing.

4.3. *Time of Filing.* A document will be deemed timely filed if electronically filed prior to midnight Eastern Time. However, if the time of day is of the essence, the assigned judge may order that the document be filed by a time certain. New cases are deemed filed the day the Clerk's Office receives the complaint and required filing fee.

4.4. *Attachments and Exhibits.* A Filing User must submit in electronic form all documents referenced as exhibits or attachments in accordance with the Court's CM/ECF Users Manual unless the Court otherwise orders. A Filing User shall submit as exhibits or attachments only those excerpts of the referenced documents that are directly germane to the matter under the Court's consideration. Excerpted material must be clearly and prominently identified as such. Filing Users who file excerpts of documents as exhibits or attachments under these Administrative Procedures do so without prejudice to their right to timely file additional excerpts or the complete document. Responding parties may also timely file the complete document or additional excerpts that they believe are directly germane to the matter under the Court's consideration.

All attachments must be described in sufficient detail so the Court and opposing counsel can easily identify and distinguish the filed attachments. Vague or general descriptions are insufficient (i.e. "Exhibit 1"). Rather, each attachment shall have a descriptive title identifying, with specificity, the document that is being filed (i.e. "Exhibit 12 Mulligan County Fire Investigation Report.") Failure to adequately describe attachments may result in the document being rejected by the Court.

4.5. *Large Documents*. Due to the length of time it takes to download a large file, documents larger than four megabytes (approximately ninety pages of .pdf scanned documents) must be filed electronically in separate four-megabyte segments. For more information on the electronic filing of large documents, please consult the Court's CM/ECF Users Manual, which is available on the Court's web page at www. nynd.uscourts.gov/cmecf/.

A party who believes a document is too lengthy to electronically image, i.e., "scan," may contact the Clerk's Office for permission to file that document conventionally. If the Clerk's Office grants permission to conventionally file the document, the Filing User shall electronically file a notice of conventional filing for the documents. A form notice for this purpose can be obtained from the Court's web page at www.nynd. uscourts.gov. Exhibits submitted conventionally shall be served on other parties as if they were not subject to these Administrative Procedures. For a list of hints and tips for scanning large documents, please consult the Court's web page at www.nynd. uscourts.gov.

4.6. *Legibility*. It shall be the Filing User's responsibility to verify the legibility of scanned documents before filing them electronically with the Court.

4.7. *Color Documents*. Since documents scanned in color or containing a graphic take much longer to upload, Filing Users are encouraged to configure their scanners to scan documents at 200 dpi and preferably in black and white rather than in color. However, should the Filing User elect to file a color document, caution should be taken to ensure that the document does not exceed the size limitation set forth in section 4.5 of this Order.

4.8. *Document Retention*. The Filing User shall retain all documents containing original signatures of anyone other than the Filing User for a period of not less than sixty days after all dates for appellate review have expired.

5. Service.

5.1. *Service of Process*. Rule 5(b) of the Federal Rules of Civil Procedure and Rule 49(b) of the Federal Rules of Criminal Procedure do not permit electronic service of process for purposes of obtaining personal jurisdiction, i.e., Rule 4 Service. Therefore, service of process must be effected in the traditional manner.

5.2. *Service of Electronically–Filed Documents*. Whenever a pleading or other paper is filed electronically in accordance with these Administrative Procedures, the System shall generate a "Notice of Electronic Filing" to the Filing User and any other attorney who is a Filing User and has requested electronic notice in that case.

If the recipient is a Filing User, the System's e-mailing of the "Notice of Electronic Filing" shall be the equivalent of service of the pleading or other paper by first class mail, postage prepaid.

5.3. *Certificates of Service*. A certificate of service on all parties entitled to service or notice is still required when a party files a document electronically. The certificate must state the manner in which service or notice was accomplished on each party so entitled. A sample certificate of service is available on the Court's web page at www. nynd.uscourts.gov.

5.4. *Service of Electronically–Filed Documents Upon Non–Filing Users.* A party who is not a Filing User of the System is entitled to a paper copy of any electronically-filed pleading, document, or order. The Filing User must therefore provide the non-Filing User with the pleading or document according to the Federal Rules of Civil Procedure.[4]

5.5. *Time to Respond Under Electronic Service.* In accordance with Rule 6(e) of the Federal Rules of Civil Procedure and Rule 45(c) of the Federal Rules of Criminal Procedure, service by electronic means is treated the same as service by mail for purposes of adding three days to the prescribed period to respond.

6. Signatures.

6.1. *Attorney Signatures.* Documents filed under an attorney's login and password shall constitute that attorney's signature for purposes of the Local and Federal Rules of Civil and Criminal Procedure, including but not limited to Rule 11 of the Federal Rules of Civil Procedure.

A pleading or other document requiring an attorney's signature shall be signed in the following manner, whether filed electronically or submitted on disk or CD/ROM to the Clerk's Office: "s/ (attorney name)." The correct format for an attorney signature is as follows:

> s/Judith Attorney
> Judith Attorney Bar Number: 123456
> Attorney for (Plaintiff/Defendant)
> ABC Law Firm
> 123 South Street
> Albany, NY 12207
> Telephone: (518) 555-1234
> Fax: (518) 555-5678
> E-mail: judith_attorney@law.com

6.2. *Non–Attorney Signature.* If an original document requires the signature of a non-attorney, the Filing User may scan the original document containing the original signature(s), then electronically file it on the System. Alternatively, the Filing User may convert the document into .pdf text format and submit the document using "s/" for the signature of the non-attorney.

Please note, the Filing User shall retain all documents containing original signatures of anyone other than the Filing User for a period of not less than sixty days after all dates for appellate review have expired. Should the authenticity of the document be questioned, the presiding judge may require the Filing User to produce the original document.

6.3. *Multiple Signatures.* A document requiring signatures of more than one party must be filed electronically either by (1) submitting a scanned document containing all necessary signatures; (2) representing the consent of the other parties on the document; or (3) in any other manner that the Court approves.

6.4. *Authenticity Disputes.* A non-filing signatory or party who disputes the authenticity of an electronically-filed document with a non-attorney signature or the authenticity of the signature on that document must file an objection to the document within ten days of receiving the Notice of Electronic Filing, or, if a non-Filing User, within ten days of receiving the document.

7. Fees Payable to the Clerk. Any fee required for filing a pleading or paper in this Court is payable to the Clerk of the Court. The Court will not maintain electronic billing or debit accounts for attorneys or law firms. Effective January 1, 2007, payment for filing fees will be mandatory through CM/ECF's Internet Credit Card Payment site—a secure Treasury Site known as (Pay.Gov[2]) . The Filing User will be prompted to enter credit card information while filing the initial pleading. Any document that requires a filing fee (e.g. Notice of Appeal, Motion for Pro Hac Vice Admission) may also be paid by credit card through Pay.Gov.

8. Orders. The assigned judge or the Clerk's Office shall electronically file all signed orders. Upon filing, the System will send a "Notice of Electronic Filing" to all Filing Users in that case. The Clerk's Office will send a paper copy of the order along with the "Notice of Electronic Filing" to non-Filing Users in the case. Any order signed electronically has the same force and effect as if the judge had affixed the judge's signature to a paper copy of the order and the order had been entered on the docket conventionally.

8.1. *Text–Only Orders.* The assigned judge or the Clerk's Office, if appropriate, may grant routine orders by a text-only entry upon the docket. In such cases, no .pdf document will issue; the text-only entry shall constitute the Court's only order on the matter. These text-only orders shall have the same force and effect as if the judge had affixed the judge's signature to a paper copy of the order and the order had been entered on the docket conventionally.

The System will generate a "Notice of Electronic Filing" as described in Section 1.5 of these Administrative Procedures. The Clerk's Office will send a paper copy of the text-only order to non-Filing Users in the case.

8.2. *Submitting a Proposed Order or Stipulation.* A document that is submitted in .pdf format cannot be modified; therefore, a proposed order or stipulation must be in a word processing format. The chambers of the assigned judge may request that a proposed order and/or a stipulation be e-mailed to the courtroom deputy for the presiding judge in either WordPerfect or Microsoft Word format. Please attach your proposed order and/or stipulation to an Internet e-mail sent to the appropriate e-mail address as listed below:

> Chief Judge Scullin NYND_FJS_ECF_NOTICES@nynd.uscourts.gov
> Judge Kahn NYND_LEK_ECF_NOTICES@nynd.uscourts.gov
> Judge Hurd NYND_DNH_ECF_NOTICES@nynd.uscourts.gov
> Judge Mordue NYND_NAM_ECF_NOTICES@nynd.uscourts.gov
> Judge Sharpe NYND_GLS_ECF_NOTICES@nynd.uscourts.gov
> Judge Munson NYND_HGM_ECF_NOTICES@nynd.uscourts.gov
> Judge McCurn NYND_NPM_ECF_NOTICES@nynd.uscourts.gov
> Judge McAvoy NYND_TJM_ECF_NOTICES@nynd.uscourts.gov
> Mag. Judge DiBianco NYND_GJD_ECF_NOTICES@nynd.uscourts.gov
> Mag. Judge Homer NYND_DRH_ECF_NOTICES@nynd.uscourts.gov
> Mag. Judge Peebles NYND_DEP_ECF_NOTICES@nynd.uscourts.gov
> Mag. Judge Treece NYND_RFT_ECF_NOTICES@nynd.uscourts.gov
> Mag. Judge Lowe NYND_GHL_ECF_NOTICES@nynd.uscourts.gov
> Prisoner Pro Se NYND_ILU_ECF_NOTICES@nynd.uscourts.gov

9. Correcting Docket Entries. Once a document is submitted and becomes part of the case docket (i.e., the Filing User receives a Notice of Electronic Filing), only the Clerk's Office can make corrections to that docket entry. In other words, the System will not permit the Filing User to make changes to the document(s) or docket entry filed in error once the transaction has been accepted.

Please consult the Court's CM/ECF Users Manual for detailed instructions on correcting docket errors. (See www.nynd.uscourts.gov/cmecf/). A document incorrectly filed in a case may be the result of posting the wrong .pdf document to a docket entry or selecting the wrong document type from the menu or entering the wrong case number and not catching the error before the transaction is completed. The Filing User should not attempt to refile the document.

As soon as possible after an error is discovered, the Filing User should contact the Clerk's Office with the case number and document number for which it is requesting a correction. If appropriate, the Court will make an entry indicating that the document was filed in error. The Clerk's Office will notify the Filing User if the document needs to be refiled.

10. Technical Failures.

10.1. *Technical Failure of the System.* The Clerk's Office shall deem the Court's CM/ECF site to be subject to a technical failure on a given day if the site is unable to accept filings continuously or intermittently over the course of any period of time greater than one hour after 10:00 a.m. that day. Known systems outages will be posted on the Court's web page, if possible.

If the Court's CM/ECF site experiences a technical failure, a Filing User may submit documents to the Court that day in an alternate manner provided that the documents are accompanied by the Filing User's affidavit stating that the Filing User attempted to file electronically at least two times in one hour increments after 10:00 a.m. that day. The following methods are acceptable alternate means for filing documents in case of a technical failure:

A) via electronic mail in a PDF attachment sent to the e-mail address for technical failures (See www.nynd.uscourts.gov/cmecf/); or

B) in person, by bringing the document to the Clerk's Office on paper accompanied by a 3.5″ disk or CD/ROM that contains the document in .pdf format.

A Filing User, whose filing is untimely as the result of a technical failure of the Court's CM/ECF site, may seek appropriate relief from the Court. However, Filing Users are cautioned that, in some circumstances, the Court lacks the authority to grant an extension of time to file (e.g., Rule 6(b) of the Federal Rules of Civil Procedure).

10.2. *Technical Failure of the Filing User's System.* Problems with the Filing User's system, such as phone line problems, problems with the Filing User's Internet Service Provider ("ISP"), or hardware or software problems, will not constitute a technical failure under these Administrative Procedures nor excuse an untimely filing. A Filing User who cannot file documents electronically because of a problem on the Filing User's system must file the documents conventionally along with an affidavit explaining the reason for not filing the documents electronically.

11. Public Access and Privacy Concerns.

11.1. *Social Security Case Information.* The public may retrieve information from the System at the Court's Internet site by obtaining a PACER login and password. See Section 13.2 for more information regarding PACER. In accordance with the policy of the Judicial Conference, social security cases are not available for public view over the Internet. Although docket sheets will be available to the Public via PACER, only counsel in the case may view documents which have been filed electronically.

11.2. *Sensitive Information.* As the public may access certain case information over the Internet through the Court's Internet site, sensitive information should not be included in any document filed with the Court unless such inclusion is necessary and relevant to the case.

Parties shall refrain from including, or shall redact where inclusion is necessary, the following personal identifiers from all pleadings filed with the Court, including exhibits thereto, whether filed electronically or in paper form, unless the Court orders otherwise.

1. Social security numbers. If an individual's social security number must be included in a document, use only the last four digits of that number.

2. Names of minor children. If the involvement of a minor child must be mentioned, use only the initials of that child.

3. Dates of birth. If an individual's date of birth must be included in a document, use only the year.

4. Financial account numbers. If financial account numbers are relevant, use only the last four digits of those numbers.

5. Home Addresses. If a home address must be used, use only the City and State.

In addition, caution shall be exercised when filing documents that contain the following:

1) personal identifying number, such as a driver's license number;

2) medical records, treatment and diagnosis;

3) employment history;

4) individual financial information; and

5) proprietary or trade secret information.

Counsel is strongly urged to discuss this issue with all their clients so that an informed decision about the inclusion of certain information may be made. The responsibility for redacting these personal identifiers rests solely with counsel and the parties. The Clerk will not review each pleading for compliance with this Rule. Counsel and the parties are cautioned that failure to redact these personal identifiers may subject them to the Court's full disciplinary power.

11.3. *Filing Under the E–Government Act of 2002.* In compliance with the E-Government Act of 2002, a party wishing to file a document containing the personal data identifiers listed above may

a. file an unredacted version of the document under seal, or

b. file a reference list under seal. The reference list shall contain the complete personal data identifier(s) and the redacted identifier(s) used in its (their) place in the filing. All references in the case to the redacted identifiers included in the reference list will be construed to refer to the corresponding complete personal data identifier. The reference list must be filed under seal and may be amended as of right. Please refer to section 12.2 of this Order for the proper procedure for filing a document under seal.

12. Documents that will continue to be traditionally filed.

12.1. *Pro Se Filers.* Pro se filers shall file paper originals of all complaints, pleadings, motions, affidavits, briefs, and other documents which must be signed or which require either verification or an unsworn declaration under any rule or statute. The Clerk's Office will scan these original documents into an electronic file in the System but will also maintain a paper file.

Pro se filers may also provide the Court with a 3.5″ disk or CD/ROM containing their documents as either .pdf text documents or .pdf scanned documents.

12.2. *Sealed Documents, Sealed Cases, Documents Presented for In Camera Review, and Documents Lodged with the Court.* If a party wishes to file one of the above listed documents, the party must file a motion or application to achieve the desired action. The motion or application, along with the documents the party is requesting to be sealed or lodged with the Court, shall be filed in a traditional manner in a sealed envelope marked "sealed." Unless the motion is being filed ex parte, the filing party shall conventionally serve all parties with the papers being filed with the Court.

If the Court grants the motion or application, the assigned judge will enter electronically the order authorizing the filing of the documents in the appropriate manner (e.g., under seal, lodged with the Court). The Clerk's Office will then file the documents in the appropriate manner.

If the Court denies the motion or application, the Court will issue an order that directs the parties to file the documents electronically.

13. **Public Access to the System Docket.**

13.1. *Public Access at the Court.* Electronic access to the electronic docket and documents filed in the System is available for viewing to the public at no charge at the Clerk's Office during regular business hours. A copy fee for an electronic reproduction is required in accordance with 28 U.S.C. § 1930.

13.2. *Internet Access.* Remote electronic access to the System for viewing purposes is limited to subscribers to the Public Access to Court Electronic Records ('PACER') system. The Judicial Conference of the United States has ruled that a user fee will be charged for remotely accessing certain detailed case information, such as filed documents and docket sheets in civil cases.[3] Application forms and information on PACER can be found on the Court's web page at www.nynd.uscourts.gov.[4]

13.3. *Conventional Copies and Certified Copies.* Conventional copies and certified copies of electronically filed documents may be purchased at the Clerk's Office. The fee for copying and certifying will be in accordance with 28 U.S.C. § 1914.

[1] L.R 83.1(a)(5) waives the biennial registration fee for all attorneys employed by federal, state and local public sector entities.

[2] Note—If the Pay.Gov system is down for any reason, new civil complaints can still be filed at any office of the Clerk by providing the Clerk with your initiating documents on a disc in .pdf format. For additional information on Pay.Gov, please visit our website at www.nynd.uscourts.gov.

[3] According to a memorandum from the Administrative Office of the United States Courts dated October 21, 2004, non-judiciary CM/ECF users will be charged a fee of eight cents per page beginning January 1, 2005, to access electronic data such as docket sheets and case documents obtained remotely through the PACER system. A cap of thirty pages per document has been approved. The access fee does not apply to official recipients of electronic documents, i.e., parties legally required to receive service or to whom the Filing User has directed service in the context of service under the Federal Rules of Civil Procedure. Filing Users will receive the initial electronic copy of a document free to download as they see fit, but if they remotely access the document again, they will be charged eight cents per page.

[4] To determine whether another party is a Filing User, the filing party can select the System's "Utilities" category, and then click on "Mailing Information for a Case" on the pull-down menu. The filing party then enters the case number and the System information will appear, stating whether or not the filer must mail a copy of the documents or if the System will electronically generate a 'Notice of Electronic Filing' to a particular party.

[Amended December 20, 2006.]

NOTICE REGARDING PRIVACY AND PUBLIC ACCESS TO ELECTRONIC CIVIL AND CRIMINAL CASE FILES

Effective January 1, 2004, the Office of the Clerk will accept electronically-filed documents and will make the content of those documents available on the Court's Internet webpage via PACER (Public Access to Court Electronic Records). Any subscriber to PACER will be able to read, download, store and print the full contents of the electronically-filed documents. The Clerk's Office is not posting documents sealed or otherwise restricted by court order (*See also General Order #22*).

You should not include sensitive information in any document filed with the Court unless such inclusion is necessary and relevant to the case. You must remember that any personal information not otherwise protected will be made available over the Internet via PACER. If sensitive information must be included, the following personal identifiers must be partially redacted from the document, whether it is filed traditionally or electronically.

• Social Security Numbers. If an individual's social security number must be included in a document, only the last four digits of that number should be used.

• Names of Minor Children. If the involvement of a minor child must be mentioned, only the initials of that child should be used.

• Dates of Birth. If an individual's of birth must be included in a document, only the year should be used.

• Financial Account Numbers. If financial account numbers are relevant, only the last four digits of these numbers should be used.

● Home Addresses. If home addresses must be used, use only the City and State.

In compliance with the E–Government Act, a party wishing to file a document containing the personal data identifiers listed above may file an unredacted document under seal. The Court shall retain this document as part of the record. The Court may, however, still require the party to file a redacted copy for the electronic[1] public file.

In addition, exercise caution when filing documents that contain the following:

● personal identifying number, such as a driver's license number

● medical records, treatment and diagnosis

● employment history

● individual financial information

● proprietary or trade secret information

● information regarding an individual's cooperation with the government

Counsel is strongly urged to share this notice with all clients so that an informed decision about the inclusion, redaction and/or exclusion of certain materials may be made. *If is the sole responsibility of counsel and the parties* to be sure that all documents comply with the rules of this Court requiring redaction of personal identifiers. The Clerk will not review each document for compliance with this rule. (*See also NDNY Local Civil Rule 8.1 and Criminal Rule 12.1(g)*).

Effective January 1, 2004.

[1] Please note that transcripts of the administrative record in social security proceedings and state court records relating to habeas corpus petitions are exempt from this requirement and shall not be made available in electronic format.

NOTICE TO MEMBERS OF THE NORTHERN DISTRICT BAR REGARDING ELECTRONIC AVAILABILITY OF CIVIL AND CRIMINAL TRANSCRIPTS

Transcripts of proceedings before the U.S. District Judges and Magistrate Judges in the Northern District of New York have been electronically filed in CM/ECF since **February 13, 2006**. Effective, **April 28, 2008**, this procedure changes slightly as outlined below.

Electronic transcripts, once ordered by a party or attorney and produced by the Court Reporter, will be e-filed and available for viewing at the Clerk's Office public terminal, but may NOT be copied or reproduced by the Clerk's Office for a period of 90 days. After the expiration of the 90–day deadline, if no redactions have been made, the restrictions on the transcript will be removed. The transcript will be available remotely to view, download or print a copy

from PACER at \$.08 per page or from the Clerk's Office at a rate of \$.10 per page. During the initial 90–day period, individuals wishing to purchase a copy of the transcript must do so through the Court Reporter. Once an attorney in the case has purchased a transcript, the attorney will be given access to the transcript through the court's CM/ECF system.

This policy will apply to all transcripts of proceedings or parts of proceedings ordered on or after April 28, 2008, regardless of when the proceeding took place. Please read this policy carefully. This policy establishes a procedure for counsel to request the redaction from the transcript of specific personal data identifiers before the transcript is made electronically available to the general public.

PLEASE READ THIS POLICY CAREFULLY

The policy establishes a procedure for counsel to request the redaction from the transcript of specific personal data identifiers before the transcript is made electronically available to the general public. The party who calls a witness to the stand, or referred to and read from a document submitted in evidence, is responsible for requesting redaction. If a judge asks a question requiring later redaction, the party who called the witness remains responsible for the redaction.

√ A party must file a **Notice of Intent to Request Redaction** within **five** (5) business days of the filing of the official transcript by the court reporter. **NOTE**: If a party fails to request redaction within this time frame, the transcript may be made electronically available without redaction. A copy of the officially filed transcript will be available for review from the clerk's office public terminal or for purchase from the court reporter during this five-day period. This copy of the transcript(s) may be in paper or electronic format. **Reference**: A Notice of Intent to Request Redaction form is available on the court's website at www.nynd.uscourts.gov.

√ If a party files a Notice of Intent To Request Redaction, the transcript will not be made remotely electronically available to the general public until the redactions are performed. **NOTE**: A copy of the officially filed transcript will be available for review from the clerk's office public terminal or purchase from the court reporter / transcriber during this time.

√ Following the filing of a Notice of Intent to Request Redaction, the parties have **twenty-one** (21) calendar days from the filing of the transcript with the clerk, or longer if ordered by the court, **the parties must file a Redaction Request indicating where the personal identifiers appear in the transcript by page and line and how they are to be redacted**. For example, if a party wanted to redact the Social Security number 123–45–6789 appearing on page 12, line 9 of the transcript, the statement would read: "Redact the Social Security number on page 12, line 9 to read xxx-xx–6789." A party is only responsible for reviewing and indicating the redactions in the testimony of the witnesses it called and its own statements (e.g. opening statements and closing arguments). **Only the personal identifiers listed in the Judicial Conference Policy on the Electronic Availability of Transcripts may be automatically redacted (*see attachment*).** If a party wants to redact other information, that party should move the court for further redaction by separate motion served on all parties and the court reporter or transcriber within the twenty-one (21) day period. **NOTE**: Counsel appointed pursuant to the Criminal Justice Act may claim compensation, at the applicable rate, for the time spent reviewing the transcript and preparing the request for redaction, as well as for costs associated with obtaining a copy of the transcript.

NOTE: If a party fails to file a Redaction Request within this time frame, the transcript will be made remotely electronically available to the general public without redaction following the expiration of the 90–day deadline.

REQUESTS FOR TRANSCRIPTS

√ Any party ordering a transcript shall serve a copy of the Request for Transcript form on all other parties. A request for Transcript form is available on the court's website at www.nynd.uscourts.gov.

Please direct all questions concerning the court's policy to our CM/ECF Help Desk.

Help Desk Numbers

(315) 234–8687—**Syracuse**

(518) 257–1815—**Albany**

(607) 779–2671—**Binghamton**

(315) 266–1195—**Utica**

Attachment

Attachment 1. Electronic Availability of Transcripts of Court Proceedings

Courts making electronic documents remotely available to the public, whether documents are filed electronically or converted to electronic form, shall make electronic transcripts of proceedings remotely available to the public if such transcripts are otherwise prepared.

Within five business days of the filing by the court reporter/transcriber of the official transcript with the clerk's office pursuant to 28 U.S.C. § 753, each party shall inform the court, by filing a notice of redaction with the clerk, of the party's intent to redact personal data identifiers from the electronic transcript of the court proceeding. Such personal data identifiers include: Social Security numbers; financial account numbers; names of minor children; dates of birth; and home addresses of individuals. The filing of this notice triggers the procedures set out below. If no such notice is filed within the allotted time, the court will assume redaction of personal data identifiers from the transcript is not necessary, and the transcript will be made electronically available after the 90–day period.

If a notice of redaction is filed by any party, following the filing of the official transcript with the clerk's office, the official transcript is not to be made remotely electronically available to the general public. Within 21 calendar days of the filing of the transcript, or longer if the court so orders, the parties shall submit to the court reporter/transcriber a statement indicating where the following personal data identifiers appear in the transcript: Social Security numbers; financial account numbers; names of minor children; dates of birth; and home addresses of individuals.

The court reporter/transcriber shall partially redact these personal data identifiers from the electronic transcript as follows:

- Social Security numbers to the last four digits;
- financial account numbers to the last four digits;
- dates of birth to the year;
- names of minor children to the initials; and
- home addresses to the city and state.

During the 21–day period, or longer if the court so orders, attorneys may move the court for any additional redactions to the transcript. The transcript shall not be electronically disseminated until the court has ruled upon any such motion.

Effective April 28, 2008.

CHAPTER 12 BANKRUPTCY RULES SUPPLEMENT

Pub. Note: The Bankruptcy Judges of the Northern District have approved the Chapter 12 Interim Rules suggested by the Committee on Rules of Practice and Procedure in February, 1987. The Chapter 12 Interim Rules are reproduced in this volume following the Rules for the Division of Business Among District Judges for the Southern and Eastern Districts, ante.

*

LOCAL BANKRUPTCY RULES FOR THE UNITED STATES BANKRUPTCY COURT FOR THE NORTHERN DISTRICT OF NEW YORK

Effective January 1, 1998

Including Amendments Received Through
September 15, 2008

Research Note

These rules may be searched electronically on Westlaw in the NY-RULES database; updates to these rules may be found on Westlaw in NY-RULESUPDATES. For search tips, and a detailed summary of database content, consult the Westlaw Scope Screen of each database.

Rule

1001–1. Short Title—Applicability.
1002–1. Petition—General.
1003–1. Involuntary Petitions [Filing Requirements].
1004–1. Petition—Partnership.
1006–1. Fees—Advance Payment or Advance Permission to Charge on File Credit Card.
1006–2. Fees—Installment Payments.
1007–1. Statement of Social Security Number.
1007–2. Mailing—List or Matrix.
1007–3. Notice to Creditors Omitted From or Incorrectly Listed on Master Mailing Matrix.
1009–1. Amendments to Lists, Schedules, Statements & Mailing Matrices.
1011–1. Responsive Pleading—Consent to Involuntary Petition.
1014–1. Interdistrict Transfer of Cases or Proceedings.
1015–1. Joint Administration and Consolidation.
1017–3. Dismissed Case—Motion to Vacate Order of Dismissal or to Reinstate.
1019–1. Conversion—Procedure Following.
1073–1. Assignment of Cases and Adversary Proceedings/Intra–District.
2002–1. Noticing to Creditors & Other Interested Parties.
2014–1. Employment of Professionals.
2015–2. Debtor in Possession Duties.
2015–6. Debtor in Possession Duties—Chapter 11 Affidavit.
2016–1. Compensation of Professionals.
2016–2. Chapter 13—Compensation of Professionals.
2090–1. Attorneys—Admission to Practice/Designation for Service.
2091–1. Attorneys—Withdrawals—Other than by Substitution.
2092–1. Attorneys—Substitution.
3001–1. Claims and Equity Security Interests—Asset Cases.
3001–2. Claims and Equity Security Interests—No Asset Cases.
3002–1. Third Party Processing of Claims (Claims Agents).

Rule

3007–1. Claims—Objections.
3012–1. Valuation of Collateral.
3015–1. Chapters 12 & 13—Plan.
3015–2. Chapters 12 and 13—Amendments or Modifications to Plans.
3015–3. Chapters 12 and 13—Confirmation.
3015–4. Chapters 12 and 13—Objections to Confirmation.
3015–5. Chapter 13—Administration of Payroll Deduction Orders.
3016–1. Chapter 11—Plan.
3016–2. Disclosure Statement—General.
3017–1. Disclosure Statement—Approval.
3018–1. Ballots—Voting on Plans.
3019–1. Chapter 11—Amendments to Plans.
3020–1. Chapter 11—Confirmation.
3021–1. Chapter 11—Affidavit Reporting Post Confirmation Disbursements.
3022–1. Chapter 11—Final Report/Decree.
4001–1. Automatic Stay—Relief From.
4001–3. Obtaining Credit.
4001–4. Chapters 12 and 13—Obtaining Credit.
4002–2. Address of Debtor.
4080–1. Chapters 12 and 13—Emergency Refund or Credit.
5005–1. Place of Filing.
5005–4. Electronic Filing.
5005–5. Electronic Case Filing (ECF) Passwords.
5005–6. Privacy.
5010–1. Reopening Cases.
5011–1. Withdrawal of Reference.
5073–1. Photography, Recording Devices & Broadcasting.
5080–1. Fees—General.
6004–1. Sale of Estate Property.
6004–2. Chapters 12 and 13—Sale or Other Disposition of Estate Property.
6005–1. Appraisers and Auctioneers.
6007–1. Abandonment [Disposition of Property].
7003–1. Cover Sheet.
7004–2. Summons.

Rule
7016–1. Pretrial Procedures.
7026–1. Discovery—General.
7026–2. Discovery Motions.
7033–1. Interrogatories to Parties.
7056–1. Summary Judgment.
7067–1. Registry Fund.
7090–1. Discontinuance and Settlement of Actions Objecting to Discharge and Dischargeability of Debts.
7091–1. Adjournments.
8005–1. Stay Pending Appeal [Supersedeas Bond].
8016–2. Notice of Order or Judgment—Appeal.
9001–1. Definitions.
9004–1. Papers—Requirements of Form.
9004–2. Caption—Papers, General.
9010–1. Attorneys—Notice of Appearance.
9010–3. Attorneys—Debtor Corporations.
9011–1. Attorneys—Duties.
9011–2. Pro Se Parties.
9011–3. Signatures and Electronic Filing.
9013–1. Motion Practice.
9013–2. Briefs & Memoranda of Law.
9013–3. Certificate of Service—Motions.
9013–4. Default Motion Practice.
9013–5. Orders, Including Ex Parte Orders, Orders to Show Cause and Orders Shortening Time.
9015–1. Jury Trial.
9019–2. Alternative Dispute Resolution (ADR).
9021–1. Judgments & Orders—Entry of.
9022–1. Judgments & Orders—Notice of.

Rule
9025–1. Sureties.
9027–1. Removal and Remand.
9034–1. Notice to and Service upon the United States Trustee.
9070–1. Exhibits.

APPENDICES
App.
I. Assignment Location and Hearing Location*.
II. Mediation Program for the U.S. Bankruptcy Court, Northern District of New York.

ADMINISTRATIVE ORDERS
Order
02–03. Procedural Rules for Electronic Case Filing.
03–01. Electronic Case Filing.
05–02. Adoption of Interim Bankruptcy Rules[1].
05–03. Disbursement of § 1326 Pre–Confirmation Adequate Protection Payments in Chapter 13 Cases Filed on and after October 17, 2005.
07–04. Increase to Transcript Fee Rates.
07–05. Issuance of Chapter 13 Discharges.
08–01. Debtor Counsel Fees in Chapter 13 Cases Filed in the Albany Division.

FEDERAL RULES OF BANKRUPTCY PROCEDURE INTERIM BANKRUPTCY RULES

RULE 1001–1. SHORT TITLE— APPLICABILITY

(a) Short Title. These local rules shall be known as the Local Bankruptcy Rules for the Northern District of New York and may be referred to and cited in papers filed in this court as Local Bankruptcy Rule __-__ or LBR__-__.

(b) Applicability. The Local Bankruptcy Rules supplement the Federal Rules of Bankruptcy Procedure. Except for those cases filed in Poughkeepsie by residents of Columbia, Green and Ulster counties, these Local Bankruptcy Rules shall govern all proceedings in bankruptcy cases hereafter filed in the Northern District of New York. As to Northern District cases pending by debtors who are residents of Columbia, Green and Ulster counties which were previously assigned to the judge sitting in Poughkeepsie, the Local Bankruptcy Rules for the Southern District of New York shall govern.

[Effective January 1, 1998. Amended effective October 24, 2005.]

Comment

Under the authority of Fed. R. Bankr. P. 9029, the district court may make and amend rules of practice and procedure not inconsistent with the Federal Rules of Bankruptcy Procedure and which do not prohibit or limit the use of the official forms.

These Local Bankruptcy Rules, effective October 24, 2005, supersede and rescind the Local Bankruptcy Rules adopted October 27, 1994 and January 1, 1998. A numbering system is employed which corresponds each rule to the most closely associated Federal Rule of Bankruptcy Procedure, in conformity with the Uniform Numbering System prescribed by the Judicial Conference of the United States.

There may be administrative orders issued by a judge which may have the effect of modifying or abrogating one or more of these Local Bankruptcy Rules. A list of administrative orders will be available on the court's internet web site which can be located at http://www.nynb.uscourts.gov.

RULE 1002–1. PETITION—GENERAL

(a) Electronic Case Filing and Signatures. Under Electronic Case Filing (ECF) and the Case Management (CM) system, original paper documents are no longer routinely accepted for filing. The requirement that petitions, verifications, resolutions, declarations, etc. be signed is met by an electronic signature. An electronic signature is considered to be the original signature upon the filed documents for all purposes under the Bankruptcy Code, relevant federal and state statutes, and applicable federal rules. Pro Se debtors will be permitted to file petitions and other documents conventionally.

(b) Where to File. Petitions may be filed electronically with the clerk or in any office of the clerk. Attorney filers may also use public scanners and computers located at the Public Intake Counter.

(c) Number of Copies to be Filed. The filing of multiple copies of petitions, lists, schedules and statements is not required.

(d) Corporate Resolution. A voluntary petition filed by a corporation shall be accompanied by a copy of the corporate resolution or other appropriate authorization, duly attested to, authorizing such filing.

(e) LLC Authority. A voluntary petition filed by a limited liability company shall be accompanied by a copy of the appropriate authorization, duly attested to, authorizing such filing.

(f) Deficient Petitions and Papers—Notice of Deficient Filing. The Clerk can issue a notice specifying deficiencies.

(g) Dismissal of Petition. The failure to comply with the requirements of this rule may subject the case to dismissal. The petition may be dismissed/stricken without a hearing if:

(1) the petition is not signed by the debtor(s);

(2) the party filing the petition does not pay the filing fee with the petition or does not file an application to pay filing fees in installments, if eligible to do so;

(3) the debtor does not file the master mailing matrix with the petition;

(4) a voluntary petition is filed without the debtor's social security number being provided.

[Effective January 1, 1998. Amended effective October 24, 2005.]

Comment

Although Fed. R. Bankr. P. 5005(a)(1) requires the clerk to accept papers for filing which are not in proper form, subsection (g) of this local rule makes clear that the court may take appropriate action to enforce this rule.

RULE 1003–1. INVOLUNTARY PETITIONS [FILING REQUIREMENTS]

(a) Number of Copies. The filing of multiple copies of petitions, lists, schedules and statements is not required.

(b) Matrix. An involuntary petition shall be accompanied by a matrix, in proper form as set forth in Local Bankruptcy Rule 1007–2(a), containing the name and address, including zip codes and any post office addresses of all petitioning creditors, any attor-

neys for petitioning creditors and other parties in interest.

(c) Certification of Matrix. The matrix required by subsection (b) shall be certified in the manner directed in Local Bankruptcy Rule 1007–2(f).

(d) Noncompliance. The failure to comply with the requirements of this rule may subject the case to dismissal.

[Effective January 1, 1998. Amended effective October 24, 2005.]

Comment

Although Fed. R. Bankr. P. 5005(a)(1) requires the clerk to accept papers for filing which are not in proper form, subsection (d) of this rule makes clear that the court may take appropriate action to enforce this rule.

RULE 1004–1. PETITION—PARTNERSHIP

(a) Partnership Declaration. A voluntary petition filed by a partnership shall be accompanied by appropriate authorization, duly attested to by all general partners, authorizing such filing.

(b) LLP Authority. A voluntary petition filed by a limited liability partnership shall be accompanied by a copy of the appropriate authorization, duly attested to, authorizing such filing.

(c) Noncompliance. The failure to comply with the requirements of this rule may subject the case to dismissal.

[Effective January 1, 1998. Amended effective October 24, 2005.]

Comment

This rule should be read in conjunction with Fed. R. Bankr. P. 1004, which permits a voluntary petition to be signed by less than all general partners, if all general partners consent.

Although Fed. R. Bankr. P. 5005(a)(1) requires the clerk to accept papers for filing which are not in proper form, subsection (c) of this local rule makes clear that the court may take appropriate action to enforce this rule.

RULE 1006–1. FEES—ADVANCE PAYMENT OR ADVANCE PERMISSION TO CHARGE ON FILE CREDIT CARD

The Clerk is not required to render any service for which a fee is legally collectible unless the fee for the particular service is paid in advance or an on file credit card is available. The use of any on file credit card is only for the purpose of making payment for electronically filed documents.

[Effective January 1, 1998. Amended effective October 24, 2005.]

RULE 1006–2. FEES–INSTALLMENT PAYMENTS

Unless otherwise ordered by the court, the clerk shall not be required to render any service for which a fee is prescribed, either by statute or by the Judicial Conference of the United States, including the acceptance of a document for filing, unless the fee for that service is paid in advance, or an order is granted pursuant to Fed. R. Bankr. P. 1006(b)(1) to pay the filing fee for a voluntary petition by an individual in installments.

Comment

Filing fees for the commencement of a case under the respective chapters of the Bankruptcy Code are set forth in 28 U.S.C. § 1930(a). Filing fees for the commencement of an adversary proceeding are authorized by 28 U.S.C. § 1930(b) and set forth in the Judicial Conference Schedule of Fees.

RULE 1007–1. STATEMENT OF SOCIAL SECURITY NUMBER

(a) Verified Statement of Full Social Security Number. FRBP 1007(f) requires the debtor to submit a verified statement (Official Form B21) of his or her full social security number. The statement is not filed in the case and does not become a part of the court record or the public record.

(b) Submission with Conventionally Filed Petitions. When petitions are filed conventionally with the court the debtor is required to submit the original signed statement to the court contemporaneously with the filing of the petition.

(c) Submission with Electronically Filed Petitions. When petitions are filed electronically, the debtor is required to sign the statement of full social security number. The debtor's attorney is required to retain the original with his or her records. The form is not to be filed electronically with the petition and is not required to be submitted to the court.

(d) Amendment of Social Security Number. When the debtor's attorney files a petition electronically and incorrectly enters the debtor's social security number into the ECF system, or if the petition is filed with an incorrect social security number, the debtor's attorney must take steps to correct the error. The attorney shall:

(1) Submit, in paper, to the court an Amended Statement of Social Security number indicating the full and correct social security number. Indicate both the incorrect social security number and the corrected social security number.

(2) Serve all creditors, the Chapter 7 or 13 trustee, and the United States trustee with the amended statement.

(3) File with the court a completed certificate of service by mail, certifying service of the amended

statement upon all creditors, the Chapter 7 or 13 trustee and the United States trustee. Attach to the certificate of service a list of all creditors, their names and addresses as well as the Chapter 7 or 13 trustee name and address. The certificate of service can be filed electronically.

(4) If the error affects the last four digits of the social security number, in addition to submitting an amended statement of social security number with the court, also file an amended petition with the court showing the corrected last four digits of the social security number. The amendment is to be noticed and served as indicated in steps 2 and 3 above. The amended petition can be filed electronically.

[Effective January 1, 1998. Amended effective October 24, 2005.]

RULE 1007–2. MAILING— LIST OR MATRIX

(a) Matrix. Any list of creditors, schedule of liabilities or list of equity security holders required to be filed pursuant to Fed. R. Bankr. P. 1007 shall be accompanied by a matrix containing the name and address of all creditors and other parties in interest. Each such matrix shall be submitted in proper form compatible with the court's automated case management system (CM/ECF). The two letter state identifier as prescribed by the United States Post Office shall be used with no periods included. Zip codes MUST appear on the same line as the city/state.

(b) Reliance Upon the Matrix. The clerk may rely upon the matrix as filed, and any amendments thereto, for purposes of providing notice as required by these Local Bankruptcy Rules and the Federal Rules of Bankruptcy Procedure.

(c) Matrix Format. The matrix must be formatted and addressed as follows. Adherence to this format will greatly reduce the number of noticing errors. Each creditor entry must consist of no more than five total lines.

● Complete address, clearly typed

● Left justified in a single column down the left edge of the paper

● Each creditor's address must be single spaced

● Creditor's city, state and zip code must all appear together on the final line of each creditor's address

● Do not include account numbers in any part of the address

● Single space required between each address

● State must appear in a two letter, capitalized format

● Each line must contain no more than 40 characters including spaces and punctuation.

(d) Examples of Proper Format for Matrix.

MBNA
P O Box 15019
Wilmington, DE 19886–5019

Wells Fargo Financial
5 Gateway Drive
Suite 5000
Columbia, MD 21046

(e) Matrix of Twenty Largest Unsecured Creditors. The list of the twenty largest unsecured creditors filed pursuant to Fed. R. Bankr. P. 1007(d) shall be accompanied by a separate matrix, in proper form, as set forth in subsection (a) above, listing only those unsecured creditors.

(f) Certification of Matrix. Whenever a matrix is required to be submitted pursuant to subsections (a) or (e) of this rule, subsection (b) of Local Bankruptcy Rule 1003–1, subsection (d) of Local Bankruptcy Rule 1009–1, subsection (c) of Local Bankruptcy Rule 1015–1, subsection (d) of Local Bankruptcy Rule 1019–1 or as otherwise required by the court, the proponent or attorney for the proponent must certify that the matrix contains the names, addresses and zip codes of all creditors and entities which appear in the schedules of liabilities, list of creditors, list of equity security holders, list of twenty largest unsecured creditors or amendments thereto. The certification shall conform substantively to the following:

CERTIFICATION OF MAILING MATRIX

I (we), _____, the attorney for the debtor/petitioner (or, if appropriate, the debtor(s) or petitioners(s)) hereby certify under the penalties of perjury that the above/attached mailing matrix has been compared to and contains the names, addresses and zip codes of all persons and entities, as they appear on the schedules of liabilities/list of creditors/list of equity security holders, or any amendment thereto filed herewith.

Dated:_____

_____
Attorney for Debtor/Petitioner
(debtor(s)/Petitioner(s))

(g) Noncompliance. The failure to comply with the requirements of this rule may subject the case to dismissal.

[Effective January 1, 1998. Amended effective October 24, 2005.]

Comment

This rule requires that matrices be compatible with the court's automated case management system The creditor matrix is to be prepared with word processing software or bankruptcy preparation software, in a single column format with a one inch left margin (not centered). Creditors are single spaced with a double space separating one creditor from the next. The city, state and zip code must all be on the last line. The creditor matrix file is saved as an ASCII Text (.txt) file and uploaded to the System per the User Manual.

Refer to Local Bankruptcy Rule 9034–1(c) for the addresses of the United States trustee.

Although Fed. R. Bankr. P. 5005(a)(1) requires the clerk to accept papers for filing which are not in proper form, subsection (g) of this local rule makes clear that the court may take appropriate action to enforce this rule.

RULE 1007–3. NOTICE TO CREDITORS OMITTED FROM OR INCORRECTLY LISTED ON MASTER MAILING MATRIX

If a debtor files schedules or an amended mailing matrix after filing the petition, and if the debtor's schedules or amended mailing matrix include one or more creditors that were not included, or were listed incorrectly on the debtor's master mailing matrix filed with the petition, the debtor must comply with the following procedures:

(a) Notice of Amendment to Add Creditors. If a debtor adds a creditor to the case or corrects the name or address of a creditor by amending either the schedules, the list of creditors or matrix previously filed, the debtor must serve upon that creditor copies of the following:

(1) the amendment;

(2) copy of the original Notice for Meeting of Creditors;

(3) Statement of Social Security Number (Official Bankruptcy Form B21);

(4) any matters previously noticed by the clerk;

(5) a proof of claim form, if applicable;

(6) any other documents filed in the case which affects the rights of the creditor;

(7) a copy of each order that establishes or extends a bar date for claims or for complaints to determine the dischargeability of certain debts or to object to the discharge of the debtor.

(b) Certificate of Compliance. With the schedules and amended mailing matrix, the debtor must file a certificate of compliance with this Rule, together with a dated and clearly titled amended mailing matrix that lists only the names and correct mailing addresses of each newly scheduled creditor.

CERTIFICATION OF COMPLIANCE WITH LBR 1007–3

I (we) ___, the attorney for the debtor/petitioner (or if appropriate, the debtor(s) or petitioners(s)) hereby certify under the penalties of perjury that on date , schedules or an amended mailing matrix were filed.

The amended mailing matrix, which is clearly titled AMENDED matrix lists only the names and correct mailing address of each newly scheduled creditor or the corrected names and corrected mailing address of each creditor who was listed incorrectly on the master mailing matrix filed with the petition.

I further certify that newly listed creditors and/or corrected creditors have been noticed as required by LBR 1007–3(a).

Dated:_____

[Effective October 24, 2005.]

RULE 1009–1. AMENDMENTS TO LISTS, SCHEDULES, STATEMENTS & MAILING MATRICES

(a) Caption. Each amendment to the petition, lists, schedules, statements and mailing matrices shall contain a caption complying with Fed. R. Bankr. P. 1005 and Fed. R. Bankr. P. 9004(b) and include the word **"AMENDED"** in the designation of the character of the paper.

(b) List of Creditors and Schedules of Liabilities. Amendments to the list of creditors and schedules of liabilities shall include only the additional creditors.

(c) Schedules of Assets and Liabilities. Any amendment to the schedules of assets and liabilities which affects the amount claimed shall be totaled on both the amended schedule(s) as well as on the amended summary of schedules.

(d) Mailing Matrix. Any amendment to the schedules of liabilities or list of creditors which adds a party not previously listed shall include an amended, certified mailing matrix, listing, without duplication, only the additional creditor(s) with complete mailing address(es).

(e) Amended List of Creditors. If the petition is filed with a list of debtor's creditors and their addresses in lieu of completed schedules as permitted by Fed. R. Bankr. P. 1007(c), and thereafter, the debtor includes an additional creditor in the completed schedules "D", "E" or "F" who was not previously included in the original list of creditors, it shall be treated as an amendment and it shall be incumbent upon the debtor to file an amended list of creditors.

(f) Notice of Amendments. In the event the petition, lists, schedules, statements or mailing matrices

are amended pursuant to Fed. R. Bankr. P. 1009, the debtor shall forthwith serve notice of such amendment upon the United States trustee, case trustee, and any entity affected thereby, and file a certificate of service reflecting the same.

(g) Notice of Amendment to Add Creditors. If a debtor adds a creditor to the case by amending either the schedules, the list of creditors or matrix previously filed, the debtor must serve upon that creditor copies of the following:

(1) the amendment;

(2) Notice for Meeting of Creditors;

(3) Statement of Social Security Number (Official Bankruptcy Form B21);

(4) any matters previously noticed by the clerk;

(5) a proof of claim form, if applicable;

(6) any other documents filed in the case which affects the rights of the creditor.

(h) Certificate of Service. Upon filing an amendment, a certificate reflecting service of notice of the amendment shall be filed simultaneously with the clerk and any trustee appointed in the case.

(i) Amendment to Claim of Exemption. An amendment to a claim of exemption pursuant to Fed. R. Bankr. P. 4003(a) shall be filed and served by the debtor or dependent of the debtor on the trustee, the United States trustee and all creditors. The certificate of service required by subsection (h) of this rule shall be filed with the amendment to claim of exemption.

(j) Filing Fees. The fee for amending a list or schedule, required by 28 U.S.C. Sec. 1930(b) and the appendix, must be paid at the time of the filing of the amendment.

[Effective January 1, 1998. Amended effective October 24, 2005.]

Comment

Amendments shall be filed in the form prescribed in Local Bankruptcy Rule 9004–1 and in accordance with Local Bankruptcy Rules 1007–1 and 1007–2.

No amendment by interlineation shall be permitted. The entire page or pages that the amendment affects shall be redrafted with the amendment redlined, underlined, or boxed in, and in such manner that the amended page(s) will be complete without referring to the page or pages that have been amended. (Note: When an amendment is submitted electronically and the submitting party uses the highlight function to indicate the amendment, the party should choose red highlighting (not yellow) to ensure the amendment continues to be easily identifiable if printed.)

RULE 1011–1. RESPONSIVE PLEADING— CONSENT TO INVOLUNTARY PETITION

A consent to an involuntary petition filed against a corporation, limited liability company or limited liability partnership shall be accompanied by a copy of the corporate resolution or other appropriate authorization, duly attested to, authorizing such consent.

A consent to an involuntary petition filed against a partnership shall be accompanied by appropriate authorization, duly attested to by all general partners, authorizing such consent.

[Effective January 1, 1998. Amended effective October 24, 2005.]

RULE 1014–1. INTERDISTRICT TRANSFER OF CASES OR PROCEEDINGS

After the expiration of ten days from the date of entry of an order transferring a case or proceeding from this district to another district, the clerk shall promptly mail to the court to which the case is transferred: (1) certified copies of the docket and order of transfer and (2) the originals of all other papers on file in the case or proceeding.

If the documents in a transferred case or proceeding are only available in electronic format in the CM/ECF system, the district receiving a transferred case or proceeding from the Northern District of New York will be directed to obtain the required documents from PACER.

[Effective January 1, 1998. Amended effective October 24, 2005.]

Comment

Transfer of cases (reassignment) between judges within the district is governed by Local Bankruptcy Rule 1073–1(d).

RULE 1015–1. JOINT ADMINISTRATION AND CONSOLIDATION

(a) Motion. Unless otherwise ordered by the court, motions for joint administration or consolidation shall be presented in each of the subject cases, shall be served on all creditors and parties in interest and shall designate one of the subject cases as the main case.

(b) Husband and Wife Joint Cases. In all cases filed by a husband and wife under 11 U.S.C. § 302, the court will presume joint administration of the case and, in an asset case, the consolidation of the assets and liabilities shall be combined in a single pool to pay creditors unless and until a motion is made by a party in interest to terminate the consolidation, which motion shall be made returnable prior to or at the final hearing. At the request of one or both of the joint debtors, and upon payment of the required fee, the joint bankruptcy case may be divided into two separate cases, after which either debtor may convert his or her individual case or move the court for separate dismissal.

(c) Matrix. Prior to the entry of an order of joint administration or consolidation, movant shall request copies from the clerk or through PACER of the matrices for each of the cases affected by the order. Movant shall submit a supplemental certified matrix containing only those parties not already included on the matrix from the main case, without duplications or omissions. The matrix must be in compliance with the filing requirements as set forth in Local Bankruptcy Rule 1007–2 and shall be filed with a proposed order of consolidation or joint administration no later than five days from the hearing date. This requirement shall not apply to the consolidation of a joint case under subsection (b) of this rule.

(d) Order. An order of joint administration or consolidation shall identify the main case and will be filed in each of the affected cases.

(e) Caption, Docket Entries and Filing. Prior to the entry of an order of consolidation or joint administration, all papers shall be captioned by their individual titles.

(1) *Consolidation.* Once separate cases have been ordered consolidated, they will be treated as one case for all purposes, with a single case number, caption, claims register and docket.

(2) *Joint Administration.* Subsequent to the entry of an order of joint administration, all papers shall be captioned in the case or cases to which they pertain and shall be entered and filed in the main case. When documents pertain to all of the jointly administered cases, there shall be no special designation on the docket or claims register. When documents pertain to one or more of the jointly administered cases but not all such cases, the docket or claims register will identify the specific case or cases to which the items relate. The clerk may rely upon the document's caption in determining the case or cases to which a particular document applies.

(f) Noncompliance. Failure to comply with subsections (c) and (d) of this rule is cause for the court to vacate its oral order and deny the relief requested.

[Effective January 1, 1998. Amended effective October 24, 2005.]

Comment

Consolidation includes substantive consolidation.

RULE 1017–3. DISMISSED CASE— MOTION TO VACATE ORDER OF DISMISSAL OR TO REINSTATE

(a) A motion to vacate or reconsider an order of dismissal shall be filed no later than ten days after the entry of the dismissal order and shall be served upon all creditors and parties in interest unless pursuant to Federal Rule of Bankruptcy Procedure 9024.

(b) In addition to the requirements outlined in subsection (a), a motion filed in a case dismissed for failure of the debtor to make payments shall state with particularity:

(1) the circumstances which explain why the required payments were not made;

(2) the circumstances which have changed that would permit the debtor to make future payments;

(3) the date and manner of the proposed future payments by the debtor to the trustee; and

(4) any new debt incurred from the date of dismissal.

(c) Any order reinstating a dismissed case shall be prepared by the debtor and served upon all creditors and parties in interest. The debtor shall also file a certificate of service of the order with the court.

[Effective January 1, 1998. Amended effective October 24, 2005.]

Comment

This rule applies to dismissed cases awaiting closing. If closing of the case has occurred, parties must proceed under 11 U.S.C. § 350 and Fed. R. Bankr. P. 5010 which necessitates the payment of a fee for reopening the case pursuant to 28 U.S.C. § 1930(b). According to the Bankruptcy Court Fee Schedule promulgated by the Administrative Office of the U.S. Courts, the fee to be charged for reopening is the filing fee in effect for commencing a new case on the date of reopening. This rule applies to cases in which an order of dismissal has been entered on the docket but the case has not yet been closed in CM/ECF.

RULE 1019–1. CONVERSION— PROCEDURE FOLLOWING

(a) Filing of Additional Lists, Schedules, Statements. In accord with Fed. R. Bankr. P. 1019, the previously filed petition, lists, schedules, statements and claims actually filed shall be deemed filed in the converted case. Only the lists, schedules and any other statements necessary to complete the filing requirements in the newly converted case shall be submitted for filing.

(b) Number of Lists, Schedules, Statements. Unless otherwise ordered by the court, any lists, schedules or statements due upon entry of an order or notice of conversion, including the schedule of unpaid debts incurred after commencement of the superseded case, shall be filed according to the requirements of Local Bankruptcy Rule 1007–1.

(c) Timeliness of Filing Schedule of Unpaid Debts. When the schedule of unpaid debts is filed in a case converted to chapter 7 within the period prescribed by Fed. R. Bankr. P. 1019(5), the clerk shall notice the creditors listed on the schedule regarding the filing of post petition claims pursuant to Fed. R. Bankr. P. 1019(6). When the schedule is untimely

filed, the filer shall provide the foregoing notice, and promptly file proof of service thereof with the clerk.

(d) Supplemental Matrix. Any lists, schedules or statements filed as a result of a conversion which include creditors not previously listed within the case matrix, shall be accompanied by a supplemental certified matrix prepared as directed by Local Bankruptcy Rule 1007–2, listing, without duplication, only those additional creditors.

(e) Small Business Election Upon Conversion to Chapter 11. Immediately upon the conversion of a chapter 7, chapter 12 or chapter 13 case to chapter 11, the debtor must apprise the court in writing of its eligibility for treatment as a "Small Business," and whether it elects treatment as such. Failure of the debtor to supply this information shall result in the presumption that the debtor is not a Small Business.

(f) Debtor's Affidavit Upon Conversion to Chapter 11. In addition to the contents specified in Local Bankruptcy Rule 2015–2, the debtor's affidavit shall set forth:

(1) if the case was originally commenced under chapter 7, 12 or 13, the name and address of any trustee appointed in such chapter 7, 12 or 13 case and the names and addresses of the members of any creditors' committee elected in the chapter 7 case; and

(2) the names and addresses of the members of any committee and any attorney for such committee, organized prior to the order for relief in a chapter 11 case, and a brief description of the circumstances surrounding the formation of any committee, including the date of formation.

[Effective January 1, 1998. Amended effective October 24, 2005.]

Comment

As provided in Fed. R. Bankr. P. 1007(c), a previously filed petition, list, schedule and statement in a case is deemed filed in a superseding case. Conversely, Fed. R. Bankr. P. 1019 addresses the effect of previously filed lists, schedules and statements in prior chapter 11, 12 and 13 cases when they are converted to chapter 7.

Subsection (a) of this rule mimics these provisions as to all other conversions. This rule makes clear that upon conversion, only the additional lists, schedules and statements required by the new chapter are to be filed.

This rule should be read in conjunction with Local Bankruptcy Rules 1007–1, 1007–2, 1007–3 and 2015–2.

RULE 1073–1. ASSIGNMENT OF CASES AND ADVERSARY PROCEEDINGS/INTRA–DISTRICT

(a) Assignment of Cases and Proceedings to Albany. All cases filed by residents of Albany, Clinton, Essex, Franklin, Fulton, Jefferson, Montgomery, Rensselaer, Saratoga, Schenectady, Schoharie, St.

Lawrence, Warren and Washington counties will be assigned to the judge sitting in Albany.

Cases filed by residents of Columbia, Greene and Ulster counties will be treated as Northern District cases and assigned to the judge sitting in Albany when filed in the Northern District of New York.

(b) Assignment of Cases and Proceedings to Utica. All cases filed by residents of Broome, Cayuga, Chenango, Cortland, Delaware, Hamilton, Herkimer, Lewis, Madison, Oneida, Onondaga, Oswego, Otsego, Tioga and Tompkins counties will be assigned to the judge sitting in Utica.

(c) Assignment—General. Except as otherwise provided in the Code and Federal Rules of Bankruptcy Procedure, the assignment of a case to a judge includes the assignment of all proceedings arising under Title 11 or arising in or related to a case under Title 11.

(d) Intradistrict Transfer. Irrespective of the case assignment, any judge may transfer to another judge within the district any case, contested matter or adversary proceeding. If a case is transferred from the judge sitting in Poughkeepsie to either Albany or Utica, these Local Bankruptcy Rules shall govern.

(e) Objections to Assignment. Objections to assignment of cases, adversary proceedings or contested matters shall be filed with the judge assigned to the case. However, objections based solely on an alleged incorrect assignment made by the clerk's office shall be filed with the chief judge of the court.

[Effective January 1, 1998. Amended effective October 24, 2005.]

Comment

Cases filed by residents of Columbia, Greene and Ulster counties are treated as Southern District cases when filed in the Southern District of New York. They are assigned to the judge sitting in Poughkeepsie and governed by the Local Bankruptcy Rules for the Southern District of New York, as provided by Local Bankruptcy Rule 1001–1(b).

Erroneous or misinterpreted information may result in the incorrect assignment of a case. The clerk may advise the court if it appears that the case has been improperly assigned. Appropriate adjustment can be made pursuant to subsection (d) of this rule. The intentional furnishing of incorrect information may subject the person who provided such information to disciplinary rules or sanctions.

Reference is made to the attached appendix listing the counties comprising the Northern District of New York, which provides limited guidance with respect to where the court will hold hearings.

Interdistrict transfer of cases is governed by Local Bankruptcy Rule 1014–1.

RULE 2002–1. NOTICING TO CREDITORS & OTHER INTERESTED PARTIES

(a) Notice to All Creditors. Unless the court otherwise provides, the court directs the proponent, excepting the office of the United States trustee, to give notice of:

(1) a proposed use, sale or lease of property other than in the ordinary course of business;

(2) the hearing on approval of a compromise or settlement of a controversy;

(3) in chapter 7, 11, and 12 cases, the hearing on the dismissal or conversion of the case to another chapter;

(4) the time fixed to accept or reject a proposed modification of a plan;

(5) except as limited by subsection (b), a hearing on all applications for compensation or reimbursement of expenses totaling in excess of $500.

(6) the time fixed for filing objections and the hearing to consider approval of a disclosure statement;

(7) the time fixed for filing objections and the hearing to consider confirmation of a plan;

(8) the notice of entry of an order confirming a chapter 11 plan; and

(9) in a chapter 7 case, the notice of the trustee's final report.

(b) Limited Notice. Where an official Creditor Committee has been appointed and as permitted by Fed. R. Bankr. P. 2002(I), required notices of hearing on the actions described below can be limited to committees or their authorized agents, the United States trustee and to the creditors and equity security holders who file with the court a request that all notices be mailed to them.

(1) Approval of a compromise or settlement;

(2) Application for compensation or reimbursement of expenses totaling less than $25,000.

(c) Certificate of Service. A certificate reciting all parties upon whom service of any notice has been made and stating the manner in which service was made shall be filed within five days of effecting service and no later than seven days prior to the return date of the hearing. For the purpose of preparing address labels, a copy of the updated matrix can be obtained from PACER or upon request from the clerk.

(d) Notices to Committees. Except as the court may otherwise designate, pursuant to Fed. R. Bankr. P. 9007, service of notice upon a committee may be made by serving the committee chairperson and the duly appointed attorney for the committee, if any, or other authorized agent. Upon application by a party in interest, the court may designate additional entities to whom notice shall be given.

(e) Return Address on Court Generated Notices. The clerk shall place the name and address of the debtor's attorney of record, or that of the pro se debtor, as the case may be, as the return address on all notices sent out by the court to all creditors and other parties in interest.

(f) Duty to Re-notice on Returned Mail. Should any such notices referred to in subsection (c) above be returned, debtor's counsel or the pro se debtor shall promptly send out the notice to any corrected address noted thereon for the given party in interest.

(g) Duty of Party in Interest to Notify Clerk of Change of Address. Any change of address of an interested party should be filed with the clerk and such notice of the change must contain the debtor's name, case number, the party's name and original address given to the court, together with the party's complete new mailing address.

[Effective January 1, 1998. Amended effective October 24, 2005.]

Comment

This rule is intended to facilitate the service of papers. Reference is made to Local Bankruptcy Rules 4002–2 and 9011–2 for requirements for designation of address and change of address for debtors and pro se parties, respectively.

The proponent of a notice under subsection (a)(1), (2), (3), (5) or (8) is referenced to LBR 9013–1(m) for form of the notice.

RULE 2014–1. EMPLOYMENT OF PROFESSIONALS

(a) Requirements of the Application, Affidavit and Order. Authority to employ a professional shall be sought by presentation of an application, affidavit and proposed order. The original application and original affidavit are to be submitted conventionally to the court, unless the application is filed electronically pursuant to Local Rule 9013–4, Default Motion Practice. The proposed order is also to be submitted conventionally.

(1) *Application.* An order approving the employment of a professional person pursuant to 11 U.S.C. § 327 shall be made only on application by the trustee, debtor in possession or committee. The original application shall be submitted conventionally to the court. The application shall fully disclose:

(a) the reason the professional should be hired;

(b) the professional services to be rendered;

(c) the proposed terms and conditions of employment including any arrangement for retainer;

(d) the source of any retainer;

(e) the hourly rates for professionals and para-professionals;

(f) any contingent fee arrangement and;

(g) all of the professional's connections with the debtor or any party in interest, including disclosure of the terms of any guaranty agreement with respect to payment of the professional's fee by a third party.

A copy of any written retainer agreement, and of any written guaranty agreement, shall be submitted with, and appended to the application.

(2) *Affidavit.* The application shall be accompanied by an original affidavit of the professional, setting forth any facts which might reasonably lead to the conclusion that the professional may not be disinterested or may hold an interest adverse to the debtor as defined in 11 U.S.C. § 101(14).

(3) *Order.* The order of appointment shall clearly state that no fees will be paid to the professional, including the use of any retainer received for post petition services without prior approval of the court.

(4) *Motions Pursuant to 11 U.S.C. § 327(e)—Albany Only.* All motions pursuant to 11 U.S.C. 327(e) in Chapter 7 and Chapter 11 cases shall be noticed pursuant to Local Bankruptcy Rule 9013–4. In addition to service on the United States trustee, the Court requires service on the debtor and attorney for the debtor. Ex Parte applications and orders should not be submitted.

(b) Auctioneers. In addition to the requirements of subsection (a)(1) of this rule, an application seeking an order of appointment of an auctioneer shall:

(1) set forth in the application that the auctioneer is duly licensed, the license number and the place of the auctioneer's business;

(2) provide a copy of the surety bond referred to in Local Bankruptcy Rule 6005–1(c) intended to cover the assets of the estate; and

(3) where a blanket bond has been approved by the United States trustee and is on file with the court, shall disclose whether or not the applicant has been appointed as auctioneer in any other case, including case name(s) and case number(s) thereof, and set forth whether or not the applicant has or will, within a reasonable period of time, come into possession of property of any other estate in which the applicant has been appointed auctioneer, together with a reasonable estimation of the value of all such property.

[Effective January 1, 1998. Amended effective October 24, 2005.]

Comment

This rule is intended to supplement Fed. R. Bankr. P. 2014(a), and information required by this rule must be submitted contemporaneous with the information required therein. As required by Local Bankruptcy Rule 9034–1, the United States trustee must be served with a copy of the application and proposed order. Fed. R. Bankr. P. 5002 sets forth certain restrictions applicable to professional appointments. Debtor's counsel must comply with the continuing disclosure requirements of Fed. R. Bankr. P. 2016(b).

Subsection (a)(3) requires that the proposed order approving the appointment make clear the necessity of obtaining court approval before any fees for post petition services are paid. This includes the application of any prepetition retainer received to cover post petition services.

When an application for employment is approved by the court, the appointment may be deemed effective as of the date of the initial receipt of the application by the court, or by office of the United States trustee, as provided by Fed. R. Bankr. P. 5005(c).

RULE 2015–2. DEBTOR IN POSSESSION DUTIES

(a) **Monthly Statements of Operation Required in Chapter 7 (Operating) and Chapter 11 Cases.** The operating reports mandated by 11 U.S.C. §§ 704(8) and 1106 must be filed monthly, and, in addition to being filed directly with the court, the United States trustee and any governmental unit charged with responsibility for collection or determination of any tax arising out of the operations, shall be served upon any official committee or its attorney.

(1) *Signature.* The operating reports filed in accordance with subsection (a) of this rule must bear an original signature of the debtor or of the chapter 7 or chapter 11 trustee, verifying the accuracy of the information contained therein.

(2) *Failure to File Monthly Operating Reports.* Failure to file the required operating reports may be cause for the court to deny any affirmative relief sought by the debtor including, but not limited to, approval of a pending disclosure statement as provided by Local Bankruptcy Rule 3016–2 and confirmation of a plan.

(b) **Reporting Requirements for Chapter 12 and 13 Debtors Engaged in Business.** In the event the debtor engages in the operation of a business enterprise, including a family farm pursuant to 11 U.S.C. § 1201, as a result of which the debtor is required to collect taxes or for which the debtor incurs tax liabilities in the ordinary course of the operation of the debtor's business, the debtor shall:

(1) file with the trustee's office, a summary of business operations on such form as promulgated by the trustee or a copy of their most recent federal tax return when requested by the trustee and in such intervals as required by the trustee;

(2) maintain a bank account which serves solely as a separate tax account (the Tax Account) for the deposit of all tax funds (including, but not limited to, funds held in trust for employee's withholding taxes, sales taxes and employer business taxes, with the exception of income taxes) which may be collected by the debtor and for which the debtor may become liable during the pendency of this case. Such tax funds are to be withdrawn from the Tax Account only for the remittance to the appropriate taxing authority or to a federal tax depository, and, the debtor shall provide proof of compliance to the trustee upon request;

(3) within two business days from the date on which any salaries are paid to the debtor's employees, deposit that portion of such salaries as is required to be withheld for social security taxes and the employer's portion of social security taxes and disability and unemployment insurance taxes to the Tax Account, and, the debtor shall provide proof of compliance to the trustee upon request;

(4) in those cases in which the debtor is required to collect sales taxes, deposit the sales taxes in the Tax Account not later than the Monday following each week for that week's sales tax liability, and, the debtor shall provide proof of compliance to the trustee upon request;

(5) deposit any other taxes which the debtor is required to collect, or for which the debtor incurs liability in the ordinary course of the operation of the debtor's business (such as federal excise taxes) into the Tax Account no later than Wednesday of the week following the week in which such taxes were collected or in which the liability was incurred, and, the debtor shall provide proof of compliance to the trustee upon request;

(6) during the pendency of the case, timely file all required federal and state tax returns and;

(7) during the pendency of the case, make required periodic deposits of federal and state taxes to a tax depository and provide the appropriate taxing authority with verification that such deposits were made within three days from the date of any such deposit.

[Effective January 1, 1998. Amended effective October 24, 2005.]

Comment

This rule addresses the requirement of filing monthly operating reports in chapter 7 cases when a business is authorized to be operated, in chapter 11 and 12 cases and in chapter 13 business cases.

Pursuant to Fed. R. Bankr. P. 5003(e) the practitioners are referred to the Clerk's registry for the addresses for the filing of tax returns and remittance of payments.

RULE 2015–6. DEBTOR IN POSSESSION DUTIES—CHAPTER 11 AFFIDAVIT

A debtor's affidavit shall be filed in each chapter 11 case and in any case converted to chapter 11 from chapter 7, 12 or 13.

(a) **Contents of Affidavit.** A debtor in a chapter 11 case shall file an original affidavit setting forth:

(1) the nature of the debtor's business and a concise statement of the circumstances leading to the debtor's filing under chapter 11;

(2) if the debtor failed to file its summary of schedules with the initial filing, a summary of the debtor's assets and liabilities;

(3) a list of all property of the debtor in the possession or custody of any custodian, public officer, mortgagee, pledgee, assignee of rents or secured creditor or agent for any such person, giving the name, address and telephone number of such person and the court, if any, in which a proceeding relating thereto is pending;

(4) if the debtor failed to file its schedule A (real property) or schedule G (statement of executory contracts and unexpired leases) with the initial filing, a list of premises owned, under lease or held under other arrangement from which the debtor operates its business; and

(5) if the debtor failed to file its statement of financial affairs with the initial filing, the location of the debtor's substantial assets, the location of its books and records and the nature, location and value of assets, if any, held by the debtor outside the territorial limits of the United States.

(b) Additional Information Required if Business Continues. If the debtor intends to continue the operation of its business, the affidavit shall so state and set forth:

(1) the estimated amount of the weekly payroll payable to employees (exclusive of the officers, partners, stockholders and directors) for the 30 day period following the filing of the chapter 11 petition;

(2) the amount paid and proposed to be paid for services for the 30 day period following the filing of the chapter 11 petition:

(A) if a corporation, to officers, stockholders and directors;

(B) if an individual or a partnership, to the individual or the members of the partnership; and

(C) if a consultant has been retained, to such consultant.

(3) a schedule setting forth for the 30 days following the filing of the petition: estimated cash receipts and disbursements, net cash gain or loss, accrued but unpaid obligations, other than professional fees, and any other information relevant to an understanding of the foregoing.

(c) When to File. In a voluntary chapter 11 case, the affidavit shall be filed within five days of the filing of the petition. In an involuntary chapter 11 case, the affidavit shall be filed within five days after entry of the order for relief or after the filing of a consent to the petition, whichever is earlier.

(d) Waiver of Requirements. On application of the debtor and notice to the United States trustee showing that it is impracticable or impossible to furnish any of the foregoing information, the court may dispense with any of the foregoing provisions, except that the affidavit shall contain the information required by paragraphs (1) and (2) of subsection (a) of this rule.

[Effective January 1, 1998. Amended effective October 24, 2005.]

Comment

This rule supplements Fed. R. Bankr. P. 1007 and should be read in conjunction with Local Bankruptcy Rule 1019–1(f) when a case converts to chapter 11.

RULE 2016–1. COMPENSATION OF PROFESSIONALS

(a) Applications for Interim and Final Compensation. Applications for compensation shall comply with all requirements, including those related to format, outlined in Fed. R. Bankr. P. 2016(a) and the United States Trustee Fee Guidelines.

(b) Filing and Paper Copy Requirements. Applications for compensation are to be filed electronically. A paper copy marked ECF Case—Chambers Copy is to be provided to the Court. In addition, the U.S. Trustee is also to be provided with a paper copy of the application. The Chambers copy and the U.S. Trustee copy are to include all the items listed in subsections (b)(1) through (b)(9) of this local rule. Each application shall include:

(1) the date the applicant was appointed by the court and, if applicable, the method of compensation, the maximum compensation and any rate of compensation fixed in the order appointing applicant;

(2) a statement as to whether all services for which compensation is requested were performed for, or on behalf of, the party retaining applicant or on behalf of any other person or paraprofessional;

(3) a summary of the professional and paraprofessional services rendered including, in concise form:

(A) a factual explanation of the nature and extent of services performed, the results obtained, and the size of the estate; and

(B) in addition, if an interim fee request, an explanation of the status of the case, a projection as to the percentage of work which the current application covers in relation to the overall case and any other matters which will enable the court to determine the reasonable value of such services;

(4) an exhibit consisting of contemporaneous daily time records for all professionals and paraprofessionals, arranged in a project billing format as suggested by the United States Trustee Fee Guidelines except that applications seeking compensation less than

$10,000 exclusive of expenses are exempt from the project billing requirement. Entries in the time records:

(A) must be legible and applicant shall define any codes, symbols, abbreviations or non-legal technical terms used in the time records; and

(B) must be sufficiently specific to permit the court to evaluate the reasonableness of the time allocated for the particular service. Failure to separately identify the time expended on each service with a single time entry may provide a basis for the court to deny compensation for that service;

(5) a statement specifying the amounts, if any, within the total request that were previously received from any source, including guarantors, with or without court authorization;

(6) a statement as to whether applicant has entered into any agreement to fix fees or to share compensation as prohibited by 18 U.S.C. § 155 and 11 U.S.C. § 504;

(7) a statement describing the estate's ability to pay the fees requested and the status of fees owed to other administrative claimants of equal priority to the extent the professional is employed pursuant to 11 U.S.C. §§ 327 or 1103 and compensation is sought from the estate and not a third party;

(8) a specific description of the basis and justification for the request in terms related to the benefit of the services to the estate to the extent an enhancement of fees beyond those supported by the time records is sought; and

(9) an itemization of expenses incurred, conforming with subsection (c) of this rule.

(c) **Reimbursement of Expenses.** All requests for reimbursement of expenses shall be separately supported in the application by a detailed, itemized listing. Each category of expenses shall be separately totaled. A summary of all expense categories shall be included, which total should equal the aggregate request.

(1) The following expenses may be reimbursable if adequately supported in the application:

(A) duplication of documents at actual cost at a rate not to exceed 20 cents per page or, if the photocopies were made by an entity unrelated to the applicant, at the rate charged by the entity as supported by a photocopy of the invoice appended to the application;

(B) computer legal research at a rate not to exceed the cost of said service incurred by the applicant;

(C) long distance travel expenses, if adequately described, including the mode of transportation, the date, destination, and purpose of the trip, and, if by automobile, the number of miles traveled, the rate

used, and substantiation of incidental expenses including lodging, tolls and parking; and

(D) facsimile transmission charges for outgoing transmissions to long distance numbers, reimbursable at either the actual toll charge or $1.00 per page.

(2) The applicant shall certify that all expenses for which reimbursement is sought were incurred on behalf of the client and no other person and that the reimbursement, if allowed in full, will not exceed the amount that applicant paid for the items.

(3) The following expenses may be considered unreasonable unless separately justified through a detailed itemization and explanation by the applicant including, but not limited to, why they were necessary and that the hourly rates charged by the professionals do not support said expenses as an overhead item within the applicant's office:

(A) travel to and from the courthouse within a 25–mile radius;

(B) any charges for typing, word processing and clerical assistance;

(C) a travel mileage rate in excess of that which the Administrator of General Services has prescribed for official travel of employees of the Federal Government, as amended from time to time, and set forth in 41 C.F.R. Part 101–7 under authority of 5 U.S.C. § 5704; and

(D) meal expenses incurred while on long-distance travel.

(d) **Certification.** Each applicant shall certify that the person or entity on whose behalf the applicant is employed, including the debtor, the creditors' committee or the trustee, has been served with the application for compensation and reimbursement of expenses.

(e) **Applications for Final Compensation in Chapter 11 Cases.** At the time of the hearing on the approval of the disclosure statement or at some later time, the court may fix the time by which all applications for final compensation must be filed. Absent such directive, all applications for allowance of fees and expenses must be filed prior to or with the report of substantial consummation.

(1) *Estimate of Future Services.* An application for final compensation may include a reasonable estimate of the hours it is anticipated will be expended and the expenses incurred through the closing of the case. The estimate shall identify the specific tasks to be performed with an allocation of hours for each task.

(2) *Supplementary Exhibit.* Any estimate of future services and expenses shall be subject to later substantiation in the form of a supplementary exhibit, to be filed both on the return date of the hearing on the application for final compensation and with the application for final decree. The exhibit shall be filed in

conformity with subsection (b)(4) governing professional compensation and Fed. R. Bankr. P. 2016(a). The supplementary exhibit must account for the actual services, hours and expenses which were estimated in the previously submitted application.

[Effective January 1, 1998. Amended effective October 24, 2005.]

Comment

This rule provides a procedure for the court to fix final compensation of professionals in order to determine the total administrative expenses chargeable to the estate while at the same time compensating and monitoring services required after confirmation through the closing of the case. Subsection (e) is intended to clarify that professionals who are required to be appointed by the court in order to be paid must receive court approval of fees and expenses for services rendered during the case, before the case is closed. Failure to file the supplementary exhibit required by subsection (e)(2) in a timely manner may result in an order of the court directing a party to disgorge compensation allowed on the basis of previously submitted estimates.

Compensation of auctioneers is addressed by Local Bankruptcy Rule 6005–1.

The travel mileage rate changes referred to in subsection (c)(3)(c) of this rule shall be posted at the clerk's office filing counters. The expenses specifically addressed in this rule are not intended to be either an exclusive or exhaustive list of potentially reimbursable expenses.

United States Trustee Fee Guidelines are available on request through the office of the United States trustee in Albany or Utica, New York.

RULE 2016–2. CHAPTER 13—COMPENSATION OF PROFESSIONALS

(a) Applications for Compensation. Unless otherwise determined by the court, if all or part of the compensation to the debtor's counsel as approved at the time of confirmation of a chapter 13 plan is to be paid through the chapter 13 trustee, and such compensation is not paid in full from a maximum of a sum equal to the aggregate of the first ten plan payments (net of trustee commissions) to be distributed by the trustee, then any remaining compensation will share equally thereafter with other creditors or at such percentage as may be fixed by the court.

(b) Notice to All Parties in Interest. Notwithstanding any other provision of this rule, if the compensation for debtor's counsel is an amount greater than one-third of the amount to be funded through the chapter 13 plan, the compensation is subject to approval upon a hearing held on notice to all parties in interest as provided for under Fed. R. Bankr. P. 2002(a) (6).

(c) Ex Parte Application for Postconfirmation Fees. An application that seeks allowance of fees and expenses totaling $1000 or less postconfirmation may be presented ex parte if it has the endorsed approval of the debtor and the chapter 13 trustee. If the application lacks the requisite approval, or if such postconfirmation fee will cause the total of compensation to debtor's counsel to exceed the monetary limit of Local Bankruptcy Rule 2002–1(b), the fee must be approved after a hearing as provided in Fed. R. Bankr. P. 2002(a)(6). When additional compensation for postpetition services is approved by the court, said compensation shall be paid through the chapter 13 plan.

(d) Supplemental Application for Compensation. The chapter 13 trustee may request, at any time, a supplemental statement pursuant to 11 U.S.C. § 329(a) and Fed. R. Bankr. P. 2016(a) to determine whether a hearing should be scheduled to consider whether payments to an attorney are excessive pursuant to Fed. R. Bankr. P. 2017.

[Effective January 1, 1998. Amended effective October 24, 2005.]

RULE 2090–1. ATTORNEYS—ADMISSION TO PRACTICE/DESIGNATION FOR SERVICE

(a) Admission. Any attorney who is admitted to practice before the district court of the Northern District of New York is also admitted to practice before this court.

(1) *Pro Hac Vice.* A member in good standing of the bar of any state or of any United States district court not otherwise admitted to practice before the court, may be permitted to practice on motion in this court only for a limited purpose in a particular case, adversary proceeding, contested matter or action. An attorney seeking admission pro hac vice shall provide a certificate of good standing in support of counsel's motion for admission, as evidence of admission to the bar of the highest court of any state or of any United States district court, and shall pay to the district court Clerk the administrative fee required to practice ex parte or on motion.

(b) Designation for Service. A judge may require an attorney who does not have an office in the Northern District of New York to designate a resident member of the bar of the Northern District of New York for service of process or papers.

[Effective January 1, 1998. Amended effective October 24, 2005.]

RULE 2091–1. ATTORNEYS—WITHDRAWALS—OTHER THAN BY SUBSTITUTION

(a) Withdrawal Other Than by Substitution. An attorney who has appeared as the attorney of record for a debtor may be relieved of representation only by order of the court after notice and a hearing. Withdrawal may be permitted upon submission of an affidavit stating satisfactory reasons for withdrawal and a statement of the status of the case. Notice of the requested withdrawal in every instance shall be given to the debtor, the United States trustee, the trustee, any § 1104 trustee, any appointed committee and any party having filed a notice of appearance.

(b) Other Attorneys of Record. Withdrawal of other attorneys of record may be accomplished by providing written notice to the court and to all creditors and interested parties. Withdrawing counsel shall furnish and file a certificate of service with the court in accordance with this rule.

[Effective January 1, 1998. Amended effective October 24, 2005.]

RULE 2092–1. ATTORNEYS— SUBSTITUTION

(a) Substitution. A debtor's attorney may be substituted by order of the court after such notice and hearing as the court may direct. Substitution may be allowed upon submission of an affidavit stating satisfactory reasons for substitution and a statement of the status of the case, or, upon the submission of a stipulation signed by debtor(s), the attorney to be relieved and the substituted attorney.

(b) Other Attorneys of Record. Substitution of other attorneys of record may be accomplished by providing written notice to the court and to all creditors and interested parties. Substituted counsel shall furnish and file a certificate of service with the court in accordance with this rule.

[Effective January 1, 1998.]

RULE 3001–1. CLAIMS AND EQUITY SECURITY INTERESTS—ASSET CASES

In all chapter 11, 12 and 13 cases, and in a chapter 7 case noticed as an asset case, any entity filing a proof of claim shall properly identify the case to which such claim relates by stating the applicable case name and number assigned thereto. Wage claims shall contain only the last four numbers of the claimant's social security number. Amended or additional proofs of claim filed after the bar date shall be served upon the appointed Chapter 7, 12, or 13 Trustee and upon the debtor's attorney, as well as filed with the Clerk.

[Effective January 1, 1998. Amended effective October 24, 2005.]

Comment

Proper identification of the debtor estate by name and case number is essential for the clerk to properly process a claim being asserted.

RULE 3001–2. CLAIMS AND EQUITY SECURITY INTERESTS—NO ASSET CASES

In a chapter 7 case noticed as a no asset case, no proof of claim shall be filed.

[Effective October 24, 2005.]

Comment

At the time of filing, if it appears that there are no assets from which a distribution can be paid to creditors, the case shall be designated as "no asset". The notice to creditors will direct creditors not to file a proof of claim unless and until a subsequent notice is received. If it should later develop that the trustee uncovers assets from which a dividend might be paid, the designation of the case will be changed from no asset to an asset case. In that event, the clerk will notify all creditors of a deadline set for the filing of proofs of claim and creditors must then file claims on or before the deadline.

RULE 3002–1. THIRD PARTY PROCESSING OF CLAIMS (CLAIMS AGENTS)

(a) Request for Claims Agent. In cases in which hundreds or thousands of creditors exist, the court may permit third parties to perform the docketing and processing of claims at the estate's expense. The request to employ third party claims processors is to be brought on by motion.

(b) Docketing of Claims in CM/ECF. Claims agents receiving claims for docketing are required to stamp claims with the date received, scan the claims and docket them to the Court's CM/ECF system. Claims are to be docketed by the claims agent within 24 hours of receipt.

(c) Electronic Format of Claims Register. Claims agents are required to keep claims registers in electronic format in the court's CM/ECF system.

(d) Transfer of Claims. Claims agents are responsible for processing all transfer of claims forms and providing notice of the transfer as required by Fed. R. Bankr. P. 3001. Claims agents are also required to give notice of the filing of a claim in the name of a creditor by a debtor or trustee as required by Fed. R. Bankr. P. 3004.

(e) Retention of Original Claims and Transmission to the FRC. The claims agent is to retain all original claims until the case is closed unless otherwise ordered by the court. Upon the closing of a case, the claims agent will be required to transmit claims registers and claims to the Federal Record Center.

[Effective October 24, 2005.]

RULE 3007–1. CLAIMS—OBJECTIONS

(a) Claim Objections in Chapter 11 Cases. Unless otherwise ordered by the court or provided by the plan, objections to claims in chapter 11 cases must be filed and served no later than ten days after the entry of an order of confirmation.

(b) Claim Objections in Chapter 12 and 13 Cases. Absent a court order approving an extension of time, objections to claims in chapter 12 and 13 cases must be filed and served within 90 days of the trustee's service of the "Notice of Claims Filed" in the Albany court and within 90 days of the trustee's service of the "Notice to Allow Claims" in the Utica court. The Notice of Claims served by the trustees in Albany shall be filed with the Clerk.

(1) *Debtor's Objection to Additional or Amended Claim.* Unless the court orders otherwise, if an amended claim is filed or a claim is filed pursuant to Local Bankruptcy Rule 3001-1, objections must be served within 90 days of the service of the Notice of Additional or Amended Claim by the trustee.

(2) *Secured Claims.* An entity holding an allowed secured claim that obtains relief from stay shall not continue to receive the payments provided for in the confirmed plan once the trustee receives the order granting the relief. Funds to be distributed by the trustee on the allowed claim may recommence only upon the consent of the parties or upon application and Order of the Court.

(3) *Amended Secured Claims.* The affected creditor referred to in subsection (b)(2) shall retain the right to file an amended claim. The amended claim shall state:

(A) the date and terms of the disposal of the secured property;

(B) the name of the entity to whom the secured property was transferred;

(C) the consideration received therefor; and

(D) a detail of all charges claimed in retaking, holding and disposing of the property.

[Effective January 1, 1998. Amended effective October 24, 2005.]

Comment

Subsection (a) of this rule sets a date by which objections to claims must be filed in chapter 11 cases in order to expedite the resolution of administrative matters remaining after confirmation. In many chapter 11 cases, a plan proponent should and will file objections to claims earlier and well in advance of confirmation in order to have objections resolved prior to confirmation.

Subsection (b) of this rule presumes that a creditor who has obtained relief from the stay will proceed to recover the collateral securing its loan thereby obviating the necessity of continued payments on the secured portion of the claim. Despite stay relief, however, the rule encourages the parties to resolve outstanding issues to allow continued payment on the secured claim under the terms of the confirmed plan.

RULE 3012–1. VALUATION OF COLLATERAL

The following rules shall apply with respect to the valuation of collateral in chapter 13 cases.

(a) Debtor's Duty to Make Property Available for Appraisal. Unless otherwise ordered by the court, within ten days of a written request by a party in interest, the debtor must make available any item of personalty for appraisal. The appraisal shall be conducted at the debtor's residence absent specific contrary agreement of the parties. It shall be the affirmative duty of the debtor to contact the party in interest requesting the appraisal to arrange for the appraisal or to seek a protective order.

(b) Failure to Appear at Valuation Hearing. Unless otherwise determined by the court, if the debtor appears but the creditor fails to appear at any valuation hearing, the court may find that the value of the collateral is as set forth in the debtor's schedules. If an objecting creditor appears at a valuation hearing and the debtor fails to appear, the court may find the value of the collateral is the value as appraised by the creditor.

[Effective January 1, 1998. Amended effective October 24, 2005.]

RULE 3015–1. CHAPTERS 12 & 13—PLAN

(a) Disclosure of Minimum Percentage Payment to Unsecured Creditors. The debtor's plan shall state the specific minimum percentage to be paid to unsecured creditors.

(b) Payment of Real Property Taxes Through the Plan. If the debtor proposes to pay delinquent real property taxes through the plan, then, for each parcel affected, debtor's counsel shall supply to the chapter 12 or 13 trustee not later than the date scheduled for the § 341 meeting of creditors, the following:

(1) tax map section, block and lot numbers or other identifying numbers of the real property at issue, the name(s) in whom the parcel is assessed and a copy of the tax map; and

(2) name, title and address of each real estate tax collector to whom the trustee is to pay taxes, together with the taxing entity of each (e.g., county name, school district name, city or village).

(c) Service of Plan Filed After Petition. If a debtor elects to file a plan after the filing of the petition pursuant to Fed. R. Bankr. P. 3015, the debtor's attorney, or, if pro se, the debtor, must serve the plan or a complete summary of the proposed plan, together with a notice of the hearing on confirmation, on each creditor, the trustee and the United States trustee. The debtor's attorney or the pro se debtor must also file an appropriate certificate of service with the court and provide a copy to the trustee. The certificate of service shall be filed within five days of effecting service and no later than seven days prior to the return date of the confirmation hearing.

[Effective January 1, 1998. Amended effective October 24, 2005.]

RULE 3015–2. CHAPTERS 12 AND 13—AMENDMENTS OR MODIFICATIONS TO PLANS

(a) If a debtor or other proponent in a chapter 12 or chapter 13 case wishes to amend a proposed plan or modify a confirmed plan, the debtor or other proponent shall:

(1) serve a copy of the notice of the amendment or modification on the trustee, the United States trustee and all creditors;

(2) file the original notice with the clerk within ten days after service;

(3) file a certificate of service with the clerk and provide a copy to the trustee within ten days after service; and

(4) file an original amended or modified plan with the clerk and serve a copy on the trustee and United States trustee.

(b) A notice of plan amendment or modification shall include, but is not limited to, the following disclosures:

(1) a clear statement of the amendment or modification, with specific reference to the provisions of the previously filed plan that are being amended or modified;

(2) any change in the dividend to be paid to unsecured creditors, indicating the specific numerical change in the dividend;

(3) any change in the time for final payment under the plan;

(4) any change in the plan payment;

(5) any effect on the specific treatment of secured creditors under the plan; and

(6) the exact reasons for the amendment or modification, including specific and detailed changes in the budget of the debtor, or other circumstances of the debtor that would justify the amendment or modification.

(c) For a preconfirmation amended plan, notice of the amended plan shall not be later than 20 days prior to the date fixed for the hearing on confirmation of the plan, or any adjournment thereof. The notice shall

advise detrimentally affected parties of any adjourned confirmation hearing date and time.

[Effective January 1, 1998. Amended effective October 24, 2005.]

Comment

This rule is intended to supplement 11 U.S.C. §§ 1223, 1323, 1229 and 1329 and Fed. R. Bankr. P. 2002(a)(5) and 3015. The procedure for postconfirmation modifications can be found in Local Bankruptcy Rule 9013–4(b)(21).

RULE 3015–3. CHAPTERS 12 AND 13—CONFIRMATION

The confirmation order shall be prepared and submitted by the trustee. Upon written request, the trustee shall serve a copy of the proposed confirmation order upon any requesting party prior to or at the time of its submission to the court. Within ten days of the service of the order, debtor's counsel or any other entity served with the order, shall notify the trustee of any objections to the terms of the order.

[Effective January 1, 1998. Amended effective October 24, 2005.]

RULE 3015–4. CHAPTERS 12 AND 13—OBJECTIONS TO CONFIRMATION

(a) Service of Objection. Any objection to confirmation must be in writing, filed with the clerk and served on the debtor, debtor's attorney and the trustee no later than five business days before the scheduled hearing on confirmation.

(b) Appearance Required Upon Written Objection. If a written objection is served, all parties shall be present at the confirmation hearing. If the objecting creditor or creditor's counsel fails to appear at the confirmation hearing, the court may treat the objecting party's absence as a waiver of the objection. If debtor's counsel is absent, the court may deny confirmation.

(c) Objections to confirmation shall:

1. Specify the number and letter section(s) of Title 11 of the United States Code upon which the objection is grounded;

2. allege the specific facts which support the objections to confirmation; and

3. summarize the creditor's claims against the debtor including the alleged classification (secured, unsecured, priority or administrative) and the amount of the claim(s).

(d) Separate Pleading Required. Objection(s) to confirmation shall be treated as responsive pleadings only and may not be combined with any motion seeking any affirmative relief other than denial of confirmation.

[Effective January 1, 1998.]

Comment

This rule is intended to address the procedure by which objections to confirmation in chapter 12 and 13 cases are framed for consideration by the court. Since objections to confirmation are frequently resolved by the insertion of special provisions in the order of confirmation, subsection (c) of this rule facilitates the process of "settling" the terms of the confirmation order prior to its entry by the court.

RULE 3015–5. CHAPTER 13—ADMINISTRATION OF PAYROLL DEDUCTION ORDERS

(a) Implementation of Payroll Deduction Order. Proposed Payroll Deduction Orders in pending Chapter 13 cases shall be prepared and submitted by the debtor's attorney or the Chapter 13 Trustee. Payroll Deduction Orders shall be produced with word processing software and contain the debtor's name, case number, redacted social security number (last four digits), employer's name, employer's address, the amount of the deduction, and the address where Chapter 13 plan payments should be sent.

(b) Termination of Payroll Deduction Order. Upon completion of a Chapter 13 plan, an Order Ceasing Payroll Deduction shall be prepared and submitted by the debtor's attorney or the Trustee.

(c) Amended Payroll Deduction Orders. In the event the debtor changes employment during the course of the Chapter 13 case, and a new Payroll Deduction Order is desired, the debtor's attorney or the Trustee must prepare and submit a new Payroll Deduction Order, which must be clearly marked "Amended".

[Effective October 24, 2005.]

RULE 3016–1. CHAPTER 11—PLAN

The jurisdictional statement in the chapter 11 plan shall reflect the fact that the court will retain jurisdiction until there is substantial consummation of the plan. The court may find a plan to be substantially consummated at the time the first payment is made pursuant to the plan if the other conditions of 11 U.S.C. § 1101(2) are satisfied.

[Effective January 1, 1998.]

RULE 3016–2. DISCLOSURE STATEMENT— GENERAL

A proposed disclosure statement submitted for court approval shall contain on its face the following language, or words of similar import, in boldface type:

THIS IS NOT A SOLICITATION OF ACCEPTANCE OR REJECTION OF THE PLAN. ACCEPTANCE OR REJECTION MAY NOT BE SOLICITED UNTIL A DISCLOSURE STATEMENT HAS BEEN APPROVED BY THE BANKRUPTCY COURT. THIS DISCLOSURE STATEMENT IS BEING SUBMITTED FOR APPROVAL BUT HAS NOT BEEN APPROVED BY THE COURT.

[Effective January 1, 1998.]

RULE 3017–1. DISCLOSURE STATEMENT—APPROVAL

(a) Amended Disclosure Statement. Any amended disclosure statement shall be prepared with any additions bolded and deletions crossed out. The amended disclosure statement shall be filed with the clerk, with a copy to chambers, and served on the United States trustee and other parties in interest.

(b) Condition of Approval. Except for good cause shown, no order shall be entered approving the disclosure statement unless all operating statements have been filed and served pursuant to Fed. R. Bankr. P. 2015(a)(3) and Local Bankruptcy Rule 2015–2.

[Effective January 1, 1998. Amended effective October 24, 2005.]

RULE 3018–1. BALLOTS— VOTING ON PLANS

(a) Filing and Review. All chapter 11 ballots transmitted to creditors for the purpose of voting to accept or reject the proposed plan of reorganization shall be filed with the proponent of the plan. Ballots received shall be made available for review, upon request, by any party in interest.

(b) Certification. At least three business days prior to the hearing on confirmation, the proponent of a plan shall certify to the court the amount and number of allowed claims or interests of each class accepting or rejecting the plan in accordance with 11 U.S.C. § 1126. The ballots received by the proponent of the plan must be submitted to the court as an exhibit to the certification. A copy of the certification shall be served by the proponent on the debtor, trustee, if any, United States trustee and any court approved committee. On the basis of the certification, the court may find that the plan is subject to confirmation. If an issue is raised as to the proponent's compliance with 11 U.S.C. § 1126, the court may hold an evidentiary hearing prior to any confirmation hearing.

Failure to timely file the required certification and ballots is cause for the court to postpone the hearing on confirmation.

[Effective January 1, 1998.]

Subsection (b) of this rule imposes a certification requirement that permits the court to rely on such certification in determining whether a plan has been accepted or rejected pursuant to 11 U.S.C. § 1126.

RULE 3019–1. CHAPTER 11—AMENDMENTS TO PLANS

In the event that the proponent of a chapter 11 plan files a modification of the plan after transmittal of the approved disclosure statement and before acceptance of the plan, the proponent shall file and serve a copy of the plan, as modified, on the debtor, trustee, if any, the United States trustee and any creditors' or equity security holders' committee appointed pursuant to Title 11 of the United States Code. On notice to such entities, the court shall determine whether the modification adversely affects the treatment of the claim of any creditor or the interest of any equity security holder who has not accepted the modification in writing. If the modification is not adverse, the plan, as modified, shall be deemed accepted by all creditors and equity security holders who accept the plan. If the modification is adverse, the requirements of Fed. R. Bankr. P. 3017 shall apply to the modified plan and any amendment of the disclosure statement made necessary by the modification. The proponent of the modified plan shall file a certificate of service with the clerk after service of the notice of the hearing on the modified plan upon affected entities.

[Effective January 1, 1998. Amended effective October 24, 2005.]

Comment

Pursuant to 11 U.S.C. § 1127(a), the proponent of a chapter 11 plan may modify such plan at any time before confirmation. While Fed. R. Bankr. P. 3019 governs modification of a plan after acceptance and before confirmation, this rule governs modification subsequent to the transmission of an approved disclosure statement and before acceptance.

RULE 3020–1. CHAPTER 11—CONFIRMATION

(a) Objection to Confirmation. An objection to the confirmation of a chapter 11 plan shall be served and filed not later than five business days prior to the first date set for the hearing to consider confirmation of a plan, or by such other date as the court may fix.

(b) Withdrawal of Objection. In the event an objection to confirmation of a plan is withdrawn or abandoned, the plan shall not be confirmed unless the plan's proponent, together with counsel, state on the record or by affidavit the consideration promised or given, directly or indirectly, for the withdrawal or failure to prosecute the objection.

(c) Motions to Confirm by "Cram–Down". If the proponent of the plan intends to seek confirmation of the plan as to one or more classes pursuant to 11 U.S.C. § 1129(b), the proponent shall file and serve upon the member or members of such class or classes, not less than seven business days prior to the hearing to consider confirmation, notice of its intent to seek confirmation of the plan as to such class or classes pursuant to 11 U.S.C. § 1129(b). Such notice shall be accompanied by an affidavit setting forth the facts and circumstances necessary to establish that the plan's treatment of such class or classes complies with the applicable provisions of 11 U.S.C. § 1129(b).

[Effective January 1, 1998.]

Comment

Subsection (a) of this rule designates a fixed time for filing and service of an objection to confirmation as permitted by Fed. R. Bankr. P. 3020(b)(1). Subsection (c) sets forth the required procedure for requesting the court to "cram-down" a given class which has not accepted the plan.

RULE 3021–1. CHAPTER 11—AFFIDAVIT REPORTING POST CONFIRMATION DISBURSEMENTS

(a) Requirement. The proponent of the plan or the disbursing agent defined by the plan or designated by the court shall file with the court and serve upon the United States Trustee an affidavit reporting all cash disbursements for each month after confirmation of the plan.

(b) Time for Filing. The affidavit shall be due on the 15th day of the month following the reported month. The duty to file the monthly affidavit shall cease upon entry of the final decree pursuant to Fed. R. Bankr. P. 3022, the conversion of the case to another chapter, or the dismissal of the case, unless otherwise ordered by the court.

(c) Contents. The monthly affidavit shall disclose all disbursements, including but not limited to:

(1) the total amount of payments made for the reported month pursuant to the plan, with a subtotal of payments for each class defined in the plan, and a statement explaining whether the total amount paid to the class complies with the terms of the plan, is in a lesser amount or whether there is good faith dispute about the amount owed;

(2) the administrative expenses paid; and

(3) the total of cash disbursements made in the ongoing operation of the debtor's business, if any.

[Effective October 24, 2005.]

RULE 3022–1. CHAPTER 11—FINAL REPORT/DECREE

(a) Disbursing Agent. At the time of confirmation of the chapter 11 plan, the court may designate an individual to serve as disbursing agent for the purpose of making the first payment pursuant to the plan. Any designated disbursing agent shall be named in the order of confirmation.

(b) Report of Substantial Consummation. The proponent of the plan shall file a report of substantial consummation which provides a basis for the court to find that the proponent of the plan has satisfied the criteria of 11 U.S.C. § 1101(2).

The report of substantial consummation shall be accompanied by a motion for final decree on notice to all creditors and parties in interest. Unless otherwise ordered by the court, the final report form, a proposed final decree, the cancelled checks representing the distributions made pursuant to the confirmed plan and the supplementary exhibit to the application for final compensation required by Local Bankruptcy Rule 2016–1 are not required to be served with the motion but must be filed with the court.

Based on the information received, the court shall ascertain whether the case has been fully administered and entertain the entry of the proposed final decree closing the case. Pursuant to Fed. R. Bankr. P. 3022, factors the court may consider in determining whether the estate has been fully administered include: (1) whether the order confirming the plan has become final; (2) whether deposits required by the plan have been distributed; (3) whether the property proposed by the plan to be transferred has been transferred; (4) whether the debtor or the successor of the debtor under the plan has assumed the business or the management of the property dealt with by the plan; (5) whether payments under the plan have commenced; and (6) whether all motions, contested matters and adversary proceedings have been finally resolved.

(c) Time for Filing. The court may require the report of substantial consummation to be filed as early as the time that all checks have cleared as to the first payment made under the plan. In no event shall the report be filed later than 180 days after entry of a final order confirming a plan unless the court, for cause shown, extends the time upon motion filed and served within the original 180 day period.

[Effective January 1, 1998. Amended effective October 24, 2005.]

Comment

The court may name the debtor, debtor's attorney or some other individual to serve as disbursing agent with respect to making the first payment under the plan. Any compensation to a disbursing agent must be preapproved by the court.

Section 350(a) of the Code and Fed. R. Bankr. P. 3022 provide that the court shall enter a final decree closing a case when it is fully administered, on the court's own motion or on motion of a party in interest. Those authorities, however, provide no deadline for such motions. It has been the experience of the court that there has often been an inordinate and unnecessary delay in filing such motions. This rule is intended to remedy that problem.

The court may administratively close the case after the first payment is made under the plan and the required report and accompanying documents are filed by the plan proponent. Under this rule, the plan proponent must file the report not later than 180 days after confirmation or as otherwise directed by the court.

The final report shall be signed and sworn to or affirmed and shall include the proper caption, but is not limited to, the following information:

1. Administrative expenses:

Trustee compensation (if applicable) $_____
Attorney for trustee compensation
(if applicable) $_____
Attorney for debtor compensation $_____
Other professionals compensation $_____
All expenses $_____
Total administrative expenses $_____

2. Percentage of claims paid:

Percentage of claims paid to general unsecured creditors _____%

I hereby certify under penalty of perjury as provided by 28 U.S.C. § 1746 that the foregoing statements contained herein are true and correct.

Once jurisdiction has been divested by the bankruptcy court, in the event of a subsequent default by the debtor under the terms of its confirmed plan, aggrieved creditors have the remedy of suit on the plan and order of confirmation. The debtor's confirmed plan creates obligations of the debtor to creditors which have been substituted for the debtor's prepetition obligations. These obligations are valid and enforceable in state and federal courts which otherwise have jurisdiction over the parties and their claims.

RULE 4001–1. AUTOMATIC STAY—RELIEF FROM

See Local Bankruptcy Rule 9013–4 (Default Motion Practice).

[Effective January 1, 1998.]

RULE 4001–3. OBTAINING CREDIT

If authority for obtaining credit or incurring debt is sought pursuant to 11 U.S.C. § 364(c) or (d), the notice of motion shall expressly state whether priority over any or all administrative expenses specified in 11 U.S.C. §§ 503(b)(2) or 507(b) is sought, and the names of those creditors specifically affected thereby.

[Effective January 1, 1998.]

RULE 4001–4. CHAPTERS 12 AND 13—OBTAINING CREDIT

(a) The debtor shall make written application to the trustee for approval to incur any non-emergency consumer debt that does not involve a material modification of the debtor's budget. The debtor shall not file the application with the clerk. If approved by the trustee, the trustee shall file the approval and the application with the clerk. If not approved by the trustee, the debtor may then file a motion to incur nonemergency consumer debt and the motion shall contain as an attachment the trustee's denial.

(b) If a motion is required, the motion shall be on notice to the trustee, the United States trustee and all creditors.

[Effective January 1, 1998.]

Comment

This rule facilitates the process whereby a chapter 12 or 13 debtor may incur ordinary credit of a nonemergency nature which does not materially affect the debtor's budget. This could involve, for example, a debtor incurring credit to finance an automobile during the life of a plan.

RULE 4002–2. ADDRESS OF DEBTOR

If the address of the debtor or the debtor's attorney is changed at any time during the administration of the case, the debtor shall immediately provide written notice of such change to the clerk, the United States trustee, any trustee or committee and any other parties affected thereby.

[Effective January 1, 1998.]

Comment

See also Local Bankruptcy Rules 9011–1 and 9011–2.

RULE 4080–1. CHAPTERS 12 AND 13—EMERGENCY REFUND OR CREDIT

(a) Written Request to Trustee. The trustee is authorized to issue an emergency refund or allow an emergency credit in chapter 12 or 13 cases from property of the estate in an amount not to exceed one monthly payment or credit per case, per year, provided:

(1) that the request for such refund or credit is in writing;

(2) that the request is signed by the debtor (both debtors in a joint case) or by the debtor's counsel;

(3) that exigent circumstances support such emergency refund or credit; and

(4) that the issuance of the refund or allowance of the credit will not substantially affect distributions to creditors.

(b) Form of Emergency Refund or Credit. In the trustee's discretion, the trustee may issue an emergency refund check or allow the debtor to forego the next monthly payment.

[Effective January 1, 1998.]

RULE 5005–1. PLACE OF FILING

All petitions, motions, pleadings, memoranda of law, or other documents required to be in writing must be filed electronically or in the office of the clerk where the assigned judge sits. After regular business hours on weekdays, on Saturdays, Sundays and legal holidays, the clerk or court, when good cause is shown, may make arrangements to permit the filing of pleadings or other papers at locations other than the official courthouses within the district.

[Effective January 1, 1998. Amended effective October 24, 2005.]

RULE 5005–4. ELECTRONIC FILING

All papers, with the exception of those listed in the Administrative Procedure, shall be filed electronically using the Electronic Case Filing System. Documents may not be filed by facsimile transmission, electronic mail transmission or on disk.

[Effective January 1, 1998. Amended effective October 24, 2005.]

RULE 5005–5. ELECTRONIC CASE FILING (ECF) PASSWORDS

(a) Requirement to Have Password for Electronic Filing. An ECF password is required to file any document electronically. Attorneys, creditors and claims agents may receive ECF passwords to file papers electronically.

(b) Attorney Password—Within District. An attorney password allows an attorney to electronically file all types of documents. Each attorney admitted to practice in this court must submit to the Bankruptcy Court a completed Attorney/Participant Registration Form (Form A), a Credit Card Blanket Authorization Form (Form C) and be trained on the ECF system before the attorney will be allowed to have a password. Training is available from either the Bankruptcy Court for the Northern District of New York or the District Court for the Northern District of New York.

(c) Attorney Password—Out of District. Out of district attorneys authorized to file electronically in another court will be provided with a password to the ECF system upon submission to the Bankruptcy Court of the Out of District Attorney Registration Form (Form B), a Credit Card Blanket Authorization Form (Form C) and the successful completion of the court's on-line ECF test. The test covers aspects of the local rules and the Administrative Procedure.

(d) Creditor/Limited Use Password. Creditors who are not represented by an attorney and claims agents may obtain a creditor/limited use password. The limited use password will allow the filing of proofs of claim, objections to claim, transfers of claim, objections to transfer of claim, requests to reclassify claims, withdrawals of claim, notices of appearance, creditors request for notice, reaffirmation agreements and certificates of service.

(e) Registration Forms for Obtaining Passwords. Registration forms are contained in the Administrative Procedure and are available at the court's website: www.nynb.uscourts.gov. Forms received by e-mail or fax will not be processed. All signed original Attorney Participant or Out of District Attorney Registration Forms shall be mailed or delivered to:

> IT Manager
> United States Bankruptcy Court
> James T. Foley U.S. Court House
> 445 Broadway
> Suite 330
> Albany, NY 12207

(f) Credit Card Blanket Authorization Forms. All signed original Credit Card Blanket Authorization Forms shall be mailed or delivered in an envelope marked CONFIDENTIAL and addressed as follows:

> Budget Analyst
> United States Bankruptcy Court
> James T. Foley U.S. Court House
> 445 Broadway
> Suite 330
> Albany, NY 12207

(g) Scheduling of Training. Training on ECF will be scheduled according to the order in which the completed Registration Form and Credit Card Blanket Authorization Form are received by the court.

(h) Login and Password Serves as Signature. The filing of a document in the CM/ECF system by an attorney or creditor who uses the assigned login and password constitutes a signature for purposes of Bankruptcy Rule 9011.

[Effective October 24, 2005.]

RULE 5005–6. PRIVACY

(a) Personal Identifiers. Except as required by Bankruptcy Rules 1005, 1007(f) and 2002(a)(1) (effective 12/1/2003) and unless ordered by the court, parties are to refrain from including, or are to partially redact when inclusion is necessary, the following personal data identifiers from papers filed with the court, including any exhibits thereto:

(1) *Social Security Numbers.* If an individual's social security number must be included in a pleading, only the last four digits of the number should be used. This instruction does not apply to Tax ID numbers.

(2) *Names of Minor Children.* If the involvement of a minor child must be mentioned, only the initials of the child should be used.

(3) *Dates of Birth.* If an individual's date of birth must be included in a pleading, only the year should be used.

(4) *Financial Account Numbers.* If the financial account numbers are relevant, only the last four digits of these numbers should be used.

(b) Responsibility. The responsibility for redacting personal identifiers rests solely with the counsel and the parties. The clerk will not review each pleading or other paper for compliance with this rule and will not redact personal identifiers.

[Effective October 24, 2005.]

RULE 5010–1. REOPENING CASES

A motion to reopen a case pursuant to Fed. R. Bankr. P. 5010 shall be in writing and shall be accompanied by the appropriate filing fee. Unless otherwise ordered by the court, the motion shall be brought on notice to the former trustee, the United States trustee and, when the moving party is not the debtor, to the debtor.

If the case has been transmitted to the Federal Records Center for storage, a separate retrieval fee must accompany the motion. The filing fee but not a retrieval fee may be waived by the court if a case is reopened to correct an administrative error or on account of actions relating to discharge.

[Effective January 1, 1998. Amended effective October 24, 2005.]

Comment

The requirement to reopen a closed case by motion and payment of the appropriate filing fee applies to both conventionally filed cases and electronically filed cases.

RULE 5011–1. WITHDRAWAL OF REFERENCE

(a) Form of Request and Place for Filing. A request for withdrawal in whole or in part of the reference of a case or proceeding, other than a sua sponte request by the Bankruptcy Judge, shall be by timely motion of a party and in accordance with Local Rule 9013–1. The Bankruptcy Judge may not conduct hearings on a withdrawal motion, but the motion should be filed with the bankruptcy clerk and a fee should be collected. The fee is equal to the civil action filing fee under 28 U.S.C. Sec. 1914(a). All such motions shall clearly and conspicuously state that: RELIEF IS SOUGHT FROM A UNITED STATES DISTRICT JUDGE as per Fed. R. Bankr. P. 5011(a).

(b) Stay. The filing of a motion to withdraw the reference does not stay proceedings in the bankruptcy court. The procedures relating to stay shall be the same as set forth in Fed. R. Bankr. P. 8005.

(c) Responses to Motions to Withdraw the Reference. Opposing parties shall file with the bankruptcy clerk and serve on all parties to the matter to which withdrawal of the reference has been requested, their written responses to the motion to withdraw the reference, within 11 days of service of a copy of the motion.

(d) Designation of Record. Upon the entry by the bankruptcy clerk of an order by a United States District Judge granting the motion and where the order is to the bankruptcy case, the moving party shall file a list designating those portions of the record of the proceedings in the bankruptcy court that the moving party believes will be reasonably necessary or pertinent. If the record designated by any party includes a transcript of any proceeding or a part thereof, that party shall immediately after filing the designation deliver to the reporter and file with the bankruptcy clerk a written request for the transcript and make satisfactory arrangements for payment of its cost. Where the order is to an adversary proceeding, the Court shall designate the entire record of the adversary proceeding.

(e) Transmittal to and Proceedings in District Court. When the record is complete for purposes of transmittal, the bankruptcy clerk shall promptly transmit to the district clerk any remaining portions of the record designated. Upon transmittal of the record, documents pertaining to the matter under review by the district court shall be filed with the Clerk of the district court, but all documents relating to other matters in the bankruptcy case or adversary proceeding shall continue to be filed with the bankruptcy clerk. The district court may, at its discretion, retain the entire matter withdrawn or may refer part or all of it back to the Bankruptcy Judge with or without instructions for further proceedings.

[Effective October 24, 2005.]

RULE 5073–1. PHOTOGRAPHY, RECORDING DEVICES & BROADCASTING

(a) Prohibition. All photographing, oral or video tape recording, and radio or television broadcasting is prohibited in the courtroom during the progress of or in connection with judicial proceedings, whether or not court is actually in session. None of the foregoing activities are allowed in the jury rooms, the offices of the judges, or in any room, hallway or corridor of the floor of the building in which the courtrooms are located.

(b) Exception. The court may except ceremonial, investiture and educational proceedings and the ac-

tions of its personnel while acting in an official capacity.

(c) Official Court Reporters. Official court reporters are not prohibited by this rule from making sound recordings for the sole purpose of discharging their official duties. No recording made for that purpose shall be used for any other purposes by any person. Personnel of the court are not prohibited by this rule from making sound recordings in the course of their work.

[Effective January 1, 1998. Amended effective October 24, 2005.]

RULE 5080–1. FEES—GENERAL

Unless otherwise ordered by the court, the clerk shall not be required to render any service for which a fee is prescribed, either by statute or by the Judicial Conference of the United States, including the acceptance of a document for filing, unless the fee for that service is paid in advance or an order is entered pursuant to 28 U.S.C. § 1915(a) granting in forma pauperis status for an adversary proceeding or appeal.

[Effective January 1, 1998.]

Comment

Filing fees for adversary proceedings and appeals are authorized by 28 U.S.C. § 1930(b) and set forth in the Judicial Conference Schedule of Fees.

Upon application and order of the court, adversary proceedings and appeals may be filed in forma pauperis. As required by 28 U.S.C. § 1915(a), a party seeking to proceed in forma pauperis must file an affidavit: (1) advising that the person is unable to pay the fee or give security therefor and (2) stating the nature of the appeal and the affiant's belief as to entitlement to relief.

RULE 6004–1. SALE OF ESTATE PROPERTY

(a) Appraisal Filed With the Court Prior to Sale. Unless otherwise ordered by the court, when an appraiser has been appointed by the court, the appraisal of the property shall be filed no later than two days prior to the return date of the motion to approve the sale of the property. Property subject to an appraisal shall not be sold until after the appraisal has been filed with the clerk and served upon the United States trustee.

(b) Access and Confidentiality of Filed Appraisal. Prior to the sale, the appraisal should never be filed electronically. The appraisal shall be submitted in a sealed envelope marked "confidential—appraisal." The envelope shall also include the complete caption of the case/proceeding and identification of the property appraised. The clerk, the United States trustee and the appraiser shall maintain the confidentiality of the appraisal, unless otherwise directed by the court.

(c) Sale Outside the Ordinary Course of Business in a Chapter 11 Case. In a chapter 11 case, if the debtor or trustee seeks authority to sell property of the estate pursuant to 11 U.S.C. § 363(b) prior to the entry of an order of confirmation, the notice of motion shall contain a clear and conspicuous statement to that effect. In addition to the information required under Fed. R. Bankr. P. 2002(c), the notice of the hearing shall specify the extent to which, if any, the proceeds of sale shall be used to benefit each class of creditors, the extent of the debtor's liabilities and the estimated net value of any of the remaining assets not subject to the proposed sale. The notice shall further articulate the business justification for disposing of estate assets outside the ordinary course of business before a disclosure statement has been approved or a plan confirmed.

[Effective January 1, 1998. Amended effective October 24, 2005.]

Comment

This rule requires special notice of a proposed sale outside the ordinary course of business. Since the proposed sale is outside the normal procedural route for proposal, adoption and confirmation of a proposed plan, it requires special scrutiny by the court. See Committee of Equity Security Holders v. Lionel Corp. (In re Lionel Corp.), 722 F.2d 1063 (2d Cir. 1983).

RULE 6004–2. CHAPTERS 12 AND 13—SALE OR OTHER DISPOSITION OF ESTATE PROPERTY

(a) Motions for Sale of Real Property. The debtor shall file a motion for approval of the sale of real property after a contract of sale is procured. The motion shall be on notice to all parties in interest and shall state the following:

(1) whether or not the debtor's plan has been confirmed;

(2) the address of the property;

(3) whether or not the property is the debtor's residence;

(4) the sale price;

(5) if the property has been appraised and, if so, when and by whom;

(6) the name of each mortgage or lienor and the approximate payoff for each lien;

(7) the approximate amount of unpaid real estate taxes;

(8) the name of any realtors and the proposed real estate commission, and, if none, the marketing efforts;

(9) the proposed attorney's fee payable upon sale, a list and explanation of other proposed deductions from the sale proceeds and the approximate amount of closing costs;

(10) a summary of the total deductions from the sale proceeds and the approximate amount of the sale proceeds to be paid into the plan; and

(11) whether or not the plan provided for a sale.

(b) Disposition of Personal Property Valued at Less Than $2,500. To sell or otherwise dispose of personal property with a value of $2,500 or less, the debtor shall make written application to the trustee and any other creditor with a lien on the property. The debtor shall not file the application with the clerk. If approved by the trustee, the debtor may dispose of or sell the property in accordance with the terms and conditions approved by the trustee. The trustee shall file the approval and application with the clerk. If not approved by the trustee, the debtor may file a motion to dispose of or sell property of the estate, other than real property, and the motion shall contain as an attachment a copy of the trustee's denial. Said motion, if necessary, shall be on notice to all parties in interest.

(c) Fees. All professionals attendant to the sale of real property must have their fees approved by the court prior to payment.

[Effective January 1, 1998.]

RULE 6005–1. APPRAISERS AND AUCTIONEERS

The following shall apply to auctioneers only.

(a) Compensation. Unless otherwise ordered by the court for cause shown, compensation and reimbursement of expenses shall be allowed to an auctioneer for sale of property as hereinafter specified.

(1) The maximum allowable commissions on the gross proceeds of each sale are as follows:

(A) 10% of any gross proceeds of sale on the first $100,000 or less;

(B) 5% of any amount in excess of $100,000 but not in excess of $200,000; and

(C) 2.5% of any amount in excess of $200,000.

(2) The auctioneer shall be reimbursed for reasonable and necessary expenses directly related to the sale, including bond or blanket bond premium cost attributable to said sale, labor, printing, advertising and insurance, but excluding worker's compensation, social security, unemployment insurance or other payroll taxes. If directed by the trustee to transport goods, the associated costs shall be reimbursable. Unless the court orders otherwise, an auctioneer shall be reimbursed for a blanket bond at the rate of $100 per case or 10% of the gross proceeds from an auction, whichever is less, less any amounts previously reimbursed for said bond.

(b) Purchase Prohibited. An auctioneer or officer, director, stockholder, agent or employee of an auctioneer shall not purchase directly or indirectly, or have a financial interest in, the purchase of any property of the estate which the auctioneer has been employed to sell.

(c) Bond. An auctioneer employed with court approval shall not act until a surety bond in favor of the United States of America is provided in each estate, at the auctioneer's expense, to be approved by and in such sum as may be fixed by the court, conditioned upon: (1) the faithful and prompt accounting for all monies and property which may come into the possession of the auctioneer; (2) compliance with all rules, orders and decrees of the court; and (3) the faithful performance of duties in all respects. In lieu of a bond in each case, an auctioneer may be permitted to file a blanket bond covering all cases in which the auctioneer may act. Such blanket bond shall be at the expense of the auctioneer, shall be in favor of the United States of America and shall be in an amount sufficient to cover the aggregate appraised value of all property to be sold.

(d) Report of Sale. The auctioneer shall file a report with the clerk and serve the United States trustee within 30 days after conclusion of the sale. The report of sale shall set forth: (1) the time, date and place of sale; (2) the gross amount realized by the sale; (3) an itemized statement of commissions sought under this rule and disbursements made, including the name of the payee and the original receipts or cancelled checks, or copies thereof, substantiating the disbursements. Where labor charges are included, the report shall specify the name(s) of the person(s) employed, the hourly wage and the number of hours worked by each person. If the cancelled checks are not available at the time the report is filed, then the report shall so state, and the cancelled checks shall be filed as soon as they become available; (4) where the auctioneer has a blanket insurance policy covering all sales conducted for which original receipts and cancelled checks are not available, an explanation of how the insurance expense charged to the estate was allocated; (5) the names of all purchasers at the sale; (6) the sign-in sheet, indicating the number of people attending the sale; (7) the disposition of any items for which there were no bid; (8) the terms and conditions of sale read to the audience immediately prior to the commencement of the sale; (9) a statement of the manner and extent of advertising the sale and the availability of the items for inspection prior to the sale; (10) the amount of sales tax collected; and (11) such other information as the court may require.

(e) Proceeds of the Amount of Sale. Unless otherwise ordered by the court, the proceeds of sale less the auctioneer's reimbursable expenses, shall be turned over to the trustee as soon as practicable and not later than 20 days from the date of sale or shall be deposited in a separate interest-bearing account. The court retains the jurisdiction to review the auction-eer's reimbursable expenses for reasonableness. In the event, the court determines that a portion of the expenses deducted from the proceeds of the sale are unreasonable, the auctioneer shall be required to return those funds to the trustee.

(f) Application for Commissions and Expenses. An auctioneer shall apply to the court for approval of commissions and expenses on not less than 20 days notice as required by Fed. R. Bankr. P. 2002 and Local Bankruptcy Rule 2002–1. No such application shall be granted unless the report referred to in subsection (d) of this rule has been filed.

[Effective January 1, 1998.]

RULE 6007–1. ABANDONMENT [DISPOSITION OF PROPERTY]

(a) The trustee may place in storage, at the expense of the estate, the debtor's books, records and papers. Upon issuance of the final decree, the trustee may return the debtor's books, records and papers to the debtor or its principal(s).

(b) The trustee may dispose of all the debtor's records in the trustee's possession, including debtor's books, records and papers, after issuance of the final decree, providing that debtor's books, records and papers have been first offered to the debtor.

(c) The trustee may retain those documents and materials which, in the trustee's judgment, may be useful in supporting performance of the trustee's duties.

[Effective January 1, 1998.]

RULE 7003–1. COVER SHEET

A complaint filed to commence an adversary proceeding shall be accompanied by an Adversary Proceeding Cover Sheet (Form B 104, Administrative Office of the U.S. Courts).

[Effective January 1, 1998.]

RULE 7004–2. SUMMONS

Complaints may be electronically filed. A summons, however, must be presented conventionally to the clerk's office. If the summons is in proper form, the clerk's office will sign, seal and issue the summons to the plaintiff for service on the defendant. The plaintiff or third-party plaintiff or their counsel will be responsible for serving the summons and the complaint. A summons, or a copy of the summons if addressed to multiple defendants, shall be provided by the plaintiff in sufficient numbers for each defendant to be served.

[Effective January 1, 1998. Amended effective October 24, 2005.]

Comment

Practitioners are referred to Fed. R. Bankr. P. 7004 for acceptable methods of service.

RULE 7016–1. PRETRIAL PROCEDURES

Insofar as Fed.R.Civ.P. 16(b), made applicable to bankruptcy by Fed. R. Bankr. P. 7016, mandates a scheduling order, it shall not be applicable to adversary proceedings.

[Effective January 1, 1998. Amended effective October 24, 2005.]

Comment

The court will issue pretrial orders, as appropriate. This rule should be read in conjunction with Local Bankruptcy Rule 7026–1.

RULE 7026–1. DISCOVERY—GENERAL

(a) **Required Disclosure.** The affirmative disclosure required to be made by a party under Fed. R.Civ.P. 26(a)(1), (2) and (3) as incorporated by Fed. R. Bankr. P. 7026, without awaiting a discovery request, shall be operative unless specifically ordered in a given proceeding.

(b) **Meeting of Parties.** Unless otherwise ordered by the court, the provisions of Fed.R.Civ.P. 26(d) and (f), as incorporated by Fed. R. Bankr. P. 7026, insofar as they mandate an actual meeting of the parties 14 days before a scheduling conference, require the submission of a written report and prohibit a party from seeking discovery from any source prior to any such meeting, shall not apply to contested matters or adversary proceedings.

[Effective January 1, 1998. Amended effective October 24, 2005.]

Comment

This provision permits the court to limit the provisions of Fed.R.Civ.P. 26, as made applicable to bankruptcy by Fed. R. Bankr. P. 7026, on a case by case basis As a general rule, however, the times specified within the federal rule do not easily conform to the time frame within which contested matters governed by Fed. R. Bankr. P. 9014 are heard, nor, for how adversary proceedings are handled.

This rule should be read in conjunction with Local Bankruptcy Rule 7016–1.

RULE 7026–2. DISCOVERY MOTIONS

(a) **Required Affidavit.** No discovery motion shall be heard by the court unless counsel for the movant files with the court an affidavit at or prior to the hearing on the motion certifying that counsel for the movant has conferred with counsel for the opposing party in a good faith effort to resolve by agreement the issues raised by the motion and that counsel have been unable to reach such an agreement. If part of the issues have been resolved by agreement, the affidavit

shall identify the issues so resolved and the issues remaining unresolved.

(b) **Decision Without Hearing.** A routine motion to compel answers to interrogatories and to compel compliance with a request for production under Fed. R.Civ.P. 34, wherein it has been averred that no response or objection has been timely served, may be summarily granted or denied by the court without awaiting response.

[Effective January 1, 1998.]

RULE 7033–1. INTERROGATORIES TO PARTIES

The automatic limitation to 25 in number of written interrogatories which may be served upon a party contained in Fed.R.Civ.P. 33(a) as incorporated by Fed. R. Bankr. P. 7033 shall apply in bankruptcy proceedings, unless ordered otherwise or consented to by the parties.

[Effective January 1, 1998. Amended effective October 24, 2005.]

Comment

Revision of Fed.R.Civ.P. 33 to limit the number of interrogatories to "25 in number including all discrete subparts" corresponded to the simultaneous revision of Fed.R.Civ.P. 26(a)(1)-(3) requiring affirmative disclosure of much of the information previously obtained by interrogatory.

RULE 7056–1. SUMMARY JUDGMENT

On a motion for summary judgment pursuant to Fed.R.Civ.P. 56, there shall be annexed to the notice of motion a separate, short and concise statement of the material facts as to which the moving party contends there is no genuine issue, with specific citations to the record.

The papers opposing a motion for summary judgment shall include a separate, short and concise statement of the material facts as to which it is contended that there exists a genuine issue, with specific citations to the record where the factual issues arise. All material facts set forth in the statement served by the moving party shall be deemed admitted unless controverted by the statement served by the opposing party.

The motion for summary judgment may be denied if the moving party fails to file and serve the statement required by this Local Rule.

[Effective January 1, 1998. Amended effective October 24, 2005.]

RULE 7067–1. REGISTRY FUND

(a) **Orders for Deposit of Funds Into the Registry.** When the clerk is to hold any money pursuant to a directive by the court in connection with any pending case or proceeding, the order directing the establishment of the registry account shall specify:

(1) the amount of the funds to be deposited;

(2) the name and location of the depository institution to receive the funds;

(3) the type of account in which the monies are to be deposited and the current interest payable on the account;

(4) the term of the deposit tailored to individual circumstances and maximized to avoid repeated renewals; and

(5) that deposits and withdrawals from the account can only be made upon further order of the court except for the imposition and collection of the registry fee.

(b) Deposits In Excess of $100,000. If the amount of the deposit is in excess of $100,000, the clerk's office must have 30 days advance notice prior to the receipt of the monies in order to arrange proper collateralization.

(c) Registry Fee. The clerk shall deduct from any interest paid on registry funds a registry fee as authorized by the Judicial Conference of the United States and set by the Director of the Administrative Office. The fee shall be collected periodically as interest accrues and shall be immediately deposited upon collection in the United States Treasury.

(d) Orders For Withdrawal of Registry Funds. At the time of intended disbursement of registry monies, an order is to be submitted to the court which shall contain the following information:

(1) the name and address of the person(s) to receive the monies;

(2) the amount of principal and interest each is to receive; and

(3) the social security number or taxpayer ID number for each recipient of funds.

[Effective January 1, 1998.]

Comment

This rule helps to implement Fed. R Bankr. P. 7067 pertaining to the deposit of money into court. Since the Federal Deposit Insurance Corporation only insures deposits up to $100,000, if the deposit exceeds that sum the depository designated must have sufficient collateral to pledge as outlined in 31 C.F.R. Part 202 (Treasury Circular 176).

The fee charged against interest earned on the registry funds has been 10% since December 1, 1990. It is subject to change and is published periodically by the Director of the Administrative Office in the Federal Register.

Social security and/or taxpayer ID numbers of the payees are required in the order of disbursement for the depository institution's tax reporting records.

RULE 7090–1. DISCONTINUANCE AND SETTLEMENT OF ACTIONS OBJECTING TO DISCHARGE AND DISCHARGEABILITY OF DEBTS

No adversary proceeding to determine the dischargeability of a debt or objection to discharge shall be settled, discontinued or withdrawn except upon court approval and in the case of an objection to discharge after notice to the trustee, the United States trustee and such other persons as the court may direct in accordance with Fed. R. Bankr. P. 7041.

Court approval is conditioned upon full disclosure as to the circumstances of any settlement, including the terms of any agreement entered into between the creditor and the debtor. If the action is not settled or withdrawn in the presence of the court on the record, then plaintiff shall file a proposed order of discontinuance accompanied by a stipulation fully disclosing the circumstances of any settlement and any consideration promised or given, directly or indirectly, for the withdrawal of the action. The court may alternatively direct the defendant to prepare and file the stipulation required by this rule.

[Effective January 1, 1998.]

Comment

See 18 U.S.C. § 152 and Fed. R. Bankr. P. 7041. This rule shall also apply without regard to whether a dispute is settled through mediation.

RULE 7091–1. ADJOURNMENTS

Requests for adjournments of dates fixed for trials and evidentiary hearings shall be presented to the judge to whom the case has been assigned on notice to all parties affected.

(a) Utica Only. Trials and evidentiary hearings may be adjourned one time on consent of the parties. The consent letter shall be sent to Courtroom Services. A further adjournment shall not be granted, except for good cause shown. Any further request should be sent to Courtroom Services.

(b) Albany Only. Trial and evidentiary hearing adjournments shall not be granted, except upon a showing to the court of exceptional circumstances. Any such request shall be sent to Chambers.

All correspondence to Chambers and/or Courtroom Services regarding adjournments shall be electronically filed. The electronic filing is then to be followed with a fax to Chambers and/or Courtroom Services.

[Effective January 1, 1998. Amended effective October 24, 2005.]

RULE 8005–1. STAY PENDING APPEAL [SUPERSEDEAS BOND]

(a) Amount When Money Judgment Only. A supersedeas bond, where the judgment is for a sum of money only, shall be in the amount of the judgment, plus 11% to cover interest and such damages for delay as may be awarded, plus an amount to be determined by the court, to cover costs.

(b) Amount Fixed by the Court. When the stay may be effected solely by the giving of the supersedeas bond, but the judgment or order is not solely for a sum of money, the court, on notice, shall fix the amount of the bond. In all other cases, it may, on notice, grant a stay on such terms as to security and otherwise as it may deem proper.

(c) Objections. Upon approval, a supersedeas bond shall be filed with the clerk, and a copy thereof, with notice of filing, promptly served on all parties affected thereby. If the appellee raises objections to the form of the bond, or to the sufficiency of the surety, the court shall hold a hearing on expedited notice to all parties.

[Effective January 1, 1998. Amended effective October 24, 2005.]

RULE 8016–2. NOTICE OF ORDER OR JUDGMENT—APPEAL

An order or judgment of an appellate court, when filed in the office of the clerk, shall automatically become the order or judgment of the court and be entered as such by the clerk without further order.

[Effective January 1, 1998.]

RULE 9001–1. DEFINITIONS

In these Local Rules of Bankruptcy Practice:

(1) "administrative order" means any order signed by the bankruptcy judges amending, modifying or supplementing procedures of the United States Bankruptcy Court for the Northern District of New York;

(2) "administrative procedure" means any procedure published by the United States Bankruptcy Court for the Northern District of New York which may amend, modify or supplement local rules and orders of the Court;

(3) "Appellate Court" means the district court where the appeal was taken;

(4) "Bankruptcy Code" or "Code" refers to the Bankruptcy Reform Act of 1978, as amended and set forth in Title 11 of the United States Code;

(5) "Chief Judge" means that individual designated to serve by the district court pursuant to 28 U.S.C. § 154(b);

(6) "clerk" means clerk or deputy clerk of the court;

(7) "conventionally" refers to paper documents submitted to the clerk for filing or lodging;

(8) "court" means the United States Bankruptcy Court for the Northern District of New York established by 28 U.S.C. § 151 and § 152 or, with respect to a case which has not been referred, means the district court;

(9) "district clerk" means clerk or deputy clerk of the district court;

(10) "district court" means the United States District Court for the Northern District of New York;

(11) "district judge" means any United States District Judge appointed to or sitting by designation in the district court;

(12) "District Rules" means the Local Rules of the United States District Court for the Northern District of New York, as amended;

(13) "ECF" means Electronic Case Filing;

(14) "Fed. R. Bankr. P." means the Federal Rules of Bankruptcy Procedure and Official Bankruptcy Forms promulgated pursuant to 28 U.S.C. § 2075 in effect on the effective date of these Local Rules of Bankruptcy Practice and as thereafter amended or enacted;

(15) "judge" means any bankruptcy judge appointed to or sitting by designation in the court or, with respect to a case which has not been referred, it means district judge;

(16) "System" means the Electronic Filing System and is also known as the Electronic Case Filing (ECF) System.

(17) "United States trustee" means the United States trustee, acting United States trustee, assistant United States trustee or attorney therefor for the Northern District of New York, Region 2; and

(18) "United States Trustee Fee Guidelines" means the United States Trustee Guidelines for Reviewing Applications For Compensation and Reimbursement of Expenses Filed Under 11 U.S.C. § 330 adopted by The Executive Office for United States Trustees on January 30, 1996, or as subsequently revised. These Guidelines adopted in 1996 superseded those previously issued on March 22, 1995.

The meanings of other words and phrases used in these Local Bankruptcy Rules shall, unless inconsistent with the context, be construed in accordance with the Bankruptcy Code and Federal Rules of Bankruptcy Procedure.

[Effective January 1, 1998. Amended effective October 24, 2005.]

Comment

These definitions apply only to the interpretation of these Local Bankruptcy Rules.

RULE 9004–1. PAPERS—REQUIREMENTS OF FORM

(a) In conformity with the District Rules and as required by the Judicial Conference, all papers presented for filing must be on standard 8½ x 11 inch white, opaque paper, plainly typed or written on one side and properly paginated at the bottom of each page, with not less than one and one-half spaces between lines except for quoted material.

(b) Backers are not required on proposed orders submitted to the Court.

[Effective January 1, 1998. Amended effective October 24, 2005.]

RULE 9004–2. CAPTION—PAPERS, GENERAL

Papers presented for filing shall bear the name of the court, the title of the case, case number and chapter number assigned thereto, the debtor's redacted social security number and/or employer identification number, and, if pertinent to an adversary proceeding, the adversary proceeding name and assigned number. The papers shall additionally identify the document by a short title.

[Effective January 1, 1998.]

Comment

Signing and verification of papers is governed by Fed. R. Bankr. P. 1008 and 9011. It requires that all papers filed on behalf of a party must be signed by an individual attorney and state an office address and telephone number. A party not represented by an attorney shall sign all papers and state the party's address and telephone number.

RULE 9010–1. ATTORNEYS—NOTICE OF APPEARANCE

Unless otherwise specifically provided, the filing and service of a notice of appearance in a case (as distinguished from the filing of a notice of appearance in an adversary proceeding) containing a request for service of copies of papers filed in the case will be deemed to be a request for only such papers and notices which these Local Bankruptcy Rules or the Federal Rules of Bankruptcy Procedure require to be served on any party requesting the same.

[Effective January 1, 1998.]

Comment

There is no basis in the Bankruptcy Code or the Federal Rules of Bankruptcy Procedure for a party to require service upon it of all papers served in a case. This rule allows a party to avoid the unnecessary expense of service upon a party not otherwise entitled to service. Service of papers in an adversary proceeding is governed by Fed.R.Bankr.P. 7005.

RULE 9010–3. ATTORNEYS—DEBTOR CORPORATIONS

(a) A debtor corporation shall not be permitted to file a petition or proceed under chapters 7, 9, 11 or 12 without representation by an attorney duly admitted to the Northern District of New York.

(b) In the event that counsel for a debtor corporation is permitted to withdraw, the case is subject to automatic dismissal unless new counsel is substituted.

[Effective January 1, 1998.]

Comment

This rule should be read in conjunction with Local Bankruptcy Rule 9011–1.

RULE 9011–1. ATTORNEYS—DUTIES

Unless otherwise determined by the court, an attorney for debtor is required to represent the debtor in all matters related to the bankruptcy case including, but not limited to, defending adversary proceedings commenced pursuant to 11 U.S.C. §§ 523 and 727, attending section 341 meetings, opposing motions to lift stay when appropriate and attending contested confirmation hearings.

[Effective January 1, 1998.]

RULE 9011–2. PRO SE PARTIES

An individual appearing pro se shall file with such individual's initial notice or pleading a designation of the individual's residence address and mailing address, if different, and telephone number where the party can be reached during daytime hours. An individual appearing pro se who is not a resident of the Northern District of New York may be required by the court to designate a mailing address within the Northern District of New York. This requirement shall not apply to an individual who has appeared solely for the purpose of filing a proof of claim or interest.

[Effective January 1, 1998.]

RULE 9011–3. SIGNATURES AND ELECTRONIC FILING

(a) Original Signature and Electronic Filing. Petitions, lists, schedules and statements, amendments, pleadings, affidavits, and other documents which must contain original signatures or which require verification under Fed. R. Bankr. P. 1008 or an unsworn declaration as provided in 28 U.S.C. § 1746, may be filed electronically by attorneys registered in the System.

(b) Format of Electronic Signature. A pleading or other document electronically filed shall indicate a signature, in the format /s/name unless the document has been scanned and shows the actual signature.

(c) Unregistered Attorneys Using a Registered Attorney's Login. Attorneys who are not registered with the Bankruptcy Court of the Northern District of New York and who do not have a login and password provided by the Court are not permitted to electronically file documents using the login and password of a registered attorney. The attorney login name and attorney name shown on a filed document must match.

(d) Retention of Original Signature. A copy containing an original signature must be retained by the filer for a minimum of two (2) years after the closing of the case and all time periods for appeals have expired unless the Court orders a different period. In adversary proceedings, the parties shall maintain the original documents for minimum of two (2) years after the proceeding ends and all time periods for appeals have expired unless the Court orders a different period. These retention periods do not affect or replace any other periods required by other applicable laws or rules. Upon request of the court, the filer must provide original documents for review. Compliance with Fed. R. Bankr. P. 9011 is required.

(e) Electronic Signature on Stipulations or Other Documents Requiring Multiple Signatures. The following procedure applies when a stipulation, which does nor require an order or another document requires two or more signatures:

1. The filer shall initially confirm that the content of the document is acceptable to all persons required to sign the document and shall obtain the physical signatures of all parties on the document. For purposes of this rule, physical, facsimile or electronic signatures are permitted. Compliance with Fed. R. Bankr. P. 9011 is required.

2. The filer shall file the document electronically, indicating each signature using the format /s/name unless the document has been scanned and shows the actual signature.

3. The filing party originating the document shall maintain the original signed document as provided for in subsection (d) above.

[Effective October 24, 2005.]

RULE 9013-1. MOTION PRACTICE

(a) Time and Manner. Unless otherwise ordered by the court, notice of any motion to be heard by the court shall be provided in the time and manner prescribed by the Federal Rules of Bankruptcy Procedure, Local Bankruptcy Rules, and the Administrative Procedure.

(b) Identification of Hearing Date and Time on Motions. In addition to being located in the body of the notice of hearing, information regarding the hearing date, hearing time and hearing place is to be placed at the top of the page on all motions. The information is to be placed immediately above the case number information as shown in the example below.

Example

UNITED STATES BANKRUPTCY COURT
HEARING DATE: October 21, 1997
NORTHERN DISTRICT OF NEW YORK
HEARING TIME: 10:00 A.M.

HEARING PLACE:
Syracuse

In re:

EASTER ISLAND PIZZA, Inc.

Case No. XX—XXXXX

Chapter 11

Debtor.

OBJECTION BY THE UNITED STATES TRUSTEE

TO THE DEBTOR'S APPLICATION TO ASSUME LEASES OF NON–RESIDENTIAL REAL PROPERTY

(c) Service of Motions. Whenever a pleading or other paper is filed electronically, the System will generate a "Notice of Electronic Filing" to the filing party and any other party who has requested electronic notice in that case.

If a recipient of service is a registered participant in the System, the Clerk's e-mailing of the "Notice of Electronic Filing" shall be the equivalent of service of the pleading or other paper by first class mail, postage prepaid.

Service of the "Notice of Electronic Filing" on a party who is not a registered participant in the System may be accomplished by e-mail, subject to the additional service requirements of the paragraph below.

A party who is not a registered participant of the System is entitled to a paper copy of any electronically filed pleading or paper. The filing party must therefore, provide the nonregistered party with the pleading according to the Fed. R. Bankr. P. and these local rules.

A certificate of service on all parties entitled to service or notice is still required when a party files a document electronically. The certificate must state the manner in which service or notice was accomplished on each party so entitled. Sample language for a Certificate of Service can be found in the Administrative Procedure.

(d) Chambers Copy. A Chambers Copy in paper format for chambers is required for the following matters. The copy must be clearly marked as ECF CASE—CHAMBERS COPY. The front page of each Chambers Copy must indicated the date and time of the relevant hearing and is to be submitted contemporaneously with the electronic filing of the motion. The Chambers Copy need not contain a copy of the original signature. Unless directed by the Court, copies should not be faxed to Chambers or Courtroom Services. Copies should be sent via the mail or hand delivered.

Utica Chambers:

(1) Notice of Hearing, Motion, application and certificate of service, and Chapter 7 Final Meeting Notices;

(2) All pleadings filed in an adversary proceeding;

(3) Pretrial statements;

(4) Memoranda of Law or documents filed in regard to a submitted matter;

(5) All documents regarding an appeal, withdrawal of reference, or Fed. R. Bankr. P. 9033 objections.

Albany Chambers:

(1) Notice of Hearing, Motions, applications, and certificates of services, excluding Ch. 13 Standing Trustee's motions to dismiss, motions to determine/expunge claim, motions to determine value and Chapter 7 Final Meeting Notices;

(2) Opposition, response, or any pleading relating to a hearing;

(3) Opposition to disclosure statements in a chapter 11;

(4) Opposition to confirmation of a plan regarding any chapter;

(5) Pretrial statements;

(6) Memoranda of Law or documents filed in regard to a submitted matter.

(e) Timeliness of Service. The filing of documents electronically does not alter the filing deadline for that document. Generally, filings are considered timely if received by the Court before midnight on the date set as a deadline, unless the judge or LBR specifically require an earlier filing, such as close of business. Any motions filed electronically on the last day for filing pursuant to LBR 9013–1 must be filed by 4:00 PM Eastern Standard Time.

Unless otherwise specified in the Federal Rules of Bankruptcy Procedure (particularly Fed. R. Bankr. P. 2002, 3007 and 4007), these Local Bankruptcy Rules, the Administrative Procedure or as ordered by the court, all motions shall be served at least 15 days before the return date of the hearing. All written motions in Chapters 12 and 13 cases shall be served upon the trustee. The moving party shall file the original motion papers, electronically or conventionally, with the clerk's office ten days prior to the return date of the motion and file a certificate of service, electronically or conventionally, no later than seven days prior to the return date of the motion. Failure to file the original motion papers and proof of service may result in the motion not appearing on the court's calendar.

(f) Answering Papers.

(1) Unless otherwise ordered by the court for cause shown, answering papers in opposition shall be filed and served for every written motion other than one which may be considered ex parte or on shortened notice as ordered by the court. Answering papers and any opposing memoranda shall be served and filed so as to be received no later than three business days before the return date of the motion and shall identify the hearing date, time and place at the top of the page.

(2) In the event the court hears oral opposition without papers and adjourns the hearing, answering papers substantiating the oral opposition shall be filed and served within three business days of the original hearing date.

(3) Any answering papers filed electronically or conventionally on the last day for filing pursuant to LBR 9013–1(f)(1) must be filed by 4:00 PM Eastern Standard Time.

(g) Reduction of Time. A request for an order reducing any specified notice period shall be made by application to the appropriate judge for an expedited hearing on the motion pursuant to Fed. R. Bankr. P. 9006(c). Such application shall contain a clear and specific showing by affidavit of good and sufficient reasons for reduction of the notice period.

(h) Notification to Court Regarding Expedited Matters. In expedited matters occurring in Albany, the movant shall contact Courtroom Services staff or Chambers staff by phone as soon as possible after filing the item needing expedited treatment.

In expedited matters occurring in Utica, the movant shall contact the Judge's Judicial Assistant only by phone before filing the item needing expedited treatment. Compliance with Fed. R. Bankr. P. 9006 is required.

(i) Rule or Statutory Basis. A request for an order, whether brought on by motion or application, shall specify the rule or statute upon which the motion or application is predicated, and the authority for the entry of the proposed order. Failure to provide the basis for relief sought is cause for the court to deny the relief requested.

(j) Adjournment. Unless otherwise ordered by the court, any party who intends to seek an adjournment of a motion or any proceeding relating thereto shall make the request to the court, after attempting to obtain consent of opposing counsel, stating the reasons why adjournment is requested and whether any previous requests for adjournment have been made. Any such request must be made no later than three days prior to the return date, except for good cause shown.

The party obtaining the adjournment shall confirm such adjournment in writing, file the written confirmation with the court and send copies to all parties who have filed and served responding papers. Adjournments will not be automatically granted on stipulation of counsel but may be granted by the court on a showing of good cause.

Any adjournment letters and status conference requests filed conventionally or electronically shall also be faxed to Chambers in Albany and Courtroom Services in Utica.

(k) Withdrawal. Any movant who does not intend to pursue a motion shall notify in writing the court and all parties who have filed and served responding papers at the earliest possible date.

(*l*) Consent to Relief. Any movant who has obtained consent to the relief requested of all necessary parties shall notify the court at the earliest possible date. Where the parties have agreed to a stipulation, a separate proposed order must be submitted for approval by the court. Consensual Orders in Chapter 12 and 13 cases shall provide for the Trustee's consent and signature thereon.

(m) Motion for Relief. Where a motion is made for the relief set forth in subsection (a)(1), (2), (3), (5) or (8) of Local Bankruptcy Rule 2002–1 and the object of the motion and its purposes are clearly and unambiguously stated in the notice of motion, accompanying affidavits, applications or exhibits need not be served on all parties or creditors. The notice of motion, however, must clearly indicate that any party is entitled to receive said applications, exhibits or affidavits without charge from the movant upon request and must provide parties or creditors with exact information on how to request and obtain accompanying affidavits, application or exhibits.

Complete copies of all motions and accompanying applications, affidavits or exhibits shall be served upon the United States trustee's office, any official committees, opposing counsel and any party which may directly be adversely affected by the granting of the requested relief. Pursuant to the Administrative Pro-

cedure and Local Rule 9070–1 (Exhibits Attached to Pleading) attachments may be summarized and only the relevant excerpts electronically filed.

[Effective January 1, 1998. Amended effective October 24, 2005.]

Comment

Pursuant to Fed. R. Bankr. P. 9006(a), the day of service or mailing is excluded when computing the notice period. The 15 day service requirement provided by subsection (e) of this rule does not apply to motions for cram-down as governed by Local Bankruptcy Rule 3020–1(c).

RULE 9013–2. BRIEFS & MEMORANDA OF LAW

See Local Bankruptcy Rule 9013–1(f)(1) (Motion Practice: Answering Papers).

[Effective January 1, 1998. Amended effective October 24, 2005.]

RULE 9013–3. CERTIFICATE OF SERVICE—MOTIONS

See Local Bankruptcy Rule 9013–1(c) (Motion Practice: Service).

[Effective January 1, 1998. Amended effective October 24, 2005.]

RULE 9013–4. DEFAULT MOTION PRACTICE

(a) Default Motions. All motions listed in subsection (b), if pursued on a default basis, shall clearly and conspicuously contain the following paragraph (which may be single-spaced):

PURSUANT TO BANKRUPTCY RULE 9014 AND LOCAL BANKRUPTCY RULE 9013–1, IF YOU INTEND TO OPPOSE THE MOTION, YOU MUST SERVE ON THE MOVANT'S COUNSEL AND FILE WITH THE CLERK OF THE BANKRUPTCY COURT, WRITTEN OPPOSITION TO THE MOTION NOT LATER THAN THREE (3) BUSINESS DAYS PRIOR TO THE RETURN DATE OF THIS MOTION. IN THE EVENT NO WRITTEN OPPOSITION IS SERVED AND FILED, NO HEARING ON THE MOTION WILL BE HELD BEFORE THE COURT ON THE RETURN DATE, AND THE COURT WILL CONSIDER THE MOTION AS UNOPPOSED.

(1) *Timely Opposition not Filed.* If no opposition is timely filed with the clerk and served upon movant's counsel as outlined in the above notice, the motion will not appear on the motion calendar of the court on the return date, and the motion will be considered by the court without the necessity of any appearance by movant's counsel.

(2) *Proposed Order.* Unless otherwise ordered by the court, all proposed orders shall be submitted *after* the return date of the motion.

(3) *Timely Opposition Filed.* If written opposition to the motion is served and filed at least three business days prior to the return date, the motion will appear on the court's motion calendar on the return date and movant will be required to appear in support of the motion.

(b) The default motion practice provided in subsection (a) applies to the following motions:

(1) Abandonment of Property (11 U.S.C. § 554(b));

(2) Allowance of Administrative Expenses Other Than Professional Fees (11 U.S.C. § 503(b));

(3) Allowance of administrative expenses for professional fees in a Chapter 13 case which are not in excess of $500.00, provided however, that said fees are requested for services rendered in connection with a motion brought by default under this Rule;

(4) Approve Settlement of Adversary or Contested Matter (Fed. R. Bankr. P. 9019);

(5) Assume or Reject Executory Contract (11 U.S.C. § 365);

(6) Avoid Judicial Lien and Non–Purchase Money Security Interest (11 U.S.C. § 522(f));

(7) Change Venue (28 U.S.C. § 1412);

(8) Compel Turnover of Property by the Trustee (11 U.S.C. § 542);

(9) Convert or Dismiss Case (11 U.S.C. §§ 706, 707, 1112(b), 1208, 1307);

(10) Disallow or Modify Claim (11 U.S.C. § 502(b));

(11) Dismissal for Failure to Pay Filing Fee (Fed. R. Bankr. P. 1006(a));

(12) Extend Time to Assume or Reject a Nonresidential Lease (11 U.S.C. § 365(d)(4));

(13) Extend Time to File Complaint (Fed. R. Bankr. P. 4004(b), 4007(c));

(14) Extend Time to File Plan and Disclosure (11 U.S.C. § 1121(d));

(15) Extend Time to File Plan—Chapter 12 (11 U.S.C. § 1221);

(16) Extend Time to Pay Filing Fee (Fed. R. Bankr. P. 1006(b));

(17) Fed. R. Bankr. P. 2004 Exam;

(18) Hardship Discharge (11 U.S.C. §§ 1228(b) and 1328(b));

(19) Objection to Claimed Exemption (Fed. R. Bankr. P. 4003(b));

(20) Obtain Credit (11 U.S.C. § 364(b), (c), (d));

(21) Postconfirmation Modification of Chapter 12 or 13 Plans (11 U.S.C. §§ 1229, 1329);

(22) Reopen Case (Fed. R. Bankr. P. 5010);

(23) Terminate or Modify Automatic Stay and/or co-debtor stay, provided, however, that the proposed Order includes a provision that any surplus proceeds obtained by the creditor will be turned over to the Chapter 7, 12 or 13 Trustee (11 U.S.C. § 362(d));

(24) Use Cash Collateral (11 U.S.C. § 363(e));

(25) Withdraw as Attorney (Local Bankruptcy Rule 2091–1); and

(26) Revoke/Reconsider Order of Dismissal, Fed. R. Bankr. P. 9024.

(27) In Albany, the following matters are also included in default motion practice.

● Retention Applications in Chapter 7 Cases (11 U.S.C. 327(e)

● Motion to waive appearance at § 341 meeting.

(c) The provisions of Local Bankruptcy Rules 9013–1, 9013–2, and 9013–3 also apply to default motion practice.

(d) The default motion practice only applies to motions listed in subsection (b). All other motions will continue to require the appearance of movant's counsel, regardless of the existence of any written opposition.

[Effective January 1, 1998. Amended effective October 24, 2005.]

Comment

Essential to the court granting the default motion is a timely filed certificate of service reflecting proper service of the default motion. In this regard, particular reference is made to Fed. R. Bankr. P. 6007 and to the provisions of Fed. R. Bankr. P. 7004(b)(1)-(10), which are applicable to contested matters pursuant to Fed. R. Bankr. P. 9014, and Local Bankruptcy Rule 9034–1.

Cross-reference: Local Bankruptcy Rule 4001–1.

RULE 9013–5. ORDERS, INCLUDING EX PARTE ORDERS, ORDERS TO SHOW CAUSE AND ORDERS SHORTENING TIME

(a) Ex Parte Orders. No ex parte order shall be granted unless based on an affidavit or motion showing cause for ex parte relief as well as cause for the relief requested and stating whether a previous application for similar relief has been made.

All ex parte orders must be submitted conventionally to the Court. An application or motion underlying an ex parte order must also be filed conventionally.

(b) Proposed Orders. All proposed orders shall be submitted, unless otherwise ordered by the court, after the return date of the hearing or trial. All proposed orders shall be submitted conventionally to the Court. Once the Court begins receiving orders electronically (through E–Orders), all orders shall be submitted electronically unless otherwise directed by these rules (e.g., ex parte orders). DO NOT ATTEMPT TO ELECTRONICALLY FILE A PLEADING WHICH CONTAINS A PROPOSED ORDER IN THE BODY OF THE PLEADING.

(c) Proposed Order as Exhibit. A proposed order can be included with an electronically filed pleading if the proposed order is clearly marked as an EXHIBIT only. A proposed order submitted as an exhibit will not be signed by the Court.

(d) Orders to Show Cause and Orders Shortening Time. No order to show cause to bring on a motion or order shortening time will be granted except upon a clear and specific showing by affidavit of good and sufficient reasons why procedure other than by notice of motion is necessary or in the case of a genuine emergency. The Court will not grant orders to show cause or orders shortening time to bring a matter before the Court on less than the minimum number of days notice required by the applicable rule where the reason given is, in the opinion of the Court, law office failure. Law office failure does not provide good and sufficient cause. The papers shall also state whether previous application for similar relief has been made.

(e) Prior Notice. Unless the purpose of an order to show cause would be defeated by prior notice, any party seeking an order to show cause which contains temporary restraining relief shall give an opposing party or, if known, counsel for an opposing party, at least 24 hours prior notice, if possible, of the presentation of the application and order and shall notify an opposing party, via counsel, if known, of the date and time of the proposed presentment of said order to show cause to the court.

(f) Application and Order to Pay Filing Fees in Installments. The only exception to the above sections is the Application and Order to pay Filing Fees in Installments. This may be filed electronically.

(g) Original Signature of Judge. Any order filed electronically by the Court without the actual original signature of a judge has the same force and effect as if the judge had affixed the judge's signature to a paper copy of the order and it had been entered on the docket in a conventional manner.

(h) Ministerial Orders. Any ministerial order filed electronically by the Clerk without the actual original signature of the Clerk has the same force and effect as if the Clerk had affixed his/her signature to a paper

copy of the order and it had been entered on the docket in a conventional manner.

[Effective January 1, 1998. Amended effective October 24, 2005.]

Comment

If the underlying relief for which the order to show cause is sought falls within one of the ten categories listed in Fed. R. Bankr. P. 7001, the application for an order to show cause must be brought within the context of a pending, filed adversary proceeding.

As incorporated by Fed. R. Bankr. P. 7065, Fed.R.Civ.P. 65(b)(2) shall be strictly adhered to in any case in which a temporary restraining order is sought.

RULE 9015–1. JURY TRIAL

If the right to a jury trial applies and a timely demand has been filed pursuant to Fed.R.Civ.P. 38(b), the parties may consent to have a jury trial conducted by a bankruptcy judge under 28 U.S.C. § 157(e) by jointly or separately filing a statement of consent within fifteen days after the last date to file a pleading.

[Effective January 1, 1998.]

Comment

As of the effective date of these Local Bankruptcy Rules, the bankruptcy judges were specially designated to conduct jury trials in all proceedings commenced in cases filed under Title 11 of the United States Code by General Order #44 of the United States District Court for the Northern District of New York.

RULE 9019–2. ALTERNATIVE DISPUTE RESOLUTION (ADR)

The mediation procedure developed by the court, as set forth in the appendix to these rules and incorporated by reference, is intended to facilitate the resolution of disputes without litigation.

[Effective January 1, 1998.]

RULE 9021–1. JUDGMENTS & ORDERS—ENTRY OF

(a) Orders and Judgments. Unless otherwise ordered by the court, any oral order of the court, including any order resulting from a default motion under Local Rule 9013–4(b), shall be reduced to writing and submitted by the prevailing party no later than 30 days from the date of ruling.

(b) Noncompliance. Failure to comply with subsection (a) of this rule is cause for the court to vacate its oral order, deny the relief requested and mark the matter off the calendar.

(c) Settlement of Judgment or Order. Unless otherwise ordered by the court, to settle a judgment or to settle an order shall mean the following:

(1) *Service.* The prevailing party or other party as directed by the court shall serve a proposed order or judgment upon the opposing party(ies) who have appeared or have requested service thereof within 15 days of the hearing. Any counter proposal must be served no later than seven days from the date of service. Counsel who served the proposed order or judgment shall submit it to the court, together with any counter proposal.

(2) *Required Notice.* All proposed orders or judgments shall be served together with a separate notice which shall clearly and conspicuously contain the following paragraph (which may be single-spaced):

THE ATTACHED PROPOSED ORDER IS BEING SERVED UPON YOU ON (DATE). PURSUANT TO LOCAL BANKRUPTCY RULE 9021–1, IF YOU INTEND TO SUBMIT ANY COUNTER PROPOSAL, YOU MUST SERVE UPON THE UNDERSIGNED A WRITTEN COUNTER PROPOSAL TO THE ORDER OR JUDGMENT ATTACHED HERETO NOT LATER THAN SEVEN DAYS FROM SERVICE HEREOF. IN THE EVENT THAT NO WRITTEN COUNTER PROPOSAL IS RECEIVED, THE ORDER OR JUDGMENT ATTACHED HERETO SHALL BE SUBMITTED TO THE COURT. IF A COUNTER PROPOSAL IS TIMELY RECEIVED, IT SHALL BE SUBMITTED, TOGETHER WITH THE PROPOSED ORDER, TO THE COURT.

(3) *Submission.* In the event counsel having served the proposed order or judgment does not receive any written counter proposal, then the proposed order or judgment, together with the original notice and a certificate of service, shall be submitted to the court. If a written counter proposal is timely received, it shall be submitted, together with the proposed order, to the court.

[Effective January 1, 1998. Amended effective October 24, 2005.]

Comment

The procedure outlined in subsection (c) is intended to afford the parties the opportunity to review any proposed order or judgment prior to submission. Three days should be added to the times otherwise provided in subsection (c) if notice is given by mail.

RULE 9022–1. JUDGMENTS & ORDERS—NOTICE OF

(a) Notice of Entry. Whenever notice of entry of a contested order or judgment is required by Fed. R. Bankr. P. 9022, the party submitting said order or judgment shall provide the clerk with a list of the names and addresses of the parties contesting the entry thereof, including the name and address of the submitting party, and the names and addresses of their respective attorneys.

(b) Delivery of Notice of Entry. The clerk must mail or deliver by electronic means to the contesting parties, a copy of a judgment or order showing the date the judgment or order was entered. Immediately upon the entry of an order or judgment in a case or proceeding assigned to the Electronic Filing System, the clerk will transmit to Filing Users in the case or proceeding, in electronic form, a Notice of Electronic Filing. Electronic transmission of the Notice of Electronic Filing constitutes the notice required by Fed. R. Bankr. P. 9022. The clerk must give notice in paper form to persons who have not consented to electronic service in accordance with the Federal Rules of Bankruptcy Procedure and these local rules.

[Effective January 1, 1998. Amended effective October 24, 2005.]

RULE 9025–1. SURETIES

(a) Execution by Surety Only. Whenever a bond, undertaking or stipulation is required, it shall be sufficient if the instrument is executed by the surety or sureties only.

(b) Security for Bond. Except as otherwise provided by law, every bond, undertaking or stipulation must be secured by: (1) the deposit of cash or government bonds in the amount of the bond, undertaking or stipulation or (2) the undertaking of a corporate surety holding a certificate of authority from the United States Secretary of the Treasury.

(c) Affidavit by Individual Surety. In the case of a bond, undertaking or stipulation executed by individual sureties, each surety shall attach an affidavit of justifications, giving the full name, occupation, residence and business addresses, and showing that the individual is qualified as an individual surety under subsection (b) of this rule.

(d) Persons Who May Not Act as Surety. Members of the bar, administrative officers, or employees of this court, the marshal, deputies or assistants, may not act as surety in any case, adversary proceeding, contested matter or action pending in this court.

[Effective January 1, 1998.]

RULE 9027–1. REMOVAL AND REMAND

(a) Notice of Removal. The party filing a Notice of Removal shall give written Notice of Removal to all adverse parties and shall file a copy of the application with the Clerk of the court from which the civil action or proceeding was removed. This notice shall effect the removal, and the parties shall proceed no further in that court unless and until the case is remanded or the Bankruptcy Court orders otherwise.

(b) Procedure after Removal. Within ten (10) days after filing a notice of removal from a state or federal court to this Court, pursuant to Fed.R.Bankr.P. 9027 the party filing the notice shall file with the Clerk of the Bankruptcy Court copies of all additional records and proceedings in the state court, together with his/her counsel's verification that they are true and complete copies of all the records and proceedings in the state court proceeding. The copies need not be certified by the state court and the added cost of certification will not be allowed as a cost item under 28 U.S.C. § 1920(4) unless certification is required after an opposing party challenges the accuracy of the copies.

(c) List of Parties. Any party removing a civil action to this Court shall file with the Bankruptcy Clerk a list containing the name of each party to the removed case, and the names, addresses and telephone numbers of their counsel, or the party, if pro se.

(d) Remand. If at any time before final judgment it appears that the civil action or proceeding was removed improvidently or without jurisdiction, the Bankruptcy Court shall remand the case and may order the payment of just costs. A certified copy of the order of remand shall be mailed by the Bankruptcy Clerk to the Clerk of the court from which the civil action or proceeding was removed, and that court may thereupon proceed with the case.

(e) Service. Service of the notice of removal or remand shall be served on all parties to the removed or remanded case, in the manner provided for in Fed. R. Bankr. P. 7004.

[Effective October 24, 2005.]

RULE 9034–1. NOTICE TO AND SERVICE UPON THE UNITED STATES TRUSTEE

(a) Notice. In addition to the notice required to be given to the Office of the United States trustee pursuant to Fed. R. Bankr. P. 2002(k) and Fed. R. Bankr. P. 9034(k), notice of the following matters should also be given to the United States trustee:

(1) All papers, including pleadings, motions and objections relating to the performance of any chapter 7, 12 or 13 trustee or any trustee or examiner appointed pursuant to 11 U.S.C. § 1104 with respect to his/her duties as trustee or examiner. This includes, but is not limited to, all motions to compel trustee to turnover property, to remove trustee and to compel trustee to distribute assets of the estate;

(2) All papers relating to motions under 11 U.S.C. § 362(d) except those relating to personal property in cases pending under chapters 7, 12 and 13 of the Bankruptcy Code; and

(3) All operating reports required under Local Bankruptcy Rule 2015–2.

(b) Service. The time and manner of service shall be in conformity with these Local Bankruptcy Rules, the Administrative Procedure and the Federal Rules of Bankruptcy Procedure and shall be effected contemporaneous with service upon all other parties in interest.

(c) Address. Where notice to or service upon the United States trustee is required and is completed by mail, the following addresses shall be used:

Utica cases:
Office of the United States Trustee
Northern District of New York
10 Broad Street, Room 105
Utica, NY 13501
Albany cases:
Office of the United States Trustee
Northern District of New York
74 Chapel Street, Suite 200
Albany, NY 12207

[Effective January 1, 1998.]

Comment

This rule is intended to supplement the requirements of notice to the United States trustee pursuant to Fed. R. Bankr. P. 2002(k), 5005(b) and 9034(k). These addresses are subject to change and should be verified.

RULE 9070–1. EXHIBITS

(a) Exhibits Attached to Pleadings. Exhibits and other attachments capable of being electronically imaged should be scanned unless the court permits conventional filing. Attachments may be summarized and only the relevant excerpts electronically filed. The size of an electronic file should be no larger than 2 MB. Attachments larger than 2 MB must be split into separate PDF files and the multiple files attached to the pleading.

(b) Marking. Exhibits offered into evidence must be submitted in hard copy. In an adversary proceeding or a contested matter, counsel for the respective parties shall, to the maximum extent possible, stipulate as to the admissibility of exhibits and present exhibits to the courtroom deputy for marking prior to the trial or evidentiary hearing in accordance with the court's scheduling order.

(c) Retention and Return. Unless otherwise ordered by the court, exhibits shall be retained by the clerk. Following decision or verdict and upon expiration of the time allowed for appeal, or following any appeal, exhibits shall be returned to the party who presented them.

[Effective January 1, 1998. Amended effective October 24, 2005.]

APPENDICES

APPENDIX I. ASSIGNMENT LOCATION AND HEARING LOCATION*

County	County Code	Usual Assignment Location	Usual Hearing Location
Albany	36001	Albany	Albany
Broome	36007	Utica	Binghamton
Cayuga	36011	Utica	Syracuse
Chenango	36017	Utica	Binghamton
Clinton	36019	Albany	Plattsburgh
Columbia	36021	Albany	Albany
Cortland	36023	Utica	Syracuse
Delaware	36025	Utica	Binghamton
Essex	36031	Albany	Plattsburgh
Franklin	36033	Albany	Plattsburgh
Fulton	36035	Albany	Albany
Greene	36039	Albany	Albany
Hamilton	36041	Utica	Utica
Herkimer	36043	Utica	Utica
Jefferson	36045	Albany	Watertown
Lewis	36049	Utica	Watertown
Madison	36053	Utica	*Syracuse or Utica
Montgomery	36057	Albany	Albany
Oneida	36065	Utica	Utica
Onondaga	36067	Utica	Syracuse
Oswego	36075	Utica	Syracuse
Otsego	36077	Utica	Binghamton
Rensselaer	36083	Albany	Albany
St. Lawrence	36089	Albany	Watertown
Saratoga	36091	Albany	Albany
Schenectady	36093	Albany	Albany
Schoharie	36095	Albany	Albany
Tioga	36107	Utica	Binghamton
Tompkins	36109	Utica	Binghamton
Ulster	36111	Albany	Albany
Warren	36113	Albany	Albany
Washington	36115	Albany	Albany

1 Madison county hearings are held in Utica and Syracuse depending upon majority of creditors and their locations.

Note: Assignment Location and Hearing Location are subject to change without notice on a case by case basis if the Court deems it necessary for ease of administration.

[Effective November 2, 1998.]

* Suggested title added by Publisher.

APPENDIX II. MEDIATION PROGRAM FOR THE U.S. BANKRUPTCY COURT, NORTHERN DISTRICT OF NEW YORK

1.0 PRELIMINARY STATEMENT

Litigation in bankruptcy cases frequently imposes significant economic and other burdens on parties and often delays resolution of disputes. Alternate dispute resolution procedures have the potential to reduce delay, cost, stress and other burdens often associated with litigation. Mediation, in particular, allows parties more active involvement in determining the resolution of their disputes without sacrificing the quality of justice to be rendered or the right of the litigants to a full trial on all issues not resolved through mediation. Mediation is a process in which an impartial person, the mediator, facilitates communication between disputing parties and counsel to promote understanding, reconciliation and settlement.

Mediation enables litigants to take control of their dispute and encourages amicable resolutions. The mediator may, among other things, suggest alternatives, analyze issues, question perceptions, use logic, conduct private caucuses and stimulate negotiations between opposing sides. The mediator is an advocate for settlement and uses the mediation process to ensure that the parties fully explore all areas of agreement. The mediator does not serve as a judge or arbitrator and has no authority to render decisions on questions of fact or law or to force settlements.

2.0 ASSIGNMENT OF MATTERS TO MEDIATION

A matter may be assigned to mediation only by order of the Court ("Order of Assignment"). Upon motion of a party to the matter or the United States trustee, written stipulation, or by sua sponte order the court may assign to mediation any dispute arising in an adversary proceeding, contested matter or otherwise in a bankruptcy case. Federal Rules of Bankruptcy Procedure 7016 hereby is made applicable to all matters in which mediation is requested.

3.0 EFFECT OF MEDIATION ON PENDING MATTERS

The assignment of a matter to mediation does not relieve the parties to that matter from complying with any other court orders or applicable provisions of the United States Code, the Federal Rules of Bankruptcy Procedure, or the local rules of this court. Unless otherwise ordered by the court, the assignment to mediation does not delay or stay discovery, pretrial, hearing dates, or trial schedules.

4.0 THE MEDIATOR

4.1 Registration of Mediators/Mediation Administrator. The clerk of the court shall establish and maintain a register of persons (the Panel) qualified under this section and designated by the court to serve as mediators in the Mediation Program.

4.2 Application and Certification of Mediators.

4.2.1 *Application and Qualification Requirements.* Each applicant shall submit to the Mediation Administrator a statement of professional qualifications, experience, training, and other information demonstrating, in the applicant's opinion, why the applicant should be designated to the Panel. The applicant shall have completed eight hours of formal mediation training. The applicant shall submit the statement in the form attached hereto as Form A. The statement also shall set forth whether the applicant has been removed from any professional organization, or has resigned from any professional organization while an investigation into allegations of professional misconduct was pending, and the circumstances of such removal or resignation. This statement shall constitute an application for designation to the Mediation Program.

4.2.2 *Court Certification.* The court in its sole discretion shall grant or deny an application submitted pursuant to subsection 4.2.1 of this rule. If the court grants the application, the applicant's name shall be added to the Panel, subject to removal pursuant to section 4.4 of this rule.

4.2.3 *Reaffirmation of Qualifications.* Each applicant accepted for designation to the Panel shall reaffirm annually the continued existence and accuracy of the qualifications, statements and representations made in the application. Failure to comply with this section shall be grounds for removal under section 4.4.

4.3 Mediator's Oath or Affirmation. Upon appointment to the Panel or selection as a mediator, every mediator must sign a written oath or affirmation (see 28 U.S.C. § 453), as if the person were a judge, and file the oath or affirmation with the Mediation Administrator.

4.4 Ethical Standards for Mediators. All mediators shall adhere to the Standards of Conduct for Mediators as promulgated by the American Arbitration Association ("AAA standards"). A failure to adhere to the AAA standards may constitute sufficient cause for the removal from the Panel. Such failure will not void any consensual agreement between the parties unless both parties consent to the rescission of the agreement or, on motion of any party to the mediation or, sua sponte, the court finds that the mediator's conflict of interest or failure to abide by the AAA standards caused actual prejudice to a party.

4.5 Removal from Panel. A person shall be removed from the Panel either at the person's written request to the Mediation Administrator or by court order for cause. If removed by court order, the personal shall not be returned to the Panel absent a court order obtained on motion to the Mediation Administrator supported by an affidavit sufficiently explaining the circumstances of such removal and the reasons justifying the return of the person to the Panel.

5.0 APPOINTMENT OF MEDIATOR

5.1.1 *Selection by Parties.* Within 15 calendar days of the date of service of the Order of Assignment of a matter to mediation, the parties to the matter to be mediated shall select a mediator, and an alternate mediator, and shall present the court with a proposed order of appointment. If such selection is not from the Panel, the parties shall submit with the proposed order of appointment a stipulation by the parties that the person is not on the Panel but is qualified to mediate the matter. If the court approves the parties' selection, immediately after entry of the order of appointment, the court shall notify the parties, the mediator and the alternate mediator of the appointment.

5.1.2 *Selection/Appointment by Court.* If the parties cannot agree upon a mediator within 15 calendar days of the date of service of the Order of Assignment, the court shall appoint a mediator and an alternate mediator from the Panel and shall notify the parties, the mediator, and the alternate mediator of such appointment.

5.2.1 *Inability of Mediator to Serve.* If the mediator is unable to serve due to a conflict or other reason precluding acceptance of the appointment, the mediator shall file and serve on all parties to the mediation and on the alternate mediator, within five calendar days after receipt of the notice of appointment, a notice of inability to accept the appointment. The alternate mediator then shall become the mediator if the alternate does not file and serve on all parties to the mediation a notice of inability to accept the appointment within five calendar days after receipt of the original mediator's notice of inability to accept the appointment. If neither the mediator nor the alternate mediator can serve, the court shall appoint another mediator and alternate mediator.

5.2.2 *Mediator's Prior Service.* A mediator has the option of declining to accept the mediation based on having served as a mediator on four previous occasions within a period of one year.

5.3 Disqualification of Mediator.

5.3.1 *Disqualifying Events.* Any person selected as a mediator may be disqualified for bias or prejudice in the same manner that a judge may be disqualified under 28 U.S.C. § 144. Any person selected as a mediator shall be disqualified in any matter where 28 U.S.C. § 455 would require disqualification if that person were a judge. Any member of the bar who is certified and designated as a mediator pursuant to this rule shall not solely for that reason be disqualified from appearing or acting as counsel in any other matter or case pending before this court.

5.3.2 *Inquiry by Mediator; Disclosure.* Promptly after receiving notice of appointment, the mediator shall make inquiry sufficient to determine whether there is a basis for disqualification under subsection 5.3.1 of this rule. The inquiry shall include, but shall not be limited to, a search for conflicts of interest in the manner prescribed by the applicable rules of professional conduct for attorney mediators, and by the applicable rules pertaining to the mediator's profession for non-attorney mediators. Within seven calendar days after receiving notice of appointment, the mediator shall file with the court and serve on the parties to the mediation either (a) a statement that there is no basis for disqualification under subsection 5.3.1 and that the mediator has no actual or potential conflict of interest or (b) a notice of withdrawal.

5.3.3 *Objection Based on Conflict of Interest.* A party to the mediation who believes that the assigned mediator and/or the alternate mediator has a conflict of interest promptly shall bring the issue to the attention of the mediator and/or the alternate mediator, as applicable, and to other parties to the mediation. If the mediator does not withdraw, the issue shall be brought to the court's attention by the mediator or any of the parties to the mediation. The court shall take such action as the court deems necessary or appropriate to resolve the alleged conflict of interest.

5.4 Mediator's Liability. There shall be no liability on the part of, and no cause of action shall arise against, any person who is appointed as a mediator pursuant to this rule on account of any act or omission in the course and scope of such person's duties as a mediator. See e.g. Wagshal v. Foster, 28 F.3d 1249 (D.C. Cir. 1994).

6.0 COMPENSATION

6.1 Compensation of Mediator. The mediator shall serve on a pro bono basis and shall not require compensation or reimbursement of expenses. It is anticipated that the mediation shall not exceed six hours in length. If, at the conclusion of the six hours of mediation, it is determined by the mediator and the parties to the mediation that additional time will be necessary and productive in order to complete the mediation, then:

(1) If the mediator consents to continue to serve on a pro bono basis, the parties to the mediation may agree to continue the mediation conference; or

(2) If the mediator does not consent to continue to serve on a pro bono basis, the mediator's fees and expenses shall be on such terms as are satisfactory to the mediator and the parties to the mediation, subject to prior court approval if the estate is to be charged. The parties to the mediation shall share equally all mediation fees and expenses unless the parties to the mediation agree otherwise. The court may, in the interest of justice, determine a different allocation. In no case will compensation exceed an hourly rate of $150 per hour.

7.0 THE MEDIATION

7.1 Time and Place of Mediation Conference. After consulting with all counsel and pro se parties, the mediator shall schedule a convenient time and place for the mediation conference, and promptly give all counsel and pro se parties at least 14 calendar days' written notice of the time and place of the mediation conference. The mediator shall schedule the mediation to begin as soon as practicable.

7.2 Submission Materials. Not less than seven calendar days before the mediation conference, each party shall submit directly to the mediator, and serve on all counsel and pro se parties, any materials (the "Submission") the mediator directs to be prepared and assembled. The mediator shall so direct not less than 14 calendar days before the mediation conference. Prior to the mediation conference, the mediator may talk with the participants to determine what materials would be helpful. The Submissions shall not be filed with the court and the court shall not have access to them.

7.3 Attendance at Mediation Conference.

7.3.1 *Persons Required to Attend.* The following persons personally must attend the mediation conference:

(1) Each party that is a natural person;

(2) If the party is not a natural person, a representative who is not the party's attorney of record and who has full authority to negotiate and settle the matter on behalf of the party;

(3) If the party is a governmental entity that requires settlement approval by an elected official or legislative body, a representative who has authority to recommend a settlement to the elected official or legislative body;

(4) The attorney who has primary responsibility for each party's case; and

(5) Other interested parties such as insurers or indemnitors, or one or more of their representatives, whose presence is necessary for a full resolution of the matter assigned to mediation.

7.3.2 *Excuse.* A person required to attend the mediation is excused from appearing if all parties and the mediator agree that the person need not attend. The court for cause may excuse a person's attendance.

7.3.3 *Failure to Attend.* Willful failure to attend any mediation conference, and any other material violation of this rule, shall be reported to the court by the mediator and may result in the imposition of sanctions by the court. Any such report of the mediator shall comply with the confidentiality requirements of section 8.1 of this rule.

7.4 Mediation Conference Procedures. The mediator may establish procedures for the mediation conference.

8.0 CONFIDENTIALITY OF MEDIATION PROCEEDINGS

8.1 Protection of Information Disclosed at Mediation. The mediator and the participants in mediation are prohibited from divulging, outside of the mediation, any oral or written information disclosed by the parties or by witnesses in the course of the mediation. No person may rely on or introduce as evidence in any arbitral, judicial, or other proceedings, evidence pertaining to any aspect of the mediation effort, including but not limited to: (a) views expressed or suggestions made by a party with respect to a possible settlement of the dispute; (b) the fact that another party had or had not indicated willingness to accept a proposal for settlement made by the mediator; (c) proposals made or views expressed by the mediator; (d) statements or admissions made by a party in the course of the mediation; and (e) documents prepared for the purpose of, in the course of, or pursuant to the mediation. In addition, without limiting the foregoing, Rule 408 of the Federal Rules of Evidence and any applicable federal or state statute, rule, common law or judicial precedent relating to the privileged nature of settlement discussions, mediation or other alternative dispute resolution procedure shall apply. Information otherwise discoverable or admissible in evidence, however, does not become exempt from discovery, or inadmissible in evidence, merely by being used by a party in a mediation.

8.2 Discovery from Mediator. The mediator shall not be compelled to disclose to the court or to any person outside the mediation conference any of the records, reports, summaries, notes, communications, or other documents received or made by a mediator while serving in such capacity. The mediator shall not testify or be compelled to testify in regard to the mediation in connection with any arbitral, judicial or other proceeding. The mediator shall not be a necessary party in any proceedings relating to the mediation. Nothing contained in this section shall prevent the mediator from reporting the status, but not the substance, of the mediation effort to the court in writing, from filing a report as required by section 9.1, or from complying with the obligations set forth in section 10.

8.3 Protection of Proprietary Information. The parties, the mediator, and all mediation participants shall protect proprietary information during and after the mediation conference.

8.4 Preservation of Privileges. The disclosure by a party of privileged information to the mediator does not waive or otherwise adversely affect the privileged nature of the information.

9.0 RECOMMENDATIONS BY MEDIATOR

The mediator is not required to prepare written comments or recommendations to the parties. Mediators may present a written settlement recommendation memorandum to attorneys or pro se litigants, but not to the court.

10.0 POST MEDIATION PROCEDURES

10.1 Preparation of Orders. If a settlement is reached at a mediation, a party designated by the mediator shall submit a fully executed stipulation and proposed order to the court within twenty calendar days after the end of the mediation. If the party fails to prepare the stipulation and order, the court may impose appropriate sanctions.

10.2 Mediator's Certificate of Completion. Promptly after the mediation conference, the mediator shall file with the court, and serve on the parties and the Mediation Administrator, a certificate in the form provided by the court showing compliance or noncompliance with the mediation conference requirements of this rule and whether or not a settlement has been reached. Regardless of the outcome of the mediation conference, the mediator shall not provide the court with any details of the substance of the conference.

10.3 Mediator's Report. In order to assist the Mediation Administrator in compiling useful data to evaluate the Mediation Program, and to aid the court in assessing the efforts of the members of the Panel, the mediator shall provide the Mediation Administrator with an estimate of the number of hours spent in the mediation conference and other statistical and evaluative information on a form provided by the court. The mediator shall provide this report whether or not the mediation conference results in settlement.

11.0 WITHDRAWAL FROM MEDIATION

Any matter assigned to mediation pursuant to this rule may be withdrawn from mediation by the court at any time upon determination that the matter is not suitable for mediation. In addition, where mediation is brought about either by sua sponte order or motion, a party may withdraw from the mediation at any time after attending the first scheduled mediation conference only upon notice and motion. In order to withdraw, the withdrawing party shall, no later than five business days prior to any subsequently scheduled mediation activity, file with the court a motion seeking to withdraw from the mediation, briefly stating the reasons for the request and serve on the Mediator Administrator, mediator and other parties (or their counsel). The method of service of the motion for withdrawal shall provide for actual receipt by the parties and the mediator no later than three business days prior to the next scheduled mediation activity. The court shall rule upon the motion without argument. All mediation activity shall be stayed pending an order from the court.

12.0 TERMINATION OF MEDIATION

Upon the filing of a mediator's certificate pursuant to section 10.2 or the entry of an order withdrawing a matter from mediation pursuant to section 11.0, the mediation will be deemed terminated, and the mediator excused and relieved from further responsibilities in the matter without further court order. If the mediation conference does not result in a resolution of all of the disputes in the assigned matter, the matter shall proceed to trial or hearing pursuant to the court's scheduling order.

13.0   REEVALUATION/REVISION PROCEDURE

The purpose and administration of this rule shall be reviewed and reevaluated at such time and in such manner as the court deems appropriate.

[Effective November 2, 1998. Amended effective October 24, 2005.]

ADMINISTRATIVE ORDERS

ADMINISTRATIVE ORDER NO. 02–03.   PROCEDURAL RULES FOR ELECTRONIC CASE FILING

Federal Rule of Civil Procedure, hereafter FRCP, 83 and Federal Rules of Bankruptcy Procedure, hereafter FRBP, 5005(a)(2), 9011, and 9029 authorize this Court to establish practices and procedures for the filing, signing, and verification of pleadings and papers by electronic means; and

The *Administrative Procedures for Filing, Signing, and Verifying Pleadings and Papers by Electronic Means*, hereafter *Administrative Procedures*, have been reviewed by this Court; and

The *Administrative Procedures* are consistent with and further the responsibility of the Clerk of Court for the control of the Court's docket under FRBP 5003, including safeguarding the integrity of the Court's docket; and

The *Administrative Procedures* do not impose fees inconsistent with the present fee structure adopted by the Judicial Council of the United States pursuant to 28 U.S.C. § 1930; and

The *Administrative Procedures* provide adequate procedures for filing pleadings and papers and provide access to review and retrieve records and dockets of this Court by parties who are not able to access the Electronic Case Filing System over the Internet, thereby complying with the requirements contained in 11 U.S.C. § 107(a); and

The *Administrative Procedures* do not impair the ability of the Clerk of the Court to perform statistical reporting responsibilities for both the Court and the Administrative Office of the United States Courts; and

The *Administrative Procedures* are consistent with notice requirements of the FRBP and the Local Bankruptcy Rules for the Northern District of New York, hereafter LBR.

IT IS ORDERED that:

1.   Introduction and Definitions.

a.   The Clerk of the Bankruptcy Court for the Northern District of New York is authorized to implement, publish, and update the *Administrative Procedures* for the district, including but not limited to the procedures for registration of attorneys and other participants, and for the distribution of logins and passwords to permit electronic filing and notice of pleadings and other papers.

b.   Continued adherence to the *Northern District of New York Local Bankruptcy Rules* is not precluded by electronic filing. In the event of a conflict between the *Northern District of New York Local Bankruptcy Rules* and the *Administrative Procedures*, the *Administrative Procedure*, as relating to the electronic filing of petitions, pleadings and other papers, shall govern.

c.   "Electronic Case Files", as referred to in the *Administrative Procedures*, are petitions, pleadings, and other papers that are stored in a fixed electronic format instead of on paper. This Court accepts documents only in the *Portable Document Format* (PDF) and creditor matrices in ASCII DOS Text format (TXT).

d.   "Conventional Case Files", as referred to in the *Administrative Procedures*, are petitions, pleadings, and other papers that are filed with the Court in "paper format". All filing requirements as provided in the FRBP and the LBR shall prevail unless otherwise noted in the *Administrative Procedures*.

e. "Filer", as referred to in the *Administrative Procedures*, is defined as the attorney of record or the actual party in interest, if not represented by counsel, who transmits any pleading or document to the Court.

2. Electronic Filing of Documents.

a. The electronic filing of a pleading or other paper in accordance with the Electronic Filing Procedures shall constitute entry of that pleading or other paper on the docket kept by the clerk under FRBP 5003.

b. The Office of the Clerk shall enter all orders, decrees, judgments, and proceedings of the court in accordance with the Electronic Filing Procedures, which shall constitute entry of the order, decree, judgment, or proceeding on the docket kept by the clerk under FRBP 5003 and 9021.

c. For filings that require a fee to be paid, the Office of the Clerk will automatically draw payment from the credit card account that will be provided with the attorney registration.

d. A "Chambers Copy" in paper format for chambers is required for the following matters. The copy must be clearly marked as **"ECF CASE–CHAMBERS COPY"** and must be submitted in compliance with the requirements of LBR 9013–1. The Chambers Copy need not contain a copy of the original signature. Unless directed by the Court, copies should not be faxed to Chambers or Courtroom Services. Copies should be sent via the mail or hand delivered.

(1) Utica Chambers:

(a) Notice of Hearing, Motion, application and certificate of service;

(b) Opposition, response, or any pleading relating to a hearing;

(c) Opposition to disclosure statements in a chapter 11;

(d) Opposition to confirmation of a plan regarding any chapter;

(e) All pleadings filed in an adversary proceeding;

(f) Pretrial statements;

(g) Memorandums of Law or documents filed in regard to a submitted matter;

(h) All documents regarding an appeal, withdrawal of reference, or FRBP 9033 objections.

(2) Albany Chambers:

(a) Notice of Hearing, Motions, applications, and certificate of services, excluding Ch. 13 Standing Trustee's motions to dismiss, motions to determine/expunge claim, and motions to determine value;

(b) Opposition, response, or any pleading relating to a hearing;

(c) Opposition to disclosure statements in a chapter 11;

(d) Opposition to confirmation of a plan regarding any chapter;

(e) Pretrial statements;

(f) All documents regarding an appeal, withdrawal of reference, or FRBP 9033 objections;

(g) Memorandums of Law or documents filed in regard to a submitted matter

3. Logins and Passwords.

a. Each attorney admitted to practice in the Northern District of New York and currently in good standing, and other filers shall be entitled to a single Electronic Case Filing System login and password to permit him/her to electronically file and electronically receive pleadings and other documents.

b.   Login and password registration forms are available in the Office of the Clerk and on the Court's Internet site, *www.nynb.uscourts.gov.*

c.   A trustee or standing trustee who also serves as private counsel should submit two separate Attorney Registration Forms and will receive two separate logins and passwords; one in his/her role as trustee and one in his/her role as private counsel.

d.   No attorney shall knowingly permit or cause to permit his/her password to be utilized by anyone other than an authorized employee of his/her law firm.

e.   No person shall knowingly utilize or cause another person to utilize the password of a registered attorney unless such person is an authorized employee of the law firm.

f.   Misuse of the Electronic Case Filing System login and password may result in revocation of the login and password of the attorney or party and/or the imposition of sanctions.

4.   Signatures.

a.   The electronic filing of a petition, pleading, motion, or other paper by an attorney or participant who is a registered user in the Electronic Case Filing System shall constitute the signature of that filer under FRBP 9011.

b.   Any pleading, affidavit or other document filed electronically shall contain an electronic signature of the filer, e.g., "/s/ name."

5.   Notice of Electronic Filing and Service.

a.   Whenever a pleading or other paper is filed electronically, a *Notice of Electronic Filing* will be automatically generated by the Electronic Case Filing System at the time of the filing and sent electronically to the party filing the pleading or other paper, as well as to all parties in the case who are registered participants in the Electronic Case Filing System or have otherwise consented to electronic service.

b.   If the recipient of notice or service is a registered participant in the Electronic Case Filing System or has otherwise consented to electronic service, service of the *Notice of Electronic Filing* shall be the equivalent of service of the pleading or other paper by first class mail, postage prepaid.

c.   Pleadings or other documents which are not filed electronically shall be served in accordance with the FRBP and the LBR except as otherwise provided by Order of the Court.

d.   Participation in the Electronic Case Filing System by receipt of a login and password from the Court shall constitute a request for service and notice electronically pursuant to FRBP 9036. Participants in the Electronic Case Filing System, by receiving a login and password from the Court, agree that notice and service by electronic means constitutes proper service.

e.   A summons and the appropriate number of copies must be filed with the Court conventionally. Service of a summons and a complaint filed in an adversary proceeding shall continue to be made conventionally pursuant to FRBP 7004. Service of a summons and an involuntary bankruptcy petition shall continue to be made pursuant to FRBP 1010 and 7004.

f.   Service by electronic means is not effective if the party making service learns that the attempted service did not reach the person to be served.

6.   The provisions of this Order shall apply to all electronically filed cases and proceedings and cases and proceedings converted to the Electronic Case Filing System in the U.S. Bankruptcy Court for the Northern District of New York. Amendments to this Order may be entered from time to time in keeping with the needs of the Court.

7.   The effective date of this General Order is January 2, 2003.

IT IS SO ORDERED.

Dated: December 13, 2002; revised January 31, 2006.

ADMINISTRATIVE PROCEDURES FOR FILING, SIGNING AND VERIFYING PLEADINGS AND PAPERS BY ELECTRONIC MEANS

Exhibit to Administrative Order No. 02–03

I. REGISTRATION FOR THE ELECTRONIC FILING *SYSTEM*.

A. *DESIGNATION OF CASES.*

1. On January 2, 2003, all documents submitted for filing in this district, no matter when a case was originally filed, shall be filed electronically using the Electronic Case Filing System (hereafter *System*) or shall be scanned and uploaded to the *System*.

2. Parties proceeding pro se shall not be required to file electronically. All filing requirements as provided in the *Fed. R. Bankr. P.* and the *Local Bankruptcy Rules* will prevail.

B. *MANDATORY ELECTRONIC CASE FILINGS.* Petitions, pleadings, motions and all other documents filed in all cases after July 1, 2004 must be filed electronically pursuant to Administrative Order No. 03–01.

C. *LOGINS AND PASSWORDS.* Each attorney admitted to practice in the Northern District of New York, an out of district attorney in good standing in their district, or a participant in any case or proceeding shall be eligible for a *System* login and password from the Bankruptcy Court. The login and password permit the attorney or party to participate in the electronic retrieval and filing of pleadings and other papers in accordance with the *System*. Registration for a login and password is governed by Section I.D.

D. *REGISTRATION.*

1. Each attorney admitted to practice in the Northern District of New York or a participant desiring to file pleadings or other papers electronically must:

• Complete and sign an Attorney/Participant Registration Form (Form A),

• Attend the necessary training required by the Court.

• **Note:** Registered Electronic Case Filing participants of the United States District Court for the Northern District of New York can receive a login and password to the Bankruptcy Court ECF System by completing Form A **and** completing the court's on-line test with a passing score of at least 80.

The above mentioned forms are also available on the Court's web site at www. nynb.uscourts.gov.

2. An Out of District attorney desiring to file pleadings or other papers electronically must:

• Complete and sign an Out of District Attorney Registration Form (Form B);

• Be a registered Electronic Case Filing participant in a United States Bankruptcy Court in another state or district and;

• Complete the court's on-line test with a passing score of at least 80.

3. All signed original Attorney/Participant or Out of District Attorney Registration Forms shall be mailed or delivered to:

IT Manager
United States Bankruptcy Court
James T. Foley U. S. Court House
445 Broadway, Suite 330
Albany, NY 12207.

4. To ensure that the Clerk's Office has correctly entered a registering attorney's or participant's Internet e-mail address in the *System*, the Clerk's Office will send the attorney or participant an Internet e-mail message which will contain either the date and time of his/her training session at the Clerk's Office or instructions on completing the certification requirements remotely. The attorney or participant may indicate on his/her registration form the name(s) of his/her support staff that he/she would like included in the same training. The login and password will **only** be given to the registering attorney or participant at his/her training session.

5. A registered participant should change the court-assigned password. This change can be made by accessing the menu option "Maintain Your ECF Account" under Utilities. In the event a filer believes that the security of an existing password has been compromised and in order to prevent unauthorized access to the *System* by use of that password, the registered participant shall immediately change his/her password in the *System* and thereafter provide notice to the Albany NDNY Help Desk and confirm by facsimile to the IT Manager. If a registered participant forgets his/her password, the IT Manager will assign a new password.

6. [Deleted.]

7. A registered attorney or participant may withdraw from using the *System* by providing the Clerk's Office with notice of withdrawal. Such notice must be in writing, and mailed or delivered to the Clerk. Upon receipt, the Clerk's Office will immediately cancel his/her password and will delete his/her name from any applicable electronic service list. The mailing address is:

Clerk
United States Bankruptcy Court
James T. Foley U. S. Court House
445 Broadway, Suite 330
Albany, NY 12207.

8. If any of the information on the Attorney/Participant or Out of District Attorney Registration Form changes, e.g., mailing address, e-mail address, etc., the registered participant must submit the appropriate amended form addressed to the IT Manager as indicated in section I.D.3. above.

II. ELECTRONIC FILING, SERVICE OF DOCUMENTS, AND TIMELINESS.

A. *FILING.*

1. The Administrative Procedures for Electronic Case Filing and the Administrative Order for Electronic Case Filing are to be read in conjunction with the Local Bankruptcy Rules for the Northern District of New York. Continued adherence to the Northern District of New York Local Bankruptcy Rules is not precluded by electronic filing. In the event of a conflict between the Northern District of New York Local Bankruptcy Rules and the Administrative Procedure, the Administrative Procedure, as relating to the electronic filing of petitions, pleadings, and other papers, shall govern.

2. Registered filers shall submit electronically all petitions, motions, pleadings, briefs, memoranda of law, proofs of claim or other documents required to be filed with the court in connection with a case or proceeding, except as provided by this procedure, in Portable Document Format (.pdf).

3. The creditor matrix is to be prepared with bankruptcy software or with word processing software, in a single column format with a one inch left margin (not centered). Creditors are to be single spaced (each on no more than 5 lines with no more than 40 characters per line) with a double space separating one creditor from the next. The city, state and zip code must all be on the last line.

The word processing file is to be saved as a Text (.txt) file and uploaded to the *System* per the user's manual.

An example of the proper format for a matrix is as follows:

MBNA
P.O. Box 15019
Wilmington DE 19886–5019
Wells Fargo Financial
5 Gateway Drive
Suite 5000
Columbia MD 21046

4. Applications for compensation are to be filed electronically. A paper copy marked *ECF Case—Chambers Copy* is to be provided to the Court. In addition, the U.S. Trustee is also to be provided with a paper copy of the application. The Chambers copy and the U.S. Trustee copy are to include all the items listed in subsections (b)(1) through (b)(9) of Local Bankruptcy Rule 2016–1.

5. A "Chambers Copy" in paper format for chambers is required for the following matters. The copy must be clearly marked as **"ECF CASE—CHAMBERS COPY"** and must be submitted in compliance with the requirements of Local Bankruptcy Rule 9013–1 and should be submitted immediately after papers are filed electronically. The Chambers Copy need not contain an original signature. Unless directed by the Court, copies should not be faxed to Chambers or Courtroom Services. Copies should be sent via the mail or hand delivered.

Note: The "Chambers Copy" is to be submitted to the actual physical location of the judge assigned to the case. Chambers copies for Judge Gerling are to be submitted to Utica and chambers copies for Judge Littlefield are to be submitted to Albany.

    a. Utica Chambers:

(1) Notices of Hearing, Motions, applications and certificates of service and Chapter 7 Final Meeting Notices;

(2) All pleadings filed in an adversary proceeding;

(3) Pretrial statements;

(4) Memoranda of Law or documents filed in regard to a submitted matter;

(5) All documents regarding an appeal, withdrawal of reference, or Fed. R. Bankr. P. 9033 objections.

    b. Albany Chambers:

(1) Notices of Hearing, Motions, applications, and certificates of service, excluding Ch. 13 Standing Trustee's motions to dismiss, motions to determine/expunge claim, motions to determine value and Chapter 7 Final Meeting Notices;

(2) Opposition, responses, or any pleading relating to a hearing;

(3) Opposition to disclosure statements in a chapter 11;

(4) Opposition to confirmation of a plan regarding any chapter, excluding Chapter 13 Trustee objections;

(5) Pretrial statements;

(6) Memoranda of Law or documents filed in regard to a submitted matter.

6. It is no longer necessary to submit a paper summons to the Clerk's Office to have it signed, sealed, and issued for service on the defendant(s). CM/ECF will electronically generate the initial summons in an adversary proceeding. The electronic summons will contain the Clerk's signature and Court seal. Multiple copies can be printed for service upon the defendant(s). Proof of service will still be required.

7. The Clerk's Office shall not maintain a paper court file in any case filed after the effective date of these procedures except as otherwise provided by this procedure. The official court record shall be an electronic file maintained on the Court's file server.

8. Any documents received in paper format in Chambers or the Clerk's Office may be shredded when it is determined that they are no longer needed.

9. Adjournment letters and status conference requests are to be filed electronically. They shall also be faxed to Chambers in Albany.

10. In expedited matters occurring in **Albany**, the movant shall contact Courtroom Services staff or Chambers staff by phone as soon as possible after filing the item needing expedited treatment.

11. In expedited matters occurring in **Utica**, the movant shall contact the judge's Judicial Assistant by phone *before* filing the item needing expedited treatment. Compliance with Fed. R. Bankr. P. 9006 is required.

B. *SERVICE.*

1. Whenever a pleading or other paper is filed electronically, in accordance with these procedures, the *System* shall generate a "Notice of Electronic Filing," (attached to this procedure as Form E), to the filing party and any other party who has requested electronic notice in that case.

a. If the recipient is a registered participant in the *System*, the Clerk's e-mailing of the "Notice of Electronic Filing" shall be the equivalent of service of the pleading or other paper by first class mail, postage prepaid.

b. Service of the "Notice of Electronic Filing" on a party who is not a registered participant in the *System* may be accomplished by e-mail, subject to the additional service requirements of Paragraph II.B.3 below.

c. There is no opt out option to electronic service via the "Notice of Electronic Filing".

2. A certificate of service on all parties entitled to service or notice is still required when a party files a document electronically. The certificate must state the manner in which service or notice was accomplished on each party so entitled. Sample language for a "Certificate of Service" is attached to these procedures as Form C.

3. A party who is not a registered participant of the *System* is entitled to a paper copy of any electronically filed pleading or paper. The filing party must therefore provide the non registered party with the pleading or paper according to the Fed. R. Bankr. P. and Local Bankruptcy Rules.

C. *SECTION 341(a) MEETING OF CREDITORS.* The attorney for the debtor or the pro se debtor shall bring to the Section 341(a) meeting of creditors the electronically filed petition, schedules, lists and statement of affairs bearing the original signatures.

D. *TIMELINESS.*

1. Filing of documents electronically does not alter the filing deadline for that document.

2. Generally, electronic filings are considered timely if received by the Court before midnight on the date set as a deadline, unless the judge or Local Bankruptcy Rules specifically require an earlier filing, such as close of business.

3. Any answering papers filed electronically on the last day for filing pursuant to Local Bankruptcy Rule 9013–1(e) must be filed by 4:00 PM Eastern Standard Time.

4. Any motions filed electronically on the last day for filing pursuant to Local Bankruptcy Rule 9013–1(e) must be filed by 4:00 PM Eastern Standard Time.

5. Due to variations in time zones, timeliness is established based on the Eastern time zone where the Northern District of New York is located.

6. A filer whose document is made untimely as the result of a technical failure of the Court's CM/ECF site, as prescribed in Section X. of this procedure, may seek appropriate relief from the court.

III. SIGNATURES.

A. Petitions, lists, schedules and statements, amendments, pleadings, affidavits, and other documents which must contain original signatures or which require verification under Fed. R. Bankr. P. 1008 or an unsworn declaration as provided in 28 U.S.C. § 1746, may be filed electronically by attorneys registered in the *System*.

B. Attorneys who are not registered with the Bankruptcy Court for the Northern District of New York and who do not have a login and password provided by the Court are not permitted to electronically file documents using the login and password of a registered attorney. The attorney login and name shown on a filed document must match.

C. The pleading or other document electronically filed shall indicate a signature in the format "/s/ *name*," unless the document has been scanned and shows the original signature.

D. A copy containing an original signature must be retained by the filer for a minimum of two (2) years after the closing of the case and all time periods for appeals have expired unless the Court orders a different period. In adversary proceedings, the parties shall maintain the original documents for a minimum of two (2) years after the proceeding ends and all time periods for appeals have expired unless the Court orders a different period. These retention periods do not affect or replace any other periods required by other applicable laws or rules. Upon request of the Court, the filer must provide original documents for review. Compliance with Fed. R. Bankr. P. 9011 is required.

E. The following procedure applies when a stipulation, which does not require an order, or another document requires two or more signatures:

1. The filer shall initially confirm that the content of the document is acceptable to all persons required to sign the document and shall obtain the physical signatures of all parties on the document. For purposes of this rule, physical, facsimile or electronic signatures are permitted. Compliance with Fed. R. Bankr. P. 9011 is required.

2. The filer shall file the document electronically, indicating each signature in the format "/s/ *name*," unless the document has been scanned and shows the actual signature

3. The filing party originating the document shall maintain the original signed document as provided for in Section III. D. above.

IV. FEES.

A. Filing fees are to be paid through the on-line payment program in CM/ECF. The Court will no longer manually charge an attorney's credit card for filing fees incurred through CM/ECF.

B. Only VISA, MASTERCARD, AMERICAN EXPRESS, DISCOVER, AND DINER'S CLUB credit cards will be accepted.

C. Filing fees are to be paid through the on-line payment program on the same day they are incurred. Failure to pay filing fees will result in your ECF account being automatically locked. Participants will be unable to file on-line until fees are paid in full. PACER access to view dockets will be unaffected.

D. [Deleted.]

E. Except as otherwise provided, all registered participants of the *System* shall be subject to the fees set forth in the Fee Schedule for Electronic Public Access (EPA Fee Schedule), adopted by the Judicial Conference of the United States.

F.   Attorneys of record and registered participants in a case receive one free electronic viewing of all filed documents through PACER from which he or she can save or print the document.   Additional PACER access to the pleading is subject to PACER fees.

G.   Filing fees will not be refunded unless so ordered by the Court.   Requests for refunds are to be made by motion or application and order.

V.   ATTACHMENTS.

A.   Registered participants must submit all documents referenced as attachments including but not limited to leases, notes and the like in Portable Document Format (PDF), unless the court permits conventional filing.   Attachments may be summarized (Form D) and only the relevant excerpts electronically filed.

B.   The size of the electronic file shall be no larger than 2 megabytes.   Attachments larger than 2 megabytes must be split into separate PDF files and the multiple PDF files attached to the pleading.

C.   If an attachment is not available in electronic form, it is preferred that such documents, or the relevant portions thereof, be electronically imaged, i.e., scanned, and filed using the Portable Document Format (PDF).   Excerpted material must be clear and prominently identified as such.   The file size limits as stated in section V.B. above are required.

D.   The filing party of electronic excerpts of documents as attachments do so without prejudice to their right to timely file additional excerpts or complete attachments.

E.   The filing party must promptly provide excerpted documents in full if the Court or a responding party makes such a request.

VI.   SEALED DOCUMENTS.

A.   A motion to file a document under seal may be filed electronically unless prohibited by law.

B.   Documents ordered to be placed under seal must be filed conventionally, and NOT electronically, unless specifically authorized by the Court.

C.   The filing party must submit to the clerk a paper copy of the signed order attached to the documents to be sealed by the clerk.

VII.   ORDERS.

A.   **All proposed orders, with the below exceptions, may be submitted conventionally to the Court until the effective date of March 1, 2006, unless the Court allows otherwise.   Effective March 1, 2006, all proposed orders, with the exception of those listed below, must be submitted electronically using the E–Orders feature of CM/ECF.**   Registered users will be notified when and how to file orders electronically.   Once the Court begins receiving orders electronically, all orders shall be submitted electronically, *after the return date of the hearing or trial*, unless otherwise ordered by the Court.

B.   All ex parte orders must be submitted conventionally to the Court.   An application or motion underlying an ex parte order must also be filed conventionally, unless otherwise ordered by the Court.

C.   All Orders to Show Cause and Orders Shortening time along with any supporting documentation, i.e., application, motion, notice, must be conventionally submitted to the Court.   In Utica the Court requires that you notify Chambers *before* submitting Orders to Show Cause and/or Orders Shortening Time.

D.   Proposed orders may not be combined with the application or motion into one document.   The application or motion must be entered on the docket prior to submitting the order.   **DO NOT ATTEMPT TO ELECTRONICALLY FILE A PLEADING WHICH CONTAINS A PROPOSED ORDER IN THE BODY OF THE PLEADING.**

E. A copy of a proposed order can be included as an attachment to an electronically filed pleading if the proposed order is clearly marked as an "EXHIBIT" only. This copy will not be considered by the Court and will not be signed by the Court.

F. The only exception to sections VII (A), VII (B), VII (C), and VII (D) above is the Application and Order to pay Filing Fees in Installments (Official Form 3A). It may be filed electronically.

G. Any order filed electronically by the Court without the original signature of a judge has the same force and effect as if the judge had affixed his/her signature to a paper copy of the order and it had been entered on the docket in a conventional manner.

H. Any ministerial order filed electronically by the Clerk without the original signature of the Clerk has the same force and effect as if the Clerk had affixed his/her signature to a paper copy of the order and it had been entered on the docket in a conventional manner.

VIII. DOCKET ENTRIES.

A. A filer who electronically submits a pleading or other document shall be responsible for designating a docket entry for the document by using one of the docket event categories prescribed by the court. This action constitutes an entry on the official court docket as provided in Fed. R. Bankr. P. 5003.

B. The Clerk shall enter all orders and judgments in the *System*, which constitute docketing of the order and judgment for all purposes. The Clerk's notation in the appropriate docket of an order or judgment shall constitute the entry of the order or judgment as provided in Fed. R. Bankr. P. 5003.

IX. CORRECTING DOCUMENTS FILED IN ERROR.

A. Once a document is submitted and becomes part of the case docket, corrections to the docket are made only by the Clerk's Office.

B. A document incorrectly filed in a case may be the result of posting the wrong PDF file to a docket entry, or selecting the wrong document type from the menu, or entering the wrong case number and not catching the error before the transaction is completed. **Do not attempt to re-file the document if an error in filing is discovered.**

C. As soon as possible after an error is discovered, the filer shall contact the Help Desk in the clerk's office which has jurisdiction over the case or proceeding. Be sure to have the case number and document number for which the correction is being requested. If appropriate, the clerk will make an entry indicating that the document was filed in error. You will be advised *if* you need to re-file the document. The *System* will not permit you to make changes to the document(s) or docket entry filed in error once the transaction has been accepted.

X. TECHNICAL FAILURES.

A. The Clerk's Office shall deem this district's CM/ECF site to be subject to technical failure on any given day if the site is unable to accept filings continuously or intermittently over the course of any period of time greater than one hour after 12:00 p.m. (noon) that day. Known systems outages will be posted on our web site, if possible.

B. Problems on the filer's end, such as with phone lines, filer's Internet Service Provider (ISP), or hardware or software, will not constitute a technical failure under these procedures nor excuse an untimely filing. A filer who cannot file a document electronically because of a problem on the filer's end must file the document conventionally.

XI. SECURITY OF THE *SYSTEM*. Each electronically filed paper shall be assigned a special identification number which can be traced, if necessary, to detect post filing alterations to a document.

XII. PRIVACY.

A. To address the privacy concerns created by Internet access to court documents, filers may modify or partially redact certain personal data identifiers appearing in pleadings or other papers. This data and the suggested modifications are as follows:

    1. Minors' Names: Use the minors' initials;

    2. Financial Account Numbers: Identify the name or type of account and the financial institution where maintained, but use only the last four numbers of the account number;

    3. Social Security Numbers: Documents filed with the Court should only contain the last four digits of the Social Security number. Attorneys are required to obtain the debtor's full social security number and maintain the originally signed "Form 21. Statement of Social Security Number" in their files.

    4. Dates of Birth: Use only the year; and

    5. Other data as permitted by order of the court.

B. Information posted on the *System* must not be downloaded for uses inconsistent with the privacy rights of any person.

XIII. PUBLIC ACCESS TO THE *SYSTEM* DOCKET.

A. Electronic access to the electronic docket and documents filed in the *System* is available for viewing to the public at no charge at each Clerk's Office public counter during regular business hours. A fee for a paper copy of an electronic document is required in accordance with 28 U.S.C. § 1930.

B. Although any person can retrieve and view the documents in the *System* and access information from it without charge at the Clerk's Office, electronic access to the *System* for viewing purposes is otherwise limited to subscribers to the Public Access to Court Electronic Records ("PACER") *System* and, in accordance with the ruling of the Judicial Conference of the United States, a user fee will be charged for accessing detailed case information, such as reviewing filed documents and docket sheets, but excluding review of calendars and similar general information.

C. Conventional copies and certified copies of the electronically filed documents may be purchased at the Clerk's Office. The fee for copying and certification will be in accordance with 28 U.S.C. § 1930.

FORM A. ATTORNEY OR PARTICIPANT REGISTRATION FORM

UNITED STATES BANKRUPTCY COURT
NORTHERN DISTRICT OF NEW YORK

ELECTRONIC CASE FILING SYSTEM
ATTORNEY OR PARTICIPANT REGISTRATION FORM

LIVE SYSTEM

This form shall be used to register an attorney or participant on the U.S. Bankruptcy Court for the Northern District of New York Electronic Case Filing (ECF) System (hereinafter *System*). A registered participant will have privileges to submit documents electronically, and to view and retrieve docket sheets and documents for all cases assigned to the Northern District's ECF *System*. (**NOTE: A PACER account is necessary for access to files and documents.** You may register for a PACER account either online at http://pacer.psc.uscourts.gov or by calling 1–800–676–6856).

First/Middle/Last Name: _____

Bar ID #: _____

State of Admission: _____

Admitted to Practice in U.S. District Court for the NDNY: _____

Firm Name, if applicable: _____

Mailing Address: _____

_____

Voice Phone Number: _____

Fax Phone Number: _____

Internet E–MAIL Address: _____

Send Notices to these additional E–MAIL Addresses: _____

_____

Send Electronic Notice (check one) ___ Each Filing ___ End of Day Summary

Send Electronic Notice in the following format (check one):

___HTML for *Netscape*, ISP mail service, i.e., *AOL, Hotmail, Yahoo,* etc.

___ Text for cc:Mail, Groupwise, Outlook, Outlook Express, other (please list) ___

In order to schedule you for the appropriate training class, please indicate your type of legal practice.

Debtor___, Creditor___, Trustee___, Other (please specify)_____

Name(s) of support staff you would like trained with you: _____

_____

By submitting this registration form the applicant agrees to adhere to the following:

1. This access is for use only in ECF cases filed in the U.S. Bankruptcy Court for the Northern District of New York. It may be used to file and view electronic documents, docket sheets, and reports. **NOTE: A PACER account is necessary for this access and the registration information is referenced above.**

2. The Fed.R.Bankr.P. 9011 requires that every pleading, motion, and other paper (except lists, schedules, statements, or amendments thereto) filed with the Court be signed by at least one attorney of record or, if the party is not represented by an attorney, by the party. The unique password issued to a participant identifies that participant to the Court each time he or she logs onto the *System*. The use of a participant's password constitutes the signature for the purposes of Fed. R.Bankr.P. 9011 on any document or pleading filed electronically using that participant's password. Therefore, a participant must protect and secure the password issued by the Court. If there is any reason to suspect the password has been compromised, it is the duty of the participant to immediately change his or her password through the "Utilities" menu in the *System*. After doing so, the participant should contact the ECF Help Desk to report the suspected password compromise.

3. Registration shall constitute a request and an agreement to receive service of pleadings and other papers electronically pursuant to Fed.R.Bankr.P. 9036, where service of pleadings and other papers is otherwise permitted by first class mail, postage prepaid.

4. I understand that by submitting an application for a password I agree to adhere to all of the rules and regulations in the NDNY Administrative Order for Filing, Signing, and Verifying Pleadings and Papers by Electronic Means currently in

effect, and any changes or additions that may be made to such Administrative Order.

_____

Applicant's Signature

_____

Last Four Digits of Social Security
Number (for security purposes)

Privacy Disclaimer: The Court may periodically send out announcements and updates by mail that are pertinent to ECF practice. However, the information contained within this application will not be sold or otherwise distributed by this office to outside sources.

Please return this form to the New York Northern Office at:

U.S. Bankruptcy Court
Attn: IT Manager
James T. Foley US Courthouse
445 Broadway, Suite 330
Albany, New York 12207

_____

FORM B.   OUT OF DISTRICT ATTORNEY REGISTRATION FORM

UNITED STATES BANKRUPTCY COURT
NORTHERN DISTRICT OF NEW YORK

ELECTRONIC CASE FILING SYSTEM
OUT OF DISTRICT ATTORNEY REGISTRATION FORM

LIVE SYSTEM

This form shall be used to register an out of district attorney on the U.S. Bankruptcy Court for the Northern District of New York Electronic Case Filing (ECF) System (hereinafter *System*) by attorneys who (1) **reside and practice outside of this district** and/or (2) represent parties in New York on **a pro hac vice basis**. A registered participant will have privileges to submit documents electronically, and to view and retrieve docket sheets and documents for all cases assigned to the Northern District ECF *System*. (**NOTE: A PACER account is necessary for access to files and documents.** You may register for a PACER account either online at http://pacer.psc.uscourts.gov or by calling 1–800–676–6856).

First/Middle/Last Name: _____

Bar ID #: _____

State of Admission: _____

Admitted to Practice in the U.S. District Court for: _____

Firm Name, if applicable: _____

Mailing Address: _____

_____

_____

Voice Phone Number: _____

Fax Phone Number: _____

Internet E–MAIL Address: _____

Send Notices to these additional E–MAIL Addresses: _____

_____

Send Electronic Notice (check one) ___Each Filing ___End of Day Summary

Send Electronic Notice in the following format (check one):

___ HTML for *Netscape*, ISP mail service, i.e., *AOL, Hotmail, Yahoo*, etc.

___ Text for cc:Mail, GroupWise, Outlook, Outlook Express, other (please list)

If "in-house" training is required, please indicate your type of legal practice. Debtor___, Creditor___, Trustee___, Other (please specify)_____

Name(s) of support staff you would like trained with you: _____

_____

In order to qualify for an account on the *system*, the out-of-district attorney/participant must certify that he or she meets one of the following conditions. **Please check the applicable box(es):**

☐ I am registered as an ECF participant in the United States Bankruptcy Court in another state or district. Please indicate court or district(s): _____

☐ I have read the NDNY Administrative Order and Procedure regarding ECF and have completed training as required by the NDNY Administrative Procedure.

By submitting this registration form the applicant agrees to adhere to the following:

1. This access is for use only in ECF cases filed in the U.S. Bankruptcy Court for the Northern District of New York. It may be used to file and view electronic documents, docket sheets, and reports. **NOTE: A PACER account is necessary for this access and the registration information is referenced above.**

2. The Fed.R.Bankr.P. 9011 requires that every pleading, motion, and other paper (except lists, schedules, statements, or amendments thereto) filed with the Court be signed by at least one attorney of record or, if the party is not represented by an attorney, by the party. The unique password issued to a participant identifies that participant to the Court each time he or she logs onto the *System*. The use of a participant's password constitutes the signature for the purposes of Fed. R.Bankr.P. 9011 on any document or pleading filed electronically using that participant's password. Therefore, a participant must protect and secure the password issued by the Court. If there is any reason to suspect the password has been compromised, it is the duty of the participant to immediately change his or her password through the "Utilities" menu in the *System*. After doing so, the participant should contact the ECF Help Desk to report the suspected password compromise.

3. Registration shall constitute a request and an agreement to receive service of pleadings and other papers electronically pursuant to Fed.R.Bankr.P. 9036, where service of pleadings and other papers is otherwise permitted by first class mail, postage prepaid.

4. I understand that by submitting an application for a password I agree to adhere to all of the rules and regulations in the NDNY Administrative Procedures for Filing, Signing and Verifying Pleadings and Papers by Electronic Means currently in effect, and any changes or additions that may be made to such Administrative Order.

_____

Applicant's Signature

_____

Last Four Digits of Social Security Number (for security purposes)

Privacy Disclaimer: The Court may periodically send out announcements and updates by mail that are pertinent to ECF practice. However, the information contained within this application will not be sold or otherwise distributed by this office to outside sources.

Please return this form to the New York Northern Office at:

U.S. Bankruptcy Court
Attn: IT Manager
James T. Foley US Courthouse
445 Broadway, Suite 330
Albany, New York 12207

FORM C.   CERTIFICATE OF SERVICE (SAMPLE FORMAT)

UNITED STATES BANKRUPTCY COURT
NORTHERN DISTRICT OF NEW YORK

In Re:

Case No.
Chapter

Debtor(s).

CERTIFICATE OF SERVICE

I hereby certify that on, _____ (Date), I electronically filed the foregoing with the Clerk of the Bankruptcy Court using the CM/ECF system which sent notification of such filing to the following:

And, I hereby certify that I have mailed by the United States Postal Service the document to the following non CM/ECF participants:

/s/name

FORM D.   SUMMARY OF ATTACHMENT(S) AND CERTIFICATE OF SERVICE (SAMPLE FORMAT)

UNITED STATES BANKRUPTCY COURT
FOR THE NORTHERN DISTRICT OF NEW YORK

In Re:

Case No.
Chapter

Debtor(s).

SUMMARY OF ATTACHMENT(S) AND CERTIFICATE OF SERVICE

The following attachment(s) in reference to _____ are available upon request:

1. ....
2. ....
3. ....

Respectfully submitted

/s/ name

ATTORNEY FOR _____

Copy of the above served this
____ day of _____, ___ on:
[respondent parties if motion]
[debtor's (s') attorney and trustee if claim]

FORM E.   NOTICE OF ELECTRONIC FILING (SAMPLE FORMAT)

* * *NOTE TO PUBLIC ACCESS USERS* * *You may view the filed documents once without charge. To avoid later charges, download a copy of each document during this first viewing.

U.S. Bankruptcy Court
Northern District of New York
Notice of Electronic Filing

The following transaction was received from Perry Mason entered on 9/11/2002 at 2:58 PM EDT and filed on 9/11/2002.

Case Name: Marilyn L Smith

Case Number: YY–NNNNN

Document Number: 1

Docket Text:

Motion for Relief from Stay. Receipt Number 12345, Fee Amount $75, Filed by Citibank. (Chest, Lynn)

The following document(s) are associated with this transaction:

Document description: Main Document

Original filename: C:\Documents and Settings\Administrator\Desktop\PDF Demo Documents\Motion.PDF

Electronic document Stamp:

[STAMP bkecfStamp_ID=l007484561 [Date—9/11/2002] [FileNumber=4026–0] [86313f869eeff877698b3d96   decaf4c49fb8bbcd658df10d0   b534645133b8a0e9c4679l af784aef258b6d0e64 cbcec71f26525f5c4 ea2l496447779953ca0505]]

YY-NNNNN Notice will be electronically mailed to:

Perry Mason *perry_mason@email.com*

YY-NNNNN Notice will not be electronically mailed to:

Joseph Trustee, Esq.
350 Norton St.
Anytown, NY 12345

SAMPLE UNSIGNED E–ORDER

THIS AREA IS LEFT BLANK FOR THE SIGNATURE OF
THE JUDGE. ALLOW AT LEAST FOUR INCHES
AT THE TOP FOR THE SIGNATURE.

UNITED STATES BANKRUPTCY COURT
NORTHERN DISTRICT OF NEW YORK

In re __John Debtorman,_____)	
)	
Debtor(s))	Case No. 06–10001
)	
)	
)	Chapter 7
_____)	

ORDER VACATING FINAL DECREE

IT APPEARING that the Final Decree filed in the above-entitled case on <u>May 31, 2005</u> was filed in error as there are still matters pending in the case, It is hereby ORDERED that said Final Decree is hereby vacated.

ADMINISTRATIVE ORDER NO. 03–01. ELECTRONIC CASE FILING

Federal Rule of Civil Procedure 83 and Bankruptcy Rule 5005(a)(2), 9011 and 9029 authorize this Court to establish practices and procedures for the filing, signing and verification of pleadings and papers by electronic means. Accordingly,

IT IS ORDERED that petitions, pleadings, motions and other documents filed in **all** cases on or after July 1, 2004 must be filed electronically pursuant to electronic filing procedures established by the Clerk of Court and contained in the Administrative Procedures for Filing, Signing and Verifying Pleadings and Papers by Electronic Means dated December 13, 2002.

IT IS ORDERED that the electronic filing of a petition, pleading, motion, proof of claim or other document by a person constitutes the signature of that person under Bankruptcy Rule 9011.

IT IS FURTHER ORDERED that no person will knowingly permit his/her password to be used by anyone to whom they have not given authorization.

IT IS FURTHER ORDERED that no person will knowingly use the password of another person without that person's authorization.

IT IS FURTHER ORDERED that this Administrative Order is to be read in conjunction with the Administrative Procedures for Filing, Signing and Verifying Pleadings and Papers by Electronic Means dated December 13, 2002, the Administrative Order for Electronic Case Filing (Administrative Order No. 02–03), and the Local Bankruptcy Rules for the Northern District of New York.

Dated: November 19, 2003.

ADMINISTRATIVE ORDER NO. 05-02. ADOPTION
OF INTERIM BANKRUPTCY RULES[1]

Whereas, on April 20, 2005 the Bankruptcy Abuse Prevention and Consumer Protection Act of 2005 (the Act) was enacted into law; and

Whereas, most provisions of the Act are effective on October 17, 2005; and

Whereas, the Advisory Committee on Bankruptcy Rules has prepared Interim Rules designed to implement the substantive and procedural changes mandated by the Act; and

Whereas, the Committee on Rules of Practice and Procedure of the Judicial Conference of the United States has also approved these Interim Rules and recommends the adoption of the Interim Rules to provide uniform procedures for implementing the Act; and

Whereas, the general effective date of the Act has not provided sufficient time to promulgate rules after appropriate public notice and an opportunity for comment;

NOW THEREFORE, IT IS ORDERED that pursuant to 28 U.S.C. section 2071, Rule 83 of the Federal Rules of Civil Procedure, and Rule 9029 of the Federal Rules of Bankruptcy Procedure, the attached Interim Rules are adopted in their entirety without change by a majority of the judges of this Court to be effective October 17, 2005 to conform with the Act. For cases and proceedings not governed by the Act, the Federal Rules of Bankruptcy Procedure and the Local Rules of this Court, other than the Interim Rules, shall apply. The Interim Rules shall remain in effect until further order of the court.

Dated: August 26, 2005.

[1] The Interim Bankruptcy Rules follow the Administrative Orders of the United States Bankruptcy Court for the Northern District of New York, post.

ADMINISTRATIVE ORDER NO. 05-03. DISBURSEMENT OF § 1326 PRE-CONFIRMATION ADEQUATE PROTECTION PAYMENTS IN CHAPTER 13 CASES FILED ON AND AFTER OCTOBER 17, 2005

Whereas a need exists to clarify and simplify the manner in which § 1326 pre-confirmation adequate protection payments will be made in Chapter 13 cases filed on and after October 17, 2005.

NOW, therefore, this 12th day of October, 2005, IT IS HEREBY ORDERED, as follows:

The Chapter 13 plan shall provide that § 1326 pre-confirmation adequate protection payments will be paid through the Chapter 13 Trustee. The plan shall list creditor name, address, account number, and monthly payment amount for each creditor receiving § 1326(a)(1) pre-confirmation adequate protection payments.

The debtor shall commence plan payments to the Trustee within 30 days after the order for relief or the order converting the case to Chapter 13. Said payment shall include the amounts necessary to pay pre-confirmation adequate protection payments plus the statutory Trustee's fees. The debtor shall not reduce plan payments to the Trustee under § 1326(a)(1)(C) as a result of these adequate protection payments, without an order of this Court.

A creditor may file a motion requesting a change in the amount of § 1326(a)(1) pre-confirmation payments pursuant to § 1326(a)(3). Until the creditor's motion is resolved, the Chapter 13 Trustee shall continue to make pre-confirmation adequate protection payments to such creditor as set forth herein.

The Chapter 13 Trustee is authorized to pay § 1326(a)(1) pre-confirmation payments in an amount as set forth in the proposed plan, however, no such payments shall be made to a creditor until a proof of claim is filed. Pre-confirmation payments shall be made to the creditors with the Trustee's first monthly disbursement at least 30 days after the petition date and following filing of the claim. At the time of such payments, the Chapter 13 Trustee is authorized to retain an administrative fee for effecting the payments described herein and shall collect such fee at the time of making the payment from the funds on hand with the Trustee. The allowed fee shall be equal to the percentage fee established by the Attorney General pursuant to 28 U.S.C. § 586(e)(1)(B) in effect at the time of disbursement. The trustee shall apply each § 1326(a)(1) pre-confirmation payments to the principal outstanding on the creditor's claim.

If the case is dismissed prior to confirmation, the creditor shall receive from the Trustee, any § 1326 pre-confirmation adequate protection payments due and owing from funds collected by the Trustee under § 1326(a)(1)(A) less statutory trustee fees and specifically allowed § 503(b) claims, including debtor's attorney fees.

This Order shall be effective October 17th, 2005.

ADMINISTRATIVE ORDER NO. 07–04.   INCREASE TO TRANSCRIPT FEE RATES

The Judicial Conference of the United States, at its September 2007 session, approved an increase of ten percent to the maximum original and copy transcript fee rates, to be effective in fiscal year 2008. The Judicial Conference also approved a new rate for the delivery of transcripts within 14 days and agreed that the rate be set at the mid-point between the rates authorized for expedited (7–day) and ordinary (30–day) delivery. It is hereby

ORDERED, that this Court adopts a revised schedule of Maximum Rates for all categories of transcript, as attached hereto. Transcripts ordered prior to the effective date of this Order shall be billed at the rates in effect at the time the transcript order was placed with the Electronic Court Recorder Operator. The rates reflected in the attachment shall remain in effect until further order of this Court.

Dated: November 20th, 2007.

Attachment

Maximum Transcript Fee Rates—All Parties Per Page

	Original	First Copy to Each Party	Each Add'l Copy to the Same Party
Ordinary Transcript (30 day) A transcript to be delivered within thirty (30) calendar days after receipt of an order.	$3.65	$.90	$.60
14–Day Transcript A transcript to be delivered within fourteen (14) calendar days after receipt of an order.	$4.25	$.90	$.60
Expedited Transcript (7 day) A transcript to be delivered within seven (7) calendar days after receipt of an order.	$4.85	$.90	$.60

	Original	First Copy to Each Party	Each Add'l Copy to the Same Party
Daily Transcript A transcript to be delivered following adjournment and prior to the normal opening hour of the court on the following morning whether or not it actually is a court day.	$6.05	$1.20	$.90
Hourly Transcript A transcript of proceedings ordered under unusual circumstances to be delivered within two (2) hours.	$7.25	$1.20	$.90
Realtime Transcript A draft unedited transcript produced by a certified realtime reporter as a byproduct of realtime to be delivered electronically during proceedings or immediately following adjournment.	$3.05	$1.20	

ADMINISTRATIVE ORDER NO. 07–05. ISSUANCE OF CHAPTER 13 DISCHARGES

The Bankruptcy Abuse Prevention and Consumer Protection Act of 2005 (BAPCPA) requires the debtor to meet certain requirements before a discharge can be issued in a chapter 13 case. In order to provide for the efficient processing of chapter 13 cases under BAPCPA, the Court has adopted a new local form entitled "Chapter 13 Debtor(s) Affidavit Demonstrating Entitlement to Discharge." In compliance with 11 U.S.C. Section 1328, the court hereby **ORDERS** that:

1. A debtor seeking entry of a discharge under 11 U.S.C. Section 1328(a) in a case filed on or after October 17, 2005, shall file the local form "Chapter 13 Debtor(s) Affidavit Demonstrating Entitlement to Discharge" and Official Form B23, "Debtor's Certification of Completion of Post Petition Instructional Course Concerning Personal Financial Management."

2. Upon the timely filing of the "Chapter 13 Debtor(s) Affidavit Demonstrating Entitlement to Discharge" and Official Form B23, the Clerk's Office will schedule a default hearing on the debtor's request for a discharge.

3. If no objections to the discharge are filed pursuant to Bankruptcy Rule 9014 and Local Bankruptcy Rule 9013–1 and the debtor is otherwise eligible to receive a discharge, the Court may issue a discharge in the case.

4. If either the "Chapter 13 Debtor(s) Affidavit Demonstrating Entitlement to Discharge" or Official Form B23 are not timely filed, the case will be closed without a discharge.

5. If a case is closed without a discharge, the debtor must file a motion to reopen the case and pay a fee equal to the filing fee for a chapter 13 petition in order to obtain a discharge. The fee to reopen a case to obtain a discharge cannot be waived.

This Order is effective immediately.

Dated: December 11th, 2007.

ADMINISTRATIVE ORDER NO. 08–01. DEBTOR COUNSEL FEES IN CHAPTER 13 CASES FILED IN THE ALBANY DIVISION

WHEREAS, a need exists to be certain that debtors understand (1) their rights and responsibilities to the court, to the Chapter 13 Trustee, and to creditors of their estate, (2) the importance of honest and continual communication with their attorney to make their case successful, and (3) the fees being charged for their case by their attorney; and

WHEREAS, a need exists to be certain that debtors' attorneys understand what legal services they are expected to provide when a chapter 13 case is filed in the Albany Division of the Northern District of New York. NOW, after due deliberation, it is hereby,

ORDERED, as follows:

Chapter 13 debtor counsel shall set forth the amount of the legal fee to be charged for services rendered to the debtor both in the 2016(b) Statement and chapter 13 plan filed with the court. The fee requested shall constitute a flat fee for all services rendered and to be rendered in connection with the case in accordance with this court's *Rights and Responsibilities of Chapter 13 Debtors and their Attorneys* (form attached) (the "Flat Fee"), unless otherwise specified in the 2016(b) Statement. Except as otherwise ordered by the court, after a hearing held on notice to all parties in interest, the Flat Fee, whether paid through the chapter 13 plan or directly by the debtor, shall not be more than $3,700, nor more than 50% of the amount to be funded through the chapter 13 plan.

If the 2016(b) Statement provides that the fee required does not constitute a Flat Fee, no fee shall be awarded absent entry of a separate order. In those instances, counsel shall request approval by filing and serving an appropriate Application for Compensation pursuant to 11 U.S.C. § 331. All such applications shall be accompanied by the appropriate narrative of services rendered and contemporaneous time records.

Nothing contained herein is meant to limit the rights of the Chapter 13 Trustee or an interested party to object to the fees or method of payment sought by debtor's counsel.

This Order shall be effective with respect to all chapter 13 cases filed with the Albany Division on or after April 1, 2008.

Dated: February 21 2008.

United States Bankruptcy Court
for the Northern District of New York
Albany Division

RIGHTS AND RESPONSIBILITIES OF CHAPTER 13 DEBTORS AND THEIR ATTORNEYS

It is important for Chapter 13 debtors to understand their rights and responsibilities. It is also important that the debtors know that communicating with their attorney(s) is essential to successfully completing their plan. Debtors should also know that they may expect certain services to be performed by their attorney.

In order to assure that debtors and their attorneys understand their rights and responsibilities in the bankruptcy process, the following guidelines approved by the Court are hereby agreed to by the debtors and their attorneys, **unless the Court orders otherwise:**

(Nothing in this Agreement shall be construed to excuse an attorney from any ethical duties or responsibilities under FRBP 9011 or applicable non-bankruptcy law.)

BEFORE THE CASE IS FILED

The debtor agrees to:

1. Provide the attorney with accurate financial information and timely provide all requested documentation.

2. Discuss with the attorney the debtor's objectives in filing the case.

The attorney agrees to:

1. Meet with the debtor to review the debtor's debts, assets, liabilities, income, and expenses.

2. Counsel the debtor regarding the advisability of filing either a Chapter 7 or Chapter 13 case, outlining the procedures with the debtor, and answering the debtor's questions.

3. Explain what payments will be made directly by the debtor and what payments will be made through the debtor's Chapter 13 plan, with particular attention to mortgage and vehicle loan payments, as well as any other claims which accrue interest.

4. Explain to the debtor how, when, and where to make the Chapter 13 plan payments.

5. Explain to the debtor how the attorney's fees are paid and provide an executed copy of this document to the debtor.

6. Explain to the debtor that the first plan payment must be made to the Trustee within 30 days of the date the plan is filed.

7. Advise the debtor of the requirement to attend the 341 Meeting of Creditors, and instruct the debtor as to the date, time, and place of the meeting.

8. Advise the debtor of the necessity of maintaining liability and hazard insurance on all real property as well as liability, collision, and comprehensive insurance on vehicles securing loans or leases.

9. Timely prepare and file the debtor's petition, plan, statements, and schedules.

AFTER THE CASE IS FILED

The debtor agrees to:

1. Keep the Trustee and attorney informed of the debtor's address and telephone number.

2. Inform the attorney of any wage garnishments or attachments of assets which occur or continue after the filing of the case.

3. Contact the attorney promptly if the debtor loses his/her job or has other financial problems.

4. Let the attorney know if the debtor is sued during the case.

5. Inform the attorney if any tax refunds the debtor is entitled to are seized or not returned to the debtor by the IRS or Franchise Tax Board.

6. Contact the attorney before buying, selling, or refinancing any property, and before entering into any loan agreements to find out what approvals are required.

The attorney agrees to:

1. Appear at the 341 Meeting of Creditors with the debtor.

2. Respond to objections to plan confirmation and, where necessary, prepare an amended plan.

3. Prepare, file, and serve necessary modifications to the plan which may include suspending, lowering, or increasing plan payments.

4. Prepare, file, and serve necessary amended statements and schedules, in accordance with information provided by the debtor.

5. Prepare, file, and serve such motions as are needed during the case including, but not limited to, motions to avoid liens, sell property, approve settlements, approve new debt, etc.

6. Timely review all filed proofs of claim.

7. Timely object to all improper and invalid proofs of claim based upon information and documentation provided by the debtor if such objection is necessary and beneficial to the debtor or to the estate.

8. Represent the debtor in connection with motions for relief from stay and for dismissal or conversion of the case.

9. Where appropriate, prepare, file, and serve necessary motions to partially or wholly avoid liens on real property or personal property pursuant to sections 506 or 522.

10. Communicate with the debtor by telephone or by being available for office appointments to discuss pending issues or matters of concern.

11. Provide such other legal services as are necessary for the proper administration of the present case before the Bankruptcy Court.

Approval for legal fees in the total sum of $_____ will be requested by the attorney. The attorney has received $_____ prepetition (the initial retainer) and requests payment of the balance of $_____ through the Chapter 13 plan.

Legal fees to be paid to the attorney shall be a "flat fee" for all services to be rendered in this case. Additional fees may be awarded and paid to the attorney if an extraordinary level of service is provided. If such occurs, the attorney shall apply to the Court for any additional fees and all such fees shall be paid through the plan unless otherwise ordered. The attorney may not receive fees directly from the debtor other than the initial retainer, without court approval.

If the debtor disputes the legal services provided or charged by the attorney, the debtor must advise the Court or the Chapter 13 Trustee in writing and request that the matter be set for a hearing.

The attorney may move to withdraw pursuant to Local Bankruptcy Rule 2091–1, or the client may discharge the attorney at any time.

Dated:

_____
Debtor

Dated:

_____
Debtor

Dated:

_____
Attorney for Debtor(s)

FEDERAL RULES OF BANKRUPTCY PROCEDURE
INTERIM BANKRUPTCY RULES
INTERIM RULE 1006.   FILING FEE

(a) General Requirement. Every petition shall be accompanied by the filing fee except as provided in subdivisions (b) and (c) of this rule. For the purpose of this rule, "filing fee" means the filing fee prescribed by 28 U.S.C. § 1930(a)(1)-(a)(5) and any other fee prescribed by the Judicial Conference of the United States under 28 U.S.C. § 1930(b) that is payable to the clerk upon the commencement of a case under the Code.

(b) Payment of Filing Fee in Installments.

(1) *Application to Pay Filing Fee in Installments.* A voluntary petition by an individual shall be accepted for filing if accompanied by the debtor's signed application, prepared as prescribed by the appropriate Official Form, stating that the debtor is unable to pay the filing fee except in installments.

* * * * *

(3) *Postponement of Attorney's Fees.* All installments of the filing fee must be paid in full before the debtor or chapter 13 trustee may make further payments to an attorney or any other person who renders services to the debtor in connection with the case.

(c) Waiver of Filing Fee. A voluntary chapter 7 petition filed by an individual shall be accepted for filing if accompanied by the debtor's application requesting a waiver under 28 U.S.C. § 1930(f), prepared as prescribed by the appropriate Official Form.

Amended, on an interim basis, effective October 17, 2005.

COMMITTEE NOTE
October 17, 2005

Subdivision (a) is amended to include a reference to new subdivision (c), which deals with fee waivers under 28 U.S.C. § 1930(f), which was added in 2005.

Subdivision (b)(1) is amended to delete the sentence requiring a disclosure that the debtor has not paid an attorney or other person in connection with the case. Inability to pay the filing fee in installments is one of the requirements for a fee waiver under the 2005 revisions to 28 U.S.C. § 1930(f). If the attorney payment prohibition were retained, payment of an attorney's fee would render many debtors ineligible for installment payments and thus enhance their eligibility for the fee waiver. The deletion of this prohibition from the rule, which was not statutorily required, ensures that debtors who have the financial ability to pay the fee in installments will do so rather than request a waiver.

Subdivision (b)(3) is amended in conformance with the changes to (b)(1) to reflect the 2005 amendments. The change is meant to clarify that (b)(3) refers to payments made after the debtor has filed the bankruptcy case and after the debtor has received permission to pay the fee in installments. Otherwise, the subdivision may conflict with intent and effect of the amendments to subdivision (b)(1).

INTERIM RULE 1007.   LISTS, SCHEDULES, STATEMENTS, AND OTHER DOCUMENTS; TIME LIMITS

(A) List of Creditors and Equity Security Holders, and Corporate Ownership Statement.

* * * * *

(4) *Chapter 15 Case.* Unless the court orders otherwise, a foreign representative filing a petition for recognition under chapter 15 shall file with the petition a list containing the name and address of all administrators in foreign proceedings of the debtor, all parties to any litigation in which the debtor is a party and that is pending in the United States at the time of the filing of the petition, and all entities against whom provisional relief is being sought under § 1519 of the Code.

(5) *Extension of Time.* Any extension of time for the filing of lists required by this subdivision may be granted only on motion for cause shown and on notice to the United States trustee and to any trustee, committee elected under § 705 or appointed under § 1102 of the Code, or other party as the court may direct.

(B) Schedules, Statements, and Other Documents Required.

(1) Except in a chapter 9 municipality case, the debtor, unless the court orders otherwise, shall file the following schedules, statements, and other documents, prepared as prescribed by the appropriate Official Forms, if any:

(A) schedules of assets and liabilities;

(B) a schedule of current income and expenditures;

(C) a schedule of executory contracts and unexpired leases;

(D) a statement of financial affairs;

(E) copies of all payment advices or other evidence of payment, if any, with all but the last four digits of the debtor's social security number redacted, received by the debtor from an employer within 60 days before the filing of the petition; and

(F) a record of any interest that the debtor has in an account or program of the type specified in § 521(c) of the Code.

(2) An individual debtor in a chapter 7 case shall file a statement of intention as required by § 521(a) of the Code, prepared as prescribed by the appropriate Official Form. A copy of the statement of intention shall be served on the trustee and the creditors named in the statement on or before the filing of the statement.

(3) Unless the United States trustee has determined that the credit counseling requirement of § 109(h) does not apply in the district, an individual debtor must file a statement of compliance with the credit counseling requirement, prepared as prescribed by the appropriate Official Form which must include one of the following:

(A) an attached certificate and debt repayment plan, if any, required by § 521(b);

(B) a statement that the debtor has received the credit counseling briefing required by § 109(h)(1) but does not have the certificate required by § 521(b);

(C) a certification under § 109(h)(3); or

(D) a request for a determination by the court under § 109(h)(4).

(4) Unless § 707(b)(2)(D) applies, an individual debtor in a chapter 7 case with primarily consumer debts shall file a statement of current monthly income prepared as prescribed by the appropriate Official Form, and, if the debtor has current monthly income greater than the applicable median family income for the applicable state and household size, the calculations in accordance with § 707(b), prepared as prescribed by the appropriate Official Form.

(5) An individual debtor in a chapter 11 case shall file a statement of current monthly income, prepared as prescribed by the appropriate Official Form.

(6) A debtor in a chapter 13 case shall file a statement of current monthly income, prepared as prescribed by the appropriate Official Form, and, if the debtor has current monthly income greater than the median family income for the applicable state and family size, a calculation of disposable income in accordance with § 1325(b)(3), prepared as prescribed by the appropriate Official Form.

(7) An individual debtor in a chapter 7 or chapter 13 case shall file a statement regarding completion of a course in personal financial management, prepared as prescribed by the appropriate Official Form.

(8) If an individual debtor in a chapter 11, 12, or 13 case has claimed an exemption under § 522(b)(3)(A) in an amount in excess of the amount set out in § 522(q)(1) in property of the kind described in § 522(p)(1), the debtor shall file a statement as to whether there is pending a proceeding in which the debtor may be found guilty of a felony of a kind described in § 522(q)(1)(A) or found liable for a debt of the kind described in § 522(q)(1)(B).

(c) **Time Limits.** In a voluntary case, the schedules, statements, and other documents required by subdivision (b)(1), (4), (5), and (6) shall be filed with the petition or within 15 days thereafter, except as otherwise provided in subdivisions (d), (e), (f), and (h) of this rule. In an involuntary case, the list in subdivision (a)(2), and the schedules, statements, and other documents required by subdivision (b)(1) shall be filed by the debtor within 15 days of the entry of the order for relief. In a voluntary case, the documents required by paragraphs (A), (C), and (D) of subdivision (b)(3) shall be filed with the petition. Unless the court orders otherwise, if the debtor has filed a statement under subdivision (b)(3)(B), the documents required by subdivision (b)(3)(A) shall be filed within 15 days of the order for relief. In a chapter 7 case, the debtor shall file the statement required by subdivision (b)(7) within 45 days after the first date set for the meeting of creditors under § 341 of the Code, and in a chapter 13 case no later than the date when the last payment was made by the debtor as required by the plan or the filing of a motion for a discharge under § 1328(b). The debtor shall file the statement required by subdivision (b)(8) no earlier than the date of the last payment made under the plan or the date of the filing of a motion for a discharge under §§ 1141(d)(5)(B), 1228(b), or 1328(b) of the Code. Lists, schedules, statements, and other documents filed prior to the conversion of a case to another chapter shall be deemed filed in the converted case unless the court directs otherwise. Except as provided in § 1116(3), any extension of time for the filing of the schedules, statements, and other documents required under this rule may be granted only on motion for cause shown and on notice to the United States trustee, any committee elected under § 705 or appointed under § 1102 of the Code, trustee, examiner, or other party as the court may direct. Notice of an extension shall be given to the United States trustee and to any committee, trustee, or other party as the court may direct.

* * * * *

Amended, on an interim basis, effective October 17, 2005; October 1, 2006.

COMMITTEE NOTE
October 17, 2005

The title of this rule is expanded to refer to "documents" in conformity with the 2005 amendments to § 521 and related provisions of the Bankruptcy Code that include a wider range of documentary requirements.

Subdivision (a) is amended to require that any foreign representative filing a petition for recognition to commence a case under chapter 15, which was added to the Code in 2005, file a list of entities with whom the debtor is engaged in litigation in the United States. The foreign representative filing the petition for recognition also must list any entities against whom provisional relief is being sought as well as all administrators in foreign proceedings of the debtor. This should ensure that the entities most interested in the case, or their representatives, will receive notice of the petition under Rule 2002(q).

Subdivision (b)(1) addresses schedules, statements, and other documents that the debtor must file unless the court orders otherwise and other than in a case under Chapter 9. This subdivision is amended to include documentary requirements added by the 2005 amendments to § 521 that apply to the same group of debtors and have the same time limits as the existing requirements of (b)(1). Consistent with the E–Government Act of 2002, Pub. L. No. 107–347, 116 Stat. 2921 (2002), the payment advices should be redacted before they are filed.

Subdivision (b)(2) is amended to conform the renumbering of the subsections of § 521.

Subdivisions (b)(3) through (b)(7) are new. They implement the 2005 amendments to the Bankruptcy Code. Subdivision (b)(3) provides a procedure for filing documents relating to the nonprofit credit counseling requirement provided by the 2005 amendments to § 109.

Subdivision (b)(4) addresses the filing of information about current monthly income, as defined in § 101, for certain chapter 7 debtors and, if required, additional calculations of expenses required by the 2005 revisions to § 707(b).

Subdivision (b)(5) addresses the filing of information about current monthly income, as defined in § 101, for individual chapter 11 debtors. The 2005 amendments to § 1129(a)(15) condition plan confirmation for individual debtors on the commitment of disposable income as defined in § 1325(b)(2), which is based on current monthly income.

Subdivision (b)(6) addresses the filing of information about current monthly income, as defined in § 101, for chapter 13 debtors and, if required, additional calculations of expenses. These changes are necessary because the 2005 amendments to § 1325 require that determinations of disposable income start with current monthly income.

Subdivision (b)(7) reflects the 2005 amendments to §§ 727 and 1328 that condition the receipt of a discharge on the completion of a personal financial management course, with certain exceptions.

Subdivision (b)(8) is amended to require an individual debtor in a case under chapter 11, 12, and 13 to file a statement that there are no reasonable grounds to believe that the restrictions on a homestead exemption as set out in § 522(q) of the Code are applicable. Sections 1141(d)(5)(C), 1228(f), and 1328(h) each provide that the court shall not enter a discharge order unless it finds that there is no reasonable cause to believe that § 522(q) applies. Requiring the debtor to submit a statement to that effect in cases under chapters 11, 12, and 13 in which an exemption is claimed in excess of the amount allowed under § 522(q)(1) provides the court with a basis to conclude, in the absence of any contrary information, that § 522(q) does not apply. Creditors receive notice under Rule 2002(f)(11) of the time to request postponement of the entry of the discharge so that they can challenge the debtor's assertions in the Rule 1007(b)(8) statement in appropriate cases.

Subdivision (c) is amended to include time limits for the filing requirements added to subdivision (b) due to the 2005 amendments to the Bankruptcy Code, and to make conforming amendments. Separate time limits are provided for the documentation of credit counseling and for the statement of the completion of the financial management course.

Subdivision (c) of the rule is also amended to recognize the limitation on the extension of time to file schedules and statements when the debtor is a small business debtor. Section 1116(3), added to the Bankruptcy Code in 2005, establishes a specific standard for courts to apply in the event that the debtor in possession or the trustee seeks an extension for filing these forms for a period beyond 30 days after the order for relief.

October 1, 2006

Subdivision (b)(3) of the rule is amended to require the debtor to file an Official Form relating to the credit counseling requirement provided by the 2005 amendments to § 109. Official Form 1 includes statements that warn the debtor of the consequences of failing to comply with the credit counseling requirement. The rule also provides that the debtor may file a statement that the debtor has received credit counseling but has not yet received a certificate from the credit counseling provider. Subdivision (c) is amended to permit the debtor to file the certificate and debt repayment plan within 15 days after the filing of the petition if a Rule 1007(b)(3)(B) statement is filed.

Other changes are stylistic.

INTERIM RULE 1009. AMENDMENTS OF VOLUNTARY PETITIONS, LISTS, SCHEDULES AND STATEMENTS

* * * * *

(b) Statement of Intention. The statement of intention may be amended by the debtor at any time before the expiration of the period provided in § 521(a) of the Code. The debtor shall give notice of the amendment to the trustee and to any entity affected thereby.

687

* * * * *

Amended, on an interim basis, effective October 17, 2005.

COMMITTEE NOTE
October 17, 2005

Subdivision (b) is amended to conform to the 2005 amendments to § 521 of the Code.

INTERIM RULE 1010. SERVICE OF INVOLUNTARY PETITION AND SUMMONS; PETITION FOR RECOGNITION OF A FOREIGN NONMAIN PROCEEDING

On the filing of an involuntary petition or a petition for recognition of a foreign nonmain proceeding the clerk shall forthwith issue a summons for service. When an involuntary petition is filed, service shall be made on the debtor. When a petition for recognition of a foreign nonmain proceeding is filed, service shall be made on the debtor, any entity against whom provisional relief is sought under § 1519 of the Code, and on any other parties as the court may direct. The summons shall be served with a copy of the petition in the manner provided for service of a summons and complaint by Rule 7004(a) or (b). If service cannot be so made, the court may order that the summons and petition be served by mailing copies to the party's last known address, and by at least one publication in a manner and form directed by the court. The summons and petition may be served on the party anywhere. Rule 7004 (e) and Rule 4 (*l*) F.R.Civ.P. apply when service is made or attempted under this rule.

Amended, on an interim basis, effective October 17, 2005.

COMMITTEE NOTE
October 17, 2005

This rule is amended to implement the 2005 amendments to the Bankruptcy Code, which repealed § 304 of the Code and replaced it with chapter 15 governing ancillary and other cross-border cases. Under chapter 15, a foreign representative commences a case by filing a petition for recognition of a pending foreign nonmain proceeding. The amendment requires service of the summons and petition on the debtor and any entity against whom the representative is seeking provisional relief. Until the court enters a recognition order under § 1517, no stay is in effect unless the court enters some form of provisional relief under § 1519. Thus, there is no need to serve all creditors of the debtor upon filing the petition for recognition. Only those entities against whom specific provisional relief is sought need to be served. The court may direct that service be made on additional entities as appropriate.

This rule does not apply to a petition for recognition of a foreign main proceeding.

INTERIM RULE 1011. RESPONSIVE PLEADING OR MOTION IN INVOLUNTARY AND CROSS–BORDER CASES

(a) Who May Contest Petition. The debtor named in an involuntary petition or a party in interest to a petition for recognition of a foreign proceeding may contest the petition. In the case of a petition against a partnership under Rule 1004, a nonpetitioning general partner, or a person who is alleged to be a general partner but denies the allegation, may contest the petition.

* * * * *

Amended, on an interim basis, effective October 17, 2005.

COMMITTEE NOTE
October 17, 2005

The rule is amended to reflect the 2005 amendments to the Bankruptcy Code, which repealed § 304 of the Code and added chapter 15. Section 304 covered cases ancillary to foreign proceedings, while chapter 15 of the Code governs ancillary and other cross-border cases and introduces the concept of a petition for recognition of a foreign proceeding.

INTERIM RULE 1017. DISMISSAL OR CONVERSION OF CASE; SUSPENSION

* * * * *

(e) Dismissal of an Individual Debtor's Chapter 7 Case or Conversion to a Case Under Chapter 11 or 13 for Abuse. The court may dismiss or, with the debtor's consent, convert an individual debtor's case for abuse under § 707(b) only on motion and after a hearing on notice to the debtor, the trustee, the United States trustee, and any other entities as the court directs. (1) Except as otherwise provided in § 704(b)(2), a motion to dismiss a case for abuse under § 707(b) or (c) may be filed only within 60 days after the first date set for the meeting of creditors under § 341(a), unless, on request filed before the time has expired, the court for cause extends the time for filing the motion to dismiss. The party filing the motion shall set forth in the motion all matters to be considered at the hearing. A motion to dismiss under § 707(b)(1) and (3) shall state with particularity the circumstances alleged to constitute abuse.

* * * * *

Amended, on an interim basis, effective October 17, 2005.

COMMITTEE NOTE
October 17, 2005

Subdivisions (e) and (e)(1) are amended to implement the 2005 revisions to § 707 of the Code. These revisions permit conversion of a chapter 7 case to a case under chapter 11 or 13, change the basis for dismissal or conversion from "substantial abuse" to "abuse," authorize parties other than the United States trustee to bring motions under § 707(b) under certain circumstances, and add § 707(c) to create an explicit ground for dismissal based on the request of a victim of a crime of violence or drug trafficking. The conforming amendments to subdivision (e) preserve the time limits already in place for § 707(b) motions, except to the extent that § 704(b)(2) sets the deadline for the United States trustee to act. In contrast to the grounds for a motion to dismiss under § 707(b)(2), which are quite specific, the grounds under § 707(b)(1) and (3) are very general. Subdivision (e) therefore requires that motions to dismiss under §§ 707(b)(1) and (3) state with particularity the circumstances alleged to constitute abuse to enable the debtor to respond.

INTERIM RULE 1019. CONVERSION OF CHAPTER 11 REORGANIZATION CASE, CHAPTER 12 FAMILY FARMER'S DEBT ADJUSTMENT CASE, OR CHAPTER 13 INDIVIDUAL'S DEBT ADJUSTMENT CASE TO A CHAPTER 7 LIQUIDATION CASE

* * * * *

(2) New Filing Periods. A new time period for filing a motion under § 707(b) or (c), a claim, a complaint objecting to discharge, or a complaint to obtain a determination of dischargeability of any debt shall commence under Rules 1017, 3002, 4004, or 4007, provided that a new time period shall not commence if a chapter 7 case had been converted to a chapter 11, 12, or 13 case and thereafter reconverted to a chapter 7 case and the time for filing a motion under § 707(b) or (c), a claim, a complaint objecting to discharge, or a complaint to obtain a determination of the dischargeability of any debt, or any extension thereof, expired in the original chapter 7 case.

* * * * *

Amended, on an interim basis, effective October 17, 2005.

COMMITTEE NOTE
October 17, 2005

Subdivision (2) is amended to provide a new filing period for motions under § 707(b) and (c) of the Code when a case is converted to chapter 7.

INTERIM RULE 1020.   SMALL BUSINESS CHAPTER 11 REORGANIZATION CASE

(a) **Small Business Debtor Designation.** In a voluntary chapter 11 case, the debtor shall state in the petition whether the debtor is a small business debtor. In an involuntary chapter 11 case, the debtor shall file within 15 days after entry of the order for relief a statement as to whether the debtor is a small business debtor. Except as provided in subdivision (c), the status of the case with respect to whether it is a small business case shall be in accordance with the debtor's statement under this subdivision, unless and until the court enters an order finding that the debtor's statement is incorrect.

(b) **Objecting To Designation.** Except as provided in subdivision (c), the United States trustee or a party in interest may file an objection to the debtor's statement under subdivision (a) not later than 30 days after the conclusion of the meeting of creditors held under § 341(a) of the Code, or within 30 days after any amendment to the statement, whichever is later.

(c) **Appointment of Committee of Unsecured Creditors.** If the United States trustee has appointed a committee of unsecured creditors under § 1102(a)(1), the case shall proceed as a small business case only if, and from the time when, the court enters an order determining that the committee has not been sufficiently active and representative to provide effective oversight of the debtor and that the debtor satisfies all the other requirements for being a small business. A request for a determination under this subdivision may be filed by the United States trustee or a party in interest only within a reasonable time after the failure of the committee to be sufficiently active and representative. The debtor may file a request for a determination at any time as to whether the committee has been sufficiently active and representative.

(d) **Procedure for Objection or Determination.** Any objection or request for a determination under this rule shall be governed by Rule 9014 and served on the debtor, the debtor's attorney, the United States trustee, the trustee, any committee appointed under § 1102 or its authorized agent, or, if no committee of unsecured creditors has been appointed under § 1102, on the creditors included on the list filed under Rule 1007(d), and on such other entities as the court may direct.

Amended, on an interim basis, effective October 17, 2005.

COMMITTEE NOTE
October 17, 2005

Under the Bankruptcy Code, as amended in 2005, there are no provisions permitting or requiring a small business debtor to elect to be treated as a small business. Therefore, there is no longer any need for a rule on elections to be considered a small business.

The 2005 amendments to the Code include several provisions relating to small business cases under chapter 11. Section 101 of the Code includes definitions of "small business debtor" and "small business case." The purpose of the new language in this rule is to provide a procedure for informing the parties, the United States trustee, and the court of whether the debtor is a small business debtor, and to provide procedures for resolving disputes regarding the proper characterization of the debtor. Because it is important to resolve such disputes early in the case, a time limit for objecting to the debtor's self-designation is imposed. Rule 9006(b)(1), which governs enlargement of time, is applicable to the time limits set forth in this rule.

690

An important factor in determining whether the debtor is a small business debtor is whether the United States trustee has appointed a committee of unsecured creditors under § 1102 of the Code, and whether such a committee is sufficiently active and representative. Subdivision (c), relating to the appointment and activity of a committee of unsecured creditors, is designed to be consistent with the Code's definition of "small business debtor."

INTERIM RULE 1021. HEALTH CARE BUSINESS CASE

(a) Health Care Business Designation. Unless the court orders otherwise, if a petition in a case under chapter 7, chapter 9, or chapter 11 states that the debtor is a health care business, the case shall proceed as a case in which the debtor is a health care business.

(b) Motion. The United States trustee or a party in interest may file a motion for a determination as to whether the debtor is a health care business. The motion shall be transmitted to the United States trustee and served on the debtor, the trustee, any committee elected under § 705 or appointed under § 1102 of the Code or its authorized agent, or, if the case is a chapter 9 municipality case or a chapter 11 reorganization case and no committee of unsecured creditors has been appointed under § 1102, on the creditors included on the list filed under Rule 1007(d), and such other entities as the court may direct. The motion shall be governed by Rule 9014.

Amended, on an interim basis, effective October 17, 2005.

COMMITTEE NOTE
October 17, 2005

Section 101(27A) of the Code, added in 2005, defines a health care business. This rule provides procedures for identifying the debtor as a health care business. The debtor in a voluntary case, or petitioning creditors in an involuntary case, will usually make the identification by checking the appropriate box on the petition. If a party in interest or the United States trustee disagrees with the determination by the debtor or the petitioning creditors as to whether the debtor is a health care business, this rule provides procedures for resolving the dispute.

INTERIM RULE 2002. NOTICES TO CREDITORS, EQUITY SECURITY HOLDERS, ADMINISTRATORS IN FOREIGN PROCEEDINGS, PERSONS AGAINST WHOM PROVISIONAL RELIEF IS SOUGHT IN ANCILLARY AND OTHER CROSS–BORDER CASES, UNITED STATES, AND UNITED STATES TRUSTEE

(a) Twenty–Day Notices to Parties in Interest. Except as provided in subdivisions (h), (i), (*l*), (p), and (q) of this rule, the clerk, or some other person as the court may direct, shall give the debtor, the trustee, all creditors and indenture trustees at least 20 days' notice by mail of:

* * * * *

(b) Twenty–Five–Day Notices to Parties in Interest. Except as provided in subdivision (*l*) of this rule, the clerk, or some other person as the court may direct, shall give the debtor, the trustee, all creditors and indenture trustees not less than 25 days notice by mail of (1) the time fixed for filing objections and the hearing to consider approval of a disclosure statement or, under § 1125(f), to make a final determination whether the plan provides adequate information so that a separate disclosure statement is not necessary; and (2) the time fixed for filing objections and the hearing to consider confirmation of a chapter 9, chapter 11, or chapter 13 plan.

(c) Content of Notice.

(1) *Proposed Use, Sale, or Lease of Property.* Subject to Rule 6004 the notice of a proposed use, sale, or lease of property required by subdivision (a)(2) of this rule shall include the time and place of any public sale, the terms and conditions of any private sale and the time fixed for filing objections. The notice of a proposed use, sale, or lease of property, including real estate, is sufficient if it generally describes the property. The notice of a proposed sale or lease of personally identifiable information under § 363(b)(1)(A) or (B) of the Code shall state whether the sale is consistent with a policy prohibiting the transfer of the information.

* * * * *

(f) Other Notices. Except as provided in subdivision (*l*) of this rule, the clerk, or some other person as the court may direct, shall give the debtor, all creditors, and indenture trustees notice by mail of: (1) the order for relief; (2) the dismissal or the conversion of the case to another chapter, or the suspension of proceedings under § 305; (3) the time allowed for filing claims pursuant to Rule 3002; (4) the time fixed for filing a complaint objecting to the debtor's discharge pursuant to § 727 of the Code as provided in Rule 4004; (5) the time fixed for filing a complaint to determine the dischargeability of a debt pursuant to § 523 of the Code as provided in Rule 4007; (6) the waiver, denial, or revocation of a discharge as provided in Rule 4006; (7) entry of an order confirming a chapter 9, 11, or 12 plan; (8) a summary of the trustee's final report in a chapter 7 case if the net proceeds realized exceed $1,500; (9) a notice under Rule 5008 regarding the presumption of abuse; (10) a statement under § 704(b)(1) as to whether the debtor's case would be presumed to be an abuse under § 707(b); and (11) the time to request a delay in the entry of the discharge under §§ 1141(d)(5)(C), 1228(f), and 1328(h). Notice of the time fixed for accepting or rejecting a plan pursuant to Rule 3017(c) shall be given in accordance with Rule 3017(d).

* * * * *

(g) Addressing Notices.

* * * * *

(2) Except as provided in § 342(f) of the Code, if a creditor or indenture trustee has not filed a request designating a mailing address under Rule 2002(g)(1), the notices shall be mailed to the address shown on the list of creditors or schedule of liabilities, whichever is filed later. If an equity security holder has not filed a request designating a mailing address under Rule 2002(g)(1), the notices shall be mailed to the address shown on the list of equity security holders.

* * * * *

(p) Notice to a Foreign Creditor.

(1) If, at the request of a party in interest or the United States trustee, or on its own initiative, the court finds that a notice mailed within the time prescribed by these rules would not be sufficient to give a creditor with a foreign address to which notices under these rules are mailed reasonable notice under the circumstances, the court may order that the notice be supplemented with notice by other means or that the time prescribed for the notice by mail be enlarged.

(2) Unless the court for cause orders otherwise, a creditor with a foreign address to which notices under this rule are mailed shall be given at least 30 days'

notice of the time fixed for filing a proof of claim under Rule 3002(c) or Rule 3003(c).

(q) Notice of Petition for Recognition of Foreign Proceeding and of Court's Intention to Communicate with Foreign Courts and Foreign Representatives.

(1) *Notice of Petition for Recognition.* The clerk, or some other person as the court may direct, shall forthwith give the debtor, all administrators in foreign proceedings of the debtor, all entities against whom provisional relief is being sought under § 1519 of the Code, all parties to any litigation in which the debtor is a party and that is pending in the United States at the time of the filing of the petition, and such other entities as the court may direct, at least 20 days' notice by mail of the hearing on the petition for recognition of a foreign proceeding. The notice shall state whether the petition seeks recognition as a foreign main proceeding or foreign nonmain proceeding.

(2) *Notice of Court's Intention to Communicate with Foreign Courts and Foreign Representatives.* The clerk, or some other person as the court may direct, shall give the debtor, all administrators in foreign proceedings of the debtor, all entities against whom provisional relief is being sought under § 1519 of the Code, all parties to any litigation in which the debtor is a party and that is pending in the United States at the time of the filing of the petition, and such other entities as the court may direct, notice by mail of the court's intention to communicate with a foreign court or foreign representative as prescribed by Rule 5012.

Amended, on an interim basis, effective October 17, 2005.

COMMITTEE NOTE
October 17, 2005

Subdivision (b) is amended to provide for 25 days' notice of the time for the court to make a final determination whether the plan in a small business case can serve as a disclosure statement. Conditional approval of a disclosure statement in a small business case is governed by Rule 3017.1 and does not require 25 days' notice. The court may consider this matter in a hearing combined with the confirmation hearing in a small business case.

Subdivision (c)(1) is amended to require that a trustee leasing or selling personally identifiable information under § 363(b)(1)(A) or (B) of the Code, as amended in 2005, include in the notice of the lease or sale transaction a statement as to whether the lease or sale is consistent with a policy prohibiting the transfer of the information.

Section 1514(d) of the Code, added in 2005, requires that such additional time as is reasonable under the circumstances be given to creditors with foreign addresses with respect to notices and the filing of a proof of claim. Thus, subdivision (p)(1) is added to the rule to give the court flexibility to direct that notice by other means shall supplement notice by mail, or to enlarge the notice period, for creditors with foreign addresses. If cause exists, such as likely delays in the delivery of mailed notices in particular locations, the court may order that notice also be given by e-mail, facsimile, or private courier. Alternatively, the court may enlarge the notice period for a creditor with a foreign address. It is expected that in most situations involving foreign creditors, fairness will not require any additional notice or extension of the notice period. This rule recognizes that the court has discretion to establish procedures to determine, on its own initiative, whether relief under subdivision (p) is appropriate, but that the court is not required to establish such procedures and may decide to act only on request of a party in interest.

Subdivisions (f)(9) and (10) are new. They reflect the 2005 amendments to §§ 342(d) and 704(b) of the Bankruptcy Code. Section 342(d) requires the clerk to give notice to creditors shortly after the commencement of the case as to whether a presumption of abuse exists. Subdivision (f)(9) adds this notice to the list of notices that the clerk must give. Subdivision (f)(10) implements the amendment to § 704(b) which requires the court to provide a copy to all creditors of a statement by the United States trustee or bankruptcy administrator as to whether the debtor's case would be presumed to be an abuse under § 707(b) not later than five days after receiving it.

Subdivision (f)(11) is also added to provide notice to creditors of the debtor's filing of a statement in a chapter 11, 12, or 13 case that there is no reasonable cause to believe that § 522(q) applies in the case. If a creditor disputes that assertion, the creditor can request a delay of the entry of the discharge in the case.

Subdivision (g)(2) of the rule is amended because the 2005 amendments to § 342(f) of the Code permit creditors in chapter 7 and 13 individual debtor cases to file a notice with any bankruptcy court of the address to which the creditor wishes all notices to be sent. This provision does not apply in cases of nonindividuals in chapter 7 and in cases under chapters 11 and 12, so Rule 2002(g)(2) still operates in those circumstances. It also continues to apply in cases under chapters 7 and 13 if the creditor has not filed a notice under § 342(f). The amendment to Rule 2002(g)(2) therefore only limits that subdivision when a creditor files a notice under § 342(f).

Subdivision (p)(2) is added to the rule to grant creditors with a foreign address to which notices are mailed at least 30 days' notice of the time within which to file proofs of claims if notice is mailed to the foreign address, unless the court orders otherwise. If cause exists, such as likely delays in the delivery of notices in particular locations, the court may extend the notice period for creditors with foreign addresses. The court may also shorten the additional notice time if circumstances so warrant. For example, if the court in a chapter 11 case determines that supplementing the notice to a foreign creditor with notice by electronic means, such as e-mail or facsimile, would give the creditor reasonable notice, the court may order that the creditor be given only 20 days' notice in accordance with Rule 2002(a)(7).

Subdivision (q) is added to require that notice of the hearing on the petition for recognition of a foreign proceeding be given to the debtor, all administrators in foreign proceedings of the debtor, entities against whom provisional relief is sought, and entities with whom the debtor is engaged in litigation at the time of the commencement of the case. There is no need at this stage of the proceedings to provide notice to all creditors. If the foreign representative should take action to commence a case under another chapter of the Code, the rules governing those proceedings will operate to provide that notice is given to all creditors.

The rule also requires notice of the court's intention to communicate with a foreign court or foreign representative under Rule 5012.

INTERIM RULE 2003. MEETING OF CREDITORS OR EQUITY SECURITY HOLDERS

(a) Date and Place. Except as provided in § 341(e) of the Code, in a chapter 7 liquidation or a chapter 11 reorganization case, the United States trustee shall call a meeting of creditors to be held no fewer than 20 and no more than 40 days after the order for relief. In a chapter 12 family farmer debt adjustment case, the United States trustee shall call a meeting of creditors to be held no fewer than 20 and no more than 35 days after the order for relief. In a chapter 13 individual's debt adjustment case, the United States trustee shall call a meeting of creditors to be held no fewer than 20 and no more than 50 days after the order for relief. If there is an appeal from or a motion to vacate the order for relief, or if there is a motion to dismiss the case, the United States trustee may set a later date for the meeting. The meeting may be held at a regular place for holding court or at any other place designated by the United States trustee within the district convenient for the parties in interest. If the United States trustee designates a place for the meeting which is not regularly staffed by the United States trustee or an assistant who may preside at the meeting, the meeting may be held not more than 60 days after the order for relief.

* * * * *

Amended, on an interim basis, effective October 17, 2005.

COMMITTEE NOTE
October 17, 2005

If the debtor has solicited acceptances to a plan before commencement of the case, § 341(e), which was added to the Bankruptcy Code in 2005, authorizes the court, on request of a party in interest and after notice and a hearing, to order that a meeting of creditors not be convened. The rule is amended to recognize that a meeting of creditors might not be held in those cases.

INTERIM RULE 2007.1 APPOINTMENT OF TRUSTEE OR EXAMINER IN A CHAPTER 11 REORGANIZATION CASE

* * * * *

(b) Election of Trustee.

* * * * *

(3) *Report of Election and Resolution of Disputes.*

(A) Report of Undisputed Election. If no dispute arises out of the election, the United States trustee shall promptly file a report certifying the election, including the name and address of the person elected and a statement that the election is undisputed. The report shall be accompanied by a verified statement of the person elected setting forth the person's connections with the debtor, creditors, any other party in interest, their respective attorneys and accountants, the United States trustee, or any person employed in the office of the United States trustee.

(B) Dispute Arising Out of an Election. If a dispute arises out of an election, the United States trustee shall promptly file a report stating that the election is disputed, informing the court of the nature of the dispute, and listing the name and address of any candidate elected under any alternative presented by the dispute. The report shall be accompanied by a verified statement by each candidate elected under each alternative presented by the dispute, setting forth the person's connections with the debtor, creditors, any other party in interest, their respective attorneys and accountants, the United States trustee, or any person employed in the office of the United States trustee. Not later than the date on which the report of the disputed election is filed, the United States trustee shall mail a copy of the report and each verified statement to any party in interest that has made a request to convene a meeting under § 1104(b) or to receive a copy of the report, and to any committee appointed under § 1102 of the Code.

(c) Approval of Appointment. An order approving the appointment of a trustee or an examiner under § 1104(d) of the Code, shall be made on application of the United States trustee. The application shall state the name of the person appointed and, to the best of the applicant's knowledge, all the person's connections with the debtor, creditors, any other parties in interest, their respective attorneys and accountants, the United States trustee, or persons employed in the office of the United States trustee. The application shall state the names of the parties in interest with whom the United States trustee consulted regarding the appointment. The application shall be accompanied by a verified statement of the person appointed setting forth the person's connections with the debtor, creditors, any other party in interest, their respective attorneys and accountants, the United States trustee, or any person employed in the office of the United States trustee.

Amended, on an interim basis, effective October 17, 2005.

COMMITTEE NOTE
October 17, 2005

Under § 1104(b)(2) of the Code, as amended in 2005, if an eligible, disinterested person is elected to serve as trustee in a chapter 11 case, the United States trustee is directed to file a report certifying the election. The person elected does not have to be appointed to the position. Rather, the filing of the report certifying the election itself constitutes the appointment. The section further provides that in the event of a dispute in the election of a trustee, the court must resolve the matter. The rule is amended to be consistent with § 1104(b)(2).

When the United States trustee files a report certifying the election of a trustee, the person elected must provide a verified statement, similar to the statement required of professional persons under Rule 2014, disclosing connections with parties in interest and certain other persons connected with the case. Although court approval of the person elected is not required, the disclosure of the person's connections will enable parties in interest to determine whether the person is disinterested.

INTERIM RULE 2007.2   APPOINTMENT OF PATIENT CARE OMBUDSMAN IN A HEALTH CARE BUSINESS CASE

(a) **Order to Appoint Patient Care Ombudsman.** In a chapter 7, chapter 9, or chapter 11 case in which the debtor is a health care business, the court shall order the appointment of a patient care ombudsman under § 333 of the Code, unless the court, on motion of the United States trustee or a party in interest filed not later than 20 days after the commencement of the case or within another time fixed by the court, finds that the appointment of a patient care ombudsman is not necessary for the protection of patients under the specific circumstances of the case.

(b) **Motion for Order to Appoint Ombudsman.** If the court has ordered that the appointment of an ombudsman is not necessary, or has ordered the termination of the appointment of an ombudsman, the court, on motion of the United States trustee or a party in interest, may order the appointment at any time during the case if the court finds that the appointment of an ombudsman has become necessary to protect patients.

(c) **Appointment of Ombudsman.** If a patient care ombudsman is appointed under § 333, the United States trustee shall promptly file a notice of the appointment, including the name and address of the person appointed. Unless the person appointed is a State Long–Term Care Ombudsman, the notice shall be accompanied by a verified statement of the person appointed setting forth the person's connections with the debtor, creditors, patients, any other party in interest, their respective attorneys and accountants, the United States trustee, and any person employed in the office of the United States trustee.

(d) **Termination of Appointment.** On motion of the United States trustee or a party in interest, the court may terminate the appointment of a patient care ombudsman if the court finds that the appointment is not necessary for the protection of patients.

(e) **Motion.** A motion under this rule shall be governed by Rule 9014. The motion shall be transmitted to the United States trustee and served on the debtor, the trustee, any committee elected under § 705 or appointed under § 1102 of the Code or its authorized agent, or, if the case is a chapter 9 municipality case or a chapter 11 reorganization case and no committee of unsecured creditors has been appointed under § 1102, on the creditors included on the list filed under Rule 1007(d), and such other entities as the court may direct.

Amended, on an interim basis, effective October 17, 2005.

COMMITTEE NOTE
October 17, 2005

Section 333 of the Code, added in 2005, requires the court to order the appointment of a health care ombudsman within the first 30 days of a health care business case, unless the court finds that the appointment is not necessary for the protection of patients. The rule recognizes this requirement and provides a procedure by which a party may obtain a court order finding that the appointment of a patient care ombudsman is unnecessary. In the absence of a timely motion under subdivision (a) of this rule, the court will enter an order directing the United States trustee to appoint the ombudsman.

Subdivision (b) recognizes that, despite a previous order finding that a patient care ombudsman is not necessary, circumstances of the case may change or newly discovered evidence may demonstrate the necessity of an ombudsman to protect the interests of patients. In that event, a party may move the court for an order directing the appointment of an ombudsman.

When the appointment of a patient care ombudsman is ordered, the United States trustee is required to appoint a disinterested person to serve in that capacity. Court approval of the appointment is not required, but subdivision (c) requires the person appointed, if not a State

Long–Term Care Ombudsman, to file a verified statement similar to the statement filed by professional persons under Rule 2014 so that parties in interest will have information relevant to disinterestedness. If a party believes that the person appointed is not disinterested, it may file a motion asking the court to find that the person is not eligible to serve.

Subdivision (d) permits parties in interest to move for the termination of the appointment of a patient care ombudsman. If the movant can show that there no longer is any need for the ombudsman, the court may order the termination of the appointment.

INTERIM RULE 2015. DUTY TO KEEP RECORDS, MAKE REPORTS, AND GIVE NOTICE OF CASE OR CHANGE OF STATUS

* * * * *

(d) Foreign Representative. In a case in which the court has granted recognition of a foreign proceeding under chapter 15, the foreign representative shall file any notice required under § 1518 of the Code within 15 days after the date when the representative becomes aware of the subsequent information.

(e) Transmission of Reports. In a chapter 11 case the court may direct that copies or summaries of annual reports and copies or summaries of other reports shall be mailed to the creditors, equity security holders, and indenture trustees. The court may also direct the publication of summaries of any such reports. A copy of every report or summary mailed or published pursuant to this subdivision shall be transmitted to the United States trustee.

Amended, on an interim basis, effective October 17, 2005.

COMMITTEE NOTE
October 17, 2005

The rule is amended to fix the time for the filing of notices under § 1519 which was added to the Code in 2005. Former subdivision (d) is renumbered as subdivision (e).

INTERIM RULE 2015.1 PATIENT CARE OMBUDSMAN

(a) Reports. Unless the court orders otherwise, a patient care ombudsman, at least 10 days before making a report under § 333(b)(2) of the Code, shall give notice that the report will be made to the court. The notice shall be transmitted to the United States trustee, posted conspicuously at the health care facility that is the subject of the report, and served on the debtor, the trustee, all patients, and any committee elected under § 705 or appointed under § 1102 of the Code or its authorized agent, or, if the case is a chapter 9 municipality case or a chapter 11 reorganization case and no committee of unsecured creditors has been appointed under § 1102, on the creditors included on the list filed under Rule 1007(d), and such other entities as the court may direct. The notice shall state the date and time when the report will be made, the manner in which the report will be made, and, if the report is in writing, the name, address, telephone number, e-mail address, and website, if any, of the person from whom a copy of the report may be obtained at the debtor's expense.

(b) Authorization to Review Confidential Patient Records. A motion by a health care ombudsman under § 333(c) to review confidential patient records shall be governed by Rule 9014, served on the patient and any family member or other contact person whose name and address has been given to the trustee or the debtor for the purpose of providing information regarding the patient's health care, and transmitted to the United States trustee subject to applicable nonbankruptcy law relating to patient privacy. Unless the court orders otherwise, a hearing on the motion may be commenced no earlier than 15 days after service of the motion.

Amended, on an interim basis, effective October 17, 2005.

COMMITTEE NOTE
October 17, 2005

This rule is new. It implements § 333, added to the Code in 2005. Subdivision (a) is designed to give parties in interest, including patients or their representatives, sufficient notice so that they will be able to review written reports or attend hearings at which reports are made. The rule permits a notice to relate to a single report or to periodic reports to be given during the case. For example, the ombudsman may give notice that reports will be made at specified intervals or dates during the case.

Subdivision (a) of the rule requires that the notice be posted conspicuously at the health care facility in a place where it will be seen by patients and their families or others visiting the patient. This may require posting in common areas and patient rooms within the facility. Because health care facilities and the patients they serve can vary greatly, the locations of the posted notice should be tailored to the specific facility that is the subject of the report.

Subdivision (b) requires the ombudsman to notify the patient and the United States trustee that the ombudsman is seeking access to confidential patient records so that they will be able to appear and be heard on the matter. This procedure should assist the court in reaching its decision both as to access to the records and appropriate restrictions on that access to ensure continued confidentiality. Notices given under this rule are subject to provisions under applicable federal and state law that relate to the protection of patients' privacy, such as the Health Insurance Portability and Accountability Act of 1996, Pub. L. No. 104–191 (HIPAA).

INTERIM RULE 2015.2 TRANSFER OF PATIENT IN HEALTH CARE BUSINESS CASE

Unless the court orders otherwise, if the debtor is a health care business, the trustee may not transfer a patient to another health care business under § 704(a)(12) of the Code unless the trustee gives at least 10 days' notice of the transfer to the patient care ombudsman, if any, and to the patient and any family member or other contact person whose name and address has been given to the trustee or the debtor for the purpose of providing information regarding the patient's health care subject to applicable nonbankruptcy law relating to patient privacy.

Adopted, on an interim basis, effective October 17, 2005.

COMMITTEE NOTE
October 17, 2005

This rule is new. Section 704(a)(12), added to the Code in 2005, authorizes the trustee to relocate patients when a health care business debtor's facility is in the process of being closed. The Code permits the trustee to take this action without the need for any court order, but the notice required by this rule will enable a patient care ombudsman appointed under § 333, or a patient who contends that the trustee's actions violate § 704(a)(12), to have those issues resolved before the patient is transferred.

This rule also permits the court to enter an order dispensing with or altering the notice requirement in proper circumstances. The facility could be closed immediately, or very quickly, such that 10 days' notice would not be possible in some instances. In that event, the court may shorten the time required for notice.

Notices given under this rule are subject to provisions under applicable federal and state law that relate to the protection of patients' privacy, such as the Health Insurance Portability and Accountability Act of 1996, Pub. L. No. 104–191 (HIPAA).

INTERIM RULE 3002. FILING PROOF OF CLAIMS OR INTEREST

* * * * *

(c) **Time for Filing.** In a chapter 7 liquidation, chapter 12 family farmer's debt adjustment, or chapter 13 individual's debt adjustment case, a proof of claim is timely filed if it is filed not later than 90 days after the first date set for the meeting of creditors called under § 341(a) of the Code, except as follows:

(1) A proof of claim filed by a governmental unit, other than for a claim resulting from a tax return filed under § 1308, is timely filed if it is filed not later than 180 days after the date of the order for relief. On motion of a governmental unit before the expiration of such period and for cause shown, the court may extend the time for filing of a claim by the governmental unit. A proof of claim filed by a governmental unit for a claim resulting from a tax return filed under § 1308 is timely filed if it is filed not later than 180 days after the date of the order for relief or 60 days after the date of the filing of the tax return, whichever is later.

* * * * *

(6) If notice of the time for filing a proof of claim has been mailed to a creditor at a foreign address, on motion filed by the creditor before or after the expiration of the time, the court may extend the time by not more than 60 days if the court finds that the notice was not sufficient under the circumstances to give the creditor a reasonable time to file a proof of claim.

Amended, on an interim basis, effective October 17, 2005.

COMMITTEE NOTE
October 17, 2005

Subdivision (c)(1) is amended to reflect the addition of § 1308 to the Bankruptcy Code in 2005. This provision requires that chapter 13 debtors file tax returns during the pendency of the case, and imposes bankruptcy-related consequences if debtors fail to do so. Subdivision (c)(1) provides additional time for governmental units to file a proof of claim for tax obligations with respect to tax returns filed during the pendency of a chapter 13 case.

Paragraph (c)(6) is added to give the court discretion to extend the time for filing a proof of claim for a creditor who received notice of the time to file the claim at a foreign address, if the court finds that the notice was not sufficient, under the particular circumstances, to give the foreign creditor a reasonable time to file a proof of claim. This amendment is designed to comply with § 1514(d), which was added to the Code in 2005 and requires that the rules and orders of the court provide such additional time as is reasonable under the circumstances for foreign creditors to file claims in cases under all chapters of the Code.

INTERIM RULE 3003. FILING PROOF OF CLAIM OR EQUITY SECURITY INTEREST IN CHAPTER 9 MUNICIPALITY OR CHAPTER 11 REORGANIZATION CASES

* * * * *

(c) Filing Proof of Claim.

(1) *Who May File.* Any creditor or indenture trustee may file a proof of claim within the time prescribed by subdivision (c)(3) of this rule.

(2) *Who Must File.* Any creditor or equity security holder whose claim or interest is not scheduled or scheduled as disputed, contingent, or unliquidated shall file a proof of claim or interest within the time prescribed by subdivision (c)(3) of this rule; any creditor who fails to do so shall not be treated as a creditor with respect to such claim for the purposes of voting and distribution.

(3) *Time for Filing.* The court shall fix and for cause shown may extend the time within which proofs of claim or interest may be filed. Notwithstanding the expiration of such time, a proof of claim may be filed to the extent and under the conditions stated in Rule 3002(c)(2), (c)(3), (c)(4), and (c)(6).

(4) *Effect of Filing Claim or Interest.* A proof of claim or interest executed and filed in accordance with this subdivision shall supersede any scheduling of that claim or interest pursuant to § 521(a)(1) of the Code.

(5) *Filing by Indenture Trustee.* An indenture trustee may file a claim on behalf of all known or unknown holders of securities issued pursuant to the trust instrument under which it is trustee.

* * * * *

Amended, on an interim basis, effective October 17, 2005.

COMMITTEE NOTE
October 17, 2005

The rule is amended to implement § 1514(d), which was added to the Code in 2005, by making the new Rule 3002(c)(6) applicable in chapter 9 and chapter 11 cases. Section 1514(d) requires that creditors with foreign addresses be provided such additional time as is reasonable under the circumstances to file proofs of claims.

INTERIM RULE 3016. FILING OF PLAN AND DISCLOSURE STATEMENT IN A CHAPTER 9 MUNICIPALITY OR CHAPTER 11 REORGANIZATION CASE

* * * * *

(b) Disclosure Statement. In a chapter 9 or 11 case, a disclosure statement under § 1125 or evidence showing compliance with § 1126(b) of the Code shall be filed with the plan or within a time fixed by the court, unless the plan is intended to provide adequate information under § 1125(f)(1). If the plan is intended to provide adequate information under § 1125(f)(1), it shall be so designated and Rule 3017.1 shall apply as if the plan is a disclosure statement.

* * * * *

Amended, on an interim basis, effective October 17, 2005.

COMMITTEE NOTE
October 17, 2005

Subdivision (b) is amended to recognize that, in 2005, § 1125(f)(1) was added to the Code to provide that the plan proponent in a small business case need not file a disclosure statement if the plan itself includes adequate information and the court finds that a separate disclosure statement is unnecessary. If the plan is intended to provide adequate information in a small business case, it may be conditionally approved as a disclosure statement under Rule 3017.1 and is subject to all other rules applicable to disclosure statements in small business cases.

INTERIM RULE 3017.1 COURT CONSIDERATION OF DISCLOSURE STATEMENT IN A SMALL BUSINESS CASE

(a) Conditional Approval of Disclosure Statement. In a small business case, the court may, on application of the plan proponent or on its own initiative, conditionally approve a disclosure statement filed in accordance with Rule 3016. On or before conditional approval of the disclosure statement, the court shall:

(1) fix a time within which the holders of claims and interests may accept or reject the plan;

(2) fix a time for filing objections to the disclosure statement;

(3) fix a date for the hearing on final approval of the disclosure statement to be held if a timely objection is filed; and

(4) fix a date for the hearing on confirmation.

(b) **Application of Rule 3017.** Rule 3017(a), (b), (c), and (e) do not apply to a conditionally approved disclosure statement. Rule 3017(d) applies to a conditionally approved disclosure statement, except that conditional approval is considered approval of the disclosure statement for the purpose of applying Rule 3017(d).

(c) **Final Approval.**

(1) *Notice.* Notice of the time fixed for filing objections and the hearing to consider final approval of the disclosure statement shall be given in accordance with Rule 2002 and may be combined with notice of the hearing on confirmation of the plan.

(2) *Objections.* Objections to the disclosure statement shall be filed, transmitted to the United States trustee, and served on the debtor, the trustee, any committee appointed under the Code and any other entity designated by the court at any time before final approval of the disclosure statement or by an earlier date as the court may fix.

(3) *Hearing.* If a timely objection to the disclosure statement is filed, the court shall hold a hearing to consider final approval before or combined with the hearing on confirmation of the plan.

Amended, on an interim basis, effective October 17, 2005.

COMMITTEE NOTE
October 17, 2005

Section 101 of the Code, as amended in 2005, defines a "small business case" and "small business debtor,"and eliminates any need to elect that status. Therefore, the reference in the rule to an election is deleted.

As provided in the amendment to Rule 3016(b), a plan intended to provide adequate information in a small business case under § 1125(f)(1) may be conditionally approved and is otherwise treated as a disclosure statement under this rule.

INTERIM RULE 3019.   MODIFICATION OF ACCEPTED PLAN BEFORE OR AFTER CONFIRMATION IN A CHAPTER 9 MUNICIPALITY OR CHAPTER 11 REORGANIZATION CASE

(a) In a chapter 9 or chapter 11 case, after a plan has been accepted and before its confirmation, the proponent may file a modification of the plan. If the court finds after hearing on notice to the trustee, any committee appointed under the Code, and any other entity designated by the court that the proposed modification does not adversely change the treatment of the claim of any creditor or the interest of any equity security holder who has not accepted in writing the modification, it shall be deemed accepted by all creditors and equity security holders who have previously accepted the plan.

(b) If the debtor is an individual, a request to modify the plan under § 1127(e) of the Code shall identify the proponent and shall be filed together with the proposed modification. The clerk, or some other person as the court may direct, shall give the debtor, the trustee, and all creditors not less than 20 days' notice by mail of the time fixed for filing objections and, if an objection is filed, the hearing to consider the proposed modification, unless the court orders otherwise with respect to creditors who are not affected by the proposed modification. A copy of the notice shall be transmitted to the United States trustee. A copy of the proposed modification shall be included with the notice. Any objection to the proposed modification shall be filed and served on the debtor, the proponent of the modification, the trustee, and any other entity designated by the court, and shall be transmitted to the United States trustee. An objection to a proposed modification is governed by Rule 9014.

Amended, on an interim basis, effective October 17, 2005.

COMMITTEE NOTE
October 17, 2005

Section 1127 was amended in 2005 to provide for modification of a confirmed plan in a chapter 11 case of an individual debtor. The rule is amended to establish the procedure for filing and objecting to a proposed modification of a confirmed plan.

701

INTERIM RULE 4002.   DUTIES OF DEBTOR

(a) In General. In addition to performing other duties prescribed by the Code and rules, the debtor shall:

(1) attend and submit to an examination at the times ordered by the court;

(2) attend the hearing on a complaint objecting to discharge and testify, if called as a witness;

(3) inform the trustee immediately in writing as to the location of real property in which the debtor has an interest and the name and address of every person holding money or property subject to the debtor's withdrawal or order if a schedule of property has not yet been filed pursuant to Rule 1007;

(4) cooperate with the trustee in the preparation of an inventory, the examination of proofs of claim, and the administration of the estate; and

(5) file a statement of any change of the debtor's address.

(b) Individual Debtor's Duty to Provide Documentation.

(1) *Personal Identification.* Every individual debtor shall bring to the meeting of creditors under § 341:

(A) a picture identification issued by a governmental unit, or other personal identifying information that establishes the debtor's identity; and

(B) evidence of social security number(s), or a written statement that such documentation does not exist.

(2) *Financial Information.* Every individual debtor shall bring to the meeting of creditors under § 341 and make available to the trustee the following documents or copies of them, or provide a written statement that the documentation does not exist or is not in the debtor's possession:

(A) evidence of current income such as the most recent payment advice;

(B) unless the trustee or the United States trustee instructs otherwise, statements for each of the debtor's depository and investment accounts, including checking, savings, and money market accounts, mutual funds and brokerage accounts for the time period that includes the date of the filing of the petition; and

(C) documentation of monthly expenses claimed by the debtor when required by § 707(b)(2)(A) or (B).

(3) *Tax Return.* At least 7 days before the first date set for the meeting of creditors under § 341, the debtor shall provide to the trustee a copy of the debtor's Federal income tax return for the most recent tax year ending immediately before the commencement of the case and for which a return was filed, including any attachments, or a transcript of the tax return, or provide a written statement that the documentation does not exist.

(4) *Tax Returns Provided to Creditors.* If a creditor, at least 15 days before the first date set for the meeting of creditors under § 341, requests a copy of the debtor's tax return that is to be provided to the trustee under subdivision (b)(3), the debtor shall provide to the requesting creditor a copy of the return, including any attachments, or a transcript of the tax return, or provide a written statement that the documentation does not exist at least 7 days before the first date set for the meeting of creditors under § 341.

(5) The debtor's obligation to provide tax returns under Rule 4002(b)(3) and (b)(4) is subject to procedures for safeguarding the confidentiality of tax information established by the Director of the Administrative Office of the United States Courts.

Amended, on an interim basis, effective October 17, 2005.

COMMITTEE NOTE
October 17, 2005

This rule is amended to implement the directives of § 521(a)(1)(B)(iv) and (e)(2) of the Code, which were added by the 2005 amendments. These Code amendments expressly require the debtor to file with the court, or provide to the trustee, specific documents. The amendments to the rule implement these obligations and establish a time frame for creditors to make requests for a copy of the debtor's Federal income tax return. The rule also requires the debtor to provide documentation in support of claimed expenses under § 707(b)(2)(A) and (B).

Subdivision (b) is also amended to require the debtor to cooperate with the trustee by providing materials and documents necessary to assist the trustee in the performance of the trustee's duties. Nothing in the rule, however, is intended to limit or restrict the debtor's duties under § 521, or to limit the access of the Attorney General to any information provided by the debtor in the case. The rule does not require that the debtor create documents or obtain documents from third parties; rather, the debtor's obligation is to bring to the meeting of creditors under § 341 the documents which the debtor possesses. Any written statement that the debtor provides indicating either that documents do not exist or are not in the debtor's possession must be verified or contain an unsworn declaration as required under Rule 1008.

Because the amendment implements the debtor's duty to cooperate with the trustee, the materials provided to the trustee would not be made available to any other party in interest at the § 341 meeting of creditors other than the Attorney General. Some of the documents may contain otherwise private information that should not be disseminated. For example, pay stubs and financial account statements might include the social security numbers of the debtor and the debtor's spouse and dependents, as well as the names of the debtor's children. The debtor should redact all but the last four digits of all social security numbers and the names of any minors when they appear in these documents. This type of information would not usually be needed by creditors and others who may be attending the meeting. If a creditor perceives a need to review specific documents or other evidence, the creditor may proceed under Rule 2004.

Tax information produced under this rule is subject to procedures for safeguarding confidentiality established by the Director of the Administrative Office of the United States Courts.

INTERIM RULE 4003.   EXEMPTIONS

* * * * *

(b) Objecting to a Claim of Exemptions.

(1) Except as provided in paragraph (2), a party in interest may file an objection to the list of property claimed as exempt within 30 days after the meeting of creditors held under § 341(a) is concluded or within 30 days after any amendment to the list or supplemental schedules is filed, whichever is later. The court may, for cause, extend the time for filing objections if, before the time to object expires, a party in interest files a request for an extension.

(2) An objection to a claim of exemption based on § 522(q) shall be filed before the closing of the case. If an exemption is first claimed after a case is reopened, an objection shall be filed before the reopened case is closed.

(3) Copies of the objections shall be delivered or mailed to the trustee, the person filing the list, and the attorney for that person.

* * * * *

Amended, on an interim basis, effective October 17, 2005.

COMMITTEE NOTE
October 17, 2005

Subdivision (b) is amended to reflect the 2005 addition of subsection (q) to § 522 of the Bankruptcy Code. Section 522(q) imposes a $125,000 limit on a state homestead exemption if the debtor has been convicted of a felony or owes a debt arising from certain causes of action. Other revised provisions of the Bankruptcy Code, such as § 727(a)(12) and § 1328(h), suggest that the court may consider issues relating to § 522 late in the case, and the 30-day period for objections would not be appropriate for this provision. A new subdivision (b)(2) is added to provide a separate time limit for this provision.

INTERIM RULE 4004. GRANT OR DENIAL OF DISCHARGE

* * * * *

(c) Grant of Discharge.

(1) In a chapter 7 case, on expiration of the time fixed for filing a complaint objecting to discharge and the time fixed for filing a motion to dismiss the case under Rule 1017(e), the court shall forthwith grant the discharge unless:

* * * * *

(F) a motion to extend the time for filing a motion to dismiss the case under Rule 1017(e) is pending,

(G) the debtor has not paid in full the filing fee prescribed by 28 U.S.C. § 1930(a) and any other fee prescribed by the Judicial Conference of the United States under 28 U.S.C. § 1930(b) that is payable to the clerk upon the commencement of a case under the Code, unless the court has waived the fees under 28 U.S.C. § 1930(f);

(H) the debtor has not filed with the court a statement regarding completion of a course in personal financial management as required by Rule 1007(b)(7);

(I) a motion to delay or postpone discharge under § 727(a)(12) is pending; or

(J) a presumption that a reaffirmation agreement is an undue hardship has arisen under § 524(m); or

(K) a motion to delay discharge, alleging that the debtor has not filed with the court all tax documents required to be filed under § 521(f), is pending.

* * * * *

(3) If the debtor is required to file a statement under Rule 1007(b)(8), the court shall not grant a discharge earlier than 30 days after the filing of the statement.

Amended, on an interim basis, effective October 17, 2005.

COMMITTEE NOTE
October 17, 2005

Subdivision (c)(1)(G) is amended to reflect the fee waiver provision added in 2005 to 28 U.S.C. § 1930.

Subdivision (c)(1)(H) is new. It reflects the 2005 addition to the Bankruptcy Code of §§ 727(a)(11) and 1328(g), which require that individual debtors complete a course in personal financial management as a condition to the entry of a discharge. Including this requirement in the rule helps prevent the inadvertent entry of a discharge when the debtor has not complied with this requirement. If a debtor fails to file the required statement regarding a personal financial management course, the clerk will close the bankruptcy case without the entry of a discharge.

Subdivision (c)(1)(I) is new. It reflects the 2005 addition to the Bankruptcy Code of § 727(a)(12). This provision is linked to § 522(q). Section 522(q) limits the availability of the homestead exemption for individuals who have been convicted of a felony or who owe a debt arising from certain causes of action within a particular time frame. The existence of reasonable cause to believe that § 522(q) may be applicable to the debtor constitutes grounds for withholding the discharge.

Subdivision (c)(1)(J) is new. It reflects the 2005 revisions to § 524 of the Bankruptcy Code that alter the requirements for approval of reaffirmation agreements. Section 524(m) sets forth circumstances under which a reaffirmation agreement is presumed to be an undue hardship.

This triggers an obligation to review the presumption and may require notice and a hearing. Subdivision (c)(1)(J) has been added to prevent the discharge from being entered until the court approves or disapproves the reaffirmation agreement in accordance with § 524(m).

Subdivision (c)(1)(K) is new. It implements § 1228(a) of Public Law No. 109–8.

The rule is also amended by adding subdivision (c)(3) that postpones the entry of the discharge of an individual debtor in a case under chapter 11, 12, or 13 if there is a question as to the applicability of § 522(q) of the Code. The postponement provides an opportunity for a creditor to file a motion to limit the debtor's exemption under that provision.

INTERIM RULE 4006. NOTICE OF NO DISCHARGE

If an order is entered denying or revoking a discharge or if a waiver of discharge is filed, the clerk, after the order becomes final or the waiver is filed, or, in the case of an individual, if the case is closed without the entry of an order of discharge, shall promptly give notice thereof to all parties in interest in the manner provided in Rule 2002.

Amended, on an interim basis, effective October 17, 2005.

COMMITTEE NOTE
October 17, 2005

Rule 4006 is amended to reflect the 2005 revisions to the Bankruptcy Code requiring that individual debtors complete a course in personal financial management as a condition to the entry of a discharge. If the debtor fails to complete the course, no discharge will be entered, but the case may be closed. The amended rule provides notice to parties in interest, including the debtor, that no discharge was entered.

INTERIM RULE 4007. DETERMINATION OF
DISCHARGEABILITY OF A DEBT

* * * * *

(c) **Time for Filing Complaint Under § 523(C) in a Chapter 7 Liquidation, Chapter 11 Reorganization, Chapter 12 Family Farmer's Debt Adjustment Case, or Chapter 13 Individual's Debt Adjustment Case; Notice of Time Fixed.** Except as provided in subdivision (d), a complaint to determine the dischargeability of a debt under § 523(c) shall be filed no later than 60 days after the first date set for the meeting of creditors under § 341(a). The court shall give all creditors no less than 30 days' notice of the time so fixed in the manner provided in Rule 2002. On motion of a party in interest, after hearing on notice, the court may for cause extend the time fixed under this subdivision. The motion shall be filed before the time has expired.

(d) **Time for Filing Complaint Under § 523(A)(6) in Chapter 13 Individual's Debt Adjustment Case; Notice of Time Fixed.** On motion by a debtor for a discharge under § 1328(b), the court shall enter an order fixing the time to file a complaint to determine the dischargeability of any debt under § 523(a)(6) and shall give no less than 30 days' notice of the time fixed to all creditors in the manner provided in Rule 2002. On motion of any party in interest after hearing on notice the court may for cause extend the time fixed under this subdivision. The motion shall be filed before the time has expired.

* * * * *

Amended, on an interim basis, effective October 17, 2005.

COMMITTEE NOTE
October 17, 2005

Subdivision (c) is amended to reflect the 2005 amendments to § 1328(a) of the Bankruptcy Code. This revision expands the exceptions to discharge upon completion of a chapter 13 plan.

Subdivision (c) extends to chapter 13 the same time limits applicable to other chapters of the Code with respect to the two exceptions to discharge that have been added to § 1328(a) and that are within § 523(c).

The amendment to subdivision (d) reflects the 2005 amendments to § 1328(a) that expands the exceptions to discharge upon completion of a chapter 13 plan, including two out of three of the provisions that fall within § 523(c). However, the 2005 revisions to § 1328(a) do not include a reference to § 523(a)(6), which is the third provision to which § 523(c) refers. Thus, the need for subdivision (d) is now limited to that provision.

INTERIM RULE 4008. DISCHARGE AND REAFFIRMATION HEARING

Not more than 30 days following the entry of an order granting or denying a discharge, or confirming a plan in a chapter 11 reorganization case concerning an individual debtor and on not less than 10 days' notice to the debtor and the trustee, the court may hold a hearing as provided in § 524(d) of the Code. A motion by the debtor for approval of a reaffirmation agreement shall be filed before or at the hearing. The debtor's statement required under § 524(k) shall be accompanied by a statement of the total income and total expense amounts stated on schedules I and J. If there is a difference between the income and expense amounts stated on schedules I and J and the statement required under § 524(k), the accompanying statement shall include an explanation of any difference.

Amended, on an interim basis, effective October 17, 2005.

COMMITTEE NOTE
October 17, 2005

Rule 4008 is amended to reflect the 2005 addition of §§ 524(k)(6)(A) and 524(m) to the Bankruptcy Code. These provisions require that a debtor file a signed statement in support of a reaffirmation agreement, and authorize a court to review the agreement if, based on the assertions on the statement, the agreement is presumed to be an undue hardship. The rule revision requires that an accompanying statement show the total income and expense amounts stated on schedules I and J and an explanation of any discrepancies. This will allow the court to evaluate the reaffirmation for undue hardship as § 524(m) requires. A corresponding change has been made to Rule 4004(c) to prevent the entry of a discharge until the court has approved or disapproved the reaffirmation agreement in accordance with § 524(m).

INTERIM RULE 5003. RECORDS KEPT BY THE CLERK

* * * * *

(e) Register of Mailing Addresses of Federal and State Governmental Units and Certain Taxing Authorities. The United States or the state or territory in which the court is located may file a statement designating its mailing address. The United States, state, territory, or local governmental unit responsible for the collection of taxes within the district in which the case is pending may file a statement designating an address for service of requests under § 505(b) of the Code, and the designation shall describe where further information concerning additional requirements for filing such requests may be found. The clerk shall keep, in the form and manner as the Director of the Administrative Office of the United States Courts may prescribe, a register that includes the mailing addresses designated under this subdivision, but the clerk is not required to include in the register more than one mailing address for each department, agency, or instrumentality of the United States or the state or territory. If more than one address for a department, agency, or instrumentality is included in the register, the clerk shall also include information that would enable a user of the register to determine the circumstances when each address is applicable, and mailing notice to only one applicable address is sufficient to provide effective notice. The clerk shall update the register annually, effective January 2 of each year. The mailing address in the register is conclusively presumed to be a proper address for the governmental unit, but the failure to use that mailing address does not invalidate any notice that is otherwise effective under applicable law.

* * * * *

Amended, on an interim basis, effective October 17, 2005.

COMMITTEE NOTE
October 17, 2005

The rule is amended to implement the addition of § 505(b)(1) to the Code in 2005, which allows taxing authorities to designate addresses to use for the service of a request under that subsection.

INTERIM RULE 5008.   NOTICE REGARDING PRESUMPTION OF ABUSE IN CHAPTER 7 CASES OF INDIVIDUAL DEBTORS

In a chapter 7 case of an individual with primarily consumer debts in which a presumption of abuse has arisen under § 707(b), the clerk shall give to creditors notice of the presumption of abuse in accordance with Rule 2002 within 10 days after the date of the filing of the petition. If the debtor has not filed a statement indicating whether a presumption of abuse has arisen, the clerk shall give notice to creditors within 10 days after the date of the filing of the petition that the debtor has not filed the statement and that further notice will be given if a later filed statement indicates that a presumption of abuse has arisen. If a debtor later files a statement indicating that a presumption of abuse has arisen, the clerk shall give notice to creditors of the presumption of abuse as promptly as practicable.

Amended, on an interim basis, effective October 17, 2005.

COMMITTEE NOTE
October 17, 2005

This rule is new. The 2005 revisions to § 342 of the Bankruptcy Code require that clerks give written notice to all creditors not later than 10 days after the date of the filing of the petition that a presumption of abuse has arisen under § 707(b). A statement filed by the debtor will be the source of the clerk's information about the presumption of abuse. This rule enables the clerk to meet its obligation to send the notice within the statutory time period set forth in § 342. In the event that the court receives the debtor's statement after the clerk has sent the first notice, and the debtor's statement indicates a presumption of abuse, this rule requires that the clerk send a second notice.

INTERIM RULE 5012.   COMMUNICATION AND COOPERATION WITH FOREIGN COURTS AND FOREIGN REPRESENTATIVES

Except for communications for scheduling and administrative purposes, the court in any case commenced by a foreign representative shall give at least 20 days' notice of its intent to communicate with a foreign court or a foreign representative. The notice shall identify the subject of the anticipated communication and shall be given in the manner provided by Rule 2002(q). Any entity that wishes to participate in the communication shall notify the court of its intention not later than 5 days before the scheduled communication.

Amended, on an interim basis, effective October 17, 2005.

COMMITTEE NOTE
October 17, 2005

This rule is new. It implements § 1525 which was added to the Code in 2005. The rule provides an opportunity for parties in the case to take appropriate action prior to the communication between courts or between the court and a foreign representative to establish procedures for the manner of the communication and the right to participate in the communica-

707

tion. Participation in the communication includes both active and passive participation. Parties wishing to participate must notify the court at least 5 days before the hearing so that ample time exists to make arrangements necessary to permit the participation.

INTERIM RULE 6004. USE, SALE, OR LEASE OF PROPERTY

* * * * *

(g) Sale of Personally Identifiable Information.

(1) *Motion.* A motion for authority to sell or lease personally identifiable information under § 363(b)(1)(B) shall include a request for an order directing the United States trustee to appoint a consumer privacy ombudsman under § 332. The motion shall be governed by Rule 9014 and shall be served on any committee elected under § 705 or appointed under § 1102 of the Code, or if the case is a chapter 11 reorganization case and no committee of unsecured creditors has been appointed under § 1102, on the creditors included on the list of creditors filed under Rule 1007(d), and on such other entities as the court may direct. The motion shall be transmitted to the United States trustee.

(2) *Appointment.* If a consumer privacy ombudsman is appointed under § 332, no later than 5 days before the hearing on the motion under § 363(b)(1)(B), the United States trustee shall file a notice of the appointment, including the name and address of the person appointed. The United States trustee's notice shall be accompanied by a verified statement of the person appointed setting forth the person's connections with the debtor, creditors, any other party in interest, their respective attorneys and accountants, the United States trustee, or any person employed in the office of the United States trustee.

(h) Stay of Order Authorizing Use, Sale, or Lease of Property. An order authorizing the use, sale, or lease of property other than cash collateral is stayed until the expiration of 10 days after entry of the order, unless the court orders otherwise.

Amended, on an interim basis, effective October 17, 2005.

COMMITTEE NOTE
October 17, 2005

This rule is amended to implement §§ 332 and 363(b)(1)(B), which were added to the Code in 2005.

INTERIM RULE 6011. DISPOSAL OF PATIENT RECORDS IN HEALTH CARE BUSINESS CASE

(a) Notice by Publication Under § 351(1)(A). A notice regarding the claiming or disposing of patient records under § 351(1)(A) shall not identify patients by name or other identifying information, but shall:

(1) identify with particularity the health care facility whose patient records the trustee proposes to destroy;

(2) state the name, address, telephone number, e-mail address, and website, if any, of a person from whom information about the patient records may be obtained and how those records may be claimed; and

(3) state the date by which patient records must be claimed, and that if they are not so claimed the records will be destroyed.

(b) Notice by Mail Under § 351(1)(B). Subject to applicable nonbankruptcy law relating to patient privacy, a notice regarding the claiming or disposing of patient records under § 351(1) (B) shall, in addition to including the information in subdivision (a), direct that a patient's family member or other representative who receives the notice inform the patient of the notice, and be mailed to the patient and any family member or other contact person whose name and address have been given to the trustee or the debtor for the purpose of providing information regarding the patient's health care, and to insurance companies known to have provided health care insurance to the patient.

(c) Proof of Compliance With Notice Requirement. Unless the court orders the trustee to file proof of compliance with § 351(1)(B) under seal, the trustee shall not file, but shall maintain, the proof of compliance for a reasonable time.

(d) Report of Destruction of Records. The trustee shall file, not later than 30 days after the destruction of patient records under § 351(3), a report certifying that the unclaimed records have been destroyed and explaining the method used to effect the destruction. The report shall not identify patients by name or other identifying information.

Adopted, on an interim basis, effective October 17, 2005.

COMMITTEE NOTE
October 17, 2005

This rule is new. It implements § 351(1), which was added to the Code in 2005. That provision requires the trustee to notify patients that their patient records will be destroyed if they remain unclaimed for one year after the publication of a notice in an appropriate newspaper. The Code provision also requires that individualized notice be sent to each patient and to the patient's family member or other contact person.

The variety of health care businesses and the range of current and former patients present the need for flexibility in the creation and publication of the notices that will be given. Nevertheless, there are some matters that must be included in any notice being given to patients, their family members, and contact persons to ensure that sufficient information is provided to these persons regarding the trustee's intent to dispose of patient records. Subdivision (a) of this rule lists the minimum requirements for notices given under § 351(1)(A), and subdivision (b) governs the form of notices under § 351(1)(B). Notices given under this rule are subject to provisions under applicable federal and state law that relate to the protection of patients' privacy, such as the Health Insurance Portability and Accountability Act of 1996, Pub. L. No. 104–191 (HIPAA).

Subdivision (c) directs the trustee to maintain proof of compliance with § 351(1)(B), but it prohibits filing the proof of compliance unless the court orders the trustee to file it under seal because the proof of compliance may contain patient names that should or must remain confidential.

Subdivision (d) requires the trustee to file a report with the court regarding the destruction of patient records. This certification is intended to ensure that the trustee properly completed the destruction process. However, because the report will be filed with the court and ordinarily will be available to the public under § 107, the names, addresses, and other identifying information of the patient shall not be included in the report to protect patient privacy.

INTERIM RULE 8001.   MANNER OF TAKING APPEAL; VOLUNTARY DISMISSAL; CERTIFICATION TO COURT OF APPEALS

* * * * *

(f) Certification for Direct Appeal to Court of Appeals.

(1) *Timely Appeal Required.* A certification of a judgment, order, or decree of a bankruptcy court to a court of appeals under 28 U.S.C. § 158(d)(2) shall not be treated as a certification entered on the docket within the meaning of § 1233(b)(4)(A) of Public Law No. 109–8 until a timely appeal has been taken in the manner required by subdivisions (a) or (b) of this rule and the notice of appeal has become effective under Rule 8002.

(2) *Court Where Made.* A certification that a circumstance specified in 28 U.S.C. § 158(d)(2)(A)(i)-(iii) exists shall be filed in the court in which a matter is pending for purposes of 28 U.S.C. § 158(d)(2) and this rule. A matter is pending in a bankruptcy court until the docketing, in accordance with Rule 8007(b), of an appeal taken under 28 U.S.C. § 158(a)(1) or (2), or the grant of leave to appeal

under 28 U.S.C. § 158(a)(3). A matter is pending in a district court or bankruptcy appellate panel after the docketing, in accordance with Rule 8007(b), of an appeal taken under 28 U.S.C. § 158(a)(1) or (2), or the grant of leave to appeal under 28 U.S.C. § 158(a)(3).

(A) Certification by Court on Request or Court's Own Initiative.

(i) Before Docketing or Grant of Leave to Appeal. Only a bankruptcy court may make a certification on request or on its own initiative while the matter is pending in the bankruptcy court.

(ii) After Docketing or Grant of Leave to Appeal. Only the district court or bankruptcy appellate panel involved may make a certification on request of the parties or on its own initiative while the matter is pending in the district court or bankruptcy appellate panel.

(B) Certification by All Appellants and Appellees Acting Jointly. A certification by all the appellants and appellees, if any, acting jointly may be made by filing the appropriate Official Form with the clerk of the court in which the matter is pending. The certification may be accompanied by a short statement of the basis for the certification, which may include the information listed in subdivision (f)(3)(C) of this rule.

(3) *Request for Certification; Filing; Service; Contents.*

(A) A request for certification shall be filed, within the time specified by 28 U.S.C. § 158(d)(2), with the clerk of the court in which the matter is pending.

(B) Notice of the filing of a request for certification shall be served in the manner required for service of a notice of appeal under Rule 8004.

(C) A request for certification shall include the following:

(i) the facts necessary to understand the question presented;

(ii) the question itself;

(iii) the relief sought;

(iv) the reasons why the appeal should be allowed and is authorized by statute or rule, including why a circumstance specified in 28 U.S.C. § 158(d)(2)(A)(i)-(iii) exists; and

(v) an attached copy of the judgment, order, or decree complained of and any related opinion or memorandum.

(D) A party may file a response to a request for certification or a cross-request within 10 days after the notice of the request is served, or another time fixed by the court.

(E) The request, cross request, and any response shall not be governed by Rule 9014 and shall be submitted without oral argument unless the court otherwise directs.

(F) A certification of an appeal under 28 U.S.C. § 158(d)(2) shall be made in a separate document served on the parties.

(4) *Certification on Court's Own Initiative.*

(A) A certification of an appeal on the court's own initiative under 28 U.S.C. § 158(d)(2) shall be made in a separate document served on the parties in the manner required for service of a notice of appeal under Rule 8004. The certification shall be accompanied by an opinion or memorandum that contains the information required by subdivision (f)(3)(C)(i)-(iv) of this rule.

(B) A party may file a supplementary short statement of the basis for certification within 10 days after the certification.

Amended, on an interim basis, effective October 17, 2005.

COMMITTEE NOTE
October 17, 2005

Subdivision (f) is added to the rule to implement the 2005 amendments to 28 U.S.C. § 158(d). That section authorizes appeals directly to the court of appeals, with that court's consent, upon certification that a ground for the appeal exists under § 158(d)(2)(A)(i)-(iii). Certification can be made by the court on its own initiative or in response to a request of a party. Certification also can be made by all of the appellants and appellees. An uncodified provision in Public Law No. 109–8, § 1233(b)(4), requires that, not later than 10 days after a certification is entered on the docket, there must be filed with the circuit clerk a petition requesting permission to appeal. Given the short time limit to file the petition with the circuit clerk, subdivision (f)(1) provides that entry of a certification on the docket does not occur until an effective appeal is taken under Rule 8003(a) or (b).

The rule adopts a bright-line test for identifying the court in which a matter is pending. Under subdivision (f)(2), the bright-line chosen is the "docketing" under Rule 8007(b) of an appeal of an interlocutory order or decree under 28 U.S.C. § 158(a)(2) or a final judgment, order or decree under 28 U.S.C. § 158(a)(1), or the granting of leave to appeal any other interlocutory judgment, order or decree under 28 U.S.C. § 158(a)(3), whichever is earlier.

To ensure that parties are aware of a certification, the rule requires either that it be made on the Official Form (if being made by all of the parties to the appeal) or on a separate document (whether the certification is made on the court's own initiative or in response to a request by a party). This is particularly important because the rule adopts the bankruptcy practice established by Rule 8001(a) and (b) of requiring a notice of appeal in every instance, including interlocutory orders, of appeals from bankruptcy court orders, judgments, and decrees. Because this requirement is satisfied by filing the notice of appeal that takes the appeal to the district court or bankruptcy appellate panel in the first instance, the rule does not require a separate notice of appeal if a certification occurs after a district court or bankruptcy appellate panel decision.

INTERIM RULE 8003.   LEAVE TO APPEAL

* * * * *

(d) If leave to appeal is required by 28 U.S.C. § 158(a) and has not earlier been granted, the authorization of a direct appeal by a court of appeals under 28 U.S.C. § 158(d)(2) shall be deemed to satisfy the requirement for leave to appeal.

Amended, on an interim basis, effective October 17, 2005.

COMMITTEE NOTE
October 17, 2005

The rule is amended to add subdivision (d) to solve the jurisdictional problem that could otherwise ensue when a district court or bankruptcy appellate panel has not granted leave to appeal under 28 U.S.C. § 158(a)(3). If the court of appeals accepts the appeal, the requirement of leave to appeal is deemed satisfied. However, if the court of appeals does not authorize a direct appeal, the question of whether to grant leave to appeal remains a matter to be resolved by the district court or the bankruptcy appellate panel.

INTERIM RULE 9006.   TIME

* * * * *

(b) Enlargement.

(1) *In General.* Except as provided in paragraphs (2) and (3) of this subdivision, when an act is required or allowed to be done at or within a specified period by these rules or by a notice given thereunder or by order of court, the court for cause shown may at any time in its discretion (1) with or without motion or notice order the period enlarged if the request therefor is made before the expiration of the period originally prescribed or as extended by a previous order or (2) on motion made after the expiration of the specified period permit the act to be done where the failure to act was the result of excusable neglect.

(2) *Enlargement Not Permitted.* The court may not enlarge the time for taking action under Rules 1007(d), 2003(a) and (d), 7052, 9023, and 9024.

(3) *Enlargement Limited.* The court may enlarge the time for taking action under Rules 1006(b)(2), 1007(c) with respect to the time to file schedules and statements in a small business case, 1017(e), 3002(c), 4003(b), 4004(a), 4007(c), 8002 and 9033, only to the extent and under the conditions stated in those rules.

* * * * *

Amended, on an interim basis, effective October 17, 2005.

COMMITTEE NOTE
October 17, 2005

Section 1116(3) of the Code, as amended in 2005, places specific limits on the time for filing schedules and a statement of affairs in small business cases. The rule is amended to recognize that extensions of time for filing these documents are governed by Rule 1007(c), which is amended to recognize restrictions on expanding the time to file these documents in small business cases.

INTERIM RULE 9009.   FORMS

The Official Forms prescribed by the Judicial Conference of the United States shall be observed and used with alterations as may be appropriate. Forms may be combined and their contents rearranged to permit economies in their use. The Director of the Administrative Office of the United States Courts may issue additional forms for use under the Code. The forms shall be construed to be consistent with these rules and the Code. References in the Official Forms to these rules shall include the Interim Rules approved by the Committee on Rules of Practice and Procedure to implement Public Law No. 109–8.

Amended, on an interim basis, effective October 17, 2005.

COMMITTEE NOTE
October 17, 2005

The Official Forms refer to the Federal Rules of Bankruptcy Procedure. This rule is amended so that the reference to rules in the Official Forms includes the Interim Rules that implement the provisions of the Bankruptcy Abuse Prevention and Consumer Protection Act of 2005 (Public Law Number 109–8).

RULES OF THE UNITED STATES DISTRICT COURT FOR THE WESTERN DISTRICT OF NEW YORK

Including Amendments Received Through
September 15, 2008

Research Note

These rules may be searched electronically on Westlaw in the NY-RULES database; updates to these rules may be found on Westlaw in NY-RULESUPDATES. For search tips, and a detailed summary of database content, consult the Westlaw Scope Screen of each database.

LOCAL RULES OF CIVIL PROCEDURE

Rule
1.1. Title.
1.2. The "Court".
5.1. Filing Cases.
5.2. Pro Se Actions.
5.3. Habeas Corpus.
5.4. Sealing of Complaints and Documents in Civil Cases.
5.5. Payment of Fees in Advance.
5.6. Filing by Facsimile or Electronic Means.
7.1. Service and Filing of Papers.
7.2. Motion to Settle an Order.
7.3. Oral Argument.
10. Form of Papers.
11. Sanctions.
16.1. Pre–Trial Procedures in Civil Cases.
16.2. Arbitration.
23. Class Actions.
24. Notice of Claim of Unconstitutionality.
26. General Rules Governing Discovery.
29. Stipulations.
30. Depositions.
34. Limitation on Requests to Produce Documents or Things.
37. Mandatory Procedure for All Discovery Motions.
38. Requests for Jury Trials in Cases Removed from State Court.
41.1. Settlements and Approval of Settlements on Behalf of Infants, Incompetents and Decedents' Estates.
41.2. Dismissal for Failure to Prosecute.
47.1. Jury Trials—Civil Actions.
47.2. Jurors.
54. Costs.
55. Default Judgment.
56.1. Statements of Facts on Motion for Summary Judgment.
56.2. Notice to Pro Se Litigants Opposing Summary Judgment.
58. Satisfaction of Judgments.
65. Temporary Restraining Orders and Preliminary Injunctions.

Rule
67. Deposits of Money Into Court.
72.1. Authority of Magistrate Judges.
72.2. Assignment of Matters to Magistrate Judges.
72.3. Review and Appeal of Magistrate Judges' Actions.
76.1. Appeals.
76.2. Bankruptcy Appeals; Dismissal for Failure to Perfect.
77.1. Sessions of Court.
77.2. Orders.
77.3. Copies of Local Rules.
77.4. Copies of Orders.
78. Motions.
79. Exhibits.
81. Removed Actions.
83.1. Attorney Admission to Practice.
83.2. Attorneys of Record—Appearance and Withdrawal.
83.3. Discipline of Attorneys.
83.4. Contempts.
83.5. Cameras and Recording Devices.
83.6. Student Practice Rule.
83.7. Student Law Clerks.
83.8. Modification of Rules.

LOCAL RULES OF CRIMINAL PROCEDURE

Rule
1.1. Title.
1.2. The "Court".
6. Grand Jury.
7. Filing Cases.
12.1. Procedures for Criminal Cases.
12.2. Motions.
15. Procedures for Depositions by other than Stenographic Means.
23. Free Press—Fair Trial Directives.
24.1. Jury Trials in Criminal Cases.
24.2. Jurors.
26. Exhibits.
32. Presentence Report.
44. Appointment of Counsel.
46. Deposits of Money Into Court.
49.1. Service and Filing of Papers.

Rule

49.2. Form of Papers.

49.3. Stipulations.

49.4. Orders.

49.5. Appeals.

49.6. Copies of Orders.

49.7. Documents to Be Provided by the U.S. Attorney's Office.

49.8. Filing by Facsimile or Electronic Means.

50. Speedy Trial.

53. Cameras and Recording Devices.

55.2. Sealing of Documents in Criminal Cases.

56. Sessions of Court.

57.1. Copies of Local Rules.

57.2. Attorney Admission, Appearance and Discipline and Student Law Clerks and Practice.

58.1. Assignment of Matters to Magistrate Judges.

58.2. Review and Appeal of Magistrate Judges' Actions.

58.3. Forfeiture of Collateral in Lieu of Appearance in Petty Offense Matters.

59. Modification of Rules.

ELECTRONIC CASE FILING

Notice of Electronic Availability of Case File Information Amended to Comply with the August 2, 2004 Amendments to the E–Government Act of 2002.

Administrative Procedures for Electronic Case Filing in the Western District of New York.

CIVIL AND CRIMINAL APPENDICES

App.

A. Civil Justice Expense and Delay Reduction Plan—Western District.

B. Jury Plan.

C. Guidelines Governing Reimbursement from the District Court Fund of Expenses Incurred by Court Appointed Counsel.

D. First Amended Plan for the Management of Court Reporters.

E. Notice of Right to Consent to Disposition of a Civil Case by a United States Magistrate.

F. Form: Consent to Proceed Before a United States Magistrate.

G. Criminal Justice Act Plan.

H. Revised Plan for Prompt Disposition of Criminal Cases.

I. Standing Order Governing Claims under the Racketeer Influenced and Corrupt Organizations Act.

J. Order: In the Matter of Applications for Leave to Proceed In Forma Pauperis in Civil Rights and Habeas Corpus Cases by State and Local Prisoners.

CHAPTER 12 BANKRUPTCY RULES SUPPLEMENT

LOCAL RULES OF CIVIL PROCEDURE

RULE 1.1 TITLE

These rules shall be known as the Local Rules of Civil Procedure for the United States District Court for the Western District of New York. These rules supplement the Federal Rules of Civil Procedure and are numbered in accordance therewith.

RULE 1.2 THE "COURT"

Wherever in these rules reference is made to the "Court", "Judge", or similar term, such term shall be deemed to include a Magistrate Judge unless the context requires otherwise.

RULE 5.1 FILING CASES

(a) Every civil action shall be filed with the Clerk. The Clerk shall assign each civil action to a District Judge and a Magistrate Judge.

(b) For purposes of assigning cases other than those filed by pro se inmate litigants, the Western District of New York is divided into two areas. Cases arising in the eight western counties: Allegany, Cattaraugus, Chautauqua, Erie, Genesee, Niagara, Orleans and Wyoming (the "Buffalo area"), shall ordinarily be assigned to a District Judge and a Magistrate Judge in Buffalo. Cases arising in the nine eastern counties: Chemung, Livingston, Monroe, Ontario, Schuyler, Seneca, Steuben, Wayne and Yates (the "Rochester area"), shall ordinarily be assigned to a District Judge and a Magistrate Judge in Rochester. The assignment within these areas shall ordinarily be by random selection.

(c) Cases filed by pro se inmate litigants shall be assigned to either a District Judge or Magistrate Judge. All cases filed by a pro se plaintiff/petitioner shall be assigned to the same District Judge or Magistrate Judge to whom any case previously filed by the same plaintiff/petitioner had been assigned. In the event that the assignment is to a Magistrate Judge, the parties shall be advised of the assignment and their right to consent to final disposition of the case by the Magistrate Judge pursuant to 28 U.S.C. § 636(c). If one or more of the parties refuse or fail to consent to proceed to disposition by the Magistrate Judge, the case will be randomly assigned to a District Judge, who may refer any matters concerning the case to the original Magistrate Judge pursuant to 28 U.S.C. § 636(b).

(d) A completed civil cover sheet on a form available from the Clerk shall be submitted with every complaint, notice of removal or other document initiating a civil action. This requirement is solely for administrative purposes; matters appearing on the civil cover sheet have no legal effect in the action.

(e) In a civil proceeding, any non-governmental corporate party must file two copies of a statement identifying all its parent companies and any publicly held corporation that owns 10% or more of its stock or stating that it has no parent companies. For purposes of this rule, a parent company means a publicly held corporation that controls the party (directly or through others) or owns 10% or more of the party's stock. A party must file the disclosure statement with its first appearance, pleading, petition, motion, response, or other request addressed to the Court. A party must promptly file a supplemental disclosure statement upon any change in this information.

(f) It shall be the continuing duty of each attorney appearing in any civil case to bring promptly to the attention of the Clerk all facts which said attorney believes are relevant to a determination that said case and one or more pending civil or criminal cases should be heard by the same judge, in order to avoid unnecessary duplication of judicial effort. As soon as the attorney becomes aware of such relationship, said attorney shall notify the Clerk by letter, who shall transmit that notification to the judges to whom the cases have been assigned. If counsel fails to comply with this rule, the Court may assess reasonable costs directly against counsel whose action has obstructed the effective administration of the Court's business.

(g) Pursuant to 28 U.S.C. § 157, all cases under Title 11 of the United States Code and all proceedings arising under Title 11 or arising in or related to a case under Title 11 are referred to the United States Bankruptcy Court for the Western District of New York. Any party seeking to file papers asserting a claim under Title 11 shall, at the time of filing, notify the Clerk in writing that the papers contain such a claim. For purposes of this section, the requirement for written notification shall be satisfied by a letter addressed to the Clerk with copies to all counsel or parties, if acting pro se.

(h) Any party asserting a claim, cross-claim or counterclaim under the Racketeer Influenced & Corrupt Organizations Act ("RICO"), 18 U.S.C. § 1961, et seq., shall file and serve a "RICO Case Statement" under separate cover as described below. This statement shall be filed contemporaneously with those papers first asserting the party's RICO claim, cross-claim or counterclaim, unless, for exigent circumstances, the Court grants an extension of time for filing the RICO Case Statement. A party's failure to file a statement may result in dismissal of the party's RICO claim, cross-claim or counterclaim. The RICO Case Statement must include those facts upon which the party is relying and which were obtained as a result of the reasonable inquiry required by Federal Rule of Civil Procedure 11. In particular, the statement shall be in a form which uses the numbers and letters as set forth below, and shall state in detail and with specificity the following information.

(1) State whether the alleged unlawful conduct is in violation of 18 U.S.C. §§ 1962(a), (b), (c) and/or (d).

(2) List each defendant and state the alleged misconduct and basis of liability of each defendant.

(3) List the alleged wrongdoers, other than the defendants listed above, and state the alleged misconduct of each wrongdoer.

(4) List the alleged victims and state how each victim was allegedly injured.

(5) Describe in detail the pattern of racketeering activity or collection of unlawful debts alleged for each RICO claim. A description of the pattern of racketeering shall include the following information:

(A) List the alleged predicate acts and the specific statutes which were allegedly violated;

(B) Provide the dates of the predicate acts, the participants in the predicate acts, and a description of the facts surrounding the predicate acts;

(C) If the RICO claim is based on the predicate offenses of wire fraud, mail fraud, or fraud in the sale of securities the "circumstances constituting fraud or mistake shall be stated with particularity." Fed. R. Civ. P. 9(b). Identify the time, place and contents of the alleged misrepresentations, and the identity of persons to whom and by whom the alleged misrepresentations were made;

(D) State whether there has been a criminal conviction for violation of each predicate act;

(E) State whether civil litigation has resulted in a judgment in regard to each predicate act;

(F) Describe how the predicate acts form a "pattern of racketeering activity"; and

(G) State whether the alleged predicate acts relate to each other as part of a common plan. If so, describe in detail.

(6) Describe in detail the alleged enterprise for each RICO claim. A description of the enterprise shall include the following information:

(A) State the names of the individuals, partnerships, corporations, associations, or other legal entities, which allegedly constitute the enterprise;

(B) Describe the structure, purpose, function and course of conduct of the enterprise;

(C) State whether any defendants are employees, officers or directors of the alleged enterprise;

(D) State whether any defendants are associated with the alleged enterprise;

(E) State whether you are alleging that the defendants are individuals or entities separate from the alleged enterprise, or that the defendants are the enterprise itself, or members of the enterprise; and

   (F) If any defendants are alleged to be the enterprise itself, or members of the enterprise, explain whether such defendants are perpetrators, passive instruments, or victims of the alleged racketeering activity.

(7) State and describe in detail whether you are alleging that the pattern of racketeering activity and the enterprise are separate or have merged into one entity.

(8) Describe the alleged relationship between the activities of the enterprise and the pattern of racketeering activity. Discuss how the racketeering activity differs from the usual and daily activities of the enterprise, if at all.

(9) Describe what benefits, if any the alleged enterprise receives from the alleged pattern of racketeering.

(10) Describe the effect of the activities of the enterprise on interstate or foreign commerce.

(11) If the complaint alleges a violation of 18 U.S.C. § 1962(a), provide the following information:

   (A) State who received the income derived from the pattern of racketeering activity or through the collection of an unlawful debt; and

   (B) Describe the use or investment of such income.

(12) If the complaint alleges a violation of 18 U.S.C. § 1962(b), describe in detail the acquisition or maintenance of any interest in or control of the alleged enterprise.

(13) If the complaint alleges a violation of 18 U.S.C. § 1962(c), provide the following information:

   (A) State who is employed by or associated with the enterprise; and

   (B) State whether the same entity is both the liable "person" and the "enterprise" under § 1962(c).

(14) If the complaint alleges a violation of 18 U.S.C. § 1962(d), describe in detail the alleged conspiracy.

(15) Describe the alleged injury to business or property.

(16) Describe the direct causal relationship between the alleged injury and the violation of the RICO statute.

(17) List the damages sustained for which each defendant is allegedly liable.

(18) List all other federal causes of action, if any, and provide the relevant statute numbers.

(19) List all pendent state claims, if any.

(20) Provide any additional information that you feel would be helpful to the Court in processing your RICO claim.

[Amended effective May 1, 2003.]

RULE 5.2   PRO SE ACTIONS

   (a) In any action based upon social security claims, employment discrimination, and non-prisoner or prisoner civil rights, in which a plaintiff files pro se (which means without assistance of an attorney), the complaint should be filed on the forms provided in the Clerk's office or found on the Court's web site at www.nywd.uscourts.gov. A complaint not filed on the appropriate form may be returned to the plaintiff for refiling on the proper form if a Judge of the Court so directs. Leave to amend the complaint at a later date shall be freely granted in accordance with Federal Rule of Civil Procedure 15.

   (b) Habeas corpus petitions under 28 U.S.C. §§ 2241, 2254 and 2255 shall be filed on forms available in the Clerk's office upon the petitioner's request or found on the Court's web site at www.nywd. uscourts.gov. Section 2255 cases are to be filed without charge. A petition not filed on the appropriate form may be returned to the petitioner for refiling on the proper form if a Judge of the Court so directs.

   (c) An indigent pro se plaintiff or petitioner (28 U.S.C. §§ 2241 or 2254) may seek in forma pauperis status to file his or her action without payment of fees by filing the form affidavit available in the Clerk's office or found on the Court's web site at www.nywd. uscourts.gov, along with the complaint/petition. The case will be given a civil docket number and the in forma pauperis application will be submitted to a Judge of the Court. If the Judge denies in forma pauperis status, the plaintiff/petitioner will by written order be given notice that the case will be dismissed without prejudice if the fee is not paid by the date specified in the order.

   (d) A party appearing pro se must furnish the Court with a current address at which papers may be served on the litigant. Papers sent to this address will be assumed to have been received by plaintiff.

   In addition, the Court must have a current address at all times. Thus, a pro se litigant must inform the Court immediately in writing of any change of address. Failure to do so may result in dismissal of the case with prejudice.

   (e) It is the responsibility of all pro se litigants to become familiar with, to follow, and to comply with the Federal Rules of Civil Procedure and the Local Rules of Civil Procedure, including those rules with special provisions for pro se litigants such as Local Rules 5.2(b), 7.1(a)(2), and 16.1. Failure to comply with the Federal Rules of Civil Procedure and Local Rules of

Civil Procedure may result in the dismissal of the case with prejudice.

[Amended effective May 1, 2003.]

RULE 5.3 HABEAS CORPUS

Petitions under 28 U.S.C. §§ 2254 and 2255 shall be filed pursuant to the Rules Governing Section 2254 Cases in the United States District Courts and the Rules Governing Section 2255 Proceedings for the United States District Courts.

[Amended effective May 1, 2003.]

RULE 5.4 SEALING OF COMPLAINTS AND DOCUMENTS IN CIVIL CASES

(a) Except when otherwise required by statute or rule, there is a presumption that Court documents are accessible to the public and that a substantial showing is necessary to restrict access.

(b) Upon the proper showing, cases may be sealed in their entirety, or only as to certain parties or documents, when they are initiated, or at various stages of the proceedings. The Court may, on its own motion, enter an order directing that a document, party or entire case be sealed. A party seeking to have a document, party or entire case sealed shall submit an application, under seal, setting forth the reasons for sealing, together with a proposed order for approval by the assigned Judge. The proposed order shall include language in the "ORDERED" paragraph stating the referenced document(s) to be sealed. Upon approval of the sealing order by the assigned Judge, the Clerk shall seal the document(s). Upon denial of a sealing application, the Clerk shall notify the party of such decision. The party shall have five business days from the date of the notice to withdraw the document(s) submitted for sealing or appeal the decision denying the sealing request. If the party fails to withdraw the document(s) or otherwise appeal after the expiration of five business days, the document(s) shall be filed by the Clerk and made a part of the public record.

(c) When the sealing of a civil complaint is appropriate under either statute or this rule, the Clerk shall inscribe in the public records of the Court only the case number, the fact that a complaint was filed under seal, the name of the District Judge or Magistrate Judge who ordered the seal, and (after assignment of the case to a District Judge and a Magistrate Judge in the normal fashion) the names of the assigned District Judge and the assigned Magistrate Judge.

(d) A complaint presented for filing with a motion to seal and a proposed order shall be treated as a sealed case, pending approval of the order.

(e) Documents authorized to be filed under seal or pursuant to a protective order must be presented to the Clerk in envelopes bearing sufficient identification. The envelopes shall not be sealed until the documents inside have been filed and docketed by the Clerk's office.

(f) Unless an order of the court otherwise directs, all sealed documents will remain sealed after final disposition of the case. The party desiring that a sealed document be unsealed after disposition of the case must seek such relief by motion on notice.

[Amended effective May 1, 2003.]

RULE 5.5. PAYMENT OF FEES IN ADVANCE

(a) The Clerk shall not be required to render any service for which a fee is prescribed by statute or by the Judicial Conference of the United States unless the fee for the particular service is paid to him or her in advance. A schedule of fees is available in the office of the Clerk and on the Court's website at *www. nywd.uscourts.gov*.

(b) Pursuant to 28 U.S.C. § 1915, the Court may authorize the commencement, prosecution or defense of any action or appeal therefrom without prepayment of fees, costs or security therefor by a person who is unable to pay such fees, costs or security in accordance with Local Rule of Civil Procedure 5.2(c).

[Renumbered effective May 1, 2003.]

RULE 5.6. FILING BY FACSIMILE OR ELECTRONIC MEANS

(a) The Clerk's Office will not accept any facsimile transmission unless ordered by the Court.

(b) Pursuant to Federal Rule of Civil Procedure 5(e), the Clerk's Office will accept papers filed, signed, or verified by electronic means that are consistent with technical standards, if any, that the Judicial Conference of the United States establishes. All electronic filings shall be governed by the Court's General Order Governing Electronic Filing.

(c) Service by electronic means is addressed in Local Rule of Civil Procedure 7.1(k).

[Adopted effective December 15, 2003.]

RULE 7.1 SERVICE AND FILING OF PAPERS

(a) All pleadings, notices and other papers shall be served and filed in accordance with the Federal Rules of Civil Procedure. The party or a designee shall declare, by affidavit, sworn statement or certification, that he or she has provided all other parties in the action with all documents being filed with the Court.

(1) Pursuant to Federal Rule of Civil Procedure 5(d), disclosures under Federal Rule of Civil Procedure 26(a)(1) and (2) and depositions, interrogatories, requests for documents or to permit entry upon land, requests for admissions, and answers and responses thereto shall not be filed with the Clerk's office until they are used in a proceeding or the Court otherwise orders. Notwithstanding, all discovery materials in pro se cases shall be filed with the Court.

(2) A party seeking or opposing any relief under the Federal Rules of Civil Procedure shall file only such portion(s) of a deposition, interrogatory, request for documents, request for admission, or other material that is pertinent to the application.

(3) A party seeking to include in a record on appeal material which was not previously filed shall apply to the Court for an order requiring the Clerk to file such material. The party may make such application by motion or by stipulation of counsel.

(b) All orders, whether issued on notice or ex parte, together with the papers on which they were granted, shall be filed forthwith.

(c) Except for papers filed in connection with a summary judgment motion, the timing for which is set forth in Rule 56.1(e), a moving party who wishes to file reply papers shall file and serve the notice of motion and supporting papers at least fifteen business days prior to the return date of the motion. The notice of motion shall also state that the moving party intends to file and serve reply papers and that the opposing party is therefore required to file and serve opposing papers at least eight business days prior to the return date. Reply papers shall be filed and served at least three business days before the return date. Under all other circumstances, and except as ordered otherwise by the Court, notices of motion together with supporting affidavits and memoranda shall be served on the parties and filed with the Clerk at least ten business days prior to the return date of the motion. Answering affidavits and memoranda shall be served and filed at least three business days prior to the return date. Sur-reply papers shall not be permitted unless otherwise ordered by the Court.

(d) A party seeking to shorten the notice requirements prescribed in subparagraph (c) must make a motion for an expedited hearing setting forth the reasons why an expedited hearing is required. The motion for an expedited hearing may, for cause shown, be made ex parte, and must be accompanied by:

(1) the motion that such party is seeking to have heard on an expedited basis, together with supporting affidavits and memorandum of law; and

(2) a proposed order granting an expedited hearing, with dates for service of the motion (by personal service or overnight mail), responding papers, and the hearing left blank to be filled in by the Court.

Immediately after filing the motion for an expedited hearing (and accompanying documents) with the Clerk's office, counsel for the moving party shall personally deliver courtesy copies of such motion to chambers and await further instructions from the Court. In the event that the moving party is represented by out-of-town counsel who is unable to personally deliver courtesy copies, counsel shall mail such courtesy copies directly to chambers and shall contact chambers by telephone to request a waiver of this requirement.

(e) Absent leave of Court or as otherwise specified in this rule, upon any motion filed pursuant to Federal Rules of Civil Procedure 12, 56 or 65(a), the moving party shall file and serve with the motion papers a memorandum of law and an affidavit in support of the motion and the opposing party shall file and serve with the papers in opposition to the motion an answering memorandum and a supporting affidavit. Failure to comply with this subdivision may constitute grounds for resolving the motion against the non-complying party.

(f) Without prior approval of the Court, briefs or memoranda in support of or in opposition to any motion shall not exceed twenty-five pages in length and reply briefs shall not exceed ten pages in length and shall comply with the requirements of Local Rule of Civil Procedure 10. Applications to exceed these page limits shall be made in writing by letter to the Court, with copies to all counsel, at least three business days before the date on which the brief must be filed.

(g) Good cause shall be shown for the making of any application ex parte. The papers in support of such application shall state attempts made to resolve the dispute through a motion on notice and/or state why notice of the application for relief may not be given.

(h) No filed document shall be removed from the Court except on order of the Court.

(i) Unless otherwise specified by statute or rules or requested by the Court, only the original of any papers shall be accepted for filing. Parties requesting date-stamped copies of documents filed with the Clerk must provide a self-addressed, adequately-sized envelope with proper postage affixed.

(j) Service of all papers other than a subpoena or a summons and complaint shall be permitted by dispatching the paper to the attorney by overnight delivery service at the address designated by the attorney for that purpose, or if none is designated, at the attorney's last known address. Service by overnight delivery service shall be complete upon deposit of the paper enclosed in a properly addressed wrapper into the custody of the overnight delivery service for overnight delivery, prior to the latest time designated by the overnight delivery service for overnight delivery.

Where a period of time prescribed by either the Federal Rules of Civil Procedure or these rules is measured from the service of a paper and service is by overnight delivery, one business day shall be added to the prescribed period. "Overnight delivery service" means any delivery service which regularly accepts items for overnight delivery to any address within the jurisdiction of the Court.

(k) No papers shall be served by electronic means unless, in accordance with Federal Rule of Civil Procedure 5(b)(2)(D), the party or parties being served has filed a written consent to accept service by this means. An attorney's registration as a user of the Court's Electronic Case Filing System constitutes consent to accept service electronically. When a document is filed electronically, the Court's system will generate a Notice of Electronic Filing, which will be transmitted by the Court via e-mail to the filer and all parties who have consented to electronic service. The Notice of Electronic Filing, which serves as the Court's date-stamp and proof of service, will contain a hyperlink to the filed document. Transmission of the Notice of Electronic Filing to the registered e-mail address constitutes service of a pleading, document, order or notice upon any attorney in the case who has consented to electronic service. For cases which are a part of the Court's Electronic Case Filing System, only service of the Notice of Electronic Filing by the Court's system is sufficient to constitute electronic service. Those parties or attorneys within the case who have not consented to electronic service must be provided notice of the filing in paper form in accordance with the Federal Rules of Civil Procedure.

[Amended effective May 1, 2003; December 15, 2003.]

RULE 7.2 MOTION TO SETTLE AN ORDER

When counsel are unable to agree as to the form of a proposed order, the prevailing party may move, upon three days notice to all parties, to settle the order. Costs and attorneys' fees may be awarded against an attorney whose unreasonable conduct is deemed to have required the bringing of such a motion.

RULE 7.3 ORAL ARGUMENT

In its discretion, the Court may require written briefs before hearing argument on motions made other than pursuant to Federal Rules of Civil Procedure 12, 56 and 65(a) [See Local Rule of Civil Procedure 7.1(e)], and may notify the parties that oral argument shall not be heard on any given motion.

RULE 10. FORM OF PAPERS

(a) All text and footnotes in pleadings, motions, legal memoranda and other papers shall be plainly and legibly written, typewritten in a font size at least 12–point type, printed or reproduced, without erasures or interlineations materially defacing them, in ink on durable white 8½″ x 11″ paper of good quality and fastened. All text in such documents shall be double-spaced.

(b) All papers shall be endorsed with the name of the Court, the title of the case, the proper docket number and the name or nature of the paper, in sufficient detail for identification. In any initial or amended pleading, counsel, or litigants acting pro se, must print or type the names of all parties in the case caption with accurate capitalization and spacing. Additionally, counsel or litigants acting pro se must number the parties in the case caption. All papers shall be signed by an attorney or by the litigant if appearing pro se, and the name, address and telephone number of each attorney or litigant so appearing shall be typed or printed thereon. All papers shall be dated and paginated.

[Effective May 1, 2003.]

RULE 11. SANCTIONS

(a) Dismissal or Default. Failure of counsel for any party, or a party proceeding pro se, to appear before the Court at a conference, or to complete the necessary preparations, or to be prepared to proceed to trial at the time set may be considered an abandonment of the case or a failure to prosecute or defend diligently and an appropriate order for sanctions may be entered against the defaulting party with respect to either a specific issue or the entire case.

(b) Imposition of Costs on Attorneys. Upon finding that sanctions pursuant to section (a) would be either inadequate or unjust as to the parties, the Judge may, in accordance with 28 U.S.C. § 1927, assess reasonable costs directly against counsel whose action has obstructed the effective administration of the Court's business.

(c) Assessment of Jury Costs. In any civil case in which a settlement is reached or in which the Court is notified of settlement later than the close of business on the last business day before jurors are to appear for jury selection, the Court, in its discretion, may impose the Court's costs of compensating the jurors for their needless appearance against one or more of the parties, or against one or more counsel, as to the Court appears proper. Funds so collected shall be deposited by the Clerk into the Treasury of the United States.

RULE 16.1 PRE–TRIAL PROCEDURES IN CIVIL CASES

(a) Discovery Conferences and Scheduling Orders.

(1) After issue is joined, the Court shall schedule a Rule 16 pre-trial discovery conference ("first discovery

conference") to be held within sixty days of issue being joined in all cases except an action, petition or proceeding:

(A) for review on an administrative record;

(B) to enforce or quash an administrative summons or subpoena;

(C) by the United States to recover benefit payments or collect on a student loan;

(D) ancillary to proceedings in other courts;

(E) to enforce an arbitration award;

(F) brought by a pro se prisoner involving civil rights;

(G) involving social security; and

(H) involving habeas corpus.

(2) Prior to the first discovery conference, the parties shall confer as required by Federal Rule of Civil Procedure 26(f) and Local Rule of Civil Procedure 26, and shall file with the Court a written report consistent with the requirements of Federal Rule of Civil Procedure 26(f).

(3) At the first discovery conference, counsel for each party shall also be prepared to discuss meaningfully the following matters:

(A) possibility of settlement;

(B) factual and legal bases for all claims and defenses, and the identity of issues in dispute or those that can be agreed upon;

(C) specific relief requested;

(D) intended discovery and proposed methods to limit and/or decrease time and expense thereof, including the willingness of the parties as a courtesy to exchange discovery demands electronically in addition to the service of paper copies;

(E) willingness to consent to the referral of any or all matters to a Magistrate Judge pursuant to 28 U.S.C. § 636 and Local Rule of Civil Procedure 72.2;

(F) suitability of case for alternative dispute resolution, and identity of the process thereof;

(G) the need for adopting special procedures for managing difficult actions involving complex issues, multiple parties or difficult legal questions;

(H) the appropriateness of an advanced trial date and limited discovery in an uncomplicated action; and

(I) the use of experts during discovery and at trial.

(4) Pursuant to Federal Rule of Civil Procedure 16(b), following the first discovery conference, the Court shall issue an order providing:

(A) a discovery cut-off date;

(B) a date for a settlement conference ("first settlement conference") to be held before the Court;

(C) a time limitation on the joinder of other parties;

(D) a time limitation on the commencement of third-party practice;

(E) a time limitation on the filing of all pre-trial motions;

(F) a time limitation on the disclosure of expert witnesses;

(G) any other matter decided or agreed upon at the first discovery conference;

(H) an advanced trial date and limited discovery in an appropriate, uncomplicated action, and

(I) that no further or additional discovery, joinder, third-party practice, or non-dispositive motions shall be permitted after the close of discovery except by leave of the Court for good cause shown in writing; provided, however, that if the Court so directs, a request for an extension of the deadline for the completion of discovery shall be signed by both the attorney and the party making the request.

(5) Additional pretrial conferences may be scheduled in the discretion of the Court, sua sponte, or at the request of a party. At any subsequent discovery conference, the attorneys shall provide a status update and a time-table for the remaining discovery to be completed within the discovery period.

(b) Settlement Conferences.

(1) Prior to the first settlement conference, the parties shall exchange a written settlement demand and a response. The settlement demand shall be provided to the opposing party or parties at least ten calendar days prior to the first settlement conference, and a response to the demand shall be provided at least five calendar days prior to the first settlement conference, in order to allow the parties meaningful opportunity to consider and discuss the settlement proposals.

(2) At the first settlement conference, the attorneys shall be present and shall be prepared to state their respective positions to the Court. Each plaintiff shall communicate a demand for settlement to the Court, and each defendant shall be prepared to communicate a response. The attorneys shall have consulted with their respective clients regarding their settlement positions prior to the settlement conference. Likewise, in cases involving insurance coverage, defense counsel shall have consulted with the insurance carrier regarding its position prior to this settlement conference. Each party shall submit in writing, or be prepared to discuss, the undisputed facts and legal issues relevant to the case, and the legal and factual issues about which the party believes there is a dispute.

(3) If a settlement is not reached at the first settlement conference, the Court may schedule additional settlement conferences from time to time as appropriate.

(4) Upon notice by the Court, representatives of the parties with authority to bind them in settlement discussions, or the parties themselves, must be present or available by telephone during any settlement conference.

(c) **Pre-trial Conference.**

(1) Within thirty days after the close of discovery, the District Judge, or if the parties have consented to disposition by the Magistrate Judge, the Magistrate Judge, shall hold a pre-trial conference for the purpose of setting a cut-off date for remaining motions, setting a firm trial date, and discussing settlement. Except for good cause shown in writing, such motion cut-off date shall not be more than ninety days after the date of the discovery cut-off and not less than 120 days prior to the trial date. Nothing contained in this rule shall be read as precluding or discouraging dispositive motions at any time during the pendency of a case.

(2) The Court, when appropriate in light of the particular action, may discuss the following additional topics at the pre-trial conference:

(A) simplification of the legal and factual issues, including the elimination of frivolous claims or defenses;

(B) the desirability of amendments to the pleadings;

(C) the possibility of avoiding unnecessary proof through the use of admissions, stipulations, or advance rulings from the Court on the admissibility of evidence;

(D) the use, limitations, and restrictions on the use of expert testimony; and

(E) any other issue the Court may direct the parties to prepare to discuss at the pre-trial conference.

(d) Counsel for each party, no later than ten days before the date of the final pre-trial conference, shall file with the Court and serve upon counsel for all other parties, a pre-trial statement which shall include the following:

(1) a detailed statement of contested and uncontested facts, and of the party's position regarding contested facts;

(2) a detailed statement as to the issues of law involved and any unusual questions relative to the admissibility of evidence together with supporting authority;

(3) proposed jury instructions, if any;

(4) a list of witnesses (other than rebuttal witnesses) expected to testify, together with a brief statement of their anticipated testimony and their addresses;

(5) a brief summary of the qualifications of all expert witnesses, and a concise statement of each expert's expected opinion testimony and the material upon which that testimony is expected to be based;

(6) a list of exhibits anticipated to be used at trial, except exhibits which may be used solely for impeachment or rebuttal;

(7) a list of any deposition testimony to be offered in evidence;

(8) an itemized statement of each element of special damages and other relief sought; and

(9) such additional submissions as the Court directs.

(e) **Marking Exhibits.** Prior to the final pre-trial conference, counsel shall meet to mark and list each exhibit contained in the pre-trial statements. At the conference, counsel shall produce a copy of each exhibit for examination by opposing counsel and for notice of any objection to its admission in evidence.

(f) **Final Pre-trial Conference.**

(1) A final pretrial conference shall be held at the direction of the Court within thirty days of the trial date. Trial counsel shall be present at this conference and shall be prepared to discuss all aspects of the case and any matters which may narrow the issues and aid in its prompt disposition, including:

(A) the possibility of settlement;

(B) motions in limine;

(C) the resolution of any legal or factual issues raised in the pre-trial statement of any party;

(D) stipulations (which shall be in writing); and

(E) any other matters that counsel or the Court deems appropriate.

(2) Following the final pre-trial conference, a pre-trial order may be entered as directed by the Court, and the case certified as ready for trial.

(g) **Attorneys Binding Authority.** Each party represented by an attorney shall be represented at each pre-trial, discovery or settlement conference by an attorney who has the authority to bind that party regarding all matters previously identified by the Court for discussion at the conference and all reasonably related matters.

[Amended effective May 1, 2003.]

RULE 16.2 ARBITRATION

(a) **Purpose and Scope.** This rule governs the consensual arbitration of civil actions as provided by 28

U.S.C. § 651, et seq. Its purpose is to promote the speedy, fair and economical resolution of controversies by informal procedures.

Under this rule, the parties in a civil action may consent to a hearing before an impartial arbitrator or panel of arbitrators who will make a decision as to the issues presented and render an award based upon that decision. Unless the parties otherwise agree, arbitration in this Court is nonbinding and parties shall have an opportunity to request a trial de novo.

(b) Actions Subject to this Rule. This rule shall apply to all civil actions which are filed after the effective date of this rule and by court order to any pending action.

(c) Notification of Right to Proceed to Arbitration. After issue is joined, the Clerk shall notify the parties in all civil actions that they may consent to arbitration under this rule.

(d) Procedure for Consenting to Arbitration. Parties may consent to arbitration at any time before trial. Such consent must be given freely and knowingly and no party or attorney shall be prejudiced for refusing to participate in arbitration. If no consent is achieved, no Judge or Magistrate Judge to whom the action is or may be assigned shall be advised of the identity of any party or attorney who opposed the use of arbitration.

(1) *Form of Consent.* The form of consent shall be prescribed by the Clerk and shall offer the parties the option of waiving the right to demand trial de novo, thus making the results of the arbitration proceeding binding upon them. The plaintiff shall be responsible for securing the execution of the consent form and for filing such form with the Clerk. The Clerk shall not accept for filing any consent form unless it has been signed by all parties to the action or their counsel.

No court approval of the election to arbitrate is required, unless any party or necessary witness is expected to be incarcerated at the time of arbitration.

(2) *Authority of Assigned Judge.*

(A) Every action subject to this rule shall be assigned to a Judge and a Magistrate Judge upon filing in the normal course in accordance with Local Rule of Civil Procedure 5.1 and the assigned Judge and Magistrate Judge shall have authority, in his or her discretion, to conduct status, pretrial and settlement conferences, hear motions, and supervise the action in all other respects in accordance with these rules and the Federal Rules of Civil Procedure, notwithstanding the referral of the action to arbitration.

(B) The Court, upon good cause shown, may modify any of the time periods for any action required under this rule.

(e) Arbitration Hearing: Scheduling. After the last responsive pleading is filed in a case wherein the parties have consented to arbitration and such consent has been approved by the Court when necessary, and after selection of the arbitrator(s), the Arbitration Clerk shall send a notice to counsel setting forth the date, time and location for the arbitration hearing. In the event a third party has been brought into the action, the notice shall be sent after filing of the last responsive pleading in the third-party action.

If the parties have filed a request for an immediate hearing, subject to the schedule of the arbitrator(s), one shall be scheduled within thirty days of filing the request. In cases in which the parties have not requested an immediate hearing, the arbitration hearing shall be scheduled no later than 180 days from the date the last responsive pleading was filed. Notwithstanding the foregoing, the arbitration proceeding shall not, in the absence of the parties' consent, commence until thirty days after the disposition by the Court of any motion to dismiss the complaint, motion for judgment on the pleadings, or motion to join necessary parties, if the motion was filed and served within twenty days after the filing of the last responsive pleading. The specified time periods may be modified by the Court for good cause shown.

(f) Arbitration Hearing: Prehearing Procedures.

(1) *Disclosure.* Upon entry of the order designating the arbitrator(s), the Arbitration Clerk shall send to each arbitrator a copy of all the pleadings, a copy of the order designating the arbitrator(s), a copy of the court docket sheet and a copy of the Guidelines for Arbitrators. The arbitrator(s) shall forthwith inform all parties, in writing, as to whether the arbitrator(s) or any firm or member of any firm with which the arbitrator(s) is affiliated has (either as a party or attorney), at any time within the past five years, been involved in litigation with or represented any party to the arbitration, or any agency, division or employee of such party.

(2) *Delivery of Exhibits and Witness Lists.* At least ten days prior to the arbitration hearing, each counsel shall deliver to the arbitrator(s) and to adverse counsel premarked copies of all exhibits, including expert reports and all portions of depositions and interrogatories (except documents intended solely for impeachment purposes) to which reference will be made at the hearing and a list of all witnesses who are to testify at the hearing. Failure to deliver any exhibit within the prescribed time period may result in the preclusion of that exhibit at the arbitration hearing.

(3) *Continuances.* A matter shall not be adjourned absent extraordinary circumstances and the decision of the arbitrator(s) shall be final. Except as otherwise provided herein, the Arbitration Clerk must be notified immediately of any request for a continuance or

any other situation or settlement of the case that would affect the hearing date.

(g) Arbitration Hearing: Conduct of Hearing.

(1) *Place of Holding Hearing.* Hearings shall be held at any location within the Western District of New York designated by the arbitrator(s). Hearings may be held in any courtroom or other room in any federal courthouse made available to the arbitrator(s) by the Clerk. When no such room is made available, the hearing shall be held at any suitable location selected by the arbitrator(s).

(2) *Nature of the Proceeding.* The arbitration hearing shall be conducted informally unless the parties agree to, and the Court approves, a more formal proceeding. Suitable instances for a more formal proceeding include matters in which the parties are bearing the expenses of an expert arbitrator which exceed the fees provided for herein, in which the parties have waived the right to demand a trial de novo, or in which the case will turn strictly on the quality of full testimony and other proofs and the Court agrees that a formal arbitration hearing is likely to substantially contribute to the just conclusion of the litigation. In receiving evidence, the arbitrator(s) shall be guided by the Federal Rules of Evidence but shall not thereby be precluded from receiving evidence which he or she considers to be relevant and trustworthy and which is not privileged.

(3) *Authority of Arbitrator(s).* The arbitrator(s) may make reasonable rules and issue orders necessary for the fair and efficient conduct of the hearing and may administer oaths and affirmations.

(4) *Testimony.* Necessary testimony shall be given under oath or affirmation and each party shall have the right to cross-examine witnesses except as herein provided.

(5) *Subpoenas.* Attendance of witnesses and production of documents may be compelled in accordance with Federal Rule of Civil Procedure 45.

(6) *Absence of a Party.* The arbitration hearing may proceed in the absence of any party who after notice fails to be present.

(7) *Transcripts.* A party may cause a transcript or recording to be made of the hearing at its expense but shall, at the request and expense of an opposing party, make a copy available to that party.

(8) *Communication with the Arbitrator(s).* There shall be no ex parte communication between an arbitrator and any counsel or party on any matter relating to the action except for purposes of scheduling or continuing the hearing.

(h) Award and Judgment.

(1) *Award.* The arbitrator(s) shall file the award with the Clerk no more than ten days following the close of the hearing. The award shall state the name or names of the prevailing party or parties and the party or parties against which it is rendered, and the precise amount of money and other relief, if any, awarded including prejudgment interest, costs, fees and attorney's fees if authorized by statute or otherwise. The award shall be in writing and signed by the arbitrator or by at least two members of a panel. No panel member shall participate in the award without having attended the hearing. Arbitrators are not required to issue an opinion explaining the award, but they may do so.

As soon as the award is filed, the Clerk shall serve copies on the parties.

(2) *Judgment.* Unless a party files a demand for trial de novo within thirty days of the filing of the award, the Clerk shall enter judgment on the award in accordance with Federal Rule of Civil Procedure 58. A judgment so entered shall have the same force and effect as a judgment of the Court in a civil action, except that it shall not be subject to review in any other court by appeal or otherwise. In cases involving multiple claims or parties, any part of an award for which a party does not request a trial de novo in accordance with this rule shall become part of the final judgment with the same force and effect as a judgment of the Court in a civil action, except that it shall not be subject to review in any other court by appeal or otherwise.

(3) *Sealing of Award.* The contents of an arbitration award shall not be made known to any Judge or Magistrate Judge who might be assigned to preside at the trial of the case or rule on potentially case-dispositive motions until the Clerk has entered a final judgment in the action, the action has been otherwise terminated, or except to prepare the report required by § 903(b) of the Judicial Improvements and Access to Justice Act.

(i) Trial De Novo.

(1) *Demand.* Within thirty days after the arbitration award is filed, any party may demand a trial de novo in the District Court on any or all issues presented at the arbitration hearing. If one party requests a trial de novo on fewer than all issues of the case, any other party may, within ten days after the original demand for trial de novo is filed, request a trial de novo on any or all other issues. The party demanding trial de novo shall serve a written demand for a trial de novo upon each counsel of record and upon any party not represented by counsel.

(2) *Restoration to the Docket.* Upon filing a demand for a trial de novo, the action shall be restored to the Court's docket, trial ready, and treated for all purposes as if it had not been referred to arbitration. The parties shall meet with the Judge or Magistrate Judge to determine a schedule for trial and other proceedings. Any right of trial by jury that a party otherwise would have had is preserved.

(3) *Withdrawal of Demand.* Withdrawal of a demand for trial de novo shall be filed with the Clerk and simultaneously served on all parties. Withdrawal of a demand for a trial de novo shall reinstate the arbitrator's award, unless within ten days thereafter any other party requests a trial de novo.

(4) *Evidence.* No evidence that an arbitration proceeding has occurred, the nature or amount of any award, or any other matter concerning the conduct of the arbitration proceeding shall be admitted at the trial de novo.

(5) *Costs.* [Abrogated].

(j) Arbitrators.

(1) *Certification Of Arbitrators.* The Chief Judge or a Judge or Judges authorized by the Chief Judge (the "Certifying Judge") shall certify as many arbitrators as he or she determines to be necessary under this rule and shall have complete discretion and authority to thereafter withdraw the certification of any arbitrator at any time.

An individual may be certified to serve as an arbitrator if he or she: (1) is a member of the bar of the State of New York; (2) is admitted to practice before this Court; and (3) is determined by the Certifying Judge to be competent to perform the duties of an arbitrator. Any member of the bar possessing these qualifications who desires to obtain certification to act as an arbitrator shall complete an application form and file it with the Arbitration Clerk. The Arbitration Clerk shall forward such applications to the Certifying Judge for review. The Clerk shall maintain a list of the names and addresses of all persons certified to act as arbitrators in this Court. Any person whose name appears thereon may ask at any time to have his or her name removed or, if selected to serve, may decline to serve but remain on the roster.

Alternatively, the parties to an action who have consented to arbitration may jointly request certification of an individual who possesses expertise in a field relevant to the particular action (an "expert arbitrator"). The Certifying Judge may, in his or her discretion, certify such an individual to act as an arbitrator for purposes of that particular action only.

Each individual certified to act as an arbitrator shall take the oath required by 28 U.S.C. § 453. An arbitrator is an independent contractor and is subject to the provisions of 18 U.S.C. §§ 201–211 to the same extent as such provisions apply to a special government employee of the Executive Branch. A person may not be barred from the practice of law because he or she is an arbitrator.

(2) *Selection of Arbitrators.* The parties may elect to proceed to arbitration before a single arbitrator or a panel of three arbitrators to be selected from the list of certified arbitrators maintained by the Clerk, or may jointly request the Court's permission to proceed to arbitration before a single expert arbitrator of their choice.

If the parties choose to proceed to arbitration before an arbitrator or arbitrators from the list maintained by the Clerk, selection of the arbitrator(s) shall be conducted at random by the Clerk or his or her designee. Not more than one member or associate of a firm or association of attorneys shall be appointed to the same panel of arbitrators.

The Clerk shall promptly send notice of the selection of the arbitrator(s) to the person or persons who are selected to serve as arbitrator(s) and to the parties.

On motion made to the Court not later than twenty days before a scheduled arbitration hearing, the Court may disqualify a person selected to be an arbitrator for bias or prejudice as provided in 28 U.S.C. § 144. Further, persons selected to be arbitrators shall disqualify themselves if they could be required to do so under 28 U.S.C. § 455 if they were a justice, judge or magistrate judge.

(3) *Compensation of Arbitrators.* Pursuant to 28 U.S.C. section 658(a), arbitrators shall be paid $250 per case if the parties utilize a single arbitrator, or $100 per arbitrator per case if the parties elect to proceed before a panel of arbitrators. The costs thereof are to be shared equally by the parties to the arbitration. In the event that the parties elect to proceed to arbitration before a single expert arbitrator of their selection, the parties are responsible for any fees assessed by the arbitrator that exceed the fees provided for in this rule.

[Amended effective May 1, 2003; April 26, 2004.]

RULE 23. CLASS ACTIONS

(a) The title of any pleading purporting to commence a class action shall bear the legend "Class Action" next to its caption.

(b) The complaint (or other pleading asserting a claim for or against a class) shall contain next after the jurisdictional grounds and under the separate heading "Class Action Allegations,":

(1) a reference to the portion or portions of Federal Rule of Civil Procedure 23 under which it is claimed that the action is properly maintainable as a class action, and

(2) appropriate allegations thought to justify the claim, including, but not necessarily limited to:

(A) the size (or approximate size) and definition of the alleged class;

(B) the basis on which the party or parties claim to be an adequate representative of the class;

(C) the alleged questions of law and fact claimed to be common to the class; and

(D) in actions claimed to be maintainable as class actions under Federal Rule of Civil Procedure 23(b)(3), allegations thought to support the findings required by that subsection.

(c) Within sixty days after issue having been joined in any class action, counsel for the parties shall meet with a District Judge or Magistrate Judge and a scheduling order shall issue providing for orderly discovery; such order may initially limit discovery only as to facts relevant to the certification of the alleged class.

(d) Within 120 days after the filing of a pleading alleging a class action, unless this period is extended on motion for good cause filed prior to the expiration of said 120–day period or in the scheduling order, the party seeking class certification shall move for a determination under Federal Rule of Civil Procedure 23(c)(1) as to whether the case is to be maintained as a class action. The motion shall include, but is not limited to, the following:

(1) a brief statement of the case;

(2) a statement defining the class sought to be certified, including its geographical and temporal scope;

(3) a description of the party's particular grievance and why that claim qualifies the party as a member of the class as defined;

(4) a statement describing any other pending actions in any court against the same party alleging the same or similar causes of actions, about which the party or counsel seeking class action certification is personally aware;

(5) in cases in which a notice to the class is required by Federal Rule of Civil Procedure 23(c)(2), a statement of what the proposed notice to the members of the class should include and how and when the notice will be given, including a statement regarding security deposit for the cost of notices; and

(6) a statement of any other matters that the movant deems necessary and proper to the expedition of a decision on the motion and the speedy resolution of the case on the merits.

The other parties shall respond to said motion in accordance with the provisions of these rules.

(e) In ruling upon a motion for class certification, the Court may allow the action to be so maintained, may disallow and strike the class action averments, or may order postponement of the determination pending discovery or such other preliminary procedures as appear to be appropriate and necessary under the circumstances. Whenever possible, where the determination is ordered to be postponed, a date shall be fixed for renewal of the motion before the same Judge.

(f) The burden shall be upon any party seeking to maintain a case as a class action to show that the action is properly maintainable as such. If the Court determines that an action may be maintained as a class action, the party obtaining that determination shall, unless otherwise ordered by the Court, initially bear the expenses of and be responsible for giving such notice as the Court may order to members of the class.

(g) Failure to move for class determination and certification within the time required herein shall constitute and signify an intentional abandonment and waiver of all class action allegations contained in the pleading and the action shall proceed as an individual, non-class action thereafter. If any motion for class determination or certification is filed after the deadline provided herein, it shall not have the effect of reinstating the class allegations unless and until it is acted upon favorably by the Court upon a finding of excusable neglect and good cause.

(h) The attorneys for the parties are governed by the New York State Lawyer's Code of Professional Responsibility as adopted from time to time by the Appellate Divisions of the State of New York concerning contact with and solicitation of potential class members.

(i) No class action allegation shall be withdrawn, deleted, or otherwise amended without court approval. Furthermore, no class action shall be compromised without court approval and notice of the proposed compromise shall be given to all members of the class in such manner as the court directs.

(j) Six months from the date of issue having been joined and every six months thereafter until the action is terminated, counsel in all class actions shall file with the Clerk a joint case status report indicating whether any motions are pending, what discovery has been completed, what discovery remains to be conducted, the extent of any settlement negotiations that have taken place and the likelihood of settlement, and whether the matter is ready for trial.

(k) The foregoing provisions shall apply, with appropriate adaptations, to any counterclaim or cross-claim alleged to be brought for or against a class.

RULE 24. NOTICE OF CLAIM OF UNCONSTITUTIONALITY

If at any time prior to the trial of any action, suit, or proceeding, to which neither the United States, an individual state, nor any agency, officer or employee of either is a party, a party draws in question the constitutionality of an Act of Congress or a state statute affecting the public interest, such party shall forthwith and in writing notify the Court of the existence of such question and specifically identify the statute and the respects in which it is claimed to be unconstitutional. This will enable the Court to comply with the requirements of 28 U.S.C. § 2403.

RULE 26. GENERAL RULES GOVERNING DISCOVERY

(a) Actions, Petitions and Proceedings Exempted From Mandatory Initial Disclosure and Discovery Conference Requirements. The following actions, petitions and proceedings are exempted from the mandatory initial disclosure and discovery conference requirements of Federal Rule of Civil Procedure 26(a) and (f):

(1) for review on an administrative record;

(2) to enforce or quash an administrative summons or subpoena;

(3) by the United States to recover benefit payments or collect on a student loan;

(4) ancillary to proceedings in other courts;

(5) to enforce an arbitration award;

(6) brought by a pro se prisoner involving civil rights;

(7) involving Social Security; and

(8) involving habeas corpus.

(b) Rule 26(f) Discovery Conference. In addition to the matters required to be addressed at the discovery conference among counsel contemplated by Federal Rule of Civil Procedure 26(f), the following topics shall also be discussed:

(1) possibility of settlement;

(2) factual and legal bases for all claims and defenses, and the identity of issues in dispute or those that can be agreed upon;

(3) specific relief requested;

(4) intended discovery and proposed methods to limit and/or decrease time and expense thereof, including the willingness of the parties as a courtesy to exchange discovery demands electronically in addition to the service of paper copy;

(5) willingness to consent to the referral of any or all matters to a Magistrate Judge pursuant to 28 U.S.C. § 636 and Local Rule of Civil Procedure 72.2;

(6) suitability of case for alternative dispute resolution, and identity of the process thereof;

(7) the need for adopting special procedures for managing difficult actions involving complex issues, multiple parties or difficult legal questions; and

(8) the appropriateness of an advanced trial date and limited discovery in an uncomplicated action.

(c) Timing and Sequence of Discovery. Subject to the requirements of Federal Rule of Civil Procedure 26(a)(1), a party may not seek discovery, absent agreement of the parties or court order, from any source before the parties have met and conferred as required by Federal Rule of Civil Procedure 26(f).

(d) Form of Interrogatories, Requests to Produce or Inspect and Requests for Admission. The parties shall number each interrogatory or request sequentially, regardless of the number of sets of interrogatories or requests. In addition to service pursuant to Federal Rule of Civil Procedure 5, the party to whom interrogatories or discovery requests are directed shall, whenever practicable, be supplied with an electronic courtesy copy, whether by computer disk or electronic mail, containing each interrogatory and/or request in sequential format. In answering or objecting to interrogatories, requests for admission, or requests to produce or inspect, the responding party shall first state verbatim the propounded interrogatory or request and immediately thereafter the answer or objection.

(e) Uniform Definitions for all Discovery Requests.

(1) The full text of the definitions and rules of construction set forth in paragraphs (3) and (4) is deemed incorporated by reference into all discovery requests. No discovery request shall use broader definitions or rules of construction than those set forth in paragraphs (3) and (4). This rule shall not preclude (a) the definition of other terms specific to the particular litigation, (b) the use of abbreviations, or (c) a more narrow definition of a term defined in paragraph (3).

(2) This rule is not intended to broaden or narrow the scope of discovery permitted by the Federal Rules of Civil Procedure.

(3) The following definitions apply to all discovery requests:

Communication. The term "communication" means the transmittal of information (in the form of facts, ideas, inquiries or otherwise).

Document. The term "document" is defined to be synonymous in meaning and equal in scope to the usage of this term in Federal Rule of Civil Procedure 34(a), including, without limitation, electronic or computerized data compilations. A draft or nonidentical copy is a separate document within the meaning of this term.

Identify (with respect to persons). When referring to a person, "to identify" means to give, to the extent known, the person's full name, present or last known address, and when referring to a natural person, additionally, the present or last known place of employment. Once a person has been identified in accordance with this subparagraph, only the name of that person need be listed in response to subsequent discovery requesting the identification of that person.

Identify (with respect to documents). When referring to documents, "to identify" means to give, to the extent known, the (i) type of document; (ii) general subject matter; (iii) date of the document; and (iv) author(s), addressee(s) and recipients(s).

Parties. The terms "plaintiff" and "defendant," as well as a party's full or abbreviated name or a pronoun referring to a party, mean the party and, where applicable, its officers, directors, employees, partners, corporate parent, subsidiaries or affiliates. This definition is not intended to impose a discovery obligation on any person who is not a party to the litigation.

Person. The term "person" is defined as any natural person or any business, legal or governmental entity or association.

Concerning. The term "concerning" means relating to, referring to, describing, evidencing or constituting.

(4) The following rules of construction apply to all discovery requests:

All/Each. The terms "all" and "each" shall be construed as all and each.

And/Or. The connectives "and" and "or" shall be construed either disjunctively or conjunctively as necessary to bring within the scope of the discovery request all responses that might otherwise be construed to be outside of its scope.

Number. The use of the singular form of any word includes the plural and vice versa.

(f) Assertion of Claim of Privilege.

(1) Where a claim of privilege is asserted in objecting to any means of discovery or disclosure, including but not limited to a deposition, and an answer is not provided on the basis of such assertion,

(A) The attorney asserting the privilege shall identify the nature of the privilege (including work product) which is being claimed and, if the privilege is governed by state law, indicate the state's privilege rule being invoked; and

(B) The following information shall be provided in the objection, unless to divulge such information would cause disclosure of the allegedly privileged information:

(i) For documents: (I) the type of document, e.g., letter or memorandum; (II) the general subject matter of the document; (III) the date of the document; and (IV) such other information as is sufficient to identify the document for a subpoena duces tecum, including, where appropriate, the author of the document, the addressees of the document, and any other recipients shown in the document, and, where not apparent, the relationship of the author, addressees, and recipients to each other;

(ii) For oral communications: (I) the name of the person making the communication and the names of persons present while the communication was made and, where not apparent, the relationship of the persons present to the person making the communication; (II) the date and place of communication; and (III) the general subject matter of the communication.

(2) Where a claim of privilege is asserted during a deposition, and information is not provided on the basis of such assertion, the information set forth in paragraph (1) above shall be furnished (a) at the deposition, to the extent it is readily available from the witness being deposed or otherwise, and (b) to the extent the information is not readily available at the deposition, in writing within ten business days after the deposition session at which the privilege is asserted, unless otherwise ordered by the Court.

(3) Where a claim of privilege is asserted in response to discovery or disclosure other than at a deposition, and information is not provided on the basis of such assertion, the information set forth in paragraph (1) above shall be furnished in writing at the time of the response to such discovery or disclosure, unless otherwise ordered by the Court.

(g) Non-filing of Discovery Materials. See Local Rules of Civil Procedure 7.1(a)(1), and 56.1(d).

(h) Cooperation Among Counsel in the Discovery Context. See the Civility Principles of the United States District Court for the Western District of New York.

[Adopted effective May 1, 2003.]

RULE 29. STIPULATIONS

All stipulations affecting a case before the Court, except stipulations which are made in open court and recorded by the court reporter, shall be in writing and signed, and shall be filed. Except to prevent injustice, any stipulation which fails to satisfy these requirements shall not be given effect.

RULE 30. DEPOSITIONS

(a) Fair Notice. Absent agreement of the parties or court order, each notice to take the deposition of a party or other witness shall be served at least twenty days prior to the date set for examination.

(b) Production of Documents in Connection with Depositions. Consistent with the requirements of Federal Rules of Civil Procedure 30 and 34, a party seeking production of documents of another party or witness in connection with a deposition shall schedule the deposition to allow for the production of the documents at least seven calendar days in advance of the deposition. Upon receipt of the documents, the party noticing the deposition shall immediately inform counsel for all other noticed parties that the requested documents have been produced and shall make the produced documents available for inspection and re-production by counsel for all other noticed parties. If documents which have been so requested are not produced at least seven days prior to the deposition, the party noticing the deposition may either adjourn the deposition until a minimum of seven days after such documents are produced or, without waiving the right to have access to the documents, proceed with the deposition on the originally scheduled date.

(c) Procedures for Videotaped Depositions. A deposition by other than stenographic means (i.e., without the use of a stenographic record) may be taken only upon order of the Court. A deposition to be recorded on video tape and by stenographic means requires no prior order (except as required by subparagraph (8) of this rule). The following procedures shall be followed:

(1) The deposition notice shall state that the deposition will be recorded both stenographically and on video tape. At the deposition, the operator of the camera shall be identified; however, nothing shall preclude utilization of an employee of the attorney who noticed the deposition from acting as the camera operator.

(2) The camera shall be directed at the witness at all times showing a head and shoulders view, except that close-up views of exhibits are permitted where requested by the questioning attorney.

(3) Prior to trial, counsel for the party seeking to use the deposition at trial shall approach opposing counsel and attempt to resolve voluntarily all objections made at the deposition.

(4) Unresolved objections shall be submitted to the Court by way of a motion in limine made by the party seeking to use the deposition at trial. The motion may be made at any time after the deposition, but shall be made no later than one week before trial or in compliance with any date established by applicable order of the Court. The objected-to portion(s) of the transcript shall be annexed to such motion papers.

(5) In accordance with the Court's ruling on objections, the party seeking to use the deposition shall notify opposing counsel of the pages and line numbers of the deposition transcript which the party plans to delete from the video tape. The party seeking to use the video tape deposition at trial shall then edit the tape accordingly, and shall bear the expenses of editing. If the Court overrules an objection made during the deposition, such objection need not be deleted. If requested, an instruction from the Court at the time the deposition is shown regarding objections heard on the tape will be given.

(6) At least three days before showing the tape, the party seeking to use the tape at trial shall deliver a copy of the edited tape to opposing counsel. Opposing counsel may only object at that time if the edited version does not comply with the Court's ruling and the agreement of counsel set forth above, or if the quality of the tape is such that it will be difficult for the jury to understand. Such objections, if any, must be made in writing and served at least 24 hours before the tape is to be shown.

(7) The party seeking to use the video tape deposition must provide the equipment necessary to do so in court.

(8) See Local Rule of Civil Procedure 54 with respect to videotaping costs being allowed as a component of taxable costs.

[Amended effective May 1, 2003.]

RULE 34. LIMITATION ON REQUESTS TO PRODUCE DOCUMENTS OR THINGS

Any party may serve upon any other party requests for the production of documents or things not exceeding 25 in number, including all discrete subparts. Service of requests for production of more than 25 documents or things is permitted only upon the parties' written stipulation or upon leave of the Court. Leave to serve additional requests shall be granted to the extent consistent with the principles of Federal Rule of Civil Procedure 26(b)(2).

[Adopted effective May 1, 2003.]

RULE 37. MANDATORY PROCEDURE FOR ALL DISCOVERY MOTIONS

To promote the efficient administration of justice and unless ordered otherwise, no motion for discovery and/or production of documents under Federal Rules of Civil Procedure 26–37 shall be heard unless moving counsel notifies the Court by written affidavit that sincere attempts to resolve the discovery dispute have been made. Such affidavit shall detail the times and places of the parties' meetings, correspondence or discussions concerning the discovery dispute, and the names of all parties participating therein.

RULE 38. REQUESTS FOR JURY TRIALS IN CASES REMOVED FROM STATE COURT

In any action removed to this Court from the courts of the State of New York, a party entitled to a trial by jury under Federal Rule of Civil Procedure 38 shall be afforded a jury trial if a demand is filed and served as provided by Federal Rule of Civil Procedure 81(c).

[Amended effective May 1, 2003.]

RULE 41.1 SETTLEMENTS AND APPROVAL OF SETTLEMENTS ON BEHALF OF INFANTS, INCOMPETENTS AND DECEDENTS' ESTATES

(a) Settlement. When a case is settled, the parties shall, within ten days, file in the office of the Clerk a signed agreement for judgment or stipulation for dismissal as appropriate, unless the Judge extends the time. If no such agreement is filed, the Judge may enter an order dismissing the case as settled, without costs, and on the merits.

(b) Settlements of Actions on Behalf of Infants or Incompetents.

(1) An action by or on behalf of an infant or an incompetent shall not be settled or compromised, voluntarily discontinued, dismissed or terminated without leave of court. The proceeding upon an application to settle or compromise such an action shall conform, as nearly as possible to Sections 1207 and 1208 of New York's Civil Practice Law and Rules, but the Judge, for cause shown, may dispense with any New York State requirement.

(2) The Judge shall determine whether such application requires a hearing and whether the presence of the infant or incompetent together with his or her legal representative is required at such hearing.

(3) The Judge shall authorize payment of a reasonable attorney's fee and proper disbursements from the amount recovered in such an action, whether realized by settlement, execution or otherwise, and shall determine such fee and disbursements, after due inquiry as to all charges against the fund.

(4) The Judge shall order the balance of the proceeds of the settlement or recovery to be distributed pursuant to Section 1206 of New York's Civil Practice Law and Rules, or upon good cause shown, pursuant to such plan as the Judge deems necessary to protect the interests of the infant or incompetent.

(c) Settlements of Actions Brought on Behalf of Decedents' Estates.

(1) Actions brought on behalf of decedents' estates shall not be settled or compromised, or voluntarily discontinued, dismissed or terminated, without leave of court. The application to settle or compromise shall include a signed affidavit or petition by the estate representative and a signed affidavit of the representative's attorney addressing the following:

(A) the circumstances giving rise to the claim;

(B) the nature and extent of the damages;

(C) the terms of the proposed settlement, including the attorneys' fees and disbursements to be paid out of the settlement;

(D) the circumstances of any other claims or settlements arising out of the same occurrence; and

(E) the reasons why the proposed settlement is believed to be in the best interests of the estate and distributees.

(2) Counsel shall submit a proposed order approving the settlement.

(3) The Judge shall determine whether a hearing to determine the application is necessary.

(4) After approval of the settlement, attorneys' fees and disbursements, the Judge shall direct the estate representative to make application to the appropriate Surrogate of the State of New York or analogous jurist of another state for an order of distribution of the net proceeds of the settlement pursuant to either Section 5-4.4 of New York's Estate Powers and Trusts Law or the analogous provision of the law of the appropriate state.

RULE 41.2 DISMISSAL FOR FAILURE TO PROSECUTE

(a) If a civil case has been pending for more than six months and is not in compliance with the directions of the Judge or a Magistrate Judge, or if no action has been taken by the parties in six months, the Clerk, upon the direction of the assigned Judge, shall issue a written order to the parties to show cause within thirty days why the case should not be dismissed for failure to prosecute. The parties shall respond to the order by sworn affidavits filed with the Clerk explaining in detail why the action should not be dismissed. They need not appear in person. No explanations communicated in person, over the telephone, or by letter shall be acceptable.

(b) If the parties fail to respond as required in section (a), the Judge may issue a written order dismissing the case for failure to prosecute or providing for sanctions or making other directives to the parties as justice requires.

RULE 47.1 JURY TRIALS— CIVIL ACTIONS

(a) The jury in a civil case shall consist of no fewer than six and not more than twelve members. All verdicts shall be by unanimous vote of the jurors unless all parties stipulate otherwise.

(b) Challenges shall be permitted as provided in 28 U.S.C. § 1870 and Federal Rule of Civil Procedure 47(b). The Court may for good cause excuse a juror from service during trial or deliberation, but no verdict shall be taken from a jury reduced in size to fewer than six members unless so stipulated by the parties.

(c) Unless otherwise ordered, interrogation of prospective jurors on voir dire examination shall be conducted by the Court. Counsel may submit proposed questions in writing to the Judge or Magistrate Judge prior to or during the voir dire examination. The Judge or Magistrate Judge in his or her discretion also may permit questions to be submitted orally.

(d) In a civil case in which a jury trial has been properly demanded, the jury may be selected by either the panel method or the struck method as determined by the Court.

(e) The method for selecting the jury pursuant to the panel method shall be as follows:

(1) The deputy will at random call names from the available panel and direct those persons to be seated in the jury box in the order in which they are called. The total number to be seated shall be determined by the Court.

(2) The Court will conduct voir dire in accordance with Local Rule of Civil Procedure 47.1(c). If counsel are permitted voir dire, counsel may question the jury at this time.

(3) The Court will excuse any prospective jurors for cause where appropriate, acting either sua sponte or upon application of a party, and replace them with new prospective jurors.

(4) When the Court has determined that none of the prospective jurors in the jury box should be dismissed for cause, the parties may exercise their peremptory challenges.

(5) Each side in a civil case may exercise or waive three peremptory challenges, pursuant to 28 U.S.C. § 1870. These challenges shall be exercised in three rounds, one challenge for each side in each round. If a challenge is not exercised by either party for that round, it is waived. After each round of challenges is exercised, the Clerk shall call names from the panel to replace the challenged jurors. After new jurors are seated, the procedure in Local Rule of Civil Procedure 47.1(e)(2)–(5) shall be repeated. At any time before the panel is sworn, a party may exercise a challenge as to any juror seated in the box.

(6) After all parties have exercised all of their challenges, the jury shall be sworn.

(f) The method for selecting a jury pursuant to the struck system shall be as follows:

(1) The deputy will call at random from the panel a number of prospective jurors equal to the total number of all jurors and all peremptory challenges for all parties in the action. Those persons will be seated in the jury box in the order they are called.

(2) The Court will conduct voir dire in accordance with Local Rule of Civil Procedure 47.1(c). If counsel are permitted voir dire, counsel may question the jury at this time.

(3) The Court will excuse any prospective jurors for cause where appropriate, acting either sua sponte or

upon application of a party, and replace them with new prospective jurors.

(4) When the Court has determined that none of the prospective jurors in the jury box should be dismissed for cause, the parties may exercise their peremptory challenges.

(5) Each side in a civil case may exercise or waive three peremptory challenges pursuant to 18 U.S.C. § 1870. These challenges shall be exercised in rounds, one challenge for each side in each round. No further jurors will be called to replace those jurors excused by peremptory challenges. At the conclusion of the parties' rounds, the Court shall announce those jurors who shall constitute the jury, and they shall be sworn.

(g) In a case with multiple defendants, the attorneys for defendants shall confer and jointly exercise their peremptory challenges. No additional peremptory challenges shall be provided solely because the case involves more than one defendant.

RULE 47.2   JURORS

Selection of petit jurors is made by random selection pursuant to the most recently-adopted Jury Selection Plan for the Western District of New York as approved by the Second Circuit Judicial Council. A copy of the Plan is available in the Clerk's office or on the Court's website at www.nywd.uscourts.gov.

RULE 54.   COSTS

(a) Within thirty days after entry of final judgment, a party entitled to recover costs shall submit to the Clerk, upon forms provided by the Clerk, a verified bill of costs. Upon motion filed within five days after the costs are taxed, the Clerk's action may be reviewed by the Court.

(b) Subject to the provisions of Federal Rule of Civil Procedure 54(d)(1), the expense of any party in obtaining all or any part of a transcript for the use of the Court when ordered by it, the expense of any party in necessarily obtaining all or any part of a transcript for the purposes of a new trial, or for amended findings, or for appeals, shall be a taxable cost against the unsuccessful party at the rates prescribed by the Judicial Conference of the United States.

(c) If a party proceeds in accordance with Local Rule of Civil Procedure 30 to record a deposition by stenographic means and video tape, any additional costs incurred in recording the deposition on video tape will not be taxed by the Clerk without a prior order from the Court allowing, or upon the agreement of the parties for taxation of, such costs.

(d) Unless otherwise ordered by the District Court, or Circuit Court of Appeals pursuant to Federal Rule of Appellate Procedure 8, the filing of an appeal shall not stay the taxation of costs, entry of judgment thereon, or enforcement of such judgment.

[Amended effective May 1, 2003.]

RULE 55. DEFAULT JUDGMENT

(a) By the Clerk. A party entitled to entry of default by the Clerk, pursuant to Federal Rule of Civil Procedure 55(b)(1), shall submit with the form of judgment a statement showing the principal amount due, which shall not exceed the amount demanded in the complaint, giving credit for any payments and showing the amounts and dates thereof, a computation of the interest to the day of judgment, and the costs and taxable disbursements claimed. The proposed judgment shall contain the last known address of each of the judgment creditors and judgment debtors. If there is no known address for any judgment creditor or judgment debtor, an affidavit executed by either the party at whose instance a judgment is docketed or the party's attorney shall be filed stating that the affiant has no knowledge of an address. An affidavit of the party or his or her attorney shall be appended to the statement showing:

(1) that the party against whom judgment is sought is not an infant or an incompetent person;

(2) that the party has defaulted in appearance in the action;

(3) that the amount shown by the statement is justly due and owing and that no part thereof has been paid except as therein set forth; and

(4) that the disbursements sought to be taxed have been made in the action or will necessarily be made or incurred therein.

The Clerk shall thereupon enter judgment for principal, interest and costs.

(b) By the Court. An application to the Court for the entry of a default judgment, pursuant to Federal Rule of Civil Procedure 55(b)(2), shall be accompanied by a Clerk's certificate noting the entry of the default and by a copy of the pleading to which no response has been made.

RULE 56.1 STATEMENTS OF FACTS ON MOTION FOR SUMMARY JUDGMENT

(a) Upon any motion for summary judgment, pursuant to Rule 56 of the Federal Rules of Civil Procedure, there shall be annexed to the notice of motion a separate, short, and concise statement of the material facts as to which the moving party contends there is no genuine issue to be tried. Failure to submit such a statement may constitute grounds for denial of the motion.

(b) The papers opposing a motion for summary judgment shall include a separate, short, and concise statement of the material facts as to which it is contended that there exists a genuine issue to be tried.

(c) All material facts set forth in the statement required to be served by the moving party will be deemed to be admitted unless controverted by the statement required to be served by the opposing party.

(d) Each statement of material fact by a movant or opponent must be followed by citation to evidence which would be admissible, as required by Federal Rule of Civil Procedure 56(e). All such citations shall identify with specificity the relevant page, and paragraph or line number of the authority cited. All cited authority, such as affidavits, relevant deposition testimony, responses to discovery requests, or other documents containing such evidence, shall be separately filed and served as an appendix to the statement prescribed by subsections (a) or (b), supra, in conformity with Federal Rule of Civil Procedure 56(e), and denominated "Plaintiff's/Defendant's Appendix to Local Rule 56.1 Statement of Material Facts." Any cited authority that has otherwise been served and filed in conjunction with the motion need not be included in the aforementioned appendix.

(e) Notwithstanding the provisions of Local Rule 7.1(c), the opposing party shall have thirty days after service of the motion, unless otherwise ordered by the Court, to serve and file responding papers; the moving party shall have fifteen days after service of the responding papers, unless otherwise ordered by the Court, to serve and file reply papers. Absent permission by the Court, surreply papers are not permitted.

In the event that the party opposing the original motion files a cross-motion, the original moving party shall have thirty days after service of the cross-motion, unless otherwise ordered by the Court, to serve and file responding papers in opposition to the cross-motion; the party that filed the cross-motion shall have fifteen days after service of the responding papers, unless otherwise ordered by the Court, to serve and file reply papers in support of the cross-motion.

[Amended effective May 1, 2003.]

RULE 56.2 NOTICE TO PRO SE LITIGANTS OPPOSING SUMMARY JUDGMENT

Any party moving for summary judgment against a party proceeding pro se shall serve and file as a separate document, together with the papers in support of the motion, a "Notice to Pro Se Litigant Opposing Motion For Summary Judgment" in the form indicated below. Where the pro se party is not the plaintiff, the movant shall amend the form notice as necessary to reflect that fact.

Notice to Pro Se Litigant Opposing Motion For Summary Judgment.

Plaintiff is hereby advised that the defendant has asked the Court to decide this case without a trial, based on written materials, including affidavits, submitted in support of the motion. THE CLAIMS PLAINTIFF ASSERTS IN HIS/HER COMPLAINT MAY BE DISMISSED WITHOUT A TRIAL IF HE/SHE DOES NOT RESPOND TO THIS MOTION by filing his/her own sworn affidavits or other papers as required by Rule 56(e). An affidavit is a sworn statement of fact based on personal knowledge that would be admissible in evidence at trial.

In short, Rule 56 provides that plaintiff may NOT oppose summary judgment simply by relying upon the allegations in the complaint. Rather, plaintiff must submit evidence, such as witness statements or documents, countering the facts asserted by the defendant and raising issues of fact for trial. Any witness statements, which may include plaintiff's own statements, must be in the form of affidavits. Plaintiff may file and serve affidavits that were prepared specifically in response to defendant's motion for summary judgment.

Any issue of fact that plaintiff wishes to raise in opposition to the motion for summary judgment must be supported by affidavits or by other documentary evidence contradicting the facts asserted by defendant. If plaintiff does not respond to the motion for summary judgment on time with affidavits or documentary evidence contradicting the facts asserted by defendant, the Court may accept defendant's factual assertions as true. Judgment may then be entered in defendant's favor without a trial.

Pursuant to Rules 7.1(e) and 56.1 of the Local Rules of Civil Procedure for the Western District of New York, plaintiff is required to file and serve the following papers in opposition to this motion: (1) a memorandum of law containing relevant factual and legal argument; (2) one or more affidavits in opposition to the motion; and (3) a separate, short, and concise statement of the material facts as to which plaintiff contends there exists a genuine issue to be tried, followed by citation to admissible evidence. In the absence of such a statement by plaintiff, all material facts set forth in defendant's statement of material facts not in dispute will be deemed admitted. A copy of the Local Rules to which reference has been made may be obtained from the Clerk's Office of the Court.

If plaintiff has any questions, he/she may direct them to the Pro Se Office.

Plaintiff must file and serve any supplemental affidavits or materials in opposition to defendant's motion no later than the date they are due as provided in Rule 56.1(e) of the Local Rules of Civil Procedure for the Western District of New York.

[Adopted effective May 1, 2003.]

RULE 58.　SATISFACTION OF JUDGMENTS

Satisfaction of a money judgment recovered or registered in this District shall be entered by the Clerk as follows:

(a) Upon the payment of the judgment into the registry of the Court, but such payment may only be made pursuant to a prior order of the Court authorizing such payment;

(b) Upon the filing of a satisfaction executed and acknowledged by:

(1) the judgment creditor; or

(2) his or her legal representatives or assigns, with evidence of their authority; or

(3) his or her attorney, if within five years of the entry of the judgment or decree.

(c) If the judgment creditor is the United States, upon the filing of a satisfaction executed by the United States Attorney; or

(d) Upon the registration of a certified copy of a satisfaction entered in another District.

RULE 65.　TEMPORARY RESTRAINING ORDERS AND PRELIMINARY INJUNCTIONS

(a) Temporary Restraining Orders (TRO). An Order to Show Cause is not generally available under the Federal Rules of Civil Procedure. Such relief is available upon motion for a TRO, pursuant to Federal Rule of Civil Procedure 65, and a motion for an expedited hearing, pursuant to Local Rule of Civil Procedure 7.1(d) and Federal Rule of Civil Procedure 6(d). There are two types of TROs: an ex parte TRO and a TRO issued upon notice to the adverse party. An ex parte TRO is available only in extraordinary circumstances. In most cases, the Court will require both notice to the adverse party and an opportunity to be heard before granting a TRO.

(1) *Ex Parte TRO.* A party seeking an ex parte TRO must demonstrate that the requirements of Fed. R. Civ. P. 65(b)(1) and (2) are met. An application for an ex parte TRO shall include:

(A) a copy of the complaint, if the case has been recently filed;

(B) the motion for a TRO;

(C) a memorandum of law in support of the TRO citing legal authority showing that the party is entitled to the relief requested; and

(D) a proposed order granting the TRO.

Immediately after filing the TRO application with the Clerk's office, counsel for the moving party shall personally deliver courtesy copies of the foregoing documents to chambers and await further instructions from the Court. In the event that the moving party is represented by out-of-town counsel who is unable to personally deliver courtesy copies, counsel shall mail such courtesy copies directly to chambers and shall contact chambers by telephone to request a waiver of this requirement. Because an application for a TRO will rarely by granted ex parte, a party moving under this subsection should consider appearing prepared to proceed pursuant to subsection (2) below, in the event that the Court finds that an ex parte proceeding is unwarranted.

(2) *TRO on Notice.* An application for a TRO on notice shall include:

(A) a copy of the complaint, if the case has been recently filed;

(B) the motion for a TRO;

(C) a memorandum of law in support of the TRO citing legal authority showing that the party is entitled to the relief requested;

(D) a proposed order granting the TRO; and

(E) a motion for an expedited hearing pursuant to Local Rule of Civil Procedure 7.1(d) and Federal Rule of Civil Procedure 6(d).

Immediately after filing the TRO application with the Clerk's office, counsel for the moving party shall personally deliver courtesy copies of the foregoing documents to chambers and await further instructions from the Court. In the event that the moving party is represented by out of town counsel who is unable to personally deliver courtesy copies, counsel shall mail such courtesy copies directly to chambers and shall contact chambers by telephone to request a waiver of this requirement.

(b) Preliminary Injunction. A preliminary injunction will only issue after notice and hearing, unless there is a waiver. An application for a preliminary injunction shall include:

(1) a copy of the complaint, if the case has been recently filed;

(2) the motion for a preliminary injunction;

(3) a memorandum of law in support of the motion citing legal authority showing that the moving party is entitled to the relief requested;

(4) a list of witnesses and exhibits to be presented at the preliminary injunction hearing, and a brief summary of the anticipated testimony of such witnesses; and

(5) a proposed order granting the injunctive relief.

Additionally, if the moving party seeks to have the motion heard on an expedited basis, such party shall include a motion for an expedited hearing pursuant to Local Rule of Civil Procedure 7.1(d) and Federal Rule of Civil Procedure 6(d).

(c) Security. The parties shall be prepared to address the security requirements of Federal Rule of Civil Procedure 65(c) whenever applying for injunctive relief.

[Adopted effective May 1, 2003.]

RULE 67. DEPOSITS OF MONEY INTO COURT

(a) General Orders Regarding Funds. The Court's directions to the Clerk regarding (1) the investment of monies placed in the custody of the Court or of the Clerk and (2) the assessment of court fees against such monies are contained in various General Orders of the Court and amendments thereto, available in the Clerk's offices.

(b) Monies Deposited Without a Special Order. Whenever money is permitted by statute or rule to be deposited into Court without leave of Court (e.g. in condemnation proceedings governed by Federal Rule of Civil Procedure 71A(j)) or is directed by the Court to be deposited as a condition to some form of relief (e.g. cash bail, cash bonds), General Orders shall govern the investment of such funds upon their receipt by the Clerk.

(c) Monies Deposited With a Special Order. Whenever statute or rule requires that leave of court be obtained for the deposit of money into the Court (e.g. Federal Rule of Civil Procedure 67), an order shall be promptly filed with the Clerk. If, and to the extent that, any such order fails to instruct the Clerk as to the handling of such funds, they shall be handled in accordance with the aforesaid General Orders.

(d) Court Fees. Such fees are promulgated and required by the Judicial Conference of the United States pursuant to 28 U.S.C. § 1914(b).

(e) Alternatives. Parties and others are encouraged to consider alternatives which do not involve the receipt of monies by the Clerk, such as escrow accounts, joint signature accounts in the names of counsel, and letters of credit. Such alternatives avoid the imposition of court fees and may provide greater flexibility to maximize yield for the benefit of the parties.

[Amended effective May 1, 2003.]

RULE 72.1 AUTHORITY OF MAGISTRATE JUDGES

(a) A full-time United States Magistrate Judge is authorized to exercise all powers and perform all duties conferred upon Magistrate Judges by 28 U.S.C. § 636(a), (b) and (c).

(b) Notwithstanding any other rule of this Court, a United States Magistrate Judge may be assigned such additional duties as are not inconsistent with the Constitution or laws of the United States.

RULE 72.2 ASSIGNMENT OF MATTERS TO MAGISTRATE JUDGES

(a) Upon filing, all civil cases shall be assigned by the Clerk to a District Judge and a Magistrate Judge. The District Judge to whom the case is assigned may designate the Magistrate Judge to conduct pre-trial procedures pursuant to Local Rule of Civil Procedure 16.1.

(b)(1) *Notice.* Upon the filing of a complaint, the Clerk shall provide to plaintiff or his or her representative, a notice, as approved by the Court, informing the parties of the availability of a Magistrate Judge to conduct any or all proceedings in the case and order the entry of a final judgment. Additional copies of the notice may be furnished to the parties at later stages of the proceedings and may be included with pre-trial notices and instructions. The decision of the parties shall be communicated to the Clerk of the Court. Thereafter, either the District Judge or the Magistrate Judge may again advise the parties of the availability of the Magistrate Judge, but in so doing, shall also advise the parties that they are free to withhold consent without adverse substantive consequences. This rule, however, shall not preclude a District Judge or Magistrate Judge from both informing the parties that they have the option of referring a case to a Magistrate Judge in accord with this rule and reminding the parties of such option, as appropriate throughout the progress of the case. The consent may be executed at any time prior to trial, subject to the approval of the District Judge to whom the case has been assigned.

(2) *Execution of Consent.*

(A) For cases in which the parties are represented by counsel, the Clerk shall not accept a consent form unless it has been signed by all of the parties or their attorneys in the case. The plaintiff shall be responsible for submitting such consent form, executed by all parties, to the Clerk of the Court.

(B) For cases in which one or more of the parties is proceeding pro se, the Clerk shall send a consent form to each of the parties. All parties are required to complete and return the form pursuant to the instructions thereon.

(3) *Reference.* After the consent form has been executed and submitted, the Clerk shall transmit it to the District Judge to whom the case has been assigned for approval and referral of the case to a Magistrate Judge. Once the case has been assigned to a Magistrate Judge, the Magistrate Judge shall have the authority to conduct any and all proceedings to which the parties have consented and to direct the Clerk to enter a final judgment in the same manner as if a District Judge had presided.

(4) *Additional Parties.* Any parties added to an action after reference to a Magistrate Judge shall be notified by the Clerk of their rights to consent to the exercise of jurisdiction by the Magistrate Judge and of their appellate rights pursuant to 28 U.S.C. § 636(c)(3), (4) and (5). In the event an added party does not consent to the Magistrate Judge's jurisdiction, the action shall be returned to the District Judge for further proceedings.

[Amended effective May 1, 2003.]

RULE 72.3 REVIEW AND APPEAL OF MAGISTRATE JUDGES' ACTIONS

(a) Review.

(1) Review of a Magistrate Judge's orders or of his or her proposed findings of fact and recommendations for disposition shall be governed by 28 U.S.C. § 636(b)(1). If the parties consent to trial before the Magistrate Judge, there shall be no review or appeal of interlocutory orders to the District Court.

(2) All orders of the Magistrate Judge issued pursuant to these rules, as authorized by 28 U.S.C. § 636(b)(1)(A), shall be final unless within ten days after being served with a copy of the Magistrate Judge's order, a party files with the Clerk and serves upon opposing counsel a written statement specifying the party's objections to the Magistrate Judge's order. The specific matters to which the party objects and the manner in which it is claimed that the order is clearly erroneous or contrary to law shall be clearly set out.

(3) A party may object to proposed findings of fact and recommendations for disposition submitted by a Magistrate Judge pursuant to 28 U.S.C. § 636(b)(1)(B), by filing with the Clerk and serving upon opposing counsel written objections to the proposed findings and recommendations within ten days after being served with a copy of such findings and recommendations, as provided in 28 U.S.C. § 636(b)(1)(C). The time for filing objections to the proposed findings and recommendations may be extended by direction of the District Judge. The written objections shall specifically identify the portions of the proposed findings and recommendations to which objection is made and the basis for such objection and shall be supported by legal authority.

(b) Appeal from Judgments in Civil Cases (28 U.S.C. § 636(c)(1)). Upon entry of a judgment in any civil case on consent of the parties under authority of 28 U.S.C. § 636(c)(1) and Local Rule of Civil Procedure 72.2(b), a party shall appeal directly to the United States Court of Appeals for the Second Circuit in the same manner as an appeal from any other judgment of this Court.

(c) Appeals from Other Orders of a Magistrate Judge. Appeals from any other decisions and orders of a Magistrate Judge not provided for in this rule shall be taken as provided by governing statute, rule or decisional law.

[Amended effective May 1, 2003.]

RULE 76.1 APPEALS

(a) Appellant shall file a notice of appeal in accordance with Federal Rule of Appellate Procedure 3. Such notice of appeal shall include the names of the parties to the judgment and the names and addresses of their respective attorneys of record.

(b) In addition to the original notice of appeal, appellant shall file sufficient copies to serve all counsel and the Clerk of the Circuit Court of Appeals.

(c) Counsel share the responsibility of preparing the index for the record on appeal. Upon completion, the index shall be presented to the Clerk for transmittal to the United States Court of Appeals for the Second Circuit or to the United States Supreme Court.

(d) Counsel shall, wherever possible and consistent with the Federal Rules of Appellate Procedure, stipulate to the designation of less than the entire trial record.

(e) Counsel are cautioned to examine and follow both the Federal Rules of Appellate Procedure and the Rules of the United States Court of Appeals for the Second Circuit.

RULE 76.2 BANKRUPTCY APPEALS; DISMISSAL FOR FAILURE TO PERFECT

If the appellant shall fail to perfect the appeal in the manner prescribed by Federal Rule of Bankruptcy Procedure 8006, the Clerk of the Bankruptcy Court shall forward to the Clerk of the District Court the notice of appeal, a copy of the order or judgment appealed from, a copy of the docket entries and such other papers as the Clerk of the Bankruptcy Court deems relevant to the appeal. When the partial record has been filed in the District Court, the Court may, upon motion of the appellee filed with the District Court or upon its own initiative, dismiss the appeal for non-compliance with Federal Rule of Bankruptcy Procedure 8006.

RULE 77.1 SESSIONS OF COURT

Regular and continuous sessions of the Court shall be held at Buffalo and Rochester.

Special sessions of Court may be held at such places in the District and for such periods of time as may be practicable and as the nature of the Court's business may require.

RULE 77.2 ORDERS

Orders of discontinuance or dismissal, whether by consent or otherwise, shall be presented to the Court for signature, except such orders listed herein which the Clerk may sign without submission to a Judge:

(1) Orders on consent for the substitution of attorneys in civil cases not yet scheduled for trial; and

(2) Orders on consent satisfying decrees and orders on consent canceling stipulations and bonds.

After the Court has instructed a prevailing party to submit an order, the prevailing party shall submit to the Court a proposed order which has been approved by opposing counsel and which contains the endorsement of opposing counsel: "Approved as to form and substance."

RULE 77.3 COPIES OF LOCAL RULES

Copies of these rules, and the amendments and appendices to them, shall be available upon request in the offices of the Clerk of Court in both Rochester and Buffalo. These rules are also available on the Court's website at www.nywd.uscourts.gov. Persons other than litigants who are permitted to proceed in forma pauperis in a pending case seeking to obtain a copy of these rules by mail must provide a self-addressed envelope of at least 9″ × 12″ in size with sufficient postage affixed.

RULE 77.4 COPIES OF ORDERS

The Clerk shall provide one copy of every order entered, together with notice thereof, to each law firm representing one or more parties to, or non-party movants in, the action.

[Adopted effective May 1, 2003.]

RULE 78. MOTIONS

Unless otherwise ordered by the Court:

(a) Motions and hearings on all contested matters shall be heard on the dates and times set by each individual Judge in the Western District of New York. Information regarding such dates and times may be obtained from the Clerk's office.

(b) If the Judge assigned to hold the Court shall be absent, the Clerk of the Court shall adjourn the hearings on motions or applications to some convenient day.

(c) All motions and notice thereof shall be governed by the Federal Rules of Civil Procedure. Original motion papers shall be filed in the Clerk's office, either at the United States Courthouse, Buffalo, New York or at the United States Courthouse, Rochester, New York. Refer to Local Rule of Civil Procedure 7.1 for more information on filing motion papers.

(d) Except as provided in subdivision (e), any application for adjournment of a motion shall be made by the attorney, or by an associate, to the Judge before whom the motion is to be argued. Such application shall be made to the Judge's courtroom deputy and not to the Judge's law clerk. In requesting an adjournment, the following guidelines shall be adhered to:

(1) The party seeking the adjournment shall first confer with all other parties before approaching the courtroom deputy;

(2) A suggested rescheduled date, agreeable to all parties, shall be determined, if possible; and

(3) The party seeking the adjournment shall notify the courtroom deputy in writing, unless unforeseen circumstances prohibit written notice, of the request and the suggested new date.

(e) Requests for adjournments by pro se litigants must be made in writing, by letter to the Court, with copies to all other counsel in the case.

[Amended effective May 1, 2003.]

RULE 79. EXHIBITS

(a) Prior to the beginning of a trial, the exhibits shall be marked and exhibit lists prepared as the Court directs.

(b) All exhibits offered by any party in civil or criminal proceedings, whether or not received as evidence, shall be retained after each day of trial by the party or attorney offering the exhibits, unless otherwise ordered by the Court. Immediately after the case is submitted to the trier of fact, all exhibits which were received into evidence shall be delivered to the courtroom deputy. After a verdict is rendered, responsibility for custody of all exhibits reverts back to the parties.

(c) In the event an appeal is prosecuted by any party, each party to the appeal shall promptly file with the Clerk any exhibits to be transmitted to the appellate court as part of the record on appeal. Documents of unusual bulk or weight and physical exhibits, other than documents, shall remain in the custody of the attorney producing them who shall permit their inspection by any party for the purpose of preparing the record on appeal and who shall be charged with the responsibility for their safekeeping and transportation to the Court of Appeals. Those exhibits not transmit-

ted as part of the record on appeal shall be retained by the parties who shall make them available for use by the appellate court upon request.

(d) If any party, having received notice from the Clerk concerning the removal of exhibits, fails to do so within thirty days from the date of such notice, the Clerk may destroy or otherwise dispose of those exhibits.

[Amended effective May 1, 2003.]

RULE 81. REMOVED ACTIONS

(a) Required Documents in Cases Removed from State Court. A party removing a civil action from State court to this Court must provide the following to the Clerk for filing:

(1) A completed civil cover sheet;

(2) The requisite filing fee; and

(3) A notice of removal with the following attachments:

    (A) An index of all documents which clearly identifies each document and indicates the date the document was filed in State court; and

    (B) Each document filed in the State court action, except discovery material, individually tabbed and arranged in chronological order according to the State court file date.

(4) The party filing the notice of removal or a designee shall declare, by affidavit or certification, that he or she has provided all other parties in the action with the notice of removal and attachments being filed with this Court.

(b) Jury Demands in Removed Actions. In any action removed to this Court from the courts of the State of New York, a party entitled to a trial by jury under Federal Rule of Civil Procedure 38 shall be afforded a jury trial if a demand is filed and served as provided by Federal Rule of Civil Procedure 81(c).

[Adopted effective May 1, 2003.]

RULE 83.1 ATTORNEY ADMISSION TO PRACTICE

(a) Who May Apply. A person admitted to practice before the courts of New York State, including those admitted pursuant to Rule 520.11 of the Rules of the New York Court of Appeals, may, on motion of a member of the bar of this Court, apply to be admitted to practice in this Court upon compliance with the following provisions of this rule. Qualification to appear as an attorney of record remains subject to Local Rule of Civil Procedure 83.2.

(b) Verified Petition. Each applicant for admission shall file with the Clerk of this Court at least thirty days prior to a hearing thereon (unless for good cause shown the Court shortens the time) a verified petition for admission stating:

(1) the applicant's residence and office addresses;

(2) the applicant's educational background and major areas of professional activities since initial admission to the bar;

(3) the time, place and court where initially admitted;

(4) whether the applicant has ever been held in contempt of court, or censured in a disciplinary proceeding, suspended or disbarred by any court or admonished by any disciplinary committee of the organized bar, or is the subject of any pending complaint before any court. If the answer is in the affirmative, the applicant shall file a separate confidential statement under seal specifying the court or disciplinary committee imposing the sanction, the date, the facts giving rise to the disciplinary action or complaint, the sanction imposed, and such other information, including any facts of a mitigating or exculpatory nature as may be pertinent, and such confidential statement, together with the petition, shall promptly be transmitted by the Clerk to the Chief Judge of the District for review;

(5) that the applicant has read and is familiar with:

(A) the provisions of the Judicial Code, 28 U.S.C. §§ 1330–1452, which pertain to jurisdiction of and venue in a United States District Court;

(B) the Federal Rules of Civil Procedure;

(C) the Federal Rules of Criminal Procedure;

(D) the Federal Rules of Evidence;

(E) the Local Rules of Practice for the United States District Court for the Western District of New York;

(F) the Revised Plan for the Prompt Disposition of Criminal Cases for the Western District of New York;

(G) the New York State Lawyer's Code of Professional Responsibility as adopted from time to time by the Appellate Divisions of the State of New York, and as interpreted and applied by the United States Supreme Court, the United States Court of Appeals for the Second Circuit, and this court; and

(H) the Civility Principles of the United States District Court for the Western District of New York.

(6) that the applicant agrees to adhere faithfully to the New York State Lawyer's Code of Professional Responsibility as adopted from time to time by the Appellate Divisions of the State of New York.

(c) Time for Admissions. Applications for admission shall be entertained on the scheduled motion days in Rochester and Buffalo, or on other days deemed appropriate by the Court.

(d) Affidavit of Sponsoring Attorney. The verified petition shall be accompanied by an affidavit of an attorney of this Court stating when the affiant was admitted to practice in this Court, how long and under what circumstances the affiant has known the applicant, and what the affiant knows of the applicant's character.

(e) Attorneys Admitted to Other Districts Within the State. A member in good standing of the bar of the United States District Court for the Southern, Eastern or Northern District of New York may be admitted to practice in this Court without formal application upon filing with this Court a certificate of the United States District Court for such District stating that he or she is a member in good standing of the bar of that Court, together with a completed attorney's oath and the proper fee. The certificate of good standing must be dated no earlier than six months prior to the date of submission to this Court.

(f) Attorneys Admitted to Districts Outside the State. A member in good standing of any United States District Court and of the bar of the state in which such District Court is located may apply to be admitted to practice in this Court on compliance with the provisions of parts (b), (c), (d), (g) and (l) of this rule.

(g) Oath, Pro Bono Service. Prior to being admitted to this Court, each applicant must take the oath of admission to this Court. Every member of the bar of this Court shall be available upon the Court's request for appointment to represent or assist in the representation of indigent parties. Appointments under this rule shall be made in a manner such that no attorney shall be requested to accept more than one appointment during any twelve month period.

(h) Change of Address, Etc. All attorneys admitted to practice before this Court must advise the Clerk in writing of any change in name, firm affiliation, office address or telephone number within thirty days of such change. Additionally, counsel must identify those pending cases on which he or she will remain counsel of record. The standard form for notifying the Clerk is available in both Clerk's offices or on the Court's website at *www.nywd.uscourts.gov*.

(i) Admission Pro Hac Vice. An attorney duly admitted to practice in any state, territory, district or foreign country may in the discretion of the Court be admitted *pro hac vice* to participate before the Court in any matter in which he or she may for the time be employed. Applicants for admission *pro hac vice* must provide the Court with information sufficient to satisfy all subparts of subdivision (b) of this rule. Attorneys admitted *pro hac vice* are subject to the provisions of Local Rule of Civil Procedure 83.2(a) regarding local counsel.

(j) Government Attorneys. United States Attorneys, Assistant United States Attorneys, special attorneys appointed under 28 U.S.C. §§ 541–543, attorneys of the Department of Justice under 28 U.S.C. § 515, attorneys serving as Federal Public Defenders or Assistant Federal Public Defenders and attorneys employed by a federal agency, shall be admitted to practice before the Court on any matter within the scope of such employment.

(k) Admission to Practice in Bankruptcy Matters. Practice in bankruptcy matters before either the District Judges or the Bankruptcy Judges of this District shall be limited to attorneys admitted under this rule, subsections (a)-(j). Such attorney shall certify knowledge of such sources and provisions of bankruptcy law and rule as the Bankruptcy Court shall require by local rule approved by this Court. The "local counsel" requirement of Rule 83.2 shall not apply in bankruptcy matters unless otherwise directed by a District Judge or Bankruptcy Judge in a specific matter. This subsection of this rule shall not apply to a student admitted under the Student Practice Rule of the Bankruptcy Court.

(l) Fees for Admission. Each applicant for admission to this Court shall pay the fee set by the Judicial Conference plus an additional fee set by the Court. Attorneys who are admitted *pro hac vice* shall pay to the Clerk a fee in the amount set by the Court unless such fee is waived by the presiding Judge or Magistrate Judge upon a showing of good cause. Applicants for admission should contact the Clerk's office for exact fee information. A portion of the fee charged to applicants for admission to practice before the Court and to attorneys admitted *pro hac vice* shall be deposited in the District Court Fund.

The Clerk shall be the trustee of the District Court Fund. Monies deposited in the District Court Fund shall be used only for the benefit of the bench and bar in the administration of justice, including, but not limited to, reimbursement of expenses incurred by counsel assigned to represent indigent clients pursuant to the provisions of this rule.

(m) Expenses of Assigned Counsel. *Pro bono* attorneys who are appointed pursuant to this rule and are unsuccessful in obtaining counsel fees may seek reimbursement for expenses incident to representation of indigent clients by application to the Court. Reimbursement will be permitted to the extent possible in light of available resources and pursuant to the Plan for the Administration of the District Court Fund on file with the Clerk.

(n) Civility Principles. Each applicant for admission must complete the oath attached to the Court's Civility Principles. The completed oath must be submitted with the admission application. This requirement applies to all attorneys seeking admission to the bar of this Court, whether by petition, certificate of good standing or *pro hac vice*.

[Amended effective May 1, 2003.]

RULE 83.2　ATTORNEYS OF RECORD— APPEARANCE AND WITHDRAWAL

(a) Except as set forth below, only members in good standing of the bar of this Court may appear as attorneys of record.

An attorney who does not maintain an office in this District may appear in an action, and, as appropriate, such attorney shall apply for admission pro hac vice pursuant to Local Rule of Civil Procedure 83.1. Such attorney, whether or not admitted to practice in this District, shall obtain local counsel unless such requirement is waived by the Court. An application to proceed without local counsel must be made in writing within thirty days of the attorney's initial filing and shall be granted for good cause shown and in the discretion of the Court.

(1) Except for attorneys appearing on behalf of the United States government or a department or agency thereof, or as otherwise provided in Local Rule of Civil Procedure 83.2(a), any attorney who is not a member of the bar of this Court shall, unless otherwise ordered by the Court, in each proceeding in which he or she desires to appear, have as associate counsel of record ("local counsel") a member of the bar of this Court who maintains an office within this District, with whom the Court and opposing counsel may readily communicate regarding the conduct of this case and upon whom papers may be served.

(2) In accord with Federal Rules of Civil Procedure 11 and 26(g), an attorney who is not a member of the bar of this Court may sign a pleading, motion, request for discovery, discovery response, objection thereto and other papers, provided local counsel has been appointed or the requirement thereof waived by the Court pursuant to Local Rule of Civil Procedure 83.2(a).

(3) An attorney who is not admitted to practice in this Court pursuant to Local Rule of Civil Procedure 83.1 shall not participate actively in the conduct of any trial or of any pre-trial or post-trial proceeding before this Court.

(b) An attorney appearing for a party in a civil case shall promptly file with the Clerk a written notice of appearance. No notice of appearance is required of an attorney whose name and address appear at the end of the complaint, notice of removal, pre-answer motion, or answer in a particular case.

(c) An attorney who has appeared as attorney of record for a party may withdraw by permission of the Court for good cause shown, but withdrawal shall be effective only upon order of the Court entered after service of notice of withdrawal on all counsel of record and on the attorney's client, or upon stipulation endorsed by all counsel of record and signed by the Clerk in accordance with Local Rule of Civil Procedure 77.2. An attorney is not required to disclose to other counsel the reason(s) for withdrawal.

[Amended effective May 1, 2003.]

RULE 83.3   DISCIPLINE OF ATTORNEYS

(a) In addition to any other sanctions imposed in any particular case under these local rules, any person admitted to practice in this Court may be disbarred or otherwise disciplined, for cause, after hearing. The Chief Judge of the District may appoint a Magistrate Judge or attorney(s) to investigate, advise or assist as to grievances or complaints from any source and as to applications by attorneys for relief from sanctions. Other than provided by subsections (b) and (c) of this rule, no censure, sanction, suspension or disbarment shall be applied without both notice and an opportunity to be heard and the approval of a majority of the District Judges of the Court in active and senior service, except that any Judge of this Court may for cause, revoke an admission pro hac vice previously granted by that Judge. Complaints or grievances, and any files based on them, shall be treated as confidential. Discipline shall be imposed only upon suitable order of the Court, which shall or shall not be made available to the public, or published or circulated, as the Court shall determine in its discretion.

(b)(1) Where the Court is informed that any attorney admitted to this Court has been convicted of a felony as defined in subsection (b)(3), the Chief Judge will issue an order suspending that attorney from practice before this Court. The order shall be sent to the last known business address of the attorney by certified mail. An application to set aside the order of suspension must be filed with the Court within thirty days from the issuance of the order. The Court, in its discretion, may consider the application on the papers submitted, schedule oral argument, or hold an evidentiary hearing. Upon good cause shown, a majority of the active and senior District Judges may set aside the suspension when it is in the interest of justice to do so.

(2) When the Court is informed that a judgment of conviction for a felony as defined in subsection (b)(3) is final, the name of the attorney convicted shall, by order of the Chief Judge, be struck from the roll of members of the bar of this Court. "Final" for purposes of this subsection means either that the time within which to appeal has lapsed or that the judgment of the conviction for a felony has been affirmed on direct appeal. The order of disbarment shall be sent to the last known business address of the attorney by certified mail. An application to set aside the order of disbarment must be filed with the Court within thirty days from the issuance of the order. The Court, in its discretion, may consider the application on the papers submitted, schedule oral argument, or hold an evidentiary hearing. Upon good cause

shown, a majority of the active and senior District Judges may set aside the disbarment when it is in the interest of justice to do so.

(3) For purposes of this subsection, the term felony shall mean any criminal offense classified as a felony under federal law; any criminal offense classified as a felony under New York law; or any criminal offense committed in any other state, commonwealth, or territory of the United States and classified as a felony therein which, if committed within New York State, would constitute a felony in New York State.

(c) Any attorney admitted to this Court who has been suspended, disbarred or disciplined in any way in any district, state, commonwealth or territory, or who has resigned from the bar of any such court while an investigation into allegations of misconduct by the attorney was pending, shall be disciplined to the same extent by this Court, as provided herein.

Upon receipt of a copy of an order imposing discipline on an attorney, the Chief Judge will issue an order disciplining the attorney to the same extent as imposed in the other jurisdiction. The order shall be sent to the last known business address of the attorney by certified mail. An application to set aside the order must be filed with the Court within thirty days from its issuance. The Court, in its discretion, may consider the application on the papers submitted, schedule oral argument, or hold an evidentiary hearing. A majority of the active and senior District Judges may set aside such order when an examination of the record resulting in that discipline discloses, by a clear and convincing evidence:

(1) that the procedure in the other jurisdiction was so lacking in notice or opportunity to be heard as to constitute a deprivation of due process;

(2) that there was such an infirmity of proof establishing the misconduct as to give rise to the clear conviction that this Court should not accept as final the conclusion on that subject; or

(3) that the imposition of the same discipline by this Court would result in grave injustice.

(d) Any member of the bar of this Court must notify the Clerk, within thirty days, of any discipline by or suspension or resignation from the bar of another federal court or from the bar of any state, commonwealth, or territory. Any member of the bar of this Court who is convicted of a felony as defined in subsection (b) must file with the Clerk, within thirty days, the record of such conviction.

(e) An attorney once disbarred or suspended who seeks reinstatement to practice before this Court must reapply for admission in accordance with the provisions of Local Rule of Civil Procedure 83.1.

[Amended effective May 1, 2003.]

RULE 83.4   CONTEMPTS

(a) A proceeding to adjudicate a person in civil contempt of court, including a case provided for in Federal Rules of Civil Procedure 37(b)(1) and 37(b)(2)(D), shall be commenced by the service of a notice of motion or order to show cause.

The affidavit upon which such notice of motion or order to show cause is based shall set forth with particularity the misconduct complained of, the claim, if any, for damages occasioned thereby, and such evidence as to the amount of damages as may be available to the moving party. Reasonable attorneys' fees necessitated by the contempt proceeding may be included as an item of damage. Where the alleged contemnor has appeared in the action by an attorney, the notice of motion or order to show cause and the papers upon which it is based may be served upon the attorney; otherwise, service shall be made personally, in the manner provided in Federal Rule of Civil Procedure 4 for the service of a summons. If an order to show cause is sought, such order may upon good cause shown embody a direction to the United States Marshal to arrest the alleged contemnor and hold him or her in bail in an amount fixed by the order, conditioned upon his or her appearance at the hearing and upon his or her holding himself or herself amenable thereafter to all orders of the Court for surrender.

(b) If the alleged contemnor puts in issue the alleged misconduct or the damages thereby occasioned, he or she shall upon demand be entitled to have oral evidence taken on the issues, either before the Court or before a master appointed by the Court. When by law the alleged contemnor is entitled to a trial by jury, he or she shall make a written demand therefor on or before the return day or adjourned day of the application; otherwise, he or she will be deemed to have waived a trial by jury.

(c) In the event the alleged contemnor is found to be in contempt of court, an order shall be made and entered

(1) reciting or referring to the verdict or findings of fact upon which the adjudication is based;

(2) setting forth the amount of the damages to which the complainant is entitled;

(3) fixing the fine, if any, imposed by the Court, which fine shall include the damages found, and naming the person to whom such fine shall be payable;

(4) stating any other conditions, the performance of which will operate to purge the contempt; and

(5) directing the arrest of the contemnor by the United States Marshal, and his or her confinement until the performance of the condition fixed in the order and the payment of the fine, or until the contemnor be otherwise discharged pursuant to law.

The order shall specify the place of confinement. No party shall be required to pay or to advance to the Marshal any expenses for the upkeep of the prisoner. Upon such an order, no person shall be detained in prison by reason of the non-payment of the fine for a period exceeding six months. A certified copy of the order committing the contemnor shall be sufficient warrant to the Marshal for the arrest and confinement. The aggrieved party shall also have the same remedies against the property of the contemnor as if the order awarding the fine were a final judgment.

(d) In the event the alleged contemnor shall be found not guilty of the charges made against him or her, he or she shall be discharged from the proceeding and, in the discretion of the Court, may have judgment against the complainant for his or her costs and disbursements and a reasonable counsel fee.

RULE 83.5   CAMERAS AND RECORDING DEVICES

(a) No one other than officials engaged in the conduct of court business and/or responsible for the security of the Court shall bring any camera, transmitter, receiver, portable telephone or recording device into the Court or its environs without written permission of a Judge of that Court.

Environs as used in this rule shall include the Clerk's office, all courtrooms, all chambers, grand jury rooms, petit jury rooms, jury assembly rooms, and the hallways outside such areas.

(b) The Presiding Judge may waive any provision of this rule for ceremonial occasions and for nonjudicial public hearings or gatherings.

RULE 83.6   STUDENT PRACTICE RULE

(a) A law student may, with the Court's approval, under supervision of an attorney, appear on behalf of any person, including the United States Attorney and the New York State Attorney General, who has consented in writing.

(b) The attorney who supervises a student shall:

(1) be a member of the bar of the United States District Court for the Western District of New York;

(2) assume personal professional responsibility for the student's work;

(3) assist the student to the extent necessary;

(4) appear with the student in all proceedings before the Court; and

(5) indicate in writing his or her consent to supervise the student.

(c) In order to be eligible to appear, the law student shall:

(1) be duly enrolled in a law school approved by the American Bar Association;

(2) have completed legal studies amounting to at least two semesters or the equivalent;

(3) be certified by a law school faculty member as qualified to provide the legal representation permitted by these rules. This certification may either be withdrawn by the certifier at any time by mailing a notice to the Clerk or be terminated by the Judge presiding in the case in which the student appears without notice, hearing, or cause. The termination of certification by action of a Judge shall not be considered a reflection on the character or ability of the student;

(4) be introduced to the Court by an attorney admitted to practice before this Court;

(5) neither ask for nor receive any compensation or remuneration of any kind for his or her services from the person on whose behalf he or she renders services, but this shall not prevent an attorney, legal aid bureau, law school, public defender agency, a state, or the United States from paying compensation to the eligible law student, nor shall it prevent any agency from making proper charges for his or her services;

(6) certify in writing that he or she is familiar with and will comply with the New York State Lawyer's Code of Professional Responsibility as adopted from time to time by the Appellate Divisions of the State of New York, and as interpreted and applied by the United States Supreme Court, the United States Court of Appeals for the Second Circuit, and this Court; and

(7) certify in writing that he or she is familiar with the federal procedural and evidentiary rules relevant to the action in which he or she is appearing.

(d) The law student, supervised in accordance with these rules, may:

(1) appear as counsel in Court or at other proceedings when written consent of the client (on the form available in the Clerk's office), or written consent of the United States Attorney when the client is the United States (or an officer or agency thereof) or of the Attorney General of New York when the client is the State of New York (or an officer or agency thereof) and the supervising attorney's name has been filed, and when the Court has approved the student's request to appear in the particular case to the extent that the Judge presiding at the hearing or trial permits; and

(2) prepare and sign motions, petitions, answers, briefs, and other documents in connection with the matter in which he or she has met the conditions of (d)(1) above; each such document shall also be signed by the supervising attorney.

(e) Forms for designating compliance with this rule shall be available in the Clerk's office. Completed forms shall be filed with the Clerk.

(f) Practice by students pursuant to this rule shall not be deemed to constitute the practice of law within the meaning of the rules for admission to the bar of any jurisdiction.

RULE 83.7   STUDENT LAW CLERKS

(a) A law student may serve as a student law clerk to a District Judge or Magistrate Judge of this Court.

(b) In order to so serve, the law student shall:

(1) be duly enrolled in a law school approved by the American Bar Association;

(2) have completed legal studies amounting to at least two semesters or the equivalent;

(3) neither be entitled to ask for nor receive compensation of any kind from the Court or anyone in connection with service as a student law clerk to a Judge;

(4) if required by the Judge, certify in writing that he or she will abstain from revealing any information and making any comments at any time, except to his or her faculty advisor or to court personnel as specifically permitted by the Judge to whom he or she is assigned, concerning any proceeding pending or impending in this Court while he or she is serving as a student law clerk. A copy of such certification shall be filed with the Clerk.

(c) A Judge supervising a student law clerk may terminate or limit the clerk's duties at any time without notice, hearing, or cause. Such termination or limitation shall not be considered a reflection on the character or ability of the student law clerk unless otherwise specified.

(d) An attorney in a pending proceeding may at any time request that a student law clerk not be permitted to work on or have access to information concerning that proceeding and, on a showing that such restriction is necessary, a Judge shall take appropriate steps to restrict the student law clerk's contact with the proceeding.

(e) For the purposes of Canons 3–A(4) and 3–A(6) of the Code of Judicial Conduct for United States Judges, a student law clerk is deemed to be a member of the Court's personnel.

(f) Forms designating compliance with this rule shall be available in the Clerk's office.

[Amended effective May 1, 2003.]

RULE 83.8   MODIFICATION OF RULES

Any of the foregoing rules shall, in special cases, be subject to such modification as may be necessary to meet emergencies or to avoid injustice or great hardship.

LOCAL RULES OF CRIMINAL PROCEDURE

RULE 1.1　TITLE

These rules shall be known as the Local Rules of Criminal Procedure for the United States District Court for the Western District of New York. These rules supplement the Federal Rules of Criminal Procedure and are numbered in accordance therewith.

RULE 1.2　THE "COURT"

Wherever in these local rules reference is made to the "Court", "Judge", or similar term, such term shall be deemed to include a Magistrate Judge unless the context requires otherwise.

RULE 6.　GRAND JURY

(a) Grand juries may be summoned by order of the Court at such times as the public interest requires, to serve until discharged by the Court consistent with 18 U.S.C. §§ 3321, 3322 and Federal Rule of Criminal Procedure 6.

(b) All grand jury proceedings are governed by Federal Rule of Criminal Procedure 6.

(c) All motions for relief from orders or process of the grand jury, such as motions to quash subpoenas or motions to hold a witness in contempt, shall be made returnable before the Judge who impaneled the grand jury, or his or her designee.

RULE 7.　FILING CASES

(a) Every criminal case shall be assigned by the Clerk to a Judge of the District upon the filing of the indictment or information.

(b) For purposes of case assignment, the Western District of New York is divided into two areas. Cases arising in the eight western counties: Allegany, Cattaraugus, Chautauqua, Erie, Genesee, Niagara, Orleans and Wyoming (the "Buffalo area"), shall ordinarily be assigned to a Judge in Buffalo. Cases arising in the nine eastern counties: Chemung, Livingston, Monroe, Ontario, Schuyler, Seneca, Steuben, Wayne and Yates (the "Rochester area"), shall ordinarily be assigned to a Judge in Rochester. The assignment within these areas shall ordinarily be by random selection.

RULE 12.1　PROCEDURES FOR CRIMINAL CASES

Unless otherwise ordered by the District Judge to whom a criminal case is assigned, the following procedures shall apply to criminal indictments and informations:

(a) A United States Magistrate Judge is authorized to arraign defendants and accept not guilty pleas pursuant to Federal Rules of Criminal Procedure 10 and 11.

(b) After providing the attorneys for the government and all defendants the opportunity to be heard, at arraignment or at a date set at the arraignment, the Court shall issue an order scheduling discovery and motion practice in all criminal cases. Such scheduling order shall include, but not be limited to, the following:

(1) dates and terms and conditions for providing discovery between the government and the defendants;

(2) dates for filing motions, responses thereto, and oral arguments of motions; and

(3) such other matters as the Court deems appropriate in the exercise of its discretion and supervisory powers.

(c) Unless authorized by the Court, all motions by a defendant or the government shall be made returnable on the same date.

(d) Such scheduling order may subsequently be changed only by leave of the Court.

(e) As soon as practicable after the resolution of motions, the trial attorneys in the case shall meet with the District Judge to set a trial date and schedule any required pre-trial hearing.

[Amended effective May 1, 2003.]

RULE 12.2　MOTIONS

Unless otherwise ordered by the Court:

(a) Motions and hearings on all contested matters shall be heard on the dates and times set by each individual Judge in the Western District of New York. Information regarding such dates and times may be obtained from the Clerk's office.

(b) If the Judge assigned to hold the Court shall be absent, the Clerk of the Court shall adjourn the hearings on motions or applications to some convenient day.

(c) All motions and notice thereof shall be governed by the Federal Rules of Criminal Procedure. Original motion papers shall be filed in the Clerk's office, either at the United States Courthouse, Buffalo, New

York or at the United States Courthouse, Rochester, New York. Refer to Local Rule of Criminal Procedure 49.1 for more information on filing motion papers.

(d) Except as provided in subdivision (e), any application for adjournment of a motion shall be made by the attorney, or by an associate, to the Judge before whom the motion is to be argued. Such application shall be made to the Judge's courtroom deputy and not to the Judge's law clerk. In requesting an adjournment, the following guidelines shall be adhered to:

(1) The party seeking the adjournment shall first confer with all other parties before approaching the courtroom deputy;

(2) A suggested rescheduled date, agreeable to all parties, shall be determined, if possible;

(3) The party seeking the adjournment shall notify the courtroom deputy in writing, unless unforeseen circumstances prohibit written notice, of the request and the suggested new date; and

(4) The reason for the adjournment must be placed on the record either in open court or in writing, so that the Court may make findings as may be required by the Speedy Trial Act of 1974, 18 U.S.C. §§ 3161–3174.

(e) Requests for adjournments by pro se litigants must be made in writing, by letter to the Court, with copies to all other counsel in the case.

[Amended effective May 1, 2003.]

RULE 15. PROCEDURES FOR DEPOSITIONS BY OTHER THAN STENOGRAPHIC MEANS

A deposition by other than stenographic means (i.e. without the use of a stenographic record) may be taken only upon order of the Court. A deposition to be recorded on video tape and by stenographic means requires no prior order. The following procedures shall be followed:

(a) The deposition notice shall state that the deposition will be recorded both stenographically and on video tape. At the deposition, the operator of the camera shall be identified; however, nothing shall preclude utilization of an employee of the attorney who noticed the deposition from acting as the camera operator.

(b) The camera shall be directed at the witness at all times showing a head and shoulders view, except that close-up views of exhibits are permitted where requested by the questioning attorney.

(c) Prior to trial, counsel for the party seeking to use the deposition at trial shall approach opposing counsel and attempt to resolve voluntarily all objections made at the deposition.

(d) Unresolved objections shall be submitted to the Court by way of a motion in limine made by the party seeking to use the deposition at trial. The motion may be made at any time after the deposition, but shall be made no later than one week before trial or in compliance with any date established by applicable order of the Court. The objected-to portion(s) of the transcript shall be annexed to such motion papers.

(e) In accordance with the Court's ruling on objections, the party seeking to use the deposition shall notify opposing counsel of the pages and line numbers of the deposition transcript which the party plans to delete from the video tape. The party seeking to use the video tape deposition at trial shall then edit the tape accordingly, and shall bear the expense of editing. If the Court overrules an objection made during the deposition, such objection need not be deleted. If requested, an instruction from the Court at the time the deposition is shown regarding objections heard on the tape will be given.

(f) At least three days before showing the tape, the party seeking to use the tape at trial shall deliver a copy of the edited tape to opposing counsel. Opposing counsel may only object at that time if the edited version does not comply with the Court's ruling and the agreement of counsel set forth above, or if the quality of the tape is such that it will be difficult for the jury to understand. Such objections, if any, must be made in writing and served at least 24 hours before the tape is to be shown.

(g) The party seeking to use the video tape deposition must provide the equipment necessary to do so in court.

RULE 23. FREE PRESS—FAIR TRIAL DIRECTIVES

(a) It is the duty of the lawyer or law firm, and of non-lawyer personnel employed by a lawyer's office or subject to a lawyer's supervision, private investigators acting under the supervision of a criminal defense lawyer, and government agents and police officers, not to release or authorize the release of non-public information or opinion which a reasonable person would expect to be disseminated by means of public communication, in connection with pending or imminent criminal litigation with which they are associated, if there is a substantial likelihood that such dissemination will interfere with a fair trial or otherwise prejudice the due administration of justice.

(b) With respect to a grand jury or other pending investigation of any criminal matter, a lawyer participating in or associated with the investigation (including government lawyers and lawyers for targets, subjects, and witnesses in the investigation) shall refrain from making any extrajudicial statement which a reasonable person would expect to be disseminated by means of public communication that goes beyond the public record or that is not necessary to inform the public that the investigation is underway, to describe the general scope of the investigation, to obtain assistance in the apprehension of a suspect, to warn the public of any dangers or otherwise to aid in the investigation, if there is a substantial likelihood that such dissemination will interfere with a fair trial or otherwise prejudice the administration of justice.

(c) During a jury trial of any criminal matter, including the period of selection of the jury, no lawyer or law firm associated with the prosecution or defense shall give or authorize any extrajudicial statement or interview relating to the trial or the parties or issues in the trial which a reasonable person would expect to be disseminated by means of public communication if there is a substantial likelihood that such dissemination will interfere with a fair trial; except that the lawyer or the law firm may quote from or refer without comment to public records of the Court in the case.

(d) Statements concerning the following subject matters presumptively involve a substantial likelihood that their public dissemination will interfere with a fair trial or otherwise prejudice the due administration of justice within the meaning of this rule:

(1) The prior criminal record (including arrests, indictments or other charges of crime), or the character or reputation of the accused, except that the lawyer or law firm may make a factual statement of the accused's name, age, residence, occupation and family status; and if the accused has not been apprehended, a lawyer associated with the prosecution may release any information necessary to aid in the accused's apprehension or to warn the public of any dangers the accused may present;

(2) The existence or contents of any confession, admission or statement given by the accused, or the refusal or failure of the accused to make any statement;

(3) The performance of any examinations or tests or the accused's refusal or failure to submit to an examination or test;

(4) The identity, testimony or credibility of prospective witnesses, except that the lawyer or law firm may announce the identity of the victim if the announcement is not otherwise prohibited by law;

(5) The possibility of a plea of guilty to the offense charged or a lesser offense;

(6) Information the lawyer or law firm knows is likely to be inadmissible at trial and would, if disclosed, create a substantial likelihood of prejudicing an impartial trial; and

(7) Any opinion as to the accused's guilt or innocence or as to the merits of the case or the evidence in the case.

(e) Statements concerning the following subject matters presumptively do not involve a substantial likelihood that their public dissemination will interfere with a fair trial or otherwise prejudice the due administration of justice within the meaning of this rule:

(1) An announcement, at the time of arrest, of the fact and circumstances of arrest (including time and place of arrest, resistance, pursuit and use of weapons), the identity of the investigating and arresting officer or agency and the length of investigation;

(2) An announcement, at the time of seizure, stating whether any items of physical evidence were seized and, if so, a description of the items seized (but not including any confession, admission or statement);

(3) The nature, substance or text of the charge, including a brief description of the offense charges;

(4) Quoting or referring without comment to public records of the Court in the case;

(5) An announcement of the scheduling or result of any state in the judicial process, or an announcement that a matter is no longer under investigation;

(6) A request for assistance in obtaining evidence; and

(7) An announcement, without further comment, that the accused denies the charges, and a brief description of the nature of the defense.

(f) Nothing in this rule is intended to preclude the formulation or application of more restrictive rules relating to the release of information about juvenile or other offenders, to preclude the holding of hearings or the lawful issuance of reports by legislative, administrative or investigative bodies, or to preclude any lawyer from replying to charges of misconduct that are publicly made against said lawyer.

(g) The Court, on motion of either party or on its own motion, may issue a special order governing such matters as extrajudicial statements by parties and witnesses likely to interfere with the rights of the accused to a fair trial by an impartial jury, the seating and conduct in the courtroom of spectators and news media representatives, the management and sequestration of jurors and witnesses and any other matters which the Court may deem appropriate for inclusion in such order. In determining whether to impose such a special order, the Court shall consider whether such an order will be necessary to ensure an impartial jury and must find that other, less extreme available remedies, singly or collectively, are not feasible or would not effectively mitigate the pretrial publicity and bring about a fair trial. Among the alternative remedies to be considered are: change of venue, postponing the trial, a searching voir dire, emphatic jury instructions, and sequestration of jurors.

(h) Disciplinary action may be taken against any lawyer who violates the terms of this rule.

[Adopted effective May 1, 2003.]

RULE 24.1 JURY TRIALS IN CRIMINAL CASES

Jury selection in a criminal case shall be governed by Federal Rules of Criminal Procedure 23 and 24 and by such procedures established by the trial judge.

RULE 24.2 JURORS

Selection of petit jurors is made by random selection pursuant to the most recently-adopted Jury Selection Plan for the Western District of New York, as approved by the Second Circuit Judicial Council. A copy of the Plan is available in the Clerk's office or on the Court's web site at *www.nywd.uscourts.gov.*

RULE 26. EXHIBITS

(a) Prior to the beginning of a trial, the exhibits shall be marked and exhibit lists prepared as the Court directs.

(b) All exhibits offered by any party in civil or criminal proceedings, whether or not received as evidence, shall be retained after each day of trial by the party or attorney offering the exhibits, unless otherwise ordered by the Court. Immediately after the case is submitted to the trier of fact, all exhibits which were received into evidence shall be delivered to the courtroom deputy. After a verdict is rendered, responsibility for custody of all exhibits reverts back to the parties.

(c) In the event an appeal is prosecuted by any party, each party to the appeal shall promptly file with the Clerk any exhibits to be transmitted to the appellate court as part of the record on appeal. Documents of unusual bulk or weight and physical exhibits, other than documents, shall remain in the custody of the attorney producing them who shall permit their inspection by any party for the purpose of preparing the record on appeal and who shall be charged with the responsibility for their safekeeping and transportation to the Court of Appeals. Those exhibits not transmitted as part of the record on appeal shall be retained by the parties who shall make them available for use by the appellate court upon request.

(d) If any party, having received notice from the Clerk concerning the removal of exhibits, fails to do so within thirty days from the date of such notice, the Clerk may destroy or otherwise dispose of those exhibits.

[Amended effective May 1, 2003.]

RULE 32. PRESENCE REPORT

(a) Disclosure of presentence reports shall, for sentencing purposes, be in accordance with Federal Rule of Criminal Procedure 32.

(b) No presentence reports shall be disclosed for any purpose other than sentencing in the absence of a compelling demonstration to the Court that disclosure of the report is required to meet the ends of justice.

(c) No copies of any report of presentence investigation shall be made by the government, the defendant, or any third party, except upon order of the Court.

(d) Any application to disclose such report shall be made to the sentencing Judge.

RULE 44. APPOINTMENT OF COUNSEL

(a) Pursuant to the Criminal Justice Act of 1964 as amended, 18 U.S.C. § 3006A, the Judges of the United States District Court for the Western District of New York have adopted a Plan for the adequate representation of any person otherwise financially unable to obtain representation.

(b) A panel of attorneys has been established under the Plan from which the Court may appoint counsel in a particular case. In addition to assignment from the panel of attorneys established under the Plan, the Court shall, whenever appropriate, appoint the Federal Public Defender.

(c) A copy of the Plan is available in the Clerk's office and on the Court's website at www.nywd. uscourts.gov. Reference should be made to the statute for further details, including procedures for obtaining payment for work done and/or reimbursement for expenses.

(d) It should be noted that under Rule 4(b) of the Rules of the Second Circuit Court of Appeals supplementing Federal Rules of Appellate Procedure, trial counsel has the duty to continue representing a defendant through the appellate process. Assigned counsel are advised to consider their appellate responsibilities when accepting criminal trial assignments.

[Amended effective May 1, 2003.]

RULE 46. DEPOSITS OF MONEY INTO COURT

(a) General Orders Regarding Funds. The Court's directions to the Clerk regarding (1) the investment of monies placed in the custody of the Court or of the Clerk and (2) the assessment of court fees against such monies are contained in various General Orders of the Court and amendments thereto, available in the Clerk's offices.

(b) Monies Deposited Without a Special Order. Whenever money is permitted by statute or rule to be deposited into court without leave of court (e.g., in condemnation proceedings governed by Federal Rule of Civil Procedure 71A(j)) or is directed by the Court to be deposited as a condition to some form of relief (e.g., cash bail, cash bonds), General Orders shall govern the investment of such funds upon their receipt by the Clerk.

(c) Monies Deposited With a Special Order. Whenever statute or rule requires that leave of court be obtained for the deposit of money into the Court (e.g., Federal Rule of Civil Procedure 67), an order shall be promptly filed with the Clerk. If, and to the extent that, any such order fails to instruct the Clerk as to the handling of such funds, they shall be handled in accordance with the aforesaid General Orders.

(d) Court Fees. Such fees are promulgated and required by the Judicial Conference of the United States pursuant to 28 U.S.C. § 1914(b).

(e) Alternatives. Parties and others are encouraged to consider alternatives which do not involve the receipt of monies by the Clerk, such as escrow accounts, and joint signature accounts in the names of counsel, and letters of credit. Such alternatives avoid the imposition of court fees and may provide greater flexibility to maximize yield for the benefit of the parties.

[Amended effective May 1, 2003.]

RULE 49.1 SERVICE AND FILING OF PAPERS

(a) All pleadings, notices and other papers shall be served and filed in accordance with the Federal Rules of Criminal Procedure. The party or a designee shall declare, by affidavit or certification, that he or she has provided all other parties in the action with all documents being filed with the Court.

(1) A party seeking or opposing any relief under the Federal Rules of Criminal Procedure shall file only such portion(s) of a deposition, interrogatory, request for documents, request for admission, or other material that is pertinent to the application.

(2) A party seeking to include in a record on appeal material which was not previously filed shall apply to the Court for an order requiring the Clerk to file such material. The party may make such application by motion or by stipulation of counsel.

(b) All orders, whether issued on notice or ex parte, together with the papers on which they were granted, shall be filed forthwith.

(c) Unless otherwise provided by the Court, a moving party who wishes to file reply papers shall file and serve the notice of motion and supporting papers at least fifteen business days prior to the return date of the motion. The notice of motion shall also state that the moving party intends to file and serve reply papers and that the opposing party is therefore required to file and serve opposing papers at least eight business days prior to the return date. Reply papers shall be filed and served at least three business days before the return date. Under all other circumstances, and except as ordered otherwise by the Court, notices of motion together with supporting affidavits and memoranda shall be served on the parties and filed with the Clerk at least ten business days prior to the return date of the motion. Answering affidavits and memoranda shall be served and filed at least three business days prior to the return date. Sur-reply papers shall not be permitted unless otherwise ordered by the Court.

(d) A party seeking to shorten the notice requirements prescribed in subparagraph (c) must make a motion for an expedited hearing setting forth the reasons why an expedited hearing is required. The motion for an expedited hearing may, for cause shown, be made ex parte, and must be accompanied by

(1) the motion that such party is seeking to have heard on an expedited basis, together with supporting affidavits and memorandum of law; and

(2) a proposed order granting an expedited hearing, with dates for service of the motion (by personal service or overnight mail), responding papers, and the hearing left blank to be filled in by the Court.

Immediately after filing the motion for an expedited hearing (and accompanying documents) with the Clerk's office, counsel for the moving party shall personally deliver courtesy copies of such motion to chambers and await further instructions from the Court. In the event that the moving party is represented by out-of-town counsel who is unable to personally deliver courtesy copies, counsel shall mail such courtesy copies directly to chambers and shall contact chambers by telephone to request a waiver of this requirement.

(e) Without prior approval of the Court, briefs or memoranda in support of or in opposition to any motion shall not exceed twenty-five pages in length and reply briefs shall not exceed ten pages in length and shall comply with the requirements of Local Rule of Criminal Procedure 49.2. Applications to exceed these page limits shall be made in writing by letter to the Court with copies to all counsel, at least three business days before the date on which the brief must be filed.

(f) Good cause shall be shown for the making of any application ex parte. The papers in support of such application shall state attempts made to resolve the dispute through a motion on notice and/or state why notice of the application for relief may not be given.

(g) No filed document shall be removed from the Court except on order of the Court.

(h) Unless otherwise specified by statute or rule or requested by the Court, only the original of any papers shall be accepted for filing. Parties requesting date-stamped copies of documents filed with the Clerk must provide a self-addressed, adequately-sized envelope with proper postage affixed.

(i) Service of all papers other than a subpoena or a summons and complaint shall be permitted by dispatching the paper to the attorney by overnight delivery service at the address designated by the attorney for that purpose, or if none is designated, at the attorney's last known address. Service by overnight delivery service shall be complete upon deposit of the paper enclosed in a properly addressed wrapper into the custody of the overnight delivery service for overnight delivery, prior to the latest time designated by the overnight delivery service for overnight delivery. Where a period of time prescribed by either the Federal Rules of Criminal Procedure or these rules is measured from the service of a paper and service is by overnight delivery, one business day shall be added to the prescribed period. "Overnight delivery service" means any delivery service which regularly accepts items for overnight delivery to any address within the jurisdiction of the Court.

(j) No papers shall be served by electronic means unless, in accordance with Federal Rule of Civil Procedure 5(b)(2)(D), the party or parties being served has filed a written consent to accept service by this means. An attorney's registration as a user of the Court's Electronic Case Filing System constitutes consent to accept service electronically. When a document is filed electronically, the Court's system will generate a Notice of Electronic Filing, which will be transmitted by the Court via e–mail to the filer and all parties who have consented to electronic service. The Notice of Electronic Filing, which serves as the Court's date–stamp and proof of service, will contain a hyperlink to the filed document. Transmission of the Notice of Electronic Filing to the registered e–mail address constitutes service of a pleading, document, order or notice upon any attorney in the case who has consented to electronic service. For cases which are a part of the Court's Electronic Case Filing System, only service of the Notice of Electronic Filing by the Court's system is sufficient to constitute electronic service. Those parties or attorneys within the case who have not consented to electronic service must be provided notice of the filing in paper form in accordance with the Federal Rules of Civil Procedure.

[Amended effective May 1, 2003; December 15, 2003.]

RULE 49.2 FORM OF PAPERS

(a) All text and footnotes in pleadings, motions, legal memoranda and other papers shall be plainly and legibly written, typewritten in a font size at least 12–point type, printed or reproduced, without erasures or interlineations materially defacing them, in ink on durable white 8½″ x 11″ paper of good quality and fastened. All text in such documents shall be double-spaced.

(b) All papers shall be endorsed with the name of the Court, the title of the case, the proper docket number and the name or nature of the paper, in sufficient detail for identification. In any initial or amended pleading, counsel, or litigants acting pro se, must print or type the names of all parties in the case caption with accurate capitalization and spacing. Additionally, counsel or litigants acting pro se must number the parties in the case caption. All papers shall be signed by an attorney or by the litigant if appearing pro se, and the name, address and telephone number of each attorney or litigant so appearing shall be typed or printed thereon. All papers shall be dated and paginated.

[Amended effective May 1, 2003.]

RULE 49.3 STIPULATIONS

All stipulations affecting a case before the Court, except stipulations which are made in open court and recorded by the court reporter, shall be in writing and signed, and shall be filed. Except to prevent injustice, any stipulation which fails to satisfy these requirements shall not be given effect.

RULE 49.4 ORDERS

Orders of discontinuance or dismissal, whether by consent or otherwise, shall be presented to the Court for signature. After the Court has instructed a prevailing party to submit an order, the prevailing party shall submit to the Court a proposed order which has been approved by opposing counsel and which contains the endorsement of opposing counsel: "Approved as to form and substance."

RULE 49.5 APPEALS

(a) Appellant shall file a notice of appeal in accordance with Federal Rule of Appellate Procedure 3. Such notice of appeal shall include the names of the parties to the judgment and the names and addresses of their respective attorneys of record.

(b) In addition to the original notice of appeal, appellant shall file sufficient copies to serve all counsel and the Clerk of the Circuit Court of Appeals.

(c) Counsel share the responsibility of preparing the index for the record on appeal. Upon completion, the index shall be presented to the Clerk for transmittal to the United States Court of Appeals for the Second Circuit or to the United States Supreme Court.

(d) Counsel shall, wherever possible and consistent with the Federal Rules of Appellate Procedure, stipulate to the designation of less than the entire trial record.

(e) Counsel are cautioned to examine and follow both the Federal Rules of Appellate Procedure and the Rules of the United States Court of Appeals for the Second Circuit.

RULE 49.6 COPIES OF ORDERS

The Clerk shall provide one copy of every order entered, together with notice thereof, to each law firm representing one or more parties to, or non-party movants in, the action.

[Adopted effective May 1, 2003.]

RULE 49.7 DOCUMENTS TO BE PROVIDED BY THE U.S. ATTORNEY'S OFFICE

(a) The United States Attorney's Office shall provide the Clerk with an adequate number of copies of charging instruments for distribution.

(b) The United States Attorney's Office is required to provide the Clerk with redacted copies of charging instruments and related documents when such documents are necessary.

[Adopted effective May 1, 2003.]

RULE 49.8 FILING BY FACSIMILE OR ELECTRONIC MEANS

(a) The Clerk's Office will not accept any facsimile transmission unless ordered by the Court.

(b) Pursuant to Federal Rule of Civil Procedure 5(e), the Clerk's Office will accept papers filed, signed, or verified by electronic means that are consistent with technical standards, if any, that the Judicial Conference of the United States establishes. All electronic filings shall be governed by the Court's General Order Governing Electronic Filing.

(c) Service by electronic means is addressed in Local Rule of Criminal Procedure 49.1(j).

[Adopted effective December 15, 2003.]

RULE 50. SPEEDY TRIAL

Pursuant to the requirements of Federal Rule of Criminal Procedure 50(b), the Speedy Trial Act of 1974, 18 U.S.C. §§ 3161–3174, and the Federal Juvenile Delinquency Act, 18 U.S.C. §§ 5031–5037, the Judges of the Western District of New York have adopted a "Plan for the Prompt Disposition of Criminal Cases." This Plan incorporates the time limits which must be observed for filing an indictment or information, for arraignment, and for commencement of trial. It also sets out the procedures to be followed in this District for compliance with the above statutory mandates. A copy of the Plan is available in the Clerk's office. For further details, reference should be made to the Plan and to these statutes.

[Amended effective May 1, 2003.]

RULE 53. CAMERAS AND RECORDING DEVICES

(a) No one other than officials engaged in the conduct of court business and/or responsible for the security of the Court shall bring any camera, transmitter, receiver, portable telephone or recording device into the Court or its environs without written permission of a Judge of that Court.

Environs as used in this rule shall include the Clerk's office, all courtrooms, all chambers, grand jury rooms, petit jury rooms, jury assembly rooms, and the hallways outside such areas.

(b) The Presiding Judge may waive any provision of this rule for ceremonial occasions and for non-judicial public hearings or gatherings.

RULE 55.2 SEALING OF DOCUMENTS IN CRIMINAL CASES

(a) Except when otherwise required by statute or rule, there is a presumption that Court documents are accessible to the public and that a substantial showing is necessary to restrict access.

(b) When the sealing of a criminal matter is ordered, the Clerk shall inscribe in the public records of the Court only the case number, the fact that a case was filed under seal, the name of the District Judge or Magistrate Judge who ordered the seal, and (after assignment of the case to a District Judge and a Magistrate Judge in the normal fashion) the names of the assigned District Judge and the assigned Magistrate Judge.

(c) Documents authorized to be filed under seal or pursuant to a protective order must be presented to the Clerk in envelopes bearing sufficient identification. The envelopes shall not be sealed until the documents inside have been filed and docketed by the Clerk's office.

(d) Unless an order of the Court otherwise directs, all sealed documents will remain sealed after final disposition of the case. The party desiring that a sealed document be unsealed after disposition of the case must seek such relief by motion on notice.

[Amended effective May 1, 2003.]

RULE 56. SESSIONS OF COURT

Regular and continuous sessions of the Court shall be held at Buffalo and Rochester.

Special sessions of court may be held at such places in the District and for such periods of time as may be practicable and as the nature of the Court's business may require.

RULE 57.1   COPIES OF LOCAL RULES

Copies of these rules, and the amendments and appendices to them, shall be available upon request in the offices of the Clerk of Court in both Rochester and Buffalo. Persons other than litigants who are permitted to proceed in forma pauperis in a pending case seeking to obtain a copy of these rules by mail must provide a self-addressed envelope of at least 9″ × 12″ in size with sufficient postage affixed.

RULE 57.2   ATTORNEY ADMISSION, APPEARANCE AND DISCIPLINE AND STUDENT LAW CLERKS AND PRACTICE

All rules related to attorney admission to practice, attorneys of record, discipline of attorneys, student practice and student law clerks are found in Local Rules of Civil Procedure 83.1, 83.2, 83.3, 83.6 and 83.7, all of which are incorporated by reference into these Local Rules of Criminal Procedure.

[Amended effective May 1, 2003.]

RULE 58.1   ASSIGNMENT OF MATTERS TO MAGISTRATE JUDGES

(a) **Misdemeanor Cases.** All misdemeanor cases shall be assigned, upon the filing of an information, complaint, or violation notice, or the return of an indictment, to a Magistrate Judge, who shall proceed in accordance with the provisions of 18 U.S.C. § 3401 and Federal Rule of Criminal Procedure 58. In the event the defendant does not waive trial before the District Court as provided therein, the file shall be returned to the Clerk of the Court for assignment to a District Court Judge. The Magistrate Judge, may, however, set bond, appoint counsel, and accept a plea of not guilty without a waiver being executed.

(b) **Extradition Proceedings.** A United States Magistrate Judge is authorized to conduct extradition proceedings in accordance with 18 U.S.C. § 3184.

(c) **Felony Cases.** Upon the return of an indictment or the filing of an information charging a felony, arraignment may be held before a Judge or a Magistrate Judge. Further proceedings in the case shall be in accordance with the order of the Judge to whom the case is assigned. Felony cases include those in which an instrument charges both felony and non-felony offenses.

[Amended effective May 1, 2003.]

RULE 58.2   REVIEW AND APPEAL OF MAGISTRATE JUDGES' ACTIONS

(a) **Review.**

(1) Review of a Magistrate Judge's orders or of his or her proposed findings of fact and recommendations for disposition shall be governed by 28 U.S.C. § 636(b)(1). If the parties consent to trial before the Magistrate Judge, there shall be no review or appeal of interlocutory orders to the District Court.

(2) All orders of the Magistrate Judge issued pursuant to these rules, as authorized by 28 U.S.C. § 636(b)(1)(A), shall be final unless within ten days after being served with a copy of the Magistrate Judge's order, a party files with the Clerk and serves upon opposing counsel a written statement specifying the party's objections to the Magistrate Judge's order. The specific matters to which the party objects and the manner in which it is claimed that the order is clearly erroneous or contrary to law shall be clearly set out.

(3) A party may object to proposed findings of fact and recommendations for dispositions submitted by a Magistrate Judge pursuant to 28 U.S.C. § 636(b)(1)(B), by filing with the Clerk and serving upon opposing counsel written objections to the proposed findings and recommendations within ten days after being served with a copy of such findings and recommendations, as provided in 28 U.S.C. § 636(b)(1)(C). The time for filing objections to the proposed findings and recommendations may be extended by direction of the District Judge. The written objections shall specifically identify the portions of the proposed findings and recommendations to which objection is made and the basis for such objection and shall be supported by legal authority.

(b) **Appeals From Judgments in Misdemeanor Cases (18 U.S.C. § 3402).** Appeals from a decision, order or judgment of conviction by a Magistrate Judge shall be taken pursuant to 18 U.S.C. § 3402 and Federal Rule of Criminal Procedure 58. Appeals shall be given a criminal case number and assigned by the Clerk to a District Judge. The appellant shall, within thirty days of the filing of the notice of appeal, file the record and shall also file a typewritten memorandum with the Clerk, together with two additional copies, stating the specific facts, points of law, and authorities on which the appeal is based. The appellant shall concurrently serve a copy of the memorandum on the appellee(s). The appellee(s) shall file an answering memorandum within thirty days of the filing of the appellant's memorandum. The Judge may extend these time limits upon a showing of good cause. Such good cause may include reasonable delay in the preparation of any necessary transcript. If an appellant fails to file his or her memorandum within the time provided by the rule or any extension thereof, the Court may dismiss the appeal.

(c) Appeals From Other Orders of a Magistrate Judge. Appeals from any other decisions and orders of a Magistrate Judge not provided for in this rule shall be taken as provided by governing statute, rule or decisional law.

RULE 58.3 FORFEITURE OF COLLATERAL IN LIEU OF APPEARANCE IN PETTY OFFENSE MATTERS

(a) This rule incorporates the rules of court relative to forfeiture of collateral in lieu of appearance in petty offense matters, copies of which are available in the Clerk's office.

(b) For petty offenses originating under the applicable federal statute or regulations or applicable state statute by virtue of the Assimilative Crimes Act (18 U.S.C. § 13) occurring within the territorial jurisdiction of a United States Magistrate Judge including areas within the boundaries of United States military installations, federal buildings and grounds, national forests, and property under the charge and control of the Veterans Administration, the person so charged shall post collateral and may, in lieu of appearance, waive appearance before a United States Magistrate Judge, and consent to the forfeiture of collateral. If collateral is forfeited, such action shall be tantamount to a finding of guilt.

(c) A list of petty offenses is available in the Clerk's office appended to the rules of court referred to in subdivision (a) of this local rule. Those offenses marked with an asterisk (*) and for which no amount of collateral is shown require a mandatory appearance before a United States Magistrate Judge.

(d) If a person charged with an offense under section (a) of this rule fails to post and forfeit collateral, any punishment, including fine, imprisonment or probation may, upon conviction, be imposed within the limits established by the applicable law.

(e) Nothing contained in this rule shall prohibit a law enforcement officer from arresting a person for the commission of any offense, including those for which collateral may be posted and forfeited, in which event the arrested person shall without unnecessary delay be taken before the nearest available United States Magistrate Judge or, in the event that a Magistrate Judge is not reasonably available, before a state or local judicial officer authorized by 18 U.S.C. § 3041, as provided in Federal Rule of Criminal Procedure 5.

RULE 59. MODIFICATION OF RULES

Any of the foregoing rules shall, in special cases, be subject to such modifications as may be necessary to meet emergencies or to avoid injustice or great hardship.

ELECTRONIC CASE FILING
ADMINISTRATIVE PROCEDURES FOR ELECTRONIC CASE FILING IN THE WESTERN DISTRICT OF NEW YORK
Revised: June, 2004; May, 2006; December 1, 2007
ADMINISTRATIVE PROCEDURES

The U.S. District Court for the Western District of New York permits attorneys to file documents with the Court from their own offices over the Internet. Only registered attorneys, as Officers of the Court, or their authorized employees or agents as provided in Section 1.c.iv, below, are permitted to file electronically. The term "Electronic Filing System" refers to the court's system that receives documents filed in electronic form. The term "Filing User" is used to refer to those who have a court-issued username and password to file documents electronically.

1. **Registration for the Electronic Case Filing System.**

a. *Designation of Cases.* Beginning January 1, 2004, all civil and criminal cases currently pending and newly filed, except as expressly noted herein, shall be assigned to the Electronic Case Filing System ("System"). Except as expressly provided and in exceptional circumstances preventing a Filing User from filing electronically, all petitions, motions, memoranda of law, or other pleadings and documents required to be filed with the court in connection with a case assigned to the Electronic Filing System must be electronically filed.

b. *Username and Password.* Attorneys admitted to practice in this Court and currently in good standing, including those admitted pro hac vice and attorneys authorized to represent the United States, may register as Filing Users of the court's Electronic Filing System.

c. *Registration.*

i. Registration is in a form prescribed by the clerk and requires the Filing User's name, address, telephone number, Internet e-mail address and a declaration that the attorney is admitted to the bar of this court. A completed registration form, in the form attached, must be submitted to the court by each attorney. The form may be duplicated for use. This form is also available on our web site at: www.nywd.uscourts.gov. Registration as a Filing User constitutes consent to electronic service of all documents as provided herein in accordance with the Federal Rules of Civil Procedure.

ii. All registration forms must be mailed or delivered to the Office of the Clerk, U.S. District Court, 68 Court Street, Buffalo, NY 14202.

iii. The registering attorney's username and password will be mailed to the attorney in an envelope marked "Confidential," unless the Clerk's Office is notified, in writing, at the time of registration that the attorney wishes an alternate delivery method. The attorney's username and password combination serves as a signature for purposes of Fed.R.Civ.P. 11, the Federal Rules of Civil Procedure, the local rules of this court, and any other purpose for which a signature is required in connection with proceedings before the court. The login and password issued to an individual attorney may be used only to file documents on behalf of that attorney.

iv. The Clerk's Office Help Desk Line will be activated on January 1, 2004 to assist users, in accordance with Section 2.o.ii, below.

v. A registered attorney may share his or her username and password with an authorized employee or agent of that attorney's law office or organization for purposes of filing. This does not in any way alter the fact that the attorney's username and password combination constitute that attorney's official signature on electronically filed documents.

vi. Registered attorneys will be able to change their own passwords. In the event that an attorney believes that the security of an existing password has been compromised and that a threat to the System exists, the attorney shall change their password immediately. In addition, the attorney shall give immediate notice by telephonic means to the Clerk of Court, Chief Deputy Clerk or Systems Manager and confirm by facsimile in order to prevent access to the System by use of the old password. Users may be subject to sanctions for failure to comply with this provision.

vii. A registered attorney whose e-mail address, mailing address, telephone or fax number has changed from that of the original Attorney Registration Form shall timely e-file a notice of a change of address in each of his or her pending cases, and serve a copy of the notice on all other parties. Registered attorneys are responsible for updating this information in their user accounts in the System.

viii. The Court reserves the right to revoke or otherwise restrict a registered attorney's access to the System at any time should the Court have reasonable cause to believe that the attorney has misused the System. Electronic and written notice of any such revocation or restriction shall be provided to the attorney.

ix. Once registered, a Filing User may withdraw from participation in the Electronic Filing System only by permission of the Chief Judge of the District for good cause shown. The Filing User seeking to withdraw must submit a written request to the Chief Judge explaining the reason(s) or justification(s) for withdrawal. Upon the Chief Judge's approval of the request, the Clerk of Court shall delete the Filing User's username and password from the system, and notify the Filing User of same. It is the Filing User's responsibility to notify opposing counsel in all pending cases that the Filing User has been granted permission to withdraw from the Electronic Filing System and that all future service must therefore be made by conventional means.

2. Electronic Filing and Service of Documents.

a. *Filing.*

i. Beginning January 1, 2004, all documents, except sealed papers and as expressly provided for in these guidelines, shall be electronically filed on the system. Electronic transmission of a document to the Electronic Filing System consistent with these procedures, whether accomplished by the Filing User or a Court User, together with the transmission of a Notice of Electronic Filing from the court, constitutes filing of the document for all purposes of the Federal Rules of Civil and Criminal Procedure and the local rules of this court, and constitutes entry of the document on the docket kept by the clerk under Fed.R.Civ.P. 58 and 79 and Fed.R.Crim.P. 49 and 55. A document shall not be considered filed for purposes of the Federal Rules of Civil and Criminal Procedure until the filing party receives a System-generated Notice of Electronic Filing.

(1) E-mailing a document to the Clerk's Office or to the assigned judge shall not constitute "filing" of the document.

ii. If the document to be filed requires leave of court such as an amended complaint or a document to be filed out of time, the proposed document shall be attached as an exhibit to the motion. If the motion is granted, the attorney must file the document electronically with the Court as a separate document.

iii. Courtesy copies of certain documents may be required. Filers should refer to the "Who Wants Paper" matrix published on the Court's website, www.nywd. uscourts.gov.

iv. Before filing a scanned document with the court, a Filing User must verify its legibility.

b. *Official Court Record.*

i. The Clerk's Office will not maintain a paper court file in any case begun on or after January 1, 2004, except as otherwise provided herein. The official court record shall be the electronic file as stored by the court, and any conventional documents or exhibits filed in accordance with these procedures.

ii. Original documents must be retained by the filing party and made available, upon request, to the Court and other parties for a period of five years following the expiration of all time periods for appeals.

c. *Complaints, Petitions, Summons and Charging Instruments.*

i. Complaints and petitions shall be filed, fees paid, and summonses issued and served in the traditional manner rather than electronically. Charging instruments in criminal cases shall be filed in the traditional manner rather than electronically. In addition, attorneys shall provide the complaint, petition or charging instrument in electronic format on a disk or CD, in PDF format, with signatures in accordance with Section 2.g, below. If the complaint, petition or charging instrument is not provided in electronic format on a disk or CD, in PDF format, the document or documents will be scanned and uploaded to the System by Clerk's Office staff.

d. *Attachments and Exhibits.*

i. Attachments and exhibits larger than five megabytes shall be filed electronically in separate five-megabyte segments.

ii. Filing Users must submit in electronic form all documents referenced as exhibits or attachments, except as otherwise provided herein. A Filing User must submit as exhibits or attachments only those excerpts of the referenced documents that are directly germane to the matter under consideration by the court. Excerpted material must be clearly and prominently identified as such. Filing Users who file excerpts of documents as exhibits or attachments under this rule do so without prejudice to their right to timely file additional excerpts or the complete document. Responding parties may timely file additional excerpts or the complete document that they believe are directly germane. The court may require parties to file additional excerpts or the complete document. A Filing User must request leave of the Court to file a document exhibit or attachment in non-electronic form.

iii. Exhibits such as videotapes and tape recordings shall be filed in the conventional manner with the Clerk of Court, and a Notice of Manual Filing shall be electronically filed by the filing party.

e. *Timely Filing of Documents.*

i. A document will be deemed timely filed if filed prior to midnight Eastern Time, unless otherwise ordered by the Court. A document will be considered untimely if filed thereafter. When a Court order requires that a document be filed on a weekend or holiday, the document may be filed by Close of Business the next business day without further application to the Court.

ii. A document filed electronically is deemed filed at the date and time stated on the Notice of Electronic Filing.

iii. Filing a document electronically does not alter the filing deadline for that document. Filing must be completed before midnight local time where the court is located in order to be considered timely filed that day.

f. *Service of Documents by Electronic Means.*

i. By participating in the electronic filing process, parties consent to the electronic service of all documents, and must make available electronic mail addresses for service during the registration process. Upon the filing of a document by a party, a Notice of Electronic Filing, with a hyperlink to the filed document, will be automatically generated by the electronic filing system and sent via electronic mail to the e-mail addresses of all parties participating in the electronic filing system in the case. Electronic service of the Notice of Electronic Filing constitutes service of the filed document for all purposes of the Federal Rules of Civil Procedure, Federal Rules of Criminal Procedure and the Local Rules of this Court.

ii. A certificate of service on all parties entitled to service or notice is still required when a party files a document electronically. The certificate must state the manner in which service or notice was accomplished on each party so entitled. A certificate of service should be filed as an attachment to the document. A sample certificate of service is attached to these guidelines, and is also available on the Court's website at: www.nywd.uscourts.gov.

iii. A party who is not a registered participant of the System is entitled to a paper copy of any electronically filed pleading, document, or order. The filing party must therefore provide the non-registered party with the pleading, document or order according to the Federal Rules of Civil and Criminal Procedure. When mailing paper copies of documents that have been electronically filed, the filing party may include the "Notice of Electronic Filing" to provide the recipient with proof of filing.

iv. E-mailing or faxing a pleading or document to any party shall not constitute service of the pleading or document.

g. *Signatures.*

i. Non–Attorney Signature Generally. If the original document requires the signature of a non-attorney, the filing party shall obtain the signature of the non-attorney on the document.

(1) The filing party or attorney then shall file the document electronically, or submit the document on disk to the Clerk's Office, indicating the signatory's name in the form **"s/(name)."**

(2) A non-filing signatory or party who disputes the authenticity of an electronically filed document or the authenticity of the signature on that

document must file an objection to the document within ten days of receiving the Notice of Electronic Filing.

ii. Defendant Signatures in Criminal Cases. A document containing the signature of a defendant in a criminal case will be filed in a scanned format that contains an image of the defendant's signature.

iii. Attorney Signature. The username and password required to submit documents to the Electronic Filing System serve as the Filing User's signature on all electronic documents filed with the court. They also serve as a signature for purposes of Fed.R.Civ.P. 11, the Federal Rules of Civil Procedure, the local rules of this court, and any other purpose for which a signature is required in connection with proceedings before this court. A pleading requiring an attorney's signature must include a signature block in the following format:

s/attorney's typed name
Attorney for [plaintiff/defendant]
Firm Name
Address
Telephone Number
E-mail Address

For certificates of service, affidavits, affirmations and declarations only, the signature block may be in the following format:

s/attorney's typed name

(1) Any party challenging the authenticity of an electronically filed document or the attorney's signature on that document must file an objection to the document within ten days of receiving the Notice of Electronic Filing.

iv. Multiple Signatures. The following procedure applies when a stipulation or other document requires two or more signatures:

(1) The filing party or attorney shall initially confirm that the content of the document is acceptable to all persons required to sign the document and shall obtain the signatures of all parties on the document.

(2) The filing party or attorney then shall file the document electronically indicating the signatories, e.g., **"s/Jane Doe," "s/John Smith,"** etc.

(3) A non-filing signatory or party who disputes the authenticity of an electronically filed document containing multiple signatures or the authenticity of the signatures themselves must file an objection to the document within ten days of receiving the Notice of Electronic Filing.

v. Originals of all documents containing signatures must be retained by the filing party and made available, upon request, to the Court and other parties for a period of five years following the expiration of all time periods for appeals.

h. *Fees Payable to the Clerk.*

i. Any fee required for filing of a pleading or paper in District Court is payable to the Clerk of Court by check, money order or cash. The Clerk's Office will document the receipt of fees on the docket with a text-only entry. The court will not maintain electronic billing or debit accounts for lawyers or law firms.

i. *Orders and Judgments.*

i. All signed orders and judgments, except those under seal, will be electronically filed by the Court. Any electronically signed order or judgment has the same force and effect as a conventional order or judgment.

ii. The assigned judge, if appropriate, may issue routine orders by a text-only entry upon the docket. In such cases, no PDF document will issue; the text-only entry shall constitute the court's only order on the matter.

iii.   Immediately upon the entry of an order or judgment in an action assigned to the Electronic Filing System, the clerk will transmit to Filing Users in the case, in electronic form, a Notice of Electronic Filing. Electronic transmission of the Notice of Electronic Filing constitutes the notice required by Fed.R.Civ.P. 77(d) and Fed.R.Crim.P. 49(c). The clerk must give notice in paper form to a person who has not consented to electronic service in accordance with the Federal Rules of Civil Procedure.

j.   *Proposed Orders.*

i.   Proposed orders should be attached to an Internet e-mail sent to the e-mail address of the assigned judge. The e-mail addresses are as follows:

Chief Judge Arcara...............	arcara@nywd.uscourts.gov
Judge Larimer....................	larimer@nywd.uscourts.gov
Judge Skretny	skretny@nywd.uscourts.gov
Judge Siragusa	siragusa@nywd.uscourts.gov
Judge Curtin	curtin@nywd.uscourts.gov
Judge Telesca	telesca@nywd.uscourts.gov
Judge Scott	scott@nywd.uscourts.gov
Judge Feldman	feldman@nywd.uscourts.gov
Judge Schroeder	schroeder@nywd.uscourts.gov
Judge Payson....................	payson@nywd.uscourts.gov
Judge McCarthy	mccarthy@nywd.uscourts.gov
Judge Foschio	foschio@nywd.uscourts.gov

No other documents, pleadings or electronic communications may be sent to the above e-mail addresses.

ii.   All proposed orders must be submitted in a format compatible with Word-Perfect, which is a "Save As" option in most word processing software. Judges will not accept proposed orders in PDF format.

k.   *Title of Docket Entries.*

i.   The party electronically filing a pleading or document shall be responsible for designating a docket entry title for the document by using one of the docket events prescribed by the court.

l.   *Correcting Docket Entries.*

i.   Once a document is submitted and accepted it becomes part of the case docket. The System will not permit the non-court electronic filer to make changes to the document(s) or docket entry.

ii.   A document incorrectly filed in a case may be the result of posting the wrong PDF file to a docket entry, or selecting the wrong document type from the menu, or entering the wrong case number and not catching the error before the transaction is completed. **The filing party should not attempt to re-file the document.**

iii.   A soon as possible after an error is discovered, the filing party should telephone the Court's Help Desk number with the case number and document number for which the correction is being requested. If appropriate, the court will make an entry indicating that the document was filed in error. The filing party will be advised if the document needs to be re-filed. In such cases, the Court will make a determination on the timeliness of the re-filed document.

m.   *Privacy.* In all filings, parties shall comply with Federal Rule of Civil Procedure 5.2 or Federal Rule of Criminal Procedure 49.1.

n.   *Conventional Filing of Certain Types of Cases.*

i.   Miscellaneous Civil and Miscellaneous Criminal cases traditionally filed under seal shall be filed conventionally. Such cases will not be available electronically,. except to court users, until such time as they are unsealed by order of the Court.

o. *Conventional Filing of Documents.*

i. The following procedures govern documents filed conventionally. The court, upon application, may also authorize conventional filing of other documents otherwise subject to these procedures.

(1) Documents Filed Under Seal. Unredacted documents filed with the court pursuant to the privacy provisions of Federal Rule of Civil Procedure 5.2 or Federal Rule of Criminal Procedure 49.1 shall be submitted in a sealing envelope with the following on the envelope:

[Case name and number]

Unredacted version of doc# [no.] e-filed on [date]

FILE UNDER SEAL

Except as authorized by statute or federal rule, no document shall be filed under seal without prior approval by the Court. A party seeking to file a document under seal shall deliver a paper copy of the following documents directly to the chambers of the assigned judge, without electronically filing the same:

(a) a copy of the document to be sealed;

(b) a supporting affidavit setting forth the reasons as to why the document should be placed under seal and, if appropriate, a memorandum of law ("supporting materials");

(c) a letter-size envelope ("sealing envelope") to which is affixed a label bearing the case name, case number and the words "Sealed per Order of Judge ___"; and

(d) a proposed order granting the motion to seal.

In addition, the party shall electronically file a notice of motion which shall identify the nature of the document to be sealed, but need not state the reasons why sealing is necessary. Motions by the government to file a warrant under seal are excluded from this requirement. In all other cases, a party seeking to be relieved of this requirement or seeking to file an ex parte motion to seal shall contact the chambers of the assigned judge for instructions.

If the motion to seal is granted, the assigned judge will sign the sealing envelope and electronically file an order authorizing the filing of the document under seal. The document will be maintained under seal in the Clerk's office and will not be filed electronically. The assigned judge, in his discretion, may also direct that the supporting materials be filed under seal. If the motion to seal is denied, the assigned judge shall enter an order denying the motion and return the document and supporting materials to the moving party.

(2) Transcripts of Proceedings. Transcripts of court proceedings will be conventionally filed and served since scanning that set of documents and filing or retrieving them electronically is impractical at this time. Because transcripts will not be scanned or otherwise placed on the System, the Clerk's Office will docket a text-only event stating that the transcript is available in paper form at the Clerk's Office.

(3) Magistrate Judge Consents. Pursuant to Fed.R.Civ.P. 73(b), parties' filings of consent to jurisdiction by United States Magistrate Judge will continue to be treated as non-public documents until all parties have consented. Therefore, parties must file their consent forms in paper (either mailed or delivered to the Clerk's Office), because electronic filing of a Magistrate Judge consent form will create a public document. If all parties consent to the jurisdiction of the Magistrate Judge, the Clerk will scan all consent forms which will then become public documents.

(4) Pro Se Filers. Pro Se filers shall file paper originals of all complaints, pleadings, motions, affidavits, briefs and other documents which must be signed or which require either verification or an unsworn declaration under any rule or statute. The Clerk's Office will scan these original documents into an electronic file in the System, but will also maintain a paper file.

(5) Habeas Corpus Cases. The administrative record in habeas corpus cases will be conventionally filed and served since scanning that set of documents and filing or retrieving them electronically is impractical at this time. Because the administrative record will not be scanned or otherwise placed on the System, the Clerk's Office will docket a text-only event stating that the record is available in paper form at the Clerk's Office.

(6) Social Security Cases. Absent a showing of good cause, and except as provided in Section o(i)(4) above, all documents, notices and orders in social security reviews will be filed and noticed electronically, except as noted below.

(a) An unredacted copy of the complaint, clearly marked as such, shall be provided to the Clerk to be maintained in the case file.

(b) The administrative record in Social Security cases will be conventionally filed and served since scanning that set of documents and filing or retrieving them electronically is impractical at this time. Because the administrative record will not be scanned or otherwise placed on the System, the Clerk's Office will docket a text-only event stating that the transcript is available in paper form at the Clerk's Office.

(c) All other documents in the case, including briefs, will be filed and served electronically unless the court otherwise orders.

(d) Access to electronic records in Social Security cases is governed by Federal Rule of Civil Procedure 5.2.

p. *System Availability.*

i. Although parties can file documents electronically 24 hours a day, attorneys are strongly encouraged to file all documents during normal working hours of the Clerk's Office (8:00 a.m. to 5:00 p.m. Eastern Time).

ii. The Clerk's Office has established a Help Desk Line to respond to questions regarding the electronic filing system and the registration process and to receive voice mail messages. The Help Desk Line will be staffed business days from 8:30 a.m. to 4:45 p.m. Eastern Standard Time (or Daylight Time when in effect), and will be available at all other times to record voice mail messages. Voice mail messages will be returned within one business day.

q. *Technical Failures.*

i. A Filing User whose filing is made untimely as the result of a technical failure may seek appropriate relief from the court.

3. Public Access to the System.

a. *Public Access at the Court.* A person may review at the Clerk's Office filings that have not been sealed by the court. Only a Filing User may file documents. Electronic access to the electronic docket and documents filed in the System is available to the public at no charge at the Clerk's Office during regular business hours. A copy fee for an electronic reproduction is required in accordance with 28 U.S.C. Section 1914.

b. *Internet Access.* Remote electronic access to the System for viewing purposes is limited to subscribers to the Public Access to Court Electronic Records ("PACER") system. The Judicial Conference of the United States has ruled that a user fee will be charged for remotely accessing certain detailed case information, such as filed documents and docket sheets in civil cases, but excluding review of calendars and similar general information. Parties' initial access to a document filed electronically is free of charge. Parties are encouraged to download or print the filed document when it is initially accessed via the Notice of Electronic Filing generated by the System.

    c. *Conventional Copies and Certified Copies.* Conventional copies and certified copies of electronically filed documents may be purchased at the Clerk's Office. The fee for copying and certifying will be in accordance with 28 U.S.C. Section 1914.

(Sample)

United States District Court
Western District of New York

_____

Case No.

_____

Certificate of Service

    I hereby certify that on   , I electronically filed the foregoing with the Clerk of the District Court using its CM/ECF system, which would then electronically notify the following CM/ECF participants on this case:

    1.

    2.

    And, I hereby certify that I have mailed the foregoing, by the United States Postal Service, to the following non-CM/ECF participants:

    1.

    2.

/s/ name

FIRM ADDRESS

E–MAIL ADDRESS

TELEPHONE NUMBERS

NOTICE OF ELECTRONIC AVAILABILITY OF CASE FILE INFORMATION AMENDED TO COMPLY WITH THE AUGUST 2, 2004 AMENDMENTS TO THE E–GOVERNMENT ACT OF 2002

    The United States District Court for the Western District of New York accepts electronically filed pleadings and makes the content of these pleadings available on the Court's Internet website via WebPACER.[1] Any subscriber to WebPACER will be able to read, download, store and print the full content of electronically filed documents. The Clerk's Office will not make electronically available documents that have been sealed or otherwise restricted by court order.

    You should not include sensitive information in any document filed with the Court unless such inclusion is necessary and relevant to the case. You must remember that any personal information not otherwise protected will be made available over the Internet via WebPACER. If sensitive information must be included, the following personal data identifiers must be partially redacted from the pleading, whether it is filed traditionally or electronically: **Social Security numbers, financial account numbers, dates of birth and the names of minor children.**

To comply with the E–Government Act of 2002, Pub.L. No. 107–347, a party wishing to file a document containing the personal data identifiers specified above may

(a) move for leave to file an unredacted document under seal. If the court grants the motion, the court will retain the paper document as part of the record, or

(b) file a reference list under seal. The reference list shall contain the complete personal data identifier(s) and the redacted identifier(s) used in its (their) place in the filing. All references in the case to the redacted identifiers included in the reference list will be construed to refer to the corresponding complete identifier. The reference list must be filed under seal, and may be amended as of right. It shall be retained by the court as part of the record.

The Court may, however, still require the party to file a redacted copy for the public file.

In addition, exercise caution when filing documents that contain the following:

1. Personal identifying number, such as driver's license number;

2. Medical records, treatment and diagnosis;

3. Employment history;

4. Individual financial information; and

5. Proprietary or trade secret information.

Counsel is strongly urged to share this notice with all clients so that an informed decision about the inclusion of certain materials may be made. If a redacted document is filed, it is the **sole responsibility of counsel and the parties** to be sure that all pleadings comply with the rules of this court requiring redaction of personal data identifiers. Likewise, counsel and the parties will be solely responsible for any unredacted documents filed. The clerk's office will not review documents for compliance with this rule, seal on its own motion documents containing personal identifiers, or redact documents, whether filed electronically or on paper.

Effective August 2, 2004.

[1] Remote electronic access to pleadings filed in civil social security cases is limited to counsel of record and court staff. Non-parties have direct access to the pleadings on file at the Clerk's Office.

CIVIL AND CRIMINAL APPENDICES

APPENDIX A. CIVIL JUSTICE EXPENSE AND DELAY REDUCTION PLAN—WESTERN DISTRICT

I. Introduction. In accordance with the provisions of the Civil Justice Reform Act of 1990, the Civil Justice Reform Act Advisory Group for the Western District of New York has submitted to the Court its report on the condition of the Court's docket and its recommendations for the reduction of cost and delay in civil litigation in the District. Having carefully considered the Advisory Group's Report and having concluded that the recommendations contained therein will serve to "facilitate deliberate adjudication of civil cases on the merits, monitor discovery, improve litigation management, and ensure just, speedy and inexpensive resolutions of civil disputes", 28 U.S.C. § 471, as required by the Civil Justice Reform Act, the members of the Court voted to adopt the recommended measures in the Advisory Group's fourteen-point Proposed Cost and Delay Reduction Plan.

In developing its Civil Justice Expense and Delay Reduction Plan, the Court considered each of the principles and techniques of litigation management contained in 28 U.S.C. § 473. All of those case management principles and techniques are incorporated in this Plan except those set forth at 28 U.S.C. § 473(a)(4) and (5).[1] The principles identified in those subdivisions—to encourage the use of voluntary, cooperative discovery and to require discovery motions to be accompanied by the movant's certification that he or she in good faith attempted to resolve the dispute prior to seeking Court intervention—are already included in the Court's Local Rules that were adopted in 1991.

As required by 28 U.S.C. § 472(c), this Plan calls for significant contributions by the Court, counsel and litigants. The members of the Court must actively participate in settlement negotiations and monitor the progress of cases. Additionally, the Plan requires the Judges to endeavor to meet target dates for decisions of motions and bench trials and to report all matters in which the target dates are not met. Counsel are called upon by the Plan to adhere to the schedule set by the Court, to request adjournments only in extraordinary instances, and to enter into earnest settlement discussions as early as possible in the proceedings. Finally, parties are expected to cooperate with their attorneys in complying with Court-established deadlines and to adopt reasonable settlement positions during the early stages of litigation.

The Court's Civil Justice Expense and Delay Reduction Plan will be implemented by way of amendments to the Court's Local Rules. The provisions of the Plan will become effective September 1, 1993, and will apply to all civil matters commenced on or after that date. The effective date of September 1, 1993 was selected in order to permit sufficient time for the giving of public notice and the opportunity to comment necessary to amend local rules as required by Fed.R.Civ.P. 83.

II. The Civil Justice Expense and Delay Reduction Plan for the Western District of New York.

1. Upon filing, the Clerk of the Court shall assign every civil case both to a District Judge and to a Magistrate Judge. Pursuant to 28 U.S.C. § 636(b)(1), the District Judge to whom each civil case is assigned shall immediately designate the Magistrate Judge to whom the case is assigned to hear and determine all issues involving discovery and non-dispositive motions. The first two sentences of Local Rule 6(a) are amended to provide as follows:

Every civil action shall be filed with the Clerk. It shall then be assigned by the Clerk to a Judge of the District and a Magistrate Judge.

2. Within ten days of the filing of a civil action, the Clerk shall notify the litigants in writing of their option to consent to the handling of the entire case (including dispositive motions and trial) by the Magistrate Judge. The parties and their attorneys shall also be advised that, as an alternative, they may consent to referral of only dispositive motions to the Magistrate Judge. This notice shall also include the names of the District Judge and Magistrate Judge to whom the case has been assigned.

3. If the parties consent to the handling of the entire case by the Magistrate Judge, the Magistrate Judge shall be responsible for the efficient handling of the case through disposition; otherwise, the Magistrate Judge shall be responsible for the efficient handling of the case through the close of discovery, and the case shall be referred to the District Judge at that time. If the parties consent, the Magistrate Judge may hear and decide dispositive motions; otherwise,

dispositive motions shall be heard and decided by the District Judge. The parties shall be encouraged, in all appropriate cases, to make dispositive motions. Dispositive motions may be made at any time during the pendency of a case and consistent with the time constraints provided in the case scheduling order pursuant to Fed.R.Civ.P. 16.

4. Local Rule 13, "Pre-trial Procedures in Civil Cases," is amended to provide as follows:

(a) Within sixty days of issue being joined, the Magistrate Judge shall hold a Rule 16 pre-trial discovery conference ("first discovery conference") in all cases except pro se prisoner civil rights, social security and habeas corpus cases, and shall issue an order providing for a discovery cut-off date, a date for a settlement conference ("first settlement conference") to be held before the Magistrate Judge, and a proposed trial date. The order shall also include a time limitation on the joinder of other parties, the commencement of third-party practice, and the filing of all pre-trial motions. No further or additional discovery, joinder, third-party practice, or non-dispositive motions shall be permitted thereafter except by leave of the Court for good cause shown in writing. [28 U.S.C. § 473(a)(2)].

At the first discovery conference, counsel for each party shall present a plan and schedule for discovery and the proposed management of the case. This plan and schedule may be presented orally or in writing, depending on the preference and in the discretion of the Magistrate Judge. [28 U.S.C. § 473(b)(1)].

Unless there is good cause shown in writing, the discovery cut-off date shall not be more than six months from the date of the order setting that date, the initial settlement conference shall be within ninety days after the date of the order, and the proposed trial date shall be no later than twelve months after the discovery cut-off date. A firm trial date will be set by the trial court. [28 U.S.C. § 473(a)(2), (3)].

Additional discovery conferences may be scheduled in the discretion of the Magistrate Judge, sua sponte, or at the request of a party. [28 U.S.C. § 473(a)(4)].

In an appropriate, uncomplicated action, upon issue being joined, any party may request, or the Court on its own motion may provide for, an advanced trial date and limited discovery. In such a case, a scheduling order shall issue providing for abbreviated discovery and a proposed early trial date. [28 U.S.C. § 473(a)(1)].

(b) All non-dispositive pre-trial motions as authorized by 28 U.S.C. § 636(b)(1) shall be made returnable before the Magistrate Judge, and all motion papers shall be filed with the Clerk.

(c) At the first settlement conference, the attorneys shall be present and shall be prepared to state their respective positions to the Magistrate Judge. Each plaintiff shall communicate a demand for settlement to the Magistrate Judge, and each defendant shall be prepared to communicate a response. The attorneys shall have spoken with their respective clients regarding their settlement positions prior to the settlement conference. Likewise, in cases involving insurance coverage, defense counsel shall have spoken with the insurance carrier regarding its position prior to this settlement conference. Each party shall submit in writing, or be prepared to discuss, the undisputed facts and legal issues relevant to the case, and the legal and factual issues about which the party believes there is a dispute. [28 U.S.C. § 473(b)(2)].

If a settlement is not reached at the first settlement conference, the Magistrate Judge may schedule additional settlement conferences from time to time as appropriate.

Upon notice by the Court, representatives of the parties with authority to bind them in settlement discussions, or the parties themselves, must be present or available by telephone during any settlement conference. [28 U.S.C. § 473(b)(5)].

Each settlement conference is designed to provide a neutral, non-binding evaluation program for the presentation of the legal and factual issues in a case, and the opportunity to present these issues to a judicial officer as early in the process as possible. [28 U.S.C. § 473(b)(4)].

(d) At any subsequent discovery conference held in the discretion of the Magistrate Judge, the attorneys shall provide a status update and a time-table for the remaining discovery to be completed within the discovery period.

(e) No extensions of the discovery period shall be granted, except for good cause shown in writing by order of the Magistrate Judge.

(f) After completion of discovery and motions as set forth in the scheduling order, any case in which the parties have not consented to disposition by the Magistrate Judge under 28 U.S.C. § 636 shall be referred to the District Judge assigned to the case, who shall then be responsible for the further efficient scheduling and disposition of that case; any other case shall remain with the Magistrate Judge, who will retain responsibility for the efficient scheduling and disposition of that case.

(g) Within thirty days after the close of discovery, the District Judge, or if the parties have consented to disposition by the Magistrate Judge, the Magistrate Judge, shall hold a pretrial conference for the purpose of setting a cut-off date for remaining motions, setting a firm trial date, and discussing settlement. Except for good cause shown in writing, such motion cut-off date shall not be more than ninety days after the date of the discovery cut-off and not less than 120 days prior to the trial date. Nothing contained in this Rule shall be read as precluding or discouraging dispositive motions at any time during the pendency of a case.

(h) Each District Judge or Magistrate Judge conducting a pre-trial conference, shall make an earnest effort to encourage and become involved in settlement negotiations between the parties. If the case is not resolved at such conference, the District Judge or the Magistrate Judge shall schedule further pre-trial conferences for the purpose of discussing settlement, as appropriate.

(i) If the case is not thereafter resolved, counsel for each party, no later than thirty days before the trial date, and in no event later than the final pre-trial conference, shall file with the Court and serve upon counsel for all other parties, a pre-trial statement which shall include the following:

(1) A detailed statement of contested and uncontested facts, and of the party's position regarding contested facts;

(2) A detailed statement as to the issues of law involved and any unusual questions relative to the admissibility of evidence together with supporting authority;

(3) A list of witnesses (other than rebuttal witnesses) expected to testify, together with a brief statement of their anticipated testimony and their addresses;

(4) A brief summary of the qualifications of all expert witnesses, and a concise statement of each expert's expected opinion testimony and the material upon which that testimony is expected to be based;

(5) A list of exhibits anticipated to be used at trial, except exhibits which may be used solely for impeachment or rebuttal;

(6) A list of any deposition testimony to be offered in evidence;

(7) An itemized statement of each element of special damages and other relief sought; and

(8) Such additional submissions as the District Judge or Magistrate Judge directs.

(j) A final pretrial conference shall be held at the direction of the District Judge or the Magistrate Judge within thirty days of the trial date. Trial counsel shall be present at this conference and shall be prepared to discuss all aspects of the case and any matters which may narrow the issues and aid in its prompt disposition, including:

(1) The possibility of settlement;

(2) Motions in limine;

(3) The resolution of any legal or factual issues raised in the pre-trial statement of any party;

(4) Stipulations (which shall be in writing); and

(5) Any other matters that counsel or the Court deems appropriate.

(k) Prior to the final pre-trial conference, counsel shall meet to mark and list each exhibit contained in the pre-trial statements. At the conference, counsel shall produce a copy of each exhibit for examination by opposing counsel and for notice of any objection to its admission in evidence. Following the final pre-trial conference, a pre-trial order may be entered as directed by the District Judge or the Magistrate Judge, and the case certified as ready for trial.

(*l*) Each party shall be represented at each pre-trial, discovery or settlement conference by an attorney who has the authority to bind that party regarding all matters previously identified by the Court for discussion at the conference and all reasonably related matters. [28 U.S.C. § 473(b)(2)].

(m) For purposes of procedural information, copies of standard referral orders used by each Judge in this District are available in the Clerk's office.

(n) A District Judge may also refer to the United States Magistrate Judge any other pre-trial matter as authorized by 28 U.S.C. § 636(b)(1)(A) and (B).

(o) If the Court so directs, a request for an extension of the deadline for the completion of discovery or for the postponement of the trial date shall be signed by both the attorney and the party making the request. [28 U.S.C. § 473(b)(3)].

For purposes of consistency, the Court shall adopt uniform pre-trial scheduling orders for use in conjunction with the procedure set forth above.

5. Local Rule 29(b)(1) is amended to provide that all civil cases shall be assigned by the Clerk to a District Judge and a Magistrate Judge, and that the District Judge to whom the case is assigned shall designate the Magistrate Judge to conduct pre-trial procedures pursuant to Local Rule 13. [28 U.S.C. § 473(a)(2)].

6. Local Rule 15, "Class Actions", is amended to provide as follows:

(a) The title of any pleading purporting to commence a class action shall bear the legend "Class Action" next to its caption.

(b) The complaint (or other pleading asserting a claim for or against a class) shall contain next after the jurisdictional grounds and under the separate heading "Class Action Allegations":

(1) a reference to the portion or portions of Fed.R.Civ.P. 23 under which it is claimed that the action is properly maintainable as a class action, and

(2) appropriate allegations thought to justify the claim, including, but not necessarily limited to:

(A) the size (or approximate size) and definition of the alleged class;

(B) the basis on which the party or parties claim to be an adequate representative of the class;

(C) the alleged questions of law and fact claimed to be common to the class; and

(D) in actions claimed to be maintainable as class actions under Fed.R.Civ.P. 23(b)(3), allegations thought to support the findings required by that subsection.

(c) Within sixty days after issue having been joined in any class action, counsel for the parties shall meet with a District Judge or Magistrate Judge and a scheduling order shall issue providing for orderly discovery; such order may initially limit discovery only as to facts relevant to the certification of the alleged class. [28 U.S.C. § 473(a)(2)].

(d) Within 120 days after the filing of a pleading alleging a class action, unless this period is extended on motion for good cause filed prior to the expiration of said 120–day period or in the scheduling order, the party seeking class certification shall move for a determination under Fed.R.Civ.P. 23(c)(1) as to whether the case is to be maintained as a class action. The motion shall include, but is not limited to, the following:

(1) a brief statement of the case;

(2) a statement defining the class sought to be certified, including its geographical and temporal scope;

(3) a description of the party's particular grievance and why that claim qualifies the party as a member of the class as defined;

(4) a statement describing any other pending actions in any court against the same party alleging the same or similar causes of actions, about which the party or counsel seeking class action certification is personally aware;

(5) in cases in which a notice to the class is required by Fed.R.Civ.P. 23(c)(2), a statement of what the proposed notice to the members of the class should include and how and when the notice will be given, including a statement regarding security deposit for the cost of notices; and

(6) a statement of any other matters that the movant deems necessary and proper to the expedition of a decision on the motion and the speedy resolution of the case on the merits.

The other parties shall respond to said motion in accordance with the provisions of these Rules.

(e) In ruling upon a motion for class certification, the Court may allow the action to be so maintained, may disallow and strike the class action averments, or may order postponement of the determination pending discovery or such other preliminary procedures as appear to be appropriate and necessary under the circumstances. Whenever possible, where the determination is ordered to be postponed, a date shall be fixed for renewal of the motion before the same Judge.

(f) The burden shall be upon any party seeking to maintain a case as a class action to show that the action is properly maintainable as such. If the Court determines that an action may be maintained as a class action, the party obtaining that determination shall, unless otherwise ordered by the Court, initially bear the expenses of and be responsible for giving such notice as the Court may order to members of the class.

(g) Failure to move for class determination and certification within the time required herein shall constitute and signify an intentional abandonment and waiver of all class action allegations contained in the pleading and the action shall proceed as an individual, non-class action thereafter. If any motion for class determination or certification is filed after the deadline provided herein, it shall not have the effect of reinstating the class allegations unless and until it is acted upon favorably by the Court upon the finding of excusable neglect and good cause.

(h) The attorneys for the parties are governed by the Code of Professional Responsibility of the American Bar Association as adopted by the New York State Bar Association concerning contact with and solicitation of potential class members.

(i) No class action allegation shall be withdrawn, deleted, or otherwise amended without Court approval. Furthermore, no class action shall be compromised without Court approval and notice of the proposed compromise shall be given to all members of the class in such manner as the Court directs.

(j) Six months from the date of issue having been joined and every six months thereafter until the action is terminated, counsel in all class actions shall file with the Clerk a joint case status report indicating whether any motions are pending, what discovery has been completed, what discovery remains to be conducted, the extent of any settlement negotiations that have taken place and the likelihood of settlement, and whether the matter is ready for trial. Counsel shall provide a copy of the case status report to the CJRA Attorney.

(k) The foregoing provisions shall apply, with appropriate adaptations, to any counterclaim or cross-claim alleged to be brought for or against a class.

7. In each pro se prisoner civil rights action filed after the effective date of this Plan, the Court will issue an order, within sixty days of issue being joined, setting deadlines for filing amended pleadings, completing discovery, filing dispositive motions, a trial date, and granting permission to conduct the deposition of the plaintiff at the correctional facility in which he or she is incarcerated. Absent good cause shown in writing, the deadline for filing amended pleadings shall be no later than thirty days from the date of the scheduling order, the deadline for completion of discovery shall be no longer than eight months from the date of the scheduling order (with a deadline one month earlier for filing motions related to discovery disputes), the deadline for filing dispositive motions shall be no later than ninety days after the discovery cut-off date, and the trial date shall be within twelve months of the discovery cut-off date. No modification of the dates set forth in the scheduling order shall be permitted except by leave of Court for good cause shown in writing. [28 U.S.C. § 473(a)(1)].

The Court shall continue the practice of issuing scheduling orders upon filing of petitions seeking habeas corpus relief. Absent extraordinary circumstances, the Court shall endeavor to terminate habeas corpus actions within twelve months of the date on which the initial petition is filed. [28 U.S.C. § 473(a)(1)].

8. The Court recognizes that the active involvement of a judicial officer in settlement negotiations is of paramount importance to the efficient handling of cases. Therefore, District Judges and Magistrate Judges will take an active role in encouraging the settlement of cases by bringing the parties together to discuss settlement in the presence of the Court, will make whatever recommendations the District Judge or Magistrate Judge deems appropriate, and will take any other steps necessary to promote and effect settlement within applicable legal and ethical principles. [28 U.S.C. § 473(a)(3)].

9. Each District Judge and Magistrate Judge shall give serious consideration to the effective utilization of courtroom personnel, and shall change duties or add assignments as appropriate. More specifically, the Courtroom Deputy in each Court shall immediately assume responsibility for the logistics of all conferences, motions, trial dates, and other appearances in court by the attorneys. This includes: (1) scheduling any attorney appearance; (2) ensuring that attorneys have been notified of all dates and times for trial, oral argument of motions, conferences or other appearances; (3) initial handling of all requests for adjournments; and (4) facilitating all other scheduling or

logistical difficulties encountered by the Court or counsel.

10. All pending decisions by a District Judge or Magistrate Judge shall be internally monitored by the Clerk's office and each month a report shall be issued that lists:

(a) All motions that have not been decided within sixty days of the date on which the motion is deemed submitted for decision; and

(b) All bench trials that have not been decided within 120 days of the close of proof, regardless of the submission of legal memoranda, oral argument, reopening of proof, or other potentially delaying factors.

11. Each motion shall be targeted for decision within sixty days of the date on which the motion is deemed submitted for decision, and each bench trial shall be targeted for decision within 120 days of the close of proof.

12. The position of the Civil Justice Reform Act Attorney ("CJRA Attorney"), originally created to assist the Advisory Group in the preparation of its Report and the Court in developing its Civil Justice Expense and Delay Reduction Plan, shall be a permanent position held by an attorney who has been appointed by, and serves at the pleasure of, the Court. The CJRA Attorney is authorized:

(a) To investigate, and respond to, inquiries by attorneys or litigants regarding the status of a pending motion or bench trial decision; such investigation shall ensure the anonymity of the source and shall be made with the approval of the Chief Judge, and with the assistance of the Chief Judge or the Chief Judge's office personnel, if necessary;

(b) To assist the Court in monitoring the progress of pending class actions by reviewing the joint case status reports required by Local Rule 15(j) and by serving as the liaison between counsel and the Court when necessary;

(c) To establish and administer court-annexed alternative dispute resolution programs at the direction of the Court and the Clerk of Court;

(d) To serve as an ombudsman to facilitate the implementation and success of the Court's Civil Justice Expense and Delay Reduction Plan. In this regard, the responsibilities of the CJRA Attorney will include, but not be limited to: (1) serving as liaison between members of the bar or litigants and the Court with respect to case status inquiries; (2) responding to requests for information from litigants and their counsel to ensure the efficient handling and disposition of pending civil cases; (3) educating the Court, members of the bar, litigants and other interested individuals about the Civil Justice Reform Act and the Court's Civil Justice Expense and Delay Reduction Plan and their im-

pact on federal court practice; (4) providing information to and soliciting comments from bar associations within the District as to the Court's Civil Justice Expense and Delay Reduction Plan and modifications to the Local Rules and individual judges' practice guidelines occasioned thereby; and (5) making litigants and their attorneys aware of alternative dispute resolution mechanisms or other means of intervention that allow for the prompt disposition of cases;

(e) To conduct settlement conferences, scheduling conferences, or other meetings at the request of a District Judge or Magistrate Judge, and to serve as a Special Master under Federal Rule of Civil Procedure 53 when so appointed;

(f) At the direction of the Magistrate Judges, to screen new civil filings in which Rule 16 conferences will be conducted primarily for the purpose of suggesting to the presiding Magistrate Judge any alternative dispute resolution method or other procedure that might expedite disposition. Inasmuch as the utility and cost-effectiveness of such case screening has not yet been proven, the screening program will be conducted initially as an experiment. New civil filings with selected nature of suit codes will be subject to screening by the CJRA Attorney for three month intervals over a period of twelve months. Upon completion of the twelve month experimental period, the Court and the Clerk will determine the types of civil actions that benefit most from such a procedure. Thereafter, the CJRA Attorney will screen new civil filings bearing nature of suit codes for those case types in which case screening has proven the most effective;

(g) At the direction of the Chief Judge, and in conjunction with the Clerk of the Court, to inquire into the status of all cases pending for more than three years, all motions awaiting decision for more than sixty days, and all bench trials awaiting decision for more than 120 days, including a review of the docket and the questioning of court personnel, litigants, and/or attorneys;

(h) In conjunction with the Clerk of the Court, to report to the Chief Judge on a monthly basis regarding the status of each case pending for more than three years, each motion awaiting decision for more than sixty days, and each bench trial awaiting decision for more than 120 days;

(i) In conjunction with the Clerk of the Court, to report to the Chief Judge twice yearly with respect to the general condition of the District's docket;

(j) To monitor compliance with the Court's Civil Justice Expense and Delay Reduction Plan on an ongoing basis and report in writing thereupon to the Chief Judge and the Advisory Group for purposes of the annual assessment called for by 28 U.S.C. § 475. The CJRA Attorney shall monitor compliance with the Civil Justice Expense and Delay Reduction Plan by: (1) reviewing monthly reports of motions that have not been decided within sixty days of the date on which the motion is submitted for decision; (2) reviewing monthly reports of bench trials that have not been decided within 120 days of the close of proof; (3) consulting with courtroom deputies regarding individual judges' pending caseload; (4) tracking the proceedings in "test groups" of cases to be designated periodically by the Clerk; (5) reviewing reports of cases that have been pending for longer than three years; (6) reviewing and analyzing workload statistics compiled and published by the Federal Judicial Center and the Administrative Office of the United States Courts; and (7) utilizing any other method as directed by the Court or the Clerk of Court;

(k) To coordinate the annual assessment required by 28 U.S.C. § 475 by providing the Court and the Advisory Group with a comprehensive review of the Court's civil and criminal dockets and a report on compliance with the Court's Civil Justice Expense and Delay Reduction Plan; and

(*l*) To solicit, receive and process suggestions by attorneys, litigants, court personnel or any interested individuals with respect to increasing the efficiency or decreasing the cost of litigating in the United States District Court for the Western District of New York.

These responsibilities may be modified by the Court or the Clerk of the Court as circumstances require.

13. The position of the Civil Justice Reform Act Management Analyst ("CJRA Analyst") shall be a permanent position held by an individual who is appointed by, and serves at the pleasure of, the Court. The CJRA Analyst shall be authorized:

(a) To assist in coordinating and, to evaluate the effectiveness of, programs established in accordance with the Court's Civil Justice Expense and Delay Reduction Plan;

(b) To furnish semiannual written reports to the Clerk of Court and the CJRA Attorney regarding the utilization and effectiveness of the Court's CJRA programs, along with appropriate recommendations for improved program operations or litigation management techniques;

(c) To act, together with the CJRA Attorney, as the district's liaison with other districts and agencies on CJRA matters;

(d) To support the CJRA Advisory Group and its Executive Committee in the annual assessments called for by 28 U.S.C. § 475. Such support shall include, but not be limited to: (1) scheduling meetings and sending meeting notices at the direction of the Advisory Group Chairman; (2) attending all Executive Committee and Advisory Group meet-

ings; (3) disseminating information to Advisory Group members at the direction of the Court, the Clerk of Court, the Advisory Group Chairman, or the CJRA Attorney; (4) conducting research and studies at the direction of the Advisory Group or the Executive Committee; and (5) drafting meeting reports.

(e) To develop and coordinate the implementation of methodologies to assess cost and delay in civil and criminal cases;

(f) To review and document case management practices in the District and elsewhere for the purpose of formulating recommendations for improving litigation management and further reducing cost and delay in the processing of civil cases;

(g) To prepare procedural manuals that the Court or the Clerk of Court require in conjunction with the implementation of the Court's Civil Justice Expense and Delay Reduction Plan or as may be required from time to time thereafter; and

(h) To perform such other functions as the Court and the Clerk of Court may deem appropriate in furtherance of the objectives of the Civil Justice Reform Act.

14. Each District Judge and Magistrate Judge shall encourage the use of the Court's voluntary arbitration program as governed by Local Rule 47 or other alternative dispute resolution mechanisms, where appropriate, in order to encourage and facilitate settlement. To complement its voluntary arbitration program, the Court shall establish additional court-annexed programs for alternative dispute resolution. Furthermore, the Court shall make available information regarding court-annexed and other methods of alternative dispute resolution that litigants and their counsel may pursue to effect early disposition of cases. [28 U.S.C. § 473(a)(6)].

III. Conclusion. The Civil Justice Expense and Delay Reduction Plan adopted by the Court responds to each of the problems in the Court's docket identified by the Advisory Group in its Report and Recommendations. The Court will, in conjunction with the Advisory Group, assess the condition of its docket on an annual basis as required by 28 U.S.C. § 475, and in so doing the Court will have the opportunity to discover any further problems that may arise in its docket and take corrective action with respect thereto. The annual assessments shall be made as of the first day of September for 1994 through 1997[2], the anniversary of the Plan's effective date. All annual assessments and Plan revisions will be made in accordance with the recommendations regarding CJRA annual assessments and plan revisions developed by the Court Administration and Case Management Committee of the Judicial Conference of the United States.

The Local Rules for the Western District of New York will be reprinted after they have been revised in accordance with this Plan. Copies of the Local Rules, as well as the Court's Civil Justice Expense and Delay Reduction Plan and the Advisory Group's Report and Recommendations will be available to interested individuals in the Clerk's offices in both Buffalo and Rochester.

Pursuant to 28 U.S.C. § 472(d), copies of the Advisory Group's Report and Recommendations and the Court's Civil Justice Expense and Delay Reduction Plan will be distributed to the Director of the Admin-

istrative Office of the United States Courts, the Judicial Council of the Second Circuit, and the Chief Judge of each of the other United States District Courts located within the Second Circuit.

1 Where particular Plan provisions embody any of the principles and techniques enumerated in 28 U.S.C. § 473, such is noted parenthetically.

2 The Civil Justice Reform Act of 1990, Title I, Pub.L. 101–650, § 103(b)(2), 104 Stat. 5096, provides that the requirements contained in 28 U.S.C. §§ 471–478 shall remain in effect until December 1, 1997.

APPENDIX B. JURY PLAN

Pursuant to the Jury Selection and Service Act of 1968, Public Law 99–274, 28 U.S.C. Sec. 1863 et seq., as amended [the Act], the following plan is hereby adopted by this Court, subject to approval by a reviewing panel and to such rules and regulations as may be adopted from time to time by the Judicial Conference of the United States.

1. Management and Supervision of Jury Selection Process. It is hereby established that the Clerk of the Court of the Western District of New York shall manage the jury selection process under the supervision and control of the Chief Judge. The functions of the Clerk under this Plan, or any portion thereof, may be delegated by the Clerk to any other person authorized by the Court to assist the Clerk in such regard.

2. Policy. It shall be the policy in the Western District of New York that all litigants in federal court entitled to trial by jury shall have the right to grand and petit juries selected at random from a fair cross-section of the community in the division wherein the Court convenes. It is further the policy of this District that all citizens not otherwise disqualified under law shall have the opportunity to be considered for service on grand and petit juries in the division wherein the Court convenes and that no citizen shall be excluded from service as a grand or petit juror in such division on account of race, color, religion, sex, national origin, or economic status. As stated in section 5, this Court, in an effort to broaden representation among prospective jurors, shall commence drawing names from voter registration lists merged with New York State Department of Motor Vehicles records, beginning in 1994 with the refilling of the Buffalo master jury wheel, and in 1995 with the Rochester master jury wheel.

3. Divisions. There being no statutory divisions in the Western District of New York, the District is hereby divided into two divisions for jury selection purposes only, as defined in Section 1869(e) of the Act, as follows:

Buffalo Division—Counties of Erie, Genesee, Niagara, Orleans, Wyoming, Chautauqua, Cattaraugus, and Allegany—for sessions of Court held at Buffalo.

Rochester Division—Counties of Livingston, Monroe, Ontario, Seneca, Wayne, Yates, Steuben, Schuyler, and Chemung—for sessions of Court held at Rochester.

4. Master Jury Wheel. The Clerk of the Court shall maintain a master jury wheel for each of the divisions within the District. The minimum number of names to be placed initially in the master jury wheels shall be as follows:

Buffalo Division—15,000 names

Rochester Division—12,000 names

The Chief Judge may order additional names to be placed in the master jury wheels from time to time as necessary.

5. Manner of Random Selection. As noted in section 2, the Court will draw names from voter registration lists and New York State Department of Motor Vehicle records commencing in 1994 with the refilling of the Buffalo master jury wheel and in 1995 with the Rochester master jury wheel. The motor vehicle records will supplement the voter registration lists to the extent possible using records provided by the State of New York as such records are prepared in the normal course of business. The Court takes notice that in the event two or more source lists are used, one person's name may appear more than once. A system will be developed, before any selection procedures begin, to eliminate as reasonably as possible such duplications. The list or lists used to select names for the master wheel shall hereafter be referred to as the "combined source list". Accordingly, names of petit and grand jurors serving in this District shall be selected by randomized procedure from the combined source list.

This plan's reference to random selection shall mean that in any selection procedure, only the first name shall be chosen by a purely random method and that each subsequent name for that drawing may be systematically taken at regular intervals throughout the remainder of the combined source list. This random selection procedure insures (a) that names chosen will represent all segments of the source file from which drawn; (b) that the mathematical odds of any single name being picked are substantially equalized; and (c) that the possibility of human discretion or choice affecting the selection of any individual's name is eliminated.

The Clerk of the Court shall determine the number of names to be randomly selected from each county within a division as that county's pro rata share of the minimum number of names set forth in section 4 for that division; it shall do the same when any additional names are ordered by the Chief Judge pursuant to section 4. Each county shall be substantially, proportionately represented in the master jury wheel according to the number of names contained in its combined source list.

The Clerk of the Court shall make the random selection by taking the number of names in each county's combined source list and adding them together to give the total number of names in the combined source list in that division. That total shall then be divided into the number of names in the combined source list in each separate county to give the percentage of the total that each county represents. These percentages will then be multiplied by the total number of names needed for the division to give the proportionate number of names needed from each county. The Clerk shall proceed to make the initial selection of names from the combined source list of each county.

A. *Determining the "Quotient" for Each County.* The Clerk of the Court shall determine the "quotient" by taking the total number of names in a county's combined source list and dividing that number by the number of names needed from that county. The number obtained will be the "quotient." The "quotient" is the ratio of total names to selected names. For example, if the Clerk of the Court should determine that 200 names are needed from Orleans County, whose combined source list contains a total of 20,000 persons, the "quotient" to be used would be 20,000 divided by 200 or 100. The Clerk of the Court would therefore take every 100th name in that county's combined source list.

B. *Determining a "Starting Number".* After determining the "quotient", the Clerk of the Court shall establish a starting number. This number will locate on the combined source list the first name to be selected for each county. The "starting number" will be manually drawn by lot from numbered cards placed in a jury wheel, drum, or box. Cards used for this drawing should begin with a card containing number one and end with a card containing the same number as the "quotient". In other words, the range of numbers from which a "starting number" is drawn is

exactly the same as the range between number one and whatever the "quotient" number happens to be. As an example of how both the "starting number" and "quotient" are used, if we suppose the "quotient" to be 100 and the "starting number" is 12, the first name chosen for that county would be the 12th name on its combined source list, the second name would be the 112th, the third name the 212th, etc., and continued in this manner to the end of the list.

C. *Selecting the Names by Machine Methods.* At the Clerk's option, and after consultation with the Court, the selection of names from complete source list databases in electronic media for the master jury wheel may be accomplished by a purely randomized process through a properly programmed electronic data processing system. Similarly, at the option of the Clerk and after consultation with the Court, a properly programmed electronic data processing system for pure randomized selection may be used to select names from the master wheel for the purpose of summoning persons to serve as grand or petit jurors. Such random selections of names from the source list for inclusion in the master wheel by data computer personnel must insure that each county within the jury division is substantially proportionally represented in the master jury wheel in accordance with 28 U.S.C. Section 1863(b)(3). The selection of names from the source list and the master wheel must also insure that the mathematical odds of any single name being picked are substantially equal.

In order to ensure the exercise of proper supervision and management over the automated aspects of jury selection and in accordance with statutory requirements, the operator of the computer shall comply with the instructions for random selection of grand and petit jurors by electronic machine methods contained in the Court's plan for random selection of grand and petit jurors and such additional written instructions as provided by the Court.

6. Drawing of Names From the Master Jury Wheel and Completion of Jury Qualification Form. From time to time, as ordered by the District Court, the Clerk of the Court shall publicly draw at random from the master jury wheel for a particular division the names of as many persons as may be required for jury service. The Clerk of the Court shall retain the names so drawn, and shall mail to every person whose name is drawn from the master jury wheel a one-step summons/qualification form, accompanied by instructions to fill out and return the form, duly signed and sworn, to the Clerk, by mail, within 10 days.

7. Selection, Summoning, and Assignment to Jury Panels. Upon order of the Court, if a grand jury is to be impaneled, this will be done initially from the prospective jurors reporting. Prospective jurors not designated to sit on a grand jury shall thereafter be added to the pool from which petit jurors shall be selected and shall remain available for service until selected or until the time for service expires.

Names drawn from the master jury wheel shall not be made public until summonses have been issued for said jurors, provided that the Chief Judge may order the names to be kept confidential in a case or cases when the interests of justice so require.

8. Determination of Qualification for Jury Service. The Chief Judge or other District Judge of the Court shall determine, in accordance with section 1865 of the Act and this plan, whether a person is unqualified for, exempt from, or to be excused from jury service. The Clerk or Jury Administrator may recommend to the Chief Judge or other District Judge that an individual be found unqualified for, be exempt from, or be excused from jury service.

9. Exemption From Jury Service. The District Court hereby finds that exemption of the following groups of persons or occupational classes is in the public interest and would not be inconsistent with the Act, and accordingly, members of such groups are barred from jury service:

A. Full-time members in active service in the Armed Forces of the United States;

B. Full-time members of any governmental police or regular fire department (not including non-governmental departments); and

C. Public officers of the United States, State, or local government who are elected to public office or directly appointed by one elected to office.

10. Excuses on Individual Request. The District Court hereby finds that jury service by members of the following occupational classes or groups of persons would entail undue hardship or extreme inconvenience to the members thereof, and the excuse of such members will not be inconsistent with the Act; upon individual request and after review by the presiding judge persons in the following classes shall be excused:

1. A person over 70 years of age;

2. A person who has served as a grand or petit juror within the last 2 years;

3. A person actively serving without compensation as a firefighter, rescue squad or ambulance crew member for a public agency;

4. A person having active care and custody of any children under 10 years of age or infirm persons whose health and/or safety would be jeopardized by your absence;

5. A person whose services are so essential to the operation of a business (sole proprietor) or agricultural enterprise that it must close or cease to function if you are required to perform jury duty.

Full-time, actively practicing in one of these occupations:

6. Attorney;

7. Physician;

8. Dentist;

9. Registered nurse;

10. Member of the clergy or a religious order.

11. Temporary Excuses. Pursuant to 28 U.S.C. Section 1866(c), temporary excuses on the grounds of undue hardship or extreme inconvenience may be granted by the Court or, under the Court's supervision, by the Clerk of Court. The names of individuals temporarily excused shall be reinserted into the jury wheel for possible resummoning.

12. Emptying and Refilling Master Jury Wheels. After the initial filling of the master jury wheel for each division, it shall be completely emptied and refilled in the years hereinafter designated:

Buffalo Division—2000 and every second year thereafter between January 1 and September 1, using the most current voter registration lists and motor vehicle records available.

Rochester Division—2001 and every second year thereafter between January 1 and September 1, using the most current voter registration lists and motor vehicle records available.

13. One–Step Summoning and Qualification Procedure. This Court has adopted the one-step summoning and qualification procedure, as authorized by 28 U.S.C. Section 1878. Accordingly, all prospective jurors shall be qualified and summoned in a single procedure.

14. Period of Jury Service. It shall be the general policy of this Court that persons summoned to petit jury service shall serve for a period of 90 days following the date of first appearance or report, unless they shall then be serving as jurors in an uncompleted trial, or until they shall have completed service as a trial juror in one trial, whichever shall have occurred first. In the latter regard, it shall rest within the discretion of the Chief Judge, upon the recommendation of the presiding judge, to direct that such persons not be excused at the conclusion of one trial, such as where said trial was particularly brief.

15. Imposition of Charges Against Party or Counsel. In any civil case in which a settlement is reached, or in which the Court is notified of settlement, later than the close of business on the last business day before jurors are to appear for jury selection, the Court, in its discretion and as stated in Local Rule 11(c), may assess reasonable charges reflecting the costs to the government of compensating the said jurors for their needless appearance. Said charges may be assessed against one or more of the parties, or against one or more counsel, as to the Court appears proper. Said charges shall be deposited by the Clerk into the Treasury of the United States.

16. Applicability and Definitions. The provisions of this plan apply to both divisions in the District unless specifically indicated otherwise.

The definitions set forth in Section 1869 of the Act shall apply to this plan unless specifically indicated otherwise.

17. Effective Date. This plan as amended this 16th day of March, 2000, shall become effective when approved by the Judicial Council of the Second Circuit.

Filed April 17, 2000.

APPENDIX C. GUIDELINES GOVERNING REIMBURSEMENT FROM THE DISTRICT COURT FUND OF EXPENSES INCURRED BY COURT APPOINTED COUNSEL

I. Introduction. It is the policy of this Court to encourage members of the bar to represent parties who are unable to afford counsel. In furtherance of this policy, the Court adopts these Guidelines governing the reimbursement of expenses of court-appointed counsel.

When an attorney has been appointed to represent an indigent party in a civil matter, that attorney may petition the Court for reimbursement of certain expenses. These expenses, which are defined in these Guidelines, must be incurred in the preparation and presentation of the case before this Court. Funding for this reimbursement program shall be obtained from this Court's District Court Fund and the total limit allowable, absent extraordinary circumstances, is $1,200 per client represented.

II. Limitations on Eligibility. Any costs which are recoverable under the provisions of Titles 18 or 28 of the United States Code or which have been recovered under any other plan for reimbursement or which have been waived shall not be reimbursed from the District Court Fund. In no case shall an appointed attorney for a party who has been awarded costs and/or fees pursuant to a judgment in an action before this Court be eligible for reimbursement from the District Court Fund of expenses incurred in that action which were included and reimbursed in full in the judgment awarding costs and/or fees.

Only those costs associated with the preparation or presentation of a civil action in the United States District Court for the Western District of New York shall be approved for reimbursement. No costs associated with the preparation or presentation of an appeal to the United States Court of Appeals for the Second Circuit or of a petition to the United States Supreme Court shall be reimbursed from the District Court Fund.

III. Procedure for Obtaining Reimbursement. Requests for reimbursement of expenses shall be made on the voucher form approved by the Court and available on request from the Clerk. The request shall be accompanied by sufficient documentation to permit the Court to determine that the request is appropriate and reasonable and that the amounts have actually been paid out. The request for reimbursement shall be filed with the Clerk who shall forward it to the presiding judge or, if the parties have consented to proceed before a magistrate judge pursuant to 28 U.S.C. § 636(c), the presiding magistrate judge. Requests for reimbursement of expenses may be made at any time during the pendency of the proceeding and up to thirty (30) days following either the entry of judgment on the merits in the proceeding or the entry of an order dismissing a settled action or, in cases where the represented party is seeking an award of attorneys fees and/or costs, the entry of judgment awarding or denying fees and/or costs. The presiding judge or magistrate judge may, for good cause shown, extend the time for filing a request.

In cases in which an appointed attorney has withdrawn or has been dismissed prior to the entry of a judgment, that attorney shall file a request for reimbursement within thirty (30) days of withdrawal or dismissal. Any work product or services obtained for which reimbursement of expenses is requested from the District Court Fund shall subsequently be provided to newly-appointed counsel or, where no new counsel is appointed, to the party for whom counsel was appointed.

IV. Allowable Expenses. An appointed attorney may request reimbursement of the following expenses, subject to approval by the presiding judge or magistrate judge. Approval of expenditures will not be automatic and counsel shall be prepared to support any request for reimbursement.

A. *Depositions and Transcripts.* An appointed attorney may order transcripts of depositions necessary for the preparation of the case. The cost of such shall not exceed the regular copy rate as established by the Judicial Conference of the United States and in effect at the time any transcript was filed unless another rate was previously provided for by Order of the Court. Only the cost of the original of any transcript shall be allowed.

B. *Investigative or Expert Services.* Counsel may request investigative or expert services necessary for the adequate preparation of a matter to be presented before the Court. Such services must have prior Court approval by the presiding judge or magistrate judge (if the parties have consented to proceed before a magistrate judge in accordance with 28 U.S.C. § 636(c)) in order to seek reimbursement from the District Court Fund.

C. *Travel Expenses.* Travel by privately-owned automobile may be claimed at the rate currently prescribed for federal judiciary employees who use a private automobile for conduct of official business, plus parking fees, tolls, and similar expenses. Transportation other than by privately-owned automobile may be claimed on an actual expense basis.

D. *Service of Papers and Witness Fees.* Those fees for service of papers and the appearance of witnesses that are not otherwise avoided, waived or recoverable may be reimbursed from the District Court Fund.

E. *Interpreter Services.* Costs of interpreter services not otherwise avoided, waived or recoverable may be reimbursed from the District Court Fund.

F. *Photocopying, Telephone Calls, etc.* Actual out-of-pocket expenses incurred for such items as photocopying, photographs, toll calls, telegrams and the like necessary for the preparation of a case may be reimbursed from the District Court Fund.

G. *Other Expenses.* Expenses other than those described above may be approved by the presiding judge or magistrate judge. No single expense under this section exceeding $100 shall be reimbursed absent the prior approval of the presiding judge or magistrate judge. When requesting reimbursement for any expenses under this section, a detailed description of the expenses should be attached to the petition for reimbursement filed with the Clerk.

V. **Non-allowable Expenses.** General office expenses, including personnel costs, rent, telephone services, secretarial help, office photocopying equipment and any general expense that would normally be reflected in the fee charged to a client are not reimbursable from the District Court Fund. Any costs incurred in conducting computer-assisted legal research are not reimbursable from the District Court Fund. The expense of printing briefs, regardless of the printing method utilized, is not reimbursable.

Any expense not properly documented with receipts or other proof may be disallowed by the presiding judge or magistrate judge.

Expenses which may be statutorily recovered or costs or fees taxed against a party or appointed counsel are not reimbursable from the District Court Fund.

VI. **Repayment of Advances.** In an instance where an advance for costs is made from the District Court Fund by the presiding judge or magistrate judge to an appointed attorney who subsequently obtains an award of costs from the opposing party, the appointed attorney shall, upon receipt of the monies awarded, promptly repay the District Court Fund any amount paid to him or her for expenses incurred in that action.

VII. **Processing of Requests for Reimbursement.** On receipt of the voucher form indicating amounts approved for reimbursement, the Clerk shall determine whether or not any payments have previously been made out of the Fund to cover expenses in the same proceeding. If no such payments have been made, the Clerk shall promptly issue the required check or checks in the amount indicated on the voucher form or the limit set by these Guidelines, whichever is lower. Where payments have previously been made from the Fund for expenses in the proceeding, the Clerk will determine whether the amounts authorized by the current voucher together with the amounts previously paid require consideration by the presiding judge or magistrate judge as to whether the matter presents extraordinary circumstances to justify payment in excess of the $1,200 limit set by these Guidelines. Where such consideration is required, the Clerk shall promptly transmit the voucher to the presiding judge or magistrate judge. On receipt of an approved voucher from the presiding judge or magistrate judge, the Clerk shall promptly issue the required check or checks in the amount indicated on the voucher form. If the presiding judge or magistrate judge disallowed any or all of the requested amounts, the Clerk shall promptly transmit to the submitting attorney a copy of the voucher showing the action of the Court.

These Guidelines were adopted by the Court on May 5, 1993.

APPENDIX D.　FIRST AMENDED PLAN FOR THE MANAGEMENT OF COURT REPORTERS

Filed August 25, 1988
(Replacing the Plan adopted August 8, 1983)

A. **Introduction.** The court desires through this Plan to achieve effective management of the official court reporters. The Chief Judge or his designee is fully authorized administratively to supervise the court reporters.

The Plan is designed to:

1. obtain effective day to day management and supervision of an efficient reporting service within the court.

2. make clear that the court reporters serve the court en banc and not a particular judge.

3. obtain effective utilization of the services of court reporters and an equitable distribution of their workload.

4. avoid backlogs of transcripts and assure prompt delivery of transcripts.

5. assure appointment of fully qualified court reporters and dismissal of incompetent court reporters.

6. minimize the use of contract court reporters.

7. enhance efficient operation and service to the court and litigants.

B. Appointment and Dismissal of Court Reporters. The Court shall appoint and dismiss court reporters, and in connection therewith the court shall consider the recommendations of the clerk. Court reporters shall be appointed in accordance with the provisions of the Court Reporters Act (28 USC Section 753) and the Policies and Procedures of the Administrative Office of the US Courts and the Judicial Conference of the United States. Only fully qualified court reporters shall be appointed as court reporters of the court. Court reporters who do not perform in a competent and satisfactory manner shall be subject to dismissal.

C. The Chief Judge. The Chief Judge or his designee shall co-ordinate and supervise the court reporters and their activities by means of, among other things:

(1) assignment and reassignment of court reporters for the purpose of assuring the best utilization of reporting personnel, subject to the provisions of paragraph D,

(2) periodically reviewing transcripts to assure full compliance with formal requirements of the Administrative Office of the US Courts and the Judicial Conference of the United States,

(3) periodically reviewing transcript billing to assure that authorized transcript rates are charged and that billing is in proper form and in accord with the recommendations and requirements of the Judicial Conference of the United States and adopted by order of this court,

(4) determining compliance by all court reporters with the rules and regulations concerning the recording and filing of pleas and sentences,

(5) periodically reviewing the time records of the court reporters to assure proper maintenance and accuracy,

(f)[1] periodically reviewing the records of the court reporters to assure the timely filing of all reports required by the Administrative Office of the U.S. Courts and the Judicial Conference of the United States,

(g)[1] requiring the court reporters to submit reports and information pertinent to this Plan,

(h)[1] performing such other activities relating to court reporters as shall be directed by the court.

[1] So in original.

D. Assignment of Court Reporters.

1. Court reporters shall be assigned to particular judges as a matter of convenience. Court reporters are not in the employ of a particular judge but are employed by the court en banc. The Chief Judge or his designee shall determine the availability of court reporters at all times for additional assignments. When necessary, and depending upon availability and subject to the approval of the judge to whom that reporter ordinarily is assigned, a court reporter may be temporarily reassigned to another judge of the court, to a visiting judge, to a senior judge, to a magistrate, or to another judicial officer as required, for reporting purposes.

2. Contract court reporters shall be utilized only pursuant to the policies and procedures of the Administrative Office of the US Courts. Contract reporters will not be used or paid for by the court to help official reporters alleviate transcript backlogs.

E. Hours of Attendance. The court reporters stationed at Buffalo are assigned to a "regular tour of duty" within the purview of that phrase as used in pronouncements of the Judicial Conference of the United States and the Director of the Administrative Office of the US Courts relating to entitlement to full-time status for purposes of computation of retirement and other benefits.

The court reporters stationed at Rochester are not so assigned.

F. Terminations, Staffing Reductions.

1. *Reporters Serve at Pleasure of the Court.* Court reporters serve at the pleasure of the court en banc. The court may make changes in reporting staff at will, and without regard to seniority.

2. *Death or Departure of Judge.* Because court reporters are employed by the court en banc, a reporter should continue to be employed at the pleasure of the court en banc regardless of the death, resignation, or retirement of a judge.

3. *Reduced Workload.* Should it be necessary to reduce the reporting staff because of a reduced workload, and where reduction cannot be accomplished by voluntary or involuntary relocation, attrition, or reduction of one or more reporters to part-time status, the

Court en banc shall decide which reporter is to be terminated and reasonable notice of termination will be given, and the Administrative Office will be contacted to determine whether other districts might be seeking a staff reporter.

4. *Transcript Responsibility After Severance.* A reporter who has resigned or been terminated remains responsible for producing requested transcript from the period of employment at the rates in effect at the time the transcript was ordered.

G. Transcripts. The Court Reporter shall advise the Chief Judge or his designee of any transcript order which cannot be delivered within 30 days; the Chief Judge or his designee may take appropriate action so that the transcript is produced when required. If a transcript is on order for more than 60 days, without good cause, the reporter shall take annual leave or leave without pay until this condition is cured.

Reporters shall not agree to "expedite" any transcript which will delay the preparation of transcripts for appeal. Any extension of time to file transcripts shall be obtained from the appropriate authority, i.e. the Clerk of the Court of Appeals in cases involving appeal transcripts and the Chief Judge or his designee in all other cases. Unless otherwise directed by the Chief Judge, his designee, or a judge, transcripts in civil cases generally should be prepared in the order in which requests for them are received. Preparation of criminal transcripts generally shall take precedence over preparation of civil transcripts. Reporters shall file with the clerk transcripts of proceedings within thirty days of their being prepared. If an electronic recording device was utilized, the reporter should certify the recording and file it as soon as the recording cassette, reel, etc. has been used to capacity.

H. Miscellaneous.

1. Court reporters who are assigned to a regular tour of duty shall not engage in private reporting work during normal court hours, and shall not use the facilities of the court to perform any private work. If a reporter's transcripts are current (none over thirty days old) and he or she is on annual leave or leave without pay, he or she may engage in private reporting during court hours, but may not use facilities of the court for such purpose. Court reporters who are not assigned a "regular tour of duty" may engage in private reporting during normal court hours, but may not utilize the facilities of the court. Private work of any nature at all times shall be subordinate to court work.

2. A reporter shall not use a substitute reporter without the prior approval of the clerk or the judge to whom the reporter is assigned at that time. Substitutes when authorized shall possess the qualifications of court reporters.

3. The work of court reporters shall be "noteread-able" so that the stenographic notes of one court reporter can be read by another in the event of an emergency.

4. The marking, filing, and storing of reporters' notes shall be standardized in order to assure the prompt locating of notes and withdrawal of the notes in the event the reporter-author of the notes is not available.

I. Authority of the Chief Judge. Any violation of this plan shall be referred to the Chief Judge for appropriate action.

APPENDIX E. NOTICE OF RIGHT TO CONSENT TO DISPOSITION OF A CIVIL CASE BY A UNITED STATES MAGISTRATE

In accordance with the provisions of 28 U.S.C. § 636(c), you are hereby notified that the full-time United States magistrate of this district court, in addition to his other duties, may, upon the consent of all the parties or their attorneys in a civil case, conduct any or all proceedings in a civil case, including a jury or nonjury trial, and order the entry of a final judgment. Copies of appropriate consent forms for this purpose are available from the clerk of the court.

You should be aware that your decision to consent, or not to consent, to the referral of your case to a United States magistrate for disposition is entirely voluntary and should be communicated solely to the clerk of the district court. Only if all the parties to the case consent to the reference to a magistrate will either the judge or magistrate to whom the case has been assigned be informed of your decision.

Your opportunity to have your case disposed of by a magistrate is subject to the calendar requirements of the court. Accordingly, the district judge to whom your case is assigned must approve the reference of the case to a magistrate for disposition.

Under the provisions of 28 U.S.C. § 636(c)(3), appeal from a judgment in a case heard by a magistrate will lie directly to the United States Court of Appeals for the Second Circuit unless the parties further consent to appeal to a district court judge at the time of the reference of the case to the magistrate, as provided in 28 U.S.C. § 636(c)(4).

Procedures relating to consensual reference to the magistrate are set out in Rule 36 of the Local Rules of this court and procedures relating to appeals are set out in Rule 37 of the Local Rules of this court.

Edward P. Gueth, Jr., Clerk

APPENDIX F.   FORM: CONSENT TO PROCEED
BEFORE A UNITED STATES MAGISTRATE

IN THE UNITED STATES DISTRICT COURT
FOR THE WESTERN DISTRICT OF
NEW YORK

```
                    )
                    )
                    )
                    )
                    )
                    )  Docket No. _____
                    )
                    )
                    )
                    )
                    )
                    )
```

Any appeal shall be taken to the United States court of appeals for this judicial circuit, in accordance with 28 U.S.C. § 636(c)(3), unless all parties further consent, by signing below, to take any appeal to a judge of the district court, in accordance with 28 U.S.C. § 636(c)(4).

Note: Return this form to the Clerk of Court only if it has been executed by all parties to the case.

CONSENT TO PROCEED BEFORE A
UNITED STATES MAGISTRATE

In accordance with the provisions of 28 U.S.C. § 636(c), the parties to the above-captioned civil matter hereby waive their right to proceed before a judge of the United States district court and consent to have a United States magistrate conduct any and all further proceedings in the case (including the trial) and order the entry of judgment.

ORDER OF REFERENCE

IT IS HEREBY ORDERED that the above-captioned matter be referred to United States Magistrate Edmund F. Maxwell for the conduct of all further proceedings and the entry of a judgment in accordance with 28 U.S.C. § 636(c) and the foregoing consent of the parties.

_____   _____
Date   UNITED STATES DISTRICT JUDGE

APPENDIX G.   CRIMINAL JUSTICE ACT PLAN

I.   Authority. Pursuant to the Criminal Justice Act of 1964 and the Guidelines for the Administration of the Criminal Justice Act, the United States District Court for the Western District of New York adopts this Plan for furnishing representation to any person eligible for such assistance in accordance with the CJA.

II.   Definitions.

A.   The term "CJA" means the Criminal Justice Act of 1964, 18 U.S.C. § 3006A.

B.   The term "Guidelines" means the Guidelines for the Administration of the Criminal Justice Act, Volume VII of the Guide to Judiciary Policies and Procedures, as promulgated by the Judicial Conference of the United States.

C.   The term "Court" means the Judges of the United States District Court for the Western District of New York.

D.   The term "District" means the geographical boundaries of the United States District Court for the Western District of New York.

E.   The term "Plan" means the Criminal Justice Act Plan for the United States District Court for the Western District of New York as stated herein.

F.   The term "Judge" means a United States District Judge, Senior District Judge and Magistrate Judge of the Court, unless stated otherwise.

G.   The term "Committee" means the Panel Selection Committee as established by the Plan.

H.   The term "Person(s)" shall mean any natural person or corporation.

I.   The term "Representation" includes legal counsel and investigative, expert and other services.

III.   Statement of Policy.

A.   It is the policy of the Court that the purposes of the CJA shall be fully achieved so that all persons eligible to obtain representation in criminal proceedings shall receive such assistance and that accused persons shall have the assistance of counsel including services as necessary to provide an adequate defense. The Plan shall be administered in accordance with the

Guidelines as adopted and amended by the Judicial Conference of the United States.

B. The Court, Clerk of the Court, the Federal Public Defender Organization and any attorney appointed under this Plan shall comply with the Guidelines and this Plan. The Clerk shall provide each member of a Panel, established under this Plan, or any other attorney appointed as counsel under the CJA and this Plan with a then current copy of this Plan. The Clerk shall maintain a current copy of the CJA Guidelines for use by any Panel member.

IV. Provision of Representation.

A. Representation shall be provided for any financially eligible person who:

(1) is charged with a felony or Class A misdemeanor;

(2) is a juvenile alleged to have committed an act of juvenile delinquency as defined in 18 U.S.C. § 5031;

(3) is under arrest, when such representation is required by law;

(4) is charged with a violation of probation, parole, or supervised release, or faces modification, reduction, or enlargement of a condition, or extension or revocation of a term of probation, parole or supervised release;

(5) is subject to a mental condition hearing under Chapter 313 of Title 18 of the United States Code;

(6) is in custody as a material witness;

(7) is charged with a capital offense or is seeking to set aside or vacate a death sentence under 28 U.S.C. §§ 2254 or 2255;

(8) is entitled to appointment of counsel in verification of consent proceedings pursuant to a transfer of an offender to or from the United States for the execution of a penal sentence under 18 U.S.C. § 4109;

(9) is the subject of a federal grand jury subpoena and risks self-incrimination, loss of liberty or contempt of court;

(10) is the subject of federal law enforcement investigation and faces a substantial risk of federal charges;

(11) is entitled to appointment of counsel under the Sixth Amendment to the Constitution; or

(12) faces loss of liberty in a case, and federal law requires the appointment of counsel.

B. Whenever a Judge determines that the interest of justice requires it, representation may be provided for a eligible person who:

(1) is charged with a petty offense (Class B or C misdemeanor, or an infraction) for which a sentence to confinement is authorized;

(2) is seeking relief, other than to set aside or vacate a death sentence, under 28 U.S.C. §§ 2242, 2254 or 2255; or

(3) is proposed by the United States Attorney for processing under a pretrial diversion program.

V. Federal Public Defender Organization.

A. The Court finds that the Federal Public Defender Organization of the Western District of New York previously established in this District pursuant to the CJA, is an effective component in the provision of legal assistance in this District as required by the CJA and Guidelines and shall continue to provide such services to eligible persons in this District under the CJA Guidelines and the Plan. The Federal Public Defender Organization shall be capable of providing representation throughout the District and shall maintain offices in Buffalo and Rochester, New York.

B. The Federal Public Defender shall be responsible for the supervision and management of the Federal Public Defender Organization. It will be the responsibility of the Federal Public Defender to designate the staff attorney who will handle a case assigned to the Public Defender Organization.

C. The Federal Public Defender shall comply with all reporting and other duties including reports of the Organization's activities, financial condition and budgets as required by the Administrative Office of the United States Courts and as provided in the Plan. Copies of such reports shall be furnished to the Court.

VI. Assignment of Federal Public Defender and Private Counsel Under the Plan.
Legal services to eligible persons shall be provided by both the Federal Public Defender Organization of this District and private counsel who are appointed from the Trial Panel and from the Appellate Panel as established under the Plan. It is the Court's intention that private counsel from the Trial and Appellate Panels will be assigned as counsel in a substantial portion of cases.

VII. Establishment of Panel Selection Committee.

A. *Membership.* A Panel Selection Committee shall be established by the Court. The Committee shall consist of seven members as follows:

(1) four experienced criminal defense attorneys from the private bar of the District—two from the Buffalo division of the District and two from the Rochester division;

(2) two Judges of the Court; and

(3) the Federal Public Defender for the District.

The private bar members of the Committee shall serve without compensation and at the pleasure of the Court. One of the four private attorney members of the Committee shall be the representative of the District to the National Conference of CJA Attorneys. The Federal Public Defender for the District shall be a permanent member of the Committee and shall serve as its secretary. The Committee shall select its own chairperson. The Committee may be expanded from time to time, at the discretion of the Court. Unless otherwise stated in this Plan, "the Committee" refers to the entire Committee or the Committee's designated subcommittee or representative.

B. *Duties of the Committee.* The Committee shall meet at least twice each calendar year to consider business pertinent to the administration of the Plan as determined by the Committee or as requested by the Court. Such business may include reviewing applications for admission to the Trial Panel, Appellate Panel and the respective Training Panels ("the Panels") as established by the Plan. The Committee shall review the qualifications of all such applicants, and recommend, for approval by the Court, those applicants meeting the criteria established by the Plan for admission to the Panels. The Committee may interview any applicant at its discretion. The Committee shall also review, at least once annually, the operation and administration of the Panels, and recommend to the Court any changes deemed necessary or appropriate by the Committee regarding the appointment process and management of the Panels, including removal of an attorney as a member of any Panels, and the general operation of the Plan. The Committee may also report to the Court as to the continued availability of Panel members to accept appointments. The Committee shall also consider such other matters as are referred to the Committee by the Court.

VIII. Establishment of the Trial Panel.

A. *Eligibility.* Any attorney who seeks appointment as a member of the Trial Panel must be admitted to practice before the Court and the United States Court of Appeals for the Second Circuit and be in good standing. Such attorney must certify that he or she has read and can demonstrate knowledge of the Federal Rules of Criminal Procedure, the Federal Rules of Evidence, the Federal Rules of Appellate Procedure, the United States Sentencing Guidelines, the Bail Reform Act of 1984, the Local Rules of Criminal Procedure and the Second Circuit Rules of Appellate Procedure.

Such attorney must have tried at least two felony cases to verdict in either state or federal court. Alternatively, an applicant for appointment to the Trial Panel must have appeared as defense counsel of record in at least two federal felony cases from initial appearance or arraignment through sentencing and have other significant trial experience as determined by the Committee. Unless specifically permitted by the Court, applicants shall have their principal place of business within the Western District of New York.

B. *Application for Trial Panel Membership.* An attorney who wishes to serve on the Trial Panel under this Plan must submit a written application for Trial

Panel Membership. This requirement applies to all attorneys regardless of whether they have previously taken assignments under the existing CJA Plan or not. Application forms for Trial Panel membership shall be available from the Clerk of the Court and the Federal Public Defender. Applications shall be submitted to the Federal Public Defender, who shall promptly forward all applications to the chairperson of the Committee.

C. *Disputes.* Any disputes regarding appointment to the Trial Panel must be submitted, in writing, to the Chief Judge for determination by the Court.

IX. Appellate Panel.

A. *Eligibility.* An Appellate Panel shall be created, consisting of attorneys who wish to handle post-conviction matters only. An applicant for membership on the Appellate Panel must complete a written application, available through the Federal Public Defender or the Clerk of the Court. Applicants must be members in good standing of the bar of the District, and admitted to practice before United States Court of Appeals for the Second Circuit. An applicant must certify that the applicant has read and can demonstrate knowledge of the Federal Rules of Criminal Procedure, the Federal Rules of Evidence, the Federal Rules of Appellate Procedure, the United States Sentencing Guidelines, the Bail Reform Act of 1984, the Local Rules of Criminal Procedure and the Second Circuit Rules of Appellate Procedure. An applicant must have been counsel of record in at least two state or federal direct criminal or habeas corpus appeals, which were briefed and argued by the applicant, and shall submit to the Committee a recent writing sample.

B. *Assignment.* Assignment of cases to members of the Appellate Panel shall follow the same procedure as set forth in Section XI of this Plan. Members of the Appellate Panel are subject to Section XV and XVI of this Plan.

C. *Disputes.* Any disputes regarding appointment to the Appellate Panel must be submitted, in writing, to the Chief Judge for determination by the Court.

X. **Training Panels.** The Committee shall establish a Training Panel for attorneys whose current professional experience does not meet the requirements for membership on either the Trial Panel or the Appellate Panel.

A. *Trial Panel.* The Training Panel for trial work shall consist of attorneys admitted in the District who wish to accept misdemeanor assignments and who are willing to assist members of the Trial Panel in a "second chair" capacity. Training Panel members may not receive assignments in felony cases. A Training Panel attorney may be appointed by a presiding Judge to provide legal representation for an eligible person where the criminal charge involved is solely a misdemeanor. A Training Panel attorney who assists on a "second chair" basis from jury selection through verdict in a federal felony trial may count such trial experience as the equivalent of having tried one felony case for the purpose of satisfying the requirements for membership on the Trial Panel. Prior service on the Training Panel is not a requirement for membership on the Trial Panel, nor will service on the Training Panel necessarily result in membership on the Trial Panel.

B. *Appellate Panels.* The Committee shall also establish a Training Panel for attorneys whose current professional experience does not meet the requirements for membership on the Appellate Panel. Training Panel members seeking membership on the Appellate Panel will be afforded an opportunity to assist a member of the Appellate Panel in the briefing for argument of at least one direct felony conviction or federal habeas corpus appeal under standards as may be adopted by the Committee. The rendering of satisfactory assistance in a minimum of one appeal to the Court of Appeals for the Second Circuit under this section as determined by the Committee may be substituted for service as appellate counsel of record in one federal appeal for purposes of meeting the requirements for membership on the Appellate Panel as provided in this Plan. Prior service on the Training Panel is not a requirement for membership on the Appellate Panel, nor will service on the Training Panel necessarily result in membership on the Trial Panel.

C. *Eligibility for Training Panels.* An applicant to a Training Panel must certify that he or she has read and can demonstrate knowledge of the Federal Rules of Criminal Procedure, the Federal Rules of Evidence, the Federal Rules of Appellate Procedure, the United States Sentencing Guidelines, the Bail Reform Act of 1984, the Local Rules of Criminal Procedure and the Second Circuit Rules of Appellate Procedure. Training Panel members shall comply with the requirements of Section XV of this Plan.

D. *Disputes.* Any disputes regarding eligibility for appointment to the Trial and Appellate Training Panels must be submitted, in writing, to the Chief Judge for determination by the Court.

XI. Assignment of Cases.

A. *Maintenance of Trial Panel List.* The Court shall maintain a list of attorneys eligible for assignment as members of the Trial Panel with office addresses and telephone numbers for each attorney. A copy of this list shall be provided to each Judge. The Court shall record all assignments to Trial Panel members and the Federal Public Defender.

B. *Assignments From the Trial Panel.* Upon determination by the Court of the need for the appointment of counsel under this Plan, the Judge shall obtain names from the Trial Panel in a suffi-

cient number as determined by the Judge. The Judge shall take all reasonable steps in the circumstances of the case to ensure that counsel is appointed expeditiously, that appointments from the Trial Panel are fairly distributed among all members of the Trial Panel and that information concerning the availability of counsel is maintained. It is the policy of the Court to seek a balanced distribution of appointments among the members of the Trial Panel.

XII. Appointment of Counsel.

A. In every case in which appointment of counsel pursuant to 18 U.S.C. § 3006A and this Plan is authorized, it is the duty of the Judge to advise the person of the right to counsel. The Judge shall appoint counsel promptly if the party is financially unable to obtain an attorney, unless the party waives his or her right to be represented by counsel.

B. The Judge, when making the appointment, shall, in his or her discretion, appoint either the Federal Public Defender or a member of the Trial Panel, except in special circumstances where it becomes necessary to appoint some other member of the bar of the Court. Such special circumstances include cases in which the Judge determines that the appointment of an attorney not a member of the Trial Panel is in the interest of justice, judicial economy or continuity of representation where permitted by the CJA or Guidelines and as determined by the Court, or when there are some other compelling circumstances warranting appointment of counsel who is not a member of the Federal Public Defender Office or the Trial Panel.

C. A defendant shall not have the right to select a particular attorney from the Federal Public Defender's Office or the Trial Panel or from the Appellate Panel.

D. Counsel shall be provided to eligible persons as soon as feasible after they are taken into custody, when they first appear before the Court, or when the Judge otherwise considers appointment of counsel appropriate under the CJA, whichever occurs first.

E. The determination of eligibility for representation under the CJA is a judicial function to be performed by the Court after making appropriate inquiries concerning the person's financial condition.

F. If, at any time after the appointment of counsel, the Court finds that the defendant is financially able to obtain counsel or make partial payments for the representation, the Court may terminate the appointment of counsel or direct that any funds available to the defendant be paid, in a lump sum or by periodic payments, as provided in 18 U.S.C. § 3006A(f). If, at any time after appointment, counsel obtains information that a client is financially able to make payment, in whole or in part, for legal or other services in connection with his or her representation, and the source of the attorney's information is not protected as a privileged communication, counsel shall advise the Court.

G. At any stage of the criminal proceedings, upon finding that the person is financially unable to continue to pay retained counsel, the Court may make an appointment of counsel in accordance with the general procedure set forth in this Plan. This proviso does not, however, relieve retained counsel from either his/her contractual obligations under the retainer agreement or his/her obligations under the Code of Professional Responsibility. Also, this proviso does not alter the mandate of the Local Rules which require leave of Court to withdraw once a notice of appearance has been entered.

H. Counsel appointed by a Judge shall, unless excused by order of the Court, continue to act for the represented party in all court proceedings and other matters for which counsel was assigned. In all criminal cases, counsel shall advise the defendant of the right to appeal and of the right to counsel on appeal. If requested to do so by the defendant in a criminal case, counsel shall file a timely notice of appeal and shall continue to represent the defendant on appeal unless or until counsel is relieved by the Court of Appeals. Counsel must also comply with all rules regarding appeal including, where appropriate, the preparation of a writ of certiorari and advice to a defendant regarding the right to proceed pro se.

I. The Judge before whom a case is pending may, in the interest of justice, substitute one appointed counsel for another at any stage of the proceedings.

XIII. Investigative, Expert and Other Services. Counsel, whether or not appointed under this Plan, for a party who is financially unable to obtain investigative, expert or other services necessary for an adequate defense, may request such services by ex parte application to a Judge, as provided in 18 U.S.C. § 3006A(e) and any applicable guidelines established by the Judicial Conference of the United States. Upon finding that such services are necessary for adequate representation, and that the person is financially unable to obtain them, the Judge shall authorize counsel to obtain the services.

XIV. Compensation.

A. Payments of fees and expenses to counsel appointed under this Plan, other than to the Federal Public Defender, including any payment for investigative, expert or other services incurred, shall be made in accordance with any statutory limitations and such rules, regulations and guidelines as have been or may be prescribed from time to time by the Judicial Conference of the United States, and in accordance with the policies of the Administrative Office of the United States Courts. No appointed counsel may request or accept any payment or promise of payment for assist-ing in the representation of a party, unless such payment is approved by order of the Court. Payment in excess of any maximum amount provided by statute or otherwise may be made for extended or complex representation, whenever the Court in which the representation was rendered certifies that the amount of the excess payment is necessary to provide fair compensation, and the payment is approved by the Chief Judge of the Second Circuit or his/her designee.

B. Claims for compensation of private attorneys providing representation under the Plan shall be submitted on the appropriate CJA form to the Clerk of the Court. The Clerk's office shall review the claim form for mathematical accuracy and for conformity with CJA Guidelines and, after such review, shall forward the claim form for the consideration of the presiding Judge.

C. In the event the Judge shall find that the claim for compensation as submitted should be reduced, the Judge may confer with counsel to resolve any questions concerning the claim. The Judge may also, in the Judge's discretion, refer the matter to the Committee for its review and recommendation. Any counsel whose request for fees has been reduced may promptly request review by the Judge or by the Committee which may, following a review of the request, in its discretion, submit a recommendation to the Judge regarding such request. The Judge shall make the final decision as to the fee request following consideration of counsel's submission concerning the request and the Committee's recommendation, if such has been submitted to the Judge.

XV. Continuing Legal Education.

A. The Federal Public Defender shall regularly schedule and conduct continuing legal education programs for Panel attorneys for the purpose of enhancing their professional knowledge and skills. The Federal Public Defender shall present at least two training programs each calendar year, one of which will cover the fundamentals of federal criminal defense practice, including sentencing law and practice under the federal sentencing guidelines. These programs will be conducted within the District, at a nominal cost to attendees.

B. Each Trial Panel member shall be required to attend at least one of the annual training programs presented by the Federal Public Defender, or, in the alternative, to complete a minimum of six hours of federal criminal defense continuing legal education offered by a bona fide continuing legal education program each year, at his or her own expense, as a condition of maintaining membership on the Panel. Panel members or applicants for Panel membership must certify, on or before January 1st of each year, on forms available at the Federal Public Defender's office, that they have satisfied the continuing legal education requirements as stated herein.

XVI. Removal From the Trial, Appellate or Training Panels.

A. *Mandatory Removal.* Any member of the Trial, Appellate or Training Panels who is suspended or disbarred from the practice of law by the state court to which such member is admitted or who is suspended or disbarred from this Court, shall be removed immediately from such Panels.

B. *Discretionary Removal.* A member of the Trial, Appellate or Training Panels who refuses to accept an appointment, or who refuses to participate in the Mentor Program as established under Section XVII of this Plan, or who refuses or neglects to comply with the requirements concerning Continuing Legal Education at Section XV, without good cause, may be removed from such Panels. A Panel member may also be removed from the Panel for failure to represent his or her client in a vigorous, professional and ethical manner. In the event that a Judge determines that an attorney should be removed from the Panel, the matter shall be referred to the Committee for its review and recommendation. The member attorney shall have an opportunity to appear and be heard, with or without counsel, before the Committee. The Committee shall promptly review the matter and report its recommendation to the Court. Upon consideration of the Committee's report, the Court may remove the attorney from the Panel.

C. *Re-Application.* Any attorney removed from the Panel may reapply one year after removal provided the requirements of Section VIII A of this Plan are satisfied.

XVII. Mentor Program.

A. If requested by the Committee, a Trial or Appellate Panel member shall serve as a mentor to a Training Panel member. To fulfill this requirement, the Trial Panel member shall allow the Training Panel member to observe and to participate in, if appropriate, all aspects of a federal criminal case, including client conferences, decisions concerning defense strategy, motion and trial preparation and court appearances including hearings and trials.

B. Appellate Panel members shall allow the Training Panel member to participate in client conferences, review and filing of the record on appeal, research and drafting briefs, pre-argument conferences, the observation of oral argument, and, with approval of the Court of Appeals, oral argument.

C. Trial and Appellate Panel members will be expected to agree to reasonable mentoring requests and endeavor to involve the Training Panel member as closely as possible in the substance of the representation. The Committee shall establish standards for the administration of this program.

XVIII. Death Penalty Cases.
Cases involving the death penalty, shall continue to be handled under the provisions of Section XI of the existing CJA Plan, adopted July 14, 1993, until further order of the Court.

XIX. Forms.
Where standard forms have been approved by the Judicial Conference of the United States, or an appropriate committee thereof, and have been distributed by the Administrative Office of the United States Courts, such forms shall be used by the Court, the Clerk, the Federal Public Defender Organization and appointed counsel.

XX. Transition.
For a period of six (6) months, until a sufficiently large pool of Trial Panel attorneys has been created under this new Plan, appointments of counsel will continue to be made from attorneys taking assignments under the existing Plan. All other provisions of the new Plan shall take effect upon its approval by the Judicial Council of the Second Circuit.

XXI. Effective Date.
This Plan, adopted the 20th day of March, 2001, shall take effect when approved by the Judicial Council of the Second Circuit.

Approved by the Judicial Council of the Second Judicial Circuit and filed in the District Court on April 5, 2001.

APPENDIX H. REVISED PLAN FOR PROMPT DISPOSITION OF CRIMINAL CASES

Pursuant to the Speedy Trial Act of 1974, 18 U.S.C. § 3161, et seq.

I. Introduction.

A. *Statement of Adoption by the Court.* Pursuant to the requirements of Rule 50(b) of the Federal Rules of Criminal Procedure, the Speedy Trial Act of 1974 (18 U.S.C. Chapter 208), the Speedy Trial Act Amendments Act of 1979 (Pub.L. No. 96–43, 93 Stat. 327), and the Federal Juvenile Delinquency Act (18 U.S.C. §§ 5036, 5037), the Judges of the United States District Court have adopted the following Plan to minimize undue delay and to further the prompt disposition of criminal cases. This Plan reflects the efforts and cooperation of the Court and other offices of the federal criminal justice community of the Western District of New York.

B. *Notice of Adoption by the Court.* Copies of the Plan adopted in this District pursuant to 18 U.S.C. §§ 3165, 3166 and the local Court Rules augmenting and implementing the Plan and the accompanying recommendations of the Planning Group will be available for public inspection at the offices of the Clerk of the Court, U.S. District Courthouse, Niagara Square, Buffalo, New York 14202 and U.S. Courthouse, 100 State Street, Rochester, New York 14614. Counsel representing defendants in criminal cases and defendants electing pro se representation shall be notified of the existence of the Act, this Plan and any local Court Rules that may be implemented to augment the Act and the Plan.

II. Statement of Time Limits and Procedures for Implementation. Pursuant to the requirements of Rule 50(b) of the Federal Rules of Criminal Procedure, the Speedy Trial Act of 1974 (18 U.S.C. Chapter 208), the Speedy Trial Act Amendments Act of 1979 (Pub.L. No. 96–43, 93 Stat. 327), and the Federal Juvenile Delinquency Act (18 U.S.C. §§ 5036, 5037), the Judges of the United States District Court for the Western District of New York have adopted the following time limits and procedures to minimize undue delay and to further the prompt disposition of criminal cases and certain juvenile proceedings.

1. *Applicability.*

(a) Offenses. The time limits set forth herein are applicable to all criminal offenses triable in the Court,[1] including cases triable by United States magistrate judges, except for petty offenses as defined in 18 U.S.C. § 19 and Rule 58(a) of the Federal Rules of Criminal Procedure. Except as specifically provided, they are not applicable to proceedings under the Federal Juvenile Delinquency Act. [18 U.S.C. §§ 5031–5042].

[1] 18 U.S.C. § 3172 defines "offense" as "any Federal criminal offense which is in violation of any Act of Congress . . ."

(b) Persons. The time limits are applicable to persons accused who have not been indicted or informed against as well as those who have, and the word "defendant" includes such persons unless the context indicates otherwise.

2. *Priorities in Scheduling Criminal Cases.* Preference shall be given to criminal proceedings as far as practicable as required by Rule 50(a) of the Federal Rules of Criminal Procedure. The trial of defendants in custody solely because they are awaiting trial and of high risk defendants as defined in section 5 should be given preference over other criminal cases. [18 U.S.C. § 3164(a)].

3. *Time Within Which an Indictment or Information Must Be Filed.*

(a) Time Limits. If an individual is arrested or served with a summons and the complaint charges an offense to be prosecuted in this District, any indictment or information subsequently filed in connection with such charge shall be filed within 30 days of arrest or service. [18 U.S.C. § 3161(b)].

(b) Grand Jury Not in Session. If the defendant is charged with a felony to be prosecuted in this District, and no grand jury in this District has been

in session during the 30–day period prescribed in subsection (a), such period shall be extended an additional 30 days. [18 U.S.C. § 3161(b)].

(c) Measurement of Time Periods. If a person has not been arrested or served with a summons on a Federal charge, an arrest will be deemed to have been made at such time as the person (i) is held in custody solely for the purpose of responding to a Federal charge; (ii) is delivered to the custody of a Federal official in connection with a Federal charge; or (iii) appears before a judicial officer in connection with a Federal charge.

(d) Related Procedures.

(i) At the time of the earliest appearance before a judicial officer of a person who has been arrested for an offense not charged in an indictment or information, the judicial officer shall establish for the record the date on which the arrest took place.

(ii) In the absence of a showing to the contrary, a summons shall be considered to have been served on the date of service shown on the return thereof.

4. *Time Within Which Trial Must Commence.*

(a) Time Limits. In accordance with 18 U.S.C. § 3161(c)(1), the trial of a defendant shall commence not later than 70 days after the last to occur of the following dates:

(i) The date on which an indictment or information is filed in this District;

(ii) The date on which a sealed indictment or information is unsealed; or

(iii) The date of the defendant's first appearance before a judicial officer of this District.

(b) Retrial; Trial After Reinstatement of an Indictment or Information. The retrial of a defendant shall commence within 70 days from the date the order occasioning the retrial becomes final, as shall the trial of a defendant upon an indictment or information dismissed by a trial court and reinstated following an appeal. If the retrial or trial follows an appeal or collateral attack, the Court may extend the period if unavailability of witnesses or other factors resulting from passage of time make trial within 70 days impracticable. The extended period shall not exceed 180 days. [18 U.S.C. § 3161(d)(2), (e)].

(c) Withdrawal of Plea. If a defendant enters a plea of guilty or nolo contendere to any or all charges in an indictment or information and is subsequently permitted to withdraw it, the time limit shall be determined for all counts as if the indictment or information were filed on the day the order permitting withdrawal of the plea became final. [18 U.S.C. § 3161(i)].

(d) Superseding Charges. If, after an indictment or information has been filed, a complaint, indictment, or information is filed which charges the defendant with the same offense or with an offense required to be joined with that offense, the time limit applicable to the subsequent charge will be determined as follows:

(i) If the original indictment or information was dismissed on motion of the defendant before the filing of the subsequent charge, the time limit shall be determined without regard to the existence of the original charge. [18 U.S.C. § 3161(d)(1)].

(ii) If the original indictment or information is pending at the time the subsequent charge is filed, the trial shall commence within the time limit for commencement of trial on the original indictment or information.

(iii) If the original indictment or information was dismissed on motion of the United States Attorney before the filing of the subsequent charge, the trial shall commence within the time limit for commencement of trial on the original indictment or information, but the period during which the defendant was not under charges shall be excluded from the computations. Such period is the period between the dismissal of the original indictment or information and the date the time would have commenced to run on the subsequent charge had there been no previous charge.[2] [18 U.S.C. § 3161(h)(6)].

[2] Under the rule of this paragraph, if an indictment was dismissed on motion of the prosecutor on May 1, with 20 days remaining within which trial must be commenced, and the defendant was arrested on a new complaint on June 1, the time remaining for trial would be 20 days from June 1; the time limit would be based on the original indictment, but the period from the dismissal to the new arrest would not count. Although the 30–day arrest-to-indictment time limit would apply to the new arrest as a formal matter, the short deadline for trial would necessitate earlier grand jury action.

If the subsequent charge is contained in a complaint, the formal time limit within which an indictment or information must be obtained on the charge shall be determined without regard to the existence of the original indictment or information, but earlier action may in fact be required if the time limit for commencement of trial is to be satisfied.

(e) Measurement of Time Periods. For the purposes of this section:

(i) If a defendant signs a written consent to be tried before a Magistrate Judge and no indictment or information charging the offense has been filed, the time limit shall run from the date of such consent. [18 U.S.C. § 3161(c)(1)].

(ii) In the event of a transfer to this District under Rule 20 of the Federal Rules of Criminal Procedure, the indictment or information shall be deemed filed in this District when the papers in the proceeding or certified copies thereof are received by the Clerk.

(iii) A trial in a jury case shall be deemed to commence at the beginning of voir dire.

(iv) A trial in a non-jury case shall be deemed to commence on the day the case is called, provided that some step in the trial procedure immediately follows.

(f) Related Procedures.

(i) At the time of the defendant's earliest appearance before a judicial officer of this District, the officer will take appropriate steps to assure that the defendant is represented by counsel and shall appoint counsel where appropriate under the Criminal Justice Act, Rule 44 of the Federal Rules of Criminal Procedure, and the Court's Criminal Justice Act Plan.

(ii) The Court shall have sole responsibility for setting cases for trial after consultation with counsel. At the time of arraignment or as soon thereafter as is practicable, each case will be set for trial on a day certain or listed for trial on a weekly or other short-term calendar. [18 U.S.C. § 3161(a)].

(iii) Individual calendars shall be managed so that it will be reasonably anticipated that every criminal case set for trial will be reached during the week of original setting. A conflict in schedules of Assistant United States Attorneys or defense counsel will be ground for a continuance or delayed setting only if approved by the Court and called to the Court's attention at the earliest practicable time.

(iv) In the event that a complaint, indictment, or information is filed against a defendant charged in a pending indictment or information or in an indictment or information dismissed on motion of the United States Attorney, the trial on the new charge shall commence within the time limit for commencement of trial on the original indictment or information unless the Court finds that the new charge is not for the same offense charged in the original indictment or information or an offense required to be joined therewith.

(v) All pretrial hearings shall be conducted as soon after the arraignment as possible, consistent with the priorities of other matters on the Court's criminal docket.

5. *Defendants in Custody and High–Risk Defendants.*[3]

[3] If a defendant's presence has been obtained through the filing of a detainer with state authorities, the Interstate Agreement on Detainers, 18 U.S.C., Appendix, may require that trial commence before the deadline established by the Speedy Trial Act. See *U.S. v. Mauro*, 436 U.S. 340, 356–57 n. 24 (1978).

(a) Time Limits. In accordance with 18 U.S.C. § 3164(b), notwithstanding any longer time periods that may be permitted under sections 3 and 4 of this Plan, the following time limits will also be applicable to defendants in custody and high-risk defendants as herein defined:

(i) The trial of a defendant held in custody solely for the purpose of trial on a Federal charge shall commence within 90 days following the beginning of continuous custody.

(ii) The trial of a high-risk defendant shall commence within 90 days of the designation as high-risk.

(b) Definition of "High–Risk Defendant". A high-risk defendant is one reasonably designated by the United States Attorney as posing a danger to himself or herself or any other person or to the community.

(c) Measurement of Time Periods. For the purposes of this section:

(i) A defendant is deemed to be in detention awaiting trial when he or she is arrested on a Federal charge or otherwise held for the purpose of responding to a Federal charge. Detention is deemed to be solely because the defendant is awaiting trial unless the person exercising custodial authority has an independent basis (not including a detainer) for continuing to hold the defendant.

(ii) If a case is transferred pursuant to Rule 20 of the Federal Rules of Criminal Procedure and the defendant subsequently rejects disposition under Rule 20 or the Court declines to accept the plea, a new period of continuous detention awaiting trial will begin at that time.

(iii) A trial shall be deemed to commence as provided in sections 4(e)(iii) and 4(e)(iv).

(d) Related Procedures.

(i) If a defendant is being held in custody solely for the purpose of awaiting trial, the United States Attorney shall advise the Court at the earliest practicable time of the date of the beginning of such custody.

(ii) The United States Attorney shall advise the Court at the earliest practicable time (usually at the hearing with respect to bail) if the defendant is considered by him or her to be high-risk.

(iii) If the Court finds that the filing of a "high-risk" designation as a public record may result in prejudice to the defendant, it may order the designation sealed for such period as is necessary to protect the defendant's right to a fair trial, but not beyond the time that the Court's judgment in the case becomes final. During the time the designation is under seal, it shall be made known to the defendant and his or her counsel but shall not be made known to other persons without the permission of the Court.

6. *Exclusion of Time From Computations.*

(a) Applicability. In computing any time limit under section 3, 4, or 5, the periods of delay set forth in 18 U.S.C. § 3161(h) shall be excluded. Such periods of delay shall not be excluded in computing the minimum period for commencement of trial under section 7.

(b) Records of Excludable Time. The Clerk of the Court shall enter on the docket, in the form prescribed by the Administrative Office of the United States Courts, information with respect to excludable periods of time for each criminal defendant.

(c) Stipulations.

(i) The attorney for the government and the attorney for the defendant may at any time enter into stipulations with respect to the accuracy of the docket entries recording excludable time.

(ii) To the extent that the amount of time stipulated by the parties does not exceed the amount recorded on the docket for any excludable period of delay, the stipulation shall be conclusive as between the parties unless it has no basis in fact or law. It shall similarly be conclusive as to a codefendant for the limited purpose of determining, under 18 U.S.C. § 3161(h)(7), whether time has run against the defendant entering into the stipulation.

(iii) To the extent that the amount of time stipulated exceeds the amount recorded on the docket, the stipulation shall have no effect unless approved by the Court.

(d) Pre-indictment Procedures.

(i) In the event that the United States Attorney anticipates that an indictment or information will not be filed within the time limit set forth in section 3, he or she may file a written motion with the Court for a determination of excludable time. In the event that the United States Attorney seeks a continuance under 18 U.S.C. § 3161(h)(8), he or she shall file a written motion with the Court requesting such a continuance.

(ii) The motion of the United States Attorney shall state (A) the period of time proposed for exclusion, and (B) the basis of the proposed exclusion. If the motion is for a continuance under 18 U.S.C. § 3161(h)(8), it shall also state whether or not the defendant is being held in custody on the basis of the complaint. In appropriate circumstances, the motion may include a request that some or all of the supporting material be considered ex parte and in camera.

(iii) The Court may grant a continuance under 18 U.S.C. § 3161(h)(8) for either a specific period of time or a period to be determined by reference to an event (such as recovery from illness) not within the control of the government. If the continuance is to a date not certain, the Court shall require one or both parties to inform the Court promptly when and if the circumstances that justify the continuance no longer exist. In addition, the Court shall require one or both parties to file periodic reports bearing on the continued existence of such circumstances. The Court shall determine the frequency of such reports in the light of the facts of the particular case.

(e) Post-indictment Procedures.

(i) In the event that the Court continues a trial beyond the time limit set forth in section 4 or 5, the Court shall determine whether the limit may be recomputed by excluding time pursuant to 18 U.S.C. § 3161(h).

(ii) If it is determined that a continuance is justified, the Court shall set forth its findings in the record, either orally or in writing. If the continuance is granted under 18 U.S.C. § 3161(h)(8), the Court shall also set forth its reasons for finding that the ends of justice served by granting the continuance outweigh the best interests of the public and the defendant in a speedy trial. If the continuance is to a date not certain, the Court shall require one or both parties to inform the Court promptly when and if the circumstances that justify the continuance no longer exist. In addition, the Court shall require one or both parties to file periodic reports bearing on the continued existence of such circumstances. The Court shall determine the frequency of such reports in light of the facts of the particular case.

7. *Minimum Period for Defense Preparation.* Unless the defendant consents in writing to the contrary, the trial shall not commence earlier than 30 days from the date on which the defendant first appears through counsel or expressly waives counsel and elects to proceed pro se. In circumstances in which the 70–day time limit for commencing trial on a charge in an indictment or information is determined by reference to an earlier indictment or information pursuant to section 4(d), the 30–day minimum period shall also be determined by reference to the earlier indictment or information. When prosecution is resumed on an original indictment or information following a mistrial, appeal, or withdrawal of a guilty plea, a new 30–day minimum period will not begin to run. The Court will in all cases schedule trials so as to permit defense counsel adequate preparation time in the light of all the circumstances. [18 U.S.C. § 3161(c)(2)].

8. *Time Within Which Defendant Should Be Sentenced.*

(a) Time Limit. Sentencing proceedings shall be scheduled no earlier than sixty (60) days following entry of a verdict of guilty or a plea of guilty or nolo contendere unless all the parties and the Court agree that, in the interest of justice, an earlier date should be set.

(b) Related Procedures. Presentence investigations and reports shall be prepared in accordance with Rule 32 of the Federal Rules of Criminal Procedure and the Local Procedural Guidelines To Govern Sentencing Procedures Under the Sentencing Reform Act of 1984.

9. *Juvenile Proceedings.*

(a) Time Within Which Trial Must Commence. An alleged delinquent who is in detention pending trial shall be brought to trial within 30 days of the date on which such detention was begun, as provided in 18 U.S.C. § 5036.

(b) Time of Dispositional Hearing. If a juvenile is adjudicated delinquent, a separate dispositional hearing shall be held no later than 20 court days after trial, unless the Court has ordered further study of the juvenile in accordance with 18 U.S.C. § 5037(d).

10. *Sanctions.*

(a) Dismissal or Release From Custody. Failure to comply with the requirements of Title I of the Speedy Trial Act may entitle the defendant to dismissal of the charges against him or her or to release from pretrial custody. Nothing in this Plan shall be construed to require that a case be dismissed or a defendant released from custody in circumstances in which such action would not be required by 18 U.S.C. §§ 3162 and 3164.[4]

[4] Dismissal may also be required in some cases under the Interstate Agreement on Detainers, 18 U.S.C., Appendix.

(b) High–Risk Defendants. A high-risk defendant whose trial has not commenced within the time limit set forth in 18 U.S.C. § 3164(b) shall, if the failure to commence trial was through no fault of the attorney for the government, have his or her release conditions automatically reviewed. A high-risk defendant who is found by the Court to have intentionally delayed the trial of his or her case shall be subject to an order of the Court modifying his or her nonfinancial conditions of release under Chapter 207 of Title 18, U.S.C., to ensure that he or she shall appear at trial as required. [18 U.S.C. § 3164(c)].

(c) Discipline of Attorneys. In a case in which counsel (i) knowingly allows the case to be set for trial without disclosing the fact that a necessary witness would be unavailable for trial, (ii) files a motion solely for the purpose of delay which he or she knows is frivolous and without merit, (iii) makes a statement for the purpose of obtaining a continuance which he or she knows to be false and which is material to the granting of the continuance, or (iv) otherwise willfully fails to proceed to trial without justification consistent with 18 U.S.C. § 3161, the Court may punish such counsel as provided in 18 U.S.C. § 3162(b).

(d) Alleged Juvenile Delinquents. An alleged delinquent in custody whose trial has not commenced within the time limit set forth in 18 U.S.C. § 5036 shall be entitled to dismissal of his or her case pursuant to that section unless the Attorney General shows that the delay was consented to or caused by the juvenile or his or her counsel, or would be in the interest of justice in the particular case.

11. *Persons Serving Terms of Imprisonment.* If the United States Attorney knows that a person charged with an offense is serving a term of imprisonment in any penal institution, he or she shall promptly seek to obtain the presence of the prisoner for trial, or cause a detainer to be filed, in accordance with the provisions of 18 U.S.C. § 3161(j).

12. *Effective Date.* This revision of the District's Plan was approved by the Court this 17th day of May 1994 and shall become effective upon the approval of the reviewing panel in accordance with 18 U.S.C. § 3165(d).

APPENDIX I. STANDING ORDER GOVERNING CLAIMS UNDER THE RACKETEER INFLUENCED AND CORRUPT ORGANIZATIONS ACT

The following standing order shall apply to all claims filed in this District under the Racketeer Influenced & Corrupt Organizations Act ("RICO"), 18 U.S.C. § 1961, et seq.

Any party asserting a claim, cross-claim or counterclaims under RICO, shall file a "RICO Case Statement" as described below. This statement shall be filed within 20 days of receipt of this Order in the particular action, and shall include those facts upon which the plaintiff is relying and which were obtained as a result of the "reasonable inquiry" required by Fed.R.Civ.P. 11. In particular, this statement shall be in a form which uses the numbers and letters as set forth below, and shall state in detail and with specificity the following information.

1. State whether the alleged unlawful conduct is in violation of 18 U.S.C. §§ 1962(a), (b), (c), and/or (d).

2. List each defendant and state the alleged misconduct and basis of liability of each defendant.

3. List the alleged wrongdoers, other than the defendants listed above, and state the alleged misconduct of each wrongdoer.

4. List the alleged victims and state how each victim was allegedly injured.

5. Describe in detail the pattern of racketeering activity or collection of unlawful debts alleged for each RICO claim. A description of the pattern of racketeering shall include the following information:

a. List the alleged predicate acts and the specific statutes which were allegedly violated;

b. Provide the dates of the predicate acts, the participants in the predicate acts, and a description of the facts surrounding the predicate acts;

c. If the RICO claim is based on the predicate offenses of wire fraud, mail fraud, or fraud in the sale of securities, the "circumstances constituting fraud or mistake shall be stated with particularity." Fed. R.Civ.P. 9(b). Identify the time, place and contents of the alleged misrepresentations, and the identity of persons to whom and by whom the alleged misrepresentations were made;

d. State whether there has been a criminal conviction for violation of each predicate act;

e. State whether civil litigation has resulted in a judgment in regard to each predicate act;

f. Describe how the predicate acts form a "pattern of racketeering activity"; and

g. State whether the alleged predicate acts relate to each other as part of a common plan. If so, describe in detail.

6. Describe in detail the alleged enterprise for each RICO claim. A description of the enterprise shall include the following information:

a. State the names of the individuals, partnerships, corporations, associations, or other legal entities, which allegedly constitute the enterprise;

b. Describe the structure, purpose, function and course of conduct of the enterprise;

c. State whether any defendants are employees, officers or directors of the alleged enterprise;

d. State whether any defendants are associated with the alleged enterprise;

e. State whether you are alleging that the defendants are individuals or entities separate from the alleged enterprise, or that the defendants are the enterprise itself, or members of the enterprise; and

f. If any defendants are alleged to be the enterprise itself, or members of the enterprise, explain whether such defendants are perpetrators, passive instruments, or victims of the alleged racketeering activity.

7. State and describe in detail whether you are alleging that the pattern of racketeering activity and the enterprise are separate or have merged into one entity.

8. Describe the alleged relationship between the activities of the enterprise and the pattern of racketeering activity. Discuss how the racketeering activity differs from the usual and daily activities of the enterprise, if at all.

9. Describe what benefits, if any, the alleged enterprise receives from the alleged pattern of racketeering.

10. Describe the effect of the activities of the enterprise on interstate or foreign commerce.

11. If the complaint alleges a violation of 18 U.S.C. § 1962(a), provide the following information:

a. State who received the income derived from the pattern of racketeering activity or through the collection of an unlawful debt; and

b. Describe the use or investment of such income.

12. If the complaint alleges a violation of 18 U.S.C. § 1962(b), describe in detail the acquisition or mainte-

nance of any interest in or control of the alleged enterprise.

13. If the complaint alleges a violation of 18 U.S.C. § 1962(c), provide the following information:

a. State who is employed by or associated with the enterprise; and

b. State whether the same entity is both the liable "person" and the "enterprise" under § 1962(c).

14. If the complaint alleges a violation of 18 U.S.C. § 1962(d), describe in detail the alleged conspiracy.

15. Describe the alleged injury to business or property.

16. Describe the direct causal relationship between the alleged injury and the violation of the RICO statute.

17. List the damages sustained for which each defendant is allegedly liable.

18. List all other federal causes of action, if any, and provide the relevant statute numbers.

19. List all pendent state claims, if any.

20. Provide any additional information that you feel would be helpful to the Court in processing your RICO claim.

ALL OF THE ABOVE IS SO ORDERED.

Dated: January 22, 1991.

APPENDIX J. ORDER: IN THE MATTER OF APPLICATIONS FOR LEAVE TO PROCEED IN FORMA PAUPERIS IN CIVIL RIGHTS AND HABEAS CORPUS CASES BY STATE AND LOCAL PRISONERS

It appearing to the Court that changes are required in processing applications to proceed in forma pauperis in civil rights and habeas corpus cases brought by state and local prisoners, the following procedures are hereby adopted:

1. Whenever a state or local prisoner submits a civil rights complaint or petition for habeas corpus and requests in forma pauperis status, the prisoner shall request from the appropriate official of the institution where he (the masculine pronoun is used throughout only for convenience) is confined, a certified copy of his trust fund account for the three-month period preceding submission of the complaint/petition, or from the date of arrival at that institution, whichever is shorter.

If the prisoner has been confined for less then three (3) months at that institution, he is to furnish additional information as follows:

In the case of a state prisoner who has transferred from another state institution, he must request from the Central Office of the Department of Correctional

Services in Albany a statement of his account for that three-month period. In the case of a state prisoner who has recently transferred to his present institution from a county jail or a federal penitentiary, he is to furnish the name of the penal institution from which he has been transferred, if applicable. In the case of a local prisoner who has been confined at that institution for less than three months, he shall furnish the name of the penal institution from which he has been transferred, if applicable.

In these events the Court in its discretion may seek further information from the prior institution.

2. The certified copies of the trust fund account information and the other information where required are to be submitted together with the application to proceed in forma pauperis and a partial filing fee or request for exemption according to procedures set forth below at Paragraphs 3–5.

3. A prisoner will be allowed to proceed in forma pauperis conditioned upon payment of a partial filing fee based on the income received at the correctional

facilities during the three-month period preceding submission of the complaint/petition. The partial filing fee required to be submitted by the prisoner shall be ten percent (10%) of the amounts deposited to his account within the preceding three months unless fixed at a lesser amount by a United States Judge or Magistrate following his consideration of any affidavit of special circumstances filed by the prisoner. In no event shall the fee exceed $5.00 for habeas corpus petitions and $120.00 for civil rights cases.

4. If the prisoner claims exceptional circumstances such as to render him unable to pay the filing fee, he shall include in addition to the aforementioned papers, an affidavit of special circumstances justifying a different payment or an exemption from the partial filing fee requirement.

5. (a). If the filing fee described above is submitted with the complaint/petition and accompanying papers, the complaint/petition shall be filed and referred to the Judge or Magistrate to whom the case is assigned for further consideration. If the application is approved, the Judge or Magistrate shall direct service of the complaint/petition by the United States Marshal.

(b). When an affidavit of special circumstances is submitted which in the opinion of the Judge or Magistrate warrants exemption from the partial filing fee, the complaint/petition will be filed.

In the event that an affidavit of special circumstances is submitted and the Judge or Magistrate rejects such application as not warranting exemption from the filing fee, the complaint/petition will be filed and the prisoner will have forty-five (45) days within which to comply with the partial filing fee requirement. The Judge or Magistrate shall direct service of the complaint/petition when the designated partial filing fee has been paid.

If the prisoner fails to comply with the filing fee Order within forty-five (45) days and has not been granted an extension of time within which to comply, the Judge may dismiss the case or a Magistrate may recommend that the action be dismissed and the entire file shall be forwarded to the assigned Judge for consideration of such recommendation.

This Order is effective as of October 1, 1989.

IT IS SO ORDERED.

CHAPTER 12 BANKRUPTCY RULES SUPPLEMENT

Historical and Statutory Notes

Pub. Note: The Bankruptcy Judges of the Western District have approved the Chapter 12 Interim Rules suggested by the Committee on Rules of Practice and Procedure in February, 1987. The Chapter 12 Interim Rules are reproduced in this volume following the Rules for the Division of Business Among District Judges for the Southern and Eastern Districts, ante.

*

LOCAL RULES OF BANKRUPTCY PROCEDURE
FOR THE
WESTERN DISTRICT OF NEW YORK

Effective May 13, 1997

Including Amendments Received Through
September 15, 2008

Research Note

These rules may be searched electronically on Westlaw in the NY-RULES database; updates to these rules may be found on Westlaw in NY-RULESUPDATES. For search tips, and a detailed summary of database content, consult the Westlaw Scope Screen of each database.

Rule

1001. Scope of Local Rules of Bankruptcy Procedure.
1007. Number of Copies of Lists, Schedules and Statements.
1009. Amendments to Voluntary Petitions, Lists, Schedules and Statements.
1014. Change of Venue.
1015. Consolidation or Joint Administration.
1019. Conversion—Procedure Following [Reserved].
1020. Chapter 11 Small Business Cases, General.
1072. Places of Holding Court.
1073. Assignment of Cases.
2002. Notices to Creditors, Equity Security Holders, United States, and United States Trustee.
2007. Trustees and Examiners.
2008. Notice to Trustee of Selection.
2010. Qualification by Trustee; Proceeding on Bond.
2014. Employment of Professionals.
2015. Trustees, Debtors–In–Possession Duties [Reserved].
2016. Compensation of Professionals.
2020. Service on the Office of the United States Trustee.
2081. Chapter 11.
2090. Attorneys—Admission to Practice.
2091. Attorneys—Withdrawal.
3001. Claims and Equity Security Interests—General.
3007. Objections to Claims.
4001. Relief From Automatic Stay; Cash Collateral and Financing Orders.
4008. Discharge and Reaffirmation Hearing.
5073. Photography, Recording Devices & Broadcasting.
5080. Fees—General.
5081. Fees—Form of Payment.
6004. Use, Sale or Lease of Property.
6007. Abandonment.
6070. Tax Returns & Tax Refunds.
7004. Service of Process.
7016. Pre–Trial Procedures.
7024. Unconstitutionality, Claim of.
7026. Discovery.

Rule

7040. Assignment of Adversary Proceedings.
7054. Costs–Taxation/Payment.
7055. Default–Failure to Prosecute.
7069. Judgment, Payment of.
8008. Appeals.
9004. Form of Papers.
9006. Time Periods.
9010. Attorneys—Notice of Appearance.
9013. Motions: Form and Service.
9014. Contested Matters.
9015. Jury Trials.
9022. Judgments and Orders, Notice of.
9024. Relief from Judgment or Order.
9070. Exhibits.
9071. Stipulations.

APPENDICES

App.

1. Conversion Table of Former Bankruptcy Rules, Standing Orders, and General Orders to Current Local Rules of Bankruptcy Procedure.
2. USDC Order of Reference.
3. Implementation of the Act of July 10, 1984, Public Law 98–353.
4. Reaffirmation of the Orders Implementing the Act of July 10, 1984, Public Law 98–353.
5. Order of Appointment of Chief Bankruptcy Judge.

ELECTRONIC CASE FILING

Administrative Procedures for Filing, Signing and Verifying Pleadings and Papers by Electronic Means.

ADMINISTRATIVE ORDERS

Order

1. Procedural Rules for Electronic Case Filing (ECF).

Order

3. Implementation of Bankruptcy Rule Amendments Concerning Privacy and Public Access to Electronic Case Files.
4. Procedural Rules Concerning Electronic Filing of Claims and Related Documents of Creditor/Limited Filer Activities.
5. Mandatory Electronic Filing of Documents by Internet Transmission.
6. Electronic Transmission of Notices by the Clerk and Elimination of Redundant Paper Notices for Registered CM/ECF E–Filers.

STANDING ORDERS

"Refund" of Filing Fees.
Notice to Creditors in Chapter 13 Cases.

Order

Debtors Asserting an Exception to the Limitation of the Automatic Stay Under 11 U.S.C. § 362(*l*) and Procedure for Receiving Rent Deposits.
Chapter 13 Cases Governed by the Bankruptcy Abuse Prevention and Consumer Protection Act of 2005.
Notice of Preferred Addresses Under 11 U.S.C. § 342(f) and National Creditor Registration Service.
Adoption of Interim Bankruptcy Rules to Implement Changes Made by the 2005 Bankruptcy Reform Legislation[1].
Common Default Statement.
Adoption of Interim Bankruptcy Rule 1007 and Revisions to Official Forms Implementing the Bankruptcy Abuse Prevention and Consumer Protection Act of 2005.
Implementation of Increase to Transcript Fee Rates and New Transcript Delivery Category.

RULE 1001. SCOPE OF LOCAL RULES OF BANKRUPTCY PROCEDURE

1001–1. Title and Numbering Sequence.

These local rules, to be known as the "Local Rules of Bankruptcy Procedure" for the Western District of New York, supplement the Federal Rules of Bankruptcy Procedure, and shall govern bankruptcy practice in the United States District Court and United States Bankruptcy Court for the Western District of New York, and supersede all previous Local Bankruptcy Rules.

[Former Rule 1]

[Effective May 13, 1997.]

RULE 1007. NUMBER OF COPIES OF LISTS, SCHEDULES AND STATEMENTS

1007–1. Number of Copies.

A. For conventionally filed cases, an original and three (3) copies of a petition, lists, schedules and statements under chapter 7 or chapter 13 of the Bankruptcy Code and amendments thereto shall be filed. These documents shall be filed in the order prescribed by the Clerk of the U.S. Bankruptcy Court.

B. For conventionally filed cases, an original and six (6) copies of a petition, lists, schedules and statements under chapter 9, chapter 11, or chapter 12 of the Bankruptcy Code and amendments thereto shall be filed. An original and six (6) copies of chapter 11 disclosure statements and plans shall be filed.

C. "Courtesy copies" for the Court, in paper format, of Voluntary Chapter 7 Petitions, Schedules Lists and Statements are not required to be provided by Filing Users electronically filing Voluntary Chapter 7 Petitions.

D. For electronically-filed cases, the filer is directed to provide one paper copy each of the petition, statements, lists, schedules, etc., directly to each of the United States Trustee and the assigned case Trustee, immediately upon notification of the Trustee assignment.

[Former Rule 11A & B] [SO 8/14/85]

1007–2. Master Mailing Matrix. In addition to the list of creditors required by Rule 1007(a) Fed. R.Bankr.P., in all cases a list of creditors shall be filed by the debtor, or such party as may be ordered, in a form specified by the Bankruptcy Clerk which shall be known as the matrix. The matrix shall be supplemented or modified by the responsible party, to include all parties that are required to be given notice, so the Clerk can rely on the matrix in the performance of his or her duties.

[Former Rule 18B]

[Effective May 13, 1997. Amended effective June 16, 2003.]

RULE 1009. AMENDMENTS TO VOLUNTARY PETITIONS, LISTS, SCHEDULES AND STATEMENTS

1009–1. Amendments. Amendments to voluntary petitions, lists (including the mailing matrix), schedules and statements must have a completed "Amendment Cover Sheet" affixed to the front thereof in a form prescribed by the Clerk. (A paper cover sheet is required for conventional filings, a cover sheet in .pdf form is required to be attached for electronic filings.) No purported amendment of any type will be acknowledged, recognized or processed as such by the Office of the Clerk in the absence of an Amendment Cover Sheet. The term "amendment" includes the delayed initial filing of a schedule, statement, list or other document that discloses the existence of parties-in-interest who were not disclosed in the list of creditors that accompanied the petition. Guidelines regarding amendments are available in the Bankruptcy Court Clerk's Office.

The title of the cover sheet has been changed and its required use expanded to include additional categories of documents, in addition to amendments. A "Cover Sheet for Schedules, Statements, Lists and/or Amendments" must be completed and attached to the front of the following types of documents:

    a. Amendments to previously-filed document(s);

    b. Schedules, Statements, Lists, etc. not previously filed;

    c. Schedules, Statements, Lists, etc. filed pursuant to Fed.R.Bankr.P. Rule 1019 upon the conversion from one chapter to another.

An affidavit of services listing all parties served must be filed with the types of documents identified above. None of the document types identified above will be acknowledged, recognized or processed as such by the Office of the Clerk in the absence of a "Cover Sheet for Schedules, Lists, Statements, and/or Amendments." A paper cover sheet is required for conventional filings, a cover sheet in .pdf format is required to be attached for electronic filings.

[General Orders 3/21/88 & 1/18/92]

[Effective May 13, 1997. Amended effective June 16, 2003.]

RULE 1014. CHANGE OF VENUE

1014–1. Reassignment of Cases. If the convenience or best interests of creditors would be served by the scheduling of a case in a geographical area served by another Judge, the assigned Bankruptcy Judge may reassign the case, on application of a party in interest.

[Former Rule 10B]

[Effective May 13, 1997.]

RULE 1015. CONSOLIDATION OR JOINT ADMINISTRATION

1015–1.

A. Upon the entry of an Order of Joint Administration of two or more related cases, the Clerk shall:

    1. Designate any one of said cases to be the lead case for purposes of docketing and filing.

    2. Enter the Order of Joint Administration simultaneously on the dockets of all cases covered by the Order and file a copy of the Order of Joint Administration in the case file of all cases covered by the Order, except the lead case.

    3. File the original of the Order of Joint Administration in the case file of the lead case.

    4. Thereafter, maintain only the lead case file and docket for all activity affecting any of the jointly-administered cases.

B. The party which obtained the Order for Joint Administration shall, within ten (10) days of the entry of said Order, file with the Court a consolidated matrix comprising a total mailing list of all interested parties in all the jointly administered cases, without duplication.

C. Adequate safeguards shall be established by the Clerk to assure that parties interested in examining the docket or file of a case that is not the lead case will be directed thereby to the docket and file of the lead case for further matters affecting the case in question. Furthermore, to the extent that a docketable paper or event clearly pertains to less than all of the jointly-administered cases, the docket entry made on the lead docket shall so indicate this to enable parties to more readily examine the activities in any one of the jointly-administered cases.

D. Notwithstanding the above, the Clerk may require parties in interest, or request the Court to seek, obtain, or execute separate documents for each case where necessary for purposes of clarity, statistical reporting, case closing or other similar cause.

[Former Rule 17A thru D]

[Effective May 13, 1997.]

RULE 1019. CONVERSION—PROCEDURE FOLLOWING [RESERVED]

[Former Rule 20]

RULE 1020. CHAPTER 11 SMALL BUSINESS CASES, GENERAL

[Former Rule 41]

    1020–1.

A. *Election to Be Considered a Small Business in a Chapter 11 Reorganization Case:* In a chapter 11 reorganization case, a debtor that is a small business may elect to be considered a small business by filing a written statement of election no later than 60 days after the date of the order for relief or by a later date as the Court, for cause, may fix.

B. *Approval of Disclosure Statement:*

    1. Conditional Approval: If the debtor is a small business and has made a timely election to be considered a small business in a chapter 11 case, the Court may, on application of the plan proponent, conditionally approve a disclosure statement filed in accordance with Rule 3016 Fed.R.Bankr.P. On or before conditional approval of the disclosure statement, the Court shall:

    (a) fix a time within which the holders of claims and interests may accept or reject the plan;

(b) fix a time for filing objections to the disclosure statement;

(c) fix a date for the hearing on final approval of the disclosure statement to be held if a timely objection is filed; and

(d) fix a date for the hearing on confirmation.

2. Application of Rule 3017 Fed.R.Bankr.P.: If the disclosure statement is conditionally approved, Rule 3017(a), (b), (c) and (e) Fed.R.Bankr.P. do not apply. Conditional approval of the disclosure statement is considered approval of the disclosure statement for the purpose of applying Rule 3017(d) Fed.R.Bankr.P.

3. Objections and Hearing on Final Approval: Notice of the time fixed for filing objections and the hearing to consider final approval of the disclosure statement shall be given in accordance with Rule 2002 Fed.R.Bankr.P. and may be combined with notice of the hearing on confirmation of the plan. Objections to the disclosure statement shall be filed, transmitted to the United States Trustee, and served on the debtor, the trustee, any committee appointed under the Bankruptcy Code and any other entity designated by the Court at any time before final approval of the disclosure statement or by an earlier date as the Court may fix. If a timely objection to the disclosure statement is filed, the Court shall hold a hearing to consider final approval before or combined with the hearing on confirmation of the plan.

[Former Rule 41]

[Effective May 13, 1997.]

RULE 1072. PLACES OF HOLDING COURT

1072–1. Sessions of Court. Regular and continuous sessions of the Bankruptcy Court shall be held at Buffalo and Rochester. Special sessions of the Court shall be held at Mayville, Olean, Niagara Falls, Batavia and Watkins Glen at such times as may be necessary.

[Former Rule 8]

1072–2. Scheduling of Cases and Proceedings as Among Places of Holding Court. Giving due regard to the convenience of a debtor, creditors, and equity holders, as well as to the availability of Court support services, the Judge assigned to the case or, if delegated to the Clerk, the Clerk may schedule hearings and trials in a case at a place of holding Court other than that which is in closest proximity to the debtor's residence or of place of business.

[Former Rule 10E]

[Effective May 13, 1997.]

RULE 1073. ASSIGNMENT OF CASES

1073–1. Assignment of Bankruptcy Cases to Bankruptcy Judges.

A. Upon filing, the Clerk shall assign each bankruptcy case to a specific Bankruptcy Judge in accordance with the following directives:

1. As to cases arising in Erie County, assignment shall be made by random selection as between the two Bankruptcy Judges stationed at Buffalo, utilizing a formula assuring an equitable distribution of those cases based upon their total case loads.

2. As to cases arising in Niagara, Orleans, Genesee, and Wyoming Counties, to a Bankruptcy Judge stationed at Buffalo as specified by the Chief Judge.

3. As to cases arising in Chautauqua, Cattaraugus, and Allegany Counties, to a Bankruptcy Judge stationed at Buffalo as specified by the Chief Judge.

4. As to cases arising in Monroe, Chemung, Livingston, Ontario, Schuyler, Seneca, Steuben, Wayne, and Yates Counties, to a Bankruptcy Judge stationed at Rochester.

5. General Provisions:

a. For the purposes of these subsections, a business debtor's case shall be deemed to have arisen in the county in which the principal place of business is located if there is a principal place of business within the district.

b. If these rules of assignment result in a disproportionate load of cases falling upon a Bankruptcy Judge, they may be changed upon a majority vote of the Judges.

c. Any case inadvertently assigned to a Judge in contravention of this rule shall be reassigned by the Chief Judge.

B. *Exigencies.* To expedite the flow of cases, proceedings or matters, the Judges may agree to the reassignment of cases, matters, or proceedings to meet exigencies arising in the conduct of a given Judge's calendar. In the absence of the Judge assigned to a case, adversary proceeding, or contested matter, any other Judge may act.

[Former Rule 10A(1) thru A(5) and Former Rule 10D]

[Effective May 13, 1997.]

RULE 2002. NOTICES TO CREDITORS, EQUITY SECURITY HOLDERS, UNITED STATES, AND UNITED STATES TRUSTEE

2002–1.

A. A party filing a motion which requires notice to creditors and/or a creditors' committee in addition to service upon adverse parties shall arrange with the

Clerk for such noticing and schedule the hearing accordingly.

B.[1]　Notices to creditors required by 2002(a) Fed. R.Bankr.P. in chapter 13 cases will be issued and served by the Standing Chapter 13 Trustee. The Chapter 13 Trustee will file an affidavit of service with the Court to evidence service of each notice. The cost of issuing such notices shall be considered an administrative expense of each Chapter 13 Office.

C.　Debtors-in-Possession (or plan proponent if other than the debtor) are directed to serve the Notice of the Hearing on Confirmation of a Plan complete with a copy of the Disclosure Statement, Plan and Ballot and upon confirmation of a plan, the notice of entry of the Order Confirming the Plan pursuant to the requirements of Rule 2002(d)(6) Fed.R.Bankr.P.

[Former Rule 14G] [SO 4/22/86]

[Effective May 13, 1997.]

[1] See, also, "Standing Order. Notice to Creditors in Chapter 13 Cases."

RULE 2007. TRUSTEES AND EXAMINERS

Rule 2007-1.　[Reserved]

[Former Rule 18]

2007-1.1.　Election of Trustee in a Chapter 11 Reorganization Case.

A.　*Request for an Election:* A request to convene a meeting of creditors for the purpose of electing a trustee in a chapter 11 reorganization shall be filed and transmitted to the United States Trustee in accordance with Rule 5005 Fed.R.Bankr.P. within the time prescribed by § 1104(b) of the Bankruptcy Code. Pending Court approval of the person elected, a person appointed trustee under § 1104(d) shall serve as trustee.

B.　*Matter of Election and Notice:* An election of a trustee under § 1104(b) of the Code shall be conducted in the manner provided in Rules 2003(b)(3) and 2006 Fed.R.Bankr.P. Notice of the meeting of creditors convened under § 1104(b) shall be given in the manner and within the time provided for notices under 2002(a) Fed.R.Bankr.P. A proxy for the purpose of voting in the election may be solicited by a committee appointed under § 1102 of the Code and by any other party entitled to solicit a proxy under Rule 2006 Fed.R.Bankr.P.

C.　*Application for Approval of Appointment and Resolution of Disputes:* If it is not necessary to resolve a dispute regarding the election of the trustee or if all disputes have been resolved by the Court, the United States Trustee shall promptly appoint the person elected to be trustee and file an application for approval of the appointment of the elected person under Rule 2001.1(b) Fed.R.Bankr.P., except that the application does not have to contain names of parties

in interest with whom the United States Trustee has consulted.

If it is necessary to resolve a dispute regarding the election, the United States Trustee shall promptly file a report informing the Court of the dispute. If no motion for the resolution of the dispute is filed within 10 days after the date of the creditors' meeting called under § 1104(b), a person appointed by the United States Trustee in accordance with § 1104(d) of the Code and approved in accordance with Rule 2007(b) Fed.R.Bankr.P. shall serve as trustee.

[Rule 40]

[Effective May 13, 1997.]

RULE 2008. NOTICE TO TRUSTEE OF SELECTION

2008-1.　Filing of Blanket Trustee Designation in Chapter 13 Cases.　The Court will accept a blanket designation for standing Chapter 13 Trustees in lieu of a separate designation for each chapter 13 case filed in the Western District of New York. A separate designation must be filed in the event of a substitution of trustee so designated under the blanket designation.

[SO 4/23/96]

[Effective May 13, 1997.]

RULE 2010. QUALIFICATION BY TRUSTEE; PROCEEDING ON BOND

2010-1.　Trustee's Reimbursement of Blanket Bond Premiums.

A.　The trustee shall issue one check or money order for the entire bond premium and provide a copy of that check to the Office of the United States Trustee.

B.　The trustee may be reimbursed from that trustee's estates pending on the date of issuance of the premium check, at the bond premium rate, or,

C.　In the alternative, the trustee may allocate the premium paid pro rata to those cases comprising the substantial majority (in dollar amount) of assets under the trustees administration on the date of issuance of the premium check. The trustee shall issue reimbursement checks from the individual estates according to their pro rata share.

D.　In no event shall the aggregate amount of the reimbursement checks exceed the amount of the premium paid.

[SO 7/31/90]

[Effective May 13, 1997.]

RULE 2014. EMPLOYMENT OF PROFESSIONALS

2014–1. Definition. "Counsel for the estate." An attorney who has obtained an order of the Court approving his or her employment as attorney for a chapter 11 debtor-in-possession or for a chapter 7, 12, or 13 trustee is counsel for the estate of the debtor. Corporate debtors must be represented by an attorney of record. Papers, including petitions, filed by a corporate debtor which has no attorney of record, may be received but later dismissed, sua sponte, by the Judge to whom the case is assigned.

[Former Rule 5A]

2014–2. Duty of Counsel for the Estate With Regard to Estate's Employment of Other Professionals.

A. Appraisers, auctioneers, accountants, brokers, special counsels, consultants, independent managers, and other professional persons employed by the debtors' estates are often unfamiliar with the requirements of bankruptcy law regarding the need for prior Court approval of their employment; regarding the record keeping and reporting requirements applicable to sustain their claim to subsequent compensation from the estate; and regarding the risk that there may be insufficient assets in the estate to satisfy such claims. Whether or not a professional person is familiar with such considerations, it is necessary and desirable that the responsibility for obtaining Court approval of such employment and for advising professionals of the responsibilities and risks of such employment be placed on the attorney for the estate.

B. Whenever the estate employs any other professional whose employment requires Court approval under the Bankruptcy Code or Rules, it is the duty of counsel for the estate to ensure that such approval is properly sought, and to advise the professional of the requirements and risks, if any, pertaining to the professional's ability to subsequently obtain compensation and reimbursement of expenses from the estate.

C. Estate counsel who fails to satisfy such duties may be determined by the Court to be personally responsible for any compensation and reimbursement of expenses lost to any professional as a result thereof.

[Former Rule 5B]

2014–3. Duty of Attorney Commencing a Chapter 11 Case on Behalf of a Debtor Which Is a Corporation.

A. A corporation which is a debtor-in-possession must be represented by an attorney duly admitted to practice before this Court and duly approved to serve as counsel for the estate by order of the Court.

B. It is the duty of an attorney who commences a chapter 11 case (whether by original petition or by obtaining an order of conversion to such chapter) on behalf of a corporate debtor to ensure that the debtor properly seeks approval of estate counsel promptly upon such commencement, or, in the alternative, to file with the Court an affidavit reciting that he or she has advised the debtor that the case would be dismissed or converted for absence of a counsel for the estate, reciting the diligent efforts made by the attorney both before and after the commencement of the chapter 11 case in assisting the debtor in obtaining such counsel, and explaining why such counsel was not obtained.

C. An attorney who fails in such duties may be found personally liable to any party who is damaged by the failure of the estate to be suitably represented.

[Former Rule 5C]

[Effective May 13, 1997.]

RULE 2015. TRUSTEES, DEBTORS–IN–POSSESSION DUTIES [RESERVED]

[Former Rule 18]

RULE 2016. COMPENSATION OF PROFESSIONALS

2016–1. Professional Persons—Compensation and Reimbursement of Expenses. In all cases under Title 11, requests for interim or final compensation shall be in a form prescribed by the Bankruptcy Clerk, who shall, at a minimum, require the applicant to include a one page face sheet bearing the caption of the case, the name and address of the applicant or applicants, the dates upon which the case was filed and the applicant was appointed, the nature and the date or the period of services rendered, a typewritten time sheet with a description of services rendered, and the amount of compensation or expense reimbursement sought. (If both compensation and reimbursement are sought, the amounts shall be separately stated.) The application should also include a statement of prior applications and prior allowances.

A. All supporting documentation shall be attached to the application and, if it is an application for interim compensation, it shall also contain an affidavit or unsworn declaration reciting why the applicant should not be required to await the filing of a final report in the case. The Court may take judicial notice of any facts of record warranting denial of the application as having been prematurely made.

B. All applications must be filed at least twenty-five (25) days prior to a calendar at which the application is to be considered.

C. Non-appearance of an applicant at the scheduled hearing shall be deemed to be a consent to the disposition of the application on the filed papers and record, if any, of the hearing.

To aid the Court and any party in interest in reviewing compensation statements filed by attorneys:

(a) The "compensation" paid or to be paid to an attorney shall include all legal fees and all charges of whatever character paid or to be paid by the debtor or other entity. Charges shall be identified and, if not self explanatory, justified.

(b) Basic services to be performed are:

(1) Analysis of the financial situation and rendering advice and assistance to the client in determining whether to file a petition under Title 11, United States Code;

(2) Preparation and filing of the petition, lists, statements or schedules in a chapter 7 or 13 case;

(3) Representation of the debtor at the § 341 meeting;

(4) Amend lists, statements or schedules to comport with developments which may have occurred before or at the § 341 meeting;

(5) Motions under § 522(f) to avoid liens on exempt property;

(6) Motions, such as motions for abandonment, or proceedings to clear title to real property owned by the debtor;

(7) Removal of garnishments or wage assignments;

ADDITIONAL SERVICES REQUIRED IN CHAPTER 7 CASES

(8) Negotiate, prepare and file reaffirmation agreements;

(9) Motions under § 722 to redeem exempt personal property from liens;

ADDITIONAL SERVICES REQUIRED IN CHAPTER 13 CASES

(10) Attend confirmation hearings;

(11) Negotiate valuation of secured claims and/or present evidence thereon at confirmation hearing.

(c) If, in the attorneys judgment, the performance of the above basic services required or will require unusual expenditures of time he or she should so state and annex time sheets or projections of time supporting the claim.

[Former Rules 38 & 39] [SO 7/30/90]

2016–2. Applications for Fees by the Attorney for the Debtor in Chapter 7 Cases.

A. The expeditious administration of chapter 7 estates is hindered by the delays by debtors' attorneys in the filing of applications for allowances from the estate under 11 U.S.C. Sec. 330. Therefore, the failure to file any fee allowance application by such an attorney before fifteen (15) days after the mailing of the Rule 2002(f)(9) Fed.R.Bankr.P. notice of the trustee's final report in any case shall be deemed a waiver of the allowance.

B. All actual compensation and disbursements whether charged by attorneys to the debtor, debtor's estate or any entity paying on behalf of the debtor or debtor's estate prior to or during the pendency of a case must be fully disclosed in a supplemental statement filed in accordance with Rule 2016(b) Fed. R.Bankr.P. [A disclosed fee which is to be charged in the event of a contingent future service, and which is charged, shall be disclosed in a supplemental statement].

C. Supplemental statements by attorneys as to compensation sought from the estate shall be supported by time sheets and detail as to any disbursements charged and shall be accompanied by a motion [notice thereof to be given by the requesting party to parties in interest in accordance with Rule 2002(a)(7) Fed.R.Bankr.P.].

[Former Rule 39] [SO 6/12/84; SO 7/30/90]

[Effective May 13, 1997.]

RULE 2020. SERVICE ON THE OFFICE OF THE UNITED STATES TRUSTEE

2020–1. Duties of Clerk of Court.

A. For conventionally filed cases, the Clerk of the Court shall ensure that the Office of the United States Trustee for the district is placed on the mailing matrix in each case filed with the Court and is sent notices (including notices of appeal) issued by the Clerk or such other person as the Court may direct.

B. For conventionally filed cases, the Clerk's office shall collect enough copies of petitions, statements, schedules, and amendments thereof to furnish the Office of the United States Trustee with two (2) copies of each.

C. For electronically-filed cases, the filer is directed to provide one paper copy each of the petition, statements, lists, schedules, etc., directly to each of the United States Trustee and the assigned case Trustee, immediately upon notification of the Trustee assignment.

[Former Rule 15A & B]

2020–2. Duties of Parties.

A. Parties shall serve a copy of all documents initiating a request for a Court order or judgment, except proofs of claim or interest, on the Office of the United States Trustee. This includes but is not limited to all pleadings in adversary proceedings and contested matters.

[Former Rule 15C]

[Effective May 13, 1997. Amended effective June 16, 2003.]

RULE 2081. CHAPTER 11

[Former Rule 19]

2081–1. Chapter 11 Reports. [Reserved]

RULE 2090. ATTORNEYS—ADMISSION TO PRACTICE

2090–1. Admission to Bankruptcy Practice and Attorneys of Record.

A. *Prior Admission.* A person admitted to practice in the United States District Court for the Western District of New York before October 1, 1979, is admitted for bankruptcy practice in the Western District of New York. A person subsequently admitted to bankruptcy practice under prior local bankruptcy rules is admitted for bankruptcy practice in the Western District of New York.

B. *Who May Apply.* A person admitted to practice before the United States District Court for the Western District of New York.

C. *Verified Petition.* Each applicant for admission shall file with the Clerk of the Bankruptcy Court a verified petition for admission stating:

(1) Applicant's residence and office address;

(2) That the applicant has been admitted to practice before the United States District Court for the Western District of New York and the date of said admission;

(3) That the applicant has read and is familiar with:

(a) The provisions of Judicial Code 28 U.S.C., section 1334, sections 151 through 158, and sections 1408 through 1412, and section 1452, which pertain to jurisdiction over and venue of bankruptcy cases, proceedings and matters.

(b) The Bankruptcy Code, Title 11 U.S.C.;

(c) The Federal Rules of Bankruptcy Procedure;

(d) The Local Rules of Bankruptcy Procedure for the Western District of New York.

D. *Other Admission Prerequisites.* Upon the filing of the aforesaid verified petition, taking of the oath, and signing of the attorneys' roll, a person shall be admitted for bankruptcy practice and the Clerk shall issue a certificate to that effect.

E. *Admission Pro Hac Vice.* An attorney duly admitted to practice in any state, territory, district, or foreign country may be admitted pro hac vice to participate in a bankruptcy case or proceeding before the District or Bankruptcy Court under such terms or conditions as may be appropriate.

F. *Government Attorneys.* An attorney duly appointed to represent the United States is permitted to appear on any matter within the scope of his or her employment.

G. Only members admitted under LBR 2090 may represent a debtor, be approved for employment as counsel in a bankruptcy case, or appear before the District or Bankruptcy Court in the litigation of adversary proceedings and contested matters.

H. An attorney who has not obtained District or Bankruptcy Court approval to represent a party when required by Bankruptcy Codes and Rules may not appear in representation of that party.

I. An attorney who accepts employment by a debtor in connection with the filing of a case under Title 11, United States Code, has the duty to render complete and competent service, to file with the Court a statement disclosing all payments rendered from a debtor or debtor-in-possession, and may not withdraw from that undertaking without the permission of the District or Bankruptcy Court.

J. Applications to approve employment as attorney of record (whenever Court approval of such employment is required by statute or rule) *must* include the following:

(1) an application, signed by the party seeking to retain counsel, which sets forth the reason this attorney should be hired, the services this attorney will provide, the arrangements reached with regard to when and how the attorney will be paid, the prior relationship between the applicant and the attorney, and the fact that no fees are to be paid unless and until there is specific Court approval;

(2) an affidavit from the attorney setting forth when he or she was admitted to practice in New York State and to bankruptcy practice in the Western District of New York, his or her qualifications; a statement of disinterestedness sufficient to persuade the Court that there is no conflict of interest; attorney's prior relationship with the debtor-client and the date upon which the petition was filed;

(3) an Order appointing counsel which clearly sets forth that no fees are to be paid without Court approval and the date from which the appointment is effective.

K. An attorney who seeks an order approving employment may do so ex parte unless the initial postpetition services date back more than thirty (30) days. The attorney otherwise shall file a motion and notice all parties in interest of the motion and hearing date. The attorney must submit the application and notice to the Clerk of the Bankruptcy Court and obtain approval that they are adequate as to form and content before mailing the notices. The attorney shall prepare and mail such applications, unless the Court orders otherwise.

[Former Rule 2A thru F; Former Rule 3A thru E]

2090–2. Attorneys—Discipline and Disbarment.

A. Any person admitted to bankruptcy practice in the Western District of New York may be disbarred from practice or otherwise disciplined after hearing, after such notice as the District or Bankruptcy Court may direct. Any member of the bar who has been disbarred in a state in which he or she was admitted to practice shall have his or her name stricken from the roll of attorneys or, if suspended from practice for a period at said bar, shall be suspended automatically for a like period from bankruptcy practice in the Western District of New York.

B. Discipline and/or suspension from practice specifically may be directed against any attorney who conducts himself or herself in a manner demonstrating inability to properly represent his or her clients' interests. [See "Malpractice in Bankruptcy—Observations from the Bench" in Commercial Law Journal (March 1985) pp. 95–100, Hon. Harold Lavien, U.S. Bankruptcy Judge for the District of Mass.]

[Former Rule 4A & B]

[Effective May 13, 1997.]

RULE 2091. ATTORNEYS— WITHDRAWAL

2091–1. Withdrawal.

A. Withdrawal shall be permitted only by order granted upon:

(1) motion to withdraw, served upon the withdrawing attorney's client and such other parties as the Court directs; or

(2) if satisfactory to the Court, stipulation of counsel and parties affected thereby.

B. An attorney who has appeared in a case under chapters 7 and 13 as the attorney of record for the debtor may be displaced without order of the Court by filing with the Court a Notice of Substitution of Attorney. The successor attorney shall file with the Court a Statement of Compensation pursuant to Rule 2016 Fed.R.Bankr.P. within ten (10) days of the Notice of Substitution of Attorney.

C. An order granting permission to withdraw or to substitute shall become effective upon ten (10) days notice to all attorneys of record unless the Court specifically directs that the order shall become effective upon entry.

[Former Rule 3F & G]

[Effective May 13, 1997.]

RULE 3001. CLAIMS AND EQUITY SECURITY INTERESTS— GENERAL

3001–1. Transfer or Claim. The Clerk of Court is to accept for filing a waiver of notice of a claim other than for security after proof filed when said notice is signed by the transferring entity and further notice need not be made. When said waiver of notice is accompanied by a properly completed assignment of claim form, the Clerk of Court shall substitute the transferee for the transferor.

[O 7/15/94]

[Effective May 13, 1997.]

RULE 3007. OBJECTIONS TO CLAIMS

3007–1. Rochester and Watkins Glen objections to claims may be granted without a hearing after the Court has considered the objection and determined the sufficiency of the claim and the objection, unless a request for a hearing is served and filed within the time permitted. Guidelines designed to comply with this procedure are available in the Bankruptcy Court Clerk's Office.

[SO 5/20/93]

[Effective May 13, 1997.]

RULE 4001. RELIEF FROM AUTOMATIC STAY; CASH COLLATERAL AND FINANCING ORDERS

4001–1.

A. *Applicability of Local Bankruptcy Rule 9013.* Except as otherwise provided herein, Local Bankruptcy Rule 9013 applies to motions for relief from stay, use of cash collateral, adequate protection, and financing orders.

B. *Motions for Relief From Stay.* The thirty (30) days within which the Court must preliminarily rule on such a motion under 11 U.S.C. § 362(e) shall be computed from the date on which a motion is served on opposing parties and filed with the Court. In addition to those parties listed in Rule 4001 Fed.R.Bankr.P., notice shall be given to the debtor, attorney for the debtor, trustee or examiner, the United States Trustee, to any persons requesting special notice under Rule 2002(i) Fed.R.Bankr.P., and any chapter 11 creditors' committee or other official committee duly appointed in a chapter 11 case.

[SO 8/4/83]

4001–2. [Reserved].

[Former Rules 18 & 24]

Cash Collateral or Adequate Protection Agreements. All requests for orders approving adequate protection or cash collateral agreements or stipulations shall be sought by written motion and notice of motion, and shall be the subject of a hearing. The party seeking the order shall prepare and serve the motion and notice of motion. Notice shall be given to the parties to the agreement, all parties having any other interest in the collateral, and the creditors' committee, if any, and the United States Trustee. If there is no creditors' committee, notice shall be given to the twenty largest creditors. At the hearing, after inquiry into the content and consequences of the agreement, the Court may direct a further hearing on notice to all creditors or all parties-in-interest. The Court will entertain without a hearing, requests for an order approving a cash collateral agreement or a stipulation which provides for nothing more than a replacement lien on post-petition assets, in an amount equal to the amount of cash collateral used.

[Effective May 13, 1997.]

RULE 4008. DISCHARGE AND REAFFIRMATION HEARING

4008–1. Reaffirmation agreements submitted must be accompanied by Form B240 (or a form which substantially conforms to Form B240) and must be completed and signed. Debtors will no longer be required to attend a discharge hearing, except as provided below. Discharge Hearing Calendars will be conducted on a regular basis throughout the district, at which debtors may present themselves for a full explanation of the meaning of discharge and of reaffirmation. Times and places of such calendars are available from the Clerk.

A. *Pro Se Debtors.* A discharge hearing must be attended by a pro se debtor filing a reaffirmation agreement. The Clerk will issue an informational letter to the debtor and a form to request a § 524(d) hearing.

B. *Reaffirmation Agreement Accompanied by Attorney's Declaration.* The debtor shall not be required to attend a discharge hearing if the debtor is represented by an attorney who attaches a declaration prepared pursuant to § 524(c)(3).

C. *Reaffirmation Agreement Not Accompanied by Attorney's Declaration.* A discharge hearing must be attended by the debtor if a reaffirmation agreement is not accompanied by a completed Attorney's Declaration. The Clerk will issue an information letter to the debtor and a form to request a § 524(d) hearing.

[GO 11/21/86]

[Effective May 13, 1997.]

RULE 5073. PHOTOGRAPHY, RECORDING DEVICES & BROADCASTING

5073–1. Cameras and Recording Devices.

A. The taking of photographs, or making of oral or video tape recordings, or radio or television broadcasting in a courtroom during the progress of or in connection with judicial proceedings, whether or not

Court is actually in session, is prohibited. None of the foregoing activities is allowed in the jury rooms, the offices of the Judges or Court reporters, or in any room, hallway or corridor of the floor of the building in which the courtrooms are located, except with the express consent of the Court.

B. The Court may except ceremonial and investitive proceedings from this prohibition.

C. Court reporters are not prohibited by this rule from making sound recordings for the sole purpose of discharging their official duties. No recording made for that purpose shall be used for any other purpose by any person. Likewise, personnel of the Court are not prohibited by Section A of this rule from making sound recordings in the course of their work.

[Former Rule 9]

[Effective May 13, 1997.]

RULE 5080. FEES—GENERAL

5080–1. Payment of Fees. The Bankruptcy Clerk, unless otherwise ordered by the Court, shall not be required to render any service for which a fee is prescribed by statute or by the Judicial Conference of the United States unless the fee for such service is paid in advance and as specified in LBR Rule 5081.

[Former Rule 22]

[Effective May 13, 1997.]

RULE 5081. FEES—FORM OF PAYMENT

5081–1. Form of Payments. Fees must be tendered in cash or by certified check, bank draft, or money order. The Clerk may specify other forms of payment.

[Former Rule 22]

[Effective May 13, 1997.]

RULE 6004. USE, SALE OR LEASE OF PROPERTY

6004–1. Statement, Form, and Notice.

A. Except as to sales in the ordinary course of operating a business, the trustee or debtor in possession shall file with the Bankruptcy Court a statement identifying any estate property proposed to be sold and the date and manner of such sale. The statement shall contain sufficient detail to enable creditors to make an informed judgment as to the wisdom of the proposed disposition. At a minimum, the statement shall contain a description of the property. A statement of sale shall contain a description of the manner and terms of sale, the name of the buyer and purchase price, if known. If the case is a chapter 11 case, a statement as to whether the sale is all or substantially all of the debtor's assets, and the effect the sale will have upon the debtor's ability to reorganize.

B. Except as provided in Rule 6004(c) Fed. R.Bankr.P., and subdivision C hereof, notice of the filing of the statement and a summary thereof shall be sent to all creditors. The notice also shall advise creditors that they may obtain a hearing on the proposed disposition by filing a written demand for a hearing with the Court within twenty (20) days of the notice date.

C. Where the statement discloses a sale of all or substantially all of the assets, the Clerk shall set the matter for hearing and notice shall be sent to all creditors.

[Former Rule 25 and Rule 26 (RESERVED)] [SO 8/9/83]

[Effective May 13, 1997.]

RULE 6007. ABANDONMENT

6007–1. Statement, Form and Notice.

A. The trustee or debtor in possession shall file with the Bankruptcy Court a statement identifying any estate property proposed to be abandoned and the date and manner of such abandonment. That statement shall contain sufficient detail to enable creditors to make an informed judgment as to the wisdom of the proposed disposition. At a minimum, the statement shall contain a description of the property.

B. Notice of the filing of the abandonment statement and a summary thereof shall be sent to all creditors. The notice also shall advise creditors that they may obtain a hearing on the proposed disposition by filing a written demand for a hearing with the Court within twenty (20) days of the notice date.

[Former Rule 25; parts of A & B]

[Effective May 13, 1997.]

RULE 6070. TAX RETURNS & TAX REFUNDS

6070–1.

A. *In General.* The failure of a debtor in an asset case under any chapter of Title 11 of the United States Code to file any required tax return promptly after filing the petition or after conversion may constitute "cause" for dismissal or conversion of the case upon a request by a party in interest and after hearing on notice.

B. *As to "Estimated" Tax Claims.* Concurrent with the debtor's duty to file tax returns is the duty to assure that improper distributions are not made upon "estimated" tax claims resulting from the Debtor's failure to file returns.

Overpayment of taxes by allowance of unduly-high "estimated" tax claims may occur to the prejudice of other unsecured creditors, whose percentage distribution may be reduced for the benefit of the excessive "priority" tax claim.

Underpayment of taxes by allowance of unduly-low "estimated" tax claims leaves the Debtor liable for the deficiency after he or she emerges from bankruptcy. And it may have resulted in a windfall for other creditors.

When the tax claim is an "estimated" claim only because no return was filed, the burden must be placed on the Debtor to take steps to avoid prejudice to other creditors (and the Debtor may wish to take steps to protect himself or herself as well.)

At the least, the Debtor shall within 30 days of service of a copy of an "estimated" tax claim that is "estimated" because of non-filing of returns, object to such claim under Rule 3007 Fed.R.Bankr.P. even if the Debtor does not disagree with the amount. A copy of the proposed return or other evidence of the amount of the liability shall accompany the objection. If the Debtor is not served with a copy of the "estimated claim", then the objection must be filed within 30 days after the closing of the 180 day opportunity for the filing of tax claims under § 502.

At the hearing on the objection the Debtor shall appear and shall be prepared to tender the tax return thereat or to provide evidence to the Court as to a proper "estimate" of the tax claim, whether higher, lower, or the same as that filed by the taxing entity.

The Court will thus "estimate" the claim for the purpose of allowance but will not at that hearing determine the Debtor's tax liability under § 505 or the applicable tax laws. The duty to file a return and the risk of additional liability remains at all times on the Debtor, and any discharge shall not discharge the unpaid balance of any actual tax liability, interest or penalties. Determination of tax liability under § 505 requires an Adversary Proceeding.

If the objection required by this rule is not made, the case may on motion on notice to the Debtor and counsel be converted or dismissed, as to the Court appears proper.

The taxing entities may assert other remedies, such as objections to confirmation of a plan. If a plan is confirmed "pending" the estimation of the tax claims as above, then confirmation shall be without prejudice to any objections properly arising out of the hearing on the claim, such as (but not limited to) objections based on feasibility, projected disposable income, or lack of good faith.

[Former Rule 42]

[Effective May 13, 1997.]

RULE 7004.   SERVICE OF PROCESS

7004–1.   Service Upon the United States in Contested Matters.

A.   Rule 9014 Fed.R.Bankr.P. requires that a motion be served "in the manner provided for service of a summons and complaint by Rule 7004 Fed.R.Bankr. P." of those Rules.   Rule 7004(a) Fed.R.Bankr.P. [by incorporating Rule 4(d) of the Federal Rules of Civil Procedure and Rule 7004(b)(4), (5)] require:

1.   that the United States be served whenever an officer or agency of the United States is served; and

2.   that service upon the United States is obtained by serving the United States Attorney for the District in which the action is brought, together with mailing a copy of the process to the Attorney General of the United States at Washington, D.C.

[Former Rule 16]

[Effective May 13, 1997.]

RULE 7016.   PRE–TRIAL PROCEDURES

7016–1.   Pre-trial Conferences in Adversary Proceedings.

A.   At the pre-trial conference required by Rule 7016 Fed.R.Bankr.P., counsel shall be prepared to report on the following matters:

(1) status of the pleadings and joinder of other parties or actions;

(2) anticipated discovery proceedings and the time required for the completion thereof;

(3) unusual problems of law or fact which may arise;

(4) anticipated motions;

(5) narrowing of the issues and stipulation as to matters which avoid unnecessary proof;

(6) the time when the case will be ready for trial;

(7) such other matters as may aid in disposition of the case.

B.   Upon the completion of the conference, an order will be entered by the Bankruptcy Court setting the time within which all pre-trial motions and discovery are to be completed and imposing such additional requirements as may be appropriate.   Thereafter, further discovery shall not be permitted except by leave of the Court for good cause shown.

[Former Rule 27]

7016–2.   Authority of Clerk.

The authority of this Court to set pre-trial conferences in adversary proceedings and other disputed matters is hereby delegated non-exclusively to the Clerk, who shall, in directing litigants to appear thereat, give them notice that such direction is by order of the Court and that the Court may impose sanctions, including a default judgment for failure to appear.

[Former Rule 28] [SO 5/7/84]

[Effective May 13, 1997.]

RULE 7024.   UNCONSTITUTIONALITY, CLAIM OF

7024–2.   Notice of Claim of Unconstitutionality.

If at any time prior to the trial of any adversary proceeding or contested matter, to which neither the United States, an individual state, nor any agency, officer or employee of either is a party, a party draws in question the constitutionality of an Act of Congress or a state statute affecting the public interest, the party shall, in writing, notify the Bankruptcy Court of the existence of such question and specifically identify the statute and the respects in which it is claimed to be unconstitutional.   See, 28 U.S.C. § 2403(a) and (b).

[Former Rule 23]

[Effective May 13, 1997.]

RULE 7026.   DISCOVERY

7026–1.   Cooperation of Counsel.

No motion for discovery and production of documents under Rules 7026 through 7037 Fed.R.Bankr.P. shall be heard unless and until moving counsel certify that they have attempted to resolve the discovery dispute on their own.

[Former Rule 29]

[Effective May 13, 1997.]

RULE 7040.   ASSIGNMENT OF ADVERSARY PROCEEDINGS

Rule 7040–1.

The assignment of the bankruptcy case to a Judge includes, subject to LBR 1073–1(B) herein, the assignment of adversary proceedings and contested matters arising in the case.

[Former Rule 10C]

[Effective May 13, 1997.]

RULE 7054.   COSTS–TAXATION/PAYMENT

7054–1.   Costs in the Bankruptcy Case.

A.   A party entitled to recover costs shall file with the Bankruptcy Clerk, upon forms provided by the Clerk, a verified bill of costs.   The date on which the parties will appear before the Clerk for taxation of the costs and proof of service of a copy upon the party liable for the costs shall be endorsed thereon.   The Clerk's action may be reviewed by the Court if a motion to retax the costs is filed within five (5) days after the costs are taxed.

B. Standards for Taxing Costs

(1) The Clerk's filing fee is allowable if paid by the claimant.

(2) Fees of the marshal as set forth in 28 U.S.C. § 1921 are allowable to the extent actually incurred. Fees for service of process by someone other than the marshal are allowable to the extent that they do not exceed those permitted by 28 U.S.C. § 1921.

(3) Reporters' transcripts:

(a) The cost of transcripts necessarily obtained for an appeal are allowable.

(b) The cost of a transcript of a statement by a Judge from the bench which is to be reduced to a formal order prepared by counsel is allowable.

(c) The cost of other transcripts is not normally allowable unless, before it is incurred, it is approved by a Judge or stipulated to be recoverable by counsel.

(4) Depositions:

(a) The cost of an original and one copy of any deposition used for any purpose in connection with the case is allowable.

(b) The expenses of counsel in attending depositions are not allowable.

(c) The cost of reproducing exhibits to depositions is allowable where the cost of the deposition is allowable.

(d) Notary fees incurred in connection with taking depositions are allowable.

(e) The attendance fee of a reporter when a witness fails to appear is allowable if the claimant made use of available process to compel the attendance of the witness.

(5) Reproduction and Exemplification:

(a) The cost of reproducing and certifying or exemplifying government records for use in the case is allowable.

(b) The cost of reproducing documents used for any purpose in connection with the trial is allowable.

(c) The cost of reproducing copies of motions, pleadings, notices and other routine case papers is not allowable.

(d) The cost of reproducing trial exhibits is allowable to the extent that a Judge requires copies to be provided.

(e) The cost of preparing charts, diagrams and other visual aids to be used as exhibits is allowable if such exhibits are reasonably necessary to assist the jury or the Court in understanding the issues at the trial.

(f) The cost of reproducing the required number of copies of the Clerk's record on appeal is allowable.

(6) Witness Expenses. Per diem, subsistence and mileage payments for witnesses are allowable to the extent reasonably necessary. No other witness expenses, including fees for expert witnesses, are allowable.

(7) Such other costs, not heretofore provided for, authorized under Rule 39, Federal Rules of Appellate Procedure, are allowable.

(8) Premiums on undertaking bonds and costs of providing security required by law, by order of a Judge, or otherwise necessarily incurred are allowable.

(9) The certificate of counsel required by 28 U.S.C. § 1924 shall be prima facie evidence of the facts recited therein. The burden is on the opposing party to establish that a claim is incorrectly stated, unnecessary or unreasonable.

[Former Rule 34]

[Effective May 13, 1997.]

RULE 7055. DEFAULT–FAILURE TO PROSECUTE

7055–1. Procedure for Granting of Default Judgments.

Before seeking default judgment, plaintiff's attorney should make certain that he or she has (1) properly and timely served the defendant, and (2) filed an accurate certificate of service. Then, once the time to answer has expired, he or she may seek entry of default judgment, following the procedures described below.

When the underlying action is a core matter, the Clerk of the Bankruptcy Court may enter the default judgment if:

A. the underlying action is a core matter; and

B. the default judgment is for a sum certain.

In order to obtain a default judgment, in this circumstance, the attorney for the plaintiff is to file (1) an application for default judgment addressed to the Clerk of Court; (2) a certificate of default; (3) a request for judgment by default and affidavit of amount due; and (4) an affidavit of non-military service.

When the underlying action is a non-core matter

A. The Bankruptcy Judge to whom the matter has been assigned may execute a recommendation that default judgment be entered, without requiring a hearing, if the judgment is for a sum certain. When it is a non-core matter at issue, final judgment—even default judgment—must be entered in the District Court.

In order to obtain such a recommendation, the plaintiff's attorney is to file: (1) a recommendation for default judgment addressed to the Bankruptcy Judge; (2) an affidavit of non-military service; (3) an order to transmit record in a non-core proceeding to District Court, combined with findings of fact, conclusions of law and recommendation regarding plaintiff's request for entry of default judgment; (4) an affidavit of amount due; and (5) judgment (for execution by a U.S. District Judge).

B. When the Bankruptcy Judge, on the basis of the submitted recommendation for default judgment, determines that a hearing is necessary, the Clerk will inform the parties of the date of that hearing. (For example, if the defendant appeared, but did not answer, the defendant has a right to be heard on the question of the amount of damages.) After that hearing, the plaintiff's attorney is to submit a revised order to transmit, a revised affidavit of amount due, and a judgment (for execution by the U.S. District Judge).

Appropriate sample forms are available from the Bankruptcy Court Clerk.

The Clerk of Court shall enter the fact of default in an adversary proceeding only when requested to do so by the nondefaulting party. Upon entry of the fact of default under Fed.R.Civ.P. Rule 55(a), the nondefaulting party may seek judgment by default from the Clerk or the Court as appropriate under Fed.R.Civ.P. Rule 55(b), (d), and (e). Where relief has been sought against multiple parties not all of whom have failed to plead or defend, the fact of default may be entered as to any party who failed to plead or defend, but no judgment by default shall be entered against such party until the case shall have been decided with respect to the nondefaulting parties, unless the Court orders otherwise. A plaintiff entitled to a default for the failure to answer a complaint must request entry of the fact of default, and make suitable request for judgment, within 60 days after the last day to answer. Failure to make these requests will result in the entry of an order placing the proceeding on a calendar for a hearing on the question of why the complaint should not be dismissed for want of prosecution.

[Former Rule 33] [SO 12/5/83; SO 4/19/84]

[Effective May 13, 1997.]

RULE 7069. JUDGMENT, PAYMENT OF

7069–1. Interest on Judgments.

Interest on Judgments entered in the United States Bankruptcy Court for the Western District of New York shall be based on the rate applicable in the Federal District Court, pursuant to Title 28 U.S.C. § 1961.

Satisfaction of Judgments. [Reserved].

[Former Rules 35 & 36 (Reserved)] [GO 1/3/84]

[Effective May 13, 1997.]

RULE 8008. APPEALS

8008–1. Filing Papers—Appeal.

Upon filing a notice of appeal, the appellant shall furnish the Clerk with a sufficient number of copies thereof for mailing.

[Former Rule 14F]

[Effective May 13, 1997.]

RULE 9004. FORM OF PAPERS

9004–1. Form of Papers.

All pleadings and other papers shall be plainly and legibly written, preferably typewritten, printed or reproduced; shall be without erasures or interlineations materially defacing them; shall be in ink or its equivalent on durable, white paper of good quality; and, except for exhibits, shall be on letter size paper.

To assist the Court in its efforts to scan all documents and make them electronically available, the requirement to securely fasten and two-hole punch all pleadings and other papers in durable covers is hereby discontinued for all filings, both electronic and conventional (paper). Documents should be fastened using a device which can be easily removed, such as a large paper clip or clamp. However, "Courtesy Copies" of electronically filed documents submitted to the Court should be bound with exhibits clearly marked.

[Former Rule 13A]

9004–2. Caption.

All pleadings and other papers shall be captioned with the name of the Court, the title of the case, the proper docket number or numbers, including the initial at the end of the number indicating the Judge to whom the matter has been assigned, and a description of their nature. All pleadings and other papers, unless excepted under Rule 9011 Fed.R.Bankr.P., shall be dated, signed and have thereon the name, address and telephone number of each attorney, or if no attorney, then the litigant appearing.

[Former Rule 13B]

9004–3.

Papers not conforming with this rule generally shall be received by the Bankruptcy Clerk, but the effectiveness of any such papers shall be subject to determination of the Court.

[Former Rule 13D]

[Effective May 13, 1997. Amended effective June 16, 2003.]

RULE 9006. TIME PERIODS

9006–1. Reduction.

If a party wishes to shorten the notice requirements prescribed by Rule 9013 Fed.R.Bankr.P., the party must make written application to the appropriate Judge for an expedited hearing.

[Former Rule 14D]

[Effective May 13, 1997.]

RULE 9010. ATTORNEYS—NOTICE OF APPEARANCE

9010–1. Student Law Clerks.

A. An eligible law student may, with the approval of his or her law school dean or a member of the law school faculty and of a Bankruptcy Judge of the Western District of New York, serve as a part-time student law clerk to that Bankruptcy Judge.

B. In order to so serve, the law student shall:

(1) be duly enrolled in a law school approved by the American Bar Association;

(2) have completed legal studies amounting to at least two semesters or the equivalent;

(3) be enrolled in a course or program at his or her law school offering academic credit for serving as a part-time law clerk to a Judge or be certified by the dean of his or her law school for non-credit clinical experience;

(4) be supervised by a member of a law school faculty. This faculty advisor shall, to the extent possible, review all aspects of the student's work before it is submitted to the Judge;

(5) be certified by the dean or a faculty member of his or her law school as being of good character and competent legal ability. This certification may be withdrawn by the certifier at any time by mailing a notice to the Judge supervising the student. Termination of certification by the certifier shall not reflect on a student's character or ability unless otherwise specified. A copy of such certification and decertification shall be filed with the Clerk of the Court;

(6) neither be entitled to ask for nor receive compensation of any kind from the Court or anyone in connection with service as a part-time law clerk to a Judge;

(7) certify in writing, which certification shall be filed with the Clerk of the Bankruptcy Court, that he or she:

(a) has read and is familiar with and will comply with the Code of Professional Responsibility, and relevant provisions of the Code of Judicial Conduct for United States Judges, and

(b) will abstain from revealing any information and making any comment at any time, except to his or her faculty advisor or to the Court personnel as specifically permitted by the Judge to whom he or she is assigned, concerning any proceeding pending or impending in this Court while he or she is serving as a part-time clerk.

C. A Judge supervising a part-time clerk may terminate or limit the clerk's duties at any time without notice or hearing and without showing of cause. Such termination or limitation shall not be considered a reflection on the character or ability of the part-time clerk unless otherwise specified.

D. An attorney in a pending proceeding may at any time request that a part-time clerk not be permitted to work on or have access to information concerning that proceeding and, on a showing that such restriction is necessary, a Judge shall take appropriate steps to restrict the clerk's contact with the proceeding.

E. For the purpose of Canons 3–A(4) and 3–A(6) of the Code of Judicial Conduct for United States Judges, a part-time law clerk is deemed to be a member of the Court's personnel.

F. Forms for designating compliance with the rule are available in the Clerk's office.

[Former Rule 6]

9010–2. Student Practice.

A. An eligible law student, with the Court's approval, under supervision of an attorney, may appear on behalf of any person, including the United States Attorney, who has consented in writing.

B. The attorney who supervises a student shall:

(1) be admitted to bankruptcy practice in the United States District and Bankruptcy Courts for the Western District of New York;

(2) assume personal professional responsibility for the student's work;

(3) assist the student to the extent necessary;

(4) appear with the student in all proceedings before the Court;

(5) indicate in writing his or her consent to supervise the student.

C. In order to appear, the student shall:

(1) be duly enrolled in a law school approved by the American Bar Association;

(2) have completed legal studies amounting to at least two semesters or the equivalent;

(3) be certified by either the dean or a faculty member of his or her law school as qualified to provide the legal representation permitted by these rules. This certification may be withdrawn by the certifier at any time by mailing a notice to the Clerk

or by termination by the Judge presiding in the case in which the student appears without notice or hearing and without showing of cause. The loss of certification by action of a Judge shall not be considered a reflection on the character or ability of the student;

(4) be introduced to the Court by an attorney admitted to bankruptcy practice before the Court;

(5) neither ask for nor receive any compensation or remuneration of any kind for his or her services from the person on whose behalf he or she renders services, but this shall not prevent an attorney, legal aid bureau, law school, a state or the United States from paying compensation to the eligible law student, nor shall it prevent any agency from making proper charges for its services;

(6) certify in writing that he or she is familiar with and will comply with the Code of Professional Responsibility of the American Bar Association;

(7) certify in writing that he or she is familiar with the procedural and evidentiary rules relevant to the action in which he or she is appearing.

D. The law student, supervised in accordance with these rules, may:

(1) appear as counsel in Court or at other proceeding when written consent of the client (on the form available in the Clerk's Office) or of the United States Attorney, when the client is the United States, and the supervising attorney have been filed, and when the Court has approved the student's request to appear in the particular case to the extent that the Judge presiding at the hearing or trial permits;

(2) prepare and sign motions, petitions, answers, briefs, and other documents in connection with any matter in which he or she had met the conditions of "1" above; each such document also shall be signed by the supervising attorney.

E. Forms for designating compliance with this rule shall be available in the Bankruptcy Court Clerk's Office. Completed forms shall be filed with the Bankruptcy Clerk.

F. Participation by students under the rule shall not be deemed a violation in connection with the rules for admission to the bar of any jurisdiction concerning practice of law before admission to that bar.

[Former Rule 7]

[Effective May 13, 1997.]

RULE 9013. MOTIONS: FORM AND SERVICE

9013–1.

A. All pleadings, notices and other papers shall be served and filed in accordance with the Federal Rules of Bankruptcy Procedure and these Local Rules.

B. Except as otherwise provided by rule or ordered by the Court, notices of motion along with supporting affidavits and memoranda shall be served on the parties and filed with the Bankruptcy Clerk at least five (5) days prior to the return date of the motion [eight (8) days if served by mail]. Motion dates may be obtained from the Clerk. Discretionary responses to motions (those not required by order) shall be filed and served upon the adverse party or parties as soon as practicable.

C. Rochester and Watkins Glen motions filed pursuant to, including but not limited to § 362, § 554, § 522(f), § 722 and § 1229 and § 1339 Modification motions may be granted by the Court by default without a hearing. Sample forms and guidelines designed to comply with this procedure are available in the Bankruptcy Court Clerk's Office.

[Former Rule 14A & C] [SO 8/4/93; SO 8/5/92; SO 3/9/93, SO 4/13/93; SO 7/25/94; SO 7/26/95]

[Effective May 13, 1997.]

RULE 9014. CONTESTED MATTERS

9014–1. Objections to Trustee's Final Report and Account in a Chapter 7 Case.

A. Parties to whom a summary of the trustee's final report and account have been sent in a chapter 7 case pursuant to Rule 2002(f)(9) Fed.R.Bankr.P. may object to the final report and account by written objection filed with the Bankruptcy Clerk and served on the Office of the United States Trustee within fifteen (15) days of the date of the summary so sent. Unless the Court orders otherwise, no trustee shall distribute dividends unless and until said fifteen (15) days have elapsed without the filing of an objection.

An objection to the trustee's final report and account is a contested matter governed by Rule 9014 Fed.R.Bankr.P.

If the summary of the final report and account is coupled with a notice of a hearing on allowances, an objection to the allowances sought may be made at or before the hearing. The party objecting shall serve a copy of the objection upon or give notice of an intention to object to the Office of the United States Trustee.

B. Responses to written questions or demands, including answers to interrogatories, depositions upon written questions, letters interrogatory or a notice demanding admissions, shall set forth each question or demand verbatim with the party's response set forth immediately thereafter. Objections to interrogatories should set forth the question, the answer and the objection thereto. Objections to responses to interrogatories should set forth the question, the answer, and the objection thereto.

C. An objection to a trustee's final report and account is a contested matter governed by Rule 9014 Fed.R.Bankr.P. Parties to whom a summary of the trustee's final report and account have been sent in a chapter 7 case pursuant to Rule 2002(f)(9) Fed. R.Bankr.P. may object to the final report and account by written objection filed with the Bankruptcy Clerk and served on the Office of the United States Trustee within fifteen (15) days of the date of the summary so sent. Unless the Court orders otherwise, no trustee shall distribute dividends unless and until said fifteen (15) days have elapsed without the filing of an objection.

If the summary of the final report and account is coupled with a notice of a hearing on allowances, an objection to the allowances sought may be made at or before the hearing. The party objecting shall serve a copy of the objection upon or give notice of an intention to object to the Office of the United States Trustee.

[Former Rule 37; Former Rule 13C]

[Effective May 13, 1997.]

RULE 9015. JURY TRIALS

A. Applicability of Certain Federal Rules of Civil Procedure. Rules 38, 39 and 47–51 Fed. R.Civ.P. and Rule 81(c) Fed.R.Civ.P. insofar as it applies to jury trials, apply in cases and proceedings, except that a demand made under Rule 38(b) Fed. R.Civ.P. shall be filed in accordance with Rule 5005 Fed.R.Bankr.P.

B. Consent to Have Trial Conducted by Bankruptcy Judge. If the right to a jury trial applies, a timely demand has been filed under Rule 38(b) Fed. R.Civ.P., and the Bankruptcy Judge has been specially designated to conduct the jury trial, the parties may consent to have a jury trial conducted by a Bankruptcy Judge under 38 USC § 157(e) by jointly or separately filing a statement of consent.

[Former Rule 31]

[Effective May 13, 1997.]

RULE 9022. JUDGMENTS AND ORDERS, NOTICE OF

9022–1. Number of Copies.

All orders and judgments shall be filed in duplicate by the party who secures them if such party desires a conformed copy be returned to them. The copies will be placed at the intake counter for pickup unless accompanied by a postage-paid, self-addressed envelope. Such party also shall furnish the Clerk with a sufficient number of additional copies thereof for mail-ing with the notice of entry, whenever notice of entry is required. All orders, whether made on notice or ex parte, together with the papers on which they were granted, shall be filed forthwith or within the time otherwise permitted by law.

Only one original proposed Order and only one original proposed Judgment need be presented to the Court, Notice of Entry sent by the Clerk's Office will be accomplished through the Bankruptcy Noticing Center. Orders and Judgments entered in unopposed matters will be mailed to the interested parties by the Clerk's Office through use of the Bankruptcy Noticing Center. It is no longer necessary for parties to provide additional copies of proposed Order for service or to be conformed and returned.

[Former Rule 14E]

[Effective May 13, 1997. Amended effective June 16, 2003.]

RULE 9024. RELIEF FROM JUDGMENT OR ORDER

General reference regarding proceedings to set aside judgments of the District Court in "Non–Core" Bankruptcy Proceedings under 28 U.S.C. § 157 is covered in the General Order regarding same entered in the U.S. District Court on September 14, 1988.

[GO 9/14/88]

[Effective May 13, 1997.]

RULE 9070. EXHIBITS

9070–1.

A. In an adversary proceeding or a contested matter, the exhibits shall be marked by counsel or the parties prior to trial or hearing.

B. Unless the Bankruptcy Court otherwise directs, exhibits (except those produced by non-parties) shall not be filed with the Bankruptcy Court Clerk but shall be retained in the custody of the respective attorneys or persons who produce them in Court. Upon submission to the trier of fact, all exhibits which were received into evidence shall be delivered to the Court. Following decision or verdict, exhibits will be returned to the parties. In the case of an appeal or other review by an appellate Court, all exhibits necessary to perfect the appeal shall be made available for inclusion in the record on appeal.

C. Exhibits produced by non-parties may be held by the Clerk or a party as the Court may direct. Whenever practicable, copies of such exhibits shall be substituted for originals. Upon expiration of the time allowed for appeal, or following an appeal, any originals retained by the Court or a party shall be returned to non-parties.

[Former Rule 30A thru C]

[Effective May 13, 1997.]

RULE 9071. STIPULATIONS

9071–1.

A. *Stipulations.* All stipulations affecting an adversary proceeding before this Court, except stipulations which are made in open Court and recorded by the court reporter, shall be in writing and signed, and shall be filed. Except to prevent injustice, no stipulation which does not satisfy these requirements shall be given in effect.

B. *Settlements.* When an adversary proceeding is settled, the parties shall file within thirty (30) days a signed agreement for judgment or stipulation for dismissal as appropriate. If no such agreement is filed, the Court may enter an order dismissing the adversary proceeding as settled, with prejudice and without costs.

[Former Rule 32]

[Effective May 13, 1997.]

APPENDICES

APPENDIX 1. CONVERSION TABLE OF FORMER BANKRUPTCY RULES, STANDING ORDERS, AND GENERAL ORDERS TO CURRENT LOCAL RULES OF BANKRUPTCY PROCEDURE

Former Local Bankruptcy Rule, General and/or Standing Order	New Local Bankruptcy Rule
1. Rule 1	LBR 1001–1
2. Rule 2	LBR 2090–1
3. Rule 3	LBR 2090–1
4. Rule 4	LBR 2090–1
5. Rule 5	LBR 2014–1; 2014–2; 2014–3
6. Rule 6	LBR 9010–1
7. Rule 7	LBR 9010–2
8. Rule 8	LBR 1072–1
9. Rule 9	LBR 5073–1
10. Rule 10	LBR 1014–1; 1072–2; 1073–1; 1073–2; 7040–1
11. Rule 11	LBR 1007–1
12. Rule 12	ABROGATED
13. Rule 13	LBR 9004–1; 9004–2; 9004–3; 9014–1
14. Rule 14	LBR 2002; 8008–1; 9006; 9013–1; 9022–1
15. Rule 15	LBR 2020–1; 2020–2
16. Rule 16	LBR 7004–1
17. Rule 17	LBR 1015–1
18. Rule 18	LBR 1007–2; 2007–1; 2015–1; 2015–2; 2015–4; 2015–5; 4001–2
19. Rule 19	LBR 2081
20. Rule 20	LBR 1019
21. Rule 21	LBR 1019
22. Rule 22	LBR 5080–1; 5081–1
23. Rule 23	LBR 7024–2
24. Rule 24	LBR 4001–2
25. Rule 25	LBR 6004–1; 6007–1
26. Rule 26	LBR 6004–1
27. Rule 27	LBR 7016–1
28. Rule 28	LBR 7016–2
29. Rule 29	LBR 7026–1
30. Rule 30	LBR 9070–1
31. Rule 31	LBR 9015–1
32. Rule 32	LBR 9071
33. Rule 33	LBR 7055–1

34.	Rule 34	LBR 7054–1
35.	Rule 35	LBR 7069–1
36.	Rule 36	LBR 7069–1
37.	Rule 37	LBR 9014–1
38.	Rule 38	LBR 2016–1
39.	Rule 39	LBR 2016–2
40.	Rule 40	LBR 2007–1
41.	Rule 41	LBR 1020–1
42.	Rule 42	LBR 6070
43.	Standing Order 8/4/83; Motions Under 11 U.S.C. § 362(d) Seeking Relief from an Automatic Stay	LBR 4001; 9013
44.	Standing Order 8/9/83; The Content of a Debtor-in-Possession's Statement of Intent to Sell Property Outside the Ordinary Course of Business	LBR 6004
45.	Standing Order 12/5/83; Defaults in Adversary Proceedings	LBR 7055
46.	General Order 1/3/84; Interest on Judgments	LBR 7069
47.	Standing Order 4/19/84; Defaults in Adversary Proceedings	LBR 7055
48.	Standing Order 5/7/84; Directing Litigants to Appear at Pre–Trial Conferences	LBR 7016–1
49.	Standing Order 6/12/84; Applications for Fees by the Attorney for the Debtor in Chapter 7 Cases	LBR 2016–1
50.	Standing Order 8/14/85; Number of Copies Required in Chapter 11 Cases	LBR 1007
51.	Standing Order 10/30/85; Cash Collateral or Adequate Protection Agreements	LBR 4001–2
52.	Standing Order 4/22/86; Issuing Notices by the Standing Chapter 13 Trustee	LBR 2002
53.	General Order 11/21/86; Discharge Hearings and Reaffirmation Agreements Under the 1986 Amendments to 11 U.S.C. 524(c) and (d)	LBR 4008
54.	Standing Order 4/29/87; Petitions: Number of copies to be filed in the Bankruptcy Court and Minimum Filing Requirements	LBR 1007–1
55.	General Order 3/21/88; Amendments to Petitions, Lists, Schedules, and Statements	LBR 1009
56.	General Order 9/14/88; Proceedings to Set Aside Judgments of the District Court in "Non–Core" Bankruptcy Proceedings Under 18 U.S.C. § 157	LBR 9024
57.	Standing Order 7/30/90; Trustee's Reimbursement of Blanket Bond Premiums	LBR 2016–1; 2016–2
58.	Standing Order 7/31/90; Compensation in Chapter 7 & 13 Cases	LBR 2010
59.	General Order & Notice 1/8/92; Amendments to Petitions, Lists, Schedules, and Statements	LBR 1009–1
60.	Standing Order 7/15/94; Waiver of Notice of Claim	LBR 3001(e)(2)
61.	Standing Order 4/23/96; Blanket Trustee Designation in Chapter 13 Cases	LBR 2008
62.	Standing Order 8/5/92; Section 362 Motions in Chapter 7 and Chapter 13 Cases in Rochester and Watkins Glen	LBR 9013
63.	Standing Order 3/9/93; Section 554 Motions in Rochester and Watkins Glen	LBR 9013

64.	Standing Order 3/9/93; Section 522(f) Motions in Rochester and Watkins Glen	LBR 9013
65.	Standing Order 4/13/93; Revised re: Section 522(f) Motions in Rochester and Watkins Glen	LBR 9013
66.	Standing Order 5/20/93; Rule 3007—Objections to Claims—Procedure in Rochester and Watkins Glen	LBR 3007
67.	Standing Order 7/25/94; Section 722 Motions in Rochester and Watkins Glen	LBR 9013
68.	Standing Order 7/26/95; Section 1229 and 1329 Modification Motions in Rochester and Watkins Glen	LBR 9013

[Effective May 13, 1997.]

APPENDIX 2.   USDC ORDER OF REFERENCE

PROCEDURE FOR THE HANDLING OF CASES UNDER AND PROCEEDINGS ARISING UNDER AND PROCEEDINGS ARISING IN OR RELATED TO A CASE UNDER TITLE 11 U.S.C.

Pursuant to § 157(a), Title 28, U.S.C., added by § 104(a) of the Act of July 10, 1984, Public Law 98–353, and subject to the remaining provisions of § 157,

IT IS ORDERED that all cases under Title 11, U.S.C. and all proceedings arising under Title 11, U.S.C. or arising in or related to a case under Title 11, U.S.C. pending on June 27, 1984 or filed on or after June 28, 1984 are referred to the bankruptcy judges for this District, to be assigned in accordance with their assignment rules.

Dated: Buffalo, NY
　　　July 13, 1984.

APPENDIX 3.   IMPLEMENTATION OF THE ACT OF JULY 10, 1984, PUBLIC LAW 98–353

Supplementing this Court's Order dated July 13, 1984 which provided "Procedure for the Handling of Cases Under and Proceedings Arising Under, and Proceedings Arising in or Related to a Case Under Title 11 U.S.C." and by way of further implementation of the Act of July 10, 1984, Public Law 98–353, it is

ORDERED, pursuant to § 154(b), Title 28, United States Code, that Beryl E. McGuire is designated Chief Judge of the Bankruptcy Court for the Western District of New York, and it is

FURTHER ORDERED that the Bankruptcy Judges of this District are authorized to promulgate local rules consistent with and necessary to the implementation of Public Law 98–353; the provisions of Title 11, United States Code, as amended; and the provisions of the Rules of Bankruptcy Procedure, as amended; and it is

FURTHER ORDERED, pursuant to § 157(b)(5), Title 28, United States Code, that personal injury tort and wrongful death claims shall be tried in the district court in which the bankruptcy case is pending, or in the district court in the district in which the claim arose, as determined by the district court in which the bankruptcy case is pending.

Dated: September 18, 1984.

APPENDIX 4.   REAFFIRMATION OF THE ORDERS IMPLEMENTING THE ACT OF JULY 10, 1984, PUBLIC LAW 98–353

In reaffirmation of the Order of this Court dated July 13, 1984, which provided "Procedure for the Handling of Cases Under and Proceedings Arising Under, and Proceedings Arising in or Related to a Case Under Title 11 U.S.C." and the Order of this Court dated September 18, 1984, which further implemented the Act of July 10, 1984, Public Law 98–353, it is

ORDERED, pursuant to § 154(b), Title 28, United States Code, that Beryl E. McGuire is designated Chief Judge of the Bankruptcy Court for the Western District of New York, and it is

FURTHER ORDERED that the Bankruptcy Judges of this District are authorized to promulgate local rules consistent with and necessary to the implementation of Public Law 98–353; the provisions of Title 11, United States Code, as amended; and the provisions of the Rules of Bankruptcy Procedure, as amended; and it is

FURTHER ORDERED, pursuant to § 157(b)(5), Title 28, United States Code, that personal injury tort and wrongful death claims shall be tried in the district court in which the bankruptcy case is pending, or in the district court in the district in which the claim arose, as determined by the district court in which the bankruptcy case is pending.

Dated: May 20, 1992.

APPENDIX 5.   ORDER OF APPOINTMENT OF CHIEF BANKRUPTCY JUDGE

The Court having been advised by the Honorable Beryl E. McGuire that he intends to resign as Chief Judge of the Bankruptcy Court for the Western District of New York effective January 1, 1993, and the Court having selected the Honorable Michael J. Kaplan as his successor pursuant to 28 U.S.C. § 154(b), it is hereby

ORDERED, that the Honorable Michael J. Kaplan* is appointed Chief Judge of the Bankruptcy Court for the Western District of New York commencing January 1, 1993, and expiring December 31, 1999.

SO ORDERED.

DATED: Rochester, New York
        December 21, 1992.

* **Publisher's Note.** So in the Court's official rules set.

ELECTRONIC CASE FILING

ADMINISTRATIVE PROCEDURES FOR FILING, SIGNING AND VERIFYING PLEADINGS AND PAPERS BY ELECTRONIC MEANS

October 18, 2004

I. REGISTRATION FOR THE ELECTRONIC FILING SYSTEM.

A. *DESIGNATION OF CASES.*

1. On June 13, 2003, all documents submitted for filing in this district, no matter when a case was originally filed, may be filed electronically using the Electronic Filing System ("System") or will be scanned and uploaded to the System.

2. Parties proceeding pro se or non-registered users will not be permitted to file electronically. All filing requirements as provided in the Federal Rules of Bankruptcy Procedure ("Fed.R.Bankr.P.") and the Local Rules of Bankruptcy Procedure ("LBR") will prevail.

B. *LOGINS AND PASSWORDS.* Attorneys admitted to the bar of this Court (including those admitted pro hac vice), United States Trustees and their assistants, private Trustees, and others as the Court deems appropriate, may register with the Court's Electronic Filing System ("Filing Users" and/or "Registered Participants"). Registration is in a form directed by the Clerk and requires the Filing User's name, address, telephone, number, Internet e-mail address, and, in the case of an attorney, a declaration that the attorney is admitted to the bar of this Court. Registration for a login and password is governed by "Section I. (C)."

Registration as a Filing User constitutes: (1) waiver of the right to receive notice by first class mail and consent to receive notice electronically; and (2) waiver of the right to service by personal service or first class mail and consent to electronic service, except with regard to service of a summons and complaint under Fed.R.Bankr.P. 7004. Waiver of service and notice by first class mail applies to notice of the entry of an order or judgment under Fed.R.Bankr.P. 9022.

Issuance of a login and password to the Filing User immediately activates access to the Court's electronic Filing System together with all procedures related thereto.

C. *REGISTRATION.*

1. Each attorney or authorized participant desiring to file pleadings or other papers electronically must complete and sign an Attorney/Participant Registration Form (Form A), or a Pro Hac Vice Registration Form (Form B), and a Credit Card Blanket Authorization Form (Form C) and attend the necessary training required by the Court. These forms are also available on our web site at www. nywb.uscourts.gov. The Court reserves the right to allow authorized participants, i.e. non-attorney filers such as creditors or governmental agencies, to become Filing Users at a future date.

2. All signed original Attorney/Participant or Pro Hac Vice Registration Forms will be mailed or delivered to the Clerk of Court, United States Bankruptcy Court, Olympic Towers, 300 Pearl Street, Buffalo, NY 14202.

3. To ensure that the Clerk's Office has correctly entered a registering attorney's or participant's Internet e-mail address in the System, the Clerk's Office will send the attorney or participant an Internet e-mail message after assigning his/her login and password. The Clerk's Office will then either mail the password information to the attorney or participant by regular, first-class mail with the envelope marked "CONFIDENTIAL," or the attorney may arrange to pick up his/her password at the Clerk's Office location designated on his/her registration form.

4. A registered participant is encouraged to change the Court-assigned password. This change can be made by accessing the menu option "Maintain Your ECF Account" under utilities. In the event that a filer believes that the security of an existing password has been compromised and in order to prevent unauthorized access to the System by use of that password, the registered participant will immediately change his/her password in the System and thereafter provide notice to the Clerk's Office's Help Desk and confirm by facsimile to the Clerk of Court. If a registered participant forgets his/her password, the Clerk of Court, through designated individuals, will assign a new password.

5. All signed original Credit Card Blanket Authorization Forms will be mailed or delivered in an envelope marked "CONFIDENTIAL" and addressed to the Financial Administrator, United States Bankruptcy Court, Olympic Towers, 300 Pearl Street, Suite 250, Buffalo, NY 14202.

6. Once registered, a registered participant may withdraw from using the System by providing the Clerk's Office with notice of withdrawal. Such notice must be in writing, and mailed or delivered to the Clerk, United States Bankruptcy Court, Olympic Towers, 300 Pearl Street, Suite 250, Buffalo, NY 14202. Upon receipt, the Clerk's Office will immediately cancel the participant's password and will delete his/her name from any applicable electronic service list.

7. If any of the information on the Attorney/Participant or Pro Hac Vice Registration Forms or the Credit Card Blanket Authorization Form changes, (e.g., mailing address, e-mail address, credit card information, etc.), the registered participant must submit the appropriate amended form addressed to the Clerk of Court and/or the Financial Administrator as indicated in Section I. (C.)(2.) and (4.) above.

II. ELECTRONIC FILING, SERVICE OF DOCUMENTS, AND TIMELINESS.

A. *FILING.*

1. Except as otherwise provided by these procedures, registered filers will submit electronically all petitions, motions, pleadings, briefs, memoranda of law, proofs of claim or other documents required to be filed with the Court in connection with a case or proceeding, in Portable Document Format ("PDF") file.

2. The creditor matrix is to be prepared with word processing software in a single column format, one inch from the left edge of each page (not centered). The name and address of each creditor must not exceed 5 lines and each line may not contain more than 40 characters, including blank spaces. "Attention" lines should be placed on the second line of the name/address. Creditor names and addresses are to be single spaced, with a double space separating each creditor. The city, state, and zip must all be on the last line. State names must be two-letter abbreviations. The word processing file must be saved as a *text ("TXT")* file and uploaded

to the Electronic Case Filing System pursuant to the CM/ECF User's Manual.

3. Notwithstanding the foregoing, anyone filing documents with the Court who is not as Filing User in the System is not required to electronically file pleadings and other papers in a case assigned to the System.

4. All summonses submitted to the Clerk of Court for filing will be presented conventionally pursuant to FRBP.

5. The Clerk's Office will not maintain a paper Court file in any case filed after the effective date of these procedures except as otherwise provided by these procedures. The official Court record will be an electronic file maintained on the Court's file server.

6. Chambers "Courtesy copies", of all documents filed electronically, are required to be provided to the Court within 2 business days of the electronic filing, *EXCEPT voluntary Chapter 7 initiating petitions, schedules and statements.* The courtesy copy must be printed on paper and clearly marked as **"ELECTRONICALLY FILED DOCU-MENT—CHAMBERS COPY"** and must be submitted in compliance with these procedures.

7. Any documents received in paper format in Chambers or the Clerk's Office will be disposed of when it is determined that they are no longer needed.

8. Any adjournment letters and status conference requests will be filed conventionally.

9. In expedited matters, the movant will contact the Courtroom Deputy in Rochester or the Judge's Secretary in Buffalo by phone as soon as possible after filing the item needing expedited treatment. Compliance with the FRBP 9006 is required.

10. The United States Trustee requires that immediately upon filing a *Chapter 11 case only*, the attorney for the debtor must provide the United States Trustee with a paper copy of the electronically filed petition, lists, schedules, statement of financial affairs, 2016(b) Statement and any amended schedules, together with an attached copy of the "Notice of Electronic Filing." The United States Trustee requires that within two days (2) of the notification of the trustee assignment, the attorney for the debtor or the pro se debtor to submit, to the *Chapter 7 Case Trustee in Buffalo and Rochester* and the *Chapter 13 Case Trustee in Rochester only*, a paper copy of the electronically filed petition, lists, schedules, statement of affairs, 2016(b) Statement, and any amended schedules, together with an attached copy of the "Notice of Electronic Filing."

Upon conversion of a case, the attorney for the debtor or the pro se debtor must provide paper copies of the electronically filed documents listed above, together with any documents filed pursuant to the Western District of New York Local Rules, to the United States Trustee within two days of the conversion and to the newly appointed case trustee within two days of notification of the trustee assignment.

B. *SERVICE.*

1. Whenever a pleading or other paper is filed electronically, in accordance with these procedures, the System will generate notice of electronic filing and send it to the filing party and any other party who has requested electronic notice in that case. Attached to these procedures as "Form F" is an example of a Notice of Electronic Filing.

2. If the recipient is a registered participant in the System, the Clerk's e-mailing of the "Notice of Electronic Filing" will be the equivalent of service of the pleading or other paper by first class mail, postage prepaid, subject to the provisions of Fed. R.Bankr.P. 7004 and 9014(b).

3. A Certificate of Service is still required when a party files a document electronically. The Certificate of Service must state the manner in which service or notice was made on each party served. Sample language for a "Certificate of Service" is attached to these procedures as "Form D."

4. A party who is not a Filing User or Registered Participant of the System is entitled to a paper copy of any electronically filed pleading or paper. The filing party must, therefore, serve the non-registered party with the pleading or paper according to the FRBP and LBR.

C. *SECTION 341(a) MEETING OF CREDITORS.* The attorney for the debtor must bring to the Section 341(a) meeting of creditors the electronically filed petition, schedules, lists and statement of affairs bearing the original signatures, as required by "Section III (B)" of these Procedures. Debtors and their attorneys will execute a "Declaration Re: Electronic Filing" at the meeting of creditors "Form G."

The attorney for the debtor must bring to the Section 341(a) meeting of creditors Official Form 21, Statement of Social Security Number(s) bearing the original signatures.

D. *TIMELINESS.*

1. Filing a document electronically does not alter the filing deadline for that document.

2. Filings are considered timely if received by the Court before midnight on the date set as a deadline, unless the judge specifically requires an earlier filing, such as close of business.

3. Due to variations in time zones, timeliness is established based on the Eastern Standard time zone where the Western District of New York is located.

4. A Filing User whose filing is made untimely as the result of a technical failure of the Court's CM/ECF site, as prescribed in Section XII of these procedures, may seek appropriate relief from the Court.

III. SIGNATURES.

A. Petitions, lists, schedules and statements, amendments, pleadings, affidavits, and other documents which must contain original signatures or which require verification under FRBP 1008 or an unsworn declaration as provided in 28 U.S.C. § 1746, will be filed electronically. THE ELECTRONIC FILING OF ANY DOCUMENT REQUIRING AN INK SIGNATURE CONSTITUTES A REPRESENTATION BY THE FILING USER THAT THE ORIGINAL SIGNATURE(S) WERE OBTAINED AND AFFIXED TO SUCH DOCUMENT(S) PRIOR TO THE ELECTRONIC FILING. VIOLATIONS OF THIS REQUIREMENT WILL BE SUBJECT TO DISCIPLINARY ACTION AGAINST THE FILING USER. The Statement of Social Security Number, Official Form 21, must be verified and signed prior to the electronic filing of the petition. Official Form 21 will *not* be electronically filed with the Court.

B. For a period of not less than five (5) years after the closing of the bankruptcy case, the Filing User originating the document must retain "verified documents," i.e., documents required to be verified under Fed.R.Bankr.P. 1008 or documents in which a person verifies, certifies, affirms, or swears under oath or penalty of perjury. (See, e.g., 28 U.S.C. § 1746 [unsworn declarations under penalty of perjury]). For a period of not less than five (5) years after the closing of the bankruptcy case, documents that are electronically filed and require original signatures other than that of the Filing User must be maintained in paper form by the Filing User. Upon request of the Court, the Filing User must provide original documents for review. Compliance with Fed.R.Bankr.P. 9011 is required.

C. The pleading or other document electronically filed must indicate a signature, i.e. "/s/ name," unless the document is a scanned PDF document and shows an original handwritten signature.

D. The following procedure applies when a stipulation or another document requires two or more signatures:

1. The Filing User must initially confirm that the content of the document is acceptable to all persons required to sign the document and must obtain the handwritten signatures of all parties on the document. For purposes of this rule, the pleading or other document electronically filed must indicate a signature, i.e., "/s/ name," unless the document is a scanned PDF document and shows an original handwritten signature. Compliance with FRBP 9011 is required.

2. The Filing User must file the document electronically, indicating each signature, i.e. "/s/ name," unless the document has been scanned and shows the actual signature

3. The Filing User originating the document must maintain the original signed document as provided for in Section III. C. above.

E. Official Form 21, Statement of Social Security Number(s) must be signed by the debtor(s) before the petition is electronically filed with the Court and retained by the debtor's attorney in accordance with the requirements of Paragraphs "A" and "B" of this Section.

IV. FEES.

A. Fees for electronic filing of any pleading or paper requiring a filing fee will be paid by the filer via credit card over the Internet.

B. Only VISA, MASTERCARD, AMERICAN EXPRESS, DISCOVER, AND DINER'S CLUB credit cards will be accepted.

C. The fee for any transaction declined by the credit card issuer for any reason must be paid to the Court in cash, check or money order by the close of business on the next business day after notification by Court staff of the deficiency. The attorney or participant has the responsibility to furnish updated credit card information to the Court.

D. Except as otherwise provided, all registered participants of the System will be subject to the fees set forth in the Fee Schedule for Electronic Public Access "EPA Fee Schedule," adopted by the Judicial Conference of the United States.

E. Registered Users in a case receive one free electronic viewing of the filed document through PACER, at the time the document is filed, without being assessed a fee. Users are encouraged to print or save the document at that time to avoid additional PACER fees. Should the Registered User not print or otherwise save the document, any subsequent PACER access to documents is subject to PACER fees.

V. ATTACHMENTS.

A. Registered participants must submit all documents referenced as attachments, or only relevant excerpts that are directly relevant to the matter under consideration by the Court, including but not limited to leases, notes and mortgages in Portable Document Format (PDF), unless the Court permits conventional filing. Attachments may be summarized using (Form E). Cover sheets are considered attachments.

B. The size of the electronic file will be limited to a manageable size so as not to degrade system performance. Attachments exceeding the recommended size requirement must be split into separate PDF files and the multiple PDF files attached to the document.

Document size limits are posted to the Court's website and will be adjusted with improvements in technology.

C. For attachments not available in electronic form, it is preferred that such documents, or the relevant portions thereof, should be electronically imaged, i.e., scanned, and filed using the Portable Document Format (PDF). Excerpted material must be clearly and prominently identified as such. The file size requirements as stated in Section V. (B.) are required.

D. Filing Users who file excerpts of documents do so without prejudice to their right to timely file additional excerpts or complete documents.

E. Filing Users must promptly provide full and complete versions of excerpted documents upon the request of the Court or responding party.

VI. SEALED DOCUMENTS.

A. A motion to file a document under seal may be filed electronically unless prohibited by law.

B. Documents ordered to be placed under seal must be filed conventionally, and NOT electronically, unless specifically authorized by the Court.

C. The filing party must file with the Clerk through conventional means a paper copy of the proposed order attached to the documents to be sealed.

VII. ORDERS.

A. Proposed Orders must be submitted conventionally to the Court, with the following exception: Proposed Orders submitted as part of the Default Motion Procedures in effect for cases filed in Rochester and Watkins Glen may be submitted electronically as a separate attachment to the motion. All other proposed Orders should be submitted to the Court within 3 business days of the granting of said Order. Document backers should not be affixed.

B. Proposed Orders may not be combined with the application or motion into one document. The application or motion must be entered on the docket prior to submitting the Order. DO NOT ELECTRONICALLY FILE A PLEADING WHICH CONTAINS A PROPOSED ORDER IN THE BODY OF THE PLEADING. Pleadings which contain a proposed Order within the body of the pleading or are not properly labeled as "proposed" will be ignored.

C. Any Order filed and docketed electronically by the Court without the original signature of a Judge has the same force and effect as if the Judge had affixed the Judge's signature to a paper copy of the Order and it had been entered on the docket in a conventional manner. Only the Court and authorized Clerk's Office Staff may file and enter Orders electronically. Orders purported to be filed electronically by filers other than the Court or authorized Clerk's Office Staff shall have no validity.

D. Any ministerial Order filed and entered electronically by the Clerk of Court without the original signature of the Judge or Clerk has the same force and effect as if the Clerk had affixed his/her signature to a paper copy of the Order and it had been entered on the docket in a conventional manner.

VIII. DOCKET ENTRIES.

A. A filer who electronically submits a pleading or other document must be responsible for designating a docket entry for the document by using one of the docket event categories prescribed by the Court. This action constitutes an entry on the official Court docket as provided in FRBP 5003.

B. The Clerk will enter all Orders and Judgments in the System, which constitute docketing of the Order and Judgment for all purposes. The Clerk's notation in the appropriate docket of an Order or Judgment will constitute the entry of the Order or Judgment as provided in FRBP 5003.

IX. CORRECTING DOCUMENTS FILED IN ERROR.

A. Once a document is submitted and becomes part of the case docket, corrections to the docket are made only by the Clerk's Office.

B. A document incorrectly filed in a case may be the result of posting the wrong PDF file to a docket entry, or selecting the wrong document type from the menu, or entering the wrong case number and not catching the error before the transaction is completed. Do not attempt to re-file the document.

C. As soon as possible after an error is discovered, the filer must contact the Help Desk in the Clerk's Office in Buffalo or Rochester, whichever has jurisdiction over the case or proceeding. Be sure to have the case number and document number for which the correction is being requested. As appropriate, the Clerk may either make an entry indicating that the Filing User has represented that a document was filed in error or the error will be brought to the attention of the Court for proper resolution. The Filing User will be advised as to how the error will be corrected and what additional actions will need to be taken by the Filing User, such as re-filing the document or providing an affidavit of the error with service to affected parties. The System will not permit Filing Users to make changes to the document(s) or docket entry filed in error once the transaction has been accepted.

X. TECHNICAL FAILURES.

A. Technical failure of the Court's CM/ECF site which prevents the filer from being able to timely file documents may seek appropriate relief from the Court or file by conventional means available. Known systems outages [generally for maintenance and system upgrades] will be posted to the Court's web site with as much advance notification as possible.

B. Problems with the filer's system(s), such as phone line problems, problems with the filer's Internet Service Provider (ISP), or hardware or software problems, will not constitute a technical failure under these procedures. A filer who cannot file a document electronically because of a problem on the filer's end may file the document conventionally or seek other appropriate relief from the Court.

XI. SECURITY OF THE SYSTEM.

Each electronically filed paper will be assigned a special identification number which can be traced, if necessary, to detect post filing alterations to a document.

XII. PRIVACY.

A. To address the privacy concerns created by Internet access to Court documents, filers should limit certain personal identifiers appearing in pleadings or other papers. The suggested limitations are as follows:

1. Names of Minor Children: Use the minors' initials;

2. Financial Account Numbers: Identify the name or type of account and the financial institution where maintained, but use only the last four numbers of the account number;

3. Social Security Numbers except as required by statute, rule or official form;

4. Dates of Birth: Use only the year; and

5. Other data and/or information as identified by order of the Court.

6. Documents such as tax returns, bank account statements, driver licenses, copies of cancelled checks, etc. should not be filed with the Court to avoid public disclosure.

B. Information posted on the System must not be downloaded for uses inconsistent with the privacy rights of any person.

C. Pursuant to the Bankruptcy Rules, the Court is not responsible for redacting the Social Security number or other personal data from documents filed with the Court, whether in paper or electronic form. Filers are cautioned to carefully review documents being filed with the Court and redact personal data protected under the new Bankruptcy Rules. The Court staff will safeguard the original Statement of Social Security Number(s), Official Form B21, which will not be made a part of the bankruptcy case file. Additionally, the CM/ECF software will be modified to comply with the new noticing considerations and protection of the debtor(s) Social Security number in full compliance with the privacy related Rules.

XIII. PUBLIC ACCESS TO THE SYSTEM DOCKET.

A. Electronic access to the electronic docket and documents filed in the System is available for viewing to the public at no charge at each Clerk's Office's public counter during regular business hours. A fee for a paper copy of an electronic document is required in accordance with 28 U.S.C. § 1930.

B. Although any person can retrieve and view the documents in the System and access information from it without charge at the Clerk's Office, electronic access to the System for viewing purposes is otherwise limited to subscribers to the Public Access to Court Electronic Records ("PACER") System and, in accordance with the ruling of the Judicial Conference of the United States, a user fee will be charged for accessing detailed case information, such as reviewing filed documents and docket sheets, but excluding review of calendars and similar general information.

C. Conventional copies and certified copies of the electronically filed documents may be purchased at the Clerk's Office. The fee for copying and certification will be in accordance with 28 U.S.C. § 1930.

Effective October 18, 2004.

FORM A
UNITED STATES BANKRUPTCY COURT
WESTERN DISTRICT OF NEW YORK
CASE MANAGEMENT/ELECTRONIC
CASE FILES SYSTEM (CM/ECF)
ATTORNEY OR PARTICIPANT
REGISTRATION FORM
LIVE SYSTEM

This form will be used to register an attorney or participant on the U.S. Bankruptcy Court for the Western District of New York Electronic Case Files (CM/ECF) System (hereinafter System). A registered participant will have privileges to submit documents electronically, and to view and retrieve docket sheets and documents for all cases assigned to the Western District's ECF System. (NOTE: A PACER account is necessary for access to files and documents. You may register for a PACER account either online at http://pacer.psc.uscourts.gov or by calling 1–800–676–6856).

First/Middle/Last Name:

Bar ID #:

State of Admission:

Admitted to Practice in U.S. District Court for the WDNY: _____

Firm Name, if applicable

Mailing Address:

Voice Phone Number:

Fax Phone Number:

Internet E–MAIL Address:

Send Notices to these additional E–MAIL Addresses:

_____

Send Electronic Notice (check one) ☐ Each Filing ☐ End of Day Summary

Send Electronic Notice in the following format (check one):

    ☐ HTML for Netscape, ISP mail service, i.e., AOL, Hotmail, Yahoo, etc.

    ☐ Text for cc:Mail, Groupwise, Outlook, Outlook Express, other (please list)

In order to schedule you for the appropriate training class, please indicate your type of legal practice.

☐ Debtor ☐ Creditor ☐ Trustee ☐ Other (please specify)_____.

Return my login and password by:

    ☐ first class mail with the envelope marked confidential OR

    ☐ pick up at public counter in ☐ Buffalo or ☐ Rochester.

By submitting this registration form the applicant agrees to adhere to the following:

1. This access is for use only in ECF cases filed in the U.S. Bankruptcy Court for the Western District of New York. It may be used to file and view electronic documents, docket sheets, and reports. NOTE: A PACER account is necessary for this access and the registration information is referenced above.

2. The FRBP 9011 requires that every pleading, motion, and other paper (except lists, schedules, statements, or amendments thereto) filed with Court be signed by at least one attorney of record or, if the party is not represented by an attorney, by the party. The unique password issued to a participant identifies that participant to the Court each time he or she logs onto the System. The use of a participant's password constitutes the signature of the purposes of FBRP 9011 on any document or pleading filed electronically using that participant's password. Therefore, a participant must protect and secure the password issued by the Court. If there is any reason to suspect the password has been compromised, it is the duty of the participant to immediately change his or her password through the "Utilities" menu in the system. After doing so, the participant should contact the ECF Help Desk to report the suspected password compromise.

3. Registration will constitute a request and an agreement to receive service of pleadings and other papers electronically pursuant to FRBP 9036, where service of pleadings and other papers is otherwise permitted by first class mail, postage prepaid.

4. I understand that by submitting an application for a password I agree to adhere to all of the rules and regulations in the WDNY Administrative Orders for Filing, Signing, and Verifying Pleadings and Papers by Electronic Means currently in effect, and any changes or additions that may be made to such Administrative Orders. The Court may periodically post announcements and updates to the Court's website that are pertinent to CM/ECF practice.

5. I assume all responsibility and liability for the payment of all applicable filing fees due at the time the document is electronically filed.

6. I understand that prior to electronically filing any document with the Court, I must obtain the original signature of the party or parties I represent on a paper copy of the document and that I must retain the original of that signed document for the length of time set forth in the "Administrative Procedures."

7. For individual debtor cases filed electronically on or after December 1, 2003, I understand that prior to the electronic filing of a petition, I must obtain the original signature(s) of the debtor(s) I represent on a paper copy of the Statement of Social Security Number(s), (Official Form B21), and that I must retain the original of that signed document for the length of time set forth in the "Administrative Procedures." I also understand I must compare the social security number(s) provided by the debtor(s) on Official Form B21 to the numbers entered into the Court's CM/ECF System to ensure they are the same.

Applicant's Signature   Date

Last four Digits of Social Security Number (for security purposes)

Privacy Disclaimer: The information contained within this application will not be sold or otherwise distributed by this office to outside sources.

Please return this form to the New York Western Office at:

    U.S. Bankruptcy Court
    Attn: Clerk of Court
    Olympic Towers
    300 Pearl Street, Suite 250
    Buffalo, NY 14202

FORM B

UNITED STATES BANKRUPTCY COURT
WESTERN DISTRICT OF NEW YORK

CASE MANAGEMENT/ELECTRONIC
CASE FILES SYSTEM (CM/ECF)
PRO HAC VICE
ATTORNEY REGISTRATION FORM

LIVE SYSTEM

This form will be used to register an out of district attorney on the U.S. Bankruptcy Court for the Western District of New York Electronic Case Files (CM/ECF) System (hereinafter System) by attorneys who (1) reside and practice outside of this district and/or (2) represent parties in New York State on a pro hac vice basis. A registered participant will have privileges to submit documents electronically, and to view and retrieve docket sheets and documents for all cases assigned to the Western District ECF System. (NOTE: A PACER account is necessary for access to files and documents. You may register for a PACER account either online at http://pacer.psc.uscourts.gov or by calling 1–800–676–6856).

First/Middle/Last Name:

Bar ID #:

State of Admission:

Admitted to Practice in the U.S. District Court for __

Firm Name, if applicable:

Mailing Address:

Voice Phone Number:

Fax Phone Number:

Internet E–MAIL Address:

Send Notices to these additional E–MAIL Addresses:

Send Electronic Notice (check one) ☐ Each Filing ☐ End of Day Summary

Send Electronic Notice in the following format (check one):

☐ HTML for Netscape, ISP mail service, i.e., AOL, Hotmail, Yahoo, etc.

☐ Text for cc:Mail, GroupWise, Outlook, Outlook Express, other (please list)

In order to schedule you for the appropriate training class, please indicate your type of legal practice.

☐ Debtor ☐ Creditor ☐ Trustee ☐ Other (please specify) _____.

In order to qualify for an account on the system, the out-of-district attorney/participant must certify that he or she meets one of the following conditions. Please check the applicable box(es):

☐ I am registered as an ECF participant in the United States Bankruptcy Court in another state or district. Please indicate court or district(s):

☐ I have read the WDNY Administrative Orders and Procedures regarding ECF and have completed training as required by the WDNY Administrative Procedures.

By submitting this registration form the applicant agrees to adhere to the following:

1. This access is for use only in ECF cases filed in the U.S. Bankruptcy Court for the Western District of New York. It may be used to file and view electronic documents, docket sheets, and reports. NOTE: A PACER account is necessary for this access and the registration information is referenced above.

2. The FRBP 9011 requires that every pleading, motion, and other paper (except lists, schedules, statements, or amendments thereto) filed with Court be signed by at least one attorney of record or, if the party is not represented by an attorney, by the party. The unique password issued to a participant identifies that participant to the Court each time he or she logs onto the System. The use of a participant's password constitutes the signature of the purposes of FBRP 9011 on any document or pleading filed electronically using that participant's password. Therefore, a participant must protect and secure the password issued by the Court. If there is any reason to suspect the password has been compromised, it is the duty of the participant to immediately change his or her password through the "Utilities" menu in the system. After doing so, the participant should contact the ECF Help Desk to report the suspected password compromise.

3. Registration will constitute a request and an agreement to receive service of pleadings and other papers electronically pursuant to FRBP 9036, where service of pleadings and other papers is otherwise permitted by first class mail, postage prepaid.

4. I understand that by submitting an application for a password I agree to adhere to all of the rules and regulations in the WDNY Administrative Procedures for Filing, Signing and Verifying Pleadings and Papers by Electronic Means currently in effect, and any changes or additions that may be made to such Administrative Orders. The Court may periodically post announcements and updates on the Court's website that are pertinent to ECF practice.

5. I assume all responsibility and liability for the payment of all applicable filing fees due at the time the document is electronically filed.

6. I understand that prior to electronically filing any document with the Court, I must obtain the original signature of the party or parties I represent on a paper copy of the document and that I must retain the original of that signed document for the length of time set forth in the "Administrative Procedures."

7. For individual debtor cases filed electronically on or after December 1, 2003, I understand that prior to the electronic filing of a petition, I must obtain the original signature(s) of the debtor(s) I represent on a paper copy of the Statement of Social Security Number(s), (Official Form B21), and that I must retain the original of that signed document for the length of time

set forth in the "Administrative Procedures." I also understand I must compare the social security number(s) provided by the debtor(s) on Official Form B21 to the numbers entered into the Court's CM/ECF System to ensure they are the same.

Applicant's Signature   Date

Last four Digits of Social Security Number (for security purposes)

Privacy Disclaimer: The information contained within this application will not be sold or otherwise distributed by this office to outside sources.

Please return this form to the New York Western Office at: U.S. Bankruptcy Court, Attn: Clerk of Court, 300 Pearl Street, Suite 250, Buffalo, New York 14202.

FORM C

UNITED STATES BANKRUPTCY COURT
WESTERN DISTRICT OF NEW YORK

CREDIT CARD BLANKET AUTHORIZATION FORM

I hereby authorize the U.S. Bankruptcy Court for the Western District of New York to charge the bank card listed below for payment of fees, costs and expenses which are incurred by the authorized users listed below. I understand if a document requiring a fee is received without the fee, the court will automatically charge the account number listed on this form. A copy of both sides of the credit card must accompany this form. I certify that I am authorized to sign this form on behalf of my law firm.

THIS FORM MUST BE TYPED, FILLED OUT COMPLETELY WITH ORIGINAL SIGNATURES, AND DELIVERED TO THE U.S. BANKRUPTCY COURT FOR THE WESTERN DISTRICT OF NEW YORK. A new original form must be submitted to the Court upon *any* change of *any* of the information below. It is the responsibility of the cardholder to notify the Court if a card has been stolen or cancelled. If the information on the form is not current, the transaction will not be processed. This form will remain in effect until the expiration date of the credit card or the form is specifically revoked in writing. Photo identification will be requested from the authorized users listed on this form when appearing personally at the Court.

*Name as it appears on card*_____

Card Type: ☐ MasterCard ☐ Visa ☐ Discover ☐ American Express ☐ Diners Club

*Account Number:*____ AmEx ID#:___ *Expiration Date:*_____

*Cardholder Signature:*_____
*Date:*_____

Names and signatures of individuals authorized to use account number listed above for payment of fees, costs, or expenses:

Name   Signature

Name   Signature

Name   Signature

Name of Firm: _____

(Sole practitioner, type or print your name)

Billing Address:

Contact Person: _____ Phone No: _____

e-mail address: _____

Please send your form to either office. The originals will be held in a secure location in the Buffalo office.

☐ BUFFALO OFFICE
300 Pearl St., Suite 250
ATTN: Financial Dept.
Buffalo, NY 14202

☐ ROCHESTER OFFICE
2100 State St., Suite 1220
ATTN: Financial Dept.
Rochester, NY 14614

Court Use Only:

Date Received:___ CC copy attached: Y N___ Info verified: Y N___ By:___

FORM D
(SAMPLE FORMAT)

UNITED STATES BANKRUPTCY COURT
WESTERN DISTRICT OF NEW YORK

In Re:

         Case No.
         Chapter

   Debtor(s).

CERTIFICATE OF SERVICE

I hereby certify that on _____(Date), I electronically filed the foregoing with the Clerk of the Bankruptcy Court using the CM/ECF system which sent notification of such filing to the following:

    1......

    2......

3......

And, I hereby certify that I have mailed by the United States Postal Service the document to the following non CM/ECF participants:

1......

2......

3......

/s/name

FORM E
(SAMPLE FORMAT)

UNITED STATES BANKRUPTCY COURT
WESTERN DISTRICT OF NEW YORK

In Re:

Case No.
Chapter

Debtor(s).

SUMMARY OF EXHIBITS/ATTACHMENT(S)
AND CERTIFICATE OF SERVICE

The following attachment(s) in reference to _____ are available upon request:

1..............

2..............

3..............

Respectfully submitted

/s/ name

ATTORNEY FOR _____

Copy of the above served this _____ day of _____, _____ on: [respondent parties if motion] [debtor's (s') attorney and trustee if claim]

FORM F

SAMPLE NOTICE OF ELECTRONIC FILING

GENERATED BY SYSTEM WHEN A DOCUMENT IS FILED

00–00000–ABC Notice of Electronic Filing

The following transaction was received from Jim C. Doe on 01/01/2001 at 12:01 AM

Case Name: Debtor name

Case Number: 00–00000–ABC

Document Number: 14

Docket Text:

MOTION FOR RELIEF FROM STAY filed by Jim C. Doe of Creditor's law firm on behalf of Creditor. (Doe, Jim C.)

The following document(s) are associated with this transaction:

Document description: Main Document

Original filename: x:/XXX/12345.pdf

Electronic Document Stamp:

[STAMP NYWBStamp_ID=1111111111[Date=01/01/2001][File Number=11111–1][other codes]

00–00000–ABC Notice will be electronically mailed to:

Jim C. Doe   jdoe@creditors.com

Julie W. Doe   jdoe@lawfirm.com

00–00000–ABC The person(s) listed below could not be notified electronically because that person's e-mail notification service is not activated:

John Doe
123 Main St.
Nowhere, USA

Jane Doe
465 Main St.
Somewhere, USA

FORM G
UNITED STATES BANKRUPTCY COURT
WESTERN DISTRICT OF NEW YORK

In Re:

                Case No.

Debtor(s)

DECLARATION RE: ELECTRONIC FILING OF PETITION, SCHEDULES & STATEMENTS
PART I—DECLARATION OF PETITIONER

I (We) and, the undersigned debtor(s), hereby declare under penalty of perjury that the information provided in the electronically filed petition, statements, and schedules is true and correct and that I signed these documents prior to electronic filing. I consent to my attorney sending my petition, statements and schedules to the United States Bankruptcy Court. I understand that this DECLARATION RE: ELECTRONIC FILING is to be executed at the First Meeting of Creditors and filed with the Trustee. I understand that failure to file the signed original of this DECLARATION may cause my case to be dismissed pursuant to 11 U.S.C. § 707(a)(3) without further notice. I (we) further declare under penalty of perjury that I (we) signed the original Statement of Social Security Number(s), (Official Form B21), prior to the electronic filing of the petition and have verified the 9–digit social security number displayed on the Notice of Meeting of Creditors to be accurate.

☐ If petitioner is an individual whose debts are primarily consumer debts and who has chosen to file under a chapter: I am aware that I may proceed under chapter 7, 11, 12 or 13 of Title 11, United States Code, understand the relief available under each chapter, and choose to proceed under this chapter. I request relief in accordance with the chapter specified in this petition. I (We) and, the undersigned debtor(s), hereby declare under penalty of perjury that the information provided in the electronically filed petition, statements, and schedules is true and correct.

☐ If petitioner is a corporation or partnership: I declare under a penalty of perjury that the information provided in the electronically filed petition is true and correct, and that I have been authorized to file this petition on behalf of the debtor. The debtor requests relief in accordance with the chapter specified in this petition.

☐ If petitioner files an application to pay filing fees in installments: I certify that I completed an application to pay the filing fee in installments. I am aware that if the fee is not paid within 120 days of the filing date of filing the petition, the bankruptcy case may be dismissed and, if dismissed, I may not receive a discharge of my debts.
Dated:

Signed: _____ _____
    (Applicant) (Joint Applicant)

PART II—DECLARATION OF ATTORNEY

I declare under penalty of perjury that the debtor(s) signed the petition, schedules, statements, etc., including the Statement of Social Security Number(s), (Official Form B21), before I electronically transmitted the petition, schedules, and statements to the United States Bankruptcy Court, and have followed all other requirements in Administrative Orders and Administrative Procedures, including submission of the electronic entry of the debtor(s) Social Security number into the Court's electronic records. If an individual, I further declare that I have informed the petitioner (if an individual) that [he or she] may qualify to proceed under chapter 7, 11, 12 or 13 of Title 11, United States Code, and have explained the relief available under each chapter. This declaration is based on the information of which I have knowledge.

Dated:

_____

Attorney for Debtor(s)

Address of Attorney

_____

_____

SUMMARY OF UPDATES TO THE ADMINISTRATIVE PROCEDURES
EFFECTIVE DECEMBER, 2003

Section	Page	Description of Change
II.A.10.	4	**Added clarifying text:** The United States Trustee requires that immediately upon filing a petition, the attorney for the debtor or the pro se debtor must provide the United States Trustee with a paper copy of the electronically filed petition, lists, schedules, statement of financial affairs, 2016(b) Statement and any amended schedules, together with an attached copy of the "Notice of Electronic Filing." The United States Trustee requires within two days of the notification of the trustee assignment the attorney for the debtor or the pro se debtor to submit to the

Section	Page	Description of Change
		case trustee a paper copy of the electronically filed petition, lists, schedules, statement of affairs, 2016(b) Statement, and any amended schedules, together with an attached copy of the "Notice of Electronic Filing."
		Added clarifying text: Upon conversion of a case, the attorney for the debtor or the pro se debtor must provide paper copies of the electronically filed documents listed above, together with any documents filed pursuant to the Western District of New York Local Rules, to the United States Trustee **within two days of the conversion and to the newly appointed case trustee within two days of notification of the trustee assignment.**
II.C.	5	**Added text:** The attorney for the debtor must bring to the Section 341(a) meeting of creditors Official Form 21, Statement of Social Security Number(s) bearing the original signatures.
III.A.	6	**Added text:** The Statement of Social Security Number, Official Form 21, must be verified and signed prior to the electronic filing of the petition. Official Form 21 will not be electronically filed with the Court.
III.E.[new]	7	**Added text:** Official Form 21, Statement of Social Security Number(s) must be signed by the debtor(s) before the petition is electronically filed with the Court and retained by the debtor's attorney in accordance with the requirements of Paragraphs "A" and "B" of this Section.
XII.A.6.	11	**Added text:** Documents such as tax returns, bank account statements, driver licenses, copies of cancelled checks, etc. should not be filed with the Court to avoid public disclosure.
XII.C. [new]	11	**Added text:** Pursuant to the Bankruptcy Rules, the Court is not responsible for redacting the Social Security number or

Section	Page	Description of Change
		other personal data from documents filed with the Court, whether in paper or electronic form. Filers are cautioned to carefully review documents being filed with the Court and redact personal data protected under the new Bankruptcy Rules. The Court staff will safeguard the original Statement of Social Security Number(s), Official Form B21, which will not be made a part of the bankruptcy case file. Additionally, the CM/ECF software will be modified to comply with the new noticing considerations and protection of the debtor(s) Social Security number in full compliance with the privacy related Rules.
Form A	13	**New item 7:** For individual debtor cases filed electronically on or after December 1, 2003, I understand that prior to the electronic filing of a petition, I must obtain the original signature(s) of the debtor(s) I represent on a paper copy of the Statement of Social Security Number(s), (Official Form B21), and that I must retain the original of that signed document for the length of time set forth in the "Administrative Procedures." I also understand I must compare the social security number(s) provided by the debtor(s) on Official Form B21 to the numbers entered into the Court's CM/ECF System to ensure they are the same.
Form B	15	**New item 7:** For individual debtor cases filed electronically on or after December 1, 2003, I understand that prior to the electronic filing of a petition, I must obtain the original signature(s) of the debtor(s) I represent on a paper copy of the Statement of Social Security Number(s), (Official Form B21), and that I must retain the original of that signed document for the length of time set forth in the "Administrative Procedures." I also understand I must compare the social security number(s) provided by the

Section	Page	Description of Change
		debtor(s) on Official Form B21 to the numbers entered into the Court's CM/ECF System to ensure they are the same.
Form G	21	**Added text to Part I:** I (we) further declare under penalty of perjury that I (we) signed the original Statement of Social Security Number(s), (Official Form B21), prior to the electronic filing of the petition and have verified the 9–digit social security number displayed on the Notice of Meeting of Creditors to be accurate.
		Added text to Part II: I *declare under penalty of perjury*

Section	Page	Description of Change
		that the debtor(s) signed the petition, schedules, statements, etc., **including the Statement of Social Security Number(s), Official Form B21,** before I electronically transmitted the petition, schedules, and statements to the United States Bankruptcy Court, and have followed all other requirements in Administrative Orders and Administrative Procedures, **including submission of the electronic entry of the debtor(s) Social Security number into the Court's electronic records.**

ADMINISTRATIVE ORDERS

ADMINISTRATIVE ORDER NO. 1. PROCEDURAL RULES FOR ELECTRONIC CASE FILING (ECF)

Federal Rule of Civil Procedure, ("FRCP"), 83 and Federal Rules of Bankruptcy Procedure, ("FRBP"), 5005(a)(2), 9011, and 9029 authorize this Court to establish practices and procedures for the filing, signing, and verification of pleadings and papers by electronic means; and

The *"Administrative Procedures for Filing, Signing, and Verifying Pleadings and Papers by Electronic Means," ("Administrative Procedures")*, have been reviewed by this Court; and

The *Administrative Procedures* are consistent with and further the responsibility of the Clerk of Court for the control of the Court's docket under FRBP 5003, including safeguarding the integrity of the Court's docket; and

The *Administrative Procedures* do not impose fees inconsistent with the present fee structure adopted by the Judicial Council of the United States pursuant to 28 U.S.C. § 1930; and

The *Administrative Procedures* provide adequate procedures for filing pleadings and papers and provide access to review and retrieve records and dockets of this Court by parties who are not able to access the Electronic Case Filing System over the Internet, thereby complying with the requirements contained in 11 U.S.C. § 107(a); and

The *Administrative Procedures* do not impair the ability of the Clerk of the Court to perform statistical reporting responsibilities for both the Court and the Administrative Office of the United States Courts; and

The *Administrative Procedures* are consistent with notice requirements of the FRBP and the Local Bankruptcy Rules for Western District of New York, (" LBR").

IT IS ORDERED that:

1. Introduction and Definitions.

a. The Clerk of the Bankruptcy Court for the Western District of New York is authorized to implement, publish, and update the *Administrative Procedures* for the district, including but not limited to the procedures for registration of attorneys and other participants, and for the distribution of logins and passwords to permit electronic filing and notice of pleadings and other papers.

b. In the event of a conflict between the *Western District of New York Local Bankruptcy Rules* and the *Administrative Procedures* regarding the electronic filing of petitions, pleadings and other papers, the *Administrative Procedures* shall govern.

c. "Electronic Case Files," as referred to in the *Administrative Procedures,* are petitions, pleading, and other papers that are stored in a fixed electronic format instead of on paper. This Court accepts documents only in the *Portable Document Format* ("PDF") and creditor matrices in ASCII DOS Text format (".TXT").

d. "Conventional Case Files", as referred to in the *Administrative Procedures*, are petitions, pleading, and other paper that are filed with the Court in "paper format". All filing requirements as provided in the FRBP and the LBR shall apply unless otherwise provided in the *Administrative Procedures*.

e. "Filer", as referred to in the *Administrative Procedures*, is defined as the attorney of record or the actual party in interest, if not represented by counsel, who transmits any pleading or document to the Court.

2. Electronic Filing of Documents.

a. The electronic filing of a pleading or other paper in accordance with the Electronic Filing Procedures shall constitute entry of that pleading or other paper on the docket kept by the Clerk of Court pursuant to FRBP 5003.

b. The Office of the Clerk will enter all orders, decrees, judgments, and proceedings of the court in accordance with the Electronic Filing Procedures, which shall constitute entry of the order, decree, judgment, or proceeding on the docket kept by the Clerk pursuant to FRBP 5003 and 9021.

c. For electronic filings that require a fee to be paid, the filer will complete the payment process over the Internet using a valid credit card account with a sufficient available credit limit.

3. Logins and Passwords.

a. Each attorney admitted to practice in the Western District of New York and currently in good standing, and other authorized filers shall be entitled to a single Electronic Case Filing System login and password to permit him/her to electronically file and electronically receive pleadings and other documents.

b. Login and password registration forms are available in the Office of the Clerk and on the Court's Internet site; www.nywb.uscourts.gov.

c. A trustee or standing trustee who also serves as private counsel should submit two separate Attorney Registration Forms and will receive two separate logins and passwords; one for the role of trustee and one for their role of private counsel.

d. No attorney, trustee or other authorized user will knowingly permit or cause to permit their password to be utilized by anyone other than an authorized employee of their law firm or organization.

e. No person shall knowingly utilize or cause another person to utilize the password of a registered attorney or other authorized user unless such person is an authorized employee of said law firm or organization.

f. Misuse of the Electronic Case Filing System login and password may result in revocation of the login and password of the attorney or party and/or the imposition of sanctions.

4. **Signatures.**

a. The electronic filing of a petition, pleading, motion, or other paper by an attorney or participant who is a registered user in the Electronic Case Filing System shall constitute the signature of that filer for purposes of FRBP 9011.

b. The signature of the debtor(s) acknowledging that the debtor(s) authorized the electronic filing of the bankruptcy case and the petition, schedules and statements filed with the Court shall be accomplished by the execution of a Declaration Re: Electronic Filing at the § 341 Meeting of Creditors.

c. Any petition, pleading, affidavit or other document filed electronically shall contain an electronic signature of the filer, e.g., *"/s/ name,"* or a facsimile of the filer's signature. The electronic filing of any document requiring an original signature constitutes a representation by Filing User that the original signature(s) of the parties to such document(s) were already obtained by the Filing User prior to the electronic filing. Violations of this requirement will result in disciplinary action against the Filing User.

5. **Notice of Electronic Filing and Service.**

a. Whenever a pleading or other paper is filed electronically, a *"Notice of Electronic Filing"* will be automatically generated by the Electronic Case Filing System at the time of the filing and sent electronically to the party filing the pleading or other paper, as well as to all parties in the case who are registered participants in the Electronic Case Filing System or have otherwise consented to electronic service.

b. If the recipient of notice or service is a registered participant in the Electronic Case Filing System or has otherwise consented to electronic service, service of the *Notice of Electronic Filing* shall be the equivalent of service of the pleading or other paper by first class mail, postage prepaid.

c. The filing party shall serve the pleading or other paper upon all other persons entitled to notice or service in accordance with the applicable rules, or, if service by first class mail is permitted under the

rules, the filing party may make service in accordance with subparagraph "f" below.

d. Participation in the Electronic Case Filing System by receipt of a login and password from the Court shall constitute a request for service and notice electronically pursuant to FRBP 9036. Participants in the Electronic Case Filing System, by receiving a login and password from the Court, agree that notice and service by electronic means constitutes proper service.

e. A summons and the appropriate number of copies must be filed with the Court conventionally. Service of a summons and a complaint filed in an adversary proceeding shall continue to be made pursuant to FRBP 7004. Service of a summons and an involuntary bankruptcy petition shall continue to be made pursuant to FRBP 1010 and 7004.

f. Pleadings or other documents which are not filed electronically shall be served in accordance with the FRBP and the LBR except as otherwise provided by Order of the Court.

g. Service by electronic means is not effective if the party making service learns that the attempted service did not reach the person to be served.

6. The provisions of this Order shall apply to all electronically filed cases and proceedings and cases and proceedings converted to the Electronic Case Filing System in the U.S. Bankruptcy Court for the Western District of New York. Amendments to this Order may be entered from time to time as deemed necessary by the Court.

7. The effective date of this Administrative Order is June 16, 2003.

IT IS SO ORDERED.

Effective June 16, 2003.

ADMINISTRATIVE ORDER NO. 3. IMPLEMENTATION OF BANKRUPTCY RULE AMENDMENTS CONCERNING PRIVACY AND PUBLIC ACCESS TO ELECTRONIC CASE FILES

The Judicial Conference of the United States has proposed changes to the Federal Rules of Bankruptcy Procedure ["FRBP"]to protect the privacy of debtors, including limitations on inclusion of Social Security Numbers on court documents. These changes will take effect on December 1, 2003, unless Congress acts to overturn the Bankruptcy Rule Amendments before that date.

The proposed amendment of FRBP Rule 1005 requires, among other things, that the title of the bankruptcy case include only the last four digits of the debtor's Social Security Number. The proposed change to FRBP Rule 1007(f) requires the debtor to *submit* to the Clerk of Court a verified statement listing the debtor's full Social Security Number or that the debtor does not have a Social Security Number. However, the debtor(s)' Social Security Number will not become part of the Court's file. "Statement of Social Security Number(s)" (Official Form 21) has been proposed as the document on which the debtor will provide his or her full Social Security Number to the Clerk of Court, although that form will not be filed with the Court.

IT IS HEREBY ORDERED that:

1.   For bankruptcy petitions filed electronically, the completed and verified "Statement of Social Security Number(s)" (Official Form 21) as required by FRBP 1007(f), must be signed by the debtor(s) prior to the electronic filing of the petition and must be retained in paper form by the debtor(s)' attorney in accordance with this Court's Administrative Orders and Administrative Procedures for Filing, Signing and Verifying Pleadings and Papers by Electronic Means. The original Statement of Social Security Number will not be filed electronically and is to be brought to the "Meeting of Creditors."

2.   For bankruptcy petitions filed conventionally in paper format, the signed original "Statement of Debtor's Social Security Number(s) "(Official Form 21) as required by FRBP 1007(f), must be *submitted* with the filing of the petition. The term *"submitted"* as used in FRBP 1007(f) means that Official Form 21 will require special handling by the Clerk's Office to ensure that the document is not available to the public and will neither be filed in the bankruptcy case nor retained in electronic format attached to the case docket.

3.   The Clerk of Court will make necessary modifications to the Administrative Procedures for Electronic Case Filing and related forms to incorporate local procedures to ensure full compliance with privacy related rules.

4.   The Clerk of Court will make necessary modifications to the electronic case filing system (CM/ECF) to ensure that notices and information provided through electronic means are in full compliance with the privacy related rules.

The effective date of this Administrative Order is December 1, 2003 concurrent with the enactment of various proposed amendments to the Federal Rules of Bankruptcy Procedure.

IT IS SO ORDERED.

Dated: October 20, 2003.

ADMINISTRATIVE ORDER NO. 4. PROCEDURAL RULES CONCERNING ELECTRONIC FILING OF CLAIMS AND RELATED DOCUMENTS OF CREDITOR/LIMITED FILER ACTIVITIES

Supplement to CM/ECF Administrative Orders 1, 2, and 3

Federal Rule of Civil Procedure ("FRCP") 83 and Federal Rules of Bankruptcy Procedure ("FRBP")

5005(a)(2) and 9029 authorize this Court to establish practices and procedures for the filing, signing, and verification of documents by electronic means.

By Administrative Order No. 1, dated May 28, 2003, this Court established practices and procedures, as set forth in the "Administrative Procedures for Filing, Signing, and Verifying Pleadings and Papers by Electronic Means," as revised December 1, 2003, ("Revised Electronic Filing Procedures") pertaining to the Court's Case Management/Electronic Case Files ("CM/ECF") System.

The Practice under the Revised Electronic Filing Procedures limited to attorneys admitted to practice before this Court the ability to obtain a CM/ECF login and password. The use by such attorneys of that login and password constitutes the signature of the attorney for all purposes, including, but not limited to, Rule 11 of the FRBP and FRCP.

To enable creditors, particularly large-volume institutional creditors, to utilize CM/ECF to electronically file documents related to claims, the Court will now permit creditors and limited filer users to access CM/ECF for the limited purpose of electronically filing certain documents relating to claims, notices of appearance and reaffirmation agreements ("Limited Access Filers"). To obtain a limited-access login and password to the CM/ECF System, an individual must apply to the Court in writing and complete such training as the Court may require.

The Administrative Procedures for Filing, Signing and Verifying Pleadings and Papers by Electronic Means, together with the Administrative Orders entered in regard to Electronic Case Filing, apply in all respects to the Limited Access Filers. The user login and password required to file documents using the CM/ECF System serve as the Filing User's signature on all documents electronically filed with the Court. The user login and password also serve as a signature, with the same force and effect as a written signature, for purposes of the Federal Rules of Bankruptcy Procedure, including, but not limited to, Rules 9001 and 3001, the Local Rules of this Court, and any other purpose for which a signature is required in connection with proceedings before or filings with the Court. Limited Access Filers bear the responsibility of keeping the limited-access password secure and have the duty to immediately notify the Court in the event the Limited Access Filer obtains greater access to CM/ECF than the limited-access password is intended to permit or if the Limited Access Filer believes that the security of the password has been compromised.

The Clerk of the Court may cancel the password of any individual who does not comply in all respects with this Standing Order and/or the provisions contained in the Revised Electronic Filing Procedures or any other Order of this Court regarding electronic filing of documents using the CM/ECF System.

Dated: February 2, 2004.

ADMINISTRATIVE ORDER NO. 5. MANDATORY ELECTRONIC FILING OF DOCUMENTS BY INTERNET TRANSMISSION

In and by "Administrative Order No. 1," dated May 28, 2003 and effective June 16, 2003, this Court adopted and approved "Administrative Procedures for Filing, Signing and Verifying Pleadings and Papers by Electronic Means," revised December 1, 2003 ("Administrative Procedures"). The Court having determined that it is necessary to substantially reduce the volume of paper filings made with the Court, given the increasing case load and the demonstrated reliability of electronic filing using the Case Management/Electronic Case Files (CM/ECF) System, it is hereby

ORDERED, that effective October 1, 2004, the Clerk of Court shall no longer be required to accept for filing any paper submission, except by contrary direction of a Judge of this Court or for papers submitted in connection with pro bono services rendered through VLP, NLPS, VLPS or the like.

Dated: May 14, 2004.

ADMINISTRATIVE ORDER NO. 6. ELECTRONIC TRANSMISSION OF NOTICES BY THE CLERK AND ELIMINATION OF REDUNDANT PAPER NOTICES FOR REGISTERED CM/ECF E–FILERS

In and by "Administrative Order No. 1," dated May 28, 2003 and effective June 16, 2003, this Court adopted and approved "Administrative Procedures for Filing, Signing, and Verifying Pleadings and Papers by Electronic Means," revised December 1, 2003 ("Administrative Procedures"). Notices required to be provided by the Clerk of the Court are not sent to "Registered CM/ECF E–Filers" both electronically through the Case Management/Electronic Case Files (CM/ECF) System and in a redundant paper mode through Bankruptcy Noticing Center ("BNC"). The Court has observed that (1) many attorneys e-filing papers through CM/ECF have indicated that receipt of the redundant paper notices is burdensome, wasteful, and unnecessary, (2) the cost for producing and mailing redundant paper notices through the BNC is an unnecessary budgetary expenditure that should be avoided, and (3) the formal process of amending Bankruptcy Rule 9036 to eliminate the electronic return receipt requirement is underway. In order to accommodate the requests of counsel to eliminate redundant paper notice and in an effort to reduce mailing expenses to the Judiciary budget, it is hereby

ORDERED, that effective December 1, 2004, the Clerk of the Court will discontinue the practice of sending redundant paper notices to registered CM/ECF e-filers through the BNC, except for the "Notice of the Meeting of Creditors" which will continue to be sent in paper through the BNC, and the electronic transmission of notices by the Clerk will be deemed complete upon transmission, and it is further

ORDERED that the Clerk of Court will establish an opt-out procedure to ensure that redundant paper notices are sent through the BNC to any registered CM/ECF e-filer requesting such, in writing.

Dated: October 18, 2004.

STANDING ORDERS

STANDING ORDER. "REFUND" OF FILING FEES

All requests for the refund of the payment of fees collected without authority or due to administrative error on the part of the Clerk's Office must be submitted in the form of an application or motion and proposed order and filed in the appropriate case. If approved, refunds will be processed through the electronic credit card system. The motion must specify which of the two circumstances identified in the paragraph below of this Standing Order warrant consideration of the relief requested.

The Clerk of Court is hereby delegated the authority to (1) refund any duplicate filing fee collected as a result of a "pay.gov" error and (2) delete any fee due (prior to payment) of a duplicate fee or a fee not due. The Clerk's office will not notify parties of duplicate payments already received or if payment was made without a fee being due.

IT IS ORDERED that refunds will not be permitted on fees due upon filing, even if the party files the document in error and even if the court dismisses the case or pleading.

IT IS ORDERED.

DATED: April 14, 2006.

STANDING ORDER. NOTICE TO CREDITORS IN CHAPTER 13 CASES

The Court orders the following interim amendment to Local Rule 2002–1(B) with respect to certain Chapter 13 notices:

1. Effective for Chapter 13 cases filed on or after November 17, 2005, the Clerk will provide creditors with notice of the initial § 341 meeting and hearing on confirmation of the Chapter 13 Plan ("Plan"), together with a copy of the plan, if filed with the Petition.

2. Effective November 17, 2005, any Chapter 13 Plan and any Modified or Amended Chapter 13 Plan filed after the date that the petition was filed must be timely served on the Chapter 13 Trustee and all creditors in the case **by the debtor,** together with the notice of hearing on confirmation. The Chapter 13 Trustee will provide the debtor with the hearing date/time/location and a notice ready form. The debtor must file a certificate of service within 48 hours of completion of service required by this Rule.

3. Effective November 17, 2005, pursuant to Bankruptcy Rule 2002, the Clerk, unless otherwise directed by the Court, will give the debtor, the trustee, all creditors and indenture trustees notice by mail or electronic means in Chapter 13 cases, notwithstanding the provisions contained in this Standing Order.

IT IS FURTHER ORDERED, that pursuant to 11 U.S.C. § 1342(b), **for Chapter 13 cases filed in Erie, Niagara, Genesee, Orleans, Wyoming, Allegany, Chautauqua, or Cattaraugus only,** the confirmation hearing on the debtor's Plan will be scheduled for same date as the first meeting of creditors, unless an objection is filed by a party-in-interest.

IT IS ORDERED.

DATED: October 21, 2005.

STANDING ORDER (REVISED). DEBTORS ASSERTING AN EXCEPTION TO THE LIMITATION OF THE AUTOMATIC STAY UNDER 11 U.S.C. § 362(*l*) AND PROCEDURE FOR RECEIVING RENT DEPOSITS

WHEREAS, the Bankruptcy Abuse Prevention and Consumer Protection Act of 2005 amended 11 U.S.C. § 101 et seq. ("Code") including the automatic stay provision of 11 U.S.C. § 362 in regards to actions to recover possession of residential property occupied by a Debtor by the enactment of 11 U.S.C. § 362(*l*), and

WHEREAS, the Court requires uniformity in the procedure for the deposit of rent by Debtors and transmittal of rent to Lessors under § 362(*l*)(1)(B) and § 362(*l*)(5)(D) of the Code, it is hereby

ORDERED, that any deposit of rent made by or on behalf of a Debtor, pursuant to § 362(*l*)(1)(B) of the Code, must be in the form of a **certified check or money order payable to the order of the Lessor,** and delivered to the Clerk of Court upon filing of the Petition and the Certification made under § 362(*l*)(1)(A) of the Code, and it is further

ORDERED, that the debtor must file a copy of the Judgment of Eviction together with the Petition, and it is further

ORDERED, that upon the Clerk's receipt of a **certified check or money order payable to the order of the Lessor**, with a copy of the Judgment of Eviction, tendered by a Debtor pursuant to § 362(*l*)(1) of the Code, the Clerk is directed to promptly transmit the certified check or money order to the Lessor, by certified mail/return receipt requested, to the address listed on the petition.

Dated: October 17, 2005.

STANDING ORDER. CHAPTER 13 CASES GOVERNED BY THE BANKRUPTCY ABUSE PREVENTION AND CONSUMER PROTECTION ACT OF 2005

Upon the deliberation of 11 U.S.C. § 1326 as amended by the Bankruptcy Abuse Prevention and Consumer Protection Act of 2005 (BAPCPA), pursuant to § 1326(a)(1), the Court orders that:

1) Adequate Protection Payments required to be made by the debtor pursuant to § 1326(a)(1)(C) shall be paid from plan payments paid to the Trustee upon commencement of the case;

2) That within 15 days of the filing of the order for relief the debtor shall file a statement with this Court detailing how each pre-confirmation adequate protection payment was calculated;

3) Such notice shall also be sent by written notice to any creditor who prior to the filing of said statement has filed with the Court either a proof of claim or a notice of appearance;

4) For the purposes of this Order, unless the parties agree otherwise, adequate protection for motor vehicles shall equal (a) at a minimum the retail value of said motor vehicle pursuant to 11 USC § 506 without interest, divided by 60; or (b) in the alternative, the statement may designate the proposed monthly payment to said creditor in the plan as adequate protection if it is at least equal to the designated monthly payment in subsection (a).

5) Nothing in this Order shall prevent an affected creditor from bringing a motion pursuant to § 1326(a)(3) for an order changing said adequate protection payments;

6) Nothing in this Order shall prevent the parties from stipulating to different treatment of the adequate protection payments to be made pursuant to § 1326. For the purposes of these stipulations, a stipulation entered into prior to the filing of the petition shall be effective if filed with the Court within 15 days of the order for relief;

7) Upon the filing of the statement of adequate protection described above, the Trustee shall be authorized to commence payment of adequate protection payments pursuant to said statement to the affected creditors; and

8) From the disbursements so made, the Chapter 13 Trustee shall be allowed his compensation and expenses at the rate set by the United States Trustee.

DATED: October 12, 2005.
    Rochester, NY

STANDING ORDER. NOTICE OF PREFERRED ADDRESSES UNDER 11 U.S.C. § 342(f) AND NATIONAL CREDITOR REGISTRATION SERVICE

Upon the deliberation of 11 U.S.C. § 342(f) as provided by the Bankruptcy Abuse Prevention and Consumer Protection Act of 2005 (BAPCPA), the Court orders the following with respect to notice of preferred addresses and the establishment of the National Creditor Registration Service, effective October 17, 2005:

A. Notwithstanding Rule 2002(g)(1)–(3), an entity and a notice provider may agree that when the notice provider is directed by the court to give a notice, to that entity, the notice provider will give the notice to the entity in the manner agreed to and at the address or addresses the entity supplies to the notice provider. That address is conclusively presumed to be a proper address for the notice. The notice provider's failure to use the supplied address does not invalidate any notice that is otherwise effective under applicable law.

B. The filing of a notice of preferred address pursuant to 11 U.S.C. § 342(f) by a creditor directly with the entity that provides noticing services for the Bankruptcy Courts will constitute the filing of such a notice with the Court.

C. Registration with the National Creditor Registration Service must be accomplished through the entity that provides noticing services for the Bankruptcy Courts. Forms and registration information are available at *www.ncruscourts.gov.*

IT IS SO ORDERED.

DATED: October 12, 2005.

STANDING ORDER. ADOPTION OF INTERIM BANKRUPTCY RULES TO IMPLEMENT CHANGES MADE BY THE 2005 BANKRUPTCY REFORM LEGISLATION[1]

WHEREAS, on April 20, 2005 the Bankruptcy Abuse Prevention and Consumer Protection Act of 2005 (the Act) was enacted into law; and

WHEREAS, most provisions of the Act are effective on October 17, 2005; and

WHEREAS, the Advisory Committee on Bankruptcy Rules has prepared Interim Rules designed to implement the substantive and procedural changes mandated by the Act; and

WHEREAS, the Committee on Rules of Practice and Procedure of the Judicial Conference of the United States has also approved these Interim Rules and recommends the adoption of the Interim Rules to provide uniform procedures for implementing the Act; and

WHEREAS, the general effective date of the Act has not provided sufficient time to promulgate rules after appropriate public notice and an opportunity for comment;

NOW THEREFORE, pursuant to 11 U.S.C. section 2071, Rule 83 of the Federal Rules of Civil Procedure, and Rule 9029 of the Federal Rules of Bankruptcy Procedure, the attached Interim Rules are adopted in their entirety without change by a majority of the judges of this Court to be effective October 17, 2005 to conform with the Act. For cases and proceedings not governed by the Act, the Federal Rules of Bankruptcy Procedure and the Local Rules of this Court, other than the Interim Rules shall apply. The Interim Rules shall remain in effect until further Order of this Court.

IT IS SO ORDERED

Dated: September 9, 2005.

1 The Interim Bankruptcy Rules follow the Administrative Orders of the United States Bankruptcy Court for the Northern District of New York, ante.

STANDING ORDER. COMMON DEFAULT STATEMENT

The multiple default statements currently in use in Rochester and Watkins Glen have been blended into a "common default statement". The "common default statement" amends and supersedes the default statements required by the Standing Orders dated August 5, 1992, March 9, 1993 (Revised April 13, 1993), May 20, 1993, July 25, 1994, July 26, 1995, June 1, 1998 and June 29, 1999.

(A) COMMON DEFAULT STATEMENT

(1) Default motion papers filed on or after September 1, 2000 shall include the "common default statement" in **bold** print.

PURSUANT TO FRBP 9014 AND THE STANDING ORDERS IMPLEMENTING DEFAULT PROCEDURES IN ROCHESTER AND WATKINS GLEN: IF YOU INTEND TO OPPOSE THE MOTION: (1) AT A MINIMUM YOU MUST SERVE IF THEY ARE NOT THE MOVING PARTY: (A) THE MOVANT'S COUNSEL; (B) THE DEBTOR AND DEBTOR'S COUNSEL; (C) IN A CHAPTER 11 CASE, THE CREDITORS' COMMITTEE AND ITS ATTORNEY, OR IT THERE IS NO COMMITTEE, THE 20 LARGEST CREDITORS; AND (D) ANY TRUSTEE; AND (2) FILE WITH THE CLERK OF THE BANKRUPTCY COURT WRITTEN OPPOSITION TO THE MOTION NOT LATER THAN THREE (3) BUSINESS DAYS PRIOR TO THE RETURN DATE OF THE MOTION

PURSUANT TO FRBP 9006(a). IN THE EVENT NO WRITTEN OPPOSITION IS SERVED AND FILED, NO HEARING ON THE MOTION WILL BE HELD ON THE RETURN DATE AND THE COURT WILL CONSIDER THE MOTION AS UNOPPOSED.

(2) With the exception of the default language statement, the requirements and procedures specific to each default motion type recited in the above Standing Orders are in effect and remain unchanged.

EXHIBIT A

Rochester's standard Objection to Claim Notice of Hearing and Order form has been revised to include the modified default statement.

EXHIBIT B. A COMPREHENSIVE LIST OF ALL DEFAULT PROCEDURES IN ROCHESTER AND WATKINS GLEN

This procedural guide has been updated to reflect the revision to the default statement.

Dated August 8, 2000.

STANDING ORDER. ADOPTION OF INTERIM BANKRUPTCY RULE 1007 AND REVISIONS TO OFFICIAL FORMS IMPLEMENTING THE BANKRUPTCY ABUSE PREVENTION AND CONSUMER PROTECTION ACT OF 2005

Whereas, on April 20, 2005, the Bankruptcy Abuse Prevention and Consumer Protection Act of 2005 (the Act) was enacted into law; and

Whereas, the Judicial Conference approved, on September 19, 2006, an amendment to Interim Bankruptcy Rule 1007 *; and

Whereas, the Judicial Conference also approved proposed revisions to Official Forms ** 1, 5, 6, 9, 22A, 22C, and new Exhibit D to Official Form 1. The effective date of the revised Official Forms is October 1, 2006.

NOW THEREFORE, pursuant to 11 U.S.C. Section 2071, Rule 83 of the Federal Rules of Civil Procedure and Rule 9029 of the Federal Rules of Bankruptcy Procedure, the amendment to Interim Rule 1007 is adopted in its entirety without change by a majority of the Judges of this Court to be effective October 17, 2006 to conform with the Act and the effective date of the revised Official Forms and amendments implementing new statistical reporting requirements mandated by the Bankruptcy Abuse Prevention and Consumer Protection Act of 2005 is October 1, 2006. For cases and proceedings not governed by the Act, the Federal Rules of Bankruptcy Procedure and the Local Rules of this Court other than the Interim Rules, shall apply. The Interim

Rules and revisions to the Official Forms shall remain in effect until further Order of this Court.

IT IS SO ORDERED.

Dated: September 26, 2006.

* The text of the Interim Bankruptcy Rules appears in this publication following the Administrative Orders of the United States Bankruptcy Court for the Northern District of New York, ante.

** The Official Forms are not included in this publication.

STANDING ORDER. IMPLEMENTATION OF INCREASE TO TRANSCRIPT FEE RATES AND NEW TRANSCRIPT DELIVERY CATEGORY

WHEREAS, the Judicial Conference, at its September 2007 session, approved an increase of ten percent to the maximum original and copy transcript fee rates to be effective in fiscal year 2008, and also approved a new rate for the delivery of transcripts within 14 days and agreed that the rate be set at the mid-point between the rates authorized for expedited (7–day) and ordinary (30–day) delivery, it is hereby

ORDERED, that this Court adopts a revised Schedule of Maximum Rates for all categories of transcript, as attached hereto. Transcripts ordered prior to the effective date of this Order shall be billed at the rates in effect at the time the transcript order was placed with the official court reporter.

SO ORDERED.

Dated: November 1, 2007.

Attachment

Maximum Transcript Fee Rates—All Parties Per Page

	Original	First Copy to Each Party	Each Add'l Copy to the Same Party
Ordinary Transcript (30 day) A transcript to be delivered within thirty (30) calendar days after receipt of an order.	$3.65	$.90	$.60
14–Day Transcript A transcript to be delivered within fourteen (14) calendar days after receipt of an order.	$4.25	$.90	$.60
Expedited Transcript (7 day) A transcript to be delivered within seven (7) calendar days after receipt of an order.	$4.85	$.90	$.60
Daily Transcript A transcript to be delivered following adjournment and prior to the normal opening hour of the court on the following morning whether or not it actually is a court day.	$6.05	$1.20	$.90
Hourly Transcript A transcript of proceedings ordered under unusual circumstances to be delivered within two (2) hours.	$7.25	$1.20	$.90

	Original	First Copy to Each Party	Each Add'l Copy to the Same Party
Realtime Transcript			
A draft unedited transcript produced by a certified realtime reporter as a byproduct of realtime to be delivered electronically during proceedings or immediately following adjournment.	$3.05	$1.20	

RULES OF PROCEDURE OF THE JUDICIAL PANEL ON MULTIDISTRICT LITIGATION

Renumbered and Amended Effective November 2, 1998

Including Amendments Effective July 30, 2007

I. GENERAL RULES/RULES FOR MULTIDISTRICT LITIGATION UNDER 28 U.S.C. § 1407

Rule
1.1. Definitions.
1.2. Practice.
1.3. Failure to Comply with Rules.
1.4. Admission to Practice Before the Panel and Representation in Transferred Actions.
1.5. Effect of the Pendency of an Action Before the Panel.
1.6. Transfer of Files.
5.1. Keeping Records and Files.
5.11. Place of Filing of Papers.
5.12. Manner of Filing of Papers.
5.13. Filing of Papers: Computer Generated Disk Required.
5.2. Service of Papers Filed.
5.3. Corporate Disclosure Statement.
6.2. Applications for Extensions of Time.
7.1. Form of Papers Filed.

Rule
7.2. Motion Practice.
7.3. Show Cause Orders.
7.4. Conditional Transfer Orders for "Tag–Along Actions".
7.5. Miscellaneous Provisions Concerning "Tag–Along Actions".
7.6. Termination and Remand.
16.1. Hearing Sessions and Oral Argument.
16.2. Notice of Presentation or Waiver of Oral Argument, and Matters Submitted on the Briefs [Repealed].

II. RULES FOR MULTICIRCUIT PETITIONS FOR REVIEW UNDER 28 U.S.C. § 2112(a)(3)

17.1. Random Selection.
25.1. Filing of Notices.
25.2. Accompaniments to Notices.
25.3. Service of Notices.
25.4. Form of Notices.
25.5. Service of Panel Consolidation Order.

I. GENERAL RULES/RULES FOR MULTIDISTRICT LITIGATION UNDER 28 U.S.C. § 1407

RULE 1.1. DEFINITIONS

As used in these Rules "Panel" means the members of the Judicial Panel on Multidistrict Litigation appointed by the Chief Justice of the United States pursuant to Section 1407, Title 28, United States Code.

"Clerk of the Panel" means the official appointed by the Panel to act as Clerk of the Panel and shall include those deputized by the Clerk of the Panel to perform or assist in the performance of the duties of the Clerk of the Panel.

"Chairman" means the Chairman of the Judicial Panel on Multidistrict Litigation appointed by the Chief Justice of the United States pursuant to Section 1407, or the member of the Panel designated by the Panel to act as Chairman in the absence or inability of the appointed Chairman.

A "tag-along action" refers to a civil action pending in a district court and involving common questions of fact with actions previously transferred under Section 1407.

(Former Rule 1 adopted May 3, 1993, eff. July 1, 1993; renumbered Rule 1.1 Sept. 1, 1998, eff. Nov. 2, 1998.)

RULE 1.2. PRACTICE

Where not fixed by statute or rule, the practice shall be that heretofore customarily followed by the Panel.

(Former Rule 5 adopted May 3, 1993, eff. July 1, 1993; renumbered Rule 1.2 Sept. 1, 1998, eff. Nov. 2, 1998.)

RULE 1.3. FAILURE TO COMPLY WITH RULES

The Clerk of the Panel may, when a paper submitted for filing is not in compliance with the provisions of these Rules, advise counsel of the deficiencies and a date for full compliance. If full compliance is not accomplished within the established time, the non-

829

complying paper shall nonetheless be filed by the Clerk of the Panel but it may be stricken by order of the Chairman of the Panel.

(Former Rule 4 adopted May 3, 1993, eff. July 1, 1993; renumbered Rule 1.3 and amended Sept. 1, 1998, eff. Nov. 2, 1998.)

RULE 1.4. ADMISSION TO PRACTICE BEFORE THE PANEL AND REPRESENTATION IN TRANSFERRED ACTIONS

Every member in good standing of the Bar of any district court of the United States is entitled without condition to practice before the Judicial Panel on Multidistrict Litigation. Any attorney of record in any action transferred under Section 1407 may continue to represent his or her client in any district court of the United States to which such action is transferred. Parties to any action transferred under Section 1407 are not required to obtain local counsel in the district to which such action is transferred.

(Former Rule 6 adopted May 3, 1993, eff. July 1, 1993; renumbered Rule 1.4 Sept. 1, 1998, eff. Nov. 2, 1998.)

RULE 1.5. EFFECT OF THE PENDENCY OF AN ACTION BEFORE THE PANEL

The pendency of a motion, order to show cause, conditional transfer order or conditional remand order before the Panel concerning transfer or remand of an action pursuant to 28 U.S.C. § 1407 does not affect or suspend orders and pretrial proceedings in the district court in which the action is pending and does not in any way limit the pretrial jurisdiction of that court. A transfer or remand pursuant to 28 U.S.C. § 1407 shall be effective when the transfer or remand order is filed in the office of the clerk of the district court of the transferee district.

(Former Rule 18 adopted May 3, 1993, eff. July 1, 1993; renumbered Rule 1.5 Sept. 1, 1998, eff. Nov. 2, 1998.)

RULE 1.6. TRANSFER OF FILES

(a) Upon receipt of a certified copy of a transfer order from the clerk of the transferee district court, the clerk of the transferor district court shall forward to the clerk of the transferee district court the complete original file and a certified copy of the docket sheet for each transferred action.

(b) If an appeal is pending, or a notice of appeal has been filed, or leave to appeal has been sought under 28 U.S.C. § 1292(b) or a petition for an extraordinary writ is pending, in any action included in an order of transfer under 28 U.S.C. § 1407, and the original file or parts thereof have been forwarded to the court of appeals, the clerk of the transferor district court shall notify the clerk of the court of appeals

of the order of transfer and secure the original file long enough to prepare and transmit to the clerk of the transferee district court a certified copy of all papers contained in the original file and a certified copy of the docket sheet.

(c) If the transfer order provides for the separation and simultaneous remand of any claim, cross-claim, counterclaim, or third-party claim, the clerk of the transferor district court shall retain the original file and shall prepare and transmit to the clerk of the transferee district court a certified copy of the docket sheet and copies of all papers except those relating exclusively to separated and remanded claims.

(d) Upon receipt of an order to remand from the Clerk of the Panel, the transferee district court shall prepare and send to the clerk of the transferor district court the following:

(i) a certified copy of the individual docket sheet for each action being remanded;

(ii) a certified copy of the master docket sheet, if applicable;

(iii) the entire file for each action being remanded, as originally received from the transferor district court and augmented as set out in this rule;

(iv) a certified copy of the final pretrial order, if applicable; and

(v) a "record on remand" to be composed of those parts of the files and records produced during coordinated or consolidated pretrial proceedings which have been stipulated to or designated by counsel as being necessary for any or all proceedings to be conducted following remand. It shall be the responsibility of counsel originally preparing or filing any document to be included in the "record on remand" to furnish on request sufficient copies to the clerk of the transferee district court.

(e) The Clerk of the Panel shall be notified when any files have been transmitted pursuant to this Rule.

(Former Rule 19 adopted May 3, 1993, eff. July 1, 1993; renumbered Rule 1.6 and amended Sept. 1, 1998, eff. Nov. 2, 1998.)

RULE 5.1. KEEPING RECORDS AND FILES

(a) The records and files of the Panel shall be kept by the Clerk of the Panel at the offices of the Panel. Records and files may be temporarily or permanently removed to such places at such times as the Panel or the Chairman of the Panel shall direct. The Clerk of the Panel may charge fees, as prescribed by the Judicial Conference of the United States, for duplicating records and files. Records and files may be transferred whenever appropriate to the Federal Records Center.

(b) In order to assist the Panel in carrying out its functions, the Clerk of the Panel shall obtain the complaints and docket sheets in all actions under consideration for transfer under 28 U.S.C. § 1407 from the clerk of each district court wherein such actions are pending. The Clerk of the Panel shall similarly obtain any other pleadings and orders that could affect the Panel's decision under 28 U.S.C. § 1407.

(Former Rule 2 adopted May 3, 1993, eff. July 1, 1993; renumbered Rule 5.1 and amended Sept. 1, 1998, eff. Nov. 2, 1998.)

RULE 5.11. PLACE OF FILING OF PAPERS

All papers for consideration by the Panel shall be submitted for filing to the Clerk of the Panel by mailing or delivering to:

Clerk of the Panel
Judicial Panel on Multidistrict Litigation
Thurgood Marshall Federal Judiciary Building
One Columbus Circle, N.E., Room G–255, North Lobby
Washington, D.C. 20002–8004

No papers shall be left with or mailed to a Judge of the Panel.

(Former Rule 3 adopted May 3, 1993, eff. July 1, 1993; renumbered Rule 5.11 and amended Sept. 1, 1998, eff. Nov. 2, 1998.)

RULE 5.12. MANNER OF FILING OF PAPERS

(a) An original of the following papers shall be submitted for filing to the Clerk of the Panel: a proof of service pursuant to Rule 5.2(a) and (b) of these Rules, a notice of appearance pursuant to Rule 5.2(c) and (d) of these Rules, a corporate disclosure statement pursuant to Rule 5.3 of these Rules, a status notice pursuant to Rules 7.2(f), 7.3(e) and 7.4(b) of these Rules, a notice of opposition pursuant to Rules 7.4(c) and 7.6(f)(ii) of these Rules, a notice of related action pursuant to Rules 7.2(i), 7.3(a) and 7.5(e) of these Rules, an application for extension of time pursuant to Rule 6.2 of these Rules, or a notice of presentation or waiver of oral argument pursuant to Rule 16.1(d) of these Rules. An original and ~~eleven~~ four* copies of all other papers shall be submitted for filing to the Clerk of the Panel. The Clerk of the Panel may require that additional copies also be submitted for filing.

(b) When papers are submitted for filing, the Clerk of the Panel shall endorse thereon the date for filing.

(c) Copies of motions for transfer of an action or actions pursuant to 28 U.S.C. § 1407 shall be filed in each district court in which an action is pending that will be affected by the motion. Copies of a motion for remand pursuant to 28 U.S.C. § 1407 shall be filed in the Section 1407 transferee district court in which any action affected by the motion is pending.

(d) Papers requiring only an original may be faxed to the Panel office with prior approval of the Clerk of the Panel. No papers requiring multiple copies shall be accepted via fax.

(Former Rule 7 adopted May 3, 1993, eff. July 1, 1993; renumbered Rule 5.12 and amended Sept. 1, 1998, eff. Nov. 2, 1998; amended Apr. 2, 2001, eff. Apr. 2, 2001; paragraph (a) suspended in part by Order filed April 19, 2005.)

  * Publisher's Note: April 19, 2005, the Judicial Panel on Multidistrict Litigation issued an Order reducing the number of copies from eleven to four. The Order reads as follows:

   IT IS HEREBY ORDERED that, because the Panel is utilizing papers and electronic distribution of those papers, Panel Rule 5.12(a), Manner of Filing Papers, R.P.J.P.M.L., 199 F.R.D. 425, 429 (2001), is partially suspended insofar as papers submitted for filing requiring an original and eleven copies shall be reduced to four copies along with an original.

RULE 5.13. FILING OF PAPERS: COMPUTER GENERATED DISK REQUIRED

(a) Whenever an original paper and eleven copies is required to be submitted for filing to the Clerk of the Panel pursuant to Rule 5.12(a) of these Rules, and where a party is represented by counsel, one copy of that paper must also be submitted on a computer readable disk and shall be filed at the time the party's paper is filed. The disk shall contain the entire paper exclusive of computer non-generated exhibits. The label of the disk shall include i) "MDL #___," ii) an abbreviated version of the MDL descriptive title, or other appropriate descriptive title, if not yet designated by the Panel, iii) the identity of the type of paper being filed (i.e. motion, response, reply, etc.), iv) the name of the counsel who signed the paper, and v) the first named represented party on the paper.

(b) The paper must be on a disk in Adobe Acrobat (PDF) format.

(c) One copy of the disk may be served on each party separately represented by counsel. If a party chooses to serve a copy of the disk, the proof of service, as required by Rule 5.2 of these Rules, must indicate service of the paper in both paper and electronic format.

(d) A party may be relieved from the requirements of this Rule by submitting a written application for a waiver, in a timely manner in advance of submission of the paper, certifying that compliance with the Rule would impose undue hardship, that the text of the paper is not available on disk, or that other unusual circumstances preclude compliance with this Rule. The requirements of this Rule shall not apply to parties appearing pro se. Papers embraced by this Rule and submitted by counsel after June 1, 2000 without a computer disk copy or Panel-approved waiver of the requirements of this Rule shall be governed by Rule 1.3 of these Rules.

(Added May 22, 2000, eff. June 1, 2000; and amended July 30, 2007, eff. July 30, 2007.)

RULE 5.2. SERVICE OF PAPERS FILED

(a) All papers filed with the Clerk of the Panel shall be accompanied by proof of previous or simultaneous service on all other parties in all actions involved in the litigation. Service and proof of service shall be made as provided in Rules 5 and 6 of the Federal Rules of Civil Procedure. The proof of service shall indicate the name and complete address of each person served and shall indicate the party represented by each. If a party is not represented by counsel, the proof of service shall indicate the name of the party and the party's last known address. The proof of service shall indicate why any person named as a party in a constituent complaint was not served with the Section 1407 pleading. The original proof of service shall be filed with the Clerk of the Panel and copies thereof shall be sent to each person included within the proof of service. After the "Panel Service List" described in subsection (d) of this Rule has been received from the Clerk of the Panel, the "Panel Service List" shall be utilized for service of responses to motions and all other filings. In such instances, the "Panel Service List" shall be attached to the proof of service and shall be supplemented in the proof of service in the event of the presence of additional parties or subsequent corrections relating to any party, counsel or address already on the "Panel Service List."

(b) The proof of service pertaining to motions for transfer of actions pursuant to 28 U.S.C. § 1407 shall certify that copies of the motions have been mailed or otherwise delivered for filing to the clerk of each district court in which an action is pending that will be affected by the motion. The proof of service pertaining to a motion for remand pursuant to 28 U.S.C. § 1407 shall certify that a copy of the motion has been mailed or otherwise delivered for filing to the clerk of the Section 1407 transferee district court in which any action affected by the motion is pending.

(c) Within eleven days of filing of a motion to transfer, an order to show cause or a conditional transfer order, each party or designated attorney shall notify the Clerk of the Panel, in writing, of the name and address of the attorney designated to receive service of all pleadings, notices, orders and other papers relating to practice before the Judicial Panel on Multidistrict Litigation. Only one attorney shall be designated for each party. Any party not represented by counsel shall be served by mailing such pleadings to the party's last known address. Requests for an extension of time to file the designation of attorney shall not be granted except in extraordinary circumstances.

(d) In order to facilitate compliance with subsection (a) of this Rule, the Clerk of the Panel shall prepare and serve on all counsel and parties not represented by counsel, a "Panel Service List" containing the names and addresses of the designated attorneys and the party or parties they represent in the actions under consideration by the Panel and the names and addresses of the parties not represented by counsel in the actions under consideration by the Panel. After the "Panel Service List" has been received from the Clerk of the Panel, notice of subsequent corrections relating to any party, counsel or address on the "Panel Service List" shall be served on all other parties in all actions involved in the litigation.

(e) If following transfer of any group of multidistrict litigation, the transferee district court appoints liaison counsel, this Rule shall be satisfied by serving each party in each affected action and all liaison counsel. Liaison counsel designated by the transferee district court shall receive copies of all Panel orders concerning their particular litigation and shall be responsible for distribution to the parties for whom he or she serves as liaison counsel.

(Former Rule 8 adopted May 3, 1993, eff. July 1, 1993; renumbered Rule 5.2 and amended Sept. 1, 1998, eff. Nov. 2, 1998.)

RULE 5.3. CORPORATE DISCLOSURE STATEMENT

(a) Any nongovernmental corporate party to a matter before the Panel shall file a statement identifying all its parent corporations and listing any publicly held company that owns 10% or more of the party's stock.

(b) A party shall file the corporate disclosure statement within eleven days of the filing of a motion to transfer or remand, an order to show cause, or a motion to vacate a conditional transfer order or a conditional remand order.

(c) Once a corporate disclosure statement by a party has been filed in an MDL docket pursuant to subsection (b) of this Rule, such a party is required to update the statement to reflect any change in the information therein i) until the matter before the Panel is decided, and ii) within eleven days of the filing of any subsequent motion to transfer or remand, order to show cause, or motion to vacate a conditional transfer order or a conditional remand order in that docket.

(Added Apr. 2, 2001, eff. Apr. 2, 2001.)

RULE 6.2. APPLICATIONS FOR EXTENSIONS OF TIME

Any application for an extension of time to file a pleading or perform an act required by these Rules must be in writing, must request a specific number of additional days and may be acted upon by the Clerk of the Panel. Such an application will be evaluated in relation to the impact on the Panel's calendar as well as on the basis of the reasons set forth in support of the application. Any party aggrieved by the Clerk of the Panel's action on such application may submit its objections to the Panel for consideration. Absent exceptional circumstances, no extensions of time shall be granted to file a notice of opposition to either a conditional transfer order or a conditional remand order. All applications for extensions of time shall be filed and served in conformity with Rules 5.12, 5.2 and 7.1 of these Rules.

(Former Rule 15 adopted May 3, 1993, eff. July 1, 1993; renumbered Rule 6.2 and amended Sept. 1, 1998, eff. Nov. 2, 1998.)

RULE 7.1. FORM OF PAPERS FILED

(a) Averments in any motion seeking action by the Panel shall be made in numbered paragraphs, each of which shall be limited, as far as practicable, to a statement of a single factual averment.

(b) Responses to averments in motions shall be made in numbered paragraphs, each of which shall correspond to the number of the paragraph of the motion to which the responsive paragraph is directed. Each responsive paragraph shall admit or deny wholly or in part the averment of the motion, and shall contain the respondent's version of the subject matter when the averment or the motion is not wholly admitted.

(c) Each pleading filed shall be:

(i) flat and unfolded;

(ii) plainly written, typed in double space, printed or prepared by means of a duplicating process, without erasures or interlineations which materially deface it;

(iii) on opaque, unglazed, white paper (not onionskin);

(iv) approximately 8–1/2 x 11 inches in size; and

(v) fastened at the top-left corner without side binding or front or back covers.

(d) The heading on the first page of each pleading shall commence not less than three inches from the top of the page. Each pleading shall bear the heading "Before the Judicial Panel on Multidistrict Litigation," the identification "MDL Docket No.___" and the descriptive title designated by the Panel for the litigation involved. If the Panel has not yet designated a title, an appropriate descriptive title shall be used.

(e) The final page of each pleading shall contain the name, address and telephone number of the attorney or party in active charge of the case. Each attorney shall also include the name of each party represented.

(f) Except with the approval of the Panel, each brief submitted for filing with the Panel shall be limited to twenty pages, exclusive of exhibits. Absent exceptional circumstances, motions to exceed page limits shall not be granted.

(g) Exhibits exceeding a cumulative total of 50 pages shall be fastened separately from the accompanying pleading.

(h) Proposed Panel orders shall not be submitted with papers for filing.

(Former Rule 9 adopted May 3, 1993, eff. July 1, 1993; renumbered Rule 7.1 and amended Sept. 1, 1998, eff. Nov. 2, 1998; amended Apr. 2, 2001, eff. Apr. 2, 2001.)

RULE 7.2. MOTION PRACTICE

(a) All requests for action by the Panel under 28 U.S.C. § 1407 shall be made by written motion. Every motion shall be accompanied by:

(i) a brief in support thereof in which the background of the litigation and factual and legal contentions of the movant shall be concisely stated in separate portions of the brief with citation of applicable authorities; and

(ii) a schedule giving

(A) the complete name of each action involved, listing the full name of each party included as such on the district court's docket sheet, not shortened by the use of references such as "et al." or "etc.";

(B) the district court and division in which each action is pending;

(C) the civil action number of each action; and

(D) the name of the judge assigned each action, if known.

(b) The Clerk of the Panel shall notify recipients of a motion of the filing date, caption, MDL docket number, briefing schedule and pertinent Panel policies.

(c) Within twenty days after filing of a motion, all other parties shall file a response thereto. Failure of a party to respond to a motion shall be treated as that party's acquiescence to the action requested in the motion.

(d) The movant may, within five days after the lapse of the time period for filing responsive briefs, file a single brief in reply to any opposition.

(e) Motions, their accompaniments, responses, and replies shall also be governed by Rules 5.12, 5.2 and 7.1 of these Rules.

(f) With respect to any action that is the subject of Panel consideration, counsel shall promptly notify the Clerk of the Panel of any development that would partially or completely moot the matter before the Panel.

(g) A joinder in a motion shall not add any action to the previous motion.

(h) Once a motion is filed, any other pleading that purports to be a "motion" in the docket shall be filed by the Clerk of the Panel as a response unless the "motion" adds an action. The Clerk of the Panel, upon designating such a pleading as a motion, shall acknowledge that designation by the distribution of a briefing schedule to all parties in the docket. Response time resulting from an additional motion shall ordinarily be extended only to those parties directly affected by the additional motion. An accelerated briefing schedule for the additional motion may be set by the Clerk of the Panel to conform with the hearing session schedule established by the Chairman.

(i) Any party or counsel in a new group of actions under consideration by the Panel for transfer under Section 1407 shall promptly notify the Clerk of the Panel of any potential tag-along action in which that party is also named or in which that counsel appears.

(Former Rule 10 adopted May 3, 1993, eff. July 1, 1993; renumbered Rule 7.2 and amended Sept. 1, 1998, eff. Nov. 2, 1998; amended Apr. 2, 2001, eff. Apr. 2, 2001.)

RULE 7.3. SHOW CAUSE ORDERS

(a) When transfer of multidistrict litigation is being considered on the initiative of the Panel pursuant to 28 U.S.C. § 1407(c)(i), an order shall be filed by the Clerk of the Panel directing the parties to show cause why the action or actions should not be transferred for coordinated or consolidated pretrial proceedings. Any party or counsel in such actions shall promptly notify the Clerk of the Panel of any other federal district court actions related to the litigation encompassed by the show cause order. Such notification shall be made for additional actions pending at the time of the issuance of the show cause order and whenever new actions are filed.

(b) Any party may file a response to the show cause order within twenty days of the filing of said order unless otherwise provided for in the order. Failure of a party to respond to a show cause order shall be treated as that party's acquiescence to the Panel action contemplated in the order.

(c) Within five days after the lapse of the time period for filing a response, any party may file a reply limited to new matters.

(d) Responses and replies shall be filed and served in conformity with Rules 5.12, 5.2 and 7.1 of these Rules.

(e) With respect to any action that is the subject of Panel consideration, counsel shall promptly notify the Clerk of the Panel of any development that would partially or completely moot the matter before the Panel.

(Former Rule 7.3 adopted May 3, 1993, eff. July 1, 1993; renumbered Rule 7.3 and amended Sept. 1, 1998, eff. Nov. 2, 1998.)

RULE 7.4. CONDITIONAL TRANSFER ORDERS FOR "TAG–ALONG ACTIONS"

(a) Upon learning of the pendency of a potential "tag-along action," as defined in Rule 1.1 of these Rules, an order may be entered by the Clerk of the Panel transferring that action to the previously designated transferee district court on the basis of the prior hearing session(s) and for the reasons expressed in previous opinions and orders of the Panel in the litigation. The Clerk of the Panel shall serve this order on each party to the litigation but, in order to afford all parties the opportunity to oppose transfer, shall not send the order to the clerk of the transferee district court for fifteen days from the entry thereof.

(b) Parties to an action subject to a conditional transfer order shall notify the Clerk of the Panel within the fifteen-day period if that action is no longer pending in its transferor district court.

(c) Any party opposing the transfer shall file a notice of opposition with the Clerk of the Panel within the fifteen-day period. If a notice of opposition is received by the Clerk of the Panel within this fifteen-day period, the Clerk of the Panel shall not transmit said order to the clerk of the transferee district court until further order of the Panel. The Clerk of the Panel shall notify the parties of the briefing schedule.

(d) Within fifteen days of the filing of its notice of opposition, the party opposing transfer shall file a motion to vacate the conditional transfer order and brief in support thereof. The Chairman of the Panel shall set the motion for the next appropriate hearing session of the Panel. Failure to file and serve a motion and brief shall be treated as withdrawal of the opposition and the Clerk of the Panel shall forthwith transmit the order to the clerk of the transferee district court.

(e) Conditional transfer orders do not become effective unless and until they are filed with the clerk of the transferee district court.

(f) Notices of opposition and motions to vacate such orders of the Panel and responses thereto shall be governed by Rules 5.12, 5.2, 7.1 and 7.2 of these Rules.

(Former Rule 12 adopted May 3, 1993, eff. July 1, 1993; renumbered Rule 7.4 and amended Sept. 1, 1998, eff. Nov. 2, 1998; amended Apr. 2, 2001, eff. Apr. 2, 2001.)

RULE 7.5.   MISCELLANEOUS PROVISIONS CONCERNING "TAG–ALONG ACTIONS"

(a) Potential "tag-along actions" filed in the transferee district require no action on the part of the Panel and requests for assignment of such actions to the Section 1407 transferee judge should be made in accordance with local rules for the assignment of related actions.

(b) Upon learning of the pendency of a potential "tag-along action" and having reasonable anticipation of opposition to transfer of that action, the Panel may direct the Clerk of the Panel to file a show cause order, in accordance with Rule 7.3 of these Rules, instead of a conditional transfer order.

(c) Failure to serve one or more of the defendants in a potential "tag-along action" with the complaint and summons as required by Rule 4 of the Federal Rules of Civil Procedure does not preclude transfer of such action under Section 1407. Such failure, however, may be submitted by such a defendant as a basis for opposing the proposed transfer if prejudice can be shown. The inability of the Clerk of the Panel to serve a conditional transfer order on all plaintiffs or defendants or their counsel shall not render the transfer of the action void but can be submitted by such a party as a basis for moving to remand as to such party if prejudice can be shown.

(d) A civil action apparently involving common questions of fact with actions under consideration by the Panel for transfer under Section 1407, which was either not included in a motion under Rule 7.2 of these Rules, or was included in such a motion that was filed too late to be included in the initial hearing session, will ordinarily be treated by the Panel as a potential "tag-along action."

(e) Any party or counsel in actions previously transferred under Section 1407 or under consideration by the Panel for transfer under Section 1407 shall promptly notify the Clerk of the Panel of any potential "tag-along actions" in which that party is also named or in which that counsel appears.

(Former Rule 13 adopted May 3, 1993, eff. July 1, 1993; renumbered Rule 7.5 and amended Sept. 1, 1998, eff. Nov. 2, 1998; amended Apr. 2, 2001, eff. Apr. 2, 2001.)

RULE 7.6.   TERMINATION AND REMAND

In the absence of unusual circumstances—

(a) Actions terminated in the transferee district court by valid judgment, including but not limited to summary judgment, judgment of dismissal and judgment upon stipulation, shall not be remanded by the Panel and shall be dismissed by the transferee district court. The clerk of the transferee district court shall send a copy of the order terminating the action to the Clerk of the Panel but shall retain the original files and records unless otherwise directed by the transferee judge or by the Panel.

(b) Each action transferred only for coordinated or consolidated pretrial proceedings that has not been terminated in the transferee district court shall be remanded by the Panel to the transferor district for trial. Actions that were originally filed in the transferee district require no action by the Panel to be reassigned to another judge in the transferee district at the conclusion of the coordinated or consolidated pretrial proceedings affecting those actions.

(c) The Panel shall consider remand of each transferred action or any separable claim, cross-claim, counterclaim or third-party claim at or before the conclusion of coordinated or consolidated pretrial proceedings on

    (i) motion of any party,

    (ii) suggestion of the transferee district court, or

    (iii) the Panel's own initiative, by entry of an order to show cause, a conditional remand order or other appropriate order.

(d) The Panel is reluctant to order remand absent a suggestion of remand from the transferee district court. If remand is sought by motion of a party, the motion shall be accompanied by:

    (i) an affidavit reciting

      (A) whether the movant has requested a suggestion of remand from the transferee district court, how the court responded to any request, and, if no such request was made, why;

      (B) whether all common discovery and other pretrial proceedings have been completed in the action sought to be remanded, and if not, what remains to be done; and

      (C) whether all orders of the transferee district court have been satisfactorily complied with, and if not, what remains to be done; and

    (ii) a copy of the transferee district court's final pretrial order, where such order has been entered.

Motions to remand and responses thereto shall be governed by Rules 5.12, 5.2, 7.1 and 7.2 of these Rules.

(e) When an order to show cause why an action or actions should not be remanded is entered pursuant to subsection (c), paragraph (iii) of this Rule, any party may file a response within twenty days of the filing of said order unless otherwise provided for in the order. Within five days of filing of a party's response, any party may file a reply brief limited to new matters. Failure of a party to respond to a show cause order regarding remand shall be treated as that party's acquiescence to the remand. Responses and replies shall be filed and served in conformity with Rules 5.12, 5.2 and 7.1 of these Rules.

(f) Conditional Remand Orders.

(i) When the Panel has been advised by the transferee district judge, or otherwise has reason to believe, that pretrial proceedings in the litigation assigned to the transferee district judge are concluded or that remand of an action or actions is otherwise appropriate, an order may be entered by the Clerk of the Panel remanding the action or actions to the transferor district court. The Clerk of the Panel shall serve this order on each party to the litigation but, in order to afford all parties the opportunity to oppose remand, shall not send the order to the clerk of the transferee district court for fifteen days from the entry thereof.

(ii) Any party opposing the remand shall file a notice of opposition with the Clerk of the Panel within the fifteen-day period. If a notice of opposition is received by the Clerk of the Panel within this fifteen-day period, the Clerk of the Panel shall not transmit said order to the clerk of the transferee district court until further order of the Panel. The Clerk of the Panel shall notify the parties of the briefing schedule.

(iii) Within fifteen days of the filing of its notice of opposition, the party opposing remand shall file a motion to vacate the conditional remand order and brief in support thereof. The Chairman of the Panel shall set the motion for the next appropriate hearing session of the Panel. Failure to file and serve a motion and brief shall be treated as a withdrawal of the opposition and the Clerk of the Panel shall forthwith transmit the order to the clerk of the transferee district court.

(iv) Conditional remand orders do not become effective unless and until they are filed with the clerk of the transferee district court.

(v) Notices of opposition and motions to vacate such orders of the Panel and responses thereto shall be governed by Rules 5.12, 5.2, 7.1 and 7.2 of these Rules.

(g) Upon receipt of an order to remand from the Clerk of the Panel, the parties shall furnish forthwith to the transferee district clerk a stipulation or designation of the contents of the record or part thereof to be remanded and furnish the transferee district clerk all necessary copies of any pleading or other matter filed so as to enable the transferee district clerk to comply with the order of remand.

(Former Rule 14 adopted May 3, 1993, eff. July 1, 1993; renumbered Rule 7.6 and amended Sept. 1, 1998, eff. Nov. 2, 1998; amended Apr. 2, 2001, eff. Apr. 2, 2001.)

RULE 16.1.   HEARING SESSIONS AND ORAL ARGUMENT

(a) Hearing sessions of the Panel for the presentation of oral argument and consideration of matters taken under submission without oral argument shall be held as ordered by the Panel. The Panel shall convene whenever and wherever desirable or necessary in the judgment of the Chairman. The Chairman shall determine which matters shall be considered at each hearing session and the Clerk of the Panel shall give notice to counsel for all parties involved in the litigation to be so considered of the time, place and subject matter of such hearing session.

(b) Each party filing a motion or a response to a motion or order of the Panel under Rules 7.2, 7.3, 7.4 or 7.6 of these Rules may file simultaneously therewith a separate statement limited to one page setting forth reasons why oral argument should, or need not, be heard. Such statements shall be captioned "Reasons Why Oral Argument Should [Need Not] Be Heard," and shall be filed and served in conformity with Rules 5.12 and 5.2 of these Rules.

(c) No transfer or remand determination regarding any action pending in the district court shall be made by the Panel when any party timely opposes such transfer or remand unless a hearing session has been held for the presentation of oral argument except that the Panel may dispense with oral argument if it determines that:

(i) the dispositive issue(s) have been authoritatively decided; or

(ii) the facts and legal arguments are adequately presented in the briefs and record, and the decisional process would not be significantly aided by oral argument.

Unless otherwise ordered by the Panel, all other matters before the Panel, such as a motion for reconsideration, shall be considered and determined upon the basis of the papers filed.

(d) In those matters in which oral argument is not scheduled by the Panel, counsel shall be promptly advised. If oral argument is scheduled in a matter the Clerk of the Panel may require counsel for all parties who wish to make or to waive oral argument to file and serve notice to that effect within a stated time in conformity with Rules 5.12 and 5.2 of these Rules. Failure to do so shall be deemed a waiver of oral argument by that party. If oral argument is scheduled but not attended by a party, the matter shall not be rescheduled and that party's position shall be treated as submitted for decision by the Panel on the basis of the papers filed.

(e) Except for leave of the Panel on a showing of good cause, only those parties to actions scheduled for oral argument who have filed a motion or written response to a motion or order shall be permitted to appear before the Panel and present oral argument.

(f) Counsel for those supporting transfer or remand under Section 1407 and counsel for those opposing such transfer or remand are to confer separately prior to the oral argument for the purpose of organizing their arguments and selecting representatives to present all views without duplication.

(g) Unless otherwise ordered by the Panel, a maximum of twenty minutes shall be allotted for oral argument in each matter. The time shall be divided equally among those with varying viewpoints. Counsel for the moving party or parties shall generally be heard first.

(h) So far as practicable and consistent with the purposes of Section 1407, the offering of oral testimony before the Panel shall be avoided. Accordingly, oral testimony shall not be received except upon notice,

motion and order of the Panel expressly providing for it.

(i) After an action or group of actions has been set for a hearing session, consideration of such action(s) may be continued only by order of the Panel on good cause shown.

(Former Rule 16 adopted May 3, 1998, eff. July 1, 1993; renumbered Rule 16.1 and amended Sept. 1, 1998, eff. Nov. 2, 1998; amended Apr. 2, 2001, eff. Apr. 2, 2001.)

RULE 16.2 NOTICE OF PRESENTATION OR WAIVER OF ORAL ARGUMENT, AND MATTERS SUBMITTED ON THE BRIEFS [REPEALED]

(Former Rule 17 adopted May 3, 1993, eff. July 1, 1993; renumbered Rule 16.2 and amended Sept. 1, 1998, eff. Nov. 2, 1998; repealed eff. Apr. 2, 2001.)

II. RULES FOR MULTICIRCUIT PETITIONS FOR REVIEW UNDER 28 U.S.C. § 2112(a)(3)

RULE 17.1. RANDOM SELECTION

(a) Upon filing a notice of multicircuit petitions for review, the Clerk of the Panel or designated deputy shall randomly select a circuit court of appeals from a drum containing an entry for each circuit wherein a constituent petition for review is pending. Multiple petitions for review pending in a single circuit shall be allotted only a single entry in the drum. This random selection shall be witnessed by the Clerk of the Panel or a designated deputy other than the random selector. Thereafter, an order on behalf of the Panel shall be issued, signed by the random selector and the witness,

(i) consolidating the petitions for review in the court of appeals for the circuit that was randomly selected; and

(ii) designating that circuit as the one in which the record is to be filed pursuant to Rules 16 and 17 of the Federal Rules of Appellate Procedure.

(b) A consolidation of petitions for review shall be effective when the Panel's consolidation order is filed at the offices of the Panel by the Clerk of the Panel.

(Former Rule 24 adopted May 3, 1993, eff. July 1, 1993; renumbered Rule 17.1 Sept. 1, 1998, eff. Nov. 2, 1998.)

RULE 25.1. FILING OF NOTICES

(a) An original of a notice of multicircuit petitions for review pursuant to 28 U.S.C. § 2112(a)(3) shall be submitted for filing to the Clerk of the Panel by the affected agency, board, commission or officer. The term "agency" as used in Section II of these Rules shall include agency, board, commission or officer.

(b) All notices of multicircuit petitions for review submitted by the affected agency for filing with the Clerk of the Panel shall embrace exclusively petitions for review filed in the courts of appeals within ten days after issuance of an agency order and received by the affected agency from the petitioners within that ten-day period.

(c) When a notice of multicircuit petitions for review is submitted for filing to the Clerk of the Panel, the Clerk of the Panel shall file the notice and endorse thereon the date of filing.

(d) Copies of notices of multicircuit petitions for review shall be filed by the affected agency with the clerk of each circuit court of appeals in which a petition for review is pending that is included in the notice.

(Former Rule 20 adopted May 3, 1993, eff. July 1, 1993; renumbered Rule 25.1 and amended Sept. 1, 1998, eff. Nov. 2, 1998.)

RULE 25.2. ACCOMPANIMENTS TO NOTICES

(a) All notices of multicircuit petitions for review shall be accompanied by:

(i) a copy of each involved petition for review as the petition for review is defined in 28 U.S.C. § 2112(a)(2); and

(ii) a schedule giving

(A) the date of the relevant agency order;

(B) the case name of each petition for review involved;

(C) the circuit court of appeals in which each petition for review is pending;

(D) the appellate docket number of each petition for review;

(E) the date of filing by the court of appeals of each petition for review; and

(F) the date of receipt by the agency of each petition for review.

(b) The schedule in Subsection (a)(ii) of this Rule shall also be governed by Rules 25.1, 25.3 and 25.4(a) of these Rules.

(Former Rule 21 adopted May 3, 1993, eff. July 1, 1993; renumbered Rule 25.2 and amended Sept. 1, 1998, eff. Nov. 2, 1998.)

RULE 25.3. SERVICE OF NOTICES

(a) All notices of multicircuit petitions for review shall be accompanied by proof of service by the affected agency on all other parties in all petitions for review included in the notice. Service and proof of service shall be made as provided in Rule 25 of the Federal Rules of Appellate Procedure. The proof of service shall state the name and address of each person served and shall indicate the party represented by each. If a party is not represented by counsel, the proof of service shall indicate the name of the party and his or her last known address. The original proof of service shall be submitted by the affected agency for filing with the Clerk of the Panel and copies thereof shall be sent by the affected agency to each person included within the proof of service.

(b) The proof of service pertaining to notices of multicircuit petitions for review shall certify that copies of the notices have been mailed or otherwise delivered by the affected agency for filing to the clerk of each circuit court of appeals in which a petition for review is pending that is included in the notice.

(Former Rule 22 adopted May 3, 1993, eff. July 1, 1993; renumbered Rule 25.3 Sept. 1, 1998, eff. Nov. 2, 1998.)

RULE 25.4. FORM OF NOTICES

(a) Each notice of multicircuit petitions for review shall be

(i) flat and unfolded;

(ii) plainly written, typed in double space, printed or prepared by means of a duplicating process, without erasures or interlineations which materially deface it;

(iii) on opaque, unglazed white paper (not onionskin);

(iv) approximately 8–1/2 x 11 inches in size; and

(v) fastened at the top-left corner without side binding or front or back covers.

(b) The heading on the first page of each notice of multicircuit petitions for review shall commence not less that three inches from the top of the page. Each notice shall bear the heading "Notice to the Judicial Panel on Multidistrict Litigation of Multicircuit Petitions for Review," followed by a brief caption identifying the involved agency, the relevant agency order, and the date of the order.

(c) The final page of each notice of multicircuit petitions for review shall contain the name, address and telephone number of the individual or individuals who submitted the notice on behalf of the agency.

(Former Rule 23 adopted May 3, 1993, eff. July 1, 1993; renumbered Rule 25.4 and amended Sept. 1, 1998, eff. Nov. 2, 1998.)

RULE 25.5. SERVICE OF PANEL CONSOLIDATION ORDER

(a) The Clerk of the Panel shall serve the Panel's consolidation order on the affected agency through the individual or individuals, as identified in Rule 25.4(c) of these Rules, who submitted the notice of multicircuit petitions for review on behalf of the agency.

(b) That individual or individuals, or anyone else designated by the agency, shall promptly serve the Panel's consolidation order on all other parties in all petitions for review included in the Panel's consolidation order, and shall promptly submit a proof of that service to the Clerk of the Panel. Service and proof of that service shall also be governed by Rule 25.3 of these Rules.

(c) The Clerk of the Panel shall serve the Panel's consolidation order on the clerks of all circuit courts of appeals that were among the candidates for the Panel's random selection.

(Former Rule 25 adopted May 3, 1993, eff. July 1, 1993; renumbered Rule 25.5 and amended Sept. 1, 1998, eff. Nov. 2, 1998.)

CONVERSION TABLE

Renumbered Rule	Previous Rule
1.1	1
1.2	5
1.3	4
1.4	6
1.5	18
1.6	19
5.1	2
5.11	3
5.12	7
5.13	—
5.2	8
5.3	—
6.2	15
7.1	9
7.2	10
7.3	11
7.4	12
7.5	13

Renumbered Rule	Previous Rule	Renumbered Rule	Previous Rule
7.6	14	25.2	21
16.1	16, 16.2 & 17	25.3	22
17.1	24	25.4	23
25.1	20	25.5	25

*

FEDERAL COURTS MISCELLANEOUS FEE SCHEDULES

COURT OF APPEALS FEE SCHEDULE

(Issued in accordance with 28 U.S.C. § 1913)

(Eff. 01/01/2007)

The following are fees to be charged for services provided by the courts of appeals. No fees are to be charged for services rendered on behalf of the United States, with the exception of those specifically prescribed in items 2, 4 and 5. No fees under this schedule shall be charged to federal agencies or programs which are funded from judiciary appropriations, including, but not limited to, agencies, organizations, and individuals providing services authorized by the Criminal Justice Act, 18 U.S.C. § 3006A, and Bankruptcy Administrator programs.

(1) For docketing a case on appeal or review, or docketing any other proceeding, $450. A separate fee shall be paid by each party filing a notice of appeal in the district court, but parties filing a joint notice of appeal in the district court are required to pay only one fee. A docketing fee shall not be charged for the docketing of an application for the allowance of an interlocutory appeal under 28 U.S.C. § 1292(b), unless the appeal is allowed. A docketing fee shall not be charged for the docketing of a direct bankruptcy appeal or a direct bankruptcy cross appeal when the fee has been collected by the bankruptcy court in accordance with Item 15 or Item 21 of the Bankruptcy Court Miscellaneous Fee Schedule.

(2) For every search of the records of the court and certifying the results thereof, $26. This fee shall apply to services rendered on behalf of the United States if the information requested is available through electronic access.

(3) For certifying any document or paper, whether the certification is made directly on the document, or by separate instrument, $9.

(4) For reproducing any record or paper, 50 cents per page. This fee shall apply to paper copies made from either: (1) original documents; or (2) microfiche or microfilm reproductions of the original records. This fee shall apply to services rendered on behalf of the United States if the record or paper requested is available through electronic access.

(5) For reproduction of recordings of proceedings, regardless of the medium, $26, including the cost of materials. This fee shall apply to services rendered on behalf of the United States if the reproduction of the recording is available electronically.

(6) For reproduction of the record in any appeal in which the requirement of an appendix is dispensed with by any court of appeals pursuant to Rule 30(f), F.R.A.P., a flat fee of $71.

(7) For each microfiche or microfilm copy of any court record, where available, $5.

(8) For retrieval of a record from a Federal Records Center, National Archives, or other storage location removed from the place of business of the court, $45.

(9) For a check paid into the court which is returned for lack of funds, $45.

(10) Fees to be charged and collected for copies of opinions shall be fixed, from time to time, by each court, commensurate with the cost of printing.

(11) The court may charge and collect fees commensurate with the cost of providing copies of the local rules of court. The court may also distribute copies of the local rules without charge.

(12) The clerk shall assess a charge for the handling of registry funds deposited with the court, to be assessed from interest earnings and in accordance with the detailed fee schedule issued by the Director of the Administrative Office of the United States Courts.

(13) Upon the filing of any separate or joint notice of appeal or application for appeal from the Bankruptcy Appellate Panel, or notice of the allowance of an appeal from the Bankruptcy Appellate Panel, or of a writ of certiorari, $5 shall be paid by the appellant or petitioner.

(14) The court may charge and collect a fee of $200 per remote location for counsel's requested use of videoconferencing equipment in connection with each oral argument.

(15) For original admission of attorneys to practice, $150 each, including a certificate of admission. For a duplicate certificate of admission or certificate of good standing, $15.

DISTRICT COURT FEE SCHEDULE

(Issued in accordance with 28 U.S.C. 1914)

(Eff. 06/01/2004)

Following are fees to be charged for services provided by the district courts. No fees are to be charged for services rendered on behalf of the United States, with the exception of those specifically prescribed in items 2, 4 and 5. No fees under this schedule shall be charged to federal agencies or programs which are funded from judiciary appropriations, including, but not limited to, agencies, organizations, and individuals providing services authorized by the Criminal Justice Act, 18 U.S.C. § 3006A, and Bankruptcy Administrator programs.

(1) For filing or indexing any document not in a case or proceeding for which a filing fee has been paid, $39.

(2) For every search of the records of the district court conducted by the clerk of the district court or a deputy clerk, $26 per name or item searched. This fee shall apply to services rendered on behalf of the United States if the information requested is available through electronic access.

(3) For certification of any document or paper, whether the certification is made directly on the document or by separate instrument, $9. For exemplification of any document or paper, twice the amount of the fee for certification.

(4) For reproducing any record or paper, $.50 per page. This fee shall apply to paper copies made from either: (1) original documents; or (2) microfiche or microfilm reproductions of the original records. This fee shall apply to services rendered on behalf of the United States if the record or paper requested is available through electronic access.

(5) For reproduction of recordings of proceedings, regardless of the medium, $26, including the cost of materials. This fee shall apply to services rendered on behalf of the United States, if the reproduction of the recording is available electronically.

(6) For each microfiche sheet of film or microfilm jacket copy of any court record, where available, $5.

(7) For retrieval of a record from a Federal Records Center, National Archives, or other storage location removed from the place of business of the court, $45.

(8) For a check paid into the court which is returned for lack of funds, $45.

(9) For an appeal to a district judge from a judgment of conviction by a magistrate in a misdemeanor case, $32.

(10) For original admission of attorneys to practice, $50 each, including a certificate of admission. For a duplicate certificate of admission or certificate of good standing, $15.

(11) The court may charge and collect fees commensurate with the cost of providing copies of the local rules of court. The court may also distribute copies of the local rules without charge.

(12) The clerk shall assess a charge for the handling of registry funds deposited with the court, to be assessed from interest earnings and in accordance with the detailed fee schedule issued by the Director of the Administrative Office of the United States Courts.

(13) For filing an action brought under Title III of the Cuban Liberty and Democratic Solidarity (LIBERTAD) Act of 1996, P.L. 104–114, 110 Stat. 785 (1996), $5,431. (This fee is in addition to the filing fee prescribed in 28 U.S.C. § 1914(a) for instituting any civil action other than a writ of habeas corpus.)

BANKRUPTCY COURT FEE SCHEDULE

(Issued in accordance with 28 U.S.C. 1930(b))

(Eff. 1/1/2007)

Following are fees to be charged for services provided by the bankruptcy courts. No fees are to be charged for services rendered on behalf of the United States, with the exception of those specifically prescribed in items 1, 3, and 5, or to bankruptcy administrators appointed under Public Law No. 99–554, § 302(d)(3)(I). No fees under this schedule shall be charged to federal agencies or programs which are funded from judiciary appropriations, including, but not limited to, agencies, organizations, and individuals providing services authorized by the Criminal Justice Act, 18 U.S.C. § 3006A.

(1) For reproducing any record or paper, $.50 per page. This fee shall apply to paper copies made from either: (1) original documents; or (2) microfiche or microfilm reproductions of the original records. This fee shall apply to services rendered on behalf of the United States if the record or paper requested is available through electronic access.

(2) For certification of any document or paper, whether the certification is made directly on the document or by separate instrument, $9. For exemplification of any document or paper, twice the amount of the charge for certification.

(3) For reproduction of recordings of proceedings, regardless of the medium, $26, including the cost of materials. This fee shall apply to services rendered on behalf of the United States, if the reproduction of the recording is available electronically.

(4) For amendments to a debtor's schedules of creditors, lists of creditors, matrix, or mailing lists, $26 for each amendment, provided the bankruptcy judge may, for good cause, waive the charge in any case. No fee is required when the nature of the amendment is to change the address of a creditor or an attorney for a creditor listed on the schedules or to add the name and address of an attorney for a listed creditor.

(5) For every search of the records of the bankruptcy court conducted by the clerk of the bankruptcy court or a deputy clerk, $26 per name or item searched. This fee shall apply to services rendered on behalf of the United States if the information requested is available through electronic access.

(6) For filing a complaint, $250. If the United States, other than a United States trustee acting as a trustee in a case under Title 11, or a debtor is the plaintiff, no fee is required. If a trustee or debtor in possession is the plaintiff, the fee should be payable only from the estate and to the extent there is any

estate realized. If a child support creditor or its representative is the plaintiff, and if such plaintiff files the form required by § 304(g) of the Bankruptcy Reform Act of 1994, no fee is required.

(7) For filing or indexing any document not in a case or proceeding for which a filing fee has been paid, $39.

(8) In all cases filed under title 11, the clerk shall collect from the debtor or the petitioner a miscellaneous administrative fee of $39. This fee may be paid in installments in the same manner that the filing fee may be paid in installments, consistent with the procedure set forth in Federal Rule of Bankruptcy Procedure 1006.

(9) Upon the filing of a petition under Chapter 7 of the Bankruptcy Code, the petitioner shall pay $15 to the clerk of the court for payment to trustees serving in cases as provided in 11 U.S.C. § 330(b)(2). An application to pay the fee in installments may be filed in the manner set forth in Federal Rule of Bankruptcy Procedure 1006(b).

(10) Upon the filing of a motion to convert a case to Chapter 7 of the Bankruptcy Code, the movant shall pay $15 to the clerk of court for payment to trustees serving in cases as provided in 11 U.S.C. § 330(b)(2). Upon the filing of a notice of conversion pursuant to Section 1208(a) or Section 1307(a) of the Code, $15 shall be paid to the clerk of the court for payment to trustees serving in cases as provided in 11 U.S.C. § 330(b)(2). If the trustee serving in the case before the conversion is the movant, the fee shall be payable only from the estate that exists prior to conversion. For filing a motion to convert or a notice of conversion, a fee shall be charged in the amount of the difference between the current filing fee for the chapter under which the case was originally commenced and the current filing fee for the chapter to which the case is requested to be converted. If the filing fee for the chapter to which the case is requested to be converted is less than the fee paid at the commencement of the case, no refund shall be provided. A fee shall not be assessed under this item for converting a Chapter 7 or 13 case to a Chapter 11 case as the fee for these actions is collected pursuant to statute under 28 U.S.C. 1930(a).

(11) For filing a motion to reopen a Bankruptcy Code case, a fee shall be collected in the same amount as the filing fee prescribed by 28 U.S.C. 1930(a) for commencing a new case on the date of reopening. The reopening fee should be charged when a case is closed

without a discharge being entered. If the motion to reopen is made for a Chapter 7 case, an additional fee of $15 shall be paid to the clerk of the court for payment to trustees serving in cases as provided in 11 U.S.C. 330(b)(2). For filing a motion to reopen a Chapter 15 case, a fee shall be charged in the same amount as the filing fee required under Item 16 of this schedule for commencing a new case on the date of reopening. The reopening fee will not be charged if the reopening is necessary: (1) to permit a party to file a complaint to obtain a determination under Rule 4007(b), or, (2) when a creditor is violating the terms of the discharge under 11 U.S.C. 524. The court may waive this fee under appropriate circumstances or may defer payment of the fee from trustees pending discovery of additional assets. If payment is deferred, the fee shall be waived if no additional assets are discovered.

(12) For each microfiche sheet of film or microfilm jacket copy of any court record, where available, $5.

(13) For retrieval of a record from a Federal Records Center, National Archives, or other storage location removed from the place of business of the court, $45.

(14) For a check paid into the court which is returned for lack of funds, $45.

(15) For docketing a proceeding on appeal or review from a final judgment of a bankruptcy judge pursuant to 28 U.S.C. § 158(a) and (b), $250. A separate fee shall be paid by each party filing a notice of appeal in the bankruptcy court, but parties filing a joint notice of appeal in the bankruptcy court are required to pay only one fee. If a trustee or debtor in possession is the appellant, the fee should be payable only from the estate and to the extent there is any estate realized. Upon notice from the court of appeals that a direct appeal from the bankruptcy court has been authorized, the appellant shall pay an additional $200.

(16) For filing a Chapter 15 proceeding, the fee shall be the same amount as the fee for a case commenced under Chapter 11 of Title 11 as required by 28 U.S.C. § 1930(a)(3).

(17) The court may charge and collect fees commensurate with the cost of providing copies of the local rules of court. The court may also distribute copies of the local rules without charge.

(18) The clerk shall assess a charge for the handling of registry funds deposited with the court, to be assessed from interest earnings and in accordance with the detailed fee schedule issued by the Director of the Administrative Office of the United States Courts.

(19) When a joint case filed under § 302 of Title 11 is divided into two separate cases at the request of the debtor(s), a fee shall be charged equal to the current filing fee for the chapter under which the joint case was commenced. If the motion to divide the case is made for a Chapter 7 case, an additional fee of $15 shall be paid to the clerk of the court for payment to trustees serving in cases as provided in 11 U.S.C. § 330(b)(2).

(20) For filing a motion to terminate, annul, modify, or condition the automatic stay provided under § 362(a) of Title 11, a motion to compel abandonment of property of the estate pursuant to Rule 6007(b) of the Federal Rules of Bankruptcy Procedure, or a motion to withdraw the reference of a case or proceeding under 28 U.S.C. § 157(d), $150. No fee is required for a motion for relief from the co-debtor stay or for a stipulation for court approval of an agreement for relief from a stay. If a child support creditor or its representative is the movant, and if such movant files the form required by § 304(g) of the Bankruptcy Reform Act of 1994, no fee is required.

(21) For docketing a cross appeal from a bankruptcy court determination, $250. If a trustee or debtor in possession is the appellant, the fee should be payable only from the estate and to the extent there is any estate realized. Upon notice from the court of appeals that a direct cross from the bankruptcy court has been authorized, the cross appellant shall pay an additional $200.

JUDICIAL PANEL ON MULTIDISTRICT LITIGATION FEE SCHEDULE

Following are fees to be charged for services provided by the Judicial Panel on Multidistrict Litigation. No fees are to be charged for services rendered on behalf of the United States, with the exception of those specifically prescribed in items 1 and 3. No fees under this schedule shall be charged to federal agencies or programs which are funded from judiciary appropriations, including, but not limited to, agencies, organizations, and individuals providing services authorized by the Criminal Justice Act, 18 U.S.C. § 3006A.

(1) For every search of the records of the court conducted by the clerk of the court or a deputy clerk, $26 per name or item searched. This fee shall apply to services rendered on behalf of the United States if the information requested is available through electronic access.

(2) For certification of any document or paper, whether the certification is made directly on the document or by separate instrument, $9.

(3) For reproducing any record or paper, $.50 per page. This fee shall apply to paper copies made from either: (1) original documents; or (2) microfiche or microfilm reproductions of the original records. This fee shall apply to services rendered on behalf of the United States if the record or paper requested is available through electronic access.

(4) For retrieval of a record from a Federal Records Center, National Archives, or other storage location removed from the place of business of the court, $45.

(5) For a check paid into the Panel which is returned for lack of funds, $45.

ELECTRONIC PUBLIC ACCESS FEE SCHEDULE

(Issued in accordance with 28 U.S.C. 1913, 1914, 1926, 1930, 1932)

(Eff. 3/11/2008)

As directed by Congress, the Judicial Conference has determined that the following fees are necessary to reimburse expenses incurred by the judiciary in providing electronic public access to court records. These fees shall apply to the United States unless otherwise stated. No fees under this schedule shall be charged to federal agencies or programs which are funded from judiciary appropriations, including, but not limited to, agencies, organizations, and individuals providing services authorized by the Criminal Justice Act, 18 U.S.C. 3006A, and bankruptcy administrator programs.

I. For electronic access to court data via a federal judiciary Internet site: eight cents per page, with the total for any document, docket sheet, or case-specific report not to exceed the fee for thirty pages- provided however that transcripts of federal court proceedings shall not be subject to the thirty-page fee limit. Attorneys of record and parties in a case (including pro se litigants) receive one free electronic copy of all documents filed electronically, if receipt is required by law or directed by the filer. No fee is owed under this provision until an account holder accrues charges of more than $10 in a calendar year. Consistent with Judicial Conference policy, courts may, upon a showing of cause, exempt indigents, bankruptcy case trustees, individual researchers associated with educational institutions, courts, section 501(c)(3) not-for-profit organizations, court appointed pro bono attorneys, and pro bono ADR neutrals from payment of these fees. Courts must find that parties from the classes of persons or entities listed above seeking exemption have demonstrated that an exemption is necessary in order to avoid unreasonable burdens and to promote public access to information. Any user granted an exemption agrees not to sell for profit the data obtained as a result. Any transfer of data obtained as the result of a fee exemption is prohibited unless expressly authorized by the court. Exemptions may be granted for a definite period of time and may be revoked at the discretion of the court granting the exemption.

II. For printing copies of any record or document accessed electronically at a public terminal in the courthouse: ten cents per page. This fee shall apply to services rendered on behalf of the United States if the record requested is remotely available through electronic access.

III. For every search of court records conducted by the PACER Service Center, $26 per name or item searched.

IV. For the PACER Service Center to reproduce on paper any record pertaining to a PACER account, if this information is remotely available through electronic access, 50 cents per page.

V. For a check paid to the PACER Service Center which is returned for lack of funds, $45.

JUDICIAL CONFERENCE POLICY NOTES

Courts should not exempt local, state or federal government agencies, members of the media, attorneys or others not members of one of the groups listed above. Exemptions should be granted as the exception, not the rule. A court may not use this exemption language to exempt all users. An exemption applies only to access related to the case or purpose for which it was given. The prohibition on transfer of information received without fee is not intended to bar a quote or reference to information received as a result of a fee exemption in a scholarly or other similar work.

The electronic public access fee applies to electronic court data viewed remotely from the public records of individual cases in the court, including filed documents and the docket sheet. Electronic court data may be viewed free at public terminals at the courthouse and courts may provide other local court information at no cost. Examples of information that can be provided at no cost include: local rules, court forms, news items, court calendars, opinions, and other information—such as court hours, court location, telephone listings—determined locally to benefit the public and the court.

†

McKinney's
New York
Rules of Court

Federal

2009
Including Amendments Received Through
January 1, 2009

PRESORTED
STANDARD
U.S. POSTAGE PAID
WEST

CHANGE SERVICE REQUESTED

WEST
620 OPPERMAN DRIVE
P.O. BOX 64779
ST. PAUL, MN 55164–0779

WEST®
A Thomson Reuters business

Mat #40843825

Copyright is not claimed as to any part of the original work prepared by a United States Government officer or employee as part of that person's official duties.

This publication was created to provide you with accurate and authoritative information concerning the subject matter covered; however, this publication was not necessarily prepared by persons licensed to practice law in a particular jurisdiction. The publisher is not engaged in rendering legal or other professional advice, and this publication is not a substitute for the advice of an attorney. If you require legal or other expert advice, you should seek the services of a competent attorney or other professional.

West's and Westlaw are registered in the U.S. Patent and Trademark Office.

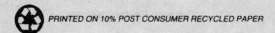 *PRINTED ON 10% POST CONSUMER RECYCLED PAPER*

PREFACE

This supplement contains amendments received through January 1, 2009.

THE PUBLISHER

January, 2009.

*

TABLE OF CONTENTS

	Page
Local Rules of the Court of Appeals for the Second Circuit	1
Local Rules of the United States District Courts for the Southern and Eastern Districts	5
United States Bankruptcy Court for the Southern District	11
United States Bankruptcy Court for the Eastern District	35
Local Rules of Practice of the United States District Court for the Northern District	39
Local Rules of Bankruptcy Procedure for the Western District	111
Federal Courts Miscellaneous Fee Schedules	115

*

LOCAL RULES OF THE COURT OF APPEALS FOR THE SECOND CIRCUIT

Including Second Circuit Amendments
Received Through January 1, 2009

PART 1. LOCAL RULES RELATING TO THE ORGANIZATION OF THE COURT

§ 0.17 Fees

The clerk charges fees and costs in accordance with 28 U.S.C. § 1913, as posted on this court's website. When fees are payable to this court, the payee name is "United States Court of Appeals for the Second Circuit".

[December 1, 1994. Amended October 17, 2005; January 9, 2009.]

§ 0.23 Dispositions by Summary Order [Superseded]

[Superseded by Second Circuit Local Rule 32.1.]

PART 2. FEDERAL RULES OF APPELLATE PROCEDURE AND LOCAL RULES SUPPLEMENTING FEDERAL RULES OF APPELLATE PROCEDURE

INTERIM LOCAL RULE 25.1
FILING AND SERVICE

(a) Documents in Digital Format.

1. *Document Defined.* For the purposes of this rule, document includes every paper submitted to the court, including forms, letters, motions, petitions and briefs but not appendices (which are governed by the requirements set forth in Local Rule 25.2).

2. *Submission Requirement.* Every document filed by a party represented by counsel must be submitted in a Portable Document Format (PDF), in addition to the required number of paper copies, unless counsel certifies that submission of the paper as a PDF document would constitute extreme hardship. A party not represented by counsel is encouraged, but not required, to submit a PDF version of every document, in addition to filing the required number of paper copies.

3. *Submission of Documents.*

(A) The PDF version of a document must be submitted as an e-mail attachment to electronic mailboxes designated according to case type. Case type is determined by the two-letter code found at the end of the docket number assigned to a case. The code, and respective mailboxes, are:

(i) ag, bk, op—agencycases@ca2.uscourts.gov. Cases involving an administrative agency, board. commission or office; tax court; bankruptcy; original proceedings; and, cases in which the United States is a party;

(ii) cr—<**criminalcases@ca2.uscourts.gov**>. Criminal cases; and

(iii) cv—<**civilcases@ca2.uscourts.gov**>. Counseled civil cases.

(B) Documents in a case that is not yet assigned a docket number must be submitted to <newcases@ca2.uscourts.gov>.

(C) A party who is pro se and a party with counsel in a pro se case may submit documents to an electronic mail box designated exclusively for pro se filers: <**prosecases@ca2.uscourts.gov**>.

(D) The e-mail in which the document is attached must set forth the following identifying information in the "Subject" or "Re" header box: the docket number; the name of the party on whose behalf the document is filed; that party's designation in the case, i.e., appellant, petitioner; and, the type of document, i.e., form, letter; and the date the document is submitted to the Court. If the document pertains to a case not yet assigned a docket number in this court, the district court docket or agency number should be included in the header box. An example of a subject line: #01–2345–cv, ABC Corp, Appellant, Letter.

4. *Content.* The PDF document must contain the entire paper. Including exhibits and any supplemental material that is bound with the paper copy filed with the court. The exhibits or supplemental material may be attached to the e-mail as a separate, clearly identified, document. A manual signature need not be included on the PDF copy.

5. *Time for Filing.* The PDF version of a document submitted pursuant to this rule must be e-mailed no later than the time for filing the required copies of the paper with the clerk.

6. *Virus Protection.* Each party submitting a PDF document must provide a signed certificate which certifies that the PDF document has been scanned for viruses and that no virus has been detected. The signed certificate must be filed along with the paper copies of the document with the clerk. A PDF version of the certificate, which need not include a manual signature, must be attached to the e-mail that includes the PDF document.

7. *Corrections.* If a document is corrected, a new e-mail attachment with the corrected version must be submitted, and the identifying information in the header box shall identify the document as corrected and include the date the corrected version of the document is submitted to the clerk.

8. *E-mail Service.* The PDF version of a document must be e-mailed to all parties represented by counsel and to those parties not represented by counsel who elected to submit PDF paper.

(b) Documents in Other Formats.

1. *Filing Requirement.* Any party, whether represented by counsel or not, who does not provide a document in PDF format, must file one unbound copy (papers not stapled or otherwise attached) of each multi-page document with the clerk. The use of paper clips or rubber bands is permitted. When only the original document is filed, the paper that comprises the document must be unbound.

[Adopted on an interim basis effective December 1, 2005. Amended effective May 27, 2008; January 20, 2009.]

INTERIM LOCAL RULE 25.2 APPENDIX ON CD–ROM

A party represented by counsel must submit every appendix on a CD–ROM, and serve a CD–ROM version on all opposing counsel, in addition to filing the required number of paper copies, unless counsel certifies that submitting a CD–ROM version of the appendix would constitute extreme hardship. A party not represented by counsel is encouraged, but not required, to submit and serve a CD–ROM version of the appendix, in addition to filing the required number of paper copies.

[Adopted on an interim basis effective January 20, 2009.]

LOCAL RULE 32.1 DISPOSITIONS BY SUMMARY ORDER

(a) Use of Summary Orders. The demands of contemporary case loads require the court to be conscious of the need to utilize judicial time effectively. Accordingly, in those cases in which decision is unanimous and each judge of the panel believes that no jurisprudential purpose would be served by an opinion (i.e., a ruling having precedential effect), the ruling may be by summary order instead of by opinion.

(b) Precedential Effect of Summary Orders. Rulings by summary order do not have precedential effect.

(c) Citation of Summary Orders.

(1) Citation to summary orders filed after January 1, 2007, is permitted.

(A) In a brief or other paper in which a litigant cites a summary order, in each paragraph in which a citation appears, at least one citation must either be to the Federal Appendix or be accompanied by the notation: "(summary order)".

(B) Service of Summary Orders on Pro Se Parties. A party citing a summary order must serve a copy of that summary order together with the paper in which the summary order is cited on any party not represented by counsel unless the summary order is available in an electronic database which is publicly accessible without payment of fee (such as the database available at http://www.ca2. uscourts.gov/). If no copy is served by reason of the availability of the order on such a database, the citation must include reference to that database and the docket number of the case in which the order was entered.

(2) Citation to summary orders filed prior to January 1, 2007, is not permitted in this or any other court, except in a subsequent stage of a case in which the summary order has been entered, in a related case, or in any case for purposes of estoppel or res judicata.

(d) **Legend.** Summary orders filed after January 1, 2007, shall bear the following legend:

SUMMARY ORDER

Rulings by summary order do not have precedential effect. Citation to summary orders filed after January 1, 2007, is permitted and is governed by this court's Local Rule 32.1 and Federal Rule of Appellate Procedure 32.1. In a brief or other paper in which a litigant cites a summary order, in each paragraph in which a citation appears, at least one citation must either be to the Federal Appendix or be accompanied by the notation: "(summary order)". A party citing a summary order must serve a copy of that summary order together with the paper in which the summary order is cited on any party not represented by counsel unless the summary order is available in an electronic database which is publicly accessible without payment of fee (such as the database available at http://www.ca2.uscourts.gov/). If no copy is served by reason of the availability of the order on such a database, the citation must include reference to that database and the docket number of the case in which the order was entered.

COMMENT

Summary orders are issued in cases in which a precedential opinion would serve no jurisprudential purpose because the result is dictated by pre-existing precedent. Such orders are prepared chiefly for the guidance and information of counsel and parties, and the district court (or other adjudicator) that issued the ruling from which the appeal is taken, all of whom are familiar with the facts, procedural history, and issues presented for review. Summary orders are therefore often abbreviated, and may omit material required to convey a complete, accurate understanding of the disposition and/or the principles of law upon which it rests. Like the great majority of the circuits, the court has chosen to make summary orders non-precedential. Denying summary orders precedential effect does not mean that the court considers itself free to rule differently in similar cases. Non-precedential summary order are used to avoid the risk that abbreviated explanations in summary orders might result in distortions of case law. Resolving some cases by summary order allows the court to devote more time to opinions whose publication will be jurisprudentially valuable.

Effective June 26, 2007.

INTERIM LOCAL RULE 34. ORAL ARGUMENT AND SUBMISSION ON BRIEFS

(a) **Party's Statement and Submission on Briefs.**

(1) *Request for Oral Argument.* An opportunity for oral argument will be provided only upon request made pursuant to this subsection (a). This subsection (a) does not apply to appeals placed on the Non-Argument Calendar pursuant to Interim Local Rule 0.29.

(2) *Counseled Appeals.* For an appeal in which all parties are represented by counsel: counsel for all parties must confer (by any convenient means) and must file, within 14 days after the due date of the last brief, a joint statement indicating whether the parties—specifying which, if fewer than all—seek oral argument, or whether the parties agree to submit the case for decision on the briefs. Unless the Court directs otherwise, failure to timely file the joint statement will result in submission of the case for decision on the briefs.

(3) *Pro Se Appeals.* For an appeal in which at least one party appears pro se: after the due date of the last brief, the Clerk of Court will mail to each party a questionnaire asking whether the party would like to have the case decided on the briefs, or whether the party seeks oral argument. All parties must return the questionnaire within 14 days of its date. Failure

by a party to timely return the questionnaire will be deemed to mean that the party does not seek oral argument.

(b) Determination by Court Not to Hear Oral Argument. If the court, acting sua sponte, contemplates deciding an appeal without hearing oral argument, each of the parties will be given an opportunity to file a statement setting forth reasons for hearing oral argument. Subject to subsection (a), oral argument will be allowed in all cases except those in which a panel of three judges, after examination of the briefs and record, shall be of the unanimous view that oral argument is not needed for one of the following reasons:

(1) the appeal is frivolous;

(2) the dispositive issue or set of issues has been recently authoritatively decided; or

(3) the facts and legal arguments are adequately presented in the briefs and record, and the decisional process would not be significantly aided by oral argument.

(c) Number of Counsel. Only one counsel will be heard for each party on the argument of a case, except by leave of the court.

(d) Time Allotments. The judge scheduled to preside over the panel will set the time allowed for argument by each party after considering the appellant's brief and each party's request for argument time. Normally, ten or fifteen minutes will be allotted to each side. Parties on the same side of an appeal may be obliged to divide the time allotted to their side. Arguments in pro se appeals are normally five minutes per side. The clerk will notify counsel and pro se parties of all such time allotments.

(e) Postponement of Argument. Except in the event of an emergency, such as unforeseen illness of counsel, an application to postpone the date for oral argument will ordinarily not be favorably entertained. Engagement of counsel in courts (other than the Supreme Court of the United States) or administrative hearings will not be considered good cause for postponement. The date for oral argument may not be postponed by stipulation.

[December 1, 1994. Amended effective August 27, 2007.]

LOCAL RULES OF THE UNITED STATES DISTRICT COURTS FOR THE SOUTHERN AND EASTERN DISTRICTS OF NEW YORK

Including Amendments Received Through January 1, 2009

LOCAL CIVIL RULES

RULE 1.5 DISCIPLINE OF ATTORNEYS

(a) Committee on Grievances. The chief judge shall appoint a committee of the board of judges known as the Committee on Grievances, which under the direction of the chief judge shall have charge of all matters relating to the discipline of attorneys. The chief judge shall appoint a panel of attorneys who are members of the bar of this court to advise or assist the Committee on Grievances. At the direction of the Committee on Grievances or its chair, members of this panel of attorneys may investigate complaints, may prepare and support statements of charges, or may serve as members of hearing panels.

(b) Grounds for Discipline or Other Relief. Discipline or other relief, of the types set forth in paragraph (c) below, may be imposed, by the Committee on Grievances, after notice and opportunity to respond as set forth in paragraph (d) below, if any of the following grounds is found by clear and convincing evidence:

(1) Any member of the bar of this court has been convicted of a felony or misdemeanor in any federal court, or in a court of any state or territory.

(2) Any member of the bar of this court has been disciplined by any federal court or by a court of any state or territory.

(3) Any member of the bar of this court has resigned from the bar of any federal court or of a court of any state or territory while an investigation into allegations of misconduct by the attorney was pending.

(4) Any member of the bar of this court has an infirmity which prevents the attorney from engaging in the practice of law.

(5)* In connection with activities in this court, any attorney is found to have engaged in conduct violative of the New York State Lawyer's Code of Professional Responsibility as adopted from time to time by the Appellate Divisions of the State of New York, and as interpreted and applied by the United States Supreme Court, the United States Court of Appeals for the Second Circuit, and this court.

(6) Any attorney not a member of the bar of this court has appeared at the bar of this court without permission to do so.

(c) Types of Discipline or Other Relief.

(1) In the case of an attorney admitted to the bar of this court, discipline imposed pursuant to paragraph (b)(1), (b)(2), (b)(3), or (b)(5) above may consist of a letter of reprimand or admonition, censure, suspension, or an order striking the name of the attorney from the roll of attorneys admitted to the bar of this court.

(2) In the case of an attorney not admitted to the bar of this court, discipline imposed pursuant to paragraph (b)(5) or (b)(6) above may consist of a letter of reprimand or admonition, censure, or an order precluding the attorney from again appearing at the bar of this court.

(3) Relief required pursuant to paragraph (b)(4) above shall consist of suspending the attorney from practice before this court.

(d) Procedure.

(1) If it appears that there exists a ground for discipline set forth in paragraph

5

(b)(1), (b)(2), or (b)(3), notice thereof shall be served by the Committee on Grievances upon the attorney concerned by first class mail, directed to the address of the attorney as shown on the rolls of this court and to the last known address of the attorney (if any) as shown in the complaint and any materials submitted therewith. Service shall be deemed complete upon mailing in accordance with the provisions of this paragraph.

In all cases in which any federal court or a court of any state or territory has entered an order disbarring or censuring an attorney or suspending the attorney from practice, whether or not on consent, the notice shall be served together with an order by the clerk of this court, to become effective twenty-four days after the date of service upon the attorney, disbarring or censuring the attorney or suspending the attorney from practice in this court upon terms and conditions comparable to those set forth by the other court of record. In all cases in which an attorney has resigned from the bar of any federal court or of a court of any state or territory while an investigation into allegations of misconduct by the attorney was pending, even if the attorney remains admitted to the bar of any other court, the notice shall be served together with an order entered by the clerk for this court, to become effective twenty-four days after the date of service upon the attorney, deeming the attorney to have resigned from the bar of this court. Within twenty days of the date of service of either order, the attorney may file a motion for modification or revocation of the order. Any such motion shall set forth with specificity the facts and principles relied upon by the attorney as showing cause why a different disposition should be ordered by this court. The timely filing of such a motion will stay the effectiveness of the order until further order by this court. If good cause is shown to hold an evidentiary hearing , the Committee on Grievances may proceed to impose discipline or to take such other action as justice and this rule may require.

In all other cases, the notice shall be served together with an order by the Committee on Grievances directing the attorney to show cause in writing why discipline should not be imposed. If the attorney fails to respond in writing to the order to show cause, or if the response fails to show good cause to hold an evidentiary hearing, the Committee on Grievances may proceed to impose discipline or to take such other action as justice and this rule may require. If good cause is shown to hold an evidentiary hearing, the Committee on Grievances may direct such a hearing pursuant to paragraph (d)(4) below.

(2) In the case of a ground for discipline set forth in paragraph (b)(2) or (b)(3) above, discipline may be imposed unless the attorney concerned establishes by clear and convincing evidence (i) that there was such an infirmity of proof of misconduct by the attorney as to give rise to the clear conviction that this court could not consistent with its duty accept as final the conclusion of the other court, or (ii) that the procedure resulting in the investigation or discipline of the attorney by the other court was so lacking in notice or opportunity to be heard as to constitute a deprivation of due process, or (iii) that the imposition of discipline by this court would result in grave injustice.

(3) Complaints in writing alleging any ground for discipline or other relief set forth in paragraph (b) above shall be directed to the chief judge, who shall refer such complaints to the Committee on Grievances. The Committee on Grievances, by its chair, may designate an attorney, who may be selected from the panel of attorneys established pursuant to paragraph (a) above, to investigate the complaint, if it deems investigation necessary or warranted, and to prepare a statement of charges, if the Committee deems that necessary or warranted. Complaints, and any files based on them, shall be treated as confidential unless otherwise ordered by the chief judge for good cause shown.

(4) A statement of charges alleging a ground for discipline or other relief set forth in paragraph (b)(4), (b)(5), or (b)(6) shall be served upon the attorney concerned by certified mail, return receipt requested, directed to the address of the attorney as shown on the rolls of this court and to the last known address of the attorney (if any) as shown in the complaint and any materials submitted therewith, together with an order by the Committee on Grievances directing the attorney to show cause in writing why discipline or other relief should not be imposed. Upon the respondent attorney's answer to the charges the matter will be designated by the Committee on Grievances for a prompt evidentiary hearing before a magistrate judge of the court or before a panel of three

attorneys, who may be selected from the panel of attorneys established pursuant to paragraph (a) above. The magistrate judge or panel of attorneys conducting the hearing may grant such pre-hearing discovery as they determine to be necessary, shall hear witnesses called by the attorney supporting the charges and by the respondent attorney, and may consider such other evidence included in the record of the hearing as they deem relevant and material. The magistrate judge or panel of attorneys conducting the hearing shall report their findings and recommendations in writing to the Committee on Grievances and shall serve them upon the respondent attorney and the attorney supporting the charges. After affording the respondent attorney and the attorney supporting the charges an opportunity to respond in writing to such report, or if no timely answer is made by the respondent attorney, or if the Committee on Grievances determines that the answer raises no issue requiring a hearing, the Committee on Grievances may proceed to impose discipline or to take such action as justice and this rule may require.

(e) **Reinstatement.** Any attorney who has been suspended or precluded from appearing in this court or whose name has been struck from the roll of the members of the bar of this court may apply in writing to the chief judge, for good cause shown, for the lifting of the suspension or preclusion or for reinstatement to the rolls. The chief judge shall refer such application to the Committee on Grievances. The Committee on Grievances may refer the application to a magistrate judge or hearing panel of attorneys (who may be the same magistrate judge or panel of attorneys who previously heard the matter) for findings and recommendations, or may act upon the application without making such a referral. Absent extraordinary circumstances, no such application will be granted unless the attorney seeking reinstatement meets the requirements for admission set forth in Local Civil Rule 1.3(a).

(f) **Remedies for Misconduct.** The remedies provided by this rule are in addition to the remedies available to individual judges and magistrate judges under applicable law with respect to lawyers appearing before them. Individual judges and magistrate judges may also refer any matter to

the chief judge for referral to the Committee on Grievances to consider the imposition of discipline or other relief pursuant to this rule.

(g) **Notice to Other Courts.** When an attorney is known to be admitted to practice in the court of any state or territory, or in any other federal court, and has been convicted of any crime or disbarred, precluded from appearing, suspended or censured in this court, the clerk shall send to such other court or courts a certified copy of the judgment of conviction or order of disbarment, preclusion, suspension or censure, a certified copy of the court's opinion, if any, and a statement of the attorney's last known office and residence address.

[Source: Former Local General Rule 4.]

Amended effective May 2, 2001; April 15, 2005; May 18, 2007.

* Publisher's Note: On or about December 18, 2008, the Court issued the following notice:

COURT NOTICE

The Courts have adopted revisions to Local Rule 1.5(b)(5). Prior to its taking effect the public is invited to comment.

Proposed New Local Rule 1.5(b)(5):

In connection with activities in this court, any attorney is found to have engaged in conduct violative of the New York State Lawyer's Code of Professional Responsibility as adopted from time to time by the Appellate Divisions of the State of New York. In interpreting the Code, in the absence of binding authority from the United States Supreme Court or the United States Court of Appeals for the Second Circuit, this court, in the interests of comity and predictability, will give due regard to decisions of the New York Court of Appeals and other New York State courts, absent significant federal interests.

Background and Reason for Recommendation:

A "Report on Deference by Federal Courts Sitting in New York to State Court Interpretations of Attorney Ethics Rules," prepared by the Advisory Group to the New York Federal-State Judicial Council, recommends that federal courts sitting in New York modify their current approach and adopt a special comity-based deference to state court interpretations of New York attorney conduct rules, in particular the already decided or predictively likely interpretations of the New York Court of Appeals. Under this special deference standard, New York federal courts would follow state court decisions construing New York attorney ethics rules as a matter of comity absent an overriding federal policy interest. Such an overriding policy interest would include undue restriction on the constitutional privilege to participate in federal court litigation in New York without being admitted in New York.

There are three reasons for the recommended change: (1) most other federal districts accord deference to state court interpretations of state attorney ethics rules, (2) the lack of such deference can result in conflicting rules in federal and state courts, and (3) an even more conclusive Erie-style adherence to highest state court decisions is favored by various committees of the Judicial Conference of the United States, including the Committee on Rules of Practice and Procedure, commonly referred to as the "Standing Committee." The Advisory Group recommends that the federal courts

sitting in New York should adopt a greater degree of deference to the interpretations of the New York State Lawyer's Code of Professional Conduct by the New York state courts, and in particular by the New York Court of Appeals.

Comments to the above are to be submitted, in writing, on or before the close of business, Friday, January 16, 2009 which is the effective date of the amendments to Local Rule 1.5(b)(5).

ADMINISTRATIVE ORDERS—EASTERN DISTRICT

ADMINISTRATIVE ORDER 2004–05. REQUESTS TO SEAL DOCUMENTS

WHEREAS the Court intends to establish a uniform procedure for the submission of requests by litigants or counsel who wish to file a document under seal; and

WHEREAS no civil case document submitted for filing, except for documents not served on defendants pursuant to provisions of the False Claims Act, 31 U.S.C. § 3730(b), will be sealed absent the express authorization of the assigned district judge or magistrate judge; and

WHEREAS in criminal cases, except for an indictment or an information sealed by the grand jury, no documents submitted by either the government or defense counsel after the public filing of an indictment or information will be sealed absent the express authorization of the assigned district judge or magistrate judge; it is

ORDERED as follows:

1.) The moving litigant or counsel who wishes to file a document under seal must provide to the Clerk's Office, on the form annexed, either a.) the case caption, docket number, assigned judge, and date of the order that authorized filing under seal; or, b.) if there is no such preexisting order, the statute, regulation, or other legal basis that authorizes filing under seal.

2.) The United States Attorney's Office may continue to follow existing procedures for sealing criminal case documents of all kinds pre-indictment; this Administrative Order and form will apply only to requests to seal documents made by either the government or defense counsel after the public filing of an indictment or information.

3.) Nothing in this Administrative Order is intended to preclude the right of any party to bring a formal motion before the assigned judicial officer for leave to file a particular document or documents under seal and/or ex parte.

4.) Any party or person who believes that a filing should not have been made under seal, may raise that question with the Court by letter, with copies served on all parties.

SO ORDERED.

Dated: April 20, 2004.

APPLICATION FOR LEAVE TO FILE DOCUMENT UNDER SEAL

TO: Clerk's Office

UNITED STATES DISTRICT COURT
EASTERN DISTRICT OF NEW YORK

APPLICATION FOR LEAVE
TO FILE DOCUMENT UNDER SEAL
* * * * *

_____

   v.

                           _____

                       Docket Number

_____

* * * * *

SUBMITTED BY: Plaintiff _____ Defendant _____ DOJ _____

Name: _____

Firm Name: _____

Address: _____

Phone Number: _____

E–Mail Address: _____

INDICATE UPON THE PUBLIC DOCKET SHEET: YES ? NO ?

If yes, state description of document to be entered on docket sheet: _____

_____

_____

A) If pursuant to a prior Court Order:

Docket Number of Case in Which Entered: _____

Judge/Magistrate Judge: _____

Date Entered: _____

_____

B) If a new application, the statute, regulation, or other legal basis that authorizes filing under seal: _____

_____

ORDERED SEALED AND PLACED IN THE CLERK'S OFFICE, MAY NOT BE UNSEALED UNLESS ORDERED BY THE COURT.

DATED: _____, NEW YORK

_____

U.S. DISTRICT JUDGE/U.S. MAGISTRATE JUDGE

RECEIVED IN CLERK'S OFFICE: _____ DATE

MANDATORY CERTIFICATION OF SERVICE:

A.) ___ A copy of this application either has been or will be promptly served upon all parties to this action, B.) ___ Service is excused by 31 U.S.C. 3730(b), or by the following other statute or regulation: _____ ; or C.) ___This is a criminal document submitted, and flight public safety, or security are significant concerns. (Check one)

_____   _____

DATE   SIGNATURE

*

UNITED STATES BANKRUPTCY COURT FOR THE SOUTHERN DISTRICT OF NEW YORK

Including Amendments Received Through
January 1, 2009

GENERAL ORDERS OF THE BANKRUPTCY COURT FOR THE SOUTHERN DISTRICT OF NEW YORK

GENERAL ORDER M–361. VACATING GENERAL ORDER M–308 (ADOPTION OF INTERIM BANKRUPTCY RULES AND FORMS)

WHEREAS, the Judicial Conference of the United States—in 2005—promulgated Interim Rules and Official Forms (collectively, the "2005 Interim Rules") to implement the Bankruptcy Abuse Prevention and Consumer Protection Act of 2005 (the "Act");

WHEREAS, this Court, by means of **General Order M–308** (signed October 11, 2005), adopted the 2005 Interim Rules in their entirety and mandated that such rules were to apply to cases governed by the Act (unless otherwise ordered by the Court):

WHEREAS, new and amended Federal Rules of Bankruptcy Procedure ("2008 Rules Amendments") are to take effect on December 1, 2008 assuming there is no Congressional action on the 2008 Rules Amendments before such date; and

WHEREAS, the 2008 Rules Amendments, after their effective date, are to supersede the 2005 Interim Rules; it is hereby

ORDERED that General Order M–308 is vacated, effective December 1, 2008.

Dated: New York, New York
November 24, 2008

GENERAL ORDER M–362. ADOPTION OF MODEL CHAPTER 13 PLAN AND CONFIRMATION ORDER

By resolution of the Board of Judges of the United States Bankruptcy Court for the Southern District of New York, it is decided that in all cases filed under Chapter 13 of the Bankruptcy Code, the debtor's plan shall conform to the model Plan and the debtor's confirmation order shall conform to the model Confirmation Order adopted by the judges of this court, copies of which are attached to this order. The relevant provisions of Federal Rule of Bankruptcy Procedure 3015 and Local Rules of Bankruptcy Procedure 3015–1 and 3015–2 shall govern as to when a plan shall be filed, served and modified in a Chapter 13 case.

The model Plan and Confirmation Order shall be available in the clerk's office and on the court's web site. The court may modify the model Plan and Confirmation Order from time to time by duly adopted General Order, making the revised model Plan and Confirmation Order available in the clerk's office and on the court's web site no less than 30 days before its effective date.

Furthermore, the Chapter 13 Standing Trustee shall prepare and file a statement detailing whether Debtor's proposed plan meets the Best Interest of Creditors' Test and, if applicable, a Section 1325(b) Analysis ("Plan Analysis Statement"). The Plan Analysis Statement shall be filed on the Court's docket twenty (20) days after the deadline to file proof(s) of claim. A Chapter 13 Plan may be confirmed prior to the filing of the Plan Analysis Statement if it appears to the satisfaction of the court that the Chapter 13 Plan is confirmable.

NOW, THEREFORE, IT IS ORDERED that the model Chapter 13 Plan and Confirmation Order shall apply to all Chapter 13 plans filed and all Chapter 13 confirmation orders signed on or after January 5, 2009.

Dated: New York, New York
 November 26, 2008.

Last Updated: 11/26/2008

Attorney name

Firm name (if applicable)

Attorney address

Attorney city, state zip

Attorney phone number, Attorney fax number

Attorney e-mail

UNITED STATES BANKRUPTCY COURT
SOUTHERN DISTRICT OF NEW YORK

--- x

In re   Case No. –   (   )

            ,   **CHAPTER 13 PLAN**

                            Debtor(s).
SSN xxx-xx-___   SSN xxx-xx- ___
--- x

Plan Definitions: If this is a joint case, use of the term "Debtor" shall also mean Debtors. The term "Trustee" shall always refer to Jeffrey L. Sapir, the Chapter 13 Standing Trustee for this court, or his substitute. The term "Bankruptcy Rule" shall refer to the Federal Rules of Bankruptcy Procedure. The term "Local Rule" shall refer to the Local Rules of Bankruptcy Procedure of the United States Bankruptcy Court for the Southern District of New York. The term "Petition" refers to Debtor's bankruptcy petition filed with the court on _____, 20___. The term "Real Property Used as a Principal Residence" includes cooperative apartments.

☐ This is an Amended or Modified Plan. The reasons for filing this Amended or Modified Plan are:

_____

In all respects, this Plan shall comply with the provisions of the Bankruptcy Code, Bankruptcy Rules and Local Rules.

Section A Plan Payments and Payment Duration	The future earnings of Debtor are submitted to the supervision and control of the Trustee. Debtor will make the first Plan payment no later than thirty (30) days after the date this Petition was filed. The Debtor shall make ___ [number] monthly payments to the Trustee as follows:

$ ___ each month, from [month] _____, 20___ through [month] _____, 20___.
$ ___ each month, from [month] _____, 20___ through [month] _____, 20___.
$ ___ each month, from [month] _____, 20___ through [month] _____, 20___.

☐ Lump-sum payment(s) in the following amount(s):

$ _____ on _____, 20___; or, if applicable (See Section I(3) below), tax refunds as follows: ___ % or amount not to exceed $ _____ for each of the following years:

_____

Pursuant to 11 U.S.C. § 1325(b)(4), the applicable commitment period is ___ months.

Payment Terms	The Debtor will pay the amounts listed above to the Trustee by bank check, certified check, teller's check, or money order sent to the following address:

        Jeffrey L. Sapir, Esq., Chapter 13 Trustee
        399 Knollwood Road, Suite 102
        White Plains, New York 10603

OPTIONAL: Debtor may pay his or her Plan payments to the Trustee by way of an
employer pay order, pursuant to 11 U.S.C. § 1325(c). If Debtor selects this option, please
check here: ☐

Upon selecting this option, Debtor hereby consents to the **immediate** entry of an order
directing Debtor's employer to deduct from Debtor's wages the amount specified in this
section and transmit that amount directly to the Trustee on Debtor's behalf. Debtor also
agrees to notify the Trustee immediately upon change or termination of employment. A
proposed order outlining Debtor's intention shall be submitted to the court for consideration upon the filing of this Plan.

☐ Non–Debtor Contributions. Identify the source and monthly amount to be contributed
to the Plan from any person or entity other than the Debtor (a "Non–Debtor Contributor"): _____

Prior to confirmation of this Plan, each Non–Debtor Contributor must either (1) file an
affidavit with the court confirming the amounts that will be contributed to the Plan or (2)
consent to entry of an employer pay order for the amount to be contributed to the Plan.

Section B Trustee's Fee	Pursuant to 28 U.S.C. § 586(e), the Trustee may collect the percentage fee from all payments and property received, not to exceed 10%.
Section C Loss Mitigation (Optional)	☐ By checking this box, the Debtor expresses an interest in discussing loss mitigation (such as a loan modification, loan refinance, short sale, or surrender in full satisfaction) concerning the Debtor's Real Property Used as a Principal Residence. List the property and/or the Secured Creditor(s) below

*This section
applies only
to the Debtor's
Real Property
Used as a
Principal
Residence.*   _____

The Debtor hereby permits the Secured Creditor(s) listed above to contact (check
all that apply):

    ☐ The Debtor directly.
    ☐ Debtor's bankruptcy counsel.
    ☐ Other: _____.

(Debtor is not required to dismiss this bankruptcy Petition during the loss mitigation
discussions. Any agreement reached during the loss mitigation discussions may be
approved pursuant to an amended plan, and the terms may be set forth in Section H,
below.)

Section D Treatment of Claims	Except as otherwise ordered by the court, the Trustee will make disbursements to creditors after the court enters an order confirming this Plan. Unless otherwise provided in Section H (below), disbursements by the Trustee shall be pro rata as outlined below.
☐ See Section H, Varying Provisions.	
Category 1 Attorney's Fees pursuant to 11 U.S.C. § 507(a)(2).	**Attorney's fees.** Counsel for the Debtor has received a prepetition retainer of $ _____, to be applied against fees and costs incurred. Fees and costs exceeding the retainer shall be paid from funds held by the Chapter 13 Trustee as an administrative expense after application to and approval by the court pursuant to Bankruptcy Rule 2016.
☐ Not Applicable.	
Category 2 Claims Secured by a Mortgage on the Debtor's Real Property Used as a Prin- cipal Residence ☐ Not Applicable.	Category 2 applies only to claims secured by a mortgage on the Debtor's Real Property Used as a Principal Residence. Category 2 Definitions: For the purposes of this Category 2, any reference to the term "Secured Creditor" means mortgagees, a creditor whose interest is secured by a mortgage on Debtor's real property, a holder and/or servicer of a claim secured by a lien, mortgage and/or deed of trust and/or any other similarly situated creditor, servicing agent and/or their assigns. The term "Mortgage" shall include references to mortgages, liens, deeds of trust and any other similarly situated interest in the Debtor's Real Property Used as a

Principal Residence. The term "Contract" shall refer to any contract or similar agreement pertaining to the Mortgage. The term "Prepetition Arrearages" shall refer to an amount owed by the Debtor to the Secured Creditor prior to the filing of Debtor's petition. The term "Post–Petition Payment" means any payment that first becomes due and payable by the Debtor to the Secured Creditor after the filing of the petition pursuant to the Mortgage or Contract.

☐ See Section H, Varying Provisions.

Confirmation of this Plan shall impose an affirmative duty on the Secured Creditor and Debtor to do all of the following, as ordered:

(a) Prepetition Arrearages.

(i) For purposes of this Plan, Prepetition Arrearages shall include all sums included in the allowed claim and shall have a "0" balance upon entry of the Discharge Order in this case. In the event that a Secured Creditor listed in this section fails to timely file a proof of claim in this case, by this Plan the Debtor shall be deemed to have timely filed a proof of claim on behalf of each such Secured Creditor pursuant to 11 U.S.C. § 501(c), in the amount set forth below in Section D, Category 2(a)(iv).

(ii) No interest will be paid on Prepetition Arrearages unless otherwise stated.

(iii) Payments made by the Trustee on Debtor's Prepetition Arrearages shall be applied **only** to those Prepetition Arrearages and not to any other amount owed by Debtor to the Secured Creditor.

(iv) Information Regarding the Arrearages.

Secured Creditor & Property Description	Value of Collateral and Valuation Method	Arrearage Amount	Arrearage Owed As Of
[Name or state "none"]	$[Value] [Valuation method]	$[Amount]	[Date]
[Address and Brief property description]			
[Add rows as needed]			

(v) If Debtor pays the amount(s) specified in section (iv) (above), while making all required Post–Petition Payments (see below), Debtor's mortgage will be reinstated according to its original terms, extinguishing any right of the Secured Creditor to recover any amount alleged to have arisen prior to the filing of Debtor's petition.

(b) Post–Petition Payments.

Debtor shall pay the following Post–Petition Payments directly to the Secured Creditor listed below during the pendency of the Plan:

Secured Creditor & Property Description	Payment Amount	Payment Timing
[Name or state "none"] [Address Where Post–Petition Payments will be sent]	$[Amount]	[How Often Payment is Due]
[Add rows as needed]		

A Secured Creditor receiving Post–Petition Payments directly from the Debtor pursuant to this section must comply with Section E(1), below, with regard to any Notice of Contract Change (as defined in Section E(1)). The Debtor shall make the Post–Petition Payments in the amount set forth on the most recent Notice of Contract Change.

(c) Return and/or Reallocation of Distribution Payment Made to Secured Creditor.

If a Secured Creditor withdraws its claim, the sum allocated towards the payment of the Secured Creditor's claim shall be distributed by the Trustee to Debtor's remaining creditors. If the Secured Creditor has received monies from the Trustee (Distribution Payment) and returns those monies to the Trustee, the monies returned shall be distributed to the Debtor's remaining creditors. If Debtor has proposed a plan that repays his or her creditors in full, then these monies will be returned to the Debtor.

(d) Important Additional Provisions.

Secured Creditors in Category 2 must comply with the "Additional Terms Applicable to Creditors and Secured Creditors" in Section E, below, regarding the following: (1) any claim for additional amounts during the pendency of the Debtor's case due to a change in the terms of the Mortgage; (2) any claim for Outstanding Obligations (defined below) that may arise during the pendency of the Debtor's case; or (3) any claim for compensation of services rendered or expenses incurred by the Secured Creditor during the pendency of the Debtor's case. Failure to comply with Section E may result in disallowance of such claims.

Category 3
Executory Contracts & Unexpired Leases

Pursuant to 11 U.S.C. § 1322(b), Debtor assumes or rejects the following unexpired lease(s) or executory contract(s). For an executory contract or unexpired lease with an arrearage to cure, the arrearage will be cured in the Plan with regular monthly payments to be paid directly to the creditor or landlord ("Creditor") by the Debtor. The arrearage amount will be adjusted to the amount set forth in the Creditor's proof of claim, unless an objection to such amount is filed, in which event it shall be adjusted to the amount allowed by the court.

☐ Not
Applicable.

☐ See Section
H, Varying
Provisions.

(a) Assumed.

Creditor & Property Description	Estimated Arrearage Amount	Arrearage Through Date
[Creditor name or state "none"]	$*[Amount]*	*[Date]*
[Address and brief property description]		
[Add rows as needed]		

(b) Rejected.

Creditor & Property Description	Estimated Arrearage Amount	Arrearage Through Date
[Creditor name or state "none"]	$*[Amount]*	*[Date]*
[Address and brief property description]		
[Add rows as needed]		

(c) Post–Petition Payments for Assumed Executory Contracts and Unexpired Leases.

Debtor shall make the following Post–Petition Payments directly to the Creditor:

Creditor & Property Description	Payment Amount	Payment Timing
[Creditor name or state "none"]	$*[Amount to be paid]*	*[How Often Payment is Due]*
[Address Post–Petition Payments will be sent]		
[Add rows as needed]		

A Creditor receiving Post–Petition Payments directly from the Debtor pursuant to this section must comply with Section E(1), below, with regard to any Notice of Contract Change (as defined in Section E(1)). The Debtor shall make the Post–Petition Payments in the amount set forth on the most recent Notice of Contract Change.

(d) Important Additional Provisions.

Creditors in Category 3 must comply with the "Additional Terms Applicable to Creditors and Secured Creditors" in Section E, below, regarding any of the following: (1) any claim for additional amounts during the pendency of the Debtor's case due to a change in the terms of the executory contract or unexpired lease; (2) any claim for Outstanding Obligations (defined below) that may arise during the pendency of the Debtor's case; or

15

(3) any claim for compensation of services rendered or expenses incurred by the Creditor during the pendency of the Debtor's case. Failure to comply with Section E may result in disallowance of such claims.

Category 4 Claims Secured by Personal Property, a Combination of Personal and Real Property, and Real Property Not Used as Debtor's Principal Residence

Category 4 applies to claims secured by personal property, a combination of personal and real property, and real property not used as the Debtor's principal residence.

Category 4 Definitions: The term "Secured Claim" shall refer to claims secured by personal property, a combination of personal and real property, and real property not used as the Debtor's principal residence. For purposes of this Category 4, any reference to the term "Secured Creditor" shall include, in addition to the definition of Secured Creditor in Category 2, any creditor whose interest is secured by an interest in any of the Debtor's property.

(a) List of Category 4 Claims.

☐ Not Applicable.

Pursuant to 11 U.S.C. § 1325(a), the Secured Creditor listed below shall be paid the amount shown as their Secured Claim under this Plan. However, if the amount listed in the Secured Creditor's proof of claim is less than the amount of the Secured Claim listed below, the lesser of the two amounts will be paid. In the event that a Secured Creditor listed below fails to timely file a proof of claim in this case, by this Plan the Debtor shall be deemed to have timely filed a proof of claim on behalf of each such Secured Creditor, in the amount set forth below.

☐ See Section H, Varying Provisions.

Creditor and Property Description	Debt Amount	Value of Collateral and Valuation Method	Amount To Be Paid on Claim	Interest Rate
[name, property address and description or state "none"]	*$[Amount]*	*$[value] [valuation method]*	*$[Amount to be paid or amount to pay debt in full]*	*[Interest rate, even if zero]*

[Add rows as needed]

(b) Adequate Protection.

If applicable, adequate protection shall be provided as follows: _____

[describe and provide the basis for calculation, or state not applicable]

(c) Post–Petition Payments.

Debtor shall pay the following Post–Petition Payments directly to the Secured Creditor listed below during the pendency of the Plan:

Secured Creditor & Property Description	Payment Amount	Payment Timing
[Name or state "none"] *[Address Where Post–Petition Payments will be sent]*	*$[Amount]*	*[How Often Payment is Due]*

[Add rows as needed]

A Secured Creditor receiving Post–Petition Payments directly from the Debtor pursuant to this section must comply with Section E(1), below, with regard to any Notice of Contract Change (as defined in Section E(1)). The Debtor shall make the Post–Petition Payments in the amount set forth on the most recent Notice of Contract Change.

(d) Return and/or Reallocation of Distribution Payment Made to Secured Creditor.

If a Secured Creditor withdraws its claim, the sum allocated towards the payment of the Secured Creditor's claim shall be distributed by the Trustee to Debtor's remaining creditors. If the Secured Creditor has received monies from the Trustee (Distribution Payment) and returns those monies to the Trustee, the monies returned shall be distributed to the Debtor's remaining creditors. If Debtor has proposed a plan that repays his or her creditors in full, then these monies will be returned to the Debtor.

(e) Important Additional Provisions.

Secured Creditors in Category 4 must comply with the "Additional Terms Applicable to Creditors and Secured Creditors" in Section E, below, regarding the following: (1) any claim for additional amounts during the pendency of the Debtor's case due to a change in the terms of the Contract; (2) any claim for Outstanding Obligations (defined below) that may arise during the pendency of the Debtor's case; or (3) any claim for compensation of services rendered or expenses incurred by the Secured Creditor during the pendency of the Debtor's case. Failure to comply with Section E may result in disallowance of such claims.

Category 5
Priority, Unsecured Claims

All allowed claims entitled to *pro rata* priority treatment under 11 U.S.C. § 507 shall be paid in full in the following order:

(a) Unsecured Domestic Support Obligations.

☐ Not Applicable.

☐ See Section H, Varying Provisions.

Debtor shall remain current on all such obligations that come due after filing the Debtor's Petition. Unpaid obligations incurred before the Petition date are to be cured by the Plan payments.

Creditor Status	Estimated Arrearages
[Status, e.g., child, spouse, former spouse or domestic partner]	$*[Amount Owed through Date]*

[Add rows as needed]

(b) Other Unsecured Priority Claims.

Creditor	Type of Priority Debt	Amount Owed
[Creditor name or state "none"]	*[description]*	$*[Amount]*

[Add rows as needed]

Category 6
Codebtor Claims

☐ Not Applicable.

☐ See Section H, Varying Provisions.

Category 6 Definition: The term "Codebtor" refers to _____

The following Codebtor claims are to be paid pro rata until the allowed amounts of such claims are paid in full.

Creditor	Codebtor Name	Estimated Debt Amount
[Creditor name or state "none"]	*[Codebtor Name]*	$ *[Amount]*

[Add rows as needed]

Category 7
Nonpriority, Unsecured Claims.

☐ Not Applicable.

☐ See Section H, Varying Provisions.

Allowed unsecured, nonpriority claims shall be paid pro rata from the balance of payments made under the Plan.

Section E
Additional Terms Applicable to Creditors and Secured Creditors

Section E Definitions: The definitions in Section D also apply to this Section. The term "Agreement" includes any executory contract, unexpired lease, Mortgage (as defined in Section D) or Contract (as defined in Section D).

(1) Notice of Contract Change.

(a) At any time during the pendency of Debtor's case, a Creditor or Secured Creditor must file on the Claims Register and serve upon the Trustee, Debtor, and Debtor's counsel (if applicable), at least thirty (30) days before the change is to take place, or a payment at a new amount is due, a notice (the "Notice of Contract Change") outlining any change(s) in the amount owed by Debtor under any Agreement, including any change(s) in the interest rate, escrow payment requirement, insurance premiums, change in payment address or other similar matters impacting the amount owed by Debtor under such Agreement (each a "Contract Change"). Additional amounts owed by the Debtor due to a Contract Change **may be disallowed by the Court** to the extent the amounts (i) were not reflected in a Notice of Contract Change filed as required by this subsection, and (ii) exceed the amount set forth in the proof of claim filed by the Creditor or Secured Creditor or deemed filed under this Plan.

(b) Within thirty (30) days of receipt of the Notice of Contract Change (defined above), Debtor shall either adjust the Post–Petition Payment to the amount set forth in the Notice of Contract Change, or file a motion with the court, objecting to the payment amount listed in the Notice of Contract Change and the stating reasons for the objection.

(2) Notice of Outstanding Obligations.

(a) At any time during the pendency of the Debtor's case, a Creditor or Secured Creditor shall file on the Claims Register and serve upon the Trustee, Debtor, and Debtor's counsel (if applicable) a notice containing an itemization of any obligations arising after the filing of this case that the Creditor or Secured Creditor believes are recoverable against the Debtor or against the Debtor's property (the "Outstanding Obligations"). Outstanding Obligations include, but are not limited to, all fees, expenses, or charges incurred in connection with any Agreement, such as any amounts that are due or past due related to unpaid escrow or escrow arrearages; insurance premiums; appraisal costs and fees; taxes; costs associated with the maintenance and/or upkeep of the property; and other similar items. Within thirty (30) days after the date such Outstanding Obligations were incurred, a Notice of Outstanding Obligations shall be filed on the Claims Register, sworn to by the Creditor or Secured Creditor pursuant to 28 U.S.C. § 1746, referencing the paragraph(s) (or specific section(s) and page number(s)) in the Agreement that allows for the reimbursement of the services and/or expenses.

(b) The Debtor reserves the right to file a motion with the court, objecting to the amounts listed in the Notice of Outstanding Obligations and stating the reasons for the objection. The bankruptcy court shall retain jurisdiction to resolve disputes relating to any Notice of Outstanding Obligations.

(3) Application for Reimbursement of Costs and Fees of Professionals. Pursuant to Bankruptcy Rule 2016 and Local Rule 2016–1, a Creditor or Secured Creditor must file an application with the court if it wishes to be compensated from the Debtor or the estate for services rendered or expenses incurred by its professionals after Debtor's filing of this Petition and before the issuance of the Notice of Discharge. The application shall include a detailed statement setting forth (1) the services rendered, time expended and expenses incurred, and (2) the amounts requested. The application shall include a statement sworn to by the Creditor or Secured Creditor pursuant to 28 U.S.C. § 1746 that references the paragraph number(s) (or specific section(s) and page number(s)) in the Agreement that allows for the reimbursement of the services and/or expenses. A Creditor or Secured Creditor may request approval of multiple fees and expenses in a single application, and any application under this subsection must be filed not later than thirty (30) days after the issuance of the Notice of Discharge in this case. **Failure to comply with the provisions in this subsection may result in disallowance by the Court of such fees and expenses.** The Debtor reserves the right to object to any application filed under this subsection. This subsection will not apply to the extent that the court has previously approved a Creditor or Secured Creditor's fees or expenses pursuant to an order or conditional order.

Section F Lien Retention	Except those expunged by order after appropriate notice pursuant to a motion or adversary proceeding, a Secured Creditor shall retain its liens as provided in 11 U.S.C. § 1325(a).
Section G Surrendered Property	Debtor surrenders the following property and upon confirmation of this Plan or as otherwise ordered by the court, bankruptcy stays are lifted as to the collateral to be surrendered.
☐ Not Applicable.	

Claimant	Property To Be Surrendered
[Name or state "none"]	*[Brief description of property]*
[Add rows as needed]	

Section H Varying Provisions	The Debtor submits the following provisions that vary from the Local Plan Form, Sections (A) through (G):

[Please state "none," or state the provision with reference to relevant paragraphs.]

Section I
Tax Returns,
Operating
Reports and
Tax Refunds

(1) Tax Returns. While the case is pending, the Debtor shall timely file tax returns and pay taxes or obtain appropriate extensions and send a copy of either the tax return or the extension to the Trustee pursuant to 11 U.S.C. § 521(f) within thirty (30) days of filing with the taxing authority.

(2) Operating Reports. If Debtor is self-employed or operates a business either individually or in a corporate capacity, Debtor shall provide the Trustee with monthly operating reports throughout the entirety of the case.

(3) Tax Refunds. The Debtor may voluntarily elect to contribute tax refunds as lump-sum payments in Section A of this Plan. Unless the Debtor has proposed a plan that repays his or her creditors in full, the court may order the Debtor to contribute a portion of the tax refunds to the Plan. The amount to be contributed shall be determined by the court on a case-by-case basis.

Section J
Funding Short-
fall

Debtor will cure any funding shortfall before the Plan is deemed completed.

Section K
Debtor's Duties

(1) *Insurance.* Debtor shall maintain insurance as required by law, contract, security agreement or Order of this court.

(2) *Payment Records to Trustee.* Debtor shall keep and maintain records of payments made to Trustee.

(3) *Payment Records to Secured Creditor(s).* Debtor shall keep and maintain records of post-petition payments made to Secured Creditor(s).

(4) *Donation Receipts.* Where applicable, Debtor shall keep a record of all charitable donations made during the pendency of this case and maintain receipts received.

(5) *Domestic Support Obligation(s).* Debtor shall maintain a record of all domestic support obligation payments paid directly to the recipient pursuant to a separation agreement, divorce decree, applicable child support collection unit order or other court's order. The Debtor must also complete and sign the "Certification Regarding Domestic Support Obligations" required by General Order M–338. The Certification should be returned to the Trustee when submitting the last payment under this Plan.

(6) *Change in Address.* Debtor must notify the court and the Trustee if the address or contact information changes during the pendency of the case. Notification must be made in writing within fifteen (15) days of when the change takes place.

(7) *Disposal of Property.* Debtor shall not sell, encumber, transfer or otherwise dispose of any Real Property or personal property with a value of more than $1,000 without first obtaining court approval.

Debtor's Signature   Dated: _____, New York
                         _____, 20___.

_____   _____
           Debtor   Debtor

_____   _____
         Address   Address

Attorney's
Signature

_____   _____
     Attorney for Debtor   Date

Attorney
Certification

I, the undersigned attorney for the Debtor, hereby certify that the foregoing chapter 13 Plan conforms to the pre-approved chapter 13 plan promulgated pursuant to [Local Bankruptcy Rule ___] of the United States Bankruptcy Court for the Southern District of New York.

_____   _____
     Attorney for Debtor   Date

Attorney name

Firm name (if applicable)

Attorney address

Attorney city, state zip

Attorney phone number, Attorney fax number

Attorney e-mail

-- x

In re   Case No. –   (   )

,

Debtor(s).

SSN xxx-xx- ___   SSN xxx-xx- ___

-- x

ORDER CONFIRMING CHAPTER 13 PLAN

Definitions: If this is a joint case, use of the term "Debtor" shall also mean Debtors. The term "Trustee" shall always refer to Jeffrey L. Sapir, the Chapter 13 Standing Trustee for this court, or his substitute. The term "Bankruptcy Rule" shall refer to the Federal Rules of Bankruptcy Procedure. The term "Local Rule" shall refer to the Local Rules of Bankruptcy Procedure of the United States Bankruptcy Court for the Southern District of New York. The term "Petition" refers to Debtor's bankruptcy petition filed with the court on _____, 20___. **Other definitions used in the Debtor's Plan apply to this Order.**

The Debtor's plan was filed on _____, and (if applicable) was modified on _____ (the "Plan"). The Plan or a summary of the Plan was transmitted to creditors pursuant to Bankruptcy Rule 3015 and Local Rule 3015–1(c) and 3015–2. The Court finds that the Plan meets the requirements of 11 U.S.C. § 1325.

IT IS ORDERED THAT:

The Plan is hereby **CONFIRMED**, and the following provisions shall apply:

PAYMENTS

The Debtor shall make ___ [number] monthly payments to the Trustee as follows:

$____ each month, from [month] _____, 20___ through [month] _____, 20___.

$____ each month, from [month] _____, 20___ through [month] _____, 20___.

$____ each month, from [month] _____, 20___ through [month] _____, 20___.

☐ Lump-sum payment(s) in the following amount(s): $_____ on _____, 20___; and/or

☐ Tax refunds as follows: ___ % or amount not to exceed $_____ for each of the following years: _____.

Unless the Debtor consented in the Plan to entry of a pay order, the Debtor will pay the amounts listed above to the Trustee by bank check, certified check, teller's check, or money order sent to the following address:

Jeffrey L. Sapir, Esq., Chapter 13 Trustee
399 Knollwood Road, Suite 102
White Plains, New York 10603

DISBURSEMENTS

Disbursements by the Trustee shall be pro rata as outlined below, and as set forth more fully in the Plan.

Category 1 (Attorney's Fees). The following fees, in excess of the pre-petition retainer received, have been approved by a separate application filed pursuant to Bankruptcy Rule 2016 and have been approved by the court: _____.

Category 2 (Claims Secured by a Mortgage on the Debtor's Real Property Used as a Principal Residence). By this Order, an affirmative duty is imposed on the Secured Creditor and Debtor to do all of the following:

(a) Prepetition Arrearages.

(i) For purposes of this Plan, Prepetition Arrearages shall include all sums included in the allowed claim and shall have a "0" balance upon entry of the Discharge Order in this case.

(ii) No interest will be paid on Prepetition Arrearages unless otherwise stated.

(iii) Payments made by the Trustee on Debtor's Prepetition Arrearages shall be applied **only** to those Prepetition Arrearages and not to any other amount owed by Debtor to the Secured Creditor.

(iv) Information Regarding the Arrearages.

[Insert Table in Section D, Category 2(a)(iv) of the Plan, if applicable.]

☐ Not Applicable.

(v) If Debtor pays the amount(s) specified in section (iv) (above), while making all required Post–Petition Payments (see below), Debtor's mortgage will be reinstated according to its original terms, extinguishing any right of the Secured Creditor to recover any amount alleged to have arisen prior to the filing of Debtor's petition.

(b) Post–Petition Payments.

Debtor shall pay the following Post–Petition Payments directly to the Secured Creditor listed below during the pendency of the Plan:

[Insert Table in Section D, Category 2(b) of the Plan, if applicable.]

☐ Not Applicable.

A Secured Creditor receiving Post–Petition Payments directly from the Debtor pursuant to this section must comply with Section E(1) of the Plan, with regard to any Notice of Contract Change (as defined in Section E(1)). The Debtor shall make the Post–Petition Payments in the amount set forth on the most recent Notice of Contract Change.

(c) Return and/or Reallocation of Distribution Payment Made to Secured Creditor.

If a Secured Creditor withdraws its claim, the sum allocated towards the payment of the Secured Creditor's claim shall be distributed by the Trustee to Debtor's remaining creditors. If the Secured Creditor has received monies from the Trustee (Distribution Payment) and returns those monies to the Trustee, the monies returned shall be distributed to the Debtor's remaining creditors. If Debtor has proposed a plan that repays his or her creditors in full, then these monies will be returned to the Debtor.

Category 3 (Executory Contracts and Unexpired Leases). Pursuant to 11 U.S.C. § 1322(b), Debtor assumes or rejects the following unexpired lease(s) or executory contract(s). For an executory contract or unexpired lease with an arrearage to cure, the arrearage will be cured as provided below, with regular monthly payments to be paid directly to the creditor or landlord ("Creditor") by the Debtor.

(a) Assumed.

[Insert Table in Section D, Category 3(a) of the Plan, if applicable.]

☐ Not Applicable.

(b) Rejected.

[Insert Table in Section D, Category 3(b) of the Plan, if applicable.]

☐ Not Applicable.

(c) Post–Petition Payments for Assumed Executory Contracts and Unexpired Leases.

[Insert Table in Section D, Category 3(c) of the Plan, if applicable.]

☐ Not Applicable.

A Creditor receiving Post–Petition Payments directly from the Debtor pursuant to this section must comply with Section E(1) of the Plan, with regard to any Notice of Contract Change (as defined in Section E(1)). The Debtor shall make the Post–Petition Payments in the amount set forth on the most recent Notice of Contract Change.

Category 4 (Claims Secured by Personal Property, a Combination of Personal and Real Property, and Real Property Not Used as Debtor's Principal Residence).

(a) List of Category 4 Claims.

[Insert Table in Section D, Category 4(a) of the Plan, if applicable.]

☐ Not Applicable.

(b) Adequate Protection. The Secured Creditor received the following amounts as adequate protection post-petition and prior to confirmation: _____.

☐ Not Applicable.

(c) Post–Petition Payments.

Debtor shall pay the following Post–Petition Payments directly to the Secured Creditor listed below during the pendency of the Plan:

[Insert Table in Section D, Category 4(c) of the Plan, if applicable.]

☐ Not Applicable.

A Secured Creditor receiving Post–Petition Payments directly from the Debtor pursuant to this section must comply with Section E(1) in the Plan, with regard to any Notice of Contract Change (as defined in Section E(1)). The Debtor shall make the Post–Petition Payments in the amount set forth on the most recent Notice of Contract Change.

(d) Return and/or Reallocation of Distribution Payment Made to Secured Creditor. If a Secured Creditor withdraws its claim, the sum allocated towards the payment of the Secured Creditor's claim shall be distributed by the Trustee to Debtor's remaining creditors. If the Secured Creditor has received monies from the Trustee (Distribution Payment) and returns those monies to the Trustee, the monies returned shall be distributed to the Debtor's remaining creditors. If Debtor has proposed a plan that repays his or her creditors in full, then these monies will be returned to the Debtor.

Category 5 (Priority, Unsecured Claims). All allowed claims entitled to pro rata priority treatment under 11 U.S.C. § 507 shall be paid in full in the following order:

(a) Unsecured Domestic Support Obligations.

Debtor shall remain current on all such obligations that come due after filing the Debtor's Petition. Unpaid obligations incurred before the Petition date are to be cured as follows:

[Insert Table in Section D, Category 5(a) of the Plan, if applicable.]

☐ Not Applicable.

(b) Other Unsecured Priority Claims.

[Insert Table in Section D, Category 5(b) of the Plan, if applicable.]

☐ Not Applicable.

Category 6 (Codebtor Claims). The following Codebtor (as defined in the Plan) claims are to be paid pro rata until the allowed amounts of such claims are paid in full.

[Insert Table in Section D, Category 6 of the Plan, if applicable.]

☐ Not Applicable.

Category 7 (Nonpriority, Unsecured Claims). Allowed unsecured, nonpriority claims shall be paid pro rata from the balance of payments made under the Plan.

☐ Not Applicable.

WARNING TO CREDITORS

Section E of the Plan requires Secured Creditors and Creditors (as defined in the Plan) receiving distributions above and/or listed in Category 2, 3 and 4 of the Plan to file (1) a **Notice of Contract Change** (defined in Section E of the Plan), (2) a claim for Outstanding Obligations (a **Notice of Outstanding Obligations**, defined in Section E of the Plan), and (3) pursuant to Bankruptcy Rule 2016 and Local Rule 2016–1, an **application for reimbursement of costs and fees** incurred by their professionals post-petition and prior to the issuance of a Notice of Discharge in this case. *Failure to comply with Section E of the Plan may result in disallowance of such claims.*

DEBTOR'S DUTIES

Tax Returns. While the case is pending, the Debtor shall timely file tax returns and pay taxes or obtain appropriate extensions and send a copy of either the tax return or the extension to the Trustee pursuant to 11 U.S.C. § 521(f) within thirty (30) days of filing with the taxing authority.

Operating Reports. If Debtor is self-employed or operates a business either individually or in a corporate capacity, Debtor shall provide the Trustee with monthly operating reports throughout the entirety of the case.

Insurance. Debtor shall maintain insurance as required by law, contract, security agreement or Order of this court.

Payment Records to Trustee. Debtor shall keep and maintain records of payments made to Trustee.

Payment Records to Secured Creditor(s). Debtor shall keep and maintain records of post-petition payments made to Secured Creditor(s).

Donation Receipts. Where applicable, Debtor shall keep a record of all charitable donations made during the pendency of this case and maintain receipts received.

Domestic Support Obligation(s). Debtor shall maintain a record of all domestic support obligation payments paid directly to the recipient pursuant to a separation agreement, divorce decree, applicable child support collection unit order or other court's order. The Debtor must also complete and sign the "Certification Regarding Domestic Support Obligations" required by General Order M–338. The Certification should be returned to the Trustee when submitting the last payment under this Plan.

Change in Address. Debtor must notify the court and the Trustee if the address or contact information changes during the pendency of the case. Notification must be made in writing within fifteen (15) days of when the change takes place.

Disposal of Property. Debtor shall not sell, encumber, transfer or otherwise dispose of any real property or personal property with a value of more than $1,000 without first obtaining court approval.

ADDITIONAL AND VARYING PROVISIONS

The following, additional provisions are hereby incorporated as part of the Plan:

_____

☐ Not Applicable.

Debtor will cure any funding shortfall before the Plan is deemed completed.

Property of the estate is hereby vested in the Debtor except where the Plan specifically provides otherwise.

CONFIRMATION ORDER CONTROLS

Additional provisions set forth in the Plan shall apply unless they are inconsistent with a specific provision of this Order. If any provision of the Plan is inconsistent with this Order, the provisions of this Order shall control.

Dated: _____

GENERAL ORDER M–363.   IN RE: ADOPTION
OF INTERIM RULE 1007–I

WHEREAS, the National Guard and Reservists Debt Relief Act of 2008 (the "Act"), Pub. L. No. 110–438, has amended 11 U.S.C. § 707(b) to provide a temporary exclusion from the application of the means test for certain members of the National Guard and Reserves in chapter 7 cases that are commenced in the three-year period beginning December 19, 2008 (the effective date of the Act); and

WHEREAS, the Judicial Conference of the United States has approved and recommended the adoption of proposed Interim Rule 1007–I through a local rule or standing order;

NOW THEREFORE, the United States Bankruptcy Court for the Southern District of New York adopts Interim Rule 1007–I, which shall apply only to chapter 7 cases commenced during the three-year period beginning December 19, 2008.

Dated: December 9, 2008
New York, New York

Interim Rule 1007–I.   Lists, Schedules, Statements, and Other Documents;   Time Limits;   Expiration of Temporary Means Testing Exclusion

* * * * *

   (b) **Schedules, Statements, and Other Documents Required.**

* * * * *

   (4) Unless either: (A) § 707(b)(2)(D)(i) applies, or (B) § 707(b)(2)(D)(ii) applies and the exclusion from means testing granted therein extends beyond the period specified by Rule 1017(e), an individual debtor in a chapter 7 case shall file a statement of current monthly income prepared as prescribed by the appropriate Official Form, and, if the current monthly income exceeds the median family income for the applicable state and household size, the information, including calculations, required by § 707(b), prepared as prescribed by the appropriate Official Form.

* * * * *

   (c) **Time Limits.** In a voluntary case, the schedules, statements, and other documents required by subdivision (b)(1), (4), (5), and (6) shall be filed with the petition or within 15 days thereafter, except as otherwise provided in subdivisions (d), (e), (f), and (h), and (n) of this rule.   In an involuntary case, the list in subdivision (a)(2), and the schedules, statements, and other documents required by subdivision (b)(1) shall be filed by the debtor within 15 days of the entry of the order for relief.   In a voluntary case, the documents required by paragraphs (A), (C), and (D) of subdivision (b)(3) shall be filed with the petition.   Unless the court orders otherwise, a debtor who has filed a statement under subdivision (b)(3)(B), shall file the documents required by subdivision (b)(3)(A) within 15 days of the order for relief.   In a chapter 7 case, the debtor shall file the statement required by subdivision (b)(7) within 45 days after the first date set for the meeting of creditors under § 341 of the Code, and in a chapter 11 or 13 case no later than the date when the last payment was made by the debtor as required by the plan or the filing of a motion for a discharge under § 1141(d)(5)(B) or § 1328(b) of the Code.   The court may, at any time and in its discretion, enlarge the time to file the statement required by subdivision (b)(7).   The debtor shall file the statement required by subdivision (b)(8) no earlier than the date of the last payment made under the plan or the date of the filing of a motion for a discharge under §§ 1141(d)(5)(B), 1228(b), or 1328(b) of the Code.   Lists, schedules, statements, and other documents filed prior to the conversion of a case to another chapter shall be deemed filed in the converted case unless the court directs otherwise.   Except as provided in § 1116(3), any extension of time to file schedules, statements, and other documents required under this rule may be granted only on motion for cause shown and on notice to the United States trustee, any committee elected under § 705 or appointed under § 1102 of the Code, trustee, examiner, or other party as the court may direct. Notice of an extension shall be given to the United States trustee and to any committee, trustee, or other party as the court may direct.

* * * * *

(n) Time Limits for, and Notice to, Debtors Temporarily Excluded from Means Testing.

(1) An individual debtor who is temporarily excluded from means testing pursuant to § 707(b)(2)(D)(ii) of the Code shall file any statement and calculations required by subdivision (b)(4) no later than 14 days after the expiration of the temporary exclusion if the expiration occurs within the time specified by Rule 1017(e) for filing a motion pursuant to § 707(b)(2).

(2) If the temporary exclusion from means testing under § 707(b)(2)(D)(ii) terminates due to the circumstances specified in subdivision (n)(1), and if the debtor has not previously filed a statement and calculations required by subdivision (b)(4), the clerk shall promptly notify the debtor that the required statement and calculations must be filed within the time specified in subdivision (n)(1).

Committee Note

This rule is amended to take account of the enactment of the National Guard and Reservists Debt Relief Act of 2008, which amended § 707(b)(2)(D) of the Code to provide a temporary exclusion from the application of the means test for certain members of the National Guard and reserve components of the Armed Forces. This exclusion applies to qualifying debtors while they remain on active duty or are performing a homeland defense activity, and for a period of 540 days thereafter. For some debtors initially covered by the exclusion, the protection from means testing will expire while their chapter 7 cases are pending, and at a point when a timely motion to dismiss under § 707(b)(2) can still be filed. Under the amended rule, these debtors are required to file the statement and calculations required by subdivision (b)(4) no later than 14 days after the expiration of their exclusion.

Subdivisions (b)(4) and (c) are amended to relieve debtors qualifying for an exclusion under § 707(b)(2)(D)(ii) from the obligation to file a statement of current monthly income and required calculations within the time period specified in subdivision (c).

Subdivision (n)(1) is added to specify the time for filing of the information required by subdivision (b)(4) by a debtor who initially qualifies for the means test exclusion under § 707(b)(2)(D)(ii), but whose exclusion expires during the time that a motion to dismiss under § 707(b)(2) may still be made under Rule 1017(e). If, upon the expiration of the temporary exclusion, a debtor has not already filed the required statement and calculations, subdivision (n)(2) directs the clerk to provide prompt notice to the debtor of the time for filing as set forth in subdivision (n)(1).

GENERAL ORDER M–364. IN RE: ADOPTION OF LOSS MITIGATION PROGRAM PROCEDURES

By resolution of the Board of Judges of the United States Bankruptcy Court for the Southern District of New York, it is decided that a uniform, comprehensive, court-supervised loss mitigation program will facilitate consensual resolutions for individual debtors whose residential real property is at risk of loss to foreclosure. A loss mitigation program will avoid the need for various types of bankruptcy litigation, reduce costs to debtors and secured creditors, and enable debtors to reorganize or otherwise address their most significant debts and assets under the United States Bankruptcy Code. Accordingly, the "Loss Mitigation Program Procedures" annexed to this order are adopted, pursuant to 11 U.S.C. § 105(a).

It is also decided that the Loss Mitigation Program Procedures and forms for requesting loss mitigation shall be available in the clerk's office and on the court's web site. The Court may modify the Loss Mitigation Program Procedures from time to time by duly adopted General Order, making the revised Loss Mitigation Program Procedures available in the clerk's office and on the court's web site immediately.

NOW, THEREFORE, IT IS ORDERED that the Loss Mitigation Program Procedures are adopted, effective January 5, 2009.

Dated: New York, New York
      December 18, 2008.

LOSS MITIGATION PROGRAM PROCEDURES

I. PURPOSE

The Loss Mitigation Program is designed to function as a forum for debtors and lenders to reach consensual resolution whenever a debtor's residential property is at risk of foreclosure. The Loss Mitigation Program aims to facilitate resolution by opening the lines of communication between the debtors' and lenders' decision-makers. While the Loss Mitigation Program stays certain bankruptcy deadlines that might interfere with the negotiations or increase costs to the loss mitigation parties, the Loss Mitigation Program also encourages the parties to finalize any agreement under bankruptcy court protection, instead of seeking dismissal of the bankruptcy case.

II. LOSS MITIGATION DEFINED

The term "loss mitigation" is intended to describe the full range of solutions that may avert either the loss of a debtor's property to foreclosure, increased costs to the lender, or both. Loss mitigation commonly consists of the following general types of agreements, or a combination of them: loan modification, loan refinance, forbearance, short sale, or surrender of the property in full satisfaction. The terms of a loss mitigation solution will vary in each case according to the particular needs and goals of the parties.

III. ELIGIBILITY

The following definitions are used to describe the types of parties, properties and loans that are eligible for participation in the Loss Mitigation Program:

A. Debtor. The term "Debtor" means any individual debtor in a case filed under Chapter 7, 11, 12 or 13 of the Bankruptcy Code, including joint debtors.

B. Property. The term "Property" means any real property or cooperative apartment used as a principal residence in which an eligible Debtor holds an interest.

C. Loan. The term "Loan" means any mortgage, lien or extension of money or credit secured by eligible Property or stock shares in a residential cooperative, regardless of whether or not the Loan (1) is considered to be "subprime" or "non-traditional," (2) was in foreclosure prior to the bankruptcy filing, (3) is the first or junior mortgage or lien on the Property, or (4) has been "pooled," "securitized," or assigned to a servicer or to a trustee.

D. Creditor. The term "Creditor" refers to any holder, mortgage servicer or trustee of an eligible Loan.

IV. ADDITIONAL PARTIES

A. Other Creditors. Where it may be necessary or desirable to obtain a global resolution, any party may request, or the bankruptcy court may direct, that multiple Creditors participate in loss mitigation.

B. Co–Debtors and Third Parties. Where the participation of a co-debtor or other third party may be necessary or desirable, any party may request, or the bankruptcy court may direct, that such party participate in loss mitigation, to the extent that the bankruptcy court has jurisdiction over the party, or if the party consents to participation in loss mitigation.

C. Chapter 13 Trustee. The Chapter 13 Trustee has the duty in Section 1302(b)(4) of the Bankruptcy Code to "advise, other than on legal matters, and assist the debtor in performance under the plan." Any party may request, or the bankruptcy court may direct, the Chapter 13 Trustee to participate in loss mitigation to the extent that such participation would be consistent with the Chapter 13 Trustee's duty under the Bankruptcy Code.

D. Mediator. At any time, a Debtor or Creditor participating in the Loss Mitigation Program may request, or the bankruptcy court may order, the appointment of an independent mediator from the United States Bankruptcy Court for the Southern District of New York's Register of Mediators, which may be viewed at http://www.nysb.uscourts. gov/mediators.html. A mediator will assist in loss mitigation in accordance with these Procedures and with the United States Bankruptcy Court of the Southern District of New York Amended General Order for the Adoption of Procedures Governing Mediation of Matters in Bankruptcy Cases and Adversary Proceedings dated January 17, 1995 (General Order M–143), as amended on October 20, 1999 (General Order M–211).

V. COMMENCEMENT OF LOSS MITIGATION

Parties are encouraged to request loss mitigation as early in the case as possible, but loss mitigation may be initiated at any time, by any of the following methods:

A. By the Debtor.

1. In Section C of the Model Chapter 13 Plan, a Chapter 13 Debtor may indicate an interest in discussing loss mitigation with a particular Creditor The Creditor shall have 21 days to object. If no objection is filed, the bankruptcy court may enter an order (a "Loss Mitigation Order").

2. A Debtor may file a request for loss mitigation with a particular Creditor. The Creditor shall have 14 days to object. If no objection is filed, the bankruptcy court may enter a Loss Mitigation Order.

3. If a Creditor has filed a motion requesting relief from the automatic stay pursuant to Section 362 of the Bankruptcy Code (a "Lift–Stay Motion"), at any time prior to the conclusion of the hearing on the Lift–Stay Motion, the Debtor may file a request for loss mitigation. The Debtor and Creditor shall appear at the scheduled hearing on the Lift– Stay Motion, and the bankruptcy court will consider the loss mitigation request and any opposition by the Creditor.

B. By a Creditor. A Creditor may file a request for loss mitigation. The Debtor shall have 7 days to object. If no objection is filed, the bankruptcy court may enter a Loss Mitigation Order.

C. By the Bankruptcy Court. The bankruptcy court may enter a Loss Mitigation Order at any time, provided that the parties that will be bound by the Loss Mitigation Order (the "Loss Mitigation Parties") have had notice and an opportunity to object.

D. Opportunity to Object. Where any party files an objection, a Loss Mitigation Order shall not be entered until the bankruptcy court has held a hearing to consider the objection. At the hearing, a party objecting to loss mitigation must present specific reasons why it believes that loss mitigation would not be successful. If a party objects on the grounds that loss mitigation has been requested in bad faith, the assertion must be supported by objective reasons.

VI. LOSS MITIGATION ORDER

A. Deadlines. A Loss Mitigation Order shall contain deadlines for all of the following:

1. The date by which the Loss Mitigation Parties shall designate contact persons and disclose contact information, if this information has not been previously provided.

2. The date by which each Creditor must initially contact the Debtor.

3. The date by which each Creditor must transmit any information request to the Debtor.

4. The date by which the Debtor must transmit any information request to each Creditor.

5. The date by which a written report must be filed or the date and time set for a status conference at which a verbal report must be provided. Whenever possible, in a Chapter 13 case the status conference will coincide with the first date set for confirmation

of the Chapter 13 plan, or an adjourned confirmation hearing. Where a written report is required, it should generally be filed not later than 7 days after the conclusion of the initial loss mitigation session.

6.   The date when the loss mitigation period will terminate, unless extended.

B.   Effect.   Whenever a Loss Mitigation Order is entered, the following shall apply to the Loss Mitigation Parties:

1.   Each Creditor is authorized to contact the Debtor directly. It shall be presumed that such communications do not violate the automatic stay.

2.   Except where necessary to prevent irreparable injury, loss or damage, a Creditor shall not file a Lift–Stay Motion during the loss mitigation period. Any Lift–Stay Motion filed by the Creditor prior to the entry of the Loss Mitigation Order shall be adjourned to a date after the last day of the loss mitigation period, and the stay shall be extended pursuant to Section 362(e) of the Bankruptcy Code.

3.   In a Chapter 13 case, the deadline by which a Creditor must object to confirmation of the Chapter 13 plan shall be extended to permit the Creditor an additional 14 days after the termination of loss mitigation, including any extension of the loss mitigation period.

4.   All communications and information exchanged by the Loss Mitigation Parties during loss mitigation will be inadmissible in any subsequent proceeding pursuant to Federal Rule of Evidence 408.

VII.   DUTIES UPON COMMENCEMENT OF LOSS MITIGATION

Upon entry of a Loss Mitigation Order, the Loss Mitigation Parties shall have the following duties:

A.   Good Faith.   The Loss Mitigation Parties shall negotiate in good faith. A party that fails to participate in loss mitigation in good faith may be subject to sanctions.

B.   Contact Information.

1.   *The Debtor.*   Unless the Debtor has already done so in the Chapter 13 plan or as part of a request for loss mitigation, the Debtor shall provide written notice to each Creditor, indicating the manner in which the Creditor should contact the Debtor.

2.   *The Creditor.*   Unless a Creditor has already done so as part of a request for loss mitigation, each Creditor shall provide written notice to the Debtor, identifying the name, address and direct telephone number of the contact person who has full settlement authority.

C.   Status Report.   The Loss Mitigation Parties shall provide either a written or verbal report to the bankruptcy court regarding the status of loss mitigation within the time set by the bankruptcy court in the Loss Mitigation Order. The status report shall state whether one or more loss mitigation sessions have been conducted, whether a resolution was reached, and whether one or more of the Loss Mitigation Parties believe that additional loss mitigation sessions would be likely to result in either a partial or complete resolution. A status report may include a request for an extension of the loss mitigation period.

D.   Bankruptcy Court Approval.   The Loss Mitigation Parties shall seek bankruptcy court approval of any resolution or settlement reached during loss mitigation.

VIII.   LOSS MITIGATION PROCESS

A.   Initial Contact.   Following entry of a loss mitigation order, the contact person designated by each Creditor shall contact the Debtor and any other Loss Mitigation Party within the time set by the bankruptcy court. The Debtor may contact any other Loss Mitigation Party at any time. The purpose of the initial contact is to create a framework for the discussion at the loss mitigation session and to ensure that each of the Loss Mitigation Parties will be prepared to participate in the loss mitigation session—it is not intended to limit additional issues or proposals that may arise during the session. During the initial contact phase, the Loss Mitigation Parties should discuss the following:

1. The time and method for conducting the loss mitigation sessions.

2. The types of loss mitigation solutions under consideration by each party.

3. A plan for the exchange of required information prior to the loss mitigation session, including the due date for the Debtor to complete and return any information request or other loss mitigation paperwork that each Creditor may require. *All information should be provided at least 7 days prior to the loss mitigation session.*

B. Loss Mitigation Sessions. Loss mitigation sessions may be conducted in person, telephonically or via video conference. At the conclusion of each loss mitigation session, the Loss Mitigation Parties should discuss whether additional sessions are necessary and set the time and method for conducting any additional sessions, including a schedule for the exchange of any further information or documentation that may be required.

C. Bankruptcy Court Assistance. At any time during the loss-mitigation period, a Loss Mitigation Party may request a settlement conference or status conference with the bankruptcy court.

D. Settlement Authority. Each Loss Mitigation Party must have a person with full settlement authority present during a loss mitigation session. During a status conference or settlement conference with the bankruptcy court, the person with full settlement authority must either attend the conference in person or be available by telephone or video conference beginning 30 minutes prior to the start of the conference.

IX. DURATION, EXTENSION AND EARLY TERMINATION

A. Initial Period. The initial loss mitigation period shall be set by the bankruptcy court in the Loss Mitigation Order.

B. Extension.

1. *Agreement.* The Loss Mitigation Parties may agree to an extension of the loss mitigation period. The Loss Mitigation Parties shall request an extension in writing, filed on the docket in the main bankruptcy case and served on all parties in interest, who shall have three days to object to a request for extension of the loss mitigation period. The bankruptcy court may grant a request for extension of the loss mitigation period for cause.

2. *No Agreement.* Where a Loss Mitigation Party does not consent to the request for an extension of the loss mitigation period, the bankruptcy court shall schedule a hearing to consider whether further loss mitigation sessions are likely to be successful. The bankruptcy court may order a reasonable extension if it appears that (1) a further loss mitigation session is likely to result in a complete or partial resolution that will provide a substantial benefit to a Loss Mitigation Party, (2) the party opposing the extension has not participated in good faith or has failed in a material way to comply with these Procedures, or (3) the party opposing the extension would not be prejudiced.

C. Early Termination.

1. *Upon Request of a Loss Mitigation Party.* A Loss Mitigation Party may request that the loss mitigation period be terminated and shall state the reasons for the request. Except where immediate termination is necessary to prevent irreparable injury, loss or damage, the request shall be made on notice to all other Loss Mitigation Parties, and the bankruptcy court may schedule a hearing to consider the termination request.

2. *Dismissal of the Bankruptcy Case.*

    a. Other than at the request of a Chapter 13 Debtor, or the motion of the United States Trustee or Trustee for failure to comply with requirements under the Bankruptcy Code: Except where a Chapter 13 Debtor requests voluntary dismissal, or upon motion, a case shall not be dismissed during the loss mitigation period unless the Loss Mitigation Parties have provided the bankruptcy court with a status report that is satisfactory to the court. The bankruptcy court may schedule a further status conference with the Loss Mitigation Parties prior to dismissal of the case.

    b. Upon the request of a Chapter 13 Debtor: **A Debtor is not required to request dismissal of the bankruptcy case as part of any resolution or settlement that is**

offered or agreed to during the loss mitigation period. Where a Chapter 13 Debtor requests voluntary dismissal of the bankruptcy case during the loss mitigation period, the Debtor's dismissal request shall indicate whether the Debtor agreed to any settlement or resolution from a Loss Mitigation Party during the loss mitigation period or intends to accept an offer of settlement made by a Loss Mitigation Party during the loss mitigation period.

c. Notice: If a bankruptcy case is dismissed for any reason during the loss-mitigation period, the Clerk of the Court shall file a notice on the docket indicating that loss mitigation efforts were ongoing at the time the bankruptcy case was dismissed.

X. SETTLEMENT

The bankruptcy court will consider any agreement or resolution reached during loss mitigation (a "Settlement") and may approve the Settlement, subject to the following provisions:

1. Implementation. A Settlement may be noticed and implemented in any manner permitted by the Bankruptcy Code and Federal Rules of Bankruptcy Procedure ("Bankruptcy Rules"), including, but not limited to, a stipulation, sale, plan of reorganization or amended plan of reorganization.

2. Fees, Costs or Charges. If a Settlement provides for a Creditor to receive payment or reimbursement of any fee, cost or charge that arose from loss mitigation, such fees, costs or charges shall be disclosed to the Debtor and to the bankruptcy court prior to approval of the Settlement.

3. Signatures. Consent to the Settlement shall be acknowledged in writing by (1) the Creditor representative who participated in loss mitigation, (2) the Debtor, and (3) the Debtor's attorney, if applicable.

4. Hearing. Where a Debtor is represented by counsel, a Settlement may be approved by the bankruptcy court without further notice, or upon such notice as the bankruptcy court directs, unless additional notice or a hearing is required by the Bankruptcy Code or Bankruptcy Rules. Where a Debtor is not represented by counsel, a Settlement shall not be approved until after the bankruptcy court has conducted a hearing at which the Debtor shall appear in person.

5. Dismissal Not Required. A Debtor is not required to request dismissal of the bankruptcy case in order to effectuate a Settlement. In order to ensure that the Settlement is enforceable, the Loss Mitigation Parties should seek bankruptcy court approval of the Settlement. Where the Debtor requests or consents to dismissal of the bankruptcy case as part of the Settlement, the bankruptcy court may approve the Settlement as a "structured dismissal," if such relief complies with the Bankruptcy Code and Bankruptcy Rules.

XI. COORDINATION WITH OTHER PROGRAMS

[Provision may be added in the future to provide for coordination with other loss mitigation programs, including programs in the New York State Unified Court System.]

UNITED STATES BANKRUPTCY COURT
SOUTHERN DISTRICT OF NEW YORK
---x

In re: Chapter ____

_____,   Case No. ____–_____ (____)

Debtor(s).
---x

LOSS–MITIGATION REQUEST—BY THE DEBTOR

I am a Debtor in this case. I hereby request loss mitigation with respect to *[Identify the property, loan and creditor(s) for which you are requesting loss mitigation]*:

_____

_____

_____

SIGNATURE

I understand that if the Court orders loss mitigation in this case, I will be expected to comply with the Loss Mitigation Procedures. I agree to comply with the Loss Mitigation Procedures, and I will participate in loss mitigation in good faith. I understand that loss mitigation is voluntary for all parties, and that I am not required to enter into any agreement or settlement with any other party as part of this loss mitigation. I also understand that no other party is required to enter into any agreement or settlement with me. I understand that **I am not required to request dismissal of this case** as part of any resolution or settlement that is offered or agreed to during the loss mitigation period.

Sign: _____ Date: _____, 2008

Print Name: _____

Telephone Number: _____

E-mail address (if any): _____

_____

UNITED STATES BANKRUPTCY COURT
SOUTHERN DISTRICT OF NEW YORK

---x

In re: Chapter ____

_____,   Case No. ____–_____ (____)

Debtor(s).

---x

LOSS–MITIGATION REQUEST—BY A CREDITOR

I am a creditor (including a holder, servicer or trustee of a mortgage or lien secured by property used by the Debtor as a principal residence) of the Debtor in this case. I hereby request loss mitigation with respect to *[Identify the property, loan and creditor(s) for which you are requesting loss mitigation]*:

_____

_____

_____

SIGNATURE

I have reviewed the Loss Mitigation Procedures, and I understand that if the Court orders loss mitigation in this case, I will be bound by the Loss Mitigation Procedures. I agree to comply with the Loss Mitigation Procedures, and I will participate in loss mitigation in good faith. If loss mitigation is ordered, I agree to provide the Court with a written or verbal status report stating whether or not the parties participated in one or more loss mitigation sessions, whether or not a settlement was reached, and whether negotiations are ongoing. I agree that **I will not require the Debtor to request or cause dismissal of this case** as part of any resolution or settlement that is offered or agreed to during the loss mitigation period.

Sign: _____ Date: _____, 2008

Print Name: _____

Title: _____

Firm or Company: _____

Telephone Number: _____

E-mail address (if any): _____

UNITED STATES BANKRUPTCY COURT
SOUTHERN DISTRICT OF NEW YORK
--x
In re: Chapter ____

_____,   Case No. ____—_____ (____)

          Debtor(s).
--x

LOSS–MITIGATION ORDER

☐ A Loss Mitigation Request[1] was filed by the debtor on *[Date]* _____, 2009.

☐ A Loss Mitigation Request was filed by a creditor on *[Date]* _____, 2009.

☐ The Court raised the possibility of loss mitigation, and the parties have had notice and an opportunity to object.

Upon the foregoing, it is hereby

ORDERED, that the following parties (collectively, the "Loss Mitigation Parties") are directed to participate in loss mitigation:

  1.   The Debtor

  2.   _____, the Creditor with respect to _____ *[describe Loan and/or Property]*.

  3.   *[Additional parties, if any]*

It is further **ORDERED**, that the Loss Mitigation Parties shall comply with the Loss Mitigation Procedures annexed to this Order; and it is further

ORDERED, that the Loss Mitigation Parties shall observe the following deadlines:

  1.   Each Loss Mitigation Party shall designate contact persons and disclose contact information by _____ *[suggested time is 7 days]*, unless this information has been previously provided. As part of this obligation, **a Creditor shall furnish each Loss Mitigation Party with written notice of the name, address and direct telephone number of the person who has full settlement authority.**

  2.   Each Creditor that is a Loss Mitigation Party shall contact the Debtor within **14 days of the date of this Order.**

  3.   Each Loss Mitigation Party must make their information request, if any, within **14 days of the date of this Order.**

  4.   Each Loss Mitigation Party shall respond to an information request within **14 days after an information request is made, or 7 days prior to the Loss Mitigation Session, whichever is earlier.**

  5.   The Loss Mitigation Session shall be scheduled not later than _____ *[suggested time is within 35 days of the date of the order]*.

  6.   The loss mitigation period shall terminate on _____ *[suggested time is within 42 days of the date of the order]*, unless extended as provided in the Loss Mitigation Procedures.

It is further **ORDERED**, that a status conference will be held in this case on _____ *[suggested time is within 42 days of the date of the order]* (the "Status

Conference"). The Loss Mitigation Parties shall appear at the Status Conference and provide the Court with a verbal Status Report unless a written Status Report that is satisfactory to the Court has been filed not later than 7 days prior to the date of the Status Conference and requests that the Status Conference be adjourned or cancelled; and it is further

ORDERED, that at the Status Conference, the Court may consider a Settlement reached by the Loss Mitigation Parties, or may adjourn the Status Conference if necessary to allow for adequate notice of a request for approval of a Settlement; and it is further

ORDERED, that any matters that are currently pending between the Loss Mitigation Parties (such as motions or applications, and any objection, opposition or response thereto) are hereby adjourned to the date of the Status Conference to the extent those matters concern (1) relief from the automatic stay, (2) objection to the allowance of a proof of claim, (3) reduction, reclassification or avoidance of a lien, (4) valuation of a Loan or Property, or (5) objection to confirmation of a plan of reorganization; and it is further.

ORDERED, that the time for each Creditor that is a Loss Mitigation Party in this case to file an objection to a plan of reorganization in this case shall be extended until 14 days after the termination of the loss mitigation period, including any extension of the Loss Mitigation period.

Dated: Poughkeepsie, New York

_____, 2009

BY THE COURT

_____
United States Bankruptcy Judge

1 All capitalized terms have the meanings defined in the Loss Mitigation Procedures.

*

UNITED STATES BANKRUPTCY COURT
FOR THE EASTERN DISTRICT OF NEW YORK

Including Amendments Received Through
January 1, 2009

RULE 5005–1. FILING AND TRANSMITTAL OF PAPERS IN NON–ELECTRONIC CASES [SUPERCEDED]

[Effective July 1, 1997; amended effective May 28, 2008. Superceded effective January 1, 2009. See, now, General Order No. 536.]

SELECTED ORDERS

GENERAL ORDER NO. 534. NEW RULES AND AMENDMENTS TO THE FEDERAL RULES OF BANKRUPTCY PROCEDURE EFFECTIVE DECEMBER 1, 2008

WHEREAS, the Advisory Committee on Bankruptcy Rules prepared Interim Rules for use by the courts while it studied the Bankruptcy Abuse Prevention and Consumer Protection Act of 2005 (Pub. L. No. 109-08, 119 Stat. 23) and prepared permanent national rules through the customary three-year rulemaking process, and

WHEREAS, on September 27, 2005, this Court by General Order of the Court No. 497, In the Matter of Adoption of Interim Bankruptcy Rules, adopted the Interim Rules in their entirety without change by a majority of the Judges of this Court effective October 17, 2005, and

WHEREAS, on September 29, 2006, this Court by Administrative Order No. 506, In the Matter of Adoption of Amended Interim Bankruptcy Rule 1007, Effective October 1, 2006, adopted amended Rule 1007 of the Interim Rules, and

WHEREAS, the following new rules and amendments to the Federal Rules of Bankruptcy Procedure will take effect on December 1, 2008, unless Congress acts to the contrary: Bankruptcy Rules 1005, 1006, 1007, 1009, 1010, 1011, 1015, 1017, 1019, 1020, 2002, 2003, 2007.1, 2015, 3002, 3003, 3016, 3017.1, 3019, 4002, 4003, 4004, 4006, 4007, 4008, 5001, 5003, 6004, 7012, 7022, 7023.1, 8001, 8003, 9006, 9009, and 9024, and new Bankruptcy Rules 1021, 2007.2, 2015.1, 2015.2, 2015.3, 5008, and 6011, and

WHEREAS, the above rule amendments and new rules implement the substantive and procedural changes to the Bankruptcy Code made by the Bankruptcy Abuse Prevention and Consumer Protection Act of 2005, and

WHEREAS, except for Interim Rule 5012, (Communication of and Cooperation with Foreign Courts and Foreign Representatives), which is under study, the amendments and new rules supersede the Interim Rules adopted as local rules of this court, it is

ORDERED, that the Interim Rules adopted by this court by General Order of the Court No. 497, and Administrative Order No. 506, are hereby rescinded effective December 1, 2008, and it is

FURTHER ORDERED, that this court will retain Interim Rule 5012 [see text of Interim Rule 5012 below] until it is replaced by a permanent national rule.

Dated: Brooklyn, New York
November 25, 2008.

INTERIM RULE 5012. COMMUNICATION AND COOPERATION WITH FOREIGN COURTS AND FOREIGN REPRESENTATIVES

Except for communications for scheduling and administrative purposes, the court in any case commenced by a foreign representative shall give at least 20 days' notice of its intent to communicate with a foreign court or a foreign representative. The notice shall identify the subject of the anticipated communication and shall be given in the manner provided by Rule 2002(q). Any entity that wishes to participate in the communication shall notify the court of its intention not later than 5 days before the scheduled communication.

Amended, on an interim basis, effective October 17, 2005.

COMMITTEE NOTE
October 17, 2005

This rule is new. It implements § 1525 which was added to the Code in 2005. The rule provides an opportunity for parties in the case to take appropriate action prior to the communication between courts or between the court and a foreign representative to establish procedures for the manner of the communication and the right to participate in the communication. Participation in the communication includes both active and passive participation. Parties wishing to participate must notify the court at least 5 days before the hearing so that ample time exists to make arrangements necessary to permit the participation.

GENERAL ORDER NO. 535. ADOPTION OF INTERIM BANKRUPTCY RULE 1007–I, LISTS, SCHEDULES, STATEMENTS, AND OTHER DOCUMENTS; TIME LIMITS; EXPIRATION OF TEMPORARY MEANS TESTING EXCLUSION

WHEREAS, on october 20, 2008, the President signed the National Guard and Reservists Debt Relief Act of 2008 (the "Act"), Pub. L. No. 110–438, and

WHEREAS, the Act amends 11 U.S.C. § 707(b)(2)(D) to provide a temporary exclusion from the bankruptcy means test for certain members of the National Guard and Reserves called to active duty or homeland defense activity following September 11, 2001, for at least 90 days, and applies only to cases commenced in the three-year period beginning on December 19, 2008 (the effective date of the Act), and

WHEREAS, the Judicial Conference of the United States has approved and recommended the adoption of Interim Rule 1007–I through a local rule or standing order, it is

ORDERED, that the United States Bankruptcy Court for the Eastern District of New York adopts Interim Rule 1007–I, which shall apply only to chapter 7 cases commenced during the three-year period beginning December 19, 2008.

Dated: December 18, 2008.

Interim Rule 1007–I. Lists, Schedules, Statements, and Other Documents; Time Limits; Expiration of Temporary Means Testing Exclusion

* * * * *

(b) **Schedules, Statements, and Other Documents Required.**

* * * * *

(4) Unless either: (A) § 707(b)(2)(D)(i) applies, or (B) § 707(b)(2)(D)(ii) applies and the exclusion from means testing granted therein extends beyond the period specified by Rule 1017(e), an individual debtor in a chapter 7 case shall file a statement of current monthly income prepared as prescribed by the appropriate Official Form, and, if the current monthly income exceeds the median family income for the applicable state and household size, the information, including calculations, required by § 707(b), prepared as prescribed by the appropriate Official Form.

* * * * *

(c) **Time Limits.** In a voluntary case, the schedules, statements, and other documents required by subdivision (b)(1), (4), (5), and (6) shall be filed with the petition or within 15 days thereafter, except as otherwise provided in subdivisions (d), (e), (f), and (h), and (n) of this rule. In an involuntary case, the list in subdivision (a)(2), and the schedules, statements, and other documents required by subdivision (b)(1) shall be filed by the debtor within 15 days of the entry of the order for relief. In a voluntary case, the documents required by paragraphs (A), (C), and (D) of subdivision (b)(3) shall be filed with the petition. Unless the court orders otherwise, a debtor who has filed a statement under subdivision (b)(3)(B), shall file the documents required by subdivision (b)(3)(A) within 15 days of the order for relief. In a chapter 7 case, the debtor shall file the statement required by subdivision (b)(7) within 45 days after the first date set for the meeting of creditors under § 341 of the Code, and in a chapter 11 or 13 case no later than the date when the last payment was made by the debtor as required by the plan or the filing of a motion for a discharge under § 1141(d)(5)(B) or § 1328(b) of the Code. The court may, at any time and in its discretion, enlarge the time to file the statement required by subdivision (b)(7). The debtor shall file the statement required by subdivision (b)(8) no earlier than the date of the last payment made under the plan or the date of the filing of a motion for a discharge under §§ 1141(d)(5)(B), 1228(b), or 1328(b) of the Code. Lists, schedules, statements, and other documents filed prior to the conversion of a case to another chapter shall be deemed filed in the converted case unless the court directs otherwise. Except as provided in § 1116(3), any extension of time to file schedules, statements, and other documents required under this rule may be granted only on motion for cause shown and on notice to the United States trustee, any committee elected under § 705 or appointed under § 1102 of the Code, trustee, examiner, or other party as the court may direct. Notice of an extension shall be given to the United States trustee and to any committee, trustee, or other party as the court may direct.

* * * * *

(n) Time Limits for, and Notice to, Debtors Temporarily Excluded from Means Testing.

(1) An individual debtor who is temporarily excluded from means testing pursuant to § 707(b)(2)(D)(ii) of the Code shall file any statement and calculations required by subdivision (b)(4) no later than 14 days after the expiration of the temporary exclusion if the expiration occurs within the time specified by Rule 1017(e) for filing a motion pursuant to § 707(b)(2).

(2) If the temporary exclusion from means testing under § 707(b)(2)(D)(ii) terminates due to the circumstances specified in subdivision (n)(1), and if the debtor has not previously filed a statement and calculations required by subdivision (b)(4), the clerk shall promptly notify the debtor that the required statement and calculations must be filed within the time specified in subdivision (n)(1).

Committee Note

This rule is amended to take account of the enactment of the National Guard and Reservists Debt Relief Act of 2008, which amended § 707(b)(2)(D) of the Code to provide a temporary exclusion from the application of the means test for certain members of the National Guard and reserve components of the Armed Forces. This exclusion applies to qualifying debtors while they remain on active duty or are performing a homeland defense activity, and for a period of 540 days thereafter. For some debtors initially covered by the exclusion, the protection from means testing will expire while their chapter 7 cases are pending, and at a point when a timely motion to dismiss under § 707(b)(2) can still be filed. Under the amended rule, these debtors are required to file the statement and calculations required by subdivision (b)(4) no later than 14 days after the expiration of their exclusion.

Subdivisions (b)(4) and (c) are amended to relieve debtors qualifying for an exclusion under § 707(b)(2)(D)(ii) from the obligation to file a statement of current monthly income and required calculations within the time period specified in subdivision (c).

Subdivision (n)(1) is added to specify the time for filing of the information required by subdivision (b)(4) by a debtor who initially qualifies for the means test exclusion under § 707(b)(2)(D)(ii), but whose exclusion expires during the time that a motion to dismiss under § 707(b)(2) may still be made under Rule 1017(e). If, upon the expiration of the temporary exclusion, a debtor has not already filed the required statement and calculations, subdivision (n)(2) directs the clerk to provide prompt notice to the debtor of the time for filing as set forth in subdivision (n)(1).

GENERAL ORDER NO. 536. ELECTRONIC CASE FILING OF DOCUMENTS IN NON–ELECTRONIC CASES

WHEREAS, the Court having established, by General Order No. 473, dated December 26, 2002, electronic filing procedures applicable to all bankruptcy cases and adversary proceedings filed on or after January 1, 2003, and

WHEREAS, E.D.N.Y. Local Bankruptcy Rule 5005–1, *Filing and Transmittal of Papers in Non–Electronic Cases*, requires the filing of all papers in any non-electronic case to be filed in the office of the Clerk located where the Judge who is assigned to the matter regularly sits, and

WHEREAS, it is in the Court's best interest to reduce the volume of paper filings submitted to the Court, and to allow practitioners the ability to file electronically in these cases, it is

ORDERED, that effective, January 1, 2009, all pending cases in the Eastern District of New York will be deemed electronic cases, and any document filed by an attorney on or after January 1, 2009, may be filed via the Internet, and it is further

ORDERED, that this Order supercedes Section II, A, 7, *Administrative Procedures on Electronic Filing and Service of Documents*, approved by this Court's General Order No. 473, and E.D.N.Y. Local Bankruptcy Rule 5005–1.

Dated: December 18, 2008.

LOCAL RULES OF PRACTICE OF THE UNITED STATES DISTRICT COURT FOR THE NORTHERN DISTRICT OF NEW YORK

Including Amendments Received Through January 1, 2009

LOCAL RULES OF PRACTICE

SECTION I. SCOPE OF RULES—ONE FORM OF ACTION

RULE 1.1. SCOPE OF THE RULES

(a) Title and Citation. These are the Local Rules of Practice for the United States District Court for the Northern District of New York. They shall be cited as "L.R. ___."

(b) Effective Date; Transitional Provision. These Rules became effective on **January 1, 2009.** Recent amendments are noted with the phrase (Amended January 1, 2009).

(c) Scope of the Rules; Construction. These Rules supplement the Federal Rules of Civil and Criminal Procedure. They shall be construed to be consistent with those Rules and to promote the just, efficient and economical determination of every action and proceeding.

(d) Sanctions and Penalties for Noncompliance. Failure of an attorney or of a party to comply with any provision of these Rules, General Orders of this District, Orders of the Court, or the Federal Rules of Civil or Criminal Procedure shall be a ground for imposition of sanctions.

(e) Definitions.

1. The word "court," except where the context otherwise requires, refers to the United States District Court for the Northern District of New York.

2. The word "judge" refers either to a United States District Judge or to a United States Magistrate Judge.

3. The words "assigned judge," except where the context otherwise requires, refer to the United States District Judge or United States Magistrate Judge exercising jurisdiction with respect to a particular action or proceeding.

4. The words "Chief Judge" refer to the Chief Judge or a judge temporarily performing the duties of Chief Judge under 28 U.S.C. § 136(e).

5. The word "clerk" refers to the Clerk of the Court or to a deputy clerk whom the Clerk designates to perform services of the general class provided for in Fed. R. Civ. P. 77.

6. The word "marshal" refers to the United States Marshal of this District and includes deputy marshals.

7. The word "party" includes a party's representative.

8. Reference in these Rules to an attorney for a party is in no way intended to preclude a party from appearing pro se, in which case reference to an attorney applies to the pro se litigant.

9. Where appropriate, the "singular" shall include the "plural" and vice versa.

[Amended effective January 1, 1999; January 1, 2004; January 1, 2005; January 1, 2006; January 1, 2007; January 1, 2008; January 1, 2009.]

RULE 5.4. CIVIL ACTIONS FILED IN FORMA PAUPERIS; APPLICATIONS FOR LEAVE TO PROCEED IN FORMA PAUPERIS

(a) On receipt of a complaint or petition and an application to proceed in forma pauperis, and supporting documentation as required for prisoner litigants, the Clerk shall promptly file the complaint or petition without the payment of fees and assign the action in accordance with L.R. 40.1. The Clerk shall then forward the complaint or petition, application and supporting documentation to the assigned judicial officer for a determination of the in forma pauperis application and the sufficiency of the complaint or petition and, if appropriate, to direct service by the Marshal. Prior to the Marshal serving process pursuant to 28 U.S.C. § 1915 (d) and L.R. 5.1(h), the Court shall review all actions filed pursuant to 28 U.S.C. § 1915(g) to determine whether sua sponte dismissal is appropriate. The granting of an in forma pauperis application shall not relieve a party of the obligation to pay all other fees for which that party is responsible regarding the action, including but not limited to copying and/or witness fees.

(b) Whenever a fee is due for a civil action subject to the Prison Litigation Reform Act ("PLRA"), the prisoner must comply with the following procedure:

1. (A) Submit a signed, fully completed and properly certified in forma pauperis application; and

(B) Submit the authorization form issued by the Clerk's office.

2. (A)(i) If the prisoner **has not** fully complied with the requirements set forth in paragraph 1 above, and the action is not subject to sua sponte dismissal, a judicial officer shall, by Court order, inform the prisoner about what he or she must submit in order to proceed with such action in this District ("Order").

(ii) The Order shall afford the prisoner **thirty (30) days** in which to comply with the terms of same. If the prisoner fails to comply fully with the terms of such Order within such period of time, the Court shall dismiss the action.

(B) If the prisoner **has** fully complied with the requirements set forth in paragraph 1 above, and the action is not subject to sua sponte dismissal, the judicial officer shall review the in forma pauperis application. The granting of the application shall in no way relieve the prisoner of the obligation to pay the full amount of the filing fee.

3. After being notified of the filing of the civil action, the agency having custody of the prisoner shall comply with the provisions of 28 U.S.C. § 1915(b) regarding the filing fee due for the action.

[Amended effective January 1, 1999; February 7, 2008; January 1, 2009.]

RULE 7.1. MOTION PRACTICE

Introduction—Motion Dates and Times. Unless the Court directs otherwise, the moving party shall make its motion returnable at the **next regularly scheduled motion date at least thirty-one days from the date the moving party files and serves its motion.** The moving party shall select a return date in accordance with the procedures set forth in subdivision (b). If the return date the moving party selects is not the next regularly scheduled motion date, or if the moving party selects no return date, the Clerk will set the proper return date and notify the parties.

Information regarding motion dates and times is specified on the case assignment form that the Court provides to the parties at the commencement of the litigation or the parties may obtain this form from the Clerk's office or at the Court's webpage at "**www.nynd.uscourts.gov.**"

The Court hereby directs the Clerk to set a proper return date in motions that pro se litigants submit for filing that do not specify a return date or fail to allow for sufficient time pursuant to this Rule. Generally, the return date that the Clerk selects should not exceed 30 days from the date of filing. Furthermore, the Clerk shall forward a copy of the revised or corrected notice of motion to the parties.

(a) Papers Required. Except as otherwise provided in this paragraph, all motions and opposition to motions require a memorandum of law, supporting affidavit, and proof of service on all the parties. See L.R. 5.1(a). Additional requirements for specific types of motions, including cross-motions, see L.R. 7.1(c), are set forth in this Rule.

1. *Memorandum of Law.* No party shall file or serve a memorandum of law that exceeds twenty-five (25) pages in length, unless that party obtains leave of the judge hearing the motion prior to filing. All memoranda of law shall contain a table of contents and, wherever possible, parallel citations. Memoranda of law that contain

citations to decisions exclusively reported on computerized databases, e.g., Westlaw, Lexis, Juris, shall include copies of those decisions.

When a moving party makes a motion based upon a rule or statute, the moving party must specify in its moving papers the rule or statute upon which it bases its motion.

A memorandum of law is required for all motions except the following:

(A) a motion pursuant to Fed. R. Civ. P. 12(e) for a more definite statement;

(B) a motion pursuant to Fed. R. Civ. P. 15 to amend or supplement a pleading;

(C) a motion pursuant to Fed. R. Civ. P. 17 to appoint next friend or guardian ad litem;

(D) a motion pursuant to Fed. R. Civ. P. 25 for substitution of parties;

(E) a motion pursuant to Fed. R. Civ. P. 37 to compel discovery; and

(F) a motion pursuant to Fed. R. Civ. P. 55 for default.

2. *Affidavit.* An affidavit must not contain legal arguments but must contain factual and procedural background that is relevant to the motion the affidavit supports.

An affidavit is required for all motions except the following:

(A) a motion pursuant to Fed. R. Civ. P. 12(b)(6) for failure to state a claim upon which relief can be granted;

(B) a motion pursuant to Fed. R. Civ. P. 12(c) for judgment on the pleadings; and

(C) a motion pursuant to Fed. R. Civ. P. 12(f) to strike a portion of a pleading.

3. *Summary Judgment Motions.* Any motion for summary judgment shall contain a Statement of Material Facts. The Statement of Material Facts shall set forth, in numbered paragraphs, each material fact about which the moving party contends there exists no genuine issue. Each fact listed shall set forth a specific citation to the record where the fact is established. The record for purposes of the Statement of Material Facts includes the pleadings, depositions, answers to interrogatories, admissions and affidavits. It does not, however, include attorney's affidavits. Failure of the moving party to submit an accurate and complete Statement of Material Facts shall result in a denial of the motion.

The moving party shall also advise pro se litigants about the consequences of their failure to respond to a motion for summary judgment. See also L.R. 56.2.

The opposing party shall file a response to the Statement of Material Facts. The non-movant's response shall mirror the movant's Statement of Material Facts by admitting and/or denying each of the movant's assertions in matching numbered paragraphs. Each denial shall set forth a specific citation to the record where the factual issue arises. The non-movant's response may also set forth any additional material facts that the non-movant contends are in dispute in separately numbered paragraphs. The Court shall deem admitted any facts set forth in the Statement of Material Facts that the opposing party does not specifically controvert.

4. *Motions to Amend or Supplement Pleadings or for Joinder or Interpleader.* A party moving to amend a pleading pursuant to Fed. R. Civ. P. 14, 15, 19–22 must attach an unsigned copy of the proposed amended pleading to its motion papers. Except if the Court otherwise orders, the proposed amended pleading must be a complete pleading, which will supersede the original pleading in all respects. A party shall not incorporate any portion of its prior pleading into the proposed amended pleading by reference.

The motion must set forth specifically the proposed amendments and identify the amendments in the proposed pleading, either through the submission of a red-lined version of the original pleading or other equivalent means.

Where a party seeks leave to supplement a pleading pursuant to Fed. R. Civ. P. 15(d), the party must limit the proposed supplemental pleading to transactions or occurrences or events which have occurred since the date of the pleading that the party seeks to supplement. The party must number the paragraphs in the proposed pleading consecutively to the paragraphs contained in the pleading that it seeks to supplement. In addition to the pleading requirements set forth above, the party requesting leave to supplement must set forth specifically the proposed supplements and identify the supplements in the proposed pleading, either through the submission of a red-lined version of the original pleading or other equivalent means.

Caveat: The granting of the motion does not constitute the filing of the amended pleading. After the Court grants leave, unless the Court otherwise orders, the moving party must file and serve the original signed amended pleading within ten (10) days of the Order granting the motion.

(b) Motions.

1. *Dispositive Motions.* The moving party must file all motion papers with the Court and serve them upon the other parties not less than **THIRTY–ONE DAYS** prior to the return date of the motion. The Notice of Motion must state the return date that the moving party has selected.

The party opposing the motion must file its opposition papers with the Court and serve them upon the other parties not less than **SEVENTEEN DAYS** prior to the return date of the motion.

The moving party must file its reply papers, which may not exceed (10) pages and with the Court and serve them upon the other parties not less than **ELEVEN DAYS** prior to the return date of the motion.

A surreply is not permitted.

Parties shall file all original motion papers, including memoranda of law and supporting affidavits, if any, in accordance with the *Administrative Procedures for Electronic Case Filing* (General Order #22) and/or the case assignment form provided to the parties at the commencement of the litigation. The parties need not provide a courtesy copy of their motion papers to the assigned judge unless the assigned judge requests a copy.

2. *Non–Dispositive Motions.* Prior to making any non-dispositive motion before the assigned Magistrate Judge, the parties must make **good faith efforts among themselves to resolve or reduce all differences relating to the non-dispositive issue.** If, after conferring, the parties are unable to arrive at a mutually satisfactory resolution, the party seeking relief must then request a court conference with the assigned Magistrate Judge.

A court conference is a prerequisite to filing a non-dispositive motion before the assigned Magistrate Judge. In the Notice of Motion, the moving party is required to set forth the date that the court conference with the Magistrate Judge was held regarding the issues being presented in the motion. Failure to include this information in the Notice of Motion may result in the Court rejecting the motion papers.

Actions which involve an incarcerated, pro se party are not subject to the requirement that a court conference be held prior to filing a non-dispositive motion.

Unless the Court orders otherwise, the moving party must file all motion papers with the Court and serve them upon the other parties not less than **THIRTY–ONE DAYS** prior to the return date of the motion.

The party opposing the motion must file its Opposition papers with the Court and serve them upon the other parties not less than **SEVENTEEN DAYS** prior to the return date of the motion.

Reply papers and adjournments are not permitted without the Court's prior permission.

3. *Failure To Timely File or Comply.* The Court shall not consider any papers required under this Rule that are not timely filed or are otherwise not in compliance with this Rule unless good cause is shown. Where a properly filed motion is unopposed and the Court determines that the moving party has met its burden to demonstrate entitlement to the relief requested therein, the non-moving party's failure to file or serve any papers as this Rule requires shall be deemed as consent to the granting or denial of the motion, as the case may be, unless good cause is shown.

Any party who does not intend to oppose a motion, or a movant who does not intend to pursue a motion, shall promptly notify the Court and the other parties of such intention. They should provide such notice at the earliest practicable date, but in any event no less than **FOURTEEN CALENDAR DAYS** prior to the scheduled return date of the motion, unless for good cause shown. **Failure to comply with this Rule may result in the Court imposing sanctions.**

(c) **Cross–Motions.** A party may file and serve cross-motions at the time it files and serves its opposition papers to the original motion, i.e., not less than **SEVENTEEN DAYS** prior to the return date of the motion. If a party makes a cross-motion, it must join its cross motion brief with its opposition brief, and this combined brief may not exceed twenty-five (25) pages in length, exclusive of exhibits. A separate brief in opposition to the original motion is not permissible.

The original moving party may reply in further support of the original motion and in opposition to the cross-motion with a reply/opposition brief that does not exceed twenty-five (25) pages in length, exclusive of exhibits. The original moving party must file its reply/opposition papers with the Court and serve them on the other parties not less than **ELEVEN DAYS** prior to the return date of the original motion.

The cross-moving party may not reply in further support of its cross-motion without the Court's prior permission.

(d) Discovery Motions. The following steps are required prior to making any discovery motion pursuant to Rules 26 through 37 of the Federal Rules of Civil Procedure.

1. Parties must make good faith efforts among themselves to resolve or reduce all differences relating to discovery prior to seeking court intervention.

2. The moving party must confer in detail with the opposing party concerning the discovery issues between them in a good faith effort to eliminate or reduce the area of controversy and to arrive at a mutually satisfactory resolution. Failure to do so may result in denial of a motion to compel discovery and/or imposition of sanctions.

3. If the parties' conference does not fully resolve the discovery issues, the party seeking relief must then request a court conference with the assigned Magistrate Judge. Incarcerated, pro se parties are not subject to the court conference requirement prior to filing a motion to compel discovery. The assigned Magistrate Judge may direct the party making the request for a court conference to file an affidavit setting forth the date(s) and mode(s) of the consultation(s) with the opposing party and a letter that concisely sets forth the nature of the dispute and a specific listing of each of the items of discovery sought or opposed. Immediately following each disputed item, the party must set forth the reason why the Court should allow or disallow that item.

4. Following a request for a discovery conference, the Court may schedule a conference and advise all parties of a date and time. The assigned Magistrate Judge may, in his or her discretion, conduct the discovery conference by telephone conference call, initiated by the party making the request for the conference, by video conference, or by personal appearance.

5. Following a discovery conference, the Court may direct the prevailing party to submit a proposed order on notice to the other parties.

6. If a party fails or refuses to confer in good faith with the requesting party, thus requiring the request for a discovery conference, the Court, at its discretion, may subject the resisting party to the sanction of the imposition of costs, including the attorney's fees of opposing party in accordance with Fed. R. Civ. P. 37.

7. A party claiming privilege with respect to a communication or other item must specifically identify the privilege and the grounds for the claimed privilege. The parties may not make any generalized claims of privilege.

8. The parties shall file any motion to compel discovery that these Rules authorize no later than **TEN CALENDAR DAYS** after the discovery cut-off date. See L.R. 16.2. A party shall accompany any motion that it files pursuant to Fed. R. Civ. P. 37 with the discovery materials to which the motion relates if the parties have not previously filed those materials with the Court.

(e) Order to Show Cause. All motions that a party brings by Order to Show Cause shall conform to the requirements set forth in L.R. 7.1(a)(1) and (2). **Immediately after filing an Order to Show Cause, the moving party must telephone the Chambers of the presiding judicial officer and inform Chambers staff that it has filed an Order to Show Cause.** Parties may obtain the telephone numbers for all Chambers from the Clerk's office or at the Court's webpage at "www.nynd.uscourts.gov." The Court shall determine the briefing schedule and return date applicable to motions brought by Order to Show Cause.

In addition to the requirements set forth in Local Rule 7.1(a)(1) and (2), a motion brought by Order to Show Cause must include an affidavit clearly and specifically showing good and sufficient cause why the standard Notice of Motion procedure cannot be used. The moving party must give reasonable advance notice of the application for an Order to Show Cause to the other parties, except in those circumstances where the movant can demonstrate, in a detailed and specific affidavit, good cause and substantial prejudice that would result from the requirement of reasonable notice.

An Order to Show Cause must contain a space for the assigned judge to set forth (a) the deadline for filing and serving supporting papers, (b) the deadline for filing and serving opposing papers, and (c) the date and time for the hearing.

(f) Temporary Restraining Order. A party may seek a temporary restraining order by Notice of Motion or Order to Show Cause, as appropriate. Filing procedures and requirements for supporting documents are the same as set forth in this Rule for other motions. The moving party must serve any application for a temporary restraining order on all other parties unless Fed. R. Civ. P. 65 otherwise permits. L.R. 7.1(b)(2) governs motions for injunctive relief, other than those brought by Order to Show Cause. L.R. 7.1(e) governs motions brought by Order to Show Cause.

(g) Motion for Reconsideration. Unless Fed. R. Civ. P. 60 otherwise governs, a party may file and serve a motion for reconsideration or reargument no later than **TEN CALENDAR DAYS** after the entry of the challenged judgment, order, or decree. All motions for reconsideration shall conform with the requirements set forth in L.R. 7.1(a)(1) and (2). The briefing schedule and return date applicable to motions for reconsideration shall conform to L.R. 7.1(b)(2). A motion for reconsideration of a Magistrate Judges's determination of a non-dispositive matter shall toll the ten (10) day time period to file objections pursuant to L.R. 72.1(b). The Court will decide motions for reconsideration or reargument on submission of the papers, without oral argument, unless the Court directs otherwise.

(h) Oral Argument. The parties shall appear for oral argument on all motions that they make returnable before a district court judge, except motions for reconsideration, on the scheduled return date of the motion. In the district court judge's discretion, or on consideration of a request of any party, the district court judge may dispose of a motion without oral argument. Thus, the parties should be prepared to have their motion papers serve as the sole method of argument on the motion.

The parties shall not appear for oral argument on motions that they make returnable before a Magistrate Judge on the scheduled return date of the motion unless the Magistrate Judge sua sponte directs or grants the request of any party for oral argument.

(i) Sanctions for Vexatious or Frivolous Motions or Failure to Comply with this Rule. A party who presents vexatious or frivolous motion papers or fails to comply with this Rule is subject to discipline as the Court deems appropriate, including sanctions and the imposition of costs and attorney's fees to the opposing party.

(j) Adjournments of Dispositive Motions. After the moving party files and serves its motion papers requesting dispositive relief, but before the time that the opposing party must file and serve its opposing papers, the parties may agree to an adjournment of the return date for the motion. However, any such adjournment may not be for more than **THIRTY–ONE DAYS** from the return date that the moving party selected. In addition, the parties may agree to new dates for the filing and service of opposition and reply papers. However, the parties must file all papers with the Court and serve them upon the other parties not less than **ELEVEN DAYS** prior to the newly selected return date of the motion. If the parties agree to such an adjournment, they must file a letter with the Court stating the following: (1) that they have agreed to an adjournment of the return date for the motion, (2) the new return date, (3) the date on which the opposing party must file and serve its opposition papers, and (4) the date on which the moving party must file and serve its reply papers. The parties may not agree to any further adjournment.

If one of the parties seeks an adjournment of not more than **THIRTY–ONE DAYS** from the return date that the moving party selected, but the other parties will not agree to such an adjournment, the party seeking the adjournment must file a letter request with the Court and serve the same upon the other parties, stating the following: (1) that the parties cannot agree to an adjournment, (2) the reason that the party is seeking the adjournment, and (3) the suggested return date for the motion.

Within three days of receiving this letter request, the parties who have not agreed to an adjournment may file a letter with the Court and serve the same upon the other parties, setting forth the reasons that they do not agree to the requested adjournment. The Court will then take the request under advisement and, as soon as practicable, will enter an order granting or denying the request and, if granting the request, will set forth new dates for the filing and serving of opposition and reply papers.

If any party seeks an adjournment of the return date that is more than **THIRTY-ONE DAYS** from the return date that the moving party selected, that party must file a letter request with the Court stating the following: (1) why the party needs a longer adjournment and (2) a suggested return date for the motion. The Court will grant such an adjournment only upon a showing of exceptional circumstances. In the alternative or if the Court denies the request for an adjournment, the moving party may **withdraw its motion without prejudice** to refile at a later date. The moving party must refile its motion within the time frame set in the Uniform Pretrial Scheduling Order unless either the assigned District Judge or the assigned Magistrate Judge has granted an extension of the motion-filing deadline.

[Amended effective January 1, 1999; January 1, 2001; January 1, 2003; January 1, 2004; January 1, 2005; January 1, 2007; January 1, 2008; January 1, 2009.]

RULE 16.1. CIVIL CASE MANAGEMENT

This Court has found that the interests of justice are most effectively served by adopting a systematic, differential case management system that tailors the level of individualized and case-specific management to such criteria as case complexity, time required to prepare a case for trial, and availability of judicial and other resources.

(a) Filing of Complaint/Service of Process. Upon the filing of a complaint, the Clerk shall issue to the plaintiff General Order 25, which requires, among other things, service of process upon all defendants within sixty (60) days of the filing of the complaint. This expedited service requirement is necessary to ensure adequate time for pretrial discovery and motion practice.

(b) Assignment of District Judge/Magistrate Judge. Immediately upon the filing of a civil action, the Clerk shall assign the action or proceeding to a District Judge and may also assign the action or proceeding to a Magistrate Judge pursuant to the Court's assignment plan. When a civil action is assigned to a Magistrate Judge, the Magistrate Judge shall conduct proceedings in accordance with these Rules and 28 U.S.C. § 636 as directed by the District Judge. Once assigned, either judicial officer shall have authority to design and issue a case management order.

(c) Initial Pretrial Conference. Except for cases excluded under section II of General Order 25, an initial pretrial conference pursuant to Fed. R. Civ. P. 16 shall be held within 120 days after the filing of the complaint. The Clerk shall set the date of this conference upon the filing of the complaint. The purpose of this conference will be to prepare and adopt a case-specific management plan which will be memorialized in a case management order. See subsection (d) below. In order to facilitate the adoption of such a plan, prior to the scheduled conference, counsel for all parties shall confer among themselves as Fed. R. Civ. P. 26(f) requires and shall use the Civil Case Management Plan form contained in the General Order 2 filing packet. The parties shall file their jointly-proposed plan, or if they cannot reach consensus, each party shall file its own proposed plan with the Clerk at least ten (10) business days prior to the scheduled pretrial conference.

(d) Subject Matter of Initial Pretrial Conference. At the initial pretrial conference the Court shall consider, and the parties shall be prepared to discuss, the following:

1. Deadlines for joinder of parties, amendment of pleadings, completion of discovery, and filing of dispositive motions;

2. Trial date;

3. Requests for jury trial;

4. Subject matter and personal jurisdiction;

5. Factual and legal bases for claims and defenses;

6. Factual and legal issues in dispute;

7. Factual and legal issues upon which the parties can agree or which they can narrow through motion practice and which will expedite resolution of the dispute;

8. Specific relief requested, including method for computing damages;

9. Intended discovery and proposed methods to limit and/or decrease time and expense thereof;

10. Suitability of case for voluntary arbitration;

11. Measures for reducing length of trial;

12. Related cases pending before this or other U.S. District Courts;

13. Procedures for certifying class actions, if appropriate;

14. Settlement prospects; and

15. If the case is in the ADR track, choice of ADR method and estimated time for completion of ADR.

(e) **Uniform Pretrial Scheduling Order.** Upon completion of the initial pretrial conference, the presiding judge may issue a Uniform Pretrial Scheduling Order setting forth deadlines for joinder of parties, amendment of pleadings, production of expert reports, completion of discovery, and filing of motions; a trial ready date; the requirements for all trial submissions; and if an ADR track case, the ADR method to be used and the deadline for completion of ADR.

(f) **Enforcement of Deadlines.** The Court shall strictly enforce any deadlines that it establishes in any case management order, and the Court shall not modify these, even upon stipulation of the parties, except upon a showing of good cause.

[Amended effective January 1, 1999; January 1, 2008; February 7, 2008; January 1, 2009.]

RULE 64.1. SEIZURE OF PERSON OR PROPERTY

The Court has adopted a Uniform Procedure for Civil Forfeiture Cases, which is available from the Clerk's office or at the Court's webpage at "**www.nynd.uscourts. gov.**"

Pursuant to Title 19, United States Code, Section 1605, the United States Customs Service, Ogdensburg, New York, shall be appointed the Substitute Custodian and be responsible for the execution of warrants of arrest in rem for assets and/or property seized and forfeited under the laws administered or enforced by the United States Customs Service.

Pursuant to Fed. R. Civ. P. Supp. R. C(3)(b)(ii), personnel of the United States Customs Service, Office of Fines, Penalties and Forfeitures, 127 North Water Street, Ogdensburg, New York, shall be appointed as special process servers in all cases pertaining to assets and/or property seized and forfeited under the laws administered or enforced by the United States Customs Service, to perform the tasks of service by mail, or in person, execution of the warrants of seizure and monition, publication of the notices of the action in newspapers having general circulation in the district in which the res were seized, and filing of all returns of such process with the United States District Court Clerk's Office for the Northern District of New York.

[Amended effective January 1, 2004; January 1, 2009.]

RULE 67.1. DEPOSITS IN COURT

(a) A supersedeas bond, where the judgment is for a sum of money only, shall be in the amount of the judgment plus 11% to cover interest and any damage for delay as may be awarded, plus $250 to cover costs.

When a stay shall be effected solely by the giving of the supersedeas bond, but the judgment or order is not solely for a sum of money, the Court, on notice, shall fix the amount of the bond. In all other cases, the Court shall, on notice, grant a stay on the terms it deems proper.

On approval, a party shall file the supersedeas bond with the Clerk, and shall promptly serve a copy thereof, with notice of filing, upon all parties affected thereby. If a party raises objections to the form of the bond or to the sufficiency of the surety, the Court shall provide prompt notice of a hearing to consider such objections.

(b) **Order Directing the Investment of Funds.** Any order directing the Clerk to invest funds deposited with the registry account of the Court pursuant to 28 U.S.C. § 2041 shall include the following:

1. The amount to be invested; and

2. The type of interest-bearing account in which the funds are to be invested.

(c) Time for Investing Funds. The Clerk shall take all reasonable steps to invest the funds within ten (10) days of the filing date of the order.

(d) Fee. Unless the Court orders otherwise, the Clerk shall deduct from income earned on registry funds invested in interest-bearing accounts or instruments a fee of ten percent (10%) on amounts that are invested that are less $100 million and held for up to 5 years. For amounts that are invested and held for 5–10 years, the fee decreases to seven and one-half percent (7.5%); for amounts that are invested and held for 10–15 years, the fee decreases to five percent (5%); and for amounts that are invested and held for 15 years or more, the fee decreases to two and one-half percent (2.5%).

The Clerk shall deduct the fee before any other distribution of the account and shall deposit the fee in the Treasury of the United States, without further order of this Court. This assessment shall apply to all registry fund investments.

[Amended effective January 1, 2008; January 1, 2009.]

RULE 72.3. ASSIGNMENT OF DUTIES TO MAGISTRATE JUDGES

(a) Immediately upon the filing of a civil action or proceeding, the Clerk shall assign the action or proceeding to a District Judge and may also assign the action or proceeding to a Magistrate Judge pursuant to the Court's Assignment Plan. When a civil action or proceeding is assigned to a Magistrate Judge, the Magistrate Judge shall conduct proceedings in accordance with these Rules and 28 U.S.C. § 636 as directed by the District Judge. See L.R. 40.1.

(b) All civil cases in which the parties have executed and filed consent forms pursuant to 28 U.S.C. § 636(c) and L.R. 72.2(b) shall be transmitted to the assigned District Judge for approval and referral of the case to a Magistrate Judge, who shall then have the authority to conduct all proceedings and to direct the Clerk to enter final judgment. See L.R. 72.2(b)(3).

(c) Prisoner Cases. Any proceedings that an unrepresented prisoner commences shall, unless the Court orders otherwise, be referred to a Magistrate Judge for the purpose of reviewing applications, petitions and motions in accordance with these Rules and 28 U.S.C. § 636.

(d) Social Security Appeal Cases. Upon the filing of the complaint, the Clerk shall assign social security appeal cases in rotation to the District Judges. The assigned District Judge shall immediately refer these cases in rotation to a full-time Magistrate Judge for the purpose of review and submission of a report-recommendation relative to the complaint or, if the Magistrate Judge has been assigned to the case pursuant to 28 U.S.C. § 636(c) and L.R. 72.2(b), for final judgment.

(e) Federal Debt Collection Act Cases.

1. Any action brought pursuant to the Federal Debt Collection Act, 28 U.S.C. § 3001 et seq., shall be handled on an expedited basis and brought before a Magistrate Judge in Syracuse, New York, or to a District Judge if no Magistrate Judge is available, for an initial determination.

2. If appropriate, the Court shall issue an order directing the Clerk to issue the writ being sought, except that an application under 28 U.S.C. § 3203 for a writ of execution in a post-judgment proceeding shall not require an order of the Court.

3. Thereafter, the Clerk shall assign geographically a Magistrate Judge if no Magistrate Judge was previously assigned in accordance with General Order #12.

4. The assigned Magistrate Judge shall conduct any hearing that may be requested, decide all non-dispositive issues, and issue a report-recommendation on any and all dispositive issues.

5. The parties shall file any written objections to the report-recommendation within twenty (20) days of the filing of same. Without oral argument, the assigned District Judge shall review the report-recommendation along with any objections that the parties have filed.

6. If a party requests a hearing, the Clerk shall make a good faith effort to schedule the hearing within five (5) days of the receipt of the request or "as soon after that as possible" pursuant to 28 U.S.C. § 3101(d)(1).

[Amended effective January 1, 2001; January 1, 2006; January 1, 2008; January 1, 2009.]

RULE 76.1. BANKRUPTCY CASES

Reference to Bankruptcy Court. All cases under Title 11 of the United States Code, and all proceedings arising under Title 11, or arising in, or related to, a case under Title 11, are referred to the bankruptcy court of this District pursuant to 28 U.S.C. § 157.

In accordance with the provisions of 28 U.S.C. § 157(e), the Board of Judges has specifically designated the United States Bankruptcy Court Judges of this District to conduct jury trials in all proceedings commenced in cases filed under Title 11 of the United States Code where the right to a jury trial applies and where all the parties have expressly consented thereto.

[Amended effective January 1, 2009.]

RULE 83.1. ADMISSION TO THE BAR

(a) Permanent Admission. A member in good standing of the bar of the State of New York or of the bar of any United States District Court, or of the highest court in the state in which they reside, whose professional character is good, may be permanently admitted to practice in this Court on motion of a member of the bar of this Court in compliance with the requirements of this Rule. **An admission packet containing all the required forms is available from the Clerk's office and on the Court's webpage at "www.nynd. uscourts.gov."**

Each applicant for permanent admission must file, at least ten (10) days prior to the scheduled hearing (unless, for good cause shown, the Court shortens the time), documentation for admission as set forth below. Ordinarily, the Court entertains applications for admission only on regularly scheduled motion days. Documentation required for permanent admission includes the following:

1. *A verified petition for admission* stating the following:

- place of residence and office address;
- the date(s) when and court(s) where previously admitted;
- legal training and trial experience;
- whether the applicant has ever been held in contempt of court, censured, suspended or disbarred by any court

and, if so, the facts and circumstances connected therewith; and

- that the applicant is familiar with the provisions of the Judicial Code (Title 28 U.S.C.), which pertain to the jurisdiction of, and practice in, the United States District Courts; the Federal Rules of Civil Procedure and the Federal Rules of Evidence for the District Courts; the Federal Rules of Criminal Procedure for the District Courts; the Local Rules of the District Court for the Northern District of New York; and the N.Y.S. Lawyer's Code of Professional Responsibility. The applicant shall further affirm faithful adherence to these Rules and responsibilities.

2. *Affidavit of Sponsor.* The sponsor must be a member in good standing of the bar of the Northern District of New York who has personal knowledge of the petitioner's background and character. A form Affidavit of Sponsor is available from the Clerk's office.

3. *Attorney E–Filing Registration Form.* The E–Filing Registration Form must be in the form the Clerk prescribes, which sets forth the attorney's current office address(es); telephone and fax number(s), and e-mail address. A copy of the Attorney E–Filing Registration Form is available on the Court's webpage at **"www. nynd.uscourts.gov."** See subdivision (e) for requirements when information on the Registration Form changes.

4. *Certificate of Good Standing.* The certificate of good standing must be dated within six (6) months of the date of admission.

5. *The Required Fee.* As prescribed by and pursuant to the Judicial Conference of the United States and the Rules of this Court, the fee for admission to the bar is $150.00.

In addition to the initial admission fee, there shall be a $30.00 biennial registration fee. This fee shall be due and owning on **June 1, 2001,** and every two years thereafter unless the Board of Judges directs otherwise. Failure to remit this fee will result in the removal of the non-paying attorney from the Court's bar roll. Should the payment of this biennial fee present a significant financial hardship, an attorney may request, by submitting an application to the Chief Judge, that the biennial registration fee be waived.

The Clerk shall deposit the additional $30.00 fee required for admission to the bar and the $30.00 biennial registration fee into the District Court Fund. The Clerk shall be the trustee of the Fund, and the monies deposited in the Fund shall be used only for the benefit of the bench and bar in the administration of justice. All withdrawals from the Fund require the approval of the Chief Judge or a judge designated by the Chief Judge to authorize the withdrawals. The admission fees and biennial registration fees are waived for all attorneys in the employ of the United States Government.

The biennial registration fees only are waived for all attorneys employed by state and local public sector entities.

6. *Oath on Admission.* Applicants must swear or affirm that as attorneys and counselors of this Court, they will conduct themselves uprightly and according to law and that they will support the Constitution of the United States. The applicant signs the Oath on Admission, Form AO 153, in court at the time of the admission.

(b) Applicants who are not admitted to another United States District Court in New York State must appear with their sponsor for formal admission unless the Court, in the exercise of its discretion, waives such appearance. If the applicant is admitted to practice in New York State, the Certificate of Good Standing submitted with the application for admission must be from the appropriate New York State Appellate Division. All requirements of subdivision (a) apply.

If the applicant is from outside New York State, the Certificate of Good Standing may be from the highest court of the state or from a United States District Court. All requirements of subdivision (a) apply. An out-of-state applicant must maintain an office in the state in which they are admitted. Upon ceasing to maintain an office in that state, they automatically cease to be members of the bar of this Court.

(c) Applicants who are members in good standing of a United States District Court for the Eastern, Western, or Southern District of New York need not appear for formal admission. They must submit a Certificate of Good Standing from the United States District Court where they are members and a proposed order granting the admission. A sponsor's affidavit is not

required. All other requirements of subdivision (a) apply.

(d) Pro Hac Vice Admission. A member in good standing of the bar of any state, or of any United States District Court, may be admitted pro hac vice to argue or try a particular case in whole or in part. In addition to the requirements of L.R. 83.1(a)(1)(3) and (4), an applicant must make a Motion for Pro Hac Vice Admission, which includes the case caption of the particular case for which the applicant seeks admission. See L.R. 10.1(b). In lieu of a written motion for admission, the sponsoring attorney may make an oral motion in open court on the record. In that case, the attorney seeking pro hac vice admission must immediately complete and file the required documents as set forth above.

The pro hac vice admission fee is $30.00. The Clerk deposits all pro hac vice admission fees into the District Court Fund. See L.R. 83.1(a)(5). An attorney admitted pro hac vice must file a written notice of appearance in the case for which the attorney was admitted in accordance with L.R. 83.2.

(e) Registration Form Changes. Every attorney must file a supplemental statement setting forth any change in the information on the Registration Form within ten (10) days of the change. The attorney should make this supplemental statement by filing a new Registration Form which reflects the new information and which identifies which information changed. Failure to timely file a supplemental Registration Form may result in the Court's inability to notify that attorney of developments in the case or other sanctions in the Court's discretion. See L.R. 41.2(b). A copy of the Attorney Registration Form is available on the Court's webpage at "**www.nynd.uscourts.gov.**"

(f) Pro Bono Service. Every member of the bar of this Court shall be available upon the Court's request for appointment to represent or assist in the representation of indigent parties. The Court shall make appointments under this Rule in a manner such that the Court shall not request any attorney to accept more than one appointment during any twelve-month period.

(g) United States Attorney's Office. An attorney appointed by the United States Attorney General as a United States Attorney, an Assistant United States Attorney, or as a Special Assistant United States

Attorney under 28 U.S.C. §§ 541–543, who has been admitted to practice before any United States District Court, shall be admitted to practice in this Court upon motion of a member of the bar of this Court. Thereafter, the attorney may appear before this Court on any matter on behalf of the United States.

[Amended effective January 1, 1999; January 1, 2001; January 1, 2004; January 1, 2005; January 1, 2008; January 1, 2009.]

RULE 83.3.   PRO BONO PANEL

(a) Description of Panel.   In recognition of the need for representation of indigent parties in civil actions, this Court has established the Pro Bono Panel ("Panel") of the Northern District of New York.

1.   The Panel shall include those members of the Criminal Assigned Counsel Panel in this Court. The Court also expects any other attorney admitted to practice in this Court to participate in periodic training that the Court offers and to accept no more than one pro bono assignment per year.

2.   The Court shall maintain a list of Panel members, which shall include the information deemed necessary for the effective administration and assignment of Panel attorneys.

3.   The Court shall select Panel members for assignment upon its determination that the appointment of an attorney is warranted. The Court shall select from the Panel a member who has not received an appointment from the Court during the past year and (1) has attended a training seminar that this Court sponsors, (2) has adequate prior experience closely related to the matter assigned, or (3) has accepted criminal (CJA) assignments from the Court.

4.   Where a pro se party has one or more other cases pending before this Court in which the Court has appointed an attorney, the Court may determine it to be appropriate that the attorney appointed in the other case or cases be appointed to represent the pro se party in the case before the Court.

5.   Where the Court finds that the nature of the case requires specific expertise, and among the Panel members available for appointment there are some with the required expertise, the attorney may be selected from among those included in the group or the Court may designate a specific member of the Panel.

6.   Where the Court finds that the nature of the case requires specific expertise and none of the Panel members available for appointment has indicated that expertise, the Court may appoint an attorney with the required expertise who is not on the Panel.

(b) Application for Appointment of Attorney.

1.   Any application that a party appearing pro se makes for the appointment of an attorney shall include a form of affidavit stating the party's efforts to obtain an attorney by means other than appointment and indicating any prior pro bono appointments of an attorney to represent the party in cases brought in this Court, including both pending and terminated actions.

2.   Failure of a party to make a written application for an appointed attorney shall not preclude appointment.

3.   Where a pro se litigant, who was ineligible for an appointed attorney at the time of initial or subsequent requests, later becomes eligible by reason of changed circumstances, the Court may entertain a subsequent application, using the procedures specified above, within a reasonable time after the change in circumstances has occurred.

(c) Factors Used in Determining Whether to Appoint Counsel.   Upon receipt of an application for the appointment of an attorney, the Court shall determine whether to appoint an attorney to represent the pro se party. The Court shall make that determination within a reasonable time after the party makes the application. Factors that the Court will take into account in making the determination are as follows:

1.   The potential merit of the claims as set forth in the pleading;

2.   The nature and complexity of the action, both factual and legal, including the need for factual investigation;

3.   The presence of conflicting testimony calling for an attorney's presentation of evidence and cross-examination;

4.   The capability of the pro se party to present the case;

5.   The inability of the pro se party to retain an attorney by other means;

6. The degree to which the interests of justice shall be served by appointment of an attorney, including the benefit that the Court shall derive from the assistance of an appointed attorney;

7. Any other factors the Court deems appropriate.

(d) Order of Appointment. Whenever the Court concludes that the appointment of an attorney is warranted, the Court shall issue an order directing the appointment of an attorney to represent the pro se party. The Court shall promptly transmit the order to the Clerk. If service of the summons and complaint has not yet been made, the Court shall accompany its appointment order with an order directing service by the United States Marshal or by other appropriate method of service.

(e) Notification of Appointment. After the Court has appointed an attorney, the Clerk shall send the attorney a copy of the order of appointment. Copies of the pleadings filed to date, relevant correspondence, and all other relevant documents shall be forwarded to the Clerk's office nearest to the attorney and made available for immediate review and copying of the necessary papers without charge. In addition to notifying the attorney, the Clerk shall also notify all of the parties to the action of the appointment, together with the name, address and telephone number of the appointed attorney.

(f) Duties and Responsibilities of Appointed Counsel. On receiving notice of the appointment, the attorney shall promptly file an appearance in the action to which the appointment applies unless precluded from acting in the action or appeal, in which event the attorney shall promptly notify the Court and the putative client. Promptly following the filing of an appearance, the attorney shall communicate with the newly-represented party concerning the action. In addition to a full discussion of the merits of the dispute, the attorney shall explore with the party any possibilities of resolving the dispute in other forums, including but not limited to administrative forums. If after consultation with the attorney the party decides to prosecute or defend the action, the attorney shall proceed to represent the party in the action unless or until the attorney-client relationship is terminated as these Rules provide.

In the Court's discretion, the Court may appoint stand-by counsel to act in an advisory capacity. "Stand-by counsel" is not the party's representative; rather, the role of stand-by counsel is to provide assistance to the litigant and the Court where appropriate. The Court may in its discretion appoint counsel for other purposes.

(g) Reimbursement for Expenses. Pro Bono attorneys whom the Court appoints pursuant to this Rule may seek reimbursement for expenses incident to representation of indigent clients by application to the Court. Reimbursement or advances shall be permitted to the extent possible in light of available resources and, absent extraordinary circumstances, shall not exceed $2,000.00. Any expenses in excess of $300.00 should receive the Court's prior approval. If good cause is shown, the Court may approve additional expenses. Appointed counsel should seek reimbursement using the Pro Bono Fund Voucher and Request for Reimbursement Form and should accompany this form with detailed documentation. The Court advises counsel that if they submit a voucher seeking more than $2,000.00 without the Court's prior approval, the Court may reduce or deny the request. The Chief Judge or a judge whom the Chief Judge designates to authorize withdrawals must approve all reimbursements made by withdrawal from the District Fund. **To the extent that appointed counsel seeks reimbursement for expenses that are recoverable as costs to a prevailing party under Fed R. Civ.P.54, the appointed attorney must submit a verified bill of costs on the form the Clerk provides for reimbursement of such expenses.**

(h) Attorney's Fees. Except as provided in this subsection, an appointed attorney cannot recover attorney's fees from the Pro Bono Fund. However, in its discretion, the Court may award an appointed attorney for a prevailing party attorney's fees from the judgment or settlement to the extent that the applicable law permits. See, e.g., 28 U.S.C. § 2678 (permitting the attorney for a prevailing party under the Federal Tort Claims Act to recover up to 25% of any judgment or settlement); 42 U.S.C. § 1988(b) (authorizing an additional award of attorney's fees to prevailing parties in civil rights actions).

(i) Grounds for Relief from Appointment. After appointment, an attorney may apply to be relieved from an order of appointment only on one or more of the following grounds, or on such other grounds as the appointing judge finds adequate for good cause shown:

1. some conflict of interest precludes the attorney from accepting the responsibilities of representing the party in the action;

2. the attorney does not feel competent to represent the party in the particular type of action assigned;

3. some personal incompatibility exists between the attorney and the party or a substantial disagreement exists between the attorney and the party concerning litigation strategy; or

4. in the attorney's opinion the party is proceeding for purposes of harassment or malicious injury or the party's claims or defenses are not warranted under existing law and cannot be supported by a good faith argument for extension, modification or reversal of existing law.

(j) Application for Relief from Appointment. An appointed attorney shall make any application for relief from an order of appointment on any of the grounds set forth in this Rule to the Court promptly after the attorney becomes aware of the existence of such grounds or within such additional period as the Court may permit for good cause shown.

(k) Order Granting Relief from Appointment. If the Court grants an application for relief from an order of appointment, the Court shall issue an order directing the appointment of another attorney to represent the party. Where the application for relief from appointment identifies an attorney affiliated with the moving attorney who is able to represent the party, the order shall direct appointment of the affiliated attorney with the consent of the affiliated attorney. Any other appointment shall be made in accordance with the procedures set forth in these Rules. Alternatively, the Court shall have the discretion not to issue a further order of appointment, in which case the party shall be permitted to prosecute or defend the action pro se.

[Amended effective January 1, 1999; January 1, 2005; January 1, 2008; March 20, 2008; January 1, 2009.]

RULE 83.4. DISCIPLINE OF ATTORNEYS

(a) The Chief Judge shall have charge of all matters relating to discipline of members of the bar of this Court.

(b) Any member of the bar of this Court who is convicted of a felony in any State, Territory, other District, Commonwealth, or Possession shall be suspended from practice before this Court and, upon the judgment of conviction becoming final, shall cease to be a member of the bar of this Court.

On the presentation to the Court of a certified or exemplified copy of a judgment of conviction, the attorney shall be suspended from practicing before this Court and, on presentation of proof that judgment of conviction is final, the name of the attorney convicted shall, by order of the Court, be struck from the roll of members of the bar of this Court.

(c) Any member of the bar of the Northern District of New York who shall resign from the bar of any State, Territory, other District, Commonwealth or Possession while an investigation into allegations of misconduct is pending shall cease to be a member of the bar of this Court.

On the presentation to the Court of a certified or exemplified copy of an order accepting resignation, the name of the attorney resigning shall, by order of the Court, be struck from the roll of members of the bar of this Court.

(d) Any member of the bar of the Northern District of New York who shall be disciplined by a court in any State, Territory, other District, Commonwealth, or Possession shall be disciplined to the same extent by this Court unless an examination of the record resulting in the discipline discloses.

1. that the procedure was so lacking in notice or opportunity to be heard as to constitute a deprivation of due process;

2. that there was such an infirmity of proof establishing the misconduct as to give rise to the clear conviction that this Court should not accept as final the conclusion on that subject;

3. that this Court's imposition of the same discipline would result in grave injustice; or

4. that this Court has held that the misconduct warrants substantially different discipline.

On the filing of a certified or exemplified copy of an order imposing discipline, this Court shall, by order, discipline the attorney to the same extent. It is provided, however, that within thirty (30) days of service on the attorney of the Court's order of discipline, either the attorney or a bar association that the Chief Judge designated in the order imposing discipline shall apply to the Chief Judge for an order to show cause why the discipline imposed in this District should not be modified on the basis of one or more of the grounds set forth in this Rule. The term "bar association" as used in this Rule shall mean the following: The New York State Bar Association or any city or county bar association.

(e) The Court may disbar, suspend or censure any member of the bar of this Court who is convicted of a misdemeanor in any State, Territory, other District, Commonwealth, or Possession, upon such conviction.

Upon the filing of a certified or exemplified copy of a judgment of conviction, the Chief Judge may designate a bar association to prosecute a proceeding against the attorney. The bar association shall obtain an order requiring the attorney to show cause within thirty (30) days after service, personally or by mail, why the attorney should not be disciplined. The Chief Judge may, for good cause, temporarily suspend the attorney pending the determination of the proceeding. Upon receiving the attorney's answer to the order to show cause, the Chief Judge may set the matter for prompt hearing before a court of one or more judges or shall appoint a master to hear and to report findings and a recommendation. After a hearing and report, or if the attorney makes no timely answer or the answer raises no issue requiring a hearing, the Court shall take action as justice requires. In all proceedings, a certificate of conviction shall constitute conclusive proof of the attorney's guilt of the conduct for which the attorney was convicted.

(f) Any attorney who has been disbarred from the bar of a state in which the attorney was admitted to practice shall have his or her name stricken from the roll of attorneys of this Court or, if suspended from practice for a period at such bar, shall be suspended automatically for a like period from practice in this Court.

(g)(1) In addition to any other sanctions imposed in any particular case under these Rules, any person admitted to practice in this Court may be prohibited from practicing in this Court or otherwise disciplined for cause.

(2) Complaints alleging any cause for discipline shall be directed to the Chief Judge and must be in writing. If the Chief Judge deems the conduct alleged in the complaint sanctionable, the Chief Judge shall appoint a panel attorney to investigate and, if necessary, support the complaint. At the same time, the Chief Judge shall refer the matter to a Magistrate Judge for all pre-disposition proceedings.

(3) The Chief Judge shall appoint a panel of attorneys who are members of the bar of this Court to investigate complaints and, if the complaint is supported by the evidence, to prepare statements of charges and to support such charges at any hearing. In making appointments to the panel, the Chief Judge may solicit recommendations from the Federal Court Bar Association and other bar associations and groups. The Chief Judge shall appoint attorneys to the panel for terms not to exceed four years without limitation as to the number of terms an attorney may serve. The Court may reimburse an attorney from this panel whom the Chief Judge appoints to investigate and support a complaint in accordance with subsection (3) below ("panel attorney") for expenses incurred in performing such duties from the Pro Bono Fund to the extent and in the manner provided in L.R. 83.3(g).

(4) If the panel attorney determines after investigation that the evidence fails to establish probable cause to believe that any violation of the Code of Professional Responsibilities has occurred, the panel attorney shall submit a report of such findings and conclusions to the Chief Judge for the consideration of the active district court judges.

(5) If the panel attorney determines after investigation that the evidence establishes probable cause to believe that one or more violations of the Code of Professional Responsibilities has occurred, the panel attorney shall prepare a statement of charges alleging the grounds for discipline. The Clerk shall cause the Statement of Charges

to be served upon the attorney concerned ("responding attorney") by certified mail, return receipt requested, directed to the address of the attorney as shown on the rolls of this Court and, if different, to the last known address of the attorney as shown in any other source together with a direction from the Clerk that the responding attorney shall show cause in writing within thirty days why discipline should not be imposed.

(6) If the responding attorney fails to respond to the statement of charges, the charges shall be deemed admitted. If the responding attorney denies any charge, the assigned Magistrate Judge shall schedule a prompt evidentiary hearing. The Magistrate Judge may grant such pre-hearing discovery as deemed necessary, shall hear witnesses called by the panel attorney supporting the charges and by the responding attorney, and may consider such other evidence included in the record of the hearing that the Magistrate Judge deems relevant and material. A disciplinary charge may not be found proven unless supported by clear and convincing evidence. The Magistrate Judge shall report his or her findings and recommendations in writing to the Chief Judge and shall serve them upon the responding attorney and the panel attorney. The responding attorney and the panel attorney may file objections to the Magistrate Judge's report and recommendations within twenty days of the date thereof.

(7) An attorney may not be found guilty of a disciplinary charge except upon a majority vote of the district judges, including senior district judges, that such charge has been proven by clear and convincing evidence. Any discipline imposed shall also be determined by a majority vote of the district judges, including senior district judges, except that in the event of a tie vote, the Chief Judge shall cast a tie-breaking vote. If the District Judge submitted the complaint under subsection (2) above giving rise to the disciplinary proceeding, that judge shall be recused from participating in the decisions regarding guilt and discipline.

(8) Unless the Court orders otherwise, all documents, records, and proceedings concerning a disciplinary matter shall be filed and conducted confidentially except that, without further order of the Court, the Clerk may notify other licensing jurisdictions of the imposition of any sanctions.

(h) A visiting attorney permitted to argue or try a particular cause in accordance with L.R. 83.1 who is found guilty of misconduct shall be precluded from again appearing in this Court. On entry of an order of preclusion, the Clerk shall transmit to the court of the State, Territory, District, Commonwealth, or Possession where the attorney was admitted to practice a certified copy of the order and of the Court's opinion.

(i) Unless the Court orders otherwise, no action shall be taken pursuant to L.R. 83.4(e) and (f) in any case in which disciplinary proceedings against the attorney have been instituted in the State.

(j) The Court shall enforce the N.Y.S. Lawyer's Code of Professional Responsibilities, as adopted from time to time by the Appellate Division of the State of New York, in construing which the court as a matter of comity will follow decisions of the New York State Court of Appeals and other New York state courts absent an overarching federal interest and as interpreted and applied by the United States Court of Appeals for the Second Circuit.

(k) Nothing in this Rule shall limit the Court's power to punish contempts or to sanction counsel in accordance with the Federal Rules of Civil or Criminal Procedure or the Court's inherent authority to enforce its rules and orders.

[Amended effective January 1, 2001; January 1, 2007; January 1, 2008; January 1, 2009.]

RULE 83.8. RESERVED

[Formerly "Rule 83.8 Number of Experts in Patent Cases", reserved effective January 1, 2009.]

RULE 83.13. SEALED MATTERS

Cases may be sealed in their entirety, or only as to certain parties or documents, when they are initiated, or at various stages of the proceedings. The Court may on its own motion enter an order directing that a document, party or entire case be sealed. A party seeking to have a document, party or entire case sealed shall submit an application, under seal, setting forth the reason(s) why the document, party or entire case should be sealed, together with a proposed order for the assigned judge's approval. The proposed order shall include language in the "ORDERED" paragraph stating the referenced document(s) to be sealed and should include the phrase "including this sealing order." Upon the assigned judge's approval of the sealing order, the Clerk shall seal the document(s) and the sealing order. A complaint presented for filing with a motion to seal and a proposed order shall be treated as a sealed case, pending approval of the proposed order. Once the Court seals a document or case, it shall remain under seal until a subsequent order, upon the Court's own motion or in response to the motion of a party, is entered directing that the document or case be unsealed.

Pleadings and other papers filed under seal in civil actions shall remain under seal for sixty (60) days following final disposition of the action, i.e., final disposition of the action includes any time allowed by the federal rules to file an appeal in a civil matter, and, if an appeal is filed, sixty (60) days from the date of the filing of the mandate if the action was not remanded for further proceedings. After that time, the Court will unseal all sealed documents and place them in the case record unless the district judge or magistrate judge, upon motion, orders that the pleading or other document remain under seal or be returned to the filing party.

[Amended effective January 1, 1999; January 1, 2008; January 1, 2009.]

SECTION XI. CRIMINAL PROCEDURE

RULE 12.1 MOTIONS AND OTHER PAPERS

(a) The moving party must file all motion papers with the Court and serve them upon the other parties no less than **THIRTY-ONE CALENDAR DAYS** prior to the return date of the motion. The Notice of Motion should state the return date that the moving party selected. The moving party must specifically articulate the relief requested and must set forth a factual basis which, if proven true, would entitle the moving party to the requested relief. The opposing party must file opposing papers with the Court and serve them upon the other parties not less than **SEVENTEEN CALENDAR DAYS** prior to the return date of the motion. The moving party may file reply papers only with leave of the Court, upon a showing of necessity. If the Court grants leave, the moving party must file reply papers with the Court and serve them upon the other parties not less than **ELEVEN CALENDAR DAYS** prior to the return date of the motion.

The parties shall not file, or otherwise provide to the assigned judge, a courtesy copy of the motion papers unless the assigned judge specifically requests that they do so.

In addition, no party shall file or serve a memorandum of law which exceeds twenty-five (25) pages in length, unless the party obtains permission from the Court to do so prior to filing. All memoranda of law exceeding five (5) pages shall contain a table of contents and, wherever possible, parallel citations. A separate memorandum of law is unnecessary when the case law may be concisely cited (i.e. several paragraphs) in the body of the motion.

(b) The Court shall not hear a motion to compel discovery unless the attorney for the moving party files with the Court, simultaneously with the filing of the moving papers, a notice stating that the moving party has conferred and discussed in detail with the opposing party the issues between them in a good faith effort to eliminate or reduce the area of controversy and to arrive at a mutually satisfactory resolution.

(c) All motions and other papers filed in a criminal action or proceeding shall show on the first page beneath the file number which, if any, of the speedy trial exclusions under 18 U.S.C. § 3161 are applicable to the action sought or opposed by the motion or other paper and the amount of resulting excludable time.

(d) Adjournment of motions shall be in the Court's discretion. Any party seeking an adjournment from the Court shall first contact the opposing attorney. A party shall make any application for an adjournment of a motion in writing and shall set forth the reason for requesting the adjournment.

(e) If the parties agree that a suppression hearing is necessary and the papers conform to the requirements of L.R.Cr.P. 12.1(a), the Court will set the matter for a hearing. If the government contests whether the Court should conduct a hearing, the defendant must accompany the motion with an affidavit, based upon personal knowledge, setting forth facts which, if proven true, would entitle the defendant to relief.

(f) An affidavit of counsel is not required when filing motions in criminal cases. A certificate of service is required at the conclusion of the motion.

(g) All papers filed in criminal cases shall comply with the guidelines established in L.R.Cr.P. 1.3 regarding personal privacy protection.

[Amended effective January 1, 1999; January 1, 2001; January 1, 2004; January 1, 2008.]

RULE 57.2. RELEASE OF BOND

When a defendant has obtained release by depositing a sum of money or other collateral as bond as provided by 18 U.S.C. § 3142, the payee or depositor shall be entitled to a refund or release thereof when the conditions of the bond have been performed and the defendant has been discharged from all obligations thereon. The defendant's attorney shall prepare a motion and proposed order for the release of the bond and submit the motion to the Court for the assigned judge's signature.

Absent direction from a Judicial Officer of the Northern District indicating otherwise, Clerk's Office personnel shall not accept cash, personal checks or credit cards as collateral for bail. However, bail may be posted with other forms of legal tender, including, but not limited to, money orders and bank-certified checks.

Unless otherwise specified by court order, or upon such proof as the Court shall require, all bond refunds shall be disbursed to the individual whose name appears on the Court's receipt for payment.

[Amended effective January 1, 2009.]

SELECTED GENERAL ORDERS

GENERAL ORDER 1. PLAN FOR THE COMPOSITION, ADMINISTRATION AND MANAGEMENT OF THE PANEL OF PRIVATE ATTORNEYS AND THE OFFICE OF THE FEDERAL PUBLIC DEFENDER UNDER THE CRIMINAL JUSTICE ACT

DATED: December 12, 2005

I. Authority. Pursuant to the Criminal Justice Act of 1964, as amended, (*CJA*), section 3006A of Title 18, United States Code, and the *Guidelines for the Administration of the Criminal Justice Act and Related Statutes (CJA Guidelines), Volume VII, Guide to Judiciary Policies and Procedures* (*CJA* Guidelines), the judges of the United States District Court for the Northern District of New York, adopt this Plan for furnishing representation in federal court for any person financially unable to obtain adequate representation in accordance with the Criminal Justice Act.

II. Statement of Policy.

A. *Objectives.*

1. The objective of the Plan is to attain equality before the law for all persons. Therefore, this Plan shall be administered so that those accused of a crime, or otherwise eligible for services pursuant to the *CJA*, will not be deprived, because they are financially unable to pay for adequate representation, or for any service necessary to an adequate defense.

2. The further objective of this Plan is to particularize the requirements of the *CJA*, the Anti–Drug Abuse Act of 1988 (codified in part at § 848(q) of Title 21, United States Code), and the *CJA Guidelines* in a way that meets the needs of this District.

B. *Compliance.*

1. The Court, its Clerk, the Federal Public Defender Organization (FPD), and private attorneys appointed under the *CJA* shall comply with the *CJA Guidelines* approved by the Judicial Conference of the United States and/or its Committee on Defender Services and with this Plan.

2. The Clerk of Court shall provide each private attorney with a current copy of this Plan upon the attorney's first appointment under the *CJA* or designation as a member of the panel of private attorneys under the Criminal Justice Act (*CJA* Panel). The clerk shall maintain a current copy of the *CJA Guidelines* for the use of members of the *CJA* Panel and shall make known to such attorneys its availability.

III. Definitions.

A. "Representation" includes counsel and investigative, expert, and other services.

B. "Appointed attorney," members of the panel of private attorneys (*CJA* Panel) who are eligible and willing to be appointed to provide representation under the Criminal Justice Act, the Federal Public Defender and staff attorneys of the Federal Public Defender, and private attorneys when needed to supplement the *CJA* Panel.

IV. Provision of Representation.

A. *Circumstance.*

1. Mandatory. Representation shall be provided for any financially eligible person who:

   a. is charged with a felony or with a *Class A* misdemeanor;

   b. is a juvenile alleged to have committed an act of juvenile delinquency as defined in § 5031 of Title 18, U.S.C.;

   c. is charged with a violation of probation, or faces a change of a term or condition of probation (unless the modification sought is favorable to the probationer and the government has not objected to the proposed change);

   d. is under arrest, when such representation is required by law;

   e. is entitled to appointment of counsel in parole proceedings;

   f. is charged with a violation of supervised release or faces modification, reduction, or enlargement of a condition, or extension or revocation of a term of supervised release;

   g. is subject to a mental condition hearing under Chapter 313 of Title 18, U.S.C.;

   h. is in custody as a material witness;

   i. is seeking to set aside or vacate a death sentence under § 2254 or § 2255 of Title 28, U.S.C.;

   j. is entitled to appointment of counsel in verification of consent proceedings pursuant to a transfer of an offender to or from the United States for the execution of a penal sentence under § 4109 of Title 18, U.S.C.;

   k. is entitled to appointment of counsel under the Sixth Amendment to the Constitution; or

   l. faces loss of liberty in a case and federal law requires the appointment of counsel.

2. Discretionary. Whenever a judge or United States magistrate judge determines that the interests of justice so require, representation may be provided for any financially eligible person who:

   a. is charged with a petty offense (Class B or C misdemeanor, or an infraction), for which a sentence to confinement is authorized;

   b. is seeking relief, other than to set aside or vacate a death sentence under § 2241, § 2254, or § 2255 of Title 28, U.S.C.;

   c. is charged with civil or criminal contempt who faces the loss of liberty;

   d. has been called as a witness before a grand jury, a court, the Congress, or a federal agency or commission which has the power to compel testimony, and there is reason to believe, either prior to or during testimony, that the witness could be subject to a criminal prosecution, a civil or criminal contempt proceeding, or face loss of liberty;

    e. is proposed by the United States attorney for processing under a pretrial diversion program;

    f. is held for international extradition under Chapter 209 of Title 18, U.S.C.

Representation may also be furnished for financially eligible persons in ancillary matters appropriate to the proceedings pursuant to subsection C of the *CJA* Plan.

    B. *When Counsel Shall Be Provided.* Counsel shall be provided to eligible persons as soon as feasible after they are taken into custody, when they appear before a judge or magistrate judge, when they are formally charged or notified of charges if formal charges are sealed, or when a judge or magistrate judge otherwise considers appointment of counsel appropriate under the *CJA*, whichever occurs earliest.

    C. *Number and Qualifications of Counsel.*

    1. Number. More than one attorney may be appointed in any case determined by the court to be extremely difficult. In a capital case, the following applies:

    a. Federal Capital Prosecutions. Pursuant to 18 U.S.C. § 3005, a person charged with a capital offense is entitled to the appointment of two attorneys, at least one of whom shall be learned in the law applicable to capital cases. Pursuant to 21 U.S.C. § 848(q)(4), if necessary for adequate representation, more than two attorneys may be appointed to represent a defendant in such a case.

    b. Habeas Corpus Proceedings. Pursuant to 21 U.S.C. Section 848(q)(4), a financially eligible person seeking to vacate or set aside a death sentence in proceedings under 28 U.S.C. § 2254 or § 2255 is entitled to appointment of one or more qualified attorneys. Due to the complex, demanding, and protracted nature of death penalty proceedings, judicial officers should consider appointing at least two counsel.

    2. Qualifications. Qualifications for appointed counsel shall be determined by the court. In capital cases, the following also applies:

    a. Appointment of Counsel Prior to Judgment. Pursuant to 21 U.S.C. § 848(q)(5), at least one of the attorneys appointed must have been admitted to practice in the court in which the case will be prosecuted for not less than five years, and must have had not less than three years experience in the actual trial of felony prosecutions in that court. Pursuant to 18 U.S.C. § 3005, at least one of the attorneys appointed must be knowledgeable in the law applicable to capital cases.

    Pursuant to 18 U.S.C. § 3005, in appointing counsel in federal capital prosecutions, the court shall consider the recommendation of the Federal Public Defender.

    b. Appointment of Counsel After Judgment. Pursuant to 21 U.S.C. § 848(q)(6), at least one of the attorneys appointed must have been admitted to practice in the court of appeals for not less than five years, and must have had not less than three years experience in the handling of appeals in felony cases in the court.

    c. Attorney Qualification Waiver. Pursuant to 21 U.S.C. § 848(q)(7), the presiding judicial officer, for good cause, may appoint an attorney who may not qualify under 21 U.S.C. § 848(q)(5) or (q)(6), but who has the background, knowledge, and experience necessary to represent the defendant properly in a capital case, giving due consideration to the seriousness of the possible penalty and the unique and complex nature of the litigation.

    D. *Eligibility for Representation.*

    1. Factfinding. The determination of eligibility for representation under the *CJA* is a judicial function to be performed by a federal judge or magistrate judge after making appropriate inquiries concerning the person's financial condition.

    2. Disclosure of Change in Eligibility. If, at any time after appointment, counsel obtains information that a client is financially able to make payment, in whole or in part, for legal or other services in connection with his or her representation, and the source of the attorney's information is not protected as a privileged communication, counsel shall advise the court.

E. *Use of Financial Information.* The Government may not use as part of its direct case, other than a prosecution for perjury or false statements, any information provided by a defendant in connection with his or her request for the appointment of counsel pursuant to this Plan.

V. Federal Public Defender.

1. *Establishment.*

a. The Federal Public Defender Office for the Northern District of New York previously established on September 29, 1997, pursuant to the provisions of the *CJA*, is hereby recognized as the Federal Public Defender Organization for this district.

b. The Federal Public Defender shall be capable of providing legal services throughout the Northern District of New York.

2. *Supervision of Defender Office.* The Federal Public Defender shall be responsible for the supervision and management of the Federal Public Defender Office. Accordingly, the Federal Public Defender shall be appointed in all cases assigned to that organization for subsequent assignment to staff attorneys at the discretion of the Federal Public Defender.

VI. Private Attorneys.

A. *Establishment of CJA Panel.* The existing previously established panel of attorneys (*CJA* Panel) who are eligible and willing to be appointed to provide representation under the *CJA* will be considered for membership on the *CJA* Panel.

B. *Organization.* The Plan for the composition, administration, and management of the Panel of private attorneys under the Criminal Justice Act is found at Appendix I of this *CJA* Plan.

C. *Ratio of Appointments.* Where practical and cost effective, private attorneys from the *CJA* Panel shall be appointed in a substantial proportion of the cases in which the accused is determined to be financially eligible for representation under the *CJA*. "Substantial" shall usually be defined as approximately 25% of the appointments under the *CJA* annually throughout the district.

VII. Representation in State Death Penalty Habeas Corpus Proceedings Under 28 U.S.C. § 2254. The Court shall appoint a member or members of the Special Death Penalty Habeas Corpus Panel, or the Federal Public Defender with his or her consent, or a qualified attorney recommended by the Federal Public Defender, or any other attorney who qualifies for appointment pursuant to § 848(q) of Title 21, United States Code to represent financially eligible persons seeking habeas corpus relief in state death penalty proceedings under § 2254 of Title 28, United States Code.

VIII. Duties of Appointed Counsel.

A. *Standards.* The services to be rendered to a person represented by appointed counsel shall be commensurate with those rendered if counsel were privately employed by the person.

B. *Professional Conduct.* Attorneys appointed pursuant to the *CJA* shall conform to the highest standards of professional conduct, including but not limited to the provisions of the New York State Lawyer's Code of Professional Responsibilities, as adopted from time to time by the Appellate Divisions of the State of New York, and as interpreted and applied by the United States Court of Appeals for the Second Circuit, and any other standards for professional conduct adopted by this court.

C. *No Receipt of Other Payment.* Appointed counsel may not require, request, or accept any payment or promise of payment or any other valuable consideration for representation under the appointment, unless such payment is approved by order of the court.

D. *Continuing Representation.* Once counsel is appointed under the *CJA*, counsel shall continue the representation until the matter, including appeals or review by certiorari (as governed by the circuit *CJA* Plan provisions concerning representation on appeal), is closed; until substitute counsel has filed a notice of appearance; until an order has been entered allowing or requiring the person represented to proceed *pro se*; or until the appointment is terminated by court order.

E. *Pro Bono Panel.* In recognition of the need for representation of indigent parties in civil actions, this Court has established the Pro Bono Panel of the Northern District of New York. The Panel shall include members of the *CJA* Panel in this Court. Any other attorney admitted to practice in this Court shall also be expected to participate in periodic training as offered by the Court and to accept no more than one Pro Bono assignment per year.

IX. Duties of Law Enforcement and Related Agencies.

A. *Presentation of Accused for Appointment of Counsel.* Federal law enforcement and prosecutorial agencies, probation officers, and pretrial services officers in this district, and those acting on their behalf, shall promptly inform any person who is in custody, or who otherwise may be entitled to counsel under the *CJA*, of their right to counsel, prior to any questioning, and that counsel shall be provided without cost if the person is unable to afford counsel. If the person requests counsel, federal law enforcement and prosecutorial agencies are encouraged to inform the person promptly of the existence of the Federal Public Defender Office and how to contact it, regardless of whether the Federal Public Defender may ultimately be appointed in their defense. In instances where the person indicates that he or she is not able to secure private representation, the Federal Public Defender shall be promptly notified. In such cases in which the person indicates that he or she is not financially able to secure representation, the Federal Public Defender shall discuss with the person the right to representation and right to appointed counsel, and if appointment seems likely, assist in the completion of a financial affidavit (*CJA* Form 23) and arrange to have the person promptly presented before a magistrate judge or judge of this Court for determination of financial eligibility and appointment of counsel. Law enforcement and related agencies must also comply with the provisions of Local Rule 5.1 of the Rules of Criminal Procedure for the Northern District of New York.

B. *Pretrial Services Interview.* This Court recognizes the importance of the advice of counsel for persons subject to proceeding under 18 U.S.C. § 3142 et seq., prior to their being interviewed by a pretrial services or probation officer. Accordingly, the United States Attorney shall include notification to the accused with the issuance of any criminal summons or appearance letter of their obligation to contact the Pretrial Services Office for the Northern District of New York at least forty-eight hours prior to their scheduled appearance with the Court to arrange for a pretrial services report to be completed. If the accused does not have retained counsel, the notification shall also include contact information for the office of the Federal Public Defender. Upon execution of an arrest warrant, law enforcement and related agencies shall comply with the requirements set forth in IX.A. Early notification to the Federal Public Defender and Pretrial Services office will assist in the furnishing of appointed counsel at this stage of the proceedings to financially eligible defendants, having due regard for the importance of affording the pretrial services officer adequate time to interview the defendant and verify information prior to the initial appearance and bail hearing.

C. *Notice of Indictment or Criminal Information.* Upon the return or unsealing of an indictment, the filing of a criminal information, or the filing of a petition to modify or revoke probation, the United States Attorney shall mail or otherwise deliver a copy of the document to appointed counsel, or to the defendant if he or she is without counsel, at the address shown on defendant's bond papers or to the jail in which the defendant is incarcerated.

X. Miscellaneous.

A. *Forms.* Standard forms, pertaining to the *CJA* and approved by the Judicial Conference of the United States or its Committee on Defender Services and prescribed and distributed by the Director of the Administrative Office of the United States Courts, shall be used, where applicable, in all proceedings under this Plan.

B. *Claims.* Claims for compensation of private attorneys providing representation under the *CJA* shall be submitted on the appropriate *CJA* form to the office of the Clerk of the court. That office shall review the claim form for mathematical and technical accuracy, and for conformity with the *CJA Guidelines*, and, if correct, shall forward the claim form for the consideration of the appropriate judge or magistrate judge. The Court may also direct the Office of the Federal Public Defender to review claim forms for mathematical and technical accuracy, and for conformity with the *CJA Guidelines*. The court will exert its best effort to avoid delays in reviewing payment vouchers and in submitting them for further processing.

C. *Supersession.* This Plan supersedes all prior Criminal Justice Act Plans for this court.

XI. Effective Date. This Plan and Appendix I, the Plan for the composition, administration, and management of the Panel of private attorneys under the *CJA* shall become effective when approved by the Judicial Council of the Second Circuit.

SO ORDERED FOR THE COURT ON December 2, 2005.

APPROVED BY THE JUDICIAL COUNCIL FOR THE SECOND CIRCUIT ON December 12, 2005.

APPENDIX I. PLAN FOR THE COMPOSITION, ADMINISTRATION AND MANAGEMENT OF THE PANEL OF PRIVATE ATTORNEYS UNDER THE CRIMINAL JUSTICE ACT

I. Composition of the Panel of Private Attorneys.

A. *CJA Panel.*

1. Approval. The Court shall establish a panel of private attorneys (hereinafter referred to as the "*CJA* Panel") who are eligible and willing to be appointed to provide representation under the Criminal Justice Act. The Court shall approve attorneys for membership on the panel on a quarterly basis after receiving recommendations from the "Panel Selection Committee," established pursuant to paragraph B of this Plan. Members of the *CJA* Panel shall serve at the pleasure of the Court.

2. Size. The Court shall fix, periodically, the size of the *CJA* Panel. The panel shall be large enough to provide a sufficient number of experienced attorneys to handle the *CJA* caseload, yet small enough so that panel members will receive an adequate number of appointments to maintain their proficiency in federal criminal defense work, and thereby provide a high quality of representation.

3. Eligibility. Attorneys who serve on the *CJA* Panel must be members in good standing of the federal bar of this district, and have demonstrated experience in, and knowledge of, the Federal Rules of Criminal Procedure, the Federal Rules of Evidence, and the Sentencing Guidelines. In addition to the above, attorneys who serve on the *CJA* Panel must attend one *CJA* Training Program at least once every two years.

Subsection (b) of the Act provides, in part, that; Counsel furnishing representation under the plan shall be selected from a panel of attorneys designated or approved by the court, or from a bar association, legal aid agency, or defender organization furnishing representation pursuant to the Plan.

However, when the district judge or magistrate judge presiding over the case, or the chief judge if a district judge or magistrate judge has not yet been assigned to the case, determines that the appointment of an attorney, who is not a member of the *CJA* panel, is in the interest of justice, judicial economy or continuity of representation, or there is some other compelling circumstance warranting his or her appointment, the attorney may be admitted to the *CJA* panel *pro hac vice* and appointed to represent the *CJA* defendant. Consideration for preserving the integrity of the panel selection process suggests that such appointments should be made only in exceptional circumstances. Further, the attorney, who may or may not maintain an office in the district, should possess such qualities as would qualify him or her for admission to the district's *CJA* panel in the ordinary course of panel selection.

4. Equal Opportunity. All qualified attorneys shall be encouraged to participate in the furnishing of representation in *CJA* cases, without regard to race, color, religion, sex, age, national origin or disabling condition. Notice of the opportunity to apply for membership on the *CJA* Panel shall be provided to attorneys at the time of admission to the bar of this Court. The applications shall also be available at the office of the Clerk and on the Court's Web Page. (*www.nynd.uscourts.gov*)

5. Terms. *CJA* Panel members shall serve at the pleasure of the court. Members of the panel shall serve continuously until they resign or are removed from the panel.

6. Removal from the Panel. Membership on the *CJA* Panel is a privilege, not a right, which may be terminated at any time by the Board of Judges, as they, in their sole discretion, may determine. The Board of Judges may seek the recommendation of the *CJA* Panel Committee with respect to the removal of existing panel members.

7. Required Training. *CJA* Panel members shall be required to attend one *CJA* training program at least once every two years. The Office of the Federal Public Defender shall sponsor two *CJA* workshops each year. *CJA* Panel members may also satisfy the training requirement by attending a nationally sponsored *CJA* Panel training program. In lieu of attending one of the above mentioned programs, a Panel member may request to have this requirement waived by demonstrating that they have participated in a criminal law seminar of equal quality and length. Requests are to be submitted to the CJA Panel Committee in care of the Clerk of Court at the James M. Hanley Federal Building and Courthouse, 100 S. Clinton Street, Syracuse, New York 13261, and shall include the following materials:

    (a) The date, location and length of the program attended;

    (b) The agenda or syllabus of the program attended; and

    (c) The number and type of CLE credit hours earned for attending the program.

Failure to fulfill this training requirement may result in grounds for removal from the *CJA* Panel.

8. Application. Application forms for membership on the *CJA* Panel shall be made available, upon request, by the Clerk of the Court. Completed applications shall be submitted to the Clerk of the Court who will transmit the applications to the Court for review and approval on a quarterly basis. Application forms are also available on the Court's website at *www.nynd.uscourts.gov*.

B. *CJA Panel Committee.*

1. Membership. A *CJA* Panel Committee shall be established by the Court. The NDNY Committee shall consist of two magistrate judges, the Federal Public Defender, two attorneys from the Syracuse and Albany Divisions, and one from the Binghamton office. The Clerk of Court or Chief Deputy Clerk shall serve as an *ad hoc* member of the Committee to provide administrative support. The Committee shall be chaired by one of the magistrate judges appointed.

2. Duties.

    a. The Committee shall be responsible for the oversight of the *CJA* Panel and the Criminal Justice Act Plan. At least once annually, the Committee shall review the operation and administration of the panel and make recommendations to the Court as to any necessary changes to the *CJA* Plan. The Committee shall also ascertain the continued availability and willingness of each panel member to accept appointments. The Committee may also make recommendations to the Court with respect to appointment of new panel members or the removal of existing panel members. The Clerk of Court shall provide the Committee with all relevant information concerning the assignment of panel members.

    b. The Committee shall assist the Court by working with local bar associations regarding recruitment efforts in furtherance of the Equal Opportunity statement in Paragraph I.A.4 of this Plan. The Clerk of Court will assist the Committee by:

1. Notifying bar associations and advertising in legal journals to solicit participation of qualified practitioners who are female, disabled or a member of some other minority;

2. Contacting current or former members of the panel, as well as prominent local attorneys to seek recommendations for appointment to the panel of qualified applicants who are female, disabled or a member of some other minority.

C. *CJA Training Panel—2nd Chair Program.* The Court has established a *"CJA Training Pane—2nd Chair Program."* The program has been designed to help educate attorneys who do not yet have the experience required for membership on the *CJA* Panel. Training Panel members should contact the Office of the Federal Public Defender to obtain information on the 2nd Chair Program. Training Panel members are not eligible to receive appointments, and shall not be eligible to receive compensation for their services in assisting members of the Federal Public Defenders Office or members of the *CJA* Panel. Attorneys participating in the 2nd Chair Program must attend the following regular court proceedings: an initial appearance; a detention hearing; an arraignment; a hearing on a pretrial motion; a change of plea, and a sentencing hearing. In addition to observing these proceedings at the District Court, the candidate must also "demonstrate familiarity with the sentencing guidelines" as defined in the program information provided to candidates by the Office of the Federal Public Defender. Prior service on the *CJA Training Panel—2nd Chair Program* is not a requirement for membership on the *CJA* Panel, nor will service on the Training Panel guarantee admission of an attorney to the *CJA* Panel.

II. Selection for Appointment

A. *Maintenance of List and Distribution of CJA Appointments.* The Clerk of the Court shall maintain a current list of all attorneys included on the *CJA* Panel, with current office addresses, telephone and fax numbers, e:mail addresses, as well as a statement of qualifications and experience. The Clerk shall furnish a copy of this list to each judge and magistrate judge, the list shall also be made available to the Federal Public Defender. The Clerk shall also maintain a public record of assignments to private counsel, and, when appropriate, statistical data reflecting the proration of appointments between attorneys from the Federal Public Defender Organization and private attorneys, according to the formula described in the *CJA* Plan for the District.

The Clerk of Court shall also maintain a record of each refusal ("pass") by a panel attorney, and the reason for each pass. If the Clerk's Office determines that a panel member has repeatedly passed assignments, the Clerk may refer the name of the attorney to the Court. The Court shall then consider the information provided by the Clerk and make such further inquiry as it deems appropriate.

B. *Method of Selection.* Appointments from the list of private attorneys should be made on a rotational basis, subject to the Court's discretion to make exceptions due to the nature and complexity of the case, an attorney's experience, and geographical considerations. This procedure should result in a balanced distribution of appointments and compensation among the members of the *CJA* Panel, and quality representation for each *CJA* defendant.

Upon the determination of a need for the appointment of counsel, the judge or magistrate judge shall notify the Clerk of Court, or Federal Public Defender of the need for counsel and the nature of the case.

The Clerk of Court shall advise the judge or magistrate judge as to the status of distribution of cases, where appropriate, as between the Federal Public Defender and the panel of private attorneys. If the judge or magistrate judge decides to appoint an attorney from the panel, the Clerk shall determine the name of the next panel member on the list who is available for appointment, and shall provide the name to the appointing judge or magistrate judge.

In the event of an emergency, i.e., weekends, holidays, or other non-working hours of the Clerk of Court's office, the presiding judge, or magistrate judge, may appoint any attorney from the list if a member of the Federal Public Defender's Office is not available. In all cases where members of the *CJA* Panel are appointed out of sequence, the appointing judge or magistrate judge shall notify the Clerk of Court, or Federal Public Defender as to the name of the attorney appointed and the date of the appointment.

In the interests of justice, where continuity of representation is a factor or other special circumstances exist, the Court may assign an attorney who is not on the panel. Consideration for preserving the integrity of the panel selection process suggests that such appointments be made only in exceptional circumstances. Further, the attorney, who may or may not maintain an office in the district, should possess such qualities as would qualify him or her for admission to the district's *CJA* panel in the ordinary course. Such attorney if appointed must also follow the appropriate full admission to the bar or pro hac admission requirements of the district.

C. *Special Circumstances.* If after appointment, counsel learns that a client is financially able to pay all or part of the fee for legal representation and the source of the attorney's information is not a privileged communication, counsel shall so advise the presiding judge. The presiding judge will take appropriate action, including but not limited to: permitting assigned counsel to continue to represent the defendant; terminating the appointment of counsel, or ordering any funds available to the party to be paid as provided in 18 U.S.C. section 3006A(f) as the interests of justice may dictate. Any amount paid by the party will be considered by the presiding judge in determining the total compensation allowed to the attorney.

D. *Investigative, Expert and Other Services.*

1. Upon Request. Counsel for a party who is financially unable to obtain investigative, expert or other services necessary for an adequate defense may request such services *ex parte* before a judge or magistrate judge having jurisdiction over the case. Such application shall be heard *in camera* and shall not be revealed without the consent of the defendant. On finding that the services are necessary and that the person is financially unable to afford them, the judge or magistrate judge shall authorize them. An order setting forth the type, purpose, and limitations of such services will be issued by the Court. The judge or magistrate judge may establish a limit on the amount that may be expended or committed for such services within the maximum prescribed by 18 U.S.C. section 3006A(e)(3).

2. Without Prior Request. Counsel appointed pursuant to this Plan may obtain subject to later review, investigative, expert, or other services without prior judicial authorization if they are necessary for an adequate defense. The total cost of services so obtained may not exceed the maximum prescribed by 18 U.S.C. section 3006(A)(e)(2) per individual or corporation providing the services (exclusive of reasonable expenses). However, in the interests of justice and upon finding that timely procurement of necessary services could not await prior authorization, a judge or magistrate judge (in a case entirely disposed of by the magistrate judge) may approve payment for such services after they have been obtained, even if the services exceed the maximum prescribed by 18 U.S.C. section 3006(A)(e)(2).

3. Necessity of Affidavit. Statements made by or on behalf of the party in support of requests for investigative, expert, and other services shall be made or supported by affidavit and filed with the Court *in camera* for review and consideration.

E. *Compensation—Filing of Vouchers.* Claims for compensation shall be submitted on the appropriate *CJA* form accompanied by the *CJA* voucher worksheets to the office of the Clerk of Court. That office shall review the claim form for mathematical and technical accuracy, and for conformity with the *Guidelines for the Administration of the Criminal Justice Act (Volume VII, Guide to Judiciary Policies and Procedures)* and, if correct, shall forward the claim form for the consideration of the appropriate judge or magistrate judge. The Court may also direct the Office of the Federal Public Defender to review claim forms for mathematical and technical accuracy, and for conformity with the *CJA* Guidelines. The court will exert its best effort to avoid delays in reviewing payment vouchers and in submitting them for further processing.

1. Maximum Amounts for Counsel. For representation of a defendant before a magistrate judge or judge of this court, or both, the compensation paid any attorney shall not exceed the maximum prescribed by 18 U.S.C. section 3006A(d)(2).

2. Waiver of Limits on Counsel Fees. Payment in excess of any maximum amount prescribed by 18 U.S.C. section 3006A(d)(2) for counsel fees or for other services may be made for extended or complex representation whenever the judge or magistrate judge (if the representation was entirely before the magistrate judge) certifies that the amount sought is necessary to provide fair compensation and the payment is approved by the Chief Judge of the Second Circuit or such active Circuit Judge to whom the Chief Judge has delegated approval authority. Counsel claiming such excess payment shall submit a detailed memorandum justifying counsel's claim that the representation was in an extended or complex case and that the excess payment is necessary to provide fair compensation.

3. Reduction of *CJA* Payment. In any case where the judge or magistrate judge believes that the claim as submitted should be reduced for reasons other than mathematical or technical errors, the judge or magistrate judge shall notify counsel in writing and afford counsel the opportunity to be heard. Counsel shall be given the opportunity to provide information or documentation relevant to the voucher and questions or concerns raised by the judge or magistrate judge. After review of the submission by the Panel member and the completion of any steps deemed appropriate by the court, the judge or magistrate judge shall make the final decision as to the fee request consistent with this Plan, the *CJA*, and the interests of justice.

Notwithstanding the procedure described above, a judge or magistrate judge may in the first instance, contact counsel to inquire regarding questions or concerns with a claim for compensation. In the event that the matter is resolved to the satisfaction of the judge or magistrate judge and Panel member, the claim for compensation need not go through the formal written submission requirements noted above.

GENERAL ORDER 3. TRANSCRIPT FEES FOR UNITED STATES COURT REPORTERS

Pursuant to the authorization of the Judicial Conference of the United States, it is hereby

ORDERED that; the following maximum allowable transcript rates per page may be charged by Official Court Reporters for the Northern District of New York, as well as any Contract or Per Diem Court Reporter. The rates reflected below shall remain in effect until further order of this Court.

It is further **ORDERED** that; the Clerk of Court post the fee schedule in a prominent location at each office of the Clerk and post it to the Court Web page at *nynd.uscourts.gov*. Issues regarding billing by members of the public or bar should be brought to the attention of the Clerk of Court.

	Original	Copy to Each Party	Each Add'l Copy to the Same Party
Ordinary Transcript—A transcript to be delivered within thirty (30) calendar days after receipt of order.	$3.65	$.90	$.60
14–Day Transcript—A transcript to be delivered within fourteen (14) calendar days after receipt of an order.	$4.25	$.90	$.60
Expedited Transcript—(7 day) A transcript to be delivered within seven (7) calendar days after receipt of an order.	$4.85	$.90	$.60
Daily Transcript—A transcript to be delivered following adjournment and prior to the normal opening	$6.05	$1.20	$.90

	Original	Copy to Each Party	Each Add'l Copy to the Same Party

hour of the court on the following morning whether
or not it actually is a court day.

Hourly Transcript—A transcript of proceedings or- $7.25 $1.20 $.90
dered under unusual circumstances to be delivered
within two (2) hours.

Realtime Transcript—A draft unedited transcript $3.05 $1.20
produced by a certified realtime reporter as a byproduct of realtime to be delivered electronically
during proceedings or immediately following adjournment.

The Judicial Conference approved a modification to the transcript fee rates for realtime unedited transcripts provided by certified realtime reporters to establish the maximum page rate authorized for the provision of realtime services, including the production and distribution of realtime unedited transcripts. Litigants who order realtime services, and subsequently order an original certified transcript of the same proceeding, will not receive a credit toward the purchase cost of the certified transcript. A litigant who orders a copy of a realtime unedited transcript will be required to purchase a certified copy of the same pages of realtime unedited copies at the regular copy rates (ordinary, 14–day, expedited, daily, or hourly). (JCUS–MAR 1996, p. 26; JCUS–MAR 1999, p. 25; and Sep 1997, p. 12.)

Transcript in CJA Cases

In multi-defendant cases involving CJA defendants, no more than one transcript should be purchased from the court reporter on behalf of CJA defendants. One of the appointed counsel or the clerk of court should arrange for the duplication, at commercially competitive rates, of enough copies of the transcript for each of the CJA defendants for whom a transcript has been approved. The cost of such duplication will be charged to the CJA appropriation. This policy would not preclude the furnishing of duplication services by the court reporter at the commercially competitive rate.

DATED this 24th day of October, 2007, at Syracuse, New York.

As adopted in March 1996, it is the policy of the Judicial Conference that effective June 1, 1996, a new category of "realtime unedited transcript" has been established. Realtime unedited transcript is defined as "a draft transcript produced by a Certified Realtime Reporter (CRR) as a byproduct of realtime to be delivered electronically during the proceedings or immediately following adjournment." Realtime includes the following services:

● The instantaneous translation of the proceedings on a computer monitor.

● The opportunity to scroll forward and backward, search the record for key words or phrases and mark portions of the text using viewer/annotation software.

● The realtime unedited transcript on diskette delivered during the proceedings or at the end of the day.

A realtime unedited transcript must be clearly marked as such with a header or footer which appears at the top or bottom of each page of transcript stating, "Realtime Unedited Transcript Only." The realtime unedited transcript should not include an appearance page, an index, or a certification. Realtime unedited transcript sold on computer diskette may be in ASCII format, or any other format requested by the ordering party and agreed to by the court reporter. It should include any notations made to the electronic file by the ordering party during the proceedings. Diskettes may not contain any protection or programming codes that would prevent copying or transferring the data.

All parties requesting realtime services shall be responsible for providing their own personal computers, viewer/annotation software, and monitors. Upon the request of the parties, reporters may make equipment and software available at no additional charge. The Court Reporter shall provide wiring and data communications connections needed to provide realtime services to these persons.

Parties should coordinate and pre-test their equipment with the Court Reporter before official proceedings begin.

A Court Reporter providing realtime unedited transcript should offer comparable services to all parties to the proceeding. The primary purpose of realtime unedited transcript is to provide access to a draft transcript of the proceedings on diskette at the end of each day. It is not intended to be used in subsequent proceedings for impeachment or for any other purpose, including further distribution.

It should be noted that when realtime unedited transcript is provided, there may be two versions of the transcript for one proceeding–unofficial and official. The realtime unedited transcript may contain errors, some of which could change the accuracy or meaning of the testimony. A realtime unedited transcript will not satisfy the requirement for the reporter to provide or file a certified transcript with the district court clerk or as the record on appeal.

GENERAL ORDER 6. ORDER LIMITING THE POSSESSION OF FIREARMS AND WEAPONS IN THE COURTROOMS OF THE NORTHERN DISTRICT OF NEW YORK

Pursuant to the recommendation of the Judicial Conference of the United States, it is hereby

ORDERED, that the possession of firearms and weapons in any courtroom in this District shall be limited to the following people: Court Security Officers, Deputies, and employees of the United States Marshals Service, or their duly authorized agents. At his or her discretion the presiding judicial officer at any proceeding may authorize additional persons to carry firearms and weapons in the courtroom.

DATED this 29th day of March, 2002, at Syracuse, New York.

GENERAL ORDER 9. THE DISTRICT POLICY ON SEARCH AND SEIZURE

IT IS ORDERED that the District Court for the Northern District of New York hereby adopts a District Policy on Search and Seizure. The policy conforms to the model search and seizure guidelines issued by the Judicial Conference of the United States at its March 1993 meeting and supersedes the District Policy on Search and Seizure issued on December 18th, 2002.

DATED this 14th Day of March 2008, at Syracuse, New York.

GENERAL ORDER 13. RULES REGARDING STUDENT PRACTICE IN THE NORTHERN DISTRICT OF NEW YORK

1. A law student admitted as a Student Practitioner may with the court's approval, under supervision of an attorney, appear on behalf of any person, including the United States Attorney, who has consented in writing on the form prescribed by the clerk.

2. The attorney who supervises a student shall in compliance with this Rule:

(a) Be a member of the bar of the United States District Court for the Northern District of New York.

(b) Assume personal professional responsibility for the student's work.

(c) Assist the student to the extent necessary.

(d) Appear with the student in all proceedings before the court unless his presence is waived by the court.

(e) Indicate in writing his consent to supervise the student.

3. In order to appear, the student shall:

(a) Be duly enrolled in a law school approved by the American Bar Association.

(b) Have completed legal studies amounting to at least four semesters, or the equivalent.

(c) Be recommended by either the dean or a faculty member of his or her law school as a student practitioner. This recommendation may be withdrawn by the recommender at any time by mailing a notice to the Clerk or by termination by the court without notice of hearing and without showing of cause.

(d) Neither ask for nor receive any compensation or remuneration of any kind for his services from the person on whose behalf s/he renders services, but this shall not prevent an attorney, legal aid bureau, law school, public defender agency, a State, or the United States from paying compensation to the eligible law student, nor shall it prevent any agency from making proper charges for its services. Neither the student, nor anyone on the student's behalf, shall seek recovery of attorneys' fees from an adverse party for the services rendered by the student as a Student Practitioner.

(e) Certify in writing that s/he is familiar with the federal procedural and evidentiary rules as well as the local rules of this court. The student practitioner shall complete and file an application for admission as a student practitioner on the form supplied by the Clerk.

(f) Upon filing such application with the Clerk of the Court, in proper form, the Clerk shall enroll the applicant's name, address, date of admission and the fact that the applicant is a student practitioner on the automated attorney roll. The Clerk shall assign a Bar Roll number to the student and assign an attorney status code of **Student Attorney** until such time formal admission to the district is obtained. The application shall also contain information on the expected date of graduation from law school. The applications for student practitioners will be maintained by the Attorney Registration Clerk.

(g) A student practitioner may appear and render services pursuant to this Rule after approval of the application by a District Court Judge or Magistrate Judge and until the results of the first New York State bar examination subsequent to the student's graduation has been published.

4.   The law student so enrolled and supervised in accordance with these rules, may:

(a) Appear as counsel in court or at other proceedings when consent of the client or his authorized representative, or the United States Attorney when the client is the United States, and the supervising attorney have been filed, and when the court has approved the student's request to appear in the particular case.

(b) Prepare and sign motions, petitions, answers, briefs, and other documents in connection with any matter in which s/he had met the conditions of (a) above; each such document shall also be signed by the supervising attorney and shall be filed in the case file.

5.   Forms approved by the court for use in connection with this Rule shall be available in the Clerk's Office. Completed forms shall be filed with the attorney registration clerk for this district.

6.   **Effective Date.** General Order #13 as revised was approved by the Court on the 15 day of September, 2007.

**UNITED STATES DISTRICT COURT
FOR THE NORTHERN DISTRICT OF NEW YORK**

STUDENT PRACTICE AUTHORIZATION FORM

FORM TO BE COMPLETED BY THE CLIENT FOR WHOM THE LAW STUDENT IS RENDERING SERVICES; OR IF THE SERVICES ARE RENDERED FOR THE GOVERNMENT, BY THE UNITED STATES ATTORNEY OR HIS AUTHORIZED REPRESENTATIVE.

CASE TITLE:_____VS_____

CIVIL ACTION NO:_____CV_____

ASSIGNED TO JUDGE:_____

I authorize _____, a law student to appear in Court or at other proceedings on my behalf, and to prepare documents on by behalf.

_____   _____
(DATE)   (SIGNATURE OF CLIENT)

(If more than one client is involved, approvals from each shall be attached. If a class action is involved, approvals from named plaintiffs shall be attached).

TO BE COMPLETED BY THE LAW STUDENT'S SUPERVISING ATTORNEY:

I will carefully supervise all of this student's work. I authorize this student to appear in court or at other proceedings, and to prepare documents. I will accompany the student at such appearances, and sign all documents prepared by the student. I assume personal responsibility for his/her work.

_____   _____
(DATE)   (SIGNATURE OF ATTORNEY)

_____

UNITED STATES DISTRICT COURT
FOR THE NORTHERN DISTRICT OF NEW YORK
APPLICATION FOR ADMISSION AS A STUDENT PRACTITIONER PURSUANT TO GENERAL ORDER #13 OF THE NORTHERN DISTRICT.

_____

(NAME OF STUDENT)

ADDRESS AND PHONE OF ABOVE:

*Please note that this address will be the address to which all notices and correspondence are to be mailed by the Court.

_____

_____

( )-_____
(Area Code and Phone Number)

NAME OF LAW SCHOOL STUDENT IS ATTENDING:_____

NUMBER OF SEMESTERS STUDENT HAS COMPLETED:_____

ANTICIPATED GRADUATION DATE[1]:_____

_____

TO BE COMPLETED BY LAW STUDENT

I certify that I have completed at least 4 semesters of law school; that I have read and am familiar with the provisions of the Judicial Code (Title 28 USC), which pertain to the jurisdiction of, and practice in, the United States District Courts; the Federal Rules of Evidence for the District Courts; the Federal Rules of Civil and Criminal Procedure for the District Courts; the Local Rules and General Orders for the Northern District of New York; and the Code of Professional Responsibility of the American Bar Association; and will faithfully adhere thereto; and that I will receive no compensation from the person on whose behalf I am rendering services, in accordance with part 3(d) of General Order #13 pertaining to Student Practice in the Northern District of New York. I further understand that I will be assigned a Bar Roll Number by the Clerk of the Court to facilitate the keeping of an accurate roll of members of the bar of this court. Upon graduation and formal admission to the Bar for the Northern District of New York I shall complete an attorney registration statement and file such statement with the clerk of the court in accordance with Local Rule 83.1.

CERTIFICATION OF APPLICANT

_____   _____
(DATE)   (SIGNATURE OF STUDENT)

1 Student Practitioner's admission shall automatically expire upon graduation unless an application for extension is granted .

_____

TO BE COMPLETED BY THE DEAN OR A FACULTY MEMBER OF THE STUDENT'S LAW SCHOOL.

I certify that this student has completed at least four semesters of law school work and recommend that the student be admitted to the court as a student practitioner.

_____   _____
(DATE)   (SIGNATURE OF DEAN)

or

_____
(SIGNATURE OF FACULTY MEMBER)

_____

Admission Approved:

_____
(DATE)

_____ (U.S. DISTRICT JUDGE)
_____ (U.S. MAGISTRATE JUDGE)

Form to be forwarded to the attention of the Attorney Registration Clerk in the Syracuse Clerk's Office.

_____
ASSIGNED BAR ROLL NUMBER #

GENERAL ORDER 14. CIVIL RICO STATEMENT
(18 U.S.C. SECTION 1961, ET SEQ.)

FILED MARCH 7, 2003

IT IS SO ORDERED THAT:

Pursuant to the case management authority of this Court, a party filing an action in which claims have been asserted under the Racketeer Influenced and Corrupt Organizations Act hereinafter "RICO") (18 U.S.C. § 1961) shall file a RICO statement which complies with the following requirements.

Within thirty (30) days after the filing date of the complaint, the plaintiff shall file a RICO case statement which shall set forth facts the plaintiff is relying upon to initiate the complaint. The facts set forth within the RICO statement shall be based upon an inquiry reasonable under the circumstances as set forth in Fed. R. Civ. P. 11(b).

In numbered paragraphs mirroring the questions listed below, the RICO statement shall state in detail and specificity the following information.

1. State whether the alleged unlawful conduct is in violation of 18 U.S.C. Sections 1962(a),(b),(c), and/or (d).

2. List each defendant and state the alleged misconduct and basis of liability of each defendant.

3. List the alleged wrongdoers, other than the defendant(s) listed above, and state the alleged misconduct of each wrongdoer.

4. List the alleged victims and state how each victim was allegedly injured.

5. Describe in detail the pattern of racketeering activity or collection of unlawful debts alleged for each RICO claim. A description of the pattern of racketeering shall include the following information:

a. List the alleged predicate acts and the specific statutes which were allegedly violated;

b. Provide the dates of the predicate acts, the participants in the predicate acts and a description of the facts surrounding the predicate acts;

c. If the RICO claim is based on the predicate offenses of wire fraud, mail fraud, or fraud in the sale of securities, the "circumstances constituting fraud or mistake shall be stated with particularity." Fed. R. Civ. P. 9(b). Identify the time, place and contents of the alleged misrepresentations, and the identity of persons to whom and by whom the alleged misrepresentations were made;

d. State whether there has been a criminal conviction for violation of the predicate acts;

e. State whether civil litigation has resulted in a judgment in regard to the predicate acts;

f. Describe how the predicate acts form a "pattern of racketeering activity"; and

g. State whether the alleged predicate acts relate to each other as part of a common plan. If so, describe in detail.

6. Describe in detail the alleged enterprise for each RICO claim. A description of the enterprise shall include the following information:

a. State the names of the individuals, partnerships, corporations, associations, or other legal entities which allegedly constitute the enterprise;

b. Describe the structure, purpose, function and course of conduct of the enterprise;

c. State whether any defendants are employees, officers or directors of the alleged enterprise;

d. State whether any defendants are associated with the alleged enterprise;

e. State whether you are alleging that the defendants are individuals or entities separate from the alleged enterprise, or that the defendants are the enterprise itself, or members of the enterprise; and

f. If any defendants are alleged to be the enterprise itself, or members of the enterprise, explain whether such defendants are perpetrators, passive instruments, or victims of the alleged racketeering activity.

7. State and describe in detail whether you are alleging that the pattern of racketeering activity and the enterprise are separate or have merged into one entity.

8. Describe the alleged relationship between the activities of the enterprise and the pattern of racketeering activity. Discuss how the racketeering activity differs from the usual and daily activities of the enterprise, if at all.

9. Describe what benefits, if any, the alleged enterprise receives from the alleged pattern of racketeering.

10. Describe the effect of the activities of the enterprise on interstate or foreign commerce.

11. If the complaint alleges a violation of 18 U.S.C. Section 1962(a), provide the following information:

a. State who received the income derived from the pattern of racketeering activity or through the collection of an unlawful debt; and

b. Describe the use or investment of such income.

12. If the complaint alleges a violation of 18 U.S.C. Section 1962(b), describe in detail the acquisition of maintenance of any interest in or control of the alleged enterprise.

13. If the complaint alleges a violation of 18 U.S.C. Section 1962(c), provide the following information:

a. State who is employed by or associated with the enterprise; and

b. State whether the same entity is both the liable "person" and the "enterprise" under Section 1962 (c).

14. If the complaint alleges a violation of 18 U.S.C. Section 1962(d), describe in detail the alleged conspiracy.

15. Describe the alleged injury to business or property.

16. Describe the direct causal relationship between the alleged injury and the violation of the RICO statute.

17. List the damages sustained for which each defendant is allegedly liable.

18. List all other federal causes of action, if any, and provide the relevant statute numbers.

19. List all pendent state claims, if any.

20. Provide any additional information that you feel would be helpful to the Court in processing your RICO claim.

21. The information is to be filed with the Court within thirty (30) days from the filing date of the complaint. A copy of the RICO Statement shall also be served upon the defendants.

a. Failure to comply with the requirements of this order may result in the dismissal of your action without prejudice.

22. **Effective Date.** General Order #14 as revised was approved by the Court on the 7th day of March, 2003.

Filed March 7, 2003.

GENERAL ORDER 15. ELECTRONIC FILING OF DOCUMENTS— CIVIL AND CRIMINAL FORFEITURE ACTIONS

I. Civil In Rem Forfeiture Procedure.

A. *18 U.S.C. § 983—Personal Property.*

Pre-Complaint Restraining (Protective) Order

1(a) The United States may seek a pre-complaint restraining or protective order pursuant to 18 U.S.C. § 983(j). The United States Attorney's Office will contact the Clerk's Office for the United States District Court and advise that it intends to file a precomplaint restraining order. The Clerk will assign a Civil Action Number to the case and assign the matter to a United States District Judge and United States Magistrate Judge.

The United States Attorney's Office will provide to the Court Clerk's Office a disk or CD[1] containing the documents to be filed.

Civil Forfeiture—Complaint

2(a) The United States Attorney's Office will contact the Clerk's Office for the United States District Court and advise that it intends to file a civil forfeiture action on the same day.

2(b) The Clerk of the Court will assign a Civil Action Number to the case and assign the matter to a United States District Judge and a United States Magistrate Judge. The identity of the assigned judges promptly will be conveyed to the United States

Attorney's Office by a telephone call made by the U.S. Attorney's Office to the Clerk's Office.

2(c) The United States will select a date for the case to appear before the U.S. District Judge assigned to the case. The return date noted on the Warrant of Arrest of Articles in Rem and the Notice of Complaint for Forfeiture will be a regular motion date for the United States District Judge to whom the case has been assigned, and shall be at least 70 days from the time the Warrant is issued, to allow time for the United States Marshals Service to arrange for publication, service of process and arrest of the property. Before scheduling this date, however, the United States Attorney's Office will call the assigned Judge's Deputy Court Clerk to confirm that the proposed return date remains a scheduled motion day for the assigned Judge.

3(a) The United States Attorney's Office will then submit its civil forfeiture complaint paperwork, consisting of (i) civil cover sheet; (ii) Notice of Complaint for Forfeiture[2], (iii) Verified Complaint for Forfeiture, attaching Plaintiff's First Set of Interrogatories pursuant to Rule C(6) of the Supplemental Rules of Admiralty and Maritime Claims; and Warrant for Arrest of Articles in Rem[3], and on occasion, (iv) a post-complaint restraining order. Both the Notice of Complaint for Forfeiture and Warrant for Arrest of Articles in Rem will set forth the date on which the case will be returnable before the assigned Judge. This initial paperwork may be filed with the Clerk's Office for the Northern District of New York in Utica, Syracuse, Binghamton, Albany, or any other location for the United States District Court for the Northern District of New York.

3(b) The Clerk's Office shall file, date stamp and certify, as requested, the originals and copies of papers filed. The Clerk's Office shall retain copies stamped "Received" of the original Warrant for Arrest of Articles In Rem, Notice of Complaint for Forfeiture and Summons, and the originals of all other complaint paperwork filed. The original Warrant for Arrest of Articles In Rem and Notice of Complaint for Forfeiture and Summons, together with copies of all remaining papers shall be returned to a designated representative in the United States Attorney's Office in Albany, New York, Syracuse, New York, or any other United States Attorney's Office so designated. This designated individual shall forward the original Warrant for Arrest of Articles In Rem, original Notice of Complaint for Forfeiture and Summons and copies of all of the other complaint paperwork to the United States Marshals Service (or the appropriate Department of Treasury agency or Immigration and Customs Enforcement agency) to accomplish service of process, arrest of the property and publication of the notice.

3(c) On the return date, the Clerk of the Court shall call the case when the civil motion calendar is called. The Clerk shall inquire as to whether there is any "appearance" on behalf of the "defendant" property (asset) sought to be forfeited. A civil in rem forfeiture case, when scheduled for a "return on a warrant of arrest in rem," shall not under any circumstance be removed from the calendar and shall always be called at calendar call on the date published in the newspaper and announced to the public in that manner. If a Judge decides to cancel a motion day, to take cases on the calendar on submission, or is otherwise unavailable for the assigned motion day, and a civil forfeiture action(s) appear(s) on said calendar, a Court Clerk shall call the civil forfeiture case(s) and note appearances or non-appearances of any potential claimants in the forfeiture actions(s).

The U.S. Attorney's Office will provide to the Court Clerk's Office a disk or CD containing the documents to be filed. Once the functions set forth in 3(b) have been accomplished, the U.S. Marshal Service will continue to manually submit these original documents to the Court for scanning and electronic filing. Moreover, for Internal Revenue Service (IRS) and Immigration and Customs Enforcement (ICE) cases, the U.S. Attorney's Office will collect these return receipts and deliver them to the Court for scanning and electronic filing.

4. If no person enters an appearance on behalf of the "defendant" property (asset) at the time the calendar is called on the return of the warrant of arrest in rem, then the United States Attorney's Office will move the Court for a Judgment of Forfeiture on the basis that the forfeiture is uncontested. Prior to the return date, the United States

Attorney's Office shall present the proposed documents set forth below to the Judge's law clerk.

a. copies of the USM–285 Process Receipts and Returns (the originals of which should be filed with the Court by the United States Marshals Service) showing personal service; if personal service cannot reasonably be performed, service by certified mail, return receipt requested;

b. a copy of an affidavit of publication (the original of which should be filed with the Court by the United States Marshals Service);

c. an affidavit of non-military service, non-infancy and non-incompetency, which states that upon information and belief, the known potential claimant(s) are not in the military service, and are not infants or incompetents;

d. a proposed Order Directing Entry of an Uncontested Judgment of Forfeiture, directing the Clerk to enter a Judgment in a Civil Case pursuant to Rule 58 of the Federal Rules of Civil Procedure; and

e. a proposed Form of Judgment will be provided to the Court after the terms of the Order Directing Entry of an Uncontested Judgment of Forfeiture have been met.

(i) The original Affidavit of Non–Military Service, Non–Infancy and Non–Incompetency shall be electronically filed with the Court and a courtesy copy provided to the Judge; (There will be no requirement for a notary signature on the Affidavit— however, the U.S. Attorney's Office will maintain a signed, notarized Affidavit in its file).

(ii) the U.S. Attorney's Office shall inquire of the District Court Clerk's Office whether the Judge assigned to the case wishes to sign a hard copy of the Order Directing Entry of an Uncontested Judgment of Forfeiture, or wishes to utilize an electronic signature. Depending upon the answer to this inquiry, the U.S. Attorney's Office may either electronically file the Order Directing Entry of an Uncontested Judgment of Forfeiture and provide a courtesy copy to the Judge OR provide a hard copy of the Order to the Judge together with a disk or CD containing the documents to be filed.

(iii) After the terms of the Order Directing Entry of an Uncontested Judgment of Forfeiture have been satisfied, the U.S. Attorney's Office shall submit to the Court a hard copy of a letter (stating that the terms of the Order have been satisfied) and enclose a proposed Judgment to be signed by a Deputy Clerk of the Court.

5. If no verified claim or answer has been filed, but the potential claimant (or counsel for the potential claimant) has contacted the Court or the United States Attorney's Office seeking some type of adjournment or postponement, then the Court may grant an enlargement of time within which the claimant or the attorney who requested a postponement may file a verified claim and answer, but the case still will be called at the originally noticed motion date to determine whether any other person has appeared to assert a claim, and any such appearance or non-appearance will be noted in the record.

6. If an individual files a claim of ownership to the property (asset) sought to be forfeited, and such claim satisfies all of the statutory requirements for a valid claim, the Government will so advise the Court that it will accept the claim as an appearance and request that the Court issue an Order barring all further claims. This Order will either be presented to the Judge at the time of the court appearance or sent to the Judge after the Court appearance.

The U.S. Attorney's Office shall inquire of the District Court Clerk's Office whether the Judge assigned to the case wishes to sign a hard copy of the Order Barring All Further Claims, or wishes to utilize an electronic signature. Depending upon the answer to this inquiry, the U.S. Attorney's Office may either electronically file the Order Barring All Further Claims OR provide a hard copy of the Order to the Judge together with a disk or CD containing the document to be filed.

6(a) If there is a potential claimant named in the complaint who has not filed a formal claim and answer by the time of the Court appearance and who has not notified the

Government or Court of his, her or its interest in the property, then, at the return date, when the Government requests that all further claims be barred, the Government shall provide the Court with an affidavit pertaining to any individual who was named in the complaint, but never interposed a verbal or written claim to the property, stating that on information and belief the known potential claimant is not in the military service, is not an infant or incompetent person, and direct the Court to the U.S. Marshal Forms USM–285, contained in the Court's file, showing publication of notice of the forfeiture and/or proof of service of process on the individual.

The U.S. Attorney's Office shall electronically file the Affidavit of Non–Military, Non–Infancy and Non–Incompetency. (There will be no requirement for a notary signature on the Affidavit—however, the U.S. Attorney's Office will maintain a signed, notarized Affidavit in its file)

6(b) Within sixty (60) days after the filing of the Order barring all further claims, the United States of America shall contact opposing counsel and/or the pro se claimant to set out and agree upon a schedule of expiration dates dealing with joinder of parties, amendment of pleadings, discovery, filing of motions and a proposed trial date, and memorialize this agreement in a stipulation form which shall be signed by the parties and so ordered by the United States Magistrate Judge assigned to the case. In the event the parties cannot come to an agreement with regard to a schedule, the United States Attorney's Office will contact the deputy clerk to the assigned Magistrate Judge and request a discovery conference.

(i) the U.S. Attorney's Office will prepare a Stipulation pursuant to F.R.Civ.P. Rule 16(b) and a Form entitled Notice, Consent and Order of Reference—Exercise of Jurisdiction by a United States Magistrate Judge. (Pursuant to General Order #25, Forfeiture/Penalty cases are exempt from the requirement of filing a Civil Case Management Plan).

(ii) Once the Stipulation is signed by all parties and/or attorneys for parties to the action, the U.S. Attorney's Office will inquire of the District Court Clerk's Office whether the Magistrate Judge assigned to the case wishes to sign a hard copy of the Rule 16(b)Stipulation, or wishes to utilize an electronic signature. Depending upon the answer to this inquiry, the U.S. Attorney's Office may either electronically file the Rule 16(b) Stipulation and maintain a fully executed original of the Stipulation in its file and attest to the signatures contained thereon OR provide a hard copy of the Stipulation and Order to the Magistrate Judge together with a disk or CD containing the document to be filed.

(iii) Should the parties and/or attorneys for the parties to the action consent to have all further proceedings conducted by a United States Magistrate Judge, the U.S. Attorney's Office will inquire of the District Court Clerk's Office whether the District Judge assigned to the case wishes to sign a hard copy of the Notice, Consent and Order of Reference—Exercise of Jurisdiction by a United States Magistrate Judge, or wishes to utilize an electronic signature. Depending upon the answer to this inquiry, the U.S. Attorney's Office may either electronically file the Notice, Consent and Order of Reference—Exercise of Jurisdiction by a United States Magistrate Judge and maintain a fully executed original of the Consent in its file and attest to the signatures contained thereon OR provide a hard copy of the Notice, Consent and Order of Reference to the District Judge together with a disk or CD containing a copy of the document to be filed.

B. *18 U.S.C. § 985—Real Property.*

Pre-Complaint Restraining (Protective) Order—Real Property.

1. The United States may seek a pre-complaint restraining or protective order pursuant to 18 U.S.C. § 983(j). The United States Attorney's Office will contact the Clerk's Office for the United States District Court and advise that it intends to file a pre-complaint restraining order. The Clerk will assign a Civil Action Number to the case and assign the matter to a United States District Judge and United States Magistrate Judge.

The United States Attorney's Office will provide to the Court Clerk's Office a disk or CD containing the documents to be filed.

Civil Forfeiture—-Complaint

2(a) The United States Attorney's Office will contact the Clerk's Office for the United States District Court and advise that it intends to file a civil forfeiture action on the same day.

2(b) The Clerk of the Court will assign a Civil Action Number to the case and assign the matter to a United States District Judge and a United States Magistrate Judge. The identity of the assigned judges promptly will be conveyed to the United States Attorney's Office by a telephone call made by the U.S. Attorney's Office to the Clerk's Office.

2(c) The United States will select a date for the case to appear before the U.S. District Judge assigned to the case. The return date noted on the Notice of Complaint for Forfeiture and Summons will be a regular motion date for the United States District Judge to whom the case has been assigned, and shall be at least 70 days from the time the Notice is issued, to allow time to arrange for publication, service of process and posting of the property. Before scheduling this date, however, the United States Attorney's Office will call the assigned Judge's Deputy Court Clerk to confirm that the proposed return date remains a scheduled motion day for the assigned Judge.

3(a) The United States Attorney's Office will then submit its civil forfeiture complaint paperwork, consisting of a (i) Civil Cover Sheet, (ii) Notice of Complaint for Forfeiture and Summons with return date, (iii) Verified Complaint for Forfeiture, attaching Plaintiff's First Set of Interrogatories pursuant to Rule C(6) of the Supplemental Rules of Admiralty and Maritime Claims, (iv) Notice of Lis Pendens, (v) Writ of Entry (the Writ will secure the property as it will not be seized (arrested))[4] and, on occasion, (vi) a post-complaint restraining (protective) order. The initial paperwork will be filed with the Clerk's Office for the Northern District of New York in Syracuse, Binghamton, Albany, or any other location for the United States District Court for the Northern District of New York.

3(b) The Clerk's Office shall file, date stamp and certify, as requested, the originals and copies of papers filed. The Clerk's Office shall retain a copy marked "Received" of the Notice of Complaint for Forfeiture and Summons, and the originals of all other complaint paperwork filed. The original Notice of Complaint for Forfeiture and Summons, together with copies of all remaining papers shall be returned to a designated representative in the United States Attorney's Office in Albany, New York, Syracuse, New York, or any other United States Attorney's Office so designated. This designated individual shall forward the original Notice of Complaint for Forfeiture and Summons and copies of all of the other complaint paperwork to the United States Marshals Service (or the appropriate Department of Treasury agency or Immigration and Customs Enforcement agency) to accomplish service of process, posting of the property and publication of the notice.

3(c) Since seizure (arrest) of the real property will generally not occur during the pendency of the civil forfeiture action, there will be no need for the issuance of a warrant of arrest in rem. However, upon a showing of exigent circumstances by the Government that less restrictive measures such as the filing of a lis pendens or a restraining (protective) order would not suffice to protect the Government's interest in the property, the Government will, request issuance of a warrant of arrest in rem pursuant to the provisions of 18 U.S.C. § 985(d)(1).

3(d) On the return date, the Clerk of the Court shall call the case when the civil motion calendar is called. The Clerk shall inquire as to whether there is any "appearance" on behalf of the "defendant" real property sought to be forfeited. A civil in rem forfeiture case, when scheduled for a "return on the Notice of Complaint and Summons" shall not under any circumstance be removed from the calendar and shall always be called at calendar call on the date published in the newspaper and announced to the public in that manner. If a Judge decides to cancel a motion day, to take cases on the calendar on submission, or is otherwise unavailable for the assigned motion day, and a civil forfeiture action(s) appear(s) on said calendar, a Court Clerk shall call the civil forfeiture case(s) and note appearances or non-appearances of any potential claimants in the forfeiture actions(s).

The U.S. Attorney's Office will provide to the Court Clerk's Office a disk or CD containing the documents to be filed. Once the functions set forth in 3(b) have been accomplished, the U.S. Marshal Service will continue to manually submit these original documents to the Court for scanning and electronic filing. Moreover, for Internal Revenue Service (IRS) and Immigration and Customs Enforcement (ICE) cases, the U.S. Attorney's Office will collect these return receipts and deliver them to the Court for scanning and electronic filing.

4. If no person enters an appearance on behalf of the "defendant" real property at the time the calendar is called on the return of the Notice of Complaint and Summons, then the United States Attorney's Office will move the Court for a Judgment of Forfeiture on the basis that the forfeiture is uncontested. Prior to the return date, the United States Attorney's Office shall present the proposed documents set forth below to the Judge's law clerk.

　　a. copies of the USM–285 Process Receipts and Returns (the originals of which should be filed with the Court by the United States Marshals Service) showing personal service of known potential claimants; if personal service cannot reasonably be performed, service by certified mail, return receipt requested;

　　b. a copy of an affidavit of publication (the original of which should be filed with the Court by the United States Marshals Service);

　　c. an affidavit of non-military service, non-infancy and non-incompetency, which states that, upon information and belief, the known potential claimant(s) are not in the military service, and are not infants or incompetents;

　　d. a proposed Order Directing Entry of an Uncontested Judgment of Forfeiture, directing the Clerk to enter a Judgment of Forfeiture pursuant to Rule 58 of the Federal Rules of Civil Procedure; and

　　e. a proposed Form of Judgment will be provided to the Court after the terms of the Order Directing Entry of an Uncontested Judgment of Forfeiture have been met.

　　(i) the original Affidavit of Non–Military Service, Non–Infancy and Non–Incompetency shall be electronically filed with the Court and a courtesy copy provided to the Judge; (There will be no requirement for a notary signature on the Affidavit—however, the U.S. Attorney's Office will maintain a signed, notarized Affidavit in their file).

　　(ii) the U.S. Attorney's Office shall inquire of the District Court Clerk's Office whether the Judge assigned to the case wishes to sign a hard copy of the Order Directing Entry of an Uncontested Judgment of Forfeiture, or wishes to utilize an electronic signature. Depending upon the answer to this inquiry, the U.S. Attorney's Office may either electronically file the Order Directing Entry of an Uncontested Judgment of Forfeiture and provide a courtesy copy to the Judge OR provide a hard copy of the Order to the Judge together with a disk or CD containing the document to be filed.

　　(iii) After the terms of the Order Directing Entry of an Uncontested Judgment of Forfeiture have been satisfied, the U.S. Attorney's Office shall submit to the Court a hard copy of a letter (stating that the terms of the Order have been satisfied) and enclose a proposed Judgment to be signed by a Deputy Clerk of the Court.

5. If no verified claim or answer has been filed, but the potential claimant (or counsel for the potential claimant) has contacted the Court or the United States Attorney's Office seeking some type of adjournment or postponement, then the Court may grant an enlargement of time within which the claimant or the attorney who requested a postponement may file a verified claim and answer, but the case still will be called at the originally noticed motion date to determine whether any other person has appeared to assert a claim, and any such appearance or non-appearance will be noted in the record.

6. If an individual files a claim of ownership to the real property sought to be forfeited, and such a claim satisfies all statutory requirements for a valid claim, the Government will so advise the Court that it will accept the claim as an appearance and request that the Court issue an Order barring all further claims. This Order will either be presented to the Judge at the time of the court appearance or sent to the Judge after the Court appearance.

The U.S. Attorney's Office shall inquire of the District Court Clerk's Office whether the Judge assigned to the case wishes to sign a hard copy of the Order Barring All Further Claims, or wishes to utilize an electronic signature. Depending upon the answer to this inquiry, the U.S. Attorney's Office may either electronically file the Order Barring All Further Claims OR provide a hard copy of the Order to the Judge together with a disk or CD containing the document to be filed.

7. If there is a potential claimant named in the complaint who has not filed a formal claim and answer by the time of the Court appearance and who has not notified the Government or Court of his, her or its interest in the property, then, at the return date, when the Government requests that all further claims be barred, the Government shall provide the Court with an affidavit pertaining to any individual who was named in the complaint, but never interposed a verbal or written claim to the property, stating that on information and belief the known potential claimant is not in the military service, is not an infant or incompetent person, and direct the Court to the U.S. Marshal Forms USM–285, contained in the Court's file, showing publication of notice of the forfeiture and/or proof of service of process on the individual.

The U.S. Attorney's Office shall electronically file the Affidavit of Non–Military, Non–Infancy and Non–Incompetency. (There will be no requirement for a notary signature on the Affidavit—however, the U.S. Attorney's Office will maintain a signed, notarized Affidavit in their file)

8. Within sixty (60) days after the filing of the Order barring all further claims, the United States of America shall contact opposing counsel and/or the pro se claimant to set out and agree upon a schedule of expiration dates dealing with joinder of parties, amendment of pleadings, discovery, filing of motions and a proposed trial date, and memorialize this agreement in a stipulation form which shall be signed by the parties and so ordered by the United States Magistrate Judge assigned to the case. In the event the parties cannot come to an agreement with regard to a schedule, the United States Attorney's Office will contact the deputy clerk to the assigned Magistrate Judge and request a discovery conference.

(i) the U.S. Attorney's Office shall prepare a Stipulation pursuant to F.R.Civ.P. Rule 16(b)[5] and a Form entitled Notice, Consent and Order of Reference—Exercise of Jurisdiction by a United States Magistrate Judge.

(ii) Once the Stipulation is signed by all parties and/or attorneys for parties to the action, the U.S. Attorney's Office will inquire of the District Court Clerk's Office whether the Magistrate Judge assigned to the case wishes to sign a hard copy of the Stipulation, or wishes to utilize an electronic signature. Depending upon the answer to this inquiry, the U.S. Attorney's Office may either electronically file the Stipulation and maintain a fully executed original of the Stipulation in its file and attest to the signatures contained thereon OR provide a hard copy of the Stipulation to the Magistrate Judge together with a disk or CD containing a copy of the document to be filed.

(iii) Should the parties and/or attorneys for the parties to the action consent to have all further proceedings conducted by a United States Magistrate Judge, the U.S. Attorney's Office will inquire of the District Court Clerk's Office whether the District Judge assigned to the case wishes to sign a hard copy of the Notice, Consent and Order of Reference—Exercise of Jurisdiction by a United States Magistrate Judge, or wishes to utilize an electronic signature. Depending upon the answer to this inquiry, the U.S. Attorney's Office may either electronically file the Notice, Consent and Order of Reference—Exercise of Jurisdiction by a United States Magistrate Judge and maintain a fully executed original of the Consent in its file and attest to the signatures contained thereon OR provide a hard copy of the Order to the District Judge together with a disk or CD containing a copy of the document to be filed.

II. Dispositive Stipulations and Orders for Settlement and Orders Directing Entry of an Uncontested Judgment of Forfeiture.

A. Settlement Agreements. Substituted Res—United States funds remitted by a claimant that are to be forfeited to the United States in place of specific real or personal property subject to forfeiture, such as real estate or a vehicle.

After a Stipulation and Order for Settlement has been signed by the parties and "So Ordered" by the Judge assigned to the case, and as directed by the Stipulation, after the terms of the Stipulation have been satisfied, the Clerk shall issue a Judgment in a Civil Case. The U.S. Attorney's Office will submit a proposed form of Judgment to the Court. In actions where there is a substitute res forfeited in place of real or personal property, the Judgment shall direct that the substituted res be forfeited to the United States of America for disposition in accordance with law.

Once the Settlement Stipulation is signed by all parties and/or attorneys for parties to the action, the U.S. Attorney's Office will inquire of the District Court Clerk's Office whether the Judge assigned to the case wishes to sign a hard copy of the Settlement Stipulation, or wishes to utilize an electronic signature. Depending upon the answer to this inquiry, the U.S. Attorney's Office may either electronically file the Settlement Stipulation and maintain a fully executed original of the Settlement Stipulation in its file and attest to the signatures contained thereon OR provide a hard copy of the Settlement Stipulation to the Judge together with a disk or CD containing the document to be filed.

B. Order Directing Entry of an Uncontested Judgment of Forfeiture. After the Order Directing Entry of an Uncontested Judgment of Forfeiture has been signed by the Judge assigned to the case and as directed in the Order, after the terms of the Order have been satisfied, the Clerk shall issue a Judgment in a Civil Case directing forfeiture of the property to the United States of America for disposition in accordance with law. The United States Attorney's Office will submit a proposed form of judgment.

The U.S. Attorney's Office will provide a hard copy of a letter and the proposed Judgment to the assigned Judge's Courtroom Deputy Clerk.

C. Dissemination of Copies of Dispositive Pleadings. The United States Attorney's Office requires, for dissemination, six date-stamped certified copies of any dispositive pleading. The United States Attorney's Office shall provide the original dispositive pleading to the assigned Judge. The Deputy Clerk of the assigned Judge shall provide the United States with six (6) date-stamped, certified copies of the pleading.

III. Civil In Rem Seizure Warrants.

Seizure Warrants are authorized pursuant to Title 21, United States Code, Section 881(b)(4), Title 18, United States Code, Section 981(b)(2), and other applicable statutes. When federal law enforcement agencies have probable cause to believe that an item is subject to forfeiture, then they may contact the United States Attorney's Office for assistance in seeking a seizure warrant. A seizure warrant is entirely different from the Warrant of Arrest In Rem that is used in civil in rem forfeiture cases. A seizure warrant merely results in the securing of the asset by federal law enforcement, pending the institution and/or conclusion of a forfeiture proceeding.

As a general rule, an application for a Seizure Warrant is not presented to a United States District Judge, unless a United States Magistrate Judge is unavailable.

The procedure for the Clerk's Office in processing Seizure Warrants shall be identical to the process employed for processing search warrants pursuant to Rule 41 of the Federal Rules of Criminal Procedure.

(i) the United States Attorney's Office will provide to the Court Clerk's Office a disk or CD containing the documents to be filed. (If the documents are sealed, no disk or CD will be required to be furnished to the Clerk's Office until the documents are unsealed); and

(ii) instead of filing a seizure warrant pursuant to 18 U.S.C. § 983(a)(3)(B)(ii)(*l*) to preserve the Government's right to maintain custody of the property pursuant to the criminal forfeiture statutes, the United States will present a hard copy of an Application and Order Regarding Criminal Forfeiture of Property In Government Custody pursuant to 18 U.S.C. § 983(a)(3)(B)(ii)(II) to the Judge assigned to the case together with a disk or CD containing the documents to be filed.

IV. Criminal Forfeiture Procedure.

The U.S. Attorney's Office will file a notice of appearance on each criminal case containing a forfeiture allegation in the Indictment/Information. This Notice of Appearance will contain language stating that the forfeiture attorney is appearing as co-counsel concerning the criminal forfeiture aspects of the case.

A. *Criminal (Protective) Restraining Orders (21 U.S.C. § 853(e)).* Prior or subsequent to the filing of a criminal indictment/information, the United States may apply for the issuance of a protective order/restraining order/temporary restraining order pursuant to the provisions of 21 U.S.C. § 853(e), to preserve the availability of the property subject to forfeiture.

(i) the United States Attorney's Office will provide to the Court Clerk's Office a disk or CD containing the documents to be filed.

B. *Criminal Seizure Warrants (21 U.S.C. § 853(f)).* The Government may request a criminal seizure warrant authorizing the seizure of property subject to forfeiture, pursuant to 21 U.S.C. § 853(f).

(i) the seizure warrant application and affidavit will manually be filed with the Court by the U.S. Attorney's Office (manual filing will ensure that the seizure warrant will not become public before it is executed); (ii) the U.S. Attorney's Office will be provided with a certified copy of the seizure warrant by the Court for service and will retain the original seizure warrant pending its execution; (iii) the original seizure warrant and return will be manually filed with the Court by the U.S. Attorney's Office and (iv) the seizure warrant, application, affidavit and return will be electronically filed by the Court only after the seizure warrant has been executed.

C. *Preliminary Order of Forfeiture (Fed.R.Crim.P. 32.2(b)).* When a defendant pleads guilty or a special verdict is rendered by the trial jury, the United States Attorney's Office shall prepare a Preliminary Order of Forfeiture, pursuant to the provisions of Federal Rules of Criminal Procedure 32.2, and submit such Order to the U.S. District Judge assigned to the case. At the same time, a copy of the Preliminary Order of Forfeiture will be sent to defendant's counsel (or pro se defendant) for submission of any objections, if any, as to form and/or content of the order. The United States Attorney will ask the assigned Judge to hold in abeyance his signing of the Preliminary Order of Forfeiture for a period of ten (10) days from the date the U.S. Attorney's Office mails the proposed Order to defendant's counsel, to allow defendant's counsel adequate time to raise objections, if any, as to the form and content of the proposed Order. A copy of the proposed Preliminary Order of Forfeiture also will be provided to the United States Probation Department by the United States Attorney's Office.

Once the United States Attorney's Office receives the signed Preliminary Order of Forfeiture from the assigned Judge, it will publish notice of its intent to dispose of the property(ies) and provide written notice to any person known to have an interest in the property(ies). Any person, other than defendant, asserting a legal interest in the property shall within 30 days of the final publication notice or receipt of actual notice by mail, file a petition in accordance with the provisions of 21 U.S.C. § 853(n). The statute calls for a hearing to be held on the ancillary claim, however, based on the common practice in this District, no hearing will be held unless requested by a petitioner or the United States after serious, good cause efforts have been made to resolve the claim without the intervention of the Court.

If no third party files an ancillary claim within the prescribed period of time, the United States Attorney's Office, at sentencing, will provide a letter to the Court advising that (i) no ancillary claims have been filed, (ii) the Preliminary Order of Forfeiture will become final as to the defendant and (iii) no separate Final Order of Forfeiture will be prepared.

When specific property of a defendant is unavailable for forfeiture, the Government may seek a personal money judgment against a defendant at an amount to be determined by the Court. In such instances, the United States Attorney's Office will prepare a Preliminary Order of Forfeiture as described above, however, nothing further will be done until such time as property is found to satisfy this money judgment.

The United States Attorney's Office will provide to the Court Clerk's Office a disk or CD containing the documents to be filed.

D. *Ancillary Motions (Fed.R.Crim. P. 32.2(b)(3))*. The United States may file discovery motions as provided in Rule 32.2(b)(3) to identify, locate or dispose of property or may commence a proceeding that complies with any statutes governing third party rights.

The United States will electronically file said motions.

E. *Ancillary Petitions (Fed.R.Crim.P. 32.2(c))*. Procedures governing ancillary forfeiture proceedings in criminal actions are set forth in Fed. R.Crim. P. 32.2(c). The United States or an ancillary petitioner may seek permission of the Court to conduct discovery in accordance with the Federal Rules of Civil Procedure, which request shall be granted if the Court first determines that discovery is necessary or desirable to resolve factual issues. When discovery ends, a party may move for summary judgment under Fed. R.Civ.P. 56.

F. *Final Orders of Forfeiture (No Ancillary Claims Filed or Ancillary Claims Resolved) (Fed.R.Crim.P. 32.2(c))*. Once all of ancillary claims filed in the matter have been resolved (or in the instance where there are no ancillary claims filed), the United States Attorney will submit to the U.S. District Judge assigned to the case the Final Order of Forfeiture containing terms resolving ancillary claim issues. After receiving the signed Final Order of Forfeiture, the United States Attorney's Office will submit this signed Order to the United States Marshal Service (or the appropriate Department of Treasury agency or Immigration and Customs Enforcement agency), requesting that the terms of the Court's Order be implemented.

(i) Final Order of Forfeiture—Resolution of Ancillary Claim(s):

The U.S. Attorney's Office shall inquire of the District Court Clerk's Office whether the Judge assigned to the case wishes to sign a hard copy of the Final Order of Forfeiture, or wishes to utilize an electronic signature. Depending upon the answer to this inquiry, the U.S. Attorney's Office may either electronically file the Final Order of Forfeiture OR provide a hard copy of the Order to the Judge together with a disk or CD containing the document to be filed.

(ii) Preliminary Order will become the Final Order of Forfeiture No Ancillary Claims Filed (Rule 32.2(c)(2)). The U.S. Attorney's Office will electronically file its letter advising the Court that there were no ancillary claims filed and the Preliminary Order shall become the Final Order of Forfeiture.

G. *Substitute Assets (21 U.S.C. § 853(p) & F.R.Crim.P. 32.2(e))*. There may be cases where a defendant's known and recoverable property subject to forfeiture at the time of conviction is insufficient to satisfy the Forfeiture Order of a Court in this District. In such cases, and where additional property of the defendant not otherwise subject to forfeiture can be located, the United States may apply to the assigned District Judge, pursuant to Fed.R. Crim.P. 32.2 and 21 U.S.C. § 853, for an order authorizing the seizure and forfeiture of such substitute assets up to but not exceeding the remaining unsatisfied amount of the Court's Order of Forfeiture. In such cases, the United States Attorney's Office, upon notice to the defendant, will present to the United States District Judge assigned to the case a letter and Affidavit (prepared by federal law enforcement special agent) seeking an amendment of the Preliminary Order/Final Order of Forfeiture to include substitute assets. If that application is granted, the Government will follow the same procedures set forth in Sections IV(C), (D) & (E) above.

The United States Attorney's Office will provide to the Court Clerk's Office a disk or CD containing the documents to be filed.

H. *Restitution (21 U.S.C. § 853(i))*. With respect to property ordered forfeited, 21 U.S.C. § 853(i) provides, in part, a mechanism to restore forfeited property to victims of crimes or to take any other action to protect the rights of innocent persons (victims).

1. In a case where restitution is ordered and the Government has obtained any necessary approvals from the Department of Justice, the Government may present a Final Order of Forfeiture Directing Restoration of Forfeited Property to Victims to the Judge assigned to the criminal case. The Final Order of Forfeiture shall direct the United States Marshal Service/Department of Treasury agency/Immigration and Customs Enforcement agency to:

(i) liquidate any vehicles or real property,

(ii) satisfy, by payment from the net proceeds of the sale, any outstanding mortgages, liens and judgments and

(iii) remit a check made payable to the Clerk of the Court for any remaining forfeited funds after "(ii)" above has been accomplished. Said check shall contain on its face the following information:

(I) the court criminal case number and

(II) the name of the defendant to whom the restitution shall be applied.

The check shall then be deposited into a general restitution account held by the U.S. District Court Clerk's Office for the Northern District of New York and be applied toward the assigned District Judge's restitution order for that specific defendant,

OR ALTERNATIVELY

2. The Government may present a Final Judgment of Restitution in Lieu of Forfeiture. In such cases, the United States will use same procedures as set forth in paragraph '1' above.

The United States Attorney's Office will provide to the Court Clerk's Office a disk or CD containing the documents to be filed.

At Syracuse, New York this 30th day of July, 2004.

---

1 This disk or CD will be returned by the District Court Clerk's Office to the representative of the U.S. Attorney's Office who filed the documents.

2 CAFRA has replaced the Summons in a Civil Forfeiture Action and the Notice of Forfeiture Action and Seizure with a form entitled "Notice of Complaint for Forfeiture and Summons."

3 CAFRA has replaced the Warrant of Arrest in Rem with Warrant for Arrest of Articles in Rem.

4 U.S. Attorney's Office will file Writ of Entry with Civil Complaint paperwork. U.S. Attorney's Office will ask Deputy Clerk to contact Courtroom Deputy for Judge assigned to case to arrange for signing of Writ by Judge. Courtroom Deputy for Judge assigned to case will then contact U.S. Attorney's Office when Writ of Entry is signed.

5 Pursuant to General Order #25, Forfeiture/Penalty cases are exempt from the requirement to file a Civil Case Management Plan.

GENERAL ORDER 17.   PLAN FOR PROMPT DISPOSITION OF CRIMINAL CASES

Final Plan Pursuant to the Speedy Trial Act of 1974—18 U.S.C. Section 3161, et seq.

I. Introduction.

A. *Statement of Adoption by the Court.* Pursuant to the requirements of Rule 50 of the Federal Rules of Criminal Procedure, the Speedy Trial Act of 1974 (18 U.S.C. § 3161 et seq.), the Speedy Trial Act Amendments Act of 1979 (Pub.L.No. 96–43, 93 Stat.327), and the Federal Juvenile Delinquency Act (18 U.S.C. §§ 5036, 5037), the Judges of the United States District Court have adopted the following Plan to minimize undue delay and to further the prompt disposition of criminal cases and certain juvenile proceedings. This Plan reflects the efforts and cooperation of the Court and other offices of the federal criminal justice community of the Northern District of New York.

B. *Notice of Adoption by the Court.* Copies of the Plan adopted by this District pursuant to 18 U.S.C. § 3165 and § 3166 will be on file with the Clerk in the Albany, Binghamton, Syracuse, and Utica offices of the United States District Court and may be obtained from the Court's web page at www.nynd.uscourts.gov. The Clerk will advise counsel representing defendants in criminal cases and defendants electing *pro se* representation of the existence of the Speedy Trial Act, this Plan and any applicable Local Rules.

C. *Characteristics of the Northern District.* To facilitate an understanding of the problems which may affect compliance with the Speedy Trial Act, it is necessary to understand the general make-up of the District. The District is the largest in terms of territory and counties in the Second Circuit. It serves 32 of the 62 counties in New York State and covers 30,511 square miles. Its northern boundary reaches to Canada and its southern boundary extends to Pennsylvania. Although much of the District is rural, it has ten major cities and a population of nearly 3,320,000 persons. It includes the major industrial cities of Syracuse, Binghamton, Utica, and Schenectady and New York State's Capitol in Albany.

The District has staffed offices in Albany, Binghamton, Syracuse, and Utica. The Court holds continuous jury terms in Albany, Binghamton, Syracuse, and Utica. Special jury terms are scheduled throughout the year in Auburn and Watertown. The District has five authorized judgeships, five authorized magistrate judgeships, and one authorized part-time magistrate judgeship. The United States Attorney has staffed offices in Albany, Binghamton, and Syracuse. Assistant U.S. Attorneys travel to Auburn, Utica, and Watertown to conduct business. The Federal Public Defender has staffed offices in Albany and Syracuse, and travels to other court locations.

The District contains numerous major intrastate and interstate highways and abuts the Canadian border with numerous ports of entry between the two countries. Two of the United States's largest navigable bodies of water, the St. Lawrence Seaway and the Hudson River, are inside or abut the District and, through the Erie and Champlain barge canals, serve the Port of Albany, which is a major transportation and distribution center for the Northeastern United States. The Amtrak and Conrail railroads send passengers and freight to all parts of the Country. There are major repair and marshaling yards, among the largest in the Nation, located in Albany and Rensselaer Counties. The District also has international airports located in Albany, Syracuse, and Binghamton with daily flights sending passengers and freight to all parts of the Country and abroad.

II. Statement of Time Limits and Procedures for Achieving Prompt Disposition of Criminal Cases. Pursuant to the requirements of Rule 50 of the Federal Rules of Criminal Procedure, the Speedy Trial Act of 1974 (18 U.S.C. § 3161 et seq.), the Speedy Trial Act Amendments Act of 1979 (Pub.L.No. 96–43, 93 Stat. 327) and the Federal Juvenile Delinquency Act (18 U.S.C. §§ 5036, 5037), the Judges of the United States District Court for the Northern District of New York have adopted the following time limits and procedures to minimize undue delay and to further the prompt disposition of criminal cases and certain juvenile proceedings.

A. *Applicability.*

(1) Offenses. The time limits set forth herein are applicable to all criminal offenses triable in the Court,[1] including cases triable by United States Magistrate Judges, except for petty offenses as defined in 18 U.S.C. § 19 and Rule 58(a) of the Federal Rules of Criminal Procedure. Except as specifically provided, they are not applicable to proceedings under the Federal Juvenile Delinquency Act. [18 U.S.C. §§ 5031–5042]

(2) Persons. The time limits are applicable to persons accused who have neither been indicted, nor charged, as well as those who have, and the word "defendant" includes such persons unless the context indicates otherwise.

B. *Priorities in Scheduling Criminal Cases.* Preference shall be given to criminal proceedings as far as practicable. The trial of defendants in custody solely because they are awaiting trial and of high risk defendants as defined in Section 5 should be given preference over other criminal cases. [18 U.S.C. § 3164(a)].

C. *Time Within Which an Indictment or Information Must Be Filed.*

(1) Time Limits. If an individual is arrested or served with a summons and the complaint charges an offense to be prosecuted in this District, any indictment or information subsequently filed in connection with such charge shall be filed within thirty (30) days of arrest or service. [18 U.S.C. § 3161(b)]

(2) Grand Jury Not in Session. If the defendant is charged with a felony to be prosecuted in this District, and no grand jury has been in session during the thirty (30) day period prescribed in subsection (1), such period shall be extended an additional thirty (30) days. [18 U.S.C. § 3161(b)].

(3) Measurement of Time Periods. If a person has not been arrested or served with a summons on a federal charge, an arrest will be deemed to have been made at such time as the person (a) is held in custody solely for the purpose of responding to the federal charge; (b) is delivered to the custody of a federal official in connection with the federal charge; or (c) appears before a judicial officer in connection with the federal charge.

(4) Related Procedures.

(a) At the time of the earliest appearance before a judicial officer of a person who has been arrested for an offense not charged in an indictment or information, the judicial officer shall establish for the record the date on which the arrest took place. Notice of arrest shall be made in compliance with Rule 5.1 of the Local Rules of Criminal Procedure.

(b) In the absence of a showing to the contrary, a summons shall be considered to have been served on the date of service shown on the return thereof.

D. *Time Within Which Trial Must Commence.*[2]

(1) Time Limits. In accordance with 18 U.S.C. § 3161(c)(1), the trial of a defendant shall commence not later than seventy (70) days after the last to occur of the following dates:

(a) The date on which an indictment or information is filed in this District;

(b) The date of the defendant's first appearance on such charge before a judicial officer of this District and entry of a not guilty plea.

(c) If a defendant consents in writing to be tried before a magistrate judge on a complaint, the trial shall commence within seventy (70) days from the date of such consent.

(2) Retrial, Trial After Reinstatement of an Indictment or Information. The retrial of a defendant shall commence within seventy (70) days from the date the order occasioning the retrial becomes final, as shall the trial of a defendant upon an indictment or information dismissed by a trial court and reinstated following appeal. If the retrial, or trial follows an appeal or collateral attack, the Court may extend the period if unavailability of witnesses or other factors resulting from passage of time make trial within seventy (70) days impracticable. The extended period shall not exceed one hundred and eighty (180) days. [18 U.S.C. § 3161(d)(2), (e)].

(3) Withdrawal of Plea. If a defendant enters a plea of guilty or *nolo contendere* to any or all charges in an indictment or information and is subsequently permitted to withdraw it, the time limit shall be determined for all counts as if the indictment or information were filed on the day the order permitting withdrawal of the plea became final. [18 U.S.C. § 3161(i)].

(4) Superseding Charges. If, after an indictment or information has been filed, a complaint, indictment, or information is filed which charges the defendant with the same offense or with an offense required to be joined with that offense, the time limit applicable to the subsequent charge will be determined as follows:

(a) If the original indictment or information was dismissed on motion of the defendant before the filing of the subsequent charge, the time limit shall be determined without regard to the existence of the original charge. [18 U.S.C. § 3161(d)(1)].

(b) If the original indictment or information is pending at the time the subsequent charge is filed, the trial shall commence within the time limit for commencement of trial on the original indictment or information, however the time from the filing of the superceding charge until the arraignment on the new charge may be excluded from the Speedy Trial Act clock.

(c) If the original indictment or information was dismissed on motion of the United States Attorney before the filing of the subsequent charge, the trial shall commence within the time limit for commencement of trial on the original indictment or information, but the period during which the defendant was not under charges shall be excluded from the computations. Such period is the period between the dismissal of the original indictment or information and the date the time would have commenced to run on the subsequent charge had there been no previous charge.[3] [18 U.S.C. § 3161(h)(6)].

(5) Measurement of Time Periods. For the purposes of this section:

(a) In the event of a transfer to this District under Rule 20 of the Federal Rules of Criminal Procedure, the indictment or information shall be deemed filed in this District when the papers in the proceeding or certified copies thereof are received and filed by the Clerk.

(b) The day of the event that triggers the beginning of the Speedy Trial Act clock is excluded from calculation of the time which indictment or trial must occur.

(6) Related Procedures.

(a) At the time of the defendant's earliest appearance before a judicial officer of this District, the officer will take appropriate steps to assure that the defendant is represented by counsel pursuant to Local Rule 44.1 of the Local Rules of Criminal Procedure for the Northern District. The judicial officer shall appoint counsel where appropriate under the Criminal Justice Act, Rule 44 of the Federal Rules of Criminal Procedure and the Court's Criminal Justice Act Plan. [General Order #1].

(b) The Court shall have sole responsibility for setting cases for trial after consultation with counsel. At the time of arraignment or as soon thereafter as is practicable, each case will be set for trial on a day certain or listed for trial on a weekly or other short-term calendar. [18 U.S.C. § 3161(a)].

(c) Individual calendars shall be managed so that it will be reasonably anticipated that every criminal case set for trial will be reached during the week of original setting. Scheduling conflicts of the parties, are not by themselves grounds for a continuance, unless the Court has made findings that the ends of justice are served by the delay or another exclusion applies.

E. *Defendants in Custody and High–Risk Defendants.*

(1) Time Limits. In accordance with 18 U.S.C. § 3164(b), excluding the periods of delay enumerated in section 3161(h), the following time limits will also be applicable to defendants in custody and high-risk defendants as herein defined:

(a) The trial of a high-risk defendant held in custody solely for the purpose of trial on a federal charge shall commence within ninety (90) days following the beginning of continuous custody; and

(b) The trial of a released defendant shall commence within ninety (90) days of the designation as high-risk. [18 U.S.C. § 3164(b)]

(2) Measurement of Time Periods. For the purposes of this section:

(a) A defendant is deemed to be in detention awaiting trial when he or she is arrested on a federal charge or otherwise held for the purpose of responding to a federal charge. Detention is deemed to be solely because the defendant is awaiting trial unless the person exercising custodial authority has an independent basis (not including a detainer) for continuing to hold the defendant.

(b) If a case is transferred pursuant to Rule 20 of the Federal Rules of Criminal Procedure and the defendant subsequently rejects disposition under Rule 20 or the Court declines to accept the plea, a new period of continuous detention awaiting trial will begin at that time.

(c) A trial shall be deemed to commence as provided in sections D(5)(b) and (c).

(4) Related Procedures.

(a) If a defendant is being held in custody solely for the purpose of awaiting trial, upon request, the United States Attorney shall advise the Court at the earliest practicable time of the date of the beginning of such custody.

(b) The United States Attorney shall advise the Court at the earliest practicable time (usually at the hearing with respect to release or detention) if the defendant is considered by the government to be high-risk.

(c) If the Court finds that the filing of a "high-risk" designation as a public record may result in prejudice to the defendant, it may order the designation sealed for such period as is necessary to protect the defendant's right to a fair trial, but not beyond the time that the Court's judgment in the case becomes final. During the time the designation is under seal, it shall be made known to the defendant and his or her counsel but shall not be made known to other persons without the permission of the Court.

F. *Exclusion of Time from Computations.*

(1) Applicability. In computing time limits under this plan, the periods of delay set forth in 18 U.S.C. 3161(h) shall be excluded. Parties seeking a continuance and exclusion under 18 U.S.C. 3161(h)(8) may do so by motion or stipulation including information sufficient to justify and support a finding that the ends of justice served by the continuance and exclusion outweigh the best interest of the public and the defendant in a speedy trial. Oral and written orders granting a delay and exclusion under 18 U.S.C. 3161(h)(8) shall include a finding that the ends of justice served by the continuance and exclusion outweigh the best interest of the public and the defendant in a speedy trial and the reasons for such finding.

(2) Records of Excludable Time. The Clerk of the Court shall enter on the docket, in the form prescribed by the Administrative Office of the United States Courts, information with respect to excludable periods of time for each criminal defendant. With respect to proceedings prior to the filing of an indictment or information, excludable time shall be reported to the clerk by the United States Attorney.

(a) The attorney for the government and the attorney for the defendant may at any time enter into stipulations with respect to the accuracy of the docket entries recording excludable time, but the Court must make findings in support.

(b) To the extent that the amount of time stipulated exceeds the amount recorded on the docket, the stipulation shall have no effect unless approved by the court.

(3) Pre–Indictment Procedures.

(a) In the event that the United States Attorney anticipates that an indictment or information will not be filed within the time limit set forth in section C, he or she may file a written motion with the Court for a determination of excludable time. In the event that the United States Attorney seeks a continuance under 18 U.S.C. § 3161(h)(8), he or she shall file a written motion with the Court requesting such a continuance stating the basis for why the ends of justice would be served by the delay.

(b) The motion of the United States Attorney shall state (i) the period of time proposed for exclusion, and (ii) the basis of the proposed exclusion. If the motion is for a continuance under 18 U.S.C. § 3161(h)(8), it shall also state whether or not the defendant is being held in custody on the basis of the complaint. In appropriate circumstances, the motion may include a request that some or all of the supporting material be considered *ex parte* and *in camera.*

(c) The Court may grant a continuance under 18 U.S.C. § 3161(h)(8) for either a specific period of time or a period to be determined by reference to an event (such as recovery from illness) not within the control of the government. If the continuance is to a date not certain, the Court shall require one or both parties to inform the Court promptly when and if the circumstances that justify the continuance no longer exist. In addition, the Court shall require one or both parties to file periodic reports bearing on the continued existence of such circumstances. The Court shall determine the frequency of such reports in the light of the facts of the particular case. The Court must then make findings that those delays served the interest of justice.

(4) Post–Indictment Procedures.

(a) In the event that the Court extends the time limit set forth in section C or D, the Court shall determine whether the limit may be recomputed by excluding time pursuant to 18 U.S.C. § 3161(h).

(b) If it is determined that a continuance is justified, the Court shall set forth its findings in the record, either orally or in writing. If the continuance is granted under 18 U.S.C. § 3161(h)(8), the Court shall also set forth its reasons for finding that the ends of justice served by granting the continuance outweigh the best interests of the public and the defendant in a speedy trial. If the continuance is to a date not certain, the Court shall require one or both parties to inform the Court promptly when and if the circumstances that justify the continuance no longer exist. In addition, the Court may require one or both parties to file periodic reports bearing on the continued existence of such circumstances. The Court shall determine the frequency of such reports in light of the facts of the particular case. The Court must then make findings that those delays served the interest of justice.

G. *Minimum Period for Defense Preparation.* Unless the defendant consents in writing to the contrary, the trial shall not commence earlier than thirty (30) days from the date on which the defendant first appears through counsel or expressly waives counsel and elects to proceed *pro se.* In circumstances in which the seventy (70) day time limit for commencing trial on a charge in an indictment or information is determined by reference to an earlier indictment or information pursuant to section D, the thirty (30) day minimum period shall also be determined by reference to the earlier indictment or information. When prosecution is resumed on an original indictment or information following a mistrial, appeal, or withdrawal of a guilty plea, a new thirty (30) day minimum period will not begin to run. The Court will in all cases schedule trials so as to permit defense counsel adequate preparation time in light of the circumstances. [18 U.S.C. § 3161(c)(2)].

H. *Time Within Which Defendant Should Be Sentenced.*

(1) Time Limit. Sentencing proceedings shall be scheduled no earlier than seventy five (75) days following the entry of a verdict of guilty or a plea of guilty or *nolo contendere* unless all the parties and the Court agree that, in the interest of justice, an earlier date should be set.

(2) Related Procedures. Presentence investigations and reports shall be prepared in accordance with Rule 32 of the Federal Rules of Criminal Procedure and the Local Procedure as set forth at Rule 32.1 of the Local Rules of Criminal Procedure.

I. *Juvenile Procedures.*

(1) Time Within Which Trial Must Commence. An alleged delinquent who is in detention pending trial shall be brought to trial within thirty (30) days of the date on which such detention was begun, as provided in 18 U.S.C. § 5036.

(2) Time of Dispositional Hearing. If a juvenile[1] is adjudicated delinquent, a separate dispositional hearing shall be held no later than twenty (20) court days after the juvenile delinquency hearing, unless the Court has ordered further study of the juvenile in accordance with 18 U.S.C. § 5037(d).

J. *Sanctions.*

(1) Dismissal or Release from Custody. Failure to comply with the requirements of Title I of the Speedy Trial Act may entitle the defendant to dismissal of the charges against him or her or to release from pretrial custody. Nothing in this Plan shall be construed to require that a case be dismissed or a defendant released from custody in circumstances in which such action would not be required by 18 U.S.C. § 3162 and 3164.[5]

(2) High–Risk Defendants. A high-risk defendant whose trial has not commenced with the time limit set forth in 18 U.S.C. § 3164(b) shall, if the failure to commence trial was through no fault of the attorney for the government, have his or her release conditions automatically reviewed. A high-risk defendant who is found by the Court to have intentionally delayed the trial of his or her case shall be subject to an order of the Court modifying his or her nonfinancial conditions of release under this title to ensure that he or she shall appear at trial as required. [18 U.S.C. § 3164(c)].

(3) Discipline of Attorneys. In a case in which counsel (a) knowingly allows the case to be set for trial without disclosing the fact that a necessary witness would be unavailable for trial, (b) files a motion solely for the purpose of delay which he or she knows is frivolous and without merit, (c) makes a statement for the purpose of obtaining a continuance which he or she knows to be false and which is material to the granting of the continuance, or (d) otherwise willfully fails to proceed to trial without justification consistent with 18 U.S.C. § 3161, the Court may punish such counsel as provided in 18 U.S.C. § 3162(b) & (c).

(4) Alleged Juvenile Delinquents. An alleged delinquent in custody whose trial has not commenced within the time limit set forth in 18 U.S.C. § 5036 shall be entitled to dismissal of his or her case pursuant to that section unless the Attorney General shows that the delay was consented to or caused by the juvenile or his or her counsel, or would be in the interest of justice in the particular case.

K. *Persons Serving Terms of Imprisonment.* If the United States Attorney knows that a person charged with an offense is serving a term of imprisonment in any penal institution, he or she shall promptly seek to obtain the presence of the prisoner for trial, or cause a detainer to be filed, in accordance with the provisions of 18 U.S.C. § 3161(j).

L. *Effective Date.* This revision to the District's Plan was approved by the Court on the 16th day of September 2006 and shall become effective upon the approval of the reviewing panel in accordance with 18 U.S.C. § 3165(d).

Approved by the Circuit Council October 4, 2006.

---

1 18 U.S.C. § 3172 defines "offense" as "any federal criminal offense which is in violation of any Act of Congress . . . ."

2 If a defendant's presence has been obtained through the filing of a detainer with state authorities, the Interstate Agreement on Detainers, 18 U.S.C., Appendix 2, may require that trial commence before the deadline established by the Speedy Trial Act, whichever date is more stringent. *See* U.S. v. Mauro, 436 U.S. 340, 356–57, n.24 (1978).

3 Under the rules of this paragraph, if an indictment was dismissed on motion of the prosecutor on September 1st, with 20 days remaining within which trial must be commenced, and the defendant was arrested on a new complaint on October 1st, the time remaining for trial would be 20 days from October 1st. The time limit would be based on the original indictment, but the period from the dismissal to the new arrest would not count. Although the 30–day arrest-to-indictment time limit would apply to the new arrest as a formal matter, the short deadline for trial would necessitate earlier grand jury action.

4 A "juvenile" is a person who has not attained his/her eighteenth birthday, or for the purpose of proceedings and disposition under this chapter for an alleged act of juvenile delinquency, a person who has not attained his/her twenty-first birthday, and "juvenile delinquency," is the violation of law of the United States committed by a person prior to his/her eighteenth birthday which would have been a crime if committed by an adult or a violation by such person of 18 U.S.C. § 922(x). [18 U.S.C. § 5031].

5 Dismissal may also be required in some cases under the Interstate Agreement on Detainers, 18 U.S.C., Appendix II.

GENERAL ORDER 18. NORTHERN DISTRICT ORDER DIRECTING FILING OF ANSWER, ADMINISTRATIVE RECORD, BRIEFS, AND PROVIDING FOR ORAL HEARING ON APPEAL FROM SOCIAL SECURITY BENEFITS DECISION

Dated: September 12, 2003
Supersedes the January 24, 2002 and
September 19, 2001 General Orders

Appeals from a final decision of the Secretary of Health and Human Services denying plaintiff's claim for Social Security benefits have been referred to one of the Magistrate Judges pursuant to this Court's Local Rule 72.3(d) and either 28 U.S.C. Section 636(b) for review and recommendation as to disposition or 28 U.S.C. Section 636(c) for all further proceedings and entry of final judgment, and it is hereby

ORDERED, that after service of the Summons and Complaint has been effected, the defendant shall file either an answer, together with a certified copy of the transcript of the administrative proceedings, **within 100 days** of said service, or a motion to dismiss[1] **within 60 days** of said service, and it is further

ORDERED, that if a motion to dismiss is denied, the defendant shall file an answer, together with a certified copy of the transcript of the administrative proceedings, **within 30 days** of service of said denial, and it is further

ORDERED, that after the answer is filed, counsel for the parties or the party, if appearing pro se, submit briefs in accordance with the following requirements:

(1) **Within forty-five (45) days** from the filing of the answer, plaintiff shall serve and file a brief setting forth all errors which plaintiff contends entitle plaintiff to relief. The brief shall contain under the appropriate headings and in the order here indicated:

(a) A Statement of the Issues Presented for Review, set forth in separate numbered paragraphs.

(b) A Statement of the Case. This statement should indicate briefly the course of the proceeding and its disposition at the administrative level and should set forth a general statement of the facts. The statement of the facts shall include plaintiff's age, education, work experience and a summary of other evidence of record. Each statement of fact shall be supported by reference to the page in the record where the evidence may be found.

(c) An Argument. The argument may be preceded by a summary. The argument shall be divided into sections separately treating each issue and must set forth the contentions of plaintiff with respect to the issues presented and reasons therefor. Each contention must be supported by specific reference to the portion of the record relied upon and by citations to statutes, regulations, and cases supporting plaintiff's position. Cases from other districts and circuits should be cited only in conjunction with relevant cases from this jurisdiction or if authority on point from this jurisdiction does not exist. Citations to unreported district court opinions must be accompanied by a copy of the opinion.

(d) A short conclusion stating the relief sought. The issue before the Court are limited to the issues properly raised in the briefs.

(2) **Within forty-five (45) days** after service of plaintiff's brief, defendant shall serve and file a brief which responds specifically to each issue raised by plaintiff. Defendant's brief shall conform to the requirements set forth above for plaintiff's brief, except that a statement of the issues and a statement of the case need not be made unless defendant is dissatisfied with plaintiff's statement thereof.

No party shall file or serve a brief that exceeds twenty-five (25) pages in length, double spaced, unless leave of the judge hearing the appeal is obtained prior to filing the brief. All briefs shall be in the form prescribed by Local Rule 10.1(a) and shall contain a table of contents and, wherever possible, parallel citations.

IT IS FURTHER ORDERED, that upon the receipt of the defendant's Brief as provided herein, the Clerk shall forward the entire file to the assigned Magistrate Judge. The Magistrate Judge will treat the proceeding as if both parties had accompanied their briefs with a motion for judgment on the pleadings pursuant to Rule 12 (c) of the Federal Rules of Civil Procedure, and it is further

ORDERED that when a plaintiff wishes to support an appeal with new evidence, such evidence must be accompanied by a legal memorandum setting forth an argument for the acceptance of the new evidence based upon the three-part showing required by the regulations. First, a plaintiff must show that the evidence he or she wishes to submit is "new" and not simply restating information that is already in the record. Second, a plaintiff must show that the new evidence is "material." In other words, it must be shown that the evidence is relevant to the plaintiff's condition during the time period for which benefits were denied and that the evidence helps to prove that the plaintiff is in fact entitled to benefits. Third, the memorandum must include a statement setting forth good cause for the failure to present the evidence earlier. Tirado v. Bowen, 842 F.2d 595, 597 (2d Cir. 1988). See also 42 U.S.C. § 405(g) (1995). The new evidence and accompanying memorandum shall be filed and a copy shall be served upon the counsel for the Commissioner of Social Security, the United States Attorney.

Upon receipt, the United States Attorney will have **THIRTY (30) DAYS** to file opposition papers.

And it is further

ORDERED, that generally no oral argument will be heard. If, however, an oral hearing is requested and scheduled before the assigned Magistrate Judge, notice of same will be sent to the parties, and at said hearing counsel should be fully prepared to argue the facts, issues, and legal contentions in this case, and it is further

ORDERED, that the Clerk shall serve a copy of this Order upon counsel for the parties herein upon the filing of the complaint, and it is further

ORDERED, that the Clerk shall notify the parties of the name of the Magistrate Judge assigned to their proceeding.

ORDERED, that this General Order shall apply to all United States Magistrate Judges in the Northern District of New York.

NOTIFICATION OF THE CONSEQUENCES OF FAILING TO FILE A BRIEF AS REQUIRED BY PARAGRAPH (1)(a–d)

PLAINTIFF'S BRIEF IS THE ONLY OPPORTUNITY FOR PLAINTIFF TO SET FORTH THE ERRORS PLAINTIFF CONTENDS WERE MADE BY THE COMMISSIONER OF SOCIAL SECURITY THAT ENTITLE PLAINTIFF TO RELIEF. THE FAILURE TO FILE A BRIEF AS REQUIRED BY THIS ORDER WILL RESULT IN THE CONSIDERATION OF THIS APPEAL WITHOUT THE BENEFIT OF PLAINTIFF'S ARGUMENTS AND MAY RESULT IN A DECISION HEAVILY INFLUENCED BY THE COMMISSIONER'S VERSION OF THE FACTS AND SUBSEQUENT DISMISSAL OF YOUR APPEAL.
DATED September 12, 2003.

---

1 Any such motion to dismiss shall be briefed in accordance with Local Rule 7.1(b)(2) and made returnable before the assigned district judge (or magistrate judge who is conducting all proceedings pursuant to 28 U.S.C. § 636(c)).

GENERAL ORDER 19.   UNITED STATES BANKRUPTCY JUDGES OF THIS DISTRICT—DESIGNATED TO CONDUCT TRIALS [ABROGATED]

[Dated March 29, 2002; abrogated effective January 1, 2009, see, now, Local Rule 76.1.]

GENERAL ORDER 20.   PROHIBITION AGAINST CASH BEING POSTED AS COLLATERAL FOR BAIL [ABROGATED]

[Ordered effective December, 2002; abrogated effective January 1, 2009, see, now, Local Criminal Rule 57.2.]

GENERAL ORDER 23. STANDARD CONDITIONS OF PROBATION AND SUPERVISED RELEASE ADOPTED BY THIS COURT

The Court seeks to adopt standard conditions of Probation and Supervised Release for the district. These conditions would be imposed as part of each and every term of Probation or Supervised Release in addition to the mandatory conditions required by statute and whichever discretionary conditions the Court chooses to impose in each individual case. To accomplish this objective, the Court adopts this General Order 23.

The following standard conditions are adopted by the United States District Court for the Northern District of New York.

1.   The defendant shall not leave the judicial district without the permission of the Court or probation officer.

2.   The defendant shall report to the probation officer as directed by the Court or probation officer and shall submit a truthful and complete written report within the first five days of each month.

3.   The defendant shall answer truthfully all inquires by the probation officer and follow the instructions of the probation officer.

4.   The defendant shall support his dependents and meet other family responsibilities.

5.   The defendant shall work regularly at a lawful occupation unless excused by the probation officer for schooling, training, or other acceptable reasons.

6.   The defendant shall notify the probation officer ten days prior to any change in residence or employment.

7.   The defendant shall refrain from excessive use of alcohol and shall not purchase, possess, use, distribute, or administer any controlled substance, or any paraphernalia related to any controlled substance, except as prescribed by a physician.

8.   The defendant shall not frequent places where controlled substances are illegally sold, used, distributed, or administered.

9.   The defendant shall not associate with any persons engaged in criminal activity, and shall not associate with any person convicted of a felony unless granted permission to do so by the probation officer.

10.   The defendant shall permit a probation officer to visit him or her at any time at home or elsewhere and shall permit confiscation of any contraband observed in plain view of the probation officer.

11.   The defendant shall notify the probation officer within 72 hours of being arrested or questioned by a law enforcement officer.

12.   The defendant shall not enter into any agreement to act as an informer or special agent of a law enforcement agency without the permission of the Court.

13.   As directed by the probation officer, the defendant shall notify third parties of any risks that may be occasioned by the defendant's criminal record or personal history or characteristics, and shall permit the probation officer to make such notifications and to confirm the defendant's compliance with such notification requirement.

14.   The defendant shall not possess a firearm, destructive device or other dangerous weapon.

IT IS SO ORDERED.

DATED this 5th day of March, 2004, at Syracuse, New York.

GENERAL ORDER 24. AMENDED JURY PLAN FOR THE RANDOM SELECTION OF GRAND AND PETIT JURORS

CIRCUIT COUNCIL APPROVAL: October 16, 2008

The jury plan heretofore adopted by this Court for the random selection of grand and petit jurors filed with the Court on July 1st, 1968 and including the amendments to the original plan is hereby revoked and rescinded, and the following plan is hereby adopted to become effective on the date approved by the Reviewing Panel of the U.S. Court of Appeals, Second Circuit.

I. Applicability of Plan. This plan is applicable to the Northern District of New York, there being no statutory divisions in the Northern District of New York, and the cities of **Albany, Auburn, Binghamton, Malone, Syracuse, Utica & Watertown** being designated by 28 U.S.C. Section 112 as the places of holding court, the district is hereby divided into divisions for jury selection purposes, as defined in 28 U.S.C. Section 1869(e).

1. *ALBANY DIVISION:* Albany, Columbia, Greene, Rensselaer, Saratoga, Schenectady, Schoharie, Ulster, Warren & Washington.

2. *BINGHAMTON DIVISION:* Broome, Chenango, Delaware, Otsego, & Tioga.

3. *SYRACUSE/AUBURN DIVISION:* Cayuga, Cortland, Madison, Onondaga, Oswego, & Tompkins.

4. *UTICA DIVISION:* Fulton, Hamilton, Herkimer, Montgomery, & Oneida.

5. *WATERTOWN DIVISION:* Jefferson, Lewis, & St. Lawrence.

6. *MALONE DIVISION:* Clinton, Essex & Franklin.

The provisions of this plan apply to all divisions in the district.

II. Policy. This plan is adopted pursuant to and in recognition of the Congressional policy declared in Title 28, United States Code, as follows:

Section 1861—Declaration of Policy

"It is the policy of the United States that all litigants in Federal Courts entitled to trial by jury shall have the right to grand and petit juries selected at random from a fair cross section of the community in the district or division wherein the court convenes. It is further the policy of the United States that all citizens shall have the opportunity to be considered for service on the grand and petit juries in the district courts of the United States, and shall have an obligation to serve as jurors when summoned for that purpose."

Section 1862—Discrimination Prohibited

"No citizen shall be excluded from service as a grand or petit juror in the district courts of the United States on account of race, color, religion, sex, national origin, or economic status."

III. Management and Supervision of Jury Selection Process. There shall be no jury commission in this district. The Clerk of the Court shall manage the jury selection process under the supervision and control of the Chief Judge, or such other District Judge or Judges as the Chief Judge may from time to time designate. In the event of the simultaneous absence, disability, or inability to act, of the Chief Judge and any other judges designated, the active district judge who is present in the district and has been in service the greatest length of time shall be authorized to act. The use of the word "clerk" in this plan contemplates the clerk and any or all of his or her deputies and any other person authorized by the Court to assist the clerk in the performance of functions under this plan.

IV. Random Selection from Voter Lists and Lists of Licensed Motor Vehicle Driver and Master Jury Wheels. While voter registration lists represent a fair cross section of the community in each division of the Northern District of New York, an even greater number of citizens will be eligible for jury service if supplemental source lists are used. Accordingly, names of grand and petit jurors serving on or after the effective date of this plan shall be selected at random from voter registration lists of all counties in the relevant division and supplemented by, if available, lists of licensed drivers for these counties from the New York State Department of Motor Vehicles. These two lists shall be merged and duplicate records purged. The Court takes notice that when two or more source lists are used, one person's name may appear more than once. A system will be developed, before any selection procedures begin, to eliminate as reasonably as possible such duplications. Should it appear that a person mailed a jury qualification form as outlined in Section V(a) has changed residence from one division of the Court to another division of the Court, that person's questionnaire shall be reviewed for determination of qualified status to serve as a grand or petit juror in the division in which the person currently resides. If the person is found qualified, that person's name shall be placed into the qualified wheel of the division in which the person currently resides.

The clerk shall maintain a master jury wheel or a master jury box, hereinafter referred to as a master jury wheel, for each of the divisions within the district.

Pursuant to 28 U.S.C. Section 1878, at the option of the district court, jurors may be qualified and summoned in a single procedure, in lieu of the two separate procedures otherwise provided for by the Jury Selection and Service Act and this Plan.

The clerk shall make the random selection of names for the master wheels as follows. There shall be selected for the master jury wheel for each division as a minimum approximately the following number of names:

1.	ALBANY DIVISION	(20,000)
2.	BINGHAMTON DIVISION	(10,000)
3.	SYRACUSE / AUBURN DIVISION	(20,000)
4.	UTICA DIVISION	(10,000)
5.	WATERTOWN DIVISION	(5,000)
6.	MALONE DIVISION	(5,000)

These numbers are as large as they are to allow for the possibility that some juror qualification forms, hereinafter mentioned, will not be returned, that some prospective jurors may be exempt by law or excused, and that some may not meet with the statutory qualifications. The clerk, based upon the court's experience and with the approval of the chief judge, may revise the minimum number of names for any master wheel without need for amendment to this plan. Furthermore, the chief judge of this district may order additional names to be placed in the master jury wheels from time to time as necessary.

At the clerk's option, and after consultation with the court, the selection of names from a complete source list database in electronic media for the master jury wheel may be accomplished by a purely randomized process through a properly programmed electronic data processing system. Similarly, at the option of the clerk and after consultation with the court, a properly programmed electronic data processing system for pure randomized selection may be used to select names from the master wheel for the purpose of summoning persons to serve as grand or petit jurors. Such random selections of names from the source list for inclusion in the master wheel by data computer personnel must insure that the names of persons residing in each of the counties within the jury division are placed in the master jury wheel, and that each county within the jury division is substantially proportionally represented in the master jury wheel in accordance with 28 U.S.C. Section 1863(b)(3). The selection of names from the source list and the master wheel must also insure that the mathematical odds of any single name being picked are substantially equal.

The master jury wheel shall be emptied and refilled every four years between the date of the November general election and the following September.

This plan is based on the conclusion and judgment that the policy, purpose, and intent of the Jury Selection and Service Act of 1968, as amended, will be fully accomplished and implemented by the use of consolidated source lists. The consolidated lists will be comprised of the voter registration lists, and supplemented by, if available, lists of licensed drivers. The use of these source lists for an at random selection of prospective grand and petit jurors will represent a fair cross-section of the community. This determination is supported by all the information this Court has been able to obtain after diligent effort and inquiry.

V. Drawing of Names From the Master Jury Wheel: Completing of Jury Qualification Form. The plan hereby incorporates the provisions of 28 U.S.C. Section 1864, which reads as follows:

"(a) From time to time as directed by the district court, the clerk or a district judge shall publicly draw at random from the master jury wheel the names of as many persons as may be required for jury service. The clerk . . . may upon order of the court, prepare an alphabetical list of the names drawn from the master jury wheel. Any list so prepared shall not be disclosed to any person except pursuant to the district court plan or pursuant to section 1867 or 1868 of this title. The clerk . . . shall mail to every person whose name is drawn from the master wheel a juror qualification form accompanied by instructions to fill out and return the form, duly signed and sworn, to the clerk . . . by mail within ten days.

If the person is unable to fill out the form another shall do it for him or her, and shall indicate that he or she has done so and the reason therefor. In any case in which it appears that there is an omission, ambiguity, or error in a form, the clerk . . . shall return the form with instructions to the person to make such additions or corrections as may be necessary and to return the form to the clerk . . . within ten days. Any person who fails to return a completed juror qualification form as instructed may be summoned by the clerk . . . forthwith to appear before the clerk . . . to fill out a juror qualification form. A person summoned to appear because of failure to return a juror qualification form as instructed who personally appears and executes a juror qualification form before the clerk . . . may, at the discretion of the district court, except where his or her prior failure to execute and mail such form was willful, be entitled to receive for such appearance the same fees and travel allowance paid to jurors under section 1871 of this title. At the time of his or her appearance for jury service, any person may be required to fill out another juror qualification form in the presence of . . . the clerk or the court, at which time, in such cases as it appears warranted, the person may be questioned, but only with regard to his or her responses to questions contained on the form. Any information thus acquired by the clerk . . . may be noted on the juror qualification form and transmitted to the Chief Judge or such other district judge as the plan may provide.

(b) Any person summoned pursuant to subsection (a) of this section who fail to appear as directed shall be ordered by the district court forthwith to appear and show cause for his or her failure to comply with the summons. Any person who fails to appear pursuant to such order or who fails to show good cause for noncompliance with the summons may be fined not more than $100 or imprisoned not more that three days, or both. Any person who willfully misrepresents a material fact on a juror qualification form for the purpose of avoiding or securing service as a juror may be fined not more than $100 or imprisoned not more that three days, or both."

VI. Qualified Jury Wheel. The clerk shall also maintain separate qualified jury wheels for each division in the district and shall place in such wheel the names of all persons drawn at random from the master jury wheels and not disqualified, exempt, or excused pursuant to this plan. Each qualification form as called for by Section 1864, supra, shall bear the number which its addressee bears on the master wheel list. The clerk shall insure that at all times at least **300** names are contained in each such qualified jury wheel. The qualified jury wheel in each division shall be emptied within three months after the master jury wheel for that division is emptied. The qualified wheels may be refilled in one drawing, or in increments; provided, however, that each qualified wheel must always contain no fewer than 300 names.

VII. Determination of Qualification. This plan hereby incorporates the provisions of 28 U.S.C. Section 1865, which reads as follows:

"(a) The Chief Judge of the district court, or such other district court judge as the plan may provide, or the clerk under supervision of the court on his or her initiative . . . shall determine solely on the basis of information provided on the juror qualification form and other competent evidence whether a person is unqualified for, or exempt, or to be excused from jury service. The clerk shall enter such determination in the space provided on the juror qualification form (or in the database).

"(b) In making such determination the chief judge of the district court, or such other district court judge as the plan may provide, or the clerk shall deem any person qualified to serve on grand and petit juries in the district court unless he or she—

(1) is not a citizen of the United States eighteen years old who has resided for a period of one year within the judicial district;

(2) is unable to read, write, and understand the English language with a degree of proficiency sufficient to fill out satisfactorily the juror qualification form;

(3) is unable to speak the English language;

(4) is incapable, by reason of mental or physical infirmity, to render satisfactory jury service; or

(5) has a charge pending against him for the commission of, or has been convicted in a State or Federal court of record of, a crime punishable by imprisonment for more than one year and his civil rights have not been restored.

The names of persons found to be disqualified under subsections (b)(1)-(5) above shall not be placed in the qualified wheel.

Notice of persons who identify themselves as non-citizens through the juror qualification process will be provided to appropriate election officials for verifying voter registration eligibility."

VIII. Exemption From Jury Service. The Court finds and hereby states that the exemption of the following occupational classes or groups of persons is in the public interest, not inconsistent with the Act, and shall be automatically granted: (1) members in active service of the armed forces of the United States; (2) members of Fire or Police Departments of any State, District, Territory, Possession, or subdivision thereof; (3) public officers in the executive, legislative, or judicial branches of the government of the United States or an State, District, Territory, or Possession or subdivision thereof who are actively engaged in the performance of official duties (public officer shall mean a person who is either elected to public office or who is directly appointed by a person elected to public office).

The names of persons found to be exempt under this section shall not be placed in the qualified wheel.

IX. Excuses on Individual Request. This Court finds and hereby states that jury service by members of the following occupational classes or groups of persons would entail undue hardship and extreme inconvenience to the member thereof, and serious obstruction and delay in the fair and impartial administration of justice, and their excuse will not be inconsistent with the Act and may be claimed, if desired, and shall be granted by the clerk upon individual request:(1) persons having active care and custody of a child or children under (12) years of age whose health and/or safety would be jeopardized by their absence for jury service; (2) a person who is essential to the care of the aged or infirm persons; (3) all persons over 70 years of age at time of executing the jury qualification form; (4) volunteer safety personnel (personnel who serve without compensation as fire fighters, members of a rescue squad or ambulance crew for a public agency); (5) Actively practicing attorneys, physicians, dentists, clergy, and registered nurses; and (6) Sole proprietor of a business.

X. Drawing of and Assignment to Jury Pools and Disclosure of Pool Names. From time to time the Court or the clerk shall publicly draw at random from the qualified jury wheel or wheels, either manually or by use of a properly programmed data computer, such numbers of names of persons as may be required for assignment to grand or petit jury pools, and the clerk shall prepare a separate list of names of persons assigned to each grand and petit jury pool (JMS Pool Selection Report). These names may be disclosed by the clerk to parties, the public, and the press upon written request to the judge presiding over the civil or criminal trial after said list is prepared and the jurors have been summoned. The Court may, however, at any time order generally, or with respect to any particular term or terms of Court, that these names be kept confidential in any case where, in the Court's judgment, the interest of justice so requires. (28 U.S.C. Section 1863(b)(7))

Summoned jurors claiming individual excuses pursuant to Section IX, subcategories (1)–(2) and (4)–(6) above, shall be excused upon determination that such excuse is valid at the time the juror is summoned.

Due to the large geographic distribution and the variable climate of the Northern District, the Court recognizes that the distance a juror may have to travel may cause an undue hardship or extreme inconvenience to the juror. Accordingly, **upon individual request**, the court will consider an application by a prospective juror for excuse from jury service on the basis of undue hardship or excessive travel at the time of summoning. The court hereby defines excessive travel as any distance over seventy miles (one way) from the juror's residence to the courthouse.

In addition, the following persons may claim individual excuses when summoned: (1) persons over 70; (2) persons for whom jury service would entail undue hardship or extreme inconvenience, consistent with the criteria set forth in 28 U.S.C. Section 1869, (3) any person who has served as a grand or petit juror in a state or federal court during the past two years immediately preceding his/her call to serve.

When finding of undue hardship or extreme inconvenience is made upon application by a person summoned for jury service, the Court, or by the clerk under the supervision of the Court, will excuse such person from service for such period of time as the Court deems necessary, at the conclusion of which such person's name shall be placed back into the wheel and summoned again for jury service.

If a summoned juror has changed residence from one division of the Court to another division of the Court subsequent to the establishment of the division qualified jury wheel that juror shall be excused from service in the division of original residence for such period of time as the Court deems necessary. At the conclusion of that period, the persons name shall be placed back into the qualified wheel and summoned for jury service in the division of current residence.

Any person summoned for jury service who fails to appear as directed shall be ordered by the district court to appear forthwith and show cause for his failure to comply with the summons. Any person who fails to show good cause for noncompliance with a summons may be fined not more than $100 or imprisoned not more than three days or both.

XI. Public Announcement of the Place and Time When Automated Drawing of Names Will Be Made. Drawing of names of prospective jurors by automated selection methods shall be publicly made at the designated computer center. The location and approximate time of such drawings shall be publicly announced in a public place such as the bulletin board in the Office of the Clerk.

In order to ensure the exercise of proper supervision and management over the automated aspects of jury selection and its accordance with statutory requirements, the operator of the computer shall comply with the instructions for random selection of grand and petit jurors by electronic machine methods contained in this court's plan for random selection of grand and petit jurors and such additional written instructions as provided by the court.

The office of the Clerk of the Court shall retain and, when requested, provide access to the following public documents:

— the Court's "Juror Selection Plan",

— a verbal or graphically chartered description of the procedure employed in the automated selection system,

— a copy of the Court's authorization and instruction order to the person or computer service organization which carries out automated name selection tasks for the Court, and

— a copy of required public notices, showing where and when posted.

XII. Disclosure of Records.

(A) *Contents of Records.* The contents of records or papers used by the clerk in connection with the jury selection process shall not be disclosed to anyone other than court personnel except pursuant to this plan or as authorized by the Chief Judge or by the Judge designated by order of the Chief Judge to supervise this plan, or as may be necessary in the preparation or presentation of a motion under subsections (a), (b), or (c) of Section 1867 of Title 28 U.S. Code, until after the master wheel has been emptied and refilled pursuant to Section 1863(b)(4) of Title 28 U.S. Code, and all persons selected to serve as jurors before the master wheel was emptied have completed such service. The parties in a case shall be allowed to inspect, reproduce and copy such records or papers at all reasonable times during the preparation and pendency of such motion. Any person who discloses the contents of any record or paper in violation of this subsection may be fined not more than $1,000 or imprisoned not more than one year, or both.

(B) *Names of Trial Jurors.*

(1) The names of trial jurors may be released to the parties, the public, or the press at the conclusion of a trial (civil or criminal) only upon leave of the court. All requests for release of juror names must be made in writing to the presiding trial judge.

(2) Lists of potential juror names and Jury Biographical Information Sheets, provided to attorneys at the start of jury selection, are the property of the court and must be returned to the court at the conclusion of each day's proceedings.

(3) Pursuant to Rule 49 of the Federal Rules of Criminal Procedure, the names of all jurors and potential jurors will not be disclosed in the public docket or in transcripts filed with the court absent an order of the Court. Transcripts will be filed in redacted form in the public docket. All requests for unredacted transcripts should be submitted in writing to the presiding trial judge.[1]

(C) *Report on Operation of the Jury Selection Plan (AO–12).* Any party seeking disclosure of the Report on Operation of the Jury Selection Plan (AO–12), must make written application to the designated jury judge. Disclosure will be made only upon the approval of the jury judge.

XIII.   Grand Jury Panels.   One or more grand juries shall be empaneled for this district or any division of this District for terms of service at Albany, Binghamton, & Syracuse, or such other places as the court may designate and at such times as the court may order. If a grand jury is to be impaneled for service in a division only, the clerk shall draw at random from the qualified wheel of that division for the grand jury panel such number of prospective grand jurors as the chief judge, or the judge designated by the chief judge to preside over the jury division in which the grand jury is to be impaneled, may direct. If a grand jury is to be empaneled for service in the entire district, the clerk shall draw at random from the qualified wheel of each division for the grand jury panel such number of prospective grand jurors as the chief judge may direct in the same ratio that the number of registered voters or consolidated lists in each division bears to the total number of registered voters or consolidated list in the district.

Prior to the day of selection, jurors summoned to serve and report for service on a grand jury panel who do not request excusal shall, whenever there is an excess of jurors over the number required to impanel the grand jury, be selected for excusal by random drawing. Except as otherwise ordered by the Court, said jurors shall be permanently excused from service.

Each grand jury shall serve until discharged by the chief judge, but no regular, criminal grand jury shall serve for more than eighteen months unless the court extends the service of the grand jury for a period of six months or less, upon a determination that such extension is in the public interest. Special Grand Juries as defined in Title 18, Section 3331, shall serve a term of eighteen months unless an order for its discharge is entered earlier by the Court. If, at the end of an eighteen-month term or any extension thereof, the District Court determines the business of the grand jury has not been completed, the court may enter an order extending such term for up to three additional six month periods. No special grand jury term so extended shall exceed thirty-six months, except as provided in subsection (e) of Section 3333 of Title 18 U.S.C.

The court may direct that alternate jurors may be designated at the time a grand jury is selected. Alternate jurors in the order in which they were designated may thereafter be impaneled to replace excused jurors. Alternate jurors shall be drawn in the same manner and shall have the same qualification as the regular jurors and if impaneled shall be subject to the same challenges, shall take the same oath and shall have the same functions, powers, facilities and privileges as the regular grand jurors.

In the interest of achieving administrative economies the court may at any time direct that one grand jury composed of jurors drawn from the qualified wheel of only one jury division shall serve the entire judicial district.

The contents of records or papers used by the clerk in connection with the grand jury selection process may be disclosed to the United States Attorney's Office upon written request to the clerk. Names and contact information for empaneled grand jurors will be provided to the U.S. Attorney's Office without prior leave.

XIV. Challenges to the Selection Procedures. Any challenge to this plan or the court's compliance with the provisions of this plan or compliance with the provisions of the Jury Selection and Service Act of 1968 shall be made within the times and in the manner provided in section 1867 of Title 28, United States Code.

XV. Maintenance and Inspection of Records. After the master jury wheels are emptied and refilled pursuant to Section IV above and after all persons selected to serve as jurors before the master wheels are emptied have completed service, all records and papers compiled and maintained by the clerk before the master wheels are emptied shall be preserved in the custody of the clerk for four years or for such longer period as may be ordered by a judge of the court, and shall be available for public inspection for the purpose of determining the validity of the selection of any jury impaneled during the relevant period (28 U.S.C. Section 1868).

XVI. Adoption of the Plan. The plan is approved and adopted by the Judges of this District on the date entered below. The plan shall be placed into operation in accordance with the provisions of the Jury Selection Act of 1968, Section 1863(a). Work toward implementing this plan shall begin as soon as practicable after its approval by a reviewing panel consisting of the members of the Judicial Council of the 2nd Circuit and the Chief Judge of this Court, or such District Judge(s) as may be designated by him; and this plan shall take effect upon approval by the reviewing Panel of the U.S. Court of Appeals, 2nd Circuit.

Dated this 20th day of September, 2008.

1 See also FRCrP 49.1, Privacy Protection for Filings made with the Court (including committee notes).

UNITED STATES DISTRICT COURT
FOR THE
NORTHERN DISTRICT OF NEW YORK

NOTICE

THE ATTACHED FILING ORDER IS A TIME SENSITIVE DOCUMENT

This filing order is to be served on all parties to the action along with the complaint or petition for removal within **sixty (60) days** of filing the action.

The attached Civil Case Management Plan must be completed and filed with the clerk no later than **ten (10) days** prior to the conference date referenced below.

CONFERENCE DATE/TIME:_____

CONFERENCE LOCATION:_____

BEFORE MAGISTRATE JUDGE:_____

CONTENTS:

    * General Order #25 (Filing Order)

    * Case Management Plan (Attachment B)

    * Case Assignment/Motion Schedules and Filing Locations (Attachment C)

    * Consent Form to Proceed before U.S. Magistrate Judge (Attachment D)

NOTE: IF THIS IS A QUALIFYING CONTRACT, TORT, OR NON–PRISONER CIVIL RIGHTS CASE IT WILL BE DIVERTED INTO THE DISTRICT'S NON–

BINDING ALTERNATIVE DISPUTE RESOLUTION PROGRAM (ADR) FOR Arbitration, Mediation or Early Neutral Evaluation. The Clerk will indicate the appropriate track based on the Nature of Suit.

Conventional Track_____ ADR Track_____

FRM DATE—06/13/2007

GENERAL ORDER 25. DIRECTING THE EXPEDITED SERVICE OF THE SUMMONS & COMPLAINT AND FURTHER DIRECTING THE COMPLETION OF RULE 16 STIPULATION FOR THE TIMELY PROGRESSION OF CIVIL ACTIONS

I. **Purpose.** It is the policy of this court to help litigants resolve their civil disputes in a just, timely and cost-effective manner. To that end, this court has adopted an Expense and Delay Reduction Plan in accordance with the Civil Justice Reform Act of 1990. This will tailor the level of individualized case management needs to such criteria as case complexity, and the amount of time reasonably needed to prepare the case for trial.

II. **Scope.** This order applies to all civil cases filed in this court except: multi-district litigation, cases remanded from the appellate court, reinstated and reopened cases, and cases in the following nature of suit categories indicated on the civil cover sheet: Prisoner Petitions (510–550), Forfeiture/Penalty (610–690), Bankruptcy (422–423), Social Security (861–865) Contracts (only nos. 150: Recovery of Overpayment and Enforcement of Judgment 151: Medicare Act, 152: Recovery of Defaulted Student Loans, 153: Recovery of Overpayment of Veteran's Benefits, and other contract actions which involve the collection of debts owed to the United States), Real Property (only no. 220: Foreclosure, and other Statutes (only no. 900: Appeal of Fee Determination Under Equal Access to Justice).

* Note—When the Court deems it appropriate, Rule 16 Scheduling Conferences will be held in the above excepted actions.

The Court has adopted the guidelines of civility as outlined in the New York State Bar Association Guidelines on Civility in Litigation, a copy of which is available on the court's web-site at www.nynd.uscourts.gov.

III. **Service.**

A. *Timing.* When serving a Complaint or Notice of Removal, the filing party shall serve on all other parties a copy of this General Order and the attached materials. Service of process should be completed within **Sixty** (60) days from the initial filing date. This expedited service is necessary to fulfill the dictates of the Civil Justice Reform Act Expense and Delay Reduction Plan of this court and to ensure adequate time for pretrial discovery and motion practice. However, in no event shall service of process be completed after the time specified in Fed. R. Civ. P. 4, or any other Rule or Statute which may govern service of process in a given action.

B. *Filing Proof(s) of Service.* Proof(s) of service of process are to be filed with the clerk's office no later than five (5) days after service of the complaint or notice of removal with a copy of this General Order.

C. *Non-Compliance with Sixty (60) Day Service Requirement.* In the event that the filing party cannot comply with the Sixty (60) day service requirement, that party shall immediately notify the assigned Magistrate Judge and request an adjournment of the initial Rule 16 case management conference date contained in the attached Civil Case Management Plan.

If an adjournment of the conference date is granted, it shall be the responsibility of the filing party to notify all parties to the action of the new date, time and location for the case management conference. Proof of service of such notice shall then be immediately filed with the clerk's office.

IV. **Additional Parties.** Any party who, after the filing of the original complaint or notice of removal, causes a new party to be joined in the action shall promptly serve on that new party a copy of General Order 25 along with any additional Uniform Pretrial Scheduling Order that has been entered by the court.

V. Removed Cases. In cases removed to this court from a state court, the removing defendant(s) shall serve on the plaintiff(s) and all other parties, at the time of service of the notice of removal, a copy of this General Order with the attached materials. The filing of a motion for remand does not relieve the moving party of any obligation under this General Order unless the assigned judge or magistrate judge specifically grants such relief.

VI. Transferred Cases. The clerk shall serve a copy of this General Order on all parties that have appeared in any action transferred to this district. The clerk shall set a return date for the initial Rule 16 case management conference on the form attached to the General Order. It shall be the obligation of the plaintiff or plaintiff's counsel to arrange for completion of the attached Case Management Plan and to file the Plan with the clerk and to serve this General Order upon any party who had not appeared in the action at the time of transfer. Attorneys appearing in transferred cases are reminded of their obligation to be properly admitted to this district in accordance with Local Rule 83.1. Attorneys must also be registered for electronic filing. Refer to Section XII of this General Order.

VII. Materials Included with This General Order Packet.

(A) Notice of Initial Rule 16 Case Management Conference

(B) Civil Case Management Plan

(C) Case Assignment Form

(D) Notice and Consent Form to Exercise of Jurisdiction by a United States Magistrate Judge

VIII. ADR Programs. It is the mission of this court to do everything it can to help parties resolve their disputes as fairly, quickly, and efficiently as possible. We offer a wide selection of non-binding alternative dispute resolution (ADR) options—each of which provides different kinds of services so that parties can use the procedure that best fits the particular circumstances of their case.

Selected Contract, Tort and non-prisoner Civil Rights cases will be diverted into Court–Annexed non-binding Arbitration, Mediation or Early Neutral Evaluation. The Northern District of New York alternative dispute resolution programs are governed by Local Rules 83.7 (Arbitration), 83.11–1, (Mediation), and 83.12–1 (Early Neutral Evaluation). The parties are encouraged to discuss the ADR alternatives in advance of the Rule 16 Pretrial Conference. At the Rule 16 Pretrial Conference, the assigned Magistrate Judge or District Court Judge will assist the parties in the selection of an appropriate ADR alternative. In addition to Arbitration, Mediation and Early Neutral Evaluation, the court also offers the following ADR processes:

(A) *Settlement Conferences.* The parties are advised that the court will honor a request for a settlement conference at any stage of the proceeding. A representative of the parties with the authority to bind the parties must be present with counsel or available by telephone at any settlement conference.

(B) *Consent to Jury or Court Trial Before a United States Magistrate Judge.* By stipulation, the parties to any civil action may elect to have a magistrate judge (instead of the assigned Article III judge) conduct all proceedings in any civil case, including presiding over a jury or bench trial. A trial before a magistrate judge is governed by the same procedural and evidentiary rules as trial before a district judge. The right to appeal is automatically preserved to the United States Court of Appeals under the same standards which govern appeals from an Article III judge. Parties often consent to resolution of their civil disputes by magistrate judge bench or jury trial because magistrate judges have less crowded calendars.

IX. Discovery.

A. *Discovery Motions.* Prior to bringing a discovery dispute to a Magistrate Judge, the parties must confer in good faith in accordance with the provisions of Local Rule 7.1(d). In addition, no non-dispositive or discovery motions should be presented to the Court unless authorized by the Magistrate Judge after communication with the Magistrate Judge's chambers.

B. *Filing Discovery.* Parties are directed not to file discovery material unless it is being filed in accordance with Local Rule 26.2.

For additional information on local requirements related to depositions and discovery please refer to Section V. of the Local Rules of this court.

X. Motions.

A. *Motion Return Dates.* Please refer to the attached case assignment form for a complete listing of the motion return dates for the judges and magistrate judges of this court.

For additional information on local requirements related to motion practice, please refer to Local Rule 7.1.

XI. Case Management Conference. Except in actions exempted under Section II of this order, or when otherwise ordered by the court, the parties shall, as soon as practicable, meet to jointly address each item contained in the attached Case Management Plan packet. The completed plan is to be filed with the clerk not later than **ten (10) days** prior to the conference date. The NOTICE setting the date, time, and location for the initial Rule 16 conference with the court is included as part of this filing order.

The Civil Justice Reform Act Plan of this court requires the court to set "early, firm" trial dates, such that the trial is scheduled to occur within eighteen (18) months after the filing of the complaint, unless a judicial officer certifies that (I) the demands of the case and its complexity make such a trial date incompatible with serving the ends of justice; or (II) the trial cannot reasonably be held within such time because of the complexity of the case or the number or complexity of pending criminal cases.

XII. Electronic Filing. As of January 1, 2004, all documents submitted for filing by attorneys admitted to practice in the Northern District of New York shall be filed electronically using the CM/ECF system. Refer to General Order #22 for procedures for filing documents electronically. Attorneys must be registered for both PACER and CM/ECF. Consult the CM/ECF section of the court's web-site at www.nynd.uscourts.gov for PACER registration, CM/ECF registration, CM/ECF training dates, and General Order #22.

Dated: June 13, 2007.

The 3/30/95 revision clarifies the time frame for filing the case management plan. The revision also includes a provision for issuing G–25 orders on excepted actions when the court deems it appropriate to schedule a Rule 16 conference.

The 3/26/97 revision expands the scope of ADR programs offered by the Northern District of New York and removes the reference to General Order #41 which was incorporated into Local Rule 7.1(b)1 on January 1, 1997.

The 11/30/00 revision allows for the inclusion of non-prisoner civil rights cases in the ADR program.

The 04/01/02 revision modifies Section IX—Discovery motions.

The 06/18/04 revision adds Section XII—Electronic Filing.

The 06/13/2007 revision includes a modification to the civil case management plan document attached to this General Order—In re: Electronic Discovery.

CIVIL CASE MANAGEMENT PLAN

UNITED STATES DISTRICT COURT
NORTHERN DISTRICT OF NEW YORK

_____

VS   NO. _____ : _____CV _____

_____

    IT IS HEREBY ORDERED that, pursuant to Rule 16(b), Federal Rules of Civil Procedure, a status and scheduling conference will be held in this case before the Honorable_____, United States Magistrate Judge on _____, _____ at ____:___M. at the United States Courthouse, Room No_____, at_____, New York.

    Counsel for all parties or individuals appearing pro se in the above-captioned action are directed to confer in accordance with Fed. R. Civ. P. 26(f) with respect to all of the agenda items listed below. That meeting must be attended in person or, if counsel for the parties are not located in the same city and do not agree to meet in person, then by telephone, and must be held at least **twenty-one (21) days** before the scheduled Rule 16 Conference. Following that Rule 26(f) meeting, a report of the results of that meeting, in the format set forth below, must be filed with the clerk within **fourteen (14) days** after the date of the Rule 26(f) meeting or not later than **ten (10) days** prior to the scheduled Rule 16 conference with the Court, whichever date is earlier. Matters which the Court will discuss at the status conference will include the following: (insert a separate subparagraph as necessary if parties disagree):

    1) JOINDER OF PARTIES: Any application to join any person as a party to this action shall be made on or before the _____ day of _____, _____.

    2) AMENDMENT OF PLEADINGS: Any application to amend the pleadings to this action shall be made on or before the _____ day of _____, _____.

    3) DISCOVERY: All discovery in this action shall be completed on or before the _____ day of _____, _____. **(Discovery time table is to be based on the complexity of the action.)**

    4) MOTIONS: All motions, including discovery motions, shall be made on or before the _____ day of _____, _____. **(Non–Dispositive motions including discovery motions may only be brought after the parties have complied with Section IX of General Order #25.)**

    5) PROPOSED DATE FOR THE COMMENCEMENT OF TRIAL: The action will be ready to proceed to trial on or before the _____ day of _____, _____. It is anticipated that the trial will take approximately _____ days to complete. The parties request that the trial be held in _____, N.Y. **(The proposed date for the commencement of trial must be within 18 months of the filing date).**

    6) HAVE THE PARTIES FILED A JURY DEMAND: _____(YES)/_____(NO).

    7) DOES THE COURT HAVE SUBJECT MATTER JURISDICTION? ARE THE PARTIES SUBJECT TO THE COURT'S JURISDICTION? HAVE ALL PARTIES BEEN SERVED? _____

_____

_____

    8) WHAT ARE THE FACTUAL AND LEGAL BASES FOR PLAINTIFF'S CLAIMS AND DEFENDANT'S DEFENSES (INCLUDE COUNTERCLAIMS & CROSSCLAIMS, IF APPLICABLE)? _____

_____

_____

9) WHAT FACTUAL AND LEGAL ISSUES ARE GENUINELY IN DISPUTE? __

10) CAN THE ISSUES IN LITIGATION BE NARROWED BY AGREEMENT OR BY MOTIONS? ARE THERE DISPOSITIVE OR PARTIALLY DISPOSITIVE ISSUES APPROPRIATE FOR DECISION ON MOTION? _____

11) WHAT SPECIFIC RELIEF DO THE PARTIES SEEK? WHAT ARE THE DAMAGES SOUGHT? _____

12) DISCOVERY PLAN:

A. *Mandatory Disclosures.* The parties will exchange the mandatory disclosures required under Rule 26(a)(1) on or before _____

B. *Subjects of Disclosure.* The parties jointly agree that discovery will be needed to address the following subjects:

C. *Discovery Sequence.* Describe the parties' understanding regarding the timing of discovery, and state whether it is anticipated that discovery will be phased to address different issues in stages.

D. *Written Discovery.* Describe the written discovery demands which the parties contemplate serving under Rules 33, 34 and 36, including when they will be promulgated, the areas to be covered, and whether there is any need for any party to exceed the number of interrogatories permitted under Rule 33.

E. *Depositions.* Set forth the parties' expectations regarding depositions, including the approximate number to be taken, their location, a general description of the deponents, and an indication of whether any non-party fact depositions are anticipated.

F. *Experts.* Set forth the parties' expectations regarding the retention of experts, and identify any particular issues to be addressed by the court concerning the retention and exchange of the information regarding experts, including whether the parties seek a variance from the expert disclosure requirements of the form uniform pretrial scheduling order typically issued by the court (i.e., initial expert disclosure at least ninety days, responsive expert disclosures at least forty-five days, and rebuttal reports due at least thirty days, before the close of discovery).

G. *Electronic Discovery.* Set forth the parties' understanding and expectations regarding discovery of electronically stored information. This description should include any agreements reached with respect to the retention of electronically stored information and the manner in which it will be produced, if requested. The parties should also identify any agreements regarding the manner in which electronically stored information subject to claims of privilege or work product protection will be handled, and whether a court order will be requested, either on stipulation or otherwise, to address this issue. If an agreement has been reached on the entry of such an order, provide a brief description of the provisions which will be included in a proposed order.

_____
_____
_____

H. *Protective Orders.* If the parties anticipate requesting a protective order from the court pursuant to Rule 26(c), describe the basis for the request and nature of the proposed protective order.

_____
_____
_____

I. *Anticipated Issues Requiring Court Intervention.* Provide a brief description of any discovery related issues which, the parties reasonably anticipate, may require court intervention.

_____
_____
_____

13) IS IT POSSIBLE TO REDUCE THE LENGTH OF TRIAL BY STIPULATIONS, USE OF SUMMARIES OR STATEMENTS, OR OTHER EXPEDITED MEANS OF PRESENTING EVIDENCE? IS IT FEASIBLE AND DESIRABLE TO BIFURCATE ISSUES FOR TRIAL?

_____
_____
_____

14) ARE THERE RELATED CASES PENDING BEFORE THE JUDGES OF THIS COURT?

_____
_____
_____

15) IN CLASS ACTIONS, WHEN AND HOW WILL THE CLASS BE CERTIFIED?

_____
_____
_____

16) WHAT ARE THE PROSPECTS FOR SETTLEMENT? Please circle below the prospect for settlement:

1—2—3—4—5—6—7—8—9—10
(VERY UNLIKELY)* * * * * * * * * * * * * (LIKELY)
CANNOT BE EVALUATED PRIOR TO _____(DATE)
HOW CAN SETTLEMENT EFFORTS BE ASSISTED?

_____
_____

(Do not indicate any monetary amounts at this time, settlement will be explored by the Magistrate Judge at the time of the initial status conference)

COMPLETE QUESTION 17 ONLY IF YOUR FILING ORDER COVER SHEET WAS CHECKED AS AN ADR TRACK CASE. THE PROGRAMS LISTED BELOW ARE COURT–ANNEXED AND NON–BINDING.

17) IF YOUR CASE WAS SELECTED AS A QUALIFYING CONTRACT, TORT, OR NON–PRISONER CIVIL RIGHTS ACTION, PLEASE SELECT THE PREFERRED ADR METHOD.

_____ ARBITRATION
_____ MEDIATION
_____ EARLY NEUTRAL EVALUATION

Pursuant to Fed. R. Civ. P. 26(f) a meeting was held on _____ (Date) at _____ (Place) and was attended by:

_____ for plaintiff(s)

_____ for defendant(s) _____ (party name)

_____ for defendant(s) _____ (party name)

At the Rule 16(b) conference, the Court will issue an order directing the future proceedings in this action. The parties are advised that failure to comply with this order may result in the imposition of sanctions pursuant to Federal Rules of Civil Procedure 16(f).

Please detach this case management plan form and file electronically with the Clerk at least ten (10) days in advance of the conference date.

w:\genorder\go25.wpd
Case Management Plan
FRM–Date 6/13/2007

CASE ASSIGNMENT FORM

UNITED STATES DISTRICT COURT
FOR THE NORTHERN DISTRICT OF NEW YORK

CIVIL ACTION NUMBER _____

THIS ACTION HAS BEEN ASSIGNED TO THE JUDGE AND MAGISTRATE JUDGE SHOWN BELOW.

ALL CORRESPONDENCE AND FILINGS SHOULD BEAR THE INITIALS OF THE ASSIGNED JUDGE AND MAGISTRATE JUDGE IMMEDIATELY FOLLOWING THE CIVIL ACTION NUMBER. (*IE: CIVIL ACTION NO 5:02–CV–0123, FJS–GJD*)

DOCUMENTS SHOULD BE FILED IN ACCORDANCE WITH GENERAL ORDER #22.

ACTION ASSIGNED TO THE JUDGE AND MAGISTRATE
JUDGE CHECKED BELOW:

INITIALS

_____ CHIEF JUDGE NORMAN A. MORDUE   (NAM)

_____ JUDGE DAVID N. HURD   (DNH)

_____ JUDGE GARY L. SHARPE   (GLS)

_____ JUDGE GLENN T. SUDDABY   (GTS)

_____ SENIOR JUDGE NEAL P. MCCURN   (NPM)

_____ SENIOR JUDGE THOMAS J. MCAVOY   (TJM)

_____ SENIOR JUDGE FREDERICK J. SCULLIN, JR.   (FJS)

_____ SENIOR JUDGE LAWRENCE E. KAHN   (LEK)

_____ MAGISTRATE JUDGE GUSTAVE J. DIBIANCO   (GJD)

INITIALS

———— MAGISTRATE JUDGE DAVID R. HOMER   (DRH)

———— MAGISTRATE JUDGE DAVID E. PEEBLES   (DEP)

———— MAGISTRATE JUDGE RANDOLPH F. TREECE   (RFT)

———— MAGISTRATE JUDGE GEORGE H. LOWE   (GHL)

* PRO SE LITIGANTS *

SEND ALL ORIGINAL PAPERS TO THE CLERK'S
OFFICE CHECKED BELOW:

___ Clerk, U.S. District Court
Federal Building & Courthouse
P.O. Box 7367
Syracuse NY 13261–7367

___ Clerk, U.S. District Court
Federal Building & Courthouse
15 Henry Street
Binghamton NY 13901

___ Clerk, U.S. District Court
James T. Foley U.S. Courthouse
445 Broadway
Albany NY 12207–2936

___ Clerk, U.S. District Court
Alexander Pirnie Federal Building
10 Broad Street
Utica NY 13501

All papers filed with the Court must conform to Local Rule 10.1

---

* COUNSEL *

ALL DOCUMENTS SHALL BE
FILED ELECTRONICALLY
ON THE COURT'S CM/ECF SYSTEM

PLEASE REFER TO GENERAL ORDER #22
FOR PROCEDURES FOR FILING
DOCUMENTS ELECTRONICALLY

All **non-dispositive** motions are to be made returnable on a submit basis before the assigned **magistrate judge**. *Please refer to Local Rule 7.1(b)1.* **All motions filed and made returnable before magistrate judges will be taken on a submit basis unless:** the parties request oral argument and/or the court directs the parties to appear for oral argument, provided, however, that Magistrate Judge David E. Peebles requires oral argument on all motions unless the court directs otherwise.

Senior Judge McCurn will not have regular motion days during the month of August. Motions may not be filed without prior approval of the court during these periods.

MONTHLY MOTION SCHEDULES

CHIEF JUDGE NORMAN A. MORDUE
10:00 A.M.—1ST AND 3RD WEDNESDAY OF EACH MONTH AT SYRACUSE. No oral argument on scheduled motion return date, unless Judge Mordue's chambers sua sponte directs or grants the request of any party for oral argument.

SENIOR JUDGE LAWRENCE E. KAHN
9:30 A.M.—1ST AND 3RD FRIDAY OF EACH MONTH AT ALBANY.—All Motions ON SUBMIT unless otherwise notified by the Court. Any request for oral argument must be submitted to the Court, in writing, no later than 10 days prior to the motion return date.

JUDGE DAVID N. HURD
2nd Friday of each month in Utica—Civil motions at 10:00 a.m., Criminal motions at 2:00 p.m.
4th Friday of each month in Albany—Civil motions at 10:00 a.m., Criminal motions at 2:00 p.m.

JUDGE GARY L. SHARPE

9:00 a.m.—1st AND 3RD THURSDAY OF EACH MONTH AT ALBANY. Motions filed in Syracuse area cases will be taken on SUBMIT unless otherwise ordered. Motions requiring oral argument will be handled by video-conference, or in person, as directed.

MAGISTRATE JUDGE GUSTAVE J. Di-BIANCO
10:00 A.M.—LAST THURSDAY OF EACH MONTH AT SYRACUSE.

JUDGE GLENN T. SUDDABY
10:00 A.M.—1ST AND 3RD TUESDAY OF EACH MONTH AT SYRACUSE. No oral argument on scheduled motion return date, unless Judge Suddaby's chambers sua sponte directs or grants the request of any party for oral argument.

MAGISTRATE JUDGE DAVID R. HOMER
9:30 A.M.—3RD THURSDAY OF EACH MONTH AT ALBANY.

SENIOR JUDGE NEAL P. McCURN

10:00 A.M.—2ND AND 4TH TUESDAYS OF EACH MONTH AT SYRACUSE.
11:00 A.M.—1ST TUESDAY OF EACH MONTH AT ALBANY. No oral argument on scheduled motion return date, unless Judge McCurn's chambers sua sponte directs or grants the request of any party for oral argument.

MAGISTRATE JUDGE DAVID E. PEEBLES
9:30 A.M.—2ND AND 4TH WEDNESDAY OF EACH MONTH AT SYRACUSE
2:00 p.m.—1st FRIDAY OF EACH MONTH AT BINGHAMTON
Oral Argument expected on all motions unless otherwise directed.

SENIOR JUDGE THOMAS J. McAVOY

10:00 A.M.—2ND MONDAY OF EACH MONTH AT ALBANY
10:00 A.M.—4TH FRIDAY OF EACH MONTH AT BINGHAMTON

MAGISTRATE JUDGE RANDOLPH F. TREECE
9:30 A.M.—1 ST THURSDAY OF EACH MONTH AT ALBANY. No oral argument on scheduled motion return date, unless Judge Treece's chambers sua sponte directs or grants the request of any party for oral argument.

SENIOR JUDGE FREDERICK J. SCULLIN, JR.
2ND FRIDAY OF EACH MONTH IN SYRACUSE–Civil motions at 10:00 a.m., Criminal motions at 11:00 a.m.
4TH FRIDAY OF EACH MONTH IN ALBANY—Civil motions at 10:00 a.m., Criminal motions at 11:00 a.m.
BEGINNING JANUARY 1, 2006—all civil motions will be taken ON SUBMIT unless otherwise notified by the Court. Any request for oral argument must be submitted to the Court, in writing, no later than 14 days prior to the motion return date. Argument will be held on criminal motions.

MAGISTRATE JUDGE GEORGE H. LOWE

10:00 A.M.—1ST AND 3RD THURSDAY OF EACH MONTH AT SYRACUSE. No oral argument on scheduled motion return date unless Judge Lowe's chambers directs counsel to appear, sua sponte, or at the request of a party.

CONSENT TO THE EXERCISE OF CIVIL JURISDICTION BY A MAGISTRATE JUDGE

In accordance with the provisions of 28 U.S.C. Section 636(c), you are hereby notified that the United States Magistrate Judges of this district court, in addition to their other duties, may, upon consent of all the parties in a civil case, conduct any or all proceedings in the case, including a jury or non jury trial, and order the entry of a final judgment.

You should be aware that your decision to consent to the referral of your case to a United States Magistrate Judge for disposition is entirely voluntary and should be indicated by counsel endorsing the attached consent form for the plaintiff(s)and defendant(s). If the form is executed by all counsel for the parties (or by the parties if appearing pro se), it should be communicated solely to the clerk of the district court. ONLY if all the parties to the case consent to the reference to a magistrate judge will either the judge or magistrate judge to whom the case has been assigned be informed of your decision.

Your opportunity to have your case disposed of by a magistrate judge is subject to the calendar requirements of the court. Accordingly, the district judge to whom your case is assigned must approve the reference of the case to a magistrate judge for disposition.

In accordance with 28 U.S.C. Section 636(c)(3), an appeal from a judgment entered by a magistrate judge will be taken to the United States Court of Appeals for this judicial circuit in the same manner as an appeal from any other judgment of a district court. See Also L.R. 72.2(b)(1).

Copies of the consent form are available in any office of the clerk of the court and on the court web-page at www.nynd.uscourts.gov.

ATTACHED FOR YOUR CONSIDERATION IS A BLANK CONSENT FORM

AO 85 (Rev. 8/98) Notice, Consent, and Order of Reference—Exercise of Jurisdiction by a United States Magistrate Judge

UNITED STATES DISTRICT COURT

Northern District of New York

Plaintiff	NOTICE, CONSENT, AND ORDER OF REFERENCE EXERCISE OF JURISDICTION BY A UNITED STATES MAGISTRATE JUDGE
v.	Case Number:
Defendant	

NOTICE OF AVAILABILITY OF A UNITED STATES MAGISTRATE JUDGE TO EXERCISE JURISDICTION

In accordance with the provisions of 28 U.S.C. § 636(c), and Fed.R.Civ.P. 73, you are notified that a United States magistrate judge of this district court is available to conduct any or all proceedings in this case including a jury or nonjury trial, and to order the entry of a final judgment. Exercise of this jurisdiction by a magistrate judge is, however, permitted only if all parties voluntarily consent.

You may, without adverse substantive consequences, withhold your consent, but this will prevent the court's jurisdiction from being exercised by a magistrate judge. If any party withholds consent, the identity of the parties consenting or withholding consent will not be communicated to any magistrate judge or to the district judge to whom the case has been assigned.

An appeal from a judgment entered by a magistrate judge shall be taken directly to the United States court of appeals for this judicial circuit in the same manner as an appeal from any other judgment of this district court.

CONSENT TO THE EXERCISE OF JURISDICTION BY A UNITED STATES MAGISTRATE JUDGE

In accordance with the provisions of 28 U.S.C.§ 636(c) and Fed.R.Civ.P. 73, the parties in this case consent to have a United States magistrate judge conduct any and all proceedings in this case, including the trial, order the entry of a final judgment, and conduct all post-judgment proceedings.

Party Represented   Signatures   Date

_____   _____   _____

_____   _____   _____

_____   _____   _____

ORDER OF REFERENCE

IT IS ORDERED that this case be referred to _____, United States Magistrate Judge, to conduct all proceedings and order the entry of judgment in accordance with 28 U.S.C. § 636(c) and Fed. R.Civ.P. 73.

_____

Date

_____

United States District Judge

NOTE: RETURN THIS FORM TO THE CLERK OF THE COURT ONLY IF ALL PARTIES HAVE CONSENTED ON THIS FORM TO THE EXERCISE OF JURISDICTION BY A UNITED STATES MAGISTRATE JUDGE.

GENERAL ORDER 26. COURTHOUSE SECURITY AND LIMITATIONS ON THE USE OF ELECTRONIC DEVICES WITHIN UNITED STATES COURTHOUSES IN THE NORTHERN DISTRICT OF NEW YORK

Introduction: Currently the Federal Rules of Criminal Procedure and Judicial Conference Policy prohibit the taking of photographs in the courtroom during judicial proceedings or the broadcasting of judicial proceedings from the Courtroom.[1] In the past, enforcement of this policy was limited to the prohibition of cameras in the Courtroom. However, as technology advances, there are an ever-growing number of wireless communication devices that have the capability of recording and/or transmitting sound, pictures, and video. Currently, these devices include, but are not limited to, cell phones, camera phones, personal data assistants (PDA's) and laptop computers. Many of these devices are also capable of wireless internet access and have recording capabilities. In order to enforce the Federal Rules of Criminal Procedure and Judicial Conference Policy this General Order sets forth the limitations on the use of electronic devices inside United States Courthouses within the Northern District of New York.

Courthouse Security.

(1) Screening and Search. All persons entering a federal courthouse in this district and all items carried by them are subject to appropriate screening and search by a United States Marshal, Court Security Officer, or any law enforcement officer. Persons may be requested to provide identification and to state the nature of their business in the courthouse. Anyone refusing to cooperate with these security measures may be denied entrance to the courthouse.

(2) Prohibitions. The taking of photographs and the use of any broadcasting equipment within any federal courthouse are prohibited, except with the permission of the court. This prohibition shall not apply to non-court federal agency tenants within their space. When necessary, tenants will coordinate use of any such equipment with the United States Marshals Service.

Use of Electronic Devices.

(1) No one other than court officials and officers of the court engaged in the conduct of court business shall bring any cameras, video cameras, recording equipment, dictaphones, pagers, cellular phones—including camera phones, personal data assistants (PDA's) and computers into courtrooms. These devices are prohibited in all courtrooms, except with permission of the court. This prohibition also applies to jurors while in the jury deliberation rooms. Officers of the court may keep their cellular phones—including camera phones and personal data assistants (PDA's) on their person while in court as long as they are turned off. If a cellular phone or PDA goes off during a court proceeding, the attorney may be sanctioned by the presiding judge. The camera device which is included in many celluar phones shall not be used while inside a United States Courthouse. Sanctions include a fine of up to $100.00 and the loss of the privilege of keeping a cellular phone or PDA on their person while at the federal courthouse.

(2) The court will allow the use of cameras and other equipment during ceremonial proceedings, including naturalization proceedings, mock trials, or a judge's investiture.

(3) In non-ceremonial proceedings, audio and audio-visual equipment may be utilized only for the limited purpose of presentation of the evidence, perpetuation of the record of the proceedings, and security.

Grand Jury Security.

(1) The secrecy of the grand jury proceedings is a matter of preeminent concern. When a grand jury is convened, the surrounding area is restricted to law enforcement officers, involved attorneys, witnesses, and employees and customers of agencies on the premises. The United States Marshals Service may secure the floor of the grand jury session as necessary to preserve the secrecy of the grand jury and protect witnesses from any unwanted interference. No electronic devices are allowed in the Grand Jury Room without the permission of the United States Attorney.

SO ORDERED THIS 1st DAY OF DECEMBER, 2006

---

[1] FRCrP Rule 53 provides: Except as otherwise provided by a statute or these rules, the court must not permit the taking of photographs in the courtroom during judicial proceedings or the broadcasting of judicial proceedings from the courtroom. Judicial Conference Policy states that the courtroom proceedings in civil and criminal cases in the district courts may not be broadcast, televised, recorded, or photographed for the purpose of public dissemination. Guide to Judiciary Policies and Procedure, vol.1, ch.3, part E.

GENERAL ORDER 29. PROCESSING SEALED DOCUMENTS FOLLOWING THE CLOSURE OF A CIVIL CASE [ABROGATED]

[Dated March 31, 2006; abrogated effective January 1, 2009, see, now, Local Rule 83.13.]

LOCAL RULES OF BANKRUPTCY PROCEDURE
FOR THE
WESTERN DISTRICT OF NEW YORK

Including Amendments Received Through
January 1, 2009

STANDING ORDER. REPEAL OF STANDING ORDER
DATED SEPTEMBER 9, 2005 ADOPTING
INTERIM BANKRUPTCY RULES

Whereas, on December 1, 2008, new and amended Federal Rules of Bankruptcy Procedure will supersede the Interim Rules adopted by the Judges of this Court, which were effective on October 17, 2005.

IT IS HEREBY ORDERED, that the Standing Order adopting Interim Bankruptcy Rules dated September 9, 2005 is hereby repealed effective on December 1, 2008. For cases and proceedings not governed by the Act, the Federal Rules of Bankruptcy Procedure and the Local Rules of this Court will apply.

IT IS FURTHER ORDERED, that Interim Bankruptcy Rule 5012 is hereby retained until it is replaced by a permanent rule under the Federal Rules of Bankruptcy Procedure.

IT IS SO ORDERED.

DATED: October 1, 2008.

STANDING ORDER. IN THE MATTER OF ISSUANCE
OF CHAPTER 13 DISCHARGES

WHEREAS, the Bankruptcy Abuse Prevention and Consumer Protection Act of 2005 (BAPCPA) requires the debtor to meet certain requirements before a discharge can be issued in a Chapter 13 case, including those set out at 11 USC §§ 1328(h) and 522(q) ("Bankruptcy Code"); and whereas, Procedural Form B283, entitled "Chapter 13 Debtor's Certifications regarding Domestic Support Obligations and Section 522(q)," has been approved for use by the Judicial Conference of the United States to satisfy these requirements, it is therefore

ORDERED, that Procedural Form B283, entitled "Chapter 13 Debtor's Certifications regarding Domestic Support Obligations and Section 522(q)," issued by the Director of the Administrative Office of the United States Courts is required for use in this District; and it is further

ORDERED, that the Chapter 13 debtor's failure to timely file Procedural Form B283 will result in the case being closed without a discharge; and it is further

ORDERED, that parties be provided notice of an opportunity to file objections and/or request a hearing regarding the applicability of § 522(q) of the Bankruptcy Code as it relates to the issuance of a discharge. Pursuant to Bankruptcy Rule 2002(f)(11), said notice will be included in the Summary of Trustee's Case Closing Report and Account, or by separate notice issued by the Court, beginning with notices issued on or after January 1, 2009; and it is further

ORDERED, that if no objections and/or requests for a hearing are filed with respect to the possible applicability of § 1328(h), and the debtor is otherwise eligible to receive a discharge, the Court may issue a discharge in the case; and it is further

ORDERED, that if the case is closed without a discharge, the debtor must file a motion to reopen the case and pay the requisite filing fee in order to obtain a discharge. The fee to reopen a case to obtain a discharge will not be waived; and it is further

ORDERED, that these procedures become effective for all Chapter 13 cases commenced under BAPCPA for which notice of an opportunity to request a hearing was provided, as indicated above.

Dated: December 11, 2008.

STANDING ORDER. IN THE MATTER OF ADOPTION OF INTERIM BANKRUPTCY RULE 1007–I

Whereas, the National Guard and Reservists Debt Relief Act of 2008, Pub.L. 110–438, ("Act",) provides a temporary exclusion from the bankruptcy means test for Reservists and members of the National Guard called to active duty or homeland defense activity for at least 90 days after September 11, 2001, and

Whereas, the Act becomes effective on December 19, 2008, and

Whereas, the Judicial Conference has approved transmitting proposed Interim Rule 1007–I to the courts to implement the Act, and

Whereas, the Judicial Conference has also approved an amendment to Official Form 22A, which includes a new Part 1C, where qualifying debtors can invoke the temporary exclusion, such form to become effective on December 19, 2008, the same time that the Act is effective, it is therefore

ORDERED that the attached Interim Rule 1007–I is adopted in its entirety and Official Form 22A as amended is also adopted, to be effective December 19, 2008. This Interim Rule shall remain in effect until further Order of this Court.

IT IS SO ORDERED.

Dated: December 11, 2008.

Interim Rule 1007–I. Lists, Schedules, Statements, and Other Documents; Time Limits; Expiration of Temporary Means Testing Exclusion

* * * * *

(b) Schedules, Statements, and Other Documents Required.

* * * * *

(4) Unless either: (A) § 707(b)(2)(D)(i) applies, or (B) § 707(b)(2)(D)(ii) applies and the exclusion from means testing granted therein extends beyond the period specified by Rule 1017(e), an individual debtor in a chapter 7 case shall file a statement of current monthly income prepared as prescribed by the appropriate Official Form, and, if the current monthly income exceeds the median family income for the applicable state and household size, the information, including calculations, required by § 707(b), prepared as prescribed by the appropriate Official Form.

* * * * *

(c) **Time Limits.** In a voluntary case, the schedules, statements, and other documents required by subdivision (b)(1), (4), (5), and (6) shall be filed with the petition or within 15 days thereafter, except as otherwise provided in subdivisions (d), (e), (f), and (h), and (n) of this rule. In an involuntary case, the list in subdivision (a)(2), and the schedules, statements, and other documents required by subdivision (b)(1) shall be filed by the debtor within 15 days of the entry of the order for relief. In a voluntary case, the documents required by paragraphs (A), (C), and (D) of subdivision (b)(3) shall be filed with the petition. Unless the court orders otherwise, a debtor who has filed a statement under subdivision (b)(3)(B), shall file the documents required by subdivision (b)(3)(A) within 15 days of the order for relief. In a chapter 7 case, the debtor shall file the statement required by subdivision (b)(7) within 45 days after the first date set for the meeting of creditors under § 341 of the Code, and in a chapter 11 or 13 case no later than the date when the last payment was made by the debtor as required by the plan or the filing of a motion for a discharge under § 1141(d)(5)(B) or § 1328(b) of the Code. The court may, at any time and in its discretion, enlarge the time to file the statement required by subdivision (b)(7). The debtor shall file the statement required by subdivision (b)(8) no earlier than the date of the last payment made under the plan or the date of the filing of a motion for a discharge under §§ 1141(d)(5)(B), 1228(b), or 1328(b) of the Code. Lists, schedules, statements, and other documents filed prior to the conversion of a case to another chapter shall be deemed filed in the converted case unless the court directs otherwise. Except as provided in § 1116(3), any extension of time to file schedules, statements, and other documents required under this rule may be granted only on motion for cause shown and on notice to the United States trustee, any committee elected under § 705 or appointed under § 1102 of the Code, trustee, examiner, or other party as the court may direct. Notice of an extension shall be given to the United States trustee and to any committee, trustee, or other party as the court may direct.

* * * * *

(n) Time Limits for, and Notice to, Debtors Temporarily Excluded from Means Testing.

(1) An individual debtor who is temporarily excluded from means testing pursuant to § 707(b)(2)(D)(ii) of the Code shall file any statement and calculations required by subdivision (b)(4) no later than 14 days after the expiration of the temporary exclusion if the expiration occurs within the time specified by Rule 1017(e) for filing a motion pursuant to § 707(b)(2).

(2) If the temporary exclusion from means testing under § 707(b)(2)(D)(ii) terminates due to the circumstances specified in subdivision (n)(1), and if the debtor has not previously filed a statement and calculations required by subdivision (b)(4), the clerk shall promptly notify the debtor that the required statement and calculations must be filed within the time specified in subdivision (n)(1).

Committee Note

This rule is amended to take account of the enactment of the National Guard and Reservists Debt Relief Act of 2008, which amended § 707(b)(2)(D) of the Code to provide a temporary exclusion from the application of the means test for certain members of the National Guard and reserve components of the Armed Forces. This exclusion applies to qualifying debtors while they remain on active duty or are performing a homeland defense activity, and for a period of 540 days thereafter. For some debtors initially covered by the exclusion, the protection from means testing will expire while their chapter 7 cases are pending, and at a point when a timely motion to dismiss under § 707(b)(2) can still be filed. Under the amended rule, these debtors are required to file the statement and calculations required by subdivision (b)(4) no later than 14 days after the expiration of their exclusion.

Subdivisions (b)(4) and (c) are amended to relieve debtors qualifying for an exclusion under § 707(b)(2)(D)(ii) from the obligation to file a statement of current monthly income and required calculations within the time period specified in subdivision (c).

Subdivision (n)(1) is added to specify the time for filing of the information required by subdivision (b)(4) by a debtor who initially qualifies for the means test exclusion under § 707(b)(2)(D)(ii), but whose exclusion expires during the time that a motion to dismiss under § 707(b)(2) may still be made under Rule 1017(e). If, upon the expiration of the temporary exclusion, a debtor has not already filed the required statement and calculations, subdivision (n)(2) directs the clerk to provide prompt notice to the debtor of the time for filing as set forth in subdivision (n)(1).

*

FEDERAL COURTS MISCELLANEOUS FEE SCHEDULES

COURT OF APPEALS FEE SCHEDULE

(Issued in accordance with 28 U.S.C. § 1913)

(Eff. 01/01/2009)

The fees included in the Court of Appeals Miscellaneous Fee Schedule are to be charged for services provided by the courts of appeals.

- The United States should not be charged fees under this schedule, except as prescribed in Items 2, 4, and 5 when the information requested is available through remote electronic access.
- Federal agencies or programs that are funded from judiciary appropriations (agencies, organizations, and individuals providing services authorized by the Criminal Justice Act, 18 U.S.C. § 3006A, and bankruptcy administrators) should not be charged any fees under this schedule.

(1) For docketing a case on appeal or review, or docketing any other proceeding, $450.

- Each party filing a notice of appeal pays a separate fee to the district court, but parties filing a joint notice of appeal pay only one fee.
- There is no docketing fee for an application for an interlocutory appeal under 28 U.S.C. § 1292(b) or other petition for permission to appeal under Fed. R. App. P. 5, unless the appeal is allowed.

- There is no docketing fee for a direct bankruptcy appeal or a direct bankruptcy cross appeal, when the fee has been collected by the bankruptcy court in accordance with item 14 of the Bankruptcy Court Miscellaneous Fee Schedule.

(2) For conducting a search of the court of appeals records, $26 per name or item searched. This fee applies to services rendered on behalf of the United States if the information requested is available through remote electronic access.

(3) For certification of any document, $9.

(4) For reproducing any document, $.50 per page. This fee applies to services rendered on behalf of the United States if the document requested is available through remote electronic access.

(5) For reproducing recordings of proceedings, regardless of the medium, $26, including the cost of materials. This fee applies to services rendered on behalf of the United States if the recording is available through remote electronic access.

(6) For reproducing the record in any appeal in which the court of appeals does not require an appendix pursuant to Fed. R. App. P.30(f), $71.

(7) For retrieving a record from a Federal Records Center, National Archives, or other storage location removed from the place of business of the court, $45.

(8) For a check paid into the court which is returned for lack of funds, $45.

(9) For copies of opinions, a fee commensurate with the cost of printing, as fixed by each court.

(10) For copies of the local rules of court, a fee commensurate with the cost of distributing the copies. The court may also distribute copies of the local rules without charge.

(11) For filing:

- Any separate or joint notice of appeal or application for appeal from the Bankruptcy Appellate Panel, $5.
- A notice of the allowance of an appeal from the Bankruptcy Appellate Panel, $5.

(12) For counsel's requested use of the court's video-conferencing equipment in connection with each oral argument, the court may charge and collect a fee of $200 per remote location.

(13) For original admission of an attorney to practice, including a certificate of

admission, $150. For a duplicate certificate of admission or certificate of good standing, $15.

DISTRICT COURT FEE SCHEDULE

(Issued in accordance with 28 U.S.C. 1914)

(Eff. 06/01/2004)

Following are fees to be charged for services provided by the district courts. No fees are to be charged for services rendered on behalf of the United States, with the exception of those specifically prescribed in items 2, 4 and 5. No fees under this schedule shall be charged to federal agencies or programs which are funded from judiciary appropriations, including, but not limited to, agencies, organizations, and individuals providing services authorized by the Criminal Justice Act, 18 U.S.C. § 3006A, and Bankruptcy Administrator programs.

(1) For filing or indexing any document not in a case or proceeding for which a filing fee has been paid, $39.

(2) For every search of the records of the district court conducted by the clerk of the district court or a deputy clerk, $26 per name or item searched. This fee shall apply to services rendered on behalf of the United States if the information requested is available through electronic access.

(3) For certification of any document or paper, whether the certification is made directly on the document or by separate instrument, $9. For exemplification of any document or paper, twice the amount of the fee for certification.

(4) For reproducing any record or paper, $.50 per page. This fee shall apply to paper copies made from either: (1) original documents; or (2) microfiche or microfilm reproductions of the original records. This fee shall apply to services rendered on behalf of the United States if the record or paper requested is available through electronic access.

(5) For reproduction of recordings of proceedings, regardless of the medium, $26, including the cost of materials. This fee shall apply to services rendered on behalf of the United States, if the reproduction of the recording is available electronically.

(6) For each microfiche sheet of film or microfilm jacket copy of any court record, where available, $5.

(7) For retrieval of a record from a Federal Records Center, National Archives, or other storage location removed from the place of business of the court, $45.

(8) For a check paid into the court which is returned for lack of funds, $45.

(9) For an appeal to a district judge from a judgment of conviction by a magistrate in a misdemeanor case, $32.

(10) For original admission of attorneys to practice, $50 each, including a certificate of admission. For a duplicate certificate of admission or certificate of good standing, $15.

(11) The court may charge and collect fees commensurate with the cost of providing copies of the local rules of court. The court may also distribute copies of the local rules without charge.

(12) The clerk shall assess a charge for the handling of registry funds deposited with the court, to be assessed from interest earnings and in accordance with the detailed fee schedule issued by the Director of the Administrative Office of the United States Courts.

(13) For filing an action brought under Title III of the Cuban Liberty and Democratic Solidarity (LIBERTAD) Act of 1996, P.L. 104–114, 110 Stat. 785 (1996), $5,431. (This fee is in addition to the filing fee prescribed in 28 U.S.C. § 1914(a) for instituting any civil action other than a writ of habeas corpus.)

BANKRUPTCY COURT FEE SCHEDULE (28 U.S.C. 1930)

Effective 10/01/2008

The fees included in the Bankruptcy Court Miscellaneous Fee Schedule are to be charged for services provided by the bankruptcy courts.

- The United States should not be charged fees under this schedule, with the exception of those specifically prescribed in Items 1, 3 and 5 when the information requested is available through remote electronic access.
- Federal agencies or programs that are funded from judiciary appropriations (agencies, organizations, and individuals providing services authorized by the Criminal Justice Act, 18 U.S.C. § 3006A, and bankruptcy administrators) should not be charged any fees under this schedule.

(1) For reproducing any document, $.50 per page. This fee applies to services rendered on behalf of the United States if the document requested is available through electronic access.

(2) For certification of any document, $9.
   For exemplification of any document, $18.

(3) For reproduction of an audio recording of a court proceeding, $26. This fee applies to services rendered on behalf of the United States if the recording is available electronically.

(4) For filing an amendment to the debtor's schedules, lists of creditors, or mailing list, $26, except:

- The bankruptcy judge may, for good cause, waive the charge in any case.
- This fee must not be charged if -
  - the amendment is to change the address of a creditor or an attorney for a creditor listed on the schedules; or
  - the amendment is to add the name and address of an attorney for a creditor listed on the schedules.

(5) For conducting a search of the bankruptcy court records, $26 per name or item searched. This fee applies to services rendered on behalf of the United States if the information requested is available through electronic access.

(6) For filing a complaint, $250, except:

- If the trustee or debtor-in-possession files the complaint, the fee should be paid by the estate, if there is an estate.

- This fee must not be charged if -
  - the debtor is the plaintiff; or
  - a child support creditor or representative files the complaint and submits the form required by § 304(g) of the Bankruptcy Reform Act of 1994.

(7) For filing any document that is not related to a pending case or proceeding, $39.

(8) Administrative fee for filing a case under Title 11 or when a motion to divide a joint case under Title 11 is filed, $39.

(9) For payment to trustees pursuant to 11 U.S.C. § 330(b)(2), a $15 fee applies in the following circumstances:

- For filing a petition under Chapter 7.
- For filing a motion to reopen a Chapter 7 case.
- For filing a motion to divide a joint Chapter 7 case.
- For filing a motion to convert a case to a Chapter 7 case.
- For filing a notice of conversion to a Chapter 7 case.

(10) In addition to any fees imposed under Item 9, above, the following fees must be collected:

- For filing a motion to convert a Chapter 12 case to a Chapter 7 case or a notice of conversion pursuant to 11 U.S.C. § 1208(a), $45.
- For filing a motion to convert a Chapter 13 case to a Chapter 7 case or a notice of conversion pursuant to 11 U.S.C. § 1307(a), $10.

The fee amounts in this item are derived from the fees prescribed in 28 U.S.C. § 1930(a).

If the trustee files the motion to convert, the fee is payable only from the estate that exists prior to conversion.

If the filing fee for the chapter to which the case is requested to be converted is less than the fee paid at the commencement of the case, no refund may be provided.

(11) For filing a motion to reopen, the following fees apply:

- For filing a motion to reopen a Chapter 7 case, $245.
- For filing a motion to reopen a Chapter 9 case, $1000.

- For filing a motion to reopen a Chapter 11 case, $1000.

- For filing a motion to reopen a Chapter 12 case, $200.

- For filing a motion to reopen a Chapter 13 case, $235.

- For filing a motion to reopen a Chapter 15 case, $1000.

The fee amounts in this item are derived from the fees prescribed in 28 U.S.C. § 1930(a).

The reopening fee must be charged when a case has been closed without a discharge being entered.

The court may waive this fee under appropriate circumstances or may defer payment of the fee from trustees pending discovery of additional assets. If payment is deferred, the fee should be waived if no additional assets are discovered.

The reopening fee must not be charged in the following situations:

- to permit a party to file a complaint to obtain a determination under Rule 4007(b); or

- when a debtor files a motion to reopen a case based upon an alleged violation of the terms of the discharge under 11 U.S.C. § 524.

(12) For retrieval of a record from a Federal Records Center, National Archives, or other storage location removed from the place of business of the court, $45.

(13) For a check paid into the court which is returned for lack of funds, $45.

(14) For filing an appeal or cross appeal from a final judgment, $250.

This fee is collected in addition to the statutory fee of $5 that is collected under 28 U.S.C. § 1930(c) when a notice of appeal is filed.

Parties filing a joint notice of appeal should pay only one fee.

If a trustee or debtor in possession is the appellant, the fee must be payable only from the estate and to the extent there is any estate realized.

Upon notice from the court of appeals that a direct appeal or direct cross appeal has been authorized, an additional fee of $200 must be collected.

(15) For filing a case under Chapter 15 of the Bankruptcy Code, $1000.

This fee is derived from and equal to the fee prescribed in 28 U.S.C. § 1930(a)(4) for filing a case commenced under Chapter 11 of Title 11.

(16) The court may charge and collect fees commensurate with the cost of providing copies of the local rules of court. The court may also distribute copies of the local rules without charge.

(17) The clerk shall assess a charge for the handling of registry funds deposited with the court, to be assessed from interest earnings and in accordance with the detailed fee schedule issued by the Director of the Administrative Office of the United States Courts.

(18) For filing a motion to divide a joint case filed under 11 U.S.C. § 302, the following fees apply:

- For filing a motion to divide a joint Chapter 7 case, $245.

- For filing a motion to divide a joint Chapter 11 case, $1000.

- For filing a motion to divide a joint Chapter 12 case, $200.

- For filing a motion to divide a joint Chapter 13 case, $235.

These fees are derived from and equal to the filing fees prescribed in 28 U.S.C. § 1930(a).

(19) For filing the following motions, $150:

- To terminate, annul, modify or condition the automatic stay;

- To compel abandonment of property of the estate pursuant to Rule 6007(b) of the Federal Rules of Bankruptcy Procedure; or

- To withdraw the reference of a case or proceeding under 28 U.S.C. § 157(d).

This fee must not be collected in the following situations:

- For a motion for relief from the codebtor stay;

- For a stipulation for court approval of an agreement for relief from a stay; or

- For a motion filed by a child support creditor or its representative, if the form required by § 304(g) of the Bankruptcy Reform Act of 1994 is filed.

JUDICIAL PANEL ON MULTIDISTRICT LITIGATION FEE SCHEDULE

Following are fees to be charged for services provided by the Judicial Panel on Multidistrict Litigation. No fees are to be charged for services rendered on behalf of the United States, with the exception of those specifically prescribed in items 1 and 3. No fees under this schedule shall be charged to federal agencies or programs which are funded from judiciary appropriations, including, but not limited to, agencies, organizations, and individuals providing services authorized by the Criminal Justice Act, 18 U.S.C. § 3006A.

(1) For every search of the records of the court conducted by the clerk of the court or a deputy clerk, $26 per name or item searched. This fee shall apply to services rendered on behalf of the United States if the information requested is available through electronic access.

(2) For certification of any document or paper, whether the certification is made directly on the document or by separate instrument, $9.

(3) For reproducing any record or paper, $.50 per page. This fee shall apply to paper copies made from either: (1) original documents; or (2) microfiche or microfilm reproductions of the original records. This fee shall apply to services rendered on behalf of the United States if the record or paper requested is available through electronic access.

(4) For retrieval of a record from a Federal Records Center, National Archives, or other storage location removed from the place of business of the court, $45.

(5) For a check paid into the Panel which is returned for lack of funds, $45.

ELECTRONIC PUBLIC ACCESS FEE SCHEDULE

(Issued in accordance with 28 U.S.C. 1913, 1914, 1926, 1930, 1932)

(Eff. 3/11/2008)

As directed by Congress, the Judicial Conference has determined that the following fees are necessary to reimburse expenses incurred by the judiciary in providing electronic public access to court records. These fees shall apply to the United States unless otherwise stated. No fees under this schedule shall be charged to federal agencies or programs which are funded from judiciary appropriations, including, but not limited to, agencies, organizations, and individuals providing services authorized by the Criminal Justice Act, 18 U.S.C. 3006A, and bankruptcy administrator programs.

I. For electronic access to court data via a federal judiciary Internet site: eight cents per page, with the total for any document, docket sheet, or case-specific report not to exceed the fee for thirty pages- provided however that transcripts of federal court proceedings shall not be subject to the thirty-page fee limit. Attorneys of record and parties in a case (including pro se litigants) receive one free electronic copy of all documents filed electronically, if receipt is required by law or directed by the filer. No

fee is owed under this provision until an account holder accrues charges of more than $10 in a calendar year. Consistent with Judicial Conference policy, courts may, upon a showing of cause, exempt indigents, bankruptcy case trustees, individual researchers associated with educational institutions, courts, section 501(c)(3) not-for-profit organizations, court appointed pro bono attorneys, and pro bono ADR neutrals from payment of these fees. Courts must find that parties from the classes of persons or entities listed above seeking exemption have demonstrated that an exemption is necessary in order to avoid unreasonable burdens and to promote public access to information. Any user granted an exemption agrees not to sell for profit the data obtained as a result. Any transfer of data obtained as the result of a fee exemption is prohibited unless expressly authorized by the court. Exemptions may be granted for a definite period of time and may be revoked at the discretion of the court granting the exemption.

II. For printing copies of any record or document accessed electronically at a public terminal in the courthouse: ten cents per page. This fee shall apply to services rendered on behalf of the United States if the record requested is remotely available through electronic access.

III. For every search of court records conducted by the PACER Service Center, $26 per name or item searched.

IV. For the PACER Service Center to reproduce on paper any record pertaining to a PACER account, if this information is remotely available through electronic access, 50 cents per page.

V. For a check paid to the PACER Service Center which is returned for lack of funds, $45.

JUDICIAL CONFERENCE POLICY NOTES

Courts should not exempt local, state or federal government agencies, members of the media, attorneys or others not members of one of the groups listed above. Exemptions should be granted as the exception, not the rule. A court may not use this exemption language to exempt all users. An exemption applies only to access related to the case or purpose for which it was given. The prohibition on transfer of information received without fee is not intended to bar a quote or reference to information received as a result of a fee exemption in a scholarly or other similar work.

The electronic public access fee applies to electronic court data viewed remotely from the public records of individual cases in the court, including filed documents and the docket sheet. Electronic court data may be viewed free at public terminals at the courthouse and courts may provide other local court information at no cost. Examples of information that can be provided at no cost include: local rules, court forms, news items, court calendars, opinions, and other information—such as court hours, court location, telephone listings—determined locally to benefit the public and the court.

†